About the Authors

Rod Stephens started out as a mathematician but, while studying at MIT, discovered the joys of programming and has been programming professionally ever since. During his career, he has worked on an eclectic assortment of applications in such fields as telephone switching, billing, repair dispatching, tax processing, wastewater treatment, and training for professional football players.

Rod has written 14 books that have been translated into half a dozen different languages, and more than 200 magazine articles covering Visual Basic, Visual Basic for Applications, Delphi, and Java. He is currently a columnist for *Visual Basic Developer* (www.pinnaclepublishing.com).

Rod's popular *VB Helper* Web site (www.vb-helper.com) receives several million hits per month and contains thousands of pages of tips, tricks, and example code for Visual Basic programmers, as well as example code for this book.

Credits

Executive Editor
Robert Elliott

Development Editor
Kevin Shafer

Technical Editor
John Mueller

Production Editor
Felicia Robinson

Copy Editor
Foxxe Editorial Services

Editorial Manager
Mary Beth Wakefield

Vice President & Executive Group Publisher
Richard Swadley

Vice President and Publisher
Joseph B. Wikert

Project Coordinators
Michael Kruzil
Erin Smith

Graphics and Production Specialists
Carrie A. Foster
Lauren Goddard
Denny Hager
Jennifer Heleine
Barbara Moore
Melanee Prendergast
Amanda Spagnuolo
Ron Terry
Julie Trippetti

Quality Control Technician
Leeann Harney
Jessica Kramer
Carl William Pierce

Proofreading and Indexing
TECHBOOKS Production Services

Acknowledgments

Thanks to Bob Elliott, Kevin Shafer, Felicia Robinson, Kathryn Bourgoine, and all of the others who make producing any book possible.

Thanks also to technical editor John Mueller for making sure I wasn't putting my foot too deeply in my mouth and for helping to add extra depth to the book. Visit `http://www.mwt.net/~jmueller` to learn about John's books and to sign up for his free newsletter *.NET Tips, Trends & Technology eXTRA*.

Introduction

When Visual Basic first appeared, it revolutionized Windows programming. By handling many of the tedious details of processing Windows events, it enabled programmers to focus on application details instead of Windows programming trivia.

Unfortunately, early versions of Visual Basic had a few drawbacks. Protection from the underlying Windows details came at the price of reduced flexibility. Using Visual Basic meant you didn't need to mess with the sticky details of Windows event loops, but it also made working directly with those events more difficult when you really wanted to. Advanced programmers could still pry off the cover and work at this lower level, but this was somewhat dangerous. If your code didn't handle all the details correctly, it could crash the program and possibly Windows itself.

Visual Basic also followed a path different from that taken by other Windows programming languages such as C++. It provided a more productive development environment and a generally more intuitive syntax. Its syntax for object-oriented development was more restrictive, however. A developer could still build safe, reliable, extensible applications, but it took some experience and care.

Visual Studio .NET addressed many of these shortcomings. It merged the Visual Basic and C++ development environments into an even more powerful tool. It added the C# language (pronounced "C-sharp") and gave all three a common underlying run-time language called Common Language Runtime (CLR). Visual Basic .NET incorporated changes to bring the language more into line with CLR and the other languages. It included more structured error handling, new syntax for declaring and initializing variables, overloaded functions and subroutines, and a more powerful model for creating classes that include true inheritance.

Visual Basic 2005 adds new features that make Visual Basic a more powerful language than ever. It includes new language features such as unsigned data types, operator overloading, and short-circuit logical operators; object-oriented enhancements such as more flexible property procedure accessibility, generics, and custom events; and coding improvements such as Extensible Markup Language (XML) comments, better IntelliSense, and code snippets.

Visual Basic 2005 is the language's second major release. Most of the obvious bugs in the first release (surprisingly few for such a major reshaping of the language) have been ironed out, so there has never been a better time to learn the language. The first release has proven stable and the current release brings new capabilities to Visual Basic programmers. Developers waiting to see what would become of Visual Basic .NET have their answer: it is here to stay.

Should You Use Visual Basic .NET?

A Visual Basic programmer's joke asks, "What's the difference between Visual Basic .NET and C#? About three months!" The implication is that Visual Basic .NET syntax is easier to understand, and building applications with it is faster. Similarly, C# programmers have their jokes about Visual Basic .NET, implying that C# is more powerful.

In fact, Visual Basic .NET is *not* a whole lot easier to use than C#, and C# is *not* significantly more powerful. The basic form of the two languages is very similar. Aside from a few stylistic differences (Visual Basic is line-oriented; C# uses lots of braces and semicolons), the languages are comparable. Both use the Visual Studio development environment, both provide access to the .NET Framework of support classes and tools, and both provide similar syntax for performing basic programming tasks.

In fact, the languages are so similar that many of Microsoft's Web pages lump the two together. For example, the page `http://msdn.microsoft.com/library/en-us/vbcon/html/vboriWhatsNewVB70.asp` is titled "What's New in Visual Basic and Visual C#."

The main difference between these languages is one of style. If you have experience with previous versions of Visual Basic, you will probably find Visual Basic .NET easier to get used to. If you have experience with C++ or Java, you will probably find C# (or Visual C++ or Visual J#) easy to learn.

Visual Basic does have some ties with other Microsoft products. For example, ASP uses Visual Basic to create interactive Web pages. Microsoft Office applications (Word, Excel, PowerPoint, and so forth) and many third-party tools use Visual Basic for Applications (VBA) as a macro programming language. If you know Visual Basic, you have a head start in using these other languages. Active Server Pages (ASP) and Visual Basic for Application (VBA) are based on pre-.NET versions of Visual Basic, so you won't instantly know how to use them, but you'll have a big advantage if you need to learn ASP or VBA.

If you are new to programming, either Visual Basic .NET or C# is a good choice. I think Visual Basic .NET may be a little easier to learn, but I may be slightly biased because I've been using Visual Basic lately. You won't be making a big mistake either way, and you can easily switch later. Of course, if you have already bought this book, you should stick with Visual Basic to get the most benefit.

Who Should Read This Book

This book is intended for programmers of all levels. It describes the Visual Basic .NET language from scratch, so you don't need experience with previous versions of the language. The book also covers many intermediate and advanced topics. It covers topics in enough depth that even experienced developers will discover new tips, tricks, and language details. After you have mastered the language, you may still find useful tidbits throughout the book, and the reference appendices will help you look up easily forgotten details.

The chapters move quickly through the more introductory material. If you have never programmed before and are intimidated by computers, then you might want to read a more introductory book first. If you are a beginner who's not afraid of the computer, then you should have few problems learning Visual Basic .NET from this book.

If you have programmed in any other language, then fundamentals such as variable declarations, data types, and arrays should be familiar to you, so you should have no problem with this book. The index and reference appendices should be particularly useful in helping you translate from the languages you already know into the corresponding Visual Basic syntax.

How This Book Is Organized

You could divide the chapters in this book into four parts plus appendices. The chapters in each part are described here. If you are an experienced programmer, you can use these descriptions to decide which chapters to skim and which to read in detail.

Part I: Getting Started

The chapters in this part of the book explain the basics of Visual Basic .NET programming. They describe the development environment, basic program syntax, and how to interact with standard controls. More advanced topics include how to build custom controls and how to implement drag and drop.

Chapter 1, "IDE," describes the integrated development environment (IDE). It explains the IDE's windows and how to customize the IDE. It also explains tools that provide help while you're programming such features as the Object Browser and the code window's Intellisense.

Chapter 2, "Controls in General," describes general control concepts. It explains how to add controls to a form, how to read and change a control's properties at design time and at run time, and how to use some of the more complicated control properties (such as Dock and Anchor). This chapter shows how to catch and respond to events, and how to change event handlers in code.

Chapter 3, "Program and Module Structure," analyzes a simple Visual Basic program and explains the structure created by Visual Studio. It describes the program's code regions and comments, and tells how you can use similar techniques to make your code more readable and manageable.

Chapter 4, "Data Types, Variables, and Constants," explains the standard data types provided by Visual Basic. It shows how to declare and initialize variables and constants, and explains variable scope. It discusses value and reference types, passing parameters by value or reference, and creating parameter variables on the fly. It also explains how to create arrays, enumerated types, and structures.

Chapter 5, "Operators," describes the operators a program uses to perform calculations. These include mathematical operators (+, *, \), string operators (&), and Boolean operators (And, Or). The chapter explains operator precedence and type conversion issues that arise when an expression combines more than one type of operator (for example, arithmetic and Boolean).

Chapter 6, "Subroutines and Functions," explains how you can use subroutines and functions to break a program into manageable pieces. It describes routine overloading and scope.

Chapter 7, "Program Control Statements," describes the statements that a Visual Basic program uses to control code execution. These include decision statements (If Then Else, Select Case, IIF, Choose) and looping statements (For Next, For Each, Do While, While Do, Repeat Until).

Chapter 8, "Error Handling," explains error handling and debugging techniques. It describes the Try Catch structured error handler in addition to the older On Error statement inherited from earlier versions of Visual Basic. It discusses typical actions a program might take when it catches an error. It also describes techniques for preventing errors and making errors more obvious when they do occur.

Chapter 9, "Introduction to Windows Forms Controls," explains the Visual Basic's standard controls that you can use on Windows forms. It describes the most useful properties, methods, and events provided by these controls, and it gives examples showing how to use them. It also describes cases where these controls rely on each other. For example, several controls such as the ToolBar obtain images from an associated ImageList control.

Chapter 10, "Forms," explains typical uses of forms. It tells how to build partially transparent forms for use as splash, login, and About forms. It describes form cursors and icons, how to override WndProc to intercept a form's Windows messages, how to make a Multiple Document Interface (MDI) application, and how to implement a Most Recently Used (MRU) file list. It does not cover all of the Form object's properties, methods, and events in detail; those are described in Appendix H, "Form Objects."

Chapter 11, "Database Controls and Objects," explains how to use Visual Basic's standard database controls. These include database connection components that handle connections to a database, `DataSet` components that hold data within an application, and data adapter controls that move data between data connections and `DataSets`.

Chapter 12, "Custom Controls," explains how to build your own customized controls that you can then use in other applications. It covers the three main methods for creating a custom control: derivation, composition, and building from scratch. This chapter also provides several examples that you can use as a starting point for controls of your own.

Chapter 13, "Drag and Drop, and the Clipboard," explains how a Visual Basic program can support drag-and-drop operations. It tells how your program can start a drag to another application, how to respond to drag operations started by another application, and how to receive a drop from another application. This chapter also explains how a program can copy data to and from the clipboard. Using the clipboard is similar to certain types of drag-and-drop operations, so these topics fit naturally in one chapter.

Part II: Object-Oriented Programming

The chapters in this part of the book explain fundamental concepts in object-oriented programming (OOP) with Visual Basic. It also describes some of the more important classes and objects that you can use when building an application.

Chapter 14, "OOP Concepts," explains the fundamental ideas behind object-oriented programming. It describes the three main features of OOP: encapsulation, polymorphism, and inheritance. It explains the benefits of these features and tells how you can take advantage of them in Visual Basic.

Chapter 15, "Classes and Structures," explains how to declare and use classes and structures. It explains what classes and structures are, and it describes their differences. It shows the basic declaration syntax and tells how to create instances of classes and structures. It also explains some of the trickier class issues (such as private class scope, declaring events, and shared variables and methods).

Chapter 16, "Namespaces," explains namespaces. It tells how Visual Studio uses namespaces to categorize code and to prevent name collisions. It describes a project's root namespace, tells how Visual Basic uses namespaces to resolve names (such as function and class names), and tells how you can add namespaces to an application yourself.

Chapter 17, "Collection Classes," explains classes included in Visual Studio that you can use to hold groups of objects. It describes the various collection, dictionary, queue, and stack classes; tells how to make strongly typed versions of those classes; and gives some guidance on deciding which class to use under different circumstances.

Chapter 18, "Generics," explains templates that you can use to build new classes designed to work with specific data types. For example, you can build a generic binary tree and then later use it to build classes to represent binary trees of customer orders, employees, or work items.

Part III: Graphics

The chapters in this part of the book describe graphics in Visual Basic .NET. They explain the Graphics Device Interface+ (GDI+) routines that programs use to draw images in Visual Basic. They explain how to draw lines and text; how to draw and fill circles and other shapes; and how to load, manipulate, and save bitmap images. This part also explains how to generate printed output and how to send reports to the screen or to the printer.

Chapter 19, "Drawing Basics," explains the fundamentals of drawing graphics in Visual Basic .NET. It describes the graphics namespaces and the classes they contain. It describes the most important of these classes, `Graphics`, in detail. It also describes the `Paint` event handler and other events that a program should use to keep its graphics up to date.

Chapter 20, "Brushes, Pens, and Paths," explains the most important graphics classes after `Graphics`: `Pen` and `Brush`. It tells how you can use `Pens` to draw solid lines, dashed lines, lines with custom dash patterns, and lines with custom lengthwise stripe patterns. It tells how to use `Brushes` to fill areas with colors, hatch patterns, linear color gradients, color gradients that follow a path, and tiled images. This chapter also describes the `GraphicsPath` class, which represents a series of lines, shapes, curves, and text.

Chapter 21, "Text," explains how to draw strings of text. It shows how to create different kinds of fonts, determine exactly how big text will be when drawn in a particular font, and use GDI+ functions to make positioning text simple. It shows how to use a `StringFormat` object to determine how text is aligned, wrapped, and trimmed, and how to read and define tab stops.

Chapter 22, "Image Processing," explains how to load, modify, and save image files. It shows how to read and write the pixels in an image, and how to save the result in different file formats such as BMP GIF, and JPEG. It tells how to use images to provide auto-redraw features, and how to manipulate an image pixel by pixel, both using a Bitmap's `GetPixel` and `SetPixel` methods and using "unsafe" access techniques that make pixel manipulation much faster than is possible with normal GDI+ methods.

Chapter 23, "Printing," explains different ways that a program can send output to the printer. It shows how you can use the `PrintDocument` object to generate printout data. You can then use the `PrintDocument` to print the data immediately, use a `PrintDialog` control to let the user select the printer and set its characteristics, or use a `PrintPreviewDialog` control to let the user preview the results before printing.

Chapter 24, "Reporting," provides an introduction to Crystal Reports, a tool that makes generating reports in Visual Basic relatively easy. The chapter explains the basics of Crystal Reports and steps through an example that builds a simple report.

Part IV: Interacting with the Environment

The chapters in this part of the book explain how an application can interact with its environment. They show how the program can save and load data in external sources (such as the System Registry, resource files, and text files); work with the computer's screen, keyboard, and mouse; and interact with the user through standard dialog controls.

Chapter 25, "Configuration and Resources," describes some of the ways that a Visual Basic program can store configuration and resource values for use at run time. Some of the most useful of these include environment variables, the Registry, configuration files, and resource files.

Chapter 26, "Streams," explains the classes that a Visual Basic application can use to work with stream data. Some of these classes are `FileStream`, `MemoryStream`, `BufferedStream`, `TextReader`, and `TextWriter`.

Chapter 27, "File-System Objects," describes classes that let a Visual Basic application interact with the file system. These include classes such as `Directory`, `DirectoryInfo`, `File`, and `FileInfo` that make it easy to create, examine, move, rename, and delete directories and files.

Chapter 28, "Useful Namespaces," describes some of the most commonly useful namespaces defined by the .NET Framework. It provides a brief overview of some of the most important System namespaces and gives more detailed examples that demonstrate regular expressions, XML, cryptography, reflection, threading, and Direct3D.

Appendixes

The book's appendices provide a categorized reference of the Visual Basic .NET language. You can use them to quickly review the syntax of a particular command, select from among several overloaded versions of a routine, or refresh your memory of what a particular class can do. The chapters earlier in the book give more context, explaining how to perform specific tasks and why one approach might be preferred over another.

Appendix A, "Useful Control Properties, Methods, and Events," describes properties, methods, and events that are useful with many different kinds of controls.

Appendix B, "Variable Declarations and Data Types," summarizes the syntax for declaring variables. It also gives the sizes and ranges of allowed values for the fundamental data types.

Appendix C, "Operators," summarizes the standard operators such as +, <<, `OrElse`, and `Like`. It also gives the syntax for operator overloading.

Appendix D, "Subroutine and Function Declarations," summarizes the syntax for subroutine, function, and property procedure declarations.

Appendix E, "Control Statements," summarizes statements that control program flow such as `If Then`, `Select Case`, and looping statements.

Appendix F, "Error Handling," summarizes both structured and "classic" error handling. It describes some useful exception classes and gives an example showing how to build a custom exception class.

The Book's Web Site

On the book's Web site, www.vb-helper.com/vb_prog_ref.htm, you can do the following:

❑ Download the examples in this book

❑ Download other Visual Basic programming examples

❑ View updates and corrections

❑ Read other readers' comments and suggestions

This book was written using beta versions of Visual Basic 2005. Microsoft often makes changes between beta versions and the final release (the whole point of the betas is to identify areas that need fixing or modification) and sometimes even produces patch releases shortly after the main product rollout. The book's Web page will include any modifications that the examples need to handle those changes.

If you have corrections or comments of your own, please send them to me at RodStephens@vb-helper. com. I will do my best to keep the Web site as up to date as possible.

Contents

Contents

Contents

Contents

Contents

Contents

Contents

Contents

Contents

Contents

Contents

Contents

Contents

Contents

Contents

IDE

This chapter describes Visual Studio's integrated development environment (IDE). It explains the most important windows, menus, and toolbars that make up the environment, and shows how to customize them to suit your personal preferences. It also explains some of the tools that provide help while you are writing Visual Basic applications.

Even if you are an experienced Visual Basic programmer, you should at least skim this material. The IDE is *extremely* complex and provides hundreds (if not thousands) of commands, menus, toolbars, windows, context menus, and other tools for editing, running, and debugging Visual Basic projects. Even if you have used the IDE for a long time, there are sure to be some features that you have overlooked. This chapter describes some of the most important of those features, and you may discover something useful that you've never noticed before.

Even after you've read this chapter, you should periodically spend some time wandering through the IDE to see what you've missed. Every month or so, spend a few minutes exploring the menus and right-clicking on things to see what their context menus contain. As you become a more proficient Visual Basic programmer, you will find uses for tools that you may have previously dismissed or failed to understand.

It is important to remember that the Visual Studio IDE is extremely customizable. You can move, hide, or modify the menus, toolbars, and windows; create your own toolbars; dock, undock, or rearrange the toolbars and windows; and change the behavior of the built-in text editors (change their indentation, colors for different kinds of text, and so forth).

These capabilities let you display the features you need the most and hide those that are unnecessary for a particular situation. If you need to use the Properties window, you can display it. If you want to make room for a very wide form, you can make it short and wide, and move it to the bottom of the screen. If you have a collection of favorite tools and possibly some you have written yourself, you can put them all in one convenient toolbar. Or you can have several toolbars for working with code, forms in general, and database forms in particular.

This chapter describes the basic Visual Studio development environment as it is initially installed. Because Visual Studio is so flexible, your development environment may not look like the one described here. After you've moved things around a bit to suit your personal preferences, your menus and toolbars may not contain the same commands described here, and other windows may be in different locations or missing entirely.

To avoid confusion, you should probably not customize the IDE's basic menus and toolbars too much. Removing the help commands from the Help menu and adding them to the Edit menu will only cause confusion later. It's less confusing to leave the menus more or less alone. Hide any toolbars you don't want and create new customized toolbars to suit your needs. Then you can find the original standard toolbars if you decide you need them later. The section "Customize" later in this chapter has more to say about rearranging the IDE's components.

This chapter describes the Visual Studio IDE. Before you can understand how to use the IDE to manage Visual Basic projects and solutions, however, you should know what projects and solutions are.

Projects and Solutions

A *project* is a group of files that produces some specific output. This output may be a compiled executable program, a dynamic-link library (DLL) of classes for use by other projects, or a custom control for use on other Windows forms.

A *solution* is a group of one or more projects that should be managed together. For example, suppose that you are building a server application that provides access to your order database. You are also building a client program that each of your sales representatives will use to query the server application. Because these two projects are closely related, it might make sense to manage them in a single solution. When you open the solution, you get instant access to all the files in both projects.

Both projects and solutions can include associated files that are useful for building the application but that do not become part of a final compiled product. For example, a project might include the application's proposal and architecture documents. These are not included in the compiled code, but it is useful to associate them with the project.

When you open the project, Visual Studio lists those documents along with the program files. If you double-click one of these documents, Visual Studio opens the file using an appropriate application. For example, if you double-click a file with a .doc extension, Visual Studio normally opens it with Microsoft Word.

To associate one of these files with a project or solution, right-click the project in the Solution Explorer (more on the Solution Explorer shortly). Select the Add command's Add New Item entry, and use the resulting dialog to select the file you want to add.

Often a Visual Basic solution contains a single project. If you just want to build a small executable program, you probably don't need to include other programming projects in the solution.

Another common scenario is to place Visual Basic code in one project and to place documentation (such as project specifications and progress reports) in another project within the same solution. This keeps the documentation handy whenever you are working on the application but keeps it separate enough that it doesn't clutter the Visual Studio windows when you want to work with the code.

While you can add any file to a project or solution, it's not a good idea to load dozens of unrelated files. While you may sometimes want to refer to an unrelated file while working on a project, the extra clutter brings additional chances for confusion. It will be less confusing to shrink the Visual Basic IDE to an icon and open the file using an external editor such as Word or WordPad. If you won't use a file very often with the project, don't add it to the project.

IDE Overview

Figure 1-1 shows the IDE immediately after starting a new project. The IDE is extremely configurable, so it may not look much like Figure 1-1 after you have rearranged things to your own liking.

If you don't have a reason to modify the IDE's basic arrangement, you should probably leave it alone. Then when you read a magazine article that tells you to use the Project menu's Add Reference command, the command will be where it should be. Using the standard IDE layout also reduces confusion when you need to consult with another developer. It's a lot easier to share tips about using the Format menu if you haven't removed that menu from the IDE.

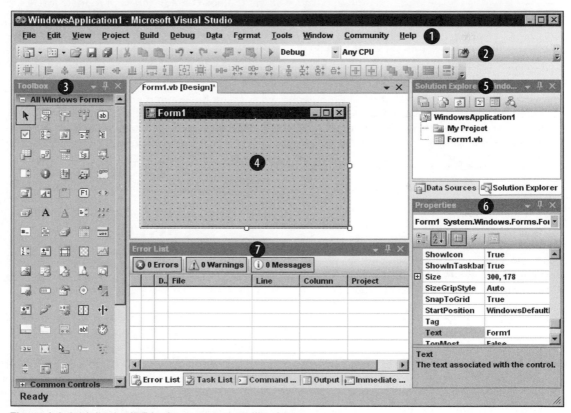

Figure 1-1: Initially the IDE looks more or less like this.

The key pieces of the IDE are labeled with numbers in Figure 1-1. The following list briefly describes each of these pieces.

❑ *(1) Menus* — The menus contain standard Visual Studio commands. These generally manipulate the current solution and the modules it contains, although you can customize the menus as needed. Visual Studio changes the menus, and their contents depending on the object you currently have selected. In Figure 1-1, a Form Designer (marked with the number 4) is open so the IDE is displaying the menus for editing forms.

❑ *(2) Toolbars* — Toolbars contain tools that you can use to perform frequently needed actions. The same commands may be available in menus, but they are easier and faster to use in toolbars. The IDE defines several standard toolbars such as Formatting, Debug, and Image Editor. You can also build your own custom toolbars to hold your favorite tools. Visual Studio changes the toolbars displayed to match the object you currently have selected.

❑ *(3) Toolbox* — The Toolbox contains tools appropriate for the item that you currently have selected and for the project type that you are working on. In Figure 1-1, a Form Designer is selected in a Windows Forms application so the Toolbox contains tools appropriate for a Form Designer. These include Windows Forms controls and components, plus tools in the other Toolbox tabs: Crystal Reports, Data, and Components (plus the General tab is scrolled off the bottom of the Toolbox). You can add other customized tabs to the Toolbox to hold your favorite controls and components. Other project types may display other tools. For example, a Web project would display Web controls and components instead of Windows Forms components.

❑ *(4) Form Designer* — A Form Designer lets you modify the graphical design of a form. Select a control tool from the Toolbox, and click and drag to place an instance of the control on the form. Use the Properties window (marked with the number 6) to change the new control's properties. In Figure 1-1, no control is selected, so the Properties window shows the form's properties.

❑ *(5) Solution Explorer* — The Solution Explorer lets you manage the files associated with the current solution. For example, in Figure 1-1, you could select Form1.vb in the Project Explorer and then click the View Code button (the icon third from the right at the top of the Solution Explorer) to open the form's code editor. You can also right-click an object in the Solution Explorer to get a list of appropriate commands for that object.

❑ *(6) Properties* — The Properties window lets you change an object's properties at design time. When you select an object in a form designer or in the Solution Explorer, the Properties window displays that object's properties. To change a property's value, simply click the property and enter the new value.

❑ *(7) Error List* — The Error List window shows errors and warnings in the current project. For example, if a variable is used and not declared, this list will say so.

If you look at the bottom of Figure 1-1, you'll notice that the Toolbox and Error List windows each have a series of tabs. The Toolbox's other tab displays the Document Outline window, which displays an outline view of a project showing its forms and components.

The Error List window's Output tab shows output printed by the application. Usually an application interacts with the user through its forms and dialogs, but it can display information here to help you debug the code. The Output window also shows informational messages generated by the IDE. For example, when you compile an application, the IDE sends messages here to tell you what it is doing and whether it succeeded.

The following sections describe the major pieces of the IDE in more detail.

Menus

The IDE's menus contain standard Visual Studio commands. These are generally commands that manipulate the project and the modules it contains. Some of the concepts are similar to those used by any Windows application (File\New, File\Save, Help\Contents), but many of the details are specific to Visual Studio programming, so the following sections describe them in a bit more detail.

The menus are customizable, so you can add, remove, and rearrange the menus and the items they contain. This can be quite confusing, however, if you later need to find a command that you have removed from its normal place in the menus. Some developers place extra commands in standard menus, particularly the Tools menu, but it is generally risky to remove standard menu items. Usually it is safest to leave the standard menus alone and make custom toolbars to hold customizations. For more information on this, see the section "Customize" later in this chapter.

Many of the menus' most useful commands are also available in other ways. Many provide shortcut key combinations that make using them quick and easy. For example, Ctrl-N opens the New Project dialog just as if you had selected the File\New Project menu command. If you find yourself using the same command very frequently, look in the menu and learn its keyboard shortcut to save time later.

Many menu commands are also available in standard toolbars. For example, the Debug toolbar contains many of the same commands that are in the Debug menu. If you use a set of menu commands frequently, you may want to display the corresponding toolbar to make using the commands easier.

Visual Studio also provides many commands through context menus. For example, if you right-click on a project in the Solution Explorer, the context menu includes an Add Reference command that displays the Add Reference dialog just as if you had invoked Project\Add Reference. Often it is easier to find a command by right-clicking an object related to whatever you want to do than it is to wander through the menus.

The following sections describe the general layout of the standard menus. You might want to open the menus in Visual Studio as you read these sections, so you can follow along.

Note that Visual Studio displays different menus and different commands in menus depending on what editor is active. For example, when you have a form open in the form editor, Visual Studio displays a Format menu that you can use to arrange controls on the form. When you have a code editor open, the Format menu is hidden because it doesn't apply to code.

File

The File menu, shown in Figure 1-2, contains commands that deal with creating, opening, saving, and closing projects and project files.

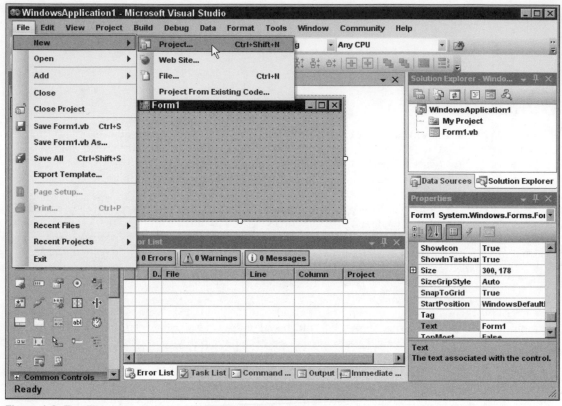

Figure 1-2: The File menu holds commands that deal with the solution and its files.

Following is a description of the commands contained in the File menu and its submenus:

❑   *New* — The New submenu shown in Figure 1-2 contains commands that let you create a new Visual Basic project, Web site project (generally ASP.NET or a Web Service), or file (text file, bitmap, Visual Basic class, icon, and many others). The Project From Existing Code command creates a new project and puts all of the files in a directory in it, optionally including subdirectories.

❑   *New\File* — The New submenu's File command displays the dialog shown in Figure 1-3. The IDE uses integrated editors to let you edit the new file. For example, the simple bitmap editor lets you set a bitmap's size, change its number of colors, and draw on it. When you close the file, Visual Studio asks if you want to save the file and lets you decide where to put it. Note that this doesn't automatically add the file to your current project. You can save the file and use the Project\Add Existing Item command if you want to do so.

❑   *Open* — The Open submenu contains commands that let you open a project or solution, Web site, or file. The Convert command displays the Convert dialog shown in Figure 1-4. From this dialog, you can launch the Visual Basic 2005 Upgrade Wizard, which can help you convert Visual Basic 6 programs to Visual Basic 2005.

❑   *Close* — This command closes the current editor. In Figure 1-2, Form1 is open in the form designer editor. This command would close this editor.

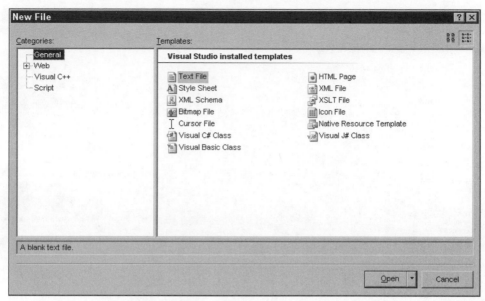

Figure 1-3: The File\New\File command displays this dialog to let you select the new file's type.

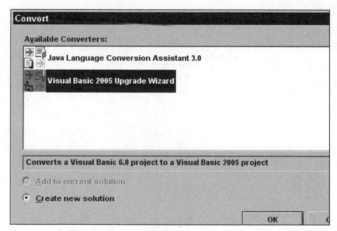

Figure 1-4: The File\Open\Convert command displays this dialog
to help you convert Visual Basic 6 applications to Visual Basic 2005.

❑ *Close Project* — This command closes the entire project and all of the files it contains. If you have a solution open, this command is labeled Close Solution.

❑ *Save Form1.vb* — This command saves the currently open file, in this example, Form1.vb.

❑ *Save Form1.vb As* — This command lets you save the currently open file in a new file.

❑ *Save All* — This command saves all modified files.

❑ *Export Template* — This command displays the dialog shown in Figure 1-5. The Export Template Wizard lets you create project or item templates that you can use later.

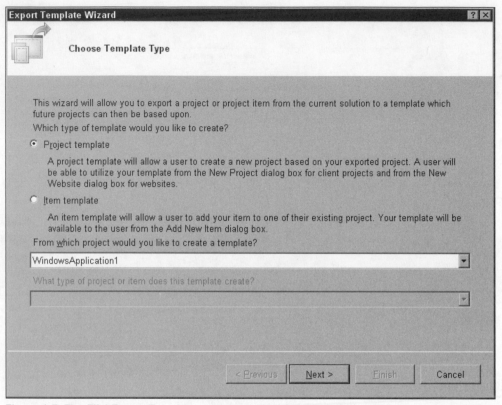

Figure 1-5: The File\Export Template command displays this dialog to help you create project or items templates that you can easily use in other projects.

❑ *Page Setup and Print* — The Page Setup and Print commands let you configure printer settings and print the current document. These commands are enabled only when it makes sense to print the current file. For example, if you are viewing a source code file or a configuration file (which is XML text), you can use these commands. If you are viewing bitmap or a form in design mode, these commands are disabled.

❑ *Recent Files and Recent Projects* — The Recent Files and Recent Projects submenus let you quickly reopen files, projects, and solutions that you have opened recently.

Edit

The Edit menu, shown in Figure 1-6, contains commands that deal with manipulating text and other objects. These include standard commands such as the Undo, Redo, Copy, Cut, and Paste commands that you've seen in other Windows applications.

Following is a description of other commands associated with the Edit menu:

❑ *Cycle Clipboard Ring* — The clipboard ring contains the last several items that you copied into the clipboard. This command copies the previous clipboard ring item to the current location. By using this command repeatedly, you can cycle through the items until you find the one you want.

Figure 1-6: The Edit menu holds commands that deal with manipulating text and other objects.

❑ *Find and Replace\Quick Find* — This command displays a find dialog where you can search the project for specific text. A drop-down lets you indicate whether the search should include only the current document, all open documents, the current project, or the entire solution. Options let you determine such things as whether the text must match case or whole words.

❑ *Find and Replace\Quick Replace* — This command displays the same dialog as the Quick except with some extra controls. It includes a text box where you can specify replacement text, and buttons that let you replace the currently found text or all occurrences of the text.

❑ *Find and Replace\Find in Files* — This command is similar to Quick Find except that it displays its results as a list in a new window. Double-click on an entry in the list to view the occurrence in its file.

❑ *Find and Replace\Replace in Files* — This command is similar to *Quick Replace* except that it displays its results as a list in a new window.

❑ *Go To* — This command lets you jump to a particular line number in the current file.

❑ *Advanced* — The Advanced submenu contains commands for performing more complex document formatting such as converting text to upper- or lowercase, controlling word wrap, and commenting, and uncommenting code.

❑ *Bookmarks* — The Bookmarks submenu lets you add, remove, and clear bookmarks, and move to the next or previous bookmark.

❑ *Outlining* — The Outlining submenu lets you expand or collapse sections of code, and turn outlining on and off.

❑ *IntelliSense* — The IntelliSense gives access to IntelliSense features. For example, its List Members command makes IntelliSense display the current object's properties, methods, and events.

View

The View menu, shown in Figure 1-7, contains commands that let you hide or display different windows and toolbars in the Visual Studio IDE.

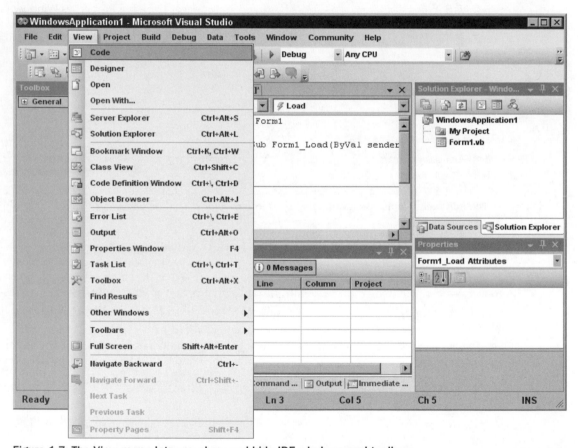

Figure 1-7: The View menu lets you show and hide IDE windows and toolbars.

Following is a description of commands associated with the View menu:

❑ *Code* — The Code command opens the selected file in a code editor window. For example, to edit a form's code, you can click on the form in the Solution Explorer and then select View\Code.

❑ *Designer* — The Designer command opens the selected file in a graphical editor if one is defined for that type of file. For example, if the file is a form, Visual Studio opens it in a graphical form editor. If the file is a class module or a code module, the View menu hides this command because Visual Studio doesn't have a graphical editor for those file types.

❑ *Open* — Opens the selected item with its default editor.

❑ *Open With* — Opens the selected item with an editor of your choosing. For example, you could open a form's code with a text editor.

❑ *Standard windows* — The next several commands shown in Figure 1-7 display the standard IDE windows Solution Explorer, Class View, Resource View, Server Explorer, Properties Window, Bookmark Window, Object Browser, Toolbox, Start Page, and Property Manager. These commands are handy if you have hidden one of the windows and want to get it back. The most useful of these windows are described later in this chapter.

❑ *Web Browser* — The Web Browser submenu lets you display and manage a Web Browser within the IDE. When the Web Browser is visible, the IDE displays a Web toolbar that lets you enter a URL, jump to one of your favorite links, or add the current page to your Web favorites. The Web Browser is particular useful for debugging Web applications because it lets you see what Web pages will look like before you publish them.

❑ *Other Windows* — The Other Windows submenu lists other standard menus that are not listed in the View menu itself. These include the Macro Explorer, Document Outline, Task List, Error List, Command Window, Output, Code Definition Window, and Object Test Bench. It also includes find results windows that list the results of searches you make using the Edit\Find and Replace commands.

❑ *Tab Order* — If a form contains controls, the Tab Order command displays the tab order on top of each control. You can click on the controls in the order you want them to have to set their tab order's quickly and easily.

❑ *Toolbars* — The Toolbars submenu lets you toggle the currently defined toolbars to hide or display them. This submenu lists the standard toolbars in addition to any custom toolbars you have created.

❑ *Full Screen* — The Full Screen command hides all toolbars and windows except for any editor windows that you currently have open. It also hides the Windows taskbar so that the IDE occupies as much space as possible. This gives you the most space possible for working with the files you have open. The command adds a small box to the title bar containing a Full Screen button that you can click to end full-screen mode.

❑ *Navigate Backward, Navigate Forward* — These commands let you move back and forth through the last several locations you visited.

❑ *Next Task, Previous Task* — These commands move through the items in the Task List.

❑ *Property Pages* — This command displays the current item's property pages. For example, if you select an application in Solution Explorer, this command displays the application's property pages similar to those shown in Figure 1-8.

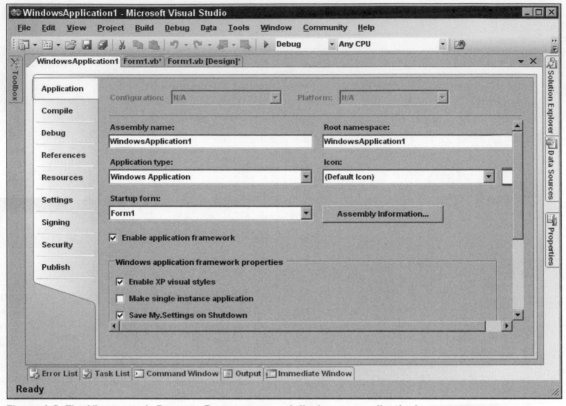

Figure 1-8: The View menu's Property Pages command displays an application's property pages.

Project

The Project menu shown in Figure 1-9 contains commands that let you add and remove items to and from the project. Which commands are available depends on the currently selected item.

Following is a description of commands associated with the Project menu:

❑ *New items* — The first several commands let you add new items to the project. These commands are fairly self-explanatory. For example, the Add Class command adds a new class module to the project. Later chapters explain how to use each of these file types.

❑ *Add New Item* — The Add New Item command displays the dialog shown in Figure 1-10. The dialog lets you select from a wide assortment of items such as text files, bitmap files, and class modules.

❑ *Add Existing Item* — The Add Existing Item command lets you browse for a file and add it to the project.

❑ *Exclude From Project* — This command removes the selected item from the project. Note that this does not delete the item's file; it just removes it from the project.

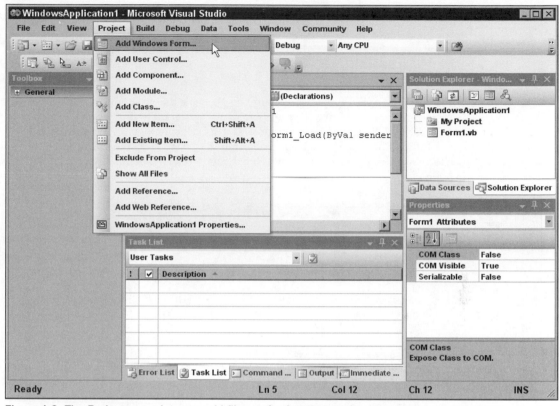

Figure 1-9: The Project menu lets you add files and references to the currently selected project.

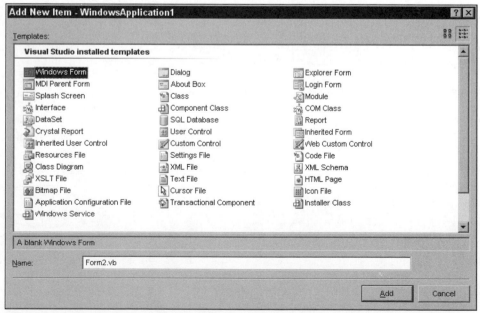

Figure 1-10: The Project menu's Add New Item command lets you add a wide variety of items to the project.

❑ *Show All Files* — The Show All Files command makes Solution Explorer list files that are normally hidden. These include resource files corresponding to forms, hidden partial classes such as designer-generated form code, resource files, and files in the `obj` and `bin` directories that are automatically created by Visual Studio when it compiles your program. Normally, you don't need to work with these files, so they are hidden. Select this command to show them. Select the command again to hide them.

❑ *Add Reference* — The Add Reference command displays the dialog shown in Figure 1-11. Select the category of the external object, class, or library that you want to find. For a .NET component, select the .NET tab. For a Component Object Model (COM) component such as an ActiveX library or control built using Visual Basic 6, select the COM tab. Select the Projects tab to add a reference to another Visual Studio project. Click the Browse tab to manually locate the file you want to reference.

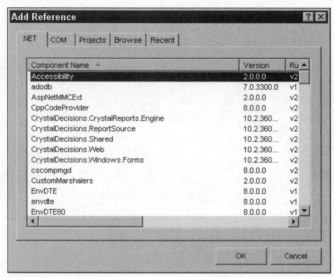

Figure 1-11: Use the Add Reference dialog to add references to external libraries.

Scroll through the list of references until you find the one you want and select it. You can use Shift-Click and Ctrl-Click to select more than one library at the same time. When you have made your selections, click OK to add the references to the project. After you have added a reference to the project, your code can refer to the reference's public objects. For example, if the file

MyMathLibrary.dll defines a class named MathTools and that class defines a public function Fibonacci, a project with a reference to this DLL could use the following code.

```
Dim math_tools As New MyMathLibrary.MathTools
MsgBox("Fib(5) = " & math_tools.Fibonacci(5))
```

❑ *Add Web Reference* — The Add Web Reference command displays the dialog shown in Figure 1-12. You can use this dialog to find Web Services and add references to them so your project can invoke them across the Internet.

❑ *WindowsApplication1 Properties* — This command displays the application's property pages shown in Figure 1-13.

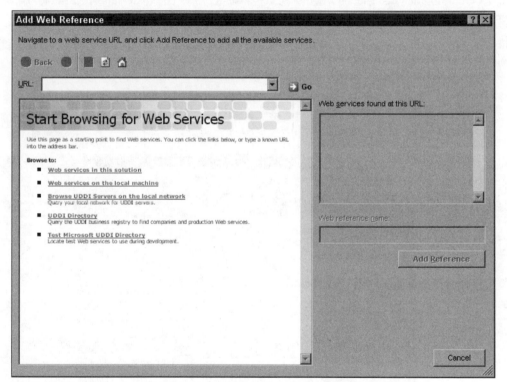

Figure 1-12: Use the Add Web Reference dialog to add references to Web Services.

In Figure 1-13, the Toolbox, Solution Explorer, Properties window, Errors List, and other secondary windows have been hidden to make more room for the large Properties page. You can see these other windows' icons lurking along the left, right, and bottom edges of the figure.

Click the tabs on the left to view and modify different types of application settings. You can leave many of the property values alone and many are set in other ways. For example, by default, the Assembly name and Root namespace values shown in Figure 1-13 are set to the name of the project when you first create it.

There are three properties on the Compile tab shown in Figure 1-14 that deserve special mention.

First, Option Explicit determines whether Visual Basic requires you to declare all variables before using them. Leaving this option turned off can sometimes lead to subtle bugs. For example, the following code is intended to print a list of even numbers between 0 and 10. Unfortunately, a typographical error makes the Debug.WriteLine statement print the value of the variable j not i. Because j is never initialized, the code prints out a bunch of blank values. If you set Option Strict to On, the compiler complains that the variable j is not declared and the problem is easy to fix.

```
For i = 1 To 10
    If i Mod 2 = 0 Then Debug.WriteLine(j)
Next i
```

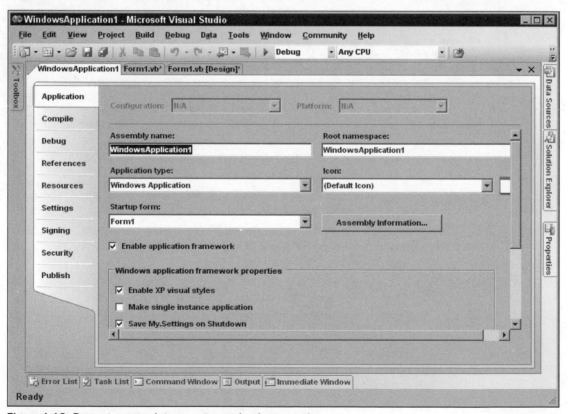

Figure 1-13: Property pages let you set a project's properties.

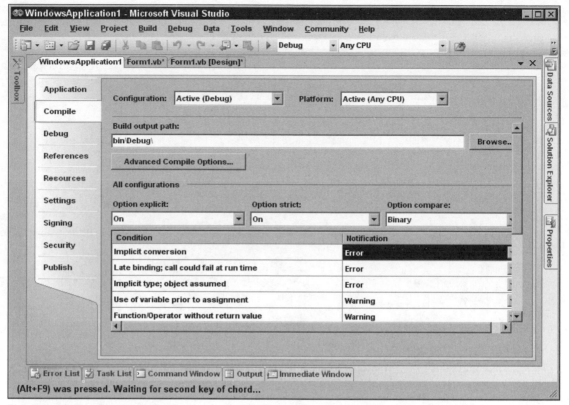

Figure 1-14: The Compile tab contains important properties for controlling code generation.

The second compiler option is Option Strict. When this option is turned off, Visual Studio allows your code to implicitly convert from one data type to another, even if the types are not always compatible. For example, Visual Basic will allow the following code to try to copy the string s into the integer i. If the value in the string happens to be a number, as in the first case, this works. If the string is not a number, as in the second case, this fails at run time.

```
Dim i As Integer
Dim s As String
s = "10"
i = s          ' This works.
s = "Hello"
i = s          ' This Fails.
```

If you set Option Strict to On, the IDE warns you that the two data types are incompatible, so you can easily resolve the problem while you are writing the code. You can still use conversion functions such as CInt, Int, and Integer.Parse to convert a string into an Integer, but you must take explicit action to do so. This makes you think about the code and reduces the chances that the conversion is just an accident. This also helps you use the correct data types and avoid unnecessary conversions that may make your program slower.

To avoid confusion and long debugging sessions, you should always set Option Explicit On and Option Strict On. You can turn them on for a project using the project page. To make them on by default for new projects, open the Tools menu and select Options. Open the Projects and Solutions folder, select the VB Defaults page, and turn the options on, as shown in Figure 1-15.

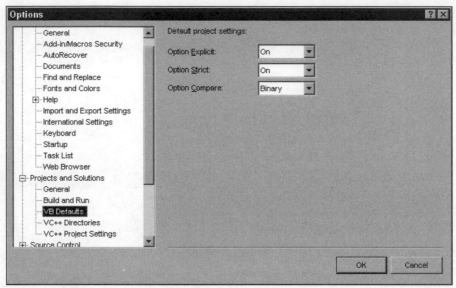

Figure 1-15: The Projects and Solutions folder's VB Defaults page lets you set default values for Option Explicit and Option Strict.

The final compiler directive, Option Compare, can take the values `Binary` or `Text`. If you set Option Compare to `Binary`, Visual Basic compares strings using their binary representations. If you set Option Compare to `Text`, Visual Basic compares strings using a case-insensitive method that depends on your computer's localization settings. Option Compare Binary is faster, but may not always produce the result you want.

If you select a solution and then invoke the Project menu's Properties command, Visual Studio displays the Solution Properties Pages dialog shown in Figure 1-16. Select an item on the left to view, and modify the corresponding values on the right.

Build

The Build menu, shown in Figure 1-17, contains commands that let you compile projects within a solution.

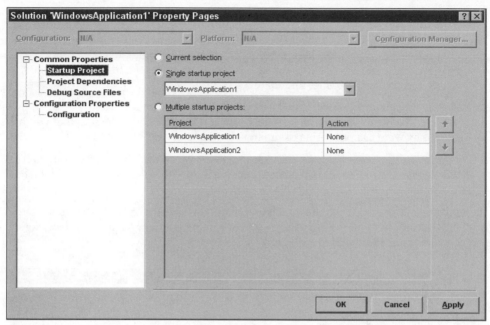

Figure 1-16. The Solution Properties Pages dialog lets you set solution properties.

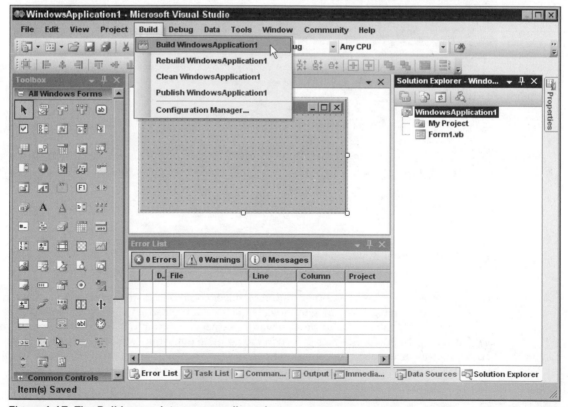

Figure 1-17: The Build menu lets you compile projects.

Following is a description of commands associated with the Build menu:

❑ *Build WindowsApplication1* — This command compiles the currently selected project, in this case the project WindowsApplication1. Visual Studio examines the project's files to see if any have changed since the last time it compiled the project. If any of the files have changed, Visual Studio recompiles those files to update the result.

❑ *Rebuild WindowsApplication1* — This command recompiles the currently selected project from scratch. The *Build WindowsApplication1* command compiles only the files that you have modified since they were last built. This command rebuilds every file.

❑ *Clean WindowsApplication1* — This command removes temporary and intermediate files that were created while building the application, leaving only the source files and the final result .exe and .dll files.

❑ *Publish WindowsApplication1* — This command displays the Publish Wizard shown in Figure 1-18. It can walk you through the process of making your application available for distribution on a local file, file share, FTP site, or Web site.

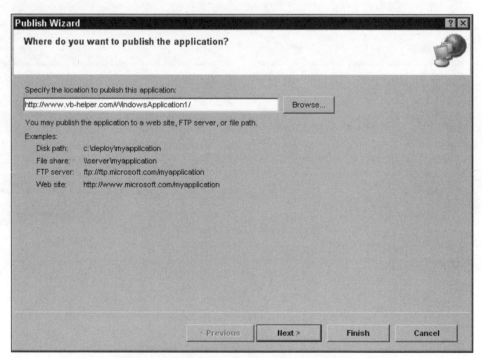

Figure 1-18: The Publish Wizard helps you deploy an application.

❑ *Configuration Manager* — The Configuration Manager command displays the dialog shown in Figure 1-19. You can use this dialog to indicate the type of build you want to use for each project (debug or release), and the platforms you want to target (for example Itanium, x64, or x86). You can also use the Build check boxes shown in the figure to determine which projects get built. You can use this feature to skip compilation of some projects within the solution. If you find that some parts of a solution are not compiling, check the Configuration Manager.

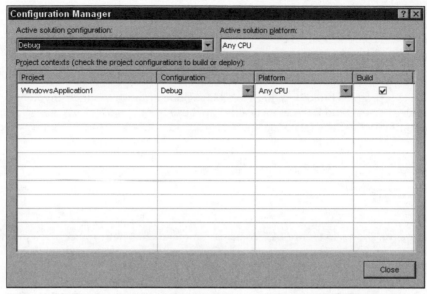

Figure 1-19: The Configuration Manager lets you manage project builds.

Release configurations use more optimizations than Debug configurations, so they provide smaller, faster executable programs. They do not include support for debugging, however, so you cannot debug a program compiled for release.

In the "Active solution configuration" drop-down, select the <New...> entry to create a new configuration. When you select this entry, Visual Studio displays the New Solution Configuration dialog shown in Figure 1-20. Enter the name you want to give the configuration, select the existing configuration from which it should copy default values, and click OK.

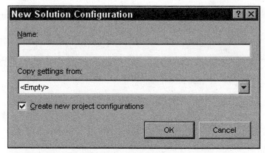

Figure 1-20: The New Solution Configuration dialog lets you create new configurations.

The "Active solution configuration" drop-down also contains an item labeled <Edit...>. If you select this entry, Visual Studio displays a dialog where you can rename or remove configurations.

Use the drop-downs and check boxes in the grid to select features for the solution's projects. For example, if the solution contains several projects, you could flag some to compile using the Debug configuration and others to compile using the Release configuration. If you then rebuilt the solution, you would be able to debug some of the projects but not all of them. This approach may be useful if you want to give some of the projects to customers in their release versions while you keep working on others.

If you uncheck a project's Build box, that project is excluded from any builds. If you build the solution, it is not compiled. Visual Studio writes its results into the Output window and counts the skipped project in its final summary line. The following line shows an example where one project was compiled and one skipped.

```
========== Build: 1 succeeded or up-to-date, 0 failed, 1 skipped ==========
```

Debug

The Debug menu, shown in Figure 1-21, contains commands that help you debug a program. These commands help you run the program in the debugger, move through the code, set and clear breakpoints, and generally follow the code's execution to see what it's doing and hopefully what it's doing wrong.

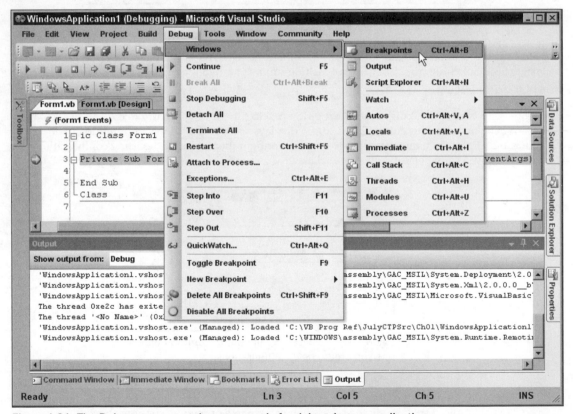

Figure 1-21: The Debug menu contains commands for debugging an application.

Effectively using these debugging techniques can make finding problems in the code much easier, so you should spend some time learning how to use these tools. They can mean the difference between finding a tricky error in minute, hours, or days.

The commands visible in the Debug window change, depending on several conditions such as the type of file you have open, whether the program is running, the line of code that contains the cursor, and whether that line contains a breakpoint. This section discusses the menu items shown in Figure 1-21. You will see other menus items under different circumstances.

The following list briefly describes the Debug menu's commands.

- ❑ *Windows* — This submenu's commands display other debugging-related windows. This submenu is described in more detail in the following section, "The Debug\Windows Submenu."

- ❑ *Continue* — This command resumes program execution. The program runs until it finishes, it reaches another breakpoint, or you stop it.

- ❑ *Break All* — This command stops execution of all programs running within the debugger. This may include more than one program if you are debugging more than one application at the same time. This can be useful, for example, if two programs work closely together.

- ❑ *Stop Debugging* — This command halts the program's execution and ends its debugging session. The program stops immediately, so it does not get a chance to execute any cleanup code.

- ❑ *Detach All* — This command detaches the debugger from any processes to which it is attached. Note that this does not stop those processes.

- ❑ *Terminate All* — This command terminates any processes to which the debugger is attached.

- ❑ *Restart* — This command stops the currently running process and restarts the startup project.

- ❑ *Attach to Process* — This command displays the dialog shown in Figure 1-22 to let you attach the debugger to a running process. Select the process to which you want to attach and click Attach.

- ❑ *Exceptions* — This command displays the dialog shown in Figure 1-23. If you check a Thrown box, the debugger stops whenever the selected type of error occurs. If you check a User-unhandled box, the debugger stops when the selected type of error occurs and the program does not catch it with error handling code. For example, suppose that your code calls a subroutine that causes a divide-by-zero exception. Use the dialog to select Common Language Runtime Exceptions/System/System.DivideByZeroException (use the Find button to find it quickly). If you check the Thrown box, the debugger stops in the subroutine when the divide-by-zero exception occurs even if the code is contained in an error handler. If you check the User-unhandled box, the debugger stops only if no error handler is active when the error occurs.

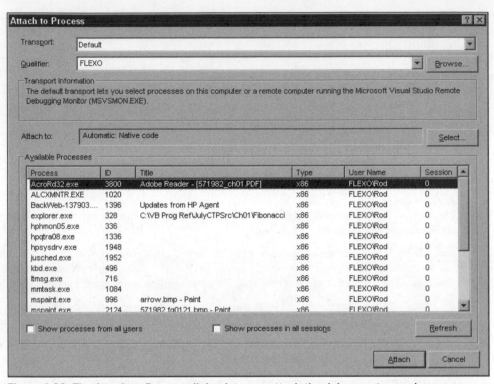

Figure 1-22: The Attach to Process dialog lets you attach the debugger to running processes.

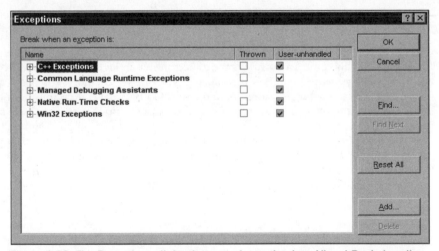

Figure 1-23: The Exceptions dialog lets you determine how Visual Basic handles uncaught exceptions.

❑ *Step Into* — This command makes the debugger execute the current line of code. If that code invokes a function, subroutine, or some other procedure, the point of execution moves into that procedure. It is not always obvious whether a line of code invokes a procedure. For example, a line of code that sets an object's property may be simply setting a value or invoking a property procedure.

❑ *Step Over* — This command makes the debugger execute the current line of code. If that code invokes a function, subroutine, or some other procedure, the debugger calls that routine but does not step into it, so you don't need to step through its code. However, if a breakpoint is set inside that routine, execution will stop at the breakpoint.

❑ *Step Out* — This command makes the debugger run until it leaves the routine it is currently executing. Execution pauses when the program reaches the line of code that called this routine.

❑ *QuickWatch* — This command displays a dialog that gives information about the selected code object. Figure 1-24 shows the dialog displaying information about a `TextBox` control named `txtDirectory`. If you look closely, you can see some of the control's properties including `TabIndex`, `TabStop`, `Tag,` and `Text`.

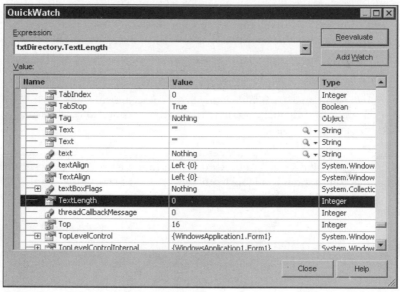

Figure 1-24: The QuickWatch dialog lets you examine an object's properties and optionally set a new watch on it.

If you double-click on a property's value, you can change it within the dialog. If you click the Add Watch button, the debugger adds the expression to the Watch window shown in Figure 1-25. You can also highlight a variable's name in the code and drag and drop it into a Watch window to create a watch very quickly. Right-click a watch in this window and select Delete Watch to remove it.

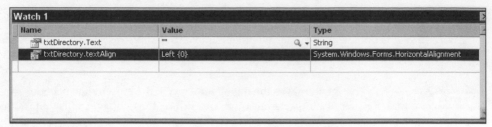

Figure 1-25: The Watch window lets you easily track expression values.

❑ *Toggle Breakpoint* — This command toggles whether the current code line contains a breakpoint. When execution reaches a line with an active breakpoint, execution pauses so you can examine the code and program variables. You can also toggle a line's breakpoint by clicking on the margin to the left of the line in the code editor. In Figure 1-21, line number 4 displays a circle containing an arrow on the left, indicating that it has a breakpoint (the circle) and that it is the current line of execution (the arrow). The following line also contains a breakpoint, and line 7 contains a disabled breakpoint, indicated by a hollow circle in the left margin.

❑ *New Breakpoint* — This submenu contains the Break At Function command. This command displays a dialog that lets you specify a function where the program should break.

❑ *Delete All Breakpoints* — This command removes all breakpoints from the entire solution.

❑ *Enable All Breakpoints* — This command reenables any disabled breakpoints. The Enable All Breakpoints command is available if any breakpoints are currently disabled. Note that you can right-click a line of code that contains a disabled breakpoint and select Enable Breakpoint to enable only that breakpoint.

❑ *Disable All Breakpoints* — This command temporarily disables all the solution's breakpoints. The breakpoints are still defined but they don't interrupt the program's execution. The Disable All Breakpoints command is available if any breakpoints are currently enabled. Note that you can right-click a line of code that contains a breakpoint and select Disable Breakpoint to disable only that breakpoint.

The Debug\Windows Submenu

The Debug menu's Windows submenu, shown in Figure 1-26, contains commands that display debugging-related windows. The following list briefly describes these commands. The two sections that follow describe some of the more complicated windows in greater detail.

❑ *Breakpoints* — This command displays the Breakpoints window shown in Figure 1-27. This dialog shows the breakpoints, their locations, and their conditions. Check or uncheck the boxes on the left to enable or disable breakpoints. Right-click a breakpoint to edit its location, condition, hit count, and action. Use the dialog's toolbar to create a new function breakpoint, delete a breakpoint, delete all breakpoints, enable or disable all breakpoints, go to a breakpoint's source code, and change the columns displayed by the dialog. Right-click on a breakpoint to change its condition (a condition that determines whether the breakpoint is activated), hit count (a count that determines whether the breakpoint is activated), and "When Hit" (action to take when activated). See the section "The Breakpoints Window" later in this chapter for more detail.

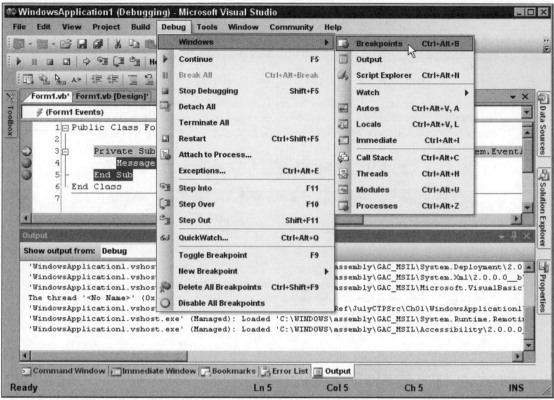

Figure 1-26: The Debug menu's Windows submenu contains commands that display debugging-related windows.

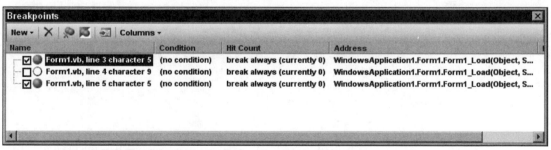

Figure 1-27: The Breakpoints window helps you manage breakpoints.

❑ *Output* — This command displays the Output window. This window displays compilation results and output produced by Debug and Trace statements.

❑ *Script Explorer* — This command displays the Script Explorer, which can help you debug script code written in VBScript or JScript.

❑ *Watch* — The Watch submenu contains the commands Watch 1, Watch 2, Watch 3, and Watch 4. These commands display four different watch windows. When you create a watch using the

Debug menu's QuickWatch command described earlier, the new watch is placed in the Watch 1 window (shown in Figure 1-25). You can click and drag watches from one watch window to another to make a copy of the watch in the second window. You can also click on the Name column in the empty line at the bottom of a watch window and enter an expression to watch. One useful IDE trick is to drag watch windows 2, 3, and 4 onto Watch 1 so that they all become tabs on the same window. Then you can easily use the tabs to group and examine four sets of watches.

❑ *Autos* — This command displays the Autos window shown in Figure 1-28. This window displays the values of local and global variables used in the current line of code and in the three lines before and after it.

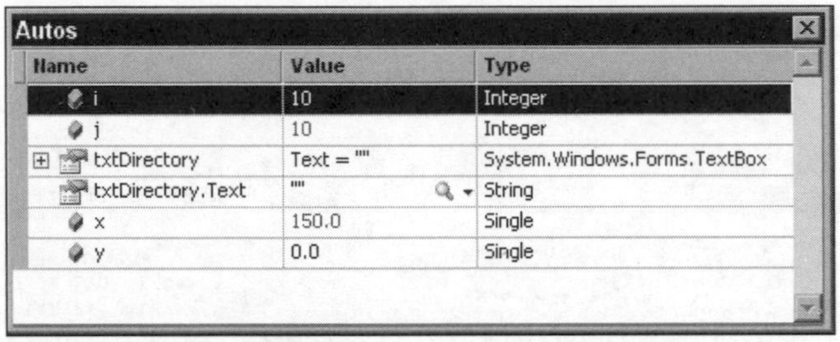

Figure 1-28: The Autos window displays the variables used in the current code statement and the three statements before and the three after.

❑ *Locals* — This command displays the Locals window shown in Figure 1-29. The Locals window displays the values of variables defined in the local context. To change a value, click on it and enter the new value. Click the plus and minus signs to the left of a value to expand or collapse it. For example, the Me entry shown in Figure 1-29 is an object with lots of properties that have their own values. Click the plus sign to expand the object's entry and view its properties. Those properties may also be objects, so you may be able to expand them further.

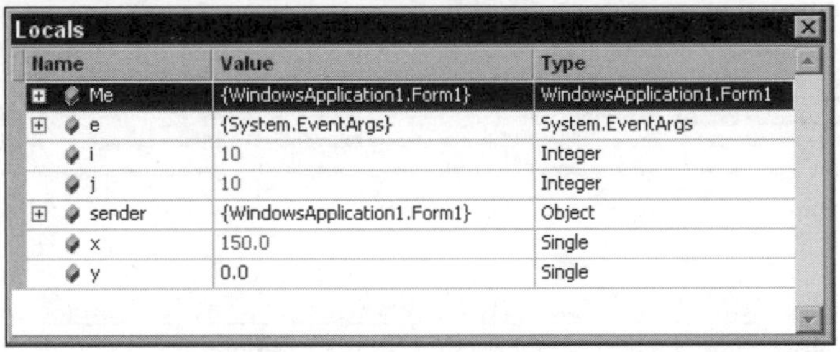

Figure 1-29: The Locals window displays the values of variables defined in the local context.

❑ *Immediate* — This command displays the Immediate window, where you can type and execute ad hoc Visual Basic statements. The section "The Command and Immediate Windows" later in this chapter describes this window in a bit more detail.

❑ *Call Stack* — This command displays the Call Stack window shown in Figure 1-30. This window lists the routines that have called other routines to reach the program's current point of execution. In this example, the program is at the line 20 in function `SearchDatabase`. That function was called by function `FindEmployee` at line 17, and that function was called by the `Form_Load` event handler. Double-click on a line to jump to the corresponding code in the program's call stack. This technique lets you move up the call stack to examine the code that called the routines that are running. This can be a very effective technique when you need to find out what code is calling a particular routine.

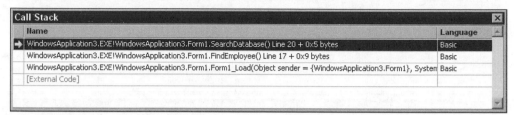

Figure 1-30: The Call Stack window shows which routines have called which to get to the program's current point of execution.

❏ *Threads* — This command displays the Threads window shown in Figure 1-31. A *thread* is a separate execution path that is running. A multithreaded application can have several threads running to perform more than one task at the same time. The Threads window lets you control the threads' priority and suspended status. The last line has the location `WindowsApplication1.Form1.SearchDatabase`, indicating that this thread is executing the `SearchDatabase` routine in the Form1 module in program `WindowsApplication1`. The arrow on the left indicates that this is the currently active thread.

ID	Name	Location	Priority	Suspend
3580				0
1260	<No Name>		Highest	0
1292	<No Name>		Normal	0
3664	<No Name>		Normal	0
2064	<No Name>		Normal	0
1892	<No Name>		Normal	0
2392	<No Name>		Normal	0
➡ 4068	<No Name>	WindowsApplication3.Form1.SearchDatabase	Normal	0

Figure 1-31: The Threads window displays information about the program's threads of execution.

Right-click a thread and select Freeze to suspend it. Select Thaw to make it resume execution. Double-click a thread or right-click it and select Switch To Thread to activate that thread.

❏ *Modules* — This command displays the Modules window shown in Figure 1-32. This window displays information about the DLL and EXE files used by the program. It shows each module's file name and path. It indicates whether the module is optimized, whether it is your code (versus an installed library), and whether debugging symbols are loaded. Scrolled off the right edge of Figure 1-32, the window shows each module's load order (lower-numbered modules are loaded first), the module's version, timestamp, and the process using the module. Click on a column to sort the modules by that column.

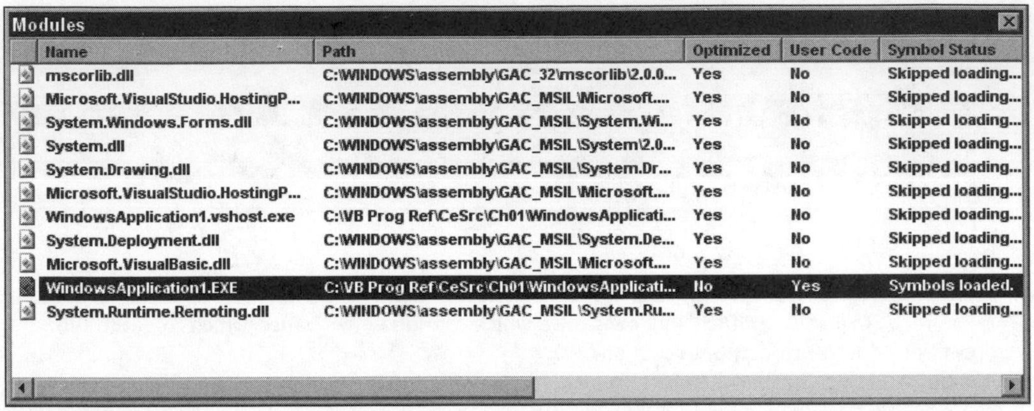

Name	Path	Optimized	User Code	Symbol Status
mscorlib.dll	C:\WINDOWS\assembly\GAC_32\mscorlib\2.0.0...	Yes	No	Skipped loading...
Microsoft.VisualStudio.HostingP...	C:\WINDOWS\assembly\GAC_MSIL\Microsoft....	Yes	No	Skipped loading...
System.Windows.Forms.dll	C:\WINDOWS\assembly\GAC_MSIL\System.Wi...	Yes	No	Skipped loading...
System.dll	C:\WINDOWS\assembly\GAC_MSIL\System\2.0...	Yes	No	Skipped loading...
System.Drawing.dll	C:\WINDOWS\assembly\GAC_MSIL\System.Dr...	Yes	No	Skipped loading...
Microsoft.VisualStudio.HostingP...	C:\WINDOWS\assembly\GAC_MSIL\Microsoft....	Yes	No	Skipped loading...
WindowsApplication1.vshost.exe	C:\VB Prog Ref\CeSrc\Ch01\WindowsApplicati...	Yes	No	Skipped loading...
System.Deployment.dll	C:\WINDOWS\assembly\GAC_MSIL\System.De...	Yes	No	Skipped loading...
Microsoft.VisualBasic.dll	C:\WINDOWS\assembly\GAC_MSIL\Microsoft....	Yes	No	Skipped loading...
WindowsApplication1.EXE	C:\VB Prog Ref\CeSrc\Ch01\WindowsApplicati...	No	Yes	Symbols loaded.
System.Runtime.Remoting.dll	C:\WINDOWS\assembly\GAC_MSIL\System.Ru...	Yes	No	Skipped loading...

Figure 1-32: The Modules window displays information about the modules used by the program.

❑   *Processes* — This window lists processes that are attached to the Visual Studio session. This includes any programs launched by Visual Studio and processes that you attached to using the Debug menu's Attach to Process command.

The Breakpoints Window

A *breakpoint* is a line of code that you have flagged to stop execution. When the program reaches that line, execution stops and Visual Studio displays the code in a code editor window. This lets you examine or set variables, see which routine called the one containing the code, and otherwise try to figure out what the code is doing.

The Breakpoints window lists all the breakpoints you have defined for the program. This is useful for a couple of reasons. First, if you define a lot of breakpoints, it can be hard to find them all later. While other commands let you disable, enable, or remove all of the breakpoints at once, there are times when you may need to find a particular breakpoint.

A common debugging strategy is to comment out broken code, add new code, and set a breakpoint near the modification so that you can see how the new code works. When you have finished testing the code, you probably want to remove either the old or new code, so you don't want to blindly remove all of the program's breakpoints. The Breakpoints window lists all of the breakpoints and, if you double-click a breakpoint in the list, you can easily jump to the code that holds it.

The Breakpoints window also lets you modify the breakpoints you have defined. Check or uncheck the boxes on the left to enable or disable breakpoints. Use the dialog's toolbar to enable or disable all breakpoints, clear all breakpoints, or jump to a breakpoint's source code.

Right-click a breakpoint and select Condition to display the dialog shown in Figure 1-33. By default, a breakpoint stops execution whenever it is reached. You can use this dialog to add an additional condition that determines whether the breakpoint activates when reached. In this example, the breakpoint stops execution only if the expression $(i = j)$ And $(i > 20)$ is True when the code reaches the breakpoint. Note that specifying a breakpoint condition can slow execution considerably.

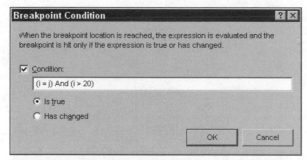

Figure 1-33: The Breakpoint Condition dialog lets you specify a condition that determines whether Visual Studio stops at the breakpoint.

Right-click a breakpoint and select Hit Count to display the Breakpoint Hit Count dialog shown in Figure 1-34. Each time the code reaches a breakpoint, it increments the breakpoint's hit count. You can use this dialog to make the breakpoint's activation depend on the hit count's value.

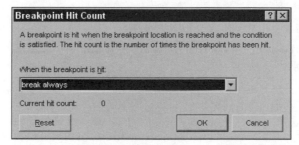

Figure 1-34: The Breakpoint Hit Count dialog lets you make a breakpoint's activation depend on the number of times the code has reached it.

From the drop-down list you can select the options "break always," "break when the hit count is equal to," "break when the hit count is a multiple of," or "break when the hit count is greater than or equal to." If you select any but the first option, you can enter a value in the text box and the program will pause execution when the breakpoint has been reached the appropriate number of times. For example, if you select the option "break when the hit count is a multiple of" and enter "2" into the text box, then execution will pause every other time it reaches the breakpoint.

Right-click a breakpoint and select When Hit to display the When Breakpoint Is Hit dialog shown in Figure 1-35. This dialog lets you specify the actions that Visual Basic takes when the breakpoint is activated. Check the "Print a message" box to make the program display a message in the Output window. Check the "Run a macro" box to make the program execute a VBA macro. Check the "Continue execution" box to make the program continue running without stopping.

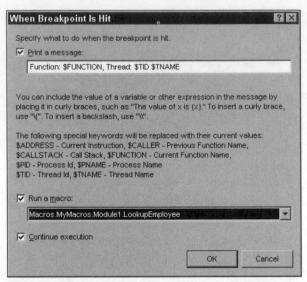

Figure 1-35: The When Breakpoint Is Hit Condition dialog lets you determine what actions Visual Basic takes when the breakpoint is activated.

The Command and Immediate Windows

The Command and Immediate windows both allow you to execute commands while the program is stopped in the debugger. One of the more useful commands in each of these windows is the `Debug.Print` statement. For example, the command `Debug.Print x` displays the value of the variable x.

You can use a question mark as an abbreviation for `Debug.Print`. The following text shows how the command might appear in the Command window. Here the > symbol is the command prompt provided by the window and 123 is the result: the value of variable x. In the Immediate window, the statement would not include the ">" character.

```
>? x
123
```

The command `>immed` tells the Command window to open the Immediate window. Conversely, the command `>cmd` tells the Immediate window to open the Command window.

While there is some overlap between these two windows, they serve two mostly different purposes. The Command window can issue commands to the Visual Studio IDE. Typically, these are commands that appear in menus or toolbars, or that could appear in menus and toolbars. For example, the following command uses the Debug menu's QuickWatch command to open a QuickWatch window for the variable `first_name`.

```
>Debug.QuickWatch first_name
```

One particularly useful command is `Tools.Alias`. This command lists command aliases defined by the IDE. For example, it indicates that `?` is the alias for `Debug.Print` and that `??` is the alias for `Debug.QuickWatch`.

The Command window includes some IntelliSense support. If you type the name of a menu, for example Debug or Tools, IntelliSense will display the commands available within that menu.

While the Command window issues commands to the IDE, the Immediate window executes Visual Basic statements. For example, suppose that you have written a subroutine named `CheckPrinter`. Then the following statement in the Immediate window executes that subroutine.

```
CheckPrinter
```

Executing subroutines in the Immediate window lets you quickly and easily test routines without writing user interface code to handle all possible situations. You can call a subroutine or function, passing it different parameters to see what happens. If you set breakpoints within the routine, the debugger will pause there.

Similarly, you can also set the values of global variables and then call routines that use them. The following Immediate window commands set the value of the `m_PrinterName` variable and then calls the `CheckPrinter` subroutine.

```
m_PrinterName = "LP_REMOTE"
CheckPrinter
```

You can execute much more complex statements in the Command and Intermediate windows. For example, suppose that your program uses the following statement to open a file for reading.

```
Dim fs As FileStream = File.OpenRead( _
    "C:\Program Files\Customer Orders\Summary" & _
    datetime.Now().ToString("yymmdd") & ".dat")
```

Suppose that the program is failing because some other part of the program is deleting the file. You can type the following code (all on one line) into the Immediate window to see if the file exists. As you step through different pieces of the code, you can use this statement again to see if the file has been deleted.

```
?System.IO.File.Exists("C:\Program Files\Customer Orders\Summary" & _
DateTime.Now().ToString("yymmdd") & ".dat")
```

The window evaluates the complicated string expression to produce a file name. It then uses the `System.IO.File.Exists` command to determine whether the file exists and displays `True` or `False` accordingly.

Data

The Data menu, shown in Figure 1-36, contains commands that deal with data and data sources. Some of the commands in this menu are only visible and enabled if you are designing a form and that form contains the proper data objects.

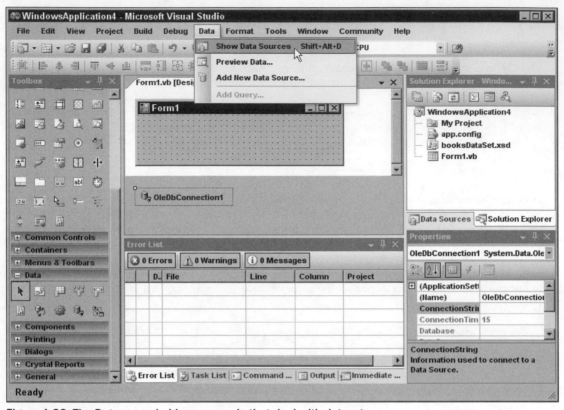

Figure 1-36: The Data menu holds commands that deal with datasets.

The following list describes commands shown in Figure 1-36:

❑   *Show Data Sources* — This command displays the Data Sources window, where you can work with the program's data sources. For example, you can drag and drop tables and fields from this window onto a form to create controls bound to the data.

❑   *Preview Data* — This command displays a dialog that lets you load data into a `DataSet` and view it at design time.

❑   *Add New Data Source* — This command displays the Data Source Configuration Wizard, which walks you through the process of adding a data source to the project.

❑   *Add Query* — This command is available when you are designing a form and have selected a data bound control such as a `DataGridView` or bound `TextBox`. This command opens a dialog where you can specify a query to add to the form. This places a `ToolStrip` on the form containing `TooStripButton` that populates the bound control by executing the query.

Format

The Format menu, shown in Figure 1-37, contains commands that arrange controls on a form. The following list describes the Format menu's submenus:

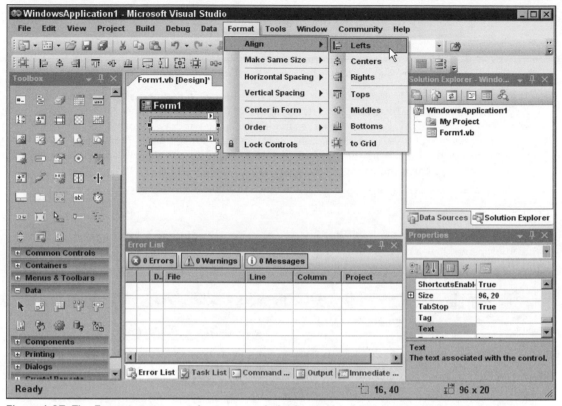

Figure 1-37: The Format menu contains commands for formatting and arranging controls on a form.

❑ *Align* — This submenu contains commands that align the controls you have selected in various ways. It contains the commands Lefts, Centers, Rights, Tops, Middles, Bottoms, and "to Grid." For example, the Lefts command aligns the controls so their left edges line up nicely. The "to Grid" command snaps the controls to the nearest grid position. This is useful if you have moved some controls off of the alignment grid, possibly by using one of the other Align commands or by changing a control's Location property in the Properties window.

❑ *Make Same Size* — This submenu contains commands that change the size of the controls you have selected. It contains the commands Width, Height, Both, and "Size to Grid." The "Size to Grid" command adjusts the selected controls' widths so that they are a multiple of the alignment grid size. The other commands give the selected controls the same width, height, or both.

❑ *Horizontal Spacing* — This submenu contains commands that change the spacing between the controls you have selected. It contains the commands Make Equal, Increase, Decrease, and Remove. For example, if you have selected three controls, the Make Equal command makes the spacing between the first two the same as the spacing between the second two. This can be handy for making columns that line up nicely.

❑ *Vertical Spacing* — This submenu contains the same commands as the Horizontal Spacing submenu except it adjusts the controls' vertical spacing rather than their horizontal spacing.

35

❑ *Center in Form* — This submenu contains commands that center the selected controls on the form. It contains the commands Horizontally and Vertically. Note that the selected controls are centered as a group; they are not centered individually on top of each other.

❑ *Order* — This submenu contains the commands Bring to Front and Send to Back, which move the selected controls to the top or bottom of the stacking order.

❑ *Lock Controls* — This command locks all of the controls on the form so that they cannot be moved or resized by clicking and dragging. You can still move and resize the controls by changing their Location and Size properties in the Properties window. Invoking this command again unlocks the controls. Locking the controls can be useful if you have spent a long time positioning them precisely. After they are locked, you can work on the controls without fear of accidentally messing up your careful design.

Tools

The Tools menu, shown in Figure 1-38, contains miscellaneous tools that do not fit particularly well in the other menus. It also contains a few duplicates of commands in other menus and commands that modify the IDE itself.

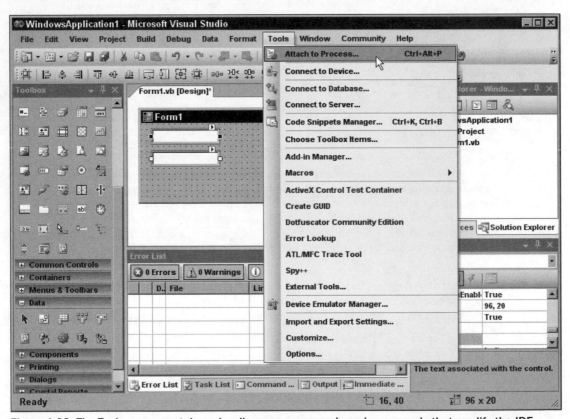

Figure 1-38: The Tools menu contains miscellaneous commands and commands that modify the IDE.

The following list describes the Tools menu's most useful commands:

❑ *Attach to Process* — This command displays the dialog shown in Figure 1-22 to let you attach the debugger to a running process. Select the process to which you want to attach and click Attach.

❑ *Connect to Device* — This command lets you connect to a physical device or emulator such as Pocket PC or Smartphone devices or emulators. You can use the devices and emulators to test software you are writing for devices other than the Windows platform where you are building the application.

❑ *Connect to Database* — This command displays the Connection Properties dialog, where you can define a database connection. The connection is added to the Server Explorer window. You can later use the connection to define data adapters and other objects that use a database connection.

❑ *Code Snippets Manager* — This command displays the Code Snippets Manager, which you can use to add and remove code snippets.

❑ *Choose Toolbox Items* — This command displays a dialog that lets you select the tools displayed in the Toolbox. For instance, by default the `OleDbDataAdapter` and `OleDbConnection` components are not included in the Toolbox. You can use this command to add them if you will use them frequently.

❑ *Add-in Manager* — This command displays the Add-in Manager, which lists the add-in projects registered on the computer. You can use the Add-in Manager to enable or disable these add-ins.

❑ *Macros* — The Macros submenu contains commands that help you create, edit, and execute macros. See the section "Macros," later in this chapter, for details.

❑ *ActiveX Control Test Container* — This command displays the ActiveX Control Test Container, which lets you test and debug ActiveX controls. You can use it to change the control's properties, call its methods, and raise its events.

❑ *Create GUID* — This command displays the Create GUID dialog shown in Figure 1-39 to let you create a new globally unique identifier (GUID, pronounced to rhyme with "squid"). Select the GUID format that you need and click New GUID to generate a new GUID. Click Copy to copy the result to the clipboard.

❑ *Dotfuscater Community Edition* — This command launches the displays the Dotfuscater Community Edition, a tool that you can use to make the intermediate language (IL) code generated by Visual Basic more obscure and harder to reverse engineer.

❑ *Error Lookup* — This command displays a small dialog where you can enter an error code and see a description of the error.

❑ *ATL/MFC Trace Tool* — If you are building Active Template Library (ATL) or Microsoft Foundation Classes (MFC) projects, this command displays a tool that lets you view debug trace messages.

❑ *Spy++* — This command launches the Spy++ tool, which lets you view the messages sent to the application.

❑ *External Tools* — This command displays a dialog that lets you add and remove commands from the Tools menu. For example, you could add a command to launch WordPad, MS Paint, WinZip, and other handy utilities from the Tools menu.

❑ *Device Emulation Manager* — This command displays the Device Emulation Manager, which lets you connect, reset, shut down, and otherwise manipulate device emulators.

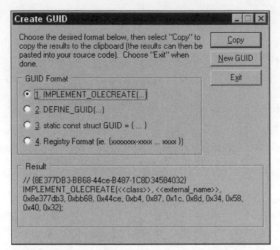

Figure 1-39: The Create GUID dialog generates GUIDs.

❏ *Import/Export Settings* — This command displays a dialog that you can use to save, restore, or reset your Visual Studio IDE settings.

❏ *Customize* — This command allows you to customize the Visual Studio IDE. See the "Customize" section later in this chapter for details.

❏ *Options* — This command allows you to specify options for the Visual Studio IDE. See the "Options" section later in this chapter for details.

Macros

The Macros submenu, shown in Figure 1-40, provides commands that help you create, edit, and execute macros that automate repetitive Visual Studio programming chores. If you must perform a series of actions many times, you can record a macro that performs them. Then you can call the macro repeatedly to perform the actions rather than executing them manually.

After you have recorded a macro, you can edit the macro's code and make changes. For example, if you want to run the code a certain number of times, you can include it in a For loop. Often, a quick inspection of the code lets you figure out how to modify the code to perform actions similar to (but not exactly the same as) the actions you originally recorded.

Most of the commands in the macros submenu are self-explanatory. Use the Record TemporaryMacro command to record a macro for quick temporary use. When you select this command, a small window pops up that contains buttons you can click to suspend, finish, or cancel recording. Visual Studio saves the commands you execute in a macro named "TemporaryMacro."

Select Run TemporaryMacro to run this macro. If you record a new TemporaryMacro, it overwrites the existing one without warning you. Select the Save TemporaryMacro command to rename the macro so you can record a new TemporaryMacro without destroying this one.

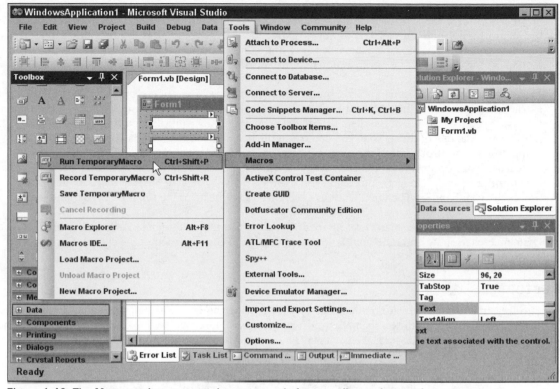

Figure 1-40: The Macros submenu contains commands for recording and executing macros.

Select the Macro Explorer command to display the window shown in Figure 1-41. If you right-click on a macro, the resulting pop-up menu lets you run, edit, rename, or delete the macro. Notice the Macro Explorer's predefined Samples section, which contains example macros that you can use or modify for your own use.

Figure 1-41: The Macro Explorer lets you edit, run, and delete macros.

Sometimes when you perform a series of programming tasks many times, there are better ways to approach the problem than writing a macro. For example, you may be able to make your program repeat the steps inside a loop. Or you may be able to extract the common code into a subroutine and then call it repeatedly rather than repeating the code many times. In these cases, your application doesn't need to contain a long sequence of repetitive code that may be hard to debug and maintain.

Macros are generally most useful when you must write similar pieces of code that cannot be easily extracted into a routine that can be shared by different parts of the application. For example, suppose that you need to write event handlers for several dozen TextBox controls. You could record a macro while you write one of them. Then you could edit the macro to make it generate the others in a loop using different control names for each event handler. You could place the bulk of the event-handling code in a separate subroutine that each event handler would call. That would avoid the need for extensive duplicated code. (In fact, you could even use the AddHandler statement to make all the controls use the same event handler. Then you wouldn't even need to write all of the separate event handlers.)

Macros are also useful for manipulating the IDE and performing IDE-related tasks. For example, you can write macros to show and hide your favorite toolbars, or to change whether the current file is opened read-only.

Customize

The Tools menu's Customize command displays the dialog shown in Figure 1-42. On the Toolbars tab, check the boxes next to the toolbars that you want to be visible. Click New to create a new toolbar where you can add your favorite tools. You can leave the toolbar floating or drag it to the edge of the IDE and dock it. If you drag it to the top, it joins the other toolbars.

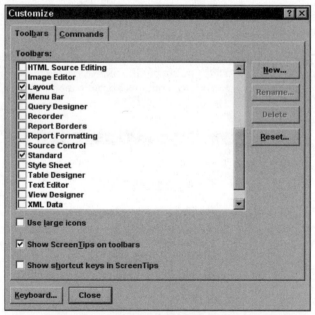

Figure 1-42: The Customize dialog's Toolbar tab lets you determine which toolbars are visible.

Click the Commands tab to see a list of categories as shown in Figure 1-43. Select a category on the left. Then click and drag a command from the list on the right. If you drop the command on a toolbar, the command is added to the toolbar. Hover over a menu to open the menu so that you can drop the command in it.

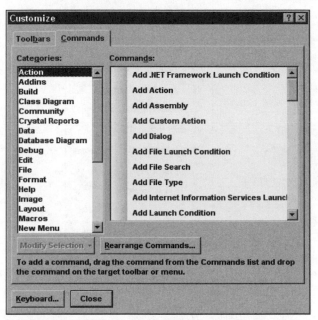

Figure 1-43: The Customize dialog's Commands tab lets you add commands to toolbars and menus.

To create a new menu, select the New Menu item in the list on the left. Then drag and drop the New Menu entry from the right list onto the IDE's menu area.

To make a command that executes a macro you have created, select the Macros category in the list on the left. Find the macro you want to use in the list on the right, and drag it onto a toolbar or menu.

To remove a command from a toolbar or menu, right-click it and select Delete. Alternatively, you can click and drag the command somewhere that it cannot be placed. For example, you can drop it on the Customize dialog or most places in the IDE other than on a menu or toolbar (code editors, the Properties window, the Toolbox). The mouse cursor changes to a box with an "X" beside it when the mouse is over one of these areas.

Modifying the IDE's standard menus and toolbars can cause confusion later. You may later discover that you need a command that you have removed from a menu, and it may take you quite a while to find it again. A better approach to modifying standard commands is to create a new custom toolbar or menu. Add the commands you want to use to the new toolbar and then hide the standard toolbar that you are replacing. Later you can restore the hidden standard toolbar if necessary.

If you right-click a command in a menu or toolbar while the Customize dialog is open, Visual Studio displays the pop-up menu shown in Figure 1-44. Click the Name text box and enter a new name to change the text displayed in the menu or toolbar.

Figure 1-44: Right-click menu and toolbar commands to change their appearances.

Use the Copy Button Image command to copy the button's image to the clipboard. Use Paste Button Image to paste a copied image onto a button. Usually you will use these two commands to copy the image from an existing button to one you are adding. However, the Paste Button Image command will paste any graphical image from the clipboard. For example, you can open a bitmap using Microsoft Paint, press Ctrl-A to select the whole image, and press Ctrl-C to copy it to the clipboard. Then you can use the Paste Button Image command to paste the image into a button. Note that the buttons are 16 by 16 pixels. If the image you copy is larger, Visual Studio shrinks it to fit.

Select the Reset Button Image command to restore the button to its default image. For a command tied to a macro, this erases the image.

Select the Edit button image command to display the simple button editor shown in Figure 1-45. If you click on a pixel that is not the selected foreground color (black in Figure 1-45), the editor changes the pixel to the foreground color. If you hold the mouse down and drag it, the editor gives the pixels you cross that color, too. If you click on a pixel that is already the foreground color, the editor erases the pixel and any others that you drag over.

If you click the Change Button Image command, a menu containing several dozen standard images pops out. Click one to assign that image to the button. A useful technique is to start with one of these images and then edit it to customize it for your command.

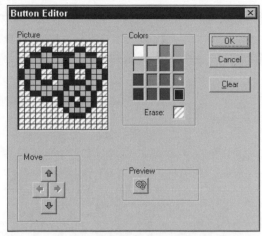

Figure 1-45: You can use Visual Studio's simple button editor to change a command's button.

The pop-up menu's Default Style command makes the command use a style that depends on whether it is in a menu or toolbar. In a menu, the command displays a button and text. In a toolbar, the command displays only a button. Ironically, a new button's default style is not Default Style. When you create a new toolbar or menu command, the button initially displays only text. You need to use the Default Style command to make the button use this style.

Text Only (Always) makes the command display only text. Text Only (in Menus) makes a command in a toolbar display a button and a command in a menu display text.

Image and Text makes the command display both an icon and text whether it is in a toolbar or a menu.

Finally, the Begin a Group command makes the IDE insert a group separator before the button.

The Customize dialog's Rearrange Commands button displays a dialog that lets you rearrange the commands in an existing menu or toolbar, and change the appearance of those commands. It's usually easier to just click and drag the commands on its menu or toolbar, however.

The Customize dialog's Keyboard button displays the dialog shown in Figure 1-46. You can use this display to view and edit keyboard shortcuts.

Enter words in the "Show commands containing" text box to filter the commands. When you click on a command, the dialog displays any keyboard shortcuts associated with it.

To make a new shortcut, click on the "Press shortcut key(s)" text box and press the keys that you want to use as a shortcut. The "Shortcut currently used by" drop-down lists any commands that already use the shortcut you entered. To make the assignment, click the Assign button.

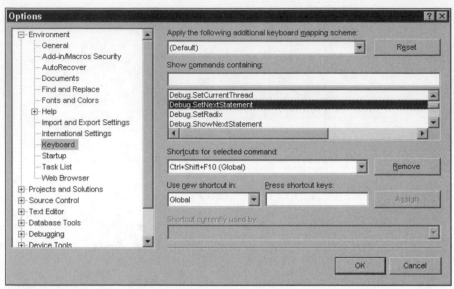

Figure 1-46: The Options dialog's Keyboard section lets you view and modify keyboard shortcuts.

Options

The Tools menu's Options command displays the dialog shown in Figure 1-47. This dialog contains a huge number of pages of options that configure the Visual Studio IDE. The Customize dialog's Keyboard button described in the previous section uses the same dialog with the Keyboard item selected in the list on the left.

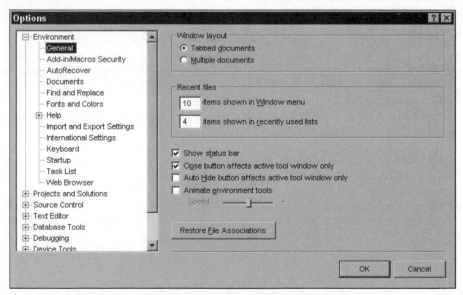

Figure 1-47: The Options dialog lets you specify IDE options.

The following list describes the Options dialog's most important categories.

❑ *Environment* — Contains general IDE settings such as whether the IDE uses an Multiple Document Interface (MDI) or Single Document Interface (SDI) interface, the number of items listed in the MRU lists, and how often the IDE saves AutoRecover information. The Fonts and Colors subsection lets you determine the colors used by the editors for different types of text. For example, comments are shown in green by default, but you can change this color.

❑ *Projects and Solutions* — Contains the default settings for Option Explicit, Option Strict, and Option Compare.

❑ *Source Control* — Contains entries that deal with the source code control system (for example, Source Safe).

❑ *Text Editor* — Contains entries that specify the text editors' features. For example, you can use these pages to determine whether delimiters are highlighted, the editor provides drag-and-drop editing, scroll bars are visible, long lines are automatically wrapped, line numbers are displayed, and the editor provides smart indentation. The Basic\VB Specific subsection lets you specify options such as whether the editor uses outlining, whether it displays procedure separators, and suggested corrections for errors.

❑ *Database Tools* — Contains database parameters such as default lengths for fields of various types.

❑ *Debugging* — Contains debugging settings such as whether the debugger displays messages as modules are loaded and unloaded, whether it should make you confirm when deleting all breakpoints, and whether it should allow Edit-and-Continue.

❑ *Device Tools* — Contains options for development on devices such as Smartphones, Pocket PCs, or Windows CE.

❑ *HTML Designer* — Contains options for configuring HTML Designer. These options determine such settings as whether the designer starts in source or design view, and whether it displays Smart Tags for controls in design view.

❑ *Windows Form Designer* — Contains settings that control the Form Designer. For example, this section lets you determine whether the designer uses a snap-to grid or snap lines.

Window

The Window menu contains commands that control Visual Studio's windows. Which commands are enabled depends on the type of window that has the focus. Figure 1-48 shows this menu when the Toolbox has the focus.

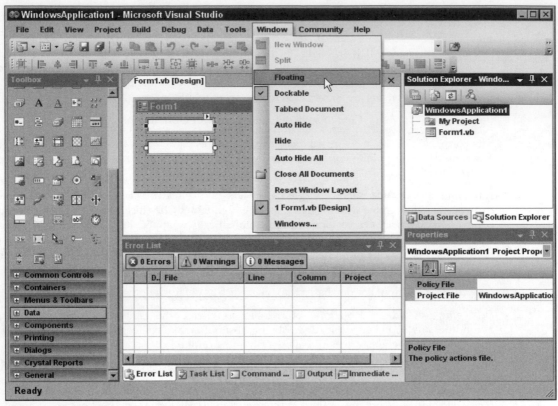

Figure 1-48: The Window menu displays commands that control Visual Studio's windows.

The following list briefly describes these commands.

❑ *New Window* — Creates a new window displaying the contents of the current code window.

❑ *Split* — Splits a code window into two panes that can display different parts of the code at the same time. This command changes to Remove Split when you use it.

❑ *Dockable, Floating, Tabbed Document* — Secondary windows such as the Toolbox, Solution Explorer, and Properties windows can be displayed as dockable, as floating, or as tabbed documents. A dockable window can be attached to the edges of the IDE or docked with other secondary windows. A floating window stays in its own independent window even if you drag it to a position where it would normally dock. A tabbed document window is displayed in the main editing area in the center of the IDE with the forms, classes, and other project files.

❑ *Auto Hide* — Puts a secondary window in Auto Hide mode. The window disappears, and its title is displayed at the IDE's nearest edge. When you click on the title or hover over it, the window reappears so that you can use it. If you click on another window, this window hides itself again automatically.

❑ *Hide* — Removes the window.

❑ *Auto Hide All* — Makes all secondary windows enter Auto Hide mode.

❑ *New Horizontal Tab Group* — Splits the main document window horizontally so that you can view two different documents at the same time.

❑ *New Vertical Tab Group* — Splits the main document window vertically so that you can view two different documents at the same time.

❑ *Close All Documents* — Closes all documents.

❑ *Reset Window Layout* — Resets the window layout to a default configuration.

❑ *Form1.vb* — The bottom part of the Window menu lists the open documents. In Figure 1-48, it lists Form1.vb in the code editor and Form1.vb [Design] in the Form Designer (Design mode). The code editor entry is checked because it is the currently active document.

❑ *Windows* — If you have too many open documents to display in the Window menu, select this command to see a list of windows in a dialog. This dialog lets you switch to another document, close one or more documents, or save documents. By using Ctrl-Click and Shift-Click you can select more than one document and quickly close them.

Community

The Community menu shown in Figure 1-49 contains commands that can help you connect with the Visual Basic programming community. These commands lead to various Microsoft Web pages where you can ask questions, send feedback, search for examples, find snippets, and so forth.

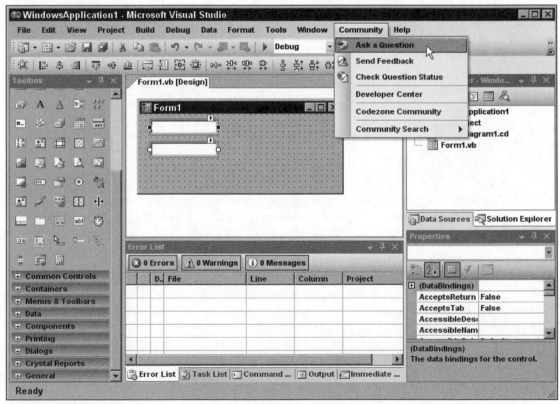

Figure 1-49: The Community menu contains commands that give access to Microsoft's Visual Basic developer community.

For other Visual Basic community resources, see the "community support" topic in the MSDN help or visit the Web page http://msdn.microsoft.com/library/en-us/vsintro7/html/vxoriAdditionalResources ForVisualStudioDevelopers.asp. Also see the Visual Studio 2005 Home Page at http://msdn.microsoft .com/vs2005/default.aspx. Microsoft may move these pages but you should be able to find them if you search Microsoft's Web site for "Additional Resources for Visual Studio Developers" and "Visual Studio 2005."

Help

The Help menu shown in Figure 1-50 displays the usual assortment of help commands. You should be familiar with most of these from previous experience.

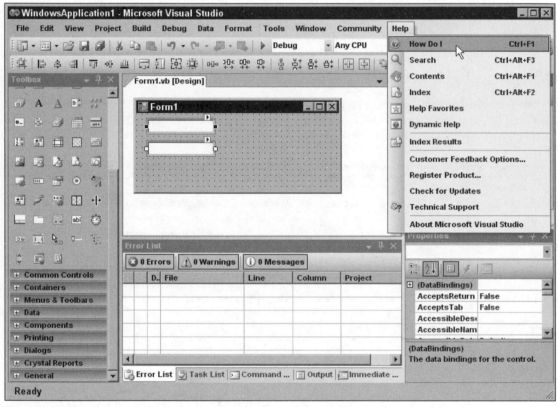

Figure 1-50: The Help menu contains commands that give you help.

One new item in the Help menu is the How Do I command. This command opens the help system and displays a page full of links to common programming topics. These topics lead to a hierarchical series of categorized tutorials on various programming topics. For example, the Visual Basic > Language > Basics > Data Types > Data Type Summary topic describes the Visual Basic data types, their storage requirements, and their ranges of allowed values.

Toolbars

Visual Studio's toolbars are easy to rearrange. Grab the four gray dots on a toolbar's left or upper edge and drag the toolbar to its new position. If you drag a toolbar to one of Visual Studio's edges, it will dock there either horizontally (on the IDE's top or bottom edge) or vertically (on the IDE's left or right edge). If you drop a toolbar away from the IDE's edges, it becomes a floating window not docked to the IDE.

You can use the menu commands described earlier in this chapter to determine which toolbars are visible, to determine what they contain, and to make custom toolbars of your own.

Many menu commands are also available in standard toolbars. For example, the Debug toolbar contains many of the same commands that are in the Debug menu. If you use a set of menu commands frequently, you may want to display the corresponding toolbar to make using the commands easier.

Secondary Windows

You can rearrange secondary windows such as the Toolbox and Solution Explorer almost as easily as you can rearrange toolbars. Click and drag the window's title area to move it. As the window moves, the IDE displays little blue icons to help you dock the window, as shown in Figure 1-51. This figure probably looks somewhat confusing, but it's fairly easy to use.

The IDE displays four docking icons near the edges of the IDE. You can see these icons near the edges of Figure 1-51. If you drop the window on one of these icons, the window docks to the corresponding edge of the IDE.

When you drag the window over another window, the IDE displays docking icons for the other window. In Figure 1-51, these are the five icons near the mouse in the middle of the screen. The four icons on the sides dock the window to the corresponding edge of the other window.

The center icon places the dropped window in a tab within the other window. If you look closely at Figure 1-51, you can see a little image of a document with two tabs on the bottom in this icon.

When you drag the mouse over one of the docking icons, the IDE displays a dark gray rectangle to give you an idea of where the window will land if you drop it. In Figure 1-51, the mouse is over the main document window's right docking icon, so the grayed rectangle shows the dropped window taking up the right half of the main document window.

If you drop a window somewhere other than on a docking icon, the window becomes free-floating.

Once you drop a window on the main document area, it becomes a tabbed document, and you cannot later pull it out. To free the window, select it and use the Window menu's Dockable or Floating command.

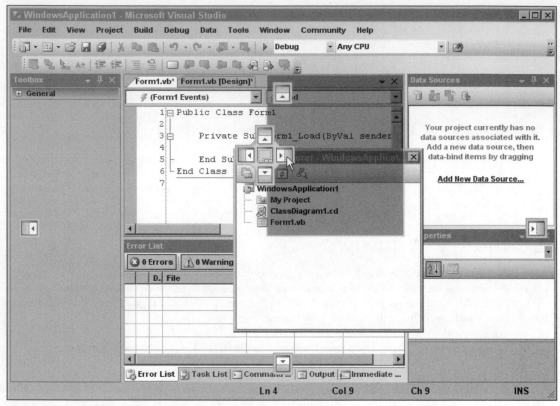

Figure 1-51: Use the IDE's docking icons to help you dock windows.

Sometimes the IDE is so cluttered with windows that it's hard to figure out exactly where the window will be dropped. It's usually fairly easy to just move the mouse around a bit and watch the grayed rectangle to see what's happening.

The windows in the Microsoft Document Explorer used by the MSDN Library and other external help files provides the same arranging and docking tools for managing its subwindows such as Index, Contents, Help Favorites, Index Results, and Search Results.

Toolbox

The Toolbox window displays a series of sections containing tools for the currently active document. These tools are grouped into sections called *tabs*, although they don't look much like the tabs on most documents. In Figure 1-52, the Toolbox displays tools for the form designer grouped into the All Windows Forms, Common Controls, Containers, Menus & Toolbars, Data, Components, Printing, Dialogs, and General tabs. In this figure, the Toolbox was enlarged greatly to show most of its contents. Most developers keep this window much smaller and docked on the left edge of the IDE.

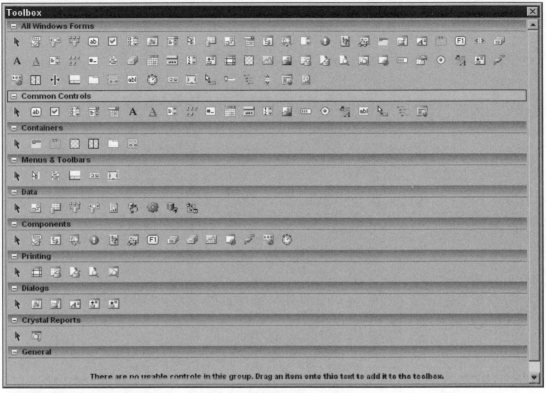

Figure 1-52: The Toolbox window can display tools by name or icon.

You can customize the Toolbox by right-clicking on it and selecting one of the commands in the context menu. The following list briefly describes these commands.

❑ *List View* — Toggles the current tab to display tools either as a list of names or a series of icons.

❑ *Show All* — Shows or hides less commonly used tool tabs such as XML Schema, Dialog Editor, DataSet, Login, WebParts, Report Items, Device Controls, and many others.

❑ *Choose Items* — displays the dialog shown in Figure 1-53. Use the .NET Framework Components tab to select .NET tools, and use the COM Components tab to select COM tools. Click the Browse button to locate tools that are not in either list.

❑ *Sort Items Alphabetically* — Sorts the items within a Toolbox tab alphabetically.

❑ *Reset Toolbox* — Restores the Toolbox to a default configuration. This removes any items you may have added by using the Choose Items command.

❑ *Add Tab* — Creates a new tab where you can place your favorite tools. You can drag tools from one tab to another. Hold down the Ctrl key while dragging to add a copy of the tool to the new tab without removing it from the old tab.

❑ *Delete Tab* — Deletes a tab.

❑ *Rename Tab* — Lets you rename a tab.

❑ *Move Up, Move Down* — Moves a tab up or down in the Toolbox. You can also click and drag the tabs to new positions.

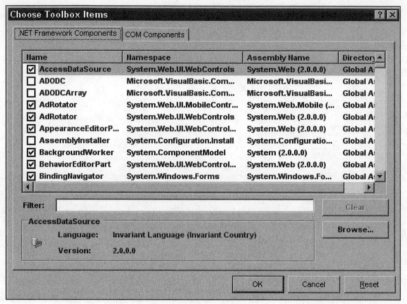

Figure 1-53: Use the Choose Toolbox Items dialog to select the tools in the Toolbox.

The Visual Basic Code Editor

Visual Studio includes editors for many different kinds of documents, including several different kinds of code. For example, it has Hypertext Markup Language (HTML), Extensible Markup Language (XML), and Visual Basic editors. These editors share some common features, such as displaying comments and keywords in different colors.

As a Visual Basic developer, you will use the Visual Basic code editor frequently, so you should spend a few minutes learning about its specialized features.

Figure 1-54 shows the code editor displaying some Visual Basic code at run time. To make referring to the code lines easier, this figure displays line numbers. To display line numbers, invoke the Tools menu's Options command, navigate to the Text Editor\Basic\General page, and check the Line Numbers box.

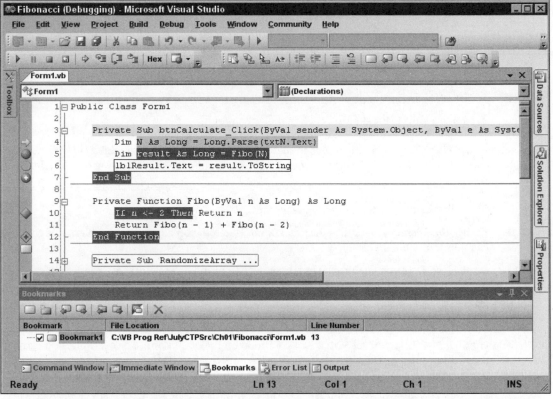

Figure 1-54: The Visual Basic code editor provides many features, including line numbers and icons that indicate breakpoints and bookmarks.

Margin Icons

The gray margin to the left of the line numbers contains icons giving information about the corresponding lines of code. The following table describes the icons on lines 4 through 11.

Line	Icon	Meaning
4	Yellow arrow	Indicates that execution is paused at this line
5	Red circle	Indicates a breakpoint
6	Hollow red circle	Indicates a disabled breakpoint
7	Red circle with plus sign	Indicates a breakpoint with a condition or hit count test
10	Red diamond	Indicates a breakpoint that executes an action when reached
11	Blue and white rectangle	Indicates a bookmark

These icons can combine to indicate more than one condition. For example, line 12 shows a blue and white rectangle to indicate a bookmark, a hollow red diamond to indicate a disabled breakpoint that performs an action, and a plus sign to indicate that the breakpoint has a condition or hit count test.

Note that the editor marks some of these lines in other ways than just an icon. It highlights the currently executing line with a yellow background. It marks lines that hold enabled breakpoints with white text on a red background.

To add or remove a simple breakpoint, click in the gray margin.

To make a more complex breakpoint, click in the margin to create a simple breakpoint. Then right-click the breakpoint icon and select one of the context menu's commands. The following list describes these commands.

- ❑ *Delete Breakpoint* — Removes the breakpoint.

- ❑ *Disable Breakpoint* — Disables the breakpoint. When the breakpoint is disabled, this command changes to Enable Breakpoint.

- ❑ *Location* — Lets you change the breakpoint's line number. Usually it is easier to click in the margin to remove the old breakpoint and then create a new one.

- ❑ *Condition* — Lets you place a condition on the breakpoint. For example, you can make the breakpoint stop execution only when the variable num_employees has a value greater than 100.

- ❑ *Hit Count* — Lets you set a hit count condition on the breakpoint. For example, you can make the breakpoint stop execution when it has been reached a certain number of times.

- ❑ *When Hit* — Lets you specify the action that the breakpoint performs when it triggers. For example, it might display a message in the Output window or run a macro.

To add or remove a bookmark, place the cursor on a line and then click the Toggle Bookmark tool. You can find this tool, which looks like the blue and white bookmark icon, in the Text Editor toolbar (under the mouse in Figure 1-54) and at the top of the Bookmarks window. Other bookmark tools let you move to the next or previous bookmark, the next or previous bookmark in the current folder, or the next or previous bookmark in the current document. The final bookmark command clears all bookmarks.

Outlining

By default, the code editor displays an outline view of code. If you look at the first line in Figure 1-54, you'll see a box with a minus sign in it just to the right of the line number. That box represents the outlining for the Form1 class. If you click this box, the editor collapses the class's definition and displays it as a box containing a plus sign. If you then click the new box, the editor expands the class's definition again.

The gray line leading down from the box leads to other code items that are outlined, and that you can expand or collapse to give you the least cluttered view of the code you want to examine. Near the bottom of Figure 1-54, you can see that the RandomizeArray subroutine has been collapsed. The ellipsis and rectangle around the routine name provided an extra indication that this code is hidden.

The editor automatically creates outlining entries for namespaces, classes and their methods, and modules and their methods. You can also use the Region statement to group a section of code for outlining. For example, you can place several related subroutines in a region so you can collapse and expand the routines as a group.

Figure 1-55 shows more examples of outlining. Line 37 begins a region named Randomization Functions that contains three collapsed subroutines. Notice that the corresponding End Region statement includes a comment giving the region's name. This is not required but it makes the code easier to understand when you are looking at the end of a region.

Line 90 contains a collapsed region named Utility Functions.

Line 96 starts a module named HelperRoutines that contains one collapsed subroutine.

Finally, Line 109 holds the collapsed ImageResources namespace.

Notice that the line numbers skip values for any collapsed lines. For example, the RandomizeIntegerArray subroutine is collapsed on line 39. This subroutine contains 15 lines (including the Sub statement), so the next visible line is labeled 54.

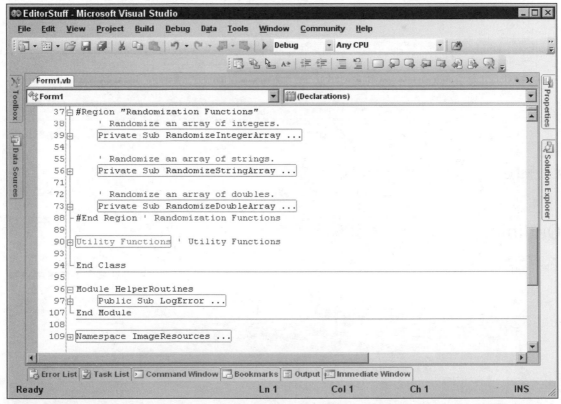

Figure 1-55: The code editor outlines namespaces, classes and their methods, modules and their methods, and regions.

Also notice that comments before a subroutine are not collapsed with the subroutine. You can make reading collapsed code easier by placing a short descriptive comment before each routine.

Tooltips

If you hover the mouse over a variable at design time, the editor displays a tooltip describing the variable. For example, if you hover over an integer variable named num_actions, the tooltip would display "Dim num_actions As Integer."

If you hover over a subroutine or function call, the tooltip displays information about that method. For example, if you hover over the RandomizeArray subroutine (which takes an array of integers as a parameter), the tooltip says, "Private Sub RandomizeArray(arr() As Integer)."

At run time, if you hover over a variable, the tooltip displays the variable's value. If the variable is complex (such as an array or structure), the tooltip displays the variable's name and a plus sign. If you click or hover over the plus sign, the tooltip expands to show the variable's members.

In Figure 1-56, the mouse hovered over variable arr. The editor displayed a plus sign and the text arr {Length = 100}. When the mouse hovered over the plus sign, the editor displayed the values shown in the figure. Moving the mouse over the up and down arrows at the top and bottom of the list makes the values scroll.

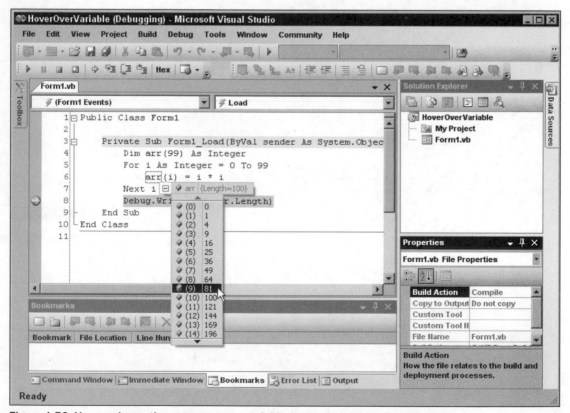

Figure 1-56: You can hover the mouse over a variable at run time to see its value.

If a variable has properties that are references to other objects, you can hover over their plus signs to expand those objects. You can continue following the plus signs to drill into the variable's object hierarchy as deeply as you like.

IntelliSense

If you start typing a line of code, the editor tries to anticipate what you will type. For example, if you type "Me." then the editor knows that you are about to use one of the current object's properties or methods.

IntelliSense displays a list of the properties and methods that you might be trying to select. As you type more of the property or method, IntelliSense scrolls to show the choices that match what you have typed.

In Figure 1-57, the code includes the text me.Set, so IntelliSense is displaying the current object's methods that begin with the string Set.

While the IntelliSense window is visible, you can use the up and down arrows to scroll through the list. While IntelliSense is displaying the item that you want to use, you can press the Tab key to accept that item. Press the Escape key to close the IntelliSense window and type the rest manually.

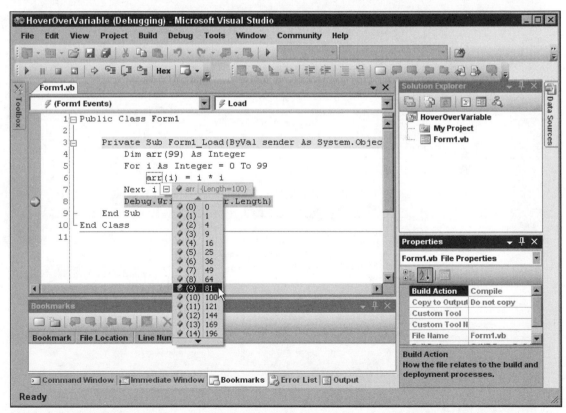

Figure 1-57: IntelliSense displays a list of properties and methods that you might be trying to type.

After you finish typing a method and its opening parenthesis, IntelliSense displays information about the method's parameters. Figure 1-58 shows parameter information for a form object's SetBounds method. This method takes four parameters: x, y, width, and height.

IntelliSense shows a brief description of the current parameter x. As you enter parameter values, IntelliSense moves on to describe the other parameters.

IntelliSense also indicates whether there are overloaded versions of the method. In Figure 1-58, IntelliSense is describing the first version of two available versions. You can use the up and down arrows on the left to move through the list of overloaded versions.

Code Coloring and Highlighting

The code editor displays different types of code items in different colors. You can change the colors used for different items by selecting the Tools menu's Options command, and opening the Environment\Fonts and Colors option page. To avoid confusion, however, you should probably leave the colors alone unless you have a good reason to change them.

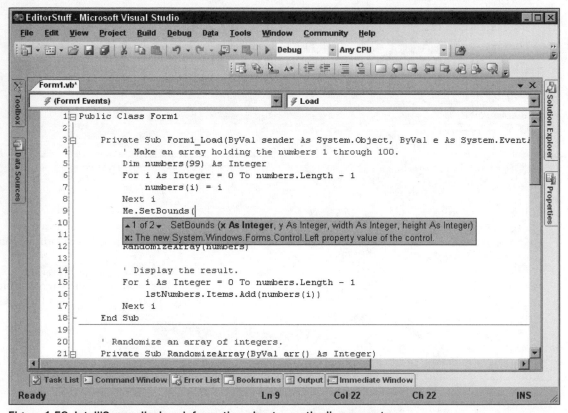

Figure 1-58: IntelliSense displays information about a method's parameters.

The following table describes some of the default colors that the code editor uses to highlight different code elements.

Item	Highlighting
Comment	Green text
Compiler error	Underlined with a wavy blue underline
Other error	Underlined with a wavy green underline
Keyword	Blue text
Preprocessor keyword	Blue text
Read-only region	Light gray background
Stale code	Purple text
User types	Navy text
User types, delegates	Navy text
User types, enums	Teal text
User types, interfaces	Navy text
User types, value types	Teal text
Warning	Underlined with a wavy purple underline

A few other items that may be worth changing have white backgrounds and black text by default. These include identifiers (variable names, types, object properties and methods, namespace names, and so forth), numbers, and strings.

When the code editor finds an error in your code, it highlights the error with a wavy underline. If you hover over the underline, the editor displays a tooltip describing the error. If Visual Studio can guess what you are trying to do, it adds a small flat rectangle to the end of the wavy error line to indicate that it may have useful suggestions.

The assignment statement i = "12" shown in Figure 1-59 has an error because it tried to assign a string value to an integer variable and that violates the Option Strict On setting. The editor displays the wavy error underline and a suggestion indicator because it knows a way to fix this error.

If you hover over the suggestion indicator, the editor displays a tooltip describing the problem and an error icon. If you click the icon, Visual Studio displays a dialog describing the error and listing the actions that you may want to take. Figure 1-60 shows the suggestion dialog for the error in Figure 1-59. If you click the text over the revised sample code, or if you double-click the sample code, the editor makes the change.

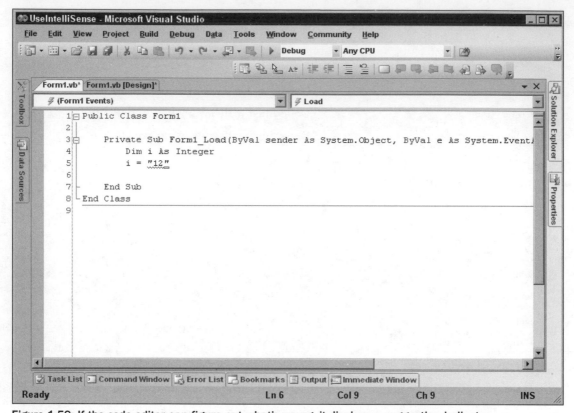

Figure 1-59: If the code editor can figure out what's wrong, it displays a suggestion indicator.

Code Snippets

A code snippet is a piece of code that you might find useful in many applications. It is stored in a snippet library so that you can quickly insert it into a new application.

Visual Studio comes with hundreds of snippets for performing standard tasks. Before you start working on a complicated piece of code, you should take a look at the snippets that are already available to you. In fact, it would be worth your time to use the Snippet Manager available from the Tools menu to take a good look at the available snippets right now before you start a new project. There's little point in you reinventing methods for calculating statistical values if someone has already done it and given you the code.

Snippets are stored in simple text files with XML tags, so it is easy to share snippets with other developers. Go to this book's Web page, `www.vb-helper.com/vbprogref.htm`, to contribute snippets and to download snippets contributed by others.

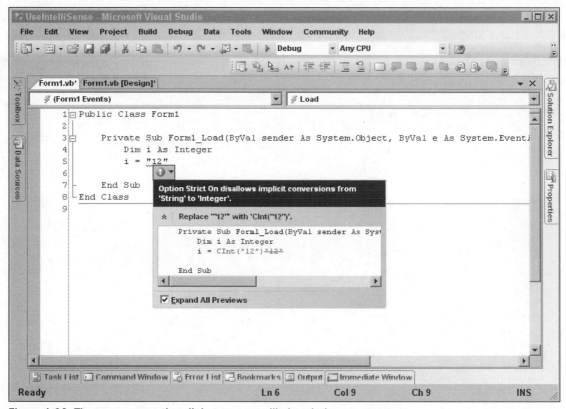

Figure 1-60: The error suggestion dialog proposes likely solutions to an error.

The following sections explain how to use snippets in your applications and how to create new snippets.

Using Snippets

To insert a snippet, right-click where you want to insert the code and select Insert Snippet to make the editor display a list of snippet categories. Double-click a category to find the kinds of snippets that you want. If you select a snippet, a tooltip pops up to describe it. Figure 1-61 shows the editor preparing to insert the snippet named "Create a public property" from the "VbProgRef CodeSnippets" category.

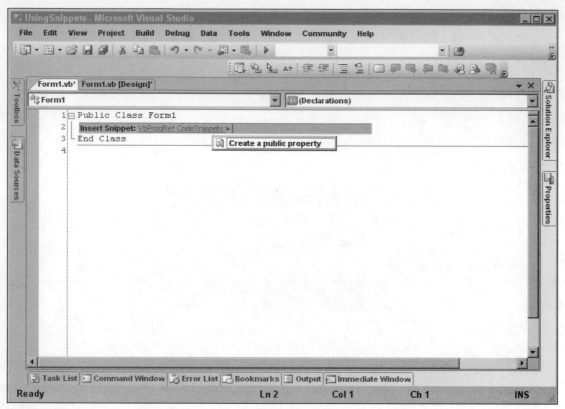

Figure 1-61: When you select a code snippet, a pop-up describes it.

Double-click on the snippet to insert it into your code. The snippet may include values that you should replace in your code. These replacement values are highlighted with a light green background, and the first value is initially selected. If you hover the mouse over one of these values, a tooltip appears to describe the value. You can use the Tab key to jump between replacement values.

Figure 1-62 shows the inserted code for this example. The text An Integer Property is highlighted and selected. Other selected text includes Integer, 0, and MyProperty. The mouse is hovering over the value An Integer Property, so the tooltip explains that value's purpose.

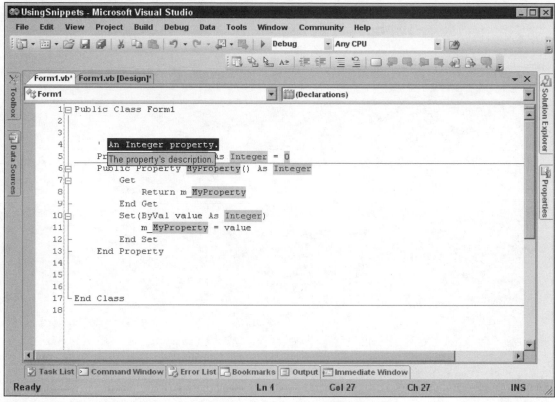

Figure 1-62: Values that you should replace in a snippet are highlighted.

Creating Snippets

To create a new snippet, you need to build an XML file containing the property tags to define the snippet and any replacements that the user should make. The following code shows the "Create a public property" snippet used in the previous section. The outer CodeSnippets and CodeSnippet tags are standard and you should not change them.

Use the Title tag in the Header section to describe the snippet.

Inside the Snippet tag, build a Declarations section describing any literal text that the user should replace. This example defines DataType, Description, DefaultValue, and PropertyName symbols. Each literal definition includes an ID, and can include a ToolTip and Description.

After the declarations, the Code tag contains the snippets source code. The syntax <![CDATA[...]]> tells XML processors to include any characters including carriage returns between the <![CDATA[and the]]> in the enclosing tag.

```
<CodeSnippets xmlns="http://schemas.microsoft.com/VisualStudio/2005/CodeSnippet">
    <CodeSnippet Format="1.0.0">
        <Header>
            <Title>Create a public property</Title>
        </Header>
        <Snippet>
            <Declarations>
                <Literal>
                    <ID>DataType</ID>
                    <ToolTip>The property's data type.</ToolTip>
                    <Default>Integer</Default>
                </Literal>
                <Literal>
                    <ID>Description</ID>
                    <ToolTip>The property's description.</ToolTip>
                    <Default>An Integer property.</Default>
                </Literal>
                <Literal>
                    <ID>DefaultValue</ID>
                    <ToolTip>The property's default value.</ToolTip>
                    <Default>0</Default>
                </Literal>
                <Literal>
                    <ID>PropertyName</ID>
                    <ToolTip>The property's name.</ToolTip>
                    <Default>MyProperty</Default>
                </Literal>
            </Declarations>
            <Code Language="VB">
                <![CDATA[
' $Description$
Private m_$PropertyName$ As $DataType$ = $DefaultValue$
Public Property $PropertyName$() As $DataType$
    Get
        Return m_$PropertyName$
    End Get
    Set(ByVal value As $DataType$)
        m_$PropertyName$ = value
    End Set
End Property
]]>
            </Code>
        </Snippet>
    </CodeSnippet>
</CodeSnippets>
```

Save the snippet's XML definition in a snippet directory. To add the directory to the list of usable snippet locations, select the Tool menu's Code Snippets Manager command to display the tool shown in Figure 1-63. Click the Add button, browse to the new snippet directory, and click OK. Now the directory and the snippets that it contains will be available in the Insert Snippet pop-ups.

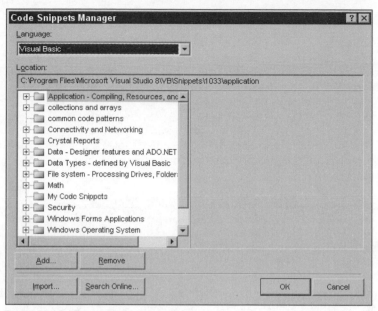

Figure 1-63: The Code Snippets Manager lets you add and remove snippet directories.

The Code Editor at Run Time

The code editor behaves slightly differently at run time and design time. Many of its design time features still work. Breakpoints, bookmarks, IntelliSense, and snippets still work.

At run time, the editor adds new tools for controlling the program's execution. Right-click on a value and select Add Watch or QuickWatch to examine and monitor the value. Use the Stop Into, Step Over, and Step Out commands on the Debug menu or toolbar to make the program walk through the code.

Right-click on a statement and select Show Next Statement to move the cursor to the next statement that the program will execute. Select Run To Cursor to make the program continue running until it reaches the cursor's current line.

Right-click and select Set Next Statement to make the program jump to a new location. You can also drag the yellow arrow indicating the next statement to a new location in the left margin. There are some restrictions on where you can move the execution position. For example, you cannot jump out of one routine and into another.

You can discover other run-time features by exploring the editor at run time. Right-click on different parts of the editor to see which commands are available in that mode.

Summary

The Visual Studio integrated development environment provides many tools for writing and debugging applications. It provides code snippets that make saving and reusing code easy. It lets you add, remove, and disable complex breakpoints that check conditions and hit counts, and that can perform customized actions. You can use regions and bookmarks to organize and find pieces of code, and you can step through the code line by line at execution time.

The IDE is extremely flexible. You can show, hide, and rearrange windows; add and remove items from menus and toolbars; and write macros to automate simple chores. Context menus attached to all sorts of objects provide help, tools, and other features that make sense for their particular objects and under different situations.

This chapter describes some of the most useful parts of the IDE, but listing every last nook and cranny would be tedious and not terribly useful. Rather than reading about the IDE further, you would be better off experimenting with it. Spend a few hours really examining all of the menus. Create a snippet with some replacement values and then insert it into your code. Step through a small program and try the Immediate and Command windows.

While you do all this, and while you're developing real applications, right-click on things to see what sort of context menus they provide. The IDE is packed with so many tools that it is sometimes hard to find the one you want. Because context menus are tied closely to the objects that you click to display them, they often provide more appropriate and focused commands than the toolbars or menus.

After you have used the IDE for a while and are comfortable with it, customize it to match your preferences. Build custom toolbars and menus to make using your favorite tools easier. When you have the tools that you use most at your fingertips, you will see just how productive Visual Studio can be.

Once you have become familiar with the IDE, you can start building applications. One way to begin is to design the application's user interface: the forms, labels, text boxes, and other controls that the user sees and manipulates to control the application. Chapter 2, "Controls in General," describes controls in general terms. It explains what controls are, how you can add them to a form, and how you can control and interact with them at design time and run time.

Controls in General

A *control* is a programming object that has a graphical component. A control sits on a form and interacts with the user, providing information and possibly allowing the user to manipulate it. Text boxes, labels, buttons, scroll bars, drop-down lists, menu items, toolstrips, and just about everything else that you can see and interact with in a Windows application is a control.

A *component* is similar to a control, except it has no visible component at run time. When you add a component to a form at design time, it appears in the *component tray* below the bottom of the form. You can select the component and use the Properties window to view and change its properties. At run time, the component is invisible to the user, although it may display a visible object such as a menu, dialog, or status icon.

Figure 2-1 shows Visual Basic's Toolbox displaying a standard assortment of 67 controls and components. The arrow tool in the upper-left corner represents the selection tool and is not a control or component.

This chapter explains controls and components in general terms. It describes different kinds of controls and components. It explains how your program can use them at design time and run time to give the user information and to allow the user to control your application.

It explains in general terms how a control's properties, methods, and events work, and it lists some of the most useful properties, methods, and events provided by the Control class. Other controls that are derived from this class inherit the use of those properties, methods, and events unless they are explicitly overridden.

Appendix G, "Standard Controls and Components," describes specific controls in greater detail.

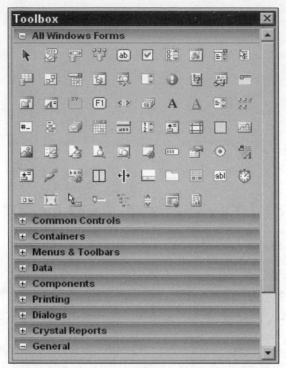

Figure 2-1: Visual Basic provides a rich assortment of controls.

Controls and Components

Most controls are graphic by nature. Buttons, text boxes, and labels provide graphical input and feedback for the user. They display data and let the user trigger program actions. Some controls (such as grid controls, tree view controls, and calendar controls) are quite powerful and provide a rich variety of tools for interacting with the user.

On the other hand, components are represented by graphical icons at design time, and they are hidden at run time. They may display some other object (such as a dialog, menu, or graphical indicator), but the component itself is hidden from the user.

Generally, your code could use a component's features at run time without requiring you to place an object on a form. For example, the program could easily call a method that displays a dialog. However, putting important functions in components rather than making them subroutine calls provides several benefits.

First, because you can add a component to a form graphically at design time, you don't need to write code to instantiate it and set its properties at run time. That would not be particularly difficult, but it would just be a little less convenient.

Adding a component to a form at design time also lets you manipulate it at design time instead of in code. You can use the Properties window to view and modify a component's properties at design time. You can also use the code editor to make event handlers for the component (event-handler creation is described in greater detail later in this chapter).

There are still times when it's useful to create controls at run time. For instance, if you don't know how many text boxes you will need until run time, you cannot create them all at design time. Fortunately, you get the best of both worlds: Visual Basic lets you create controls at either design time or run time.

Some components also provide information needed by graphical controls. For example, a program can use connection, data adapter, and data set components to define data that should be selected from a database. Then a grid control could then display the data to the user. Because the connection, data adapter, and data set objects are components, you can define all this at design time without writing code.

Figure 2-2 shows a form at design time that contains several components. The components appear in the Component Tray at the bottom of the form, not on the form's graphical surface.

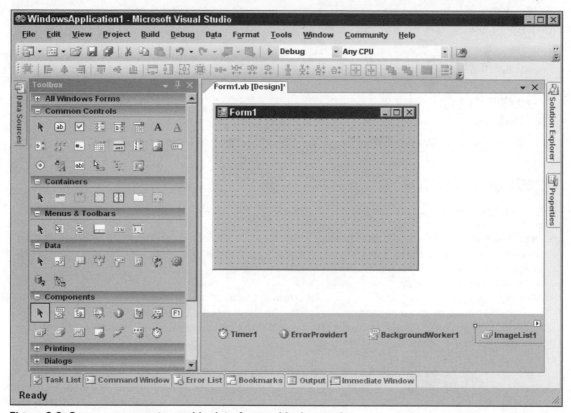

Figure 2-2: Some components provide data for graphical controls.

This example contains four components. `Timer1` fires an event periodically so the program can take some action at specified time intervals. `ErrorProvider1` displays an error icon and error messages for certain controls on the form such as `TextBoxes`. `BackgroundWorker1` performs tasks asynchronously while the main program works independently. `ImageList1` contains a series of images. Usually an `ImageList` is associated with a control such as a `Button`, `ListView`, or `TreeView`, and provides images for the control.

Aside from the lack of a graphical component on the form, working with components is about the same as working with controls. You use the Properties window to set components' properties, the code editor to define event handlers, and code to call their methods. The rest of this chapter focuses on controls, but the same concepts apply just as well to components.

Creating Controls

Usually you add controls to a form graphically at design time. In some cases, however, you may want to add new controls to a form at run time. This gives you a bit more flexibility so that you can change the program's appearance at run time in response to the program's needs or the user's commands.

For example, suppose that an application might need between 1 and 100 text boxes. Most of the time it needs only a few, but depending on the user's input, it might need a lot. You could give the form 100 text boxes and then hide the ones it didn't need, but that would be a waste of memory most of the time. By creating only the number of text boxes actually needed, you can conserve memory in the most common cases.

The following sections explain how to create controls both at design time and at run time.

Creating Controls at Design Time

To create a control at design time, double-click on a form in Solution Explorer to open it in the form editor. Decide which control you want to use from the Toolbox. If the Toolbox tab you are using is in List View mode, it displays the controls' names. If the tab displays only control icons, you can hover the mouse over a tool to see a tooltip that gives the control's name and a brief description. Figure 2-3 shows a tooltip describing the `HelpProvider` component.

After you have chosen a control, there are several ways you can add it to the form. First, you can double-click on the tool to place an instance of the control on the form at a default size in a default location. After adding the control to the form, the IDE deselects the tool and selects the pointer tool (the upper leftmost tool in the Toolbox's current tab).

A second way you can add a control to a form is to select it in the Toolbox, and then click and drag to place it on the form. If you click on the form without dragging, the IDE adds a new control at that position with a default size. After you add the control, the IDE deselects the tool and selects the pointer tool.

Third, if you click and drag a tool from the Toolbox onto the form, Visual Basic makes a new control with a default size at the position where you dropped the tool.

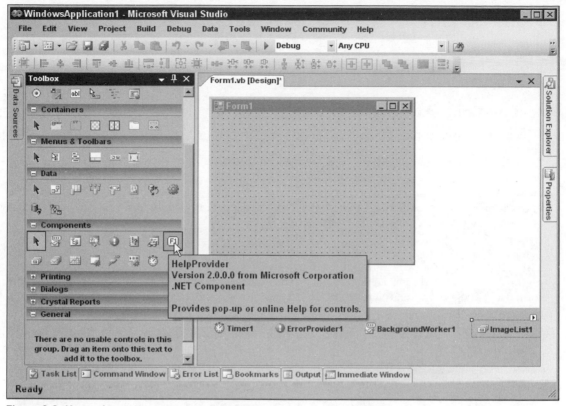

Figure 2-3. Hover the mouse over a toolbox icon to see the tool's description.

Fourth, if you plan to add many copies of the same type of control to the form, hold down the Ctrl key and click on the tool. Now the tool remains selected even after you add a control to the form. If you click and drag on the form, the IDE creates a new control at that position and keeps the tool selected so that you can immediately create another control. If you click on the form without dragging the mouse, the IDE adds a new control at that position with a default size. When you are finished adding instances of that control type, click the pointer tool to stop adding new controls.

After you have added controls to a form, there are a couple ways you can make copies of those controls. First, you can select some controls, press Ctrl-C to copy them to the clipboard, and press Ctrl-V to paste them back onto the form at a default location.

Similarly, you can copy and paste controls to other forms. For example, an application might need several dialog boxes that all display similar text in labels, pictures in picture boxes, and OK and Cancel buttons. After you create one dialog, you can copy and paste its controls onto other dialogs to build them more quickly.

The copied controls have the same property values as the originals (except for their names, which must always be unique). If you want to make a series of controls with the same properties, you can make one, set its properties, and then use copy and paste to make the others.

Another way to copy existing controls is to select them, click and drag, and hold down the Ctrl key when you drop them. This makes copies of the controls at the position where you drop them. This technique is particularly useful for making a large array of controls aligned in rows or columns. If you use Ctrl-C and Ctrl-V to copy and paste the controls, they appear in a default location and you must reposition them in a separate step. If you drag and drop while pressing the Ctrl key, you can position the copies as you make them.

Selecting Controls

Telling you to select controls to copy them begs the question, how do you select the controls? Click on a control on the form to select it. Hold down the Shift or Ctrl key while clicking to add or remove a control from the selection without removing any other controls from the current selection.

Click and drag over part of the form to select all of the controls that intersect the rectangle you define with the mouse. Hold down the Ctrl key while you click and drag to select controls without removing any currently selected controls from the selection.

Some controls can contain other controls. When you click and drag to select the controls in an area, Visual Basic selects only controls contained in the control on which you initially click. For example, Figure 2-4 shows a form that contains eight buttons. The four buttons on the left are contained in the form itself. The four buttons on the right are contained in a `Panel` control.

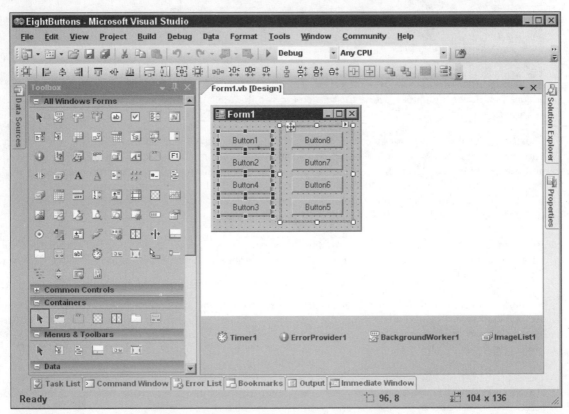

Figure 2-4: When you click and drag on a form, Visual Basic selects only controls with the same container.

If you click on an open piece of form and drag to select an area that covers every control on the form, Visual Basic selects the four buttons on the left and the `Panel` control because they are all contained in the form itself. It does not select the buttons on the right because they are contained in the `Panel` control.

If you click on the interior of the `Panel` control and then drag to surround all of the controls, Visual Basic selects only the four buttons on the right because they are contained in the `Panel` control.

If you want to select controls from more than one container, you must hold down the Ctrl key and click (or click and drag) to select the controls in several steps. In this case, you might click and drag on the form to select the buttons on the left and the `Panel` control. Next you would press Ctrl, click in the `Panel` control, and drag to select the remaining buttons. Unfortunately, clicking on the `Panel` control deselects it so you need to press Ctrl and click on the `Panel` again to reselect it. (If you want to select *all* of the controls on the form, you can also click on the form and press Ctrl-A.)

After you have selected the controls you want to manipulate, you can delete them, copy them, drag them to a new location, modify their common properties using the Properties window, and so forth.

Container Controls

As the previous section mentions, some controls can contain other controls. For example, the `GroupBox` and `Panel` controls can hold other controls.

There are several ways you can place a control in a container. If you select the container and then double-click a control's tool in the Toolbox, Visual Basic places the new control inside the container.

If you select a tool and click and drag inside a container, Visual Basic also places the new control inside the container, whether it is selected or not.

You can also click and drag a Toolbox tool onto the container, or click and drag controls from one part of the form onto the container. If you hold down the Ctrl key when you drop the controls, Visual Basic makes new copies of the controls.

Two common mistakes programmers make with containers is placing a control *above* a container when they want it *inside* the container, and vice versa. For example, you can place different controls inside different `Panel` controls and then hide or display the `Panel`s to show different controls at different times. If a control lies above a `Panel` but is not inside it, the control remains visible even if the `Panel` is not.

To tell if a control is inside a container, move the container slightly. If the control also moves, it is inside the container. If the control doesn't move, it is above the container but not inside it.

Creating Controls at Run Time

Normally, you create controls interactively at design time. Sometimes, however, it's more convenient to create new controls at run time. For example, you may want to provide different interfaces for different users. Users with different skill levels or authorizations may need to use different controls to do their jobs. Or you may not know how many pieces of data you will need to display until run time. Sometimes you can display unknown amounts of data using a list, grid, or other control that can hold a variable number of items, but other times you might like to display the data in a series of labels or text boxes. In cases such as these, you need to create new controls at run time.

The following code shows how a program might create a new `Label` control. First it declares a variable of type `Label` and initializes it with the `New` keyword. It uses the label's `SetBounds` method to position the label and sets its `Text` property to "Hello World!" The code then adds the label to the current form's `Controls` collection.

```
Dim lbl As New Label
lbl.SetBounds(10, 50, 100, 25)
lbl.Text = "Hello World!"
Me.Controls.Add(lbl)
```

Usually, a label just displays a message so you don't need to catch its events. Other controls such as buttons and scroll bars, however, are not very useful if the program cannot respond to their events.

There are two approaches you can take to catching a new control's events. First, you can declare the control's variable with the `WithEvents` keyword. Then you can open the form in the code editor, select the variable's name from the left drop-down list, and select the event from the right drop-down list to give the control an event handler.

The following code demonstrates this approach. It declares variable `btnHi` at the module level using the `WithEvents` keyword. When you click the `btnMakeHiButton` button, its event handler initializes the variable. It sets the control's position and text, and adds it to the form's `Controls` collection. When the user clicks this button, the `btnHi_Click` event handler executes and displays a message.

```
' Declare the btnHi button WithEvents.
Private WithEvents btnHi As Button

' Make the new btnHi button.
Private Sub btnMakeHiButton_Click(ByVal sender As System.Object, _
 ByVal e As System.EventArgs) Handles btnMakeHiButton.Click
    btnHi = New Button
    btnHi.SetBounds(96, 50, 75, 23)
    btnHi.Text = "Say Hi"
    Me.Controls.Add(btnHi)
End Sub

' The user clicked the btnHi button.
Private Sub btnHi_Click(ByVal sender As Object, _
 ByVal e As System.EventArgs) Handles btnHi.Click
    MessageBox.Show("Hi")
End Sub
```

This first approach works if you know how many controls you need. Then you can define variables for them all using the `WithEvents` keyword. If you don't know how many controls you need to create, however, this isn't practical. For example, suppose that you want to create a button for each file in a directory. When the user clicks on a button, the file should open. If you don't know how many files the directory might hold, you don't know how many variables you might need.

One solution to this dilemma is to use the `AddHandler` statement to add event handlers to the new controls. The following code demonstrates this approach. When you click the `btnMakeHelloButton` button, its `Click` event handler creates a new `Button` object, storing it in a locally declared variable. It sets the button's position and text and adds it to the form's `Controls` collection as before. Next, the program uses the `AddHandler` statement to make subroutine `Hello_Click` an event handler for the button's `Click` event. When the user clicks the new button, subroutine `Hello_Click` displays a message.

```
' Make a new Hello button.
Private Sub btnMakeHelloButton_Click(ByVal sender As System.Object, _
 ByVal e As System.EventArgs) Handles btnMakeHelloButton.Click
    ' Make the button.
    Dim btnHello As New Button
    btnHello.SetBounds(184, 50, 75, 23)
    btnHello.Text = "Say Hello"
    Me.Controls.Add(btnHello)

    ' Add a Click event handler to the button.
    AddHandler btnHello.Click, AddressOf Hello_Click
End Sub

' The user clicked the Hello button.
Private Sub Hello_Click(ByVal sender As System.Object, _
 ByVal e As System.EventArgs)
    MessageBox.Show("Hello")
End Sub
```

You can use the same routine as an event handler for more than one button. In that case, the code can convert the sender parameter into a `Button` object and use the button's `Name`, `Text`, and other properties to determine which button was pressed.

To remove a control from the form, simply remove it from the form's `Controls` collection. To free the resources associated with the control, set any variables that refer to it to `Nothing`. For example, the following code removes the `btnHi` control created by the first example.

```
Me.Controls.Remove(btnHi)
btnHi = Nothing
```

This code will also remove controls that you created interactively at design time, as well as controls you create during run time.

Properties

A *property* is some value associated with a control. Often, a property corresponds in an obvious way one of the control's visual or behavioral features. For example, the `Text` property represents the text that the control displays, `BackColor` represents the control's background color, `Top` and `Left` represent the control's position, and so forth.

Many properties, including `Text`, `BackColor`, `Top`, and `Left`, apply to many kinds of controls. Other properties only work with certain specific types of controls. For example, the `ToolStrip` control has an `ImageList` property that indicates the `ImageList` control containing the images the `ToolStrip` should display.

You can manipulate a control's properties interactively at design time or using code at run time.

Properties at Design Time

To modify a control's properties at design time, open its form in the Form Designer and click on the control. The Properties window displays the control's properties. Figure 2-5 shows the Properties window displaying a Button control's properties. For example, the control's Text property has the value "Make Hi Button", and its TextAlign property (which determines where the button displays its text) is set to MiddleCenter.

The drop-down at the top of the Properties window, just below the Properties title, indicates that this control is named btnMakeHiButton and that it is of the System.Windows.Forms.Button class.

You can set many properties by clicking on a property's value in the Properties window and then typing the new value. This works with simple string values such as the controls' name and Text property, and it works with some other properties where typing a value makes some sense.

For example, the HScrollBar control (horizontal scrollbar) has Minimum, Maximum, and Value properties that determine the control's minimum, maximum, and current values. You can click on those properties in the Properties window and enter new values. When you press the Enter key or move to another property, the control validates the value you typed. If you entered a value that doesn't make sense (for example, if you typed "ABC" instead of a numeric value), the IDE reports the error and lets you fix it.

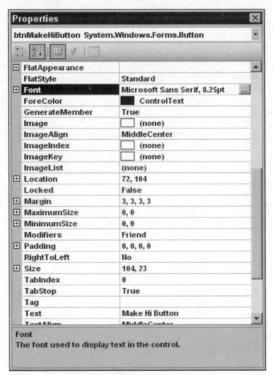

Figure 2-5: The Properties window lets you change a control's properties at design time.

Compound Properties

A few properties have compound values. The Location property includes the X and Y coordinates of the control's upper-left corner. The Size property contains the control's width and height. The Font property includes the font's name, size, boldness, and other font properties.

The Properties window displays these properties with a plus sign on the left. If you click the plus sign, the window expands the property to show the values that it contains. Figure 2-6 shows the same Properties window shown in Figure 2-5 with the Font and Location properties expanded. You can click on these subvalues and set them independently just as you can set any other property value.

When you expand a compound property, a minus sign appears to the left (see the Font and Location properties in Figure 2-6). Click this minus sign to collapse the property and hide its members.

In some cases, you can also set a compound property's values in a single step. The Location property shown in Figure 2-6 has the value "8, 8." You can type a new value (say, "16, 8") directly into the Property window.

Figure 2-6: The Properties window lets you change even complex properties at design time.

Some compound properties provide more sophisticated methods for setting the property's values. If you click the ellipsis button to the right of the Font property shown in Figure 2-6, the IDE presents the font selection dialog shown in Figure 2-7. You can use this dialog to set many of the font's properties.

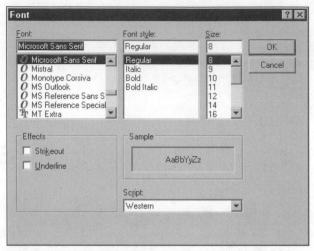

Figure 2-7: The Font property displays a dialog that lets you set the font's properties.

Restricted Properties

Some properties allow more restricted values. For example, the Visible property is a Boolean, so it can only take the values True and False. If you click on the property, a drop-down arrow appears on the right. If you click this arrow, the window displays a drop-down list where you can select one of the choices, True or False.

Many properties have enumerated values. The Button control's FlatStyle property allows the values Flat, Popup, Standard, and System. If you click the drop-down arrow to the right of this property, you'll see the list shown in Figure 2-8. You can select a new value from this list.

You can also double-click on the property to cycle through its allowed values. After you select a property, you can use the up and down arrows to move through the values.

Some properties determine at any given moment exactly what values they can take. For example, some properties contain references to other controls. The Button control's ImageList property is a reference to an ImageList component that contains the picture that the Button control should display. If you click the drop-down arrow to the right of this value, the Properties window displays a list of the ImageList components on the form that you might use for this property. This list also contains the entry (none), which you can select to remove any previous control reference in the property.

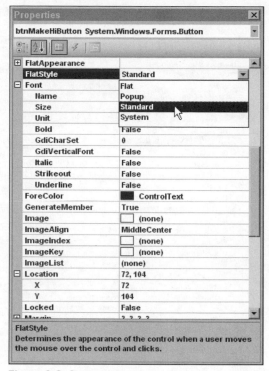

Figure 2-8: Some properties provide an enumerated list of allowed value.

Many properties take very specialized values and provide specialized property editors to let you select values easily. For example, the Anchor property lets you anchor a control's edges to the edges of its container. Normally, a control is anchored to the top and left edges of the container so that it remains in the same position even if the container is resized. If you also anchor the control on the right, its right edge moves in or out as the container gets wider or narrower. This lets you make controls that resize with their containers in certain useful ways.

If you select the Anchor property and click the drop-down arrow on the right, the Properties window displays the small graphical editor shown in Figure 2-9. Click on the skinny rectangles on the left, top, right, or bottom to anchor or unanchor the control on those sides. Press the Enter key to accept your choices or press Escape to cancel them.

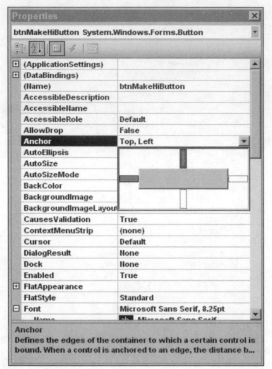

Figure 2-9: Some properties, such as `Anchor`, provide
specialized editors to let you select their values.

Other complex properties may provide other editors. These are generally self-explanatory. Click the ellipsis or drop-down arrow to the right of a property value, and experiment to see how these editors work.

You can right-click any property and select Reset from its context menu to reset the property to a default value. Many complex properties can take the value "(none)," and for those properties, selecting Reset usually sets the value to "(none)."

Collection Properties

Some properties represent collections of objects. For example, the `ListBox` control displays a list of items. Its `Items` property is a collection containing those items. The Properties window displays the value of this property as "(Collection)." If you select this property and click the ellipsis to the right, the Properties window displays a simple dialog where you can edit the text displayed by the control's items. This dialog is quite straightforward: Enter the items' text on separate lines and click OK.

Other properties are much more complex. For example, to create a `TabControl` that displays images on its tabs, you must also create an `ImageList` component. Select the `ImageList`'s `Images` property, and click the ellipsis to the right to display the dialog shown in Figure 2-10. When you click the Add button, the dialog displays a file selection dialog that lets you add an image file to the control. The list on the left shows you the images you have loaded and includes a small thumbnail picture of each image. The values on the right show you the images' properties.

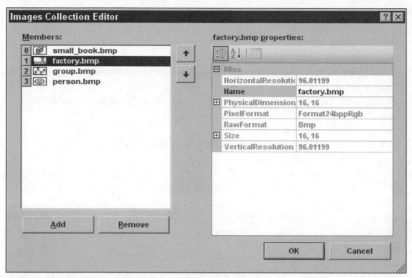

Figure 2-10: This dialog lets you load images into an `ImageList` control at design time.

After you add pictures to the `ImageList` control, create a `TabControl`. Select its `ImageList` property, click the drop-down arrow on the right, and select the `ImageList` control you created. Next, select the `TabControl`'s `TabPages` property, and click the ellipsis on the right to see the dialog shown in Figure 2-11.

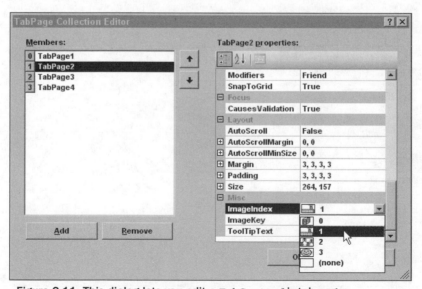

Figure 2-11: This dialog lets you edit a `TabControl`'s tab pages.

Select a tab page, click on its `ImageIndex` property, click the drop-down arrow to the right, and pick the number of the image in the `ImageList` that you want to use for this tab. Figure 2-12 shows the result.

Some properties even contain a collection of objects, each of which contains a collection of objects. For example, the `ListView` control has an `Items` property that is a collection. Each item in that collection is an object that has a `SubItems` property, which is itself a collection. When you display the `ListView` control as a list with details, an object in the `Items` collection represents a row in the view and the `SubItems` property represents the secondary values in a row.

To set these values at design time, select the control and click the ellipsis to the right of the control's `Items` property in the Properties window. Create an item in the editor, and click the ellipsis to the right of the item's `SubItems` property. Figure 2-13 shows these editors in action. The one in the back is the `Items` editor; the one in front is the `SubItems` editor.

Other complicated properties provide similarly complex editors. While they may implement involved relationships among various controls and components, they are usually easy enough to figure out with a little experimentation.

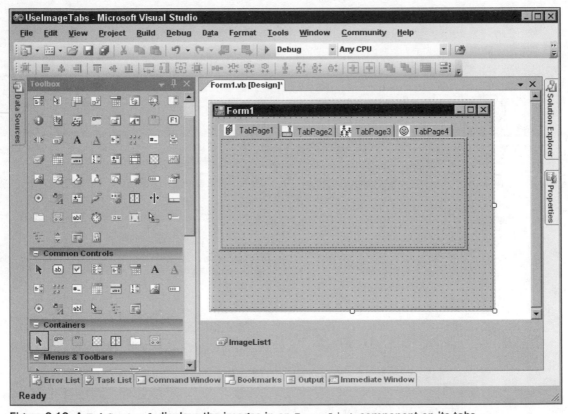

Figure 2-12: A `TabControl` displays the images in an `ImageList` component on its tabs.

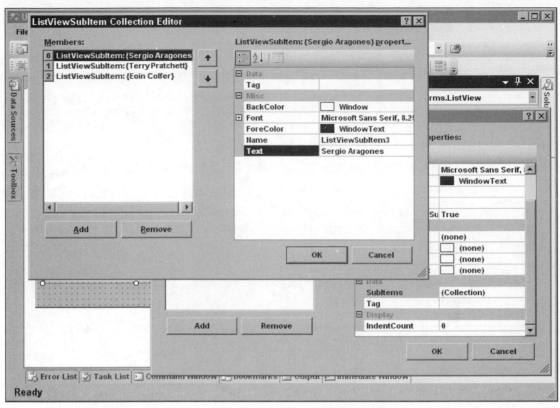

Figure 2-13: The objects in the `ListView` control's `Items` collection each have a `SubItems` property, which is also a collection.

Properties at Run Time

Visual Basic lets you set most control properties at design time, but often you will need to view and modify property values at run time. For example, you might need to change a label's text to tell the user that something has changed, disable a button because it is not applicable at a particular moment, or read the value selected by the user from a list.

As far as your code is concerned, a property is just like any other public variable defined by an object. You get or set a property by using the name of the control, followed by a dot, followed by the name of the property. For example, the following code examines the text in the `TextBox` named `txtPath`. If the text doesn't end with a `/` character, the code adds one. This code both reads and sets the `Text` property.

```
If Not txtPath.Text.EndsWith("/") Then txtPath.Text &= "/"
```

If a property contains a reference to an object, you can use the object's properties and methods in your code. The following code displays a message box indicating whether the `txtPath` control's font is bold. It examines the `TextBox`'s `Font` property. That property returns a reference to a `Font` object that has a `Bold` property.

```
If txtPath.Font.Bold Then
    MessageBox.Show("Bold")
Else
    MessageBox.Show("Not Bold")
End If
```

Note that a `Font` object's properties are read-only, so the code cannot set the value of `txtPath.Font`
`.Bold`. To change the `TextBox` control's font, the code would need to create a new font as shown in the
following code. This code passes the `Font` object's constructor a copy of the TextBox control's current
font to use as a template, and a value indicating that the new font should be bold.

```
txtPath.Font = New Font(txtPath.Font, FontStyle.Bold)
```

If a property represents a collection or array, you can loop through or iterate over the property just as if it
were declared as a normal collection or array. The following code lists the items the user has selected in
the `ListBox` control named `lstChoices`. (If the `ListBox` control's `SelectionMode` property is set to
`MuliExtended`, the user can select any or all of the items.)

```
For Each selected_item As Object In lstChoices.SelectedItems()
    Debug.WriteLine(selected_item.ToString)
Next selected_item
```

A few properties are read-only at run time, so your code can examine them but not change their values.
For example, a `Panel` control's `Controls` property returns a collection holding references to the controls
inside the `Panel`. This property is read-only at run time so you cannot set it equal to a new collection.
Note that the collection provides methods for adding and removing controls so you don't really need to
replace the whole collection, you can change the controls that it contains instead.

Note also that at design time, this collection doesn't appear in the Properties window. Instead of explicitly working with the collection, you add and remove controls interactively by dropping them in and out
of the `Panel` control.

A control's `Bottom` property is also read-only and not shown in the Properties window. It represents the
distance between the top of the control's container and the control's bottom edge. This value is really
just the control's `Top` property plus its `Height` property (`control.Bottom = control.Top + control.`
`Height`), so you can modify it using those properties instead of setting the `Bottom` property directly.

In theory, a property can also be write-only at run time. Such a property is really more like a method
than a property, however, so most controls use a method instead. In practice, read-only properties are
uncommon and write-only properties are extremely rare.

Useful Control Properties

Appendix A, "Useful Control Properties, Methods, and Events," summarizes the `Control` class's most
important properties.

All controls (including the `Form` control) inherit directly or indirectly from the `Control` class. That
means they inherit the `Control` class's properties, methods, and events, unless they take action to override the `Control` class's behavior.

While these properties are available to all controls that inherit from the Control class, many are considered "advanced," so they are not shown by the IntelliSense pop-up's Common tab. For example, a program is intended to set a control's position by using its Location property not its Left and Top properties, so Location is in the Common tab while Left and Top are only in the Advanced tab.

Figure 2-14 shows the Common tab on the IntelliSense pop-up for a Label control. It shows the Location property but not the Left property. If you click on the All tab, you can see Left and the other advanced properties. If you type the control's name and enough of the string Left to differentiate it from the Location property (in this case lblDirectory.Le), the pop-up automatically switches to the All tab.

Many of the properties described in the previous list are straightforward, but a few deserve special attention. The following sections describe some of the more confusing properties in greater detail.

Anchor and Dock

The Anchor and Dock properties allow a control to automatically resize itself when its container is resized. The Anchor property determines which of the controls edges should remain a fixed distance from the corresponding edges of the container.

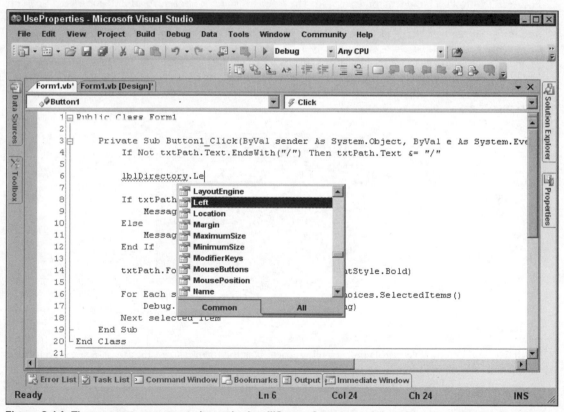

Figure 2-14: The Location property is on the IntelliSense Common tab but the Left property is not.

For example, normally a control's `Anchor` property is set to `Top`, `Left`. That means the control's top and `left` positions remain fixed when the container resizes. If the control's upper-left corner is at the point (8, 16) initially, it remains at the position (8, 16) when you resize the container. This is the normal control behavior, and it makes the control appear fixed on the container.

For another example, suppose that you set a control's `Anchor` property to `Top`, `Right`, and you place the control in the container's upper-right corner. When you resize the container, the control moves, so it remains in the upper-right corner.

If you set two opposite `Anchor` values, the control resizes itself to satisfy them both. For example, suppose that you make a button that starts 8 pixels from its container's left, right, and top edges. Then suppose that you set the control's `Anchor` property to `Top`, `Left`, `Right`. When you resize the container, the control resizes itself so that it is always 8 pixels from the container's left, right, and top edges.

In a more common scenario, you can place `Label` controls on the left with `Anchor` set to `Top`, `Left` so they remain fixed on the form. On the right, you can place `TextBoxes` and other controls with `Anchor` set to `Top`, `Left`, `Right`, so they resize themselves to take advantage of the resizing form's new width.

Figure 2-15 shows a New Customer dialog. The `Labels`, state `ComboBox`, and ZIP code `TextBox` controls all have `Anchor` set to `Top`, `Left` so they do not move when the form resizes. The two buttons have `Anchor` set to `Top`, `Right`, so they keep their positions relative to the upper-right corner of the form. The `First Name`, `Last Name`, `Street`, and `City` `TextBox` controls have `Anchor` set to `Top`, `Left`, `Right`, so they resize themselves to fill in whatever space is between the labels and the buttons. This arrangement lets the `TextBox` controls use as much of the form's available space as possible. The `Anchor` properties are set at design time and do all the work automatically, so you don't need to write any extra code to rearrange the controls at run time.

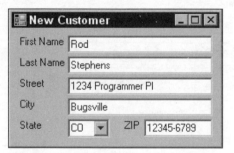

Figure 2-15: This dialog uses `Anchor`
properties to make its `TextBox` **controls**
use whatever space is available on the form.

Similarly, you can make controls that stretch vertically as the form resizes. Figure 2-16 shows a form listing customer orders. The upper `ListView` control has `Anchor` set to `Top`, `Left`, `Right`, so it keeps its initial height and fills the width of the form. The bottom `ListView` has `Anchor` set to `Top`, `Bottom`, `Left`, `Right`. It fills the width of the form and fills the form from its initial `Top` position to the bottom of the form. If the user makes the form taller, the control resizes itself to use the available space.

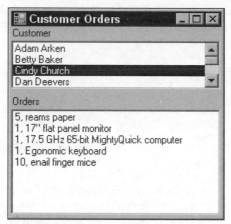

Figure 2-16: The bottom `ListView` **control resizes itself to use up any extra vertical space on the form.**

If you do not provide any `Anchor` value for either the vertical or horizontal directions, the control anchors its center to the container's center. For example, suppose that you position a button in the bottom middle of the form and you set `Anchor` to `Bottom` (omitting `Left` and `Right`). Because you placed the control in the middle of the form, the control's center coincides with the form's center. When you resize the form, the control moves so it remains centered horizontally.

If you place other controls on either side of the centered one, they will all move so they remain together centered as a group as the form resizes. Figure 2-17 shows a form containing a group of controls with `Anchor` set to `Bottom`. You may want to experiment with this property to see the effect.

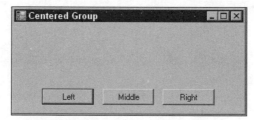

Figure 2-17: Controls with `Anchor` **set to** `Bottom` **remain centered as a group.**

At run time, you can set a control's `Anchor` property to `AnchorStyles.None` or to a Boolean combination of the values `AnchorStyles.Top`, `AnchorStyles.Bottom`, `AnchorStyles.Left`, and `AnchorStyles.Right`. For example, the following code moves the `Button1` control to the form's lower-right corner and sets its `Anchor` property to `Bottom, Right`, so it stays there.

```
Private Sub Form1_Load(ByVal sender As System.Object, _
 ByVal e As System.EventArgs) Handles MyBase.Load
    Button1.Location = New Point( _
        Me.ClientRectangle.Width - Button1.Width, _
        Me.ClientRectangle.Height - Button1.Height)
    Button1.Anchor = AnchorStyles.Bottom Or AnchorStyles.Right
End Sub
```

Dock

The Dock property determines whether a control attaches itself to one or more of its container's sides. For example, if you set a control's Dock property to Top, the control docks to the top of its container. It fills the container from left to right and is flush with the top of the container. If the container is resized, the control remains at the top, keeps its height, and resizes itself to fill the container's width. This is how a typical toolbar behaves. The effect is similar to placing the control at the top of the container so that it fills the container's width and then setting the Anchor property to Top, Left, Right.

You can set a control's Dock property to Top, Bottom, Left, Right, Fill, or None. The value Fill makes the control dock to all of its container's remaining interior space. If it is the only control in the container, that makes it fill the whole container.

If the container holds more than one control with Dock set to a value other than None, the controls are arranged according to their stacking order (also called the Z-order). The control that is first in the stacking order (would normally be drawn first at the back) is positioned first using its Dock value. The control that comes next in the stacking order is arranged second, and so on until all of the controls are positioned.

Figure 2-18 shows four TextBoxes with Dock set to different values. The first in the stacking order has Dock set to Left so it occupies the left edge of the form. The next control has Dock set to Top, so it occupies the top edge of the form's remaining area. The third control has Dock set to Right, so it occupies the right edge of the form's remaining area. Finally, the last control has Dock set to Fill so it fills the rest of the form.

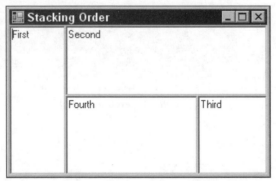

Figure 2-18: Controls with Dock not equal to None are arranged according to their stacking order.

Controls docked to an edge resize to fill the container in one dimension. For example, a control with Dock set to Top fills whatever width the container has available. A control with Dock set to Fill resizes to fill all of the form's available space.

Other than that, the Dock property does not arrange controls very intelligently when you resize the container. For example, suppose that you have two controls, one above the other. The first has Dock set to Top and the second has Dock set to Fill. You can arrange the controls so that they evenly divide the form vertically. When you make the form taller, however, the second control, with Dock set to Fill, takes up all of the new space, and the other control remains the same size.

You cannot use the Dock property to make the controls divide the form evenly when it is resized. You cannot use the Anchor property to evenly divide the form either. Instead, you need to use code similar to the following. When the form resizes, this code moves and sizes the two controls TextBox1 and TextBox2 to fill the form, evenly dividing it vertically.

```
Private Sub Form1_Load(ByVal sender As Object, _
 ByVal e As System.EventArgs) Handles Me.Load
    ArrangeTextBoxes()
End Sub

Private Sub Form1_Resize(ByVal sender As Object, _
 ByVal e As System.EventArgs) Handles Me.Resize
    ArrangeTextBoxes()
End Sub

Private Sub ArrangeTextBoxes()
    Dim wid As Integer = Me.ClientRectangle.Width
    Dim hgt1 As Integer = Me.ClientRectangle.Height \ 2
    Dim hgt2 As Integer = Me.ClientRectangle.Height - hgt1
    TextBox1.SetBounds(0, 0, wid, hgt1)
    TextBox2.SetBounds(0, hgt1, wid, hgt2)
End Sub
```

When you want to divide a form, the SplitterContainer control can also be useful. The SplitterContainer contains two panels that can hold other controls. The user can drag the divider between the two panels to adjust the size allocated to each.

Position and Size Properties

Controls contain many position and size properties, and the differences among them can be confusing. Some of the more bewildering aspects of controls are the ideas of client area, nonclient area, and display area.

A control's *client area* is the area inside the control where you can draw things or place other controls. A control's *nonclient area* is everything else. In a typical form, the borders, title bar, and menus are the nonclient area. The client area is the space inside the borders and below the menus where you can place controls or draw graphics.

A control's *display area* is the client area minus any internal decoration. For example, a GroupBox control displays an internal border and a title. While you can place controls over these, you normally wouldn't. The display area contains the space inside the GroupBox's borders and below the space where the title sits.

The following table describes properties related to the control's size and position.

Property	Data Type	Read/Write	Purpose
Bounds	Rectangle	Read/Write	The control's size and position within its container including non-client areas.
ClientRectangle	Rectangle	Read	The size and position of the client area within the control.
ClientSize	Size	Read/Write	The size of the client area. If you set this value, the control adjusts its size to make room for the nonclient area, while giving you this client size.
DisplayRectangle	Rectangle	Read	The size and position of the area within the control where you would normally draw or place other controls.
Location	Point	Read/Write	The position of the control's upper-left corner within its container.
Size	Point	Read/Write	The control's size including non-client areas.
Left, Top, Width, Height	Integer	Read/Write	The control's size and position within its container including nonclient areas.
Bottom, Right	Integer	Read	The position of the control's lower-right corner within its container.

Methods

A *method* executes code associated with a control. The method can be a function that returns a value or a subroutine that does not return a value. Methods can take parameters just like any other function or subroutine.

Because methods execute code, you cannot invoke them at design time. You can only invoke them using code at run time.

Appendix A summarizes the Control class's most important methods. Controls that inherit from the Control class also inherit these methods unless they have overridden the Control class's behavior.

Events

A control or other object raises an *event* to let the program know about some change in circumstances. Sometimes raising an event is also called "firing" or "throwing" the event. Specific control classes provide events that are relevant to their special purposes. For example, the `Button` control provides a `Click` event to let the program know when the user clicks on the button.

The program responds to an event by creating an event handler that "catches" the event and takes whatever action is appropriate. Each event defines its own event-handler format and determines the parameters that the event handler will receive. Often, these parameters give additional information about the event.

For example, when part of the form is covered and exposed, the form raises its `Paint` event. The `Paint` event handler takes as a parameter an object of type `PaintEventArgs`. That object's `gr` property is a reference to a `Graphics` object that the program can use to redraw the form's contents.

Some event handlers take parameters that are used to send information about the event back to the object that raised it. For example, the `Form` class's `FormClosing` event handler has a parameter of type `FormClosingEventArgs`. That parameter is an object with that has a property named `Cancel`. If the program sets `Cancel` to `True`, the `Form` cancels the `FormClosing` event and remains open. For example, the event handler can verify that the data entered by the user was properly formatted. If the values didn't make sense, the program can display an error message and keep the form open.

While many of a control's most useful events are specific to the control type, controls do inherit some common events from the `Control` class. Appendix A summarizes the `Control` class's most important events. Controls that inherit from the `Control` class also inherit these events unless they have overridden the `Control` class's behavior.

Creating Event Handlers at Design Time

There are a couple of ways that you can create an event handler at design time. If you open a form in the Form Designer and double-click on a control, the code editor opens and displays the control's default event handler. For example, a `TextBox` control opens its `TextChanged` event handler, a `Button` control opens its `Click` event handler, and the form itself opens its `Load` event handler.

To create some other nondefault event handler for a control, open the code window, select the control from the left drop-down list, and then select the event handler from the right drop-down list, as shown in Figure 2-19. To create an even handler for the form itself, select "(Form1 Events)" from the left drop-down and then select an event from the right drop-down.

The code window creates an event handler with the correct parameters and return value. For example, the following code shows an empty `TextBox` control's `Click` event handler (note that the first two lines are wrapped in this text and appear on one line in the code editor). Now you just need to fill in the code that you want to execute when the event occurs.

```
Private Sub TextBox1_Click(ByVal sender As Object, ByVal e As System.EventArgs) _
    Handles TextBox1.Click

End Sub
```

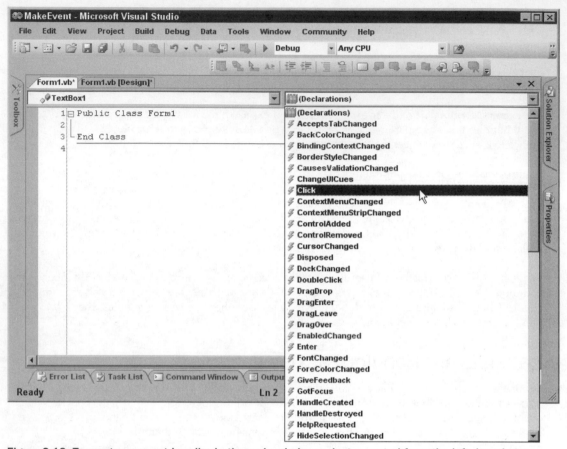

Figure 2-19: To create an event handler in the code window, select a control from the left drop-down, and then select an event from the right drop-down.

WithEvents Event Handlers

If you declare an object variable using the `WithEvents` keyword, you can catch its events. After you declare the variable, you can select it in the code designer's left drop-down, just as you can select any other control. Then you can select one of the object's events from the right drop-down.

When the code assigns an instance of an object to the variable, any event handlers defined for the variable receive the object's events.

Usually, you don't need to create `WithEvents` variables for controls because Visual Basic does it for you. However, using a variable declared `WithEvents` lets you enable and disable events quickly and easily. For example, suppose that a program wants to track a `PictureBox`'s mouse events at some times, but not at others. It could declare a `PictureBox` variable as shown in the following code.

```
Private WithEvents m_Canvas As PictureBox
```

When the program wants to receive events, it can set this variable equal to its `PictureBox` control as in this code. Now the variable's event handlers such as `m_Canvas_MouseDown`, `m_Canvas_MouseMove`, and `m_Canvas_MouseUp` are enabled.

```
m_Canvas = PictureBox1
```

When it no longer wants to receive these events, the program can set `m_Canvas` to `Nothing` as in the following statement. While `m_Canvas` is `Nothing`, it has no associated control to generate events for it.

```
m_Canvas = Nothing
```

Setting Event Handlers at Run Time

Not only can you create event handlers at design time, but you can also assign them at run time. First create the event handler. You must get the routine's parameters exactly correct for the type of event handler you want to create. For example, a `TextBox` control's `Click` event handler must take two parameters with types `System.Object` and `System.EventArgs`.

To ensure that you get the details right, you can start by creating an event handler for a normal control at design time. Select the control from the code designer's left drop-down, and then select the event from the right. Change the resulting event handler's name to something appropriate (for example, you might change `Button1_Click` to `ToolClicked`) and remove the `Handles` statement that ties the event handler to the control. You can also delete the original control if you don't need it for anything else.

Now you can use the `AddHandler` and `RemoveHandler` statements to add and remove the event handler from a control. The following code shows how a program can switch the event handler that a button executes when it is clicked.

When `RadioButton1` is checked or unchecked, its `CheckedChanged` event handler adds or removes the `ButtonHandler1` event handler from the `Button1` control's `Click` event. Similarly, when `RadioButton2` is checked or unchecked, its `CheckedChanged` event handler adds or removes the `ButtonHandler2` event handler from the `Button1` control's `Click` event.

The `ButtonHandler1` and `ButtonHandler2` event handlers simply display a message telling you which is executing. The form's `Load` event handler selects the first radio button.

```
' Add or remove ButtonHandler1.
Private Sub RadioButton1_CheckedChanged(ByVal sender As System.Object, _
  ByVal e As System.EventArgs) Handles RadioButton1.CheckedChanged
    If RadioButton1.Checked Then
        AddHandler Button1.Click, AddressOf ButtonHandler1
    Else
        RemoveHandler Button1.Click, AddressOf ButtonHandler1
    End If
End Sub

' Add or remove ButtonHandler2.
Private Sub RadioButton2_CheckedChanged(ByVal sender As System.Object, _
  ByVal e As System.EventArgs) Handles RadioButton2.CheckedChanged
    If RadioButton2.Checked Then
```

```
            AddHandler Button1.Click, AddressOf ButtonHandler2
        Else
            RemoveHandler Button1.Click, AddressOf ButtonHandler2
        End If
    End Sub

    ' Display a message telling which event handler this is.
    Private Sub ButtonHandler1(ByVal sender As System.Object, _
     ByVal e As System.EventArgs)
        MessageBox.Show("ButtonHandler1")
    End Sub

    Private Sub ButtonHandler2(ByVal sender As System.Object, _
     ByVal e As System.EventArgs)
        MessageBox.Show("ButtonHandler2")
    End Sub

    ' Start with RadioButton1 selected.
    Private Sub Form1_Load(ByVal sender As System.Object, _
     ByVal e As System.EventArgs) Handles MyBase.Load
        RadioButton1.Checked = True
    End Sub
```

You can also use `AddHandler` and `RemoveHandler` to enable and disable events as needed much as the previous section showed how to enable and disable events using variables declared with the `WithEvents` keyword.

`AddHandler` and `RemoveHandler` allow you to switch one or two events relatively easily. If you must switch many event handlers for the same control at once, however, it may be easier to use a variable declared using the `WithEvents` keyword.

Changing Design Time Event Handlers

An event handler you create for a particular control at design time is just like any other event handler subroutine at run time. You can use `RemoveHandler` to detach it from the control's events, and you can use `AddHandler` to reattach it to an event.

Typically, an event handler that you create attached to a particular control seems different from those you write separately from any control. It may follow different naming conventions (perhaps `btnTool_Click` versus `ToolClickEventHandler`), and its declaration includes a `Handles` clause that a "hand-coded" event-handling routine will not have.

This lack of symmetry may make switching these event handlers with those you create on your own a bit confusing. On the other hand, using `AddHandler` and `RemoveHandler` to remove and reattach an event handler is relatively straightforward. As long as you don't mix and match the two kinds of event handlers, this should cause no confusion.

Control "Array" Events

Visual Basic 6 and earlier versions allowed you to use control arrays. A *control array* was an array of controls with the same name that shared the same event handlers. A parameter to the event handlers gave the index of the control in the array that fired the event. If the controls perform closely related tasks, the common event handler may be able to share a lot of code for all of the controls. Visual Basic .NET does not allow control arrays, but you can get similar effects in a couple of ways.

First, suppose that you add a control to a form and give it event handlers. Then you copy and paste the control to make other controls on the form. All these controls share the event handlers you already created by default. If you look at the event handlers' code, you'll see the `Handles` statements list all of the copied controls. You can also modify an event handler's `Handles` clause manually to attach it to more than one control.

Another way to make controls share event handlers is to attach them to the controls by using the `AddHandler` statement.

An event handler's first parameter is a variable of the type `System.Object` that contains a reference to the object that raised the event. The program can use this object and its properties (for example, its `Name` property) to determine which control raised the event and take appropriate action.

Validation Events

Data validation is an important part of many applications. Visual Basic provides two events to make validating data easier: `Validating` and `Validated`.

The `Validating` event fires when the code should validate a control's data. This happens when the control has the input focus and the form tries to close, and when focus moves from the control to another control that has `CausesValidation` property set to `True`.

The `Validation` event handler can verify that the data in a control has a legal value and take appropriate action if it doesn't. For example, consider the form shown in Figure 2-20. The first `TextBox`'s `Validating` event handler checks that the control's value contains exactly five digits. If the value does not contain five digits, as is the case in the figure, the program uses an `ErrorProvider` control to flag the `TextBox`'s value as being in error and moves the input focus back to the `TextBox`. The `ErrorProvider` displays the little exclamation mark icon to the right of the control and makes the icon blink several times to get the user's attention. If the user hovers the mouse over the icon, the `ErrorProvider` displays the error text in a tooltip.

Figure 2-20: The `Validating` event fires when the focus moves to a control that has CausesValidation set to True.

The second `TextBox` control in this example has a `CausesValidation` property value of `False`. When the user moves from the first `TextBox` control to the second one, the `Validating` event does not fire and the `TextBox` control is not flagged. The third `TextBox` control has `CausesValidation` set to `True` so, when the user moves into that `TextBox` control, the first `TextBox`'s `Validating` event fires, and the value is flagged if it is invalid. The `Validating` event also fires if the user tries to close the form.

The following code shows the `Validating` event handler used by this example. Notice that the `Handles` clause lists all three `TextBoxes' Validating` events so this event handler catches the `Validating` event for all three controls.

The event handler receives the control that raised the event in its sender parameter. It uses `DirectCast` to convert that generic Object into a `TextBox` object and passes it to the `ValidateFiveDigits` subroutine. It also passes the `e.Cancel` parameter, so the subroutine can cancel the action that caused the event if necessary.

`ValidateFiveDigits` checks the `TextBox's` contents and sets its `cancel_event` parameter to `True` if the text has nonzero length and is not exactly five digits. This parameter is passed by reference so this changes the original value of `e.Cancel` in the calling event handler. That will restore focus to the `TextBox` control that raised the event and that contains the invalid data.

If `cancel_event` is `True`, then the value is invalid so the program uses the `ErrorProvider` component named ErrorProvider1 to assign an error message to the `TextBox` control.

If `cancel_event` is `False`, then the value is valid so the program blanks the `ErrorProvider's` message for the `TextBox` control.

The event handler receives the control that raised the event in its sender parameter. It uses `DirectCast` to convert that generic `Object` into a `TextBox` object and passes it to the `ValidateFiveDigits` subroutine. It also passes the `e.Cancel` parameter, so the subroutine can cancel the action that caused the event if necessary.

`ValidateFiveDigits` checks the `TextBox's` contents and sets its cancel_event parameter to `True` if the text has nonzero length and is not exactly five digits. This parameter is passed by reference, so this changes the original value of `e.Cancel` in the calling event handler. That will restore focus to the `TextBox` that raised the event and that contains the invalid data.

If `cancel_event` is `True`, the value is invalid, so the program uses the `ErrorProvider` component named ErrorProvider1 to assign an error message to the `TextBox` control.

If `cancel_event` is `False`, then the value is valid so the program blanks the `ErrorProvider's` message for the `TextBox`.

```
' Validate the TextBox's contents.
Private Sub TextBox1_Validating(ByVal sender As Object, _
 ByVal e As System.ComponentModel.CancelEventArgs) _
 Handles TextBox1.Validating, TextBox2.Validating, TextBox3.Validating
    ' Get the TextBox.
    Dim text_box As TextBox = DirectCast(sender, TextBox)

    ' Validate the control's value.
    ValidateFiveDigits(text_box, e.Cancel)
End Sub

' Verify that the TextBox contains five digits.
Private Sub ValidateFiveDigits(ByVal text_box As TextBox, _
 ByRef cancel_event As Boolean)
    If text_box.Text.Length = 0 Then
```

```
            ' Allow a zero-length string.
            cancel_event = False
        Else
            ' Allow five digits.
            cancel_event = Not (text_box.Text Like "#####")
        End If

        ' See if we're going to cancel the event.
        If cancel_event Then
            ' Invalid. Set an error.
            ErrorProvider1.SetError(text_box, _
                text_box.Name & " must contain exactly five digits")
        Else
            ' Valid. Clear any error.
            ErrorProvider1.SetError(text_box, "")
        End If
End Sub
```

The event handler receives the control that raised the event in its sender parameter. It uses DirectCast to convert that generic Object into a TextBox object and passes it to the ValidateFiveDigits subroutine. It also passes the e.Cancel parameter, so the subroutine can cancel the action that caused the event if necessary.

ValidateFiveDigits checks the TextBox's contents and sets its cancel_event parameter to True if the text has nonzero length and is not exactly five digits. This parameter is passed by reference, so this changes the original value of e.Cancel in the calling event handler. That will restore focus to the TextBox that raised the event and that contains the invalid data.

If cancel_event is True, the value is invalid, so the program uses the ErrorProvider component named ErrorProvider1 to assign an error message to the TextBox control.

If cancel_event is False, then the value is valid so the program blanks the ErrorProvider's message for the TextBox control.

Separated Validation

A control's Validated event fires after the focus successfully leaves the control, either to another control with CausesValidation set to True or when the form closes. The control should have already validated its contents in its Validating event, hence the event name Validated.

This event doesn't really have anything directly to do with validation, however, and it fires whether or not the code has a Validating event handler and even if the control's value is invalid. The only time it will not execute is if the validation does not complete. That happens if the Validating event handler cancels the event causing the validation.

The previous section showed how to set or clear a control's error in its Validating event handler. An alternative strategy is to set errors in the Validating event handler and clear them in the Validated event handler, as shown in the following code. If the control's value is invalid, the Validating event handler cancels the event causing the validation so the Validated event does not occur. If the control's value is valid, the Validating event handler does not cancel the event and the Validated event handler executes, clearing any previous error.

```
' Validate the TextBox's contents.
Private Sub TextBox1_Validating(ByVal sender As Object, _
 ByVal e As System.ComponentModel.CancelEventArgs) _
 Handles TextBox1.Validating, TextBox2.Validating, TextBox3.Validating
    ' Validate the control's value.
    ValidateFiveDigits(DirectCast(sender, TextBox), e.Cancel)
End Sub

' Verify that the TextBox contains five digits.
Private Sub ValidateFiveDigits(ByVal text_box As TextBox, _
 ByRef cancel_event As Boolean)
    ' Cancel if nonzero length and not five digits.
    cancel_event = (text_box.Text.Length <> 0) And _
        Not (text_box.Text Like "#####")

    ' See if we're going to cancel the event.
    If cancel_event Then
        ' Invalid. Set an error.
        ErrorProvider1.SetError(text_box, _
            text_box.Name & " must contain exactly five digits")
    End If
End Sub

' Validation succeeded. Clear any error.
Private Sub TextBox1_Validated(ByVal sender As Object, _
 ByVal e As System.EventArgs) _
 Handles TextBox1.Validated, TextBox2.Validated, TextBox3.Validated
    ' Valid. Clear any error.
    ErrorProvider1.SetError(DirectCast(sender, TextBox), "")
End Sub
```

Deferred Validation

By keeping focus in the control that contains the error, the previous approaches force the user to fix problems as soon as possible. In some applications, it may be better to let the user continue filling out other fields and fix the problems later. For example, a user who is touch-typing data into a lot several fields may not look up to see the error until much later, after failing to enter many values in the invalid field and wasting a lot of time.

The following code shows one way to let the user continue entering values in other fields. The Validating event handler calls the ValidateFiveDigits subroutine much as before, but this time ValidateFiveDigits does not take the cancel_event parameter. If the TextBox's value has an error, the routine uses the ErrorProvider to assigns an error message to it and exits.

When the user tries to close the form, the FormClosing event handler executes. This routine assumes that some field contains invalid data, so it sets e.Cancel to True. It then calls function IsInvalidField for each of the controls that it wants to validate. If IsInvalidField returns True, the event handler exits, e.Cancel remains True, and the form refuses to close. If all of the fields pass validation, then the event handler sets e.Cancel to False, and the form closes.

Function IsInvalidField uses the ErrorProvider's GetError method to get a control's assigned error message. If the message is blank, the function returns False to indicate that the control's data is valid. If the message is not blank, then the function displays it in a message box, sets focus to the control, and returns `True` to indicate that the data is invalid.

When the user tries to close the form, the `FormClosing` event handler executes. This routine assumes that some field contains invalid data, so it sets `e.Cancel` to `True`. It then calls function `IsInvalidField` for each of the controls that it wants to validate. If `IsInvalidField` returns `True`, the event handler exits, `e.Cancel` remains `True`, and the form refuses to close. If all of the fields pass validation, the event handler sets `e.Cancel` to `False`, and the form closes.

Function `IsInvalidField` uses the `ErrorProvider`'s `GetError` method to get a control's assigned error message. If the message is blank, then the function returns `False` to indicate that the control's data is valid. If the message is not blank, then the function displays it in a message box, sets focus to the control, and returns `True` to indicate that the data is invalid.

```
' Validate the TextBox's contents.
Private Sub TextBox1_Validating(ByVal sender As Object, _
 ByVal e As System.ComponentModel.CancelEventArgs) _
 Handles TextBox1.Validating, TextBox2.Validating, TextBox3.Validating
    ' Validate the control's value.
    ValidateFiveDigits(DirectCast(sender, TextBox))
End Sub

' Verify that the TextBox contains five digits.
Private Sub ValidateFiveDigits(ByVal text_box As TextBox)
    ' See if the data is valid.
    If (text_box.Text.Length <> 0) And _
        Not (text_box.Text Like "#####") _
    Then
        ' Invalid. Set an error.
        ErrorProvider1.SetError(text_box, _
            text_box.Name & " must contain exactly five digits")
    Else
        ' Valid. Clear the error.
        ErrorProvider1.SetError(text_box, "")
    End If
End Sub

' See if any fields have error messages.
Private Sub Form1_FormClosing(ByVal sender As Object, _
 ByVal e As System.Windows.Forms.FormClosingEventArgs) _
 Handles Me.FormClosing
    ' Assume we will cancel the close.
    e.Cancel = True

    ' Check for errors.
    If IsInvalidField(TextBox1) Then Exit Sub
    If IsInvalidField(TextBox3) Then Exit Sub

    ' If we got this far, the data's okay.
    e.Cancel = False
End Sub

' If this control has an error message assigned to it,
```

```
' display the message, set focus to the control,
' and return True.
Private Function IsInvalidField(ByVal ctl As Control) As Boolean
    ' See if the control has an associated error message.
    If ErrorProvider1.GetError(ctl).Length = 0 Then
        ' No error message.
        Return False
    Else
        ' There is an error message.
        ' Display the message.
        MessageBox.Show(ErrorProvider1.GetError(ctl))

        ' Set focus to the control.
        ctl.Focus()
        Return True
    End If
End Function
```

When the user tries to close the form, the `FormClosing` event handler executes. This routine assumes that some field contains invalid data so it sets `e.Cancel` to `True`. It then calls function `IsInvalidField` for each of the controls that it wants to validate. If `IsInvalidField` returns `True`, the event handler exits, `e.Cancel` remains `True`, and the form refuses to close. If all of the fields pass validation, the event handler sets `e.Cancel` to `False`, and the form closes.

The function `IsInvalidField` uses the `ErrorProvider`'s `GetError` method to get a control's assigned error message. If the message is blank, the function returns `False` to indicate that the control's data is valid. If the message is not blank, then the function displays it in a message box, sets focus to the control, and returns `True` to indicate that the data is invalid.

If the focus is in a `TextBox` when the form tries to close, its `Validating` event fires before the form's `FormClosing` event so the `TextBox` control has a chance to validate its contents before the `FormClosing` event fires.

Summary

This chapter describes controls, components, and objects in general terms. It tells how to create controls and how to use their properties, methods, and events. It spends some extra time on data-validation events, as well as adding and removing event handlers.

Appendix A, "Useful Control Properties, Methods, and Events," describes the most useful properties, methods, and events provided by the `Control` class. All controls that inherit from this class also inherit these properties, methods, and events, unless they take action to override the `Control` class's behavior.

Appendix G, "Standard Controls and Components," describes the standard Windows controls in detail. This appendix can help you understand the controls and decide which is best for a particular situation.

This chapter gives some useful background for working with controls in general, but there's more to building a Visual Basic application than just controls. You also need to understand the code behind the controls that lets the program take values from controls, manipulate those values, and display a result in the controls. The next several chapters cover these topics in detail. Chapter 3, "Program and Module Structure," starts the process by explaining the files that make up a Visual Basic project and the structure contained within code files.

Program and Module Structure

A Visual Basic solution contains one or more related *projects*. A project contains files related to some topic. Usually, a project produces some kind compiled output (such as an executable program, class library, control library, and so forth). The project includes all the files related to the output, including source code files, resource files, documentation files, and whatever other kinds of files you decide to add to it.

This chapter describes the basic structure of a Visual Basic project. It explains the functions of some of the most common files and tells how you can use them to manage your applications.

This chapter also explains the basic structure of source code files. It explains regions, namespaces, and modules. It also describes some simple typographic features provided by Visual Basic such as comments, line continuation, and line labels. These features do not execute programming commands themselves, but they are an important part of how you can structure your code.

Hidden Files

Figure 3-1 shows the Solution Explorer window for a solution that contains two projects. The solution named MySolution contains two projects named WindowsApplication1 and WindowsApplication2. Each project contains a My Project item that represents the project's properties, an `app.config` file containing project configuration settings, and a form named `Form1`.

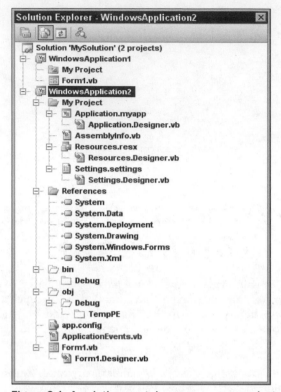

Figure 3-1: A solution contains one or more projects that contain files.

In WindowsApplication2, the Show Hidden Files button has been pushed (the second button from the left with the box around it) so that you can see all the project's files. WindowsApplication1 has similar files, but they are hidden by default.

These files are generated by Visual Basic for various purposes. For example, `Resources.resx` contains resources used by the project and `Settings.settings` contains project settings.

> *Resources are chunks of data that are distributed with the application but that are not intended to be modified by the program. These might include prompt strings, error message strings, icons, and sound files. For example, resources are commonly used for customizing applications for different languages. You build different resource files for different languages, and the program loads its prompts and error messages from the appropriate resource file. Chapter 25," Configuration and Resources," has more to say about resources.*

> *Settings are values that control the execution of the application. These might include flags telling the program what options to display or how to perform certain tasks. For example, you could build different profiles to provide settings that make the program run in a restricted demo mode or in a fully licensed mode.*

The following list describes the files contained in WindowsApplication2 and shown in Figure 3-1. The types of files generated for a project changed a bit between some of the early versions of Visual Studio 2005, so the exact files you see may be different from those shown here. This list should give you an idea of what's involved in building a project, however.

❑ *WindowsApplication2* — This folder represents the entire project. You can expand or collapse it to show and hide the project's details.

❑ *My Project* — This folder represents the project's assembly information, application-level events, resources, and configuration settings. Double-click the My project entry to view and edit these values.

❑ `Application.myapp` — This XML file defines application properties (such as whether it's a single instance program and whether its shutdown mode is `AfterMainFormCloses` or `AfterAllFormsClose`).

❑ `Application.Designer.vb` — This file contains code that works with the values defined in `Application.myapp`.

❑ `AssemblyInfo.vb` — This file contains information about the application's assembly such as copyright information, company name, trademark information, and assembly version.

❑ `Resources.resx` — This resource file contains project's resources.

❑ `Resources.Designer.vb` — This file contains Visual Basic code for manipulating resources defined in `Resources.resx`. For example, if you define a string resource named `Greeting` in `Resources.resx`, Visual Basic adds a read-only property to this module so you can read the value of Greeting as shown in the following code.

```
MessageBox.Show(My.Resources.Greeting)
```

❑ `Settings.settings` — This file contains settings that you can define to control the application.

❑ `Settings.Desginer.vb` — This file contains Visual Basic code for manipulating settings defined in `Settings.settings`, much as `Resources.Designer.vb` contains code for working with `Resources.resx`. For example, the following code uses the `UserLevel` setting.

```
If My.Settings.UserMode = "Clerk" Then ...
```

❑ *References* — This folder lists references to external components such as DLLs and COM components.

❑ *bin* — This folder is used to build the application before it is executed. It contains the compiled .exe file.

❑ *obj* — This folder is used to build the application before it is executed.

❑ `app.config` — This XML file contains configuration information for the application. It includes the information in `MySettings.settings`.

❑ `ApplicationEvents.vb` — This code file contains application-level event handlers for the MyApplication object. For example, it contains the application's `Startup`, `Shutdown`, and `NetworkAvailabilityChanged` event handlers.

❑ `Form1.vb` — This is a form file. It contains the code you write for the form, its controls, their event handlers, and so forth.

❑ `Form1.Designer.vb` — This file contains designer-generated Visual Basic code that builds the form. It initializes the form when it is created, adds the controls you placed on the form, and defines variables with the `WithEvents` keyword for the controls so that you can easily catch their events.

Some projects may have other hidden files. For example, when you add controls to a form, the designer adds a resource file to the form to hold any resources needed by the controls.

Normally, you do not need to work directly with the hidden files. You can use other tools to modify them indirectly instead. For example, the files `Resources.Designer.vb`, `Settings.Designer.vb`, and `Form1.Designer.vb` are automatically generated when you modify their corresponding source files `Resources.resx`, `Settings.settings`, and `Form1.vb`.

You don't even need to work with all of these source files directly. For example, if you double-click the My Project item, the property pages shown in Figure 3-2 appear. The Application tab shown in this figure lets you set high-level application settings such as the shutdown mode (stored in `Application.myapp`). The View Code button scrolled off the bottom of the figure lets you edit the application-level events stored in `ApplicationEvents.vb`.

The Resources tab shown in Figure 3-2 lets you view, add, and remove project references. As you can probably guess, the Resources and Settings tabs let you edit the project's resources and settings.

A particularly important section hidden away in these tabs is the assembly information. If you click the Assembly Information button shown in Figure 3-2, the dialog shown in Figure 3-3 appears.

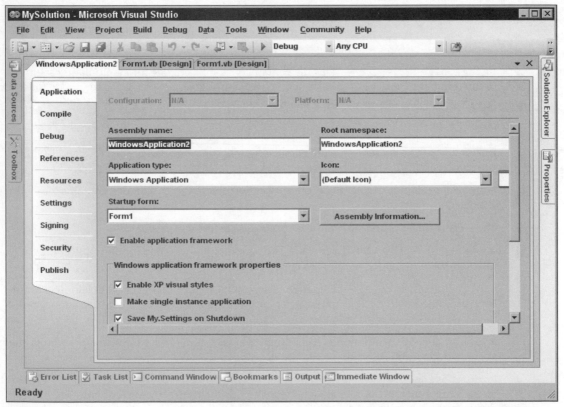

Figure 3-2: These property pages let you define project resources, settings, and general configuration.

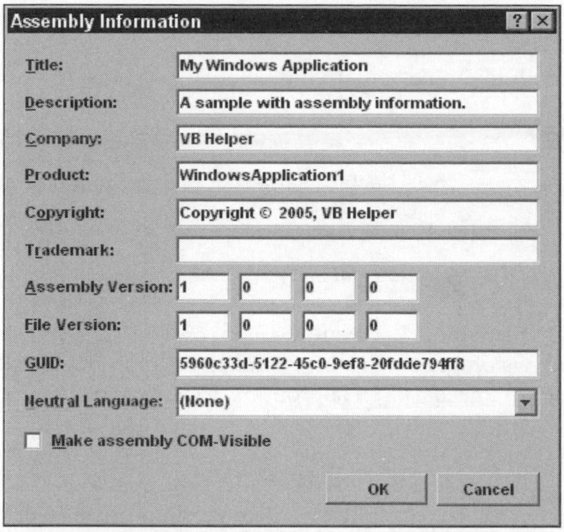

Figure 3-3: The Assembly Information dialog lets you define basic project information such as title, copyright, and version number.

An assembly is the fundamental unit of deployment and version control in Visual Studio .NET. An assembly can contain an executable application, a DLL, or control library. Usually a project is contained in a single assembly.

The Assembly Information dialog lets you define information that should be associated with the assembly, including the assembly's company name, description, copyright, trademark, name, product name, title, and version (which includes major, minor, revision, and build values).

The `My.Application.AssemblyInfo` namespace provides easy access to these values at run time. The following code shows how a program can display this information in a series of labels when it starts.

```
Private Sub Form1_Load(ByVal sender As System.Object, _
 ByVal e As System.EventArgs) Handles MyBase.Load
    lblCompanyName.Text = My.Application.Info.CompanyName
    lblDescription.Text = My.Application.Info.Description
    lblCopyright.Text = My.Application.Info.Copyright
    lblTrademark.Text = My.Application.Info.Trademark
    lblDirectoryPath.Text = My.Application.Info.DirectoryPath
    lblProductName.Text = My.Application.Info.ProductName
    lblTitle.Text = My.Application.Info.Title
    lblVersion.Text = My.Application.Info.Version.ToString
End Sub
```

Code File Structure

A form, class, or code module should contain the following sections in this order (if they are present):

❑   *Option statements* — Option Explicit, Option Strict, or Option Compare.

❑   *Imports statements* — These declare namespaces that the module will use.

❑   *A Main subroutine* — The routine that starts execution when the program runs.

❑   *Class, Module, and Namespace statements* — As needed.

Some of these items may be missing. For example, Option and Imports statements are optional. Note that an executable Windows program can start from a Main subroutine or it can start by displaying a form, in which case it doesn't need a Main subroutine. Classes and code modules don't need Main subroutines.

The following code shows a simple code module. It sets Option Explicit On (variables must be declared before used) and Option Strict On (implicit type conversions cause an error). It imports the System.IO namespace so the program can easily use classes defined there. It then defines the Employee class.

```
Option Explicit On
Option Strict On

Imports System.IO

Public Class Employee
    ...
End Class
```

Usually, you put each class or module in a separate file, but you can add more Class or Module statements to a file if you like. Figure 3-4 shows a code module that contains two classes and two modules.

Class and Module statements define top-level nodes in the code hierarchy. Click the minus sign to the left of one of these statements to collapse the code it contains. When the code is collapsed, click the plus sign to the left of it to expand the code. In Figure 3-4, the BillingTools module and Employee class are collapsed, hiding whatever code they contain.

The project can freely refer to any public class, or to any public variable or routine in a module. If two modules contain a variable or routine with the same name, the program can select the version it wants by prefixing the name with the module's name. For example, if the AccountingTools and BillingTools modules both have a subroutine named ConnectToDatabase, the following statement executes the version in the BillingTools module:

```
BillingTools.ConnectToDatabase
```

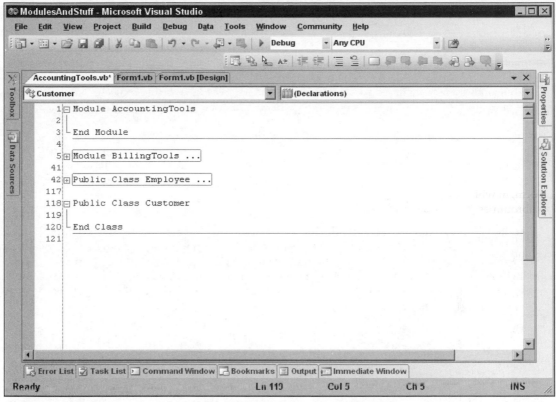

Figure 3-4: A single file can contain multiple Class and Module statements.

Code Regions

Class and Module statements define regions of code that you can expand or collapse to make the code easier to understand. Similarly, you can use the Region statement to organize your code. You can place subroutines that have a common purpose in a region so you can collapse and expand the code as needed. The following code shows a simple region:

```
#Region "Drawing Routines"
    ...
#End Region
```

Note that the IDE's search-and-replace features normally work only on expanded regions. If you collapse a region and make a global search-and-replace in the current document or the current selection, the collapsed code remains unchanged. If you make a global replace throughout the whole project, the replacement occurs within collapsed regions as well.

By itself, the End Region statement does not tell you which region it is ending. You can make your code easier to understand, particularly if you have many regions in the same module, by adding a comment after the End Region statement giving the name of the region, as shown in the following code:

```
#Region "Drawing Routines"
    ...
#End Region ' Drawing Routines
```

Sometimes it may be easier to move related pieces of code into separate files. The `Partial` keyword allows you to place parts of a class in different files. For example, you could move a form's code for loading and saving data in a separate file and use the `Partial` keyword to indicate that the code was part of the form. Chapter 15, "Classes and Structures," describes the `Partial` keyword in detail.

However, you cannot use the `Partial` keyword with modules so a module's code must all go in one file. In that case, you can use regions to similarly separate a group of related routines and make the code easier to read.

Conditional Compilation

Conditional compilation statements allow you to include or exclude code from the program's compilation. The basic conditional compilation statement is similar to a multiline `If Then Else` statement. The following code shows a typical statement. If the value `condition1` is `True`, the code in `code_block_1` is included in the compiled program. If that value is `False` but the value `condition2` is `True`, the code in `code_block_2` becomes part of the compiled program. If neither condition is `True`, the code in `code_block_3` is included in the program.

```
#If condition1 Then
    code_block_1...
#ElseIf condition2 Then
    code_block_2...
#Else
    code_block_3...
#End If
```

It is important to understand that the code not included by the conditional compilation statements is completely omitted from the executable program. At compile time, Visual Studio decides whether a block of code should be included or not. That means any code that is omitted does not take up space in the executable program. It also means that you cannot set the execution statement to omitted lines in the debugger because those lines are not present.

In contrast, a normal `If Then Else` statement includes all the code in every code block in the executable, and then decides which code to execute at run time.

Because the conditional compilation statement evaluates its conditions at compile time, those conditions must be expressions that can be evaluated at compile time. For example, they can be expressions containing values that you have defined using compiler directives (described shortly). They cannot include values generated at run time (such as the value of variables).

In fact, a conditional compilation statement evaluates its conditions at design time, so it can give feedback while you are writing the code. For example, if `Option Explicit` is set to `On`, then Visual Basic flags the following assignment statement as in error. Because the first condition is `True`, the variable X is declared as a string. `Option Explicit On` disallows implicit conversion from an integer to a string, so the IDE flags the statement as an error.

```
#If True Then
    Dim X As String
#Else
    Dim X As Integer
#End If

    X = 10
```

That much makes sense, but it's also important to realize that the code not included in the compilation is not evaluated by the IDE. If the first condition in the previous code were False, the code would work properly because variable X would be declared as an integer. The IDE doesn't evaluate the other code, so it doesn't notice that there is an error if the condition is False. You probably won't notice the error until you try to actually use the other code.

You can set conditional compilation constants in two main ways: in code and in the project's compilation settings.

Setting Constants in Code

To set conditional compilation constants explicitly in your program, use a #Const statement, as shown in the following code:

```
#Const UserType = "Clerk"

#If UserType = "Clerk" Then
    ' Do stuff appropriate for clerks...
    ...
#ElseIf UserType = "Supervisor" Then
    ' Do stuff appropriate for supervisors...
    ...
#Else
    ' Do stuff appropriate for others...
    ...
#End If
```

Note that these constants are defined only after the point at which they appear in the code. If you use a constant before it is defined, its value is False (unfortunately Option Explicit doesn't apply to these constants). That means the following code displays the value Slow followed by the value Fast:

```
#If UseFastAlgorithm Then
    MessageBox.Show("Fast")
#Else
    MessageBox.Show("Slow")
#End If

#Const UseFastAlgorithm = True

#If UseFastAlgorithm Then
    MessageBox.Show("Fast")
#Else
    MessageBox.Show("Slow")
#End If
```

To avoid possible confusion, many programmers define these constants at the beginning of the file.

Also note that your code can redefine a constant using a new #Const statement later. That means these are not really constants in the sense that their values are unchangeable.

Setting Constants with the Project's Compilation Settings

To set constants with the project's compilation settings, open Solution Explorer and double-click on My Project. Click on the Compile tab to see the form shown in Figure 3-5.

Click the Advanced Compile Options button to open the Advanced Compiler Settings dialog shown in Figure 3-6. Enter the names and values of the constants in the Custom Constants text box. Enter each value in the form ConstantName=Value. Separate multiple constants with commas.

Constants you specify on the Advanced Compiler Settings dialog are available everywhere in the project. However, your code can redefine the constant using a #Const directive. The constant has the new value until the end of the file or until you redefine it again.

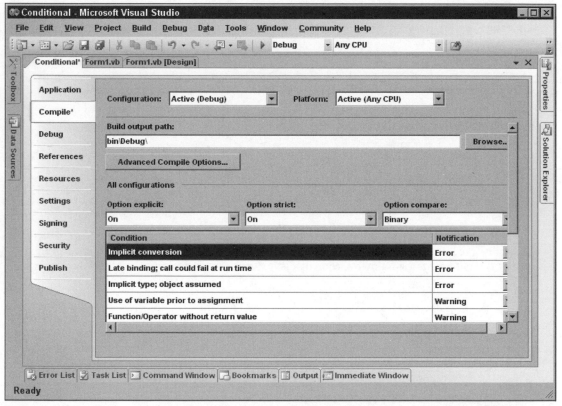

Figure 3-5: Click the Compile tab's Advanced Compile Options button to set compilation constants.

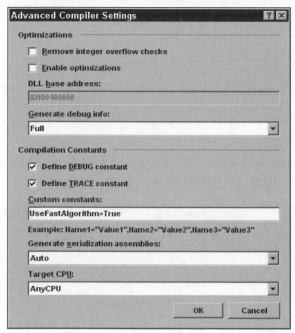

Figure 3-6: Use the Advanced Compiler Settings dialog
to define compilation constants.

Predefined Constants

Visual Basic automatically defines several conditional compilation constants that you can use to determine the code that your application compiles. The following table describes these constants.

Constant	Meaning
CONFIG	A string that gives the name of the current build. Typically, this will be `"Debug"` or `"Release"`.
DEBUG	A Boolean that indicates whether this is a debug build. By default, this value is `True` when you build a project's Debug configuration.
TARGET	A string that tells the kind of application the project builds. This can be `winexe` (Windows form application), `exe` (console application), `library` (class library), or `module` (code module).
TRACE	A Boolean that indicates whether the `Trace` object should generate output in the Output window.
VBC_VER	A number giving Visual Basic's major and minor version numbers. The value for Visual Basic 2005 is 8.0.

The following sections describe the DEBUG, TRACE, and CONFIG constants and their normal uses in more detail.

DEBUG

Normally when you make a debug build, Visual Basic sets the DEBUG constant to True. When you compile a release build, Visual Basic sets DEBUG to False. The Configuration Manager lets you select the Debug build, the Release build, or other builds that you defined yourself.

Initially, the Configuration Manager should be available, but if you find that it is not, you can activate it. Open the Tools menu and select Options command. Select the Projects and Solutions node's General entry, and check the "Show advanced build configurations" box.

After you have activated the Configuration Manager, you can open it by clicking on the project in the Solution Explorer and then selecting the Build menu's Configuration Manager command. Figure 3-7 shows the Configuration Manager. Select Debug or Release from the dropdown list, and click Close.

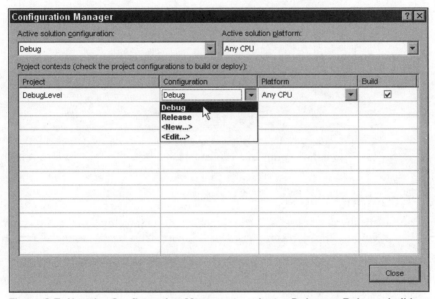

Figure 3-7: Use the Configuration Manager to select a Debug or Release build.

When the DEBUG constant is True, the Debug object's methods send output to the Output window. When the DEBUG constant is not True, the Debug object's methods do not generate any code, so the object doesn't produce any output. This makes the Debug object useful for displaying diagnostic messages during development and then hiding the messages in release builds sent to customers.

The following sections describe some of the Debug object's most useful properties and methods.

Assert

The Debug.Assert method evaluates a Boolean expression and, if the expression is False, displays an error message. This method can optionally take as parameters an error message and a detailed message to display. The following code shows how a program might use Debug.Assert to verify that the variable NumEmployees is greater than zero:

```
Debug.Assert(NumEmployees > 0, _
    "NumEmployees must be greater than zero", _
    "The program cannot generate timesheets if no employees are defined.")
```

Figure 3-8 shows the dialog displayed by this statement if NumEmployees is zero.

If you click the dialog's Abort button, the program immediately halts. If you click Retry, the program breaks into the debugger, so you can examine the code. If you click Ignore, the program continues as if the Assert statement's condition was True.

A good use for the Assert method is to verify that a routine's parameters or other variable values are reasonable before starting calculations. For example, suppose that the AssignJob subroutine assigns a repair person to a job. The routine could begin with a series of Assert statements that verify that the person exists, the job exists, the person has the skills necessary to perform the job, and so forth. It is usually easier to fix code if you catch these sorts of errors before starting a long calculation or database modification that may later fail because, for example, the repair person doesn't have the right kind of truck to perform the job.

If the DEBUG constant is not True, the Assert method does nothing. This lets you automatically remove these rather obscure error messages from the compiled executable that you send to customers. You wouldn't want a user to see the dialog Figure 3-8!

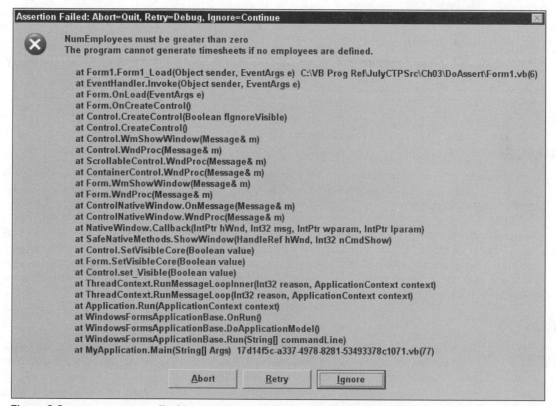

Figure 3-8: Debug.Assert displays an error message if a Boolean expression is False.

You should take some care when deciding what tests should be placed in `Assert` statements so that they are removed from the compiled executable. For example, you might use `Assert` to verify that a string entered by the user contains a valid value. When you run the compile executable, however, this test is removed, so the program does not protect itself from bad data. When you use `Assert` to verify a condition, you must be certain that the program can run safely if the `Assert` statement is removed and the condition fails.

Fail

The `Debug.Fail` method displays an error message just as `Debug.Assert` does when its Boolean condition parameter is `False`.

IndentSize, Indent, Unindent, and IndentLevel

These properties and methods determine the amount of indentation used when the `Debug` object writes into the Output window. You can use them, for example, to indent the output in subroutines to show the program's structure more clearly.

The `IndentSize` property indicates the number of spaces that should be used for each level of indentation. The `IndentLevel` property determines the current indentation level. For example, if `IndentSize` is 4 and `IndentLevel` is 2, output is indented by eight spaces.

The `Indent` and `Unindent` methods increase and decrease the indentation level by one.

Write, WriteLine, WriteIf, and WriteLineIf

These routines send output to the Output window. The `Write` method prints text and stops without starting a new line. `WriteLine` prints text and follows it with a new line.

The `WriteIf` and `WriteLineIf` methods take a Boolean parameter and act the same as `Write` and `WriteLine` if the parameter's value is `True`.

TRACE

The `Trace` object is very similar to the `Debug` object and provides the same set of properties and methods. The difference is that it generates output when the `TRACE` constant is defined rather than when the `DEBUG` constant is defined.

Normally, the `TRACE` constant is defined for both debug and release builds so `Trace.Assert` and other `Trace` object methods work in both builds. By default, DEBUG is defined only for debug builds, so you get `Debug` messages for debug builds. You can add "listener" objects to the `Trace` object (or the `Debug` object) to perform different actions on any `Trace` output. For example, a listener could write the `Trace` output into a log file.

CONFIG

The `Config` constant's value is the name of the type of build. Normally, this is either `Debug` or `Release`, but you can also create your own build configurations. You can use these for interim builds, point releases, alpha and beta releases, or any other release category you can think of.

To select the debug or release build, click on the project in the Solution Explorer and then select the Build menu's Configuration Manager command to display the dialog shown in Figure 3-7. Select <New...> from the dropdown list to display the New Solution Configuration dialog shown in Figure 3-9. Enter a name for the new configuration, select the existing configuration from which the new one should initially copy its settings, and click OK.

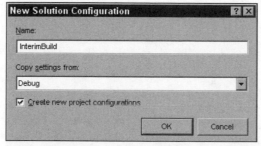

Figure 3-9: You can use the Configuration Manager to create your own configurations.

The following code shows how to use the CONFIG compiler constant to determine which build is being made and take different actions accordingly:

```
#If CONFIG = "Debug" Then
    ' Do stuff for a Debug build...
#ElseIf CONFIG = "Release" Then
    ' Do stuff for a Release build...
#ElseIf CONFIG = "InterimBuild" Then
    ' Do stuff for a custom InterimBuild...
#Else
    MsgBox("Unknown build type")
#End If
```

Note that a compilation constant's value is case-sensitive; for example, you should compare CONFIG to "Debug" not "debug" or "DEBUG."

Debugging Level Constants

Sometimes it is helpful to be able to easily adjust the level of diagnostic output a program generates. You could define the constant DEBUG_LEVEL and then send data to the Output window, depending on its value. For example, you might place level 1 Debug statements in major subroutines, level 2 statements in secondary routines, and level 3 statements throughout important routines to provide step-by-step information. Then you can define the DEBUG_LEVEL constant to quickly give you the amount of information you want.

The following code shows a small example. The IsPhoneNumberValid function determines whether its parameter looks like a valid 7- or 10-digit U.S. phone number. If DEBUG_LEVEL is at least 1, the function displays messages when it starts and when it exits. It also indents the output when it starts and unindents the output before it exits. If DEBUG_LEVEL is at least 2, the function also displays statements telling when it is about to check for 7- and 10-digit phone numbers.

```
#Const DEBUG_LEVEL = 2

    Private Function IsPhoneNumberValid(ByVal phone_number As String) As Boolean
#If DEBUG_LEVEL >= 1 Then
        Debug.WriteLine("Entering IsPhoneNumberValid(" & phone_number & ")")
        Debug.Indent()
#End If

        ' Check for a 7-digit phone number.
#If DEBUG_LEVEL >= 2 Then
        Debug.WriteLine("Checking for 7-digit phone number")
#End If
        Dim is_valid As Boolean = _
            phone_number Like "###-####"

        If Not is_valid Then
#If DEBUG_LEVEL >= 2 Then
            Debug.WriteLine("Checking for 10-digit phone number")
#End If
            is_valid = phone_number Like "###-###-####"
        End If

#If DEBUG_LEVEL >= 1 Then
        Debug.Unindent()
        Debug.WriteLine("Leaving IsPhoneNumberValid, returning " & is_valid)
#End If
        Return is_valid
    End Function
```

The following text shows the results in the Output window when DEBUG_LEVEL is set to 2.

```
Entering IsPhoneNumberValid(123-4567)
    Checking for 7-digit phone number
Leaving IsPhoneNumberValid, returning True
```

From this output, you can tell that the function examined the string "123-4567", did not need to check for a 10-digit phone number, and returned True.

For more information on debugging Visual Basic applications, see Chapter 8, "Error Handling."

Namespaces

Visual Studio uses *namespaces* to categorize code. A namespace can contain other namespaces, which can contain others, forming a hierarchy of namespaces.

You can define your own namespaces to help categorize your code. By placing different routines in separate namespaces, you can allow pieces of code to include only the namespaces they are actually using. That makes it easier to ignore the routines that the program isn't using. It also allows more than one namespace to define items that have the same names.

For example, you could define an Accounting namespace that contains the AccountsReceivable and AccountsPayable namespaces. Each of those might contain a subroutine named

ListOutstandingInvoices. The program could select one version or the other by calling either Accounting.AccountsReceivable.ListOutstandingInvoices or Accounting.AccountsPayable.ListOutstandingInvoices.

You can only use the Namespace statement at the file level or inside another namespace, not within a class or module. Within a namespace, you can define nested namespaces, classes, or modules. The following example defines the AccountingModules namespace. That namespace contains the two classes PayableItem and ReceivableItem, the module AccountingRoutines, and the nested namespace OrderEntryModules. The AccountingRoutines module defines the PayInvoice subroutine. All the classes, modules, and namespaces may define other items.

```
Namespace AccountingModules
    Public Class PayableItem
        ...
    End Class

    Public Class ReceivableItem
        ...
    End Class

    Module AccountingRoutines
        Public Sub PayInvoice(ByVal invoice_number As Long)
            ...
        End Sub
        ...
    End Module

    Namespace OrderEntryModules
        Public Class OrderEntryClerk
            ...
        End Class
        ...
    End Namespace
End Namespace
```

Code using a module's namespace does not need to explicitly identify the module. If a module defines a variable or routine that has a unique name, you do not need to specify the module's name to use that item. In this example, there is only one subroutine named PayInvoice, so the code can invoke it as AccountingModules.PayInvoice(). If the AccountingModules namespace contained another module that defined a PayInvoice subroutine, the code would need to indicate which version to use as in AccountingModules.AccountingRoutines.PayInvoice().

While modules are transparent within their namespaces, nested namespaces are not. Because the nested OrderEntryModules namespace defines the OrderEntryClerk class, the code must specify the full namespace path to the class, as in the following code:

```
Dim oe_clerk As New AccountingModules.OrderEntryModules.OrderEntryClerk
```

Note that a Visual Basic project defines its own namespace that contains everything else in the project. Normally, the namespace has the same name as the project. To view or modify this root namespace, double-click on the Solution Explorer's My Project entry to open the project property page shown in Figure 3-10. Enter the new root namespace name in text box in the upper right.

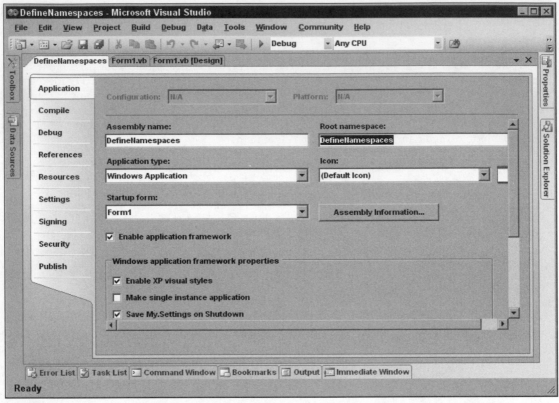

Figure 3-10: The project's Application property page lets you view or change the project's root namespace.

You can use an `Imports` statement to simplify access to a namespace inside a file. For example, suppose that you are working on the `GeneralAccounting` project that has root namespace `GeneralAccounting`. The first statement in the following code allows the program to use items defined in the `AccountingModules` namespace without prefixing them with "`AccountingModules.`" The second statement lets the program use items defined in the `AccountingModules` nested namespace `OrderEntryModules`. The last two lines of code declare variables using classes defined in those namespaces.

```
Imports GeneralAccounting.AccountingModules
Imports GeneralAccounting.AccountingModules.OrderEntryModules
...
Private m_OverdueItem As PayableItem      ' In the AccountingModules namespace.
Private m_ThisClerk As OrderEntryClerk    ' In the namespace
                                          ' AccountingModules.OrderEntryModules.
```

Typographic Code Elements

A few typographic code elements can make a program's structure a bit easier to understand. They do not execute programming commands themselves, but they are an important part of how you can structure your code. These elements include comments, line continuation and joining characters, and line labels.

Comments

Comments can help other developers (or you at a later date) understand the program's purpose, structure, and method. You start a comment by typing a single quotation mark (') that is not inside a quoted string. All of the characters starting at the quote and continuing until the end of the line are part of the comment and are ignored by Visual Basic.

If a line with a comment ends with a line continuation character (described shortly), Visual Basic ignores that character. That means the line is not continued onto the next line, so the comment ends with the current line. In other words, you cannot use line continuation characters to make a multiline comment.

In the following code, the first declaration is followed by a comment. The comment ends with a line continuation character so you might expect the second declaration to be part of the comment. That is not the case. Because this can be misleading, you should not end comments with a line continuation character. The second statement declares and initializes a string using a value that contains a single quote. Because the quote is inside a quoted string, it becomes part of the string and does not start a comment. The next single quotation mark outside of the string begins a new comment.

```
Dim num_customers As Integer     ' The number of customers in the application. _
Dim product_name As String = "Miracle Code Fixer"  ' The name of this program.
```

If you want to continue a comment on the following line, you must use another comment character, as in the following example:

```
' Return True if the address is valid. This function checks the address's
' format to see that it makes sense. It also looks up the ZIP code and
' verifies that the city is valid for that ZIP code. It does not verify
' that the street and street number exist.
Private Function IsAddressValid(ByVal address_text As String) As Boolean
...
```

To quickly comment or uncomment a large block of code, select it using the mouse and then open the Edit menu's Advanced submenu. Select the Comment Selection command to comment out the selection or select Uncomment Selection to remove the comment characters from the front of the selection. Those commands are also available more conveniently as buttons in the Text Editor toolbar. Use the View menu, Toolbars submenu's Text Editor command to show or hide this toolbar.

Another way to quickly remove a chunk of code from the program is to surround it with compiler directives, as in the following code:

```
#If False Then
    Dim A As Integer
    Dim B As Integer
    Dim C As Integer
#End If
```

Use comments to make your code clear. Comments do not slow the executable program down, so there's no good reason to exclude them.

XML Comments

A normal comment is just a piece of text that gives information to a developer trying to read your code. XML comments let you add some context to a comment. For example, you can mark a comment as a summary describing a subroutine.

Visual Studio automatically extracts XML comments to build an XML file describing the project. This file displays the hierarchical shape of the project, showing comments for the project's modules, namespaces, classes, and other elements.

The result is not particularly easy to read, but you can use it to automatically generate more useful documentation.

You can place a block of XML comments before code elements that are not contained in methods. Generally, you use them to describe a module, class, variable, property, method, or event.

To begin a comment block, place the cursor on the line before the element you want to describe and type three single quotes ('''). Visual Studio automatically inserts a template for an XML comment block. If the element that follows takes parameters, it includes sections describing the parameters, so it is in your best interest to completely define the parameters before you create the XML comment block.

The following code shows the XML comment block created for a simple subroutine. It includes a summary area to describe the subroutine, two param sections to describe the subroutine's parameters, and a remarks section to provide additional detail.

```
'''  <summary>
'''
'''  </summary>
'''  <param name="jobs"></param>
'''  <param name="employees"></param>
'''  <remarks></remarks>
Public Sub AssignJobs(ByVal jobs() As Job, ByVal employees() As Employee)

End Sub
```

Note that XML elements can span multiple lines, as the summary element does in this example.

You can add more XML comment sections to the block simply by typing them, following the convention that they should begin with three single quotes. For example, the following code adds some content for the comments in the previous code and an extra WrittenBy element that contains a date attribute:

```
'''  <summary>
'''  Assigns jobs to employees, maximizing the total value of jobs assigned.
'''  </summary>
'''  <param name="jobs">The array of Jobs to assign.</param>
'''  <param name="employees">The array of Employees to assign.</param>
'''  <remarks>The full assignment is not guaranteed to be unique.</remarks>
'''  <WrittenBy date="7/24/04">Rod Stephens</WrittenBy>
Public Sub AssignJobs(ByVal jobs() As Job, ByVal employees() As Employee)

End Sub
```

These XML comments are somewhat bulky and hard to read. In the previous example, it isn't easy to pick out the subroutine's most important summary information with a quick glance at the code. To make reading XML comments easier, Visual Basic defines an outlining section for each XML comment block. If you click the minus sign to the left of the first line in the block, the whole block collapses and shows only the summary information. If you then click the plus sign to the left of the summary, Visual Studio expands the comments to show them all.

The following code shows the beginning of an application that assigns jobs to employees. The project contains two files, a form named `Form1.vb` and a code module named `Module1.vb`. The form contains very little code. The code module defines the `Job` and `Employee` classes and the `AssignJobs` subroutine. Each of these has an XML comment block.

```
Public Class Form1

    Private m_Jobs() As Job
    Private m_Employees() As Employee

End Class

Module Module1
    Public Class Job
        Public JobNumber As Integer

        ''' <summary>
        ''' A list of skills required to perform this job.
        ''' </summary>
        ''' <remarks>Represent required equipment as skills.</remarks>
        Public SkillsRequired As New Collection

        ''' <summary>
        ''' The value of this job.
        ''' </summary>
        ''' <remarks>Higher numbers indicate more priority.</remarks>
        Public Priority As Integer
    End Class

    Public Class Employee
        Public FirstName As String
        Public LastName As String
        ''' <summary>
        ''' A list of skills this employee has.
        ''' </summary>
        ''' <remarks>Represent special equipment as skills.</remarks>
        Public Skills As New Collection
    End Class

    ''' <summary>
    ''' Assigns jobs to employees.
    ''' </summary>
    ''' <param name="jobs">Array of Jobs to assign.</param>
```

```
    ''' <param name="employees">Array of Employees to assign jobs.</param>
    ''' <remarks>The assignment maximizes total value of jobs assigned.</remarks>
    ''' <WrittenBy date="7/26/04">Rod Stephens</WrittenBy>
    Public Sub AssignJobs(ByVal jobs() As Job, ByVal employees() As Employee)

    End Sub
End Module
```

Figure 3-11 shows the Object Browser describing the `Job` class's `SkillsRequired` property. The area on the lower right shows the property's XML summary and remarks sections. This project's name is AssignJobsProject and its root namespace is AssignJobsRoot, so the complete path to the `Job` class shown in the tree view on the left is AssignJobsProject (project), AssignJobsRoot (root namespace), Module1 (module), Job (class).

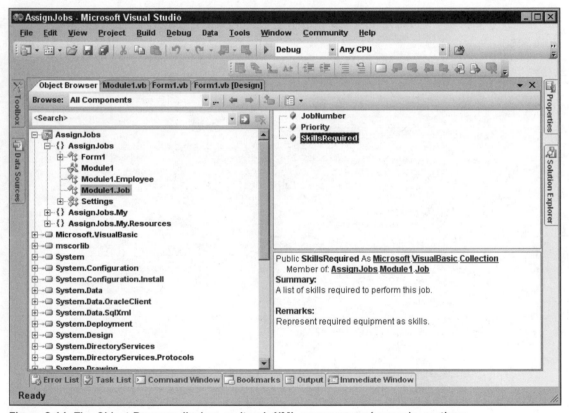

Figure 3-11: The Object Browser displays an item's XML summary and remarks sections.

When you compile the application, Visual Studio extracts the XML comments and places them in an XML file with the same name as the executable file in the project's bin\Debug directory. The following text shows the result. If you look through the document carefully, you can pick out the XML comments.

```xml
<?xml version="1.0"?>
<doc>
<assembly>
<name>
AssignJobs
</name>
</assembly>
<members>
<member name="F:AssignJobs.Module1.Job.SkillsRequired">
<summary>
 A list of skills required to perform this job.
 </summary>
<remarks>Represent required equipment as skills.</remarks>
</member><member name="F:AssignJobs.Module1.Job.Priority">
<summary>
 The value of this job.
 </summary>
<remarks>Higher numbers indicate more priority.</remarks>
</member><member name="F:AssignJobs.Module1.Employee.Skills">
<summary>
 A list of skills this employee has.
 </summary>
<remarks>Represent special equipment as skills.</remarks>
</member><member name="M:AssignJobs.Module1.AssignJobs(
  AssignJobs.Module1.Job[],AssignJobs.Module1.Employee[])">
<summary>
 Assigns jobs to employees.
 </summary>
<param name="jobs">Array of Jobs to assign.</param>
<param name="employees">Array of Employees to assign jobs.</param>
<remarks>The assignment maximizes total value of jobs assigned.</remarks>
<WrittenBy date="7/26/04">Rod Stephens</WrittenBy>
</member>
</members>
</doc>
```

Line Continuation

Line continuation characters let you break long lines across multiple shorter lines so that they are easier to read. To continue a line, end it with a space followed by an underscore (_). Visual Basic treats the following line as if it were tacked on to the end of the first line:

```vb
Dim background_color As Color = _
    Color.FromName( _
        My.Resources.ResourceManager.GetString( _
            "MainFormBackgroundColor"))
```

As the previous section explains, you cannot continue comments. A comment includes any space and underscore at the end of its line so the comment does not apply to the following line.

You can break a line just about anywhere that a space is allowed and between program elements. For example, you can break a line after the opening parenthesis in a parameter list, as shown in the following code:

```
AReallyReallyLongSubroutineNameThatTakesFiveParameters( _
    parameter1, parameter2, parameter3, parameter4, parameter5)
```

You cannot break a line inside a quoted string. If you want to break a string, end the string and restart it on the next line, as in the following example:

```
Dim txt As String = "To break a long string across multiple lines, " & _
    "end the string, add the line continuation character (space + underscore) " & _
    "and restart the string on the next line."
```

Visual Basic does not enforce its usual indentation rules on continued lines, so you can indent the lines in any way you like to make the code's structure more clear. For example, many programmers align parameters in long subroutine calls.

```
DoSomething( _
    parameter1, _
    parameter2, _
    parameter3)
```

Line Joining

Not only can you break a long statement across multiple lines, but you can also join short statements on a single line. To use two statements on a single line, separate them with a colon (:). The following line of code contains three statements that store the red, green, and blue components of a form's background color in the variables r, g, and b:

```
r = BackColor.R : g = BackColor.G : b = BackColor.B
```

Line joining is most useful when you have many lines in a row that all have a very similar structure. By scanning down the lines, you can tell if there are differences that may indicate a bug.

Use line joining with some caution. If the statements are long, or if you have a series of joined lines with dissimilar structure, combining lots of statements on a single line can make the code harder to read. If the code is easier to read with each statement on a separate line, write the code that way. Using more lines doesn't make the code run any slower.

Line Labels

You can place a label to the left of any line of code. The label can be either a name or a number, followed by a colon. The following code defines three labels. The first is named DeclareX and marks the declaration of the variable X. The second has value 10 and is located on a line containing a comment. The third label, named Done, labels a blank line.

```
DeclareX:  Dim X As Single
10:             ' Do something here.
Done:
```

You label a line if you will later want to jump to that line. For example, the GoTo, On Error GoTo, and Resume statements can make code jump to a labeled line. These are less useful in Visual Basic .NET than they were in Visual Basic 6 and previous versions that didn't have structured error handling (the Try Catch block), but they are still available.

Summary

A Visual Studio solution contains a hierarchical arrangement of items. At the top level, it contains one or more projects. Each project contains several standard items such as My Project (that represents the project as a whole), References (that records information about references to external objects), the bin and obj items (that are used by Visual Studio when building the application), and app.config (which holds configuration information). Projects also contain form, class, and other code modules.

Normally, many of these files are hidden and you do not need to edit them directly. Instead, you can double-click Solution Explorer's My Project entry and use the project's Properties pages to view and modify application values. Other hidden files store code and resources that determine a form's appearance, and you can modify them by altering the form with the Form Designer.

Within a code module, you can use modules, classes, regions, and namespaces to group related code into blocks. You can use conditional compilation statements and conditional compilation constants to easily add or remove code to or from the compiled application. The Debug and Trace objects let you generate messages and alerts, depending on whether certain predefined constants are defined.

Finally, typographic elements such as comments, line continuation, and line joining let you format the code so that it is easier to read and understand. XML comments provide additional information that is useful to the Object Browser and that you can use to automatically generate more complete documentation.

While all of these components are not required by Visual Basic, they can make the difference between understanding the code quickly and completely, and not understanding it at all. Over an application's lifetime of development, debugging, upgrading, and maintenance, this can determine a project's success.

This chapter describes structural elements that make up code files. Within those elements, you can place the code that gathers, manipulates, stores, and displays data. Chapter 4, "Data Types, Variables, and Constants," describes the variables that a program uses to hold data values. It explains how to declare variables, what types of data they can hold, and how Visual Basic converts from one data type to another.

Data Types, Variables, and Constants

Variables are among the most fundamental building blocks of a program. A *variable* is a program object that stores a value. The value can be a number, letter, string, date, structure containing other values, or an object representing both data and related actions.

Once a variable contains a value, the program can manipulate it. It can perform arithmetic operations on numbers, string operations on strings (concatenation, calculating substrings, finding a target within a string), date operations (find the difference between two dates, add a time period to a date), and so forth.

Four factors determine a variable's exact behavior:

❑ *Data type* determines the kind of the data (integer, character, string, and so forth).

❑ *Scope* defines the code that can access the variable. For example, if you declare a variable inside a For loop, only other code inside the For loop can use the variable. If you declare a variable at the top of a subroutine, all the code in the subroutine can use the variable.

❑ *Accessibility* determines what code in other modules can access the variable. If you declare a variable at the module level (outside of any subroutine in the module) and you use the Private keyword, only the code in the module can use the variable. If you use the Public keyword, code in other modules can use the variable as well.

❑ *Lifetime* determines how long the variable's value is valid. A variable inside a subroutine that is declared with a normal Dim statement is created when the subroutine begins and is destroyed when it exits. If the subroutine runs again, it creates a new copy of the variable and its value is reset. If the variable is declared with the Static keyword, however, the same instance of the variable is used whenever the subroutine runs. That means the variable's value is preserved between calls to the subroutine.

For example, a variable declared within a subroutine has scope equal to the subroutine. Code outside of the subroutine cannot access the variable. If a variable is declared on a module level outside any subroutine, it has module scope. If it is declared with the `Private` keyword, it is accessible only to code within the module. If it is declared with the `Public` keyword, then it is also accessible to code outside of the module.

Visibility is a concept that combines scope, accessibility, and lifetime. It determines whether a certain piece of code can use a variable. If the variable is accessible to the code, and the code is within the variable's scope, and the variable is within its lifetime (has been created and not yet destroyed), the variable is visible to the code.

This chapter explains the syntax for declaring variables in Visual Basic. It explains how you can use different declarations to determine a variable's data type, scope, accessibility, and lifetime. It also discusses some of the issues you should consider when selecting a type of declaration.

Constants, parameters, and property procedures all have concepts of scope and data type that are similar to those of variables, so they are also describe here.

The chapter finishes with a brief explanation of naming conventions. Which naming rules you adopt isn't as important as the fact that you adopt some. This chapter tells where you can find the conventions used by Microsoft Consulting Services. From those, you can build your own coding conventions.

Data Types

The following table summarizes Visual Basic's elementary data types.

Type	Size	Values
Boolean	2 bytes	`True` or `False`
Byte	1 byte	0 to 255 (unsigned byte)
SByte	1 byte	-128 to 127 (signed byte)
Char	2 bytes	0 to 65,535 (unsigned character)
Short	2 bytes	-32,768 to 32,767
UShort	2 bytes	0 through 65,535 (unsigned short)
Integer	4 bytes	-2,147,483,648 to 2,147,483,647
UInteger	4 bytes	0 through 4,294,967,295 (unsigned integer)
Long	8 bytes	-9,223,372,036,854,775,808 to 9,223,372,036,854,775,807
ULong	8 bytes	0 through 18,446,744,073,709,551,615 (unsigned long)
Decimal	16 bytes	0 to +/-79,228,162,514,264,337,593,543,950,335 with no decimal point. 0 to +/-7.9228162514264337593543950335 with 28 places

Type	Size	Values
Single	4 bytes	-3.4028235E+38 to -1.401298E-45 (negative values) 1.401298E-45 to 3.4028235E+38 (positive values)
Double	8 bytes	-1.79769313486231570E+308 to -4.94065645841246544E-324 (negative values) 4.94065645841246544E-324 to 1.79769313486231570E+308 (positive values)
String	variable	Depending on the platform, a string can hold approximately 0 to 2 billion Unicode characters
Date	8 bytes	January 1, 0001 0:0:00 to December 31, 9999 11:59:59 pm
Object	4 bytes	Points to any type of data
Structure	variable	Structure members have their own ranges

The System namespace also provides integer data types that specify their number of bits explicitly. For example, Int32 represents a 32-bit integer. Using these values instead of Integer emphasizes the fact that the variable uses 32 bits. That can sometimes make code clearer. For example, suppose that you need to call an application programming interface (API) function that takes a 32-bit integer as a parameter. In Visual Basic 6, a Long uses 32 bits but in Visual Basic .NET, an Integer uses 32 bits. You can make it obvious that you are using a 32-bit integer by giving the parameter the Int32 type.

The data types that explicitly give their sizes are Int16, Int32, Int64, UInt16, UInt32, and UInt64.

The Integer data type is usually the fastest of the integral types. You will generally get better performance using Integers than you will with the Char, Byte, Short, Long, or Decimal data types. You should stick with the Integer data type unless you need the extra range provided by Long and Decimal, or you need to save space with the smaller Char and Byte data types. In many cases, the space savings you will get using the Char and Byte data types isn't worth the extra time and effort, unless you are working with a very large array of values.

Note that you cannot safely assume that a variable's storage requirements are exactly the same as its size. In some cases, the program may move a variable so that it begins on a boundary that is natural for the hardware platform. For example, if you make a structure containing several Short (2-byte) variables, the program may insert 2 extra bytes between them so they can all start on 4-byte boundaries, because that may be more efficient for the hardware.

Some data types also come with some additional overhead. For example, an array stores some extra information about each of its dimensions.

Type Characters

Data type characters identify a value's data type. The following table lists Visual Basic's data type characters.

Character	Data Type
%	Integer
&	Long
@	Decimal
!	Single
#	Double
$	String

You can specify a variable's data type by adding a data type character after a variable's name when you declare it. When you use the variable later, you can omit the data type character if you like. For example, the following code declares variable num_desserts as a Long and satisfaction_quotient as a Double. It then assigns values to these variables.

```
Dim num_desserts&
Dim satisfaction_quotient#

num_desserts = 100
satisfaction_quotient# = 1.23
```

If you have Option Explicit turned off, you can include a data type character the first time you use the variable to determine its data type. If you omit the character, Visual Basic picks a default data type based on the value you assign to the variable.

If the value you assign is an integral value that will fit in an Integer, Visual Basic makes the variable an Integer. If the value is too big for an Integer, Visual Basic makes the variable a Long. If the value contains a decimal point, Visual Basic makes the variable a Double.

The following code shows the first use of three variables (Option Explicit is off). The first statement sets the variable an_integer equal to the value 100. This value fits in an Integer, so Visual Basic makes the variable an Integer. The second statement sets a_long equal to 10000000000. That value is too big to fit in an Integer, so Visual Basic makes it a Long. The third statement sets a_double to 1.0. That value contains a decimal point, so Visual Basic makes the variable a Double.

```
an_integer = 100
a_long = 10000000000
a_double = 1.0
```

If you set a variable equal to a True or False, Visual Basic makes it a Boolean.

Dates in Visual Basic are delimited with # characters. If you assign a variable to a date value, Visual Basic gives the variable the Date data type. The following code assigns Boolean and Date variables:

```
a_boolean = True
a_date = #12/31/2007#
```

In addition to data type characters, Visual Basic provides a set of *literal type characters* that determine the data type of literal values. These are values that you explicitly type into your code in statements such as assignment and initialization statements. The following table lists Visual Basic's literal type characters.

Character	Data Type
S	Short
US	UShort
I	Integer
UI	UInteger
L	Long
IL	ULong
D	Decimal
F	Single (F for "floating point")
R	Double (R for "real")
c	Char (note that this is a lower case "c")

A literal type character determines the data type of a literal value in your code and may indirectly determine the data type of a variable assigned to it. For example, suppose that the following code is the first use of the variables i and ch (with `Option Explicit` turned off). Normally, Visual Basic would make i an Integer, because the value 123 fits in an Integer. Because the literal value 123 ends with the L character, however, the value is a Long, so the variable i is also a Long.

Similarly, Visual Basic would normally make variable ch a String because the value "X" looks like a string. The "c" following the value tells Visual Basic to make this a Char variable instead, as shown here:

```
i = 123L
ch = "X"c
```

Visual Basic also lets you precede a literal integer value with &H to indicate that it is hexadecimal (base 16) or &O to indicate that it is octal (base 8). For example, the following three statements set the variable flags to the same value. The first statement uses the decimal value 100, the second uses the hexadecimal value &H64, and the third uses the octal value &O144.

```
flags = 100       ' Decimal 100.
flags = &H64      ' Hexadecimal &H64 = 6 * 16 + 4 = 96 + 4 = 100.
flags = &O144     ' Octal &O144 = 1 * 8 * 8 + 4 * 8 + 4 = 64 + 32 + 4 = 100.
```

As an aside, note that the Hex and Oct functions let you convert numeric values into hexadecimal and octal strings, respectively. In some sense, this is the opposite of what the &H and &O codes do: make Visual Basic interpret a string literal as hexadecimal or octal. The following example displays the value of the variable flags in decimal, hexadecimal, and octal:

```
Debug.WriteLine(flags)         ' Decimal.
Debug.WriteLine(Hex(flags))    ' Hexadecimal.
Debug.WriteLine(Oct(flags))    ' Octal.
```

Sometimes you must use literal type characters to make a value match a variable's data type. For example, the first assignment in the following code tries to assign the value "X" to a Char variable. This throws an error because "X" is a String value. While it is obvious to a programmer that this code is trying to assign the character X to the variable, Visual Basic thinks the types don't match. The second assignment statement works because it assigns the Char value "X"c to the variable. The next assignment fails when it tries to assign the Double value 12.34 to a Decimal variable. The final assignment works because the value 12.34D is a Decimal literal.

```
Dim ch As Char
ch = "X"            ' Error because "X" is a String.
ch = "X"c           ' Okay because "X"c is a Char.

Dim amount As Decimal
amount = 12.34      ' Error because 12.34 is a Double.
amount = 12.34D     ' Okay because 12.34D is a Decimal.
```

The following code shows another way to accomplish these assignments. This version uses the data type conversion functions CChar and CDec to convert the values into the proper data types. The following section, "Data Type Conversion," has more to say about data type conversion functions.

```
ch = CChar("X")
amount = CDec(12.34)
```

Using data type characters, literal type characters, and Visual Basic's default data type assignments can lead to very confusing code. You cannot expect every programmer to notice that a particular variable is a Single because it is followed by ! in its first use, but not in others. You can make your code less confusing by using variable declarations that include explicit data types.

Data Type Conversion

Normally, you assign a value to a variable that has the same data type as the value. For example, you assign a string value to a string variable, you assign an integer value to an integer variable, and so forth. Whether you can assign a value of one type to a variable of another type depends on whether the conversion is a narrowing or widening conversion.

Narrowing Conversions

A *narrowing conversion* is one where data is converted from one type to another type that cannot hold all of the possible values allowed by the original data type. For example, the following code copies the value from a Long variable into an Integer variable. A Long value can hold values that are too big to fit in an Integer, so this is a narrowing conversion. The value contained in the Long variable may or may not fit in the Integer.

```
Dim an_integer As Integer
Dim a_long As Long
...
an_integer = a_long
```

The following code shows a less obvious example. Here the code assigns the value in a String variable to an Integer variable. If the string happens to contain a number (for example "10" or "1.23"), the assignment works. If the string contains a non-numeric value (such as "Hello"), however, the assignment fails with an error.

```
Dim an_integer As Integer
Dim a_string As String
...
an_integer = a_string
```

Another non-obvious narrowing conversion is from a class to a derived class. Suppose that the Employee class inherits from the Person class. Then setting an Employee variable equal to a Person object, as shown in the following code, is a narrowing conversion because you cannot know without additional information whether the Person is a valid Employee. All Employees are Persons, but not all Persons are Employees.

```
Dim an_employee As Employee
Dim a_person As Person
...
an_employee = a_person
```

If you have Option Strict turned on, Visual Basic will not allow implicit narrowing conversions. If Option Strict is off, Visual Basic will attempt an implicit narrowing conversion and throw an error if the conversion fails (for example, if you try to copy the Integer value 900 into a Byte variable).

To make a narrowing conversion with Option Strict turned on, you must explicitly use a data type conversion function. Visual Basic will attempt the conversion and throw an error if it fails. The CByte function converts a numeric value into a Byte value, so you could use the following code to copy an Integer value into a Byte variable:

```
Dim an_integer As Integer
Dim a_byte As Byte
...
a_byte = CByte(an_integer)
```

If the Integer variable contains a value less than 0 or greater than 255, the value will not fit in a Byte variable so CByte throws an error.

The following table lists Visual Basic's data type conversion functions.

Function	Converts To
CBool	Boolean
CByte	Byte
CChar	Char
CDate	Date
CDbl	Double
CDec	Decimal
CInt	Integer

Table continued on following page

Function	Converts To
CLng	Long
CObj	Object
CSByte	SByte
CShort	Short
CSng	Single
CStr	String
CUInt	UInteger
CULng	ULong
CUShort	UShort

The CInt and CLng functions round fractional values off to the nearest whole number. If the fractional part of a number is exactly .5, the functions round to the nearest even whole number. For example, 0.5 rounds to 0, 0.6 rounds to 1, and 1.5 rounds to 2.

In contrast, the Fix and Int functions truncate fractional values. Fix truncates toward zero, so Fix(-0.9) is 0 and Fix(0.9) is 0. Int truncates downward, so Int(-0.9) is –1 and Int(0.9) is 0.

Fix and Int also differ from CInt and CLng because they return the same data type they are passed. CInt always returns an Integer no matter what type of value you pass it. If you pass a Long into Fix, Fix returns a Long. In fact, if you pass a Double into Fix, Fix returns a Double.

The CType function takes as parameters a value and a data type, and it converts the value into that type if possible. For example, the following code uses CType to perform a narrowing conversion from a Long to an Integer. Because the value of a_long can fit within an integer, the conversion succeeds.

```
Dim an_integer As Integer
Dim a_long As Long = 100
an_integer = Ctype(a_long, Integer)
```

The DirectCast statement changes value types much as CType does, except that it only works when the variable it is converting implements or inherits from the new type. For example, suppose that the variable dessert_obj has the generic type Object and you know that it points to an object of type Dessert. Then the following code converts the generic Object into the specific Dessert type.

```
Dim dessert_obj As Object = New Dessert("Ice Cream")
Dim my_dessert As Dessert
my_dessert = DirectCast(dessert_obj, Dessert)
```

DirectCast throws an error if you try to use it to change the object's data type. For example, the following code doesn't work, even though converting an Integer into a Long is a narrowing conversion.

```
Dim an_integer As Integer = 100
Dim a_long As Long
a_long = DirectCast(an_integer, Long)
```

The `TryCast` statement converts data types much as `DirectCast` does, except that it returns `Nothing` if there is an error, rather than throwing an error.

Data Type Parsing Methods

Each of the fundamental data types except for String has a `Parse` method that attempts to convert a string into the variable type. For example, the following two statements both try to convert the string value `txt_entered` into an Integer:

```
Dim txt_entered As String = "112358"
Dim num_entered As Integer
...
num_entered = CInt(txt_entered)              ' Use CInt.
num_entered = Integer.Parse(txt_entered)     ' Use Integer.Parse.
```

Some of these parsing methods can take additional parameters to control the conversion. For example, the numeric methods can take a parameter that gives the international number style the string should have.

The class parsing methods have a more object-oriented feel than the conversion functions. They are also a bit faster. They only parse strings, however, so if you want to convert from a Long to an Integer, you need to use `CInt` rather than `Integer.Parse`.

Widening Conversions

In contrast to a narrowing conversion, a *widening conversion* is one where the new data type is always big enough to hold the old data type's values. For example, a Long is big enough to hold any Integer value, so copying an Integer value into a Long variable is a widening conversion.

Visual Basic allows widening conversions. Note that some widening conversions can still result in a loss of data. For example, a Decimal variable can store more significant digits than a Single variable can. A Single can hold any value that a Decimal can but not with the same precision. If you assign a Decimal value to a Single variable, you may lose some precision.

Variable Declarations

The complete syntax for a variable declaration is as follows:

```
[attribute_list] [accessibility] [Shared] [Shadows] [ReadOnly] _
Dim [WithEvents] name [(bounds_list)] [As [New] type] [= initialization_expression]
```

All declarations have only one thing in common: They contain a variable's name. Other than the name, different declarations may have nothing in common. Variable declarations with different forms can use or omit any other piece of the general declaration syntax. For example, the following two declarations don't share a single keyword:

```
Dim i = 1              ' Declare a private Integer named i. (Option Explicit Off)
Public j As Integer    ' Declare a public Integer named j.
```

The many variations supported by a variable declaration make the general syntax rather intimidating. In most cases, however, declarations are straightforward. The previous two declarations are fairly easy to understand.

The following sections describe the pieces of the general declaration in detail.

attribute_list

The optional attribute list is a comma-separated list of attributes that apply to the variable. An attribute further refines the definition of a variable to give more information to the compiler and the run-time system.

Attributes are rather specialized and address issues that arise when you perform very specific programming tasks. For example, when you write code to serialize and deserialize data, you can use serialization attributes to gain more control over the process.

The following code defines the `OrderItem` class. This class declares three public variables: `ItemName`, `Quantity`, and `Price`. It uses attributes on its three variables to indicate that `ItemName` should be stored as text, `Price` should be stored as an attribute named "Cost," and `Quantity` should be stored as an attribute with its default name, "Quantity."

```
Public Class OrderItem
    <XmlText()> _
        Public ItemName As String
    <XmlAttributeAttribute(AttributeName:="Cost")> _
        Public Price As Decimal
    <XmlAttributeAttribute()> _
        Public Quantity As Integer
End Class
```

The following code shows the XML serialization of an `OrderItem` object:

```
<OrderItem Cost="1.25" Quantity="12">Cookie</OrderItem>
```

Because attributes are so specialized, they are not described in more detail here. For more information, see the sections in the online help related to the tasks you need to perform. For more information in XML serialization attributes, for example, search for "System.Xml.Serialization Namespace," or go to `http://msdn.microsoft.com/library/en-us/cpref/html/frlrfSystemXmlSerialization.asp`.

For more information on Attributes, see the "Attributes" section of the Visual Basic Language Reference or go to `http://msdn.microsoft.com/library/en-us/vbls7/html/vblrfVBSpec4_10.asp`. For a list of attributes you can use to modify variable declarations, search the online help for "Attribute Hierarchy," or go to `http://msdn.microsoft.com/library/en-us/cpref/html/frlrfsystemattributeclasshierarchy.asp`.

accessibility

A variable declaration's *accessibility* clause can take one of the following values:

❑ *Public* — You can use the Public keyword only for variables declared at the module, class, structure, namespace, or file level but not inside a subroutine. Public indicates that the variable should be available to all code inside or outside of the variable's module. This allows the most access to the variable.

❑ *Protected* — You can use the Protected keyword only at the class level, not inside a module or inside a routine within a class. Protected indicates that the variable should be accessible only to code within the same class or a derived class. The variable is available to code in the same or a derived class, even if the instance of the class is different from the one containing the variable. For example, one Employee object can access a Protected variable inside another Employee object.

❑ *Friend* — You can use the Friend keyword only for variables declared at the module, class, namespace, or file level, not inside a subroutine. Friend indicates that the variable should be available to all code inside or outside of the variable's module within the same project. The difference between this and Public is that Public allows code outside of the project to access the variable. This is generally only an issue for code and control libraries. For example, suppose that you build a code library containing dozens of routines and then you write a program that uses the library. If the library declares a variable with the Public keyword, the code in the library and the code in the main program can use the variable. In contrast, if the library declares a variable with the Friend keyword, only the code in the library can access the variable, not the code in the main program.

❑ *Protected Friend* — You can use Protected Friend only at the class level, not inside a module or inside a routine within a class. Protected Friend is the union of the Protected and Friend keywords. A variable declared Protected Friend is accessible only to code within the same class or a derived class and only within the same project.

❑ *Private* — You can use the Private keyword only for variables declared at the module, class, or structure, not inside a subroutine. A variable declared Private is accessible only to code in the same module, class, or structure. If the variable is in a class or structure, it is available to other instances of the class or structure. For example, one Customer object can access a Private variable inside another Customer object.

❑ *Static* — You can use the Static keyword only for variables declared within a subroutine or a block within a subroutine (for example, a For loop or Try Catch block). You cannot use Static with Shared or Shadows. A variable declared Static keeps its value between lifetimes. For example, if a subroutine sets a Static variable to 27 before it exits, the variable begins with the value 27 the next time the subroutine executes. The value is stored in memory, so it is not retained if you exit and restart the whole program. Use a database, the System Registry, or some other means of permanent storage if you need to save values between program runs.

Shared

You can use the Shared keyword at the module, class, structure, namespace, or file level, not within a subroutine. This keyword means that all instances of the class or structure containing the variable share the same variable.

For example, suppose that the Order class declares the Shared variable NumOrders to represent the total number of orders in the application. Then all instances of the Order class share the same NumOrders variable. If one instance of an Order sets NumOrders to 10, all instances of Order see NumOrders equals 10.

You can access a `Shared` variable either by using a specific class instance or by using the class itself. For example, the following code uses the `order1` object's `NumOrders` variable to set the value of `NumOrders` to 100. It then displays this value by using `order1` and another `Order` object named `order2`. Next, it uses the class itself to set the value of `NumOrders` and uses the class to display the result.

```
order1.NumOrders = 100              ' Use order1 to set NumOrders = 100.
MessageBox.Show(order1.NumOrders)   ' Use order1 to display 100.
MessageBox.Show(order2.NumOrders)   ' Use a different Order to Display 100.
Order.NumOrders = 101               ' Use the class to set NumOrders = 101.
MessageBox.Show(Order.NumOrders)    ' Use the class to display 101.
```

You cannot use the `Shared` keyword with the `Static` keyword. This makes sense because a `Shared` variable is in some fashion static to the class or structure that contains it. If one instance of the class modifies the variable, the value is available to all other instances. In fact, even if you destroy every instance of the class or never create any instances at all, the class itself still keeps the variable's value safe. That provides a persistence similar to that given by the `Static` keyword.

Shadows

You can use the `Shadows` keyword only for variables declared at the module, class, structure, namespace, or file level, not inside a subroutine. `Shadows` indicates that the variable hides a variable with the same name in a base class. In a typical example, a subclass provides a variable with the same name as a variable declared in one of its ancestor classes.

The following code defines a `Person` class that contains public String variables `LastName` and `EmployeeId`. The `Employee` class inherits from `Person` and declares its own version of the `EmployeeId` variable. It uses the `Shadows` keyword so this version covers the version defined by the `Person` class. Note that `Shadows` works here even though the two versions of `EmployeeId` have different data types: Long versus String. An `Employee` object gets the Long version, and a `Person` object gets the String version.

The `Manager` class inherits from the `Employee` class and defines its own version of the `LastName` variable. A `Manger` object uses this version, while an `Employee` or `Person` object uses the version defined by the `Person` class.

Having defined these three classes, the program works with them to demonstrate shadowing. First, it creates a `Manager` object, and sets its `LastName` variable to `Manager Last Name` and its `EmployeeId` variable to 1. The `LastName` value is stored in the `Manager` class's version of the variable declared with the `Shadows` keyword. The `EmployeeId` value is stored in the `EmployeeId` variable declared with the `Shadows` keyword in the `Employee` class.

The program then creates an `Employee` variable and makes it point to the `Manager` object. This makes sense because `Manager` inherits from `Employee`. A `Manager` is a type of `Employee` so an `Employee` variable can point to a `Manager` object. The program sets the `Employee` object's `LastName` variable to `Employee Last Name` and its `EmployeeId` variable to 2. The `LastName` value is stored in the `Person` class's version of the variable. The `EmployeeId` value is stored in the `EmployeeId` variable declared with the `Shadows` keyword in the `Employee` class. Because the `Manager` class does not override this declaration with its own shadowing declaration of `EmployeeId`, this value overwrites the value stored by the `Manager` object.

Next, the program creates a Person variable and makes it point to the same Manager object. Again this makes sense because a Manager is a type of Person so a Person variable can point to a Manager object. The program sets the Person object's LastName variable to "Person Last Name" and its EmployeeId variable to "A." The Person class does not inherit, so the program stores the values in the versions of the variables defined by the Person class. Because the Employee class does not override the Person class's declaration of LastName with its own shadowing declaration, this value overwrites the value stored by the Employee object.

Finally, the program prints the values of the EmployeeId and LastName variables for each of the objects.

```
Public Class Person
    Public LastName As String
    Public EmployeeId As String
End Class

Public Class Employee
    Inherits Person
    Public Shadows EmployeeId As Long
End Class

Public Class Manager
    Inherits Employee
    Public Shadows LastName As String
End Class

Private Sub TestShadows()
    Dim mgr As New Manager
    mgr.LastName = "Manager Last Name"
    mgr.EmployeeId = 1

    Dim emp As Employee = CType(mgr, Employee)
    emp.LastName = "Employee Last Name"
    emp.EmployeeId = 2

    Dim per As Person= CType(mgr, Person)
    per.LastName = "Person Last Name"
    per.EmployeeId = "A"

    Debug.WriteLine(mgr.EmployeeId & ": " & mgr.LastName)
    Debug.WriteLine(emp.EmployeeId & ": " & emp.LastName)
    Debug.WriteLine(per.EmployeeId & ": " & per.LastName)
End Sub
```

The following output shows the program's results. Notice that the Employee object's value for EmployeeId (2) overwrote the value saved by the Manager object (1) and that the Person object's value for LastName (Person Last Name) overwrote the value saved by the Employee object (Employee Last Name).

```
2: Manager Last Name
2: Person Last Name
A: Person Last Name
```

Normally, you don't need to access shadowed versions of a variable. If you declare a version of `LastName` in the `Employee` class that shadows a declaration in the `Person` class, you presumably did it for a good reason (unlike in the previous example which does it just to show how it's done), and you don't need to access the shadowed version directly.

However, if you really do need to access the shadowed version, you can use variables from ancestor classes to do so. For example, the previous example creates `Employee` and `Person` objects pointing to a `Manager` object to access that object's shadowed variables.

Within a class, you can similarly cast the `Me` object to an ancestor class. For example, the following code in the `Manager` class makes a `Person` variable pointing to the same object and sets its `LastName` value:

```
Public Sub SetPersonEmployeeId(ByVal employee_id As String)
    Dim per As Person = CType(Me, Person)
    per.EmployeeId = employee_id
End Sub
```

Code in a class can also use the `MyBase` keyword to access the variables defined by the parent class. The following code in the `Manager` class sets the object's `LastName` variable declared by the `Employee` parent class:

```
Public Sub SetManagerLastName(ByVal last_name As String)
    MyBase.LastName = last_name
End Sub
```

ReadOnly

You can use the `ReadOnly` keyword only for variables declared at the module, class, structure, namespace, or file level, not inside a subroutine. `ReadOnly` indicates that the program can read, but not modify, the variable's value.

You can initialize the variable in one of two ways. First, you can include an initialization statement in the variable's declaration, as shown in the following code:

```
Public Class EmployeeCollection
    Public ReadOnly MaxEmployees As Integer = 100
    ...
End Class
```

Second, you can initialize the variable in the object's constructors. The following code declares the `ReadOnly` variable `MaxEmployees`. The empty constructor sets this variable to `100`. A second constructor takes an integer parameter and sets the `MaxEmployees` to its value.

```
Public Class EmployeeCollection
    Public ReadOnly MaxEmployees As Integer

    Public Sub New()
        MaxEmployees = 100
    End Sub

    Public Sub New(ByVal max_employees As Integer)
```

```
        MaxEmployees = max_employees
    End Sub
    ...
End Class
```

After the object is initialized, the program cannot modify the ReadOnly variable. This restriction applies to code inside the module that declared the variable, as well as code in other modules. If you want to allow code inside the same module to modify the value but want to prevent code in other modules from modifying the value, you should use a property procedure instead. See the section "Property Procedures" later in this chapter for more information.

Dim

The Dim keyword officially tells Visual Basic that you want to create a variable.

You can omit the Dim keyword if you specify Public, Protected, Friend, Protected Friend, Private, Static, or ReadOnly. In fact, if you include one of these keywords, the Visual Basic editor automatically removes the Dim keyword if you include it.

If you do not specify otherwise, variables you declare using a Dim statement are Private. The following two statements are equivalent:

```
Dim num_people As Integer
Private num_people As Integer
```

For certainty's sake, many programmers explicitly specify Private to declare private variables. Using Private means that programmers don't need to remember that the Dim keyword gives a private variable by default.

One place where the Dim keyword is common is when declaring variables inside subroutines. You cannot use the Private keyword inside a subroutine (or Public, Protected, Friend, Protected Friend, or ReadOnly, for that matter), so you must use either Static or Dim.

WithEvents

The WithEvents keyword tells Visual Basic that the variable is of a specific object type that may raise events that you will want to catch. For example, the following code declares the variable Face as a PictureBox object that may raise events you want to catch:

```
Private WithEvents Face As PictureBox
```

When you declare a variable with the WithEvents keyword, Visual Basic creates an entry for it in the left drop-down in the module's code window, as shown in Figure 4-1.

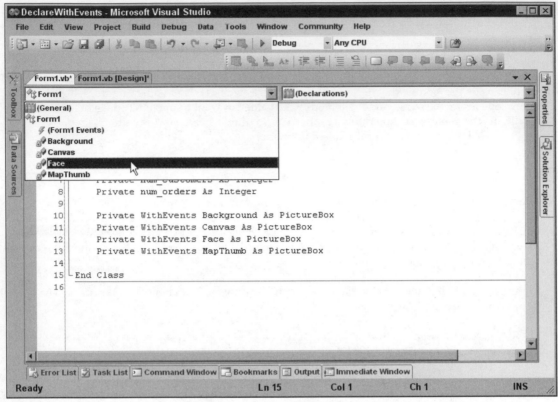

Figure 4-1: Visual Basic creates a drop-down entry for variables declared WithEvents.

If you select the object in the left drop-down list, Visual Basic fills the right drop-down with the object's events that you might want to catch, as shown in Figure 4-2.

If you select an event, Visual Basic creates a corresponding empty event handler. Letting Visual Basic automatically generate the event handler in this way is easier and safer than trying to type the event handler yourself, creating all of the required parameters by hand.

Declaring variables using the WithEvents keyword is a powerful technique. You can make the variable point to an object to catch its events. Later, if you want to process events from some other object using the same event handlers, you can set the variable to point to the new object. If you no longer want to receive that any events, you can set the variable to Nothing.

Unfortunately, you cannot declare an array using the WithEvents keyword. That means you cannot use a simple declaration to allow the same event handlers to process events from more than one object. However, you can achieve this by using the AddHandler method to explicitly set the event handler routines for a series of objects. For more information on this technique, see the section "Catching Events" in Chapter 15.

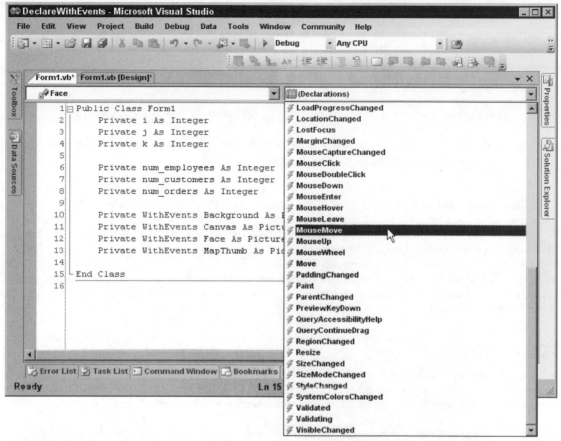

Figure 4-2: When you select an object declared `WithEvents` in the left drop-down, Visual Basic fills the right drop-down with events you might want to catch.

name

A declaration's *name* clause gives the name of the variable. This must be a valid Visual Basic identifier. The rules for valid identifiers are a bit confusing, but generally an identifier should begin with a letter or underscore, followed by any number of letters, digits, or underscores. If the identifier begins with an underscore (which is unusual), it must contain at least one other valid character (letter, digit, or underscore) so that Visual Basic doesn't confuse it with a line continuation character. Here are some examples:

`num_employees`	Valid
`NumEmployees`	Valid
`_manager`	Valid (but unusual)
`_`	Invalid (contains only a single underscore)
`__`	Valid (two underscores is valid but could be very confusing)
`1st_employee`	Invalid (doesn't begin with a letter or underscore)

Normal identifiers cannot be the same as a Visual Basic keyword. However, you can *escape* an identifier by enclosing it in square brackets. If you escape an identifier, you can give it the same name as a Visual Basic keyword. For example, in the following code, the `ParseString` subroutine takes a single parameter named `String` of type String:

```
Public Sub ParseString(ByVal [String] As String)
    Dim values() As String = Split([String])
    ...
End Sub
```

If you begin writing a call to this subroutine in the code editor, the IntelliSense popup describes this routine as `ParseString(String As String)`.

These rules let you come up with some strange and potentially confusing identifier names. For example, you can make escaped variables named `String`, `Boolean`, `ElseIf`, and `Case`. Depending on your system's settings, underscores may be hard to read either on the screen or in printouts. That may make variables such as __ (two underscores) seem to vanish and may make it hard to tell the difference between _Name and Name.

While these identifiers are all legal, they can be extremely confusing and may lead to long, frustrating debugging sessions. To avoid confusion, use escaped identifiers and identifiers beginning with an underscore sparingly.

bounds_list

A variable declaration's *bounds_list* clause specifies bounds for an array. This should be a comma-separated list of non-negative integers that give the upper bound for the array's dimensions. All dimensions have a lower bound of zero. You can optionally specify the lower bound, but it must always be zero.

The following code declares two arrays in two different ways. The first statement declares a one-dimensional array of 101 `Customer` objects with indexes ranging from 0 to 100. The second statement defines a two-dimensional array of `Order` objects. The first dimension has bounds ranging from 0 to 100 and the second dimension has bounds ranging from 0 to 10. The array's entries are those between `orders(0, 0)` and `orders(100, 10)` giving a total of 101 * 11 = 1111 entries. The last two statements define similar arrays, while explicitly declaring the arrays' lower bounds.

```
Private customers(100) As Customer
Private orders(100, 10) As Order
Private customers2(0 To 100) As Customer
Private orders2(0 To 100, 0 To 10) As Order
```

You may find that specifying the lower bound makes the code easier to read because it gives the lower bound explicitly rather than requiring you to remember that lower bounds are always 0. It can be particularly helpful for those who have used Visual Basic 6 and earlier versions because those versions of Visual Basic allowed arrays to have lower bounds other than 0.

Note that declarations of this sort that use an object data type do not instantiate the objects. For example, the first declaration in the previous example defines 101 array entries that all point to `Nothing`. They do not initially point to instances of the `Customer` class. After this declaration, the program would need to create each object reference individually, as shown in the following code:

```
Private customers(100) As Customer
For i As Integer = 0 To 100
    customers(i) = New Customer
Next i
```

Alternatively, the program can use an initialization statement to declare and initialize the objects in a single step. See the section "initialization_expression" later in this chapter for more information on initializing arrays in their declarations.

If you provide parentheses but no *bounds_list*, Visual Basic defines the array, but doesn't create it with specific bounds. Later, you can use the ReDim statement to give it bounds. Note that you can also use ReDim to change the bounds of an array that you initially give bounds. The following example declares two arrays named a1 and a2. Initially, the program allocates 11 items for array a1 but no items for array a2. The program then uses ReDim to allocate 21 entries for both arrays.

```
Dim a1(10) As Integer
Dim a2() As Integer

ReDim a1(20)
ReDim a2(0 To 20)
```

The ReDim statement cannot change the number of bounds in an array. If you want to declare but not initialize a multidimensional array, include commas as if you were defining the bounds. The following code declares a three-dimensional array and initializes its separate steps:

```
Dim a1(,,) As Integer

ReDim a1(10, 20, 30)
```

New

If you are declaring an object variable, the New keyword tells Visual Basic to create a new instance of the object. Without this keyword, Visual Basic makes an object variable that doesn't yet hold a reference to any object. It initially holds Nothing.

For example, the first line in the following code declares an Employee object variable named emp1. After that line, the variable is defined, but it doesn't point to anything. If you examine the variable, you will find that it has the value Nothing. The second line sets emp1 equal to a new Employee object. The last line creates an Employee object variable named emp2 and assigns it to a new Employee object. This does the same thing as the first and second line but in a single statement.

```
Dim emp1 As Employee
emp1 = New Employee

Dim emp2 As New Manager
```

If the object's class has constructors that take parameters, you can include the parameters after the class name. For example, suppose that the Employee class has two constructors: an empty constructor (one that takes no parameters) and a constructor that takes first and last name strings as parameters. Then, the following code creates two Employee objects using the different constructors:

```
Dim emp1 As New Employee
Dim emp2 As New Employee("Rod", "Stephens")
```

Note that you must provide parameters that match some constructor. If the class does not have a constructor that takes no arguments, you cannot use the New keyword without specifying parameters. If the Employee class didn't have an empty constructor, the first line in the previous example would be illegal.

initialization_expression

The *initialization_expression* clause gives data that Visual Basic should use to initialize the variable. The most straightforward form of initialization assigns a simple value to a variable. The following code declares the variable num_employees and assigns it the initial value zero:

```
Dim num_employees As Integer = 0
```

More complicated data types may require more complex initialization clauses. If the declaration declares an object variable, you can use the New keyword to initialize the variable. For example, the first line in the following code declares an Employee variable named emp1 and sets it equal to a new Employee object. The second statement uses the As New form of declaration to do the same thing without a separate initialization clause. This version is slightly more compact, but you can use whichever version seems most natural to you.

```
Dim emp1 As Employee = New Employee("Rod", "Stephens")
Dim emp2 As New Employee("Rod", "Stephens")
```

Initializing Arrays

Arrays have their own special initialization syntax. To declare and initialize an array in one statement, you must omit the array's bounds. Visual Basic uses the initialization data to discover the bounds.

Place the array's values inside curly braces separated by commas. The following code initializes a one-dimensional array of integers:

```
Dim fibonacci() As Integer = {1, 1, 2, 3, 5, 8, 13, 21, 33, 54, 87}
```

For a multidimensional array, put commas in the variable's parentheses to indicate the number of dimensions. Use curly braces to surround the array data. Nest each dimension of data inside the previous one, enclosing each dimension's data with braces and separating entries with commas.

This probably makes the most sense if you think of a multidimensional array as an array of arrays. For example, a three-dimensional array is an array of two-dimensional arrays. Each of the two-dimensional arrays is an array of one-dimensional arrays. You can use line continuation characters and indentation to make the array's structure more obvious.

The following code declares and initializes a two-dimensional array of integers and then prints the values:

```
Dim int_values(,) As Integer = _
{ _
    {1, 2, 3}, _
    {4, 5, 6} _
```

```
    }
    For i As Integer = 0 To 1
        For j As Integer = 0 To 2
            Debug.Write(int_values(i, j))
        Next j
        Debug.WriteLine("")
    Next i
```

The following shows this code's output:

```
123
456
```

The following code declares and initializes a three-dimensional array of strings. The text for each value gives its position in the array. For example, the value str_values(0, 1, 1) is "011." Notice how the code uses indentation to make the data a bit easier to understand. Items in the first dimension are indented one level and items in the second dimension are indented two levels. The final level is basically a one-dimensional array, which is fairly easy to understand with just commas separating its values. After initializing the array, the code loops through its entries and prints them.

```
Dim str_values(,,) As String = _
{ _
    { _
        {"000", "001", "002"}, _
        {"010", "011", "012"} _
    }, _
    { _
        {"100", "101", "102"},
        {"110", "111", "112"} _
    } _
}
Debug.WriteLine("")
For i As Integer = 0 To 1
    For j As Integer = 0 To 1
        For k As Integer = 0 To 2
            Debug.Write(str_values(i, j, k) & " ")
        Next k
    Next j
    Debug.WriteLine("")
Next i
```

The following text shows this code's output:

```
000 001 002 010 011 012
100 101 102 110 111 112
```

Note that you must provide the correct number of items for each of the array's dimensions. For example, the following declaration is invalid because the array's second row contains fewer elements than its first row:

```
Dim int_values(,) As Integer = _
{ _
    {1, 2, 3}, _
    {4, 5} _
}
```

Initializing Object Arrays

The basic syntax for initializing an array of objects is similar to the syntax you use to initialize any other array. You still omit the array bounds from the declaration and then include values inside curly braces. The values you use to initialize the array, however, are different because object variables do not take simple values such as 12 and "Test" that you would use to initialize integer or string arrays.

If you create an array of objects without an initialization clause, Visual Basic creates the object variables but does not create objects for them. Initially, all of the array's entries are Nothing.

The following code creates an array containing 11 references to Employee objects. Initially, all of the references are set to Nothing.

```
Dim employees(0 To 10) As Employee
```

If you want to initialize the objects, you must initialize each object in the array separately using Nothing or the class's constructors. The following code declares an array of Employee objects. It initializes two entries using an Employee object constructor that takes as parameters the employee's first and last names, two entries with an empty constructor, and two final entries with Nothing.

```
Dim employees() As Employee = _
{ _
    New Employee("Alice", "Andrews"), _
    New Employee("Bart", "Brin"), _
    New Employee, _
    New Employee, _
    Nothing, _
    Nothing _
}
```

To initialize higher-dimensional arrays of objects, use the syntax described in the previous section. Use Nothing or the New keyword and object constructors to initialize each array entry individually.

Multiple Variable Declarations

Visual Basic .NET allows you to declare more than one variable in a single declaration statement. For example, the following statement declares two Integer variables named num_employees and num_customers:

```
Private num_employees, num_customers As Integer
```

You can place accessibility keywords (Private, Public, and so on), Shared, Shadows, and ReadOnly only at the beginning of the declaration and they apply to all of the variables in the declaration. In the previous statement, both num_employees and num_customers are Private.

You can declare variables with different data types by including more than one `As` clause separated by commas. The following statement declares two Integer variables and one String variable:

```
Private emps, custs As Integer, cust As String
```

You cannot use an initialization statement if more than one variable share the same `As` clause, but you can include an initialization statement for variables that have their own `As` clause. In the previous example, you cannot initialize the two Integer variables, but you can initialize the String variable as shown in the following statement.

```
Private emps, custs As Integer, cust As String = "Cozmo"
```

To initialize all three variables, you would need to give them each their own `As` clauses, as shown in the following example:

```
Private emps As Integer = 5, custs As Integer = 10, cust As String = "Cozmo"
```

You can also declare and initialize multiple objects, arrays, and arrays of objects all in the same statement.

While all of these combinations are legal, they quickly become too confusing to be of much practical use. Even the relatively simple statement that follows can lead to later misunderstandings. Quickly glancing at this statement, the programmer may think that all three variables are declared as Long.

```
Private num_employees, num_customers As Integer, num_orders As Long
```

You can reduce the possibility of confusion by using one `As` clause per declaration. Then a programmer can easily understand how the variables are defined by looking at the beginning and ending of the declaration. The beginning tells the programmer the variables' accessibility and whether they are shared, shadowing other variables, or read-only. The end gives the variables' data type.

You can also keep the code simple by giving variables with initialization statements their own declarations. Then a programmer reading the code won't need to decide whether an initialization statement applies to one or all of the variables.

There's nothing particularly wrong with declaring a series of relatively short variables in a single statement, as long as you don't find the code confusing. The following statements declare five Integer variables and three Single variables. Breaking this into eight separate `Dim` statements would not make it much clearer.

```
Dim i, j, k, R, C As Integer
Dim X, Y, Z As Single
```

Option Explicit and Option Strict

The `Option Explicit` and `Option Strict` compiler options play an important role in variable declarations.

When `Option Explicit` is set to `On`, you must declare all variables before you use them. If `Option Explicit` is `Off`, Visual Basic automatically creates a new variable whenever it sees a variable that it has not yet encountered. For example, the following code doesn't explicitly declare any variables. As it executes the code, Visual Basic sees the first statement, num_managers = 0. It doesn't recognize the variable num_managers, so it creates it. Similarly, it creates the variable i when it sees it in the For loop.

```
Option Explicit Off
Option Strict Off

Public Class Form1
    ...
    Public Sub CountManagers()
        num_managers = 0
        For i = 0 To m_Employees.GetUpperBound(0)
            If m_Employees(i).IsManager Then num_managrs += 1
        Next i

        MsgBox(num_managers)
    End Sub
    ...
End Class
```

Keeping Option Explicit turned off can lead to two very bad problems. First, it silently hides typographical errors. If you look closely at the previous code, you'll see that the statement inside the For loop increments the misspelled variable num_managrs instead of the correctly spelled variable num_managers. Because Option Explicit is off, Visual Basic assumes that you want to use a new variable, so it creates num_managrs. After the loop finishes, the program displays the value of num _managers, which is zero because it was never incremented.

The second problem that occurs when Option Explicit is off is that Visual Basic doesn't really know what you will want to do with the variables it creates for you. It doesn't know whether you will use a variable as an Integer, Double, String, or PictureBox. Even after you assign a value to the variable (say, an Integer), Visual Basic doesn't know whether you will always use the variable as an Integer or whether you might later want to save a String in it.

To keep its options open, Visual Basic creates undeclared variables as generic objects. Then it can fill the variable with just about anything. Unfortunately, this can make the code much less efficient than it needs to be. For example, programs are much better at manipulating integers than they are at manipulating objects. If you are going to use a variable as an integer, creating it as an object makes the program run much slower.

In more advanced terms, integers are value types, while objects are reference types. A reference type is really a fancy pointer that represents the location of the actual object in memory. When you treat a value type as a reference type, Visual Basic performs an operation called "boxing," where it wraps the value in an object so it can use references to the boxed value. If you then perform an operation involving two boxed values, Visual Basic must unbox them, perform the operation, and then possibly box the result to store it in another reference variable. All of this boxing and unboxing has a significant overhead.

The following code executes two For loops. In the first loop, it explicitly declares its looping variable to be of type Integer. In the second loop, the code doesn't declare its looping variable, so Visual Basic automatically makes it an object when it is needed. In one test, the second loop took more than 60 times as long as the first loop.

```
Const TRIALS As Integer = 10000000
Dim start_time As DateTime
Dim stop_time As DateTime
Dim elapsed_time As TimeSpan

Dim i As Integer
start_time = Now
For i = 1 To TRIALS

Next i
stop_time = Now
elapsed_time = stop_time.Subtract(start_time)
MsgBox(elapsed_time.TotalSeconds.ToString("0.000000"))

start_time = Now
For j = 1 To TRIALS

Next j
stop_time = Now
elapsed_time = stop_time.Subtract(start_time)
MsgBox(elapsed_time.TotalSeconds.ToString("0.000000"))
```

The second compiler directive that influences variable declaration is Option Strict. When Option Strict is turned off, Visual Basic silently converts values from one data type to another, even if the types are not very compatible. For example, Visual Basic will allow the following code to try to copy the string s into the integer i. If the value in the string happens to be a number (as in the first case), this works. If the string is not a number (as in the second case), this throws an error at run time.

```
Dim i As Integer
Dim s As String
s = "10"
i = s          ' This works.
s = "Hello"
i = s          ' This Fails.
```

If you turn Option Strict on, Visual Basic warns you of possibly illegal conversions at compile time. You can still use conversion functions such as CInt, Int, and Integer.Parse to convert a string into an Integer, but you must take explicit action to do so.

To avoid confusion and ensure total control of your variable declarations, you should always turn on Option Explicit and Option Strict. (Frankly it's strange that Visual Basic doesn't have these options on by default. Or it could simply remove them completely and behave as if they were on. Possibly this is done for historical reasons or perhaps it's so because the related language VBScript doesn't allow variable declarations.)

For more information on Option Explicit and Option Strict (including instructions for turning these options on), see the "Project" section in Chapter 1.

Scope

A variable's *scope* tells which other pieces of code can access it. For example, if you declare a variable inside a subroutine, only code within that subroutine can access the variable. The four possible levels of scope are (in increasing size of scope) block, procedure, module, and namespace.

Block Scope

A *block* is a series of statements enclosed in construct that ends with some sort of End, Else, Loop, or Next statement. If you declare a variable within a block of code, the variable has block scope, and only other code within that block can access the variable. Furthermore, only code that appears after the variable's declaration can see the variable.

Variables declared in the block's opening statement are also part of the block. Note that a variable is visible within any subblock contained within the variable's scope.

The following example uses a For loop with the looping variable i declared in the For statement. The scope of variable i is block-defined by the For loop. Code inside the loop can see variable i, but code outside of the loop cannot.

Inside the loop, the code declares variable j. This variable's scope is also the For loop's block.

If i equals j, the program declares variable M and uses it. This variable's scope includes only the two lines between the If and Else statements.

If i doesn't equal j, the code declares variable N. This variable's scope includes only the two lines between the Else and End If statements.

The program then declares variable k. This variable also has block scope, but it is available only after it is declared, so the code could not have accessed it earlier in the For loop.

```
For i As Integer = 1 To 5
    Dim j As Integer = 3
    If i = j Then
        Dim M As Integer = i + j
        Debug.WriteLine("M: " & M)
    Else
        Dim N As Integer = i * j
        Debug.WriteLine("N: " & N)
    End If

    Dim k As Integer = 123
    Debug.WriteLine("k: " & k)
Next i
```

Other code constructs that define blocks include the following:

❑   *Select Case statements* — Each Case has its own block.

❑   *Try Catch statements* — The Try section and each Exception statement defines a block. Note also that the exception variable defined in each Exception statement is in its own block; for example, they can all have the same name.

```
Try
    Dim i As Integer = CInt("bad value")
Catch ex As InvalidCastException
    Dim txt As String = "InvalidCastException"
    MsgBox(txt)
Catch ex As Exception
    Dim txt As String = "Exception"
    MsgBox(txt)
End Try
```

❑ *Single-Line If Then statements* — These are strange and confusing enough that you should avoid them, but the following code *is* legal:

```
If manager Then Dim txt As String = "M" : MsgBox(txt) Else _
    Dim txt As String = "E" : MsgBox(txt)
```

❑ *While loops* — Variables declared inside the loop are local to the loop.

❑ *Using statements* — Resources acquired by the block and variables declared inside the block are local to the block. The Using statement in the following code defines two Employee objects and variable i within its block. Those variables are visible only within the block.

```
Using _
    emp1 As New Employee("Ann", "Archer"), _
    emp2 As New Employee("Bob", "Beagle")
    Dim i As Integer
    ...
End Using
```

Because block scope is the most restrictive, you should use it whenever possible to reduce the chances for confusion. The section "Restricting Scope" later in this chapter discusses more about restricting variable scope.

Procedure Scope

If you declare a variable inside a subroutine, function, or other procedure, but not within a block, the variable is visible in any code inside the procedure that follows the declaration. The variable is not visible outside of the procedure. In a sense, the variable has block scope where the block is the procedure.

A procedure's parameters also have procedure scope. For example, in the following code, the scope of the order_object and order_item parameters is the AddOrderItem subroutine:

```
Public Sub AddOrderItem(ByVal order_object As Order, ByVal order_item As OrderItem)
    order_object.OrderItems.Add(order_item)
End Sub
```

Module Scope

A variable with module scope is available to all code in its code module, class, or structure, even if the code appears before the variable's declaration. For example, the following code works even though the DisplayLoanAmount subroutine is declared before the m_LoanAmount variable that it displays:

```
Private Class Lender
    Public Sub DisplayLoanAmount()
        MsgBox(m_LoanAmount)
    End Sub

    Private m_LoanAmount As Decimal
    ...
End Class
```

To give a variable module scope, you should declare it with the Private, Protected, or Protected Friend keyword. If you declare the variable Private, it is visible only to code within the same module.

If you declare the variable Protected, it is accessible only to code in its class or a derived class. Remember that you can only use the Protected keyword in a class.

A Protected Friend variable is both Protected and Friend. That means it is available only to code that is inside the variable's class or a derived class (Protected), and that is within the same project (Friend).

These keywords apply to both variable and procedure declarations. For example, you can declare a subroutine, function, or property procedure Private, Protected, or Protected Friend.

For more information on accessibility keywords, see the section "accessibility" earlier in this chapter.

Namespace Scope

By default, a project defines a namespace that includes all the project's variables and code. However, you can use Namespace statements to create other namespaces if you like. This may be useful to help categorize the code in your application.

If you declare a variable with the Public keyword, it has namespace scope and is available to all code in its namespace, whether inside the project or in another project. It is also available to code in any namespaces nested inside the variable's namespace. If you do not create any namespaces of your own, the whole project lies in a single namespace, so you can think of Public variables as having global scope.

If you declare a variable with the Friend keyword, it has namespace scope and is available to all code in its namespace within the same project. It is also available to code in any namespaces nested inside the variable's namespace within the project. If you do not create any namespaces if your own, the whole project lies in a single namespace so you can think of Friend variables as having project scope.

For more information on the Public and Friend keywords, see the section, "accessibility," earlier in this chapter.

Restricting Scope

There are several reasons why you should give variables the most restrictive scope possible that still lets them do their jobs.

Limited scope keeps the variable localized so that programmers cannot use the variable incorrectly in far off code that is unrelated to the variable's main purpose.

Having fewer variables with global scope means programmers have less to remember when they are working on the code. They can concentrate on their current work, rather than worrying about whether variables r and c are declared globally and whether the current code will interfere with them.

Limiting scope keeps variables closer to their declarations, so it's easier for programmers to check the declaration. One of the best examples of this situation is when a For loop declares its looping variable right in the For statement. A programmer can easily see that the looping variable is an integer without scrolling to the top of the subroutine hunting for its declaration. It is also easy to see that the variable has block scope, so other variables with the same names can be used outside of the loop.

Limited scope means a programmer doesn't need to worry about whether a variable's old value will interfere with the current code, or whether the final value after the current code will later interfere with some other code. This is particularly true for looping variables. If a program declares variable i at the top of a subroutine, and then uses it many times in various loops, you might need to do a little thinking to be sure the variable's past values won't interfere with new loops. If you declare i separately in each For statement, each loop has its own version of i, so there's no way they can interfere with each other.

Finally, variables with larger scope tend to be allocated more often, so they take up memory more often. For example, block variables and nonstatic variables declared with procedure scope are allocated when they are needed and are destroyed when their scope ends, freeing their memory. A variable declared Static or with module or namespace scope is not freed until your application exits. If those variables are large arrays, they may take up a lot of memory the entire time your application is running.

Parameter Declarations

Parameter declarations for subroutines, functions, and property procedures always have nonstatic procedure scope. Visual Basic creates parameter variables when a procedure begins and destroys them when the procedure ends. The subroutine's code can access the parameters, but code outside of the routine cannot.

For example, the following subroutine takes an integer as a parameter. The subroutine calls this value employee_id. Code within the subroutine can access employee_id, while code outside of the subroutine cannot.

```
Public Sub DisplayEmployee(ByVal employee_id As Integer)
    ...
End Sub
```

While a parameter's basic scope is straightforward (nonstatic procedure scope), parameters have some special features that complicate the situation. While this isn't exactly a scoping issue, it's related closely enough to scope that it's worth covering here.

You can declare a parameter ByRef or ByVal (ByVal is the default if you use neither keyword). If you declare the variable ByVal, the routine makes its own local parameter variable with procedure scope just as you would expect.

If you declare a parameter with the ByRef keyword, the routine does not create a separate copy of the parameter variable. Instead, it uses a reference to the parameter you pass in, and any changes the routine makes to the value are reflected in the calling subroutine.

For instance, the following code includes two routines that double their parameters. Subroutine DoubleItByVal declares its parameter with the ByVal keyword. This routine makes a new variable named X and copies the value of its parameter into that variable. The parameter X is available within the subroutine, the routine multiplies it by 2, and then exits. At that point, the parameter variable goes out of scope and is destroyed.

Subroutine DoubleItByRef declares its parameter with the ByRef keyword. This routine's variable X is a reference to the variable passed into the routine. The subroutine doubles X and that doubles the variable in the calling code.

Subroutine TestParameters calls each of these routines. It declares a variable named value, passes it to subroutine DoubleItByVal, and displays the result after DoubleItByVal returns. Because DoubleItByVal declares its parameter ByVal, the variable value is not changed so the result is 10.

Subroutine TestParameters then calls subroutine DoubleItByRef and displays the result after the call returns. Subroutine DoubleItByRef declares its parameter ByRef so the variable value is changed to 20.

```
Sub DoubleItByVal(ByVal X As Single)
    X *= 2
End Sub
Sub DoubleItByRef(ByRef X As Single)
    X *= 2
End Sub
Sub TestParameters()
    Dim value As Single

    value = 10
    DoubleItByVal(value)
    Debug.WriteLine(value)

    value = 10
    DoubleItByRef(value)
    Debug.WriteLine(value)
End Sub
```

Even this more complex view of how procedures handle parameters has exceptions. If you pass a literal value or the result of an expression into a procedure, there is no variable to pass by reference, so Visual Basic must create its own temporary variable. In that case, any changes made to a ByRef parameter are not returned to the calling routine, because that code did not pass a variable into the procedure. The following code shows statements that pass a literal expression and the result of an expression into the DoubleItByRef subroutine:

```
DoubleItByRef(12)        ' Literal expression.
DoubleItByRef(X + Y)     ' Result of an expression.
```

Another case where a ByRef parameter does not modify a variable in the calling code is when you omit an optional variable. For example, the following subroutine takes an optional ByRef parameter. If you call this routine and omit the parameter, Visual Basic creates the `employee_id` parameter from scratch so the subroutine can use it in its calculations. Because you called the routine without passing it a variable, the subroutine does not update a variable.

```
Sub UpdateEmployee(Optional ByRef employee_id As Integer = 0)
    ...
End Sub
```

Probably the sneakiest way a `ByRef` variable can fail to update a variable in the calling routine is if you enclose the variable in parentheses. The parentheses tell Visual Basic to evaluate their contents as an expression, so Visual Basic creates a temporary variable to hold the result of the expression. It then passes the temporary variable into the procedure. If the procedure's parameter is declared `ByRef`, it updates the temporary variable, but not the original variable, so the calling routine doesn't see any change to its value.

The following code calls subroutine `DoubleItByRef`, passing the variable `value` into the routine surrounded with parentheses. The `DoubleItByRef` subroutine doubles the temporary variable Visual Basic creates, leaving `value` unchanged.

```
DoubleItByRef((value))
```

Keep these issues in mind when you work with parameters. Parameters have nonstatic procedure scope but the `ByRef` keyword can sometimes carry their values outside of the routine.

For more information on routines and their parameters, see Chapter 6, "Subroutines and Functions."

Property Procedures

Property procedures are routines that can represent a variable-like value. To other pieces of the program, property procedures look just like variables, so they deserve mention in this chapter.

The following code shows property procedures that implement a `Name` property. The `Property Get` procedure simply returns the value in the private variable `m_Name`. The `Property Set` procedure saves a new value in the `m_Name` variable.

```
Private m_Name As String

Property Name() As String
    Get
        Return m_Name
    End Get
    Set(ByVal Value As String)
        m_Name = Value
    End Set
End Property
```

A program could use these procedures exactly as if there was a single public `Name` variable. For example, if this code is in the `Employee` class, the following code shows how a program could set and then get the `Name` value for the `Employee` object named `emp`.

```
emp.Name = "Rod Stephens"
MessageBox.Show(cmp.Name)
```

There are several reasons why you might want to use property procedures rather than a public variable. First, the routines give you extra control over the getting and setting of the value. For example, you could use code to validate the value before saving it in the variable. The code could verify that a postal code or phone number has the proper format and throw an error if the value is badly formatted.

You can set breakpoints in property procedures. Suppose that your program is crashing because a piece of code is setting an incorrect value in a variable. If you implement the variable with property procedures, you can set a breakpoint in the `Property Set` procedure and stop whenever the program sets the value. This can help you find the problem relatively quickly.

Property procedures let you set and get values in formats other than those you want to actually use to store the value. For example, the following code defines Name property procedures that save a name in `m_FirstName` and `m_LastName` variables. If your code would often need to use the last and first names separately, you could also provide property procedures to give access to those values separately.

```
Private m_LastName As String
Private m_FirstName As String

Property MyName() As String
    Get
        Return m_FirstName & " " & m_LastName
    End Get
    Set(ByVal Value As String)
        m_FirstName = Value.Split(" "c)(0)
        m_LastName = Value.Split(" "c)(1)
    End Set
End Property
```

Finally, you can use property procedures to create read-only and write-only variables. The following code shows how to make a read-only `NumEmployees` property procedure and a write-only `NumCustomers` property procedure. (Write-only property procedures are unusual but legal.)

```
Public ReadOnly Property NumEmployees() As Integer
    Get
        ...
    End Get
End Property

Public WriteOnly Property NumCustomers() As Integer
    Set(ByVal Value As Integer)
        ...
    End Set
End Property
```

You don't need to remember all of the syntax for property procedures. If you type the first line and press Enter, Visual Basic fills in the rest of the empty property procedures. If you use the keyword `ReadOnly` or `WriteOnly`, Visual Basic only includes the appropriate procedure.

Enumerated Data Types

An *enumerated type* is a discrete list of specific values. You define the enumerated type and the values allowed. Later, if you declare a variable of that data type, it can take only those values.

For example, suppose that you are building a large application where users can have one of three access levels: clerk, supervisor, and administrator. You could define an enumerated type named `AccessLevel` that allows the values `Clerk`, `Supervisor`, and `Administrator`. Now, if you declare a variable to be of type `AccessLevel`, Visual Basic will only allow the variable to take those values.

The following code shows a simple example. It defines the `AccessLevel` type and declares the variable `m_AccessLevel` using the type. Later the `MakeSupervisor` subroutine sets `m_AccessLevel` to the value `AccessLevel.Supervisor`. Notice that the value is prefixed with the enumerated type's name.

```
Public Enum AccessLevel
    Clerk
    Supervisor
    Administrator
End Enum

Private m_AccessLevel As AccessLevel     ' The user's access level.

' Set supervisor access level.
Public Sub MakeSupervisor()
    m_AccessLevel = AccessLevel.Supervisor
End Sub
```

The syntax for declaring an enumerated type is as follows:

```
[attribute_list] [accessibility] [Shadows] Enum name [As type]
    [attribute_list] value_name [= initialization_expression]
    [attribute_list] value_name [= initialization_expression]
    ...
End Enum
```

Most of these terms, including *attribute_list* and *accessibility*, are similar to those used by variable declarations. See the section "Variable Declarations" earlier in this chapter for more information.

The *type* value must be an integral type and can be Byte, Short, Integer, or Long. If you omit this value, Visual Basic stores the enumerated type values as integers.

The *value_name* pieces are the names you want to allow the enumerated type to have. You can include an *initialization_expression* for each value if you like. This value must be compatible with the underlying data type (Byte, Short, Integer, or Long). If you omit a value's initialization expression, the value is set to one greater than the previous value. The first value is zero by default.

For example, in the previous example, `Clerk = 0`, `Supervisor = 1`, and `Administrator = 2`. The following code changes the default assignments so `Clerk = 10`, `Supervisor = 11`, and `Administrator = -1`:

```
Public Enum AccessLevel
    Clerk - 10
    Supervisor
    Administrator = -1
End Enum
```

Usually, all that's important about an enumerated type is that its values are unique, so you don't need to explicitly initialize the values.

Note that you can give enumerated values the same integer value either explicitly or implicitly. For example, the following code defines several equivalent AccessLevel values. The first three values, Clerk, Supervisor, and Administrator, default to 0, 1, and 2, respectively. The code explicitly sets User to 0, so it is the same as Clerk. The values Manager and SysAdmin then default to the next two values, 1 and 2 (the same as Supervisor and Administrator, respectively). Finally, the code explicitly sets Superuser = SysAdmin.

```
Public Enum AccessLevel
    Clerk
    Supervisor
    Administrator
    User = 0
    Manager
    SysAdmin
    Superuser = SysAdmin
End Enum
```

This code is somewhat confusing. The following version makes it more obvious that some values are synonyms for others:

```
Public Enum AccessLevel
    Clerk
    Supervisor
    Administrator

    User = Clerk
    Manager = Supervisor
    SysAdmin = Administrator
    Superuser = Administrator
End Enum
```

You can get an effect similar to enumerated types using integer variables and constants, as shown in the following code. This code does roughly the same thing as the previous examples.

```
Public Const Clerk As Integer = 0
Public Const Supervisor As Integer = 1
Public Const Administrator As Integer = 2

Private m_AccessLevel As Integer         ' The user's access level.

' Set supervisor access level.
Public Sub MakeSupervisor()
    m_AccessLevel = Supervisor
End Sub
```

Declaring an enumerated type has a couple of advantages over using integers and constants, however. First, it prevents you from assigning nonsense values to the variable. In the previous code, you could set m_AccessLevel to 10, which wouldn't make any sense.

Using an enumerated data type allows Visual Basic to verify that the value you are assigning to the variable makes sense. You can only set the variable equal to one of the values in the enumerated type or to the value stored in another variable of the same enumerated type.

If you really need to set an enumerated variable to a calculated value for some reason, you can use the CType function to convert an integer value into the enumerated type. For example, the following statement uses the value in the variable integer_value to set the value of the variable m_AccessLevel. Making you use CType to perform this type of conversion makes it less likely that you will set an enumerated value accidentally.

```
m_AccessLevel = CType(integer_value, AccessLevel)
```

Another benefit of enumerated types is that they allow Visual Basic to provide IntelliSense help. If you type m_AccessLevel =, Visual Basic provides a list of the allowed AccessLevel values.

A final benefit of enumerated types is that they provide a ToString method that returns the textual name of the value. For example, the following code displays the message "Clerk."

```
Dim access_level As AccessLevel = AccessLevel.Clerk
MessageBox.Show(access_level.ToString())
```

If you have a value that can take only a fixed number of values, you should probably make it an enumerated type. Also, if you discover that you have defined a series of constants to represent related values, you should consider converting them into an enumerated type. Then you can gain the benefits of Visual Basic's improved type checking and IntelliSense.

Constants

In many respects, a constant is a lot like a read-only variable. Both variable and constant declarations may have attributes, accessibility keywords, and initialization expressions. Both read-only variables and constants represent a value that the code cannot change after it is assigned.

The syntax for declaring a constant is as follows:

```
[attribute_list] [accessibility] [Shadows] _
Const name [As type] = initialization_expression
```

For the general meanings of the various parts of a constant declaration, see the section "Variable Declarations" earlier in this chapter. The following sections describe differences between read-only variable and constant declarations.

accessibility

When you declare a variable, you can omit the Dim keyword if you use any of the keywords Public, Protected, Friend, Protected Friend, Private, Static, or ReadOnly. You cannot omit the Const keyword when you declare a constant, because it tells Visual Basic that you are declaring a constant rather than a variable.

You cannot use the Static, ReadOnly, or Shared keywords in a constant declaration. Static implies that the value will change over time, and the value should be retained when the enclosing routine starts and stops. Because the code cannot change a constant's value, that doesn't make sense.

The ReadOnly keyword would be redundant because you already cannot change a constant's value.

You use the Shared keyword in a variable declaration within a class to indicate that the variable's value is shared by all instances of the class. If one object changes the value, all objects see the changed value. Because the program cannot change a constant's value, the value need not be shared. All objects have the same version of the constant at all times. You can think of a constant as always shared.

You can use the other accessibility keywords in a constant declaration: Public, Protected, Friend, Protected Friend, and Private.

As type

If you have Option Strict turned on, you must include the constant's data type. A constant can only be an intrinsic type (Boolean, Byte, Short, Integer, Long, Decimal, Single, Double, Char, String, Date, or Object) or the name of an enumerated type. You cannot declare a constant that is a class, structure, or array.

If you declare the constant with the Object data type, the *initialization_expression* must set the object equal to Nothing. If you want a constant that represents some other object, or a class, structure, or array, use a read-only variable instead.

Because the generic Object class doesn't raise any events, and because you cannot make a constant of some other class type, it doesn't make sense to use the WithEvents keyword in a constant declaration.

initialization_expression

The *initialization_expression* assigns the constant its never-changing value. You cannot use variables in the *initialization_expression*, but you can use conversion functions such as CInt. You can also use the values of previously defined constants and enumeration values. The expression can include type characters such as # or &H, and if the declaration doesn't include a type statement (and Option Explicit is off), the type of the value determines the type of the constant.

The following code demonstrates these capabilities. The first statement uses the CInt function to convert the value 123.45 into an integer constant. The second and third statements set the values of two Long constants to hexadecimal values. The next statement combines the values defined in the previous two using a bitwise Or. The final statement sets a constant to a value defined by the enumerated type AccessLevel.

```
Private Const MAX_VALUES As Integer = CInt(123.45)
Private Const MASK_READ As Long = &H1000&
Private Const MASK_WRITE As Long = &H2000&
Private Const MASK_READ_WRITE As Long = MASK_READ Or MASK_WRITE
Private Const MAX_ACCESS_LEVEL As AccessLevel = AccessLevel.SuperUser
```

Delegates

A *delegate* is an object that refers to a subroutine, function, or other method. The method can be an instance method provided by an object, a class's shared method, or a method defined in a code module. A delegate variable acts as a pointer to a subroutine or function. Delegate variables are sometimes called *type safe function pointers*.

The Delegate keyword defines a delegate class and specifies the parameters and return type of the method to which the delegate will refer.

The following code uses a Delegate statement to declare the StringDisplayerType to be a delegate to a subroutine that takes a string as a parameter. Next the code declares the variable m_DisplayStringRoutine to be of this type. This variable can hold a reference to a subroutine that takes a string parameter. The code then sets the variable equal to the ShowStringInOutputWindow subroutine. Finally, the code invokes the delegate's subroutine, passing it a string.

```
' Define a StringDisplayerType delegate to be a pointer to a subroutine
' that has a string parameter.
Private Delegate Sub StringDisplayerType(ByVal str As String)
...
' Declare a StringDisplayerType variable.
Dim m_DisplayStringRoutine As StringDisplayerType

' Assign the variable to a subroutine.
m_DisplayStringRoutine = AddressOf ShowStringInOutputWindow

' Invoke the delegate's subroutine.
m_DisplayStringRoutine("Hello world")
```

The delegate in the previous example holds a reference to a subroutine defined in a code module. A delegate can also hold the address of a class's shared method or an instance method. For example, suppose the Employee class defines the shared function GetNumEmployees that returns the number of employees loaded. Suppose that it also defines the instance function ToString that returns an Employee object's first and last names.

The following code uses delegates for both of these functions. First, it declares and initializes an Employee object named emp. It then defines a delegate named NumEmployeesDelegate, which is a pointer to a function that returns an integer. The btnShared_Click event handler declares a variable of this type, sets it to the address of the Employee class's shared GetNumEmployees function, and calls the function. Then the code defines a delegate named GetNameDelegate, which is a pointer to a function that returns a string. The btnInstance_Click event handler declares a variable of this type, sets it to the address of the emp object's ToString function, and then calls the function.

```
Dim emp As New Employee("Rod", "Stephens")

Private Delegate Function NumEmployeesDelegate() As Integer

Private Sub btnShared_Click(ByVal sender As System.Object, _
  ByVal e As System.EventArgs) Handles btnShared.Click
    Dim show_num As NumEmployeesDelegate
    show_num = AddressOf Employee.GetNumEmployees
```

```
    MessageBox.Show(show_num().ToString)
End Sub

Private Delegate Function GetNameDelegate() As String

Private Sub btnInstance_Click(ByVal sender As System.Object, _
 ByVal e As System.EventArgs) Handles btnInstance.Click
    Dim show_name As GetNameDelegate
    show_name = AddressOf emp.ToString
    MessageBox.Show(show_name())
End Sub
```

These examples are somewhat contrived because the code could easily invoke the subroutines and functions directly without delegates, but they show how a program can save a delegate pointing to a subroutine or function and then call it later. A real application might set the delegate variable's value and only use it much later.

A particular delegate variable could hold references to different methods, depending on the program's situation. For example, different subroutines might generate output on a form, on the printer, or into a bitmap file. The program could set a delegate variable to any of these routines. Later, the program could invoke the variable's routine without needing to know which routine will actually execute.

Another useful technique is to pass a delegate variable into a subroutine or function. For example, suppose that you are writing a subroutine that sorts an array of Customer objects. This routine could take as a parameter a delegate variable that references the function to use when comparing the objects in the array. By passing different functions into the routine, you could make it sort customers by company name, contact name, customer ID, total past sales, or anything else you can imagine.

Delegates are particularly confusing to many programmers, but understanding them is worth a little extra effort. They can add an extra dimension to your programming by essentially allowing you to manipulate subroutines and functions as if they were data.

Naming Conventions

Many development teams adopt naming conventions to make their code more consistent and easier to read. Different groups have developed their own conventions, and you cannot really say that one of them is best. It doesn't really matter which convention you adopt. What is important is that you develop some coding style that you use consistently.

One rather simple convention is to use lowercase_letters_with_underscores for variables with routine scope, MixedCaseLetters for variables with module and global scope, and ALL_CAPS for constants of any scope. Use the prefixes m_ and g_ to differentiate between module and global scope, and an abbreviation to give an object's data type. For example, the following statement defines a module-scope PictureBox variable:

```
Private m_picCanvas As PictureBox
```

Routine names are generally `MixedCase`.

Many developers carry these rules a bit further and add type prefix abbreviations to all variables, not just objects. For example, this statement declares an integer variable:

```
Dim iNumEmployees As Integer
```

If you apply these rules strictly enough, you should never need to assign one variable to another variable's value, unless the two have the same type abbreviation. If you see a statement that mixes variable types, you should examine the code more closely to see if there is a real data type mismatch problem. For example, the following statement should make the developer suspicious because it's assigning an Integer value to a Long variable.

```
mlngNumEmployees = intNumAbsent + intNumPresent
```

Some developers extend the rules to cover all programming objects, including functions and subroutines. For example, a global function that returns a string might be named `gstrGetWebmasterName`.

Generally, this scope and type information is more important the farther you are from a variable's declaration. If you declare a variable inside a subroutine, a developer can usually remember the variable's data type. If there is any doubt, it's easy to scroll up and review the variable's declaration.

In contrast, if a variable is declared globally in an obscure code module that developers rarely need to read, a programmer may have trouble remembering the variable's scope and data type. In that case, using prefixes to help the developers' memory can be important.

No matter which convention you use, the most important piece of a name is the descriptive part. The name `mblnDL` tells you that the value is a module-scope Boolean, but it doesn't tells you what the value means (and variables with such terrible names are all too common). The name `mblnDataIsLoaded` is much more descriptive. I have never seen a project that suffered because it lacked variable prefixes such as `mbln`. On the other hand, I have seen developers waste huge amounts of time because the descriptive parts of variable names were confusing.

Building an all-encompassing naming convention that defines abbreviations for every conceivable type of data, control, object, database component, menu, constant, and routine name takes a lot of time and more space than it's worth in a book such as this. For an article that describes the conventions used by Microsoft Consulting Services, go to `http://support.microsoft.com/default.aspx?scid=kb;en-us;110264`. It explains everything, including data type abbreviations, making the first part of a function name contain a verb (`GetUserName` rather than `UserName`), and commenting conventions.

Naming and coding conventions make it easier for other programmers to read your code. Look over the Microsoft Consulting Services conventions or search the Web for others. Pick the features that you think make the most sense and ignore the others. It's more important that you write consistent code than that you follow a particular set of rules.

Summary

Two of the most important things you control with a variable declaration are its data type and its visibility. Visibility combines scope (the piece of code that contains the variable such as a For loop, subroutine, or module), accessibility (the code that is allowed to access the variable determined by keywords such as Private, Public, and Friend), and lifetime (when the variable has been created and not yet destroyed).

To avoid confusion, always explicitly declare the data type and use the most limited scope possible for the variable's purpose. Turn Option Explicit and Option Strict on to allow the IDE to help you spot potential scope and type errors before they become a problem.

Parameters, property procedures, and constants have similar data type and scope issues. Once you become comfortable with variable declarations, these should give you little trouble.

One of the most important steps you can take to make your code easier to debug and maintain is to work to make your code consistent. A good naming convention can help. Review the guidelines used by Microsoft Consulting Service, and adopt the pieces that make the most sense to you.

Once you know how to declare variables, you are ready to learn how to combine them. Chapter 5, "Operators," explains the symbols such as +, -, and ^ that you can use to combine variables to produce new results.

5

Operators

An *operator* is a basic code element that performs some operation on one or more values to create a result. The values the operator acts upon are called *operands*. For example, in the following statement, the operator is + (addition), the operands are B and C, and the result is assigned to the variable A:

```
A = B + C
```

Visual Basic's operators fall into five main categories: arithmetic, concatenation, comparison, logical, and bitwise. The following sections explain these categories and the operators they contain. This chapter then discusses other operator issues such as precedence, assignment operators, and operator overloading. Also included are discussions of some specialized issues that arise when you work with strings and dates.

Arithmetic Operators

The following table lists the arithmetic operators provided by Visual Basic. Most programmers should be very familiar with these. Four that may need a little extra explanation are \, Mod, <<, and >>. The last two rows in the table manipulate bit values.

Operator	Purpose	Example	Result
^	Exponentiation	2 ^ 3	(2 to the power 3) = 2 * 2 * 2 = 8.
–	Negation	–2	–2
*	Multiplication	2 * 3	6
/	Division	3 / 2	1.5
\	Integer division	17 \ 5	3
Mod	Modulus	17 Mod 5	2
+	Addition	2 + 3	5

Table continued on following page

Operator	Purpose	Example	Result
-	Subtraction	3 - 2	1
<<	Bit left shift	10110111 << 1	01101110
>>	Bit right shift	10110111 >> 1	01011011

The \ operator performs integer division. It returns the result of dividing its first operand by the second, dropping any remainder. It's important to understand that the result is truncated toward zero, not rounded.

The Mod operator returns the remainder after dividing its first operand by its second. For example, 17 Mod 5 = 2 because 17 = 3 * 5 + 2.

The << operator shifts the bits of an integer value to the left, padding the empty bits on the right with zeros. For example, the byte value with bits 10110111 shifted 1 bit to the left gives 01101110. Shifting 10110111 2 bits to the left gives 11011100.

The >> operator shifts the bits of a value to the right, padding the empty bits on the left with zeros. For example, the byte value with bits 10110111 shifted 1 bit to the right gives 01011011. Shifting 10110111 2 bits to the right gives 00101101.

Unfortunately, Visual Basic doesn't work easily with bit values, so you cannot use a value such as 10110111 in your code. Instead, you must write this value as the hexadecimal value &HB7 or the decimal value 183. The last two entries in the table show the values in binary, so it is easier to understand how the shifts work.

The Calculator application that comes with Windows lets you easily convert between binary, octal, hexadecimal, and decimal. To start the Calculator, open the Start menu and select Programs→ Accessories→Calculator. Open the View menu and select Scientific. Now you can click the Bin, Oct, Dec, or Hex radio buttons to select a base, enter a value, and select another base to convert the value.

Concatenation Operators

Visual Basic provides two concatenation operators: + and &. Both join two strings together. Because the + symbol also represents an arithmetic operator, your code will be easier to read if you use the & symbol for concatenation. Using & can also make your code faster and lead to fewer problems because it lets Visual Basic know that the operands are strings.

Comparison Operators

Comparison operators compare one value to another and return a Boolean value (True or False), depending on the result. The following table lists the comparison operators provided by Visual Basic. The first six (=, <>, <, <=, >, and >=) are relatively straightforward. Note that the Not operator is not a comparison operator, so it is not listed here. It is described in the next section, "Logical Operators."

Operator	Purpose	Example	Result
=	Equals	A = B	True if A equals B
<>	Not equals	A <> B	True if A does not equal B
<	Less than	A < B	True if A is less than B
<=	Less than or equal to	A <= B	True if A is less than or equal to B
>	Greater than	A > B	True if A is greater than B
>=	Greater than or equal to	A >= B	True if A is greater than or equal to B
Is	Equality of two objects	emp Is mgr	True if emp and mgr refer to the same object
IsNot	Inequality of two objects	emp IsNot mgr	True if emp and mgr refer to different objects
TypeOf...Is	Object is of a certain type	TypeOf(obj) Is Manager	True if obj points to a Manager object
Like	Matches a text pattern	A Like "###-####"	True if A contains three digits, a dash, and four digits

The Is operator returns True if its two operands refer to the same object. For example, if you create an Order object and make two different variables, A and B point to it, the expression A Is B is True. Note that Is returns False if the two operands point to different Order objects that happen to have the same property values.

The IsNot operator is simply shorthand for a more awkward Not...Is construction. For example, the statement A IsNot Nothing is equivalent to Not (A Is Nothing).

The TypeOf operator returns True if its operand is of a certain type. This operator is particularly useful when a subroutine takes a parameter that could be of more than one object type. It can use TypeOf to see which type of object it has.

The Like operator returns True if its first operand matches a pattern specified by its second operand. Where the pattern includes normal characters, the string must match those characters exactly. The pattern can also include several special character sequences summarized in the following table.

Character(s)	Meaning
?	Matches any single character
*	Matches any zero or more characters
#	Matches any single digit

Table continued on following page

Character(s)	Meaning
[characters]	Matches any of the characters between the brackets
[!characters]	Matches any character not between the brackets
A-Z	When inside brackets, matches any character in the range A to Z

You can combine ranges of characters and individual characters inside brackets. For example, the pattern [a-zA-Z] matches any letter between "a" and "z" or between "A" and "Z." The following table lists some useful patterns.

Pattern	Meaning
[2-9]##-####	Seven-digit phone number
[2-9]##-[2-9]##-####	Ten-digit phone number, including area code
1-[2-9]##-[2-9]##-####	Eleven-digit phone number, beginning with 1 and area code
#####	Five-digit ZIP code
#####-####	Nine-digit ZIP + 4 code
?*@?*.?*	E-mail address

These patterns are not completely foolproof. For example, the e-mail address pattern verifies that the string contains at least one character, an "@" character, at least one other character, a dot, and at least one more character. For example, it allows RodStephens@vb-helper.com. However, it does not verify that the extension makes sense, so it allows RodStephens@vb-helper.commercial, and it allows more than one @ character, as in RodStephens@vb-helper.com@bad_value.

Regular expressions provide much more powerful pattern-matching capabilities. For more information, look up "regular expressions" in the online help.

Logical Operators

Logical operators combine two Boolean values and return True or False, depending on the result. The following table summarizes Visual Basic's logical operators.

Operator	Purpose	Example	Result
Not	Logical or bitwise negation	Not A	True if A is false
And	Logical or bitwise And	A And B	True if A and B are both true
Or	Logical or bitwise Or	A Or B	True if A or B or both are true

Operator	Purpose	Example	Result
Xor	Logical or bitwise exclusive Or	A Xor B	True if A or B but not both is true
AndAlso	Logical or bitwise And with short-circuit evaluation	A AndAlso B	True if A and B are both true (see notes)
OrElse	Logical or bitwise Or with short-circuit evaluation	A OrElse B	True if A or B or both are true (see the following notes)

The operators Not, And, and Or are relatively straightforward. The Xor operator returns true if one of its operands is true and the other one is false.

The AndAlso and OrElse operators are similar to the And and Or operators, except that they provide short-circuit evaluation. In *short-circuit evaluation*, Visual Basic is allowed to stop evaluating operands if it can deduce the final result without them. For example, consider the expression A AndAlso B. If Visual Basic evaluates the value A and discovers that it is false, the program knows that the expression A AndAlso B is also false no matter what value B has, so it doesn't need to evaluate B.

Whether the program evaluates both operands doesn't matter much if A and B are simple Boolean variables. However, assume that they are time-consuming functions, as shown in the following code. For example, the TimeConsumingFunction function might need to look up values in a database or download data from a Web site. In that case, not evaluating the second operand might save a lot of time.

```
If TimeConsumingFunction("A") AndAlso TimeConsumingFunction("B") Then ...
```

Just as AndAlso can stop evaluation if it discovers one of its operands is false, the OrElse operand can stop evaluating if it discovers that one of its operands is true. The expression A OrElse B is true if either A or B is true. If the program finds that A is true, it doesn't need to evaluate B.

Because AndAlso and OrElse do the same thing as And and Or but sometimes faster, you might wonder why you would ever use And and Or. The main reason is that the operands may have side effects. A *side effect* is some action a routine performs that is not obviously part of the routine. For example, suppose that the NumEmployees function opens an employee database and returns the number of employee records, leaving the database open. The fact that this function leaves the database open is a side effect.

Now, suppose that the NumCustomers function similarly opens the customer database, and then consider the following statement:

```
If (NumEmployees() > 0) AndAlso (NumCustomers() > 0) Then ...
```

After this code executes, you cannot be certain which databases are open. If NumEmployees returns 0, the AndAlso operator's first operand is false, so it doesn't evaluate the NumCustomers function and that function doesn't open the customer database.

The AndAlso and OrElse operators can improve application performance under some circumstances. However, to avoid possible confusion and long debugging sessions, do not use AndAlso or OrElse with operands that have side effects.

Bitwise Operators

Bitwise operators work much like logical operators do, except they compare values one bit at a time. The bitwise negation operator Not flips the bits in its operand from 1 to 0 and vice versa. The following shows an example:

```
        10110111
Not 01001000
```

The And operator places a 1 in a result bit if both of the operands have a 1 in that position. The following shows the results of combining two binary values by using the bitwise And operator:

```
        10101010
And 00110110
        00100010
```

The bitwise Or operator places a 1 bit in the result if either of its operands has a 1 in the corresponding position. The following shows an example:

```
        10101010
Or  00110110
        10111110
```

The bitwise Xor operator places a 1 bit in the result if exactly one of its operands, but not both, has a 1 in the corresponding position. The following shows an example:

```
        10101010
Xor 00110110
        10011100
```

There are no bitwise equivalents for the AndAlso and OrElse operators.

Operator Precedence

When Visual Basic evaluates a complex expression, it must decide the order in which to evaluate operators. For example, consider the expression $1 + 2 * 3 / 4 + 2$. The following text shows three orders in which you might evaluate this expression to get three different results.

```
1 + (2 * 3) / (4 + 2) = 1 + 6 / 6 = 2
1 + (2 * 3 / 4) + 2 = 1 + 1.5 + 2 = 4.5
(1 + 2) * 3 / (4 + 2) = 3 * 3 / 6 = 1.5
```

Precedence determines which operator Visual Basic executes first. For example, Visual Basic's precedence rules say the program should evaluate multiplication and division before addition, so the second equation is correct.

The following table lists the operators in order of precedence. When evaluating an expression, the program evaluates an operator before it evaluates those lower than it in the list. When operators are on the same line, or if an expression contains more than one instance of the same operator, the program evaluates them in left-to-right order.

Operator	Description
( )	Grouping (parentheses)
^	Exponentiation
–	Negation
*, /	Multiplication and division
\	Integer division
Mod	Modulus
+, –, +	Addition, subtraction, and concatenation
&	Concatenation
<<, >>	Bit shift
=, <>, <, <=, >, >=, Like, Is, IsNot, TypeOf...Is	All comparisons
Not	Logical and bitwise negation
And, AndAlso	Logical and bitwise And with and without short-circuit evaluation
Xor, Or, OrElse	Logical and bitwise Xor, and Or with and without short-circuit evaluation

Parentheses are not really operators, but they do have a higher precedence than the true operators, so they're listed to make the table complete. You can always use parentheses to explicitly dictate the order in which Visual Basic will perform an evaluation. If there's the slightest doubt about how Visual Basic will handle an expression, add parentheses to make it obvious. There's no extra charge for using parentheses, and they may avoid some unnecessary confusion.

Assignment Operators

Visual Basic has always had the simple assignment operator =. Visual Basic .NET added several new assignment operators to handle some common statements where a value was set equal to itself combined with some other value. For example, the following two statements both add the value 10 to the variable iterations.

```
iterations = iterations + 10    ' Original syntax.
iterations += 10                ' New syntax.
```

All the other assignments operators work similarly by adding an equals sign to an arithmetic operator. For example, the statement A ^= B is equivalent to A = A ^ B.

You can still use the original syntax if you like. However, the new syntax allows the compiler to perform additional optimizations that may give you better performance under some circumstances.

The complete list of assignment operators is: =, ^=, *=, /=, \=, +=, -=, &=, <<=, and >>=.

If you have Option Strict set to on, the variables must have the appropriate data types. For example, /= returns a Double, so you cannot use that operator with an Integer, as in the following code:

```
Dim i As Integer = 100
i /= 2                          ' Not allowed.
```

To perform this operation, you must explicitly convert the result into an Integer, as shown in the following statement:

```
i = CInt(i / 2)
```

This makes sense because you are trying to assign the value of floating-point division to an integer. It's less obvious why the following code is also illegal. Here the code is trying to assign an Integer result to a Single variable, so you would think it should work.

```
Dim x As Single
x \= 10                         ' Not allowed.
```

The problem isn't in the assignment, but in performing the calculation. The following statement is equivalent to the previous one, and it is also illegal:

```
x = x \ 10                      ' Not allowed.
```

The problem with both of these statements is that the \ operator takes as arguments two integers. If Option Strict is on, the program will not automatically convert a floating-point variable into an integer for the \ operator. To make this statement work, you must manually convert the variable into an Integer data type, as shown in the following example:

```
x = CLng(x) \ 10                ' Allowed.
```

While the += and &= operators will both combine strings, &= is less ambiguous, so you should use it whenever possible. It may also give you better performance because it tells Visual Basic that the operands are strings.

The StringBuilder Class

The & and &= operators are useful for concatenating a few strings together. However, if you must combine a large number of strings, you may get better performance using the StringBuilder class. This class is optimized for performing long sequences of concatenations to build big strings.

For small pieces of code, the difference between using a String and a StringBuilder is not noticeable. On one hand, if you need only to concatenate a dozen or so strings once, using a StringBuilder won't make much difference in run time. On the other hand, if you make huge strings built up in pieces, or if you build simpler strings but many times in a loop, StringBuilder may make your program run faster.

The following code concatenates the string 1234567890 a large number of times, first using a String variable and then using a StringBuilder. In one test that performed the concatenation 10,000 times to build strings 100,000 characters long, using a String took roughly 1.6 seconds. Using a StringBuilder, the program was able to build the string in roughly 0.001 seconds.

```
Private Sub btnGo_Click(ByVal sender As System.Object, _
 ByVal e As System.EventArgs) Handles btnGo.Click
    Const ADD_STRING As String = "1234567890"
    Dim num_trials As Long = Long.Parse(txtNumTrials.Text)
    Dim start_time As DateTime
    Dim stop_time As DateTime
    Dim elapsed_time As TimeSpan
    Dim txt As String
    Dim string_builder As New StringBuilder

    lblString.Text = ""
    lblStringBuilder.Text = ""
    Application.DoEvents()

    txt = ""
    start_time = Now
    For i As Long = 1 To num_trials
        txt = txt & ADD_STRING
    Next i
    stop_time = Now
    elapsed_time = stop_time.Subtract(start_time)
    lblString.Text = elapsed_time.TotalSeconds.ToString("0.000000")

    txt = ""
    start_time = Now
    For i As Long = 1 To num_trials
        string_builder.Append(ADD_STRING)
    Next i
    txt = string_builder.ToString()
    stop_time = Now
    elapsed_time = stop_time.Subtract(start_time)
    lblStringBuilder.Text = elapsed_time.TotalSeconds.ToString("0.000000")
End Sub
```

Admittedly, building such enormous strings is not a common programming task. Even when the strings are shorter, you can sometimes see a noticeable difference in performance. The following code concatenates the string 1234567890 to itself 100 times to build a string 1,000 characters long. It builds the string repeatedly for a certain number of trials. In one test building the 1,000 character string 10,000 times, using a String took around 0.95 seconds, whereas using a StringBuilder took about 0.06 seconds.

```
Private Sub btnGo_Click(ByVal sender As System.Object, _
 ByVal e As System.EventArgs) Handles btnGo.Click
    Const ADD_STRING As String = "1234567890"
    Dim num_trials As Long = Long.Parse(txtNumTrials.Text)
    Dim start_time As DateTime
    Dim stop_time As DateTime
    Dim elapsed_time As TimeSpan
    Dim txt As String
    Dim string_builder As New StringBuilder

    lblString.Text = ""
    lblStringBuilder.Text = ""
    Application.DoEvents()

    start_time = Now
    For i As Long = 1 To num_trials
        txt = ""
        For j As Long = 1 To 100
            txt = txt & ADD_STRING
        Next j
    Next i
    stop_time = Now
    elapsed_time = stop_time.Subtract(start_time)
    lblString.Text = elapsed_time.TotalSeconds.ToString("0.000000")

    txt = ""
    start_time = Now
    For i As Long = 1 To num_trials
        string_builder = New StringBuilder
        For j As Long = 1 To 100
            string_builder.Append(ADD_STRING)
        Next j
        txt = string_builder.ToString()
    Next i
    stop_time = Now
    elapsed_time = stop_time.Subtract(start_time)
    lblStringBuilder.Text = elapsed_time.TotalSeconds.ToString("0.000000")
End Sub
```

Strings and string operations are a bit more intuitive than the `StringBuilder` class, so your code will usually be easier to read if you use String variables when performance isn't a big issue. If you are building enormous strings, or are building long strings a huge number of times, the performance edge given by the `StringBuilder` class may be worth slightly more complicated-looking code.

Date and TimeSpan Operations

The Date data type is fundamentally different from other data types. When you perform an operation on most data types, you get a result that has the same data type or that is at least of some compatible data type. For example, if you subtract two Integer variables, the result is an Integer. If you divide two Integers using the / operator, the result is a Double. That's not another Integer, but it is a compatible numeric data type used because an Integer cannot always hold the result of a division.

If you subtract two Date variables, however, the result is not a Date. For example, what's August 7 minus July 20? It doesn't make sense to think of the result as a Date. Instead, Visual Basic defines the difference between two Dates as a TimeSpan. A TimeSpan measures the elapsed time between two Dates. In this example, August 7 minus July 20 is 18 days.

The following equations define the arithmetic of Dates and TimeSpans.

❑ Date – Date = TimeSpan

❑ Date + TimeSpan = Date

❑ TimeSpan + TimeSpan = TimeSpan

❑ TimeSpan – TimeSpan = TimeSpan

The TimeSpan class also defines unary negation (ts2 = -ts1), but other operations (such as multiplying a TimeSpan by a number) are not defined. However, in some cases, you can still perform the calculation if you must. For example, the following statement makes the TimeSpan ts2 equal to 12 times the duration of TimeSpan ts1.

```
ts2 = New TimeSpan(ts1.Ticks * 12)
```

A unary operator takes a single operand. For example, A = +B (unary plus), C = -D (unary negation), and E = Not F (logical unary negation) all use unary operators.

In Visual Basic 2005, the +, –, <, >, <=, >=, <>, and = operators are defined for Dates and TimeSpans. Previous versions did not define these operators, but the Date class did provide equivalent operator methods. For example, the Date class's op_Subtraction method subtracts two Dates and returns a TimeSpan.

These operator methods are still available and you may want to use them if you find using the normal operator symbols less clear. The following table lists the Date operator methods. Note that the Common Language Runtime name for the Date data type is DateTime, so you need to look for DateTime in the online help for more information on these methods.

Syntax	Meaning
result_date = Date.op_Addition (date1, timespan1)	Returns date1 plus timespan1
result_boolean = Date.op_Equality (date1, date2)	True if date1 > date2
result_boolean = Date.op_ GreaterThan(date1, date2)	True if date1 > date2
result_boolean = Date.op_ GreaterThanOrEqual(date1, date2)	True if date1 >= date2
result_boolean = Date.op_ Inequality(date1, date2)	True if date1 <> date2

Table continued on following page

Syntax	Meaning
result_boolean = Date.op_ LessThan(date1, date2)	True if date1 < date2
result_boolean = Date.op_ LessThanOrEqual(date1, date2)	True if date1 <= date2
result_timespan = Date.op_ Subtraction(date1, date2)	Returns the TimeSpan between date1 and date2
result = Date.Compare (date1, date2)	Returns a value indicating whether date1 is greater than, less than, or equal to date2

The Compare method is a bit different from the others, returning an Integer rather than a Boolean or Date. Its value is less than zero if date1 < date2, greater than zero if date1 > date2, and equal to zero if date1 = date2.

These are shared methods, so you do not need to use a specific instance of the Date data type to use them. For example, the following code displays the number of days between July 20 and August 7:

```
Dim date1 As Date = #7/20/04#
Dim date2 As Date = #8/7/04#
Dim elapsed_time As TimeSpan

    elapsed_time = Date.op_Subtraction(date2, date1)
    Debug.WriteLine(elapsed_time.Days)
```

These operators are a bit cumbersome. To make these kinds of calculations easier, the Date data type provides other methods for performing common operations that are a bit easier to read. While the operator methods take both operands as parameters, these methods take a single operand as one parameter and use the current object as the other. For example, a Date object's Add method adds a TimeSpan to the date and returns the resulting date. The following table summaries these methods.

Syntax	Meaning
result_date = date1.Add(timespan1)	Returns date1 plus timespan1
result_date = date1.AddYears (num_years)	Returns the date plus the indicated number of years
result_date = date1.AddMonths (num_months)	Returns the date plus the indicated number of months
result_date = date1.AddDays (num_days)	Returns the date plus the indicated number of days
result_date = date1.AddHours (num_hours)	Returns the date plus the indicated number of hours
result_date = date1.AddMinutes (num_minutes)	Returns the date plus the indicated number of minutes

Syntax	Meaning
result_date = date1.AddSeconds (num_seconds)	Returns the date plus the indicated number of seconds
result_date = date1.AddMilliseconds (num_milliseconds)	Returns the date plus the indicated number of milliseconds
result_date = date1.AddTicks (num_ticks)	Returns the date plus the indicated number of ticks (100-nanosecond units)
result_timespan = date1.Subtract (date2)	Returns the time span between date2 and date1
result_integer = date1.CompareTo (date2)	Returns a value indicating whether date1 is greater than, less than, or equal to date2
result_boolean = date1.Equals (date2)	Returns True if date1 equals date2

The CompareTo method returns a value less than zero if date1 < date2, greater than zero if date1 > date2, and equal to zero if date1 = date2.

Operator Overloading

Visual Basic defines operators for expressions that use standard data types such as integers and Boolean values. It defines a few operators such as Is and IsNot for objects, but operators such as * and Mod don't make sense for objects in general.

However, you can also define those operators for your structures and classes by using the Operator statement. This is a more advanced topic, so if you're new to Visual Basic, you may want to skip this section and come back to it later, perhaps after you read Chapter 15, "Classes and Structures."

The general syntax for operator overloading is:

```
[ <attributes> ] Public [ Overloads ] Shared [ Shadows ] _
  [ Widening | Narrowing ]  Operator symbol ( operands ) As type
    ...
End Operator
```

The parts of this declaration are:

❑   *attributes* — Attributes for the operator.

❑   *Public* — All operators must be Public Shared.

❑   *Overloads* — You can only use this if the operator takes two parameters that are from a base class and a derived class as its two operators. In that case, it means the operator overrides the operator defined in the base class.

❑ *Shared* — All operators must be `Public Shared`.

❑ *Shadows* — The operator replaces a similar operator defined in the base class.

❑ *Widening* — Indicates that the operator defines a widening conversion that always succeeds at run time. This operator must catch and handle all errors. The `CType` operator must include either the `Widening` or `Narrowing` keyword.

❑ *Narrowing* — Indicates that the operator defines a narrowing conversion that may fail at run time. The `CType` operator must include either the `Widening` or `Narrowing` keyword.

❑ *symbol* — The operator's symbol. This can be +, -, *, /, \, ^, &, <<, >>, =, <>, <, >, <=, >=, Mod, Not, And, Or, Xor, Like, IsTrue, IsFalse, or CType.

❑ *operands* — Declarations of the objects to be manipulated by the operator. The unary operators +, -, Not, IsTrue, and IsFalse take a single operand. The binary operators +, -, *, /, \, ^, &, <<, >>, =, <>, <, >, <=, >=, Mod, And, Or, Xor, Like, and CType take two operands.

❑ *type* — All operators must have a return type and must return a value by using a `Return` statement.

Operator overloading is subject to several constraints:

❑ Some operands come in pairs, and if you define one you must define the other. The pairs are = and <>, < and >, <= and >=, and IsTrue and IsFalse.

❑ For the standard unary or binary operators, the class or structure that defines the operator must appear in an operand. For the `CType` conversion operator, the class or structure must appear in the operand or return type.

❑ The `IsTrue` and `IsFalse` operators must return Boolean values.

❑ The second operands for the << and >> operators must be Integers.

If you define an operator, Visual Basic can automatically handle the same operator followed by the = sign. For example, if you define the + operator, Visual Basic can understand the += assignment operator.

While you cannot use the `IsTrue` and `IsFalse` operators directly, you can use them indirectly. If you define `IsTrue` for a class, Visual Basic uses it to determine whether an object should be treated as `True` in a Boolean expression. For example, the following statement uses the `IsTrue` operator to decide whether the object `c1` should be considered `True`:

```
If c1 Then ...
```

If you define the `And` and `IsFalse` operators, Visual Basic uses them to handle the `AndAlso` operator as well. For this to work, the `And` operator must return the same type of class or structure where you define it. For example, suppose you have defined `And` and `IsFalse` for the `Composite` class and suppose variables `c1`, `c2`, and `c3` are all instances of this class. Then consider the following statement:

```
c3 = c1 AndAlso c2
```

Visual Basic uses `IsFalse` to evaluate `c1`. If `IsFalse` returns `True`, the program doesn't bother to evaluate `c2`. Instead it assumes the whole statement is false and returns a `False` value. Because `IsFalse` returned `True` for `c1`, Visual Basic knows that `c1` is a false value so it sets `c3` equal to `c1`.

This is pretty confusing. It may make more sense if you think about how Visual Basic evaluates Boolean expressions that use the normal `AndAlso` operator.

Similarly, if you define the `Or` and `IsTrue` operators, Visual Basic automatically provides the `OrElse` operator.

While you generally cannot make two versions of a function in Visual Basic that differ only in their return types, you can do that for `CType` conversion operators. When the program tries to make a conversion, Visual Basic can tell by the type of the result which conversion operator to use.

The following code shows a `Complex` class that represents a complex number. It defines +, −, and * operators to implement normal addition, subtraction, and multiplication on complex numbers. It also defines =, <>, and unary negation operators, and a conversion operator that converts a `Complex` object into a Double giving its magnitude.

```
Public Class Complex
    Public Re As Double
    Public Im As Double

    ' Constructors.
    Public Sub New()
    End Sub
    Public Sub New(ByVal real_part As Double, ByVal imaginary_part As Double)
        Re = real_part
        Im = imaginary_part
    End Sub

    ' ToString.
    Public Overrides Function ToString() As String
        Return Re.ToString & " + " & Im.ToString & "i"
    End Function

    ' Operators.
    Public Shared Operator *(ByVal c1 As Complex, ByVal c2 As Complex) As Complex
        Return New Complex( _
            c1.Re * c2.Re - c1.Im * c2.Im, _
            c1.Re * c2.Im + c1.Im * c2.Re)
    End Operator
    Public Shared Operator +(ByVal c1 As Complex, ByVal c2 As Complex) As Complex
        Return New Complex( _
            c1.Re + c2.Re, _
            c1.Im + c2.Im)
    End Operator
    Public Shared Operator -(ByVal c1 As Complex, ByVal c2 As Complex) As Complex
        Return New Complex( _
```

```
                c1.Re - c2.Re, _
                c1.Im - c2.Im)
        End Operator
        Public Shared Operator =(ByVal c1 As Complex, ByVal c2 As Complex) As Boolean
            Return (c1.Re = c2.Re) AndAlso (c1.Im = c2.Im)
        End Operator
        Public Shared Operator <>(ByVal c1 As Complex, ByVal c2 As Complex) As Boolean
            Return (c1.Re <> c2.Re) OrElse (c1.Im <> c2.Im)
        End Operator
        Public Shared Operator -(ByVal c1 As Complex) As Complex
            Return New Complex(c1.Im, c1.Re)
        End Operator
        Public Shared Narrowing Operator CType(ByVal c1 As Complex) As Double
            Return System.Math.Sqrt(c1.Re * c1.Re + c1.Im * c1.Im)
        End Operator
    End Class
```

It is easy to get carried away with operator overloading. Just because you can define an operator for a class doesn't mean you should. For example, you might be able to concoct some meaning for addition with the Employee class, but it would probably be a counterintuitive operation. You would probably be better off writing a subroutine or function with a meaningful name.

Summary

A program uses operators to manipulate variables, constants, and literal values to produce new results. Visual Basic's operators fall into five main categories: arithmetic, concatenation, comparison, logical, and bitwise. In most cases, using operators is straightforward and intuitive.

Operator precedence determines the order in which Visual Basic applies operators when evaluating an expression. In cases where an expression's operator precedence is unclear, add parentheses to make the order obvious. Even if you don't change the way that Visual Basic handles the statement, you can make the code more understandable and avoid possibly time-consuming bugs.

The String data type has its own special needs. String manipulation plays a big role in many applications, so Visual Basic provides a StringBuilder class for manipulating strings more efficiently. On one hand, if your program only works with a few short strings, it probably doesn't need to use a StringBuilder, and using the String data type will probably make your code easier to understand. On the other hand, if your application builds enormous strings or concatenates a huge number of strings, you may be able to save a noticeable amount of time using the StringBuilder class.

The Date data type also behaves differently from other data types. The normal operators such as + and – have different meanings than they do for other data types. For example, a Date minus a Date gives a TimeSpan, not another Date. These operations generally make sense if you think carefully about what dates and time spans are.

Just as addition, subtraction, and the other operators have special meaning for Dates and TimeSpans, you can use operator overloading to define operators for your classes. Defining division or exponentiation may not make much sense for Employees, Customer, or Orders, but in some cases custom operators can make your code more readable. For example, you might imagine the following statement adding an `OrderItem` to a `CustomerOrder`:

```
the_order += new_item
```

This chapter explains how to use operators to combine variables to calculate new results. A typical program may perform the same set of calculations many times for different variable values. While you might be able to perform those calculations in a long series, the result would be cumbersome and hard to maintain. Chapter 6, "Subroutines and Functions," explains how you can use subroutines and functions to break a program into manageable pieces that you can then reuse to make performing all of the calculations easier and more uniform.

6

Subroutines and Functions

Subroutines and functions enable you to break an otherwise unwieldy chunk of code into manageable pieces. They enable you to extract code that you may need to use under more than one circumstance and place it in one location where you can call it as needed. This not only reduces repetition within your code; it also enables you to maintain and update the code in a single location.

A *subroutine* performs a task for the code that invokes it. A *function* performs a task and then returns some value. The value may be the result of a calculation, or a status code indicating whether the function succeeded or failed.

Together, subroutines and functions are sometimes called *routines* or *procedures*. They are also sometimes called *methods*, particularly when they are subroutines or functions belonging to a class. Subroutines are also occasionally called *sub procedures*.

This chapter describes subroutines and functions. It explains the syntax for declaring and using each in a Visual Basic application. It also provides some tips for making routines more maintainable.

Subroutines

A Sub statement defines the subroutine's name. It declares the parameters that the subroutine takes as arguments and defines the parameters' data types. Code between the Sub statement and an End Sub statement determines what the subroutine does when it runs.

The syntax for defining a subroutine is as follows:

```
[attribute_list] [inheritance_mode] [accessibility] _
Sub subroutine_name([parameters]) [ Implements interface.subroutine ]
    [ statements ]
End Sub
```

The following sections describe the pieces of this declaration.

attribute_list

The optional attribute list is a comma-separated list of attributes that apply to the subroutine. An attribute further refines the definition of a class, method, variable, or other "thing" to give more information to the compiler and the run-time system.

Attributes are specialized and address issues that arise when you perform very specific programming tasks. For example, the `Conditional` attribute means the subroutine is conditional upon the definition of some compiler constant. The following code defines the compiler constant DEBUG_LIST_CUSTOMERS. The value DEBUG_LIST_EMPLOYEES is not defined, because it is commented out.

This program's `Form1_Load` event handler calls subroutines `ListCustomers` and `ListEmployees`. `ListCustomers` is defined using the `Conditional` attribute with parameter DEBUG_LIST_CUSTOMERS. That tells the compiler to generate code for the routine only if DEBUG_LIST_CUSTOMERS is defined. Because that constant is defined, the compiler generates code for this subroutine.

Subroutine `ListEmployees` is defined using the `Conditional` attribute with parameter DEBUG_LIST_EMPLOYEES. Because that constant is not defined, the compiler does not generate code for this subroutine and, when `Form1_Load` calls it, the subroutine call is ignored.

```
#Const DEBUG_LIST_CUSTOMERS = True
' #Const DEBUG_LIST_EMPLOYEES = True

Private Sub Form1_Load(ByVal sender As System.Object, _
 ByVal e As System.EventArgs) Handles MyBase.Load
    ListCustomers()
    ListEmployees()
End Sub

<Conditional("DEBUG_LIST_CUSTOMERS")> _
Private Sub ListCustomers()
    Debug.WriteLine("ListCustomers")
End Sub

<Conditional("DEBUG_LIST_EMPLOYEES")> _
Private Sub ListEmployees()
    Debug.WriteLine("ListEmployees")
End Sub
```

The following text shows the output from this program:

```
ListCustomers
```

Visual Basic 2005 defines around 200 attributes. Many have fairly specialized purposes that won't interest you most of the time, but some are pretty useful.

Many attributes give metadata for editors and the IDE, so you will often see their effects only when you view an object in an editor or the IDE. If you are building a control or component, you can put one on a form and then see its properties in the Properties window. In that case, many kinds of attributes will be useful. If you're building an `Employee` class that's used only in code, fewer attributes are useful in any obvious way.

However, Visual Basic 2005 comes with a powerful `PropertyGrid` control that lets you display an object's properties on a form much as the Properties window displays them to a developer. That control honors all of the property-related attributes and gives them a whole new level of usefulness.

The following list describes some of the most useful attributes. Most of them are in the System. ComponentModel namespace. Check the online help to find the namespaces for the others and to learn about each attribute's parameters. Even these most useful attributes are fairly specialized and advanced so you may not immediately see their usefulness. If one of them doesn't make sense, skip it and scan the list again after you have more experience with such topics as building custom controls.

❑ *AttributeUsage* — You can build your own custom attributes by inheriting from the Attribute class. You can give your attribute class the `AttributeUsage` attribute to specify how your attribute can be used. You can determine whether an item can have multiple instances of your attribute, whether your attribute can be inherited by a derived class, and the kinds of things that can have your attribute (assembly, class, method, and so forth).

❑ *Browsable* — This indicates whether a property or event should be displayed in an editor such as the Properties window. If you pass the attribute's constructor the value `False`, the Properties window does not display the property.

❑ *Category* — This indicates the grouping that should hold the property or event in a visual designer such as the Properties window. For example, if the user clicks the Categorized button in the Properties window, the window groups the properties by category. This attribute tells which category should hold the property. Note that the category names are not magic. You can use any string you like and the Properties window will make a new category for you if necessary.

❑ *DefaultEvent* — This gives a class's default event name. If the class is a control or component and you double-click on it in a form, the code editor opens to this event. For example, the default event for a Button is Click, so when you double-click a Button at design time, the code editor opens the control's Click event handler.

❑ *DefaultProperty* — This gives a class's default property name. Suppose that the Employee component has LastName set as its default property. Then suppose that you select the form and click on the FormBorderStyle property in the Properties window. Now you click on an Employee. Because Employee doesn't have a FormBorderStyle property, the Properties window displays its default property: LastName.

❑ *DefaultValue* — This gives a property a default value. If you right-click on the property in the Properties window and select Reset, the property is reset to this value. Be sure to use a valid value. For example, don't set this to the string "unknown" if the property is an Integer.

❑ *Description* — This gives a description of the item. If a property has a `Description` and you select the property in the Properties window, the window displays the description text at the bottom.

Visual Basic 2005 carries this one step further and also allows you to use XML comments to provide a description of routines and their parameters for use by IntelliSense. For more information, see the section, "XML Comments," in Chapter 3.

❑ *Localizable* — This determines whether a property should be localizable. If this is `True`, localized values are automatically stored in the appropriate resource files. If this is `False` (the default), all locales share the same property value.

To try this out, set the form's `Localizable` property to `True` and enter a value for the property. Then set the form's `Language` property to another language and give the localizable property a new value. Visual Basic automatically applies the right value for the user's locale when it runs the program.

❑ *MergableProperty* — This indicates whether or not the property can be merged with the same property provided by other components in the Properties window. If this is `False` and you select more than one instance of a control with the property, the Properties window does not display the property.

If this is `True` and you select more than one control with the property, the Properties window displays the value if the controls all have the same value. If you enter a new value, all of the controls are updated. This is the way the `Text` property works for `TextBox`, `Label`, and many other kinds of controls.

❑ *ParenthesizePropertyName* — This indicates whether editors such as the Properties window should display parentheses around the property's name. If the name has parentheses, the Properties window moves it to the top of the list when displaying properties alphabetically or to the top of its category when displaying properties by category.

❑ *ReadOnly* — This indicates whether designers should treat this property as read-only. For example, the Properties window displays the property grayed out and doesn't let the user change its value. This attribute is a little strange in practice because `ReadOnly` is a Visual Basic keyword. If you enter just the attribute name `ReadOnly`, Visual Basic gets confused. Either use the full name `System.ComponentModel.ReadOnly` or enclose the name in square brackets as in `<[ReadOnly](True)>` . . . .

❑ *RecommendedAsConfigurable* — This indicates that a property should be tied to the configuration file. When you select the object at design time and expand the "(Dynamic Properties)" item, the property is listed. If you click the ellipsis to the right, a dialog appears that lets you map the property to a key in the configuration file.

❑ *RefreshProperties* — This indicates how an editor should refresh the object's *other* properties if *this* property is changed. The value can be `Default` (do not refresh the other properties), `Repaint` (refresh all other properties), or `All` (requery and refresh all properties).

❑ *Conditional* — This indicates that the method is callable if a compile-time constant such as `DEBUG` or `MY_CONSTANT` is defined. If the constant is not defined, code for the method is still generated and parameters in the method call are checked against the parameter types used by the method, but calls to the method are ignored at run time. If the method has more than one `Conditional` attribute, the method is callable if any of the specified compile-time constants is defined.

Note that the constant must be defined in the main program not in the component if you are building a component. Select the main program, open the Project menu, select the Properties item at the bottom, open the Configuration Properties folder, click Build, and in the "Custom constants" box enter a value such as `IS_DEFINED=True`.

You can also use the compiler directive `#if` to exclude code completely from compilation. However, if you eliminate a method in this way, any calls to the routine will generate compile-time errors because the method doesn't exist. The `Conditional` attribute lets you hide a method while still allowing the code to contain calls to it.

❑ *DebuggerHidden* — This tells debuggers whether a method should be debuggable. If DebuggerHidden is True, the IDE skips over the method and will not stop at breakpoints inside it.

❑ *DebuggerStepThrough* — This tells debuggers whether to let the developer step through a method in the debugger. If DebuggerStepThrough is True, the IDE will not step through the method, although it will stop at any breakpoints inside it.

❑ *ToolboxBitmap* — This tells the IDE where to find a control or component's Toolbox bitmap. This can be a file, or it can be a type in an assembly that contains the bitmap and the bitmap's name in the assembly. It's awkward but essential if you're developing controls or components.

❑ *NonSerializedAttribute* — This indicates that a member of a serializable class should not be serialized. This is useful for excluding values that need not be serialized.

❑ *Obsolete* — This indicates that the item (class, method, property, or whatever) is obsolete. Optionally, you can specify the message that the code editor should display to the developer if code uses the item (for example, "Use the NewMethod instead"). You can also indicate whether the IDE should treat using this item as a warning or an error.

❑ *Serializable* — This indicates that a class is serializable. All public and private fields are serialized by default. Note that some routines require a class to be serializable even though you don't use the serialization yourself. Also note that attributes in the System.Xml.Serialization namespace can provide a lot of control over serializations.

❑ *ThreadStaticAttribute* — This indicates that a Shared class variable should not be shared across threads. Different threads get their own copies of the variable and all instances of the class within each thread share the thread's copy.

inheritance_mode

The *inheritance_mode* can be one of the values Overloads, Overrides, Overridable, NotOverridable, MustOverride, Shadows, or Shared. These values determine how a subroutine declared within a class inherits from the parent class or how it allows inheritance in derived classes. The following list explains the meanings of these keywords.

❑ *Overloads* — Indicates that the subroutine has the same name as another subroutine defined for this class. The parameter list must be different in the different versions so that Visual Basic can tell them apart (if they are the same, this works just like Overrides described next). If you are overloading a subroutine defined in a parent class, you must use this keyword. If you are overloading only subroutines in the same class, you can omit the keyword. If you use the keyword in any of the overloaded subroutines, however, you must include it for them all.

❑ *Overrides* — Indicates that this subroutine replaces a subroutine in the parent class that has the same name and parameters.

❑ *Overridable* — Indicates that a derived class can override this subroutine. This is the default for a subroutine that overrides another one.

❑ *NotOverridable* — Indicates that a derived class cannot override this subroutine. You can only use this with a subroutine that overrides another one.

❏ *MustOverride* — Indicates that any derived classes must override this subroutine. When you use this keyword, you omit all subroutine code and the End Sub statement, as in the following code:

```
MustOverride Sub Draw()
MustOverride Sub MoveMap(ByVal X As Integer, ByVal Y As Integer)
MustOverride Sub Delete()
...
```

If a class contains a subroutine declared MustOverride, you must declare the class using the MustInherit keyword. Otherwise, Visual Basic won't know what to do if you call this subroutine, because it contains no code.

MustOverride is handy for defining a subroutine that derived classes must implement, but for which a default implementation in the parent class doesn't make sense. For example, suppose that you make a Drawable class that represents a shape that can be drawn and that you will derive specific shape classes such as Rectangle, Ellipse, Line, and so forth. To let the program draw a generic shape, the Drawable class defines the Draw subroutine. Because Drawable doesn't have a particular shape, it cannot provide a default implementation of that subroutine. To require the derived classes to implement Draw, the Drawable class declares it MustOverride.

❏ *Shadows* — Indicates that this subroutine replaces an item (probably a subroutine) in the parent class that has the same name, but not necessarily the same parameters. If the parent class contains more than one overloaded version of the subroutine, this subroutine shadows them all. If the derived class defines more than one overloaded version of the subroutine, they must all be declared with the Shadows keyword.

❏ *Shared* — Indicates that this subroutine is associated with the class itself, rather than with a specific instance of the class. You can invoke it using the class's name (ClassName.SharedSub) or using a specific instance (class_instance.SharedSub). Because the subroutine is not associated with a specific class instance, it cannot use any properties or methods that are provided by a specific instance. The subroutine can only use other Shared properties and methods, as well as globally available variables.

accessibility

A subroutine's *accessibility* clause can take one of these values: Public, Protected, Friend, Protected Friend, and Private. These values determine which pieces of code can invoke the subroutine. The following list explains these keywords.

❏ *Public* — Indicates that there are no restrictions on the subroutine. Code inside or outside of the subroutine's class or module can call it.

❏ *Protected* — Indicates that the subroutine is accessible only to code in the same class or in a derived class. You can only use the Protected keyword with subroutines declared inside a class.

❏ *Friend* — Indicates that the subroutine is available to all code inside or outside of the subroutine's module within the same project. The difference between this and Public is that Public allows code outside of the project to access the subroutine. This is generally only an issue for code libraries (DLLs) and control libraries. For example, suppose that you build a code library containing dozens of routines and then you write a program that uses the library. If the library declares a subroutine with the Public keyword, the code in the library and the code in the main program can use the subroutine. In contrast, if the library declares a subroutine with the `Friend` keyword, only the code in the library can access the subroutine, not the code in the main program.

❑ `Protected Friend` — Indicates that the subroutine has both `Protected` and `Friend` status. The subroutine is available only within the same project and within the same class or a derived class.

❑ `Private` — Indicates that the subroutine is available only within the class or module that contains it.

To reduce the amount of information that developers must remember, you should generally declare subroutines with the most restricted accessibility that allows them to do their jobs. If you can, declare the subroutine `Private`. Then, developers working on other parts of the application don't even need to know that the subroutine exists. They can create other routines with the same name if necessary and won't accidentally misuse the subroutine.

Later, if you discover that you need to use the subroutine outside of its class or module, you can change its declaration to allow greater accessibility.

subroutine_name

The subroutine's name must be a valid Visual Basic identifier. That means it should begin with a letter or an underscore. It can then contain zero or more letters, numbers, and underscores. If the name begins with an underscore, it must include at least one other character so that Visual Basic can tell it apart from a line continuation character.

Many developers use "camel case" when naming subroutines so a subroutine's name consists of several descriptive words with their first letters capitalized. A good method for generating subroutine names is to use a short phrase beginning with a verb and describing what the subroutine does. Some examples include `LoadData`, `SaveNetworkConfiguration`, and `PrintExpenseReport`.

Subroutine names with leading underscores can be hard to read, so you should either save them for special purposes or avoid them entirely. Names such as `_1` and `__` (two underscores) are particularly confusing.

parameters

The *parameters* section of the subroutine declaration defines the arguments that the subroutine takes as parameters. The parameter declarations define the numbers and types of the parameters. This section also gives the names by which the subroutine will know the values.

Declaring parameters is very similar to declaring variables. See Chapter 4, "Data Types, Variables, and Constants," for information on variable declarations, data types, and other related topics.

The following sections describe some of the more important details related to subroutine parameter declarations.

ByVal

If you include the optional `ByVal` keyword before a parameter's declaration, the subroutine makes its own local copy of the parameter with procedure scope. The subroutine can modify this value all it wants and the corresponding value in calling procedure isn't changed.

For example, consider the following code. The main program initializes the variable A and prints its value in the Output window. It then calls subroutine DisplayDouble, which declares its parameter X with the ByVal keyword. It doubles X and displays the new value. Because the parameter X is declared ByVal, the subroutine has its own local copy of the variable, so doubling it doesn't change the value of the variable A in the main program. When the subroutine ends and the main program resumes, it displays the value of variable A.

```
Private Sub Main()
    Dim A As Integer = 12
    Debug.WriteLine("Main: " & A)
    DisplayDouble(A)
    Debug.WriteLine("Main: " & A)
End Sub

Private Sub DisplayDouble(ByVal X As Integer)
    X *= 2
    Debug.WriteLine("DisplayDouble: " & X)
End Sub
```

The following text shows the results:

```
Main: 12
DisplayDouble: 24
Main: 12
```

ByRef

If you declare a parameter with the ByRef keyword, the subroutine does not create a separate copy of the parameter variable. Instead, it uses a reference to the original parameter passed into the subroutine and any changes the subroutine makes to the value are reflected in the calling subroutine.

Consider the following code. This code is the same as the previous example except that the DisplayDouble subroutine declares its parameter using the ByRef keyword. As before, the main program initializes the variable A and prints its value in the Output window. It then calls subroutine DisplayDouble, which doubles its parameter X and displays the new value. Because X is declared ByRef, this doubles the value of the variable A that was passed by the main program into the subroutine. When the subroutine ends and the main program resumes, it displays the new doubled value of variable A.

```
Private Sub Main()
    Dim A As Integer = 12
    Debug.WriteLine("Main: " & A)
    DisplayDouble(A)
    Debug.WriteLine("Main: " & A)
End Sub

Private Sub DisplayDouble(ByRef X As Integer)
    X *= 2
    Debug.WriteLine("DisplayDouble: " & X)
End Sub
```

The following text shows the results.

```
Main: 12
DisplayDouble: 24
Main: 24
```

Arrays Declared ByVal and ByRef

If you declare an array parameter using `ByVal` or `ByRef`, those keywords apply to the array itself, not to the array's values. In either case, the subroutine can modify the values inside the array.

The `DoubleArrayValues` subroutine shown in the following code has a parameter named `arr`. This parameter is an array of integers and is declared `ByVal`. The routine loops through the array, doubling each of its values. It then loops through the array, displaying the new values. Next, the subroutine assigns the variable `arr` to a new array of integers. It loops through the array, again displaying the new values.

```
Private Sub DoubleArrayValues(ByVal arr() As Integer)
    ' Double the values.
    For i As Integer = arr.GetLowerBound(0) To arr.GetUpperBound(0)
        arr(i) *= 2
    Next i

    ' Display the values.
    For i As Integer = arr.GetLowerBound(0) To arr.GetUpperBound(0)
        Debug.WriteLine(arr(i))
    Next i
    Debug.WriteLine("----------")

    ' Create a new array of values.
    arr = New Integer() {-1, -2}

    ' Display the values.
    For i As Integer = arr.GetLowerBound(0) To arr.GetUpperBound(0)
        Debug.WriteLine(arr(i))
    Next i
    Debug.WriteLine("----------")
End Sub
```

The following code declares an array of integers containing the values 1, 2, and 3. It invokes the subroutine `DoubleArrayValues` and then loops through the array, displaying the values after `DoubleArrayValues` returns.

```
Dim the_values() As Integer = {1, 2, 3}
DoubleArrayValues(the_values)

For i As Integer = the_values.GetLowerBound(0) To the_values.GetUpperBound(0)
    Debug.WriteLine(the_values(i))
Next i
```

The following text shows the results. The `DoubleArrayValues` subroutine lists the array's doubled values 2, 4, 6, assigns a new array to its local variable `arr`, and then displays the new values -1 and -2. When `DoubleArrayValues` returns, the main program displays its version of the values. Notice that the values were updated by `DoubleArrayValues` but that the subroutine's assignment of its `arr` variable to a new array had no effect on the main program's array `the_values`.

```
2
4
6
----------
-1
-2
----------
2
4
6
```

Now suppose that the subroutine `DoubleArrayValues` was declared with the following statement:

```
Private Sub DoubleArrayValues(ByRef arr() As Integer)
```

In this case, when `DoubleArrayValues` assigns a new array to its `arr` variable, the calling routine sees the change, so the `the_values` array receives the new array. The following text shows the new results:

```
2
4
6
----------
-1
-2
----------
-1
-2
```

Parenthesized Parameters

There are a couple ways that a subroutine can fail to update a parameter declared using the `ByRef` keyword. The most confusing occurs if you enclose a variable in parentheses when you pass it to the subroutine. Parentheses tell Visual Basic to evaluate their contents as an expression. Visual Basic creates a temporary variable to hold the result of the expression and then passes the temporary variable into the procedure. If the procedure's parameter is declared `ByRef`, the subroutine updates the temporary variable but not the original variable, so the calling routine doesn't see any change to its value.

The following code calls subroutine `DisplayDouble`, passing it the variable `A` surrounded by parentheses. Subroutine `DisplayDouble` modifies its parameter's value, but the result doesn't get back to the variable `A`.

```
Private Sub Main()
    Dim A As Integer = 12
    Debug.WriteLine("Main: " & A)
    DisplayDouble((A))
    Debug.WriteLine("Main: " & A)
End Sub

Private Sub DisplayDouble(ByRef X As Integer)
    X *= 2
    Debug.WriteLine("DisplayDouble: " & X)
End Sub
```

The following text shows the results:

```
Main: 12
DisplayDouble: 24
Main: 12
```

Chapter 4 has more to say about parameters declared with the ByVal and ByRef keywords.

Optional

If you declare a parameter with the Optional keyword, the code that uses it may omit that parameter. When you declare an optional parameter, you must give it a default value for the subroutine to use if the parameter is omitted by the calling routine.

The DisplayError subroutine in the following code takes an optional string parameter. If the calling routine provides this parameter, the subroutine displays it. If the calling routine leaves this parameter out, then DisplayError displays its default message "An error occurred." The PlaceOrder subroutine checks its the_customer parameter. If this parameter is Nothing, PlaceOrder calls DisplayError to show the message "Customer is Nothing in subroutine PlaceOrder." Next, subroutine PlaceOrder calls the_customer's IsValid function. If IsValid returns False, the subroutine calls DisplayError. This time it omits the parameter so DisplayError presents its default message.

```
Private Sub DisplayError(Optional ByVal error_message As String = _
 "An error occurred")
    MsgBox(error_message)
End Sub

Private Sub PlaceOrder(ByVal the_customer As Customer, _
 ByVal order_items() As OrderItem)
    ' See if the_customer exists.
    If the_customer Is Nothing Then
        DisplayError("Customer is Nothing in subroutine PlaceOrder")
        Exit Sub
    End If

    ' See if the_customer is valid.
    If Not the_customer.IsValid() Then
        DisplayError()
        Exit Sub
    End If

    ' Generate the order.
    ...
End Sub
```

Optional parameters must go at the end of the parameter list. If one parameter uses the Optional keyword, all of the following parameters must use it too.

Optional parameters are particularly useful for initializing values in a class's constructor. The following code shows a DrawableRectangle class. Its constructor takes as parameters the rectangle's position and size. All the parameters are optional, so the main program can omit them if it desires. Because each parameter has default values, the constructor always knows it will have the four values, so it can always initialize the object's Bounds variable.

```
Public Class DrawableRectangle
    Public Bounds As Rectangle

    Public Sub New( _
     Optional ByVal X As Integer = 0, _
     Optional ByVal Y As Integer = 0, _
     Optional ByVal Width As Integer = 100, _
     Optional ByVal Height As Integer = 100)
        Bounds = New Rectangle(X, Y, Width, Height)
    End Sub
    ...
End Class
```

Note that overloaded subroutines cannot differ only in optional parameters. If a call to the subroutine omitted the optional parameters, Visual Basic would be unable to tell which version of the subroutine to use.

Optional versus Overloading

Different developers have varying opinions on whether you should use optional parameters or over-loaded routines under various circumstances. For example, suppose that the FireEmployee method could take one or two parameters giving either the employee's name or the name and reason for dismissal. You could make this a subroutine with the reason parameter optional, or you could make one overloaded version of the FireEmployee method for each possible parameter list.

One argument in favor of optional parameters is that overloaded methods might duplicate a lot of code. However, it is easy to make each version of the method call another version that allows more parameters, passing in default values. For example, in the following code the first version of the FireEmployee method simply invokes the second version.

```
Public Sub FireEmployee(ByVal employee_name As String)
    FireEmployee(employee_name, "Unknown reason")
End Sub

Public Sub FireEmployee(ByVal employee_name As String, ByVal reason As String)
    ...
End Sub
```

Method overloading is generally superior when the different versions of the routine need to do some-thing different. You might be able to make a single routine with optional parameters take different actions based on the values of its optional parameters, but separating the code into overloaded routines will probably produce a cleaner solution.

Parameter Arrays

Sometimes it is convenient to allow a subroutine to take a variable number of parameters. For example, a subroutine might take as parameters the addresses of people who should receive e-mail. It would loop through the names to send each a message.

One approach is to include a long list of optional parameters. For example, the e-mail subroutine might set the default value for each of its parameters to an empty string. Then it would need to send e-mail to every address parameter that was not empty.

Unfortunately, this type of subroutine would need to include code to deal with each optional parameter separately. This would also place an upper limit on the number of parameters the subroutine can take (however many you are willing to type in the subroutine's parameter list).

A better solution is to use the `ParamArray` keyword to make the subroutine's final argument a parameter array. A *parameter array* contains an arbitrary number of parameter values. At run time, the subroutine can loop through the array to process the parameter values.

The `DisplayAverage` subroutine shown in the following code takes a parameter array named `values`. It checks the array's bounds to make sure it contains at least one value. If the array isn't empty, the subroutine adds the values it contains and divides by the number of values to calculate the average.

```
' Display the average of a series of values.
Private Sub DisplayAverage(ByVal ParamArray values() As Double)
    ' Do nothing if there are no parameters.
    If values Is Nothing Then Exit Sub
    If values.Length < 1 Then Exit Sub

    ' Calculate the average.
    Dim total As Double = 0
    For i As Integer = LBound(values) To UBound(values)
        total += values(i)
    Next i

    ' Display the result.
    MessageBox.Show((total / values.Length).ToString)
End Sub
```

The following code shows one way the program could use this subroutine. In this example, `DisplayAverage` would display the average of the integers 1 through 7, which is 4.

```
DisplayAverage(1, 2, 3, 4, 5, 6, 7)
```

Parameter arrays are subject to several restrictions.

- ❑ A subroutine can have only one parameter array, and it must come last in the parameter list.

- ❑ All other parameters in the parameter list must *not* be optional.

- ❑ All parameter lists are declared `ByVal`, so any changes the subroutine makes to the array's contents do not affect the calling routine.

- ❑ Parameter array values are implicitly optional, so the calling routine can provide any number of values (including zero) for the array. However, you cannot use the `Optional` keyword when you declare the parameter array.

❑   All the items in the parameter array must have the same data type. However, you can use an array that contains the generic `Object` data type and then it can hold just about anything. The downside is you may need to convert the items into a more specific type (for example, using `DirectCast` or `CInt`) to use their features.

The calling routine can pass any number of values (including zero) for the parameter array. It can also pass the value `Nothing`, in which case the subroutine's parameter array has value `Nothing`.

The program can also pass an array of the appropriate data type in place of the parameter array values. The following two calls to the `DisplayAverage` subroutine produce the same result inside the `DisplayAverage` subroutine.

```
DisplayAverage(1, 2, 3, 4, 5, 6, 7)

Dim values() As Double = {1, 2, 3, 4, 5, 6, 7}
DisplayAverage(values)
```

Implements interface.subroutine

An *interface* defines a set of properties, methods, and events that a class implementing the interface must provide. An interface is a lot like a class with all of its properties, methods, and events declared with the `MustOverride` keyword. Any class that inherits from the base class must provide implementations of those properties, methods, and events.

The `IDrawable` interface shown in the following code defines a `Draw` subroutine, a `Bounds` function, and a property named `IsVisible`. The `DrawableRectangle` class begins with the statement `Implements IDrawable`. That tells Visual Basic that the class will implement the `IDrawable` interface. If you make the class declaration, type the `Implements` statement, and then press the Enter key, Visual Basic automatically fills in the declarations you need to satisfy the interface. In this example, it creates the empty `Bounds` function, `Draw` subroutine, and `IsVisible` property procedures shown here. All you need to do is fill in the details.

Developers often begin the name of interfaces with a capital I so that it's obvious that it's an interface.

```
Public Interface IDrawable
    Sub Draw(ByVal gr As Graphics)
    Function Bounds() As Rectangle
    Property IsVisible() As Boolean
End Interface

Public Class DrawableRectangle
    Implements IDrawable

    Public Function Bounds() As System.Drawing.Rectangle _
      Implements IDrawable.Bounds

    End Function

    Public Sub Draw(ByVal gr As System.Drawing.Graphics) _
      Implements IDrawable.Draw
```

```
        End Sub

    Public Property IsVisible() As Boolean Implements IDrawable.IsVisible
        Get

        End Get
        Set(ByVal Value As Boolean)

        End Set
    End Property
End Class
```

If you look at the previous code, you can see where the subroutine declaration's "Implements *interface. subroutine*" clause comes into play. In this case, the Draw subroutine implements the IDrawable interface's Draw method.

When you type the Implements statement and press the Enter key, Visual Basic generates empty routines to satisfy the interface; then you don't need to type the "Implements *interface.subroutine*" clause yourself. Visual Basic enters this for you.

The only time you should need to modify this statement is if you change the interface's name or subroutine name or you want to use some other subroutine to satisfy the interface. For example, you could give the DrawableRectangle class a DrawRectangle method and add Implements IDrawable.Draw to its declaration. Visual Basic doesn't care what you call the routine, as long as *some* routine implements IDrawable.Draw.

statements

A subroutine's *statements* section contains whatever Visual Basic code is needed to get the routine's job done. This can include all the usual variable declarations, For loops, Try blocks, and other Visual Basic paraphernalia.

The subroutine's body cannot include module, class, subroutine, function, structure, enumerated type, or other file-level statements. For example, you cannot define a subroutine within another subroutine.

One new statement that you can use within a subroutine is Exit Sub. This command makes the subroutine immediately exit and return control to the calling routine. Within a subroutine, the Return statement is equivalent to Exit Sub.

You can use Exit Sub or Return as many times as you like to allow the subroutine to exit under different conditions. For example, the following subroutine checks whether a phone number has a 10-digit or 7-digit format. If the phone number matches a 10-digit format, the subroutine exits. Then if the phone number matches a 7-digit format, the subroutine exits. If the number doesn't match either format, the subroutine displays an error message to the user.

```
    Private Sub ValidatePhoneNumber(ByVal phone_number As String)
        ' Check for a 10-digit phone number.
        If phone_number Like "###-###-####" Then Exit Sub

        ' Check for a 7-digit phone number.
```

```
       If phone_number Like "###-####" Then Return

       ' The phone number is invalid.
       MsgBox("Invalid phone number " & phone_number, _
           MsgBoxStyle.Exclamation, _
           "Invalid Phone Number")
   End Sub
```

Functions

Functions are basically the same as subroutines, except that they return some sort of value. The syntax for defining a function is:

```
[attribute_list] [inheritance_mode] [accessibility] _
Function function_name([parameters]) [As return_type] [ Implements
interface.function ]
    [ statements ]
End Function
```

This is almost the same as the syntax for defining a subroutine. See the section "Subroutines" earlier in this chapter for information about most of this declaration's clauses.

One simple difference is that a function ends with the End Function statement rather than End Sub. Similarly a function can exit before reaching its end using Exit Function rather than Exit Sub.

The one really new piece in the declaration is the clause "As *return_type*" that comes after the function's parameter list. This tells Visual Basic the type of value that the function will return.

The function can set its return value in one of two ways. First, it can set its name equal to the value it wants to return. The Factorial function shown in the following code calculates the factorial of a number. Written N!, the factorial of N is N * (N - 1) * (N - 2) . . . * 1. The function initializes its result variable to 1, and then loops over the values between 1 and the number parameter, multiplying these values to the result. It finishes by setting its name, Factorial, equal to the result value that it should return.

```
Private Function Factorial(ByVal number As Integer) As Double
    Dim result As Double = 1

    For i As Integer = 2 To number
        result *= i
    Next i

    Factorial = result
End Function
```

A function can assign and reassign its return value as many times as it wants to before it returns. Whatever value is assigned last becomes the function's return value.

The second way a function can assign its return value is to use the `Return` keyword followed by the value that the function should return. The following code shows the `Factorial` function rewritten to use the `Return` statement:

```
Private Function Factorial(ByVal number As Integer) As Double
    Dim result As Double = 1

    For i As Integer = 2 To number
        result *= i
    Next i

    Return result
End Function
```

The `Return` statement is roughly equivalent to setting the function's name equal to the return value, and then immediately using an `Exit Function` statement. The `Return` statement may allow the compiler to perform extra optimizations, however, so it is generally preferred to setting the function's name equal to the return value.

Property Procedures

Property procedures are routines that can represent a property-like value. A normal read-write property procedure contains a function for returning the property's value and a subroutine for assigning it.

The following code shows property procedures that implement a `Value` property. The `Property Get` procedure is a function that returns the value in the private variable `m_Value`. The `Property Set` subroutine saves a new value in the `m_Value` variable.

```
Private m_Value As Single

Property Value() As Single
    Get
        Return m_Value
    End Get
    Set(ByVal Value As Single)
        m_Value = Value
    End Set
End Property
```

While the property is implemented as a pair of property procedures, the program could treat the value as a simple property. For example, suppose that the `OrderItem` class contains the previous code. Then the following code sets the `Value` property for the `OrderItem` object named `paper_item`:

```
paper_item.Value = 19.95
```

You can add property procedures to any type of object module. For example, you can use property procedures to implement a property for a form or for a class of your own.

It's less obvious that you can also use property procedures in a code module. The property procedures look like an ordinary variable to the routines that use them. If you place the previous example in a code module, the program could act as if there were a variable named Value defined in the module.

For more information on property procedures, see the section "Property Procedures" in Chapter 4.

Summary

Subroutines and functions let you break an application into manageable, reusable pieces. A subroutine performs a series of commands. A function performs a series of commands and returns a value.

Property procedures use paired functions and subroutines to provide the behavior of a simple property using routines.

These form the fundamental building blocks of the procedural part of an application. Chapters 14 through 18 explain the other half of an application's structure, the objects that encapsulate the application's behavior. Together, the program's objects and its procedural subroutines and functions define the application.

This chapter explains how to break an otherwise unwieldy expanse of code into subroutines and functions of manageable size. However, the chapters so far have not explained how to write anything other that straight-line code that executes one statement after another with no deviation. Most programs need to follow more complex paths of execution, performing some statements only under certain conditions and repeating others a given number of times. Chapter 7, "Program Control Statements," describes the statements that a Visual Basic program uses to control the flow of code execution. These include decision statements (If Then Else, Select Case, IIF, Choose) and looping statements (For Next, For Each, Do While, While Do, Repeat Until).

7

Program Control Statements

Program control statements tell an application which other statements to execute under a particular set of circumstances. They control the path that execution takes through the code. They include commands that tell the program to execute some statements but not others and to execute certain statements repeatedly.

The two main categories of control statements are *decision* (or *conditional*) *statements* and *looping statements*. The following sections describe in detail the decision and looping statements provided by Visual Basic .NET.

Decision Statements

A decision or conditional statement represents a branch in the program. It marks a place where the program can execute one set of statements or another, or possibly no statements at all, depending on some condition. These include `If`, `Choose`, and `Select Case` statements.

Single Line If Then

The single-line `If Then` statement has two forms. The first allows the program to execute a single statement if some condition is true. The syntax is as follows:

```
If condition Then statement
```

If the condition is true, the program executes the statement. In the most common form of single-line `If Then` statement, the statement is a single simple command (such as assigning a value to a variable or calling a subroutine).

The following example checks the `emp` object's `IsManager` property. If `IsManager` is true, the statement sets the `emp` object's `Salary` property to 90,000.

```
If emp.IsManager Then emp.Salary = 90000
```

The other variations on the single-line If Then statement are more confusing and generally harder to debug and maintain. To prevent unnecessary confusion, many programmers switch to the multiline If Then statement described in the next section when the simple single-statement version won't work.

The second form of single-line If Then statement uses the Else keyword. The syntax is as follows:

```
If condition Then statement1 Else statement2
```

If the condition is true, the code executes the first statement. If the condition is false, the code executes the second statement. The decision about which statement to execute is an "either-or" decision; the code executes one statement or the other, but not both.

This type of single-line If Then Else statement is very confusing if it is too long to easily see in the code editor. For longer statements, a multiline If Then Else statement is easier to understand and debug. The performance of single-line and multiline If Then Else statements is comparable (in one test, the multiline version took only about 80 percent as long), so you should use the one that seems easiest for you to read.

The statements executed by a single-line If Then statement can be simple commands (such as assigning a value to a variable). They can also be a series of simple statements separated by colons on the same line. For example, the following code tests the value of the Boolean variable is_new_customer. If is_new_customer is true, the program calls the customer object's Initialize method and then calls its Welcome method.

```
If is_new_customer Then customer.Initialize() : customer.Welcome()
```

Using more than one simple statement separated by colons like this can be perplexing. It gets even worse if you use single-line If Then Else, as shown here:

```
If order.Valid() Then order.Save() : order.Post() Else order.Delete()
```

The single-line If Then statement can also include Else If clauses. For example, the following code examines the variable X. If X is 1, the program displays a message box saying "One." If X has the value 2, the program displays a message box saying "Two." If X is not 1 or 2, the program displays a message box containing a question mark.

```
If X = 1 Then MsgBox("One") Else If X = 2 Then MsgBox("Two") Else MsgBox("?")
```

The code can include as many Else If clauses as you like, and each execution statement can be composed of multiple simple statements separated by colons. However, confusing code such as these examples can lead to puzzling bugs that are easy to avoid if you use multiline If Then statements instead.

In summary, if you can write a simple single-line If Then statement with no Else If or Else clauses, and the whole thing fits nicely on the line so that it's easy to see the whole thing without confusion, go ahead. If the statement is too long to read easily, contains Else If or Else clauses, or executes a series of statements separated by colons, you are usually better off using a multiline If Then statement. It may take more lines of code, but the code will be easier to read, debug, and maintain later.

Multiline If Then

A multiline If Then statement can execute more than one line of code when a condition is true. The syntax for the simplest form of multiline If Then statement is as follows:

```
If condition Then
    statements...
End If
```

If the condition is true, the program executes all the commands that come before the End If statement. For example, the following code shows a multiline version of one of the statements shown in the previous section. If the Boolean variable is_new_customer has value True, the program calls the customer object's Initialize method and then calls its Welcome method.

```
If is_new_customer Then
    customer.Initialize()
    customer.Welcome()
End If
```

Like the single-line If Then statement, the multiline version can include Else If and Else clauses. For possibly historical reasons, ElseIf is spelled as a single word in the multiline If Then statement. The syntax is as follows:

```
If condition1 Then
    statements1...
ElseIf condition2
    statements2...
Else
    statements3...
End If
```

If the first condition is true, the program executes the first set of statements. If the first condition is false, the code examines the second condition and, if that one is true, the code executes the second set of statements. The program continues checking conditions until it finds one that is true and it executes the corresponding code.

If the program reaches an Else statement, it executes the corresponding code. If the program reaches the End If statement without finding a true condition or an Else clause, it doesn't execute any of the statement blocks.

The following simple example shows a multiline version of the confusing single-line If Then Else statement shown in the section, "Single-Line If-Then," earlier in this chapter.

```
If order.Valid() Then
    order.Save()
    order.Post()
Else
    order.Reject()
    order.Delete()
End If
```

It is important to understand that the program exits the If Then construction immediately after it has executed the block of statements that goes with the first condition it finds that is true. It does not examine the other conditions. This saves the program some time and is particularly important if the conditions involve functions. If each test calls a relatively slow function, skipping these later tests can save the program a significant amount of time.

You need to be particularly aware of this issue if the conditions call functions that have *side effects*. A *side effect* is some change in the program's state that can affect parts of the program outside of the function. If you don't know how many of an If Then statement's conditions are executed, you cannot know which side effects may have occurred.

For example, suppose the GetEmployee function pulls data from a database to initialize an Employee object and returns that object. The following code loads Alice Adams' record and checks to see if she is a manager. If Alice is not a manager, the code loads Brian Buckley's data and sees if he is a manager. If Brian isn't a manager either, the code checks Cindy Cantrell and possibly others.

```
If GetEmployee("Alice Adams").IsManager() Then
    ...
ElseIf GetEmployee("Brian Buckley").IsManager() Then
    ...
ElseIf GetEmployee("Cindy Cantrell").IsManager() Then
    ...
ElseIf ...
    ...
End If
```

After this code finishes executing, how many Employee objects has the program loaded? Are all of the employees loaded, or are some still only in the database? The answers depend on which of these people is a manager. If Alice is a manager, the program loads only her record. If none of these people is a manager, the program loads data for everyone. If someone later in the list is a manager, the program loads some but not all of the employees. There's no easy way to tell how many Employee objects were created without knowing all the details contained in the employee data.

In this example, knowing the number of employees loaded might not be big deal. However, whenever an If Then statement uses a series of conditions with side effects, you cannot easily tell what state the program is in afterward.

You can avoid this type of potential confusion by not using routines with side effects in this sort of If Then structure. One alternative would be to load every employee and then look for one who is a manager. In this example, that may take a little longer if Alice Adams is a manager, but at least the program is in a well-known state afterwards.

Select Case

The Select Case statement lets a program execute one of several pieces of code depending on a single value. The basic syntax is as follows:

```
Select Case test_value
    Case comparison_expression1
        statements1
    Case comparison_expression2
```

```
        statements2
    Case comparison_expression3
        statements3
    ...
    Case Else
        else_statements
End Select
```

If `test_value` matches `comparison_expression1`, the program executes the statements in the block `statements1`. If `test_value` matches `comparison_expression2`, the program executes the statements in the block `statements2`. The program continues checking the expressions in the `Case` statements in order until it matches one, or it runs out of `Case` statements.

If `test_value` doesn't match any of the expressions in the `Case` statements, the program executes the code in the `else_statements` block. Note that you can omit the `Case Else` section. In that case, the program executes no code if `test_value` doesn't match any of the expressions.

For example, the following code checks the value in the `txtDessertSelection` text box and displays a message. If the text box doesn't contain one of the strings `Pie`, `Cake`, or `Cookies`, the code displays the message "You have not selected a dessert."

```
Select Case txtDessertSelection.Text
    Case "Pie"
        MessageBox.Show("You have selected pie")
    Case "Cake"
        MessageBox.Show("You have selected cake")
    Case "Cookies"
        MessageBox.Show("You have selected cookies")
    Case Else
        MessageBox.Show("You have not selected a dessert")
End Select
```

`Select Case` is functionally equivalent to an `If Then Else` statement. The following code does the same thing as the previous version:

```
If txtDessertSelection.Text = "Pie" Then
    MessageBox.Show("You have selected pie")
ElseIf txtDessertSelection.Text = "Cake" Then
    MessageBox.Show("You have selected cake")
ElseIf txtDessertSelection.Text = "Cookies" Then
    MessageBox.Show("You have selected cookies")
Else
    MessageBox.Show("You have not selected a dessert")
End If
```

`Select Case` is sometimes easier to understand than a long `If Then Else` statement. It is often faster as well, largely because `Select Case` doesn't need to reevaluate `test_value` for every `Case` statement. In the previous code, each `ElseIf` clause must find the value of `txtDessertSelection.Text`. The `Select Case` version only calculates this value once, and then compares the result to the comparison expressions in the `Case` statements. The savings in time can be significant in frequently executed code when `test_value` is extremely complicated. For example, in the following code, the test expression accesses a deeply nested series of object properties. Reevaluating this expression for each `ElseIf` statement would take a relatively long time.

```
If employee.Department.Manager.Secretary. _
   HomeAddress.Phone.SubString(0, 3) = "212" Then
   ...
ElseIf employee.Department.Manager.Secretary. _
   HomeAddress.Phone.SubString(0, 3) = "213" Then
   ...
ElseIf employee.Department.Manager.Secretary. _
   HomeAddress.Phone.SubString(0, 3) = "214" Then
   ...
End If
```

If you think a particular piece of code will be easier to understand using an `If Then Else` statement instead of a `Select Case` statement, you can speed the code up (and make it easier to read) by storing a complex `test_value` in a variable. The following code shows an improved version of the previous `If Then Else` statement:

```
Dim phone_prefix As String = employee.Department.Manager.Secretary. _
    HomeAddress.Phone.SubString(0, 3) = "123"

If phone_prefix = "212" Then
   ...
ElseIf phone_prefix = "213" Then
   ...
ElseIf phone_prefix = "214" Then
   ...
End If
```

The comparison expressions used in a `Select Case` statement are often constants. In the earlier examples, the expressions are the constant strings `Pie`, `Cake`, and `Cookies`. A comparison expression can also specify ranges using the `To` and `Is` keywords, and include a comma-separated list of expressions. These forms are described in the following sections.

To

The `To` keyword specifies a range of values that `test_value` should match. The following code examines the variable `num_items`. If `num_items` is between 1 and 10, the program calls subroutine `ProcessSmallOrder`. If `num_items` is between 11 and 100, the program calls subroutine `ProcessLargeOrder`. If `num_items` is less than 1 or greater than 100, the program beeps.

```
Select Case num_items
    Case 1 To 10
        ProcessSmallOrder()
    Case 11 To 100
        ProcessLargeOrder()
    Case Else
        Beep()
End Select
```

Is

The `Is` keyword lets you perform comparisons using `num_items`. The word `Is` takes the place of `num_items` in a comparison expression. For example, the following code does almost the same things as the previous version. If the value `num_items` is less than or equal to 10, the program calls subroutine

ProcessSmallOrder. If the first Case clause doesn't apply and num_items is less than or equal to 100, the program calls subroutine ProcessLargeOrder. If neither of these cases applies, the program beeps.

```
Select Case num_items
    Case Is <= 10
        ProcessSmallOrder()
    Case Is <= 100
        ProcessLargeOrder()
    Case Else
        Beep()
End Select
```

This version is slightly different from the previous one. If num_items is less than 1, this code calls subroutine ProcessSmallOrder while the previous version beeps.

Note also that the order of the Case clauses is important in this example. If you were to reverse the first two Case clauses, ProcessSmallOrder would never be used. Any value less than or equal to 10 is also less than or equal to 100, so any value that would satisfy the case Is <= 10 would be handled by the case Is <= 100 before the program reached the second Case clause.

You can use the operators =, <>, <, <=, >, and >= in an Is clause. (In fact, if you use a simple value in a Case clause as in Case 7, you are implicitly using Is = as in Case Is = 7.)

Comma-Separated Expressions

A comparison expression can include a series of expressions separated by commas. If the test value matches any of the comparison values, the program executes the corresponding code.

For example, the following code examines the department_name variable. If department_name is R & D, Test, or Computer Operations, the code adds the text "Building 10" to the address_text string. If department_name is Finance, Purchasing, or Accounting, the code adds Building 7 to the address. More Case clauses could check for other department_name values and the code could include an Else statement.

```
Select Case department_name
    Case "R & D", "Test", "Computer Operations"
        address_text &= "Building 10"
    Case "Finance", "Purchasing", "Accounting"
        address_text &= "Building 7"
    ...
End Select
```

Note that you cannot use comma-separated expressions in a Case Else clause. For example, the following code doesn't work:

```
Case Else, "Corporate"      ' This doesn't work.
```

However, you can simply omit any values you want to use with the Else clause. If the values don't appear in another Case clause, the program will execute the Else clause code when it finds those values. You can make the code more self-documenting by including the comparison values in a comment after the Else keyword, as in the following statement:

```
Case Else      ' Corporate
```

You can mix and match constants, `To`, and `Is` expressions in a single `Case` clause, as shown in the following example. This code checks the variable `item_code` and calls subroutine `DoSomething` if the value is less than 10, between 30 and 40 inclusive, exactly equal to 100, or greater than 200.

```
Select Case item_code
    Case Is < 10, 30 To 40, 100, Is > 200
        DoSomething()
End Select
```

Complex comparison expressions are sometimes difficult to read. If an expression is too complicated, you should consider rewriting the code to make it easier to understand. Storing values in temporary variables can help.

IIf

The `IIf` statement evaluates a Boolean expression and then returns one of two values, depending on whether the expression is true or false. This statement may look more like an assignment statement or a function call than a decision statement such as `If Then`.

The syntax is as follows:

```
variable = IIf(condition, value_if_false, value_if_true)
```

For example, the following code examines an `Employee` object's `IsManager` property. If `IsManager` is true, the code sets the employee's `Salary` to 90,000. If `IsManager` is false, the code sets the employee's `Salary` to 10,000.

```
emp.Salary = IIf(emp.IsManager, 90000, 10000)
```

Note that the `IIf` statement returns an Object data type. If you have `Option Strict` turned on, Visual Basic will not allow this statement, because it assigns a result of type Object to an Integer variable. To satisfy Visual Basic, you must explicitly convert the value into an Integer, as in the following code:

```
emp.Salary = CInt(IIf(emp.IsManager, 90000, 10000))
```

The `IIf` statement has several drawbacks. First, it is confusing. When you type an `IIf` statement, IntelliSense will remind you that its parameters give a condition, a "true value," and a "false value." When you are reading the code, however, you must remember what the different parts of the statement mean. If you use `IIf` in some other statement, the chances for confusion increase. For example, consider the following code:

```
For i = 1 To CType(IIf(employees_loaded, num_employees, 0), Integer)
    ' Process employee i.
    ...
Next i
```

Code is generally much easier to understand if you replace `IIf` with an appropriate `If Then` statement. The following code takes more lines of code but is easier to understand than the previous version:

```
If employees_loaded Then
    max_i = num_employees
Else
    max_i = 0
End If

For i = 1 To max_i
    ' Process employee i.
    ...
Next i
```

Another drawback to IIf is that it evaluates both the true and false values whether the condition is true or false. For example, consider the following code. If the Boolean use_groups is true, the code sets num_objects to the result of the CountGroups function. If use_groups is false, the code sets num_objects to the result of the CountIndividuals function. IIf evaluates both functions no matter which value it actually needs. If the functions are time-consuming or executed inside a large loop, this can waste a lot of time.

```
num_objects = CType(IIf(use_groups, CountGroups(), CountIndividuals()), Integer)
```

For an even more dangerous example, consider the following code. If data_loaded is true, this statement sets num_loaded = num_employees. If data_loaded is false, the code sets num_loaded to the value returned by the LoadEmployees function (which loads the employees and returns the number of employees it loaded).

```
num_loaded = CType(IIf(data_loaded, num_employees, LoadEmployees()), Integer)
```

IIf evaluates both the value num_employees and the value LoadEmployees() no matter what. If the employees are already loaded, IIf calls LoadEmployees() to load the employees again, ignores the returned result, and sets num_loaded = num_employees. LoadEmployees may waste quite a while loading the data that is already loaded. Even worse, the program may not be able to handle loading the data when it is already loaded.

A final drawback to IIf is that it is slower than a comparable If Then Else statement. In one test, IIf took roughly twice as long as a comparable If Then statement.

One case where you can argue that IIf is easier to understand is when you have a long series of very simple statements. In that case, IIf statements may allow you to easily see the common features in the code and notice if anything looks wrong. For example, the following code initializes several text boxes using strings. It uses an IIf statement to set a text box's value to <Missing> if the string is not yet initialized.

```
txtLastName.Text = IIf(last_name Is Nothing, "<Missing>", last_name)
txtFirstName.Text = IIf(first_name Is Nothing, "<Missing>", first_name)
txtStreet.Text = IIf(street Is Nothing, "<Missing>", street)
txtCity.Text = IIf(city Is Nothing, "<Missing>", city)
txtState.Text = IIf(state Is Nothing, "<Missing>", state)
txtZip.Text = IIf(zip Is Nothing, "<Missing>", zip)
```

The following code uses If Then statements to avoid the IIf statements. This version is a bit more difficult to read, partly because it is much longer.

```
If last_name Is Nothing Then
    txtLastName.Text = "<Missing>"
Else
    txtLastName.Text = last_name
End If
If first_name Is Nothing Then
    txtFirstName.Text = "<Missing>"
Else
    txtFirstName.Text = first_name
End If
If street Is Nothing Then
    txtStreet.Text = "<Missing>"
Else
    txtStreet.Text = street
End If
If city Is Nothing Then
    txtCity.Text = "<Missing>"
Else
    txtCity.Text = city
End If
If state Is Nothing Then
    txtState.Text = "<Missing>"
Else
    txtState.Text = state
End If
If zip Is Nothing Then
    txtZip.Text = "<Missing>"
Else
    txtZip.Text = zip
End If
```

In larger programming projects, debugging and maintenance are much bigger costs than development. Use IIf only if it makes the code easier to understand.

Choose

The IIf statement uses a Boolean expression to pick between two values. The Choose statement uses an integer to decide among any number of options. The syntax is as follows:

```
variable = Choose(index, value1, value2, value3, value4, ...)
```

If the index parameter is 1, Choose returns the first value, value1; if index is 2, Choose returns value2; and so forth. If index is less than 1 or greater than the number of values in the parameter list, Choose returns Nothing.

This statement has the same drawbacks as IIf. Sometimes Choose is more confusing than a comparable Select Case statement. If the values look dissimilar (mixing integers, objects, function calls, and so forth), involve complicated functions, or are wrapped across multiple lines, a Select Case statement may be easier to read.

However, if the Choose statement's values are short and easy to understand, and the statement contains many values, the Choose statement may be easier to read. For example, the following Choose and Select Case statements do the same thing. Because the Choose statement's values are short and easy to understand, this statement is easy to read. The Select Case statement is rather long. If the program had more choices, the Select Case statement would be even longer, making it more difficult to read.

```
fruit = Choose(index, "apple", "banana", "cherry", "date")

Select Case index
    Case 1
        fruit = "apple"
    Case 2
        fruit = "banana"
    Case 3
        fruit = "cherry"
    Case 4
        fruit = "date"
End Select
```

While it's not always clear whether a Choose statement or a Select Case statement will be easier to read, Select Case is certainly faster. In one test, Choose took more than five times as long as Select Case. If the code lies inside a frequently executed loop, the speed difference may be an issue.

Choose and Select Case are not your only options. You can also store the program's choices in an array, and then use the index to pick an item from the array. For example, the following code stores the strings from the previous example in the values array. It then uses the index to pick the right choice from the array.

```
Dim values() As String = {"apple", "banana", "cherry", "date"}

fruit = values(index - 1)
```

Notice that the code subtracts 1 from the index when using it to pick the right choice. The Choose statement indexes its values starting with 1, but arrays in Visual Basic .NET start with index 0. Subtracting 1 allows the program to use the same index values used in the previous example.

This version makes you think about the code in a different way. It requires that you know that the values array contains the names of the fruits that the program needs. If you understand the array's purpose, then the assignment statement is easy to understand.

The assignment code is even slightly faster than Select Case, at least if you can initialize the values array ahead of time.

If you find Choose easy to understand and it doesn't make your code more difficult to read in your particular circumstances, by all means use it. If Select Case seems clearer, use that. If you will need to perform the assignment many times and prebuilding an array of values makes sense, using a value array might improve your performance.

Looping Statements

Looping statements make the program execute a series of statements repeatedly. The loop can run for a fixed number of repetitions, run while some condition holds true, or run until some condition is true.

Broadly speaking, there are two types of looping statement. For loops execute a certain number of times that (in theory at least) is known. For example, a For loop may execute a series of statement exactly 10 times. Or, it may execute the statements once for each object in a certain collection. If you know how many items are in the collection, you can calculate the number of times the loop will execute.

A While loop executes while a condition is true or until a condition is met. Without a lot more information about the application, it is impossible to tell how many times the code will execute. For example, suppose that a program looks through a list of employees until it finds one who is a manager. Even if you know the number of employees in the list and the number who are managers, you cannot easily tell how many records you will need to search before you find a manager.

The following sections describe the looping statements supported by Visual Basic .NET. The next two sections describe For loops, and the sections after those describe While loops.

For Next

The For Next loop is the most common type of looping statement in Visual Basic. The syntax is:

```
For variable [As data_type] = start_value To stop_value [Step increment]
    statements
    [Exit For]
    statements
    [Continue For]
    statements
Next [variable]
```

The value variable is the looping variable that controls the loop. When the program reaches the For statement, it sets variable equal to start_value. It then compares variable to stop_value. If variable has passed stop_value, the loop exits. This is important. It means the loop may not execute even once depending on the start and stop values.

Normally, you would not intentionally write a loop that doesn't execute, but this can occur when you use variables for the start and stop values. For example, the following loop runs for the values employee_num = 1, employee_num = 2, . . . , employee_num = num_employees. If the program has not loaded any employees so num_employees = 0, the code inside the loop is not executed at all.

```
For employee_num = 1 To num_employees
    ProcessEmployee(employee_num)
Next employee_num
```

After it compares variable to stop_value, the program executes the statements inside the loop. It then adds increment to variable and starts the process over, again comparing variable to stop_value. If you omit increment, the program uses an increment of 1.

Note that `increment` can be negative or a fractional number, as in the following example:

```
For i As Double = 3 To 1 Step -0.5
    Debug.WriteLine(i)
Next i
```

If `increment` is positive, the program executes as long as `variable <= stop_value`. If `increment` is negative, the program executes as long as `variable >= stop_value`. This means that the loop would not execute infinitely if `increment` were to move `variable` away from `stop_value`. For example, in the following code `start_value = 1` and `increment = -1`. The variable i would take the values i = 1, i = 0, i = -1, and so forth, so i will never reach the `stop_value` of 2. However, because increment is negative, the loop only executes while i >= 2. Because i starts with the value 1, the program immediately exits and the loop doesn't execute at all.

```
For i As Integer = 1 To 2 Step -1
    Debug.WriteLine(i)
Next i
```

The program doesn't need for you to include the variable's name in the `Next` statement, although including the name helps make the code easier to read. If you specify the name in the `Next` statement, it must match the name you use in the `For` statement.

If you do not specify the looping variable's data type in the `For` statement and you have `Option Explicit` turned on, you must declare the variable before the loop. For example, the following loop declares the variable i outside of the loop:

```
Dim i As Integer

For i = 1 To 10
    Debug.WriteLine(i)
Next i
```

You cannot declare the same variable both inside and outside of a loop. If you declare a variable in the `For` statement, the variable's scope is limited to the loop, and code outside of the loop cannot access the variable.

Declaring the variable in the `For` statement is a good practice. It limits the scope of the variable so you don't need to remember what the variable is for in other pieces of code. It keeps the variable's declaration close to the code where it is used, so it's easier to remember the variable's data type. It also lets you more easily reuse counter variables without fear of confusion. If you have several loops that need an arbitrarily named looping variable, they can all declare and use the variable i without interfering with each other.

The program calculates its `start_value` and `stop_value` before the loop begins and it never recalculates them, even if their values change. For example, the following code loops from 1 to `this_customer.Orders(1).NumItems`. The program calculates `this_customer.Orders(1).NumItems` before executing the loop and doesn't recalculate that value even if it later changes. This saves the program time, particularly for long expressions such as this one, which could take a noticeable amount of time to reevaluate each time through a long loop.

```
For item_num As Integer = 1 To this_customer.Orders(1).NumItems
    this_customer.ProcessItem(item_num)
Next item_num
```

If you must reevaluate stop_value every time the loop executes, use a While loop.

The Exit For statement allows the program to leave a For loop before it would normally finish. For example, the following code loops through the employees array. When it finds an entry with IsManager property set to True, it saves the employee's index and uses Exit For to immediately stop looping.

```
Dim manager_index As Integer

For i As Integer = employees.GetLowerBound(0) To _
                   employees.GetUpperBound(0)
    If employees(i).IsManager Then
        manager_index = i
        Exit For
    End If
Next i
```

The Exit For statement exits only the For loop immediately surrounding the statement. For example, in the following code, variable i loops from 1 to 5. Within that loop, variable j loops from 1 to 5. If the two values are equal, the Exit For statement ends the inner loop, but the outer loop continues.

```
For i As Integer = 1 To 5
    For j As Integer = 1 To 5
        If i = j Then Exit For
        Debug.WriteLine("(" & i & ", " & j & ")")
    Next j
Next i
```

The following shows this code's result. You may want to walk through the code either mentally or in the debugger to convince yourself that this makes sense.

```
(2, 1)
(3, 1)
(3, 2)
(4, 1)
(4, 2)
(4, 3)
(5, 1)
(5, 2)
(5, 3)
(5, 4)
```

The Continue For statement makes the loop jump back to its For statement, increment its looping variable, and start the loop over again. This is particularly useful if the program doesn't need to execute the rest of the steps within the loop and wants to quickly start the next iteration.

Your code can change the value of the control variable inside the loop, but that's generally not a good idea. The For Next loop has a very specific intent, and modifying the control variable inside the loop violates that intent making the code more difficult to understand and debug. If you must modify the control variable in more complicated ways than are provided by a For Next loop, use a While loop instead. Then programmers reading the code won't expect a simple incrementing loop.

Noninteger For Next Loops

Usually a For Next loop's control variable is an integral data type such as an Integer or Long, but it can be any of Visual Basic's fundamental numeric data types. For example, the following code uses a variable declared as Single to display the values 1.0, 1.5, 2.0, 2.5, and 3.0:

```
For x As Single = 1 To 3 Step 0.5
    Debug.WriteLine(x.ToString("0.0"))
Next x
```

Because floating-point numbers cannot exactly represent every possible value, however, these data types are subject to rounding errors that can lead to unexpected results in For Next loops. The previous code works as you would expect, at least on my computer. The following code, however, has problems. Ideally, this code would display values between 1 and 2, incrementing them by 1/7. Because of rounding errors, however, the value of x after seven trips through the loop is approximately 1.85714316. The program adds 1/7 to this and gets 2.0000003065381731. This is greater than the stopping value 2, so the program exits the loop and the Debug statement does not execute for x = 2.

```
For x As Single = 1 To 2 Step 1 / 7
    Debug.WriteLine(x)
Next x
```

One solution to this type of problem is to convert the code into a loop that uses an Integer control variable. Integer variables do not have the same problems with rounding errors that floating-point numbers do, so you have more precise control over the values used in the loop.

The following code does roughly the same thing as the previous code. It uses an Integer control variable, however, so this loop executes exactly eight times as desired. The final value printed into the Output window by the program is 2.

```
Dim x As Single

x = 1
For i As Integer = 1 To 8
    Debug.WriteLine(x)
    x += CSng(1 / 7)
Next i
```

If you look at the value of variable x in the debugger, you will find that its real value during the last trip through the loop is roughly 2.0000001702989851. If this variable were controlling the For loop, the program would see that this value is greater than 2, so it would not display its final value.

For Each

A `For Each` loop iterates over the items in a collection, array, or other container class that supports `For Each` loops. The syntax is as follows:

```
For Each variable [As object_type] In group
    statements
    [Exit For]
    statements
    [Continue For]
    statements
Next [variable]
```

Here, `group` is a collection, array, or other object that supports `For Each`. As in `For Next` loops, the control variable must be either declared in or before the `For` statement.

> *To support **For Each**, the group object must implement the `System.Collections.IEnumerable` interface. This interface defines a `GetEnumerator` method that returns an enumerator. For more information, see the next section, "Enumerators."*

The control variable must be of a data type compatible with the objects contained in the group. If the group contains `Employee` objects, the variable could be an `Employee` object. It could also be a generic Object or any other class that readily converts into an `Employee` object. For example, if `Employee` inherits from the `Person` class, then the variable could be of type `Person`.

Visual Basic doesn't automatically understand what kinds of objects are stored in a collection or array until it tries to use them. If the control variable's type is not compatible with an object's type, the program generates an error when the `For Each` loop tries to assign the control variable to that object's value.

For example, the following code creates a collection containing an `Employee` object and a `Customer` object. It then uses a `For Each` loop to display the name of each object. The control variable `emp` is of type `Employee`. The first time through the loop, the program sets `emp` equal to the collection's `Employee` object and displays its name as expected. The second time through the loop, the program tries to set `emp` equal to the collection's `Customer` object. That causes an "invalid cast exception."

```
Dim people As New Collection

people.Add(New Employee("Alice Auxley"))
people.Add(New Customer("Bob Brentwood"))
For Each emp As Employee In people
    Debug.WriteLine(emp.Name)
Next emp
```

When a collection or array contains more than one type of object (as in the previous example), the control variable must be of a type that can hold all of the objects. Assuming that the `Employee` and `Customer` classes in the previous example are not derived from a common ancestor class, the code must use a control variable of type Object, as in the following code:

```
For Each person As Object In people
    Debug.WriteLine(person.Name)
Next person
```

This code works as long as the Employee and Customer classes both have a Name property. However, if you have set Option Strict On, the compiler will complain because the generic Object class does not have a Name method. To avoid this error, you need to convert the generic Object variable into a specific type that does have the Name method.

The following code shows one way to use specific object types. The program uses the TypeOf statement to check the control variable's class type. If the object has type Employee, then the code uses CType to convert the Object variable into an Employee object. It then uses that object's Name method. Similarly, if the object is a Customer, the code uses CType to convert the generic Object into a Customer and uses its Name method.

```
Dim emp As Employee
For Each person As Object In people
    If TypeOf person Is Employee Then
        emp = CType(person, Employee)
        Debug.WriteLine(emp.Name)
    ElseIf TypeOf person Is Customer Then
        Debug.WriteLine(CType(person, Customer).Name)
    End If
Next person
```

You can use the Exit For statement to jump out of a For Each loop early. The following code loops through the employees collection using TypeOf to examine each object's type. When it finds an object that has type Manager, the code saves a reference to the Manager object and uses Exit For to stop looping.

```
Dim a_manager As Manager

For Each emp As Employee in employees
    If TypeOf emp Is Manager Then
        a_manager = CType(emp, Manager)
        Exit For
    End If
Next emp
```

The Continue For statement makes the loop jump back to its For statement, fetch the next object from the collection, and start the loop over again. This is particularly useful if the program doesn't need to execute the rest of the steps within the loop and wants to quickly start the next iteration.

You should not rely on the value of the looping variable outside of the loop, even if you declare the variable before the loop begins. After the loop ends in the current version of Visual Basic .NET, the variable contains a reference to the last object the code processed. If the code uses an Exit For statement, the variable refers to whatever object the code was processing at the time. If the loop examines all the objects in the group and finishes normally, the variable refers to the last object in the collection.

This behavior is different from previous versions of Visual Basic, however. In Visual Basic 6, the looping variable is set to Nothing if the loop examines all the collection's objects and finishes normally.

To avoid confusion and possibly subtle bugs in future versions of Visual Basic, do not use the control variable outside of the loop. If you must use one of the objects in the collection later, save a reference to it in a variable declared outside of the loop, as shown in the previous example.

You cannot declare the same variable both inside and outside of a For Each loop. If you declare a variable in the For Each statement, the variable's scope is limited to the loop, and code outside of the loop cannot access the variable.

Declaring the variable in the For Each statement is a good practice. It limits the scope of the variable, so you don't need to remember what the variable is for in other pieces of code. It keeps the variable's declaration close to the code where it is used, so it's easier to remember the variable's data type. It also lets you more easily reuse counter variables without fear of confusion. If you have several loops that need an arbitrarily named looping variable, they can all declare and use the variable obj, person or whatever else makes sense without interfering with each other.

Your code can change the value of the control variable inside the loop, but that has no effect on the loop's progress through the collection or array. The loop resets the variable to the next object inside the group and continues as if you had never changed the variable's value.

To avoid confusion, you should not change the control variable's value, because that may lead other programmers to believe that you are trying to change the way the loop works through the group of objects. If you must do something more elaborate with an object, assign the control variable to a temporary variable and work with that instead. If you need to move arbitrarily through the group, consider using a While loop instead of a For Each loop.

Changes to a collection are immediately reflected in the loop. For example, if the statements inside the loop add a new object to the end of the collection, then the loop continues until it processes the new item. Similarly if the loop's code removes an item from the end of the collection (that it has not yet reached), the loop does not process that item.

The exact effect on the loop depends on whether the item added or removed comes before or after the object the loop is currently processing. For example, if you remove an item before the current item, the loop has already examined that item, so there is no change to the loop. If you remove an item after the current one, the loop doesn't examine it. If you remove the current item, the loop seems to get confused and exits without raising an error.

Additions and deletions to an array are *not* reflected in the loop. If you use a ReDim statement to add items to the end of the array, the loop does not process them. If you try to access those objects, however, the program generates an "Index was outside the bounds of the array" error.

If you use ReDim to remove items from the end of the array, the loop processes those items anyway! If you modify the values in the array, for example, you change an object's properties or set an array entry to an entirely new object, the loop sees the changes.

To avoid all these possible sources of confusion, don't modify a collection or array while a For Each loop is examining its contents.

One common scenario when dealing with collections is examining every item in the collection and removing some of them. If you use a For Each loop, removing the loop's current item makes the loop exit prematurely.

Another approach that seems like it might work (but doesn't) is to use a For Next loop, as shown in the following code. If the code removes an object from the collection, the loop skips the next item because its index has been reduced by one and the loop has already passed that position in the collection. Worse still, the control variable i will increase until it reaches the original value of employees.Count. If the loop has removed any objects, the collection no longer holds that many items. The code tries to access an index beyond the end of the collection and throws an error.

```
Dim emp As Employee

For i As Integer = 1 To employees.Count
    emp = CType(employees(i), Employee)
    If emp.IsManager Then employees.Remove(i)
Next i
```

One solution to this problem is to use a For Next loop to examine the collection's objects in reverse order, as shown in the following example. In this version, the code never needs to use an index after it has been deleted because it is counting backwards. The index of an object in the collection also doesn't change unless that object has already been examined by the loop. The loop examines every item exactly once, no matter which objects are removed.

```
For i As Integer = employees.Count To 1 Step -1
    emp = CType(employees(i), Employee)
    If emp.IsManager Then employees.Remove(i)
Next i
```

Enumerators

An *enumerator* is an object that lets you move through the objects contained by some sort of container class. For example, collections, arrays, and hash tables provide enumerators. This section discusses enumerators for collections, but the same ideas apply for other classes that provide enumerators.

You can use an enumerator to view the objects in a collection but not to modify the collection itself. You can use the enumerator to alter the objects in the collection, but you can generally not use it to add, remove, or rearrange the objects in the collection.

Initially, an enumerator is positioned before the first item in the collection. Your code can use the enumerator's MoveNext method to step to the next object in the collection. MoveNext returns True if it successfully moves to a new object or False if there are no more objects in the collection.

The Reset method restores the enumerator to its original position before the first object, so you can step through the collection again.

The Current method returns the object that the enumerator is currently reading. Note that Current returns a generic Object, so you will probably need to use CType to convert the result into a more specific data type before you use it. Invoking Current throws an error if the enumerator is not currently reading any object. That happens when the enumerator is first created and it is before the first object, and after the enumerator has moved past the last object.

The following example uses an enumerator to loop through the items in a collection named m_Employees. It declares an Employee variable named emp and an IEnumerator object named employee_enumerator. It uses the collection's GetEnumerator method to obtain an enumerator for the collection. The program then enters a While loop. If employee_enumerator.MoveNext returns True, the enumerator has successfully moved to the next object in the collection. As long as it has read an object, the program uses CType to convert the generic object returned by Current into an Employee object, and it displays the Employee object's Title, FirstName, and LastName values. When it has finished processing all of the objects in the collection, employee_enumerator.MoveNext returns False and the While loop ends.

```
Dim emp As Employee
Dim employee_enumerator As IEnumerator
employee_enumerator = m_Employees.GetEnumerator()
Do While (employee_enumerator.MoveNext)
    emp = CType(employee_enumerator.Current, Employee)
    Debug.WriteLine(emp.Title & " " & emp.FirstName & " " & emp.LastName)
Loop
```

A For Each loop provides roughly the same access to the items in a container class as an enumerator. Under some circumstances, however, an enumerator may provide a more natural way to loop through a container class than a For Each loop. For example, an enumerator can skip several items without examining them closely. You can also use an enumerator's Reset method to restart the enumeration. To restart a For Each loop, you would need to repeat the loop, possibly by placing it inside yet another loop that determined when to stop looping.

The Visual Basic documentation states that an enumerator is valid only as long as you do not modify the collection. If you add or remove an object to or from the collection, the enumerator throws an "invalid operation" exception the next time you use it. In at least some cases, however, this doesn't seem to be true, and an enumerator can still work even if you modify its collection. This could lead to extremely confusing situations, however. To avoid unnecessary confusion, do not modify a collection while you are accessing it with an enumerator.

The IEnumerable interface defines the features needed for enumerators so any class that implements the IEnumerable interface provides enumerators. Any class that supports For Each must also implement the IEnumerable interface, so any class that supports For Each also supports enumerators. A few of the classes that implement IEnumerable include the following:

Array	ArrayList	ControlCollection	Collection
CollectionBase	DataView	DictionaryBase	DictionaryEntries
Hashtable	HybridDictionary	ListDictionary	MessageQueue
OdbcDataReader	OleDbDataReader	OracleDataReader	Queue
ReadOnlyCollectionBase	SortedList	SqlDataReader	Stack
String	StringCollection	StringDictionary	TableCellCollection
TableRowCollection	XmlNode	XmlNodeList	

Iterators

An *iterator* is similar in concept to an enumerator. It also provides methods that allow you to step through the objects in some sort of container object. Iterators are more specialized than enumerators and work with a particular kind of class. While you can use a generic IEnumerator object to step through the items contained in any class that implements IEnumerable (an array, collection, hash table, or whatever), a certain iterator class is associated with a specific container class.

For example, a `GraphicsPath` object represents a series of connected lines and curves. A `GraphicsPathIterator` object can step through the line and curve data contained in a `GraphicsPath` object.

Iterators are much more specialized than enumerators. How you use them depends on what you need to do and on the kind of iterator, so they are not described in detail here.

Do Loop Statements

Visual Basic .NET supports three basic forms of `Do Loop` statements. The first form is a loop that repeats forever. The syntax is as follows:

```
Do
    statements
    [Exit Do]
    statements
    [Continue Do]
    statements
Loop
```

This kind of `Do Loop` executes the code it contains until the program somehow ends the loop. The following loop processes work orders. It calls the `WorkOrderAvailable` function to see if a work order is available. If an order is available, the code calls `ProcessWorkOrder` to process it. The code then repeats the loop to look for another work order.

```
Do
    ' See if a work order is available.
    If WorkOrderAvailable() Then
        ' Process the next work order.
        ProcessWorkOrder()
    End If
Loop
```

This example keeps checking for work orders forever. Most programs include some method for the loop to end so that the program can eventually stop. For example, the loop might use the `Exit Do` statement described shortly to end the loop if the user clicks a Stop button.

The second and third forms of `Do Loop` statements both include a test to determine whether they should continue looping. The difference between the two versions is where they place the test.

The second version of `Do Loop` places its test at the beginning, so the test is evaluated before the code is executed even once. If the test initially indicates that the loop should not continue, the statements inside the loop are never executed. The syntax is as follows:

```
Do {While | Until} condition
    statements
    [Exit Do]
    statements
    [Continue Do]
    statements
Loop
```

The final version of Do Loop places its test at the end. In this version, the statements inside the loop are executed before the loop performs its test. That means that the code is always executed at least once. The syntax is as follows:

```
Do
    statements
    [Exit Do]
    statements
    [Continue Do]
    statements
Loop {While | Until} condition
```

If the code uses the While keyword, the loop executes as long as the condition is true. If the code uses the Until keyword, the loop executes as long as the condition is false. Note that the statement Until condition is equivalent to While Not condition. Visual Basic provides these two variations so that you can pick the one that makes your code more readable. Use the one that makes the most sense to you.

The Exit Do statement allows the program to leave a loop before it would normally finish. For example, the following code uses an enumerator to look through the m_Employees collection. If it finds an Employee object that has title Manager, it exits the Do While Loop. Note that the loop eventually exits whether it finds a manager or not, so the code must later check to see if it found a manager.

```
Dim emp As Employee
Dim employee_enumerator As IEnumerator
employee_enumerator = m_Employees.GetEnumerator()
Do While (employee_enumerator.MoveNext)
    emp = CType(employee_enumerator.Current, Employee)
    If emp.Title = "Manager" Then Exit Do
Loop

' Process the Manager.
If emp.Title = "Manager" Then ...
```

The Exit Do statement exits only the Do Loop immediately surrounding the statement. For example, the following code makes the variable R run from 1 to 10. For each value of R, the program makes variable C run from 1 to 100. Within the inner loop, the program checks cost(R, C). If that value is greater than 100, the program displays R, C, and cost(R, C) and then uses Exit Do to stop the inner loop. The loop over C ends and the code continues with the next value of R.

```
R = 1
Do While R < 10
    C = 1
    Do While C < 100
        If cost(R, C) > 100 Then
            Debug.WriteLine("(" & R & ", " & C & ") = " & cost(R, C))
        End If
    Loop
Loop
```

The Continue Do statement makes the loop jump back to its Do statement and start the loop over again. This is particularly useful if the program doesn't need to execute the rest of the steps within the loop and wants to quickly start the next iteration. Unlike a For loop, the Do loop does not automatically increment a looping variable or move to the next object in a collection. The code must explicitly change the loop's condition before calling `Continue Do` or else the loop will continue forever.

While End

A `While End` loop is equivalent to a `Do While Loop`. The syntax is as follows:

```
While condition
    statements
    [Exit While]
    statements
    [Continue While]
    statements
End While
```

This is equivalent to the following:

```
Do While condition
    statements
    [Exit Do]
    statements
Loop
```

The `End While` statement exits a `While End` loop just as an `Exit Do` statement exits a `Do While Loop`.

The difference between `While End` and `Do While Loop` is stylistic, and you can use whichever seems clearer to you. Because `Do Loop` provides more flexibility, having four different versions using `While` or `Until` at the start or finish of the loop, you might want to stick to them for consistency's sake.

Previous versions of Visual Basic ended `While` loops with the `Wend` keyword, as in the following Visual Basic 6 code:

```
i = 1
While i < 5
    Debug.Print i
    i = i + 1
Wend
```

The `Wend` keyword is no longer supported, so you should use `End While` instead.

Exit and Continue

The Exit statement lets you end a loop early. The Continue statement lets you jump to the start of a loop before reaching its end.

Both of these statements work on the innermost loop of the appropriate type. For example, the following code contains a `For` loop, that contains `Do` loop, that contains a second `For` loop. Within the innermost loop, an `Exit For` statement exits the inner `For` loop. An `Exit Do` statement exits the `Do` loop. There is no simple Exit statement that can exit the outer `For` loop from this position.

```
For i As Integer = 1 To 3
    Dim j As Integer = 1
    Do While j < 3
        For k As Integer = 1 To 3
            '...
            If test1 Then Exit For ' Exits the For K loop.
            '...
            If test2 Then Exit Do ' Exits the Do.
            '...
        Next k
    Loop
Next i
```

Similarly, a Continue statement continues the innermost loop of the appropriate type: For, Do, or While.

GoTo

A GoTo statement unconditionally tells the program to jump to a specific location in the code. Because it tells the program what to do, it is a program control statement. The syntax is as follows:

```
GoTo line_label
...
line_label:
...
```

While GoTo by itself isn't a decision statement, it is often used to mimic a decision statement. For example, the following code fragment uses GoTo to mimic an If Then Else statement. It examines the purchase_total variable. If purchase_total is less than 1000, the code jumps to the line labeled SmallOrder. If purchase_total is greater than or equal to 1000, the program continues to execute the code that processes a larger order.

```
If purchase_total < 1000 Then GoTo SmallOrder
' Process a large order.
...
Exit Sub

SmallOrder:
' Process a small order.
...
```

The following code does roughly the same thing as the previous version but without the GoTo statement:

```
If purchase_total < 1000 Then
    ' Process a large order.
    ...
Else
    ' Process a small order.
    ...
End If
```

Similarly, GoTo is sometimes used to build a loop. The following code uses GoTo to jump backward in the code to call subroutine DoSomething 10 times:

```
    Dim i As Integer = 1
StartLoop:
    DoSomething()
    i += 1
    If i <= 10 Then GoTo StartLoop
```

The following code does the same thing without the GoTo statement:

```
For i As Integer = 1 To 10
    DoSomething()
Next i
```

The problem with the GoTo statement is its flexibility. By using GoTo in a haphazard way, an undisciplined programmer can make the program jump all over the place with little rhyme or reason. This can lead to "spaghetti code" (so called because a diagram showing the program's flow of control can look like a pile of spaghetti) that is extremely difficult to understand, debug, and maintain.

Many programming groups prohibit any use of GoTo because it can lead to this kind of code. Some even believe GoTo should be removed from the Visual Basic language. You can always use If Then Else statements, For Next loops, While loops, and other control statements in place of GoTo statements, so GoTo is not absolutely necessary.

However, some programmers feel that GoTo simplifies code under certain very specific circumstances. The following code begins by performing some sort of initialization. It may open databases, create temporary files, connect to the Internet, and perform other startup chores. It then executes a series of tasks, each of which may fail or otherwise make it pointless for the program to continue. If any of these steps sets the variable should_stop to True, the program uses a GoTo statement to jump to its clean up code. This code closes any open database, deletes temporary files, closes permanent files, and performs any other necessary clean up chores.

```
    ' Get started, open database, open files, etc.
    Initialize()

    ' Perform a long series of tasks.
    DoStuff1()
    If should_stop Then GoTo CleanUp

    DoStuff2()
    If should_stop Then GoTo CleanUp

    DoStuff3()
    If should_stop Then GoTo CleanUp

    ...

CleanUp:
    ' Close database, delete tempporary files, etc.
    PerformCleanUp()
```

The GoTo statement in this code lets the program jump to the clean-up code any time it needs to stop performing its tasks. That may be because a task failed, the user canceled the operation, or all the tasks are finished.

Note that this is a very specific use of GoTo. The code only jumps forward, never backward. It also only jumps to clean-up code, not to some arbitrary point in the code. These facts help make the GoTo statement easier to understand and prevent spaghetti code.

The following code does the same thing as the previous version without using GoTo. At each step, the program checks the value of should_stop to see if it should continue working through its tasks.

```
' Get started, open database, open files, etc.
Initialize()

' Perform a long series of tasks.
DoStuff1()

If Not should_stop Then DoStuff2()

If Not should_stop Then DoStuff3()

' Close database, delete tempporary files, etc.
PerformCleanUp()
```

The following code shows another version that doesn't use GoTo. This version places the code that formerly contained the GoTo statement in a new subroutine. Instead of using GoTo, this routine uses Exit Sub to stop performing tasks early if necessary.

```
Sub DoWork()
    ' Get started, open database, open files, etc.
    Initialize()

    ' Perform all of the tasks.
    PerformTasks()

    ' Close database, delete tempporary files, etc.
    PerformCleanUp()
End Sub

' Perform a long series of tasks.
Sub PerformTasks()
    DoStuff1()
    If should_stop Then Exit Sub

    DoStuff2()
    If should_stop Then Exit Sub

    DoStuff3()
    If should_stop Then Exit Sub
End Sub
```

Conceptually, an `Exit Sub` statement is little different from a `GoTo` statement. After all, it, too, is an unconditional jump command. However, `Exit Sub` has a very specific, well-known effect: It makes the program stop executing the current subroutine. It cannot make the program jump around arbitrarily, possibly leading to spaghetti code.

If you ever feel tempted to use `GoTo`, take a few moments to think about ways you might rewrite the code. If the only ways you can think of to rewrite the code are more confusing than the original version, go ahead and use `GoTo`. You should probably add some fairly detailed comments to ensure that the `GoTo` statement doesn't cause trouble later.

Summary

Control statements form the heart of any program. Decision statements determine what commands are executed, and looping statements determine how many times they are executed.

Single-line and multiline `If Then` statements, as well as `Select Case`, are the most commonly used decision statements. `IIf` and `Choose` statements are often more confusing and sometimes slower, so usually you should use `If Then` and `Select Case` statements instead. Under some specific circumstances, however, `IIf` and `Choose` may make your code more readable. Use your judgment and pick the method that makes the most sense in your application.

`For Next`, `For Each`, and `Do Loop` are the most common looping statements. Some container classes also support enumerators that let you step through the items in the container. An enumerator can be more natural than a `For Each` loop under some circumstances.

`While End` is equivalent to `Do While Loop`. You can use whichever you think makes more sense, although you might want to use `Do While Loop` because it is more consistent with the other forms of `Do Loop`.

Finally, the `GoTo` statement is often used in a decision statement or to create a loop. Unfortunately, undisciplined use of `GoTo` statements can lead to "spaghetti code" that is extremely hard to understand, debug, and maintain. To avoid later frustration, you should comment `GoTo` statements whenever possible. Some programmers use `GoTo` in very specialized cases, while others avoid it at all costs. You can always rewrite code to avoid `GoTo` statements, and usually that is better in the long run.

Using the control statements described in this chapter, you can build extremely complex and powerful applications. In fact, you can build applications that are so complex that it is difficult to ensure that they work correctly. Even a relatively simple application sometimes encounters errors. For example, it might try to use an array index that lies outside of the array's bounds or to modify a collection while using an enumerator for it. Chapter 8, "Error Handling," explains how you can protect an application from these and other unexpected errors and let it take action to correct any problems or at least not crash.

8

Error Handling

While it is theoretically possible to write a program that perfectly predicts every possible situation that it might encounter, in practice that's very difficult for nontrivial programs. For large applications, it is very difficult to plan for every eventuality. Errors in the program's design and implementation can introduce bugs that give unexpected results. Users and corrupted databases may give the application values that it doesn't know how to manage.

Similarly, changing requirements over time may introduce data that the application was never intended to handle. The "Y2K bug" is a good example. When engineers wrote accounting, auto registration, financial, inventory, and other systems in the 1960s and 1970s, they didn't think their programs would still be running in the year 2000. At the time, disk storage and memory were relatively expensive, so they stored years as 2-byte values (for example, "89" meant "1989"). When the year 2000 rolled around, the applications couldn't tell whether the value 01 meant the year 1901 or 2001. In one humorous case, an auto registration system started issuing "horseless carriage" license plates to new cars because it thought cars built in 00 must be antiques.

The Y2K problem wasn't really a bug. It was a case of software used with data that wasn't part of its original design.

This chapter explains different kinds of exceptional conditions that can arise in an application. These range from unplanned data (as in the Y2K problem) to bugs where the code is just plain wrong. With some advanced planning, you can build a robust application that can keep running gracefully, even when the unexpected happens.

Bugs versus Unplanned Conditions

Several different types of unplanned condition can derail an otherwise high-quality application. How you should handle these conditions depends on their nature.

For this discussion, a *bug* is a mistake in the application code. Some bugs become apparent right away and are easy to fix. These usually include simple typographic errors and cases where you misuse an object (for example, by using the wrong control property). Other bugs are subtler and may only be detected long after they occur. For example, a data-entry routine might place invalid characters into a rarely used field in a `Customer` object. Only later when the program tries to access that field will you discover the problem. This kind of bug is difficult to track down and fix, but there are some proactive steps you can take to make these sorts of bugs easier to find.

As an historical note, the term "bug" has been used since at least the time of the telegraph to mean some sort of defect. Probably the origin of the term in computer science was an actual moth that was caught between two relays in an early computer in 1945. For a bit more information including a picture of this first computer bug, see www.jamesshuggins.com/h/tek1/first_computer_bug.htm.

An *unplanned condition* is some predictable condition that you don't want to happen, but that you know could happen despite your best efforts. For example, there are many ways that a simple printing operation can fail. The printer might be unplugged, disconnected from its computer, disconnected from the network, out of toner, out of paper, experiencing a memory fault, clogged by a paper jam, or just be plain broken. These are not bugs, because the application software is not at fault. There is some condition outside of the program that must be fixed.

Another common unplanned condition occurs when the user enters invalid data. You may want the user to enter a value between 1 and 10 in a text box, but the user might enter 0, 9999 or "lunch" instead.

Catching Bugs

By definition, bugs are unplanned. No programmer sits down and thinks, "Perhaps I'll put a bug in this variable declaration."

Because bugs are unpredictable, you cannot know ahead of time where a bug will lie. However, you can watch for behavior in the program that indicates that a bug may be present. For example, suppose that you have a subroutine that sorts a purchase order's items by cost. If the routine receives an order with 100,000 items, something is probably wrong. If one of the items is a computer keyboard with a price of $73 trillion, something is probably wrong. If the customer who placed the order doesn't exist, something is probably wrong.

This routine could go ahead and sort the 100,000 items with prices ranging from a few cents to $73 trillion. Later, the program would try to print a 5000-page invoice with no shipping or billing address. Only then would the developers realize that there is a problem.

Rather than trying to work around the problematic data, it would be better for the sorting routine to immediately tell developers that something is wrong so that they can start trying to find the cause of the problem. Bugs are easier to find the sooner they are detected. This bug will be easier to find if the sorting routine notices it, rather than waiting until the application tries to print an invalid invoice. Your routines can protect themselves and the program as a whole by proactively validating their inputs and outputs, and reporting anything suspicious to developers.

Some developers object to making routines spend considerable effort validating data that they "know" is correct. After all, one routine generated this data and passed it to another, so you know that it is correct because the first routine did its job properly. That's only true if every routine that touches the data works perfectly. Since it's difficult for any nontrivial program to anticipate every possible condition, you cannot assume that all the routines are perfect and that the data remains uncorrupted.

Many companies these days use automated testing tools to try to flush out problems early. Regression testing tools can execute code to verify that its outcome isn't changed after you have made modifications to other parts of the application. If you build a suite of testing routines to validate data and subroutines' results, you may be able to work them into an automated testing system, too.

To prevent validation code from slowing down the application, you can use the Debug object's Assert method to check for strange conditions. When you are debugging the program, these statements throw an error if they detect something suspicious. When you make a release build to send to customers, the Debug.Assert code is removed from the application. That makes the application faster and doesn't inflict cryptic error messages on the user.

You can also use the DEBUG, TRACE, and CONFIG compiler constants to add other input and output validation code.

The following subroutine starts by validating its input. It verifies that the Order object it is passed has an Items collection and that its Customer variable is not Nothing. It also verifies that the order contains fewer than 100 items. If a larger order comes along during testing, developers can increase this number to 200 or whatever value makes sense, but there's no need to start with an unreasonably large default.

Before the subroutine exits, it loops through the sorted items to verify that they are correctly sorted. If any item has cost less than the one before, the program throws an error. Because this test is contained within an #If DEBUG Then statement, this code is removed from release builds.

```
Private Sub SortOrderItems(ByVal the_order As Order)
    ' Validate input.
    Debug.Assert(the_order.Items IsNot Nothing, "No items in order")
    Debug.Assert(the_order.Customer IsNot Nothing, "No customer in order")
    Debug.Assert(the_order.Items.Count < 100, "Too many order items")
    ...

    ' Sort the items.
    ...

    ' Validate output.
#If DEBUG Then
    ' Verify that the items are sorted.
    Dim order_item1 As OrderItem
    Dim order_item2 As OrderItem
    order_item1 = DirectCast(the_order.Items(1), OrderItem)
    For i As Integer = 2 To the_order.Items.Count
        order_item2 = DirectCast(the_order.Items(i), OrderItem)
        Debug.Assert(order_item1.Price <= order_item2.Price, _
            "Order items not properly sorted")
        order_item1 = order_item2
    Next i
#End If
End Sub
```

After you have tested the application long enough, you should have discovered most of these types of errors. When you make the release build, the compiler automatically removes the validation code, making the finished executable smaller and faster.

Catching Unexpected Conditions

While you don't want an unexpected condition to happen, with some careful thought, you can predict where an unexpected condition might occur. Typically, these situations arise when the program must work with something outside of its own code. For example, when the program needs to access a file, printer, Web page, floppy disk, or CD-ROM, that item may be unavailable. Similarly, whenever the program takes input from the user, the user may enter the wrong data.

Notice how this differs from the bugs described in the previous section. After sufficient testing, you should have found and fixed most of the bugs. No amount of testing can remove the possibility of unexpected conditions. No matter what code you use, the user may still remove a floppy disk from the drive before the program is ready.

Whenever you know that an unexpected condition might occur, you should write code to protect the program from dangerous conditions. It is generally better to test for these conditions explicitly rather than simply attempting to perform whatever action you were planning and then catching an error if one occurs. Testing for problem conditions generally gives you more complete information about what's wrong. It's also usually faster than catching an error because the structured error handling described shortly comes with considerable overhead.

For example, the following statement sets an integer variable using the value the user entered in a text box:

```
Dim num_items As Integer = Integer.Parse(txtNumItems.Text)
```

The user might enter a valid value in the text box. Unfortunately, the user may also enter something that is not a number, a value that is too big to fit in an integer, or zero or a negative number when you are expecting a positive number. The user may even leave the field blank.

The following code shows an improved version of this declaration. It checks that the field is not blank and uses the IsNumeric function to verify that the field contains a vaguely numeric value. Unfortunately, the IsNumeric function doesn't exactly match the behavior of functions such as Integer.Parse. IsNumeric returns False for values such as &H10, which is a valid hexadecimal value that Integer.Parse can correctly interpret. IsNumeric also returns True for values such as 123456789012345 that lie outside of the values allowed by integers. Because IsNumeric doesn't exactly match Integer.Parse, the program still needs to use a Try Catch block to protect itself when it actually tries to convert the string into an integer. The code finishes by verifying that the value lies within a reasonable bound. If the value passes all of these checks, the code uses the value.

```
' Check for blank entry.
Dim num_items_txt As String = txtNumItems.Text
If num_items_txt.Length < 1 Then
    MessageBox.Show("Please enter Num Items")
    txtNumItems.Focus()
    Exit Sub
End If

' See if it's numeric.
If Not IsNumeric(num_items_txt) Then
    MessageBox.Show("Num Items must be a number")
    txtNumItems.Select(0, num_items_txt.Length)
    txtNumItems.Focus()
    Exit Sub
End If

' Assign the value.
```

```
Dim num_items As Integer
Try
    num_items = Integer.Parse(txtNumItems.Text)
Catch ex As Exception
    MessageBox.Show("Error in Num Items." & vbCrLf & ex.Message)
    txtNumItems.Select(0, num_items_txt.Length)
    txtNumItems.Focus()
    Exit Sub
End Try

' Check that the value is between 1 and 100.
If num_items < 1 Or num_items > 100 Then
    MessageBox.Show("Num Items must be between 1 and 100")
    txtNumItems.Select(0, num_items_txt.Length)
    txtNumItems.Focus()
    Exit Sub
End If
```

A typical subroutine might need to read and validate many values, and retyping this code would be cumbersome. A better solution is to move it into the function shown in the following code:

```
' If the TextBox doesn't contain an integer between min_value and max_value,
' display an error message, set focus to the TextBox, and return False.
' Otherwise return True and return the integer through the ByRef
' parameter result.
Private Function IsValidInteger(ByRef result As Integer, _
 ByVal txt As TextBox, ByVal field_name As String, _
 Optional ByVal min_value As Integer = Integer.MinValue, _
 Optional ByVal max_value As Integer = Integer.MaxValue) As Boolean

    ' Check for blank entry.
    Dim num_items_txt As String = txt.Text
    If num_items_txt.Length < 1 Then
        MessageBox.Show("Please enter " & field_name & ".")
        txt.Focus()
        Return False
    End If

    ' See if it's numeric.
    If Not IsNumeric(num_items_txt) Then
        MessageBox.Show(field_name & " must be a number.")
        txt.Select(0, num_items_txt.Length)
        txt.Focus()
        Return False
    End If

    ' Assign the value.
    Try
        result = Integer.Parse(txt.Text)
    Catch ex As Exception
        MessageBox.Show("Error in " & field_name & "." & _
            vbCrLf & ex.Message)
        txt.Select(0, num_items_txt.Length)
        txt.Focus()
        Return False
```

```
        End Try

        ' Check that the value is between min_value and max_value.
        If result < min_value Or result > max_value Then
            MessageBox.Show(field_name & " must be between " & _
                min_value.ToString & " and " & max_value.ToString & ".")
            txt.Select(0, num_items_txt.Length)
            txt.Focus()
            Return False
        End If

        ' The value is okay.
        Return True
    End Function
```

Now the program can use this function, as in the following code:

```
Dim num_items As Integer
If Not IsValidInteger(num_items, txtNumItems, "Num Items", 1, 100) Then Exit Sub
...
```

You can write similar routines to validate other types of data fields such as phone numbers, e-mail addresses, street addresses, and so forth.

Global Exception Handling

Normally, you should try to catch an error as close as possible to the place where it occurs. If an error occurs in a particular subroutine, it will be easiest to fix the bug if you catch it in that subroutine.

However, bugs often arise in unexpected places. Unless you protect every subroutine with error-handling code (a fairly common strategy), a bug may arise in code that you have not protected. In early versions of Visual Basic, you could not catch the bug, so the application crashed. In Visual Basic 2005, however, you can define a global error handler to catch any bug that isn't caught by other error-handling code.

To define application-level event handlers such as this one, double-click My Project in the Project Explorer. Open the Application tab and click the View Application Events button. This opens a code window for application-level events.

In the left drop-down list, select "(MyApplication Events)." Then in the right drop-down list, you can select one of several events including NetworkAvailabilityChanged, Shutdown, Startup, StartupNextInstance, and UnhandledException. Select the last of these commands to open the UnhandledException event handler.

In the event handler, you can take whatever action is appropriate for the error. Since you probably didn't anticipate the error, there's usually little chance that the program can correct it properly. However, you can at least log the error and possibly save data before shutting down the application.

The event parameter e has an ExitApplication property that you can set to True or False to tell Visual Basic whether the application should terminate.

The following code displays a message giving the unhandled exception's error message. It then sets e.ExitApplication to False, so the program keeps running.

```
Private Sub MyApplication_UnhandledException( _
 ByVal sender As Object, ByVal e As _
 Microsoft.VisualBasic.ApplicationServices.UnhandledExceptionEventArgs) _
 Handles Me.UnhandledException
    MessageBox.Show("Exception caught globally" & vbCrLf & _
        e.Exception.Message)
    e.ExitApplication = False
End Sub
```

When you run the application in the IDE, Visual Basic stops execution in the debugger when it reaches the statement that causes the error. If you run the compiled executable, however, the UnhandledException event fires and the global error-handler runs.

Structured Error Handling

Visual Basic .NET introduced structured error handling using the Try block. The syntax is as follows:

```
Try
    try_statements...
[Catch ex As exception_type_1
    exception_statements_1...]
[Catch ex As exception_type_2
    exception_statements_2...]
...
[Catch
    final_exception_statements...]
[Finally
    finally_statements...]
End Try
```

The program executes the code in the *try_statements* block. If any of that code throws an exception, the program jumps to the first Catch statement.

If the exception matches *exception_type_1*, the program executes the code in *exception_statements_1*. The exception type might match the Catch statement's exception class exactly, or it might be a subclass of the listed class. For example, suppose that the code in the *try_statements* block performs a calculation that divides by zero. That raises a DivideByZeroException. That class inherits from the ArithmeticException class, which inherits from SystemException, which inherits from Exception. That means the code would stop at the first Catch statement it finds that looks for DivideByZeroException, ArithmeticException, or SystemException.

If the raised exception does not match the first exception type, the program checks the next Catch statement. The program keeps comparing the exception to Catch statements until it finds one that applies, or it runs out of Catch statements.

If no Catch statement matches the exception, the exception "bubbles up" to the next level in the call stack and Visual Basic moves to the routine that called the current one. If that routine has appropriate error-handling code, it deals with the error. If that routine can't catch the error, then the exception bubbles up again until Visual Basic eventually either finds error-handling code that can catch the exception, or it runs off the top of the call stack. If it runs off the call stack, Visual Basic calls the global UnhandledException event handler described in the previous section, if one exists. If there is no UnhandledException event handler, the program crashes.

If you include a Catch statement with no exception type, that block matches any exception. If the raised exception doesn't match any of the previous exception types, the program executes the *final_exception_statements* block of code. Note that the statement Catch ex As Exception also matches all exceptions, so it's just good as Catch by itself. It also gives you easy access to the exception object's properties and methods.

There are several ways you can figure out what exception classes to use in Catch statements. First, you can spend a lot of time digging through the online help. An easier method is to let the program crash and then look at the error message it produces. Figure 8-1 shows the error message a program throws when it tries to convert the non-numeric string "TextBox1" into an integer with Integer.Parse. From this message it's easy to see that the program should look for an FormatException.

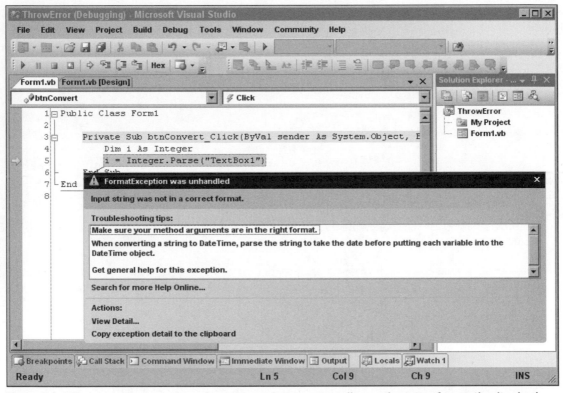

Figure 8-1: When a program crashes, the message it generates tells you the type of exception it raised.

Another way to decide what types of exceptions to catch is to place a final generic Catch ex As Exception statement at the end of the Catch list. Place code inside that Catch block that displays either the exception's type name (use TypeName) or the result of its ToString method. When you encounter new exception types, you can give them their own Catch statements and take more specific action appropriate to different exception types.

In some cases, it may not be possible to take meaningful action when you catch certain exceptions. For example, if a program uses up all of the available memory, Visual Basic throws an OutOfMemoryException. If there is no memory available, then you may have trouble doing anything useful. Similarly, if there's a problem with the file system, you may be unable to write error descriptions into a log file.

After it has finished running the code in *try_statements* and it has executed any necessary exception code in a Catch block, the program executes the code in *finally_statements*. You can use the Finally section to execute code whether the code in *try_statements* succeeds or fails.

You do not need to include any Catch statements in a Try block, but leaving them all out defeats the Try block's purpose. If the *try_statements* raise an error, the program doesn't have any error code to execute, so it sends the error up the call stack. Eventually, the program finds an active error handler or the error pops off the top of the stack and the program crashes. You may as well not bother with the Try block if you aren't going to use any Catch sections.

A Try block must include at least one Catch or Finally section, although those sections do not need to contain any code. For example, the following Try block calls subroutine DoSomething and uses an empty Catch section to ignore any errors that occur:

```
Try
    DoSomething()
Catch
End Try
```

Using an empty Finally section is legal but not terribly useful. The following code doesn't protect the program from any exceptions and doesn't do anything in the Finally block. You may as well just call the DoSomething subroutine without a Try block.

```
Try
    DoSomething()
Finally
End Try
```

Exception Objects

When a Catch statement catches an exception, its exception variable contains information about the error that raised the exception. Different exception classes may provide different features, but they all provide the basic features defined by the Exception class from which they are all derived. The following table lists the most commonly used Exception class properties and methods.

Item	Purpose
InnerException	The exception that caused the current exception. For example, suppose that you write a tool library that catches an exception and then throws a new custom exception describing the problem in terms of your library. You should set InnerException to the exception that you caught before you throw the new exception.
Message	Returns a brief message that describes the exception.
Source	Returns the name of the application or object that threw the exception.
StackTrace	Returns a string containing a stack trace giving the program's location when the error occurred.
TargetSite	Returns the name of the method that threw the exception.
ToString	Returns a string describing the exception and including the stack trace.

In the following code, the btnCalculate_Click event handler calls subroutine CalculateEmployeeSalaries within a Try block. That routine calls subroutine CheckVacationPay, which performs a calculation that divides by zero. When the program encounters the error, it looks for an active error handler in subroutine CheckVacationPay. It doesn't find one so the code travels up the call stack to subroutine CalculateEmployeeSalaries and looks for an error handler there. Again, the program doesn't find one, so it moves up the call stack to subroutine Calculate. There it finds an active Try block so it jumps to the block's Catch statements. The Catch statement here looks for a generic Exception object so it matches any exception. The code displays the exception's Message, StackTrace, and ToString values.

```
Private Sub btnCalculate_Click(ByVal sender As System.Object, _
 ByVal e As System.EventArgs) Handles btnCalculate.Click
    Try
        CalculateEmployeeSalaries()
    Catch ex As Exception
        Debug.WriteLine("***********")
        Debug.WriteLine(ex.Message)
        Debug.WriteLine("***********")
        Debug.WriteLine(ex.StackTrace)
        Debug.WriteLine("***********")
        Debug.WriteLine(ex.ToString)
        Debug.WriteLine("***********")
    End Try
End Sub

Private Sub CalculateEmployeeSalaries()
    CheckVacationPay()
End Sub

Private Sub CheckVacationPay()
    Dim i As Integer
    Dim j As Integer

    i = 1 \ j
End Sub
```

The following text shows this program's output. The exception's `Message` property returns the string "Attempted to divide by zero." The `StackTrace` method returned a series of strings listing the routines that called each other on the way to the error. The lines are broken to fit here but each appears on a single line in the program's actual output. Each line shows the file and line number where the subroutine calls occurred. This program was called `StackTraceTest` so that name prefixes all of the routine names. For instance, `StackTraceTest.Form1.CheckVacationPay` is the `CheckVacationPay` subroutine in the Form1 module in project StackTraceTest. The exception's `ToString` method returned a brief message describing the error followed by a stack trace.

```
***********
Attempted to divide by zero.
***********
    at ShowExceptionInfo.Form1.CheckVacationPay() in C:\Documents and
Settings\Rod\Local Settings\Application Data\Temporary
Projects\ShowExceptionInfo\Form1.vb:line 25
    at ShowExceptionInfo.Form1.CalculateEmployeeSalaries() in C:\Documents and
Settings\Rod\Local Settings\Application Data\Temporary
Projects\ShowExceptionInfo\Form1.vb:line 18
    at ShowExceptionInfo.Form1.btnCalculate_Click(Object sender, EventArgs e) in
C:\Documents and Settings\Rod\Local Settings\Application Data\Temporary
Projects\ShowExceptionInfo\Form1.vb:line 5
***********
System.DivideByZeroException: Attempted to divide by zero.
    at ShowExceptionInfo.Form1.CheckVacationPay() in C:\Documents and
Settings\Rod\Local Settings\Application Data\Temporary
Projects\ShowExceptionInfo\Form1.vb:line 25
    at ShowExceptionInfo.Form1.CalculateEmployeeSalaries() in C:\Documents and
Settings\Rod\Local Settings\Application Data\Temporary
Projects\ShowExceptionInfo\Form1.vb:line 18
    at ShowExceptionInfo.Form1.btnCalculate_Click(Object sender, EventArgs e) in
C:\Documents and Settings\Rod\Local Settings\Application Data\Temporary
Projects\ShowExceptionInfo\Form1.vb:line 5
***********
```

The `StackTrace` and `ToString` values can help developers find a bug, but they can be intimidating to end users. Even the abbreviated format used by the exception's `Message` property is usually not very useful to a user. If the user clicked the "Find Outstanding Invoices" button, the message "Attempted to divide by zero" doesn't really tell the user what the problem is or what to do about it.

When a program catches an error, a good strategy is to record the full `ToString` message in a log file or e-mail it to a developer. Then display a message that recasts the error message in terms that the user can understand. For example, the program might say the following: "Unable to total outstanding invoices. A bug report has been sent to the development team." The program should then try to continue as gracefully as possible. It may not be able to finish this calculation, but it should not crash, and it should allow the user to continue working on other tasks if possible.

StackTrace Objects

An exception object's `ToString` and `StackTrace` methods return textual representations of the program's stack trace. Your code can also use `StackTrace` objects to examine the program's execution position without generating an error.

In the following code, the `btnCalculate_Click` event handler calls subroutine `CalculateEmployeeSalaries`, which calls subroutine `CheckVacationPay`, which calls subroutine `ShowCallStack`. Subroutine `ShowCallStack` creates a new `CallStack` object, passing it the parameter `True` to indicate that it should generate file name and line number information for the stack trace. The `CallStack` object contains an ordered series of `StackFrame` objects that represent the programs subroutine calls. Subroutine `ShowCallStack` loops through the `StackFrame` objects, displaying the routine names, file names, and line numbers for each.

```
Imports System.Diagnostics
...
Private Sub btnCalculate_Click(ByVal sender As System.Object, _
 ByVal e As System.EventArgs) Handles btnCalculate.Click
    CalculateEmployeeSalaries()
End Sub

Private Sub CalculateEmployeeSalaries()
    CheckVacationPay()
End Sub

Private Sub CheckVacationPay()
    ShowCallStack()
End Sub

' Loop through the call stack from the bottom up.
Private Sub ShowCallStack()
    ' Create a StackTrace object with
    ' file names and line numbers.
    Dim stack_trace As New System.Diagnostics.StackTrace(True)

    ' Display the frame information.
    For i As Integer = 0 To stack_trace.FrameCount - 1
        With stack_trace.GetFrame(i)
            Debug.WriteLine( _
                "Method: " & .GetMethod().ToString & _
                ", File: '" & _
                .GetFileName() & _
                "', Line: " & .GetFileLineNumber())
        End With
    Next i
End Sub
```

The following text shows the program's output. In this example, subroutine `ShowCallStack` was called by `CheckVacationPay`, which was called by `CalculateEmployeeSalaries`, which was called by the `btnCalculate_Click` event handler. Beyond that, the code moves into the Visual Basic system code behind the scenes. Notice that the output does not include a line number or file name for the routines beyond this point. The button's `Click` event handler was called by an `OnClick` routine. This button was triggered by clicking the mouse on the button. You can move farther up the stack to see other hidden system routines all the way through the Windows message loop and back to the call to `ThreadStart`, which started the program running.

```
Method: Void ShowCallStack()
    Line: 21, File: 'C:\VB Prog Ref\CeSrc\Ch08\ShowStackTrace\Form1.vb'
Method: Void CheckVacationPay()
    Line: 14, File: 'C:\VB Prog Ref\CeSrc\Ch08\ShowStackTrace\Form1.vb'
```

```
Method: Void CalculateEmployeeSalaries()
    Line: 10, File: 'C:\VB Prog Ref\CeSrc\Ch08\ShowStackTrace\Form1.vb'
Method: Void btnCalculate_Click(System.Object, System.EventArgs)
    Line: 6, File: 'C:\VB Prog Ref\CeSrc\Ch08\ShowStackTrace\Form1.vb'
Method: Void OnClick(System.EventArgs)
    Line: 0, File: ''
Method: Void OnClick(System.EventArgs)
    Line: 0, File: ''
Method: Void PerformClick()
    Line: 0, File: ''
Method: Boolean ProcessDialogKey(System.Windows.Forms.Keys)
    Line: 0, File: ''
Method: Boolean ProcessDialogKey(System.Windows.Forms.Keys)
    Line: 0, File: ''
Method: Boolean PreProcessMessage(System.Windows.Forms.Message ByRef)
    Line: 0, File: ''
Method: Boolean PreTranslateMessage(MSG ByRef)
    Line: 0, File: ''
Method: Boolean
 System.Windows.Forms.UnsafeNativeMethods.IMsoComponent.FPreTranslateMessage(
 MSG ByRef)
    Line: 0, File: ''
Method: Boolean
 System.Windows.Forms.UnsafeNativeMethods.IMsoComponentManager.FPushMessageLoop(
 Int32, Int32, Int32)
    Line: 0, File: ''
Method: Void RunMessageLoopInner(Int32, System.Windows.Forms.ApplicationContext)
    Line: 0, File: ''
Method: Void RunMessageLoop(Int32, System.Windows.Forms.ApplicationContext)
    Line: 0, File: ''
Method: Void Run(System.Windows.Forms.ApplicationContext)
    Line: 0, File: ''
Method: Void OnRun()
    Line: 0, File: ''
Method: Void DoApplicationModel()
    Line: 0, File: ''
Method: Void Run(System.String[])
    Line: 0, File: ''
Method: Void Main(System.String[])
    Line: 76, File: '17d14f5c-a337-4978-8281-53493378c1071.vb'
Method: Int32 nExecuteAssembly(System.Reflection.Assembly, System.String[])
    Line: 0, File: ''
Method: Int32 ExecuteAssembly(System.String, System.Security.Policy.Evidence,
 System.String[])
    Line: 0, File: ''
Method: Void RunUsersAssembly()
    Line: 0, File: ''
Method: Void ThreadStart_Context(System.Object)
    Line: 0, File: ''
Method: Void Run(System.Threading.ExecutionContext,
 System.Threading.ContextCallback, System.Object)
    Line: 0, File: ''
Method: Void ThreadStart()
    Line: 0, File: ''
```

The `StackTrace` class has a `ToString` method that provides a similar output in a single string, although it omits the file names and line numbers. The `StackFrame` objects contained in the `StackTrace` object also have `ToString` methods that provide output similar to the results shown here.

Throwing Exceptions

In addition to catching exceptions, your program may need to generate its own exceptions. Because handling an exception is called "catching" it, logically, raising an exception must be "throwing" it. (This is just a silly pun. People also catch lions and colds, but I don't think many people throw them. It's as good a term as any, however, so don't worry too much about it.)

To throw an error, the program creates an instance of the type of exception it wants to generate, passing the constructor additional information describing the problem. The program can set other exception fields if you like. For example, it might set the exception's `Source` property to tell any other code that catches the error where it originated. The program then uses the `Throw` statement to raise the error. If an error handler is active somewhere in the call stack, Visual Basic jumps to that point and the error handler processes the exception.

The following code shows how the `DrawableRectangle` class can protect itself against invalid input. The class's constructor takes four arguments: an X and Y position, and a width and height. If the width is less than or equal to zero, the program creates a new `ArgumentException` object. It passes the exception's constructor a description string and the name of the argument that is invalid. After creating the exception object, the program uses the `Throw` statement to raise the error. The code checks the object's new height similarly, but it creates and throws the exception in a single statement to demonstrate another style for throwing an error.

```
Public Class DrawableRectangle
    Public Sub New(ByVal new_x As Integer, ByVal new_y As Integer, _
    ByVal new_width As Integer, ByVal new_height As Integer)
        ' Verify that new_width > 0.
        If new_width <= 0 Then
            ' Throw an ArgumentException.
            Dim ex As New ArgumentException( _
                "DrawableRectangle must have a width greater than zero", _
                    "new_width")
            Throw ex
        End If

        ' Verify that new_height> 0.
        If new_height <= 0 Then
            ' Throw an ArgumentException.
            Throw New ArgumentException( _
                "DrawableRectangle must have a height greater than zero", _
                    "new_height")
        End If

        ' Save the parameter values.
        ...
    End Sub

    ' Other code for this class omitted.
    ...
End Class
```

The following code shows how a program might use a `Try` block to protect itself while creating a new `DrawableRectangle` object:

```
Try
    Dim rect As New DrawableRectangle(10, 20, 0, 100)
Catch ex As Exception
    MessageBox.Show(ex.Message)
End Try
```

Figure 8-2 shows the error message generated by this code. The exception class composed the message based on the description and parameter name used in the call to the exception class's constructor.

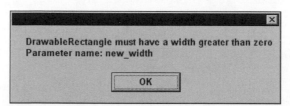

Figure 8-2: An `ArgumentException` **object generates its Message value from the description and parameter name passed to its constructor.**

When your application needs to throw an exception, it's easiest to use an existing exception class. There are a few ways to get lists of exception classes so that you can find one that makes sense for your application. First, Appendix F lists some of the more useful exception classes. The online help topic, "Introduction to Exception Handling in Visual Basic .NET," also has a good list of exception classes at the end.

Another method for finding exception classes is to open the Object Browser (select the View menu's Object Browser command) and search for "Exception." Figure 8-3 shows the Object Browser displaying roughly 400 matches, many of which are exception classes. The `System.FormatException` class is selected, so the Object Browser is showing that class's description.

When you throw exceptions, you must use your judgment about selecting these classes. For example, Visual Basic uses the `System.Reflection.AmbiguousMatchException` class when it tries to bind a subroutine call to an object's method, and it cannot determine which overloaded method to use. This happens at a lower level than your program will act, so you won't use that class for exactly the same purpose. It may be useful, for example, if your routine parses a string and, based on the string, cannot decide what action to take. In that case, you might use this class to represent the error, even though you're not using it exactly as it was originally intended.

Before you use one of these classes, look it up in the online help to make sure that it fits your purpose. If there's no good fit, you can always create your own as described in the section "Custom Exceptions," later in this chapter.

Specialized classes and libraries sometimes have their own particular exception classes. For example, serialization and cryptographic objects have their own sets of exception classes that make sense within their own domains. Usually, these are fairly specialized, so you won't need to throw them in your program unless you are reraising an error you received from a serialization or cryptographic object.

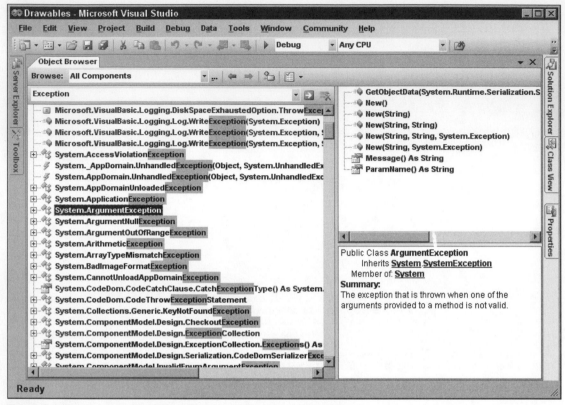

Figure 8-3: You can use the Object Browser to find exception classes.

Custom Exceptions

When your application needs to raise an exception, it's easiest to use an existing exception class. Reusing existing exception classes makes it easier for developers to understand what the exception means. It also prevents exception proliferation, where the developer needs to watch for dozens or hundreds of types of exceptions.

Sometimes, however, the predefined exceptions don't quite fit your needs. For example, suppose that you build a class that contains data that may exist for a long time. If the program tries to use an object that has not refreshed its data for a while, you want to raise some sort of "data expired" exception. You could squeeze this into the `System.TimeoutException` class, but that exception doesn't quite fit this use. The `Expired` class is a better fit, but it's part of the System.Net.Cookie namespace. Using it would require your application to include the System.Net.Cookie namespace just to define the exception class, even if the program has nothing to do with cookies.

In this case, it would be better to create your own exception class. Building a custom exception class is easy. Make a new class that inherits from the `System.ApplicationException` class. Then, provide constructor methods to let the program create instances of the class. That's all there is to it.

By convention, an exception class's name should end with the word Exception. Also by convention, you should provide at least three overloaded constructors. The first takes no parameters and initializes the exception with a default message describing the general type of error.

The other two versions take as parameters an error message, and an error message plus an inner exception object. These constructors pass their parameters to the base class's constructors to initialize the object appropriately.

For completeness, you can also make a constructor that takes as parameters a SerializationInfo object and a StreamingContext object. This version can also pass its parameters to a base class constructor to initialize the exception object. This constructor is useful if the exception will be serialized and deserialized. If you're not sure whether you need this constructor, you probably don't. If you do include it, however, you will need to import the System.Runtime.Serialization namespace in the exception class's file to define the SerializationInfo and StreamingContext classes.

The following code shows how you might define the ObjectExpiredException class:

```vb
Imports System.Runtime.Serialization

Public Class ObjectExpiredException
    Inherits System.ApplicationException

    ' No parameters. Use a default message.
    Public Sub New()
        MyBase.New("This object has expired")
    End Sub

    ' Set the message.
    Public Sub New(ByVal new_message As String)
        MyBase.New(new_message)
    End Sub

    ' Set the message and inner exception.
    Public Sub New(ByVal new_message As String, ByVal inner_exception As Exception)
        MyBase.New(new_message, inner_exception)
    End Sub

    ' Include SerializationInfo object and StreamingContext objects.
    Public Sub New(ByVal info As SerializationInfo, _
      ByVal context As StreamingContext)
        MyBase.New(info, context)
    End Sub
End Class
```

After you have defined the exception class, you can throw and catch it just as you can throw and catch any exception class defined by Visual Basic. For example, the following code throws an ObjectExpiredException.

```vb
Throw New ObjectExpiredException("This Customer object has expired.")
```

The parent class System.ApplicationException automatically handles the object's Message, StackTrace, and ToString properties so you don't need to implement them yourself.

Visual Basic Classic Error Handling

Structured error handling using the `Try` block is a relatively recent innovation, appearing in the first versions of Visual Basic .NET. Visual Basic 6 and earlier versions used a more line-oriented syntax sometimes called "Visual Basic Classic Error Handling." While the `Try` block is generally preferred, you can still use classic error handling in your Visual Basic .NET applications. In fact, you can use both styles in the same program, although not in the same routine. The section "Structured versus Classic Error Handling" later in this chapter discusses the pros and cons of each.

A classic error handler begins with an `On Error` statement that tells Visual Basic what it should do if it encounters an error. This statement can take one of four forms: `On Error GoTo` *line*, `On Error Resume Next`, `On Error GoTo 0`, and `On Error GoTo -1`.

On Error GoTo line

After this statement, if Visual Basic encounters an error, it enters error-handling mode and jumps to the indicated line. The error handler that begins at the indicated line can take whatever action is appropriate.

The following code executes the statement `On Error GoTo LoadPayrollError` and then calls subroutine `LoadPayrollFile`. If that routine causes an error, Visual Basic jumps to the line labeled `LoadPayrollError`. The error-handler code displays an error message and exits the subroutine. The program then executes the statement `On Error GoTo PrintPaychecksError` and calls the `PrintPaychecks` routine. If that routine throws an error, the code starting at the `PrintPaychecksError` label executes. After it has finished its work, the routine uses an `Exit Sub` statement to end without falling into the error-handling code.

```
Private Sub ProcessPayroll()
    ' Load the payroll file.
    On Error GoTo LoadPayrollError
    LoadPayrollFile()

    On Error GoTo PrintPaychecksError
    ' Print paychecks.
    PrintPaychecks()

    ' We're done.
    Exit Sub

LoadPayrollError:
    MessageBox.Show("Error loading the payroll file.")
    Exit Sub

PrintPaychecksError:
    MessageBox.Show("Error printing paychecks.")
    Exit Sub
End Sub
```

The program can leave error-handling mode using the statements `Exit Sub`, `Exit Function`, `Resume`, or `Resume Next`.

An `Exit Sub` or `Exit Function` statement makes the program immediately leave the routine in which the error occurred, and that's the end of error-handling mode for this error.

The Resume statement makes the program resume execution with the statement that caused the error. If the problem has not been fixed, the error will occur again and the program may enter an infinite loop. You should use the Resume statement only if there is a chance that the error has been fixed. For example, if the program tries to read from a floppy disk and the drive is empty, the program could ask the user to insert the disk and then it could try to read the disk again.

The Resume Next statement makes the program resume execution with the statement after the one that caused the error. This statement is appropriate when the program cannot fix the problem but should continue anyway. For example, suppose that a program fails to read a value from a file. It might want to continue anyway so that it can close the file in the next statement.

On Error Resume Next

After this statement, if Visual Basic encounters an error, it skips the statement that caused the error and resumes execution with the following statement. If the program doesn't care whether the statement completed, On Error Resume Next lets it continue without checking for errors.

If the program needs to take action when an error occurs, it can use the Err object to check for errors after each statement. For example, the following code uses the On Error Resume Next statement and then calls subroutine DoSomething. When the subroutine returns, the program checks the Err object's Number property to see if an error occurred. If there is an error, the program displays a message and exits the subroutine. If subroutine DoSomething did not cause an error, the program calls subroutine DoSomethingElse and performs a similar check for errors.

```
On Error Resume Next
DoSomething()
If Err.Number <> 0 Then
    MessageBox.Show("Error in DoSomething")
    Exit Sub
End If

DoSomethingElse()
If Err.Number <> 0 Then
    MessageBox.Show("Error in DoSomethingElse")
    Exit Sub
End If
...
```

A program can also use this statement to check for different kinds of errors and take appropriate action. The following example takes no special action if there is no error. If Err.Number is 11, the program tried to divide by zero. In that case, the code sets variable X to a default value. If there is some other error, the program tells the user and exits the subroutine.

```
' Try to calculate X.
On Error Resume Next
X = CalculateValue()

Select Case Err.Number
    Case 0       ' No error. Do nothing.
    Case 11      ' Divide by zero. Set a default value.
        X = 1000
```

```
        Case Else    ' Unexpected error. Tell the user.
            MessageBox.Show("Error calculating X." & vbCrLf & Err.Description)
            Exit Sub
    End Select
    ...
```

On Error GoTo 0

The `On Error GoTo 0` statement disables any active error handler. You should deactivate an error handler when it no longer applies to what the program is doing. The following code installs an error handler while it loads some data. When it is finished loading the data, it uses `On Error GoTo 0` to deactivate the error handler before it performs other tasks.

```
    On Error GoTo LoadDataError
    ' Load the data.
    ...
    ' Done loading data.
    On Error GoTo 0

    ...
    Exit Sub

LoadDataError:
    MessageBox.Show("Error loading data." & vbCrLf & Err.Description)
    Exit Sub
End Sub
```

Deactivating the error handler stops the program from taking inappropriate action for an error. In the previous example, it might confuse the user to say there was an error loading data when the program was doing something else. In other cases, the program might incorrectly try to fix problems that are not there if you leave an old error handler installed. For example, the program might ask the user to insert a floppy disk when it had already finished reading from the disk.

Deactivating old error handlers also lets the program fail if an unexpected error occurs. That lets developers discover and handle new types of failure, possibly by adding a new error handler.

On Error GoTo -1

The `On Error GoTo -1` statement is very similar to `On Error GoTo 0`. It deactivates any active error handler. However, it also ends error-handling mode if it is running. The following code shows the difference. The program uses `On Error GoTo DivideError1` to install an error handler and then executes a command that causes a "divide by zero" error.

In this code, the error-handler code uses `On Error GoTo -1` to end error-handling mode and continue execution. It then calls `On Error Resume Next` to ignore errors and performs another calculation that divides by zero. Because the `On Error Resume Next` statement is in effect, the program ignores this error.

Next, the code uses `On Error GoTo DivideError2` to install another error handler. It divides by zero again to jump to the error handler and enter error-handling mode.

This time the error handler uses the On Error GoTo 0 statement. This uninstalls the current error handler (On Error GoTo DivideError2), but does not end error-handling mode. The program then uses the On Error Resume Next statement. Unfortunately, this statement is ignored while the program is running in error-handling mode. If the program used a Resume statement to exit error-handling mode, this statement would then have an effect, but it does nothing until error-handling mode ends. Now, when the program divides by zero again, there is no active error handler, so the program crashes.

```
Dim i As Integer
Dim j As Integer = 0

    On Error GoTo DivideError1
    i = 1 \ j                    ' This raises an error.

DivideError1:                    ' We enter error-handling mode here.
    On Error GoTo -1             ' This ends error-handling mode.
    On Error Resume Next         ' Ignore errors in the future.
    i = 1 \ j                    ' This error is ignored.

    On Error GoTo DivideError2
    i = 1 \ j                    ' This raises an error.

DivideError2:                    ' We enter error-handling mode here.
    On Error GoTo 0              ' This does NOT end error-handling mode.
    On Error Resume Next         ' This statement doesn't work in error-handling mode.
    i = 1 \ j                    ' This error is not caught and crashes the program.
```

To avoid confusion, you should not use this style of error handling with error-handling code running through the body of a subroutine. Instead, place error-handling code at the end of the routine and use Exit Sub, Exit Function, Resume, or Resume Next to return to the routine's main body of code. The On Error GoTo -1 statement is usually more confusing than it's worth.

Error-Handling Mode

Undoubtedly the most confusing part of classic error handling is error-handling mode. The On Error GoTo *line* statement makes the program enter a special error-handling mode that remains in effect until the error handler calls Exit Sub, Exit Function, Resume, Resume Next, or On Error GoTo -1. While in error-handling mode, most other error-handling statements do not work as they normally do. Generally, their effects only take place when error-handling mode finally ends.

For example, consider the following code fragment. The program uses the statement On Error GoTo EquationError to install an error handler and then performs a calculation that divides by zero. The program jumps to the line labeled EquationError and enters error-handling mode. The error-handling code starts by executing the statement On Error Resume Next. Because the program is running in error-handling mode, this statement has no immediate effect. The program then performs another calculation that divides by zero. Because the code is already running in error-handling mode, it cannot jump to a new error handler, so the program crashes.

```
Private i, j As Integer

Private Sub PerformCalculation()
    On Error GoTo EquationError
```

```
    i = 1 \ j
    Exit Sub

EquationError:
    On Error Resume Next
    i = 2 \ j
    Resume Next
End Sub
```

The previous example demonstrates one of the most common mistakes programmers make when working with error-handling mode. The error-handler code must be safe, or the program will crash (or at least the error will propagate up to the calling routine).

If you really need to perform risky operations in the error handler's code, you should move that code into a subroutine. That routine can use its own error-handling code to protect itself from another error. The following example demonstrates this approach. The SetDefaultValue subroutine uses its own On Error Resume Next statement to avoid crashing if it has problems of its own.

```
Private i, j As Integer

Private Sub PerformCalculation()
    On Error GoTo EquationError
    i = 1 \ j
    Exit Sub

EquationError:
    SetDefaultValue()
    Resume Next
End Sub

Private Sub SetDefaultValue()
    On Error Resume Next
    i = 2 \ j
End Sub
```

Structured versus Classic Error Handling

The newer structured error-handling approach provided by the Try statement has several advantages over classic error handling. First, classic error handling doesn't make it immediately obvious whether a piece of code is protected by an error handler. To determine whether a statement is protected, you must look back through the code until you find an On Error statement. If you come to a labeled line, you also must track down any places where a GoTo or a Resume *line* statement could jump to that line and see what error handler might be installed at the time.

Classic error handling also doesn't make it obvious whether the code is running in error-handler mode. In some cases, it is impossible to tell until run time. The following code uses an On Error GoTo statement to protect itself and then initializes an integer from a value that the user entered in a text box. If the user enters a valid integer, the code works normally and keeps running in normal (not error-handling) mode. If the user enters a value that is not a valid integer, the program jumps to the label BadFormat and enters error-handling mode. There's no way to tell before run time whether the program will be in error-handling mode when it reaches the following comment.

```
    Dim i As Integer
    On Error GoTo BadFormat
    i = CInt(txtNumber.Text)
BadFormat:
    ' Are we in error-handling mode here?
    ...
```

Finally, you cannot nest classic error-handling code. If you must perform a risky action in an error handler, you must place the code in a separate subroutine that contains its own error-handling code to protect itself.

Structured error handling addresses these shortcomings. By looking at the enclosing `Try` or `Catch` block, you can easily tell whether a line of code is protected (inside the `Try` block) or part of an error handler (in the `Catch` block).

You can even nest `Try` statements, as shown in the following code. The program tries to initialize an integer from a value that the user entered in a text box. If the user enters an invalid value, the code moves into the first `Catch` block. There it tries to set the value of the integer using a calculation. If that calculation fails (for example, if j is 0), the next `Catch` block sets the variable to a default value.

```
' Get the user's value.
Try
    i = Integer.Parse(txtNumber.Text)
Catch ex As Exception
    ' The user's value is no good.
    ' Calculate a different value.
    Try
        i = 1 \ j
    Catch ex2 As Exception
        ' The calculated value is no good.
        ' Use a default value.
        i = 3
    End Try
End Try
```

Finally, the `Try` block doesn't have a bewildering error-handling mode. The potential for confusion there alone is probably worth using structured error handling.

One of the few advantages to classic error handling is that it is easier to ignore errors by using the `On Error Resume Next` statement. The following code uses classic error handling to execute three subroutines and ignore any errors they produce:

```
On Error Resume Next
DoSomething()
DoSomethingElse()
DoSomethingMore()
...
```

The following version shows the same code using structured error handling. This version is quite a bit more verbose.

```
Try
    DoSomething()
Catch
End Try

Try
    DoSomethingElse()
Catch
End Try

Try
    DoSomethingMore()
Catch
End Try
...
```

The Err Object

When an error occurs, Visual Basic initializes an object named Err. You can use this object's properties to learn more about the error. These properties correspond to those provided by the exception objects used by the Try statement's Catch sections. The following table lists these properties.

Property	Purpose
Description	A message describing the error.
Erl	The line number at which the error occurred.
HelpContext	The help context ID for the error.
HelpFile	The full path to the help file describing the error.
LastDLLError	A system error code generated by a call to a DLL (if appropriate).
Number	The error number. The value 0 means no error has occurred.
Source	The name of the object or application that caused the error.

The Err object also provides three useful methods for working with errors: Clear, Raise, and GetException. The Clear method clears the object's information and resets it for the next statement. If the statement following an error does not raise an error itself, the Err object may still show the previous error unless you clear it, as shown in the following code:

```
On Error Resume Next
X = Single.Parse(txtX.Text)
If Err.Number <> 0 Then
    MessageBox.Show(Err.Description)      ' Display the error.
    Err.Clear                            ' Clear the error.
End If

Y = Single.Parse(txtY.Text)
```

```
If Err.Number <> 0 Then
    MessageBox.Show(Err.Description)    ' Display the error.
    Err.Clear                          ' Clear the error.
End If
...
```

The Err object's Raise method generates an error. For example, the following statement raises error number 5, "Procedure call or argument is invalid":

```
Err.Raise(5)
```

Finally, the GetException method returns an exception object representing the Err object's error. You can use this object just as you can use any other exception object. In particular, you can use its StackTrace property to get a trace starting where the error occurred.

If you use classic error handling, you can use the Err object to learn about the error. If you use structured error handling with the Try statement, you can use the exception objects provided by Catch statements, and you can do without the Err object.

Debugging

Visual Basic provides a rich set of tools for debugging an application. Using the development environment, you can stop the program at different lines of code and examine variables, change variable values, look at the call stack, and call routines to exercise different pieces of the application. You can step through the program, executing the code one statement at a time to see what it is doing. You can even make some modifications to the source code and let the program continue running.

Chapter 1, "IDE," describes the development environment, including the tools you can use to debug an application such as breakpoints, watches, and the locals, autos, immediate, and call stack windows. See Chapter 1 for details.

In addition to setting breakpoints in the code, you can use the Stop statement to pause execution at a particular line. This can be particularly useful for detecting unexpected values during testing. For example, the following statement stops execution if the variable m_NumEmployees is less than 1 or greater than 100.

```
If (m_NumEmployees < 1) Or (m_NumEmployees > 100) Then Stop
```

Summary

In practice, it's extremely difficult to anticipate every condition that can occur within a large application. You should try to predict as many incorrect situations as possible, but you should also plan for unforeseen errors. You should write error-checking code that makes bugs obvious when they occur and recovers from them if possible. You may not be able to anticipate every possible bug, but with a little thought you can make the program detect and report obviously incorrect values. The sooner you detect a bug, the easier it is to find and fix.

You should also look for unexpected conditions (such as the user entering a phone number in a Social Security number field) and make the program react gracefully. Your program cannot control everything in its environment (such as the user's actions, printer status, and network connectivity), but it should be prepared to act when things aren't exactly the way they should be.

When you do encounter an error, you can use tools such as breakpoints, watches, and the development environment's Locals, Auto, Immediate, and Call Stack windows to figure out where the problem begins and how to fix it. You may never be able to remove every last bug from a 100,000-line program, but you can make any remaining bugs appear so rarely that the users can do their jobs in relative safety.

The chapters up to this point have focused mostly on the code that lies behind a Visual Basic application. Another major component to an application is the interface that the user sees. In Visual Basic, you assemble the user interface with forms, and controls and components added to the forms. Chapter 9, "Introduction to Windows Forms Controls," introduces the Windows forms controls and components. It describes the most commonly used controls and components and gives some guidelines for selecting those that are most appropriate for different user interface needs.

Introduction to Windows Forms Controls

Controls are an extremely important part of any interactive application. They give information to the user (Label, ToolTip, TreeView, PictureBox) and organize the information so that it's easier to understand (GroupBox, Panel, TabControl). They enable the user to enter data (TextBox, RichTextBox, ComboBox, MonthCalendar), select options (RadioButton, CheckBox, ListBox), control the application (Button, MenuStrip, ContextMenuStrip), and interact with objects outside of the application (OpenFileDialog, SaveFileDialog, PrintDocument, PrintPreviewDialog). Some controls also provide support for other controls (ImageList, ToolTip, ContextMenuStrip, ErrorProvider).

This chapter provides only a very brief description of the standard Windows Forms controls and some tips that can help you decide which control to use for different purposes. Appendix G, "Standard Controls and Components," covers the controls in much greater detail, describing each control's most useful properties, methods, and events.

Figure 9-1 shows the Visual Basic toolbox displaying the standard Windows forms controls.

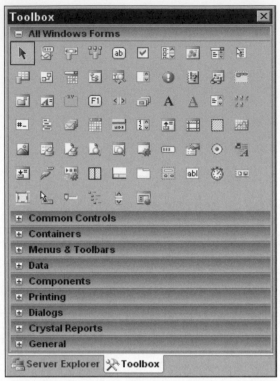

Figure 9-1: Visual Basic provides a large number of standard controls for Windows forms.

Controls Overview

The following table briefly describes the controls shown in Figure 9-1 in the order in which they appear in the figure (starting at the top, or row 1, and reading from left to right).

Control	Purpose
Row 1	
Pointer	This is the pointer tool, not a control. Click this tool to deselect any selected controls on a form. Then you can select new controls.
BackgroundWorker	Executes a task asynchronously and notifies the main program when it is finished.
BindingNavigator	Provides a user interface for navigating through a data source. For example, it provides buttons that let the user move back and forth through the data, add records, delete records, and so forth.
BindingSource	Encapsulates a form's data source and provides methods for navigating through the data.

Control	Purpose
Button	A simple push button. When the user clicks it, the program can perform some action.
CheckBox	A box that the user can check and uncheck.
CheckedListBox	A list of items with check boxes that the user can check and uncheck.
ColorDialog	Lets the user pick a standard or custom color.
ComboBox	A text box with an attached list or drop-down list that the user can use to enter or select a textual value.
ContextMenuStrip	A menu that appears when the user right-clicks on a control. You set a control's ContextMenuStrip property to this control, and the rest is automatic.
Row 2	
DataGridView	A powerful grid control that lets you display large amounts of complex data with hierarchical or Web-like relationships relatively easily.
DataSet	An in-memory store of data with properties similar to those of a relational database. It holds objects representing tables containing rows and columns, and can represent many database concepts such as indexes and foreign key relationships.
DateTimePicker	Lets the user select a date and time in one of several styles.
DirectoryEntry	Represents a node in an Active Directory hierarchy.
DirectorySearcher	Performs searches of an Active Directory hierarchy.
DomainUpDown	Lets the user scroll through a list of choices by clicking up-arrow and down-arrow buttons.
ErrorProvider	Displays an error indicator next to a control that is associated with an error.
EventLog	Provides access to Windows event logs.
FileSystemWatcher	Notifies the application of changes to a directory or file.
FlowLayoutPanel	Displays the controls it contains in rows or columns. For example, when laying out rows, it places controls next to each other horizontally in a row until it runs out of room and then it starts a new row.
Row 3	
FolderBrowserDialog	Lets the user select a folder.
FontDialog	Lets the user specify a font's characteristics (name, size, boldness, and so forth).

Table continued on following page

Row 3	
GroupBox	Groups related controls for clarity. It also defines a default RadioButton group for any RadioButtons that it contains.
HelpProvider	Displays help for controls that have help if the user sets focus on the control and presses F1.
HScrollBar	A horizontal scroll bar.
ImageList	Contains a series of images that other controls can use. For example, the images that a TabControl displays on its tabs are stored in an associated ImageList control. Your code can also pull images from an ImageList for its own use.
Label	Displays text that the user cannot modify or select by clicking and dragging.
LinkLabel	Displays a label, parts of which may be hyperlinks. When the user clicks a hyperlink, the program can take some action.
ListBox	Displays a list of items that the user can select. Depending on the control's properties, the user can select one or several items.
ListView	Displays a list of items in one of four possible views: LargeIcon, SmallIcon, List, and Details.
Row 4	
MaskedTextBox	A text box that requires the input to match a specific format (such as a phone number or ZIP code format).
MenuStrip	Represents the form's main menus, submenus, and menu items.
MessageQueue	Provides communication between different applications.
MonthCalendar	Displays a calendar that allows the user to select a range of dates.
NotifyIcon	Displays an icon in the system tray or status area.
NumericUpDown	Lets the user change a number by clicking up-arrow and down-arrow buttons.
OpenFileDialog	Lets the user select a file for opening.
PageSetupDialog	Lets the user specify properties for printed pages. For example, it lets the user specify the printer's paper tray, page size, margins, and orientation (portrait or landscape).
Panel	A control container. Using the control's Anchor and Dock properties, you can make the control resize itself so that its child controls resize themselves in turn. The control can automatically provide scroll bars and defines a RadioButton group for any RadioButtons that it contains.
PerformanceCounter	Provides access to Windows performance counters.

Row 5

PictureBox	Displays a picture. Also provides a useful drawing surface.
PrintDialog	Displays a standard print dialog. The user can select the printer, pages to print, and printer settings.
PrintDocument	Represents output to be sent to the printer. A program can use this object to print and display print previews.
PrintPreviewControl	Displays a print preview within one of the application's forms.
PrintPreviewDialog	Displays a print preview in a standard dialog.
Process	Allows the program to interact with processes, and to start and stop them.
ProgressBar	Displays a series of colored bars to show the progress of a long operation.
PropertyGrid	Displays information about an object in a format similar to the one used by the Properties window at design time.
RadioButton	Represents one of an exclusive set of options. When the user selects a RadioButton, Visual Basic deselects all other RadioButtons in the same group. Groups are defined by GroupBoxes, Panels, and the form.
RichTextBox	A text box that supports Rich Text extensions. The control can display different pieces of text with different font names, sizes, bolding, and so forth. It also provides paragraph-level formatting for justification, bullets, hanging indentation, and more.

Row 6

SaveFileDialog	Lets the user select the name of a file where the program will save data.
SerialPort	Represents a serial port and provides methods for controlling, reading, and writing it.
ServiceController	Represents a Windows service and lets you manipulate services.
SplitContainer	Lets the user drag a divider vertically or horizontally to split available space between two areas within the control.
StatusStrip	Provides an area (usually at the bottom of the form) where the application can display status messages, small pictures, and other indicators of the application's state.
TabControl	Displays a series of tabs attached to pages that contain their own controls. The user clicks a tab to display the associated page.
TableLayoutPanel	Displays the controls it contains in a grid.

Table continued on following page

Row 6	
TextBox	Displays some text that the user can edit.
Timer	Triggers an event periodically. The program can take action when the event occurs.
ToolStrip	Displays a series of buttons, drop-downs, and other tools that let the user control the application.

Row 7	
ToolStripContainer	A container that allows a ToolStrip control to dock to some or all of its edges. You might dock a ToolStripContainer to a form to allow the user to dock a ToolStrip to each of the form's edges.
ToolTip	Displays a tooltip if the user hovers the mouse over an associated control.
TrackBar	Allows the user to drag a pointer along a bar to select a numeric value.
TreeView	Displays hierarchical data in a graphical, treelike form.
VScrollBar	A vertical scroll bar.
WebBrowser	A Web browser in a control. You can place this control on a form and use its methods to navigate to a Web page. The control displays the results exactly as if the user were using a standalone browser. One handy use for this control is displaying Web-based help.

See Appendix G, "Standard Controls and Components," for detailed descriptions of the controls.

Choosing Controls

Keeping all of the intricacies of each of these controls in mind at once is a daunting task. With so many powerful tools to choose from, it's not always easy to pick the one that's best for a particular situation.

To simplify error-handling code, you should generally pick the most restrictive control that can accomplish a given task, because more restrictive controls give the user fewer options for entering invalid data.

For example, suppose that the user must pick from the choices Small, Medium, and Large. The application could let the user type a value in a TextBox control, but then the user could type Weasel. The program would need to verify that the user typed one of the valid choices and display an error message if the text was invalid. The program might also need to use precious screen real estate to list the choices so that the user can tell what to type.

A better idea would be to use a group of three RadioButtons or a ComboBox with DropDownStyle set to DropDownList. Then the user can easily see the choices available and can only select a valid choice. If the program initializes the controls with a default value rather than leaving them initially undefined, it knows that there is always a valid choice selected.

The following sections summarize different categories of controls and provide some tips about when to use each.

Containing and Arranging Controls

These controls contain, group, and help arrange other controls. These controls include `FlowLayoutPanel`, `TableLayoutPanel`, `GroupBox`, `Panel`, `TabControl`, and `SplitContainer`.

The `FlowLayoutPanel` arranges the controls it contains in rows or columns. For example, when its `FlowDirection` property is `LeftToRight`, the control arranges its contents in rows from left to right. It positions its contents in a row until it runs out of room and then it starts a new row. `FlowLayoutPanel` is particularly useful for Toolboxes and other situations where the goal is to display as many of the contained controls as possible at one time, and the exact arrangement of the controls isn't too important.

The `TableLayoutPanel` control displays its contents in a grid. All the cells in a particular row have the same height, and all the cells in a particular column have the same width. In contrast the `FlowLayoutPanel`, control simply places controls next to each other until it fills a row and then starts a new one. Figure 9-2 shows these two controls side by side.

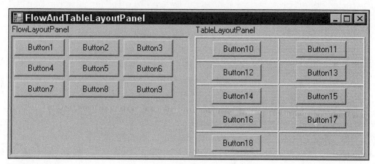

Figure 9-2: `FlowLayoutPanel` **places controls close together.** `TableLayoutPanel` **arranges controls in a grid.**

A `GroupBox` control is good for grouping related controls or the `RadioButtons` in a `RadioButton` group. (The `RadioButton` control is discussed later in this chapter in the section, "Making Selections.") It provides a visible border and caption so that it can help the user make sense out of a very complicated form.

The rule of thumb in user interface design is that a user can evaluate seven items plus or minus two at any given time. A list of five or six choices is manageable, but a list containing dozens of options can be confusing. By placing choices into categories visibly separated in `GroupBoxes`, you can make the interface much easier for the user to understand. Rather than trying to keep dozens of options straight all at once, the user can mentally break the problem into smaller pieces and consider each group of options separately.

The `Panel` control can also contain the `RadioButtons` in a `RadioButton` group. It doesn't display a visible border, however, so you must use some other method to ensure that the user can tell that the buttons form a group. For example, you could use several `Panels` in a row, each containing a column of `RadioButtons`. Then the user would select one option from each column.

One of the `Panel` control's more powerful features is its ability to automatically display scroll bars. If you set a `Panel` control's `AutoScroll` property to `True` and the `Panel` resizes so that all of its contents cannot fit, it automatically displays the scroll bars so the user can still see all of the content. Scrolling back and forth can be cumbersome for the user, however, so this is not the best way to display data if the user must view it all frequently. If the user must jump back and forth between different controls inside a scrolling `Panel`, it may be better to use a `TabControl`.

`TabControl` displays data grouped by pages. The tabs enable the user to quickly jump from page to page. The control can display scroll bars if necessary, although that makes using the control much more awkward. `TabControl` works well if the data falls into natural groupings that you can use for the tab pages. It doesn't work as well if the user must frequently compare values on one page with those on another, forcing the user to jump back and forth.

The `SplitContainer` control allows the user to divide an area between two adjacent regions. `SplitContainer` contains two `Panel` controls in which you can place your own controls. When the user drags the splitter between the two panels, the control resizes the panels accordingly. You can set the `Panels`' `AutoScroll` properties to `True` to make them automatically provide scroll bars when necessary.

`SplitContainer` is helpful when the form isn't big enough to hold all the data the program must display, and the user can trade area in one part of the form for area in another. It is particularly useful when the user must compare values in the two areas by viewing them at the same time.

While you can nest `SplitContainers` inside other `SplitContainers`, they are easiest to use when they separate only two areas. Large groups of `SplitContainers` separating many areas are usually clumsy and confusing.

These container controls help arrange the controls they contain. The `Anchor` and `Dock` properties of any controls inside the containers work relative to the containers. For example, suppose that you place a series of buttons with `Anchor = Top, Left, Right` inside a `SplitContainer` so that they are as wide as the `Panel` containing them. When you drag the splitter, the buttons automatically resize to fit the width of their `Panel`.

Making Selections

Selection controls enable the user to choose values. If you use them carefully, you can reduce the chances of the user making an invalid selection, so you can reduce the amount of error-handling code you need to write.

These controls include `CheckBox`, `CheckedListBox`, `ComboBox`, `ListBox`, `RadioButton`, `DateTimePicker`, `MonthCalendar`, `DomainUpDown`, `NumericUpDown`, `TrackBar`, `HScrollBar`, and `VScrollBar`.

`CheckBox` enables the user to select an option or not, independently of all other selections. If you want the user to select only one of a series of options, use a `RadioButton` instead. If a form requires more than, say, five to seven `CheckBoxes` that have related purposes, consider using a `CheckedListBox` instead.

The `CheckedListBox` control enables the user to select among several independent options. It is basically a series of `CheckBoxes` arranged in a list that provides scroll bars if necessary.

The ComboBox control enables the user to make one brief selection. This control is particularly useful when its DropDownStyle property is set to DropDownList because then the user must pick a value from a list. If you want to allow the user to select a value or enter one that is not on the list, set the control's DropDownStyle to Simple or DropDown. This control does roughly the same things as a simple ListBox but takes less space.

The ListBox control displays a list of items that the user can select. You can configure the control to let the user select one or more items. A ListBox takes more room than a ComboBox but can be easier to use if the list is very long. If you have a long list and want to allow the user to select many items, it is relatively easy for the user to accidentally deselect all of the previous selections by clicking on a new item. To make things easier for the user, you should consider using a CheckedListBox, which doesn't have that problem.

The RadioButton control lets the user pick one of a set of options. For example, three RadioButtons might represent the choices Small, Medium, and Large. If the user selects one, Visual Basic automatically deselects the others. This control is useful when the list of choices is relatively small, and there is a benefit to allowing the user to see all the choices at the same time. If the list of choices is long, consider using a ListBox or ComboBox.

The DateTimePicker and MonthCalendar controls enable the user to select dates and times. They validate the user's selections, so they are generally better than other controls for selecting dates and times. For example, if you use a TextBox to let the user enter month, date, and year, you must write extra validation code to ensure that the user doesn't enter February 29, 2007.

The DomainUpDown and NumericUpDown controls let the user scroll through a list of values. If the list is relatively short, a ListBox or ComboBox may be easier for the user. The DomainUpDown and NumericUpDown controls take very little space, however, so they may be helpful on very crowded forms. By holding down one of the controls' arrow buttons, the user can scroll very quickly through the values, so these controls can also be useful when they represent a long list of choices.

The TrackBar control lets the user drag a pointer to select an integer value. This is usually a more intuitive way to select a value than a NumericUpDown control, although it takes a lot more space on the form. It also requires some dexterity if the range of values allowed is large.

The HScrollBar and VScrollBar controls let the user drag a "thumb" across a bar to select an integral value much as the TrackBar does. HScrollBar, VScrollBar, and TrackBar even have similar properties. The main difference is in the controls' appearances. On one hand, the two scroll bar controls allow more flexible sizing (the TrackBar has definite ideas about how tall it should be for a given width), and they may seem more elegant to some users. On the other hand, users are familiar with their normal purpose of scrolling an area on the form, so using them as numeric selection bars may sometimes be confusing.

Entering Data

Sometimes it is impractical to use the selection controls described in the previous section. For example, the user cannot reasonably enter biographical data or comments using a ComboBox or RadioButton.

The RichTextBox, TextBox, and MaskedTextBox controls let the user enter text with few restrictions. These controls are most useful when the user must enter a large amount of textual data that doesn't require any validation.

The TextBox is less complex than the RichTextBox, so you may want to use it unless you need the RichTextBox's extra features. If you need those features (such as multiple fonts, indentation, paragraph alignment, superscripting and subscripting, multiple colors, more than one level of undo/redo, and so forth), you need to use a RichTextBox.

The MaskedTextBox is a TextBox that requires the user to enter data in a particular format. For example, it can help the user enter a phone number of the form 234-567-8901. This is useful only for short fields where the format is tightly constrained. In those cases, however, it reduces the chances of the user making mistakes.

Displaying Data

These controls display data to the user. They include Label, DataGridView, ListView, TreeView, and PropertyGrid.

The Label control displays a simple piece of text that the user can view but not select or modify. Because you cannot select the text, you cannot copy it to the clipboard. If the text contains a value that you think the user might want to copy to the clipboard and paste into another application (for example, serial numbers, phone numbers, email addresses, Web URLs, and so forth), you can use a TextBox with its ReadOnly property set to True to allow the user to select and copy the text.

The DataGridView control can display tablelike data. The control can also display several tables linked with master/detail relationships and the user can quickly navigate through the data. You can also configure this control to allow the user to update the data.

The ListView control displays data that is naturally viewed as a series of icons or as a list of values with columns providing extra detail. With a little extra work, you can sort the data by item or by detail columns.

The TreeView control displays hierarchical data in a treelike format similar to the directory display provided by Windows Explorer. You can determine whether the control allows the user to edit the nodes' labels.

The PropertyGrid control displays information about an object in a format similar to the one used by the Properties window at design time. The control enables the user to organize the properties alphabetically or by category and lets the user edit the property values. Figure 9-3 shows a PropertyGrid displaying information about an Employee object.

Figure 9-3: The `PropertyGrid` **control displays an object's properties.**

Providing Feedback

These controls provide feedback to the user. These controls include `ToolTip`, `HelpProvider`, `ErrorProvider`, `NotifyIcon`, `StatusStrip`, and `ProgressBar`. Their general goal is to tell the user what is going on without becoming so obtrusive that the user cannot continue doing other things. For example, the `ErrorProvider` flags a field as incorrect but doesn't prevent the user from continuing to enter data in other fields.

The `ToolTip` control provides the user with a brief hint about a control's purpose when the user hovers the mouse over it. The `HelpProvider` provides the user with more detailed help about a control's purpose when the user sets focus to the control and presses F1. A high-quality application provides both tooltips and F1 help for every control that could confuse the user. These features are unobtrusive and only appear if the user needs them, so it is better to err on the side of providing too much help rather than not enough.

The `ErrorProvider` control flags a control as containing invalid data. It is better to use selection controls that do not allow the user to enter invalid data, but this control is useful when that is not possible.

The `NotifyIcon` control can display a small icon in the taskbar notification area to let the user easily learn the application's status. This is particularly useful for applications that run in the background without the user's constant attention. If the application needs immediate action from the user, it should display a dialog or message box rather than relying on a `NotifyIcon`.

The taskbar notification area, also called the Windows system tray, is the small area in the task bar usually on the right that displays the current time and icons indicating the status of various running applications.

The StatusStrip control displays an area (usually at the bottom of the form) where the program can give the user some information about its state. This information can be in the form of small images or short text messages. It can contain a lot more information than a NotifyIcon, although it is visible only when the form is displayed.

The ProgressBar indicates how much of a long task has been completed. Usually, the task is performed synchronously, so the user is left staring at the form while it completes. The ProgressBar lets the user know that the operation is not stuck.

Initiating Action

These controls make the program perform some action. These controls include Button, MenuStrip, ContextMenuStrip, ToolStrip, LinkLabel, TrackBar, HScrollBar, VScrollBar and Timer. All except the Timer control let the user initiate the action.

All of these controls interact with the program through event handlers. For example, the Button control's Click event handler normally makes the program perform some action when the user clicks the button.

Other controls also provide events that can initiate action. For example, the CheckBox control provides CheckChanged and Click events that you could use to perform some action. By catching the proper events, you can use almost any control to initiate an action. Because the main intent of those controls is not to execute code, they are not listed in this section.

The Button control allows the user to tell the program to execute a particular function. A button is normally always visible on its form, so it is most useful when the user must perform the action frequently or the action is part of the program's central purpose. For actions less frequently performed, use a MenuStrip or ContextMenuStrip control.

Items in a MenuStrip control also enable the user to make the program perform an action. You must perform more steps to open the menu, find the item, and select it than you must to click a button, so a Button control is faster and easier. On the other hand, menus take up less form real estate than buttons. You can also assign keyboard shortcuts (such as F5 or Ctrl-S) to frequently used menu items, making them even easier to invoke than buttons.

A ContextMenuStrip control provides the same advantages and disadvantages as a MenuStrip control. ContextMenuStrip is available only from certain controls on the form, however, so it is useful for commands that are appropriate only within specific contexts. For example, a Save command applies to all the data loaded by a program, so it makes sense to put it in a MenuStrip. A command that deletes a particular object in a drawing only applies to that object. By placing the command in a ContextMenuStrip control attached to the object, the program keeps the command hidden when the user is working on other things. It also makes the relationship between the action (delete) and the object clear to both the user and the program.

The ToolStrip control combines some of the best features of menus and buttons. It displays a series of buttons so they are easy to use without navigating through a menu. The buttons are small and grouped at the top of the form, so they don't take up as much space as a series of larger buttons.

It is common to place buttons or ToolStrip buttons on a form to duplicate frequently used menu commands. The menu commands provide keyboard shortcuts for more advanced users and the buttons make it easy to invoke the commands for less-experienced users.

The LinkLabel control displays text much as a Label control does. It also displays some text in blue with an underline, displays a special cursor when the user moves over that text, and raises an event if the user clicks the text. That makes the control appropriate when clicking on a piece of text should perform some action. For example, on a Web page, clicking on a link typically navigates to the link's Web page.

The TrackBar, HScrollBar, and VScrollBar controls let the user drag a "thumb" across a bar to select an integral value. As mentioned in the section, "Making Selections," earlier in this chapter, you can use these controls to let the user select a numeric value. However, they can also be used to perform some action interactively. For example, the scroll bars are often used to scroll an area on the form. More generally, they are used to make the program take action based on some new value. For example, you could use a scroll bar to let the user select new red, green, and blue color components for an image. As the user changed a scroll bar's value, the program would update the image's colors.

The Timer control triggers some action at a regular interval. When the Timer control raises its Timer event, the program takes action.

Displaying Graphics

These controls display graphics, either on the screen or on a printout. These controls include Form, PictureBox, PrintPreviewControl, PrintDocument, and PrintPreviewDialog.

A Form (which can also display graphics) provides methods for drawing, but it's often better to draw in a PictureBox control instead of the form itself. That makes it easier to move the drawing if you later need to redesign the form. For example, if you decide that the picture might be too big, it is easy to move a PictureBox into a scrolling Panel control. It would be much harder to rewrite the code to move the drawing from the Form into a PictureBox later.

PrintPreviewControl displays a print preview for a PrintDocument object. The program responds to events raised by the PrintDocument object. PrintPreviewControl displays the results within a control on one of the program's forms.

The PrintPreviewDialog control displays graphics from a PrintDocument object much as a PrintPreviewControl does, but it provides its own dialog. Unless you need to arrange the print preview in some special way, it is easier to use a PrintPreviewDialog rather than build your own preview dialog with a PrintPreviewControl. The PrintPreviewDialog control provides many features that enable the user to zoom, scroll, and move through the pages of the preview document. Implementing those features yourself would be a lot of work.

Displaying Dialogs

Visual Basic provides a rich assortment of dialogs that enable the user to make standard selections. Figuring out which of these dialogs to use is usually easy because each has a very specific purpose. The following table lists the dialogs and their purposes.

Dialog	Purpose
ColorDialog	Select a color
FolderBrowserDialog	Select a folder (directory)
FontDialog	Select a font
OpenFileDialog	Select a file to open
PageSetupDialog	Specify page set up for printing
PrintDialog	Print a document
PrintPreviewDialog	Display a print preview
SaveFileDialog	Select a file for saving

Supporting Other Controls

Many of Visual Basic's controls require the support of other controls. The two controls used most by other controls are ImageList and PrintDocument. These controls also include DataConnector and DataNavigator.

The ImageList control holds images for other controls to display. Your code can also take images from an ImageList control to use in whatever way it needs.

The PrintDocument control provides support for printing and print previewing. It generates the graphics sent to the printer, PrintPreviewDialog, or PrintPreviewControl.

The DataConnector control provides a link between a data source and controls bound to the connector. The program can use the DataConnector's methods to navigate, sort, filter, and update the data, and the control updates its bound controls appropriately.

The DataNavigator control provides methods for navigating through a data source such as a DataConnector.

Third-Party Controls

Visual Basic comes with a large number of useful controls ready to go, but there are many other controls you can use if you need them. If you right-click on the Toolbox and select Choose Items, you can select from a huge list of .NET Framework and COM components available on your system.

You can also obtain other controls provided by other companies and available for purchase and sometimes for free on the Web. Many of these controls perform specialized tasks such as generating bar codes, making shaped forms, warping images, and providing special graphical effects.

Other controls extend the standard controls to provide more power or flexibility. Several controls are available that draw two- and three-dimensional charts and graphs. Other controls provide more powerful reporting services than those provided by Visual Studio's own tools.

If you use any major Web search engine to search for "windows forms controls," you will find lots of Web sites where you can download controls for free or for a price. A few places you might like to explore include:

❑ MVPs.org (www.mvps.org), a site leading to resources provided by people related to Microsoft's Most Valuable Professional (MVP) program. The Common Controls Replacement Project (ccrp.mvps.org) provides controls that duplicate and enhance standard Visual Basic 6 controls. Development on this project has stopped but some of the old Visual Basic 6 controls may give you some ideas for building controls of your own. MVPs.org is also a good general resource.

❑ Windows Forms .NET (www.windowsforms.net), Microsoft's official Windows Forms .NET community.

❑ ASP.NET (www.asp.net), Microsoft's official ASP.NET community.

❑ Download.com (www.download.com)

❑ Shareware.com (www.shareware.com)

❑ Shareware Connection (www.sharewareconnection.com)

You should use these as a starting point for your own search, not as a definitive list. You can download controls from hundreds (if not thousands) of Web sites.

Summary

Controls form the main connection between the user and the application. They allow the application to give information to the user, and they allow the user to control the application. Controls are everywhere in practically every Windows application. Only a tiny percentage of applications that run completely in the background can do without controls.

This chapter briefly describes purposes of the standard Visual Basic controls and provides a few tips for selecting the controls appropriate for different purposes. Appendix G, "Standard Controls and Components," describes the controls in much greater detail.

Even knowing all about the controls doesn't guarantee that you can produce an adequate user interface. There's a whole science to designing user interfaces that are intuitive and easy to use. A good design enables the user to get a job done naturally and with a minimum of wasted work. A bad interface can encumber the user and turn even a simple job into an exercise in beating the application into submission.

For more information on building usable applications, read some books on user-interface design. They explain standard interface issues and solutions. You can also learn a lot by studying other successful applications. Look at the layout of their forms and dialogs. You shouldn't steal their designs outright, but you can try to understand why they arrange their controls in the way they do. Look at applications that you like and find particularly easy to use. Compare them with applications that you find awkward and confusing.

This chapter provides an introduction to Windows Forms controls. These are graphical objects that can sit on a Windows form to interact with the user. In fact, forms themselves are also controls. The `Form` class inherits from the `ContainerControl` class, which inherits from the `ScrollableControl` class, which inherits from the `Control` base class. While in a sense forms are just another kind of control, they are such an important type of control that they deserve special attention. Chapter 10, "Forms," provides an introduction to forms and explains some of the special form-related issues that don't apply to other kinds of controls.

10

Forms

Visual Basic's Windows `Form` class is a descendant of the `Control` class. The inheritance trail is `Control` → `ScrollableControl` → `ContainerControl` → `Form`. That means a form *is* a type of control. Except where overridden, it inherits the properties, methods, and events defined by the `Control` class. In many ways, a form is just another kind of control (like a `TextBox` or `ComboBox`).

At the same time, `Forms` have their own special features that set them apart from other kinds of controls. You usually place controls inside a form, but you rarely place a form inside another form. `Forms` also play a very central role in most Visual Basic applications. They are the largest graphical unit with which the user interacts directly. The user can minimize, restore, maximize, and close forms. They package the content provided by the other controls so that the user can manage them in a meaningful way.

This chapter describes some of the special features of Windows forms not provided by other objects. It focuses on different ways that typical applications use forms. For example, it explains how to build multiple-document interface (MDI) applications, custom dialogs, and splash screens.

> *An MDI application displays more than one document at a time in separate windows within a larger MDI parent form. MDI applications usually provide tools for managing the child forms they contain. These let the user minimize child forms, arrange the icons for the minimized forms, tile the parent form's area with the child forms, and so forth. Visual Studio can display many windows (form designers, code editors, bitmap editors, and so forth) all within its main form, so it is an MDI application.*

> *A single-document interface (SDI) application displays only one document in each form. For example, Microsoft Paint can manage only one picture at a time, so it is an SDI application. Some SDI applications can display more than one document at a time, but each has its own separate form.*

The chapter covers the `Form` object's properties, methods, and events only in passing. For a detailed description of specific `Form` properties, methods, and events, see Appendix H, "Form Objects."

Transparency

The `Form` object provides a couple of properties that you can use to make a form partially transparent. `Opacity` determines the form's opaqueness. At design time, the Properties window shows

Opacity as a percentage where 100% means the form is completely opaque, and 0% means that the form is completely transparent. At run time, your program must treat Opacity as a floating-point value between 0.0 (completely transparent) and 1.0 (completely opaque).

A program can use an Opacity value less than 100% to let the user see what lies below the form. For example, you might build a partially transparent Search dialog so the user could see the underlying document as a search progresses.

Figure 10-1 shows a form with Opacity set to 66%. You can still see the form's borders, title bar, system menus, and button, but you can also see the Visual Basic IDE showing through from behind.

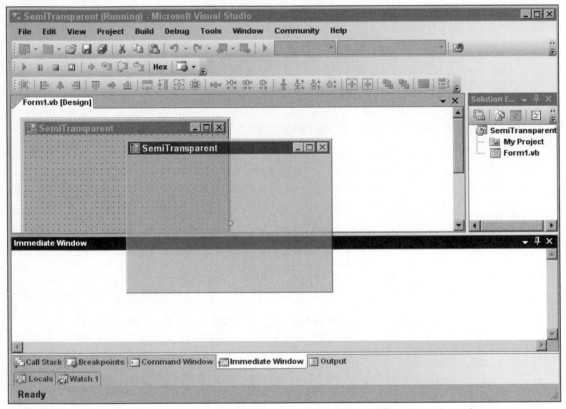

Figure 10-1: A form with Opacity set to 66% allows the Visual Basic IDE to show through.

If Opacity is greater than 0%, the form behaves normally aside from its ghostlike appearance. The user can click on it, interact with its controls, minimize and maximize it, and grab its borders to resize it.

If Opacity is 0%, the form is completely transparent and the user can only interact with the form through the keyboard. For example, the user can press the Tab key to move between the form's controls, type text, press the Spacebar to invoke a button that has the focus, and press Esc or Cancel to fire the form's Accept and Cancel buttons. However, the form and its controls will not detect mouse clicks. The user also cannot see the form (obviously), so figuring out which control has the focus can be difficult.

If Opacity is 1%, the form is still invisible, but it recognizes mouse clicks.

A second property that helps determine the form's transparency is TransparencyKey. This property is a color that tells Visual Basic which parts of the form should be completely transparent. When the form is rendered, any areas with this color as their background colors are not drawn.

Figure 10-2 shows a form with TransparencyKey set to red. Both the form and a label that says "Hole" have red backgrounds so they are transparent. The form's Paint event handler draws a blue ellipse around the inside of the form.

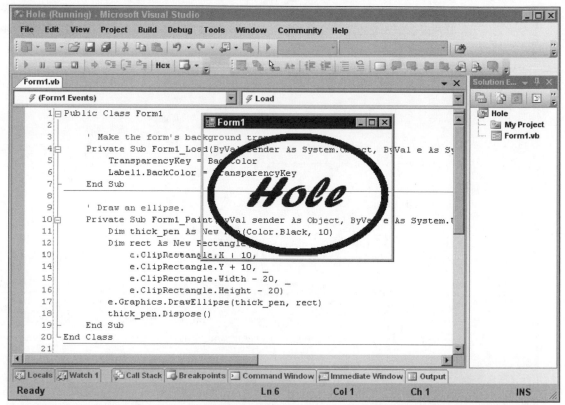

Figure 10-2: A form's TransparencyKey **property lets you make shaped forms such as this one with a hole in it.**

Not only are the transparent pixels not drawn, but the form also doesn't respond to mouse events that they would normally receive. For example, if the user clicks on a hole in the form caused by removed pixels, the mouse click falls through to whatever application lies below the hole.

TransparencyKey applies to both the form's client and nonclient areas, and to any controls on the form. That can cause some strange side effects. For example, the form, many controls, and the tops of form borders have BackColor values of SystemColors.Control. If you set TransparencyKey to SystemColors.Control, the form, control, and border backgrounds disappear.

Figure 10-3 shows a form in this rather unusual state. The form contains a button, label, and check box that all float over whatever lies beneath. If you look very closely, you may be able to see some pale-colored pixels near the text. Those are anti-aliasing pixels that would have made the text appear smoother on a light gray form. These pixels are out of place when the background behind the form is dark, as is it here.

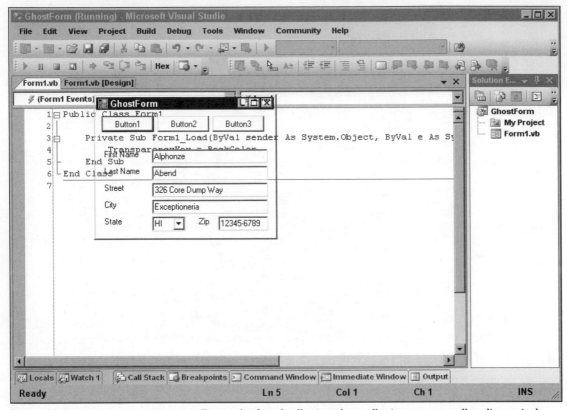

Figure 10-3: `TransparencyKey` **applies to the form's client and nonclient areas, as well as its controls.**

If you look closely at the form's Minimize, Maximize, and Close system buttons on the upper right in Figure 10-3, you'll see parts of the Visual Basic IDE showing through. If you click on part of the button that has been cut out, the click falls through to the Visual Basic IDE. If you click on the tiny pieces of the buttons that are not transparent, the buttons function normally.

The most common use for `TransparencyKey` is to create shaped forms. Set the form's `FormBorderStyle` property to `None` to remove the borders, title bar, and system buttons. Set the form's `BackColor` and `TransparencyKey` properties to a color that you don't want to appear on the form. Then draw the shape you want the form to have in some other color.

Figure 10-4 shows a form shaped like a smiley face. The form's `Paint` event handler draws the image from a bitmap file. These sorts of forms make interesting splash screens and About dialogs, although they are often too distracting for use in a program's main user interface.

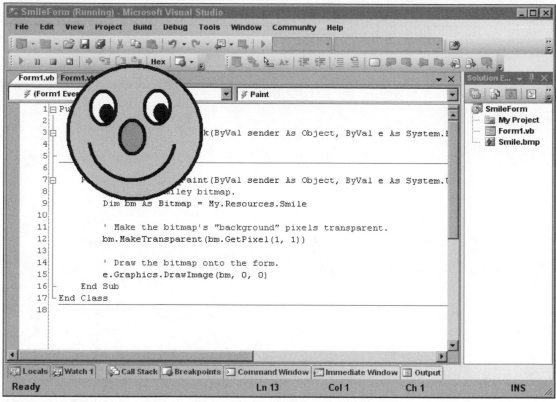

Figure 10-4: The `TransparencyKey` **property lets you make shaped forms such as this one.**

Note that this form has no title bar, borders, or system buttons, so the user cannot move, resize, minimize, maximize, or close it. To use this form as a splash screen, add a `Timer` control to make the form disappear after a few seconds. To use it as an About dialog or some other kind of dialog, add a button that closes it.

If you use `Opacity` and `TransparencyKey` together, pixels that match `TransparencyKey` are completely removed and any remaining pixels are shown according to the `Opacity` value.

About, Splash, and Login Forms

The `TransparencyKey` and `Opacity` properties enable you to build forms with unusual and interesting shapes. While these would be distracting if used for the bulk of a business application, they can add a little interest to About dialogs, splash screens, and login forms.

These three kinds of forms have quite a bit in common. Usually, they all display the application's name, version number, copyright information, trademarks, and so forth. They may also display a serial number, the name of the registered user, and a Web site or phone number where the user can get customer support.

The main difference between these forms is in how the user dismisses them. A splash screen automatically disappears after a few seconds. The user closes an About dialog by pressing an OK button. A login form closes when the user enters a valid user name and password and then clicks OK. It also closes if the user clicks Cancel, although then it doesn't display the main application.

Sometimes a splash screen is displayed while the application initializes, loads needed data, and otherwise prepares itself for work. In that case, the application removes the splash screen after initialization is complete or a few seconds have passed, whichever comes second.

The forms also differ slightly in the controls they contain. A splash screen needs a Timer control to determine when it's time to close the form. An About dialog needs a single OK button. A login form needs TextBoxes to hold the user name and password, two Labels to identify them, and OK and Cancel buttons.

Splash screens and login forms both serve to greet the user, so there's no need to provide both, but that still leaves you with the task of building two nearly identical forms: splash and About, or login and About. With a little planning, you can use a single form as a splash screen, About dialog, and login form. At run time, you can add whichever set of controls is appropriate to the form's use. Alternatively, you can build the form with all three sets of controls at design time and then hide the ones you don't need for a particular purpose.

The following code shows how a form can display itself as either a splash screen or an About dialog. The form contains both a Timer named tmrUnload and an OK button named btnAboutOk. The form's ShowSplash method enables the tmrUnload Timer control and calls Show to display the form. The Timer control's Interval property was set to 3,000 milliseconds at design time, so its Timer event fires after three seconds and closes the form.

The ShowAbout method makes the btnOk button visible and calls ShowDialog to display the form modally. A *modal* form holds the application's focus so the user cannot interact with other parts of the application until the modal form is dismissed. When the user clicks the button, the button's Click event handler closes the form.

```
' Display as a splash screen.
Public Sub ShowSplash()
    Me.tmrUnload.Enabled = True ' The Timer close the dialog.
    Me.TopMost = True           ' Keep on top of main form.
    Me.Show()                   ' Show non-modally.
End Sub


' Unload the splash screen.
Private Sub tmrUnload_Tick(ByVal sender As System.Object, _
 ByVal e As System.EventArgs) Handles tmrUnload.Tick
    Me.Close()
End Sub

' Display as an About dialog.
Public Sub ShowAbout()
    btnOK.Visible = True        ' The OK button closes the dialog.
    Me.ShowDialog()             ' Show modally.
End Sub

' Close the About dialog.
```

```
Private Sub btnOK_Click(ByVal sender As System.Object, _
  ByVal e As System.EventArgs) Handles btnOK.Click
    Me.Close()
End Sub
```

Mouse Cursors

A form's `Cursor` property determines the kind of mouse cursor the form displays. The `Form` class inherits the `Cursor` property from the `Control` class, so other controls have a `Cursor` property, too. If you want to give a particular control a special cursor, you can set its `Cursor` property. For example, if you use a `Label` control as a hyperlink, you could make it display a pointing hand similar to those displayed by Web browsers to let the user know that the control is a hyperlink.

The `Cursors` class provides several standard cursors as shared values. For example, the following statement sets a form's cursor to the system default cursor (normally an arrow pointing up and to the left):

```
Me.Cursor = Cursors.Default
```

Figure 10-5 shows the names and images of the standard cursors defined by the `Cursors` class.

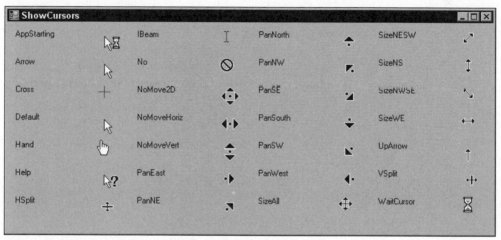

Figure 10-5: The Cursors class defines standard cursors.

Unless a control explicitly sets its own cursor, it inherits the cursor of its container. If the control is placed directly on the form, it displays whatever cursor the form is currently displaying. That means you can set the cursor for a form and all of its controls in a single step by setting the form's cursor.

Similarly, if a control is contained within a `GroupBox`, `Panel`, or other container control, it inherits the container's cursor. You can set the cursor for all the controls within a container by setting the cursor for the container.

One common use for cursors is to give the user a hint when the application is busy. The program sets its cursor to `Cursors.WaitCursor` when it begins a long task and then sets it back to `Cursors.Default` when it finishes. The following code shows an example:

```
Me.Cursor = Cursors.WaitCursor
' Perform the long task.
...
Me.Cursor = Cursors.Default
```

If the program displays more than one form, it must set the cursors for each form individually. It can set the cursors manually, or it can loop through the `My.Application.OpenForms` collection. The `SetAllCursors` subroutine shown in the following code makes setting the cursor for all forms a bit easier:

```
Private Sub SetAllCursors(ByVal the_cursor As Cursor)
    For Each frm As Form In My.Application.OpenForms
        frm.Cursor = the_cursor
    Next frm
End Sub
```

The following code uses the `SetAllCursors` subroutine while performing a long task:

```
SetAllCursors(Cursors.WaitCursor)
' Perform the long task.
...
SetAllCursors(Cursors.Default)
```

To use a custom cursor, create a new `Cursor` object using a file or resource containing cursor or icon data. Then assign the new object to the form's `Cursor` property. The following code sets a form's cursor to the program resource named `SmileIcon.ico`:

```
Me.Cursor = New Cursor(My.Resources.SmileIcon.Handle)
```

Icons

Each form in a Visual Basic application has its own icon. A form's icon is displayed on the left side of its title bar, in the system's taskbar, and by applications such as the Task Manager and Windows Explorer.

Some of these applications display icons at different sizes. For example, if you set Windows Explorer's view to Large Icons, it displays 32 × 32 pixel icons. Windows Explorer displays 16 × 16 pixel icons for its other views.

If an icon file doesn't provide whatever size Windows needs, the system shrinks or enlarges an existing image to fit. That may produce an ugly result. To get the best appearance, you should ensure that icon files include at least 16 × 16 and 32 × 32 pixel sizes. Depending on the characteristics of your system, you may also want to include other sizes.

Visual Studio's integrated icon editor enables you to define images for various color models ranging from monochrome to 256 colors, and sizes ranging from 16 × 16 to 96 × 96 pixels. It even lets you build icon images with custom sizes such as 32 × 48 pixels, although it is unlikely that Windows will need to use those.

To use this editor, open Solution Explorer and double-click on the My Project entry to open the project properties window. Select the Resources tab, open the Add drop-down, and select New Icon. Use the drawing tools to build the icons. Right-click the icon and use the Current Icon Image Types submenu to work with icons of different sizes.

To assign an icon to a form at design time, open the Form Designer and select the Icon property in the Properties window. Click the ellipsis on the right and select the icon file that you want to use.

To assign an icon to a form at run time, set the form's Icon property to an Icon object. The following code sets the form's Icon property to an icon resource named MainFormIcon.

```
Me.Icon = My.Resources.MainFormIcon
```

Some applications change their icons to provide an indication of their status. For example, a process-monitoring program might turn its icon red when it detects an error. It could even switch back and forth between to icons to make the icon blink in the taskbar.

Application Icons

Windows displays a form's icon in the form's title bar, in the taskbar, and in the Task Manager. Applications (such as Windows Explorer) that look at the application as a whole rather than at its individual forms display an icon assigned to the application not to a particular form. To set the application's icon, open Solution Explorer and double-click on the My Project entry to open the Project Properties window. In the Icon drop-down, select the icon file that you want to use or select <Browse...> to look for the file you want to use.

Notification Icons

Visual Basic applications can display one other kind of icon by using the NotifyIcon control. This control can display an icon in the system tray. The *system tray* (also called the *status area*) is the little area holding small icons that is usually placed in the lower-left part of the taskbar, and shown in Figure 10-6. The little stop light in the upper left is an icon displayed by a NotifyIcon control.

Figure 10-6: An application can use a NotifyIcon control to display status icons in the system tray.

The control's Icon property determines the icon that it displays. A typical application will change this icon to give information about the program's status. For example, a program that monitors the system's load could use its system tray icon to give the user an idea of the current load. Notification icons are particularly useful for programs that have no user interface or that run in the background so that the user isn't usually looking at the program's forms.

Notification icons also often include a context menu that appears when the user right-clicks on the icon. The items in the menu enable the user to control the application. If the program has no other visible interface, this may be the only way the user can control it.

Appendix G, "Standard Controls and Components," describes the NotifyIcon control in greater detail.

Properties Adopted by Child Controls

Some properties are adopted by many of the controls contained on a form. For example, by default, a Label control uses the same background color as the form. If you change the form's BackColor property, its Label controls change to display the same color.

Some properties adopted by a form's controls include BackColor, ContextMenu, Cursor, Enabled, Font, and ForeColor. Not all controls use all of these properties, however. For example, a TextBox only matches its form's Enabled and Font properties.

If you explicitly set one of these properties for a control, its value takes precedence over the form's settings. For example, if you set a Label control's BackColor property to red, the control keeps its red background even if you change the Form's BackColor property.

Some of these properties are also not tremendously useful to the Form object itself, but they give guidance to the form's controls. For example, a form doesn't automatically display text on its surface, so it never really uses its Font property. Its Label, TextBox, ComboBox, List, RadioButton, CheckBox, and many other controls adopt the value of this property, however, so the form's Font property serves as a central location to define the font for all of these controls. If you change the form's Font property, even at run time, all of the form's controls change to match. The change applies to all of the form's controls, even those contained within GroupBoxes, Panels, and other container controls so that they do not sit directly on the form.

These properties can also help your application remain consistent both with the controls on the form and with other parts of the application. For example, the following code draws the string "Hello World!" on the form whenever the form needs to be repainted. This code explicitly creates the Comic Sans MS font.

```
Private Sub Form1_Paint(ByVal sender As Object, _
 ByVal e As System.Windows.Forms.PaintEventArgs) Handles Me.Paint
    Dim new_font As New Font("Comic Sans MS", 20)
    e.Graphics.DrawString("Hello World!", _
        new_font, Brushes.Black, 10, 10)
    new_font.Dispose()
End Sub
```

Rather than making different parts of the program build their own fonts, you can use the forms' Font properties as shown in the following code. This makes the code simpler and ensures that different pieces of code use the same font.

```
Private Sub Form1_Paint(ByVal sender As Object, _
 ByVal e As System.Windows.Forms.PaintEventArgs) Handles Me.Paint
    e.Graphics.DrawString("Hello World!", Me.Font, Brushes.Black, 10, 100)
End Sub
```

As a nice bonus, changing the form's Font property raises a Paint event, so, if the form's font changes, this code automatically runs again and redraws the text using the new font.

Property Reset Methods

The Form class provides several methods that reset certain property values to their defaults. The most useful of those methods are ResetBackColor, ResetCursor, ResetFont, ResetForeColor, and ResetText.

If you change one of the corresponding form properties, either at design time or at run time, these methods restore them to their default values. The default values may vary from system to system, but currently on my computer BackColor is reset to Control, Cursor is reset to Default, Font is reset to 8-point regular (not bold or italic) Microsoft Sans Serif, ForeColor is reset to ControlText, and Text is reset to an empty string.

Because the controls on a form adopt many of these properties (all except Text), these methods also reset the controls on the form.

Overriding WndProc

The Windows operating system sends all sorts of messages to applications that tell them about changes in the Windows environment. Messages tell forms to draw, move, resize, hide, minimize, close, respond to changes in the Windows environment, and do just about everything else related to Windows.

All Windows applications have a subroutine tucked away somewhere that responds to those messages. That routine is traditionally called a WindowProc. A Visual Basic .NET form processes these messages in a routine named WndProc. You can override that routine to take special actions when the form receives certain messages.

For example, the following code shows how a program can ensure that a form always keeps the same aspect ration (ratio of height to width). The program overrides the form's WndProc subroutine and looks for the WM_SIZING message. This message receives as parameters a flag indicating the edge that the user is dragging to resize the form and a Rect structure giving the form's new size and location.

This code begins by defining the Rect structure. It then declares the overridden WndProc routine. That routine defines some constants and a static variable to hold the form's original aspect ratio.

Next, WndProc determines the type of message it is processing. If the message is WM_SIZING, then the routine uses the Marshal.PtrToStructure function to copy the m.LParam parameter into a Rect structure. It uses this structure to calculate the form's new width and height, and its aspect ratio.

If this is the first time the WndProc has executed, the static value fixed_aspect_ratio is zero. If the code sees that the value is zero, it saves the form's current aspect ratio in the variable fixed_aspect_ratio.

Next WndProc decides whether the form's aspect ratio is different from its original value. If the ratio has changed, then it determines which dimension (width or height) it should save. If the user is dragging one of the form's corners, the routine saves whichever of the width and height is bigger, and calculates a value for the other dimension that gives the desired aspect ratio.

If the user is dragging one of the form's sides, the program keeps the new width and calculates an appropriate height. Similarly, if the user is dragging the form's top or bottom, the program keeps the height and calculates an appropriate width.

Next, the program determines whether it should move the form's left or right side and its top or bottom edge. The program moves whichever edges the user is dragging. For example, if the user is dragging the form's lower-left corner, the program adjusts the form's left and bottom values so the upper-right corner remains stationary.

WndProc then calls Marshal.StructureToPtr to copy the Rect structure back into the m.LParam parameter.

Finally, WndProc calls MyBase.WndProc to make the parent class's original version of WndProc process the message. If the code changed the values in the Rect structure, the parent's WndProc uses the new values to resize the form.

Calling the parent class's WndProc routine is extremely important. If the program doesn't do this for every message that it does not completely handle itself, the message will not be processed. In that case, the window will not handle all of its Windows messages. It may not repaint, move, load, unload, display menus, and perform all sorts of other Windows tasks correctly.

```vb
Imports System.Runtime.InteropServices

Public Class Form1
    Public Structure Rect
        Public left As Integer
        Public top As Integer
        Public right As Integer
        Public bottom As Integer
    End Structure

    Protected Overrides Sub WndProc(ByRef m As System.Windows.Forms.Message)
        Const WM_SIZING As Long = &H214
        Const WMSZ_LEFT As Integer = 1
        Const WMSZ_RIGHT As Integer = 2
        Const WMSZ_TOP As Integer = 3
        Const WMSZ_TOPLEFT As Integer = 4
        Const WMSZ_TOPRIGHT As Integer = 5
        Const WMSZ_BOTTOM As Integer = 6
        Const WMSZ_BOTTOMLEFT As Integer = 7
        Const WMSZ_BOTTOMRIGHT As Integer = 8
        Static fixed_aspect_ratio As Double = 0

        Dim new_aspect_ratio As Double

        If m.Msg = WM_SIZING And m.HWnd.Equals(Me.Handle) Then
            ' Turn the message's lParam into a Rect.
            Dim r As Rect
            r = DirectCast( _
                Marshal.PtrToStructure(m.LParam, GetType(Rect)), _
                Rect)

            ' Get the current dimensions.
            Dim wid As Double = r.right - r.left
            Dim hgt As Double = r.bottom - r.top

            ' Get the new aspect ratio.
```

```
            new_aspect_ratio = hgt / wid

    ' The first time, save the form's aspect ratio.
    If fixed_aspect_ratio = 0 Then
        fixed_aspect_ratio = new_aspect_ratio
    End If

    ' See if the aspect ratio is changing.
    If fixed_aspect_ratio <> new_aspect_ratio Then
        ' To decide which dimension we should preserve,
        ' see what border the user is dragging.
        If m.WParam.ToInt32 = WMSZ_TOPLEFT Or _
           m.WParam.ToInt32 = WMSZ_TOPRIGHT Or _
           m.WParam.ToInt32 = WMSZ_BOTTOMLEFT Or _
           m.WParam.ToInt32 = WMSZ_BOTTOMRIGHT _
        Then
            ' The user is dragging a corner.
            ' Preserve the bigger dimension.
            If new_aspect_ratio > fixed_aspect_ratio Then
                ' It's too tall and thin. Make it wider.
                wid = hgt / fixed_aspect_ratio
            Else
                ' It's too short and wide. Make it taller.
                hgt = wid * fixed_aspect_ratio
            End If
        ElseIf m.WParam.ToInt32 = WMSZ_LEFT Or _
               m.WParam.ToInt32 = WMSZ_RIGHT _
        Then
            ' The user is dragging a side.
            ' Preserve the width.
            hgt = wid * fixed_aspect_ratio
        ElseIf m.WParam.ToInt32 = WMSZ_TOP Or _
               m.WParam.ToInt32 = WMSZ_BOTTOM _
        Then
            ' The user is dragging the top or bottom.
            ' Preserve the height.
            wid = hgt / fixed_aspect_ratio
        End If

        ' Figure out whether to reset the top/bottom
        ' and left/right.
        ' See if the user is dragging the top edge.
        If m.WParam.ToInt32 = WMSZ_TOP Or _
           m.WParam.ToInt32 = WMSZ_TOPLEFT Or _
           m.WParam.ToInt32 = WMSZ_TOPRIGHT _
        Then
            ' Reset the top.
            r.top = r.bottom - CInt(hgt)
        Else
            ' Reset the bottom.
            r.bottom = r.top + CInt(hgt)
        End If

        ' See if the user is dragging the left edge.
        If m.WParam.ToInt32 = WMSZ_LEFT Or _
```

```
                    m.WParam.ToInt32 = WMSZ_TOPLEFT Or _
                    m.WParam.ToInt32 = WMSZ_BOTTOMLEFT _
                Then
                    ' Reset the left.
                    r.left = r.right - CInt(wid)
                Else
                    ' Reset the right.
                    r.right = r.left + CInt(wid)
                End If

                ' Update the Message object's LParam field.
                Marshal.StructureToPtr(r, m.LParam, True)
            End If
        End If

        MyBase.WndProc(m)
    End Sub
End Class
```

In Visual Basic 6 and earlier versions, a program could install a custom `WindowProc` to perform roughly the same operations. This process was called *subclassing*, an unfortunate choice of name given that object-oriented languages use the term to mean "deriving one class from another" as Visual Basic does with its `Inherits` statement.

Overriding `WndProc` in Visual Basic .NET is much easier and safer than subclassing in Visual Basic 6. As you can see from the example, however, it still requires some tricks to convert the `IntPtr` stored in `m.LParam` to and from the appropriate structure. You must also figure out what messages to intercept, what `m.LParam` and `m.WParam` parameters they take, and what you can do to safely affect them.

One way to learn about messages is to insert the following `WndProc` and then perform the action that you want to study (resizing the form, in this example):

```
Protected Overrides Sub WndProc(ByRef m As System.Windows.Forms.Message)
    Debug.Print(m.ToString)
    MyBase.WndProc(m)
End Sub
```

The following statement shows the result for the `WM_SIZING` message sent to the form while the user resizes it. It at least shows the message name (`WM_SIZING`) and its numeric value (hexadecimal 0x214).

```
msg=0x214 (WM_SIZING) hwnd=0x30b8c wparam=0x2 lparam=0x590e29c result=0x0
```

Searching for the message name on Microsoft's Web site and on other programming sites usually gives you the other information you need to know (such as what `m.WParam` and `m.LParam` mean).

Note also that the `Form` class inherits the `WndProc` subroutine from the `Control` class, so all other Windows forms controls inherit it as well. That means you can override their `WndProc` routines to change their behaviors.

For example, the following code shows how the `NoCtxMnuTextBox` class works. This control is derived from the `TextBox` control. Its `WndProc` subroutine checks for `WM_CONTEXTMENU` messages and calls the base class's `WndProc` for all other messages. By failing to process the `WM_CONTEXTMENU` message, the control prevents itself from displaying the `TextBox`'s normal Copy/Cut/Paste context menu when you right-click on it.

```
Public Class NoCtxMnuTextBox
    Inherits System.Windows.Forms.TextBox

    Protected Overrides Sub WndProc(ByRef m As System.Windows.Forms.Message)
        Const WM_CONTEXTMENU As Integer = &H7B

        If m.Msg <> WM_CONTEXTMENU Then
            MyBase.WndProc(m)
        End If
    End Sub
End Class
```

SDI and MDI

A *single-document interface* (SDI) application displays a single "document" in each form. Here, a "document" can be an actual disk file, or it can be a group of related items such as those on an order, employee record, or architectural drawing. For example, Microsoft Paint and Notepad are both SDI applications. Figure 10-7 shows an SDI application showing three files in separate forms.

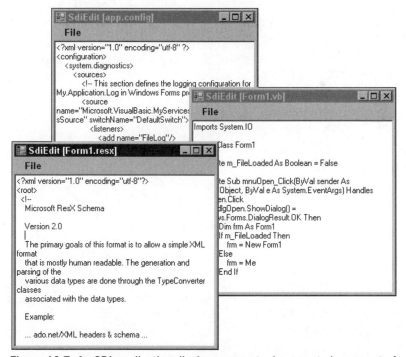

Figure 10-7: An SDI application displays separate documents in separate forms.

In contrast, a *multiple-document interface* (MDI) application displays its documents in their own forms, but then places the forms inside a container form. For example, Visual Studio can act either as an MDI application or it can display its child forms (form designers, code editors, and so forth) using tabs. The individual document windows are called *MDI child forms* and the container form is called the *MDI container* or *MDI parent* form. Figure 10-8 shows an MDI application with three MDI child forms.

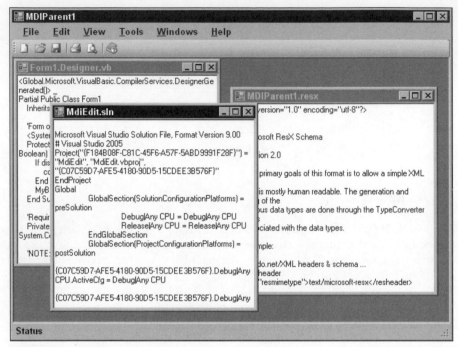

Figure 10-8: An MDI application displays documents in forms contained within an MDI container form.

The following sections describe some of the features provided by MDI forms and discuss reasons you might want to use an MDI or SDI application style.

MDI Features

The MDI container form provides several services for its child forms. It contains the forms and keeps them all together so that they are easy to find. If you move a form so that it won't fit within the container, the container automatically displays scroll bars so you can view it.

The program displays an icon in the taskbar and Task Manager for the MDI container, but not for the child forms. If you minimize the MDI container, all of the forms it contains are hidden with it. If you minimize a child form, its icon is displayed within the container, not separately in the taskbar. If you maximize an MDI child, it fills the parent form and its caption becomes part of the parent's. For example, if the MDI parent form's caption is Parent and the child's caption is Child, then when you maximize the child the parent's caption becomes "Parent - [Child]."

The MDI container also provides some methods for arranging its child forms. The following code shows how an MDI container's code can cascade the children so that they overlap nicely, tile the children vertically or horizontally, and arrange the icons of any minimized child forms.

```
Private Sub CascadeToolStripMenuItem_Click(ByVal sender As Object, _
 ByVal e As EventArgs) Handles CascadeToolStripMenuItem.Click
    Me.LayoutMdi(MdiLayout.Cascade)
End Sub

Private Sub TileVerticleToolStripMenuItem_Click(ByVal sender As Object, _
 ByVal e As EventArgs) Handles TileVerticalToolStripMenuItem.Click
    Me.LayoutMdi(MdiLayout.TileVertical)
End Sub

Private Sub TileHorizontalToolStripMenuItem_Click(ByVal sender As Object, _
 ByVal e As EventArgs) Handles TileHorizontalToolStripMenuItem.Click
    Me.LayoutMdi(MdiLayout.TileHorizontal)
End Sub

Private Sub ArrangeIconsToolStripMenuItem_Click(ByVal sender As Object, _
 ByVal e As EventArgs) Handles ArrangeIconsToolStripMenuItem.Click
    Me.LayoutMdi(MdiLayout.ArrangeIcons)
End Sub
```

Some other useful commands that you can add to an MDI application include Minimize All, Restore All, Maximize All, and Close All. You can implement these commands by looping through the MDI container's MdiChildren collection, as shown in the following code:

```
Private Sub MinimizeAllToolStripMenuItem_Click(ByVal sender As System.Object, _
 ByVal e As System.EventArgs) Handles MinimizeAllToolStripMenuItem.Click
    For Each frm As Form In Me.MdiChildren
        frm.WindowState = FormWindowState.Minimized
    Next frm
End Sub

Private Sub RestoreAllToolStripMenuItem_Click(ByVal sender As System.Object, _
 ByVal e As System.EventArgs) Handles RestoreAllToolStripMenuItem.Click
    For Each frm As Form In Me.MdiChildren
        frm.WindowState = FormWindowState.Normal
    Next frm
End Sub

Private Sub MaximizeAllToolStripMenuItem_Click(ByVal sender As System.Object, _
 ByVal e As System.EventArgs) Handles MaximizeAllToolStripMenuItem.Click
    For Each frm As Form In Me.MdiChildren
        frm.WindowState = FormWindowState.Maximized
    Next frm
End Sub

Private Sub CloseAllToolStripMenuItem_Click(ByVal sender As Object, _
 ByVal e As EventArgs) Handles CloseAllToolStripMenuItem.Click
    For Each frm As Form In Me.MdiChildren
        frm.Close()
    Next
End Sub
```

Depending on your application, you might also provide commands that operate on subsets of the child forms. Suppose that a program displays a main order record and its many related order items in MDI child forms. You might want to let the user close all the order items, while keeping the main order form open.

Many MDI programs include a Window menu that displays a list of the MDI child forms that are open. You can select one of these menu items to move that form to the top of the others.

Building an MDI child list is easy in Visual Basic. Select the main `MenuStrip` control. Then in the Properties window, set the control's `MdiWindowListItem` property to the menu that you want to hold the child list. When you open and close child windows, Visual Basic automatically updates the list.

Figure 10-9 shows a menu displaying an MDI child list. The form with the caption `MDIEdit.sln` currently has the focus, so the list displays a check mark next to that form's entry.

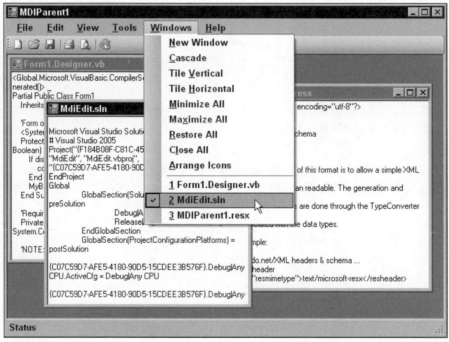

Figure 10-9: The `MenuStrip`'s `MdiWindowListItem` **property determines which menu item displays an MDI child list.**

Most "normal" Visual Basic applications use SDI and when you create a new application, you get SDI by default. To build an MDI application, start a new application as usual. Then set the startup form's `IsMdiContainer` property to `True`. In the Form Designer, this form will change appearance, so it's obvious that it is an MDI parent form.

Alternatively you can select the Project menu's Add Windows Form command. In the new form dialog, select MDI Parent Form, give the form a reasonable name, and click Add. Visual Basic adds a new MDI parent form and gives it an assortment of standard controls that you might like it to have including a menu strip containing standard menus (File, Edit, View, and so forth) and a toolbar with standard tools (new, open, save, and so forth).

At design time, an MDI child form looks just like any other form. To make the child form sit inside the MDI container, you must set its MdiParent property to the MDI container form at run time.

The following code shows how the MDI parent form in Figure 10-8 creates new MDI children. When the user selects the File menu's Open command or the toolbar's Open tool, this event handler executes and displays a file open dialog. If the user selects a file and clicks OK, the code creates a new Form1 object. It loads the selected file into the form's txtContents TextBox, sets the form's caption to the file's name (without the path), sets the form's MdiParent property to Me (the MDI parent form), and displays the form. The form is automatically shown in the MDI container and added to the MDI child list.

```
Private Sub OpenFile(ByVal sender As Object, ByVal e As EventArgs) Handles _
  OpenToolStripMenuItem.Click, OpenToolStripButton.Click
    Dim dlgOpen As New OpenFileDialog
    If dlgOpen.ShowDialog(Me) = Windows.Forms.DialogResult.OK Then
        Dim frm As New Form1
        frm.txtContents.Text = File.ReadAllText(dlgOpen.FileName)
        frm.txtContents.Select(0, 0)
        frm.Text = New FileInfo(dlgOpen.FileName).Name
        frm.MdiParent = Me
        frm.Show()
    End If
End Sub
```

Normally, the system menu in the left of a form's title area includes a Close command with the shortcut Alt-F4. This command closes the form. An MDI child's system menu also contains a Close command, but this one's shortcut is Ctrl-F4. If you select this command or invoke its shortcut, the application closes the MDI child form but not the MDI container.

The MDI child's system menu also includes a Next command that moves the focus to the MDI container's next MDI child. The menu shows this command's shortcut as Ctrl-F6. However, Ctrl-Tab works as well. Ctrl-Tab may be a bit easier to remember because it is more similar to the Alt-Tab shortcut that moves to the next application on the desktop. This is also more consistent with the shortcuts for closing forms: Alt-F4 closes a top-level form, while Ctrl-F4 closes an MDI child; Alt-Tab moves to the next desktop application, while Ctrl-Tab moves to the next MDI child form.

MDI Events

Events for an MDI child form generally occur before the corresponding MDI parent's events. For example, if you try to close an MDI form, the child forms all receive FormClosing events before the MDI parent receives its FormClosing event. Next, the MDI child forms receive FormClosed events, and finally the MDI parent receives its FormClosed event.

Note that MDI child forms also receive these events if only the child form is closing. If the user closes an MDI child form, it receives a FormClosing event followed by its FormClosed event.

If a form's FormClosing event handler sets its e.Cancel parameter to True, the close is canceled and the form remains open. The form can use this to guarantee that its data is consistent and has been saved.

For example, the following code checks the m_IsDirty variable to see if the form's data has been modified since it was loaded. If m_IsDirty is True, the program displays a message box to the user asking if it should save the changes.

If the user clicks the Yes button, the code calls subroutine SaveFile to save the changes. This routine saves the data and sets m_IsDirty to False if it is successful. If SaveFile fails (for example, if the data file is locked), it leaves m_IsDirty set to True. If the user clicks No to indicate that the program should discard the changes, the FormClosing event handler leaves e.Cancel equal to False so the form closes normally. If the user clicks the Cancel button to indicate that the form should not be closed after all, the event handler sets e.Cancel to True to keep the form open.

```
' See if it's safe to close the form.
Private Sub mdiChild_FormClosing(ByVal sender As Object, _
 ByVal e As System.Windows.Forms.FormClosingEventArgs) _
 Handles Me.FormClosing
    If m_IsDirty Then
        ' There are unsaved changes.
        ' Ask the user if we should save them.
        Select Case MessageBox.Show( _
                "The data has changed. Save the changes?", _
                "Save Changes?", _
                MessageBoxButtons.YesNoCancel, _
                MessageBoxIcon.Question)
            Case Windows.Forms.DialogResult.Yes
                ' Save the changes.
                SaveFile()

                ' See if we succeeded.
                e.Cancel = m_IsDirty
            Case Windows.Forms.DialogResult.No
                ' Discard the changes.
                ' Leave e.Cancel = False.
            Case Windows.Forms.DialogResult.Cancel
                ' Cancel the close.
                e.Cancel = True
        End Select
    End If
End Sub
```

If the user tries to close the MDI container and *any* of the MDI child forms' FormClosing event handlers sets e.Cancel to True, the close is canceled for *all* the child forms. Any child forms that have not yet received a FormClosing event do not get one. All of the children remain open, even those that set e.Cancel = False.

After the children process their FormClosing events, the MDI parent form still gets the final word. It receives a FormClosing event with its e.Cancel value set to True if *any* of the child forms set it to True. The value e.Cancel value is False if all of the child forms left it False.

The MDI parent can leave the e.Cancel alone to accept whatever value the child forms selected, or it can override the value and force the program to exit or not as it desires.

The child forms still have one chance to save their data in their `FormClosed` events. At this point, they will close, however, so they had better take action if they need to save their data.

MDI Versus SDI

MDI and SDI applications both have their advantages. In an SDI application, building and understanding the menus is simpler. A menu applies to exactly one form, and there is no merging and swapping of menus as the user changes MDI child forms.

SDI applications work particularly well when the program works with only one document at a time. Notepad, Microsoft Paint, and similar applications that only let the user work with one file at a time are SDI applications. These programs are light enough in weight that the user can easily run more than one instance of the program to view more than one file at a time if necessary.

MDI applications help the user display many related files at once without cluttering up the desktop. For example, Visual Studio can use an MDI interface to let you examine all of the files in a project side by side. Displaying all of a project's form designers, code editors, resource editors, and other files in separate windows might bury the desktop under forms and fill the taskbar with icons. Putting all of these forms inside an MDI container makes using the application easier. It lets the system represent the Visual Studio program with a single container form and a single icon. The Windows menu provides an MDI child list that makes it easier to find a particular form.

You can also build a hybrid application that displays several MDI containers, each holding any number of MDI child forms. For example, each MDI container might hold all the forms related to a particular order: customer data, order items, and so forth. This would keep these related items together. It would also enable the user to display information about more than one order at a time in separate MDI containers.

In practice, examples of this kind of hybrid application are often cumbersome and poorly designed. It would generally be simpler to build this application as a standard MDI application and let the user launch multiple instances to display more than one order's data at once, but there may be times when it is easier to build a single multiple-MDI application. For example, if the program must work with a password-protected database, the program would need only to prompt the user for a username and password once, and all the MDI containers could share the same database connection. Often, you can avoid the need for multiple forms (and hence an MDI format) by using other controls to fit more information on a single form. For example, `ComboBox`, `ListBox`, `TreeView`, `SplitterContainer`, and many other controls can display large amounts of data in a limited space, providing scroll bars as necessary.

The `TabControl` lets an application display many pages of data on a single form. For example, you might use different tabs to display the different pages that are relevant to an order: customer data, the order itself, order items, shipping and billing addresses, and so forth. This type of tabbed form placed inside an MDI container can make a very powerful application that enables the user to easily manage and understand huge amounts of information.

One drawback to many of these controls is that they make it more difficult to perform side-by-side comparisons of values. For example, suppose that a single form displays different addresses (billing, shipping, contact, and so forth) on different tabs. Then it would be difficult for the user to compare two addresses to see if they are identical. If you know that the user may want to compare two pieces of data, try to arrange them so they can both be visible at the same time.

MRU Lists

MDI and SDI interfaces provide different ways to manage documents. Another tool that helps users manage documents is a *Most Recently Used* (MRU) list. The MRU list is a series of menu items (usually at the bottom of an application's File menu) that displays the files most recently accessed by the user. If the user clicks on one of these menu items, the program reopens the corresponding file. Figure 10-10 shows an MRU list in a simple editing application.

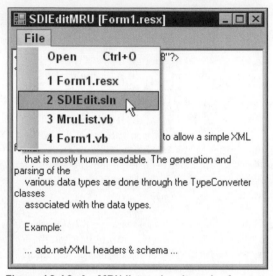

Figure 10-10: An MRU list makes it easier for users to reopen the files they have used most recently.

By convention, these menu items begin with the accelerator characters 1, 2, 3, and so forth. If you opened the File menu shown in Figure 10-10 and pressed 2, for example, the program would reopen the file SdiEdit.sln.

When the user opens a new file or saves a file with a new name, that file is placed at the top of the list. Most applications display up to four items in the MRU list and, if the list ever contains more items, the oldest are removed.

Most applications remove a file from the MRU list if the applications try to open it and fail. For example, if the user selects an MRU menu item but the corresponding file has been removed from the system, the program removes the file's menu item.

Building an MRU list isn't too difficult in Visual Basic. The following code shows a simple MruList class. The class has its own private variables to store the application's name, a reference to the main program's File menu (or whichever menu should hold the MRU list), and the maximum number of MRU list entries that it should display. It also uses private collections to hold the names of the files in the MRU list and references to the menu items it has added to the File menu.

After declaring the private variables, the class declares a public OpenFile event. It raises this event to tell the main program that the user has selected one of the MRU files.

The class's constructor takes as parameters the application's name, a reference to the File menu, and the maximum number of entries it should display. It stores those values, calls LoadMruList to load the MRU list that was saved the last time the program ran, and then calls DisplayMruList to add the MRU items to the File menu.

The subroutine LoadMruList loops through the numbers 1 to the maximum number of entries it should display and uses GetSetting to fetch a file name from the System Registry. These values are stored in the Registry area named for the application (in the section named MruList). The values themselves are named FileName1, FileName2, and so forth.

The program passes the call to GetSetting a default value of " ", so it returns a zero-length string if the value is not in the Registry. If GetSetting returns a nonblank string, the code adds it to the m_FileNames collection.

The subroutine SaveMruList saves the MRU list's current file names into the registry. It starts by using GetSetting to see if there is a FileName1 entry. If this entry is present, the program uses the DeleteSetting statement to remove the entire MruList section from the program's area in the Registry. Then SaveMruList loops through the m_FileNames collection, making the appropriate Registry entries.

The subroutine DisplayMruList builds the MRU menu items. First it loops through the m_MenuItems collection and removes any menu items that it created previously. Next, if the m_FileNames collection contains any file names, the subroutine adds a separator to the File menu. In Figure 10-10, this is the horizontal gray line above the first MRU item and below the Properties item. The routine creates this item, saves a reference to it in the m_MenuItems collection, and adds the item to the File menu.

DisplayMruList then loops through the MRU file names making their menu items. For each file, it makes a new menu item with an appropriate caption. The caption starts with an ampersand followed by a number. That makes the number appear underlined in the menu and makes the number the item's accelerator. For example, the caption "&1 Text.txt" would be displayed as "1 Test.txt." If you opened the File menu and pressed 1, this menu item would fire.

The subroutine DisplayMruList assigns the MruItem_Click event handler with the new menu item's Click event, saves a reference to the new item in the m_MenuItems collection, and then adds the item to the File menu.

The MruItem_Click event handler executes when the user clicks one of the MRU menu items. It uses DirectCast to convert the sender parameter into the ToolStripMenuItem object that raised the event. It then loops through the m_MenuItems collection looking for that item. When it finds the item, the code looks up the corresponding file name and raises the OpenFile event, passing it the file name. Note that the indexes in the m_MenuItems and m_FileNames collections differ by one, because the separator has an entry in the m_MenuItems collection but not in m_FileNames.

The subroutines Add and Remove let the main program control the MruList object. Add takes as a parameter the name of a file to add to the MRU list. It uses the FileNameIndex function to see if the file is already on the list, and it removes the file if it is present. Add then inserts the file at the front of the MRU list. If this makes the list too long, the routine removes the last entry from the m_FileNames collection. Finally, the program calls DisplayMruList to recreate the MRU list's File menu items and calls SaveMruList to update the list's registry entries.

The FileNameIndex helper function loops through the m_FileNames collection and returns a file name's index if it is present.

Finally, the subroutine Remove takes as a parameter the name of a file to remove from the MRU list. It uses FileNameIndex to get the file's index in the m_FileNames collection. If the file is present, the code removes if from the collection, calls DisplayMruList to recreate the menu items, and calls SaveMruList to update the list's registry entries.

```
Imports System.IO

Public Class MruList
    Private m_ApplicationName As String
    Private m_FileMenu As ToolStripMenuItem
    Private m_NumEntries As Integer
    Private m_FileNames As Collection
    Private m_MenuItems As Collection

    Public Event OpenFile(ByVal file_name As String)

    Public Sub New(ByVal application_name As String, _
     ByVal file_menu As ToolStripMenuItem, ByVal num_entries As Integer)
        m_ApplicationName = application_name
        m_FileMenu = file_menu
        m_NumEntries = num_entries
        m_FileNames = New Collection
        m_MenuItems = New Collection

        ' Load saved file names from the Registry.
        LoadMruList()

        ' Display the MRU list.
        DisplayMruList()
    End Sub

    ' Load previously saved file names from the Registry.
    Private Sub LoadMruList()
        Dim file_name As String
        For i As Integer = 1 To m_NumEntries
            ' Get the next file name and title.
            file_name = GetSetting(m_ApplicationName, _
                "MruList", "FileName" & i, "")

            ' See if we got anything.
            If file_name.Length > 0 Then
                ' Save this file name.
                m_FileNames.Add(file_name, file_name)
            End If
        Next i
    End Sub

    ' Save the MRU list into the Registry.
    Private Sub SaveMruList()
        ' Remove previous entries.
        If GetSetting(m_ApplicationName, "MruList", _
          "FileName1", "").Length > 0 Then
            DeleteSetting(m_ApplicationName, "MruList")
```

```vb
            End If

        ' Make the new entries.
        For i As Integer = 1 To m_FileNames.Count
            SaveSetting(m_ApplicationName, _
                "MruList", "FileName" & i, _
                m_FileNames(i).ToString)
        Next i
End Sub


' Display the MRU list.
Private Sub DisplayMruList()
    ' Remove old menu items from the File menu.
    For Each mnu As ToolStripItem In m_MenuItems
        m_FileMenu.DropDownItems.Remove(mnu)
    Next mnu
    m_MenuItems = New Collection

    ' See if we have any file names.
    If m_FileNames.Count > 0 Then
        ' Make the separator.
        Dim sep As New ToolStripSeparator()
        m_MenuItems.Add(sep)
        m_FileMenu.DropDownItems.Add(sep)

        ' Make the other menu items.
        Dim mnu As ToolStripMenuItem
        For i As Integer = 1 To m_FileNames.Count
            mnu = New ToolStripMenuItem()
            mnu.Text = "&" & i & " " & _
                New FileInfo(m_FileNames(i).ToString).Name
            AddHandler mnu.Click, AddressOf MruItem_Click
            m_MenuItems.Add(mnu)
            m_FileMenu.DropDownItems.Add(mnu)
        Next i
    End If
End Sub

' MRU menu item event handler.
Private Sub MruItem_Click(ByVal sender As System.Object, _
 ByVal e As System.EventArgs)
    Dim mnu As ToolStripMenuItem
    mnu = DirectCast(sender, ToolStripMenuItem)

    ' Find the menu item that raised this event.
    For i As Integer = 1 To m_FileNames.Count
        ' See if this is the item. (Add 1 for the separator.)
        If m_MenuItems(i + 1) Is mnu Then
            ' This is the item. Raise the OpenFile
            ' event for its file name.
            RaiseEvent OpenFile(m_FileNames(i).ToString)
            Exit For
        End If
    Next i
```

```
        End Sub

        ' Add a file to the MRU list.
        Public Sub Add(ByVal file_name As String)
            ' Remove this file from the MRU list
            ' if it is present.
            Dim i As Integer = FileNameIndex(file_name)
            If i > 0 Then m_FileNames.Remove(i)

            ' Add the item to the begining of the list.
            If m_FileNames.Count > 0 Then
                m_FileNames.Add(file_name, file_name, m_FileNames.Item(1))
            Else
                m_FileNames.Add(file_name, file_name)
            End If

            ' If the list is too long, remove the last item.
            If m_FileNames.Count > m_NumEntries Then
                m_FileNames.Remove(m_NumEntries + 1)
            End If

            ' Display the list.
            DisplayMruList()

            ' Save the updated list.
            SaveMruList()
        End Sub

        ' Return the index of this file in the list.
        Private Function FileNameIndex(ByVal file_name As String) As Integer
            For i As Integer = 1 To m_FileNames.Count
                If m_FileNames(i).ToString = file_name Then Return i
            Next i
            Return 0
        End Function

        ' Remove a file from the MRU list.
        Public Sub Remove(ByVal file_name As String)
            ' See if the file is present.
            Dim i As Integer = FileNameIndex(file_name)
            If i > 0 Then
                ' Remove the File.
                m_FileNames.Remove(i)

                ' Display the list.
                DisplayMruList()

                ' Save the updated list.
                SaveMruList()
            End If
        End Sub
    End Class
```

The following code shows how a main program can use the MruList class. This program is a simple text viewer that lets the user open and view files.

This program declares an MruList variable named m_MruList. It uses the WithEvents keyword so that it is easy to catch the object's OpenFile event.

The form's New event handler initializes the MruList object, passing it the application's name, the File menu, and the number of items the MRU list should hold.

When the user selects the File menu's Open command, the program displays an open file dialog. If the user selects a file and clicks OK, the program calls subroutine OpenFile, passing it the name of the selected file.

If the user selects a file from the MRU list, the m_MruList_OpenFile event handler executes and calls subroutine OpenFile, passing it the name of the selected file.

Subroutine OpenFile loads the file's contents into the txtContents TextBox. It then calls the MruList object's Add method, passing it the file's name. It finishes by setting the form's caption to the file's name without its directory path.

```
Imports System.IO

Public Class Form1

    Private WithEvents m_MruList As MruList

    ' Initialize the MRU list.
    Private Sub Form1_Load(ByVal sender As Object, _
     ByVal e As System.EventArgs) Handles Me.Load
        m_MruList = New MruList("SdiMruList", mnuFile, 4)
    End Sub


    ' Let the user open a file.
    Private Sub mnuFileOpen_Click(ByVal sender As System.Object, _
     ByVal e As System.EventArgs) Handles mnuFileOpen.Click
        If dlgOpen.ShowDialog() = Windows.Forms.DialogResult.OK Then
            OpenFile(dlgOpen.FileName)
        End If
    End Sub


    ' Open a file selected from the MRU list.
    Private Sub m_MruList_OpenFile(ByVal file_name As String) _
     Handles m_MruList.OpenFile
        OpenFile(file_name)
    End Sub


    ' Open a file and add it to the MRU list.
    Private Sub OpenFile(ByVal file_name As String)
        txtContents.Text = File.ReadAll(file_name)
        txtContents.Select(0, 0)
        m_MruList.Add(file_name)
        Me.Text = "[" & New FileInfo(file_name).Name & "]"
    End Sub
End Class
```

You could easily convert the MruList class into a component. If you give the component ApplicationName, FileMenu, and MaxEntries properties, you can set those values at design time. For more information about building components, see Chapter 12, "Custom Controls."

Dialogs

Using a form as a dialog is easy. Create the form and give it whatever controls it needs to do its job. Add one or more buttons to let the user dismiss the dialog. Many dialogs use OK and Cancel buttons, but you can also use Yes, No, Retry, and others. You may also want to set the form's FormBorderStyle property to FixedDialog, although that's not mandatory

Set the form's AcceptButton property to the button you want to invoke if the user presses the Enter key. Set its CancelButton property to the button you want to invoke when the user presses the Esc key.

The form's DialogResult property indicates the dialog's return value. If the main program displays the dialog by using its ShowDialog method, ShowDialog returns the DialogResult value. The following code shows how the main program can display a dialog and react to its result. It creates a new instance of the dlgEmployee form and displays it by calling its ShowDialog method. If the user clicks OK, then ShowDialog returns DialogResult.OK and the program displays the employee's name entered on the dialog. If the user clicks the Cancel button, ShowDialog returns DialogResult.Cancel and the program displays the message "Canceled."

```
Private Sub btnShowDialog_Click(ByVal sender As System.Object, _
  ByVal e As System.EventArgs) Handles btnShowDialog.Click
    Dim dlg As New dlgEmployee
    If dlg.ShowDialog() = Windows.Forms.DialogResult.OK Then
        MessageBox.Show( _
            dlg.txtFirstName.Text & " " & _
            dlg.txtLastName.Text)
    Else
        MessageBox.Show("Canceled")
    End If
End Sub
```

If the user clicks the Cancel button or closes the form by using the system menu, the form automatically sets its DialogResult property to Cancel and closes the form.

If the user clicks some other button, your event handler should set DialogResult to an appropriate value. Setting this value automatically closes the form.

You can also set a button's DialogResult property to indicate the value that the dialog should return when the user presses that button. When the user presses the button, Visual Basic sets the form's DialogResult property automatically.

The following code shows how the employee form reacts when the user clicks the OK button. It sees if the first and last name TextBox controls contain nonblank values. If either value is blank, the event handler displays an error message and returns without setting the form's DialogResult property. If both values are nonblank, the code sets DialogResult to OK, and setting DialogResult closes the form. Note that the dialog doesn't need an event handler for the Cancel button. If the user clicks Cancel, Visual Basic automatically sets the form's DialogResult to Cancel and closes the form.

```
Private Sub btnOk_Click(ByVal sender As System.Object, _
 ByVal e As System.EventArgs) Handles btnOk.Click
    ' Verify that the first name is present.
    If txtFirstName.Text.Length = 0 Then
        MessageBox.Show( _
            "Please enter a First Name", _
            "First Name Required", _
            MessageBoxButtons.OK, _
            MessageBoxIcon.Exclamation)
        txtFirstName.Select()
        Exit Sub
    End If

    ' Verify that the last name is present.
    If txtLastName.Text.Length = 0 Then
        MessageBox.Show( _
            "Please enter a Last Name", _
            "Last Name Required", _
            MessageBoxButtons.OK, _
            MessageBoxIcon.Exclamation)
        txtLastName.Select()
        Exit Sub
    End If

    ' Accept the dialog.
    Me.DialogResult = Windows.Forms.DialogResult.OK
End Sub
```

Many dialogs provide OK and Cancel buttons, so they usually set `DialogResult` to `OK` or `Cancel`. However, you can also set `DialogResult` to `Abort`, `Ignore`, `No`, `None`, `Retry`, and `Yes` if that makes sense for your program. The main program can use an `If Then` or `Select Case` statement to see which value was set.

Wizards

One common type of dialog is called a *wizard*. A wizard is a form that guides the user through a series of steps to do something. For example, building a database connection is complicated, so Visual Basic provides a data connection configuration wizard that helps the user enter the correct information for different kinds of databases. When it finishes, the wizard adds a connection object to the current form.

Figure 10-11 shows a typical wizard. The user enters data on each tab and then moves on to the next one. This wizard asks the user to enter an employee's name, identification (Social Security number and Employee ID), address and phone number, office location and extension, and privileges.

When the user has filled in all the fields, the wizard enables the OK button. When the user clicks the OK or Cancel button, control returns to the main program, which handles the result just as it handles any other dialog.

Figure 10-12 shows a different style of wizard. Instead of tabs, it uses buttons to let the user move through its pages of fields. The wizard only enables a button when the user has filled in the necessary information on the previous page. In Figure 10-12, the Office button is disabled because the user has not filled in all the fields on the Address page.

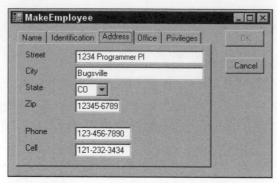

Figure 10-11: A wizard guides the user through the steps of some complicated task.

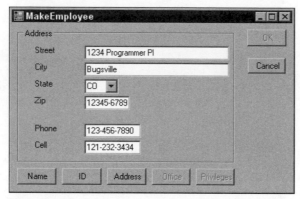

Figure 10-12: This wizard uses buttons instead of tabs to move through its pages of data.

Summary

While forms are just one kind of control, they have some very special characteristics. They form the basic pieces of an application that sit on the desktop, and they have many properties, methods, and events that set forms apart from other controls. Appendix H, "Form Objects," provides more information about form properties, methods, and events.

This chapter describes some of the more typical uses of forms. It explains how to build About, Splash, and Login Forms; manage a form's mouse cursors and icons; override WndProc to intercept a form's Windows messages; build MDI applications and tools that help the user manage MDI child forms; and make dialogs and wizards. After you master these tasks, you can build the forms that implement the large-scale pieces of an application.

Chapter 9 described standard Windows Forms controls and components. This chapter explained forms, which are specialized types of controls. Chapter 11, "Database Controls and Objects," explains controls and components that are useful in database applications. They include components to connect an application to a database and to move data between the database and the application.

Database Controls and Objects

The Windows forms controls described in Chapter 10 allow the application and the user to communicate. They let the application display data to the user, and they let the user control the application.

Visual Basic's database controls play roughly the same role between the application and a database. They move data from the database to the application, and they allow the application to send data back to the database.

Database programming is an enormous topic, and many books have been written that focus exclusively on database programming. This is such a huge field that no general Visual Basic book can adequately cover it in any real depth. However, database programming is also a very important topic, and every Visual Basic programmer should know at least something about using databases in applications.

This chapter explains how to build data sources and use drag and drop to create simple table- and record-oriented displays. It also explains the most useful controls and objects that Visual Basic provides for working with databases. While this is far from the end of the story, it will help you get started building basic database applications.

Automatically Connecting to Data

Visual Studio 2005 provides new tools that make getting started with databases easier than ever. To build a simple database program, start a new application and select the Data menu's Add New Data Source command to display the Data Source Configuration Wizard shown in Figure 11-1.

Visual Studio 2005 allows you to use databases, Web Services, and objects in your application. The most straightforward choice is Database.

Select the type of data source you want add and click Next to pick a data connection on the page shown in Figure 11-2.

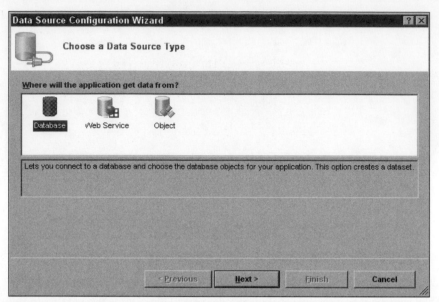

Figure 11-1: The Data Source Configuration Wizard lets you add or configure data sources.

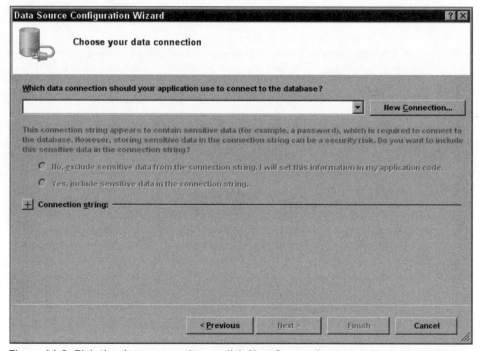

Figure 11-2: Pick the data connection or click New Connection to create a new one.

If you have previously created data connections, you can select one from the dropdown. If you have not created any data connections, click the New Connection button to open the dialog shown in Figure 11-3.

Figure 11-3: Use the Add Connection dialog to create a data connection.

If you don't like the default data source type selected by the dialog (in this example, Microsoft Access Database File), click the Change button to display the dialog shown in Figure 11-4. This dialog lets you select different kinds of databases such as Microsoft Access, ODBC data sources, SQL Server databases, and Oracle databases.

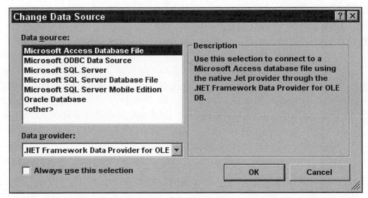

Figure 11-4: The Change Data Source dialog to select a new kind of database.

After you have selected the database type, close the Change Data Source dialog and return to the Add Connection dialog. Depending on the type of database you selected in Figure 11-4, this dialog may no longer look like Figure 11-3. For example, Figure 11-5 shows what the Add Connection dialog looks like if you select a SQL Server database.

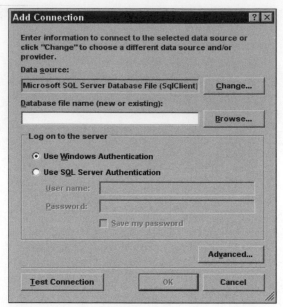

Figure 11-5: The Add Connection dialog looks like this for SQL Server databases.

Enter the necessary data in the Add Connection dialog. For a SQL Server database, select the server name, authentication method, database name, and other information.

For a Microsoft Access database, enter the file name or click the Browse button shown in Figure 11-3 and find the database file. Enter a user name and password if necessary and click OK.

When you return to the Data Source Configuration Wizard, select the new connection as shown in Figure 11-6. If you click the plus sign next to the "Connection string" label, the wizard shows the connection information it will use to connect the data source to the database.

When you click Next, the wizard tells you that you have selected a local database file that is not part of the project and it asks if you want to add it to the project. If you click Yes, the wizard adds the database to the project so it shows up in Project Explorer. If you plan to distribute the database with the application, you may want to do this to make it easier to manage the database and the Visual Basic source code together.

Next the wizard displays the dialog shown in Figure 11-7, asking if you want to save the connection string in the project's configuration file. If you leave this box checked, the wizard adds the configuration string to the project's app.config file.

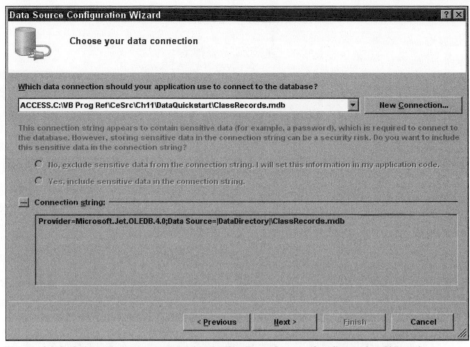

Figure 11-6: Select the new connection in the Data Source Configuration Wizard.

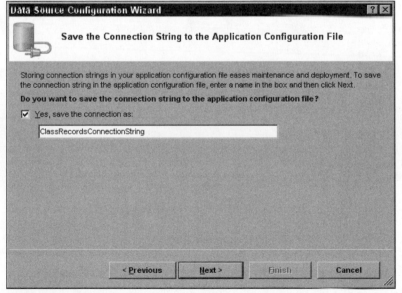

Figure 11-7: Decide whether you want to include the connection string in the configuration file.

The following shows the part of the configuration file containing the connection string.

```
<connectionStrings>
    <add name="SimpleDBApp.Settings.ClassRecordsConnectionString"
        connectionString="Provider=Microsoft.Jet.OLEDB.4.0;Data
Source=|DataDirectory|\ClassRecords.mdb"
        providerName="System.Data.OleDb" />
</connectionStrings>
```

Later, the program uses the `Settings.Default.ClassRecordsConnectionString` values to get this value and connect to the database. You can easily make the program connect to another data source by changing this configuration setting and then restarting the application.

You should never save database passwords in the configuration file. The file is stored in plain text and anyone can read it. If you need to use a password, store a connection string that contains a placeholder for the real password. Then at run time, load the connection string and replace the placeholder with a real password entered by the user.

Click Next to display the dialog shown in Figure 11-8. This page shows the objects available in the database. In this example, the database contains two tables named Students and TestScores. By clicking on the plus signs next to the objects, you can expand them to see what they contain. In Figure 11-8, the tables are expanded so you can see the fields they contain.

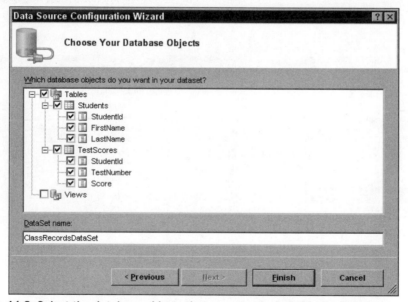

Figure 11-8: Select the database objects that you want included in the data source.

Select the database objects that you want to include in the data source. In Figure 11-8, both of the tables are selected.

When you click Finish, the wizard adds a couple objects to the application. The Solution Explorer shown in Figure 11-9 lists the database ClassRecords.mdb and the new file ClassRecordsDataSet.xsd. This is a schema definition file that describes the data source.

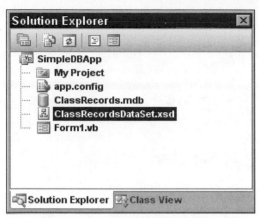

Figure 11-9: The Data Source Configuration Wizard
adds a database and schema to Solution Explorer.

If you double-click the schema file, Visual Basic opens it in the editor shown in Figure 11-10. This display shows the tables defined by the schema and their fields.

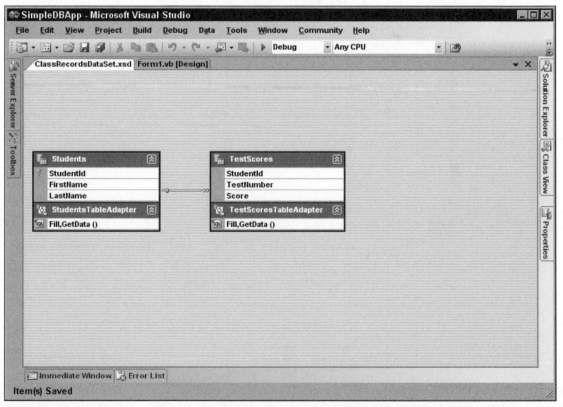

Figure 11-10: The Schema Editor shows the tables defined by the schema and their relationships.

The line between the files with the little key on the left and the infinity symbol on the right indicates that the tables are joined by a one-to-many relationship. In this example, the Students.StudentId field and TestScores.StudentId field form a foreign key relationship. That means every StudentId value in the TestScores table must correspond to some StudentId value in the Students table. If you double-click the relationship link or right-click it and select Edit Relation, the editor displays the dialog shown in Figure 11-11.

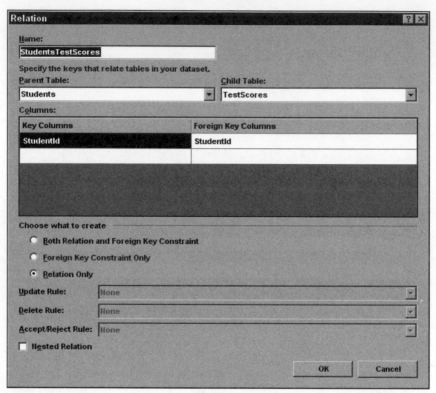

Figure 11-11: Use this dialog to edit relationships among data source tables.

At the bottom of the tables shown in Figure 11-10, you can see two data adapter objects containing the labels "Fill,GetData()." These represent data adapter objects that the program will later use to move data from and to the data source.

In addition to adding the schema file to Solution Explotet, the wizard also added a new DataSet object to the Data Sources window shown in Figure 11-12. (If this window is not visible, select the Data menu's Show Data Sources command.)

You can use the plus signs next to expand the objects contained within the DataSet. In Figure 11-12, the DataSet is expanded to show its tables, and the tables are expanded to show their fields. Notice that the TestScores table is listed below the Students table because it has a parent/child relationship with that table.

It takes a lot of words and pictures to describe this process, but using the wizard to build the data source is actually quite fast. After you have created the data source, you can build a simple user interface with no extra work. Simply drag objects from the Data Sources window onto the form.

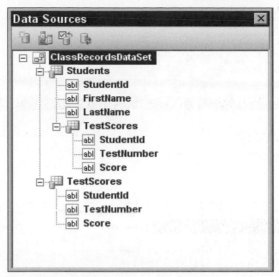

Figure 11-12: The Data Sources window lists the new data source.

If you click and drag a table from the Data Sources window onto the form, Visual Basic automatically creates `BindingNavigator` and `DataGridView` controls, and other components to display the data from the table. Figure 11-13 shows the result.

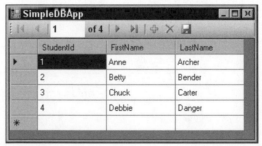

Figure 11-13: Drag and drop a table from the Data Sources window onto the form to create a simple `DataGridView`.

Instead of dragging an entire table onto the form, you can drag individual database columns. In that case, Visual Basic adds controls to the form to represent the column. Figure 11-14 shows the columns from the Students table dragged onto a form.

If you select a table in the Data Sources window, a drop-down arrow appears on the right. Open the drop-down to give the table a different display style, as shown in Figure 11-15. For example, if you set a table's style to Details and drag the table onto a form, Visual Basic displays the table's data using a record detail view similar to the one shown in Figure 11-14 instead of the grid shown in Figure 11-13.

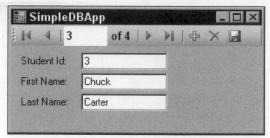

Figure 11-14: Drag and drop table columns onto a form to create a record-oriented view instead of a grid.

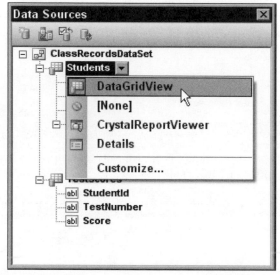

Figure 11-15: Use the drop-down in the Data Sources window to give a table a different display style.

Similarly, you can change the display styles for specific database columns. Select a column in the Data Sources window and click its drop-down arrow to make it display in a text box, label, link label, combo box, or other control. Now, when you drag the column onto a form, or when you drag the table onto the form to build a record view, Visual Basic uses this type of control to display the column's values.

Automatically Created Objects

When you drag database tables and columns from the Data Sources window onto a form, Visual Basic does a lot more than simply placing a `DataGridView` control on a form. It also creates about two dozen other controls and components. Four of the more important of these objects are the `DataSet`, `TableAdapter`, `BindingSource`, and `BindingNavigator`. You can see these components in the component area below the form in Figure 11-16.

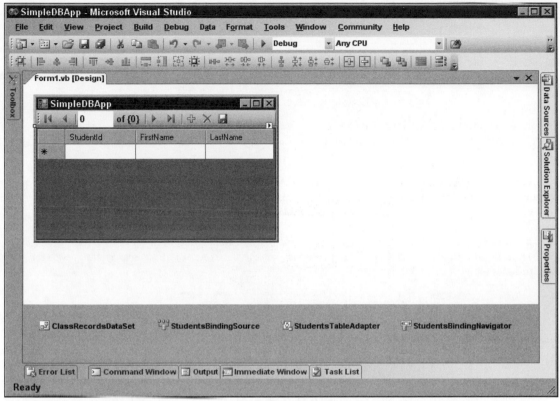

Figure 11-16: Visual Basic uses `DataSet`, `TableAdapter`, `BindingSource`, and `BindingNavigator` components to manage a `DataGridView` display.

The program stores data in a `DataSet` object. A single `DataSet` object can represent an entire database. It contains `DataTable` objects that represent database tables. Each `DataTable` contains `DataRow` objects that represent rows in a table, and each `DataRow` contains items representing column values for the row.

The `TableAdapter` object copies data between the database and the `DataSet`. It has methods for performing operations on the database (such as selecting, inserting, updating, and deleting records). Hidden inside the `TableAdapter` is a connection object that contains information on the database so that the `TableAdapter` knows where to find it.

The `BindingSource` object encapsulates all of the `DataSet`'s data and provides programmatic control functions. These perform such actions as moving through the data, adding and deleting items, and so forth.

The `BindingNavigator` provides a user interface so the user can control the `BindingSource`.

Figure 11-17 shows the relationships among the `DataSet`, `TableAdapter`, `BindingSource`, and `BindingNavigator` objects.

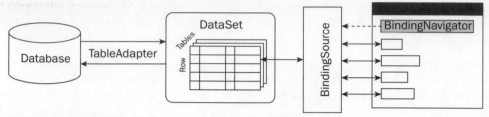

Figure 11-17: Visual Basic uses `DataSet`, `TableAdapter`, `BindingSource`, **and** `BindingNavigator` **objects to display data.**

Even all these objects working together don't quite do everything you need to make the program display data. When it creates these objects, Visual Basic also adds the following code to the form. The `Form1_Load` event handler makes the `TableAdapter` copy data from the database into the `DataSet`.

The `bindingNavigatorSaveItem_Click` event handler fires when the user clicks the `BindingNavigator`'s Save tool. This routine makes the `TableAdapter` save any changes to the Students table to the database.

```
Public Class Form1

    Private Sub Form1_Load(ByVal sender As System.Object, _
     ByVal e As System.EventArgs) Handles MyBase.Load
        'TODO: This line of code loads data into the 'ClassRecordsDataSet.Students'
        ' table. You can move, or remove it, as needed.
        Me.StudentsTableAdapter.Fill(Me.ClassRecordsDataSet.Students)

    End Sub

    Private Sub StudentsBindingNavigatorSaveItem_Click(ByVal sender As
System.Object, _
     ByVal e As System.EventArgs) Handles StudentsBindingNavigatorSaveItem.Click
        Me.Validate()
        Me.StudentsBindingSource.EndEdit()
        Me.StudentsTableAdapter.Update(Me.ClassRecordsDataSet.Students)

    End Sub
End Class
```

Visual Basic builds all this automatically, and if you ran the program at this point, it would display data and let you manipulate it. It's still not perfect, however. It doesn't perform any data validation, and it will let you close the application without saving any changes you have made to the data. It's a pretty good start for such a small amount of work, however.

Other Data Objects

If you want a simple program that can display and modify data, then the solution described in the previous sections may be good enough. In that case, you should let Visual Basic do most of the work for you, and you don't need to dig into the lower-level details of database access.

You can also use objects similar to those created by Visual Basic to build your own solutions. On one hand, you can create your own `DataSet`, `TableAdapter`, `BindingSource`, and `BindingNavigator` objects to bind controls to a database.

On the other hand, if you need to manipulate the database directly with code, it doesn't necessarily make sense to create all these objects. If you simply want to modify a record programmatically, it certainly doesn't make sense to create `DataGridView`, `BindingNavigator`, and `BindingSource` objects.

For cases such as this, Visual Basic provides several other kinds of objects that you can use to interact with databases. These objects fall into the following four categories:

❑ *Data containers* hold data after is has been loaded from the database into the application much as a `DataSet` does. You can bind controls to these objects to automatically display and manipulate the data.

❑ *Connections* provide information that lets the program connect to the database.

❑ *Data adapters* move data between a database and a data container.

❑ *Command objects* provide instructions for manipulating data. A command object can select, update, insert, or delete data in the database. It can also execute stored procedures in the database.

Data container and adapter classes are generic and work with different kinds of databases, while different types of connection and command objects are specific to different kinds of databases. For example, the connection objects `OleDbConnection`, `SqlConnection`, `OdbcConnection`, and `OracleConnection` objects work with Object Linking and Embedding Database (OLE DB); SQL Server, including Microsoft Data Engine (MSDE); Open Database Connectivity (ODBC); and Oracle databases, respectively. The SQL Server and Oracle objects work only with their specific brand of database, but they are more completely optimized for those databases and may give better performance

Aside from the different database types they support, the various objects work in more or less the same way. The following sections explain how an application uses those objects to move data to and from the database. They describe the most useful properties, methods, and events provided by the connection, transaction, data adapter, and command objects.

Later sections describe the `DataSet` and `DataView` objects and tell how you can use them to bind controls to display data automatically.

Data Overview

An application uses three basic objects to move data to and from a database: a connection, a data adapter, and a data container such as a `DataSet`. The connection object defines the connection to the database. It contains information about the database's name and location, any username and password needed to access the data, database engine information, and flags that determine the kinds of access the program will need.

The data adapter object defines a mapping from the database to the `DataSet`. It determines what data is selected from the database, and which database columns are mapped to which `DataSet` columns.

The DataSet object stores the data within the application. It can hold more than one table and can define and enforce relationships among the tables. For example, the database used in the earlier examples in this chapter has a TestScores table that has a StudentId field. The values in this field must be values listed in the Students table. This is called a *foreign key constraint*. The DataSet can represent this constraint and raise an error if the program tries to create a TestScores record with a StudentId value that does not appear in the Students table.

Once the connection, data adapter, and DataSet objects are initialized, the program can call the data adapter's Fill method to copy data from the database into the DataSet. Later it can call the data adapter's Update method to copy any changes to the data from the DataSet back into the database. Figure 11-18 shows the process.

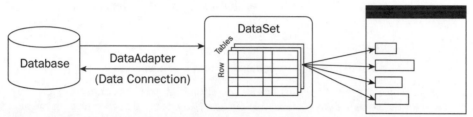

Figure 11-18: An application uses connection, data adapter, and DataSet objects to move data to and from the database.

If you compare Figure 11-18 to Figure 11-17, you'll see several similarities. Both approaches use an adapter to copy data between the database and a DataSet. At first glance, it may seem that Figure 11-17 doesn't use a connection object, but actually the TableAdapter contains a connection object internally that it uses to access the database.

One major difference is that Figure 11-17 uses a BindingSource to provide an extra layer between the DataSet and the program's controls. It also includes a DataNavigator object that lets the user control the BindingSource to move through the data.

As in the previous example, a program using the objects shown in Figure 11-18 could call the data adapter's Fill method in a form's Load event handler. Later it could call the Update method when the user clicked a Save button, in the form's FormClosing event handler, or whenever you wanted to save the data.

Connection Objects

The connection object manages the application's connection to the database. It allows a data adapter to move data in and out of a DataSet.

The different flavors of connection object (OleDbConnection, SqlConnection, OdbcConnection, OracleConnection, and so forth) provide roughly the same features, but there are some differences. Check the online help to see if a particular property, method, or event is supported by one of the flavors. The Web page http://msdn.microsoft.com/library/en-us/cpguide/html/cpconADONETConnections.asp provides links to pages that explain how to connect to SQL Server,

OLE DB, ODBC, and Oracle data sources. Other links lead to information on the `SqlConnection`, `OleDbConnection`, and `OdbcConnection` classes.

If you will be working extensively with a particular type of database (for example, SQL Server), also review the features provided by its type of connection object to see if it has special features for that type of database.

Some connection objects can work with more than one type of database. For example, the `OleDbConnection` object works with any database that supports ODBC connections. Generally, connections that work with a specific kind of database (such as `SqlConnection` and `OracleConnection`) give better performance. If you think you might later need to change databases, you can minimize the amount of work required by sticking to features that are shared by all the types of connection object.

The Toolbox window does not automatically display tools for these objects. To add them, right-click on the Toolbox tab where you want them and select Choose Items. Check the boxes next to the tools you want to add (for example, OracleCommand or OdbcConnection) and click OK.

The following table describes the most useful properties provided by the `OleDbConnection` and `SqlConnection` classes.

Property	Purpose
ConnectionString	The string that defines the connection to the database.
ConnectionTimeout	The time the object waits while trying to connect to the database. If this timeout expires, the object gives up and raises an error.
Database	Returns the name of the current database.
DataSource	Returns the name of the current database file or database server.
Provider	(`OleDbConnection` only) Returns the name of the OLE DB database provider (for example, "Microsoft.Jet.OLEDB.4.0").
ServerVersion	Returns the database server's version number. This value is available only when the connection is open and may look like "04.00.0000."
State	Returns the connection's current state. This value can be Closed, Connecting, Open, Executing (executing a command), Fetching (fetching data), and Broken (the connection was open but then broke; you can close and reopen the connection).

The `ConnectionString` property includes many fields separated by semicolons. The following text shows a typical `ConnectionString` value for an `OleDbConnection` object that will open an Access database. The text here shows each embedded field on a separate line, but the actual string would be all run together in one long line.

```
Jet OLEDB:Global Partial Bulk Ops=2;
Jet OLEDB:Registry Path=;
Jet OLEDB:Database Locking Mode=1;
Data Source="C:\Personnel\Data\Personnel.mdb";
Mode=Share Deny None;
```

```
Jet OLEDB:Engine Type=5;
Provider="Microsoft.Jet.OLEDB.4.0";
Jet OLEDB:System database=;
Jet OLEDB:SFP=False;
persist security info=False;
Extended Properties=;
Jet OLEDB:Compact Without Replica Repair=False;
Jet OLEDB:Encrypt Database=False;
Jet OLEDB:Create System Database=False;
Jet OLEDB:Don't Copy Locale on Compact=False;
User ID=Admin;
Jet OLEDB:Global Bulk Transactions=1"
```

Many of these properties are optional and you can omit them. Remembering which ones are optional (or even which fields are allowed for a particular type of connection object) is not always easy. Fortunately, it's also not necessary. Instead of typing all these fields into your code or in the connection control's ConnectString property in the Properties window, you can let Visual Basic build the string for you.

Select the View menu's Server Explorer command to display the Server Explorer shown in Figure 11-19. (Yes, the Server Explorer command displays the Server Explorer, at least in Visual Basic 2005 Beta 2. Perhaps this will be fixed before the final release.)

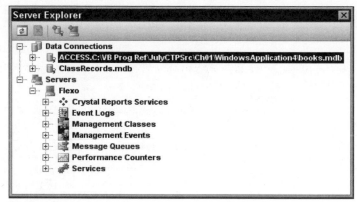

Figure 11-19: The Database Explorer can generate a connection string for you.

Right-click on the Database Connections item and select Add Connection to display the dialog shown in Figure 11-20. Use the Change button to select a different kind of database such as SQL Server or Oracle.

Enter the information necessary to connect to your selected kind of database. For a Microsoft Access Database File (OLE DB) connection, enter the database file's name or click Browse to locate it. Then click OK to create the connection.

On the Server Explorer window, click on the new connection. Then open the Properties window and select the Connection String property. You cannot change this value, but you can select it. Click on the value and press Home to move to the beginning. Then press Shift-End to select the value, and press Ctrl-C to copy it to the clipboard. Now you can paste the value into your code. The following shows the result for one database. This text is broken across two lines so it's easier to read but it comes from the Properties window all on one long line.

```
Provider=Microsoft.Jet.OLEDB.4.0;
Data Source="C:\VB Prog Ref\JulyCTPSrc\Ch11\books.mdb"
```

Figure 11-20: Use the Add Connection dialog to configure a new database connection.

The following code fragment shows how a program can create, open, use, and close an `OleDbConnection` object.

```
' To use this Imports statement, add a reference to System.Data.
Imports System.Data.OleDb

Public Class Form1
    Private Sub Form1_Load(ByVal sender As System.Object, _
    ByVal e As System.EventArgs) Handles MyBase.Load
        ' Create the connection.
        Dim conn As New OleDbConnection( _
            "Provider=Microsoft.Jet.OLEDB.4.0;" & _
            "Data Source=""C:\VB Prog Ref\JulyCTPSrc\Ch11\books.mdb"";")
"Persist Security Info=True;" & _
"Jet OLEDB:Database Password=MyPassword")

        ' Open the connection.
        conn.Open()

        ' Do stuff with the connection.
        '...

        ' Close the connection.
        conn.Close()
        conn.Dispose()
    End Sub
End Class
```

The following table describes the most useful methods provided by the `OleDbConnection` and `SqlConnection` classes.

Method	Purpose
BeginTransaction	Begins a database transaction and returns a transaction object representing it. A transaction lets the program ensure that a series of commands are either all performed or all canceled as a group. See the section "Transaction Objects" later in this chapter for more information.
ChangeDatabase	Changes the currently open database.
Close	Closes the database connection.
CreateCommand	Creates a command object that can perform some action on the database. The action might select records, create a table, update a record, and so forth.
Open	Opens the connection using the values specified in the `ConnectionString` property.

The connection object's most useful events are `InfoMessage` and `StateChange`. The `InfoMessage` event occurs when the database provider issues a warning or informational message. The program can read the message and take action or display it to the user. The `StateChange` event occurs when the database connection's state changes.

Note that the method for using a connection object shown in Figure 10-18 relies on the data adapter's `Fill` and `Update` methods, not on the connection object's `Open` and `Close` methods. `Fill` and `Update` automatically open the connection, perform their tasks, and then close the connection so that you don't need to manage the connection object yourself. For example, when the program calls `Fill`, the data adapter quickly opens the connection, copies data from the database into the `DataSet`, and then closes the database. When you use this model for database interaction, the data connections are open only very briefly.

Transaction Objects

A transaction defines a set of database actions that should be executed "atomically" as a single unit. Either all of them should occur or none of them should occur, but no action should execute without all of the others.

The classic example is a transfer of money from one account to another. Suppose that the program tries to subtract money from one account and then add it to another. After it subtracts the money from the first account, however, the program crashes. The database has lost money—a bad situation for the owners of the accounts.

On the other hand, suppose that the program performs the operations in the reverse order: first it adds money to the second account and then subtracts it from the first. This time if the program gets halfway through the operation before crashing, the database has created new money—a bad situation for the bank.

The solution is to wrap these two operations in a database transaction. If the program gets halfway through the transaction and then crashes, the database engine unwinds the transaction, so the data looks as if nothing had happened. This isn't as good as performing the whole transaction flawlessly, but at least the database is consistent and the money has been conserved.

To use transactions in Visual Basic, the program uses a connection object's BeginTransaction method to open a transaction. It then creates command objects associated with the connection and the transaction, and it executes them. When it has finished, the program can call the transaction object's Commit method to make all the actions occur, or it can call Rollback to cancel them all.

The following code shows an example. The program begins by defining a connection string. When it starts, the program uses the string to open a database connection. It calls the subroutine ShowValues and closes the connection.

The subroutine ShowValues creates a command object that selects records from the Accounts table. It executes the command and gets an OleDbDataReader to process the results. It then loops through the returned records building a string holding the records' AccountName and Balance fields, and displays the result in the program's txtValues text box.

When the user clicks the Update button, the program reopens the connection and uses its BeginTransaction method to make the transaction object trans. Next, the code defines an OleDbCommand object named cmd, setting its command text to "UPDATE People SET Balance=Balance + ? WHERE AccountName=?" Note that it passes the transaction object into the command object's constructor to make the command part of the transaction.

The question marks in the command text represent parameters to the command. The program defines the parameters' values by adding two parameter objects to the command object. It then calls the command's ExecuteNonQuery method to perform the query.

The code clears the command's parameters, adds two parameters with different values and calls the command's ExecuteNonQuery method again.

Now the program displays a message box asking whether you want to commit the transaction. If you click "Yes," then the program calls the transaction's Commit method and both of the update operations occur. If you click "No," the program calls the transaction's Rollback method and both of the update operations are canceled.

The program finishes by calling ShowValues to display the updated data and by closing the connection.

```
Imports System.Data
Imports System.Data.OleDb

Public Class Form1

    Private Const CONNECT_STRING As String = _
        "Provider=Microsoft.Jet.OLEDB.4.0;" & _
        "Data Source=C:\VB Prog Ref\" & _
            "JulyCTP\Ch11\Transactions\CustomerAccounts.mdb;" & _
        "Persist Security Info=False"

    Private Sub Form1_Load(ByVal sender As System.Object, _
     ByVal e As System.EventArgs) Handles MyBase.Load
        ' Open the connection.
        Dim connAccounts As New OleDbConnection(CONNECT_STRING)
        connAccounts.Open()

        ' Display the current balances.
        ShowValues(connAccounts)

        ' Close the connection.
        connAccounts.Close()
    End Sub

    ' Display the account values.
    Private Sub ShowValues(ByVal conn As OleDbConnection)
        Dim txt As String = ""
        Dim select_cmd As New OleDbCommand( _
            "SELECT * FROM Accounts", _
            conn)
        Dim reader As OleDbDataReader = select_cmd.ExecuteReader()
        Do While reader.Read()
            txt &= _
                reader.Item("AccountName").ToString & ": " & _
                reader.Item("Balance").ToString & vbCrLf
        Loop

        txtValues.Text = txt
    End Sub

    Private Sub btnUpdate_Click(ByVal sender As System.Object, _
     ByVal e As System.EventArgs) Handles btnUpdate.Click
        ' Open the connection.
        Dim connAccounts As New OleDbConnection(CONNECT_STRING)
        connAccounts.Open()

        ' Make the transaction.
        Dim trans As OleDbTransaction = _
            connAccounts.BeginTransaction(IsolationLevel.ReadCommitted)

        ' Make a Command for this connection.
        ' and this transaction.
        Dim cmd As New OleDbCommand( _
            "UPDATE Accounts SET Balance=Balance + ? WHERE AccountName=?", _
```

```
            connAccounts, _
            trans)

        ' Create parameters for the first command.
        cmd.Parameters.Add(New OleDbParameter("Balance", _
            Decimal.Parse(txtAmount.Text)))
        cmd.Parameters.Add(New OleDbParameter("AccountName", _
            "Alice's Software Emporium"))

        ' Execute the second command.
        cmd.ExecuteNonQuery()

        ' Create parameters for the second command.
        cmd.Parameters.Clear()
        cmd.Parameters.Add(New OleDbParameter("Balance", _
            Decimal.Parse(txtAmount.Text)))
        cmd.Parameters.Add(New OleDbParameter("AccountName", _
            "Bob's Consulting"))

        ' Execute the second command.
        cmd.ExecuteNonQuery()

        ' Commit the transaction.
        If MessageBox.Show( _
            "Commit transaction?", _
            "Commit?", _
            MessageBoxButtons.YesNo, _
            MessageBoxIcon.Question) = Windows.Forms.DialogResult.Yes _
        Then
            ' Commit the transaction.
            trans.Commit()
        Else
            ' Rollback the transaction.
            trans.Rollback()
        End If

        ' Display the current balances.
        ShowValues(connAccounts)

        ' Close the connection.
        connAccounts.Close()
    End Sub
End Class
```

Instead of clicking "Yes" or "No" when the program asks if it should commit the transaction, you can use the IDE to stop the program. If you then restart the program, you will see that neither update was processed.

In addition to the Commit and Rollback methods, transaction objects may provide other methods for performing more complex transactions. For example, the OleDbTransaction class has a Begin method that enables you to create a nested transaction. Similarly, the SqlTransaction class has a Save method that creates a "savepoint" that you can use to roll back part of the transaction. See the online help for the type of transaction object you are using to learn about these methods. The Web page `http://msdn.microsoft` `.com/library/en-us/cpguide/html/cpconperformingtransactionusingadonet.asp` gives an overview or using transactions. Links at the bottom lead to information about the `OleDbTransaction`, `SqlTransaction`, and `OdbcTransaction` classes.

Data Adapters

A data adapter transfers data between a connection and a `DataSet`. This object's most important methods are `Fill` and `Update`, which move data from and to the database. A data adapter also provides properties and other methods that can be useful. The following table describes the object's most useful properties.

Property	Purpose
DeleteCommand	The command object that the adapter uses to delete rows.
InsertCommand	The command object that the adapter uses to insert rows.
SelectCommand	The command object that the adapter uses to select rows.
TableMappings	A collection of `DataTableMapping` objects that determine how tables in the database are mapped to tables in the `DataSet`. Each `DataTableMapping` object has a `ColumnMappings` collection that determines how the columns in the database table are mapped to columns in the `DataSet` table.
UpdateCommand	The command object that the adapter uses to update rows.

There are a couple of ways you can create the command objects. For example, if you use the Data Adapter Configuration Wizard (described shortly) to build the adapter at design time, the wizard automatically creates these objects. You can select the adapter and expand these objects in the Properties window to read their properties, including the `CommandText` property that defines the commands.

Another way to create these commands is to use a command builder object. If you attach a command builder to a data adapter, the adapter uses the command builder to generate the commands it needs automatically.

The following code shows how a program could associate an `OleDbCommandBuilder` object with an `OleDbDataAdapter`. When it calls the adapter's `Update` method, the adapter uses the command builder if necessary to generate insert, update, and delete commands. The `Debug.WriteLine` statements display the text of the automatically generated commands.

```
Private Sub Form1_Load(ByVal sender As System.Object, _
  ByVal e As System.EventArgs) Handles MyBase.Load
    'TODO: This line of code loads data into the 'BooksDataSet.Books' table.
    ' You can move, or remove it, as needed.
    Me.BooksTableAdapter.Fill(Me.BooksDataSet.Books)

    ' Attach a command builder to the data adapter
    ' and display the geneated commands.
    Dim command_builder As New OleDbCommandBuilder(OleDbDataAdapter1)
```

```
        Debug.WriteLine(command_builder.GetDeleteCommand.CommandText)
        Debug.WriteLine(command_builder.GetInsertCommand.CommandText)
        Debug.WriteLine(command_builder.GetUpdateCommand.CommandText)
    End Sub
```

The following text shows the results of the previous Debug statements. The UPDATE statement is wrapped across two lines, but is one line in the Output window. The command builder generated these commands based on the select statement "SELECT Title, URL From Books" that was used to load the DataSet.

```
DELETE FROM Books WHERE ((Title = ?) AND ((? = 1 AND URL IS NULL) OR (URL = ?)))
INSERT INTO Books (Title, URL) VALUES (?, ?)
UPDATE Books SET Title = ?, URL = ? WHERE ((Title = ?) AND ((? = 1 AND URL IS NULL)
OR (URL = ?)))
```

A data adapter's TableMappings property enables you to change how the adapter maps data in the database to the DataSet. For example, you could make it copy the Employees table in the database into a DataSet table named People. You don't usually need to change the table and column names, however, and you can make these changes interactively at design time more easily than you can do this in code, so you will usually leave these values alone at run time.

To create a data adapter control at design time, open a form in the form designer, select the Toolbox's Data tab, and double-click the appropriate data adapter control. (If the data adapter you want doesn't appear in the Toolbox, right-click on the Toolbox, select Choose Items, and pick the data adapter that you want to use.)

When you create a data adapter, the Data Adapter Configuration Wizard shown in Figure 11-21 appears. The first steps are similar to those described earlier for configuring a new data source. Select a connection or click the New Connection button and define one.

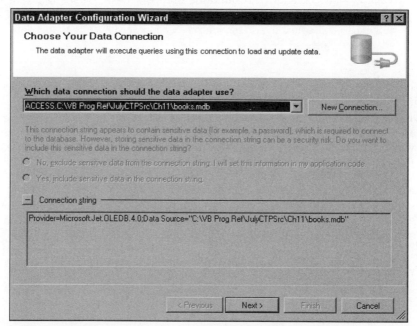

Figure 11-21: The Data Adapter Configuration Wizard helps you define a data adapter.

Click Next to display the page shown in Figure 11-22. Use the option buttons to tell select the method the adapter should to work with the data source. This type determines how the data adapter will fetch, update, delete, and insert data in the database. Select "Use SQL Statements" to make the adapter use simple SQL statements. Pick "Create new stored procedures" to make the wizard generate stored procedures in the database. Pick "Use existing stored procedures" to make the wizard use procedures you have already created. In Figure 11-22, the first choice is the only one enabled because it is the only option available to the OleDbDataAdapter attached to an Access database that was used in this example.

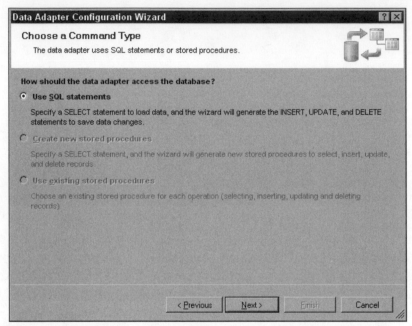

Figure 11-22: Select the method the data adapter will use to manipulate database data.

If you select "Use SQL Statements" and click Next, the form shown in Figure 11-23 appears. If you are experienced at writing SQL statements, enter the SELECT statement that you want the data adapter to use to select its data.

If you have less experience or are not familiar with the database's structure, click the Query Builder button to use the Query Builder shown in Figure 11-24. Select the database tables containing the data you want to use and click Add. Figure 11-24 shows only one table, Books, because that database contains only one table. After you have selected the tables you want, close the Add Table dialog and check the boxes next to the fields. You can use other columns in the second panel to determine how the fields are sorted. The third panel shows the SQL statement you are building. Click the Execute Query button to run the query and display the results in the bottom panel. When you are satisfied with the results, click OK.

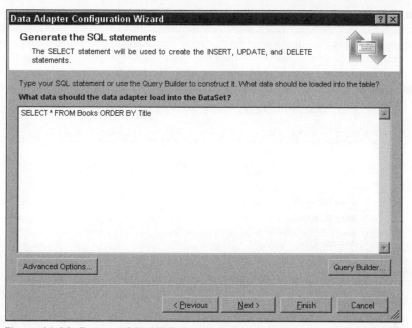

Figure 11-23: Enter an SQL SELECT statement or click the Query Builder button.

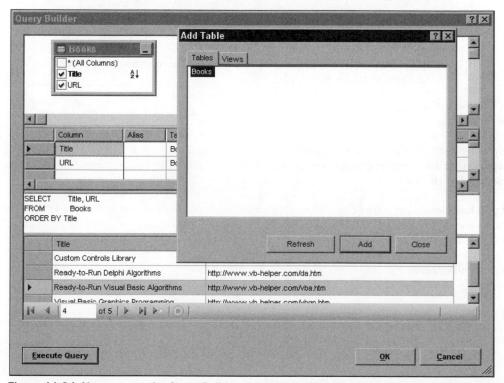

Figure 11-24: You can use the Query Builder to interactively define the data that a data adapter selects.

When you click Next, the Data Adapter Configuration Wizard displays a summary similar to the one shown in Figure 11-25. The summary describes the actions that the wizard will and will not perform. Depending on the query you use to select data, the wizard may not generate all the commands to select, update, insert, and delete data. For example, if the query joins more than one table, the wizard will be unable to figure out how to update the tables, so it won't generate insert, update, or delete commands.

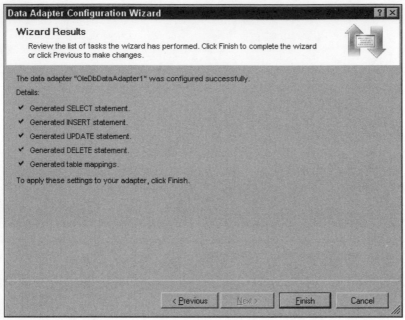

Figure 11-25: The Data Adapter Configuration Wizard displays a summary of the tasks it will perform.

When you click Finish, the wizard creates the new data adapter and a new connection object to go with it. It sets the adapter's `DeleteCommand`, `InsertCommand`, `SelectCommand`, and `UpdateCommand` properties to new command objects with appropriate `CommandText` values and with `Connection` property set to the database connection you selected. It also generates default table mappings to transform database values into `DataSet` values.

Command Objects

The command object classes (`OleDbCommand`, `SqlCommand`, `OdbcCommand`, and `OracleCommand`) define database commands. The command can be a SQL query, or some nonquery statement such as an `INSERT`, `UPDATE`, `DELETE`, or `CREATE TABLE` statement.

The object's `Connection` property gives the database connection object on which it will execute its command. `CommandText` gives the SQL text that the command represents.

The CommandType property tells the database the type of command text the command holds. This can be StoredProcedure (CommandText is the name of a stored procedure), TableDirect (CommandText is the name of one or more tables from which the database should return data), or Text (an SQL statement).

The command object's Parameters collection contains parameter objects that define any values needed to execute the command text. For example, the following code creates an OleDbCommand object to execute the SQL statement "INSERT INTO PeopleNames (FirstName, LastName) VALUES (?, ?)" The question marks are placeholders for parameters that will be added later. The code then adds two new OleDbParameter objects to the command's Parameters collection. When the code invokes the command's ExecuteNonQuery method, the adapter replaces the question marks with these parameter values in the order in which they appear in the Parameters collection. In this example, the value of txtFirstName.Text replaces the first question mark and txtLastName.Text replaces the second.

```
Private Sub btnAdd_Click(ByVal sender As System.Object, _
  ByVal e As System.EventArgs) Handles btnAdd.Click
    ' Open the connection.
    Dim conn_people As New OleDbConnection(CONNECT_STRING)
    conn_people.Open()

    ' Make a Command to insert data.
    Dim cmd As New OleDbCommand( _
        "INSERT INTO PeopleNames (FirstName, LastName) " & _
        "VALUES (?, ?)", _
        conn_people)

    ' Create parameters for the command.
    cmd.Parameters.Add(New OleDbParameter("FirstName", txtFirstName.Text))
    cmd.Parameters.Add(New OleDbParameter("LastName", txtLastName.Text))

    ' Execute the command.
    Try
        cmd.ExecuteNonQuery()
    Catch ex As Exception
        MessageBox.Show(ex.Message)
    End Try

    ' Show the data.
    ShowValues(conn_people)

    ' Close the connection.
    conn_people.Close()
    conn_people.Dispose()
End Sub
```

The command object's Transaction property gives the transaction object with which it is associated. See the section "Transaction Objects" earlier in this chapter for more information about transactions.

The command object provides three methods for executing its CommandText. ExecuteNonQuery executes a command that is not a query and that doesn't return any values.

ExecuteScalar executes a command and returns the first column in the first row selected. This is useful for commands that return a single value such as "SELECT COUNT * FROM Users."

ExecuteReader executes a SELECT statement and returns a data reader object (for example, OleDbDataReader). The program can use this object to navigate through the returned rows of data.

The command object's two other most useful methods are CreateParameter and Prepare. As you may be able to guess, CreateParameter adds a new object to the command's Parameters collection. The Prepare method compiles the command into a form that the database may be able to execute more quickly. It is often faster to execute a compiled command many times using different parameter values than it is to execute many new commands.

DataSet

DataSet is the flagship object when it comes to holding data in memory. It provides all the features you need to build, load, store, manipulate, and save data similar to that stored in a relational database. It can hold multiple tables related with complex parent/child relationships and uniqueness constraints. It provides methods for merging DataSets, searching for records that satisfy criteria, and saving data in different ways (such as into a relational database or an XML file). In many ways, it is like a complete database stored in memory rather than on a disk.

One of the most common ways to use a DataSet is to load it from a relational database when the program starts, use various controls to display the data and let the user manipulate it interactively, and then save the changes back into the database when the program ends.

In variations on this basic theme, the program can load its data from an XML file or build a DataSet in memory without using a database. The program can use controls bound to the DataSet to let the user view and manipulate complex data with little extra programming.

The following code builds and initializes a DataSet from scratch. It starts by creating a new DataSet object named Scores. It makes a DataTable named Students and adds it to the DataSet's Tables collection.

Next, the code uses the DataTable's Columns.Add method to add FirstName, LastName, and StudentId columns to the table. It then sets the StudentId column's Unique property to True to make the DataSet prohibit duplicated StudentId values.

The program then makes an array of DataColumn objects containing references to the FirstName and LastName columns. It uses the array to create a UniqueConstraint and adds it to the table's Constraints collection. This makes the DataSet ensure that each record's FirstName/LastName pair is unique.

Similarly, the program creates the TestScores table, gives it StudentId, TestNumber and Score columns, and adds a uniqueness constraint on the StudentId/TestNumber pair of columns.

Next, the code adds a relationship linking the Students table's StudentId column and the TestScores table's StudentId column.

The program then adds some Students records and some random TestScores records.

Finally, the program attaches the `DataSet` to a `DataGrid` control to display the result. The user can use the `DataGrid` to examine and modify the data just as if it had been loaded from a database.

```
Private Sub Form1_Load(ByVal sender As System.Object, _
 ByVal e As System.EventArgs) Handles MyBase.Load
    ' Make the DataSet.
    Dim scores_dataset As New DataSet("Scores")

    ' Make the Students table.
    Dim students_table As DataTable = _
        scores_dataset.Tables.Add("Students")

    ' Add columns to the Students table.
    students_table.Columns.Add("FirstName", GetType(String))
    students_table.Columns.Add("LastName", GetType(String))
    students_table.Columns.Add("StudentId", GetType(Integer))

    ' Make the StudentId field unique.
    students_table.Columns("StudentId").Unique = True

    ' Make the combined FirstName/LastName unique.
    Dim first_last_columns() As DataColumn = { _
        students_table.Columns("FirstName"), _
        students_table.Columns("LastName") _
    }
    students_table.Constraints.Add( _
        New UniqueConstraint(first_last_columns))

    ' Make the TestScores table.
    Dim test_scores_table As DataTable = _
        scores_dataset.Tables.Add("TestScores")

    ' Add columns to the TestScores table.
    test_scores_table.Columns.Add("StudentId", GetType(Integer))
    test_scores_table.Columns.Add("TestNumber", GetType(Integer))
    test_scores_table.Columns.Add("Score", GetType(Integer))

    ' Make the combined StudentId/TestNumber unique.
    Dim studentid_testnumber_score_columns() As DataColumn = { _
        test_scores_table.Columns("StudentId"), _
        test_scores_table.Columns("TestNumber") _
    }
    test_scores_table.Constraints.Add( _
        New UniqueConstraint(studentid_testnumber_score_columns))

    ' Make a relationship linking the
    ' two tables' StudentId fields.
    scores_dataset.Relations.Add( _
        "Student Test Scores", _
        students_table.Columns("StudentId"), _
        test_scores_table.Columns("StudentId"))

    ' Make some student data.
```

```
        students_table.Rows.Add(New Object() {"Art", "Ant", 1})
        students_table.Rows.Add(New Object() {"Bev", "Bug", 2})
        students_table.Rows.Add(New Object() {"Cid", "Cat", 3})
        students_table.Rows.Add(New Object() {"Deb", "Dove", 4})

        ' Make some random test scores.
        Dim score As New Random
        For id As Integer = 1 To 4
            For test_num As Integer = 1 To 10
                test_scores_table.Rows.Add( _
                    New Object() {id, test_num, score.Next(65, 100)})
            Next test_num
        Next id

        ' Attach the DataSet to the DataGrid.
        grdScores.DataSource = scores_dataset
    End Sub
```

The following table describes the DataSet object's most useful properties.

Property	Purpose
CaseSensitive	Determines whether string comparisons inside DataTable objects are case-sensitive.
DataSetName	The DataSet's name. Often, you don't need to use this for much. If you need to use the DataSet's XML representation, however, this determines the name of the root element.
DefaultViewManager	Returns a DataViewManager object that you can use to determine the default settings (sort order, filter) of DataViews you create later.
EnforceConstraints	Determines whether the DataSet should enforce constraints while updating data. For example, if you want to add records to a child table before the master records have been created, you can set Enforce-Constraints to False while you add the data. You should be able to avoid this sort of problem by adding the records in the correct order.
HasErrors	Returns True if any of the DataSet's DataTable objects contains errors.
Namespace	The DataSet's namespace. If this is nonblank, the DataSet's XML data's root node includes an xmlns attribute as in <Scores xmlns="my_namespace">.
Prefix	Determines the XML prefix that the DataSet uses as an alias for its namespace.
Relations	A collection of DataRelation objects that represent parent/child relations among the columns in different tables.
Tables	A collection of DataTable objects representing the tables stored in the DataSet.

The `DataSet`'s XML properties affect the way the object reads and writes its data in XML form. For example, if the `Namespace` property is `my_namespace` and the `Prefix` property is `pfx`, the `DataSet`'s XML data might look like the following:

```
<pfx:Scores xmlns:pfx="my_namespace">
  <Students xmlns="my_namespace">
    <FirstName>Art</FirstName>
    <LastName>Ant</LastName>
    <StudentId>1</StudentId>
  </Students>
  <Students xmlns="my_namespace">
    <FirstName>Bev</FirstName>
    <LastName>Bug</LastName>
    <StudentId>2</StudentId>
  </Students>
  . . .
  <TestScores xmlns="my_namespace">
    <StudentId>1</StudentId>
    <TestNumber>1</TestNumber>
    <Score>78</Score>
  </TestScores>
  <TestScores xmlns="my_namespace">
    <StudentId>1</StudentId>
    <TestNumber>2</TestNumber>
    <Score>81</Score>
  </TestScores>
  . . .
</pfx:Scores>
```

The following table describes the `DataSet` object's most useful methods.

Method	Purpose
AcceptChanges	Accepts all changes to the data that were made since the data was loaded, or since the last call to `AcceptChanges`. When you modify a row in the `DataSet`, the row is flagged as modified. If you delete a row, the row is marked as deleted but not actually removed. When you call `AcceptChanges`, new and modified rows are marked as `Unchanged` instead of `Added` or `Modified`, and deleted rows are permanently removed.
Clear	Removes all rows from the `DataSet`'s tables.
Clone	Makes a copy of the `DataSet` including all tables, relations, and constraints, but not including the data.
Copy	Makes a copy of the `DataSet` including all tables, relations, constraints, and the data.
GetChanges	Makes a copy of the `DataSet` containing only the rows that have been modified. This method's optional parameter indicates the type of changes that the new `DataSet` should contain (added, modified, deleted, or unchanged).

Table continued on following page

Method	Purpose
GetXml	Returns a string containing the DataSet's XML representation.
GetXmlSchema	Returns the DataSet's XML schema definition (XSD).
HasChanges	Returns True if any of the DataSet's tables contains new, modified, or deleted rows.
Merge	Merges a DataSet, DataTable, or array of DataRow objects into this DataSet.
ReadXml	Reads XML data from a stream or file into the DataSet.
ReadXmlSchema	Reads an XML schema from a stream or file into the DataSet.
RejectChanges	Undoes any changes made since the DataSet was loaded or since the last call to AcceptChanges.
WriteXml	Writes the DataSet's XML data into a file or stream. It can optionally include the DataSet's schema.
WriteXmlSchema	Writes the DataSet's XSD schema into an XML file or stream.

Several of these methods mirror methods provided by other finer-grained data objects. For example, HasChanges returns True if any of the DataSet's tables contain changes. The DataTable and DataRow objects also have HasChanges methods that return True if their more limited scope contains changes.

These mirrored methods include AcceptChanges, Clear, Clone, Copy, GetChanges, and RejectChanges. See the following sections that describe the DataTable and DataRow objects for more information.

DataTable

The DataTable class represents the data in one table within a DataSet. A DataTable contains DataRow objects representing its data, DataColumn objects that define the table's columns, constraint objects that define constraints on the table's data (for example, a uniqueness constraint requires that only one row may contain the same value in a particular column), and objects representing relationships between the table's columns and the columns in other tables. This object also provides methods and events for manipulating rows.

The following table describes the DataTable's most useful properties.

Property	Purpose
CaseSensitive	Determines whether string comparisons inside the DataTable are case-sensitive.
ChildRelations	A collection of DataRelation objects that define parent/child relationships where this table is the parent. For example, suppose the Orders table defines order records and contains an OrderId field. Suppose that the OrderItems table lists the items for an order and it also has an OrderId field. One Orders record can correspond to many OrderItems records, all linked by the same OrderId value. In this example, Orders is the parent table and OrderItems is the child table.
Columns	A collection of DataColumn objects that define the table's columns (column name, data type, default value, maximum length, and so forth).
Constraints	A collection of Constraint objects represent restrictions on the table's data. A ForeignKeyConstraint requires that the values in some of the table's columns must be present in another table (for example, the Addresses record's State value must appear in the States table's StateName column). A UniqueConstraint requires that the values in a set of columns must be unique within the table (for example, only one Student record can have a given FirstName and LastName pair).
DataSet	The DataSet object that contains this DataTable.
DefaultView	Returns a DataView object that you can use to view, sort, and filter the table's rows.
HasErrors	Returns True if any of the DataTable's rows contains an error.
MinimumCapacity	The initial capacity of the table. For example, if you know you are about to load 1000 records into the table, you can set this to 1000 to let the table allocate space all at once instead of incrementally as the records are added. That will be more efficient.
Namespace	The DataTable's namespace. If this is nonblank, the DataTable's XML records' root nodes include an xmlns attribute as in <Students xmlns="my_namespace">.
ParentRelations	A collection of DataRelation objects that define parent/child relationships where this table is the child. See the description of the ChildRelations property for more details.
Prefix	Determines the XML prefix that the DataTable uses as an alias for its namespace.
PrimaryKey	Gets or sets an array of DataColumn objects that define the table's primary key. The primary key is always unique and provides the fastest access to the records.
Rows	A collection of DataRow objects containing the table's data.
TableName	The table's name.

The DataTable's XML properties affect the way the object reads and writes its data in XML form. For example, if the Namespace property is my_namespace and the Prefix property is tbl1, one of the DataTable's XML records might look like the following:

```
<pfx:Students xmlns:pfx="my_namespace">
  <FirstName xmlns="my_namespace">Art</FirstName>
  <LastName xmlns="my_namespace">Ant</LastName>
  <StudentId xmlns="my_namespace">1</StudentId>
</pfx:Students>
```

The following list describes the DataTable object's most useful methods.

Method	Purpose
AcceptChanges	Accepts all changes to the table's rows that were made since the data was loaded or since the last call to AcceptChanges.
Clear	Removes all rows from the table.
Clone	Makes a copy of the DataTable, including all relations and constraints, but not including the data.
Compute	Computes the value of an expression using the rows that satisfy a filter condition. For example, the statement tblTestScores.Compute ("SUM(Score)", "StudentId = 1") calculates the total of the tblTestScores DataTable's Score column where the StudentId is 1.
Copy	Makes a copy of the DataTable including all relations, constraints, and data.
GetChanges	Makes a copy of the DataTable containing only the rows that have been modified. This method's optional parameter indicates the type of changes that the new DataSet should contain (added, modified, deleted, or unchanged).
GetErrors	Gets an array of DataRow objects that contain errors.
ImportRow	Copies the data in a DataRow object into the DataTable.
LoadDataRow	This method takes an array of values as a parameter. It searches the table for a row with values that match the array's primary key values. If it doesn't find such a row, it uses the values to create the row. The method returns the DataRow object it found or creates.
NewRow	Creates a new DataRow object that matches the table's schema. To add the new row to the table, you can create a new DataRow, fill in its fields, and use the table's Rows.Add method.
RejectChanges	Undoes any changes made since the DataTable was loaded or since the last call to AcceptChanges.
Select	Returns an array of DataRow objects selected from the table. Optional parameters indicate a filter expression that the selected rows must match, sort columns and sort order, and the row states to select (new, modified, deleted, and so forth).

The DataTable object also provides several useful events, which are listed in the following table.

Event	Purpose
ColumnChanged	Occurs after a value has been changed in a row.
ColumnChanging	Occurs when a value is being changed in a row.
RowChanged	Occurs after a row has changed. A user might change several of a row's columns and ColumnChanged will fire for each one. RowChanged fires when the user moves to a new row.
RowChanging	Occurs when a row is being changed.
RowDeleted	Occurs after a row has been deleted.
RowDeleting	Occurs when a row is being deleted.

DataRow

A DataRow object represents the data in one record in a DataTable. This object is relatively simple. It basically just holds data for the DataTable, and the DataTable object does most of the interesting work.

The following table describes the DataRow's most useful properties.

Property	Purpose
HasErrors	Returns True if the row's data has errors.
Item	Gets or sets one of the row's item values. Overloaded versions of this property use different parameters to identify the column. This parameter can be the column's zero-based index, its name, or a DataColumn object. An optional second parameter can indicate the version of the row so, for example, you can read the original value in a row that has been modified.
ItemArray	Gets or sets all of the row's values by using an array of generic Objects.
RowError	Gets or sets the row's error message text.
RowState	Returns the row's current state: Added, Deleted, Modified, or Unchanged.
Table	Returns a reference to the DataTable containing the row.

If a row has an error message defined by its RowError property, the DataGrid control displays a red circle containing a white exclamation point to the left of the row as an error indicator. If you hover the mouse over the error indicator, a tooltip displays the RowError text. In Figure 11-26, the third row has RowError set to "Missing registration."

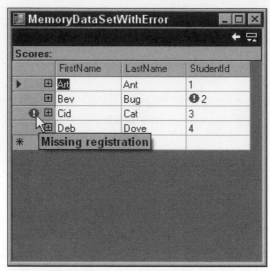

Figure 11-26: The DataGrid **control marks a** DataRow **that has a nonblank** RowError.

The following table describes the DataRow object's most useful methods.

Method	Purpose
AcceptChanges	Accepts all changes to the row that were made since the data was loaded or since the last call to AcceptChanges.
BeginEdit	Puts the row in data-editing mode. This suspends events for the row, so your code or the user can change several fields without triggering validation events. BeginEdit is implicitly called when the user modifies a bound control's value and EndEdit is implicitly called when you invoke AcceptChanges. While the row is in edit mode, it stores the original and modified values, so you can retrieve either version, accept the changes with EndEdit or cancel the changes with CancelEdit.
CancelEdit	Cancels the current edit on the row and restores its original values.
ClearErrors	Clears the row's column and row errors.
Delete	Deletes the row from its table.
GetChildRows	Returns an array of DataRow objects representing this row's child rows as specified by a parent/child data relation.
GetColumnError	Returns the error text assigned to a column.
GetParentRow	Returns a DataRow object representing this row's parent record as specified by a parent/child data relation.
GetParentRows	Returns an array of DataRow objects representing this row's parent records as specified by a data relation.

Method	Purpose
HasVersion	Returns `True` if the row has a particular version (`Current`, `Default`, `Original`, or `Proposed`). For example, while a row is being edited, it has `Current` and `Proposed` versions.
IsNull	Indicates whether a particular column contains a `NULL` value.
RejectChanges	Removes any changes made to the row since the data was loaded or since the last call to `AcceptChanges`.
SetColumnError	Sets error text for one of the row's columns. If a column has an error message, then a `DataGrid` control displays a red circle containing a white exclamation point to the left of the column's value as an error indicator. In Figure 11-26, the second row's second column has a column error set. If you hover the mouse over the error indicator, a tooltip displays the error's text.
SetParentRow	Sets the row's parent row according to a data relation.

DataColumn

The `DataColumn` object represents a column in a `DataTable`. It defines the column's name and data type, and your code can use it to define relationships among different columns.

The following table describes the `DataColumn` object's most useful properties.

Property	Purpose
AllowDBNull	Determines whether the column allows `NULL` values.
AutoIncrement	Determines whether new rows automatically generate auto-incremented values for the column.
AutoIncrementSeed	Determines the starting value for an auto-increment column.
AutoIncrementStep	Determines the amount by which an auto-incrementing column's value is incremented for new rows.
Caption	Gets or sets a caption for the column. Note that some controls may not use this value. For example, the `DataGrid` control displays the column's `ColumnName`, not its `Caption`.
ColumnMapping	Determines how the column is saved in the table's XML data. This property can have one of the values `Attribute` (save the column as an attribute of the row's element), `Element` (save the column as a subelement), `Hidden` (don't save the column), and `SimpleContent` (save the column as `XmlText` inside the row's element). If a column is hidden, the `DataGrid` control doesn't display its value. See the text following this table for an example.

Table continued on following page

Property	Purpose
ColumnName	Determines the name of the column in the DataTable. Note that data adapters use the column name to map database columns to DataSet columns, so, if you change this property without updating the table mapping, the column will probably not be filled.
DataType	Determines the column's data type. Visual Basic raises an error if you change this property after the DataTable begins loading data. Visual Basic supports the data types Boolean, Byte, Char, DateTime, Decimal, Double, Int16, Int32, Int64, SByte, Single, String, TimeSpan, UInt16, UInt32, and UInt64.
DefaultValue	Determines the default value assigned to the column in new rows.
Expression	Sets an expression for the column. You can use this to create calculated columns. For example, the expression Quantity * Price makes the column display the value of the Quantity column times the value of the Price column.
MaxLength	Determines the maximum length of a text column.
Namespace	The column's namespace. If this is nonblank, the rows' XML root nodes include an xmlns attribute as in <StudentId xmlns="my_namespace">12</StudentId>.
Ordinal	Returns the column's index in the DataTable's Columns collection.
Prefix	Determines the XML prefix that the DataColumn uses as an alias for its namespace. For example, if Namespace is my_namespace and Prefix is pfx, then a row's StudentId field might be encoded in XML as <pfx:StudentId xmlns:pfx="my_namespace">12</pfx:StudentId>.
ReadOnly	Determines whether the column allows changes after a record is created.
Table	Returns a reference to the DataTable containing the column.
Unique	Determines whether different rows in the table can have the same value for this column.

The following example defines the Students table's XML column mappings. It indicates that the table's FirstName and LastName columns should be saved as attributes of the row elements, and that the StudentId column should be saved as XmlText. Note that you cannot use the SimpleContent ColumnMapping if any other column has a ColumnMapping of Element or SimpleContent.

```
students_table.Columns("FirstName").ColumnMapping = MappingType.Attribute
students_table.Columns("LastName").ColumnMapping = MappingType.Attribute
students_table.Columns("StudentId").ColumnMapping = MappingType.SimpleContent
```

The following text shows some of the resulting XML Students records:

```
<Students FirstName="Art" LastName="Ant">1</Students>
<Students FirstName="Bev" LastName="Bug">2</Students>
<Students FirstName="Cid" LastName="Cat">3</Students>
<Students FirstName="Deb" LastName="Dove">4</Students>
```

The following code makes the FirstName and LastName columns elements of the Students rows, and it makes the StudentId an attribute:

```
students_table.Columns("FirstName").ColumnMapping = MappingType.Element
students_table.Columns("LastName").ColumnMapping = MappingType.Element
students_table.Columns("StudentId").ColumnMapping = MappingType.Attribute
```

The following text shows the resulting records:

```
<Students StudentId="1">
  <FirstName>Art</FirstName>
  <LastName>Ant</LastName>
</Students>
<Students StudentId="2">
  <FirstName>Bev</FirstName>
  <LastName>Bug</LastName>
</Students>
<Students StudentId="3">
  <FirstName>Cid</FirstName>
  <LastName>Cat</LastName>
</Students>
<Students StudentId="4">
  <FirstName>Deb</FirstName>
  <LastName>Dove</LastName>
</Students>
```

DataRelation

A DataRelation object represents a parent/child relationship between sets of columns in different tables. For example, suppose that a database contains a Students table containing FirstName, LastName, and StudentId fields. The TestScores table has the fields StudentId, TestNumber, and Score. The StudentId fields connect the two tables in a parent/child relationship. Each Students record may correspond to any number of TestScores records. In this example, Students is the parent table, and TestScores is the child table.

The following code defines this relationship. It uses the Students.StudentId field as the parent field and the TestScores.StudentId field as the child field.

```
' Make a relationship linking the two tables' StudentId fields.
scores_dataset.Relations.Add( _
    "Student Test Scores", _
    students_table.Columns("StudentId"), _
    test_scores_table.Columns("StudentId"))
```

A DataRelation can also relate more than one column in the two tables. For example, two tables might be linked by the combination of the LastName and FirstName fields.

Most programs don't need to manipulate a relation after it is created. The `DataSet`'s `Relations.Add` method shown in the previous code creates a relation and thereafter the program can usually leave it alone. However, the `DataRelation` object does provide properties and methods in case you do need to modify one. The following table describes the `DataRelation` object's most useful properties.

Property	Purpose
ChildColumns	Returns an array of `DataColumn` objects representing the child columns.
ChildKeyConstraint	Returns the `ForeignKeyConstraint` object for this relation. You can use this object to determine the relation's behavior when the program updates, deletes, or modifies the values used in the relationship. For example, if the StudentId field links the Students and TestScores tables and you delete a Students record, you can use this object to make the database automatically delete any corresponding TestScores records.
ChildTable	Returns a `DataTable` object representing the relation's child table.
DataSet	Returns a reference to the `DataSet` containing the relation.
Nested	Determines whether the child data should be nested within parent rows in the `DataSet`'s XML representation. See the text following this table for more detail.
ParentColumns	Returns an array of `DataColumn` objects representing the parent columns.
ParentKeyConstraint	Returns the `UniqueConstraint` object for this relation. This object requires that the values in the parent's columns are unique within the parent table.
ParentTable	Returns a `DataTable` object representing the relation's parent table.
RelationName	Determines the relation's name.

Normally, tables are stored separately in a `DataSet`'s XML representation, but you can use the `Nested` property to make the XML include one table's records inside another's. For example, suppose that the Students and TestScores tables are linked by a common StudentId field. If you set this relation's `Nested` property to `True`, the XML data would include the TestScores for a student within the Students record, as shown in the following:

```
<Students>
    <FirstName>Deb</FirstName>
    <LastName>Dove</LastName>
    <StudentId>4</StudentId>
    <TestScores>
        <StudentId>4</StudentId>
        <TestNumber>1</TestNumber>
        <Score>81</Score>
    </TestScores>
    <TestScores>
        <StudentId>4</StudentId>
```

```
      <TestNumber>2</TestNumber>
      <Score>68</Score>
    </TestScores>
    ...
  </Students>
```

Note that in this representation the TestScores table's StudentId value is redundant because the same value is contained in the Students element's StudentId subelement. If you set the TestScores.StudentId column's ColumnMapping value to Hidden, you can remove the redundant values and get the following result:

```
<Students>
    <FirstName>Deb</FirstName>
    <LastName>Dove</LastName>
    <StudentId>4</StudentId>
    <TestScores>
      <TestNumber>1</TestNumber>
      <Score>81</Score>
    </TestScores>
    <TestScores>
      <TestNumber>2</TestNumber>
      <Score>68</Score>
    </TestScores>
    ...
  </Students>
```

Constraints

A constraint imposes a restriction on the data in a table's columns. DataSets support two kinds of constraint objects:

❏ A ForeignKeyConstraint restricts the values in one table based on the values in another table. For example, you could require that values in the Addresses table's State field must exist in the States table's StateName field. That would prevent the program from creating an Addresses record where State is XZ.

❏ A UniqueConstraint requires that the combination of one or more fields within the same table must be unique. For example, an Employee table might require that the combination of the FirstName and LastName values be unique. That would prevent the program from creating two Employees records with the same FirstName and LastName.

The following sections describe each of these types of constraint in greater detail.

ForeignKeyConstraint

In addition to requiring that values in one table must exist in another table, a ForeignKeyConstraint can also determine how changes to one table propagate to the other. For example, suppose that the Addresses table has a ForeignKeyConstraint requiring that its State field contain a value that is present in the States table's StateName field. If you delete the States table's record for Colorado, the constraint could automatically delete all of the Addresses records that used that state's name.

The following table describes the `ForeignKeyConstraint` object's most useful properties.

Property	Purpose
AcceptRejectRule	Determines the action taken when the `AcceptChanges` method executes. This value can be `None` (do nothing) or `Cascade` (update the child fields' values to match the new parent field values).
Columns	Returns an array containing references to the constraint's child columns.
ConstraintName	Determines the constraint's name.
DeleteRule	Determines the action taken when a row is deleted. This value can be `Cascade` (delete the child rows), `None` (do nothing), `SetDefault` (change child field values to their default values), or `SetNull` (change child field values to `NULL`).
RelatedColumns	Returns an array containing references to the constraint's parent columns.
RelatedTable	Returns a reference to the constraint's parent table.
Table	Returns a reference to the constraint's child table.
UpdateRule	Determines the action taken when a row is updated. This value can be `Cascade` (update the child rows' values to match), `None` (do nothing), `SetDefault` (change child field values to their default values), or `SetNull` (change child field values to `NULL`).

The following code makes a foreign key constraint relating the Students.StudentId parent field to the TestScores.StudentId child field:

```
scores_dataset.Relations.Add( _
    "Student Test Scores", _
    students_table.Columns("StudentId"), _
    test_scores_table.Columns("StudentId"))
```

UniqueConstraint

If you want to require the values in a single column to be unique, you can set the column's `Unique` property to `True`. This automatically creates a `UniqueConstraint` object and adds it to the `DataTable`. The following code shows how a program can make the Students table's StudentId column require unique values:

```
students_table.Columns("StudentId").Unique = True
```

You can use the `UniqueConstraint` object's constructors to require that a group of fields has a unique combined value. The following code makes an array of `DataColumn` objects representing the Students table's FirstName and LastName fields. It passes the array into the `UniqueConstraint` object's constructor to require that the FirstName/LastName pair be unique in the table.

```
' Make the combined FirstName/LastName unique.
Dim first_last_columns() As DataColumn = { _
    students_table.Columns("FirstName"), _
    students_table.Columns("LastName") _
}
students_table.Constraints.Add( _
    New UniqueConstraint(first_last_columns))
```

After executing this code, the program could add two records with the same FirstName and different LastNames or with the same LastName and different FirstNames, but it could not create two records with the same FirstName and LastName values.

The following table describes the UniqueConstraint object's properties.

Property	Purpose
Columns	Returns an array of DataColumn objects representing the columns that must be unique. ConstraintName determines the name of the constraint.
IsPrimaryKey	Returns True if the columns form the table's primary key.
Table	Returns a reference to the DataTable that contains the constraint.

DataView

A DataView object represents a customizable view of the data contained in a DataTable. You can use the DataView to select some or all of the DataTable's data and display it sorted in some manner without affecting the underlying DataTable.

A program can use multiple DataViews to select and order a table's data in different ways. You can then bind the DataViews to controls such as the DataGrid control to display the different views. If any of the views modifies its data, for example by adding or deleting a row, the underlying DataTable's data is updated and any other views that need to see the change are updated as well.

The following code builds a DataTable named Contacts containing the fields FirstName, LastName, Street, City, State, and Zip. It places a uniqueness constraint on the FirstName/LastName pair and adds some rows of data to the table. It then binds the DataTable to the DataGrid control named grdAll. Next the program makes a DataView named dv_co based on the table, sets its RowFilter property to make it select rows where the State field has the value CO, and binds the DataView to the DataGrid named grdCO. Finally, the code makes another DataView with RowFilter set to select records where the FirstName field is greater than or equal to "E" and binds that DataView to the grdName DataGrid.

```
Private Sub Form1_Load(ByVal sender As System.Object, _
  ByVal e As System.EventArgs) Handles MyBase.Load
    ' Make a DataTable.
    Dim contacts_table As New DataTable("Contacts")

    ' Add columns.
    contacts_table.Columns.Add("FirstName", GetType(String))
```

```
        contacts_table.Columns.Add("LastName", GetType(String))
        contacts_table.Columns.Add("Street", GetType(String))
        contacts_table.Columns.Add("City", GetType(String))
        contacts_table.Columns.Add("State", GetType(String))
        contacts_table.Columns.Add("Zip", GetType(String))

        ' Make the combined FirstName/LastName unique.
        Dim first_last_columns() As DataColumn = { _
            contacts_table.Columns("FirstName"), _
            contacts_table.Columns("LastName") _
        }
        contacts_table.Constraints.Add( _
            New UniqueConstraint(first_last_columns))

        ' Make some contact data.
        contacts_table.Rows.Add(New Object() {"Art", "Ant", _
            "1234 Ash Pl", "Bugville", "CO", "11111"})
        contacts_table.Rows.Add(New Object() {"Bev", "Bug", _
            "22 Beach St", "Bugville", "CO", "22222"})
        contacts_table.Rows.Add(New Object() {"Cid", "Cat", _
            "3 Road Place Lane", "Programmeria", "KS", "33333"})
        contacts_table.Rows.Add(New Object() {"Deb", "Dove", _
            "414 Debugger Way", "Programmeria", "KS", "44444"})
        contacts_table.Rows.Add(New Object() {"Ed", "Eager", _
            "5746 Elm Blvd", "Bugville", "CO", "55555"})
        contacts_table.Rows.Add(New Object() {"Fran", "Fix", _
            "647 Foxglove Ct", "Bugville", "CO", "66666"})
        contacts_table.Rows.Add(New Object() {"Gus", "Gantry", _
            "71762-B Gooseberry Ave", "Programmeria", "KS", "77777"})
        contacts_table.Rows.Add(New Object() {"Hil", "Harris", _
            "828 Hurryup St", "Programmeria", "KS", "88888"})

        ' Attach grdAll to the DataTable.
        grdAll.DataSource = contacts_table
        grdAll.CaptionText = "All Records"

        ' Make a DataView for State = CO.
        Dim dv_co As New DataView(contacts_table)
        dv_co.RowFilter = "State = 'CO'"
        grdCO.DataSource = dv_co
        grdCO.CaptionText = "CO Records"

        ' Make a DataView for FirstName >= E.
        Dim dv_name As New DataView(contacts_table)
        dv_name.RowFilter = "FirstName >= 'E'"
        grdName.DataSource = dv_name
        grdName.CaptionText = "LastName >= E"
    End Sub
```

Figure 11-27 shows the result. The DataGrid on the top is bound to the DataTable and shows all the table's rows. The second DataGrid is bound to the dv_co DataView and displays records where State = CO. The bottom DataGrid is bound to the dv_name DataView, so it displays records where FirstName >= E. If you use any of these DataGrid controls to modify the data, the other grids immediately show the updates.

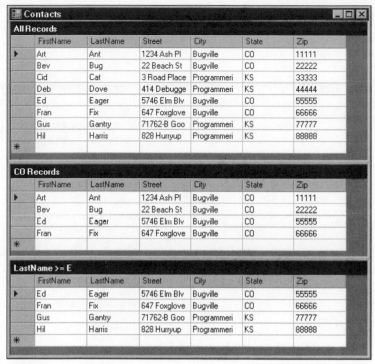

Figure 11-27: Different `DataView` **objects can show different views of the same data.**

The `DataView` class is geared more toward data display than toward storage. It basically refers to data stored in a `DataTable` object, so it doesn't provide the same features for managing relations and constraints that the `DataTable` does. It does, however, provide links to the `DataRow` objects it represents. From those objects, you can get back to the rows' `DataTable` objects if necessary.

The following table describes the `DataView` object's most useful properties.

Property	Purpose
AllowDelete	Determines whether the `DataView` allows row deletion. If this is `False`, any bound controls such as the `DataGrid` will not allow the user to delete rows.
AllowEdit	Determines whether the `DataView` allows row editing. If this is `False`, any bound controls (such as the `DataGrid`) will not allow the user to edit rows.
AllowNew	Determines whether the `DataView` allows new rows. If this is `False`, any bound controls (such as the `DataGrid`) will not allow the user to add rows.
Count	Returns the number of rows selected by the view.
Item	Returns a `DataRowView` object representing a row in the view.
RowFilter	A string that determines the records selected by the view.

Table continued on following page

Property	Purpose
RowStateFilter	The state of the records that should be selected by the view. This can be Added, CurrentRows (unchanged, new, and modified rows), Deleted, ModifiedCurrent (current version of modified rows), ModifiedOriginal (original version of modified rows), None, OriginalRows (original, unchanged, and deleted rows), and Unchanged.
Sort	A string giving the columns that should be used to sort the data. For example, "State, City, Zip" sorts by State, then City, and then Zip in descending order.
Table	Specifies the underlying DataTable object.

The following table describes some of the most useful DataView methods.

Method	Purpose
AddNew	Adds a new row to the underlying DataTable.
Delete	Deletes the row with a specific index from the underlying DataTable.
Find	Returns the index of a row that matches the view's sort key columns. This method returns -1 if no row matches the values it is passed. It raises an error if the number of values it receives does not match the number of the DataView's key values.
FindRows	Returns an array of DataRowView objects representing rows that match the view's sort key columns.

The DataView's Sort property determines not only the fields by which the data is sorted but also the key fields used by the Find method. The following code makes the dv_name DataView sort by FirstName and LastName. It then uses the Find method to display the index of a row with FirstName = Hil and LastName = Harris.

```
dv_name.Sort = "FirstName, LastName"
MessageBox.Show(dv_name.Find(New String() {"Hil", "Harris"}).ToString)
```

DataRowView

A DataRow object can hold data for more than one state. For example, if a DataTable row has been modified, its DataRow object contains the row's original data and the new modified values.

The DataRowView object represents a view of a DataRow object in a particular state. That state can be one of Current, Default, Original, or Proposed.

A DataView object holds DataRowView objects representing a view of a DataTable selecting particular rows in a particular state.

The `DataRowView` object's purpose is to represent a row in a specific state so this object is relatively simple. It basically indicates the chosen state and refers to a `DataRow`.

The following table describes the `DataRowView` objects most useful properties.

Property	Purpose
DataView	The `DataView` that contains the `DataRowView`
IsEdit	Returns `True` if the row is in editing mode
IsNew	Returns `True` if the row is new
Item	Gets or sets the value of one of the row's fields
Row	The `DataRow` object that this `DataRowView` represents
RowVersion	The version of the `DataRow` represented by this object (`Current`, `Default`, `Original`, or `Proposed`)

Simple Data Binding

Binding a simple property such as `Text` to a data source is relatively easy. First, create a `DataSet`, `DataTable`, or `DataView` to act as the data source. You can create this object at design time using controls or at run time using object variables.

If you build the data source at design time, you can also bind the property at design time. Select the control that you want to bind and open the Properties window. Expand the (DataBindings) entry and find the property you want to bind (for example, `Text`). Click the drop-down arrow on the right, and use the pop-up display to select the data source item that you want to bind to the property.

Figure 11-28 shows the pop-up binding the `txtTitle` control's `Text` property to the `dsBooks` `DataSet`'s Books table's Title field.

At run time, your code can bind a simple property to a data source by using the control's `DataBindings` collection. This collection's `Add` method takes as parameters the name of the property to bind, the data source, and the name of the item in the data source to bind.

The following statement binds the `txtUrl` control's `Text` property to the `dsBooks` `DataSet`'s Books table's URL field.

```
txtUrl.DataBindings.Add("Text", dsBooks.Books, "URL")
```

That's all there is to binding simple properties. By itself, however, this binding doesn't provide any form of navigation. If you were to bind the `Text` properties of a bunch of `TextBox` controls and run the program, you would see the data for the data source's first record and nothing else. To allow the user to navigate through the data source, you must use a `CurrencyManager` object.

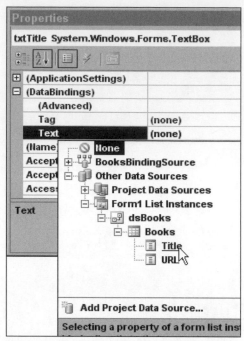

Figure 11-28: You can bind a simple control property to a data source at design time.

CurrencyManager

Some controls such as the `DataGrid` provide their own forms of navigation. If you bind a `DataGrid` to a `DataSet`, it allows the user to examine the `DataSet`'s tables, view and edit data, and follow links between the tables. A simpler control such as a `TextBox` can display only one data value at a time. You must provide some means for the program to navigate through the data source's records.

A data source manages its position within its data by using a `CurrencyManager` object. The `CurrencyManager` supervises the list of `Binding` objects that bind the data source to controls such as `TextBoxes`.

The following table describes the `CurrencyManager` object's most useful properties.

Property	Purpose
Bindings	A collection of the bindings that the object manages.
Count	Returns the number of rows associated with the `CurrencyManager`.
Current	Returns a reference to the current data object (row).

Property	Purpose
List	Returns an object that implements the IList interface that provides the data for the CurrencyManager. For example, if the data source is a DataSet or DataTable, this object is a DataView.
Position	Gets or sets the current position within the data. For example, in a DataTable this is the row number.

The CurrencyManager also provides some methods for manipulating the data. The following table describes the CurrencyManager object's most useful methods.

Method	Purpose
AddNew	Adds a new item to the data source
CancelCurrentEdit	Cancels the current editing operation
EndCurrentEdit	Ends the current editing operation, accepting any changes
Refresh	Refills the bound controls
RemoveAt	Removes the data source item at a specified index

The CurrencyManager class raises a PositionChanged event when its position in the data changes.

The following code shows how a program can use a CurrencyManager to let the user navigate through a DataTable. The code begins by declaring the DataTable and CurrencyManager objects. The form's Load event handler builds the DataTable and gives it some data. Next the event handler uses the DataBindings collections of several TextBox controls to bind them to the fields in the DataTable. The event handler finishes by saving a reference to the DataTable's CurrencyManager. The form's BindingContext property is a collection that contains references to the BindingManagerBase objects used by the controls on the form. That includes the CurrencyManager used by the DataTable. This code passes the DataTable as a parameter to the BindingContext collection to get the table's CurrencyManager. If the data source contained multiple objects (for example, a DataSet can contain multiple DataTables), you also need to pass the collection a path to the data object that you want to use.

The user can move through the DataTable by clicking the program's navigation buttons btnFirst, btnPrev, btnNext, and btnLast. The event handlers for these buttons move through the data by adjusting the CurrencyManager's Position property.

When the user clicks the Add button, the btnAdd_Click event handler calls the CurrencyManager's AddNew method to create a new record.

When the user clicks the Delete button, the btnDelete_Click event handler displays a message box asking if the user really wants to delete the record. If the user clicks "Yes," the code uses the CurrencyManager's RemoveAt method to delete the current record.

```vb
' The data source.
Private m_ContactsTable As DataTable

' The data source's CurrencyManager.
Private m_CurrencyManager As CurrencyManager

Private Sub Form1_Load(ByVal sender As System.Object, _
 ByVal e As System.EventArgs) Handles MyBase.Load
    ' Make a DataTable.
    m_ContactsTable = New DataTable("Contacts")

    ' Add columns.
    m_ContactsTable.Columns.Add("FirstName", GetType(String))
    m_ContactsTable.Columns.Add("LastName", GetType(String))
    m_ContactsTable.Columns.Add("Street", GetType(String))
    m_ContactsTable.Columns.Add("City", GetType(String))
    m_ContactsTable.Columns.Add("State", GetType(String))
    m_ContactsTable.Columns.Add("Zip", GetType(String))

    ' Make the combined FirstName/LastName unique.
    Dim first_last_columns() As DataColumn = { _
        m_ContactsTable.Columns("FirstName"), _
        m_ContactsTable.Columns("LastName") _
    }
    m_ContactsTable.Constraints.Add( _
        New UniqueConstraint(first_last_columns))

    ' Make some contact data.
    m_ContactsTable.Rows.Add(New Object() {"Art", "Ant", _
        "1234 Ash Pl", "Bugville", "CO", "11111"})
    m_ContactsTable.Rows.Add(New Object() {"Bev", "Bug", _
        "22 Beach St", "Bugville", "CO", "22222"})
    m_ContactsTable.Rows.Add(New Object() {"Cid", "Cat", _
        "3 Road Place Lane", "Programmeria", "KS", "33333"})
    m_ContactsTable.Rows.Add(New Object() {"Deb", "Dove", _
        "414 Debugger Way", "Programmeria", "KS", "44444"})
    m_ContactsTable.Rows.Add(New Object() {"Ed", "Eager", _
        "5746 Elm Blvd", "Bugville", "CO", "55555"})
    m_ContactsTable.Rows.Add(New Object() {"Fran", "Fix", _
        "647 Foxglove Ct", "Bugville", "CO", "66666"})
    m_ContactsTable.Rows.Add(New Object() {"Gus", "Gantry", _
        "71762-B Gooseberry Ave", "Programmeria", "KS", "77777"})
    m_ContactsTable.Rows.Add(New Object() {"Hil", "Harris", _
        "828 Hurryup St", "Programmeria", "KS", "88888"})

    ' Bind to controls.
    txtFirstName.DataBindings.Add("Text", m_ContactsTable, "FirstName")
    txtLastName.DataBindings.Add("Text", m_ContactsTable, "LastName")
    txtStreet.DataBindings.Add("Text", m_ContactsTable, "Street")
    txtCity.DataBindings.Add("Text", m_ContactsTable, "City")
    txtState.DataBindings.Add("Text", m_ContactsTable, "State")
    txtZip.DataBindings.Add("Text", m_ContactsTable, "Zip")

    ' Save a reference to the CurrencyManager.
    m_CurrencyManager = _
```

```
        DirectCast(Me.BindingContext(m_ContactsTable), CurrencyManager)
End Sub

Private Sub btnFirst_Click(ByVal sender As System.Object, _
 ByVal e As System.EventArgs) Handles btnFirst.Click
    m_CurrencyManager.Position = 0
End Sub

Private Sub btnPrev_Click(ByVal sender As System.Object, _
 ByVal e As System.EventArgs) Handles btnPrev.Click
    m_CurrencyManager.Position -= 1
End Sub

Private Sub btnNext_Click(ByVal sender As System.Object, _
 ByVal e As System.EventArgs) Handles btnNext.Click
    m_CurrencyManager.Position += 1
End Sub

Private Sub btnLast_Click(ByVal sender As System.Object, _
 ByVal e As System.EventArgs) Handles btnLast.Click
    m_CurrencyManager.Position = m_CurrencyManager.Count - 1
End Sub

' Add a new record.
Private Sub btnAdd_Click(ByVal sender As System.Object, _
 ByVal e As System.EventArgs) Handles btnAdd.Click
    m_CurrencyManager.AddNew()
End Sub

Private Sub btnDelete_Click(ByVal sender As System.Object, _
 ByVal e As System.EventArgs) Handles btnDelete.Click
    If MsgBox("Are you sure you want to delete this record?", _
        MsgBoxStyle.Question Or MsgBoxStyle.YesNo, _
        "Confirm Delete?") = MsgBoxResult.Yes _
    Then
        m_CurrencyManager.RemoveAt(m_CurrencyManager.Position)
    End If
End Sub
```

Figure 11-29 shows the program in action.

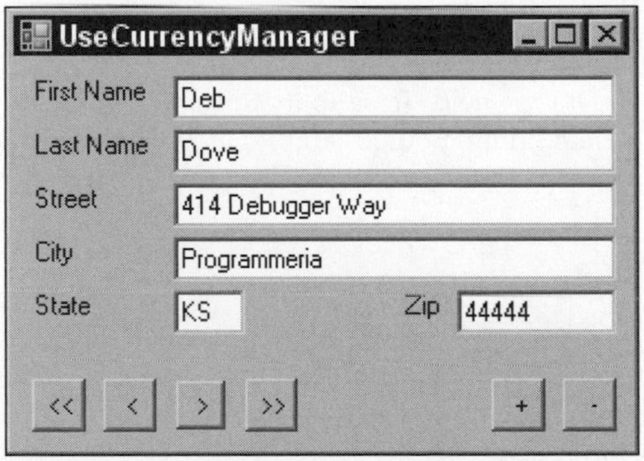

Figure 11-29: This program's buttons use a
CurrencyManager to let the user add, delete,
and navigate through a table's records.

Complex Data Binding

For some controls (such as the `TextBox` and `Label`) binding the `Text` property is good enough. Other controls, however, do not display a simple textual value.

For example, suppose that you have a database containing a Users table with fields FirstName, LastName, and UserType. The UserTypes table has fields UserTypeId and UserTypeName. The Users.UserType field contains a value that should match UserTypes.UserTypeId. The UserTypes.UserTypeName field contains values such as Programmer, Project Manager, Department Manager, Program Manager, and Lab Director.

When you build a form to display the Users table data, you would like to use a `ComboBox` to allow the user to select only the allowed choices Programmer, Project Manager, and so on. However, the Users table doesn't store those string values. Instead it stores the `UserTypeId` value corresponding to the `UserTypeName` value that the user selects. When the user picks a `UserTypes.UserTypeName` value, the `ComboBox` should look up the corresponding `UserTypes.UserTypeId` value and save it in the Users.UserType field.

Clearly the simple binding strategy used for `TextBox`es won't work here. Binding this control requires two rather complicated steps: defining the `DataSet` and binding the control. Each piece of the operation is easy, but you must do everything correctly. If you miss any detail, the `ComboBox` won't work, and Visual Basic's error messages probably won't give you enough information to figure out how to fix the problem.

The first step is building a data connection. Select the Data menu's Add New Data Source command. Use the Data Source Configuration Wizard to make a data source that selects both the Users and UserTypes tables from the database.

Next, create a `ComboBox` named `cboUserType` to the form. In the Properties window, select the control's DataSource property and click the drop-down arrow on the right. Select the `DataSet`'s UserTypes table as shown in Figure 11-30. This tells the `ComboBox` where to look up values.

When you set this property, Visual Basic also adds a `DataSet`, `BindingSource`, and `TableAdapter` to the form. These components provide access to the UserTypes table.

Set the `ComboBox`'s `DisplayMember` property to the field in the lookup table (specified by the `DataSource` property) that the control will display to the user. In this example, the field is `UserTypeName`.

Set the `ComboBox`'s `ValueMember` property to the field in the lookup table that represents the value that the `ComboBox` will need to read and write from the database. In this example, that's the `UserTypeId` field.

Next, you need to bind the `ComboBox` to the field that it must read and write in the database. In this example, that's the Users table's UserType field. To simplify this binding, add a new `BindingSource` to the form. Change its name to "UsersBindingSource" and set its `DataSource` property to the `ComputerUsersDataSet` as shown in Figure 11-31. Then set the `BindingSource`'s `DataMember` property to the Users table.

Figure 11-30: Set the `ComboBox`'s `DataSource` property to the UserTypes table.

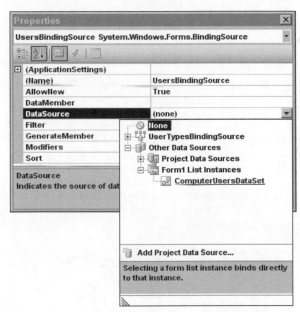

Figure 11-31: Set the `BindingSource`'s `DataSource` to the `ComputerUsersDataSet`.

The last `ComboBox` property you need to set is `SelectedValue`. Click on the `ComboBox`, open the Properties window, and expand the (DataBindings) entry at the top. Click the drop-down arrow to the right of the `SelectedValue` property and select the field that the control must read and write in the database. For this example, that's the `UsersBindingSource`'s UserType field. Figure 11-32 shows the Property window setting this property.

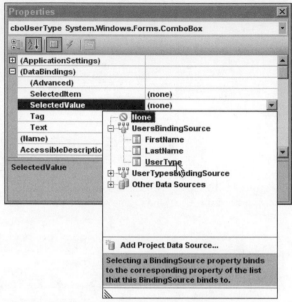

Figure 11-32: Set the `BindingSource`'s `SelectedValue` to the `UsersBindingSource`'s **UserType field.**

Next, create `TextBox` controls to display the Users table's FirstName and LastName fields. In the Properties window, open their (Data Bindings) items and set their `Text` properties to the `UserBindingSource`'s FirstName and LastName fields.

Finally, to give the user a way to navigate through the data, add a `BindingNavigator` to the form. Set this component's `BindingSuorce` property to `UserBindingSource` and the program is ready to run. Figure 11-33 shows the program in action.

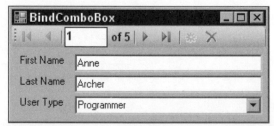

Figure 11-33: At run time, the `ComboBox` displays the field bound to its `DisplayMember` property while updating the field bound to its `SelectedValue` property.

The choices allowed by the ComboBox are taken from the values in the UserTypes table's UserTypeName field. If you select a new user value from the ComboBox, the control automatically makes the appropriate change to the Users table.

Binding a ListBox

The steps for binding a ListBox control are exactly the same as those for binding a ComboBox. Figure 11-34 shows a program that uses a Listbox to display user types. As you move through the records, the ListBox selects the appropriate user type for each user.

Figure 11-34: The steps for binding a ListBox are the same as those for binding a ComboBox.

Summary

Working with databases in Visual Basic is an enormous topic. This chapter does not cover every detail of database programming, but it does explain the basics. It tells how to build data sources and how to drag and drop tables and fields from the Data Sources window onto a form. It describes the most important database controls and objects, such as connection, data adapter, DataSet, and DataTable objects. It also explains the fundamentals of simple and complex data binding, and using CurrencyManager objects to navigate through data.

For more information on database programming in Visual Basic .NET, see a book about database programming. Database programming has changed considerably in Visual Basic 2005, so be sure to get a book that covers this version. Older books explain many of the fundamental database objects such as DataSet, DataTable, DataRow, and CurrencyManager, but they won't cover new objects such as TableAdapter, DataConnector, and DataNavigator.

If you must build and maintain large databases, you should also read books about database management. These can tell you how to design, build, and maintain a database throughout the application's lifetime. You should also read about the particular kinds of databases that you need to use. For example, if you are working with SQL Server databases, get a good book on using SQL Server.

Becoming an expert database developer is a big task, but the techniques described in this chapter should at least get you started.

Chapters 9, 10, and this chapter, describe a wide variety of controls. Chapter 9, "Introduction to Windows Forms Controls," describes the standard controls that applications use to interact with the user. Chapter 10, "Forms," describes a special kind of control: forms. This chapter describes controls that you can use to manipulate databases.

Even all of these different kinds of controls cannot satisfy every application's needs. Chapter 12, "Custom Controls," explains how you can build controls of your own to satisfy unfulfilled needs. These controls can implement completely new features or combine existing controls to provide a neat package that is easy to reuse.

Custom Controls

Visual Basic .NET provides a rich assortment of controls that you can use to build applications. However, those controls may not always be able to do what you need. In that case, you may want to build a control of your own. Building your own control lets you get exactly the behavior and appearance that you want.

Custom controls solve a couple of problems. First, they let you package a particular behavior or appearance so that you can easily reuse it later. If you need to draw one engineering diagram, you can draw it on a `PictureBox`. If you will need to draw many engineering diagrams (possibly in different applications), it would be easier to make an `EngineeringDiagram` control that you can use to make all the diagrams.

Another benefit to custom controls is that developers are familiar with controls and comfortable using them. Any experienced Visual Basic developer understands how to create instances of a control, set its properties, call its methods, and respond to its events. If you build a custom control to perform some complex task, developers already know a lot about how to use it. You just need to explain the specific features of your control.

Finally, controls can save and restore property information at design time. A developer can set properties for a control at design time, and the control uses those properties at run time. This is useful for graphical controls, where properties such as `Text`, `BackColor`, and `BorderStyle` determine the controls' appearance. It is also useful for nongraphical controls such as database connection, data adapter, `DataSet`, and `DataView` controls that use properties to determine what data is loaded and how it is arranged.

This chapter explains how to build custom controls. There are three main approaches to building custom controls. First, you can derive a control from an existing control. If a control already does most of what you want your custom control to do, you may be able to inherit from the existing control and avoid reimplementing all of its useful features.

The second way to build a custom control is to compose your control out of existing controls. For example, you might want to make a color selection control that enables the user to select red, green, and blue color components by using scroll bars, and then displays a sample of the resulting color. You could build this control using three scroll bars and a `PictureBox`. This gives you the advantages provided by the constituent controls without requiring you to reimplement their functionality.

Finally, you can build a custom control from scratch. This is the most work but gives you absolute control over everything that the control does.

This chapter explains the basics of building a control library project and testing its controls. It also describes the three approaches to building custom controls: deriving from an existing control, composing existing controls, and building a control from scratch.

A component is similar to a control that is invisible at run time. Like controls, you can place components on a form at design time. Unlike controls, however, components do not sit on the form itself. Instead, they sit in the *component tray* below the form at design time, and they are invisible to the user at run time. Most of this chapter's discussion of custom controls applies equally to custom components.

Custom Controls in General

Building a custom control requires five basic steps:

1. Create the control's project.
2. Make a Toolbox bitmap icon for the control.
3. Test the control in the UserControl Test Container.
4. Give the control properties, methods, and events.
5. Make a test project to debug the control more thoroughly.
6. Test the control at design time and run time to make sure it works.

The following sections describe these steps.

Making the Control Project

To make a new control library in Visual Basic, select the File menu's New Project command, select the Windows Control Library template, enter the project's name, and click OK. The library can contain several controls, so it may not always make sense to name the library after a single control. This example assumes that you are building a control that displays a smiley face. In that case, you might name the library FaceControls in case you want to add bored, sad, and other faces later.

Initially, Visual Basic gives the control library a single UserControl object named UserControl1. Change this file's name to something more descriptive such as SmileyFace. If you look at the file in the code editor, you should find that Visual Basic has automatically changed the control's class name to match.

Add code to the control to make it do whatever you want it to do. For a SmileyFace control, you might add properties such as FaceColor, NodeColor, and EyeColor. The control's Paint event handler will draw the smiley face.

Next use the Build menu to compile the control library. The project's bin directory contains the library's compiled .dll file.

Setting the Toolbox Icon

If you add the control to the form designer's Toolbox now, you'll see a default image that looks like a gear. To make your control display something more meaningful, you must set its Toolbox icon.

You can set the control's Toolbox icon by adding a `ToolboxBitmap` attribute to the control's class. The constructor for the `ToolboxBitmap` attribute can take as parameters the name of the bitmap file, a class that contains the bitmap resource to use, or a class and the name of a bitmap resource to use (if the class contains more than one bitmap resource). This section assumes that you will use the last method. See the online help for more information. The Web page `http://msdn.microsoft.com/library/en-us/cpref/html/frlrfSystemDrawingToolboxBitmapAttributeClassTopic.asp` describes the `ToolboxBitmapAttribute` class and its constructors.

Open Solution Explorer and double-click on the My Project entry to view the project's property pages. Click the Resources tab and open the Add Resource drop-down. Select the Add Existing File command, and select bitmap file to create a new bitmap resource. Double-click the new bitmap to open it in the integrated Bitmap Editor and modify it if necessary. Use the Properties window to make the bitmap 16 × 16 pixels in size.

Set the pixel in the lower-left corner to the color that you want to use as the Toolbox bitmap's transparent color. Visual Basic will replace the pixels having this color with the Toolbox's background color. Draw and save the bitmap, and then close it.

Click on the bitmap file in Solution Explorer, and open the Properties window. Select the file's Build Action property, click the drop-down arrow on the right, and select Embedded Resource. Now when you compile the control library, this bitmap will be embedded as a resource inside the `.dll` file.

Next, open the control's module in the code editor, and insert a `ToolboxBitmap` attribute in front of the control's class declaration, as shown in the following code. This example tells Visual Basic that the control's Toolbox icon should come from the `SmileyFaceTool` resource embedded in the `SmileyFace` class. Notice the line continuation character at the end of the first line so that the `ToolboxBitmap` statement is on the same code line as the class declaration.

```
<ToolboxBitmap(GetType(SmileyFace), "SmileyFaceTool")> _
Public Class SmileyFace
    ...
    End Class
```

Now when you build the control library, the `SmileyFace` control includes the information it needs to display its Toolbox bitmap.

Testing in the UserControl Test Container

If you use the Debug menu's Start command to "execute" a control library project, Visual Studio displays a sample control in the UserControl Test Container shown in Figure 12-1. The drop-down list at the top lets you select different controls in the project. You can use the property grid on the right to experiment with different property values to see how the control behaves.

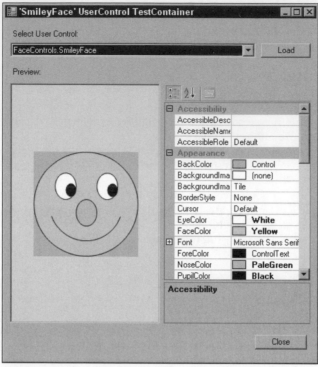

Figure 12-1: Visual Basic lets you preview controls in the UserControl Test Container.

As its name hints, the UserControl Test Container only displays UserControls. If you create a control that inherits from the Control class or from some other control, then the UserControl Test Container does not list it and will not display it. In that case, you must skip this step and move on to the next one, making a test project.

Making a Test Project

The UserControl Test Container only lets you test UserControls, not those that inherit from the Control class or some other control. It also only lets you test a control's properties. You can see the control's design time behavior, but not how its methods and events work at run time.

To test controls that are not UserControls and to test the control's run-time behavior, you must build a test project. You can either build a completely separate project, or you can add a new Windows application to the control's project.

To add an application to the control's project, open the File menu's Add submenu and select New Project. Select the Windows Application template, give the project a meaningful name (such as FaceControlsTest), and click OK. This adds the test project to the same solution that already contains the control library.

To make Visual Basic start execution with the test project, open the Solution Explorer, right-click the new project, and select Set as StartUp Project.

When you open the new project's form, the Toolbox will contain a FaceControls Components section (assuming that the control project is named FaceControls) that holds icons representing the controls defined by the control library. You can use these tools just as you would use any other control tools.

When you create separate applications that are not part of the control library's solution, you must add the controls to the Toolbox manually. To add the controls, open a form in the form designer. Right-click on the Toolbox, and select Choose Items. On the Choose Toolbox Items dialog shown in Figure 12-2, click the Browse button. Select the .dll file in the control library's bin folder, and click Open to make the controls appear in the dialog's .NET Framework Components tab. Check the boxes next to the controls (they should be checked by default), and click OK.

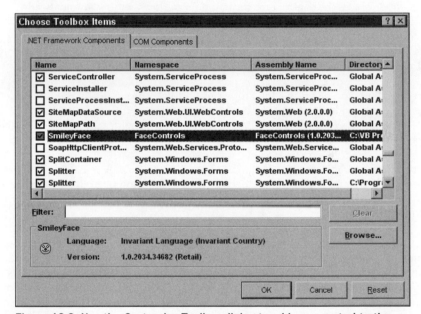

Figure 12-2: Use the Customize Toolbox dialog to add your control to the Toolbox.

If you change the control's Toolbox icon, you must rebuild the control library's .dll file. Then open the test project's form, right-click the Toolbox, select Add/Remove Items again, click the Browse button, and reselect the control library's .dll file.

Test the Control

After you add it to the Toolbox, you can use the control on the test project's form just as you can use any other control. Click on the Toolbox icon to select the control, and click and drag to place an instance of the control on the form. Double-click on the control to place an instance of the control in a default location with a default size. Initially, Visual Basic sets the controls' names to their class's name followed by a number, as in SmileyFace1, SmileyFace2, and so forth.

Use the Properties window to set the controls' properties at design time. Use code to examine and modify the controls' properties, methods, and events at run time.

Implement Properties, Methods, and Events

At this point, you can test the control, but if you haven't given it any properties, methods, and events, you can only work with the default behavior that it inherits from its parent class. If the control is to do something useful, you must give it new properties, methods, and events.

Controls implemented from scratch often use `Paint` event handlers to draw the control. Composite controls often respond to events raised by their constituent controls and take actions, which may include raising new events for the form containing the control.

When a developer places the control on a form, the Properties window automatically displays any public properties that are not read-only. This feature is remarkably intelligent. If a property has the Integer data type, the Properties window will only allow the developer to enter an integer. If a property has an enumerated type, the Properties window automatically displays a drop-down list containing the types of allowed values.

If a property has the `Font` data type, the Properties window automatically provides an ellipsis to the right of the property's value and displays a font selection dialog if the user clicks it. Similarly, if the property is a `Color`, `Image`, or `Date`, the Properties window provides an appropriate dialog or drop-down to let the user select the property's value.

If a property's data type is `OleDbDataConnection`, `DataSet`, `TextBox`, `Label`, or some other control or component type, then the Properties window provides a drop-down list that lets the developer pick from any appropriate item on the form. If the data type is `TextBox`, then the drop-down will list all of the form's `TextBox`es.

In fact, the Properties window can even handle custom controls and components that you build yourself. For example, suppose that you create a control named `EmployeeRegister`. You can then create another control that has a property of type `EmployeeRegister`. If the developer selects the control, opens the Properties window, clicks on that property, and clicks the drop-down arrow on the right, Visual Basic will display a list of any `EmployeeRegister` controls on the form.

Even more miraculously, the Properties window can handle collections of objects that you define. For example, the following code defines a `WorkItem` class. It then defines a `UserControl` class named `WorkItemLister`. This class has a property named `WorkItems` that is a collection of `WorkItem` objects.

```
Imports System.Collections.Generic

' Represents a piece of work.
<Serializable()> _
Public Class WorkItem
    ' The ItemName property.
    Private m_ItemName As String
    Public Property ItemName() As String
        Get
            Return m_ItemName
        End Get
        Set(ByVal value As String)
```

```
                m_ItemName = value
            End Set
    End Property
End Class


' UserControl that has the property.
Public Class WorkItemLister
    ' The WorkItems property.
    Private m_WorkItems As New List(Of WorkItem)
    Public Property WorkItems() As List(Of WorkItem)
        Get
            Return m_WorkItems
        End Get
        Set(ByVal value As List(Of WorkItem))
            ' Copy the new items into the
            ' m_WorkItems List.
            For Each work_item As WorkItem In value
                m_WorkItems.Add(work_item)
            Next work_item
        End Set
    End Property
End Class
```

If you add a `WorkItemLister` object to a form and select it, the Properties window lists the `WorkItems` property's value as "`(Collection)`" and displays a drop-down arrow to the right. If you click the arrow, Visual Basic displays the collection editor shown in Figure 12-3.

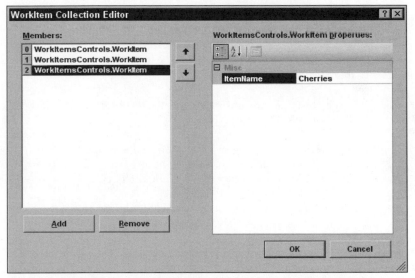

Figure 12-3: Visual Basic automatically provides collection editors for collection properties.

Assign Attributes

You can modify a control's behavior by adding attributes to its properties, methods, and events, and to its class declaration. The following code demonstrates some of the most useful control (or component) and property attributes for a `UserControl` named `EmployeeRegister`:

The `ToolboxBitmap` attribute tells Visual Basic that it can find a Toolbox bitmap for the class in the assembly containing the `EmployeeRegister` type, and that the bitmap resource's name is "`EmployeeRegisterTool`."

The `DefaultProperty` attribute sets the component's default property. If you click on an `EmployeeRegister` control in the form designer, the property named `TextValue` is initially selected in the Properties window.

Note that the `DefaultProperty` doesn't always work as advertised because the Properties window tries to display the same property when you select different controls. For example, suppose that you click on a `TextBox` control and select its `Name` property in the Properties window. If you then click on an `EmployeeRegister` control, the Properties window shows its `Name` property because `EmployeeRegister` has a `Name` property. On the other hand, if you select a `TextBox`'s `MultiLine` property and then click on an `EmployeeRegister` control, the Properties window selects the `TextValue` property because `EmployeeRegister` doesn't have a `MultiLine` property.

The `DefaultEvent` attribute indicates the component's default event. If you double-click on an `EmployeeRegister` control in the form designer, Visual Basic opens the code editor and displays the control's default event handler.

The `DesignTimeVisible` attribute determines whether the component is visible in the form designer at design time. If you set this to `False`, the control or component does not appear in the Toolbox. If a form already contains an instance of the object, a component is hidden in the component tray, although a control remains visible. You can use this attribute to build a control that the program can create and manipulate at run time but that the developer cannot create at design time.

The `TextValue` property's `Description` attribute gives the text displayed at the bottom of the Properties window when you select the property.

The `Category` attribute determines the category that contains the property when you select the Property window's Categorized button. This attribute's value can be any string. The Property window will make a new category with this name if it doesn't name an existing category.

The `Browsable` attribute determines whether the Property window displays the property. If you set this value to `False`, you cannot set the property's value at design time.

Finally the `DefaultValue` property determines the default value for the property. If you set a control's property to this value, Visual Basic does not store the property's value with the form. Later, when it reloads the form, Visual Basic does not load any value for the property. This code shows one way to initialize a property's value when it declares `Private m_TextValue As String = "Default Value"`. To avoid confusion, you should generally initialize the private variable representing a property to the same value you set with `faultValue` attribute.

If you right-click on a property in the Properties window and select the Reset command, Visual Basic sets the property to the value defined by the `DefaultValue` attribute. This is particularly useful for images and other objects where you might want to make the default value `Nothing`.

```
Imports System.ComponentModel

<ToolboxBitmap(GetType(EmployeeRegister), "EmployeeRegisterTool"), _
 DefaultProperty("TextValue"), _
 DefaultEvent("TheEvent"), _
 DesignTimeVisible(True)> _
Public Class EmployeeRegister
    ' Declare a public event.
    Public Event TheEvent()

    ' The TextValue property.
    Private m_TextValue As String = "Default Value"
    <Description("The object's text value."), _
     Category("String Values"), _
     Browsable(True), _
     DefaultValue("Default Value")> _
    Public Property TextValue() As String
        Get
            Return m_TextValue
        End Get
        Set(ByVal value As String)
            m_TextValue = value
        End Set
    End Property
End Class
```

See the online help for more information on these attributes and others that you might find useful under less common circumstances.

Manage Design Time and Run Time

A control or component can use its predefined `DesignMode` property to determine whether it is running at design time or run time and take different actions if that is appropriate. For example, a control might allow the developer to manipulate its data directly at design time but prevent the user from changing the data at run time.

The following code shows how the control can check whether it is running at design or run time:

```
If Me.DesignMode Then
    ' Let the developer manipulate the data at design time.
    ...
Else
    ' Don't let the user change the data at run time.
    ...
End If
```

Derived Controls

If an existing control does almost what you need to do, you can derive a new control from the existing one. That enables you to take advantage of all of the existing control's features while adding new ones of your own.

To make a derived control, start a control library project as usual and give the library a meaningful name. Discard the default `UserControl1` class, add a new class, and give it an appropriate `Inherits` statement. For example, the following code derives the `RowSortingListView` class from the `ListView` class:

```
Public Class RowSortingListView
    Inherits ListView

End Class
```

That's about all there is to building a derived control. Now you just need to write code that implements the new features and modifies inherited features. One particularly common task for derived controls is overriding the functionality provided by the parent control class. The `RowSortingListView` control provides a good example.

The standard `ListView` control lets a program display data items with subitems in a variety of ways. The control can display items as large icons, small icons, a list showing the items' names, or a detail list showing the items and their subitems. The list and detail displays even allow you to sort the items in ascending and descending order. Unfortunately, the `ListView` control doesn't use the subitems in the sort even to break ties. It sorts only on the main items' names.

For example, suppose that several items all have the item value Book and their first subitems contain book titles. If you set the `ListView` control's `Sorting` property to `Ascending` or `Descending`, the control will group these items together because they all have the same item value: Book. Unfortunately, the items' order in the list is arbitrary. The control does not sort the Book items by their titles.

Fortunately, the `ListView` control provides a back door for implementing custom sort orders. To implement a custom sort order, you set the `ListView` control's `ListViewItemSorter` property to an object that implements the `IComparer` interface. To satisfy the interface, this object must provide a `Compare` function that compares two `ListView` items and returns `-1`, `0`, or `1` if the first item should be considered less than, equal to, or greater than the second item.

The `ListViewComparerAllColumns` class shown in the following code implements the `IComparer` interface. Its private `m_SortOrder` variable tells the object whether to sort in ascending or descending order. The class's constructor takes a parameter that sets this value. The `Compare` function converts the generic `Objects` that it is passed into `ListViewItems`. It calls the `ListViewItemValue` helper function to get strings containing the items and their subitems separated by Tab characters. It then uses the `String` class's `Compare` method to determine which value should come first in the sort order.

```
' Implements a ListViewItem comparer
' that sorts on all columns.
Private Class ListViewComparerAllColumns
    Implements IComparer

    ' Ascending or Descending.
```

```
        Private m_SortOrder As SortOrder

        ' Initialize with a sort order.
        Public Sub New(ByVal sort_order As SortOrder)
            m_SortOrder = sort_order
        End Sub

        ' Compare two items' subitems.
        Public Function Compare(ByVal x As Object, ByVal y As Object) As Integer _
          Implements System.Collections.IComparer.Compare
            ' Get the ListViewItems.
            Dim item_x As ListViewItem = DirectCast(x, ListViewItem)
            Dim item_y As ListViewItem = DirectCast(y, ListViewItem)

            ' Get the ListViewItems' values.
            Dim values_x As String = ListViewItemValue(item_x)
            Dim values_y As String = ListViewItemValue(item_y)

            ' Compare the values.
            If m_SortOrder = SortOrder.Ascending Then
                Return String.Compare(values_x, values_y)
            Else
                Return String.Compare(values_y, values_x)
            End If
        End Function

        ' Return a delimited string containing all of
        ' the ListViewItem's values.
        Private Function ListViewItemValue(ByVal lvi As ListViewItem, _
          Optional ByVal delimiter As String = vbTab) As String
            Dim txt As String = ""
            For i As Integer = 0 To lvi.SubItems.Count - 1
                txt &= delimiter & lvi.SubItems(i).Text
            Next i
            Return txt.Substring(delimiter.Length)
        End Function
    End Class
```

The RowSortingListView control uses the ListViewComparerAllColumns class and the following code to sort its data using all of the items' values and their subitems' values. To provide the new sorting behavior, the control must override the Sorting property defined by the parent ListView class.

The control defines a private m_Sorting variable to store the property's value and declares property procedures to let the program get and set it. The property is declared with the Shadows keyword, so it hides the definition of the parent class's Sorting property. That prevents the developer or a program that uses the RowSortingListView control from using the original ListView version of the property.

The Sorting Property Get procedure simply returns the value of m_Sorting.

The Property Set procedure saves the new value. Then if the new Sorting value is None, the code sets the control's inherited ListViewItemSorter property to Nothing to remove any previously installed sorter object. If Sorting is not None, the code sets the control's ListViewItemSorter property to a new ListViewComparerAllColumns object configured to sort the items in the proper order.

```
' Reimplement the Sorting property.
Private m_Sorting As SortOrder
Public Shadows Property Sorting() As SortOrder
    Get
        Return m_Sorting
    End Get
    Set(ByVal Value As SortOrder)
        ' Save the new value.
        m_Sorting = Value

        ' Make a new ListViewItemSorter if necessary.
        If m_Sorting = SortOrder.None Then
            MyBase.ListViewItemSorter = Nothing
        Else
            MyBase.ListViewItemSorter = _
                New ListViewComparerAllColumns(m_Sorting)
        End If
    End Set
End Property
```

Adding new properties and methods that don't shadow those of base class is even easier. Simply declare the property or method as you would for any other class. You can also create new events for the derived control just as you would add events to any other class.

Shadowing Parent Features

The RowSortingListView control's code implements a Sorting property that shadows the property in its parent class. You can provide new versions of methods and events in the same way.

For example, normally, the ListView control raises a ColumnClick event when the user clicks on a column header. By default, the RowSortingListView control inherits that behavior, so it also raises the event when the user clicks on a column header.

The following code replaces the parent class's ColumnClick event with a new version. The event declaration uses the Shadows keyword so this version hides the parent's version from the program that uses the RowSortingListView control so the program cannot receive the original version of the event. The inherited version of ColumnClick passes the event handler a parameter that gives information about the event. The new version just returns the index of the column clicked. The control's ColumnClick event handler (which handles the MyBase.ColumnClick event) raises the new event handler. The control could also raise the event from some other code or not at all.

```
Public Shadows Event ColumnClick(ByVal column_number As Integer)

Private Sub RowSortingListView_ColumnClick(ByVal sender As Object, _
  ByVal e As System.Windows.Forms.ColumnClickEventArgs) Handles MyBase.ColumnClick
    RaiseEvent ColumnClick(e.Column)
End Sub
```

The following code shows how a program could handle the new event. This code simply displays the column number that the user clicked.

```
Private Sub RowSortingListView1_ColumnClick(ByVal column_number As Integer) _
 Handles RowSortingListView1.ColumnClick
    MessageBox.Show(column_number)
End Sub
```

In the same way, you can shadow a method provided by the parent class. The following code shows how the RowSortingListView class can replace its parent's Clear method. Instead of removing all of the data from the control, this version removes only items with text value "Book."

```
Public Shadows Sub Clear()
    For Each item As ListViewItem In Me.Items
        If item.Text = "Book" Then item.Remove()
    Next item
End Sub
```

Hiding Parent Features

Sometimes you might want to completely hide a parent feature rather than replace it with a new version. Hiding an event is easy. Declare a new event with the Shadows keyword as described in the previous section and then never raise the event. A program using the control can write an event handler for the event, but it will never be called.

Hiding properties and methods is a little more difficult. One approach you might try would be to create a private version of the property or method with the Shadows keyword. For example, the intent of the following code is to hide the control's inherited Clear method. The idea is that the Private keyword makes the method inaccessible to the program and the Shadows keyword hides the parent's version.

```
Private Shadows Sub Clear()
    For Each item As ListViewItem In Me.Items
        If item.Text = "A" Then item.Remove()
    Next item
End Sub
```

Unfortunately, if you use the Shadows keyword but the program cannot see the property or method (in this case, because it is private), Visual Basic exposes the parent's version. This approach won't work.

While you can't completely hide inherited properties and methods from the program using the control, you can disable them. The following code declares a shadowing version of the ListView control's Clear method. If the program invokes this method, the control throws the MissingMethodException. If the program catches the error, the exception object's error message says, "Method RowSortingListView.Clear not found." Next the code defines a shadowing version of the Tag property. It gives the property the BrowsableAttribute with the value False. This prevents the property from appearing in the Properties window at design time. If the program tries to read or set the control's Tag property at run time, the control throws a MissingFieldException. If the program catches the error, the exception object's error message says, "Field RowSortingListView.Tag not found."

```
Public Shadows Sub Clear()
    Throw New System.MissingMethodException("RowSortingListView", "Clear")
End Sub

<System.ComponentModel.BrowsableAttribute(False)> _
Public Shadows Property Tag() As Object
    Get
        Throw New System.MissingFieldException("RowSortingListView", "Tag")
    End Get
    Set(ByVal Value As Object)
        Throw New System.MissingFieldException("RowSortingListView", "Tag")
    End Set
End Property
```

Composite Controls

A *composite control* combines several existing controls into one new control. For example, the ColorScroller control shown in Figure 12-4 contains three labels, three scroll bars, and a panel. At run time, the user can drag the scroll bars to select a color's red, green, and blue components. The control displays a sample of the color in the panel on the right.

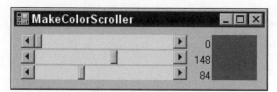

Figure 12-4: The ColorScroller **control lets the user select a color interactively by dragging scroll bars.**

To build a composite control, start a new control library project as usual. Give the library a meaningful name, and change the name of the default control UserControl1 to something more descriptive.

Next, in Solution Explorer, double-click on the control to open it in the form designer. Use the Toolbox to add constituent controls to the UserControl just as you would add controls to a form. Set the controls' design time properties using the Properties window.

Edit the UserControl's code to make the constituent controls work together to provide the behavior that you want. For the ColorScroller control shown in Figure 12-4, you would make the scroll bars' events adjust the color displayed in the sample area on the right. You can handle the constituent controls' events, get and set their property values, and invoke their methods. You can also define new properties, methods, and events for the composite control.

The following code shows how the ColorScroller control works. It starts by declaring the ColorChanged event to tell the program when the user changes the control's selected color. It then includes property procedures that define the SelectedColor property. The Property Get procedure uses the Color class's FromArgb to convert the scroll bars' values into a color. The Property Set procedure sets the control's Red, Green, and Blue properties to the components of the new Color value. The

Red Property Get procedure returns the value of the red scroll bar. The Property Set procedure sets the red scroll bar's value, displays the value in the red label, displays a sample of the current color, and raises the ColorChanged event. The Green and Blue property procedures are basically the same so they are not shown here. When the user changes the red scroll bar's value, the hbarRed_Scroll event handler sets the control's new Red property value. The event handlers for the Green and Blue scroll bars are similar, so they are not shown here.

```
Public Class ColorScroller
    ' Tell the program that the color has changed.
    Public Event ColorChanged(ByVal new_color As Color)

    ' Get or set the currently selected Color.
    Public Property SelectedColor() As Color
        Get
            Return Color.FromArgb( _
                255, _
                hbarRed.Value, _
                hbarGreen.Value, _
                hbarBlue.Value)
        End Get
        Set(ByVal value As Color)
            Red = value.R
            Green = value.G
            Blue = value.B
        End Set
    End Property

    ' Get: Return the color component value.
    ' Set: Set the scroll bar value,
    '      display the color, and
    '      raise the ColorChanged event.
    Public Property Red() As Byte
        Get
            Return CByte(hbarRed.Value)
        End Get
        Set(ByVal Value As Byte)
            hbarRed.Value = Value
            lblRed.Text = hbarRed.Value.ToString
            panSample.BackColor = SelectedColor
            RaiseEvent ColorChanged(SelectedColor)
        End Set
    End Property

    ' Green and Blue property procedures omitted...

    ' The user has changed a color value.
    ' Set the appropriate color component value.
    Private Sub hbarRed_Scroll(ByVal sender As System.Object, _
     ByVal e As System.Windows.Forms.ScrollEventArgs) Handles hbarRed.Scroll
        Red = CByte(hbarRed.Value)
    End Sub

    ' Green and Blue scroll bar Scroll event handlers omitted...
End Class
```

Composite controls are useful when you can build the behavior you want by using existing controls. They are most useful when you will need to use the combined controls many times, either in the same application or in several applications. If you need to implement these features only once, you can simply place the constituent controls right on a form and include code to handle their events.

Composite controls are also useful for keeping the related controls and their code together. This keeps some of the details of the controls and their code separate from the rest of the application. If the interactions among the controls are complex, it may make sense to build a separate UserControl to simplify the project.

Composite controls (or any control, for that matter) also provide a nice, clean separation between developers. If you build a complex control and add it to a large project, other developers can interact with the control only through the properties, methods, and events that it exposes. They cannot access the constituent controls directly, and that removes a potential source of bugs.

Controls Built from Scratch

If no existing control or group of controls can provide the behavior that you want, you can build a control completely from scratch. Start a new control library project as usual. Give the library a meaningful name and remove the default control UserControl1.

Add a new class, open it in the code editor, and add the statement "Inherits Control". Then add whatever code you need to make the control do what you want.

The following code shows how the SimpleSmiley control works. When the control receives a Paint or Resize event, it calls subroutine DrawFace, passing it the Graphics object on which it should draw. Subroutine DrawFace clears the control using the parent's background color. It then calls a series of Graphics object methods to draw a smiley face on the control's surface. This drawing code isn't terribly relevant for this discussion, so it is omitted here to save space.

```
<ToolboxBitmap(GetType(SimpleSmiley), "SmileyFaceTool")> _
Public Class SimpleSmiley
    Inherits Control

    Private Sub SimpleSmiley_Paint(ByVal sender As Object, _
     ByVal e As System.Windows.Forms.PaintEventArgs) Handles Me.Paint
        DrawFace(e.Graphics)
    End Sub
    Private Sub SimpleSmiley_Resize(ByVal sender As Object, _
     ByVal e As System.EventArgs) Handles Me.Resize
        Me.Invalidate()
    End Sub

    ' Draw the smiley face.
    Private Sub DrawFace(ByVal gr As Graphics)
        If (Me.ClientSize.Width = 0) Or _
           (Me.ClientSize.Height = 0) Then Exit Sub

        gr.Clear(Me.BackColor)
```

```
            gr.SmoothingMode = Drawing2D.SmoothingMode.HighQuality

        ' Face.
        Dim face_rect As New Rectangle(0, 0, _
            Me.ClientSize.Width - 1, _
            Me.ClientSize.Height - 1)
        gr.FillEllipse(Brushes.Yellow, face_rect)
        gr.DrawEllipse(Pens.Black, face_rect)

        ' More drawing code omitted...
    End Sub
End Class
```

When you build your own control from scratch, you can make it do just about anything that you like. The obvious drawback is that you need to write code to make it do everything that you want. If there's already a control that does almost what you need, it will generally be easier to derive a control from that one rather than building one from scratch.

If you can display the data in standard controls such as `Label`, `TextBox`, or `TreeView` controls, it would be easier to build a composite control. If you must display information by drawing it yourself anyway, a composite control won't help, so you might want to use this kind of control. For example, if you are building a mapping or drafting system, you might want to build a control from scratch to load and display maps and architectural drawings.

Components

A *component* is basically a control with no visible component at run time. Instead of appearing on the form at design time, a component appears in the component tray below the form. Figure 12-5 shows a form containing several components.

You can select a component in the component tray and then view and modify its properties in the Properties window. In Figure 12-5, the FontDialog1 component is selected, so the Properties window is displaying that component's properties.

Building a component is just as easy as building a control. To make a new component, open the Project menu and select Add Component. Leave the Component Class template selected, enter the name you want to give the component, and click OK.

Initially, Visual Basic displays the component as shown in Figure 12-6. To add instances of existing components to the new component, click and drag tools from Server Explorer or the Toolbox onto the new component.

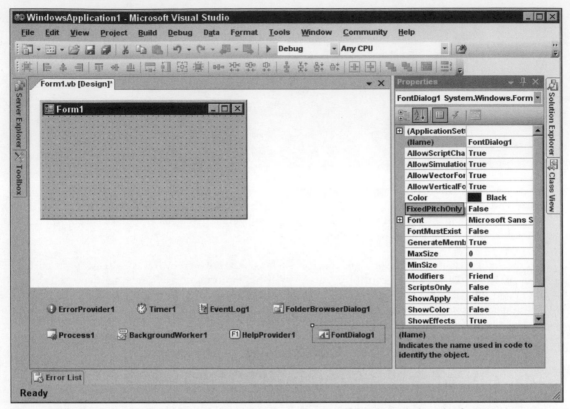

Figure 12-5: The form designer displays components in the component tray below the form.

If you click the Solution Explorer's Show All Files button and then open the component's designer-generated code file, you'll see that the class inherits from the System.ComponentModel.Component class rather than from the System.Windows.Forms.Control class.

You can add properties, methods, and events to the component just as you would add them to a control. You can also use the same attributes to modify the component and its properties and events. For example, you can give the component a Toolbox bitmap, a default property and event, add descriptions to properties, and assign properties to categories. In addition to displaying the bitmap in the Toolbox, Visual Basic also displays it in the component tray below the form when you add an instance of the component to the form.

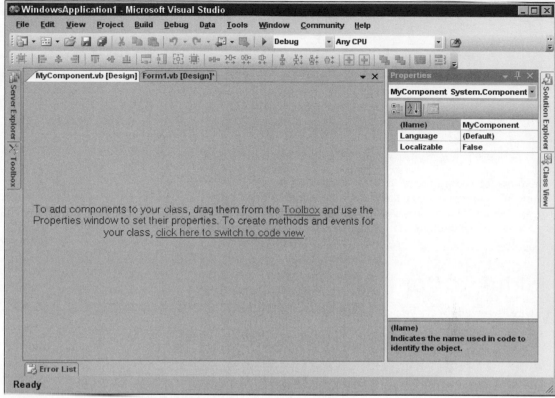

Figure 12-6: You can add existing components to a new component.

Invisible Controls

You can make a control invisible at run time by having its code set its `Visible` property to `False`. For example, the following code shows how the `InvisibleControl` class works. Whenever it needs to draw itself, the controls `DrawControl` method sets the control's `Visible` property equal to its `DesignMode` property, so the control is visible at design time and hidden at run time.

```
Public Class InvisibleControl
    Inherits Control

    Private Sub InvisibleControl_Paint(ByVal sender As Object, _
     ByVal e As System.Windows.Forms.PaintEventArgs) Handles Me.Paint
        DrawControl(e.Graphics)
    End Sub

    Private Sub InvisibleControl_Resize(ByVal sender As Object, _
     ByVal e As System.EventArgs) Handles Me.Resize
        Me.Invalidate()
```

```
        End Sub

    Private Sub DrawControl(ByVal gr As Graphics)
        Me.Visible = Me.DesignMode

        gr.Clear(Me.BackColor)
        gr.DrawEllipse(New Pen(Me.ForeColor), _
            0, 0, _
            Me.ClientRectangle.Width - 1, _
            Me.ClientRectangle.Height - 1)
    End Sub
End Class
```

If you want a control to be invisible at run time, you should consider making it a component instead of a control. Components take fewer resources and don't take up space on the form at design time. The only reason you should make a control invisible in this manner is if you want it to display some sort of complex data at design time that should be hidden from the user at run time.

Picking a Control Class

There are several ways you can build objects that sit on a form at design time. Depending on the features you need, these objects can inherit from the Component, Control, and UserControl classes. They can also inherit from an existing control class such as a Button, TextBox, or ListView.

The Component class is the simplest of these classes. It doesn't take up space on the form at design time, so it is appropriate when you don't want an object that is visible to the user. If you want a class with properties that you can set at design time, but that should be invisible at run time, build a Component.

The Control class is visible on the form at design and run time but it is simpler than the UserControl class. Unlike a UserControl, it cannot contain constituent controls. If you want a control that draws itself without using any constituent controls, make your control inherit from the Control class.

The UserControl class is visible on the form at design and run time. Unlike the Control class, it can contain constituent controls. If you want a control that uses constituent controls, make your control inherit from the UserControl class.

Finally, if some existing class provides some of the features that you need to use, make your control inherit from that class. The standard Visual Basic controls are very powerful and extensively tested, so you can save yourself a considerable amount of time by taking advantage of their existing features.

Controls and Components in Executable Projects

Most of this chapter explains how to build a control library containing any number of controls and components. You can compile the library into a .dll file and use it in executable applications.

You can also build custom controls or components within an executable project. In that case, the controls or components are compiled into the executable rather than a separate .dll file, so you cannot use them in other applications. If these are very specialized objects that you probably won't need to use in other applications, this is not a major disadvantage and saves you the trouble of installing an extra .dll file with the application.

UserControls in Executable Projects

To add a custom UserControl to a project, open the Project menu and select Add User Control. Leave the User Control template selected, enter a name for the control, and click Add. Add constituent controls to the UserControl as usual.

Initially, the control does not appear in the Toolbox, so you cannot use it on a form. Select the Build menu's Build command to compile the control and the rest of the project. Visual Basic places the new control in a Toolbox section named after the project. If the project's name is Billing, it places the control in a Toolbox section named Billing Components. Now you can use the control as usual.

Inherited UserControls in Executable Projects

To build a UserControl that inherits from an existing UserControl class, select the Project menu's Add New Item command. In the resulting dialog, select the Inherited User Control template, enter a name for the control, and click Add. The Inheritance Picker dialog shown in Figure 12-7 lists compiled components in the current project. Select the control from which you want to inherit and click OK.

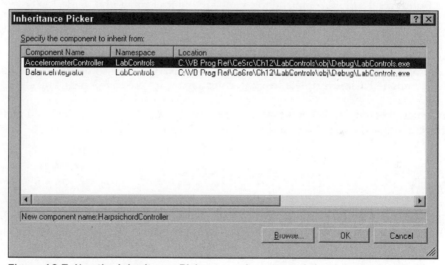

Figure 12-7: Use the Inheritance Picker to make a control that inherits from an existing UserControl.

Add properties, methods, and events to the control as usual. Select the Build menu's Build command to compile the control and add it to the Toolbox.

Alternatively, you can create a new class and add an Inherits statement that makes the class inherit from the previously built UserControl.

Controls in Executable Projects

To build a control that inherits from the `Control` class in an executable project, select the Project menu's Add Class command. Leave the Class template selected, enter a name for the control, and click Add. Add the statement `Inherits Control` to the control's code.

Add properties, methods, and events to the control as usual. For example, you may want to give the control `Paint` and `Resize` event handlers so that it can draw itself. You may also want to override the parent class's behaviors.

Select the Build menu's Build command to compile the control and add it to the Toolbox.

Inherited Controls in Executable Projects

To build a control that inherits from a predefined control, select the Project menu's Add Class command. Leave the Class template selected, enter a name for the control, and click Add. Add an `Inherits` statement that makes the class inherit from the previously built control.

Add properties, methods, and events to the control as usual. For example, you may want to give the control `Paint` and `Resize` event handlers so that it can draw itself. You may also want to override the parent class's behaviors.

Select the Build menu's Build command to compile the control and add it to the Toolbox.

Components in Executable Projects

To add a component to an executable project, select the Project menu's Add Component command. Leave the Component Class template selected, enter a name for the component, and click Add.

Add properties, methods, and events to the component as usual. Then select the Build menu's Build command to compile the component and add it to the Toolbox.

Summary

Visual Basic provides a large assortment of controls that you can use on your forms. When they don't do exactly you need, you can build others.

If an existing control does most of what you need, derive a new control from that one. If a group of controls together with their properties, methods, and events can do what you need, combine them into a composite control that inherits from the `UserControl` object. If you want to build a new control from scratch, make a class that inherits from the `Control` class. Finally, if you want an object that is available at design time but invisible at run time, build a component.

When you build a control or component, you can use attributes to give extra information to Visual Studio. The `ToolboxBitmap`, `DefaultProperty`, `DefaultEvent`, `DesignTimeVisible`, `Description`, `Category`, `Browsable`, and `DefaultValue` attributes are some of the more useful for control and component classes.

Visual Basic provides many other features that you can use to build other kinds of control-related classes and their properties. An *extender provider* class adds new properties to the other controls on a form much as the `ErrorProvider` and `ToolTip` controls do. A *type converter* (which translates data from one type to another) can translate between values and text for display in the Properties window, and can generate a customized list of choices for a property drop-down. A *UI type editor* enables you to build a graphical editor that the developer can use to view and manipulate special property values. These are more advanced topics that lie beyond the scope of this book.

Visual Basic also provides tools for designer localization, control licensing, multithreading, control containers, and much more. Most of the time, however, you can do what you want using standard controls, derived controls, composed controls, controls built from scratch, and components. If you really must offer more exotic features (such as fancy editors and wizards), read the online help or search Visual Basic discussion groups on the Web.

Chapters 9 through 12 all deal with different kinds of controls. Chapter 13, "Drag and Drop, and The Clipboard," moves away from the topic of controls and explains how an application can support drag-and-drop applications. Using the clipboard is similar to certain types of drag-and-drop operations, so Chapter 13 also explains how to use the clipboard.

Drag and Drop, and the Clipboard

The clipboard is an object where programs can save and restore data. A program can save data in multiple formats and retrieve it later, or another program might retrieve the data. Windows, rather than Visual Basic, provides the clipboard, so it is available to every application running on the system, and any program can save or fetch data from the clipboard.

The clipboard can store remarkably complex data types. For example, an application can store a representation of a complete object in the clipboard for use by other applications that know how to use that kind of object.

Drag and drop enables the user to drag information from one control to another. The controls may be in the same application or in different applications. For example, your program could let the user drag items from one list to another, or it could let the user drag files from Windows Explorer into a file list inside your program.

A drag occurs in three main steps. First, a *drag source* control starts the drag, usually when the user presses the mouse down on the control. The control starts the drag, indicating the data that it wants to drag and the type of drag operations it wants to perform (such as Copy, Link, or Move).

When the user drags over a control, that control is a possible *drop target*. The control examines the kind of data being dragged and the type of drag operation requested (such as Copy, Link, or Move). The drop target then decides whether it will allow the drop and what type of feedback it should give to the user. For example, if the user drags a picture over a label control, the label might refuse the drop and display a "no drop" icon (a circle with a line through it). If the user drags the picture over a `PictureBox` that the program is using to display images, it might display a "drop link" icon (a box with a curved arrow in it).

Finally, when the user releases the mouse, the current drop target receives the data and does whatever is appropriate. For example, if the drop target is a `TextBox` control and the data is a string, the `TextBox` control might display the string. If the same `TextBox` control receives a file name, it might read the file and display its contents.

The following sections describe drag and drop in more detail and give several examples of common drag-and-drop tasks. The section "Using the Clipboard" near the end of the chapter explains how to use the clipboard. Using it is very similar to using drag and drop, although it doesn't require as much user feedback, so it is considerably simpler.

Drag-and-Drop Events

The drag source control starts a drag operation by calling its DoDragDrop method. It passes this method the data to be dragged and the type of drag operation that the control wants to perform. The drag type can be Copy, Link, or Move.

If you are dragging to other general applications, the data should be a standard data type such as a String or Bitmap so that the other application can understand it. If you are dragging data within a single application or between two applications that you have written, you can drag any type of data. This won't necessarily work with general objects and arbitrary applications. For example, WordPad doesn't know what an Employee object is, so you can't drop an Employee on it.

As the user drags the data around the screen, Visual Basic sends events to the controls it moves over. Those controls can indicate whether they will accept the data and how they can accept it. For example, a control might indicate that it will allow a Copy, but not a Move. The following table describes the events that a drop target receives as data is dragged over it.

Event	Purpose
DragEnter	The drag is entering the control. The control can examine the type of data available and set e.Effect to indicate the types of drops it can handle. These can include All, Copy, Move, Link, and None. The control can also display some sort of highlighting to indicate that the data is over it. For example, it might display a dark border or shade the area where the new data would be placed.
DragLeave	The drag has left the control. If the control displays some sort of highlighting or other indication that the drag is over it in the DragEnter event, it should remove that highlight now.
DragOver	The drag is over the control. This event continues to fire a few times per second until the drag is no longer over the control. The control may take action to indicate how the drop will be processed much as the DragEnter event handler does. For example, as the user moves the mouse over a ListBox, the control might highlight the list item that is under the mouse to show that this item will receive the data. The program can also check for changes to the mouse or keyboard. For example, it might allow a Copy if the Ctrl key is pressed and a Move if the Ctrl key is not pressed.
DragDrop	The user has dropped the data on the control. The control should process the data.

A drop target with simple needs can specify the drop actions it will allow in its DragEnter event handler and not provide a DragOver event handler. It knows whether it will allow a drop based solely on the type of item being dropped. For example, a graphical application might allow the user to drop a bitmap on it, but not a string.

A more complex target that must track such items as the keyboard state, mouse position, and mouse button state can provide a DragOver event handler and skip the DragEnter event handler. For example, a circuit design application might check the drag's position over its drawing surface, and highlight the location where the dragged item would be positioned. As the user moved the object around, the DragOver event would continue to fire so the program could update the drop highlighting.

After the drag and drop finishes, the drag source's DoDragDrop method returns the last type of action that was displayed when the user dropped the data. That lets the drag source know what the drop target expects the source to do with the data. For example, if the drop target accepted a Move, the drag source should remove the data from its control. If the drop target accepted a Copy, the drag source should not remove the data from its control.

The following table describes the two events that the drag source control receives to help it control the drop.

Event	Purpose
GiveFeedback	The drag has entered a valid drop target. The source can take action to indicate the type of drop allowed. For example, it might allow a Copy if the target is a Label and allow Move or Copy if the target is a TextBox.
QueryContinueDrag	The keyboard or mouse button state has changed. The drag source can decide whether to continue the drag, cancel the drag, or drop the data immediately.

The following sections describe some examples that demonstrate common drag-and-drop scenarios.

A Simple Example

The following code shows one of the simplest examples possible that contains both a drag source and a drop target. To build this example, start a new project and add two Label controls named lblDragSource and lblDropTarget.

Note that the lblDropTarget control must have its AllowDrop property set to True either at design time or at run time or it will not receive any drag-and-drop events. When the user presses a mouse button down over the lblDragSource control, the MouseDown event handler calls that control's DoDragDrop method passing it the text "Here's the drag data!" and indicating that it wants to perform a Copy. When the user drags the data over the lblDropTarget control, its DragEnter event handler executes. The event handler sets the routine's e.Effect value to indicate that the control will allow a Copy operation. If the user drops the data over the lblDropTarget control, its DragDrop event handler executes. This routine uses the e.Data.GetData method to get a text data value and displays it in a message box.

```
Public Class Form1
    ' Start a drag.
    Private Sub lblDragSource_MouseDown(ByVal sender As Object, _
     ByVal e As System.Windows.Forms.MouseEventArgs) _
     Handles lblDragSource.MouseDown
        lblDragSource.DoDragDrop("Here's the drag data!", DragDropEffects.Copy)
    End Sub

    ' Make sure the drag is coming from lblDragSource.
    Private Sub lblDropTarget_DragEnter(ByVal sender As Object, _
     ByVal e As System.Windows.Forms.DragEventArgs) _
     Handles lblDropTarget.DragEnter
        e.Effect = DragDropEffects.Copy
    End Sub

    ' Display the dropped data.
    Private Sub lblDropTarget_DragDrop(ByVal sender As Object, _
     ByVal e As System.Windows.Forms.DragEventArgs) _
     Handles lblDropTarget.DragDrop
        MessageBox.Show(e.Data.GetData("Text").ToString)
    End Sub
End Class
```

As it is, this program lets you drag and drop data from the lblDragSource control to the lblDropTarget control. You can also drag data from the lblDragSource control into Word, WordPad, and any other application that can accept a drop of text data.

Similarly, the lblDropTarget control can act as a drop target for any application that provides drag sources. For example, if you open WordPad, enter some text, select it, and then click and drag it onto the lblDropTarget control, the application will display the text you dropped in a message box.

This example is a bit too simple to be really useful. If the drop target does nothing more, it should check the data it will receive and ensure that it is text. If you drag a file from Windows Explorer and drop it onto the lblDropTarget control, the e.Data.GetData method returns Nothing so the program cannot display its value. Because the program cannot display a file, it is misleading for the lblDropTarget control to display a Copy cursor when the user drags a file over it.

The following version of the lblDropTarget_DragEnter event handler uses the e.Data.GetDataPresent method to see if the data being dragged has a textual format. If a text format is available, the control allows a Copy operation. If the data does not come in a textual form, the control doesn't allow a drop.

```
' Make sure the drag is coming from lblDragSource.
Private Sub lblDropTarget_DragEnter(ByVal sender As Object, _
 ByVal e As System.Windows.Forms.DragEventArgs) Handles lblDropTarget.DragEnter
    ' See if the drag data includes text.
    If e.Data.GetDataPresent("Text") Then
        e.Effect = DragDropEffects.Copy
    Else
        e.Effect = DragDropEffects.None
    End If
End Sub
```

Now, if you drag a file from Windows Explorer onto lblDropTarget, the control displays a no-drop icon.

The lblDropTarget_DragDrop event handler doesn't need to change because Visual Basic doesn't raise the event if the control does not allow any drop operation. For example, if the user drags a file from Windows Explorer onto lblDropTarget, then that control's DragEnter event handler sets e.Effect to DragDropEffects.None, so Visual Basic doesn't raise the DragDrop event handler if the user drops the file there.

Moving between ListBoxes

The following code provides a more complete example that demonstrates many of the drag-and-drop events. It allows the user to drag items between two ListBoxes named lstUnselected and lstSelected. It also allows the user to drag an item to a specific position in its new ListBox and to drag an item from one position to another within a ListBox.

The code uses the variable m_DragSource to remember the control that started the drag. If this variable is Nothing during a drag, then the application knows that the drag was started by another application. In this example, the program ignores drags from other applications.

When the form loads, it sets the AllowDrop properties for its two ListBoxes. It then uses the AddHandler statement to give the two controls the same MouseDown, DragOver, DragDrop, and DragLeave event handlers.

When the user presses the mouse down on one of the ListBoxes, the List_MouseDown executes. If the user is pressing the right mouse button, the program casts the sender parameter into a ListBox to see which control raised the event. It uses the control's IndexFromPoint method to see which item is under the mouse and selects that item. If there is no item under the mouse, the routine exits. Next, the program saves a reference to the control in m_DragSource and calls the DoDragDrop method to start the drag for a Move operation. When DoDragDrop ends, the code sets m_DragSource to Nothing to indicate that the drag is over.

When the drag sits over one of the ListBoxes, the List_DragOver event handler executes. If m_DragSource is Nothing, then the drag event was caused by another application and the event handler exits without allowing the operation. If m_DragSource is not Nothing, the control allows a Move operation. It then uses the control's IndexFromPoint method to see which item is under the mouse and it selects that item.

If the user drags off of a ListBox, the List_DragLeave event handler unselects the item that is currently selected in that ListBox. This may help prevent some confusion about where the item will be dropped if the user releases the mouse button.

When the user drops over a ListBox, the List_DragDrop event handler executes. It uses the e.Data.GetData method to get the dropped text and calls subroutine MoveItem to move the item from the m_DragSource control to the drop target.

Subroutine MoveItem determines which item is selected in the drop target. If no item is selected, it adds the new item to the end of the target list. If an item is selected, the code inserts the new item in front of the selected item. In either case, the program selects the newly inserted item.

MoveItem then removes the original item from the drag source. If the drag source and the drop target are the same, then the code finds the first instance of the item being moved. If that is the same item that was just added, the code uses the source list's RemoveAt method to remove the next occurrence of the item. If the first item is not the one that was just added, the code removes it.

```
Public Class Form1
    ' Remember where we got it.
    Private m_DragSource As ListBox = Nothing

    ' Allow drag events.
    Private Sub Form1_Load(ByVal sender As System.Object, _
     ByVal e As System.EventArgs) Handles MyBase.Load
        lstUnselected.AllowDrop = True
        lstSelected.AllowDrop = True

        ' Add event handlers.
        AddHandler lstUnselected.MouseDown, AddressOf List_MouseDown
        AddHandler lstUnselected.DragOver, AddressOf List_DragOver
        AddHandler lstUnselected.DragDrop, AddressOf List_DragDrop
        AddHandler lstUnselected.DragLeave, AddressOf List_DragLeave

        AddHandler lstSelected.MouseDown, AddressOf List_MouseDown
        AddHandler lstSelected.DragOver, AddressOf List_DragOver
        AddHandler lstSelected.DragDrop, AddressOf List_DragDrop
        AddHandler lstSelected.DragLeave, AddressOf List_DragLeave
    End Sub

    ' Start a drag.
    Private Sub List_MouseDown(ByVal sender As Object, _
     ByVal e As System.Windows.Forms.MouseEventArgs)
        ' Make sure this is the right button.
        If e.Button <> MouseButtons.Right Then Exit Sub

        ' Select the item at this point.
        Dim this_list As ListBox = DirectCast(sender, ListBox)
        this_list.SelectedIndex = this_list.IndexFromPoint(e.X, e.Y)
        If this_list.SelectedIndex < 0 Then Exit Sub

        ' Remember where the drag started.
        m_DragSource = this_list

        ' Start the drag.
        this_list.DoDragDrop( _
            this_list.SelectedItem.ToString, _
            DragDropEffects.Move)

        ' We're done dragging.
        m_DragSource = Nothing
    End Sub

    ' Highlight the item under the mouse.
    Private Sub List_DragOver(ByVal sender As Object, _
     ByVal e As System.Windows.Forms.DragEventArgs)
```

```
        If m_DragSource Is Nothing Then Exit Sub

        e.Effect = DragDropEffects.Move
        Dim this_list As ListBox = DirectCast(sender, ListBox)
        Dim pt As Point = _
            this_list.PointToClient(New Point(e.X, e.Y))
        Dim drop_index As Integer = _
            this_list.IndexFromPoint(pt.X, pt.Y)
        this_list.SelectedIndex = drop_index
    End Sub


    ' Unhighlight the target item when the drag leaves.
    Private Sub List_DragLeave(ByVal sender As Object, ByVal e As System.EventArgs)
        Dim this_list As ListBox = DirectCast(sender, ListBox)
        this_list.SelectedIndex = -1
    End Sub


    ' Accept the drop.
    Private Sub List_DragDrop(ByVal sender As Object, _
     ByVal e As System.Windows.Forms.DragEventArgs)
        Dim this_list As ListBox = DirectCast(sender, ListBox)
        MoveItem(e.Data.GetData(DataFormats.Text).ToString, _
            m_DragSource, this_list, e.X, e.Y)
    End Sub


    ' Move the value txt from drag_source to drop_target.
    Private Sub MoveItem(ByVal txt As String, ByVal drag_source As ListBox, _
     ByVal drop_target As ListBox, ByVal X As Integer, ByVal Y As Integer)
        ' See which item is selected in the drop target.
        Dim drop_index As Integer = drop_target.SelectedIndex
        If drop_index < 0 Then
            ' Add at the end.
            drop_index = drop_target.Items.Add(txt)
        Else
            ' Add before the selected item.
            drop_target.Items.Insert(drop_target.SelectedIndex, txt)
        End If

        ' Select the item.
        drop_target.SelectedIndex = drop_index

        ' Remove the value from drag_source.
        If drag_source Is drop_target Then
            ' Make sure we don't remove the item we just added.
            Dim target_index As Integer = drag_source.FindStringExact(txt)
            If target_index = drop_index Then _
                target_index = drag_source.FindStringExact(txt, target_index)
            drag_source.Items.RemoveAt(target_index)
        Else
            ' Remove the item.
            drag_source.Items.Remove(txt)
        End If
    End Sub
End Class
```

This example shows how to drag items from one `ListBox` to another or to a new position within a single `ListBox`. The case is somewhat simpler if you don't need to worry about dragging items within a single `ListBox`. In that case, the `MoveItem` subroutine doesn't need to worry about removing the item you just added.

Moving and Copying between ListBoxes

It isn't too difficult to modify the previous example to allow the user to move or copy items between the two lists. If the user holds down the Ctrl key while dropping an item, the program copies the item and leaves the original item where it started. If the user doesn't hold down the Ctrl key while dropping the item, the program moves it as before.

The code is almost the same as in the previous example. The first change is in the way the program starts the drag in the `List_MouseDown` event handler. In the call to `DoDragDrop`, the new code allows both Move and Copy operations.

```
' Start the drag.
this_list.DoDragDrop( _
    this_list.SelectedItem.ToString, _
    DragDropEffects.Move Or DragDropEffects.Copy)
```

Instead of always allowing the Move operation, the new `DragOver` event handler uses the following code to allow a Move or Copy, depending on whether the Ctrl key is pressed:

```
' Display the Move or Copy cursor.
Const KEY_CTRL As Integer = 8
If (e.KeyState And KEY_CTRL) <> 0 Then
    e.Effect = DragDropEffects.Copy
Else
    e.Effect = DragDropEffects.Move
End If
```

Remember that the `DragOver` event handler fires periodically as long as the drag sits over the control. This not only lets the program highlight the item beneath the mouse but also lets the code change the drag effect if the user presses and releases the Ctrl key while the drag is still in progress.

The new `DragDrop` event handler must determine whether the Ctrl key was pressed when the data was dropped. The `e.Effect` parameter indicates which drag-and-drop effect was displayed when the drop occurred. The new `DragDrop` compares `e.Effect` with `DragDropEffects.Move` and passes the `MoveItem` subroutine `True` if the effect was Move.

```
' Accept the drop.
Private Sub List_DragDrop(ByVal sender As Object, ByVal e As
System.Windows.Forms.DragEventArgs)
    Dim this_list As ListBox = DirectCast(sender, ListBox)
    MoveItem(e.Data.GetData(DataFormats.Text).ToString, _
        m_DragSource, this_list, e.X, e.Y, _
        e.Effect = DragDropEffects.Move)
End Sub
```

Finally, the `MoveItem` subroutine takes a new Boolean parameter `move_item`, which indicates whether it should move the item or copy it. It is similar to the previous version, except that it does not remove the item from its original list if `move_item` is `False`.

```
' Move the value txt from drag_source to drop_target.
Private Sub MoveItem(ByVal txt As String, ByVal drag_source As ListBox, _
 ByVal drop_target As ListBox, ByVal X As Integer, ByVal Y As Integer, _
 ByVal move_item As Boolean)
    ' See which item is selected in the drop target.
    Dim drop_index As Integer = drop_target.SelectedIndex
    If drop_index < 0 Then
        ' Add at the end.
        drop_index = drop_target.Items.Add(txt)
    Else
        ' Add before the selected item.
        drop_target.Items.Insert(drop_target.SelectedIndex, txt)
    End If

    ' Select the item.
    drop_target.SelectedIndex = drop_index

    ' See if we are moving or copying.
    If move_item Then
        ' Remove the value from drag_source.
        If drag_source Is drop_target Then
            ' Make sure we don't remove the item we just added.
            Dim target_index As Integer = drag_source.FindStringExact(txt)
            If target_index = drop_index Then _
                target_index = drag_source.FindStringExact(txt, target_index)
            drag_source.Items.RemoveAt(target_index)
        Else
            ' Remove the item.
            drag_source.Items.Remove(txt)
        End If
    End If
End Sub
```

Learning Data Types Available

When the user drags data over a drop target, the target's `DragEnter` event handler decides which kinds of drop to allow. The event handler can use the `e.GetDataPresent` method to see whether the data is available in a desired data format.

`GetDataPresent` takes as a parameter a string giving the desired data type. An optional second parameter indicates whether the program will accept another format if the system can derive it from the original format. For example, the system can convert Text data into System.String data so you can decide whether to allow the system to make this conversion.

The `DataFormats` class provides a shared series of standardized string values specifying various data types. For example, `DataFormats.Text` returns the string "`Text`" representing the text data type.

If you use a `DataFormats` value, you don't need to worry about misspelling one of these formats. Some of the most commonly used `DataFormats` include `Bitmap`, `Html`, `StringFormat`, and `Text`. See the online help for other formats. The Web page `http://msdn.microsoft.com/library/en-us/cpref/html/frlrfsystemwindowsformsdataformatsmemberstopic.asp` lists the `DataFormats` class's supported formats.

`GetDataPresent` can also take as a parameter a data type. For example, the following code fragment uses `GetDataPresent` to allow a Copy operation if the drag data contains an `Employee` object.

```
If e.Data.GetDataPresent(GetType(Employee)) Then
    ' Allow Copy.
    e.Effect = DragDropEffects.Copy
Else
    ' Allow no other drops.
    e.Effect = DragDropEffects.None
End If
```

In addition to `GetDataPresent`, you can use the `e.Data.GetFormats` method to get an array of strings giving the names of the available formats. The following code shows how a program can list the formats available. It clears its `lstWithoutConversion` ListBox and then loops through the values returned by `e.Data.GetFormats` adding them to the ListBox. It passes `GetFormats` the parameter `False` to indicate that it should return only data formats that are directly available, not those that can be derived from others. The program then repeats these steps again, this time passing `GetFormats` the parameter `True` to include derived formats.

```
Private Sub lblDropTarget_DragEnter(ByVal sender As Object, _
  ByVal e As System.Windows.Forms.DragEventArgs) Handles lblDropTarget.DragEnter
    lstWithoutConversion.Items.Clear()
    For Each fmt As String In e.Data.GetFormats(False)
        lstWithoutConversion.Items.Add(fmt)
    Next fmt

    lstWithConversion.Items.Clear()
    For Each fmt As String In e.Data.GetFormats(True)
        lstWithConversion.Items.Add(fmt)
    Next fmt
End Sub
```

Dragging within an Application

Sometimes, you may want a drop target to accept only data dragged from within the same application. The following code shows one way to handle this. Before it calls `DoDragDrop`, the program sets its `m_Dragging` variable to `True`. The `lblDropTarget` control's `DragEnter` event checks `m_Dragging`. If the user drags data from a program other than this one, `m_Dragging` will be `False` and the program sets `e.Effect` to `DragDropEffects.None`, prohibiting a drop. If `m_Dragging` is `True`, that means this program started the drag, so the program allows a Copy operation. After the drag and drop finishes, the `lblDragSource` control's `MouseDown` event handler sets `m_Dragging` to `False`, so the drop target will refuse future drags from other applications.

```
Public Class Form1
    ' True while we are dragging.
    Private m_Dragging As Boolean

    ' Start a drag.
    Private Sub lblDragSource_MouseDown(ByVal sender As Object, _
     ByVal e As System.Windows.Forms.MouseEventArgs) _
     Handles lblDragSource.MouseDown
        m_Dragging = True
        lblDragSource.DoDragDrop("Some text", DragDropEffects.Copy)
        m_Dragging = False
    End Sub

    ' Only allow Copy if we are dragging.
    Private Sub lblDropTarget_DragEnter(ByVal sender As Object, _
     ByVal e As System.Windows.Forms.DragEventArgs) Handles lblDropTarget.DragEnter
        If m_Dragging Then
            e.Effect = DragDropEffects.Copy
        Else
            e.Effect = DragDropEffects.None
        End If
    End Sub

    ' Display the dropped text.
    Private Sub lblDropTarget_DragDrop(ByVal sender As Object, _
     ByVal e As System.Windows.Forms.DragEventArgs) Handles lblDropTarget.DragDrop
        MessageBox.Show(e.Data.GetData(DataFormats.Text).ToString)
    End Sub
End Class
```

There is no easy way to allow your program to drag data to its own controls, but not allow it to drag data to another program. The philosophy is that a drag source provides data for any application that can handle it.

If you don't want other applications to read data dragged from your application, you can package the data in an object and drag the object as described in the section "Dragging Objects" later in this chapter. This will make it very difficult for most applications to understand the data, even if they try to accept it.

Accepting Dropped Files

Many applications let you drop files onto them. When you drag files over a drop target, the data object contains data of several types, including FileDrop. This data is an array of strings containing the names of the files being dragged.

The following code shows how a program might process files dragged onto it. The lblDropTarget control's DragEnter event handler uses the GetDataPresent method to see if the drag contains FileDrop data, and allows the Copy operation if it does. The control's DragDrop event handler uses GetData to get the data in FileDrop format. It converts the data from a generic object into an array of strings, and then loops through the entries, adding each to the lstFiles ListBox.

```
Public Class Form1
    ' Allow Copy if there is FileDrop data.
    Private Sub lblDropTarget_DragEnter(ByVal sender As Object, _
     ByVal e As System.Windows.Forms.DragEventArgs) Handles lblDropTarget.DragEnter
        If e.Data.GetDataPresent(DataFormats.FileDrop) Then
            e.Effect = DragDropEffects.Copy
        Else
            e.Effect = DragDropEffects.None
        End If
    End Sub


    ' Display the dropped file names.
    Private Sub lblDropTarget_DragDrop(ByVal sender As Object, _
     ByVal e As System.Windows.Forms.DragEventArgs) Handles lblDropTarget.DragDrop
        lstFiles.Items.Clear()
        Dim file_names As String() = _
            DirectCast(e.Data.GetData(DataFormats.FileDrop), String())
        For Each file_name As String In file_names
            lstFiles.Items.Add(file_name)
        Next file_name
    End Sub
End Class
```

A more realistic application would do something more useful than simply listing the files. For example, it might delete them, move them into the wastebasket, copy them to a backup directory, display thumbnails of images files, and so forth.

Dragging Objects

Dragging text is simple enough. Simply pass the text into the DoDragDrop method and you're finished.

You can drag an arbitrary object in a similar manner, as long as the drag source and drop target are within the same application. If you want to drag objects between applications, however, you must use serializable objects. A *serializable* object is one that provides methods for translating the object into and out of a streamlike format. Usually, this format is text, and lately XML is the preferred method for storing text streams.

For example, consider the following Employee class:

```
Public Class Employee
    Public FirstName As String
    Public LastName As String

    Public Sub New()
    End Sub

    Public Sub New(ByVal first_name As String, ByVal last_name As String)
        FirstName = first_name
        LastName = last_name
    End Sub
End Class
```

You could serialize an `Employee` object having `FirstName` = "Rod" and `LastName` = "Stephens" with the following XML text:

```
<Employee>
  <FirstName>Rod</FirstName>
  <LastName>Stephens</LastName>
</Employee>
```

You can use drag and drop to move a serializable object between applications. The drag source converts the object into its serialization and sends the resulting text to the drop target. The drop target uses the serialization to recreate the object.

You might think it would be hard to make an object serializable. Fortunately, Visual Basic .NET provides many features for automatically discovering the structure of objects, so it can do most of the work for you. In most cases, all you need to do is add the `Serializable` attribute to the class, as shown in the following code:

```
<Serializable()> _
Public Class Employee
    Public FirstName As String
    Public LastName As String

    Public Sub New()
    End Sub

    Public Sub New(ByVal first_name As String, ByVal last_name As String)
        FirstName = first_name
        LastName = last_name
    End Sub
End Class
```

The drag source can pass objects of this type to the `DoDragDrop` method.

The following code shows how an application can act as a drag source and a drop target for objects of the `Employee` class. It starts by defining the `Employee` class. It also defines the constant `DATA_EMPLOYEE`. This value, "DragEmployee.frmDragEmployee+Employee," is the name of the data format type assigned to the `Employee` class. This name combines the project name, module name where the class is defined, and the class name.

When the user presses the mouse down over the `lblDragSource` control, its `MouseDown` event handler creates an `Employee` object, initializing it with the values contained in the `txtFirstName` and `txtLastName` text boxes. It then calls the `lblDragSource` control's `DoDragDrop` method, passing it the `Employee` object and allowing the Move and Copy operations. If `DoDragDrop` returns the value `Move`, the user performed a Move rather than a Copy, so the program removes the values from its text boxes.

When the user drags over the `lblDropTarget` control, its `DragOver` event handler executes. The routine first uses the `GetDataPresent` method to verify that the dragged data contains an `Employee` object. It then checks the Ctrl key's state. If the user is holding down the Ctrl key, then the event handler allows the Copy operation. If the user is not holding down the Ctrl key, the subroutine allows the Move operation.

If the user drops the data on the `lblDropTarget` control, its `DragDrop` event handler executes. It uses the `GetData` method to retrieve the `Employee` object. `GetData` returns a generic `Object`, so the program uses `DirectCast` to covert the result into an `Employee` object. The event handler finishes by displaying the object's `FirstName` and `LastName` properties in its text boxes.

```
Imports System.IO
Imports System.Xml.Serialization

Public Class frmDragEmployee
    Public Const DATA_EMPLOYEE As String = "DragEmployee.frmDragEmployee+Employee"
    <Serializable()> _
    Public Class Employee
        Public FirstName As String
        Public LastName As String
        Public Sub New()
        End Sub
        Public Sub New(ByVal first_name As String, ByVal last_name As String)
            FirstName = first_name
            LastName = last_name
        End Sub
    End Class

    ' Start dragging the Employee.
    Private Sub lblDragSource_MouseDown(ByVal sender As Object, _
     ByVal e As System.Windows.Forms.MouseEventArgs) _
     Handles lblDragSource.MouseDown
        Dim emp As New Employee(txtFirstName.Text, txtLastName.Text)

        If lblDragSource.DoDragDrop(emp, _
            DragDropEffects.Copy Or DragDropEffects.Move) = DragDropEffects.Move _
        Then
            ' A Move succeeded. Clear the TextBoxes.
            txtFirstName.Text = ""
            txtLastName.Text = ""
        End If
    End Sub

    ' If an Employee object is available, allow a Move
    ' or Copy depending on whether the Ctrl key is pressed.
    Private Sub lblDropTarget_DragOver(ByVal sender As Object, _
     ByVal e As System.Windows.Forms.DragEventArgs) _
     Handles lblDropTarget.DragOver
        If e.Data.GetDataPresent(DATA_EMPLOYEE) Then
            ' Display the Move or Copy cursor.
            Const KEY_CTRL As Integer = 8
            If (e.KeyState And KEY_CTRL) <> 0 Then
                e.Effect = DragDropEffects.Copy
            Else
                e.Effect = DragDropEffects.Move
            End If
        End If
    End Sub

    ' Display the dropped Employee object.
```

```
      Private Sub lblDropTarget_DragDrop(ByVal sender As Object, _
       ByVal e As System.Windows.Forms.DragEventArgs) _
       Handles lblDropTarget.DragDrop
          Dim emp As Employee = DirectCast(e.Data.GetData(DATA_EMPLOYEE), Employee)
          lblFirstName.Text = emp.FirstName
          lblLastName.Text = emp.LastName
      End Sub
  End Class
```

If you compile this program, you can run two copies of the executable program stored in the bin directory and drag from the drag source in one to the drop target in the other.

If you remove the `Serializable` attribute from the `Employees` class, the program still works if you drag from the drag source to the drop target within the same instance of the application. If you run two instances and drag from one to the other, however, the drop target gets the value `Nothing` from the `GetData` method, so the drag and drop fails.

Changing Format Names

The previous example dragged data with the rather unwieldy data format name "`DragEmployee .frmDragEmployee+Employee.`" This name identifies the class reasonably well, so it is unlikely that another application will try to load this data if it has some other definition for the `Employee` class.

On the other hand, the name is rather awkward. It is also problematic if you want to drag objects between two different applications, because each will use its project and module name to define the data format type. If you want to drag `Employee` objects between the `TimeSheet` program and the `EmployeePayroll` program, the names of the data formats generated by the two programs won't match.

The `DataObject` class provides more control over how the data is represented. Instead of dragging an `Employee` object directly, you create a `DataObject`, store the `Employee` object inside it with the data format name of your choosing, and then drag the `DataObject`.

The following code fragment shows this technique. It creates an `Employee` object as before and then creates a `DataObject`. It calls the `DataObject`'s `SetData` method, passing it the `Employee` object and the data format name.

```
Dim emp As New Employee(txtFirstName.Text, txtLastName.Text)
Dim data_object As New DataObject()
data_object.SetData("Employee", emp)

If lblDragSource.DoDragDrop(data_object, _
    DragDropEffects.Copy Or DragDropEffects.Move) = DragDropEffects.Move _
Then
    ' A Move succeeded. Clear the TextBoxes.
    txtFirstName.Text = ""
    txtLastName.Text = ""
End If
```

In general, you should try to avoid very generic names such as "Employee" for data types. Using such a simple name increases the chances that another application will use the same name for a different class. Another program will not be able to convert your `Employee` data into a different type of `Employee` class.

To ensure consistency across applications, you must define a naming convention that can identify objects across projects. To ensure that different applications use exactly the same object definitions, you might also want to define the objects in a separate DLL used by all of the applications. That simplifies the naming problem, because you can use the DLL's name as part of the object's name.

For example, suppose that you build an assortment of billing database objects such as `Employee`, `Customer`, `Order`, `OrderItem`, and so on. If the objects are defined in the module `BillingObjects.dll`, you could give the objects name such as `BillingObjects.Employee`, `BillingObjects.Customer`, and so forth.

Dragging Multiple Data Formats

The `DataObject` not only allows you to pick the data form name used by a drag; it also allows you to associate more than one piece of data with a drag. To do this, the program simply calls the object's `SetData` method more than once, passing it data in different formats.

The following code shows how a program can drag the text in a `RichTextBox` control in three data formats: RTF, plain text, and HTML. The `lblDragSource` control's `MouseDown` event handler makes a `DataObject` and calls its `SetData` method, passing it the `rchSource` control's contents in the `Rtf` and `Text` formats. It then builds an HTML string and passes that to the `SetData` method as well.

```
' Start a drag.
Private Sub lblDragSource_MouseDown(ByVal sender As Object, _
 ByVal e As System.Windows.Forms.MouseEventArgs) Handles lblDragSource.MouseDown
    ' Make a DataObject.
    Dim data_object As New DataObject

    ' Add the data in various formats.
    data_object.SetData(DataFormats.Rtf, rchSource.Rtf)
    data_object.SetData(DataFormats.Text, rchSource.Text)

    ' Build the HTML version.
    Dim html_text As String
    html_text = "<HTML>" & vbCrLf
    html_text &= "   <HEAD>The Quick Brown Fox</HEAD>" & vbCrLf
    html_text &= "   <BODY>" & vbCrLf
    html_text &= rchSource.Text & vbCrLf
    html_text &= "   </BODY>" & vbCrLf & "</HTML>"
    data_object.SetData(DataFormats.Html, html_text)

    ' Start the drag.
    lblDragSource.DoDragDrop(data_object, DragDropEffects.Copy)
End Sub
```

The following code shows how the `lblDropTarget` control's `DragEnter` event handler. If the data includes the RTF, Text, or HTML data formats, the control allows a Copy operation.

```
' Allow drop of Rtf, Text, and HTML.
Private Sub lblDropTarget_DragEnter(ByVal sender As Object, _
 ByVal e As System.Windows.Forms.DragEventArgs) Handles lblDropTarget.DragEnter
    If e.Data.GetDataPresent(DataFormats.Rtf) Or _
       e.Data.GetDataPresent(DataFormats.Text) Or _
       e.Data.GetDataPresent(DataFormats.Html) _
    Then
        e.Effect = DragDropEffects.Copy
    End If
End Sub
```

The following code shows how a program can read these formats. If the dropped data includes the RTF format, the code displays it in the `RichTextControl rchTarget`. It also displays the RTF data in the `lblRtf` Label. This lets you see the Rich Text codes. If the data includes the `Text` format, the program displays it in the `lblTarget` label. Finally, if the data includes HTML the program displays it in the `lblHtml` label.

```
' Display whatever data we can.
Private Sub lblDropTarget_DragDrop(ByVal sender As Object, _
 ByVal e As System.Windows.Forms.DragEventArgs) Handles lblDropTarget.DragDrop
    If e.Data.GetDataPresent(DataFormats.Rtf) Then
        rchTarget.Rtf = e.Data.GetData(DataFormats.Rtf).ToString
        lblRtf.Text = e.Data.GetData(DataFormats.Rtf).ToString
    Else
        rchTarget.Text = ""
        lblRtf.Text = ""
    End If

    If e.Data.GetDataPresent(DataFormats.Text) Then
        lblTarget.Text = e.Data.GetData(DataFormats.Text).ToString
    Else
        lblTarget.Text = ""
    End If

    If e.Data.GetDataPresent(DataFormats.Html) Then
        lblHtml.Text = e.Data.GetData(DataFormats.Html).ToString
    Else
        lblHtml.Text = ""
    End If
End Sub
```

Figure 13-1 shows the results. The `RichTextBox` on the top shows the original data in `rchSource`. Below the drag source and drop target labels, other controls show the dropped results. The first control is a `RichTextBox` that shows the `Rtf` data. The second control is a label displaying the Rich Text codes. The third control is a label showing the Text data, and the final control is a label showing the H data.

Figure 13-1: This program drags and drops data in Text, Rtf, and Html formats.

If you drag data from another application onto the drop target, this program displays only the data that is available. For example, if you drag data from WordPad, this program will display only Rtf and Text data, because those are the only compatible formats provided by WordPad.

Using the Clipboard

Using the clipboard is very similar to using drag and drop. To save a single piece of data, call the Clipboard object's SetDataObject method passing, it the data that you want to save. For example, the following code copies the text in the txtLastName control to the clipboard.

```
Clipboard.SetDataObject(txtLastName.Text)
```

Copying data to the clipboard in multiple formats is very similar to dragging and dropping multiple data formats. First, create a DataObject and use its SetData method to store the data exactly as before. Then call the Clipboard object's SetDataObject method, passing it the DataObject.

The following code adds Rtf, Text, and Html data to the clipboard:

```
' Copy data to the clipboard.
Private Sub btnCopy_Click(ByVal sender As System.Object, _
 ByVal e As System.EventArgs) Handles btnCopy.Click
    ' Make a DataObject.
    Dim data_object As New DataObject

    ' Add the data in various formats.
    data_object.SetData(DataFormats.Rtf, rchSource.Rtf)
```

```
        data_object.SetData(DataFormats.Text, rchSource.Text)

        ' Build the HTML version.
        Dim html_text As String
        html_text = "<HTML>" & vbCrLf
        html_text &= "  <HEAD>The Quick Brown Fox</HEAD>" & vbCrLf
        html_text &= "  <BODY>" & vbCrLf
        html_text &= rchSource.Text & vbCrLf
        html_text &= "  </BODY>" & vbCrLf & "</HTML>"
        data_object.SetData(DataFormats.Html, html_text)

        ' Copy data to the clipboard.
        Clipboard.SetDataObject(data_object)
    End Sub
```

To retrieve data from the clipboard, use the `GetDataObject` method to get an `IDataObject` representing the data. Use that object's `GetDataPresent` method to see if a data type is present, and use its `GetData` method to get data with a particular format.

The following code displays `Rtf`, `Text`, and `Html` data from the clipboard:

```
' Paste data from the clipboard.
Private Sub btnPaste_Click(ByVal sender As System.Object, _
 ByVal e As System.EventArgs) Handles btnPaste.Click
    Dim data_object As IDataObject = Clipboard.GetDataObject()

    If data_object.GetDataPresent(DataFormats.Rtf) Then
        rchTarget.Rtf = data_object.GetData(DataFormats.Rtf).ToString
        lblRtf.Text = data_object.GetData(DataFormats.Rtf).ToString
    Else
        rchTarget.Text = ""
        lblRtf.Text = ""
    End If

    If data_object.GetDataPresent(DataFormats.Text) Then
        lblTarget.Text = data_object.GetData(DataFormats.Text).ToString
    Else
        lblTarget.Text = ""
    End If

    If data_object.GetDataPresent(DataFormats.Html) Then
        lblHtml.Text = data_object.GetData(DataFormats.Html).ToString
    Else
        lblHtml.Text = ""
    End If
End Sub
```

The `IDataObject` returned by the `GetDataObject` method also provides a `GetFormats` method that returns an array of the data formats available. This array is very similar to the one returned by the `GetFormats` method provided by the `DragEnter` event described earlier in this chapter.

You can copy and paste objects using the clipboard much as you drag and drop objects. Simply make the object's class serializable and add an instance of the class to the DataObject.

The following code shows how a program can copy and paste an Employee object. The btnCopy_Click event handler makes an Employee object and a DataObject. It passes the Employee object to the DataObject's SetData method, giving it the data format name "Employee." The program then passes the DataObject to the Clipboard object's SetDataObject method. The btnPaste_Click event handler retrieves the clipboard's data object and uses its GetDataPresent method to see if the clipboard is holding data with the "Employee" format. If the data is present, the program uses the data object's GetData method to fetch the data, casts it into an Employee object, and displays the object's property values.

```
' Copy the Employee to the clipboard.
Private Sub btnCopy_Click(ByVal sender As System.Object, _
 ByVal e As System.EventArgs) Handles btnCopy.Click
    Dim emp As New Employee(txtFirstName.Text, txtLastName.Text)
    Dim data_object As New DataObject
    data_object.SetData("Employee", emp)
    Clipboard.SetDataObject(data_object)
End Sub

' Paste data from the clipboard.
Private Sub btnPaste_Click(ByVal sender As System.Object, _
 ByVal e As System.EventArgs) Handles btnPaste.Click
    Dim data_object As IDataObject = Clipboard.GetDataObject()
    If data_object.GetDataPresent("Employee") Then
        Dim emp As Employee = _
            DirectCast(data_object.GetData("Employee"), Employee)
        txtPasteFirstName.Text = emp.FirstName
        txtPasteLastName.Text = emp.LastName
    End If
End Sub
```

The following table lists the most methods provided by the Clipboard object, including several that make working with common data types easier.

Method	Purpose
Clear	Removes all data from the clipboard.
ContainsAudio	Returns True if the clipboard contains audio data.
ContainsData	Returns True if the clipboard contains data in a particular format.
ContainsFileDropList	Returns True if the clipboard contains a file drop list.
ContainsImage	Returns True if the clipboard contains an image.
ContainsText	Returns True if the clipboard contains text.
GetAudioStream	Returns the audio stream contained in the clipboard.
GetData	Returns data in a specific format.

Method	Purpose
GetDataObject	Returns the clipboard's DataObject.
GetFileDropList	Returns the file drop list contained in the clipboard.
GetImage	Returns the image contained in the clipboard.
GetText	Returns the text contained in the clipboard.
SetAudio	Saves audio bytes or an audio stream in the clipboard.
SetData	Saves data in a particular format in the clipboard.
SetDataObject	Saves the data defined by a DataObject in the clipboard.
SetFileDropList	Saves a file drop list in the clipboard. The data should be a StringCollection containing the filenames.
SetImage	Saves an image in the clipboard.
SetText	Saves text in the clipboard.

The following code retrieves file drop list data from the clipboard:

```
Private Sub btnPaste_Click(ByVal sender As System.Object, _
 ByVal e As System.EventArgs) Handles btnPaste.Click
    lstFiles.Items.Clear()
    If Clipboard.ContainsFileDropList() Then
        Dim file_names As StringCollection = Clipboard.GetFileDropList()
        For Each file_name As String In file_names
            lstFiles.Items.Add(file_name)
        Next file_name
    End If
End Sub
```

Summary

Drag and drop and the clipboard both move data from a source to a destination. The source and destination can be in the same program or in two different applications.

The clipboard lets a program save and retrieve data in a central, shared location. Data copied to the clipboard may remain in the clipboard for a long time so that the user can paste it into another application later.

Drag and drop lets the user directly copy or move date immediately. Once the operation is complete, the data is not left lying around as it is in the clipboard. A user who wants to copy the data again later must perform a new drag-and-drop operation.

Providing drag and drop with appropriate feedback is more work than using the clipboard, but it provides the user with more direct control, and it doesn't replace whatever data currently sits in the clipboard.

Together, these two tools let you provide the user with more control over the application's data. They let the user move data between different parts of an application and between different applications. While drag and drop and the clipboard are usually not the main purpose of an application, they can add to the user's experience an extra dimension of hands-on control.

The chapters in the book so far have focused on specific Visual Basic programming details. They explained the Visual Basic development environment, language syntax, standard controls and forms, custom controls, drag and drop, and the clipboard.

The chapters in the next part of the book deal with higher-level object-oriented programming (OOP) issues. They explain fundamental concepts in object-oriented development and how they apply to Visual Basic. They tell how to build and use classes and objects, and they describe some of the standard classes that Visual Basic and the .NET Framework provide to perform common programming tasks.

Chapter 14, "OOP Concepts," starts by explaining fundamental ideas behind object-oriented programming such as the three main features of OOP: encapsulation, polymorphism, and inheritance. It explains the benefits of these features and tells how you can take advantage of them in Visual Basic.

14

OOP Concepts

This chapter explains the fundamental ideas behind object-oriented programming (OOP). It describes the three main features of OOP languages: encapsulation, inheritance, and polymorphism. It explains the benefits of these features and tells how you can take advantage of them in Visual Basic.

This chapter also describes method overloading. In a sense, overloading provides another form of polymorphism. It lets you create more than one definition of the same class method, and Visual Basic decides which version to use based on the parameters the program passes to the method.

Many of the ideas described in this chapter will be familiar to you from your experiences with forms, controls, and other building blocks of the Visual Basic language. Those building blocks are object-oriented constructs in their own rights, so they provide you with the benefits of encapsulation, inheritance, and polymorphism whether you knew about them or not.

Classes

A *class* is a programming entity that gathers together all the data and behavior that characterizes some sort of programming abstraction. It wraps the abstraction in a nice, neat package with well-defined interfaces to outside code. Those interfaces determine exactly how code outside of the class can interact with the class. A class determines which data values are visible outside of the class and which are hidden. It determines the routines that the class supports and their availability (visible or hidden).

A class defines properties, methods, and events that let the program work with the class:

- ❑ A *property* is some sort of data value. It may be a simple value (such as a name or number), or it may be a more complex item (such as an array, collection, or object containing its own properties, methods, and events).

- ❑ A *method* is a subroutine or function. It is a piece of code that makes the object defined by the class do something.

- ❑ An *event* is an action notification defined by the class. An event calls some other piece of code to tell it that some condition in a class object has occurred.

For a concrete example, imagine a Job class that represents a piece of work to be done by an employee. This class might have the properties shown in the following table.

Property	Purpose
JobDescription	A string describing the job
EstimatedHours	The number of hours initially estimated for the job
ActualHours	The actual number of hours spent on the job
Status	The job's status (New, Assigned, In Progress, or Done)
ActionTaken	A string describing the work performed, parts installed, and so forth
JobCustomer	An object of the Customer class that describes the customer (name, address, phone number, service contract number, and so on)
AssignedEmployee	An object of the Employee class that describes the employee assigned to the job (name, employee ID, Social Security number, and so on)

The JobDescription, EstimatedHours, ActualHours, Status, and ActionTaken properties are relatively simple string and numeric values. The JobCustomer and AssignedEmployee properties are objects themselves with their own properties, methods, and events.

This class might provide the methods shown in the following table.

Method	Purpose
AssignJob	Assign the job to an employee.
BillJob	Print an invoice for the customer after the job is finished.
EstimatedCost	Returns an estimated cost based on the customer's service contract type and EstimatedHours.

The class could provide the events shown in the following table to keep the main program informed about the job's progress.

Event	Purpose
Created	Occurs when the job is first created
Assigned	Occurs when the job is assigned to an employee
Rejected	Occurs if an employee refuses to do the job, perhaps because the employee doesn't have the right skills or equipment to do the work
Canceled	Occurs if the customer cancels the job before it is worked
Finished	Occurs when the job is finished

Thus, in a nutshell, a class is an entity that encapsulates the data and behavior of some programming abstraction such as a `Job`, `Employee`, `Customer`, `LegalAction`, `TestResult`, `Report`, or just about anything else you could reasonably want to manipulate as a single entity.

After you have defined a class, you can make instances of the class. An *instance* of the class is an object of the class type. For example, if you define a `Job` class, you can then make an instance of the class that represents the specific job of installing a new computer for a particular customer. The process of creating an instance is called *instantiation*.

There are a couple of common analogies to describe instantiation. One compares the class to a blueprint. After you define the class, you can use it to create any number of instances of the class, much as you can use the blueprint to make any number of similar houses.

Another analogy compares a class definition to a cookie cutter. Once you define the cookie cutter, you can use it to make any number of cookies.

Note that Visual Basic is jam-packed with classes. Every type of control and component (`Form`, `TextBox`, `Label`, `Panel`, `GroupBox`, `Button`, `PictureBox`, `Timer`, and so forth) is a class. The parent classes `Control` and `Component` are classes. Even `Object`, from which all other classes derive, is a class. Whenever you work with any of these (getting or setting properties calling methods and responding to events), you are working with instances of classes.

Because all of these ultimately derive from the `Object` class, they are often simply called *objects*. If you don't know or don't care about an item's class, you can simply refer to it as an object.

> When you read the section "Polymorphism" later in this chapter, you'll see that this makes technical as well as intuitive sense. Because all classes eventually derive from the `Object` class, all instances of all classes are in fact `Objects`.

The following sections describe some of the features that OOP languages in general, and Visual Basic in particular, add to this bare-bones definition of a class.

Encapsulation

A class's *public interface* is the set of properties, methods, and events that are visible to code outside of the class. The class may also have private properties, methods, and events that it uses to do its job. For example, the `Job` class described in the previous section provides an `AssignJob` method. That method might call a private `FindQualifiedEmployee` function, which looks through an employee database to find someone who has the skills and equipment necessary to do the job. That routine is not used outside of the class, so it can be declared private.

The class may also include properties and events hidden from code outside of the class. These hidden properties, methods, and events are not part of the class's public interface.

The class *encapsulates* the programming abstraction that it represents (a `Job` in this ongoing example). Its public interface determines what is visible to the application outside of the class. It hides the ugly details of the class's implementation from the rest of the world. Because the class hides its internals in this way, encapsulation is also sometimes called *information hiding*.

By hiding its internals from the outside world, a class prevents exterior code from messing around with those internals. It reduces the dependencies between different parts of the application, allowing only those dependencies that are explicitly permitted by its public interface.

Removing dependencies between different pieces of code makes the code easier to modify and maintain. If you must change the way the Job class assigns a job to an employee, you can modify the AssignJob method appropriately. The code that calls the AssignJob routine doesn't need to know that the details have changed. It simply continues to call the method and leaves the details up to the Job class.

Removing dependencies also helps break the application into smaller, more manageable pieces. A developer who calls the AssignJob method can concentrate on the job at hand, rather than on how the routine works. This makes developers more productive and less likely to make mistakes while modifying the encapsulated code.

The simpler and cleaner a class's public interface is, the easier it is to use. You should try to hide as much information and behavior inside a class as possible while still allowing the rest of the program to do its job. Keep properties, methods, and events as simple and focused as possible. When you write code that the class needs to use to perform its tasks, do not expose that code to the outside program unless it is really necessary. Adding extra features complicates the class's public interface and makes the programmer's job more difficult.

This can be a troublesome concept for beginning programmers. Exposing more features for developers to use gives them more power, so you might think it would make their jobs easier. Actually, it makes development more difficult. Rather than thinking in terms of giving the developer more power, you should think about giving the developer more things to worry about and more ways to make mistakes. Ideally, you should not expose any more features than the developer will actually need.

Note that you can achieve many of the benefits of encapsulation without classes. Decades before the invention of object-oriented languages, programmers were making code libraries that encapsulated functionality. For example, a library of trigonometry functions would expose public function calls to calculate sines, cosines, tangents, arctangents, and so forth. To perform its calculations, the library might contain private lookup tables and helper functions that calculate series expansions. The tables and helper functions were hidden from the main program calling the library functions.

One big benefit of classes over this sort of library encapsulation is intuitiveness. When you make a class named Job, Customer, or Employee, anyone familiar with your business can make a lot of assumptions about what the class represents. Even if you don't know how the Job class works, you can probably guess what a new ReassignJob method would do. As long as everyone has a common vision of what the class does, you get an extra level of *intuitive encapsulation* that you don't necessarily get with a more procedural approach.

Inheritance

Inheritance is the process of deriving a child class from a parent class. The child class inherits all of the properties, methods, and events of the parent class. It can then modify, add to, or subtract from the parent class. Making a child class inherit from a parent class is also called *deriving* the child class from the parent, and *subclassing* the parent class to form the child class.

For example, you might define a `Person` class that includes variables named `FirstName`, `LastName`, `Street`, `City`, `State`, `Zip`, `Phone`, and `Email`. It might also include a `DialPhone` method that dials the person's phone number on the phone attached to the computer's modem.

You could then derive the `Employee` class from the `Person` class. The `Employee` class inherits the `FirstName`, `LastName`, `Street`, `City`, `State`, `Zip`, `Phone`, and `Email` variables. It then adds new `EmployeeId`, `SocialSecurityNumber`, `OfficeNumber`, `Extension`, and `Salary` variables. This class might override the `Person` class's `DialPhone` method, so it dials the employee's office extension instead of the home phone number.

You can continue deriving classes from these classes to make as many types of objects as you need. For example, you could derive the `Manager` class from the `Employee` class and add fields such as `Secretary`, which is another `Employee` object that represents the manager's secretary. Similarly, you could derive a `Secretary` class that includes a reference to a `Manager` object. You could derive `ProjectManager`, `DepartmentManager`, and `DivisionManager` from the `Manager` class, `Customer` from the `Person` class, and so on for other types of people that the application needed to use. Figure 14-1 shows these inheritance relationships graphically.

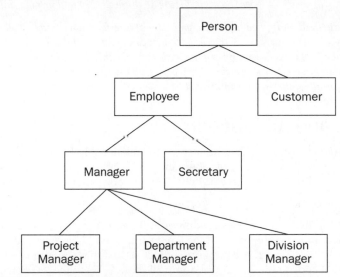

Figure 14-1: You can derive classes from other classes to form quite complex inheritance relationships.

Inheritance Hierarchies

One of the key benefits of inheritance is code reuse. When you derive a class from a parent class, the child class inherits the parent's properties, methods, and events, so the child class gets to reuse the parent's code. That means you don't need to implement separate `FirstName` and `LastName` properties for the `Person`, `Employee`, `Manager`, `Secretary`, and other classes shown in Figure 14-1. These properties are defined only in the `Person` class, and all of the other classes inherit them.

Code reuse not only saves you the trouble of writing more code but also makes maintenance of the code easier. Suppose that you build the hierarchy shown in Figure 14-1 and then decide that everyone needs a new `BirthDate` property. Instead of adding a new property to every class, you can simply add it to the `Person` class and all of the other classes inherit it.

Similarly, if you need to modify or delete a property or method, you only need to make the change in the class where it is defined, not in all of the classes that inherit it. If the `Person` class defines a `SendEmail` method and you must modify it so that it uses a particular email protocol, you only need to change the routine in the `Person` class, not in all the classes that inherit it.

Some languages allow multiple inheritance, where one class can be derived from more than one parent class. For example, suppose that you create a `Vehicle` class that defines properties of vehicles (number of wheels, horsepower, maximum speed, acceleration, and so forth) and a `House` class that defines properties of living spaces (square feet, number of bedrooms, number of bathrooms, and so forth). Using multiple inheritance, you could derive a `MotorHome` class from both the `Vehicle` and `House` classes. This class would have the features of both `Vehicles` and `Houses`.

Visual Basic does not allow multiple inheritance, so a class can have at most one parent class. That means relationships such as those shown in Figure 14-1 are treelike and form an inheritance hierarchy.

If you think you need multiple inheritance, you can use interface inheritance. Instead of defining multiple parent classes, define parent interfaces. Then you can make the child class implement as many interfaces as you like. The class doesn't inherit any code from the interfaces, but at least its behavior is defined by the interfaces. See the section "`Implements` interface" in Chapter 15, "Classes and Structures," for more information on interfaces.

Refinement and Abstraction

There are two different ways you can think about the relationship between a parent class and its child classes. First, using a top-down view of inheritance, you can think of the child classes as *refining* the parent class. They provide extra detail that differentiates among different types of the parent class.

For example, suppose that you start with a broadly defined class such as `Person`. The `Person` class would need general fields such as name, address, and phone number. It would also need more specific fields that do not apply to all types of person. For example, employees would need employee ID, Social Security number, office number, and department fields. Customers would need customer ID, company name, and discount code fields. You could dump all these fields in the `Person` class, but that would mean stretching the class to make it play two very different roles. A `Person` acting as an `Employee` would not use the `Customer` fields, and vice versa.

A better solution is to derive new `Employee` and `Customer` classes that refine the `Person` class and differentiate between the types of `Person`.

A bottom-up view of inheritance considers the parent class as *abstracting* common features out of the child classes into the parent class. Common elements in the child classes are removed and placed in the parent class. Because the parent class is more general than the child classes (it includes a larger group of objects), abstraction is sometimes called *generalization*.

Suppose that you are building a drawing application and you define classes to represent various drawing objects such as `Circle`, `Ellipse`, `Polygon`, `Rectangle`, and `DrawingGroup` (a group of objects that should be drawn together). After you work with the code for a while, you may discover that these classes share a lot of functionality. Some, such as `Ellipse`, `Circle`, and `Rectangle`, are defined by bounding rectangles. All the classes need methods for drawing the object with different pens and brushes on the screen or on a printer.

You could abstract these classes and create a new parent class named `Drawable`. That class might provide basic functionality such as a simple variable to hold a bounding rectangle. This class would also define a `DrawObject` routine for drawing the object on the screen or printer. It would declare that routine with the `MustOverride` keyword, so each child class would need to provide its own `DrawObject` implementation, but the `Drawable` class would define its parameters.

Sometimes you can pull variables and methods from the child classes into the parent class. In this example, the `Drawable` class might include `Pen` and `Brush` variables that the objects would use to draw themselves. Putting code in the parent class reduces the amount of redundant code in the child classes, making debugging and maintenance easier.

To make the classes more consistent, you could even change their names to reflect their shared ancestry. You might change their names to `DrawableEllipse`, `DrawablePolygon`, and so forth. This not only makes it easier to remember that they are all related to the `Drawable` class but also helps avoid confusion with class names such as `Rectangle` that are already used by Visual Basic.

The `Drawable` parent class also allows the program to handle the drawing objects more uniformly. It can define a collection named `AllObjects` that contains references to all the current drawing's objects. It could then loop through the collection, treating the objects as `Drawables`, and calling their `DrawObject` methods. The section "Polymorphism" later in this chapter provides more details.

Usually application architects define class hierarchies using refinement. They start with broad general classes and then refine them as necessary to differentiate among the kinds of objects that the application will need to use. These classes tend to be relatively intuitive, so you can easily imagine their relationships.

Abstraction often arises during development. As you build the application's classes, you notice that some have common features. You abstract the classes and pull the common features into a parent class to reduce redundant code and make the application more maintainable.

Refinement and abstraction are useful techniques for building inheritance hierarchies, but they have their dangers. Designers should be careful not to get carried away with *unnecessary refinement* or *over-refinement*. For example, suppose that you define a `Vehicle` class. You then refine this class by creating `Auto`, `Truck`, and `Boat` classes. You refine the `Auto` class into `Wagon` and `Sedan` classes and further refine those for different drive types (four-wheel drive, automatic, and so forth). If you really go crazy, you could define classes for specific manufacturers, body styles, and color.

The problem with this hierarchy is that it captures more detail than the application needs. If the program is a repair dispatch application, it might need to know whether a vehicle is a car or truck. It will not need to differentiate between wagons and sedans, different manufacturers, or colors. Vehicles with different colors have the same behaviors as far as this application is concerned.

Avoid unnecessary refinement by only refining a class when doing so lets you capture new information that the application actually needs to know.

Just as you can take refinement to ridiculous extremes, you can also overdo class abstraction. Because abstraction is driven by code rather than intuition, it sometimes leads to unintuitive inheritance hierarchies. For example, suppose that your application needs to mail work orders to remote employees and invoices to customers. If the WorkOrder and Invoice classes have enough code in common, you might decide to give them a common parent class named MailableItem that contains the code needed to mail a document to someone.

This type of unintuitive relationship can confuse developers. Because Visual Basic doesn't allow multiple inheritance, it can also cause problems if the classes are already members of other inheritance hierarchies. You can avoid some of those problems by moving the common code into a library and having the classes call the library code. In this example, the WorkOrder and Invoice classes would call a common set of routines for mailing documents and would not be derived from a common parent class.

Unnecessary refinement and overabstracted classes lead to overinflated inheritance hierarchies. Sometimes the hierarchy grows very tall and thin. Other times, it may include several root classes (with no parents) on top of only one or two small classes each. Either of these can be symptoms of poor designs that include more classes than necessary. If your inheritance hierarchy starts to take on one of these forms, you should spend some time reevaluating the classes. Ensure that each adds something meaningful to the application and that the relationships are reasonably intuitive. Too many classes with confusing relationships can drag a project to a halt as developers spend more time trying to understand the hierarchy than they spend implementing the individual classes.

If you are unsure whether to add a new class, leave it out. It's usually easier to add a new class later if you discover that it is necessary than it is to remove a class once developers start using it.

"Has-a" and "Is-a" Relationships

Refinement and abstraction are two useful techniques for generating inheritance hierarchies. The "has-a" and "is-a" relationships can help you understand whether it makes sense to make a new class using refinement or abstraction.

The "is-a" relationship means one object is a specific type of another class. For example, an Employee "is-a" specific type of Person object. The "is-a" relation maps naturally into inheritance hierarchies. Because an Employee "is-a" Person, it makes sense to derive the Employee class from the Person class.

The "has-a" relationship means that one object has some item as an attribute. For example, a Person object "has-a" street address, city, state, and ZIP code. The "has-a" relation maps most naturally to embedded objects. For example, you could give the Person class Street, City, State, and Zip properties.

Suppose that the program also works with WorkOrder, Invoice, and other classes that also have street, city, state, and ZIP code information. Using abstraction, you might make a HasPostalAddress class that contains those values. Then you could derive Person, WorkOrder, and Invoice as child classes. Unfortunately, that makes a rather unintuitive inheritance hierarchy. Deriving the Person, WorkOrder, and Invoice classes from HasPostalAddress makes those classes seem closely related when they are actually related almost coincidentally.

A better solution would be to encapsulate the postal address data in its own PostalAddress class and then include an instance of that class in the Person, WorkOrder, and Invoice classes. The following code shows how the Person class would include an instance of the PostalAddress class:

```
Public Class Person
    Public MailingAddress As PostalAddress
    ...
End Class
```

You make a parent class through abstraction in part to avoid duplication of code. The parent class contains a single copy of the common variables and code, so the child classes don't need to have their own separate versions for you to debug and maintain. Placing an instance of the PostalAddress class in each of the other classes provides the same benefit without confusing the inheritance hierarchy.

You can often view a particular relationship as either an "is-a" or "has-a" relationship. A Person "has-a" postal address. At the same time, a Person "is-a" "thing that has a postal address." Use your intuition to decide which view makes more sense. One hint is that "postal address" is easy to describe while "thing that has a postal address" is more awkward and ill-defined. Also, think about how the relationship might affect other classes. Do you really want Person, WorkOrder, and Invoice to be siblings in the inheritance hierarchy? Or would it make more sense for them to just share an embedded class?

Adding and Modifying Class Features

Adding new properties, methods, and events to a child class is easy. You simply declare them as you would in any other class. The parent class knows nothing about them, so the new items are added only to the child class.

The following code shows how you could implement the Person and Employee classes in Visual Basic. The Person class includes variables that define the FirstName, LastName, Street, City, State, Zip, Phone, and Email values. It also defines the DialPhone method. The version shown here simply displays the Person object's Phone value. A real application could connect to the computer's modem and dial the number.

The Employee class inherits from the Person class. It declares its own EmployeeId, SocialSecurityNumber, OfficeNumber, Extension, and Salary variables. It also defines a new version of the DialPhone method that displays the Employee object's Extension value rather than its Phone value. The DialPhone method in the Person class is declared with the Overridable keyword to allow derived classes to override it. The version defined in the Employee class is declared with the Overrides keyword to indicate that it should replace the version defined by the parent class.

```
Public Class Person
    Public FirstName As String
    Public LastName As String
    Public Street As String
    Public City As String
    Public State As String
    Public Zip As String
    Public Phone As String
    Public Email As String

    ' Dial the phone using Phone property.
    Public Overridable Sub DialPhone()
        MessageBox.Show("Dial " & Me.Phone)
    End Sub
```

```
End Class

Public Class Employee
    Inherits Person
    Public EmployeeId As Integer
    Public SocialSecurityNumber As String
    Public OfficeNumber As String
    Public Extension As String
    Public Salary As Single

    ' Dial the phone using Extension property.
    Public Overrides Sub DialPhone()
        MessageBox.Show("Dial " & Me.Extension)
    End Sub
End Class
```

A class can also *shadow* a feature defined in a parent class. When you declare a property, method, or event with the Shadows keyword, it hides any item in the parent that has the same name. This is very similar to overriding, except that the parent class does not have to declare the item as overridable and the child item needs only to match the parent item's name.

For example, the parent might define a SendMail subroutine that takes no parameters. If the child class defines a SendMail method that takes some parameters and uses the Shadows keyword, the child's version hides the parent's version.

In fact, the child and parent items don't even need to be the same kind of item. For example, the child class could make a subroutine named FirstName that shadows the parent class's FirstName variable. This type of change can be confusing, however, so usually you should only shadow items with similar items.

The following code shows how the Employee class might shadow the Person class's SendMail subroutine. The Person class displays the mailing address where it would send a letter. A real application might print a letter on a specific printer for someone to mail. The Employee class shadows this routine with one of its own, which displays the employee's office number instead of a mailing address.

```
Public Class Person
    ...
    ' Send some mail to the person's address.
    Public Sub SendMail()
        MessageBox.Show("Mail " & Street & ", " & City & ", " & State & " " & Zip)
    End Sub
End Class

Public Class Employee
    Inherits Person
    ...
    ' Send some mail to the person's office.
    Public Shadows Sub SendMail()
        MessageBox.Show("Mail " & OfficeNumber)
    End Sub
End Class
```

Interface Inheritance

When you derive one class from another, the child class inherits the properties, methods, and events defined by the parent class. It inherits both the definition of those items as well as the code that implements them.

Visual Basic also allows you to define an interface. An *interface* defines a class's behaviors, but does not provide an implementation. After you have defined an interface, a class can use the Implements keyword to indicate that it provides the behaviors specified by the interface. It's then up to you to provide the code that implements the interface.

For example, consider again the MotorHome class. Visual Basic does not allow a class to inherit from more than one parent class, but a class can implement as many interfaces as you like. You could define an IVehicle interface (by convention, interface names begin with the capital letter I) that defines properties of vehicles (number of wheels, horsepower, maximum speed, acceleration, and so forth) and an IHouse interface that defines properties of living spaces (square feet, number of bedrooms, number of bathrooms, and so forth). Now, you can make the MotorHome class implement both of those interfaces. The interfaces do not provide any code, but they do declare that the MotorHome class implements the interface's features.

Like true inheritance, interface inheritance provides polymorphism (see the next section, "Polymorphism," for more details on this topic). You can use a variable having the type of the interface to refer to objects that define the interface. For example, suppose that the Employee class implements the IPerson interface. Then you can use a variable of type IPerson to refer to an object of type Employee.

Suppose that the people collection contains Employee objects. The following code uses a variable of type IPerson to display the objects' names:

```
For Each person As IPerson In people
    Debug.WriteLine(person.FirstName & " " & person.LastName)
Next person
```

Polymorphism

Roughly speaking, *polymorphism* means treating one object as another. In OOP terms, it means that you can treat an object of one class as if it were from a parent class.

For example, suppose that Employee and Customer are both derived from the Person class. Then you can treat Employee and Customer objects as if they were Person objects because in a sense they *are* Person objects. They are specific types of Person objects. After all, they provide all of the properties, methods, and events of a Person object.

Visual Basic allows you to assign a value from a child class to a variable of the parent class. In this example, you can place an Employee or Customer object in a Person variable, as shown in the following code:

```
Dim emp As New Employee     ' Create an Employee.
Dim cust As New Customer     ' Create a Customer.
Dim per As Person            ' Declare a Person variable.
per = emp                    ' Okay. An Employee is a Person.
per = cust                   ' Okay. A Customer is a Person.
emp = per                    ' Not okay. A Person is not necessarily an Employee.
```

One common reason to use polymorphism is to treat a collection of objects in a uniform way that makes sense in the parent class. For example, suppose that the Person class defines the FirstName and LastName fields. The program could define a collection named AllPeople and add references to Customer and Employee objects to represent all the people that the program needs to work with. The code could then iterate through the collection, treating each object as a Person, as shown in the following code:

```
For Each per As Person In AllPeople
    Debug.WriteLine(per.FirstName & " " & per.LastName)
Next Per
```

You can only access the features defined for the type of variable you actually use to refer to an object. For example, if you use a Person variable to refer to an Employee object, you can only use the features defined by the Person class not those added by the Employee class.

If you know that a particular object is of a specific subclass, you can convert the variable into a more specific variable type. The following code loops through the AllPeople collection and uses the TypeOf statement to test each object's type. If the object is an Employee, the code uses DirectCast to convert the object into an Employee object. It can then use the Employee object to perform Employee-specific tasks.

Similarly, the code determines whether the object is a Customer object. If it is, the code converts the generic Person variable into a Customer variable and uses the new variable to perform Customer-specific tasks, as shown here:

```
For Each per As Person In AllPeople
    If TypeOf per Is Employee Then
        Dim emp As Employee = DirectCast(per, Employee)
        ' Do something Employee-specific.
        ...
    ElseIf TypeOf per Is Customer Then
        Dim cust As Customer = DirectCast(per, Customer)
        ' Do something Customer-specific.
        ...
    End If
Next per
```

Overloading

Visual Basic .NET allows you to give a class more than one method with the same name but with different parameters. The program decides which version of the method to use based on the parameters being passed to the method.

For example, the Person class shown in the following code has two constructors named New. The first takes no parameters and initializes the object's FirstName and LastName variables to default values. The second overloaded constructor takes two strings as parameters and uses them to initialize FirstName and LastName.

```
Public Class Person
    Public FirstName As String
    Public LastName As String

    Public Sub New()
        FirstName = "<first>"
        LastName = "<last>"
    End Sub

    Public Sub New(ByVal first_name As String, ByVal last_name As String)
        FirstName = first_name
        LastName = last_name
    End Sub
End Class
```

The following code uses these constructors. The first statement passes no parameters to the constructor, so Visual Basic uses the first version of the New method. The second statement passes two strings to the constructor, so Visual Basic uses the second constructor.

```
Dim person1 As New Person()
Dim person2 As New Person("Rod", "Stephens")
```

A common technique for providing constructors that take different numbers of arguments is to make the simpler constructors call those with more parameters. In the following code, the empty constructor calls a constructor that takes two parameters, passing it default values.

```
Public Class Person
    Public FirstName As String
    Public LastName As String

    Public Sub New()
        Me.New("<first>", "<last>")
    End Sub

    Public Sub New(ByVal first_name As String, ByVal last_name As String)
        FirstName = first_name
        LastName = last_name
    End Sub
End Class
```

Two overloaded methods cannot differ only by optional parameters. For example, the first_name and last_name parameters in the previous constructor could not both be optional. If they were, then Visual Basic could not tell which version of the New subroutine to call if the program passed it no parameters. While you cannot make the parameters optional in the second constructor, you can get a similar result by combining the two constructors, as shown in the following code:

```
Public Class Person
    Public FirstName As String
    Public LastName As String

    Public Sub New( _
     Optional ByVal first_name As String = "<first>", _
```

```
        Optional ByVal last_name As String = "<last>")
            FirstName = first_name
            LastName = last_name
        End Sub
    End Class
```

Overloaded functions also cannot differ only in their return types. For example, you cannot have two versions of a function with the same name and parameters but different return types.

If you have Option Strict set to Off, there are many circumstances where Visual Basic performs automatic type conversion. In that case, it might not be able to decide which of two functions to use if they differ only in return type. For example, suppose that one version of the TotalCost function returns an Integer and another version returns a Double. If you set a string variable equal to the result of the function, Visual Basic wouldn't know whether to use the Integer version or the Double version.

Summary

Classes are programming abstractions that group data and related behavior in nicely encapsulated packages. After you define a class, you can instantiate it to create an instance of the class. You can interact with the new object by using its properties, methods, and events.

Inheritance enables you to derive one class from another. You can then add, remove, or modify the behavior that the child class inherits from the parent class. Sometimes it makes sense to think of the classes in inheritance hierarchies in a top-down manner, so child classes refine the features of their parents. At other times, it makes sense to use a bottom-up view and think of a parent class as abstracting the features of its children.

Interface inheritance lets you define some of the features of a class without using true class inheritance. This gives you another method for using polymorphism and lets you build classes that, in a sense, appear to inherit from multiple parents.

Polymorphism enables you to treat an object as if it were of an ancestor's type. For example, if the Manager class inherits from Employee and Employee inherits from Person, then you can treat a Manager object as if it is a Manager, Employee, or Person.

In addition to these features, Visual Basic .NET allows you to overload a class's subroutines, functions, and operators. It lets you create different methods with the same name but different parameters. The compiler selects the right version of the method based on the parameters you pass to it.

These object-oriented concepts provide the general background you need to understand classes in Visual Basic. Chapter 15, "Classes and Structures," describes the specifics of classes and structures in Visual Basic .NET. It shows how to declare and instantiate classes and structures and explains the differences between the two.

15

Classes and Structures

A variable holds a single value. It may be a simple value such as an Integer or String, or a reference that points to a more complex entity. Two kinds of more complex entities are classes and structures.

Classes and structures are both *container types*. They group several related data values into a convenient package that you can manipulate as a group.

For example, an EmployeeInfo structure might contain fields that hold information about an employee (such as first name, last name, employee ID, office number, extension, and so forth). If you make an EmployeeInfo structure and fill it with the data for a particular employee, you can then move the structure around as a single unit instead of passing around a bunch of separate variables holding the first name, last name, and the rest.

This chapter explains how to declare classes and structures, and how to create instances of them (*instantiate* them). It also explains the differences between classes and structures and provides some advice about which to use under different circumstances.

Classes

A class packages data and related behavior. For example, a WorkOrder class might store data describing a customer's work order in its properties. It could contain methods (subroutines and functions) for manipulating the work order. It might provide methods for scheduling the work, modifying the order's requirements, and setting the order's priority.

The syntax for declaring a class is:

```
    [attribute_list] [Partial] [accessibility] [Shadows] [inheritance] _
Class name[(Of type_list)]
    [Inherits parent_class]
    [Implements interface]
    statements
End Class
```

The only things that all class declarations must include are the `Class` clause and the `End Class` statement. Everything else is optional. The following code describes a valid (albeit not very interesting) class:

```
Class EmptyClass
End Class
```

The following sections describe the pieces of the general declaration in detail.

attribute_list

The optional *attribute_list* is a comma-separated list of attributes that apply to the class. An attribute further refines the definition of a class to give more information to the compiler and the run-time system.

Attributes are rather specialized. They address issues that arise when you perform very specific programming tasks. For example, if your application must use drag and drop to copy instances of the class from one application to another, you must mark the class as serializable, as shown in the following code:

```
<Serializable()> _
Class Employee
    Public FirstName As String
    Public LastName As String
End Class
```

Some attributes are particular to specific kinds of classes. For example, the `DefaultEvent` attribute gives the form designer extra information about component classes. If you double-click on a component on a form, the code designer opens to the component's default event.

Because attributes are so specialized, they are not described in more detail here. For more information, see the sections in the online help that are related to the tasks you need to perform.

For more information on Attributes, see the "Attributes" section of the *Visual Basic Language Reference* or go to `http://msdn.microsoft.com/library/en-us/vbls7/html/vblrfVBSpec4_10.asp`. For a list of attributes defined by Visual Basic, search the online help for "Attribute Hierarchy" or go to `http://msdn.microsoft.com/library/en-us/cpref/html/frlrfsystemattributeclass hierarchy.asp`.

Partial

The `Partial` keyword tells Visual Basic that the current declaration defines only part of the class. The following code shows the `Employee` class broken into two pieces:

```
Partial Public Class Employee
    Public FirstName As String
    Public LastName As String
    ...
End Class

... other code, possibly unrelated to the Employee class ...

Partial Public Class Employee
```

```
        Public Email As String
        ...
    End Class
```

The program could contain any number of other pieces of the Employee class, possibly in different code modules. At compile time, Visual Basic finds these pieces and combines them to define the class.

One of the primary benefits of classes is that they hold the code and data associated with the class together in a nice package. Scattering the pieces of a class in this way makes the package less self-contained and may lead to confusion. To prevent confusion, you should avoid splitting a class unless you have a good reason to (for example, to allow different developers to work on different pieces of the class at the same time).

At least one of the pieces of the class must be declared with the Partial keyword, but in the other pieces it is optional. Explicitly providing the keyword in all of the class's partial definitions emphasizes the fact that the class is broken into pieces and may minimize confusion.

accessibility

A class's *accessibility* clause can take one of the values: Public, Protected, Friend, Protected Friend, and Private.

Public indicates that the class should be available to all code inside or outside of the class's module. This allows the most access to the class. Any code can create and manipulate instances of the class.

You can only use the Protected keyword if the class you are declaring is contained inside another class. For example, the following code defines an Employee class that contains a protected EmployeeAddress class:

```
Public Class Employee
    Public FirstName As String
    Public LastName As String
    Protected Address As EmployeeAddress

    Protected Class EmployeeAddress
        Public Street As String
        Public City As String
        Public State As String
        Public Zip As String
    End Class

    ... other code ...
End Class
```

Because the EmployeeAddress class is declared with the Protected keyword, it is only visible within the enclosing Employee class and any derived classes. For example, if the Manager class inherits from the Employee class, code within the Manager class can access the Address variable.

The Friend keyword indicates that the class should be available to all code inside or outside of the class's module *within the same project*. The difference between this and Public is that Public allows code outside of the project to access the class. This is generally only an issue for code libraries (.dll files) and control libraries. For example, suppose that you build a code library containing dozens of routines and then you write a program that uses the library. If the library declares a class with the Public keyword, the code in the library and the code in the main program can use the class. On the other hand, if the library declares a class with the Friend keyword, only the code in the library can access the class, not the code in the main program.

Protected Friend is the union of the Protected and Friend keywords. A class declared Protected Friend is accessible only to code within the enclosing class or a derived class and only within the same project.

A class declared Private is accessible only to code in the enclosing module, class, or structure. If the EmployeeAddress class were declared Private, only code within the Employee class could use that class.

If you do not specify an accessibility level, it defaults to Friend.

Shadows

The Shadows keyword indicates that the class hides the definition of some other entity in the enclosing class's base class.

The following code shows an Employee class that declares a public class OfficeInfo and defines an instance of that class named Office. The derived class Manager inherits from Employee. It declares a new version of the OfficeInfo class with the Shadows keyword. It defines an instance of this class named ManagerOffice.

```
Public Class Employee
    Public Class OfficeInfo
        Public OfficeNumber As String
        Public Extension As String
    End Class

    Public FirstName As String
    Public LastName As String
    Public Office As New OfficeInfo
End Class

Public Class Manager
    Inherits Employee

    Public Shadows Class OfficeInfo
        Public OfficeNumber As String
        Public Extension As String
        Public SecretaryOfficeNumber As String
        Public SecretaryExtension As String
    End Class

    Public ManagerOffice As New OfficeInfo
End Class
```

The following code uses the `Employee` and `Manager` classes. It creates instances of the two classes and sets their `Office.Extension` properties. Both of those values are part of the `Employee` class's version of the `OfficeInfo` class. Next, the code sets the `Manager` object's `ManagerOffice.SecretaryExtension` value.

```
Dim emp As New Employee
Dim mgr As New Manager
emp.Office.Extension = "1111"
mgr.Office.Extension = "2222"
mgr.ManagerOffice.SecretaryExtension = "3333"
```

Note that the `Manager` class contains two different objects of type `OfficeInfo`. Its `Office` property is the `Employee` class's flavor of `OfficeInfo` class. Its `ManagerOffice` value is the `Manager` class's version of `OfficeInfo`.

The presence of these different classes with the same name can be confusing. Usually, you are better off not using the `Shadows` keyword in the declarations and giving the classes different names. In this case, you could call the `Manager` class's included class `ManagerOfficeInfo`.

It is more common to use the `Shadows` keyword to allow the derived class to replace a method in the parent class.

inheritance

A class's *inheritance* clause can take the value `MustInherit` or `NotInheritable`.

`MustInherit` prohibits the program from creating instances of the class. The program should create an instance of a derived class instead. This kind of class is sometimes called an *abstract class*.

By using `MustInherit`, you can make a parent class that defines some of the behavior that should be implemented by derived classes without implementing the functionality itself. The parent class is not intended to be used itself, just to help define the children.

For example, the following code defines the `Vehicle` class with the `MustInherit` keyword. This class defines features that are common to all vehicles. It defines a `NumWheels` variable and a `Drive` subroutine declared with the `MustOverride` keyword. The real world doesn't contain generic vehicles, however. Instead, it contains cars, trucks, and other specific kinds of vehicles. The code defines a `Car` class that inherits from the `Vehicle` class. When you enter the `Inherits` statement and press `Enter`, Visual Basic automatically adds the empty `Drive` subroutine required by the `Vehicle` class.

```
Public MustInherit Class Vehicle
    Public NumWheels As Integer
    Public MustOverride Sub Drive()
End Class

Public Class Car
    Inherits Vehicle

    Public Overrides Sub Drive()

    End Sub
End Class
```

The following code uses these classes. It declares a Vehicle and a Car variable. The first assignment statement causes an error because it tries to make a new Vehicle object. This is not allowed, because Vehicle is declared with the MustInherit keyword. The program sets variable a_car to a new Car variable and then sets variable a_vehicle to a_car. This works because a Car is a type of Vehicle, so the a_vehicle variable can refer to a Car object. This lets the program handle different kinds of vehicles (Cars, Trucks, BigRigs) using the generic Vehicle type if that is convenient. In its last line, the code assigns a_vehicle directly to a new Car object.

```
Dim a_vehicle As Vehicle
Dim a_car As Car

a_vehicle = New vehicle    ' This causes an error because Vehicle is MustInherit.
a_car = New Car            ' This works.
a_vehicle = a_car          ' This works.
a_vehicle = New Car        ' This works.
```

The NotInheritable keyword does the opposite of the MustInherit keyword. MustInherit says that a class must be inherited to be instantiated. NotInheritable says no class can inherit from this one.

You can use NotInheritable to stop other developers from making new versions of the classes you have built. This isn't really necessary if you design a well-defined object model before you start programming and if everyone obeys it. NotInheritable can prevent unnecessary proliferation of classes if developers don't pay attention, however. For example, declaring the Car class NotInheritable would prevent overeager developers from deriving FrontWheelDriveCar, RedCar, and Subaru classes from the Car class.

Of type_list

The Of type_list clause makes the class generic. It allows the program to create instances of the class that work with specific data types. For example, the following code defines a generic Tree class. The class includes a public variable named RootObject that has the data type given in the class's Of data_type clause.

```
Public Class Tree(Of data_type)
    Public RootObject As data_type
    ...
End Class
```

When you read this declaration, you should think "Tree of *something*," where *something* is defined later when you make an instance of the class.

The following code fragment declares the variable my_tree to be a "Tree of Employee." It then instantiates my_tree and sets its RootObject variable to an Employee object.

```
Dim my_tree As Tree(Of Employee)
my_tree = New Tree(Of Employee)
my_tree.RootObject = New Employee
...
```

Chapter 18, "Generics," discusses generic classes further.

Inherits parent_class

The Inherits statement indicates that the class (the child class) is derived from another class (the parent class). The child class automatically inherits the parent's properties, methods, and events.

The following code defines an Employee class that contains LastName, FirstName, OfficeNumber, and Extension variables. It then derives the Manager class from the Employee class. Because it inherits from the Employee class, the Manager class automatically has LastName, FirstName, OfficeNumber, and Extension variables. It also adds new SecretaryOfficeNumber and SecretaryExtension variables. These are available to instances of the Manager class but not to the Employee class.

```
Public Class Employee
    Public FirstName As String
    Public LastName As String
    Public OfficeNumber As String
    Public Extension As String
End Class

Public Class Manager
    Inherits Employee

    Public SecretaryOfficeNumber As String
    Public SecretaryExtension As String
End Class
```

The following code makes a new Employee object and sets its Extension property to "1000." It then creates a Manager object and sets its Extension and SecretaryExtension values.

```
Dim emp As New Employee
emp.Extension = "1000"

Dim mgr As New Manager
mgr.Extension = "2000"
mgr.SecretaryExtension = "2001"
```

If a class inherits from another class, the Inherits statement must be the first statement after the Class statement that is not blank or a comment. Also note that a class can inherit from at most one parent class, so a class definition can include at most one Inherits statement.

For more information on inheritance, see the Chapter 14, "OOP Concepts."

Implements interface

The Implements keyword indicates that a class will implement an interface. An interface defines behaviors that the implementing class must provide, but it does not provide any implementation for the behaviors.

For example, the following code defines the IDomicile interface. By convention, the names of interfaces should begin with the capital letter "I." This interface defines the SquareFeet, NumBedrooms, and NumBathrooms properties, and the Clean subroutine.

The interface also defines the read-only property `FileSystemNeeded`. Usually a read-only property calculates its return from other property values. For example, `FileSystemNeeded` might return `True` if a house has more than a certain number of square feet. You can define write-only properties similarly, although they are much less common than read-only properties.

The `House` class implements the `IDomicile` interface. When you type the `Implements` statement and press `Enter`, Visual Basic automatically generates empty routines to provide the features defined by the interface.

```
Public Interface IDomicile
    Property SquareFeet() As Integer
    Property NumBedrooms() As Integer
    Property NumBathrooms() As Integer
    ReadOnly Property NeedsFireSystem() As Boolean
    Sub Clean()
End Interface

Public Class House
    Implements IDomicile

    Public Sub Clean() Implements IDomicile.Clean

    End Sub

    Public Property NumBathrooms() As Integer Implements IDomicile.NumBathrooms
        Get

        End Get
        Set(ByVal Value As Integer)

        End Set
    End Property

    Public Property NumBedrooms() As Integer Implements IDomicile.NumBedrooms
        Get

        End Get
        Set(ByVal Value As Integer)

        End Set
    End Property

    Public Property SquareFeet() As Integer Implements IDomicile.SquareFeet
        Get

        End Get
        Set(ByVal Value As Integer)

        End Set
    End Property

    Public ReadOnly Property NeedsFireSystem() As Boolean _
     Implements IDomicile.NeedsFireSystem
```

```
            Get

            End Get
        End Property
    End Class
```

An interface defines behaviors but does not supply them. When you derive a class from a parent class, the derived class inherits all the code that the parent class uses to implement its features. When you implement an interface, the behavior is defined, but not supplied for you. That makes interfaces more difficult to use than inheritance, so inheritance is generally preferred whenever it is possible.

One case where Visual Basic's inheritance is insufficient is when you need to implement multiple inheritance. In *multiple inheritance*, one child class can inherit from more than one parent class. For example, you might define a `Domicile` class and a `Boat` class, and then make the `HouseBoat` class inherit from both. You can do this in some languages but not in Visual Basic. However, you can make a class implement more than one interface.

The following code defines the `IBoat` interface. It then defines the `HouseBoat` class and uses two `Implements` statements to indicate that it implements both the `IDomicile` and `IBoat` interfaces.

```
Public Interface IBoat
    Property HasMotor() As Boolean
    Property HorsePower() As Integer
    Property Capacity() As Integer
    Sub Sail()
End Interface

Public Class HouseBoat
    Implements IDomicile
    Implements IBoat

    Public Sub Clean() Implements IDomicile.Clean

    End Sub

    Public ReadOnly Property NeedsFireSystem() As Boolean Implements
IDomicile.NeedsFireSystem
        Get

        End Get
    End Property

    Public Property NumBathrooms() As Integer Implements IDomicile.NumBathrooms
        Get

        End Get
        Set(ByVal Value As Integer)

        End Set
    End Property

    Public Property NumBedrooms() As Integer Implements IDomicile.NumBedrooms
```

```
            Get

        End Get
        Set(ByVal Value As Integer)

        End Set
    End Property

    Public Property SquareFeet() As Integer Implements IDomicile.SquareFeet
        Get

        End Get
        Set(ByVal Value As Integer)

        End Set
    End Property

    Public Property Capacity() As Integer Implements IBoat.Capacity
        Get

        End Get
        Set(ByVal Value As Integer)

        End Set
    End Property

    Public Property HasMotor() As Boolean Implements IBoat.HasMotor
        Get

        End Get
        Set(ByVal Value As Boolean)

        End Set
    End Property

    Public Property HorsePower() As Integer Implements IBoat.HorsePower
        Get

        End Get
        Set(ByVal Value As Integer)

        End Set
    End Property

    Public Sub Sail() Implements IBoat.Sail

    End Sub
End Class
```

Using an interface in place of inheritance is sometimes called *interface inheritance*. The class doesn't inherit a parent class's code, but it does inherit the definition of the features that it must provide.

Note that a class can inherit from one class and also implement one or more interfaces. To save coding, you could make one of the parent interfaces into a class. For example, if the IDomicile interface defines more behaviors than the IBoat interface, and if those behaviors are generic enough to provide help for derived classes, you could turn IDomicile into a Domicile class that implemented those features. Then the House and HouseBoat classes could inherit the Domicile class's features, and HouseBoat would implement IBoat.

If a class declaration uses any Implements statements, they must come after any Inherits statement and before any other statements (other than comments).

Structures

Structures are very similar to classes. The syntax for declaring a structure is as follows:

```
[attribute_list] [Partial] [accessibility] [Shadows] _
Structure name[(Of type_list)]
    [Implements interface]
    statements
End Structure
```

The only thing that all structure declarations must include is the Structure clause and the End Structure statement. The rest is optional.

Unlike a class, however, a structure cannot be empty. It must contain at least one variable or event declaration. The following code describes a valid structure. Its only member is a Private variable, so this structure wouldn't be of much use, but it is valid.

```
Structure EmptyStructure
    Private m_Num As Integer
End Structure
```

The structure's *attribute_list* and *accessibility* clauses, Shadows and Partial keywords, and the Implements statement are the same as those for classes. See the sections "*attribute_list*" and "*accessibility*"earlier in this chapter for details.

The are two main differences between a structure and a class: Structures cannot inherit and structures are value types rather than reference types.

Structures Cannot Inherit

A structure cannot inherit, so it cannot use the MustInherit, NotInheritable, or Inherits keywords. However, a structure can implement any number of interfaces. The following code declares the IPerson interface, which defines the FirstName and LastName properties. The Employee structure implements this interface, providing code to handle those properties and adding two new variables named OfficeNumber and Extension.

```
Public Interface IPerson
    Property FirstName() As String
    Property LastName() As String
End Interface

Public Structure Employee
    Implements IPerson

    Public OfficeNumber As String
    Public Extension As String
    Private m_FirstName As String
    Private m_LastName As String

    Public Property FirstName() As String Implements IPerson.FirstName
        Get
            Return m_FirstName
        End Get
        Set(ByVal value As String)
            m_FirstName = value
        End Set
    End Property

    Public Property LastName() As String Implements IPerson.LastName
        Get
            Return m_LastName
        End Get
        Set(ByVal value As String)
            m_LastName = value
        End Set
    End Property
End Structure
```

Structures are Value Types

The biggest difference between a structure and a class is in how each allocates memory for its data. Classes are *reference types*. That means an instance of a class is actually a reference to the object's storage in memory. When you create an instance of a class, Visual Basic actually creates a 4-byte value that points to the object's actual location in memory.

On the other hand, structures are *value types*. An instance of a structure contains the data inside the structure rather than simply pointing to it. Figure 15-1 illustrates the difference.

The difference between reference and value type has several important consequences that are described in the following sections.

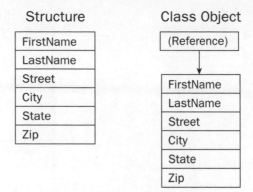

Figure 15-1: A structure object contains the data, while a class object contains a reference that points to data.

Memory Required

The difference in memory required by classes and structures is small when you consider only a single object. If you look at an array, however, the distinction is more important. An array of class objects contains references to data in some other part of memory. When you first declare the array, the references all have the value Nothing, so they don't point to any data and no memory is allocated for the data. The references take 4 bytes each, so the array uses only 4 bytes per array entry.

An array of structure instances, on the other hand, allocates space for the data inside the array. If each structure object takes up 1000 bytes of memory, then an array containing N items uses 1000 * N bytes of memory. Each structure object's memory is allocated, whether its fields contain meaningful data or not.

Figure 15-2 illustrates this situation. The array of class objects on the left uses very little memory when the references are Nothing. The array of structure objects on the right uses a lot of memory even if its elements have not been initialized.

If you must use a large array of objects where only a few at a time will have values other than Nothing, then using a class may save the program a considerable amount of memory. If you will need most of the objects to have values other than Nothing at the same time, it may be faster to allocate all the memory at once using a structure. This will also use slightly less memory, because an array of class references requires an extra 4 bytes per entry to hold the references.

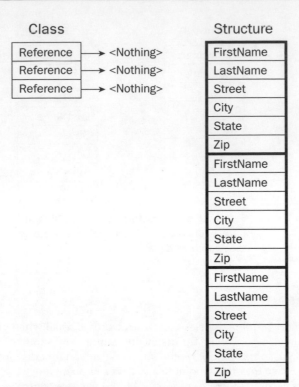

Figure 15-2: An array of class objects contains small references to data, many of which may be `Nothing`. **An array of structures takes up a significant amount of memory.**

Heap and Stack Performance

Visual Basic programs allocate variables from two pools of memory called the *stack* and the *heap*. It takes memory for value types (such as integers and dates) from the stack.

Space for reference types comes from the heap. More than one reference can point to the same chunk of memory allocated on the heap. That makes garbage collection and other heap-management issues more complex than using the stack, so using the heap is generally slower than using the stack.

Because structures are value types and classes are reference types, structures are allocated on the stack and class objects are allocated from the heap. That makes structures faster than classes. The exact difference for a particular program depends on the application.

Note that arrays are themselves reference types, so all arrays are allocated from the heap whether they contain structures or references to class objects. The memory for an array of structures is allocated all at once, however, so there is still some benefit to using structures. All the memory in an array of structures is contiguous, so the program can access its elements more quickly than it would if the memory were scattered throughout the heap.

Object Assignment

When you assign one reference type variable to another, you make a new reference to an existing object. When you are finished, the two variables point to the same object. If you change the object's fields using one variable, the fields shown by the other are also changed.

On the other hand, if you set one value type variable equal to another, Visual Basic copies the data from one to the other. If you change the fields in one object, the fields in the other remain unchanged. Figure 15-3 illustrates the difference.

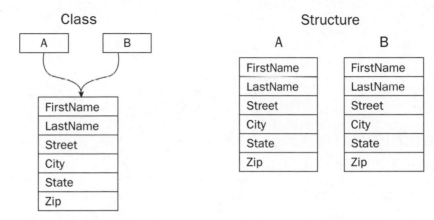

Figure 15-3: Assigning one class reference to another makes them both point to the same object. Assigning one structure variable to another makes a new copy of the data.

To see the difference in code, consider the following declarations. The CPerson class and the SPerson structure are the same, except that one is a class and the other is a structure.

```
Public Class CPerson
    Public FirstName As String
    Public LastName As String
End Class

Public Structure SPerson
    Public FirstName As String
    Public LastName As String
End Structure
```

Now consider the following code. The program creates two CPerson references and initializes the first to a new CPerson object. It sets cperson1.FirstName to "Alice" and then sets cperson2 = cperson1. The code then sets cperson2.FirstName to "Ben." Because these are reference variables, they both point to the same object, so this changes the FirstName value of the underlying object and the message box displays the text "Ben, Ben." Next the program repeats these steps using the SPerson structure instead of the CPerson class. When the code sets sperson2 = sperson1, Visual Basic copies the values from sperson1 into sperson2. At that point, both objects have a FirstName value of "Alice." The code then sets sperson2.FirstName to "Ben." Because the two structure variables refer to different objects, this does not affect sperson1 and the message box displays the text "Alice, Ben."

```
Dim cperson1 As New CPerson
Dim cperson2 As CPerson
cperson1.FirstName = "Alice"
cperson2 = cperson1
cperson2.FirstName = "Ben"
MessageBox.Show(cperson1.FirstName & ", " & cperson2.FirstName)

Dim sperson1 As New SPerson
Dim sperson2 As SPerson
sperson1.FirstName = "Alice"
sperson2 = sperson1
sperson2.FirstName = "Ben"
MessageBox.Show(sperson1.FirstName & ", " & sperson2.FirstName)
```

Parameter Passing

When you pass a parameter to a function or subroutine, you can pass it by reference using the ByRef keyword, or by value using the ByVal keyword. If you pass a parameter by reference, any changes that the routine makes are reflected in the original parameter passed into the routine.

For example, consider the following code. Subroutine TestByRef creates an integer named i and sets its value to 1. It then calls subroutine PassByVal. That routine declares its parameter with the ByVal keyword, so i is passed by value. PassByVal multiplies its parameter by 2 and ends. Because the parameter was declared ByVal, the original variable i is unchanged, so the message box displays the value 1. Next the program calls subroutine PassByRef passing it the variable i. Subroutine PassByRef declares its parameter with the ByRef keyword, so a reference to the variable is passed into the routine. PassByRef doubles its parameter and ends. Because the parameter is declared with the ByRef keyword, the value of variable i is modified so the message box displays the value 2.

```
Public Sub TestByRef()
Dim i As Integer = 1

    PassByVal(i)
    MessageBox.Show(i.ToString)     ' i = 1.

    PassByRef(i)
    MessageBox.Show(i.ToString)     ' i = 2.
End Sub

Public Sub PassByVal(ByVal the_value As Integer)
    the_value *= 2
End Sub

Public Sub PassByRef(ByRef the_value As Integer)
    the_value *= 2
End Sub
```

When you work with class references and structures, you must think a bit harder about how `ByRef` and `ByVal` work. There are four possible combinations: reference `ByVal`, structure `ByVal`, reference `ByRef`, and structure `ByRef`.

If you pass a class reference to a routine by value, the routine receives a copy *of the reference*. If it changes the reference (perhaps making it point to a new object), the original reference passed into the routine remains unchanged. It still points to the same object it did when it was passed to the routine. However, the routine can change the values in the object to which the reference points. If the reference points to a `Person` object, the routine can change the object's `FirstName`, `LastName`, and other fields. It cannot change the reference itself to make it point to a different `Person` object, but it can change the object's data.

On the other hand, suppose that you pass a structure into a routine by value. In that case, the routine receives a *copy* of the entire structure. The routine can change the values contained in its copy of the structure, but the original structure's values remain unchanged. It cannot change the original structure's fields the way it could if the parameter were a reference type.

If you pass a class reference variable by reference, then the routine can not only modify the values in the object to which the reference points but can also change the object to which it points. The routine could use the `New` keyword to make the variable point to a completely new object.

If you pass a structure by reference, the routine receives a pointer to the structure's data. If it changes the structure's data, the fields in the original variable passed into the routine is modified.

In addition to these differences in behavior, passing class references and structures by reference or by value can make differences in performance. When you pass a pointer to data, Visual Basic only needs to send the routine a 4-byte value. If you pass a structure into a routine by value, Visual Basic must duplicate the entire structure, so the routine can use its own copy. If the structure is very large, that may take a little extra time.

Boxing and Unboxing

Visual Basic allows a program to treat any variable as an object. For example, a collection class stores objects. If you add a simple value type such as an Integer to a collection, Visual Basic wraps the Integer in an object and adds that object to the collection.

The process of wrapping the Integer in an object is called *boxing*. Later, if you need to use the Integer as a value type again, the program *unboxes* it. Because structures are value types, the program must box and unbox them whenever it treats them as objects, and that adds some extra overhead.

Some operations that require boxing and possibly unboxing include assigning a structure to an `Object` variable, passing a structure to a routine that takes an `Object` as a parameter, or adding a structure to a collection class. Note that this last operation includes adding a structure to a collection used by a control or other object. For example, adding a structure to a `ListBox`'s `Items` collection requires boxing.

Note that arrays are themselves reference types, so treating an array as an object doesn't require boxing.

Class Instantiation Details

When you declare a reference variable, Visual Basic allocates space for the reference. Initially, that reference is set to `Nothing`, so it doesn't point to anything and no memory is allocated for an actual object.

You create an object by using the `New` keyword. Creating an actual object is called *instantiating* the class.

The following code shows a simple object declaration and instantiation. The first line declares the reference variable. The second line makes the variable point to a new `Employee` object.

```
Dim emp As Employee      ' Declare a reference to an Employee object.
emp = New Employee       ' Make a new Employee object and make emp point to it.
```

Visual Basic also allows you to declare and initialize a variable in a single statement. The following code shows how to declare and initialize an object reference in one statement:

```
Dim emp As Employee = New Employee     ' Declare and instantiate an Employee object.
```

Visual Basic lets you declare a variable to be of a new object type, as shown in the following statement. This version has the same effect as the previous one but is slightly more compact.

```
Dim emp As New Employee                     ' Declare and instantiate an Employee object.
```

Both of these versions that define and initialize an object in a single statement ensure that the variable is initialized right away. They guarantee that the object is instantiated before you try to use it. If you place these kinds of declarations immediately before the code where the object is used, they also make it easy to see where the object is defined.

While you can declare and instantiate a reference variable separately, value type variables are allocated when they are declared. Because structures are value types, when you declare one you also allocate space for its data, so you don't need to use the `New` keyword to initialize a structure variable.

Both classes and structures can provide special subroutines called *constructors*. A constructor is a special subroutine named `New` that Visual Basic calls when a new instance of the class or structure is created. The constructor can perform initialization tasks to get the new object ready for use.

A constructor can optionally take parameters to help in initializing the object. For example, the `Person` class shown in the following code has a constructor that takes as parameters first and last names and saves them in the control's `FirstName` and `LastName` variables.

```
Public Class Person
    Public FirstName As String
    Public LastName As String

    Public Sub New(ByVal first_name As String, ByVal last_name As String)
        FirstName = first_name
        LastName = last_name
    End Sub
End Class
```

The following code shows how a program might use this constructor to create a new `Person` object:

```
Dim author As New Person("Rod", "Stephens")
```

You can overload the `New` method just as you can overload other class methods. The different overloaded versions of the constructor must have different parameter lists so that Visual Basic can decide which one to use when it creates a new object.

The following code shows a `Person` class that provides two constructors. The first takes no parameters and sets the object's `FirstName` and `LastName` values to "<unknown>." The second version takes two strings as parameters and copies them into the object's `FirstName` and `LastName` values.

```
Public Class Person
    Public FirstName As String
    Public LastName As String

    Public Sub New()
        Me.New("<unknown>", "<unknown>")
    End Sub

    Public Sub New(ByVal first_name As String, ByVal last_name As String)
        FirstName = first_name
        LastName = last_name
    End Sub
End Class
```

The following code uses each of these constructors:

```
Dim person1 As New Person                    ' <unknown> <unknown>.
Dim person2 As New Person("Olga", "O'Toole")  ' Olga O'Toole.
```

If you do not provide any constructors for a class, Visual Basic allows the program to use the `New` keyword with no parameters. If you create any constructor, however, Visual Basic does not allow the program to use this default empty constructor (without parameters) unless you build one explicitly. For example, if the previous version of the `Person` class did not include an empty constructor, the program could not use the first declaration in the previous code that doesn't include any parameters.

You can use this feature to ensure that the program assigns required values to an object. In this case, it would mean that the program could not create a `Person` object without assigning `FirstName` and `LastName` values.

If you want to allow an empty constructor in addition to other constructors, an alternative is to create a single constructor with optional parameters. The following code shows this approach. With this class, the program could create a new `Person` object, passing its constructor zero, one, or two parameters.

```
Public Class Person
    Public FirstName As String
    Public LastName As String

    Public Sub New( _
     Optional ByVal first_name As String = "<unknown>", _
```

```
          Optional ByVal last_name As String = "<unknown>")
            FirstName = first_name
            LastName = last_name
      End Sub
End Class
```

Structure Instantiation Details

Structures handle instantiation somewhat differently from object references. When you declare a reference variable, Visual Basic does not automatically allocate the object to which the variable points. On the other hand, when you declare a value type such as a structure, Visual Basic automatically allocates space for the variable's data. That means you never need to use the New keyword to instantiate a structure.

However, the Visual Basic compiler warns you if you do not explicitly initialize a structure variable before using it. To satisfy the compiler, you can use the New keyword to initialize the variable when you declare it.

A structure can also provide constructors, and you can use those constructors to initialize the structure. The following code defines the SPerson structure and gives it a constructor that takes two parameters, the second optional:

```
Public Structure SPerson
    Public FirstName As String
    Public LastName As String

    Public Sub New( _
     ByVal first_name As String, _
     Optional ByVal last_name As String = "<unknown>")
        FirstName = first_name
        LastName = last_name
    End Sub
End Structure
```

To use a structure's constructor, you initialize the structure with the New keyword much as you initialize a reference variable. The following code allocates a SPerson structure variable using the two-parameter constructor:

```
Dim artist As New SPerson("Sergio", "Aragones")
```

You can also use structure constructors later to reinitialize a variable or set its values, as shown here:

```
' Allocate the artist variable.
Dim artist As SPerson

' Do something with artist.
...

' Reset FirstName and LastName to Nothing.
artist = New SPerson
```

```
...

' Set FirstName and LastName to Bill Amend.
artist = New SPerson("Bill", "Amend")
```

Structure and class constructors are very similar, but there are some major differences. A structure cannot declare a constructor that takes no parameters. It also cannot provide a constructor with all optional parameters, because that would allow the program to call it with no parameters. Visual Basic always allows the program to use a default empty constructor to declare a structure variable, but you cannot make it use *your* empty constructor. Unfortunately, that means you cannot guarantee that the program always initializes the structure's values as you can with a class. If you need that feature, you should use a class instead of a structure.

You also cannot provide initialization values for variables declared within a structure as you can with a class. That means you cannot use this technique to provide default values for the structure's variables.

The following code demonstrates these differences. The CPerson class defines initial values for its FirstName and LastName variables, provides an empty constructor, and provides a two-parameter constructor. The SPerson structure cannot define initial values for FirstName and LastName and cannot provide an empty constructor.

```
' Class.
Public Class CPerson
    Public FirstName As String = "<unknown>"    ' Initialization value allowed.
    Public LastName As String = "<unknown>"     ' Initialization value allowed.

    ' Empty constructor allowed.
    Public Sub New()
    End Sub

    ' Two-parameter constructor allowed.
    Public Sub New(ByVal first_name As String, ByVal last_name As String)
        FirstName = first_name
        LastName = last_name
    End Sub
End Class

' Structure.
Public Structure SPerson
    Public FirstName As String ' = "<unknown>" ' Initialization value NOT allowed.
    Public LastName As String ' = "<unknown>"  ' Initialization value NOT allowed.

    '' Empty constructor NOT allowed.
    'Public Sub New()
    'End Sub

    ' Two-parameter constructor allowed.
    Public Sub New(ByVal first_name As String, ByVal last_name As String)
        FirstName = first_name
        LastName = last_name
    End Sub
End Structure
```

Garbage Collection

When a program starts, the system allocates a chunk of memory for the program called the *managed heap*. When it allocates data for reference types (class objects), Visual Basic uses memory from this heap.

When the program no longer needs to use a reference object, Visual Basic does *not* mark the heap memory as free for later use. If you set a reference variable to Nothing so that no variable points to the object, the object's memory is no longer available to the program, but Visual Basic does not reuse the object's heap memory, at least not right away.

The *garbage collector's* optimizing engine determines when it needs to clean up the heap. If the program allocates and frees many reference objects, a lot of the heap may be full of memory that is no longer used. In that case, the garbage collector will decide to clean house.

When it runs, the garbage collector examines all the program's reference variables, parameters that are object references, CPU registers, and other items that might point to heap objects. It uses those values to build a graph describing the heap memory that the program can still access. It then compacts the objects in the heap and updates the program's references so that they can find any moved items. The garbage collector then updates the heap itself so that the program can allocate memory from the unused portion.

When it destroys an object, the garbage collector frees the object's memory and any managed resources it contains. It may not free unmanaged resources, however. You can determine when and how an object frees its managed and unmanaged resources by using the Finalize and Dispose methods.

Finalize

When it destroys an object, the garbage collector frees any managed resources used by that object. For example, suppose that an unused object contains a reference to an open file stream. When the garbage collector runs, it notices that the file stream is inaccessible to the program, so it destroys the file stream as well as the object that contains its reference.

However, suppose that the object uses an *unmanaged resource* that is outside of the scope of objects that Visual Basic understands. For example, suppose the object holds an integer representing a file handle, network connection, or channel to a hardware device that Visual Basic doesn't understand. In that case, the garbage collector doesn't know how to free that resource.

You can tell the garbage collector what to do by overriding the class's Finalize method, which is inherited from the Object class. The garbage collector calls an object's Finalize method before permanently removing the object from the heap. Note that there are no guarantees about exactly when the garbage collector calls this method, or the order in which different objects' methods are called. Two objects' Finalize methods may be called in either order even if one contains a reference to the other or if one was freed long before the other. If you must guarantee a specific order, you must provide more specific clean-up methods of your own.

The following code demonstrates the Finalize method. The Form1 class defines the public variable Running. It then defines the Junk class, which contains a variable referring to the Form1 class. This class's constructor saves a reference to the Form1 object that created it. Its Finalize method sets the Form1 object's Running value to False.

When the user clicks the form's Go button, the btnGo_Click event handler sets Running to True and starts creating Junk objects, passing the constructor this form as a parameter. The routine keeps creating new objects as long as Running is True. Note that each time it creates a new object, the old object that the variable new_obj used to point to becomes inaccessible to the program so it is available for garbage collection.

Eventually the program's heap runs low, so the garbage collector executes. When it destroys one of the Junk objects, the object's Finalize subroutine executes and sets the form's Running value to False. When the garbage collector finishes, the btnGo_Click event handler sees that Running is False, so it stops creating new Junk objects. It displays the number of the last Junk object it created and is done.

```
Public Class Form1
    Public Running As Boolean

    Private Class Junk
        Public MyForm As Form1

        Public Sub New(ByVal my_form As Form1)
            MyForm = my_form
        End Sub

        ' Garbage collection started.
        Protected Overrides Sub Finalize()
            ' Stop making objects.
            MyForm.Running = False
        End Sub
    End Class

    ' Make objects until garbage collection starts.
    Private Sub btnGo_Click(ByVal sender As System.Object, _
     ByVal e As System.EventArgs) Handles btnGo.Click
        Running = True

        Dim new_obj As Junk
        Dim max_i As Long
        For i As Long = 1 To 100000
            new_obj = New Junk(Me)

            If Not Running Then
                max_i = i
                Exit For
            End If
        Next i
        MessageBox.Show("Allocated " & max_i.ToString & " objects")
    End Sub
End Class
```

In one test, this program created 30,456 Junk objects before the garbage collector ran. In a second trial run immediately after the first, the program created 59,150 objects, and in a third it created 26,191. The garbage collector gives you little control over when it finalizes objects.

Visual Basic also calls every object's Finalize method when the program ends. Again, there are no guarantees about the exact timing or order of the calls to different objects' Finalize methods.

The following example code tests the `Finalize` method when the program ends. The `Numbered` class contains a variable `m_Number` and initializes that value in its constructor. Its `Finalize` method writes the object's number in the Output window. The `btnGo_Click` event handler creates a new `Numbered` object, giving it a new number. When the event handler ends, the `new_numbered` variable referring to the `Numbered` object goes out of scope, so the object is no longer available to the program. If you look at the Output window at this time, you will probably find that the program has not bothered to finalize the object yet. If you click the button several times and then close the application, Visual Basic calls each object's `Finalize` method. If you click the button five times, you should see five messages displayed by the objects' `Finalize` methods.

```
Public Class Form1
    Private Class Numbered
        Private m_Number As Integer
        Public Sub New(ByVal my_number As Integer)
            m_Number = my_number
        End Sub

        ' Garbage collection started.
        Protected Overrides Sub Finalize()
            ' Display the object's number.
            Debug.WriteLine("Number: " & m_Number)
        End Sub
    End Class

    ' Make objects until garbage collection starts.
    Private Sub btnGo_Click(ByVal sender As System.Object, _
     ByVal e As System.EventArgs) Handles btnGo.Click
        Static i As Integer = 0
        i += 1
        Dim new_numbered As New Numbered(i)
        Me.Text = i.ToString
    End Sub
End Class
```

If your class allocates unmanaged resources, you should give it a `Finalize` method to free them.

Dispose

Because Visual Basic doesn't keep track of whether an object is reachable at any given moment, it doesn't know when it can permanently destroy an object until the program ends or the garbage collector reclaims it. That means the object's memory and resources may remain unused for quite a while. The memory itself isn't a big issue. If the program's heap runs out of space, the garbage collector runs to reclaim some of the unused memory.

If the object contains a reference to a resource, however, that resource is not freed until the object is finalized. That can have dire consequences. You generally don't want control of a file, network connection, scanner, or other scarce system resource left to the whims of the garbage collector.

By convention, the `Dispose` subroutine frees an object's resources. Before a program frees an object that contains important resources, it can call that object's `Dispose` method to free them explicitly.

To handle the case where the program does not call Dispose, the class should also free any unmanaged resources that it holds in its Finalize subroutine. Because Finalize is executed whether the program calls Dispose or not, it must also be able to execute both the Dispose and Finalize subroutines without harm. For example, if the program shuts down some piece of unusual hardware, it probably should not shut down the device twice.

To make building a Dispose method a little easier, Visual Basic defines the IDisposable interface, which declares the Dispose method. If you enter the statement Implements IDisposable and press Enter, Visual Basic creates an empty Dispose method for you.

The following code demonstrates the Dispose and Finalize methods. The Named class has a Name variable that contains a string identifying an object. Its Finalize method simply calls its Dispose method. Dispose uses a static variable named done_before to ensure that it only performs its task only once. If it has not already run, the Dispose method displays the object's name. In a real application, this method would free whatever resources the object holds. Whether the program explicitly calls Dispose, or whether the garbage collector calls the object's Finalize method, this code is executed exactly once.

The main program has two buttons labeled Dispose and No Dispose. When you click the Dispose button, the btnDispose_Click event handler makes a Named object, giving it a new name, and then calls the object's Dispose method, which immediately displays the object's name.

When you click the No Dispose button, the btnNoDispose_Click event handler makes a new Named object with a new name and then ends without calling the object's Dispose method. Later, when the garbage collector runs or when the program ends, the object's Finalize method executes and calls Dispose, which displays the object's name.

```
Public Class Form1
    Private Class Named
        Implements IDisposable

        ' Save our name.
        Public Name As String
        Public Sub New(ByVal new_name As String)
            Name = new_name
        End Sub

        ' Free resources.
        Protected Overrides Sub Finalize()
            Dispose()
        End Sub

        ' Display our name.
        Public Sub Dispose() Implements System.IDisposable.Dispose
            Static done_before As Boolean = False
            If done_before Then Exit Sub
            done_before = True

            Debug.WriteLine(Name)
        End Sub
    End Class

    ' Make an object and dispose it.
    Private Sub btnDispose_Click(ByVal sender As System.Object, _
```

```
        ByVal e As System.EventArgs) Handles btnDispose.Click
        Static i As Integer = 0
        i += 1
        Dim obj As New Named("Dispose " & i)
        obj.Dispose()
    End Sub

    ' Make an object and do not dispose it.
    Private Sub btnNoDispose_Click(ByVal sender As System.Object, _
     ByVal e As System.EventArgs) Handles btnNoDispose.Click
        Static i As Integer = 0
        i += 1
        Dim obj As New Named("No Dispose " & i)
    End Sub
End Class
```

If your class allocates managed or unmanaged resources and you don't want to wait for the garbage collector to get around to freeing them, you should implement a `Dispose` method and use it when you no longer need an object.

Constants, Properties, and Methods

Declaring constants, properties, and methods within a class is the same as declaring them outside a class. The main difference is that the context of the declaration is the class rather than a namespace. For example, a variable declared `Private` within a class is available only to code within the class.

For information on declaring variables and constants, see Chapter 4, "Data Types, Variables, and Constants." For information on declaring methods, see Chapter 6, "Subroutines and Functions." Chapter 6 also describes property procedures, special routines that implement a property for a class.

One issue that is sometimes confusing is that the unit scope of a class is the class's *code*, not the code within a specific instance of the class. If you declare a variable within a class `Private`, then all code within the class can access the variable, whether or not that code belongs to the instance of the object that contains the variable.

For example, consider the following `Student` class. The `m_Scores` array is `Private` to the class, so you might think that a `Student` object could only access its own scores. In fact, any `Student` object can access any other `Student` object's `m_Scores` array as well. The `CompareToStudent` subroutine calculates the total score for the current `Student` object. It then calculates the total score for another student and displays the results.

```
Public Class Student
    Public FirstName As String
    Public LastName As String
    Private m_Scores() As Integer
    ...
    Public Sub CompareToStudent(ByVal other_student As Student)
        Dim my_score As Integer = 0
        For i As Integer = 0 To m_Scores.GetUpperBound(0)
```

```
            my_score += m_Scores(i)
        Next i

        Dim other_score As Integer = 0
        For i As Integer = 0 To other_student.m_Scores.GetUpperBound(0)
            other_score += other_student.m_Scores(i)
        Next i

        Debug.WriteLine("My score:    " & my_score)
        Debug.WriteLine("Other score: " & other_score)
    End Sub
    ...
End Class
```

Breaking the encapsulation provided by the objects in this way can lead to unnecessary confusion. It is generally better to try to access an object's `Private` data only from within that object. Usually, you can provide access routines that make using the object's data easier to understand.

The following version of the `Student` class includes a `TotalScore` function that returns the total of a `Student` object's scores. This function works only with its own object's scores, so it does not pry into another object's data. The `CompareToStudent` subroutine uses the `TotalScore` function to display the total score for its object and for a comparison object.

```
Public Class Student
    Public FirstName As String
    Public LastName As String
    Private m_Scores() As Integer
    ...
    Public Sub CompareToStudent(ByVal other_student As Student)
        Debug.WriteLine("My score:    " & TotalScore())
        Debug.WriteLine("Other score: " & other_student.TotalScore())
    End Sub

    ' Return the total of this student's scores.
    Private Function TotalScore() As Integer
        Dim total_score As Integer = 0
        For i As Integer = 0 To m_Scores.GetUpperBound(0)
            total_score += m_Scores(i)
        Next i

        Return total_score
    End Function
    ...
End Class
```

Function `TotalScore` is itself declared `Private`, so only code within the class can use it. In this example, the `CompareToStudent` subroutine calls another object's `Private TotalScore` function, so the separation between the two objects is not absolute, but at least `CompareToStudent` doesn't need to look directly at the other object's data.

Events

Properties let the application view and modify an object's data. Methods let the program invoke the object's behaviors and perform actions. Together, properties and methods let the program send information (data values or commands) to the object.

In a sense, events do the reverse: They let the object send information to the program. When something noteworthy occurs in the object's code, it can raise an event to tell the main program about it. The main program can then decide what to do about the event.

The following sections describe events. They explain how a class declares events and how other parts of the program can catch events.

Declaring Events

A class object can raise events whenever it needs to notify to the program of changing circumstances. Normally, the class declares the event using the `Event` keyword. The following text shows the `Event` statement's syntax:

```
[attribute_list] [accessibility] [Shadows] _
Event event_name([parameters]) [Implements interface.event]
```

The following sections describe the pieces of this declaration. Some of these are similar to earlier sections that describe constant, variable, and class declarations. By now, you should notice some familiarity in the use of the *attribute_list* and *accessibility* clauses. For more information on constant and variable declarations, see Chapter 4, "Data Types, Variables, and Constants." For more information on class declarations, see the section "Classes" earlier in this chapter.

attribute_list

The *attribute_list* defines attributes that apply to the event. For example, the following declaration defines a description that the code editor should display for the `ScoreAdded` event:

```
Imports System.ComponentModel

Public Class Student
    <Description("Occurs when a score is added to the object")> _
    Public Event ScoreAdded(ByVal test_number As Integer)
    ...
End Class
```

accessibility

The *accessibility* value can take one of the following values: `Public`, `Protected`, `Friend`, `Protected Friend`, and `Private`. These values determine which pieces of code can catch the event. Following is an explanation of these keywords:

❑   `Public` — Indicates that there are no restrictions on the event. Code inside or outside the class can catch the event.

❑   `Protected` — Indicates that the event is accessible only to code in the same class or in a derived class.

❑ *Friend* — Indicates that the event is available to all code inside or outside the class module within the same project. The difference between this and Public is that Public allows code outside of the project to access the subroutine. This is generally only an issue for code libraries (.dll files) and control libraries. For example, suppose that you build a code library containing a class that raises some events. You then you write a program that uses the class. On one hand, if the class declares an event with the Public keyword, then the code in the library and the code in the main program can catch the event. On the other hand, if the class declares an event with the Friend keyword, only the code in the library can catch the event, not the code in the main program.

❑ *Protected Friend* — Indicates that the event has both Protected and Friend status. The event is available only within the same project and within the same class or a derived class.

❑ *Private* — Indicates that the event is available only within the class that contains it. An instance of the class can catch this event, but code outside of the class cannot.

Shadows

The Shadows keyword indicates that this event replaces an event in the parent class that has the same name but not necessarily the same parameters.

parameters

The *parameters* clause gives the parameters that the event will pass to event handlers. The syntax for the parameter list is the same as the syntax for declaring the parameter list for a subroutine or function.

If an event declares a parameter with the ByRef keyword, the code that catches the event can modify that parameter's value. When the event handler ends, the class code that raised the event can read the new parameter value.

Implements interface.event

If the class implements an interface and the interface defines an event, this clause identifies this event as the one defined by the interface. For example, the IStudent interface shown in the following code defines the ScoreChanged event handler. The Student class implements the IStudent interface. The declaration of the ScoreChanged event handler uses the Implements keyword to indicate that this event handler provides the event handler defined by the IStudent interface.

```
Public Interface IStudent
    Event ScoreChanged()
    ...
End Interface

Public Class Student
    Implements IStudent

    Public Event ScoreChanged() Implements IStudent.ScoreChanged
    ...
End Class
```

Raising Events

After it has declared an event, a class raises it with the RaiseEvent keyword. It should pass the event whatever parameters were defined in the Event statement.

For example, the Student class shown in the following code declares a ScoreChange event. Its AddScore method makes room for a new score, adds the score to the Scores array, and then raises the ScoreChanged event, passing the event handler the index of the score in the Scores array.

```
Public Class Student
    Private Scores() As Integer
    ...
    Public Event ScoreChanged(ByVal test_number As Integer)
    ...
    Public Sub AddScore(ByVal new_score As Integer)
        ReDim Preserve Scores(Scores.Length)
        Scores(Scores.Length - 1) = new_score
        RaiseEvent ScoreChanged(Scores.Length - 1)
    End Sub
    ...
End Class
```

Catching Events

There are two ways that you can catch an object's events. First, you can declare the object variable using the WithEvents keyword, as shown in the following code:

```
Private WithEvents TopStudent As Student
```

In the code editor, click the left drop-down list and select the variable's name. In the right drop-down list, select the event. This makes the code editor create an empty event handler similar to the following one. When the object raises its ScoreChanged event, the event handler executes.

```
Private Sub TopStudent_ScoreChanged(ByVal test_number As Integer) _
  Handles TopStudent.ScoreChanged

End Sub
```

The second method for catching events is to use the AddHandler statement to define an event handler for the event. First, write the event handler subroutine. This subroutine must take parameters of the proper type to match those defined by the event's declaration in the class. The following code shows a subroutine that can handle the ScoreChanged event. Note that the parameter's name has been changed, but its accessibility (ByRef or ByVal) and data type must match those declared for the ScoreChanged event.

```
Private Sub HandleScoreChanged(ByVal quiz_num As Integer)

End Sub
```

If the event handler's parameter list is long and complicated, writing an event handler can be tedious. To make this easier, you can declare an object using the WithEvents keyword and use the drop-down lists to give it an event handler. Then you can edit the event handler to suit your needs (change its name, remove the Handles clause, change parameter names, and so forth).

After you build the event handler routine, use the AddHandler statement to assign the routine to a particular object's event. The following statement makes the HandleScoreChanged event handler catch the TopStudent object's ScoreChanged event:

```
AddHandler TopStudent.ScoreChanged, AddressOf HandleScoreChanged
```

Using AddHandler is particularly handy when you want to use the same event handler with more than one object. For example, you might write an event handler that validates a TextBox control's contents to ensure that it contains a valid phone number. By repeatedly using the AddHandler statement, you can make the same event handler validate any number of TextBox controls.

AddHandler is also convenient if you want to work with an array of objects. The following code shows how a program might create an array of Student objects and then use the HandleScoreChanged subroutine to catch the ScoreChanged event for all of them:

```
' Create an array of Student objects.
Const MAX_STUDENT As Integer = 30
Dim students(MAX_STUDENT) As Student
For i As Integer = 0 To MAX_STUDENT
    students(i) = New Student
Next i

' Add ScoreChanged event handlers.
For i As Integer = 0 To MAX_STUDENT
    AddHandler students(i).ScoreChanged, AddressOf HandleScoreChanged
Next i
...
```

If you plan to use AddHandler in this way, you may want to ensure that the events provide enough information for the event handler to figure out which object raised the event. For example, you might modify the ScoreChanged event so that it passes a reference to the object raising the event into the event handler. Then the shared event handler can determine which Student object had a score change.

If you add an event handler with AddHandler, you can later remove it with the RemoveHandler statement. The syntax is the same as the syntax for AddHandler, as shown here:

```
RemoveHandler TopStudent.ScoreChanged, AddressOf HandleScoreChanged
```

Declaring Custom Events

A second form of event declaration provides more control over the event. This version is quite a bit more complicated and at first can seem very confusing. Skim through the syntax and description that follows and then look at the example. Then if you go back and look at the syntax and description again, they should make more sense. This version is also more advanced and you may not need it often (if ever), so you can skip it for now if you get bogged down.

This version enables you to define routines that are executed when the event is bound to an event handler, removed from an event handler, and called. The syntax is as follows:

```
[attribute_list] [accessibility] [Shadows] _
Custom Event event_name As delegate_name [Implements interface.event]
    [attribute_list] AddHandler(ByVal value As delegate_name)
        ...
    End AddHandler
    [attribute_list] RemoveHandler(ByVal value As delegate_name)
        ...
    End RemoveHandler
    [attribute_list] RaiseEvent(delegate_signature)
        ...
    End RaiseEvent
End Event
```

The *attribute_list*, *accessibility*, Shadows, and Implements *interface.event* parts have the same meaning as in the previous, simpler event declaration. See the section "Declaring Events" earlier in this chapter for information on these pieces.

The *delegate_name* tells Visual Basic the type of event handler that will catch the event. For example, the delegate might indicate a subroutine that takes as a parameter a String variable named new_name. The following code shows a simple delegate for this routine. The delegate's name is NameChangedDelegate. It takes a String parameter named new_name.

```
Public Delegate Sub NameChangedDelegate(ByVal new_name As String)
```

For more information on delegates, see the section "Delegates" in Chapter 4, "Data Types, Variables, and Constants."

The main body of the custom event declaration defines three routines named AddHandler, RemoveHandler, and RaiseEvent. You can use these three routines to keep track of the event handlers assigned to an object (remember that the event declaration is declaring an event for a class) and to call the event handlers when appropriate.

The AddHandler routine executes when the program adds an event handler to the object. It takes as a parameter a delegate variable named value. This is a reference to a routine that matches the delegate defined for the event handler. For example, if the main program uses the AddHandler statement to add the subroutine Employee_NameChanged as an event handler for this object, then the parameter to AddHandler is a reference to the Employee_NameChanged subroutine.

Normally, the AddHandler subroutine saves the delegate in some sort of collection so that the RaiseEvent subroutine described shortly can invoke it.

The RemoveHandler subroutine executes when the program removes an event handler from the object. It takes as a parameter a delegate variable indicating the event handler that should be removed. Normally, the RemoveHandler subroutine deletes the delegate from the collection that AddHandler used to originally store the delegate.

Finally, the `RaiseEvent` subroutine executes when the object's code uses the `RaiseEvent` statement to raise the event. For example, suppose that the `Employee` class defines the `NameChanged` event. When the class's `FirstName` or `LastName` property procedure changes an `Employee` object's name, it uses the `RaiseEvent` statement to raise the `NameChanged` event. At that point, the custom `RaiseEvent` subroutine executes.

Normally, the `RaiseEvent` subroutine calls the delegates stored by the `AddHandler` subroutine in the class's collection of event delegates.

The following code shows how the `Employee` class might implement a custom `NameChanged` event. It begins with the `FirstName` and `LastName` property procedures. The `Property Set` procedures both use the `RaiseEvent` statement to raise the `NameChanged` event. This is fairly straightforward and works just as it would if the class used the simpler event declaration. Next the code defines an `ArrayList` named `m_EventDelegates` that it will use to store the event handler delegates. It then uses a `Delegate` statement to define the types of event handlers that this event will call. In this example, the event handler must be a subroutine that takes a String parameter passed by value. Now the code defines the `NameChanged` custom event. Notice that the `Custom Event` statement ends with the delegate `NameChangedDelegate`. If you type this first line and press Enter, Visual Basic creates empty `AddHandler`, `RemoveHandler`, and `RaiseEvent` subroutines for you.

Subroutine `AddHandler` displays a message and saves the delegate in the `m_EventDelegates` list. When `AddHandler` is called, the `value` parameter refers to an event handler routine that has the proper type.

The subroutine `RemoveHandler` displays a message and removes a delegate from the `m_EventDelegates` list. In a real application, this routine would need some error-handling code in case the delegate is not in `m_EventDelegates`.

When the `FirstName` and `LastName` property set procedures use the `RaiseEvent` statement, the `RaiseEvent` subroutine executes. This routine's parameter takes whatever value the class used when it used the `RaiseEvent` statement. This subroutine displays a message and then loops through all the delegates stored in the `m_EventDelegates` list, invoking each. It passes each delegate the `new_name` value it received in its parameter, with spaces replaced by plus signs.

```
Public Class Employee
    ' The FirstName property.
    Private m_FirstName As String
    Public Property FirstName() As String
        Get
            Return m_FirstName
        End Get
        Set(ByVal value As String)
            m_FirstName = value
            RaiseEvent NameChanged(m_FirstName & " " & m_LastName)
        End Set
    End Property

    ' The LastName property.
    Private m_LastName As String
    Public Property LastName() As String
        Get
            Return m_LastName
```

```
            End Get
            Set(ByVal value As String)
                m_LastName = value
                RaiseEvent NameChanged(m_FirstName & " " & m_LastName)
            End Set
    End Property

    ' List to hold the event handler delegates.
    Private m_EventDelegates As New ArrayList

    ' Defines the event handler signature.
    Public Delegate Sub NameChangedDelegate(ByVal new_name As String)

    ' Define the custom NameChanged event.
    Public Custom Event NameChanged As NameChangedDelegate
        AddHandler(ByVal value As NameChangedDelegate)
            Debug.WriteLine("AddHandler")
            m_EventDelegates.Add(value)
        End AddHandler

        RemoveHandler(ByVal value As NameChangedDelegate)
            Debug.WriteLine("RemoveHandler")
            m_EventDelegates.Remove(value)
        End RemoveHandler

        RaiseEvent(ByVal new_name As String)
            Debug.WriteLine("RaiseEvent (" & new_name & ")")
            For Each a_delegate As NameChangedDelegate In m_EventDelegates
                a_delegate(new_name.Replace(" ", "+"))
            Next a_delegate
        End RaiseEvent
    End Event
End Class
```

The following code demonstrates the NameChanged event handler. It creates a new Employee object and then uses two AddHandler statements to assign the event Employee_NameChanged handler to the object's NameChanged event. This makes the custom AddHandler subroutine execute twice and save two references to the Employee_NameChanged subroutine in the delegate list. Next, the program sets the Employee object's FirstName. The FirstName property set procedure raises the NameChanged event so the RaiseEvent subroutine executes. RaiseEvent loops through the delegate list and calls the delegates. In this example, that means the subroutine Employee_NameChanged executes twice. The program then uses a RemoveHandler statement to remove an Employee_NameChanged event handler. The custom RemoveHandler subroutine executes and removes one instance of the Employee_NameChanged subroutine from the delegate list. Next the program sets the Employee object's LastName. The LastName property set procedure uses the RaiseEvent statement so the RaiseEvent subroutine executes. Now there is only one instance of the Employee_NameChanged subroutine in the delegate list, so it is called once. Finally, the code uses the RemoveHandler statement to remove the remaining instance of Employee_NameChanged from the delegate list. The RemoveHandler subroutine executes and removes the instance form the delegate list.

```
Dim emp As New Employee
AddHandler emp.NameChanged, AddressOf Employee_NameChanged
AddHandler emp.NameChanged, AddressOf Employee_NameChanged
emp.FirstName = "Rod"
RemoveHandler emp.NameChanged, AddressOf Employee_NameChanged
emp.LastName = "Stephens"
RemoveHandler emp.NameChanged, AddressOf Employee_NameChanged
```

The following text shows the result in the Debug window. It shows where the `AddHandler`, `RaiseEvent`, and `RemoveHandler` subroutines execute. You can also see where the `Employee_NameChanged` event handler executes and displays its name.

```
AddHandler
AddHandler
RaiseEvent (Rod )
Employee_NameChanged: Rod+
Employee_NameChanged: Rod+
RemoveHandler
RaiseEvent (Rod Stephens)
Employee_NameChanged: Rod+Stephens
RemoveHandler
```

Shared Variables

If you declare a variable in a class with the `Shared` keyword, all objects of the class share a single instance of that variable. You can get or set the variable's value through any instance of the class.

For example, suppose the `Student` class declares a shared `NumStudents` variable, as shown in the following code:

```
Public Class Student
    Shared NumStudents As Integer
...
End Class
```

In this case, all instances of the `Student` class share the same `NumStudents` value. The following code creates two `Student` objects. It uses one to set the shared `NumStudents` value and uses the other to display the result.

```
Dim student1 As New Student
Dim student2 As New Student
student1.NumStudents = 100
MessageBox.Show(student2.NumStudents)
```

Because all instances of the class share the same variable, any changes to the value that you make using one object are visible to all the others. Figure 15-4 illustrates this idea. Each `Student` class instance has its own `FirstName`, `LastName`, `Scores`, and other "individual" data values, but they all share the same `NumStudents` value.

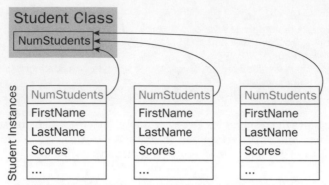

Figure 15-4: If a variable in a class is declared Shared, all instances of a class share the same value.

Because a shared variable is associated with the class as a whole and not a specific instance of the class, Visual Basic lets you refer to it using the class's name in addition to using specific instance variables. The following code defines a new Student object and uses it to set NumStudents to 100. It then uses the class name to display the NumStudents value.

```
Dim student1 As New Student
student1.NumStudents = 100
MessageBox.Show(Student.NumStudents)
```

Shared Methods

Shared methods are a little less intuitive than shared variables. Like shared variables, shared methods are accessible using the class's name. For example, the NewStudent function shown in the following code is declared with the Shared keyword. This function creates a new Student object, initializes it by adding it to some sort of database and then returns the new object.

```
Public Class Student
    ...
    ' Return a new Student.
    Public Shared Function NewStudent() As Student
        ' Instantiate the Student.
        Dim new_student As New Student

        ' Add the new student to the database.
        '...

        ' Return the new student.
        Return new_student
    End Function
    ...
End Class
```

The type of function that creates a new instance of a class is sometimes called a *factory method*. In some cases, you can use an appropriate constructor instead of a factory method. One time when a factory method is useful is when object creation might fail. If data passed to the method is invalid, some resource (such as a database) prohibits the new object (perhaps a new Student has the same name as an existing Student), or the object may come from more than one place (for example, it may either be a new object or one taken from a pool of existing objects). In those cases, a factory method can return Nothing. A constructor could raise an error, but it cannot force an object to not be created.

If you want to force the program to use a factory method rather than creating an instance of the object directly, give the class a private constructor. Code that lies outside of the class cannot use the constructor because it is private. It also cannot use the default constructor associated with the New statement because the class has an explicit constructor. The code must create new objects by using the factory method, which can use the private constructor because it's inside the class.

As is the case with shared variables, you can access a shared method by using any instance of the class or by using the class's name. The following code declares the student1 variable and initializes it by calling the NewStudent factory method using the class's name. Next, the code declares student2 and uses the student1 object's NewStudent method to initialize it.

```
Dim student1 As Student = Student.NewStudent()
Dim student2 As Student = student1.NewStudent()
```

By default, Visual Basic warns you if you try to access a shared member by using a specific variable such as student1 rather than the class name.

One oddity of shared methods is that they can use class variables and methods only if they are also shared. If you think about accessing a shared method through the class name rather than an instance of the class, this makes sense. If you don't use an instance of the class, then there is no instance to give the method data.

In the following code, the Student class declares the variable NumStudents with the Shared keyword so shared methods can use that value. It declares the instance variables FirstName and LastName without the Shared keyword, so shared methods cannot use those values. The shared NewStudent method starts by incrementing the shared NumStudents value. It then creates a new Student object and initializes its FirstName and LastName values. It can initialize those values because it is using a specific instance of the class and that instance has FirstName and LastName values.

```
Public Class Student
    Public Shared NumStudents As Integer
    Public FirstName As String
    Public LastName As String
    ...
    ' Return a new Student.
    Public Shared Function NewStudent() As Student
        ' Increment the number of Students loaded.
        NumStudents += 1

        ' Instantiate the Student.
        Dim new_student As New Student
        new_student.FirstName = "<unknown>"
        new_student.LastName = "<unknown>"

        ' Add the new student to the database.
```

```
        ...

        ' Return the new student.
        Return new_student
    End Function
    ...
End Class
```

Figure 15-5 illustrates the situation. The shared `NewStudent` method is contained within the class itself and has access to the `NumStudents` variable. If it wanted to use a `FirstName`, `LastName`, or `Scores` value, however, it needs to use an instance of the class.

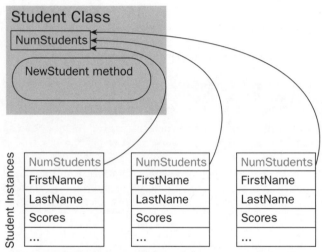

Figure 15-5: A shared method can only access other shared variables and methods.

Summary

Classes and structures are very similar. Both are container types that group related variables, methods, and events in a single entity.

Most developers use classes exclusively, primarily because structures are relatively new and developers are more familiar with classes. Structures also have the additional restriction that they cannot take advantage of inheritance.

Another significant factor when picking between classes and structures, however, is their difference in type. Classes are reference types, while structures are value types. This gives them different behaviors when defining and initializing objects, and when passing objects to routines by value and by reference.

Once you understand the differences between classes and structures, you can pick the one that is more appropriate for your application.

If you build enough classes and structures, you may start to have naming collisions. It is common for developers working on different projects to define similar business classes such as `Employee`, `Customer`, `Order`, and `InventoryItem`. While these objects may be similar, they may differ in important details. The `Customer` class defined for a billing application might include lots of account and billing address information, while a repair assignment application might focus on the customer's equipment and needs.

Having two `Customer` classes around can result in confusion and programs that cannot easily interact with each other. Namespaces can help categorize code and differentiate among classes. You can define separate namespaces for the billing and repair assignment applications, and use them to tell which version of the `Customer` class you need for a particular purpose.

Chapter 16 describes namespaces in detail. It explains how to create namespaces and how to use them to refer to classes created in other modules.

16

Namespaces

In large applications, it is fairly common to have name collisions. One developer might create an `Employee` class, while another makes a function named `Employee` that returns the employee ID for a particular person's name. Or two developers might build different `Employee` classes that have different properties and different purposes. When multiple items have the same name, this is called a *namespace collision* or *namespace pollution*.

These sorts of name conflicts are most common when programmers are not working closely together. For example, different developers working on the payroll and human resources systems might both define `Employee` classes.

Namespaces enable you to classify and distinguish among programming entities that have the same name. For instance, you might build the payroll system in the Payroll namespace and the human resources system in the HumanResources namespace. Then, the two `Employee` classes would have fully qualified names `Payroll.Employee` and `HumanResources.Employee`, so they could coexist peacefully.

The following code shows how an application would declare these two types of `Employee` objects:

```
Dim payroll_emp As Payroll.Employee
Dim hr_emp As HumanResources.Employee
```

Namespaces can contain other namespaces, so you can build a hierarchical structure that groups different entities. You can divide the Payroll namespace into pieces to give developers working on that project some isolation from each other.

Namespaces can be confusing at first, but they are really fairly simple. They just break the code up into manageable pieces so that you can group parts of the program and tell different parts from each other.

This chapter describes namespaces. It explains how to use namespaces to categorize programming items and how to use them to select the right versions of items with the same name.

The Imports Statement

Visual Studio defines an enormous number of variables, classes, routines, and other entities to provide tools for your applications. It categorizes them in namespaces to prevent name collisions and to make it easier for you to find the items you need.

Visual Studio's root namespaces are named Microsoft and System. The Microsoft namespace includes the CSharp, JScript, VisualBasic, and Vsa namespaces that support different programming languages. The Microsoft namespace also includes the Win32 namespace, which provides classes that handle operating system events and that manipulate the registry.

The System namespace contains a huge number of useful programming items, including many nested namespaces. For example, the System.Drawing namespace contains classes related to drawing, System.Data contains classes related to databases, System.Threading holds classes dealing with multithreading, and System.Security includes classes for working with security and cryptography.

Note that these namespaces are not necessarily available to your program at all times. For example, by default, the Microsoft.JScript namespace is not available to Visual Basic programs. To use it, you must first add a reference to the `Microsoft.JScript.dll` library.

Visual Studio includes so many programming tools that the namespace hierarchy is truly enormous. Namespaces are refined into subnamespaces, which may be further broken into more namespaces until they reach a manageable size. While this makes it easier to differentiate among all of the different programming entities, it makes the fully qualified names of some classes rather cumbersome.

For example, the following code draws a rectangle inside a form. Fully qualified names such as `System.Drawing.Drawing2D.DashStyle.DashDotDot` are so long that they make the code hard to read.

```
Private Sub DrawDashedBox(ByVal gr As System.Drawing.Graphics)
    Dim my_pen As New System.Drawing.Pen(System.Drawing.Color.Blue, 5)
    my_pen.DashStyle = System.Drawing.Drawing2D.DashStyle.DashDotDot

    Dim rect As System.Drawing.Rectangle = Me.ClientRectangle
    rect.X += 10
    rect.Y += 10
    rect.Width -= 20
    rect.Height -= 20
    gr.Clear(Me.BackColor)
    gr.DrawRectangle(my_pen, rect)
End Sub
```

You can use the `Imports` statement at the top of the file to make using namespaces easier. After you import a namespace, your code can use the items it contains without specifying the namespace.

The following version of the previous code imports the System.Drawing and System.Drawing.Drawing2D namespaces, so it doesn't need to mention the namespaces in its object declarations. This version is much easier to read.

```
Imports System.Drawing
Imports System.Drawing.Drawing2D
...
Private Sub DrawDashedBox(ByVal gr As Graphics)
    Dim my_pen As New Pen(Color.Blue, 5)
    my_pen.DashStyle = DashStyle.DashDotDot

    Dim rect As Rectangle = Me.ClientRectangle
    rect.X += 10
    rect.Y += 10
    rect.Width -= 20
    rect.Height -= 20
    gr.Clear(Me.BackColor)
    gr.DrawRectangle(my_pen, rect)
End Sub
```

Figure 16-1 shows the results.

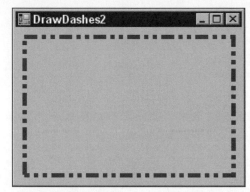

Figure 16-1: The `Imports` **statement greatly simplifies the code that draws this dashed rectangle.**

A file can include any number of `Imports` statements. The statements must appear at the beginning of the file, and they define namespace shortcuts for the entire file. If you want different pieces of code to use different sets of `Imports` statements, you must place the pieces of code in different files. If the pieces of code are in the same class, use the `Partial` keyword so you can split the class into several files.

If a program imports more than one namespace that defines the same class, it must use fully qualified names to select the right versions. For example, suppose that the Payroll and HumanResources modules both define `Employee` classes. Then you must use the fully qualified names `Payroll.Employee` and `HumanResources.Employee` to differentiate between the two.

The complete syntax for the Imports statement is as follows:

```
Imports [alias =] namespace[.element]
```

The following sections describe namespace aliases and elements in detail.

Automatic Imports

Visual Basic lets you quickly import a namespace for all of the modules in a project. In Solution Explorer, double-click My Project. Click on the References tab to display the page shown in Figure 16-2.

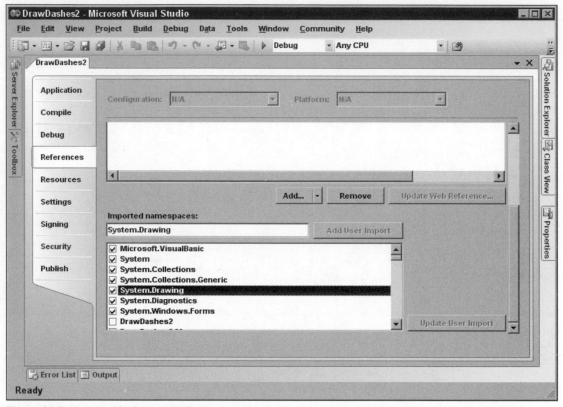

Figure 16-2: Use the My Project References tab to import namespaces for every module in a project.

In the Imported Namespaces list at the bottom, check the box next to the namespaces that you want to import. The program's files will be able to use the objects defined in these namespaces, even though they do not include Imports statements.

This is most useful when most of the program's modules need to import the same namespaces. Including the Imports statement in the files makes it easier for developers to see which namespaces are available, however, so you might want to do this instead, particularly if you use unusual namespaces.

By default, Visual Basic loads imports for the type of application you are building. For example, when you start a Windows form application, Visual Basic imports the following namespaces:

❑ Microsoft.VisualBasic

❑ System

❑ System.Collections

❑ System.Collections.Generic

❑ System.Drawing

❑ System.Diagnostics

❑ System.Windows.Forms

You can use the upper half of the References property page to manage project references. Use the Add and Remove buttons (scrolled off to the right in Figure 16-2) to add and remove references.

Click the Unused References button (scrolled off to the right in Figure 16-2) to see a list of referenced libraries not currently used by the project. Before you distribute the program, you can remove the unused references.

Namespace Aliases

You can use the *alias* clause to define a shorthand notation for the namespace. For instance, the following code imports the System.Drawing.Drawing2D namespace and gives it the alias D2. Later, it uses D2 as shorthand for the fully qualified namespace.

```
Imports D2 = System.Drawing.Drawing2D
...
Dim dash_style As D2.DashStyle = D2.DashStyle.DashDotDot
```

An `Imports` statement with an alias is more restrictive than an `Imports` statement without one. The previous code defines a namespace alias, so the code *must* use the alias to access the namespace. On one hand, if you remove the occurrences of D2 from the declaration of the `dash_style` variable, Visual Basic will not understand what the `DashStype` type and the `DashStyle.DashDotDot` value mean. On the other hand, if you omit the alias from the `Imports` statement, the previous code works without the occurrences of D2.

You can get the best of both worlds by importing the namespace twice, once with an alias and once without. The following code imports the System.Drawing.Drawing2D namespace twice. In the declaration of the variable `dash_style`, the variable's type `DashStyle` does not use the namespace alias, but the initialization value `D2.DashStyle.DashDotDot` does.

```
Imports System.Drawing.Drawing2D
Imports D2 = System.Drawing.Drawing2D
...
Dim dash_style As DashStyle = D2.DashStyle.DashDotDot
```

This technique is handy if you need to use two namespaces that define different classes with the same name. Normally, if two namespaces define classes with the same name, you must use the fully qualified class names so that Visual Basic can tell them apart. You can use aliases to indicate the namespaces more concisely.

Suppose that the JobClasses and FinanceStuff namespaces both define an `Employee` class. If you declare a variable using the unqualified class `Employee`, Visual Basic would not know which version to use. The following code shows how you can declare fully qualified versions of the `Employee` class:

```
Imports MyApplication.JobClasses
Imports MyApplication.FinanceStuff
...
Dim job_emp As MyApplication.JobClasses.Employee
Dim finance_emp As MyApplication.FinanceStuff.Employee
...
```

You can use aliases to simplify these declarations. You could use `Job` as an alias for MyApplication .JobClasses and `Finance` as an alias for MyApplication.FinanceStuff.

Now suppose that the JobClasses namespace also defines the `Dispatcher` class. The FinanceStuff namespace does not define a `Dispatcher` class, so there is no name conflict between the namespaces. You could use the `Job` alias to refer to the `Dispatcher` class, or you could import the JobClasses namespace again without an alias as shown in the following code:

```
Imports MyApplication.JobClasses
Imports Job = MyApplication.JobClasses
Imports Finance = MyApplication.FinanceStuff
...
Dim job_emp As Job.Employee
Dim finance_emp As Finance.Employee
Dim job_dispatcher As Dispatcher
...
```

Namespace Elements

In addition to importing a namespace, you can import an element within the namespace. This is particularly useful for enumerated types.

For example, the following code imports the System.Drawing.Drawing2D namespace, which defines the `DrawStyle` enumeration. It declares the variable `dash_style` to be of the `DashStyle` type and sets its value to `DashStyle.DashDotDot`.

```
Imports System.Drawing.Drawing2D
...
Dim dash_style As DashStyle = DashStyle.DashDotDot
...
```

The following code also imports the System.Drawing.Drawing2D.DashStyle enumeration. That allows it to set the value of the `dash_style` variable to `DashDotDot` without needing to specify the name of the enumeration (`DashStyle`).

```
Imports System.Drawing.Drawing2D
Imports System.Drawing.Drawing2D.DashStyle
...
Dim dash_style As DashStyle = DashDotDot
...
```

The Root Namespace

Every project has a root namespace, and every item in the project is contained directly or indirectly within that namespace. To view or change the project's root namespace, open Solution Explorer and double-click the My Projects entry. View or modify the root namespace on the Application tab shown in Figure 16-3.

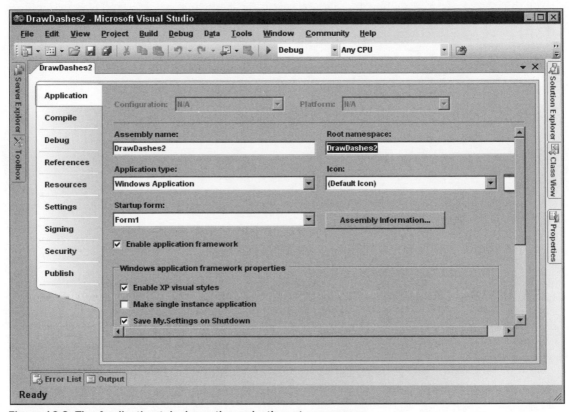

Figure 16-3: The Application tab shows the project's root namespace.

Making Namespaces

You can create new namespaces nested within the root namespace to further categorize your code. The easiest way to create a namespace is by using the Namespace statement. The following code declares a namespace called SchedulingClasses. It includes the definition of the TimeSlot class and possibly other classes.

```
Namespace SchedulingClasses
    Public Class TimeSlot
        ...
    End Class
    ...
End Namespace
```

After defining this namespace, code inside the namespace can refer to the new class as simply `TimeSlot`. Code outside of the namespace can refer to the class using the namespace as shown in the following code (assuming MyApplication is the project's root namespace):

```
Dim time_slot As New MyApplication.SchedulingClasses.TimeSlot
```

You can nest namespaces within other namespaces to any depth. In fact, because all of your application's code is contained within the root namespace, any namespace you create must be contained within another namespace. There is no way to make a namespace that is not contained within the root namespace.

If you want to make a namespace that lies outside of the application's root namespace, you must create a library project. Then the code in that project lies within its own root namespace.

The following code defines the DispatchClasses namespace. That namespace contains the AppointmentClasses and JobClasses namespaces, each of which defines some classes.

```
Namespace DispatchClasses
    Namespace AppointmentClasses
        Public Class AppointmentWindow
            ...
        End Class
        ...
    End Namespace

    Namespace JobClasses
        Public Class SkilledJob
            ...
        End Class
        ...
    End Namespace
End Namespace
```

The following code shows how an application could create references to `AppointmentWindow` and `SkilledJob` objects using the class's fully qualified names:

```
Dim appt As New MyApplication.DispatchClasses.AppointmentClasses.AppointmentWindow
Dim job As New MyApplication.DispatchClasses.JobClasses.SkilledJob
```

A `Namespace` statement can only appear at the namespace level. You cannot create a namespace within a module, class, or structure.

Inside a namespace, you can define other namespaces, classes, structures, modules, enumerated types, and interfaces. You cannot directly define variables, properties, subroutines, functions, or events. Those items must be contained within some other entity (such as a class, structure, module, or interface).

You can use more than one `Namespace` statement to define pieces of the same namespace. For example, the following code uses a `Namespace` statement to make the OrderEntryClasses namespace, and it defines the `Employee` class inside it. Later, the code uses another `Namespace` statement to add the `Customer` class to the same namespace. In this case, the single namespace contains both classes.

```
Namespace OrderEntryClasses
    Public Class Employee
        ...
    End Class
End Namespace
...
Namespace OrderEntryClasses
    Public Class Customer
        ...
    End Class
End Namespace
```

Scattering pieces of a namespace throughout your code will probably confuse other developers. One case where it might make sense to break a namespace into pieces would be if you want to put different classes in different code files, either to prevent any one file from becoming too big or to allow different programmers to work on the files at the same time. In that case, it might make sense to place related pieces of the application in the same namespace but in different files.

Classes, Structures, and Modules

Modules, classes, and structures create their own name contexts that are similar in some ways to namespaces. For example, a class can contain the definition of another class and a structure can contain the definition of another structure, as shown in the following code:

```
Public Class Class1
    Public Class Class2
        ...
    End Class
End Class

Public Structure Struct1
    Public Name As String

    Public Structure Struct2
        Public Name As String
    End Structure
End Structure
```

You can access public module members and shared class or structure members using a fully qualified syntax similar to the one used by namespaces. For example, the following code creates the GlobalValues module and defines the public variable MaxJobs within it. Later, the program can set MaxJobs using its fully qualified name.

```
Module GlobalValues
    Public MaxJobs As Integer
    ...
End Module
...
MyApplication.GlobalValues.MaxJobs = 100
```

While these cases look very similar to namespaces, they really are not. One big difference is that you cannot use a `Namespace` statement inside a class, structure, or module.

IntelliSense gives another clue that Visual Basic treats classes, structures, and modules differently from namespaces. The IntelliSense popup shown in Figure 16-4 displays curly braces {} next to the FinanceStuff and JobClasses namespaces, but it displays different icons for the classes `Employer` and `Form1`, and the module `Module1`.

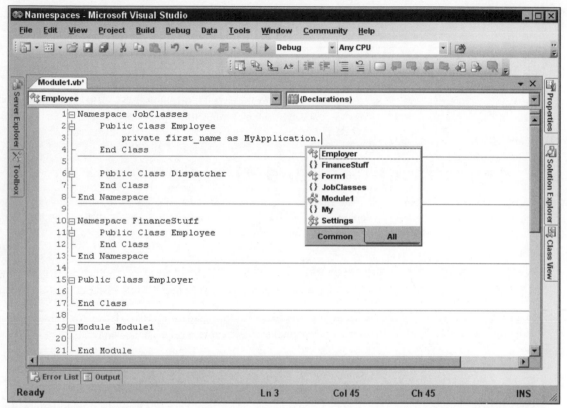

Figure 16-4: IntelliSense displays curly braces {} to the left of namespaces such as FinanceStuff and JobClasses.

Resolving Namespaces

Normally, Visual Basic does a pretty good job of resolving namespaces, and you don't need to worry too much about the process. If you import a namespace, you can omit the namespace in any declarations that you use. If you have not imported a namespace, you can fully qualify declarations that use the namespace and you're done. There are some in-between cases, however, that can be confusing. To understand them, it helps to know a bit more about how Visual Basic resolves namespaces.

When Visual Basic sees a reference that uses a fully qualified namespace, it looks in that namespace for the item it needs and that's that. It either succeeds or fails. For example, the following code declares a variable of type `System.Collections.Hashtable`. Visual Basic looks in the System.Collections namespace and tries to find the `Hashtable` class. If the class is not there, the declaration fails.

```
Dim hash_table As New System.Collections.Hashtable
```

When Visual Basic encounters a qualified namespace, it first assumes that it is fully qualified. If it cannot resolve the reference as described in the previous paragraph, it tries to treat the reference as partially qualified and it looks in the current namespace for a resolution. For example, suppose you declare a variable as shown in the following code:

```
Dim emp As JobClasses.Employee
```

In this case, Visual Basic searches the current namespace for a nested namespace called JobClasses. If it finds such a namespace, it looks for the `Employee` class in that namespace.

If Visual Basic cannot resolve a namespace using these methods, it moves up the namespace hierarchy and tries again. For example, suppose that the current code is in the MyApplication.JobStuff .EmployeeClasses.TimeSheetRoutines namespace. Now, suppose that the `SalaryLevel` class is defined in the MyApplication.JobStuff namespace and consider the following code:

```
Dim salary_level As New SalaryLevel
```

Visual Basic examines the current namespace MyApplication.JobStuff.EmployeeClasses.TimeSheetRoutines and doesn't find a definition for `SalaryLevel`. It moves up the namespace hierarchy and searches the MyApplication.JobStuff.EmployeeClasses namespace, again failing to find `SalaryLevel`. It moves up the hierarchy again to the MyApplication.JobStuff namespace, and there it finally finds the `SalaryLevel` class.

Movement up the namespace hierarchy can sometimes be a bit confusing. It may lead Visual Basic to resolve references in an ancestor of the current namespace, in some sort of "uncle/aunt" namespace, or in a "cousin" namespace.

For example, consider the namespace hierarchy shown in Figure 16-5. The root namespace MyApplication contains the namespaces BusinessClasses and AssignmentStuff. BusinessClasses defines the `Employee` and `Customer` classes. AssignmentStuff contains the `AssignmentGlobals` module, which defines the `MakeAssignment` subroutine and a different version of the `Employee` class.

Now, suppose that the `Customer` class contains the following subroutine:

```
Public Sub AssignEmployee()
    AssignmentStuff.AssignmentGlobals.MakeAssignment(Me)
    ...
End Sub
```

This code lies in the MyApplication.BusinessClasses namespace. Visual Basic cannot find a meaning for the AssignmentStuff namespace locally in that context, so it moves up the namespace hierarchy to MyApplication, where it finds the AssignmentStuff namespace. Within that namespace, it finds the AssignmentGlobals module and the `MakeAssignment` subroutine that it contains.

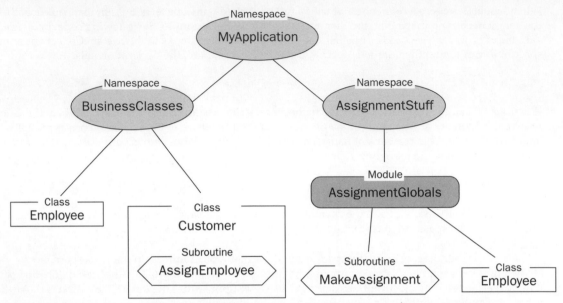

Figure 16-5: Visual Basic may move all over the namespace hierarchy to resolve a declaration.

Visual Basic can also peer into modules as if their public contents were part of the namespace itself. That means you can rewrite the previous code in the following slightly simpler version:

```
Public Sub AssignEmployee()
    AssignmentStuff.MakeAssignment(Me)
    ...
End Sub
```

In this example, there is only one `MakeAssignment` subroutine, so there's little doubt that Visual Basic has found the correct one. If different namespaces define items with the same names, the situation can be somewhat more confusing. Suppose that the `Customer` class declares an object that is from the `Employee` class defined in the MyApplication.AssignmentStuff namespace, as shown in the following code:

```
Dim emp As New AssignmentStuff.Employee
```

If you understand how Visual Basic performs namespace resolution, you can figure out that the object is of the `Employee` class defined in the MyApplication.AssignmentStuff namespace. This isn't completely obvious, however.

If you add `Imports` statements to the program, the situation gets more confusing. Suppose that the program imports the AssignmentStuff namespace and then the `Customer` class declares a variable of type `Employee`. Because this code is in the BusinessClasses namespace, Visual Basic uses that namespace's version of `Employee`. If the code is in some other namespace (such as MyApplication), the program uses the imported AssignmentStuff version of the class.

Finally, suppose that the program imports both BusinessClasses and AssignmentStuff.AssignmentGlobals and then makes the following declaration in another namespace. In this case, Visual Basic cannot decide which version of the class to use, so it generates an error.

```
Dim emp As Employee
```

This example is so confusing, however, that you would probably be better off restructuring the namespaces and possibly renaming one of the versions of the Employee class rather than trying to figure out how Visual Basic is resolving the namespaces.

You can simplify these issues by avoiding duplicate names across all namespaces. When you do use duplicate namespaces, you can use fully qualified namespaces to avoid ambiguity. You can also use `Imports` statements to make namespace aliases and then use the aliases to avoid ambiguity more concisely.

Summary

Namespaces are everywhere in Visual Basic. Every piece of code you write is contained in some namespace, even if it is only the application's root namespace. Despite their pervasiveness, many developers never need to use namespaces explicitly, so they find them somewhat mystical.

Namespaces are really quite simple, however. They merely divide programming items into a hierarchy. They allow you to categorize related items and resolve name collisions in different parts of the application.

You can use the `Imports` statement to allow the program to refer to items in a namespace without giving its fully qualified name. A namespace alias lets you explicitly specify an item's namespace in an abbreviated form. This is particularly useful to resolve ambiguous names that appear in more than one namespace included in `Imports` statements.

This chapter describes namespaces in general. Chapter 17, "Collection Classes," describes some of the useful classes for grouping object classes, including those in the System.Collections and System.Collections.Generic namespaces.

Collection Classes

Visual Basic .NET includes a large assortment of prebuilt classes that store and manage groups of objects. These collection classes provide a wide variety of different features, so the right class for a particular purpose depends on your application.

For example, an array is good for storing objects in a particular fixed order. An `ArrayList` enables you to add, remove, and rearrange its objects much more easily than an array does. A `Queue` lets a program easily add items and remove them in first in, first out order. In contrast, a `Stack` lets the program remove items in last in, first out order.

This chapter describes these different kinds of collection classes and provides tips for selecting the right one for various purposes.

What Is a Collection?

The word "collection" means a group of objects that should be kept together. Unfortunately, that's such a useful concept that Visual Basic adopted the word and made a specific `Collection` class. The `Collection` class *does* keep a group of objects together, but it reserves for its own use the perfect word for these kinds of groups of objects.

That leads to some ambiguity when you talk about collection classes. Do you mean the `Collection` class? Or do you mean some other class that groups objects? Even the Visual Basic documentation has this problem and sometimes uses "collection classes" to mean classes that group things together.

This chapter describes the `Collection` class as well as other "collection classes."

One of the most basic Visual Basic entities that groups objects is an *array*. An array stores data values or references to objects in a simple, block of memory with one entry directly following another. The `Array` class does provide some special methods for manipulating arrays (such as reversing, sorting, or searching the array).

The Collection class provides a few specific features for working with its group of objects. It allows you to add an item to the Collection, optionally specifying a key for the item. You can then search for the item or remove the item using its key or its index in the Collection.

One of the key features of the Collection class is that it supports enumerators and For Each loops. That lets you easily loop over the objects in a Collection without worrying about the number of objects it contains.

Other classes derived from the Collection class provide additional features. For example, the HashTable class can store a large number of objects with associated keys very efficiently. The Queue class makes it easy to work with objects on a first in, first out (FIFO) basis, while the Stack class helps you work with objects in a last in, first out order (LIFO).

The remainder of this chapter describes these classes in detail.

Arrays

Visual Basic .NET provides two basic kinds of arrays. First, it provides the normal arrays that you get when you declare a variable by using parentheses. For example, the following code declares an array of Integers named squares. The array contains 11 items with indexes ranging from 0 to 10. The code loops over the items, setting each one's value. Next, it loops over the values again, adding them to a string. When it has finished building the string, the program displays the result.

```
Private Sub ShowSquares()
    Dim squares(10) As Integer

    For i As Integer = 0 To 10
        squares(i) = i * i
    Next i

    Dim txt As String = ""
    For i As Integer = 0 To 10
        txt &= squares(i).ToString & vbCrLf
    Next i
    MessageBox.Show(txt)
End Sub
```

Visual Basic's Array class provides another kind of array. This kind of array is actually an object that provides methods for managing the items stored in the array.

The following code shows the previous version of the code rewritten to use an Array object. This version creates the array by using the Array class's shared CreateInstance method, passing it the data type that the array should contain and the number of items that it should hold. The code then loops over the items using the array's SetValue method to set the items' values. If you have Option Strict turned off, the code can set the items' values exactly as before by using the statement squares(i) = i * i. If Option Strict is on, you need to use SetValue. Next, the program loops over the items again, using the array's GetValue method to add the item values to a string. If Option Strict is off, you can use the same syntax as before: txt &= squares(i).ToString & vbCrLf. If Option Strict is on, you need to use the array's GetValue method. After building the string, the program displays it in a message box as before.

```
Private Sub ShowSquares()
    Dim squares As Array = _
        Array.CreateInstance(GetType(Integer), 11)

    For i As Integer = 0 To 10
        squares.SetValue(i * i, i)
    Next i

    Dim txt As String = ""
    For i As Integer = 0 To 10
        txt &= squares.GetValue(i).ToString & vbCrLf
    Next i
    MessageBox.Show(txt)
End Sub
```

The following sections describe the similarities and differences between normal arrays and `Array` objects.

Array Dimensions

Both normal variable arrays and `Array` objects can support multiple dimensions. The following statement declares a three-dimensional array with 11 items in the first dimension, 11 in the second, and 21 in the third. It then sets the value for the item in position (1, 2, 3).

```
Dim values(10, 10, 20) As Integer
values(1, 2, 3) = 100
```

The following code does the same thing with an `Array` object:

```
Dim values As Array = _
    Array.CreateInstance(GetType(Integer), 11, 21, 31)
    values.SetValue(100, 1, 2, 3)
```

If Option Strict is off, the code can use the same syntax for getting and setting the `Array` item's value. The following code sets the (1, 2, 3) item's value to 100 and then displays its value:

```
Option Explicit Off
...
values(1, 2, 3) = 100
Debug.WriteLine(values(1, 2, 3))
```

Lower Bounds

A normal array of variables always has lower bound 0 in every dimension. The following code declares an array with indexes ranging from 0 to 10:

```
Dim values(10) As Integer
```

You can fake a variable array that has nonzero lower bounds, but it requires extra work on your part. You must add or subtract an appropriate amount from each index to map the indexes you want to use to zero-based indexes.

The following code fragment uses an index variable i that ranges from 100 to 110. The code subtracts 100 from each index to map the values 100 to 110 to the values 0 to 10. If you wanted a multi-dimensional array with nonzero lower bounds, you would need to add or subtract from the indexes in each dimension.

```
For i As Integer = 100 To 110
    values(i - 100) = i
Next i
```

Array objects can handle nonzero lower bounds for you. The following code creates a two-dimensional array with indexes ranging from 1 to 10 in the first dimension, and 101 to 120 in the second dimension. First, it defines an array containing the lower bounds it wants to use for each dimension. Next, it defines an array containing the number of elements it wants for each dimension.

The code then calls the Array class's shared CreateInstance method, passing it the data type of the array's objects, the array of dimension lengths, and the array of lower bounds. The CreateInstance method uses the arrays of lower bounds and dimensions to create an Array object with the appropriate bounds.

```
Dim lower_bounds() As Integer = {1, 101}
Dim dimension_lengths() As Integer = {10, 20}
Dim values As Array = _
    Array.CreateInstance(GetType(Integer), dimension_lengths, lower_bounds)
```

The following code sets the values in this array:

```
For i As Integer = 1 To 10
    For j As Integer = 101 To 120
        values.SetValue(i * 100 + j, i, j)
    Next j
Next i
```

If Option Explicit is off, the program can use the following simpler syntax:

```
For i As Integer = 1 To 10
    For j As Integer = 101 To 120
        values(i, j) = i * 100 + j
    Next j
Next i
```

Resizing

You can use the ReDim statement to change a normal array's dimensions. Add the Preserve keyword if you want the array to keep its existing values, as shown here:

```
Dim values(100) As Integer
...
ReDim Preserve values(200)
```

An Array object cannot resize itself, but it is relatively easy to copy an Array object's items to another Array object. The following code creates a values array containing 101 items with indexes ranging from 0 to 100. Later, it creates a new Array object containing 201 items and uses the values array's CopyTo method to copy its values into the new array. The second parameter to CopyTo gives the index in the destination array where the copy should start placing values.

```
Dim values As Array = _
    Array.CreateInstance(GetType(Integer), 101)
...
Dim new_array As Array = _
    Array.CreateInstance(GetType(Integer), 201)
values.CopyTo(new_array, 0)
values = new_array
```

The Array class's shared Copy method allows you greater control. It lets you specify the index in the source array where the copy should start, the index in the destination array where the items should be copied, and the number of items to be copied.

While building a new Array object and copying items into it is more cumbersome than using ReDim to resize a variable array, the process is surprisingly fast.

Speed

There's no doubt that arrays of variables are much faster than Array objects. In one test, setting and getting values in an Array object took more than 100 times as long as performing the same operations in a variable array.

If your application performs only a few hundred or a thousand array operations, the difference is unimportant. If your application must access array values many millions of times, you may need to consider using an array of variables even if the Array class would be more convenient for other reasons (such as nonzero lower bounds).

Microsoft has also optimized one-dimensional variable arrays, so they are faster than multidimensional arrays. The difference is much less dramatic than the difference between variable arrays and Array classes, however.

The following code compares the speeds of a one-dimensional array and a two-dimensional array. After some setup, it creates a one-dimensional array, fills it with values, and displays the elapsed time.

Next, the program erases the first array to free its memory. If you don't do this, then the second array might use up all of the system's memory and force the program to swap data to the disk. That greatly slows the program and makes the two-dimensional array seem even slower than it really is.

The program then creates the two-dimensional array, fills it with values, and displays the elapsed time. It repeats these steps for one- and two-dimensional Array objects as well.

```
Private Sub btnGo_Click(ByVal sender As System.Object, _
 ByVal e As System.EventArgs) Handles btnGo.Click
    Dim start_time As DateTime
    Dim stop_time As DateTime
    Dim elapsed_time As TimeSpan

    ' Clear any previous results.
    lbl1D.Text = ""
```

```
lbl2D.Text = ""
lbl1Dclass.Text = ""
lbl2Dclass.Text = ""
Cursor = Cursors.WaitCursor
Refresh()

' Get the number of items.
Dim num_items As Integer = Integer.Parse(txtNumItems.Text)

' One-dimensional array.
Dim array1(0 To num_items - 1) As Integer
start_time = Now
For i As Integer = 0 To num_items - 1
    array1(i) = i
Next i
stop_time = Now
elapsed_time = stop_time.Subtract(start_time)
lbl1D.Text = elapsed_time.TotalSeconds().ToString
lbl1D.Refresh()

' Free the first array's memory.
Erase array1

' Two-dimensional array.
Dim array2(0 To 0, 0 To num_items - 1) As Integer
start_time = Now
For i As Integer = 0 To num_items - 1
    array2(0, i) = i
Next i
stop_time = Now
elapsed_time = stop_time.Subtract(start_time)
lbl2D.Text = elapsed_time.TotalSeconds().ToString

' Free the second array's memory.
Erase array2

' One-dimensional Array.
Dim array3 As Array = _
    Array.CreateInstance(GetType(Integer), num_items)
start_time = Now
For i As Integer = 0 To num_items - 1
    array3.SetValue(i, i)
Next i
stop_time = Now
elapsed_time = stop_time.Subtract(start_time)
lbl1Dclass.Text = elapsed_time.TotalSeconds().ToString
lbl1Dclass.Refresh()

' Free the Array's memory.
array3 = Nothing

' Two-dimensional Array.
Dim array4 As Array = _
    Array.CreateInstance(GetType(Integer), 1, num_items)
```

```
        start_time = Now
        For i As Integer = 0 To num_items - 1
            array4.SetValue(i, 0, i)
        Next i
        stop_time = Now
        elapsed_time = stop_time.Subtract(start_time)
        lbl2Dclass.Text = elapsed_time.TotalSeconds().ToString


        Cursor = Cursors.Default
    End Sub
```

Figure 17-1 shows the results. Variable arrays are much faster than array classes. One-dimensional variable arrays generally seem to be slightly faster than two-dimensional arrays.

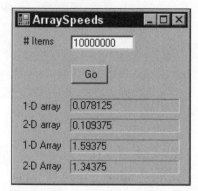

Figure 17-1: Variable arrays are faster than array classes.

Other Array Class Features

The `Array` class provides several other useful shared methods that were not available in Visual Basic 6 and earlier versions. For example, the `IndexOf` and `LastIndexOf` methods return the position of a particular item in an `Array` object's items. The following code creates an `Array` object and fills it with integers. It then displays the indexes of the first occurrence of the value 6 and the last occurrence of the value 3.

```
Dim values As Array = _
    Array.CreateInstance(GetType(Integer), 11)
For i As Integer = 0 To 10
    values.SetValue(i, i)
Next i

MessageBox.Show(Array.IndexOf(values, 6).ToString)
MessageBox.Show(Array.LastIndexOf(values, 3).ToString)
```

Methods such as `IndexOf` and `LastIndexOf` would be a strong argument supporting `Array` objects over normal arrays of variables if it weren't for one somewhat surprising fact: Those same methods work with regular arrays of variables, too! The following code is similar to the previous example, except that it uses an array of variables instead of an `Array` object:

481

```
Dim values(10) As Integer
For i As Integer = 0 To 10
    values(i) = i
Next i

MessageBox.Show(Array.IndexOf(values, 6).ToString)
MessageBox.Show(Array.LastIndexOf(values, 3).ToString)
```

The following sections describe some of the `Array` class's other useful shared methods. All of these work both for arrays of variables and `Array` objects.

Array.Reverse

The `Array.Reverse` method reverses the order of the items in an array. The following code demonstrates this method. It builds and initializes an array of integers, calls `Array.Reverse`, and then displays the items in their new order.

```
Dim values(10) As Integer
For i As Integer = 0 To 10
    values(i) = i
Next i

Array.Reverse(values)

Dim txt As String
For i As Integer = 0 To 10
    txt &= values(i) & " "
Next i
MessageBox.Show(txt)
```

There's nothing particular confusing about this method. It can easily reverse its items even if the items are not things that you can reasonably compare. For example, it can reverse an array of integers, strings, `StockOption` objects, or `TreeView` controls.

Array.Sort

The `Array.Sort` method sorts the items in the array. To sort the items, this method must compare them to each other. That means the items must be things that can be reasonably compared (such as integers, strings, or dates). More precisely, the method can sort the items if they implement the `IComparable` interface, meaning they contain the means to compare themselves to each other.

The following code shows a `Person` class that implements the `IComparable` interface. The class defines two public strings `FirstName` and `LastName`. For convenience, it also defines a constructor and a `ToString` function. The code then defines the `CompareTo` function that is required by the `IComparable` interface. This function should compare the value of the current object (object1) to the value of the object passed as a parameter (object2) and return the following: -1 if object1 should come before object2, 0 if neither object must come before the other, and 1 if object2 should come before object1. The `String.Compare` function makes exactly that calculation for two strings, so the `CompareTo` function uses it to compare the two `Person` objects' names. You could use a more complicated `CompareTo` function to order just about anything.

```
Public Class Person
    Implements IComparable

    Public FirstName As String
    Public LastName As String

    Public Sub New(ByVal first_name As String, ByVal last_name As String)
        FirstName = first_name
        LastName = last_name
    End Sub

    Public Overrides Function ToString() As String
        Return LastName & ", " & FirstName
    End Function

    Public Function CompareTo(ByVal obj As Object) As Integer _
      Implements System.IComparable.CompareTo
        Dim other_Person As Person = DirectCast(obj, Person)
        Return String.Compare(Me.ToString, other_Person.ToString)
    End Function
End Class
```

The following code makes and sorts an array of `Person` objects:

```
' Make the array of Person objects.
Dim people(4) As Person
people(0) = New Person("Rod", "Stephens")
people(1) = New Person("Sergio", "Aragones")
people(2) = New Person("Terry", "Pratchett")
people(3) = New Person("Homer", "Simpson")
people(4) = New Person("Eoin", "Colfer")

' Sort.
Array.Sort(people)

' Display the results.
Dim txt As String = ""
For i As Integer = 0 To people.GetUpperBound(0)
    txt &= people(i).ToString() & vbCrLf
Next i
MessageBox.Show(txt)
```

You can also sort objects that do not implement the `IComparable` interface if you pass the `Sort` method an object that can sort them. The following code defines a `Manager` class that is similar to the `Employee` class without the `IComparable` interface. It also defines a `ManagerComparer` class that implements the `IComparer` interface. This class's `Compare` method takes two objects as parameters and returns -1, 0, or 1 to indicate which should come before the other.

```
Public Class Manager
    Public FirstName As String
    Public LastName As String

    Public Sub New(ByVal first_name As String, ByVal last_name As String)
        FirstName = first_name
```

```
            LastName = last_name
        End Sub

        Public Overrides Function ToString() As String
            Return LastName & ", " & FirstName
        End Function
End Class

Public Class ManagerComparer
    Implements IComparer

    Public Function Compare(ByVal x As Object, ByVal y As Object) As Integer _
      Implements System.Collections.IComparer.Compare
        Dim mgr1 As Manager = DirectCast(x, Manager)
        Dim mgr2 As Manager = DirectCast(y, Manager)

        Return String.Compare(mgr1.ToString, mgr2.ToString)
    End Function
End Class
```

The call to `DirectCast` converts its parameters from one type to another. In this code, it converts the variables *x* and *y* into *Manager* objects.

Note that `DirectCast` only works if the variables are of the new type. In this case, we know that variables *x* and *y* are *Manager* objects that have been passed to the *Compare* function as *Object* variables.

If the variables have some other type that can be converted into the desired type, you would need to use *CType* instead of *DirectCast*. For example, suppose that *x* and *y* were *Supervisor* objects and *Supervisor* is a subclass of *Manager*. Then you could convert *x* and *y* into *Manager* objects because a *Supervisor* is a type of *Manager*, but you would need to use *CType* instead of *DirectCast*.

The following code uses a `ManagerComparer` object to sort an array of `Manager` objects:

```
' Make the array of Manager objects.
Dim managers(4) As Manager
managers(0) = New Manager("Rod", "Stephens")
managers(1) = New Manager("Sergio", "Aragones")
managers(2) = New Manager("Terry", "Pratchett")
managers(3) = New Manager("Homer", "Simpson")
managers(4) = New Manager("Eoin", "Colfer")

' Make a comparer.
Dim manager_comparer As New ManagerComparer

' Sort.
Array.Sort(managers, manager_comparer)

' Display the results.
Dim txt As String = ""
For i As Integer = 0 To managers.GetUpperBound(0)
    txt &= managers(i).ToString() & vbCrLf
Next i
MessageBox.Show(txt)
```

Other overloaded versions of the Sort method let you sort two arrays (one containing keys and the other values) in tandem or sort only parts of the array.

Array.BinarySearch

If the array contains items that are sorted, and the items implement the IComparable interface, the Array.BinarySearch method uses a binary search algorithm to locate a specific item within the array.

For example, suppose that the array contains Person objects as defined in the previous section. Then you could use the following code to find the object representing "Rod Stephens" in the people array. The code starts by using Array.Sort to sort the array. If you know that the array is already sorted, the program can skip this step. Next the program makes a new Person object that has the name "Rod Stephens." The program needs this object to represent the target. The program calls the ArrayBinarySearch method to find the index of the object with the target name and saves the result in the variable target_index. It then uses that index to assign the target_person variable to the corresponding Person object in the array.

```
' Sort the array.
Array.Sort(people)

' Find Rod Stephens.
Dim target_person As New Person("Rod", "Stephens")
Dim target_index As Integer = Array.BinarySearch(people, target_person)
target_person = people(target_index)
MessageBox.Show(target_person.ToString)
```

Binary search is extremely fast. To understand why, you must understand how the algorithm works. The details are tricky, but the idea is straightforward. At each step, the program picks the item in the middle of the part of the array that it is considering and compares it to the target item. If the target comes before the middle item, then the algorithm repeats the search in the first half of the items. If the target comes after the middle item, the algorithm repeats the search in the second half of the items.

Figure 17-2 illustrates a binary search for the value 12. The program starts considering the whole array. It picks the item in the middle with value 9 and compares it to the target 12. The target value 12 is greater than 9, so the routine discards the items on the left and considers those with values 12 through 22.

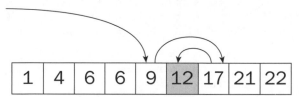

Figure 17-2: Binary search quickly locates a target value in an array.

Next, the program picks the middle item from those remaining and compares it to the target. The middle value 17 is greater than 12, so the program discards the items to the right and considers the remaining items to the left. In this example, only one item remains and it has the target value 12.

In this example, a binary search needs to examine only three items to find the target value 12. More generally, each time it examines an item, the program removes half of the remaining items from consideration. If the array contains N items, then the algorithm only needs to repeat this process $\text{Log}_2(N)$ times before it has found the target or eliminated every item from consideration. For example, if the array contains $1,048,576 = 2^{20}$ items, then the program will need to examine only around 20 items before it finds the target. That's pretty fast! An array large enough to really slow binary search down would be so large that you probably couldn't store it all in your computer's memory at once anyway. For such huge arrays, you would be better off storing the data in a database and using a database engine to search it.

Collections

Visual Basic's collection classes basically hold items and don't provide a lot of extra functionality. Other classes described later in this chapter provide more features.

The following sections describe Visual Basic's simple collection classes: `ArrayList`, `StringCollection`, and `NameValueCollection`. They also describe strongly typed collections that you can build to make code that uses these classes a bit easier to debug and maintain.

ArrayList

The `ArrayList` class is a resizable array. You can add and remove items from any position in the list and it resizes itself accordingly. The following table describes some of the class's more useful properties and methods.

Property/Method	Purpose
Add	Adds an item at the end of the list.
AddRange	Adds the items in an object implementing the `ICollection` interface to the end of the list.
BinarySearch	Returns the index of an item in the list. The items must implement the `IComparable` interface, or you must provide the `Sort` method with an `IComparer` object.
Capacity	Gets or sets the number of items that the list can hold. For example, if you know that you will need to add 1000 items to the list, you may get better performance by setting `Capacity` to 1000 before starting, rather than letting the object grow incrementally as you add the items.
Clear	Removes all of the items from the list. The `Capacity` property remains unchanged, so the `ArrayList` keeps any space it has previously allocated to improve performance.
Contains	Returns `True` if a specified item is in the list.
CopyTo	Copies some or the entire list into a one-dimensional `Array` object.
Count	The number of items currently in the list. This is always less than or equal to `Capacity`.
GetRange	Returns an `ArrayList` containing the items in part of the list.
IndexOf	Returns the zero-based index of the first occurrence of a specified item in the list.

Property/Method	Purpose
Insert	Adds an item at a particular position in the list.
InsertRange	Adds the items in an object implementing the ICollection interface to a particular position in the list.
Item	Returns the item at a particular position in the list.
LastIndexOf	Returns the zero-based index of the last occurrence of a specified item in the list.
Remove	Removes the first occurrence of a specified item from the list.
RemoveAt	Removes the item at the specified position in the list.
RemoveRange	Removes the items in the specified positions from the list.
Reverse	Reverses the order of the items in the list.
SetRange	Replaces the items in part of the list with new items taken from an ICollection object.
Sort	Sorts the items in the list. The items must implement the IComparable interface, or you must provide the Sort method with an IComparer object.
ToArray	Copies the list's items into a one-dimensional array.
TrimToSize	Reduces the list's allocated space so that it is just big enough to hold its items. This sets Capacity = Count.

The ToArray method can copy the items into an array of objects, an array of a specific type, or an Array object (holding objects). The following code demonstrates each of these. ToArray returns a generic array of Object even if the objects are some other data type such as strings, so the second method must use a DirectCast statement to convert the result into an array of strings, if Option Strict is On.

```
' Declare and initialize the ArrayList.
Dim array_list As New ArrayList
array_list.Add("Apple")
array_list.Add("Banana")
array_list.Add("Cherry")
...

' Array of objects.
Dim obj_array() As Object
obj_array = array_list.ToArray()

' Array of strings.
Dim string_array() As String
string_array = DirectCast(array_list.ToArray(GetType(String)), String())

' Array object of objects.
Dim astring_array As Array
astring_array = array_list.ToArray()
```

A single `ArrayList` object can hold objects of many different kinds. The following code creates an `ArrayList` and adds a string, `Form` object, integer, and `Bitmap` to it. It then loops through the items in the list and displays their types.

```
Dim array_list As New ArrayList
array_list.Add("What?")
array_list.Add(Me)
array_list.Add(1001)
array_list.Add(New Bitmap(10, 10))
For Each obj As Object In array_list
    Debug.WriteLine(obj.GetType.ToString)
Next obj
```

The following text shows the results:

```
System.String
UseArrayList.Form1
System.Int32
System.Drawing.Bitmap
```

The value displayed for the second item depends on the name of the project (in this case, "UseArrayList").

StringCollection

A `StringCollection` is similar to an `ArrayList`, except that it can hold only strings. Because it works only with strings, this class provides some extra type checking that the `ArrayList` does not. If your program tries to add an `Employee` object to a `StringCollection`, the collection raises an error.

To take advantage of this extra error checking, you should always use a `StringCollection` instead of an `ArrayList` if you are working with strings. Of course, if you need other features (such as the fast lookups provided by a `Hashtable`), you should use one of the classes described in the following sections.

Strongly Typed Collections

A *strongly typed collection* is a collection class built to work with a particular data type. An `ArrayList` can store objects of any data type. A `StringCollection` is strongly typed to work only with strings. That gives you extra error checking that makes finding and fixing programming mistakes easier. If the program tries to insert an `IncidentReport` object into a `StringCollection`, the collection immediately raises an error and the problem is relatively easy to find.

Similarly, you can define your own collection classes that are strongly typed. For example, you could make an `OrderCollection` class that holds `Order` items. If the program tries to add a `Manager` or `Secretary` object to it, the collection raises an error.

To build a strongly typed collection "from scratch," create a new class that inherits from `System.Collections.CollectionBase`. Inheriting from this class automatically gives your class an `ArrayList` object named `List`. It also gives your class some inherited routines that do not depend on the type of object you want the collection to hold. For example, the `RemoveAt` method removes the object at a specific index in the list. It doesn't care whether the collection holds `Employee` objects, bitmaps, or Pizzas, so the parent class `CollectionBase` can implement it for you.

Your class can implement other methods for adding and retrieving items in the collection. For example, it can implement the Add, Remove, and Item methods.

Fortunately, you don't need to build these methods from scratch. You can simply delegate them to the inherited List object. For example, the Add method can simply call List.Add, as shown in the following code:

```
' Add an Employee.
Public Sub Add(ByVal value As Employee)
    List.Add(value)
End Sub
```

This code does nothing other than call the List object's methods. The only magic here is that the EmployeeCollection class's Add method takes a parameter of a particular type (Employee), while the List object's Add method takes a generic Object as a parameter. It is the EmployeeCollection class's insistence on Employee objects that makes the collection strongly typed.

The Add and Item methods are about the minimum useful feature set you can provide for a strongly typed collection class.

The following table lists the standard methods provided by a strongly typed collection class. The third column indicates whether the CollectionBase parent class automatically provides the method, or whether you must delegate the method to the List object.

Method	Purpose	Provided By
Add	Adds an item to the collection	List
Capacity	Returns the amount of space in the collection	CollectionBase
Clear	Removes all items from the collection	CollectionBase
Contains	Returns True if the collection contains a particular item	List
CopyTo	Copies items from the collection into an array	List
Count	Returns the number of items in the collection	CollectionBase
IndexOf	Returns the index of an item	List
InnerList	Returns an ArrayList holding the collection's objects	CollectionBase
Insert	Inserts an item at a specific position	List
Item	Returns the item at a specific position	List
List	Returns an IList holding the collection's objects	CollectionBase
Remove	Removes an item	List
RemoveAt	Removes the item at a specific position	CollectionBase

You can also add other more specialized methods if they would be useful in your application. For example, you could add methods for working with object field values rather than with the objects themselves. You might make an overloaded version of the Item method that takes as parameters a first and last name and returns the corresponding Employee object if it is in the list. You could also modify the simple Add method shown previously so that it doesn't allow duplicates. And, you could make an Add function that takes first and last names as parameters, creates a new Employee object using those names, and returns the new object.

The following code shows a complete EmployeeCollection class. Most of its methods are straightforward delegations to the List object. The most interesting method is the Item property. This method is implemented as a read-only property, so it can include the Default keyword (which is not allowed on functions). This keyword marks Item as the class's default property and that allows a program to access it by providing an index to an object of the class as in emp_collection(3). Notice that the Item property procedure uses DirectCast to convert the generic Object stored in List into an Employee object.

```
' A strongly typed collection of Employees.
Public Class EmployeeCollection
    Inherits CollectionBase

    ' Add an Employee.
    Public Sub Add(ByVal value As Employee)
        List.Add(value)
    End Sub

    ' Return True if the collection contains this employee.
    Public Function Contains(ByVal value As Employee) As Boolean
        Return List.Contains(value)
    End Function

    ' Return this Employee's index.
    Public Function IndexOf(ByVal value As Employee) As Integer
        Return List.IndexOf(value)
    End Function

    ' Insert a new Employee.
    Public Sub Insert(ByVal index As Integer, ByVal value As Employee)
        List.Insert(index, value)
    End Sub

    ' Return the Employee at this position.
    Default Public ReadOnly Property Item(ByVal index As Integer) As Employee
        Get
            Return DirectCast(List.Item(index), Employee)
        End Get
    End Property

    ' Remove an Employee.
    Public Sub Remove(ByVal value As Employee)
        List.Remove(value)
    End Sub
End Class
```

An additional benefit that comes with inheriting from the CollectionBase class is For Each loop support. The following code shows how a program might use this EmployeeCollection class. It creates the collection and adds five Employee objects to the list. It then uses a For Each loop to display the Employees.

```
Dim emp_list As New EmployeeCollection
emp_list.Add(New Employee("Ann", "Anderson"))
emp_list.Add(New Employee("Bart", "Baskerville"))
emp_list.Add(New Employee("Candy", "Cant"))
emp_list.Add(New Employee("Durk", "Distant"))
emp_list.Add(New Employee("Edwina", "Evers"))

For Each emp As Employee In emp_list
    Debug.WriteLine(emp.ToString)
Next emp
```

Generics provide another method for building strongly typed collections. See the section "Generics" later in this chapter for more information on generic collections. For more general information on generics, see Chapter 18, "Generics."

Read-Only Strongly Typed Collections

The CollectionBase class enables you to build a strongly typed collection class that allows a program to store and retrieve values. In some cases, you might want a function to return a collection of objects that the calling program cannot modify. For example, suppose that your function returns a list of your company's production locations. You don't want the program to modify the list because it cannot change the locations. In this case, you can build a read-only strongly typed collection.

You can do this much as you build a strongly typed collection. Instead of deriving the new collection class from CollectionBase, however, derive it from the ReadOnlyCollectionBase class. Provide read-only Item methods, but do not provide any Add or Remove methods. The class itself can access its inherited InnerList object to add and remove items, but it must not give the program using your class access to that object.

Your program still needs a way to get objects into the collection, however. One method is to build the collection class in a separate library project and give it initialization methods declared with the Friend keyword. Other code in the library project could use those methods while the main program could not.

Another technique is to pass initialization data to the class's constructor. Your code creates the collection and returns it to the main program. The main program cannot change the collection's contents. It can create an instance of the collection of its own, but it cannot modify the one you built.

NameValueCollection

The NameValueCollection class is a collection that can hold more than one string value for a particular key (name). For example, you might use employee names as keys. The string values associated with a particular key could include extension, job title, employee ID, and so forth.

Of course, you could also store the same information by putting extension, job title, employee ID, and the other fields in an object or structure, and then storing the objects or structures in some sort of collection class such as an ArrayList. A NameValueCollection, however, is very useful if you don't know ahead of time how many strings will be associated with each key.

The following table describes some of the NameValueCollection's most useful properties and methods.

Property/Method	Description
Add	Adds a new name/value pair to the collection. If the collection already holds an entry for the name, it adds the new value to that name's values.
AllKeys	Returns a string array holding all of the key values.
Clear	Removes all names and values from the collection.
CopyTo	Copies items starting at a particular index into a one-dimensional Array object. This copies only the items (see the Item property) not the keys.
Count	Returns the number of key/value pairs in the collection.
Get	Gets the item for a particular index or name as a comma-separated list of values.
GetKey	Returns the key for a specific index.
GetValues	Returns a string array containing the values for a specific name or index.
HasKeys	Returns True if the collection contains any non-null keys.
Item	Gets or sets the item for a particular index or name as a comma-separated list of values.
Keys	Returns a collection containing the keys.
Remove	Removes a particular name and all of its values.
Set	Sets the item for a particular index or name as a comma-separated list of values.

The following code demonstrates some of these features. It creates a NameValueCollection and fills it with values. It associates the name Food with the values Sandwich, Salad, and Taco. It associates the name Dessert with the values Ice Cream, Pie, Cake, and Cookie. Next, the code loops through the collection's keys. For each key, it displays the key's name, uses the collection's GetValues method to get an array containing the corresponding values, and then displays those values. The code then displays the values again in comma-separated lists. It again loops through the collection's keys, this time using the Item method to display each key's list of values.

```
Dim nvc As New NameValueCollection
nvc.Add("Food", "Sandwich")
nvc.Add("Food", "Salad")
nvc.Add("Food", "Taco")
nvc.Add("Dessert", "Ice Cream")
nvc.Add("Dessert", "Pie")
nvc.Add("Dessert", "Cake")
nvc.Add("Dessert", "Cookie")

Dim values() As String
For Each key As String In nvc.Keys
```

```
        Debug.WriteLine(key & ":")
        values = nvc.GetValues(key)
        For Each value As String In values
            Debug.WriteLine("    " & value)
        Next value
    Next key

    Debug.WriteLine("*****")
    For Each key As String In nvc.Keys
        Debug.WriteLine(key & ": " & nvc.Item(key))
    Next key
```

The following text shows the result:

```
Food:
    Sandwich
    Salad
    Taco
Dessert:
    Ice Cream
    Pie
    Cake
    Cookie
*****
Food: Sandwich,Salad,Taco
Dessert: Ice Cream,Pie,Cake,Cookie
```

Note that there is no easy way to remove a particular value from a name. For example, it's not trivial to remove the value Pie from the name Dessert. The following statement shows one method, although you would need to modify it slightly if you didn't know whether the Pie entry was last in the list (so it might or might not be followed by a comma):

```
nvc.Item("Dessert") = nvc.Item("Dessert").Replace("Pie,", "")
```

Dictionaries

A *dictionary* is a collection that associates keys with values. You look up a key, and the dictionary provides you with the corresponding value. This is similar to the way a NameValueCollection works, except that a dictionary's keys and values need not be strings, and a dictionary associates each key with a single value object.

Visual Studio provides several different kinds of dictionary classes that are optimized for different uses. Their differences come largely from the ways in which they store data internally. While you don't need to understand the details of how the dictionaries work internally, you do need to know how they behave so that you can pick the best one for a particular purpose.

Because all of the dictionary classes provide the same service (associating keys with values), they have roughly the same properties and methods. The following table describes some of the most useful of these.

Property/Method	Description
Add	Adds a key/value pair to the dictionary.
Clear	Removes all key/value pairs from the dictionary.
Contains	Returns True if the dictionary contains a specific key.
CopyTo	Copies the dictionary's data starting at a particular position into a one-dimensional array of DictionaryEntry objects. The DictionaryEntry class has Key and Value properties.
Count	Returns the number of key/value pairs in the dictionary.
Item	Gets or sets the value associated with a key.
Keys	Returns a collection containing all of the dictionary's keys.
Remove	Removes the key/value pair with a specific key.
Values	Returns a collection containing all of the dictionary's values.

The following sections describe Visual Studio's different dictionary classes in more detail.

ListDictionary

A ListDictionary stores its data in a linked list. In a linked list, each item is held in an object that contains its data plus a reference or *link* to the next item in the list. Figure 17-3 illustrates a linked list. This list contains the key/value pairs Appetizer/Salad, Entrée/Sandwich, Drink/Water, and Dessert/Cupcake. The link out of the Dessert/Cupcake item is set to Nothing, so the program can tell when it has reached the end of the list. A reference variable inside the ListDictionary class, labeled Top in Figure 17-3, points to the first item in the list.

Adding and removing items in a linked list is simple. To add a new item at the top of the list, you create a new item, set its link to point to the item that is currently at the top, and then make the list's Top variable point to the new item.

To remove a target item from the list, you find the item before the target and set its link to point to the item after the target. This is a lot easier than removing an item from the middle of an array of contiguous items and then shifting everything over to fill in the hole.

Figure 17-4 shows the linked list from Figure 17-3 with a new Side/Fries item added at the top and the Drink/Water item removed.

Linked lists make adding and removing items from the dictionary easy. By using links, the list can rearrange itself without your needing to slide items back and forth, as you might in a contiguous array.

Unfortunately, if the list grows long, finding items can take a long time. To find an item in the list, the program starts at the top and works its way down, following the links between items, until it finds the one it wants. If the list is short, that doesn't take very long. If the list holds 100,000 items, this means potentially a 100,000-item crawl from top to bottom. That means a ListDictionary object's performance degrades if it contains too many items.

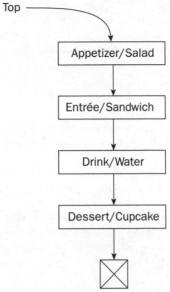

Figure 17-3: Each item in a linked list keeps a reference to the next item in the list.

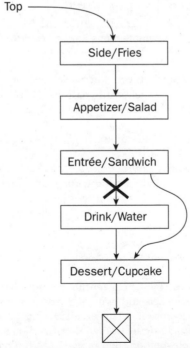

Figure 17-4: Adding and removing items from a linked list is relatively easy.

If you only need to store a few hundred items in the dictionary and you don't need to access them frequently, a ListDictionary is fine. If you need to store 100,000 entries, or if you need to access the dictionary's entries a huge number of times, you may get better performance using a "bigger" object such as a Hashtable. A Hashtable has more overhead than a ListDictionary but is faster at accessing its entries.

Hashtable

A Hashtable looks a lot like a ListDictionary on the outside, but internally it stores its data in a very different way. Rather than using a linked list, this class uses a hash table to hold data.

A hash table is a data structure that allows extremely fast access to items using their keys. It works by mapping an object's key into a bucket by calculating the key's *hash value*.

For example, suppose that you want to make a dictionary associating Employee objects with their Social Security numbers. You could make an array holding 10 buckets and then map employees to bucket numbers using the last digit of their Social Security numbers. Employee 123-45-6789 goes in bucket 9, employee 111-22-3333 goes in bucket 3, and employee 865-29-8361 goes in bucket 1, as shown in Figure 17-5.

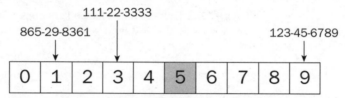

Figure 17-5: A Hashtable maps key values into buckets.

This kind of hash table is easy to enlarge. If you add a few dozen employees, you might use 100 buckets and map Social Security numbers using their last two digits. Then employee 123-45-6789 goes in bucket 89, employee 111-22-3333 goes in bucket 33, and employee 865-29-8361 goes in bucket 61.

More employees? Make more buckets! You can use 1000, 10,000, or more buckets if necessary.

To find an employee's data in the dictionary, you need only to calculate the hash value (last digits of Social Security number) and then look in that bucket. For a large dictionary, this is much faster than digging through a linked list. If you have 10,000 employees perfectly divided one to a bucket in a table of 10,000 buckets, you need only to look in one bucket to find the data you want. That's a lot faster than slogging through a 10,000-item linked list.

Of course, there is a catch. Actually, there are two catches.

First, if you have too many employees, you are eventually going to find two that map to the same bucket. Suppose that you have 10 buckets and two employees with Social Security numbers 732-45-7653 and 145-76-4583. These both map to bucket 3. This is called a *key collision*, and the hash table must use some sort of *collision resolution policy* to figure out what to do when two keys map to the same bucket. This policy is generally some simple method such as making a linked list in the bucket or letting the second item spill over into the following bucket. Whatever collision resolution scheme you use, it takes a little extra time to search through full buckets.

You can make the buckets less full if you use more of them. In this example, if you switched to 100 buckets, the two employees would map to buckets 53 and 83, so no collision occurs. That makes looking up these items faster.

The second catch is that you can make a hash table faster by adding more buckets, but using more buckets means using more space. When a hash table starts to fill up, collisions are common, so performance suffers. Add more space and performance improves, but there's a lot of "wasted" space not occupied by any data.

Those are the advantages and disadvantages of the Hashtable class. A Hashtable gives better performance than a ListDictionary, but takes more space.

In addition to the usual dictionary properties and methods, the Hashtable has a few that help manage the internal hash table that it uses to store its items.

One overloaded version of the Hashtable's constructor takes a parameter that tells how many items the table should initially be able to hold. If you know you are going to load 1000 items, you might make the table initially hold room for 1500. Then the program could add all the items without filling the table too much, so it would still give good performance. If you don't set an initial size, the hash table might need to resize itself many times before it could hold 1000 items, and that will slow it down.

Another version of the constructor lets you specify the hash table's *load factor*. The load factor is a number between 0.1 and 1.0 that gives the largest ratio of elements to buckets that the Hashtable will allow before it enlarges its internal table. For example, suppose that the hash table's capacity is 100 and its load factor is 0.8. Then when it holds 80 elements, the Hashtable will enlarge its internal table.

HybridDictionary

A HybridDictionary is a cross between a ListDictionary and a Hashtable. If the dictionary is small, the HybridDictionary stores its data in a ListDictionary. If the dictionary grows too large, HybridDictionary switches to a Hashtable.

If you know that you will only need a few items, you can use a ListDictionary. If you know you will need to use a very large number of items, you can use a Hashtable. If you are unsure whether you will have few or many items, you can hedge your bet with a HybridDictionary.

Strongly Typed Dictionaries

Just as you can make strongly typed collections, you can also make strongly typed dictionaries. The idea is exactly the same. You derive your strongly typed class from a class that supports basic dictionary functionality. In this case, that parent class is DictionaryBase, and it provides a Dictionary object that your class can use to implement its dictionary features.

Next, you implement dictionary methods such as Add, Item, Keys, and so forth. Your code requires specific data types and uses the parent class's Dictionary variable to do all the hard work through delegation.

The following table lists the standard methods provided by a strongly typed dictionary class. The third column indicates whether the DictionaryBase parent class automatically provides the method or whether you must delegate the method to the Dictionary object.

Method	Purpose	Provided By
Add	Adds a key/value pair to the dictionary	Dictionary
Clear	Removes all key/value pairs from the dictionary	DictionaryBase
Contains	Returns True if the dictionary contains a specific key	Dictionary
CopyTo	Copies elements from the dictionary into an Array of DictionaryEntry objects	DictionaryBase
Count	Returns the number of key/value pairs in the dictionary	DictionaryBase
Dictionary	Returns a Dictionary holding the dictionary's key/value pairs	DictionaryBase
InnerHashtable	Returns a Hashtable holding the dictionary's key/value pairs	DictionaryBase
Item	Returns the value corresponding to a specific key	Dictionary
Keys	Returns an ICollection containing the dictionary's keys	Dictionary
Remove	Removes the key/value pair for a specific key	Dictionary
Values	Returns an ICollection containing the dictionary's values	Dictionary

As is the case with strongly typed collections, you can add other more specialized methods if they would be useful in your application.

The following code shows an EmployeeDictionary class with keys that are strings and values that are Employee objects. The Add method takes a string and an Employee object as parameters, and passes them on to the Dictionary object's Add method. The Item property procedure gets or sets an item using a string key and an Employee object as a value. The property's get procedure uses the Dictionary object's Item method to get the object for a particular key. It uses DirectCast to turn the resulting generic Object into an Employee. The property's set procedure uses the Dictionary object's Item method to set the value for the key. The Keys and Values properties' get procedures simply pass their requests on to the Dictionary object. (Actually, the DictionaryBase class could provide these functions, since they return generic collections rather than, for example, collections of strings or Employee objects. For whatever reason, DictionaryBase doesn't do that.) Finally, the Contains and Remove methods take strongly typed string parameters and pass their requests along to the Dictionary object.

```
Public Class EmployeeDictionary
    Inherits System.Collections.DictionaryBase

    ' Add a Dictionary entry.
    Public Sub Add(ByVal new_key As String, ByVal new_employee As Employee)
        Dictionary.Add(new_key, new_employee)
    End Sub
```

```
        ' Return an object with the given key.
        Default Public Property Item(ByVal key As String) As Employee
            Get
                Return DirectCast(Dictionary.Item(key), Employee)
            End Get
            Set(ByVal Value As Employee)
                Dictionary.Item(key) = Value
            End Set
        End Property

        ' Return a collection containing the Dictionary's keys.
        Public ReadOnly Property Keys() As ICollection
            Get
                Return Dictionary.Keys
            End Get
        End Property

        ' Return a collection containing the Dictionary's values.
        Public ReadOnly Property Values() As ICollection
            Get
                Return Dictionary.Values
            End Get
        End Property

        ' Return True if the Dictionary contains this Employee.
        Public Function Contains(ByVal key As String) As Boolean
            Return Dictionary.Contains(key)
        End Function

        ' Remove this entry.
        Public Sub Remove(ByVal key As String)
            Dictionary.Remove(key)
        End Sub
End Class
```

The following code uses the EmployeeDictionary class. It makes a new EmployeeDictionary object and adds some Employee objects to it. It then uses the Item method to locate a particular object and display its data.

```
Dim dict As New EmployeeDictionary
dict.Add("123-45-6789", New Employee("Al", "Ankh"))
dict.Add("111-22-3333", New Employee("Bertie", "Bithoin"))
dict.Add("365-76-5476", New Employee("Carl", "Catabalpas"))
dict.Add("832-77-6847", New Employee("Dee", "Divers"))

Dim emp As Employee = dict.Item("365-76-5476")
MessageBox.Show(emp.ToString)
```

Other Strongly Typed Derived Classes

How a class stores its data internally is generally not a developer's concern. As long as it does its job, you shouldn't care whether the DictionaryBase class stores its data in a linked list, hash table, or some other data structure. (Although the DictionaryBase class has an InnerHashtable method that returns its data in a Hashtable form, so perhaps that's a hint.)

499

However, if you really want a strongly typed class that you know uses a `ListDictionary` instead of a hash table (or whatever `CollectionBase` uses), you could derive a strongly typed class from the `ListDictionary` class.

The following code shows the `EmployeeListDictionary` class, which is derived from the `ListDictionary` class. It uses the `Shadows` keyword to replace the `ListDictionary` class's `Add`, `Item`, `Contains`, and `Remove` methods with new strongly typed versions. Those methods simply pass their requests along to the base class `ListDictionary`.

```vb
Public Class EmployeeListDictionary
    Inherits ListDictionary

    ' Add a Dictionary entry.
    Public Shadows Sub Add(ByVal new_key As String, ByVal new_employee As Employee)
        MyBase.Add(new_key, new_employee)
    End Sub

    ' Return an object with the given key.
    Default Public Shadows Property Item(ByVal key As String) As Employee
        Get
            Return DirectCast(MyBase.Item(key), Employee)
        End Get
        Set(ByVal Value As Employee)
            MyBase.Item(key) = Value
        End Set
    End Property

    ' Return True if the Dictionary contains this Employee.
    Public Shadows Function Contains(ByVal key As String) As Boolean
        Return MyBase.Contains(key)
    End Function

    ' Remove this entry.
    Public Shadows Sub Remove(ByVal key As String)
        MyBase.Remove(key)
    End Sub
End Class
```

StringDictionary

The `StringDictionary` class uses a hash table to manage keys and values that are all strings. Because it uses a hash table, it can handle very large data sets quickly.

Its methods are strongly typed to require strings, so they provide extra type checking that can make finding potential bugs easier. For that reason, you should use a `StringDictionary` instead of a generic `ListDictionary` or `Hashtable` if you want to work exclusively with strings.

SortedList

The `SortedList` class acts as a `Hashtable`/`Array` hybrid. When you access a value by key, it acts as a hash table. When you access a value by index, it acts as an array containing items sorted by key value.

For example, suppose that you add a number of `Job` objects to a `SortedList` named `jobs` using their priorities as keys. Then `jobs(0)` always returns the job with the smallest priority value.

The following code shows an example. It makes a `SortedList` and then adds four items with priorities. Notice that it adds leading zeros to priorities less than 10, so their alphabetical order is the same as their numeric order. It then loops through the jobs displaying their keys and values. Next, the code clears the `SortedList` and creates similar items using integer values instead of strings as keys. Again it loops through the items displaying their keys and values.

```
Dim jobs As New SortedList
jobs.Add("02", "Two")
jobs.Add("10", "Ten")
jobs.Add("01", "One")
jobs.Add("06", "Six")

For i As Integer = 0 To jobs.Count - 1
    Debug.WriteLine(jobs.GetKey(i).ToString() & ": " & _
        jobs.GetByIndex(i).ToString())
Next i

jobs.Clear()
jobs.Add(2, "Two")
jobs.Add(10, "Ten")
jobs.Add(1, "One")
jobs.Add(6, "Six")

For i As Integer = 0 To jobs.Count - 1
    Debug.WriteLine(jobs.GetKey(i).ToString() & ": " & _
        jobs.GetByIndex(i).ToString())
Next i
```

The following text shows the results:

```
01: One
02: Two
06: Six
10: Ten
1: One
2: Two
6: Six
10: Ten
```

This code clears the `SortedList` before adding the second set of values with numeric keys. If it did not, the list would have raised an error when it tried to compare numeric and textual key values.

CollectionsUtil

Normally `Hashtables` and `SortedLists` are case-sensitive. The `CollectionsUtil` class provides two shared methods, `CreateCaseInsensitiveHashtable` and `CreateCaseInsensitiveSortedList`, that create `Hashtables` and `SortedLists` objects that are case-insensitive.

The following code creates a normal case-sensitive `SortedList`. It then adds two items with keys that differ only in their capitalization. This works because a case-sensitive `SortedList` treats the two keys as different values. The code then creates a case-insensitive `SortedList`. When it tries to add the same two items, the list raises an exception, complaining that it already has an object with key value "Sport."

```
Dim sorted_list As SortedList

' Use a normal, case-sensitive SortedList.
sorted_list = New SortedList
sorted_list.Add("Sport", "Volleyball")
sorted_list.Add("sport", "Golf")          ' Okay because Sport <> sport.

' Use a case-insensitive SortedList.
sorted_list = CollectionsUtil.CreateCaseInsensitiveSortedList()
sorted_list.Add("Sport", "Volleyball")
sorted_list.Add("sport", "Golf")          ' Error because Sport = sport.
```

If you can use case-insensitive `Hashtables` and `SortedLists`, you should generally do so. This prevents the program from adding two entries that are supposed to be the same but have different capitalization. For example, if one routine spells a key value "Law Suit" and another spells it "law suit," the case-insensitive `Hashtable` or `SortedList` will quickly catch the error.

Stacks and Queues

Stacks and *queues* are specialized data structures that are useful in many programming applications. These objects are useful for storing objects temporarily before you process them and remove them from the stack or queue. Visual Basic's `Stack` and `Queue` classes implement stacks and queues.

Usually, items are removed shortly after they are added. For example, an algorithm might fill a stack with objects to process and then, as long as the stack is not empty, remove one and process it. Processing one job might add others to the stack, which would be processed later. The process would continue until the stack was empty.

The difference between a stack and a queue is the order in which they return the items stored in them. The following two sections describe stacks and queues and explain the ways in which they return items.

Stack

A stack returns items in last in, first out (LIFO, pronounced "life-o") order. Because of the LIFO behavior, a stack is sometimes called a *LIFO list* or simply a *LIFO*.

Adding an item to the stack is called *pushing the item onto the stack* and removing an item is called *popping the item off of the stack*. These operations have the names push and pop because a stack is like a spring-loaded stack of plates in a cafeteria or buffet. You push new plates down onto the top of the stack and the plates sink into the counter. You pop the top plate off and the stack rises to give you the next plate.

Figure 17-6 illustrates this kind of stack. If you haven't seen this sort of thing before, don't worry about it. Just remember that push adds an item and pop removes the top item.

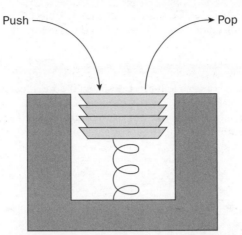

Figure 17-6: A Stack lets you remove items in last in, first out (LIFO) order.

Normally, you use a Stack object's Push and Pop methods to add and remove items, but the Stack class also provides some "cheating" methods that let you peek at the Stack's top object or convert the Stack into an array. The following table describes the Stack class's most useful properties and methods.

Property/Method	Purpose
Clear	Removes all items from the Stack.
Contains	Returns True if the Stack contains a particular object.
CopyTo	Copies some or all of the Stack's objects into a one-dimensional array.
Count	Returns the number of items in the Stack.
Peek	Returns a reference to the Stack's top item without removing it from the Stack.
Pop	Returns the Stack's top item and removes it from the Stack.
Push	Adds an item to the top of the Stack.
ToArray	Returns a one-dimensional array containing references to the objects in the Stack. The Stack's top item is placed first in the array.

A Stack allocates memory to stores its items. If you Push an object onto a Stack that is completely full, the Stack must resize itself to make more room and that slows the operation down.

To make memory management more efficient, the Stack class provides three overloaded constructors. The first takes no parameters and allocates a default initial capacity. The second takes as a parameter the number of items it should initially be able to hold. If you know that you will add 10,000 items to the Stack, you can avoid a lot of resizing by initially allocating room for 10,000 items.

The third version of the constructor takes as a parameter an object that implements the ICollection interface. The constructor allocates enough room to hold the items in the collection and copies them into the Stack.

The following code uses a stack to reverse the characters in a string. It gets the string from the txtInput TextBox and creates a stack. For each letter in the string, it adds the letter to the stack.

Next, while the stack is not empty, the program removes the top letter from the stack and adds it to the result string. Because the letters are popped off the stack in LIFO order, the result is the reverse of the original string.

```
Dim txt As String = txtInput.Text
Dim letter_stack As New Stack

' Add the letters to the stack.
For i As Integer = 0 To txt.Length - 1
    Debug.WriteLine(i)
    letter_stack.Push(txt.Substring(i, 1))
Next

' Remove the letters from the stack.
txt = ""
Do While letter_stack.Count > 0
    txt &= DirectCast(letter_stack.Pop(), String)
Loop

' Display the result.
lblResult.Text = txt
```

Queue

A queue returns items in first in, first out (FIFO, pronounced "fife-o") order. Because of the FIFO behavior, a queue is sometimes called a *FIFO list* or simply a *FIFO*.

A queue is similar to a line at a customer service desk. The first person in line is the first person to leave it when the service desk is free. Figure 17-7 illustrates a queue.

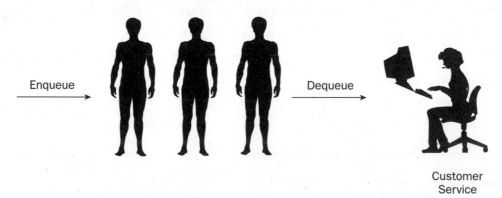

Figure 17-7: In a queue, items are removed in first in, first out (FIFO) order.

Queues are particularly useful for processing items in the order in which they were created. For example, an order-processing application might keep orders in a queue so that customers who place orders first are satisfied first (or at least their order is shipped first, whether they are satisfied or not).

Historically, the routines that add and remove items from a queue are called Enqueue and Dequeue. The following table describes these methods and the Queue class's other most useful properties and methods.

Property/Method	Purpose
Clear	Removes all items from the Queue.
Contains	Returns True if the Queue contains a particular object.
CopyTo	Copies some or all of the Queue's objects into a one-dimensional array.
Count	Returns the number of items in the Queue.
Dequeue	Returns the item that has been in the Queue the longest and removes it from the Queue.
Enqueue	Adds an item to the back of the Queue.
Peek	Returns a reference to the Queue's oldest item without removing it from the Queue.
ToArray	Returns a one-dimensional array containing references to the objects in the Queue. The Queue's oldest item is placed first in the array.
TrimToSize	Frees empty space in the Queue to set its capacity equal to the number of items it actually contains.

A Queue object stores its items in a circular array, as shown in Figure 17-8. The array isn't really circular; the Queue just pretends it is. If it goes past the last item in the normal one-dimensional array, the Queue wraps around to the first item as if the array were circular.

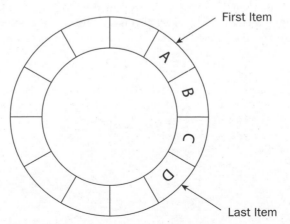

Figure 17-8: A Queue stores its items in a circular array.

Counters keep track of where the first and last items in the Queue are stored. When you Dequeue an item, the Queue returns the first item and moves the first item pointer to the next item in the array. When you Enqueue an item, the Queue places the new item after the last item and updates the last item pointer.

If you Enqueue an item when the Queue's array is full, the Queue must resize its array to make more room and that slows down the operation. To make memory management more efficient, the Queue class provides four overloaded constructors. The first takes no parameters and allocates a default initial capacity. If the Queue is full, it enlarges its array by a default growth factor.

The second constructor takes as a parameter its initial capacity. If you know that you will add 600 items to the Queue, you can save some time by initially allocating room for 600 items. With this constructor, the Queue also uses a default growth factor.

The third constructor takes as a parameter an object that implements the ICollection interface. The constructor allocates enough room to hold the items in the collection and copies them into the Queue. It also uses a default growth factor.

The final version of the constructor takes as parameters an initial capacity and a growth factor between 1.0 and 10.0. A larger growth factor will mean that the Queue resizes itself less often, but it may contain many empty array entries.

Queues are useful for scheduling items in a FIFO order. For example, a shared network computer uses a queue. Users on different computers send jobs to the printer, and they are printed in FIFO order.

The following code shows how a program might use a queue to arrange strings for output. When you click the btnAdd1 Button control, the program takes the text from the txtInput1 TextBox control and adds it to the queue. It then calls subroutine DisplayQueue to show the items currently in the queue. Other Button event handlers not shown similarly take strings from other TextBox controls and add them to the queue.

When you click the btnDequeue Button, the program removes the first entry from the queue and adds it to the lstResult ListBox. It then calls DisplayQueue again to show the queue's contents.

Subroutine DisplayQueue uses the queue's ToArray method to fetch the items in the queue. It loops through the items, adding them to a ListBox, so you can see what's in the queue. Note that the code uses DirectCast to convert the generic Object array entries into Strings.

```
' Create the queue.
Private m_Queue As New Queue

' Add an item to the queue.
Private Sub btnAdd1_Click(ByVal sender As System.Object, _
 ByVal e As System.EventArgs) Handles btnAdd1.Click
    m_Queue.Enqueue(txtInput1.Text)
    DisplayQueue()
End Sub

' Other routines for adding items to the queue.
...
```

```
' Remove the first item from the queue.
Private Sub btnDequeue_Click(ByVal sender As System.Object, _
 ByVal e As System.EventArgs) Handles btnDequeue.Click
    Dim txt As String = DirectCast(m_Queue.Dequeue(), String)
    lstResult.Items.Add(txt)
    DisplayQueue()
End Sub

' Display the items in the queue.
Private Sub DisplayQueue()
    lstQueue.Items.Clear()
    For Each str As String In m_Queue.ToArray()
        lstQueue.Items.Add(str)
    Next str

    ' Enable or disable the Dequeue button.
    btnDequeue.Enabled = (m_Queue.Count > 0)
End Sub
```

Generics

The System.Collections.Generic namespace provides several generic collection classes that you can use to build strongly typed collections. These collections work with a specific data type that you supply in a variable's declaration. For example, the following code makes a List that holds strings:

```
Imports System.Collections.Generic

...
Dim places As New List(Of String)
places.Add("Chicago")
```

The places object's methods are strongly typed and work only with strings, so they provide extra error protection that a less specialized collection doesn't provide. To take advantage of this extra protection, you should use generic collections or strongly typed collections derived from the CollectionBase class whenever possible.

When you derive a strongly typed collection from the CollectionBase class, you can add extra convenience functions to it. For example, an EmployeeCollection class could include an overloaded version of the Add method that accepts first and last names as parameters, makes a new Employee object, and adds it to the collection.

You cannot directly modify a generic collection class, but you can derive an enhanced collection from one. For example, the following code defines an EmployeeCollection class that inherits from the generic Collection(Of Employee). It then adds an overloaded version of the Add method that takes first and last names as parameters.

```
Imports System.Collections.Generic

Public Class EmployeeList
    Inherits List(Of Employee)
```

```
        Public Overloads Sub Add(ByVal first_name As String, ByVal last_name As String)
            Dim emp As New Employee(first_name, last_name)
            MyBase.Add(emp)
        End Sub
    End Class
```

The following table lists the some of the most useful classes defined by the System.Collections.Generic namespace.

Collection	Purpose
Comparer	Compares two objects of the specific type and returns -1, 0, or 1 to indicate whether the first is less than, equal to, or greater than the second
Dictionary	A strongly typed dictionary
LinkedList	A strongly typed linked list
LinkedListNode	A strongly typed node in a linked list
List	A strongly typed list
Queue	A strongly typed queue
SortedDictionary	A strongly typed sorted dictionary
SortedList	A strongly typed sorted list
Stack	A strongly typed stack

For more information on generics (including instructions for writing your own generic classes), see Chapter 18, "Generics."

Summary

This chapter describes five types of objects: arrays, collections, dictionaries, stacks, and queues. It also explains how to convert any of these into strongly typed classes and how to use generic collections.

Arrays store objects sequentially. They allow fast access at any point in the array. The Array class lets you make arrays indexed with nonzero lower bounds, although they provide slower performance than arrays of variables, which require lower bounds of zero. The Array class provides several useful methods for working with Array objects and normal variable arrays, including Sort, Reverse, IndexOf, LastIndexOf, and BinarySearch.

Collections store data in ways that are different from those used by arrays. An ArrayList stores items in a linked list. That works well for short lists, but slows down when the list grows large. A StringCollection holds a collection of strings. StringCollection is an example of a strongly typed collection (it holds only strings). The NameValueCollection class is a specialized collection that can hold more than one string value for a given key value.

Dictionaries associate key values with corresponding data values. You look up the key to find the data much as you might look up a word in the dictionary to find its definition. The ListDictionary class stores its data in a linked list. It is fast for small data sets but slow when it contains too much data. A Hashtable, on the other hand, has substantial overhead, but is extremely fast for large dictionaries. A HybridDictionary acts as a ListDictionary if it doesn't contain too much data, and switches to a Hashtable when it gets too big. The StringDictionary class is basically a Hashtable that is strongly typed to work with strings. The SortedList class is a Hashtable/Array hybrid that lets you access values by key or in sorted order.

Stacks provide access to items in last in, first out (LIFO) order, while Queues give access to their items in first in, first out (FIFO) order.

The generic Dictionary, LinkedList, List, Queue, SortedDictionary, SortedList, and Stack classes enable you to use strongly typed data structures without going to the trouble of building your own strongly typed classes.

All of these classes, plus other strongly typed collections that you can derive from the CollectionBase, DictionaryBase, and other classes, providing significant flexibility and options, so you can pick the class that best satisfies your needs. Deciding which class is best can be tricky, but making the right choice can mean the difference between a program that processes a large data set in seconds, hours, or not at all. Spend some time reviewing the different characteristics of the class so that you can make the best choice possible.

This chapter explains how you can use the generic collection classes provided by the System.Collections .Generic namespace to build strongly typed collection classes of several useful types. Chapter 18, "Generics," explains how you can build generic classes of your own. Using generics, you can build strongly typed classes that manipulate objects in any way you can imagine.

Generics

Classes are often described as cookie cutters for creating objects. You define a class, and then you can use it to make any number of objects that are instances of the class.

Similarly, a *generic* is like a cookie cutter for creating classes. You define a generic, and then you can use it to create any number of classes that have similar features.

For example, Visual Basic comes with a generic List class. You can use it to make lists of strings, lists of integers, lists of Employee objects, or lists of just about anything else.

This chapter explains generics. It shows how you define generics of your own and how you can use them.

Advantages of Generics

A generic class is tied to one or more specific data types. For example, you can build a list of OrderItem objects, a hash table containing PurchaseOrders identified by number, or a Queue that contains Customer objects.

Tying generics to specific data types gives them a few advantages over more traditional classes:

❑ *Strong typing* — Methods can take parameters and return values that have the class's instance type. For example, a List(Of String) can only hold string values, and its Item method returns string values. This makes it more difficult to accidentally add the wrong type of object to the collection.

❑ *IntelliSense* — By providing strong typing, a class built from a generic lets Visual Studio provide IntelliSense. If you make a List(Of Employee), Visual Studio knows that the items in the collection are Employee objects, so it can give you appropriate IntelliSense.

❑ *No boxing* — Because the class manipulates objects with a specific data type, Visual Basic doesn't need to convert items to and from the plain Object data type. For example, if a program stores TextBox controls in a normal collection, the program must convert the TextBox controls to and from the Object class when it adds and uses items in the collection. Avoiding these steps makes the code more efficient.

❑ *Code reuse* — You can use a generic class with more than one data type. For example, if you have built a generic `PriorityQueue` class, then you can make a `PriorityQueue` holding `Employee`, `Customer`, `Order`, or `Objection` objects. Without generics, you would need to build four separate classes to build strongly typed priority queues for each of these types of objects. Reusing this code makes it easier to write, test, debug, and maintain the code.

Defining Generics

Visual Basic allows you to define generic classes, structures, interfaces, procedures, and delegates. The basic syntax is similar, so once you understand how to make generic classes, the others should be fairly easy.

To define a generic class, make a class declaration as usual. After the class name, add a parenthesis, the keyword `Of`, and a placeholder for a data type. For example, the following code shows the outline of a generic `MostRecentList` class. Its declaration takes one type that the class internally names `ItemType`. This is similar to a variable name that you would give to a subroutine. The class's code can use the name `ItemType` to refer to the type associated with the instance of the generic class.

```
Public Class MostRecentList(Of ItemType)
    ...
End Class
```

For example, suppose that you want to make a list that can act as a most recently used (MRU) file list. It should be able to hold at most four items. New items are added at the top of the list, and the others are bumped down one position with the last item being dropped if the list contains too many items. If you add an existing item to the list, it jumps to the top of the list.

The following code shows a generic `MostRecentList` class. The `Of ItemType` clause indicates that the class will take a single type that it internally names `ItemType`. The class stores its items in a private list named `m_Items`. It declares this list using the generic list class defined in the System.Collections.Generic namespace, and it indicates that this is a list that will hold `ItemType` objects. This refers to the `ItemType` parameter used in the generic `MostRecentList` class's declaration. If the program makes a `MostRecentList` of strings, `m_Items` is a list of strings.

In this code, the `Item` property procedures simply let the main program get and set the values in the `m_Items` list. The `MaxItems` property lets the program determine the number of items that the list can hold. The property set routine saves the new size and then resizes the `m_Items` list appropriately if necessary. The `Count` property returns the number of items currently in the list. The subroutine `Add` first removes the new item if it is already in the list. It then adds the new item at the top of the list and removes the last item if the list now contains too many items. The `Remove` and `RemoveAt` routines simply call the `m_Items` .list's `Remove` and `RemoveAt` methods.

```
Imports System.Collections.Generic

' A list of at most MaxItems items.
Public Class MostRecentList(Of ItemType)
    ' The Item property.
    Private m_Items As New List(Of ItemType)
```

```
            Public Property Item(ByVal index As Integer) As ItemType
                Get
                    Return m_Items(index)
                End Get
                Set(ByVal value As ItemType)
                    m_Items(index) = value
                End Set
            End Property

            ' The MaxItems property.
            Private m_MaxItems As Integer = 4
            Public Property MaxItems() As Integer
                Get
                    Return m_MaxItems
                End Get
                Set(ByVal value As Integer)
                    m_MaxItems = value

                    ' Resize appropriately.
                    Do While m_Items.Count > m_MaxItems
                        m_Items.RemoveAt(m_Items.Count - 1)
                    Loop
                End Set
            End Property

            ' The current number of items.
            Public ReadOnly Property Count() As Integer
                Get
                    Return m_Items.Count
                End Get
            End Property

            ' Add an item to the top of the list.
            Public Sub Add(ByVal value As ItemType)
                ' Remove the item if it is present.
                If m_Items.Contains(value) Then m_Items.Remove(value)

                ' Add the item to the top of the list.
                m_Items.Insert(0, value)

                ' Make sure there are at most MaxItems items.
                If m_Items.Count > m_MaxItems Then m_Items.RemoveAt(m_Items.Count - 1)
            End Sub

            ' Remove an item.
            Public Sub Remove(ByVal value As ItemType)
                m_Items.Remove(value)
            End Sub

            ' Remove an item at a specific position.
            Public Sub RemoveAt(ByVal index As Integer)
                m_Items.RemoveAt(index)
            End Sub
        End Class
```

The following code creates a new `MostRecentList` of strings and then adds some values to it:

```
Dim the_items As New MostRecentList(Of String)
the_items.Add("Apple")
the_items.Add("Banana")
the_items.Add("Cherry")
the_items.Add("Date")
the_items.Add("Banana")
the_items.Add("Fig")
```

After this code executes, the list contains the values in the following order: Fig, Banana, Date, Cherry.

Generic Constructors

You can give constructors to a generic class just as you can give them to any other class. For example, the following constructor initializes the `MostRecentList` class's `MaxItem` property:

```
' Initialize MaxItems for the new list.
Public Sub New(ByVal max_items As Integer)
    MaxItems = max_items
End Sub
```

To use the constructor, the main program adds normal parameters after the type parameters in the object declaration. The following statement creates a new `MostRecentList` of strings, passing its constructor the value 4:

```
Dim the_items As New MostRecentList(Of String)(4)
```

Multiple Types

If you want the class to work with more than one type, you can add other types to the declaration separated by commas. For example, suppose that you want to create a list of data items associated with two keys. You might want to be able to look up customer data using customer ID or customer name.

The following code defines the generic `PairDictionary` class. This class acts as a dictionary that associates a key value with a pair of data values. Notice how the `Class` declaration includes three data types named `KeyType`, `DataType1`, and `DataType2`.

The `PairDictionary` class defines its own private `DataPair` class to hold data pairs. The `DataPair` class has two public variables of types `DataType1` and `DataType2`. Its only method is a constructor that makes initializing the two variables easier.

The `PairDictionary` class then declares a generic `Dictionary` object named `m_Dictionary` using the key type `KeyType` and data type `DataPair`. It delegates most of its work to the `m_Dictionary` object.

`PairDictionary` then provides `Count`, `Add`, `Clear`, `ContainsKey`, `GetItem`, `SetItem`, `Keys`, and `Remove` methods. Notice how it delegates these to the `m_Dictionary` object and how it uses the `DataPair` class to store values in `m_Dictionary`.

```
Imports System.Collections.Generic

' A Dictionary that associates
' a pair of data values with each key.
Public Class PairDictionary(Of KeyType, DataType1, DataType2)
    ' A structure to hold paired data.
    Private Structure DataPair
        Public Data1 As DataType1
        Public Data2 As DataType2
        Public Sub New(ByVal data_value1 As DataType1, _
          ByVal data_value2 As DataType2)
            Data1 = data_value1
            Data2 = data_value2
        End Sub
    End Structure

    ' A Dictionary to hold the paired data.
    Private m_Dictionary As New Dictionary(Of KeyType, DataPair)

    ' Return the number of data pairs.
    Public ReadOnly Property Count() As Integer
        Get
            Return m_Dictionary.Count
        End Get
    End Property

    ' Add a key and data pair.
    Public Sub Add(ByVal key As KeyType, ByVal _
      data_value1 As DataType1, _
      ByVal data_value2 As DataType2)
        m_Dictionary.Add(key, New DataPair(data_value1, data_value2))
    End Sub

    ' Remove all data.
    Public Sub Clear()
        m_Dictionary.Clear()
    End Sub

    ' Return True if the PairDictionary contains this key.
    Public Function ContainsKey(ByVal key As KeyType) As Boolean
        Return m_Dictionary.ContainsKey(key)
    End Function

    ' Return a data pair.
    Public Sub GetItem(ByVal key As KeyType, _
      ByRef data_value1 As DataType1, _
      ByRef data_value2 As DataType2)
        Dim data_pair As DataPair = m_Dictionary.Item(key)
        data_value1 = data_pair.Data1
        data_value2 = data_pair.Data2
    End Sub

    ' Set a data pair.
    Public Sub SetItem(ByVal key As KeyType, _
```

```
        ByVal data_value1 As DataType1, _
        ByVal data_value2 As DataType2)
        m_Dictionary.Item(key) = _
            New DataPair(data_value1, data_value2)
    End Sub

    ' Return a collection containing the keys.
    Public ReadOnly Property Keys() As System.Collections.ICollection
        Get
            Return m_Dictionary.Keys()
        End Get
    End Property

    ' Remove a particular entry.
    Public Sub Remove(ByVal key As KeyType)
        m_Dictionary.Remove(key)
    End Sub
End Class
```

The following code creates an instance of the generic `PairDictionary` class that uses integers as keys and strings for both data values. It adds three entries to the `PairDictionary` and then retrieves and displays the entry with key value 32.

```
' Create the PairDictionary and add some data.
Dim pair_dictionary As New PairDictionary(Of Integer, String, String)
pair_dictionary.Add(10, "Ann", "Archer")
pair_dictionary.Add(32, "Bill", "Beach")
pair_dictionary.Add(17, "Cynthia", "Campos")
' Print the values for index 32.
Dim value1 As String = ""
Dim value2 As String = ""
pair_dictionary.GetItem(32, value1, value2)
Debug.WriteLine(value1 & ", " & value2)
```

Constrained Types

To get the most out of your generic classes, you should make them as flexible as possible. Depending on what the class will do, however, you may need to constrain the types used to create instances of the generic.

For example, consider the generic `MostRecentList` class described earlier in this chapter. It stores at most a certain number of objects in a list. When you add an object to the list, the class first removes the object from the list if it is already present.

That works with simple data types such as integers and strings. However, suppose that you want the list to hold `Employee` objects. When you add a new `Employee` object, the list tries to remove the item if it is already present in its `m_Items` list. However, you are adding a *new* instance of the `Employee` class. The object may have the same values as an object that is already in the list, but the list won't know that because the values are stored in two different objects.

What the list needs is a way to compare objects in the list to see if they are equal. It can then look through the list and remove an existing item if it matches the new one.

One way to allow the list to compare items is to guarantee that the items implement the IComparable interface. Then the program can use their CompareTo methods to see if two objects match.

The following code shows a new version of MostRecentList. Instead of calling the m_Items list's Remove method directly, the Add method now calls the class's Remove method. That method loops through the list using each item's CompareTo method to see if the item matches the target item. If there is a match, the program removes the item from the list.

```
Public Class MostRecentList(Of ItemType As IComparable)
    ...
    ' Add an item to the top of the list.
    Public Sub Add(ByVal value As ItemType)
        ' Remove the item if it is present.
        Remove(value)

        ' Add the item to the top of the list.
        m_Items.Insert(0, value)

        ' Make sure there are at most MaxItems items.
        If m_Items.Count > m_MaxItems Then m_Items.RemoveAt(m_Items.Count - 1)
    End Sub

    ' Remove an item.
    Public Sub Remove(ByVal value As ItemType)
        ' Find the item.
        For i As Integer = m_Items.Count - 1 To 0 Step -1
            If value.CompareTo(m_Items(i)) = 0 Then
                m_Items.RemoveAt(i)
            End If
        Next i
    End Sub
    ...
End Sub
```

A type's As clause can specify any number of interfaces and at most one class from which the type must be derived. It can also include the keyword New to indicate that the type used must provide a constructor that takes no parameters. If you include more than one constraint, the constraints should be separated by commas and enclosed in brackets.

The following code defines the StrangeGeneric class that takes three type parameters. The first type must implement the IComparable interface and must provide an empty constructor. The second type has no constraints and the third type must be a class that inherits from Control.

```
Public Class StrangeGeneric(Of Type1 As {IComparable, New}, Type2, _
    Type3 As Control)
    ...
End Class
```

The following code declares an instance of the StrangeGeneric class:

```
Dim my_strange_generic As New StrangeGeneric(Of Integer, Employee, Button)
```

Constraining a type gives Visual Basic more information about that type, so it lets you use the properties and methods defined by the type. In the previous code, for example, if a variable is of type `Type3`, then Visual Basic knows that it inherits from the `Control` class, so you can use `Control` properties and methods such as `Anchor`, `BackColor`, `Font`, and so forth.

Using Generics

The previous sections have already shown a few examples of how to use a generic class. The program declares the class and includes whatever data types are required in parentheses. The following code shows how a program might create a generic list of strings:

```
Imports System.Collections.Generic
...
Dim names As New List(Of String)
```

To use a generic class's constructor, add a second set of parentheses and any parameters after the type specifications. The following statement creates an `IntStringList` object, passing it the types Integer, String, and Employee. It calls the class's constructor, passing it the value 100.

```
Dim the_employees As New IntStringList(Of Integer, String, Employee)(100)
```

If the program needs to use only a few generic classes (for example, a single collection of strings), this isn't too bad. If the program needs to use many instances of the class, however, the code becomes cluttered.

For example, suppose that the `TreeNode` class shown in the following code represents a node in a tree. Its `MyData` field holds some piece of data and its `Children` list holds references to child nodes.

```
Public Class TreeNode(Of DataType)
    Public MyData As DataType
    Public Children As New List(Of TreeNode(Of DataType))

    Public Sub New(ByVal new_data As DataType)
        MyData = new_data
    End Sub
End Class
```

The following code uses this class to build a small tree of `Employee` objects:

```
Dim root As New TreeNode(Of Employee)(New Employee("Annabelle", "Ant"))
Dim child1 As New TreeNode(Of Employee)(New Employee("Bert", "Bear"))
Dim child2 As New TreeNode(Of Employee)(New Employee("Candice", "Cat"))

root.Children.Add(child1)
root.Children.Add(child2)
```

Repeating the nodes' data types in the first three lines makes the code rather cluttered. Two techniques that you can use to make the code a bit simpler are using an imports alias and deriving a new class. Both of these let you create a simpler name for the awkward class name `TreeNode(Of Employee)`.

Imports Aliases

Normally, you use an `Imports` statement to make it easier to refer to namespaces and the symbols they contain. However, the `Imports` statement also lets you define an alias for a namespace entity. To use this to make using generics easier, create an `Imports` statement that refers to the type of generic class you want to use and give it a simple alias.

For example, the following code is in the `DataTreeTest` namespace. It uses an `Imports` statement to refer to a `TreeNode` of `Employee`. It gives this entity the alias `EmployeeNode`. Later, the program can use the name `EmployeeNode` to create a `TreeNode` of `Employee`.

```
Imports EmployeeNode = DataTreeTest.TreeNode(Of DataTreeTest.Employee)
...
Dim root As New EmployeeNode(New Employee("Annabelle", "Ant"))
Dim child1 As New EmployeeNode(New Employee("Bert", "Bear"))
Dim child2 As New EmployeeNode(New Employee("Candice", "Cat"))

root.Children.Add(child1)
root.Children.Add(child2)
...
```

Derived Classes

A second method that simplifies using generics is to derive a class from the generic class. The following code derives the `EmployeeNode` class from `TreeNode(Of Employee)`. Later, it creates instances of this class to build the tree.

```
Public Class EmployeeNode
    Inherits TreeNode(Of Employee)
    Public Sub New(ByVal new_data As Employee)
        MyBase.New(new_data)
    End Sub
End Class
...
Dim root As New EmployeeNode(New Employee("Annabelle", "Ant"))
Dim child1 As New EmployeeNode(New Employee("Bert", "Bear"))
Dim child2 As New EmployeeNode(New Employee("Candice", "Cat"))

root.Children.Add(child1)
root.Children.Add(child2)
...
```

Predefined Generic Classes

The System.Collections.Generic namespace defines several generic classes. These are basically collection classes that are strongly typed to work with the data type you specify. See the section "Generics" near the end of Chapter 17, "Collection Classes," for more information and a list of the predefined generic collection classes.

Summary

A class abstracts the properties and behaviors of a set of objects to form a template that you can use to make objects that implement those properties and behaviors. After you define the class, you can make many instances of it and they all have the features defined by the class.

Generics take abstraction one level higher. A generic class abstracts the features of a set of classes defined for specific data types. It determines the properties and methods that any class in the generic group provides. After you define the generic class, you can easily make classes that work with different data types but that all provide the common set of features defined by the generic.

By defining common functionality, generic classes let you reuse code to perform similar actions for different data types. By allowing you to parameterize the class instances with a data type, they let you build strongly typed classes quickly and easily. That, in turn, lets Visual Basic provide IntelliSense to make programming faster and easier.

Together these benefits, easier code reuse, strong typing, and IntelliSense support, help you write, test, debug, and maintain code more easily.

Chapters 1 through 13 explained Visual Basic programming details. They explained the Visual Basic development environment, language syntax, standard controls and forms, custom controls, drag and drop, and the clipboard.

Chapters 14 through 18 describe object-oriented concepts such as classes, structures, namespaces, and generics.

The chapters in the next part of the book deal with graphics programming. They explain how to draw lines, ellipses, curves, and text. They show how to use different colors, line styles, and brush types. They also explain how to manipulate bitmapped images, print, and generate reports.

Chapter 19, "Drawing Basics," explains the fundamentals of drawing graphics in Visual Basic 2005. It provides the information you need to start drawing simple shapes and curves.

19

Drawing Basics

Visual Basic .NET provides a large assortment of objects for drawing and for controlling drawing attributes. The `Graphics` object provides methods that enable you to draw and fill rectangles, ellipses, polygons, curves, lines, and other shapes. `Pen` and `Brush` objects determine the appearance of lines (solid, dashed, dotted) and filled areas (solid colors, hatched, filled with a color gradient).

This chapter provides an overview of the drawing process and a survey of the most important drawing namespaces and their classes. It describes in detail the most central of these classes, `Graphics`, and provides examples showing how to use it.

Chapter 20, "Brushes, Pens, and Paths," describes some of the other important drawing classes in greater detail.

If you are new to graphics, this chapter and those that follow may involve a lot of new concepts and unfamiliar terms. The examples available on the book's Web site will help make many of the concepts more concrete. If you find some term confusing, you can find additional details by using Microsoft's advanced search page `http://search.microsoft.com/search/search.aspx?st=a&View=en-us`. You can also consult online glossaries such as the Webopedia (`www.webopedia.com`) and Wikipedia (`www.wikipedia.org`).

Drawing Overview

Whenever you draw something in Visual Basic, you must use a `Graphics` object. This object represents the surface where you are drawing, whether it is a `PictureBox`, `Form`, or `PrintDocument`. Sometimes you will have to create a `Graphics` object, and other times (as in a `Paint` event handler) one is provided for you.

The Graphics Device Interface+ (GDI+), or the .NET version of GDI drawing routines use two classes, `Pen` and `Brush`, to determine the appearance of whatever they are drawing.

A `Pen` object determines how lines are drawn. A `Pen` sets a line's color, thickness, dash style, end cap style, and other properties. The `Pen` applies to all lines drawn by a GDI+ routine. For example, the `DrawPolygon` subroutine draws a series of lines, and its `Pen` parameter determines how all the lines are drawn.

A `Brush` object determines how areas are filled. A `Brush` sets the area's fill color, hatch pattern (a pattern of lines, dots, checks, or other shapes), color gradient (shading from one color to another), and texture (image tiled over the area). Chapter 20 provides more advanced details of these and provides figures showing examples. The `Brush` applies to GDI+ routines that fill closed areas such as `FillRectangle`, `FillEllipse`, and `FillPolygon`.

The basic steps for drawing a simple shape are:

1.   Obtain a `Graphics` object.

2.   Define a `Brush` object and fill with it.

3.   Define a `Pen` object and draw with it.

For example, the `Paint` event handler shown in the following code runs when the form needs to redraw itself. The `Paint` event handler's `e.Graphics` parameter gives the `Graphics` object on which the program should draw. When the event handler is finished, Visual Basic copies the contents drawn in this `Graphics` object onto the parts of the form that must be redrawn. The event handler creates an orange `SolidBrush` object. `SolidBrush` is a class derived from the `Brush` class, so it will serve as a `Brush`. The program uses the brush to fill the circle bounded by the square with upper-left corners at (10, 10) and 100 pixels wide and 100 pixels tall. The code then creates a pen representing a 10-pixel wide blue line and uses it to draw the outline of the same circle.

```
Private Sub Form1_Paint(ByVal sender As Object, _
  ByVal e As System.Windows.Forms.PaintEventArgs) Handles MyBase.Paint
    Dim circle_brush As New SolidBrush(Color.Orange)
    e.Graphics.FillEllipse(circle_brush, 10, 10, 100, 100)

    Dim circle_pen As New Pen(Color.Blue, 10)
    e.Graphics.DrawEllipse(circle_pen, 10, 10, 100, 100)
End Sub
```

Whenever the form is hidden and exposed, partially covered and exposed, minimized and restored or maximized, or resized to expose a new part of the form, the `Paint` event handler executes and redraws the circle. Figure 19-1 shows the result. You can't see the colors in the book, but you can see that the solid circle has a thick border.

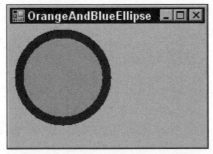

Figure 19-1: This program uses `SolidBrush` and `Pen` objects to draw an orange circle with a wide blue outline.

The `Graphics` object's filling and drawing methods provide several overloaded versions. Most can take an object parameter that defines the shape to draw. For example, the `FillEllipse` and `DrawEllipse` methods can take a `Rectangle` as a parameter to define the ellipse's bounding rectangle.

This provides a convenient method for ensuring that the filled and drawn areas match exactly. The following code draws the same circle as the previous example, but it uses a `Rectangle` to define the circle. It uses the same `Rectangle` for its calls to `FillEllipse` and `DrawEllipse`, so it's easy to tell that they define exactly the same circle. If you modify this code to change the circle, you don't need to remember to change its coordinates everywhere they occur, because the circle is defined in only one place (the `Rectangle`).

```
Private Sub Form1_Paint(ByVal sender As Object, _
 ByVal e As System.Windows.Forms.PaintEventArgs) Handles MyBase.Paint
    Dim rect As New Rectangle(10, 10, 100, 100)
    Dim circle_brush As New SolidBrush(Color.Orange)
    e.Graphics.FillEllipse(circle_brush, rect)

    Dim circle_pen As New Pen(Color.Blue, 10)
    e.Graphics.DrawEllipse(circle_pen, rect)
End Sub
```

All GDI+ drawing is based on these simple steps, but there are a lot of variations. `Pens` and `Brushes` can be much more complicated. For example, you can fill a polygon with a color gradient that follows a path you define and then outline it with a custom dash pattern. The `Graphics` object also provides some fairly exotic drawing routines such as `DrawBezier`, which draws a Bézier curve.

A Bézier curve is a smooth curve guided by a set of four control points. The curve starts at the first point and ends at the last. The middle two points control the curve's direction and curvature. The section "`DrawBezier`" later in this chapter gives more information on Bézier curves and Figure 19-7 shows an example.

The following sections describe the namespaces containing the most useful GDI+ objects. Chapter 20, "Brushes, Pens, and Paths," provides additional details and contains pictures of the results produced by many of these objects.

Drawing Namespaces

Before jumping into GDI+ graphics, it's worth taking a moment to learn which namespaces contain which objects. By default, the System.Drawing namespace is imported into new applications automatically, so you don't need to explicitly import it to work with `Graphics`, `Pen`, `Brush`, and the other basic drawing objects. However, if you want to create custom dash patterns (long dashes, dot-dash-dot), linear gradient color fills (shading from one color to another and possibly to others), or advanced image files (JPEG, GIF, TIFF), you must know which namespaces to import into your application.

System.Drawing

The System.Drawing namespace contains the most important and basic GDI+ classes. These classes include `Graphics`, `Pen`, `Brush`, `Font`, `FontFamily`, `Bitmap`, `Icon`, and `Image`. The following table describes the most useful System.Drawing classes.

Class	Description
Graphics	This is without doubt the most important object you'll use when creating graphics. A Graphics object represents the surface you're going to draw on. That could be a PictureBox, form, bitmap in memory, or whatever. The Graphics object provides the methods for drawing lines, rectangles, ellipses, and so forth.
Pen	This class represents the drawing characteristics of a line, including the line's color, thickness, dash style, and so forth.
Pens	This class provides a large number of predefined pens with different colors and width 1. For example, you can use Pens.Blue as a standard blue pen.
Brush	This class represents how solid areas are filled. It determines whether the area is solidly colored, hatched, filled with a pattern, and so forth.
Brushes	This class provides a large number of predefined solid brushes with different colors. For example, you can use Brushes.Green to fill an area with green.
SolidBrush	This class represents a solid brush. When you want to fill an object with a solid color, you use a SolidBrush. This is by far the most common type of fill for most applications.
Bitmap	This class represents a bitmap image defined by pixel data rather than drawn lines.
Icon	This class represents a Windows icon similar to a bitmap.
Metafile	This class represents a graphic metafile that contains graphical operations that a program can record, save to a file, load from a file, and play back later.
Image	This is an abstract base class from which Bitmap, Icon, and Metafile inherit. Some routines can work with any of these kinds of objects, so they take an Image parameter. (In brief, a *bitmap* is a typical picture. An icon has additional transparency and possibly hot-spot information so it can act as a form or application icon or mouse pointer. A *metafile* contains drawing instructions that some applications can use to scale the picture smoothly.)
Font	This class represents a particular font. It defines the font's name, size, and style (such as italic or bold).
FontFamily	This class represents a group of typefaces with similar characteristics.
Region	This class defines a shape created from rectangles and paths. You can fill a region, use it to perform hit testing, or clip a drawing to a region.

The System.Drawing namespace also defines some structures that a program can use for drawing. The following table describes the most useful of these structures.

Structure	Description
Color	This object defines a color's red, green, and blue components as values between 0 and 255, plus an *alpha* value that indicates the color's transparency. An alpha value of 0 means the object is completely transparent, while a value of 255 means it is totally opaque.
Point	This object defines a point's X and Y coordinates.
Size	This object defines a width and height.
Rectangle	This object defines a rectangle using a Point and a Size.

GDI+ routines work in pixels on the screen, printer, or whatever object they are drawing on, so the Point, Size, and Rectangle structures hold integral coordinates and sizes. However, the System.Drawing namespace also defines PointF, SizeF, and RectangleF classes to work with floating-point values.

The Color class provides a large number of predefined color values. For example, Color.PaleGreen defines a light green color. You can use these predefined colors instead of creating a new color object.

System.Drawing.Drawing2D

The System.Drawing.Drawing2D namespace contains most of the other objects you'll need to draw more advanced two-dimensional graphics. Some of these classes refine the more basic drawing classes, or define values for those classes. For example, the HatchBrush class represents a specialized type of Brush that fills with a hatch pattern. The following table describes this namespace's most useful classes.

Class	Description
HatchBrush	This class defines a Brush that fills an area with a hatch pattern. It defines the pattern, a foreground color, and a background color.
LinearGradientBrush	This class defines a Brush that fills an area with a linear color gradient. By default the fill shades smoothly from one color to another along a line that you define, but it can also represent multicolor gradients. (Chapter 20 has more to say about LinearGradientBrushes, and Figure 20-11 shows some examples.)
Blend	This class represents a blend pattern for a LinearGradientBrush or PathGradientBrush. For example, suppose that you define a gradient running from red to yellow. Normally the gradient is smooth and linear, but you can use a Blend to change this. For example, you might want the color to change from red to yellow very quickly, so it is 80 percent yellow only 20 percent of the way across the gradient. (The effects of a Blend are subtle but you can see them in Figure 20-11.)
PathGradientBrush	This class is similar to a LinearGradientBrush except its gradient follows a path rather than a line. (Figure 20-12 shows some examples.)

Table continued on following page

Class	Description
ColorBlend	This class defines colors and positions for LinearGradientBrush or PathGradientBrush. This lets you make the colors vary between several different colors along the brush's path. (Figure 20-11 shows an example.)
GraphicsPath	This class represents a series of connected lines and curves. You can draw, fill, or clip to a GraphicsPath. For example, you could add text to a GraphicsPath and then draw its outline or clip a drawing so that it only shows within the text's path. (Figure 20-13 shows a GraphicsPath filled with TextureBrush.)
Matrix	This class represents a 3×3 transformation matrix. You can use matrices to translate, scale, and rotate graphics operations. See the section "Transformations Basics" later in this chapter for more information.

The System.Drawing.Drawing2D namespace also defines some enumerations that are useful for more advanced drawing. The following able describes the most useful of these enumerations.

Enumeration	Description
DashCap	These values determine how the ends of a dash in a dashed line are drawn. DashCap values include Flat, Round, and Triangle. These give the same appearance as the Flat, Round, and Triangle LineCaps shown in Figure 19-2.
DashStyle	These values determine how a dashed line is drawn. DashStyle values include Dash, DashDot, DashDotDot, Dot, Solid, and Custom. If you set a Pen's DashStyle property to DashStyle.Custom, then you should also set its DashPattern property to an array telling the Pen how many to pixels to draw and skip. For example, the array {10, 20, 5, 2} means draw 10, skip 2, draw 5, skip 2, and then repeat as necessary.
LineCap	These values determine how the ends of a line are drawn. Values include ArrowAnchor, DiamondAnchor, Flat, NoAnchor, Round, RoundAnchor, Square, SquareAnchor, Triangle, and Custom. If LineCap is Custom, you should use a CustomLineCap object to define the cap. Figure 19-2 shows the standard LineCaps.
LineJoin	These values determine how lines are joined by a GDI+ method that draws connected lines. For example, the DrawPolygon and DrawLines methods use this property. Values include Bevel, Miter, Round, and MiterClipped. Figure 19-3 shows the first three values. MiterClipped produces either a mitered or beveled corner, depending on whether the miter's length exceeds a certain limit.
HatchStyle	These values define the hatch style used by a HatchBrush object to fill an area. This enumeration includes 54 values, so they are not all listed here. Figure 19-4, however, lists them and shows samples.

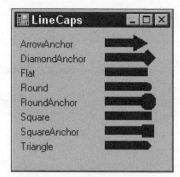

Figure 19-2: The `LineCap` enumeration determines how a line's endpoint is drawn.

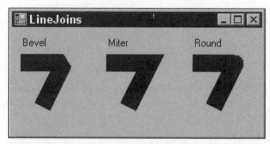

Figure 19-3: The `LineJoin` enumeration determines how lines are joined.

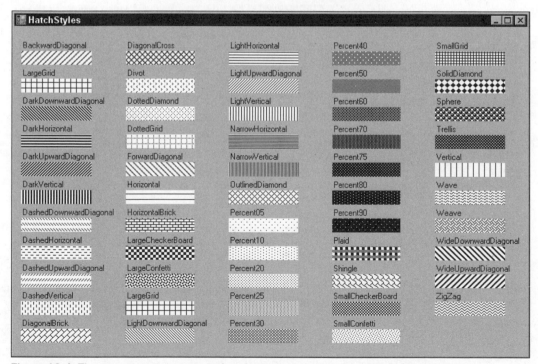

Figure 19-4: The `HatchStyle` enumeration determines how a HatchBrush fills an area.

System.Drawing.Imaging

The System.Drawing.Imaging namespace contains classes that deal with more advanced bitmap graphics. It includes classes that define image file formats such as GIF and JPG, classes that manage color palettes, and classes that define metafiles. The following table describes this namespace's most useful classes.

Class	Description
ImageFormat	This class specifies an image's format. This can be one of bmp, emf, exif, gif, icon, jpeg, memory bitmap, png, tiff, or wmf. (For descriptions of these image format types, try searching for them at Web sites such as Webopedia (www.webopedia.com). The page www.webopedia.com/DidYouKnow/Internet/2002/JPG_GIF_PNG.asp discusses the differences between the three most common Web image formats: GIF, JPEG, and PNG. Microsoft's Web site has a comparison of the BMP, GIF, JPEG, Exif, PNG, and TIFF formats at msdn.microsoft.com/library/en-us/gdicpp/GDIPlus/aboutGDIPlus/imagesbitmapsandmetafiles/typesofbitmaps.asp.
ColorMap	This class defines a mapping from old color values to new ones. You can use ColorMaps to change some colors in an image to others.
ColorPalette	This class represents a palette of color values. (A *palette* is a collection of color values that are used in a particular image. For example, 8-bit color images can contain only 256 different colors. The image's color palette lists the colors used and an 8-bit numeric value gives each pixel's color index in the palette. Recently, higher color models such as 16-, 24-, and 32-bit color have become more common. In those color models, the bits give each pixel's red, green, and blue color components directly rather than referring to a color palette, so no palette is needed.)
Metafile	This class represents a graphic metafile that contains drawing instructions. You can create, save, reload, and play back metafile information.
MetafileHeader	This class defines the attributes of a Metafile object. (A *metafile* lets a program define a drawing in terms of lines, curves, and filled areas rather than using pixels in a bitmap. This lets the program later redraw the image scaled, rotated, or otherwise transformed smoothly without the distortion that would occur in a bitmapped image.)
MetaHeader	This class contains information about a Windows metafile (WMF).
WmfPlaceableFileHeader	This class defines how a metafile should be mapped to an output device. You can use this to ensure that the metafile is properly sized when you import it into a drawing program such as CorelDRAW!.

System.Drawing.Text

The System.Drawing.Text namespace contains only three classes. These three classes provide a somewhat awkward method for learning about the fonts installed on the system or the fonts installed for an application. The following table describes these three classes.

Class	Description
FontCollection	A base class for the derived InstalledFontCollection and PrivateFontCollection classes. It provides a method that returns an array of FontFamily objects.
InstalledFontCollection	This is derived from the FontCollection class. This class's Families method returns an array containing FontFamily objects representing the fonts installed on the system.
PrivateFontCollection	This is also derived from the FontCollection class. Objects from this class represent fonts installed by an application from font files. The program can use this object to install fonts just for the use of the application and not for the rest of the system. This class provides methods for installing and listing the application's fonts.

It is rather odd that this class is defined just to provide one method that returns an array of FontFamily objects. It would have made more sense to give the FontCollection class a method such as ListInstalledFonts or to give the InstalledFontCollection class a shared method that creates such a FontCollection object. That's not the way these classes work, however.

To list the system's fonts, a program creates an instance of the InstalledFontCollection and uses that object's Families method to get an array of the installed FontFamily objects. The program can then loop through the array to list the fonts. The following code demonstrates this method:

```
Private Sub Form1_Load(ByVal sender As System.Object, _
  ByVal e As System.EventArgs) Handles MyBase.Load
    ' Get the installed fonts collection.
    Dim installed_fonts As New InstalledFontCollection

    ' Get an array of the system's font familiies.
    Dim font_families() As FontFamily = installed_fonts.Families()

    ' Display the font families.
    For Each font_family As FontFamily In font_families
        lstFonts.Items.Add(font_family.Name)
    Next font_family
    lstFonts.SelectedIndex = 0
End Sub
```

Figure 19-5 shows the result.

Figure 19-5: An `InstalledFontCollection` **object provides access to an array of** `FontFamily` **objects representing the fonts installed on the system.**

The System.Drawing.Text namespace also defines the `TextRenderingHint` enumeration. *Anti-aliasing* is a process that uses pixels of different shades to make jagged edges and curves appear smoother. You can set a `Graphics` object's `TextRenderingHint` property to tell Visual Basic whether it should use anti-aliasing to smooth the text. The following table describes the `TextRenderingHint` enumeration values.

Enumeration Value	Description
`AntiAlias`	Characters are drawn anti-aliased without hinting.
`AntiAliasGridFit`	Characters are drawn anti-aliased with hinting to improve stems and curves.
`ClearTypeGridFit`	Characters are drawn using ClearType glyphs with hinting. This takes advantage of ClearType font features. (In this context, a *glyph* is the image of a letter. Some fonts are drawn as glyphs and others such as TrueType fonts are drawn as outlines. TrueType was developed jointly by Microsoft and Apple. ClearType is a newer type of glyph font developed by Microsoft.)
`SingleBitPerPixel`	Characters are drawn without anti-aliasing or hinting. This is the fastest and lowest-quality setting.
`SingleBitPerPixelGridFit`	Characters are drawn without anti-aliasing, but with hinting.
`SystemDefault`	Characters are drawn using the system default setting.

The following code shows how a program can display text with and without anti-aliasing. First it creates a large font. It sets the Graphics object's TextRenderingHint property to AntiAliasGridFit and draws some text. Then it sets TextRenderingHint to SingleBitPerPixel and draws the text again.

```
Private Sub Form1_Paint(ByVal sender As Object, _
  ByVal e As System.Windows.Forms.PaintEventArgs) Handles MyBase.Paint
    ' Make a big font.
    Dim the_font As New Font(Me.Font.FontFamily, _
        40, FontStyle.Bold, GraphicsUnit.Pixel)

    ' Draw without anti-aliasing.
    e.Graphics.TextRenderingHint = TextRenderingHint.AntiAliasGridFit
    e.Graphics.DrawString("Alias", _
        the_font, Brushes.Black, 5, 5)

    ' Draw with anti-aliasing.
    e.Graphics.TextRenderingHint = TextRenderingHint.SingleBitPerPixel
    e.Graphics.DrawString("Alias", _
        the_font, Brushes.Black, 5, 50)
End Sub
```

Figure 19-6 shows the result, greatly enlarged to emphasize the difference. Notice how the anti-aliased version uses different shades of gray to make the text appear smoother.

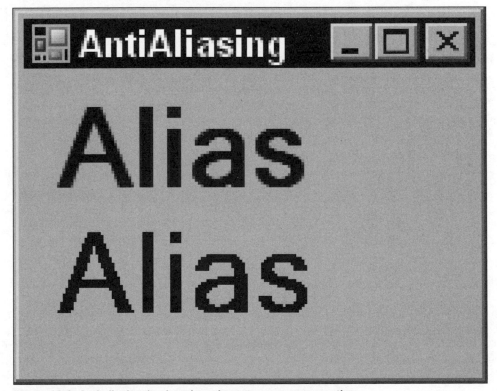

Figure 19-6: Anti-aliasing (top) makes characters appear smoother.

System.Drawing.Printing

The System.Drawing.Printing namespace contains objects for printing and managing the printer's characteristics.

Normally, to generate a printed document, you create a `PrintDocument` object. You set the object's properties to define printing attributes and then call its `Print` method. As it prints, the `PrintDocument` object generates `PrintPage` events that let you draw on the printout's pages.

Other classes in this namespace define properties for the `PrintDocument` object. The following table describes the most useful of these property objects.

Class	Description
PageSettings	This class defines the page settings for either an entire `PrintDocument` or for a particular page. This object has properties that are `Margins`, `PaperSize`, `PaperSource`, `PrinterResolution`, and `PrinterSettings` objects.
Margins	This class defines the margins for the printed page through its `Top`, `Bottom`, `Left`, and `Right` properties.
PaperSize	This class defines the paper's size. You can set the object's `Kind` property to a standard value such as `A2`, `Legal`, or `Letter`. Alternatively, you can set the object's `Height` and `Width` properties explicitly.
PaperSource	This class defines the printer's paper source. You can set this object's `Kind` property to such values as `AutomaticFeed`, `Upper`, `Middle`, `Lower`, `Envelope`, and `ManualFeed`.
PrinterResolution	This class defines the printer's resolution.
PrinterSettings	This class defines the printer's settings. You can use this class to get setting values such as whether the printer can print double-sided (`CanDuplex`), the names of the installed printers (`InstalledPrinters`), and the printer's supported resolutions (`PrinterResolutions`). You can use other properties to control the printer. For example, you can set the number of copies (`Copies`), set the minimum and maximum page number the user can select in a print dialog (`MinimumPage` and `MaximumPage`), and determine whether the printer collates its output (`Collate`).

Graphics

Whenever you draw in Visual Basic .NET, you need a `Graphics` object. A `Graphics` object represents a drawing surface, whether it is a `Form`, `PictureBox`, `Bitmap` in memory, metafile, or printer surface.

The `Graphics` class provides many methods for drawing shapes and filling areas. It also includes properties and methods that modify the graphics results. For example, its transformation methods let you scale, translate, and rotate the drawing output.

The following sections describe the `Graphics` object's properties and methods for drawing, filling, and otherwise modifying the drawing.

Drawing Methods

The `Graphics` object provides many methods for drawing lines, rectangles, curves, and other shapes. The following table describes these methods.

Method	Description
DrawArc	Draws an arc of an ellipse.
DrawBezier	Draws a Bézier curve. See the section "DrawBezier" later in this chapter for an example.
DrawBeziers	Draws a series of Bézier curves. See the section "DrawBezier" later in this chapter for an example.
DrawClosedCurve	Draws a closed curve that joins a series of points, connecting the final point to the first point. See the section "DrawClosedCurve" later in this chapter for an example.
DrawCurve	Draws a smooth curve that joins a series of points. This is similar to a `DrawClosedCurve`, except that it doesn't connect the final point to the first point.
DrawEllipse	Draws an ellipse. To draw a circle, draw an ellipse with a width equal to its height.
DrawIcon	Draws an `Icon` onto the `Graphics` object's drawing surface.
DrawIconUnstretched	Draws an `Icon` object onto the `Graphics` object's drawing surface without scaling. If you know that you will not resize the icon, this may be faster than the `DrawIcon` method.
DrawImage	Draws an `Image` object onto the `Graphics` object's drawing surface. Note that `Bitmap` is a subclass of `Image`, so you can use this method to draw a `Bitmap` on the surface.
DrawImageUnscaled	Draws an `Image` object onto the drawing surface without scaling. If you know that you will not resize the image, this may be faster than the `DrawImage` method.
DrawLine	Draws a line.
DrawLines	Draws a series of connected lines. If you need to draw a series of connected lines, this is much faster than using `DrawLine` repeatedly.
DrawPath	Draws a `GraphicsPath` object. See the section "DrawPath" later in this chapter for an example.

Table continued on following page

Method	Description
DrawPie	Draws a pie slice taken from an ellipse.
DrawPolygon	Draws a polygon. This is similar to DrawLines, except that it connects the last point to the first point.
DrawRectangle	Draws a rectangle.
DrawRectangles	Draws a series of rectangles. If you need to draw a series of rectangles, this is much faster than using DrawRectangle repeatedly.
DrawString	Draws text on the drawing surface.

The following sections provide examples of some of the more complicated of these drawing methods.

DrawBezier

The DrawBezier method draws a Bézier curve. A Bézier curve is a smooth curve defined by four control points. The curve starts at the first point and ends at the last point. The line between the first and second points gives the curve's initial direction. The line connecting the third and fourth points gives its final direction as it enters the final point.

The following code draws a Bézier curve. It starts by defining the curve's control points. It then draws dashed lines connecting the points, so you can see where the control points are in the final drawing. You would omit this step if you just wanted to draw the curve. Next the program sets the Graphics object's SmoothingMode property to HighQuality, so the program draws a smooth, anti-aliased curve. The SmoothingMode property is described in the section "SmoothingMode" later in this chapter. The program creates a black pen three pixels wide and draws the Bézier curve.

```
Private Sub Form1_Paint(ByVal sender As Object, _
  ByVal e As System.Windows.Forms.PaintEventArgs) Handles MyBase.Paint
    ' Define the Bezier curve's control points.
    Dim pts() As Point = { _
        New Point(10, 10), _
        New Point(200, 10), _
        New Point(50, 200), _
        New Point(200, 150) _
    }

    ' Connect the points with dashed lines.
    Dim dashed_pen As New Pen(Color.Black, 0)
    dashed_pen.DashStyle = Drawing2D.DashStyle.Dash
    For i As Integer = 0 To 2
        e.Graphics.DrawLine(dashed_pen, pts(i), pts(i + 1))
    Next i

    ' Draw the Bezier curve.
    e.Graphics.SmoothingMode = Drawing2D.SmoothingMode.HighQuality
    Dim bez_pen As New Pen(Color.Black, 3)
    e.Graphics.DrawBezier(bez_pen, pts(0), pts(1), pts(2), pts(3))
End Sub
```

Figure 19-7 shows the result. You can see in the picture how the control points determine the curve's end points and the direction it takes at them.

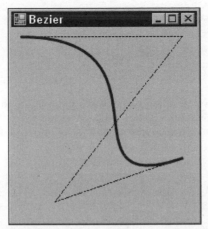

Figure 19-7: The `DrawBezier` method draws a smooth curve controlled by four control points.

DrawBeziers

The `DrawBeziers` method draws a series of Bézier curves with common end points. It takes as parameters an array of points that determine the curves' end points and interior control points. The first four entries in the array represent the first curve's starting point, its two interior control points, and the curve's end point. The next curve uses the first curve's end point as its starting point, provides two interior control points, and its own end point. This pattern repeats for each of the curves. To draw N curves, the array should contain $3 * N + 1$ points.

The following code draws two Bézier curves. It defines seven points ($3 * 2 + 1 = 7$) and connects them with dashed lines. It sets the `Graphics` object's `SmoothingMode` property and calls the `DrawBeziers` method.

```
Private Sub Form1_Paint(ByVal sender As Object, _
  ByVal e As System.Windows.Forms.PaintEventArgs) Handles MyBase.Paint
    ' Define the Bezier curve's control points.
    Dim pts() As Point = { _
        New Point(10, 10), _
        New Point(200, 10), _
        New Point(50, 200), _
        New Point(200, 150), _
        New Point(250, 50), _
        New Point(250, 200), _
        New Point(100, 250) _
    }

    ' Connect the points with dashed lines.
    Dim dashed_pen As New Pen(Color.Black, 0)
    dashed_pen.DashStyle = Drawing2D.DashStyle.Dash
```

```
    For i As Integer = 0 To pts.Length - 2
        e.Graphics.DrawLine(dashed_pen, pts(i), pts(i + 1))
    Next i

    ' Draw the Bezier curve.
    e.Graphics.SmoothingMode = Drawing2D.SmoothingMode.HighQuality
    Dim bez_pen As New Pen(Color.Black, 3)
    e.Graphics.DrawBeziers(bez_pen, pts)
End Sub
```

Figure 19-8 shows the result. Notice that the two Bézier curves share a common end point, but they do not meet smoothly. To make them meet smoothly, you would need to ensure that the last two points in the first curve and the first two points in the second curve (one of which is the same as the last point in the first curve) all lie along the same line.

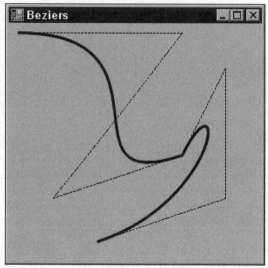

Figure 19-8: The `DrawBeziers` method draws a series of Bézier curves with common end points.

DrawClosedCurve

Using the `DrawBeziers` method, you can draw a series of connected curves, but joining them smoothly is difficult. The `DrawClosedCurve` method connects a series of points with a smooth curve.

The following code draws a closed curve. It defines a series of points, sets the `Graphics` object's `SmoothingMode` property, and calls `DrawClosedCurve` to draw the curve. It the loops through the curve's control points, drawing a box over each so you can see where they are.

```
Private Sub Form1_Paint(ByVal sender As Object, _
  ByVal e As System.Windows.Forms.PaintEventArgs) Handles MyBase.Paint
    ' Define the curve's control points.
    Dim pts() As Point = { _
        New Point(10, 50), _
        New Point(200, 30), _
```

```
        New Point(20, 200), _
        New Point(200, 150), _
        New Point(250, 50), _
        New Point(250, 200), _
        New Point(100, 250) _
    }

    ' Draw the closed curve.
    e.Graphics.SmoothingMode = Drawing2D.SmoothingMode.HighQuality
    Dim curve_pen As New Pen(Color.Black, 3)
    e.Graphics.DrawClosedCurve(curve_pen, pts)

    ' Draw rectangles on the control points.
    For i As Integer = 0 To pts.Length - 1
        e.Graphics.FillRectangle(Brushes.White, pts(i).X - 2, pts(i).Y - 2, 5, 5)
        e.Graphics.DrawRectangle(Pens.Black, pts(i).X - 2, pts(i).Y - 2, 5, 5)
    Next i
End Sub
```

Figure 19-9 shows the result. Notice that the curve is smooth and that it passes through each of the control points exactly. If you just want to connect a series of points smoothly, it is easier to use a closed curve than Bézier curves.

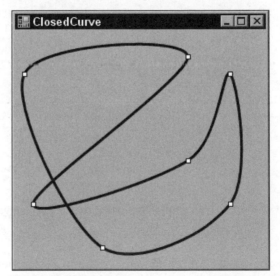

Figure 19-9: The `DrawClosedCurve` **method draws a smooth curve connecting a series points.**

The `DrawCurve` method is similar to `DrawClosedCurve`, except that it doesn't connect the last point to the first.

Overloaded versions of the `DrawClosedCurve` method take a tension parameter that indicates how tightly the curve bends. Usually this value is between 0 and 1. The value 0 makes the method connect the curve's points with straight lines. The value 1 draws a nicely rounded curve. Tension values greater than 1 produce some strange (but sometimes interesting) results.

The following code draws closed curves with tension set to 0.0, 0.25, 0.5, 0.75, and 1.0. It uses progressively thicker lines so you can see which curves are which.

```
For tension As Single = 0 To 1 Step 0.25
    Dim curve_pen As New Pen(Color.Black, tension * 4 + 1)
    e.Graphics.DrawClosedCurve(curve_pen, pts, tension, _
        Drawing2D.FillMode.Alternate)
Next tension
```

Figure 19-10 shows the result. You can see the curves growing smoother as the tension parameter increases and the pen thickens.

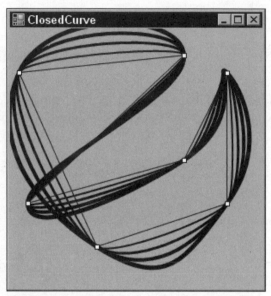

Figure 19-10: The DrawClosedCurve **method can take a tension parameter that determines how tightly the curve bends.**

Overloaded versions of the DrawCurve method also take tension parameters.

DrawPath

The DrawPath method draws a GraphicsPath object as shown in the following code. The program creates a new, empty GraphicsPath object and uses its AddString method to add a string to the path. This method takes as parameters a string, FontFamily, font style, font size, point where the text should start, and a string format. The code sets the Graphics object's SmoothingMode property to draw anti-aliased curves. It then calls the FillPath method to fill the area defined by the GraphicsPath object with white and uses the DrawPath method to draw the path's outline in black.

```
Private Sub Form1_Paint(ByVal sender As Object, _
  ByVal e As System.Windows.Forms.PaintEventArgs) Handles MyBase.Paint
    ' Create a GraphicsPath.
    Dim graphics_path As New Drawing2D.GraphicsPath
```

```
    ' Add some text to the path.
    graphics_path.AddString("GraphicsPath", _
        New FontFamily("Times New Roman"), _
        CInt(FontStyle.Bold), _
        80, New Point(10, 10), _
        StringFormat.GenericTypographic)

    ' Draw the path.
    e.Graphics.SmoothingMode = SmoothingMode.AntiAlias
    e.Graphics.FillPath(Brushes.White, graphics_path)
    e.Graphics.DrawPath(New Pen(Color.Black, 3), graphics_path)
End Sub
```

Figure 19-11 shows the result.

Figure 19-11: The `DrawPath` method draws the outline defined by a `GraphicsPath` **object.**

You can use `GraphicsPath` objects to make all sorts of interesting effects. For example, you could fill a `GraphicsPath` with a color gradient, hatch pattern, or bitmap.

Filling Methods

The `Graphics` object provides many methods for filling areas. These correspond exactly to the drawing methods that define a closed shape. For example, `DrawRectangle` draws a rectangle and `FillRectangle` fills one.

Corresponding draw and fill methods take exactly the same parameters, except that the drawing methods use a `Pen` object while the filling methods use a `Brush` object. For example, the following statements fill and draw a `GraphicsPath` object. The only difference in the parameters is the `Pen` or `Brush`.

```
    e.Graphics.FillPath(Brushes.White, graphics_path)
    e.Graphics.DrawPath(Pens.Black, graphics_path)
```

The `Graphics` object provides the following methods for filling areas: `FillClosedCurve`, `FillEllipse`, `FillPath`, `FillPie`, `FillPolygon`, `FillRectangle`, and `FillRectangles`. These methods work the same way as the corresponding drawing methods (`DrawClosedCurve`, `DrawEllipse`, `DrawPath`, `DrawPie`, `DrawPolygon`, `DrawRectangle`, and `DrawRectangles`), except they fill an area with a brush rather than drawing it with a pen. See the section "Drawing Methods" earlier in this chapter for descriptions of these methods.

Other Graphics Properties and Methods

The following table describes the `Graphics` object's most useful properties and methods, other than those that draw or fill shapes.

Properties/Methods	Description
AddMetafileComment	If the `Graphics` object is attached to a metafile, this adds a comment to it. Later, if an application enumerates the metafile's records, it can view the comments.
Clear	Clears the `Graphics` object and fills it with a specific color. For example, a form's `Paint` event handler might use the statement `e.Graphics.Clear(Me.BackColor)` to clear the form using its background color.
Clip	Determines the `Region` object used to clip a drawing on the `Graphics` surface. Any drawing command that falls outside of this `Region` is clipped off and not shown in the output.
Dispose	Releases the resources held by the `Graphics` object. You can use this method to free the resources of an object that you no longer need sooner than they would be freed by garbage collection. For a more detailed discussion, see the section "Dispose" in Chapter 15, "Classes and Structures."
DpiX	Returns the horizontal number of dots per inch (DPI) for this `Graphics` object's surface.
DpiY	Returns the vertical number of DPI for this `Graphics` object's surface.
EnumerateMetafile	If the `Graphics` object is attached to a metafile, this sends the metafile's records to a specified *callback* subroutine one at a time.
ExcludeClip	Updates the `Graphics` object's clipping region to exclude the area defined by a `Region` or `Rectangle`.
FromHdc	Creates a new `Graphics` object from a handle to a device context (DC). (A *device context* is a structure that defines an object's graphic attributes: pen, color, fill, and so forth. Usually, you can use the GDI+ drawing routines and ignore DCs. They are more useful if you need to use older GDI functions.)
FromHwnd	Creates a new `Graphics` object from a window handle (hWnd).
FromImage	Creates a new `Graphics` object from an `Image` object. This is a very common way to make a new `Graphics` object to manipulate a bitmap.
InterpolationMode	Determines whether drawing routines use anti-aliasing when drawing images. See the section "InterpolationMode" later in this chapter for an example.

Properties/Methods	Description
IntersectClip	Updates the Graphics object's clipping region to be the intersection of the current clipping region and the area defined by a Region or Rectangle. (The *clipping region* determines where GDI+ will draw output. If a line falls outside of the clipping region, GDI+ doesn't draw the part that sticks out. Normally, an image's clipping region includes its whole visible area, but you can redefine it so that, for example, parts of the visible area are not drawn.)
IsVisible	Returns True if a specified point is within the Graphics object's visible clipping region.
MeasureCharacterRanges	Returns an array of Region objects that show where each character in a string will be drawn.
MeasureString	Returns a SizeF structure that gives the size of a string drawn on the Graphics object with a particular font.
MultiplyTransform	Multiplies the Graphics object's current transformation matrix by another transformation matrix.
PageScale	Determines the amount by which drawing commands are scaled. For example, if you set this to 2, then every coordinate and measurement is scaled by a factor of 2 from the origin.
PageUnits	Determines the units of measurement. This can be Display (1/75 inch), Document (1/300 inch), Inch, Millimeter, Pixel, or Point (1/72 inch).
RenderingOrigin	Determines the point used as a reference when hatching. Normally this is (0, 0), so all HatchBrushes use the same RenderingOrigin and, if you draw two overlapping hatched areas, their hatch patterns line up. If you change this property, you can make their hatch patterns not line up.
ResetClip	Resets the object's clipping region, so the drawing is not clipped.
ResetTransformation	Resets the object's transformation matrix to the identity matrix, so the drawing is not transformed.
Restore	Restores the Graphics object to a state saved by the Save method. See the section "Saving and Restoring Graphics" later in this chapter for an example.
RotateTransform	Adds a rotation to the object's current transformation. This rotates all drawing by a specified amount. See the section "Transformation Basics" later in this chapter for an example.
Save	Saves the object's current state in a GraphicsState object, so you can later restore it by calling the Restore method. See the section "Saving and Restoring Graphics" later in this chapter for an example.

Table continued on following page

Properties/Methods	Description
ScaleTransform	Adds a scaling transformation to the Graphics object's current transformation. This scales all drawing by a specified factor in the X and Y directions. See the section "Transformation Basics" later in this chapter for an example.
SetClip	Sets or merges the Graphics object's clipping area to another Graphics object, a GraphicsPath object, or a Rectangle. Only parts of drawing commands that lie within the clipping region are displayed.
SmoothingMode	Determines whether drawing routines use anti-aliasing when drawing lines and curves. See the section "SmoothingMode" later in this chapter for an example.
TextRenderingHint	Determines whether text is drawn with anti-aliasing and hinting. See the section "TextRenderingHint" later in this chapter section and the section, "System.Drawing.Text" earlier in this chapter for more details.
Transform	Gets or sets the Graphics object's transformation matrix. This matrix represents all scaling, translation, and rotation applied to the object.
TransformPoints	Applies the object's current transformation to an array of points.
TranslateTransform	Adds a translation transformation to the Graphics object's current transformation. This offsets all drawing a specified distance in the X and Y directions. See the section "Transformation Basics" later in this chapter for an example.

The following sections give examples of some of the more important (but confusing) Graphics properties and methods.

Anti-Aliasing

Aliasing is an effect caused when you draw lines, curves, and text that do not line up exactly with the screen's pixels. For example, if you draw a vertical line, it neatly fills in a column of pixels. If you draw a line at a 45-degree angle, it also fills a series of pixels that are nicely lined up, but the pixels are a bit farther apart and that makes the line appear lighter on the screen. If you draw a line at some other angle (for example, 30 degrees), then the line does not line up exactly with the pixels. The line will contain some runs of two or three pixels in a horizontal group. The result is a line that is lighter than the vertical line and that is noticeably jagged.

A similar affect occurs when you resize an image. If you enlarge an image by simply drawing each pixel as a larger block of the same color, the result is blocky. If you shrink an image by removing some pixels, the result may have tears and gaps.

Anti-aliasing is a process that smoothes out lines, text, and images. Instead of drawing a series of pixels that all have the same color, the drawing routines give pixels different shades of color to make the result smoother.

The Graphics object provides three properties that control anti-aliasing for lines and curves, text, and images: SmoothingMode, TextRenderingHint, and InterpolationMode.

SmoothingMode

The SmoothingMode property controls anti-aliasing for drawn lines and curves, and for filled shapes. This property can take the values AntiAlias, Default, HighQuality, HighSpeed, and None. The following code shows how a program might draw a circle's outline and a filled circle using the HighQuality SmoothingMode:

```
gr.SmoothingMode = SmoothingMode.HighQuality
gr.DrawEllipse(Pens.Black, 10, 10, 20, 20)
gr.FillEllipse(Brushes.Black, 30, 10, 20, 20)
```

Figure 19-12 shows the effects of each of the SmoothingModes. It's not clear whether there's any difference between the Default, HighSpeed, and None modes, or between HighQuality and AntiAlias, at least on this computer. The HighQuality and AntiAlias modes are noticeably smoother than the others, however.

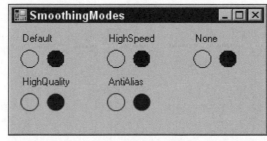

Figure 19-12: The Graphics **object's** SmoothingMode **property controls anti-aliasing for lines, curves, and filled shapes.**

TextRenderingHint

The TextRenderingHint property controls anti-aliasing for text. This property can take the values AntiAlias, AntiAliasGridFit, ClearTypeGridFit, SingleBitPerPixel, SingleBitPerPixel GridFit, and SystemDefault. The following code shows how a program can draw text using the TextRenderingHint value AntiAliasGridFit:

```
gr.TextRenderingHint = TextRenderingHint.AntiAliasGridFit
gr.DrawString("TextRenderingHint", Me.Font, Brushes.Black, 10, 10)
```

Figure 19-13 shows the effects of each of the TextRenderingHint values. The TextRenderingHint value SingleBitPerPixel produces a poor result. SystemDefault and SingleBitPerPixelGridFit give an acceptable result (the default appears to be AntiAliasGridFit on this computer). AntiAlias and AntiAliasGridFit give the best results.

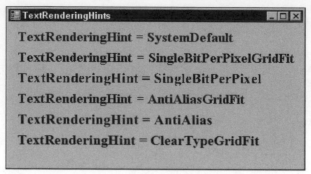

Figure 19-13: The `Graphics` object's `TextRenderingHint` property controls anti-aliasing for text.

Most of the differences are quite subtle. The "grid fit" versions use hinting about where the characters are positioned to try to improve stems and curves. If you look extremely closely (perhaps with a magnifying glass), you can see that the base of the initial "T" is a bit cleaner and more solid in the `AntiAliasGridFit` and `ClearTypeGridFit` modes than in the `AntiAlias` mode. The "grid fit" modes also provide text that is slightly more compact horizontally than the `AntiAlias` mode. In any case, each of the last three versions provides a very high-quality result.

InterpolationMode

The `InterpolationMode` property controls anti-aliasing when a program shrinks or enlarges an image. This property can take the values `Bicubic`, `Bilinear`, `Default`, `High`, `HighQualityBicubic`, `HighQualityBilinear`, `Low`, and `NearestNeighbor`.

The following code shows how a program can draw images using the `InterpolationMode` value `HighQualityBilinear`. The program starts by creating a `Bitmap` object and a `Graphics` object associated with it. It then uses the `Graphics` object to draw a smiley face on the `Bitmap`. The program uses the form's `Graphics` object's `DrawImage` method to draw the `Bitmap` onto the form at its full size. It then draws the `Bitmap` at a reduced size and draws the center of the `Bitmap` enlarged.

```
Private Sub Form1_Paint(ByVal sender As Object, _
  ByVal e As System.Windows.Forms.PaintEventArgs) Handles MyBase.Paint
    ' Draw a smiley face in the rectangle (0, 0) - (100, 100).
    Dim bm As New Bitmap(101, 101)
    Dim gr As Graphics = Graphics.FromImage(bm)
    gr.FillEllipse(Brushes.Yellow, 0, 0, 99, 99)     ' Face.
    gr.DrawEllipse(Pens.Black, 0, 0, 99, 99)
    gr.DrawArc(Pens.Black, 20, 20, 60, 60, 0, 180)   ' Smile.
    gr.FillEllipse(Brushes.Black, 40, 40, 20, 25)    ' Nose
    gr.FillEllipse(Brushes.White, 25, 15, 20, 25)    ' Left eye.
    gr.DrawEllipse(Pens.Black, 25, 15, 20, 25)
    gr.FillEllipse(Brushes.Black, 35, 20, 10, 15)
    gr.FillEllipse(Brushes.White, 55, 15, 20, 25)    ' Right eye.
    gr.DrawEllipse(Pens.Black, 55, 15, 20, 25)
    gr.FillEllipse(Brushes.Black, 65, 20, 10, 15)

    ' Display at full scale at (10, 10)-(110, 110).
    e.Graphics.DrawImage(bm, 10, 10)
```

```
        ' Display shrunk to fit the rectangle (120, 10)-(170, 60).
        e.Graphics.InterpolationMode = InterpolationMode.Bilinear
        e.Graphics.DrawImage(bm, 120, 10, 50, 50)

        ' Display the Bitmap rectangle (35, 35)-(65, 65)
        ' enlarged to fit the rectangle (180, 10)-(230, 60).
        Dim src_rect As New Rectangle(35, 35, 30, 30)
        Dim dest_rect As New Rectangle(180, 10, 50, 50)
        e.Graphics.DrawImage(bm, dest_rect, src_rect, GraphicsUnit.Pixel)
        e.Graphics.DrawRectangle(Pens.Red, dest_rect)
    End Sub
```

Figure 19-14 shows the effects of each of the `InterpolationMode` values. The large smiley face in the upper left shows the original image. Each of the other images shows the face shrunk and enlarged. It's hard to see the differences between the enlarged images (although the `NearestNeighbor` example is noticeably blockier than the others), but you can easily see breaks in the lower-quality shrunken versions.

Figure 19-14: The `Graphics` object's `InterpolationMode` property controls anti-aliasing for shrunk or enlarged images.

The `InterpolationMode` value `NearestNeighbor` gives the worst result when both shrinking and enlarging. The others give comparable results when enlarging. You can't see it in the book, but on the screen you can see very small differences between them.

When shrinking the image, however, `Default`, `Low`, `Bilinear`, and `Bicubic` all show ugly aliasing affects. Pieces of the lines are missing, so the lines appear broken.

The values `High`, `HighQualityBilinear`, and `HighQualityBicubic` produce much smoother results. You probably can't tell in the book without a microscope, but on the screen `HighQualityBilinear` gives a slightly better result than `HighQualityBicubic` and `High` (which is probably the same as `HighQualityBicubic` on this computer). These tiny differences will probably depend on the image you are shrinking. For example, most of these effects are much less noticeable when you enlarge and shrink photographs instead of drawn images.

Speed Considerations

The anti-aliasing settings for all three of these properties provide smoother results, but they are slower. For a few lines, strings, and images, the difference in performance won't be an issue. However, if you build a more intensive application (such as a mapping program that draws several thousand street segments on the form), you may notice a difference in speed.

Transformation Basics

Graphical transformations modify the coordinates and sizes you use to draw graphics to produce a result that is scaled, translated, or rotated. For example, you could apply a scaling transformation that multiples by 2 in the X direction and 3 in the Y direction. If you then drew a line between the points (10, 10) and (20, 20), the result drawn on the screen would connect the points (10 * 2, 10 * 3) = (20, 30) and (20 * 2, 20 * 3) = (40, 60). This stretches the line so it is larger overall, but it stretches its height more than its width (a factor of 3 versus a factor of 2). Notice that this also moves the line farther from the origin [from (10, 10) to (20, 30)]. In general, a scaling transformation moves an object farther from the origin unless it lies on the origin.

You don't really need to understand all the details of the mathematics of transformations to use them, but a little background is quit helpful.

In two dimensions, you can represent scaling, translation, and rotation with 3×3 matrices. You represent a point with a vector of three entries, two for the X and Y coordinates and a final 1 that gives the vector three entries so that it matches the matrices.

When you multiply a point's coordinates by a transformation matrix, the result is the transformed point.

To multiply a point by a matrix, you multiply the point's coordinates by the corresponding entries in the matrix's columns. The first transformed coordinate is the point's coordinates times the first column, the second transformed coordinate is the point's coordinates times the second column, and the third transformed coordinate is the point's coordinates times the third column.

The following calculation shows the result when you multiple a generic vector *<A, B, C>* by a matrix. When you work with two-dimensional transformations, the value *C* is always 1.

```
                | m11 m12 m13 |
  <A, B, C> *   | m21 m22 m23 |
                | m31 m32 m33 |
  = <A * m11 + B * m21 + C * m31,
     A * m12 + B * m22 + C * m32,
     A * m13 + B * m23 + C * m33>
```

The following matrix represents scaling by a factor of *Sx* in the X direction and a factor of *Sy* in the Y direction:

```
| Sx  0  0 |
|  0 Sy  0 |
|  0  0  1 |
```

The following example shows the point (10, 20) multiplied by a matrix that represents scaling by a factor of 2 in the X direction and 3 in the Y direction. The result is the vector <20, 60, 1>, which represents the point (20, 60) as you should expect.

```
                 | 2 0 0 |
   <10, 20, 1> * | 0 3 0 |
                 | 0 0 1 |
   = <10 * 2 + 20 * 0 + 1 * 0,
      10 * 0 + 20 * 3 + 1 * 0,
      10 * 0 + 20 * 0 + 1 * 1>
   = <20, 60, 1>
```

The following matrix represents translation through the distance *Tx* in the X direction and *Ty* in the Y direction:

```
| 1  0  Tx |
| 0  1  Ty |
| 0  0  1  |
```

The following matrix represents rotation through the angle *t*:

```
|  Cos(t)   Sin(t)   0 |
| -Sin(t)   Cos(t)   0 |
|    0         0      1 |
```

Finally, the following transformation, called the *identity transformation*, leaves the point unchanged. If you multiply a point by this matrix, the result is the same as the original point.

```
| 1 0 0 |
| 0 1 0 |
| 0 0 1 |
```

You can work through some examples to verify that these matrices represent translation, scaling, rotation, and the identity, or consult an advanced graphics programming book for proofs.

One of the most useful and remarkable properties of matrix/point multiplication is that it is associative. If p is a point and $T1$ and $T2$ are transformation matrices, $p * T1 * T2 = (p * T1) * T2 = p * (T1 * T2)$.

This result means that you can multiply any number of transformation matrices together to create a single combined matrix that represents all of the transformations applied one after the other. You can then apply this single matrix to all the points that you need to draw. This can save a considerable amount of time over multiplying each point by a long series of matrices one at a time.

The Graphics object maintains a current transformation matrix at all times, and it provides several methods that let you add more transformations to that matrix. The ScaleTransform, TranslateTransform, and RotateTransform methods add a new transformation to the current transformation. These methods take parameters that specify the amount by which points should be rotated, scaled, translated, or rotated.

A final parameter indicates whether you want to prepend the new transformation on the left (MatrixOrder.Prepend) or append it on the right (MatrixOrder.Append) of the current transformation. If you prepend the new transformation on the left, that transformation is applied before any that are already part of the current transformation. If you append the new transformation on the right, that transformation is applied after any that are already part of the current transformation.

Strangely, the default if you omit this parameter is to prepend the new transformation on the left. That means the new transformation applies to the point before any other transformations that you have previously applied. That, in turn, means that you must compose a combined transformation backward. If you want to rotate, then scale, then translate, you need to prepend the translation first, the scaling second, and the rotation last. That seems very counterintuitive.

A more natural approach is to explicitly set this final parameter to MatrixOrder.Append so that later transformations are applied after existing ones.

The following code shows how a program can use transformations to draw a complex result with a simple drawing routine. Subroutine DrawArrow draws an arrow within the rectangle 0 <= X <= 4, 0 <= Y <= 4. If you were to call this routine without any transformations, you would see a tiny arrow four pixels long and four pixels wide drawn in the upper-left corner of the form.

This form's Paint event handler uses the ScaleTransform method to give the Graphics object a transformation that scales by a factor of 30 in both the X and Y directions. It then calls the DrawArrow routine, passing it the parameter HatchStyle.Horizontal. The result is an arrow near the upper-left corner but 30 times larger than the original arrow and filled with a horizontal hatch pattern.

Next the program uses the TranslateTransform method to add a transformation that translates 150 pixels in the X direction and 60 pixels vertically. It appends this transformation so that the drawing is first scaled (the scaling transformation is still part of the Graphics object's current transformation) and then translated. It calls DrawArrow again, passing it the parameter HatchStyle.Vertical, so the result is an arrow 30 times larger than the original, moved 150 pixels to the right and 60 pixels down, and filled with a vertical hatch pattern.

Finally, the program uses the RotateTransform method to add a transformation that rotates the drawing by 30 degrees clockwise around the origin in the upper-left corner. It again appends the transformation so that the drawing is first scaled, then translated, and then rotated. It calls DrawArrow, passing it the parameter HatchStyle.Cross, so the result is an arrow 30 times larger than the original, moved 150 pixels to the right and 60 pixels down, rotated 30 degrees, and filled with a crosshatch pattern.

```
' Draw an arrow outline.
Private Sub DrawArrow(ByVal gr As Graphics, ByVal hatch_style As HatchStyle)
    Dim pts() As Point = { _
        New Point(0, 1), _
        New Point(2, 1), _
        New Point(2, 0), _
        New Point(4, 2), _
        New Point(2, 4), _
        New Point(2, 3), _
        New Point(0, 3) _
    }
    gr.FillPolygon(New HatchBrush(hatch_style, Color.Black, Color.White), pts)
    gr.DrawPolygon(New Pen(Color.Black, 0), pts)
End Sub

Private Sub Form1_Paint(ByVal sender As Object, _
  ByVal e As System.Windows.Forms.PaintEventArgs) Handles MyBase.Paint
```

```
    ' Scale by a factor of 30.
    e.Graphics.ScaleTransform(30, 30, MatrixOrder.Append)
    DrawArrow(e.Graphics, HatchStyle.Horizontal)

    ' Translate 150 horizontally and 60 vertically.
    e.Graphics.TranslateTransform(150, 60, MatrixOrder.Append)
    DrawArrow(e.Graphics, HatchStyle.Vertical)

    ' Rotate 30 degrees.
    e.Graphics.RotateTransform(30, MatrixOrder.Append)
    DrawArrow(e.Graphics, HatchStyle.Cross)
End Sub
```

Figure 19-15 shows the result.

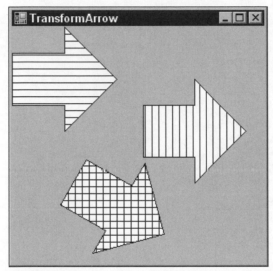

Figure 19-15: This program draws arrows scaled, translated, and rotated.

It is very important to realize that the order in which you apply transformations matters. You cannot change the order of scaling, translation, and rotation and expect the result to be the same.

The following code demonstrates this fact. This version of the DrawArrow subroutine draws a larger arrow that is not positioned in the upper-left corner of the screen. It fills the arrow with white and then outlines it in black. It then draws some text inside the arrow.

The form's Paint event handler sets the form's font, enables font anti-aliasing, and uses the DrawArrow subroutine to draw the untransformed arrow. Next, it uses a transformation to translate 150 pixels the X direction and 50 pixels in the Y direction, and draws the arrow again containing the text "A1." It then adds a rotation transformation to rotate 45 degrees and draws the arrow again, now containing the text "A2."

The program then uses the Graphics object's ResetTransformation method to remove the translation and rotation. It rotates 45 degrees and draws the arrow containing the text "B1." Finally, it translates the same distances as before and draws the arrow one last time, containing the text "B2."

```
' Draw an arrow outline containing some text.
Private Sub DrawArrow(ByVal gr As Graphics, ByVal txt As String)
    ' Draw the arrow.
    Dim pts() As Point = { _
        New Point(80, 20), _
        New Point(120, 20), _
        New Point(120, 10), _
        New Point(140, 30), _
        New Point(120, 50), _
        New Point(120, 40), _
        New Point(80, 40) _
    }
    gr.FillPolygon(Brushes.White, pts)
    gr.DrawPolygon(Pens.Black, pts)

    ' Draw the text.
    Dim layout_rectangle As New RectangleF(80, 20, 50, 20)
    Dim string_format As New StringFormat
    string_format.LineAlignment = StringAlignment.Center
    string_format.Alignment = StringAlignment.Center
    gr.DrawString(txt, Me.Font, Brushes.Black, _
        layout_rectangle, string_format)
End Sub

Private Sub Form1_Paint(ByVal sender As Object, _
 ByVal e As System.Windows.Forms.PaintEventArgs) Handles MyBase.Paint
    ' Set the font and font anti-aliasing properties.
    Me.Font = New Font("Times New Roman", 20, FontStyle.Bold, GraphicsUnit.Pixel)
    e.Graphics.TextRenderingHint = TextRenderingHint.AntiAliasGridFit

    ' Draw the original arrow.
    DrawArrow(e.Graphics, "")

    ' Translate 150 horizontally and 50 vertically.
    e.Graphics.TranslateTransform(150, 50, MatrixOrder.Append)
    DrawArrow(e.Graphics, "A1")

    ' Rotate 45 degrees.
    e.Graphics.RotateTransform(45, MatrixOrder.Append)
    DrawArrow(e.Graphics, "A2")

    ' Reset the transformation.
    e.Graphics.ResetTransform()

    ' Rotate 45 degrees.
    e.Graphics.RotateTransform(45, MatrixOrder.Append)
    DrawArrow(e.Graphics, "B1")

    ' Translate 150 horizontally and 50 vertically.
    e.Graphics.TranslateTransform(150, 50, MatrixOrder.Append)
    DrawArrow(e.Graphics, "B2")
End Sub
```

Figure 19-16 shows the result. The translation followed by rotation gives the arrow labeled "A2." The rotation followed by translation gives the arrow labeled "B2." It's clear from the figure that these are not even close to the same results.

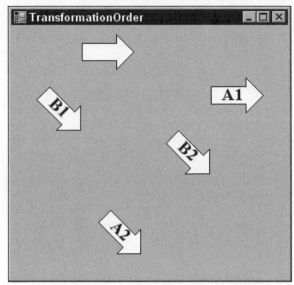

Figure 19-16: A translation followed by a rotation (A1 and A2) is not the same as a rotation followed by a translation (B1 and B2).

The Graphics object's methods for working with transformations include MultiplyTransform, PageScale, PageUnits, ResetTransformation, RotateTransform, ScaleTransform, Transform, TransformPoints, and TranslateTransform. See the section "Other Graphics Properties and Methods," earlier in this chapter for descriptions of those methods.

Notice also that the transformations apply to text as well as drawn lines and filled shapes.

Advanced Transformations

You can build very complex transformations by combining simple ones. For example, you can scale around an arbitrary point by combining simple translation and scaling transformations.

A normal scaling transformation moves an object farther away from the origin. If you scale the point (10, 20) by a factor of 20 in the X and Y directions, you get the point (200, 400), which is much father from the origin. Similarly, if you scale all the points in a shape, all the points move farther from the origin.

To scale the object around some point other than the origin, first translate it so the point of rotation is centered at the origin. Then scale it and translate it back to its original position.

The following code scales a diamond around its center. The DrawDiamond subroutine draws a diamond centered at the point (125, 125). The form's Paint event handler calls DrawDiamond to draw the original diamond. It then translates to move the diamond's center to the origin, scales by a factor of 2 vertically and horizontally, and then reverses the first translation to move the origin back to the diamond's original center.

```
Private Sub DrawDiamond(ByVal gr As Graphics)
    Dim pts() As Point = { _
        New Point(75, 125), _
        New Point(125, 75), _
        New Point(175, 125), _
        New Point(125, 175) _
    }
    gr.DrawPolygon(Pens.Black, pts)
End Sub

Private Sub Form1_Paint(ByVal sender As Object, _
 ByVal e As System.Windows.Forms.PaintEventArgs) Handles MyBase.Paint
    ' Draw the original diamond.
    DrawDiamond(e.Graphics)

    ' Translate to center at the origin.
    e.Graphics.TranslateTransform(-125, -125, MatrixOrder.Append)

    ' Scale by a factor of 2.
    e.Graphics.ScaleTransform(2, 2, MatrixOrder.Append)

    ' Translate the center back to where it was.
    e.Graphics.TranslateTransform(125, 125, MatrixOrder.Append)

    ' Draw the diamond.
    DrawDiamond(e.Graphics)
End Sub
```

Figure 19-17 shows the result.

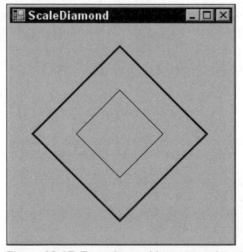

Figure 19-17: To scale an object at a point other than the origin, translate it to the origin, scale it, and then translate it back.

Notice that the lines' widths have also been scaled by a factor of 2 in this figure. The Pen object's Width property is a Single, so you can use fractional pen widths if necessary. For example, if you want to scale an object by a factor of 4 and you want the result to have a line width of 2, you can set the Pen's Width to 0.5 and let it scale.

If you want the final result to have a line width of 1, you can also set the Pen's Width to 0. This value tells the GDI+ routines to use a single pixel line width, no matter how the drawing is scaled.

Note also that the line width will not go below 1 if you use a scaling transformation to reduce the size of the drawing.

A particularly useful transformation maps a specific rectangle in world coordinates (the coordinates in which you draw) to a specific rectangle in device coordinates (the coordinates on the drawing surface). For example, you might graph a function in the world coordinates -1 <= X <= 1, -1 <= Y <= 1 and want to map it to the drawing surface rectangle 10 <= X <= 200, 10 <= Y <= 200.

To do this, you can first translate to center the world coordinate rectangle at the origin, scale to resize the rectangle to match the size of the device coordinate rectangle, and then translate to move the origin to the center of the device coordinate rectangle.

The MapRectangles subroutine shown in the following code maps a world coordinate rectangle into a device coordinate rectangle for a Graphics object. It begins by resetting the Graphics object's transformation to clear out anything that may already be in there. Next, the routine translates the center of the world coordinate rectangle to the origin, scales to stretch the world coordinate rectangle to the device coordinate rectangle's size, and then translates to move the origin to the center of the device-coordinate rectangle.

```
' Map a world coordinate rectangle to a device coordinate rectangle.
Private Sub MapRectangles(ByVal gr As Graphics, _
 ByVal world_rect As Rectangle, ByVal device_rect As Rectangle)
    ' Reset the transformation.
    gr.ResetTransform()

    ' Translate to center the world coordinate
    ' rectangle at the origin.
    gr.TranslateTransform( _
        CSng(-(world_rect.X + world_rect.Width / 2)), _
        CSng(-(world_rect.Y + world_rect.Height / 2)), _
        MatrixOrder.Append)

    ' Scale.
    gr.ScaleTransform( _
        CSng(device_rect.Width / world_rect.Width), _
        CSng(device_rect.Height / world_rect.Height), _
        MatrixOrder.Append)

    ' Translate to move the origin to the center
    ' of the device coordinate rectangle.
    gr.TranslateTransform( _
        CSng(device_rect.X + device_rect.Width / 2), _
        CSng(device_rect.Y + device_rect.Height / 2), _
        MatrixOrder.Append)
End Sub
```

The following code shows how a program can use this subroutine to position a drawing. The `DrawSmiley` subroutine draws a smiley face within the area $0 <= X <= 1, 0 <= Y <= 1$. The `Paint` event handler creates a `Rectangle` representing the device coordinates where it wants to draw the smiley face. It draws the rectangle so that you can see where the target is. The code then creates a world coordinate rectangle representing the area where the `DrawSmiley` subroutine draws the face. It calls subroutine `MapRectangles` to make the necessary transformation and calls `DrawSmiley` to draw the transformed face.

```
' Draw a smiley face in the rectangle
' 0 <= X <= 1, 0 <= Y <= 1.
Private Sub DrawSmiley(ByVal gr As Graphics)
    Dim the_pen As New Pen(Color.Black, 0)
    gr.FillEllipse(Brushes.Yellow, 0, 0, 1, 1)                  ' Face.
    gr.DrawEllipse(the_pen, 0, 0, 1, 1)
    gr.DrawArc(the_pen, 0.2, 0.2, 0.6, 0.6, 0, 180)            ' Smile.
    gr.FillEllipse(Brushes.Black, 0.4, 0.4, 0.2, 0.25)        ' Nose
    gr.FillEllipse(Brushes.White, 0.25, 0.15, 0.2, 0.25)      ' Left eye.
    gr.DrawEllipse(the_pen, 0.25, 0.15, 0.2, 0.25)
    gr.FillEllipse(Brushes.Black, 0.35, 0.2, 0.1, 0.15)
    gr.FillEllipse(Brushes.White, 0.55, 0.15, 0.2, 0.25)      ' Right eye.
    gr.DrawEllipse(the_pen, 0.55, 0.15, 0.2, 0.25)
    gr.FillEllipse(Brushes.Black, 0.65, 0.2, 0.1, 0.15)
End Sub

Private Sub Form1_Paint(ByVal sender As Object, _
 ByVal e As System.Windows.Forms.PaintEventArgs) Handles MyBase.Paint
    ' Draw the target rectangle.
    Dim device_rect As New Rectangle(50, 50, 150, 150)
    e.Graphics.DrawRectangle(Pens.Black, device_rect)

    ' Map between world and device coordinate rectangles.
    Dim world_rect As New Rectangle(0, 0, 1, 1)
    MapRectangles(e.Graphics, world_rect, device_rect)

    ' Draw the smiley face.
    DrawSmiley(e.Graphics)
End Sub
```

Figure 19-18 shows the result. Notice that the smiley face fits the target device coordinate rectangle nicely.

The previous example uses subroutine `MapRectangles` to scale and translate a drawing, but the routine can also stretch or flip the drawing. The program shown in Figure 19-19 is exactly the same as the previous example, except that it uses the following statement to define its device coordinate rectangle:

```
Dim device_rect As New Rectangle(50, 50, 50, 150)
```

Subroutine `MapRectangles` can be particularly handy if you need to graph an equation. Normally, in device coordinates, the origin is in the upper-left corner and Y values increase downward. When you draw a graph, however, the origin is in the lower-left corner and Y values increase upward. You could work out how to modify the equation you are trying to draw so that it comes out in the proper orientation, but it's much easier to use subroutine `MapRectangles` to flip the Y coordinates.

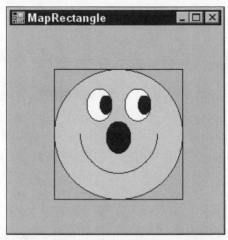

Figure 19-18: This program uses the `MapRectangles` subroutine to map a smiley face in world coordinates into a rectangle in device coordinates.

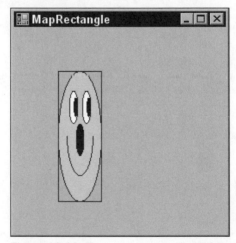

Figure 19-19: The `MapRectangles` subroutine can stretch a drawing by different amounts vertically and horizontally.

To invert the Y coordinates, set the device coordinate `Rectangle` structure's Y property to the largest Y coordinate you want to use, and set its height to the negative of the height you really want to use. For example, suppose that you want the graph to fill the device coordinate rectangle 50 <= X <= 200, 50 <= Y <= 200. The rectangle has width and height 150, so you would use the following statement to map the coordinate windows:

```
Dim device_rect As New Rectangle(50, 200, 150, -150)
```

Figure 19-20 shows the same smiley face program used in the previous examples drawn with this mapping. This doesn't particularly help the smiley face program because the DrawSmiley subroutine was written for a coordinate system where Y increases downward. It is more useful in situations such as graphing, where it is more natural for Y to increase upward.

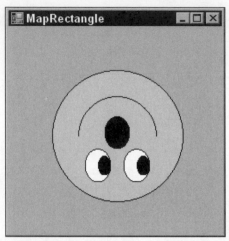

Figure 19-20: The MapRectangles subroutine can flip a drawing's
Y coordinates so that they increase upward instead of downward.

Notice that the target rectangle is not drawn in Figure 19-20 as it was in the previous two versions. The DrawRectangle subroutine won't draw rectangles with widths or heights less than 1, so the target rectangle doesn't appear.

You could also use subroutine MapRectangles to flip a drawing's X coordinates, although the need for that is much less common.

Saving and Restoring Graphics State

The Graphics object's Save method takes a snapshot of the object's graphic state and stores it in a GraphicsState object. Later, you can pass this GraphicsState object to the Graphics object's Restore method to return to the saved state.

Note that you can pass a particular GraphicsState object to the Restore method only once. If you want to use the same state again, you can call the Save method to save it again right after you restore it. That's the approach used by the following code. The program creates transformations that scale by a factor of 90 and then translate to move the origin to the center of the form. It then starts a loop to draw a rectangle rotated by angles between 5 degrees and 90 degrees.

Within the loop it calls the Save method to record the Graphics object's current state. That state includes the initial scaling and translation. The loop then adds a rotation transformation to the Graphics object. It passes the RotateTransform method the value MatrixOrder.Prepend, so the rotation is added to the *front* of the transformation matrix. That makes the combined transformation apply the rotation before the scaling and translation. In other words, drawings are rotated, then scaled, and then translated.

The loop then draws the rectangle -1 <= X <= 1, -1 <= Y <= 1, and then calls Restore to restore the saved graphics state that holds just the scaling and translation.

```
Private Sub Form1_Paint(ByVal sender As Object, _
  ByVal e As System.Windows.Forms.PaintEventArgs) Handles MyBase.Paint
    ' Scale by a factor of 90.
    e.Graphics.ScaleTransform(90, 90, MatrixOrder.Append)

    ' Translate to center on the form.
    e.Graphics.TranslateTransform( _
        Me.ClientRectangle.Width \ 2, _
        Me.ClientRectangle.Height \ 2, _
        MatrixOrder.Append)

    For i As Integer = 5 To 90 Step 5
        ' Save the state.
        Dim graphics_state As GraphicsState = e.Graphics.Save()

        ' Rotate i degrees.
        e.Graphics.RotateTransform(i, MatrixOrder.Prepend)

        ' Draw a rectangle.
        e.Graphics.DrawRectangle(New Pen(Color.Black, 0), -1, -1, 2, 2)

        ' Restore the saved state.
        e.Graphics.Restore(graphics_state)
    Next i
End Sub
```

Figure 19-21 shows the result.

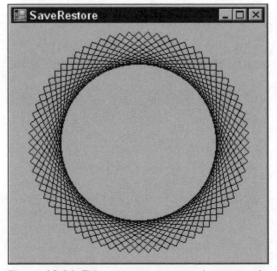

Figure 19-21: This program saves and restores the Graphics object's state containing a scaling and translation, adding an extra rotation as needed.

There are usually many other ways to achieve the same affect in graphics programming. While changing the order of transformations generally does not give the same result, you can always use different sets of transformations to produce the same outcome.

The following code shows a simpler `For` loop that creates the same result as the previous version. Rather than using `Restore` to remove the `Graphics` object's current rotation and replacing it with a new one, this version simply adds another 5-degree rotation to the current rotation. For example, a single 10-degree rotation is the same as two 5-degree rotations.

```
For i As Integer = 5 To 90 Step 5
    ' Rotate 5 degrees.
    e.Graphics.RotateTransform(5, MatrixOrder.Prepend)

    ' Draw a rectangle.
    e.Graphics.DrawRectangle(New Pen(Color.Black, 0), -1, -1, 2, 2)
Next i
```

Normally, you would not use `Save` and `Restore` if such a simple solution is available without them. `Save` and `Restore` are more useful when you want to perform several operations using the same transformation and other transformations are interspersed.

The following code shows yet another version. This code creates the initial transformation including the scaling and translation, and then saves the `Graphics` object's `Transfom` property in a transformation matrix variable. Then, in its `For` loop, the code sets the `Graphics` object's `Transfom` property to this saved matrix before applying the new rotation.

```
' Save the transformation.
Dim trans As Matrix = e.Graphics.Transform

For i As Integer = 5 To 90 Step 5
    ' Restore the saved transformation.
    e.Graphics.Transform = trans

    ' Rotate i degrees.
    e.Graphics.RotateTransform(i, MatrixOrder.Prepend)

    ' Draw a rectangle.
    e.Graphics.DrawRectangle(New Pen(Color.Black, 0), -1, -1, 2, 2)
Next i
```

Drawing Events

When part of a control must be redrawn, it generates a `Paint` event. For example, if you minimize a form and then restore it, partially cover a form with another form, or enlarge a form, parts of the form must be redrawn.

The `Paint` event handler provides a parameter e of type `PaintEventArgs`. That parameter's `Graphics` property holds a reference to a `Graphics` object that the event handler should use to redraw the control. This `Graphics` object has its clipping region set to the part of the control that must be redrawn. For example, if you make a form wider, the `Graphics` object is clipped, so it only draws on the new piece of form on the right that was just exposed. Clipping the Graphics object makes drawing a faster because the GDI+ routines can ignore drawing commands outside of the clipping region more quickly than it can draw them.

Clipping the Graphics object sometimes leads to unexpected results, particularly if the Paint event handler draws something that depends on the form's size. The following code draws a rectangle with an X in it filling the form whenever the form resizes:

```
Private Sub Form1_Paint(ByVal sender As Object, _
  ByVal e As System.Windows.Forms.PaintEventArgs) Handles MyBase.Paint
    e.Graphics.Clear(Me.BackColor)
    e.Graphics.DrawRectangle(Pens.Black, 0, 0, _
        Me.ClientSize.Width - 1, _
        Me.ClientSize.Height - 1)
    e.Graphics.DrawLine(Pens.Black, 0, 0, _
        Me.ClientSize.Width - 1, _
        Me.ClientSize.Height - 1)
    e.Graphics.DrawLine(Pens.Black, _
        Me.ClientSize.Width - 1, 0, _
        0, Me.ClientSize.Height - 1)
End Sub
```

Figure 19-22 shows the result after the form has been resized several times. Each time the form resizes, the Paint event handler draws the newly exposed region, but the existing drawing remains, giving the appearance of stacked envelopes.

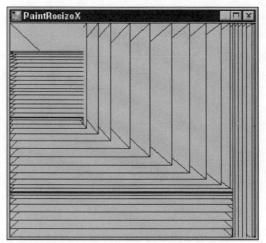

Figure 19-22: Paint **event handlers that adjust their drawings based on the form's size may produce unexpected results.**

Some computers generate Paint events every time the mouse moves during a resize, so the newly exposed areas are filled with a densely packed series of lines.

Paint event handlers also don't execute when the form shrinks. If the form shrinks, no new areas are exposed, so no Paint events fire.

Paint event handlers work well if the image on the control does not depend on the control's size. For example, if you want to draw an ellipse with bounds 10 <= X <= 300, 10 <= Y <= 10, then a Paint event handler works nicely.

If a drawing depends on the control's size, you must also draw the picture in the control's Resize event handler. The Resize event handler does not receive a Graphics object representing the control as a parameter, however, but you can use the control's CreateGraphics method to make one.

If you only draw in the Resize event handler, the image will not refresh if the control needs repainting. The solution is to draw the control in both the Paint and Resize event handlers. To avoid duplicating code, you can move the drawing statements into a separate subroutine and then call it from both the Paint and Resize event handlers. Because the Paint event handler provides a Graphics object for drawing, but the Resize event handler does not, you should pass the Graphics object on which this routine should draw into the routine. The following code shows an improved version of the previous example. Its Paint event handler calls subroutine DrawGraphics, passing it the event handler's Graphics object. The Resize event handler calls DrawGraphics, passing it a new Graphics object created for the form. Subroutine DrawGraphics uses its Graphics object parameter to draw a rectangle and an X filling the form.

```
Private Sub Form1_Paint(ByVal sender As Object, _
  ByVal e As System.Windows.Forms.PaintEventArgs) Handles MyBase.Paint
    DrawGraphics(e.Graphics)
End Sub

Private Sub Form1_Resize(ByVal sender As Object, _
  ByVal e As System.EventArgs) Handles MyBase.Resize
    DrawGraphics(Me.CreateGraphics())
End Sub

Private Sub DrawGraphics(ByVal gr As Graphics)
    gr.Clear(Me.BackColor)
    gr.DrawRectangle(Pens.Black, 0, 0, _
        Me.ClientSize.Width - 1, _
        Me.ClientSize.Height - 1)
    gr.DrawLine(Pens.Black, 0, 0, _
        Me.ClientSize.Width - 1, _
        Me.ClientSize.Height - 1)
    gr.DrawLine(Pens.Black, _
        Me.ClientSize.Width - 1, 0, _
        0, Me.ClientSize.Height - 1)
End Sub
```

When the form shrinks, only the Resize event handler fires. Similarly, if some or all of the form is hidden and then exposed, only the Paint event handler executes.

When the form is enlarged, however, the Resize event fires and draws the entire form. Then the Paint event handler fires and redraws the newly exposed areas. For simple images, this is not a problem. For very complex images that take a long time to draw, the user may see a noticeable delay or flicker.

Visual Basic provides an alternative strategy that allows a form to redraw itself only once when it is exposed or resized. As shown in the following code, first, set the form's ResizeRedraw property to True to indicate that the form should redraw itself when it is resized. Next use the form's SetStyle method to set the `AllPaintingInWmPaint` style to `True`. This tells Visual Basic that the form does all of its drawing in its `Paint` event handler. Now, when the form resizes, Visual Basic raises the `Paint` event in addition to the `Resize` event, so the program can do all of its drawing in the `Paint` event and not worry about why the `Resize` event.

```
Private Sub Form1_Load(ByVal sender As System.Object, _
 ByVal e As System.EventArgs) Handles MyBase.Load
    Me.ResizeRedraw = True
    Me.SetStyle(ControlStyles.AllPaintingInWmPaint, True)
End Sub

Private Sub Form1_Paint(ByVal sender As Object, _
 ByVal e As System.Windows.Forms.PaintEventArgs) Handles Me.Paint
    e.Graphics.Clear(Me.BackColor)
    e.Graphics.DrawRectangle(Pens.Black, 0, 0, _
        Me.ClientSize.Width - 1, _
        Me.ClientSize.Height - 1)
    e.Graphics.DrawLine(Pens.Black, 0, 0, _
        Me.ClientSize.Width - 1, _
        Me.ClientSize.Height - 1)
    e.Graphics.DrawLine(Pens.Black, _
        Me.ClientSize.Width - 1, 0, _
        0, Me.ClientSize.Height - 1)
End Sub
```

Another way to minimize drawing time is to make the drawing on a `Bitmap` and then set a `PictureBox`'s `Image` property to the result. When part of the `PictureBox` is exposed, it automatically redisplays the image without needing a `Paint` event handler. The section "Implementing 'AutoRedraw'" in Chapter 22, "Image Processing," describes technique in greater detail.

Summary

Visual Basic .NET provides a huge number of graphical classes. This chapter provides an overview of these classes. It also focuses on the most important graphics class: `Graphics`. The `Graphics` class provides methods that let you draw and fill rectangles, ellipses, polygons, curves, lines, and other shapes. `Pen` and `Brush` objects determine the appearance of lines (solid, dashed, dotted) and filled areas (solid colors, hatched, filled with a color gradient). Other `Graphics` properties and methods let you determine the types of anti-aliasing used when drawing different kinds of objects, and how drawings are transformed.

Chapter 20, "Brushes, Pens, and Paths," describes the next two most important graphics classes: `Brush` and `Pen`. It also explains the `GraphicsPath` object that you can use to draw and fill paths consisting of lines, shapes, curves, and text.

Brushes, Pens, and Paths

After `Graphics`, `Pen` and `Brush` are the two most important graphics classes. Whenever you perform any drawing operation that does not manipulate an image's pixels directly, you use a `Pen` or a `Brush`.

❑   `Pen`s control the appearance of lines. They determine a line's color, thickness, dash style, and caps.

❑   `Brush`es control the appearance of filled areas. They can fill an area with solid colors, hatched colors, a tiled image, or different kinds of color gradients.

This chapter describes `Pen`s and `Brush`es in detail. It shows how to use these classes to draw and fill all sorts of interesting shapes.

This chapter also describes the `GraphicsPath` class that represents a series of lines, shapes, curves, and text. You can fill a `GraphicsPath` using `Pen`s and `Brush`es.

Pen

The `Pen` object determines how lines are drawn. It determines the lines' color, thickness, dash style, join style, and end cap style.

A program can explicitly create `Pen` objects, but often it can simply use one of the more than 280 pens that are predefined by the `Pens` class. For example, the following code draws a rectangle using a hot pink line that's one pixel wide:

```
gr.DrawRectangle(Pens.HotPink, 10, 10, 50, 50)
```

`Pen`s are scaled by transformations applied to a `Graphics` object, however, so the result is not necessarily one pixel thick. If the `Graphics` object applies a transformation that scales by a factor of 10, the resulting line will have thickness 10.

One solution to this problem is to create a new `Pen` object setting its thickness to 0.1, as shown in the following code. The thickness is scaled to 0.1 * 10 = 1.

```
gr.DrawRectangle(New Pen(Color.HotPink, 0.1), 10, 10, 50, 50)
```

Another solution is to create a pen with thickness 0. The GDI+ routines always draw lines with 0 thickness one pixel wide.

The `Pen` class provides several overloaded constructors, which are described in the following table.

Constructors	Description
Pen(*brush*)	Creates a pen of thickness 1 using the indicated `Brush`. Lines are drawn as rectangles filled with the `Brush`. This makes the most sense for relatively thick lines, so the fill is visible. It produces sometimes irregular dashed or dotted results for thin lines.
Pen(*color*)	Creates a pen of thickness 1 using the indicated color.
Pen(*brush, thickness*)	Creates a pen with the indicated thickness (a `Single`) using a `Brush`.
Pen(*color, thickness*)	Creates a pen with the indicated thickness (a `Single`) using the indicated color.

The following table describes some of the `Pen` class's most useful properties and methods.

Property or Method	Purpose
Alignment	Determines whether the line is drawn inside or centered on the theoretical perfectly thin line specified by the drawing routine. See the section "Alignment" later in this chapter for examples.
Brush	Determines the `Brush` used to fill lines.
Color	Determines the lines' color.
CompoundArray	Lets you draw lines that are striped lengthwise. See the section "CompoundArray" later in this chapter for examples.
CustomEndCap	Determines the line's end cap. See the section "Custom Line Caps" later in this chapter for examples.
CustomStartCap	Determines the line's start cap. See the section, "Custom Line Caps," later in this chapter for examples.
DashCap	Determines the cap drawn at the ends of dashes. This can be `Flat`, `Round`, or `Triangle`.
DashOffset	Determines the distance from the start of the line to the start of the first dash.
DashPattern	An array of `Singles` that specifies a custom dash pattern. The array entries tell how many pixels to draw, skip, draw, skip, and so forth. Note that these values are scaled if the pen is not one pixel wide.

Property or Method	Purpose
DashStyle	Determines the line's dash style. This value can be Dash, DashDot, DashDotDot, Dot, Solid, or Custom. If you set the DashPattern property, this value is set to Custom. Note that the dashes and gaps between them are scaled if the pen is not one pixel wide.
EndCap	Determines the cap used at the end of the line. This value can be ArrowAnchor, DiamondAnchor, Flat, NoAnchor, Round, RoundAnchor, Square, SquareAnchor, Triangle, and Custom. If LineCap is Custom, you should use a CustomLineCap object to define the cap. Figure 20-1 shows the standard LineCap values.
LineJoin	Determines how lines are joined by a GDI+ method that draws connected lines. For example, the DrawPolygon and DrawLines methods use this property. This value can be Bevel, Miter, and Round. Figure 20-2 shows these values.
MultiplyTransform	Multiplies the Pen's current transformation by another transformation matrix. See the section, "Pen Transformations," later in this chapter for more information and examples.
ResetTransform	Resets the Pen's transformation to the identity transformation. See the section, "Pen Transformations," later in this chapter for more information and examples.
RotateTransform	Adds a rotation transformation to the Pen's current transformation. See the section, "Pen Transformations," later in this chapter for more information and examples.
ScaleTransform	Adds a scaling transformation to the Pen's current transformation. See the section, "Pen Transformations," later in this chapter for more information and examples.
SetLineCap	This method takes parameters that let you specify the Pen's StartCap, EndCap, and LineJoin properties at the same time.
StartCap	Determines the cap used at the start of the line. See the EndCap property for details.
Transform	Determines the transformation applied to the initially circular "pen tip" used to draw lines. The transformation lets you draw with an elliptical tip. See the section, "Pen Transformations," later in this chapter for more information and examples.
TranslateTransform	Adds a translation transformation to the Pen's current transformation. Pens ignore any translation component in their transformations, so this method does has no effect on the Pen's final appearance and was probably added for consistency and completeness. See the section, "Pen Transformations," later in this chapter for more information and examples.
Width	The width of the pen. This value is scaled if the pen is transformed either by its own transformation or by the transformation of the Graphics object that uses it.

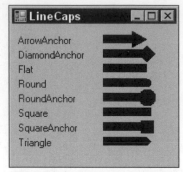

Figure 20-1: The `LineCap` enumeration determines how a line's endpoints are drawn.

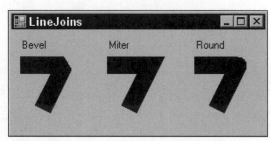

Figure 20-2: The `LineJoin` enumeration determines how lines are joined.

The following sections describe some of the `Pen` class's more confusing properties and methods.

Alignment

The `Alignment` property determines whether thick lines for closed curves are drawn inside or centered on the theoretical perfectly thin line specified by the drawing routine. This property can take the values `Center` or `Inset`.

The following code draws a circle with a thick white line and its pen's `Alignment` set to `Center`. It then draws the same circle with a thin black line. Next, the code repeats these steps, drawing its thick white circle with `Alignment` set to `Inset`.

```
Private Sub Form1_Paint(ByVal sender As Object, _
  ByVal e As System.Windows.Forms.PaintEventArgs) Handles MyBase.Paint
    Dim the_pen As New Pen(Color.White, 20)

    the_pen.Alignment = PenAlignment.Center
    e.Graphics.DrawEllipse(the_pen, 25, 25, 100, 100)
    e.Graphics.DrawEllipse(Pens.Black, 25, 25, 100, 100)

    the_pen.Alignment = PenAlignment.Inset
    e.Graphics.DrawEllipse(the_pen, 150, 25, 100, 100)
    e.Graphics.DrawEllipse(Pens.Black, 150, 25, 100, 100)
End Sub
```

Figure 20-3 shows the result.

The `Alignment` property applies only to closed figures such as ellipses, rectangles, and polygons. Open figures such as line segments, arcs, and unclosed curves are always drawn centered.

The `PenAlignment` enumeration also defines the values `Left`, `Right`, and `Outset`, but these have the same effect as the value `Center`.

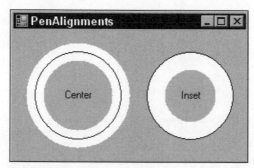

Figure 20-3: A `Pen`'s `Alignment` property determines whether the line is drawn on or inside its theoretical perfectly thin line.

CompoundArray

The `CompoundArray` property lets a program draw lines that are striped lengthwise. This property is an array of `Single` values that determine where the solid and empty parts of the line lie as a fraction of the line's width. For example, an array containing the values {0.0, 0.25, 0.75, 1.0} makes the first quarter of the line solid (0.0–0.25), the next half of the line not drawn (0.25–0.75), and the last quarter of the line solid (0.75–1.0).

The following code demonstrates the `CompoundArray` property. It creates a thick pen, sets its `CompoundArray` property to draw a line with a thin empty stripe down the middle, and draws a line. Next, the code sets the `CompoundArray` property to draw three equally sized and spaced stripes, and draws a rectangle and circle. Finally, the code sets the `Graphics` object's `SmoothingMode` property to `AntiAlias`, resets `CompoundArray` to draw a line with two thin empty stripes and draws another circle.

```
Private Sub Form1_Paint(ByVal sender As Object, _
  ByVal e As System.Windows.Forms.PaintEventArgs) Handles MyBase.Paint
    Dim the_pen As New Pen(Color.Black, 10)

    the_pen.CompoundArray = New Single() {0.0, 0.45, 0.55, 1.0}
    e.Graphics.DrawLine(the_pen, 10, 20, 400, 20)

    the_pen.CompoundArray = New Single() {0.0, 0.2, 0.4, 0.6, 0.8, 1.0}
    e.Graphics.DrawRectangle(the_pen, 20, 50, 100, 100)
    e.Graphics.DrawEllipse(the_pen, 150, 50, 100, 100)

    the_pen.CompoundArray = New Single() {0.0, 0.1, 0.2, 0.8, 0.9, 1.0}
    e.Graphics.SmoothingMode = Drawing2D.SmoothingMode.AntiAlias
    e.Graphics.DrawEllipse(the_pen, 300, 50, 100, 100)
End Sub
```

Figure 20-4 shows the result.

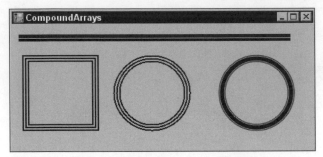

Figure 20-4: A Pen's CompoundArray **property lets you draw lines that are striped lengthwise.**

Custom Line Caps

The Pen class's CustomEndCap and CustomStartCap properties let you define your own end caps for lines. To make a custom cap, make a GraphicsPath object that defines the cap's drawing commands. This object should use a coordinate system where X increases to the left of the line, and Y increases in the direction of the line, as shown in Figure 20-5.

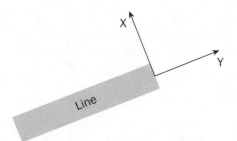

Figure 20-5: When building a custom line cap, X increases to the line's left and Y increases in the line's direction.

Next, create a CustomLineCap object, passing its constructor the GraphicsPath object. Pass the GraphicsPath as the first parameter if it defines a fill for the cap. Pass it as the second parameter if it defines drawn lines for the cap. Pass Nothing for the other parameter.

You can use the CustomLineCap object's properties and methods to modify its appearance. For example, its StrokeJoin property determines the style used to join the lines in the GraphicsPath, and its SetStrokeCaps method lets you specify the end caps for the lines in the GraphicsPath.

The following code shows an example. It defines an array of points that defines lines that make an X. It makes a GraphicsPath object and uses its AddLines method to add the lines to it. It then creates a CustomLineCap object, passing its constructor this GraphicsPath. The code makes a Pen and sets its CustomStartCap and CustomEndCap properties to the CustomLineCap object. It then draws four lines with different widths.

```
Private Sub Form1_Paint(ByVal sender As Object, _
 ByVal e As System.Windows.Forms.PaintEventArgs) Handles MyBase.Paint
    ' Make a GraphicsPath that draws an X.
    Dim pts() As Point = { _
        New Point(-2, -2), _
        New Point(0, 0), _
        New Point(-2, 2), _
        New Point(0, 0), _
        New Point(2, 2), _
        New Point(0, 0), _
        New Point(2, -2) _
    }

    Dim cap_path As New GraphicsPath
    cap_path.AddLines(pts)

    ' Make the CustomLineCap.
    Dim x_cap As New CustomLineCap(Nothing, cap_path)

    ' Draw some lines with x_cap.
    Dim the_pen As New Pen(Color.Black, 1)
    the_pen.CustomStartCap = x_cap
    the_pen.CustomEndCap = x_cap
    e.Graphics.DrawLine(the_pen, 50, 10, 200, 10)

    the_pen.Width = 5
    e.Graphics.DrawLine(the_pen, 50, 40, 200, 40)

    the_pen.Width = 10
    e.Graphics.DrawLine(the_pen, 50, 100, 200, 100)

    the_pen.Width = 20
    e.Graphics.DrawLine(the_pen, 50, 200, 200, 200)
End Sub
```

Figure 20-6 shows the result.

Pen Transformations

The Pen class has properties and methods that let you define a transformation. The Pen applies this transformation to its initially circular "tip" when drawing lines. The Pen ignores any translation component in the transformation, so the result is always an ellipse. (With some thought, you can probably convince yourself that any combination of scaling and rotation applied to a circle always gives an ellipse.) When the program draws with the transformed pen, its lines may have thick and thin elements similar to the ones you get when you draw with a calligraphy pen.

The following code uses a transformed Pen to draw a circle. It begins by defining some constants to make working with the circle easier. It defines the circle's center (Cx, Cy) and its radius R. It also defines a constant to represent the Pen's Width. Next, the program creates a new Pen with the desired width. It applies a scaling transformation to the pen, scaling by a factor of 4 in the Y direction. For the purposes of scaling Pens, the X and Y directions match those on the screen. This transformation stretches the Pen's tip vertically on the screen. Next, the program rotates the Pen's tip by 45 degrees.

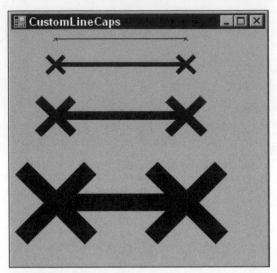

Figure 20-6: This program uses a `CustomLineCap` that draws an X at the end of lines.

The program sets the `Graphics` object's `SmoothingMode` property to `AntiAlias` and draws a circle centered at (*Cx*, *Cy*) with radius *R*.

Next, the program draws some ellipses showing where the Pen's tip was while it was drawing the circle. It starts by applying the same scaling and rotation transformations to the `Graphics` object. The program will later draw a circle with a diameter equal to the line's thickness and centered at the origin. These transformations give the circle the same shape as the `Pen`'s transformed tip. The final step is to translate these ellipses so that they lie along the path of the circle drawn earlier with the transformed `Pen`.

The program uses a loop to make an angle vary from 0 to 2 * *PI* radians in steps of *PI* /8. For each angle, the code saves the `Graphics` object's state so it doesn't lose the scaling and rotation it already applied. It then applies a translation transformation to move the origin to a point on the circle drawn earlier. The center of the circle is at (*Cx*, *Cy*). The points on the circle are offset from that point by *R* * Cos(angle) in the X direction and *R* * Sin(angle) in the Y direction.

Having defined all these transformations, the program draws a white ellipse centered at the origin and with diameter matching the `Pen`'s width. The transformations scale, rotate, and translate the ellipse to match one of the `Pen`'s tip positions while it drew the large ellipse. Finally, the code restores the saved graphics state so it is ready for the next trip through the loop.

```
Private Sub Form1_Paint(ByVal sender As Object, _
  ByVal e As System.Windows.Forms.PaintEventArgs) Handles MyBase.Paint
    Const Cx As Integer = 120
    Const Cy As Integer = 120
    Const R As Integer = 100
    Const PEN_WID As Integer = 10
```

```
' Draw a circle with a transformed Pen.
Dim the_pen As New Pen(Color.Black, PEN_WID)
the_pen.ScaleTransform(1, 4, MatrixOrder.Append)
the_pen.RotateTransform(45, MatrixOrder.Append)
e.Graphics.SmoothingMode = SmoothingMode.AntiAlias
e.Graphics.DrawEllipse(the_pen, Cx - R, Cx - R, R * 2, R * 2)

' Draw "Pen tips" on the circle.
e.Graphics.ScaleTransform(1, 4, MatrixOrder.Append)
e.Graphics.RotateTransform(45, MatrixOrder.Append)

For angle As Single = 0 To 2 * PI Step PI / 8
    Dim graphics_state As GraphicsState = e.Graphics.Save
    e.Graphics.TranslateTransform( _
        CSng(Cx + R * Cos(angle)), _
        CSng(Cy + R * Sin(angle)), _
        MatrixOrder.Append)
    e.Graphics.DrawEllipse(Pens.White, _
        -PEN_WID / 2, -PEN_WID / 2, PEN_WID, PEN_WID)
    e.Graphics.Restore(graphics_state)
Next angle
End Sub
```

Figure 20-7 shows the result. The small white ellipses show the positions that the Pen's tip took while drawing the large black ellipse. This picture should give you a good intuition for how transformed Pens work.

Figure 20-7: The white circles show where the Pen's transformed tip was as it drew the large black circle.

Brush

The `Brush` object determines how areas are filled when you draw them using the `Graphics` object's methods `FillClosedCurve`, `FillEllipse`, `FillPath`, `FillPie`, `FillPolygon`, `FillRectangle`, and `FillRectangles`. Different types of `Brushes` fill areas with solid colors, hatch patterns, and color gradients.

The `Brush` class itself is an abstract or `MustInherit` class, so you cannot make instances of the `Brush` class itself. Instead, you can create instances of one of the derived classes `SolidBrush`, `TextureBrush`, `HatchBrush`, `LinearGradientBrush`, and `PathGradientBrush`. The following table briefly describes these classes.

Class	Purpose
SolidBrush	Fills areas with a single solid color
TextureBrush	Fills areas with a repeating image
HatchBrush	Fills areas with a repeating hatch pattern
LinearGradientBrush	Fills areas with a linear gradient of two or more colors
PathGradientBrush	Fills areas with a color gradient that follows a path

The following sections describe these classes in more detail and provide examples.

SolidBrush

A `SolidBrush` fills areas with a single solid color. This class is extremely simple. It provides a single constructor that takes a parameter giving the brush's color. It's only commonly useful property is `Color`, which determines the brush's color.

A program can create a `SolidBrush` using its constructor, or it can use one of the 280+ predefined solid brushes defined by the `Brushes` class. The following code demonstrates both techniques. First, it creates a red `SolidBrush` and uses it to fill a rectangle. Then, it uses the `Brushes` class's `Blue` property to get a standard blue solid brush and fills another rectangle with that brush.

```
Private Sub Form1_Paint(ByVal sender As Object, _
  ByVal e As System.Windows.Forms.PaintEventArgs) Handles MyBase.Paint
    Dim red_brush As New SolidBrush(Color.Red)
    e.Graphics.FillRectangle(red_brush, 10, 10, 200, 100)

    Dim blue_brush As Brush = Brushes.Blue
    e.Graphics.FillRectangle(blue_brush, 10, 120, 200, 100)
End Sub
```

TextureBrush

A `TextureBrush` fills areas with an image, usually a Bitmap. The following table describes this class's most useful properties and methods.

Property or Method	Purpose
Image	The image that the brush uses to fill areas.
MultiplyTransform	Multiplies the brush's current transformation by another transformation matrix.
ResetTransform	Resets the brush's transformation to the identity transformation.
RotateTransform	Adds a rotation transformation to the brush's current transformation.
ScaleTransform	Adds a scaling transformation to the brush's current transformation.
Transform	A transformation that the brush applies to its image before using it to fill areas.
TranslateTransform	Adds a translation transformation to the brush's current transformation.
WrapMode	Determines how the brush wraps the image. This property can take the values Clamp (use a single copy that overlaps the origin of the shape's bounding rectangle), Tile (tile normally), TileFipX (tile flipping every other column of images over horizontally), TileFlipY (tile flipping every other row of images over vertically), and TileFlipXY (tile flipping every other column horizontally and every other row vertically). Figure 20-8 shows examples of these settings.

If you look closely at Figure 20-8, you'll see that the images do not always begin in the upper-left corner of the shape being filled. The brush essentially sets its tiling origin to the form's upper-left corner and then spaces its images accordingly.

If you want to move the tiling origin, you can apply a translation transformation to the brush to move the image to the new origin. The following code creates a TextureBrush using a PictureBox's Image property to define its image and sets WrapMode to TileFlipXY. It translates the brush to the point (50, 100) and then fills a rectangle with upper-left corner at this same point. This ensures that the first copy of the brush's image is placed exactly in the rectangle's upper-left corner. It also ensures that the first image is not flipped vertically or horizontally.

```
' Make a TextureBrush using the smiley face.
Dim texture_brush As New TextureBrush(picSmiley.Image)
texture_brush.WrapMode = System.Drawing.Drawing2D.WrapMode.TileFlipXY

texture_brush.TranslateTransform(50, 100)
DrawSample(e.Graphics, texture_brush, 50, 100)
```

The following code uses a transformed TextureBrush. First, it generates points to define a star-shaped polygon and creates a TextureBrush using a PictureBox's Image property to define its image. Next, the program scales the brush by a factor of 2 in the X direction, making the smiley face wider than normal. It then rotates the brush by 30 degrees, fills the star-shaped polygon with the brush, and then outlines the polygon in black.

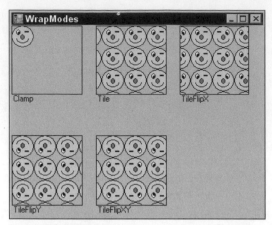

Figure 20-8: The TextureBrush's WrapMode
property determines how the brush tiles its image.

```
Private Sub Form1_Paint(ByVal sender As Object, _
 ByVal e As System.Windows.Forms.PaintEventArgs) Handles MyBase.Paint
    ' Generate points to draw a star shape.
    Dim cx As Integer = Me.ClientSize.Width \ 2
    Dim cy As Integer = Me.ClientSize.Height \ 2
    Dim r1 As Integer = Min(cx, cy) - 10
    Dim r2 As Integer = Min(cx, cy) \ 2
    Dim pts(9) As Point
    For i As Integer = 0 To 9 Step 2
        pts(i).X = cx + CInt(r1 * Cos(i * PI / 5 - PI / 2))
        pts(i).Y = cy + CInt(r1 * Sin(i * PI / 5 - PI / 2))
        pts(i + 1).X = cx + CInt(r2 * Cos((i + 1) * PI / 5 - PI / 2))
        pts(i + 1).Y = cy + CInt(r2 * Sin((i + 1) * PI / 5 - PI / 2))
    Next i

    ' Make a TextureBrush using the smiley face.
    Dim texture_brush As New TextureBrush(picSmiley.Image)
    texture_brush.ScaleTransform(2, 1, MatrixOrder.Append)
    texture_brush.RotateTransform(30, MatrixOrder.Append)

    e.Graphics.FillPolygon(texture_brush, pts)
    e.Graphics.DrawPolygon(Pens.Black, pts)
End Sub
```

Figure 20-9 shows the result. Notice that not only is the image transformed, but the tiled rows and columns are also transformed.

HatchBrush

A TextureBrush gives you complete control over every pixel in the filled area. You could build your own images to use as hatch patterns, but it's generally easier to use the HatchBrush class.

HatchBrush is a relatively simple class. Its three most useful properties are BackgroundColor, ForegroundColor, and HatchStyle. ForegroundColor and BackgroundColor determine the colors the brush uses. HatchStyle can take one of 54 values. Figure 20-10 lists the HatchStyle values and shows samples.

Figure 20-9: This star is filled with a
TextureBrush that is scaled and rotated.

The following code shows how a program can fill a rectangle with a HatchBrush. It makes a brush using the LargeConfetti style with a blue foreground and light blue background. It calls a Graphics object's FillRectangle method to fill a rectangle with this brush, and then calls DrawRectangle to outline the rectangle in black.

```
Dim the_brush As New HatchBrush(HatchStyle.LargeConfetti, _
    Color.Blue, Color.LightBlue)
gr.FillRectangle(the_brush, 10, 10, 200, 200)
gr.DrawRectangle(Pens.Black, 10, 10, 200, 200)
```

LinearGradientBrush

A LinearGradientBrush fills areas with a linear gradient of two or more colors. The simplest of these brushes shades an area smoothly from one color to another along a specified direction. For example, a rectangle might be red at one end and shade smoothly to blue at the other.

With some extra work, you can specify exactly how the colors blend from one to the other. For instance, you could make the colors blend quickly at the start and then slowly across the rest of the rectangle.

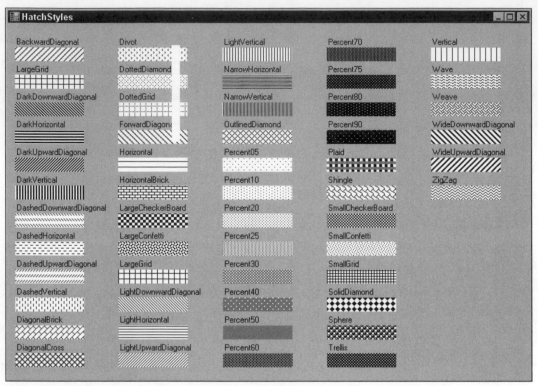

Figure 20-10: The `HatchStyle` enumeration determines which of 54 patterns a `HatchBrush` uses to fill an area.

You can also specify more than two colors for the brush. You could make the colors blend from red to green to blue.

The following table describes the `LinearGradientBrush`'s most useful properties and methods.

Property or Method	Purpose
Blend	A `Blend` object that determines how quickly the colors blend across the brush. By default, this is a simple linear blending.
InterpolationColors	A `ColorBlend` object that determines the colors (possibly more than two) that the brush blends and their positions within the blend.
LinearColors	An array of two colors that determines the starting and ending colors for a simple linear blend.
MultiplyTransform	Multiplies the brush's current transformation by another transformation matrix.
ResetTransform	Resets the brush's transformation to the identity transformation.

Property or Method	Purpose
RotateTransform	Adds a rotation transformation to the brush's current transformation.
ScaleTransform	Adds a scaling transformation to the brush's current transformation.
SetBlendTriangularShape	Makes the brush use a midpoint gradient where the color blends from the start color to the end color, and then back to the start color. You could do something similar with the Blend property, but this is easier.
SetSigmaBellShape	Makes the brush's color gradient change according to a bell curve instead of linearly.
Transform	A transformation that the brush applies to its gradient before using it to fill areas.
TranslateTransform	Adds a translation transformation to the brush's current transformation.
WrapMode	Determines how the brush wraps when it doesn't completely fill the area. This property can take the values Clamp, Tile, TileFipX, TileFlipY, and TileFlipXY. Because the brush is infinitely tall in the direction perpendicular to the line that determines its direction, not all of these values make a difference for all brushes.

Figure 20-11 shows an assortment of LinearGradientBrushes.

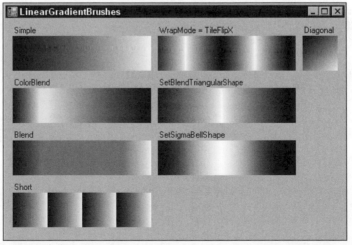

Figure 20-11: LinearGradientBrushes can produce all these effects and more.

The following code fills the rectangles shown in Figure 20-11. As you step through the code, refer to the figure to see the result.

The code begins by making a relatively straightforward `LinearGradientBrush` shading from black to white along the line starting at (9, 10) and ending at (210, 10). It then fills a rectangle with the brush. Notice that the points defining the brush determine the brush's drawing origin. The rectangle's X coordinates cover the same range as those of the brush, so the brush's origin lines up nicely with the rectangle. If the two did not line up, then the brush would finish its gradient before it reached the end of the rectangle and it would need to wrap. Usually, you will want the brush to line up with the object it is filling. You can arrange that by carefully defining the brush to fit over the object or by using a transformation to make it fit.

Next, the code creates a `ColorBlend` object. It passes the object's constructor the value 3 to indicate that it will use three colors. The code sets the `ColorBlend` object's `Colors` property to an array containing the three colors black, white, and black. This example uses black and white, so the result will show up well in the book, but you could use any colors here such as orange, hot pink, and blue. Next, the code sets the `ColorBlend` object's `Positions` property to an array of `Singles` that define the positions within the blend where the colors should be located. In this example, the first color (black) begins 0.0 of the way through the blend, the second color (white) sits 0.2 or 20 percent of the distance through the blend, and the third color (black again) sits at the end of the blend. You can see in Figure 20-11 that the white area is to the left of the center in this rectangle.

The code then creates a `Blend` object, passing its constructor the parameter 4 to indicate that the program will set four blend points. It sets the object's `Factors` property to an array of Singles that determine the fraction of the blend that should occur at the four points. It then sets the object's `Positions` property to an array that sets the positions of the blend points. In this example, the point 0.0 of the distance through the blend has factor 0.0, so the blend has not begun and that point has the start color. The point 0.2 of the distance through the blend has a factor of 0.5, so the blend should be half done at that point. The point 0.8 of the distance through the blend has a factor of 0.5, so the blend should still be only half done at that point. Finally, the point at the end of the blend should have the end color. The result is a blend that changes quickly initially, remains fixed for a stretch in the middle, and then finishes quickly. (An optical illusion makes the area on the left of the "flat" region in the middle appear brighter than it really is, and the area on the right appears darker than it really is.)

Next, the program makes a `LinearGradientBrush` that is defined by points too close together to cover its whole rectangle. The brush repeats its gradient as many times as necessary to cover the rectangle.

The program then changes the previous brush's `WrapMode` property to `TileFlipX`. When the brush must repeat its gradient to fill the rectangle, it reverses the start and end colors to produce a series of gradient bands.

Next, the program calls a brush's `SetBlendTriangularShape` method. This makes the gradient shade from the start color to the end color and back. The `SetBlendTriangularShape` method's parameter gives the position in the gradient where the end color should occur. You could get a similar affect using a `Blend`, but this method is easier for this kind of fill.

The program then calls the brush's `SetSigmaBellShape` method. It uses the same position parameter 0.5 as the previous call to `SetBlendTriangularShape`, so it places the end color in the middle of the gradient. The effect is similar to the triangular brush, except that the colors vary according to a bell curve instead of linear relationship. These two rectangles are lined up vertically in Figure 20-11, so it is easy to see the difference.

The code defines the final brush with a line that is not horizontal, so its gradient moves diagonally across its rectangle.

```
Private Sub Form1_Paint(ByVal sender As Object, _
 ByVal e As System.Windows.Forms.PaintEventArgs) Handles MyBase.Paint
    Dim y As Integer = 10
    Dim x As Integer = 10
    Dim wid As Integer = 200
    Dim hgt As Integer = 50

    ' Make a rectangle that shades from black to white.
    e.Graphics.DrawString("Simple", Me.Font, Brushes.Black, x, y)
    y += 15
    Dim black_white_brush As New _
        LinearGradientBrush( _
            New Point(x, y), New Point(x + wid, y), _
            Color.Black, Color.White)
    e.Graphics.FillRectangle(black_white_brush, _
        x, y, wid, hgt)
    y += hgt + 10

    ' ColorBlend.
    e.Graphics.DrawString("ColorBlend", Me.Font, Brushes.Black, x, y)
    y += 15
    Dim color_blend As New ColorBlend(3)
    color_blend.Colors = New Color() {Color.Red, Color.Green, Color.Blue}
    color_blend.Colors = New Color() {Color.Black, Color.White, Color.Black}
    color_blend.Positions = New Single() {0.0, 0.2, 1.0}
    black_white_brush.InterpolationColors = color_blend
    e.Graphics.FillRectangle(black_white_brush, _
        x, y, wid, hgt)
    y += hgt + 10

    ' Make a brush that makes 50 percent of the color change
    ' in the first 20 percent of the distance, stays there
    ' until 80 percent of the distance, and then finishes
    ' in the remaining distance.
    e.Graphics.DrawString("Blend", Me.Font, Brushes.Black, x, y)
    y += 15
    Dim the_blend As New Blend(4)
    the_blend.Factors = New Single() {0.0, 0.5, 0.5, 1.0}
    the_blend.Positions = New Single() {0.0, 0.2, 0.8, 1.0}
    black_white_brush.Blend = the_blend
    e.Graphics.FillRectangle(black_white_brush, _
        x, y, wid, hgt)
    y += hgt + 10

    ' This brush's line is too short to cross the whole rectangle.
    e.Graphics.DrawString("Short", Me.Font, Brushes.Black, x, y)
    y += 15
    Dim short_brush As New _
        LinearGradientBrush( _
            New Point(x, y), New Point(x + 50, y), _
            Color.Black, Color.White)
    e.Graphics.FillRectangle(short_brush, _
```

```
        x, y, wid, hgt)
    y += hgt + 10

    x += wid + 10
    y = 10

    ' Change the brush's WrapMode.
    e.Graphics.DrawString("WrapMode = TileFlipX", Me.Font, Brushes.Black, x, y)
    y += 15
    short_brush.WrapMode = WrapMode.TileFlipX
    e.Graphics.FillRectangle(short_brush, _
        x, y, wid, hgt)
    y += hgt + 10

    ' Trangular brush.
    e.Graphics.DrawString("SetBlendTriangularShape", Me.Font, Brushes.Black, x, y)
    y += 15
    black_white_brush.SetBlendTriangularShape(0.5)
    e.Graphics.FillRectangle(black_white_brush, _
        x, y, wid, hgt)
    y += hgt + 10

    ' Sigma bell shape.
    e.Graphics.DrawString("SetSigmaBellShape", Me.Font, Brushes.Black, x, y)
    y += 15
    black_white_brush.SetSigmaBellShape(0.5, 1)
    e.Graphics.FillRectangle(black_white_brush, _
        x, y, wid, hgt)
    y += hgt + 10

    ' A diagonal brush.
    x += wid + 10
    y = 10
    wid = hgt
    e.Graphics.DrawString("Diagonal", Me.Font, Brushes.Black, x, y)
    y += 15
    Dim diag_brush As New _
        LinearGradientBrush( _
            New Point(x, y), New Point(x + wid, y + hgt), _
            Color.Black, Color.White)
    e.Graphics.FillRectangle(diag_brush, _
        x, y, wid, hgt)
    y += hgt + 10
End Sub
```

PathGradientBrush

A `PathGradientBrush` object fills areas with a color gradient that blends colors from a center point to the points along a path. For example, you might shade from white in the middle of an ellipse to blue along its edges.

The `Blend`, `InterpolationColors`, `SetBlendTriangularShape`, `SetSigmaBellShape`, and other properties and methods that deal with the characteristics of the blend work along lines running from the center point to the points on the path. For example, you can use this object's `Blend` property to determine how quickly colors blend across the brush. In the `LinearGradientBrush` class, this property determines how the colors blend from one side of the brush to the other. In a `PathGradientBrush`, it controls how the colors blend from the center point to the path's points.

The following table describes the `PathGradientBrush`'s most useful properties and methods.

Property or Method	Purpose
Blend	A `Blend` object that determines how quickly the colors blend across the brush. By default, this is a simple linear blending.
CenterColor	Determines the color at the center point.
CenterPoint	Determines the location of the center point. By default, this point is set to the center of the path.
InterpolationColors	A `ColorBlend` object that determines the colors (possibly more than two) that the brush blends and their positions within the blend.
MultiplyTransform	Multiplies the brush's current transformation by another transformation matrix.
ResetTransform	Resets the brush's transformation to the identity transformation.
RotateTransform	Adds a rotation transformation to the brush's current transformation.
ScaleTransform	Adds a scaling transformation to the brush's current transformation.
SetBlendTriangularShape	Makes the brush use a midpoint gradient where the color blends from the start color to the end color and then back to the start color. You could do something similar with the `Blend` property, but this is easier.
SetSigmaBellShape	Makes the brush's color gradient change according to a bell curve instead of linearly.
SurroundColors	An array of `Colors` that correspond to the points on the path. The color gradient blends from the `CenterColor` to these colors around the edge of the path. If there are more points in the path than colors, the final color is repeated as needed. Note that curves such as ellipses define a large number of colors that you do not explicitly specify, so making these colors match up with points on the curve can be difficult. This property is easier to understand for polygons.
Transform	A transformation that the brush applies to its gradient before using it to fill areas.
TranslateTransform	Adds a translation transformation to the brush's current transformation.

Table continued on following page

581

Property or Method	Purpose
WrapMode	Determines how the brush wraps when it doesn't completely fill the area. This property can take the values Clamp, Tile, TileFipX, TileFlipY, and TileFlipXY. Because the brush is infinitely tall in the direction perpendicular to the line that determines its direction, not all of these values make a difference for all brushes.

Figure 20-12 shows an assortment of PathGradientBrushes.

The following code fills the shapes shown in Figure 20-12. As you step through the code, refer to the figure to see the result.

The code first creates an array of Point objects initialized to form a rectangle. It passes those points to the constructor for a PathGradientBrush and then uses the brush to fill that rectangle. This is about the simplest PathGradientBrush you can build, so it's worth studying a bit before moving on to more confusing examples. Notice that the color shades smoothly from black in the center to white on the rectangle's edges (those are the default colors).

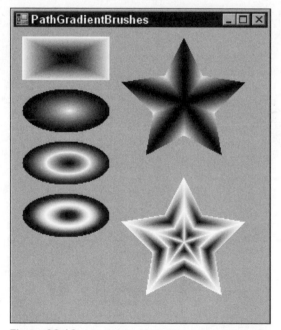

Figure 20-12: PathGradientBrush**es can produce all these effects and more.**

Next, the program makes a GraphicsPath object and adds an ellipse to it. It passes the GraphicsPath to the PathGradientBrush's constructor. It then sets the brush's CenterColor and SurroundColors properties. The `SurroundColors` array doesn't contain enough values for every point on the elliptical path, so the last color (black) is repeated as much as necessary. The program fills the ellipse with this brush.

The code then creates a new `GraphicsPath` object, adds a new ellipse, and uses it to make a `PathGradientBrush` as before. It also sets the brush's `CenterColor` and `SurroundColors` properties as before. The program then calls the brush's `SetBlendTriangularShape` method to make the colors along the lines from the center point to the path's edges blend from the end color to the start color and back. The parameter 0.5 makes the start color appear halfway from the center point to the edge.

Next, the program repeats these same steps, except that it calls the brush's `SetSigmaBellShape` method instead of `SetBlendTriangularShape`. The result is similar to the previous result, except that the colors vary according to a bell curve instead of a linear relationship.

The code then generates an array of points that defines a star shape. It creates a new `GraphicsPath` object and calls its `AddPolygon` method to add the star. It passes this `GraphicsPath` object to the `PathGradientBrush`'s constructor to make the brush use the star as its path. The program then sets the brush's `SurroundPoints` property to an array containing the `Colors` it should use for each of the star's points. The code fills the star using this brush to draw a star where the tips of the star are black and the rest of the shape's points vary from white to black.

Finally, the program repeats the previous steps to define a new star-shaped brush. It creates a new `Blend` object and sets its `Position` and `Factors` properties to indicate how the gradient should progress from the center point to the shape's edges. The `Positions` values give locations along a line from the center to an edge point. The `Factors` values indicate how far the blend should have progressed for the corresponding point. For example, this code's second entries for those arrays are 0.25 and 1.0 to indicate that the point one quarter of the distance from the center point to an edge point should have blended completely to the end color. This example sets its `Factors` values so the color blends from the start color to the end color several times.

```
Private Sub Form1_Paint(ByVal sender As Object, _
  ByVal e As System.Windows.Forms.PaintEventArgs) Handles MyBase.Paint
    Dim x As Integer = 10
    Dim y As Integer = 10
    Dim wid As Integer = 100
    Dim hgt As Integer = 50

    ' Fill a rectangle.
    Dim rect_pts() As Point = { _
        New Point(x, y), _
        New Point(x + wid, y), _
        New Point(x + wid, y + hgt), _
        New Point(x, y + hgt) _
    }
    Dim path_brush As New PathGradientBrush(rect_pts)
    e.Graphics.FillPolygon(path_brush, rect_pts)
    y += hgt + 10

    ' Fill an ellipse setting CenterColor and SurroundColors.
    Dim ellipse_path As New GraphicsPath
    ellipse_path.AddEllipse(x, y, wid, hgt)
```

```
path_brush = New PathGradientBrush(ellipse_path)
path_brush.CenterColor = Color.White
path_brush.SurroundColors = New Color() {Color.Black}
e.Graphics.FillEllipse(path_brush, x, y, wid, hgt)
y += hgt + 10

' Fill an ellipse using SetBlendTriangularShape.
ellipse_path = New GraphicsPath
ellipse_path.AddEllipse(x, y, wid, hgt)
path_brush = New PathGradientBrush(ellipse_path)
path_brush.CenterColor = Color.White
path_brush.SurroundColors = New Color() {Color.Black}
path_brush.SetBlendTriangularShape(0.5)
e.Graphics.FillEllipse(path_brush, x, y, wid, hgt)
y += hgt + 10

' Fill an ellipse using SetSigmaBellShape.
ellipse_path = New GraphicsPath
ellipse_path.AddEllipse(x, y, wid, hgt)
path_brush = New PathGradientBrush(ellipse_path)
path_brush.CenterColor = Color.White
path_brush.SurroundColors = New Color() {Color.Black}
path_brush.SetSigmaBellShape(0.5, 1)
e.Graphics.FillEllipse(path_brush, x, y, wid, hgt)
y += hgt + 10

' Fill a star shape.
x += wid + 10
y = 10
wid = 150
hgt = 150
Dim cx As Integer = x + wid \ 2
Dim cy As Integer = y + hgt \ 2
Dim r1 As Integer = CInt(wid * 0.5)
Dim r2 As Integer = CInt(hgt * 0.25)
Dim star_pts(9) As Point
For i As Integer = 0 To 9 Step 2
    star_pts(i).X = cx + CInt(r1 * Cos(i * PI / 5 - PI / 2))
    star_pts(i).Y = cy + CInt(r1 * Sin(i * PI / 5 - PI / 2))
    star_pts(i + 1).X = cx + CInt(r2 * Cos((i + 1) * PI / 5 - PI / 2))
    star_pts(i + 1).Y = cy + CInt(r2 * Sin((i + 1) * PI / 5 - PI / 2))
Next i
Dim star_path As New GraphicsPath
star_path.AddPolygon(star_pts)
Dim star_brush As New PathGradientBrush(star_pts)
star_brush.CenterColor = Color.Black
star_brush.SurroundColors = New Color() { _
    Color.Black, Color.White, _
    Color.Black, Color.White, _
    Color.Black, Color.White, _
    Color.Black, Color.White, _
    Color.Black, Color.White _
}
e.Graphics.FillPolygon(star_brush, star_pts)
y += hgt + 10
```

```
                ' Fill a star shape.
                cx = x + wid \ 2
                cy = y + hgt \ 2
                r1 = CInt(wid * 0.5)
                r2 = CInt(hgt * 0.25)
                For i As Integer = 0 To 9 Step 2
                    star_pts(i).X = cx + CInt(r1 * Cos(i * PI / 5 - PI / 2))
                    star_pts(i).Y = cy + CInt(r1 * Sin(i * PI / 5 - PI / 2))
                    star_pts(i + 1).X = cx + CInt(r2 * Cos((i + 1) * PI / 5 - PI / 2))
                    star_pts(i + 1).Y = cy + CInt(r2 * Sin((i + 1) * PI / 5 - PI / 2))
                Next i
                star_path = New GraphicsPath
                star_path.AddPolygon(star_pts)
                star_brush = New PathGradientBrush(star_pts)
                star_brush.CenterColor = Color.White
                star_brush.SurroundColors = New Color() { _
                    Color.White, Color.Black, _
                    Color.White, Color.Black, _
                    Color.White, Color.Black, _
                    Color.White, Color.Black, _
                    Color.White, Color.Black _
                }
                Dim star_blend As New Blend
                star_blend.Positions = New Single() {0.0, 0.25, 0.5, 0.75, 1.0}
                star_blend.Factors = New Single() {0.0, 1.0, 0.0, 1.0, 0.0}
                star_brush.Blend = star_blend
                e.Graphics.FillPolygon(star_brush, star_pts)
                y += hgt + 10
        End Sub
```

GraphicsPath Objects

A GraphicsPath object represents a path defined by lines, curves, text, and other drawing commands. A GraphicsPath can even include other GraphicsPath objects.

You can use a Graphics object's DrawPath and FillPath methods to draw or fill a GraphicsPath. For example, the following code creates a GraphicsPath object and adds a string to it. It creates a TextureBrush from a PictureBox's image and uses the FillPath method to fill the path with the TextureBrush. It finishes by calling the DrawPath method to outline the path in black.

```
    Private Sub Form1_Paint(ByVal sender As Object, _
     ByVal e As System.Windows.Forms.PaintEventArgs) Handles MyBase.Paint
        ' Make a GraphicsPath containing text.
        Dim txt As String = "Path"
        Dim graphics_path As New GraphicsPath
        graphics_path.AddString(txt, _
            New FontFamily("Times New Roman"), _
            FontStyle.Bold, 150, _
            New Point(0, 0), _
            New StringFormat)
```

```
      ' Fill the path with an image.
      Dim smiley_brush As New TextureBrush(picSmiley.Image)
      e.Graphics.FillPath(smiley_brush, graphics_path)
      e.Graphics.DrawPath(Pens.Black, graphics_path)
   End Sub
```

Figure 20-13 shows the result.

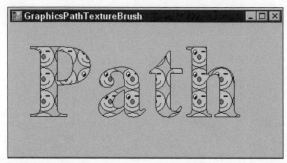

Figure 20-13: A program can use a `Graphics` object's `FillPath` and `DrawPath` methods to fill and draw a `GraphicsPath` object.

In addition to drawing and filling a `GraphicsPath`, you can also use one to define a region. The following code creates a `GraphicsPath` representing text much as the previous example does. It then sets the form's `Region` property equal to a new `Region` object created from the `GraphicsPath`. This restricts the form to the region. Any pieces of the form that lie outside of the textual path are chopped off, so they are not drawn and mouse events in those areas fall through to whatever lies below the form.

When you use a path to define a form's region, the path is taken relative to the form's origin, which is not the same as the origin of the form's client area. The form's origin is at the upper-left corner of the form, including its borders and title bar. To allow for this difference in origins, the code uses the `PointToScreen` method to get the screen coordinates of the client area's origin.

The code applies a translation transformation to the `Graphics` object so the client area origin is mapped to the form's origin. It then sets the `Graphics` object's `SmoothingMode`, fills the path with white, and then outlines the path with a thick black pen.

```
   Private Sub Form1_Paint(ByVal sender As Object, _
    ByVal e As System.Windows.Forms.PaintEventArgs) Handles MyBase.Paint
      ' Make a GraphicsPath containing text.
      Dim txt As String = "Path"
      Dim graphics_path As New GraphicsPath
      graphics_path.AddString(txt, _
          New FontFamily("Times New Roman"), _
          FontStyle.Bold, 150, _
          New Point(0, 0), _
          New StringFormat)

      ' Set the form's region to the path.
      Me.Region = New Region(graphics_path)
```

```
        ' Fill the path with white and outline it in black.
        Dim origin As Point = Me.PointToScreen(New Point(0, 0))
        e.Graphics.TranslateTransform(Me.Left - origin.X, Me.Top - origin.Y)
        e.Graphics.SmoothingMode = SmoothingMode.AntiAlias
        e.Graphics.FillPath(Brushes.White, graphics_path)
        e.Graphics.DrawPath(New Pen(Color.Black, 5), graphics_path)
    End Sub
```

Figure 20-14 shows the result. Here the form is sitting above the Visual Basic development environment.

Because the 5-pixel wide line around the path is centered on the edge of the form's region, half of it is cut off.

Notice also that the path used in this example cut the form's borders and title bar off, so the user has no way to resize, move, or close this form. If you use this technique in an application, be sure to at least provide some method for the user to close the form. For example, you could provide a button or context menu. Or you could unload the form if the user clicked on it or pressed a certain key while the form had the input focus.

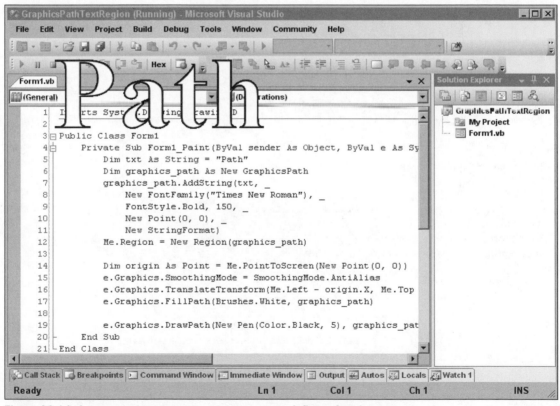

Figure 20-14: A program can use a `GraphicsPath` to define a form's `Region`.

One more use for `GraphicsPaths` is to define clipping regions. The following code creates a `GraphicsPath` containing text much as the previous examples do. It then calls the `Graphics` object's `SetClip` method to make this path the form's clipping region. Next, the program draws 200 lines between randomly generated points on the form. Only the parts of the lines inside the clipping region are drawn.

```
Private Sub Form1_Paint(ByVal sender As Object, _
 ByVal e As System.Windows.Forms.PaintEventArgs) Handles MyBase.Paint
    ' Make a GraphicsPath containing text.
    Dim txt As String = "Path"
    Dim graphics_path As New GraphicsPath
    graphics_path.AddString(txt, _
        New FontFamily("Times New Roman"), _
        FontStyle.Bold, 150, _
        New Point(0, 0), _
        New StringFormat)
    e.Graphics.SetClip(graphics_path)

    ' Fill the ClientRectangle with white.
    e.Graphics.FillRectangle(Brushes.White, Me.ClientRectangle)

    ' Draw a bunch of random lines on the form.
    Dim rnd As New Random
    Dim x1, y1, x2, y2 As Integer
    For i As Integer = 1 To 200
        x1 = rnd.Next(0, Me.ClientSize.Width - 1)
        y1 = rnd.Next(0, Me.ClientSize.Height - 1)
        x2 = rnd.Next(0, Me.ClientSize.Width - 1)
        y2 = rnd.Next(0, Me.ClientSize.Height - 1)
        e.Graphics.DrawLine(Pens.Black, x1, y1, x2, y2)
    Next i
End Sub
```

Figure 20-15 shows the result.

Figure 20-15: A program can use a `GraphicsPath` object to define a clipping region.

The `GraphicsPath` class provides many methods for adding lines, curves, text, and other shapes to the path. These methods include `AddArc`, `AddBezier`, `AddBeziers`, `AddClosedCurve`, `AddCurve`, `AddEllipse`, `AddLine`, `AddLines`, `AddPath`, `AddPie`, `AddPolygon`, `AddRectangle`, `AddRectangles`, and `AddString`. These are roughly analogous to the `Draw` and `Fill` methods provided by the `Graphics` object. For example, `DrawEllipse` draws an ellipse, `FillEllispe` fills an ellipse, and `AddEllipse` adds an ellipse to a path.

The following table describes the `GraphicsPath` object's other most useful properties and methods.

Property or Method	Purpose
CloseAllFigures	Closes all open figures by connecting their last points with their first points, and then starts a new figure.
CloseFigure	Closes the current figure by connecting its last point with its first point, and then starts a new figure. For example, if you draw a series of lines and arcs, this method closes the figure.
FillMode	Determines how the path handles overlaps when you fill it. This property can take the values `Alternate` and `Winding`. Figure 20-16 shows the difference.
Flatten	Converts any curves in the path into a sequence of lines. For example, this lets you explicitly calculate colors for every point in the path when setting a `PathGradientBrush`'s `SurroundColors` property.
GetBounds	Returns a `RectangleF` structure representing the path's bounding box.
GetLastPoint	Returns the last `PointF` structure in the `PathPoints` array.
IsOutlineVisible	Returns `True` if the indicated point lies beneath the path's outline.
IsVisible	Returns `True` if the indicated point lies within the path's interior.
PathData	Returns a `PathData` object that encapsulates the path's graphical data. It holds arrays similar to those returned by the `PathPoints` and `PathTypes` properties.
PathPoints	Returns an array of `PointF` structures giving the points in the path.
PathTypes	Returns an array of `Bytes` representing the types of the points in the path.
PointCount	Returns the number of points in the path.
Reset	Clears the path data and resets `FillMode` to `Alternate`.
Reverse	Reverses the order of the path's data.
StartFigure	Starts a new figure so future data is added to the new figure. Later, calling `CloseFigure` will close this figure, but not the previous one.
Transform	Applies a transformation matrix to the path.
Warp	Applies a warping transformation to the path. The transformation is defined by mapping a parallelogram to a rectangle.
Widen	Enlarges the curves in the path to enclose a line drawn by a specific pen.

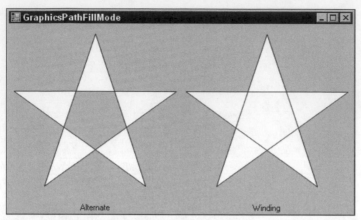

Figure 20-16: These polygonal paths were filled with white and drawn with black. The GraphicsPath **object's** FillMode **property determines how the areas between the lines are filled.**

Garbage-Collection Issues

Objects such as brushes contain references to memory and graphics resources. If you allocate a lot of brushes and then let them go out of scope, they become candidates for garbage collection. Later, when the system decides it needs to free some memory, it walks through all of the objects that you have previously allocated and determines which ones are not reachable by your code. It frees those objects and makes their memory available for future use.

Unfortunately, if those objects contain references to other objects, the garbage collector may think those second-hand objects are still referenced by the original object, so it will not collect them until it runs a second time.

For example, suppose that your program allocates a brush, uses it, and lets it fall out of scope. When the garbage collector runs, it sees that the brush refers to some resources, so it doesn't reclaim them. It sees that your program is no longer using the brush, however, so it frees that memory. The next time the garbage collector runs, the brush is gone, so nothing refers to the brush's secondary resources and the garbage collector can free those, too.

While the garbage collector eventually frees all of the memory, it takes longer than necessary. It ties up memory longer and that may force more frequent garbage collection.

You can speed up the process greatly by explicitly calling the brush object's Dispose method. Dispose makes the brush free its internal resources and prepare for garbage collection. Now, when the garbage collector runs, it frees both the brush and its secondary resources in a single pass.

The following code shows how to use the Dispose method. When the form loads, this code makes a new Bitmap object to fit the form. It attaches a Graphics object to the Bitmap, makes a HatchBrush and `Pen`, and uses them to draw a filled ellipse on the `Bitmap`. The program then sets the form's `BackgroundImage` property to the `Bitmap`. Finally, the code calls the `Dispose` method for the `HatchBrush`, `Pen`, and `Graphics` objects.

```
Private Sub Form1_Load(ByVal sender As System.Object, _
 ByVal e As System.EventArgs) Handles MyBase.Load
    ' Make a new bitmap to fit the form.
    Dim bm As New Bitmap(Me.ClientRectangle.Width, Me.ClientRectangle.Height)
    Dim gr As Graphics = Graphics.FromImage(bm)
    gr.Clear(Me.BackColor)

    ' Fill an ellipse.
    Dim hatch_brush As New HatchBrush(HatchStyle.LargeConfetti, _
        Color.Blue, Color.Yellow)
    Dim rect As New Rectangle(10, 10, _
        Me.ClientRectangle.Width - 20, _
        Me.ClientRectangle.Height - 20)
    gr.FillEllipse(hatch_brush, rect)

    ' Outline the ellipse.
    Dim thick_pen As New Pen(Color.Black, 5)
    gr.DrawEllipse(thick_pen, rect)

    ' Set the result as the form's BackgroundImage.
    Me.BackgroundImage = bm

    ' Free resources.
    hatch_brush.Dispose()
    thick_pen.Dispose()
    gr.Dispose()
End Sub
```

Whenever you can call an object's `Dispose` method, you should. This lets the garbage collector reclaim memory more efficiently.

You cannot always call `Dispose`, however. If you call `Dispose` on an object that is still needed by some other object, the program will crash. For example, the previous code uses a `Bitmap` object. It's not obvious from the code, but the form's `BackgroundImage` property continues to reference that object after this subroutine exits. If the program calls the `Bitmap`'s `Dispose` method, then the form later throws an "`Invalid parameter used`" exception.

Summary

Visual Basic .NET provides a huge variety of objects for drawing graphics. The three most important drawing classes are `Graphics`, `Pen`, and `Brush`.

The `Graphics` object represents the canvas on which you will draw. It provides methods that let you draw and fill all sorts of shapes including lines, rectangles, ellipses, polygons, text, and curves. It also provides methods for transforming those commands to translate, scale, and rotate the results.

The `Pen` object determines the appearance of lines. It sets the lines' color, thickness, dash style, fill pattern, and caps.

Various kinds of brush objects determine the appearance of filled areas. They can fill areas with solid colors, tiled images, hatch patterns, linear color gradients, and color gradients that follow a path.

These classes and the others described in this chapter give you powerful tools for drawing graphics of practically unlimited complexity and sophistication.

This chapter discusses the brushes, pens, and paths that you use to draw lines, curves, and other shapes. Chapter 21, "Text," explains how to draw text. While you can display simple text in a `Label`, `TextBox`, or other control, when you draw text using GDI+ routines you have greater control over exactly how the text is drawn.

21

Text

Text is different from the lines, rectangles, ellipses, and other kinds of shapes that a program typically draws. A program normally draws and fills a rectangle in separate steps. On the other hand, a program typically draws text in a single step, usually with a solid color.

Text also differs in the way it is drawn by the GDI+ routines. To draw a line, rectangle, or ellipse, the program specifies the shape's location, and the GDI+ routines draw it accordingly. Text is not specified by simple location data. A program can specify the text's general location but has only limited control over its size. Different characters may have different widths in a particular font, so strings containing the same number of characters may have different sizes when displayed.

Even if you know every character's nominal size, you may not be able to add them up to calculate the size of a string. Fonts sometimes use special algorithms that adjust the spacing between certain pairs of letters to make the result look better. For example, a font might decrease the spacing between the characters A and W when they appear next to each other (as in AW) to allow the W to lean over the A.

This chapter describes some of the tools that Visual Basic provides for controlling text. It explains how to draw text aligned and formatted in various ways, and how to measure text so that you can figure out more exactly where it will appear.

Note that several examples use the `Graphics` object's `TextRenderingHint` property to make text appear smoother. For more information on this property, see the section "System.Drawing.Text" in Chapter 19, "Drawing Basics."

Drawing Text

The `Graphics` object's `DrawString` method draws text. It provides several overloaded versions that let you specify the string, font, positioning, and alignment information.

One of the simplest versions of `DrawString` takes only four parameters: the text to draw, the font to use, the brush to use when filling the text, and the position where the text should start. The following code draws some text starting at the point (10, 10) on the form. It then draws a circle around this point.

```
Private Sub Form1_Paint(ByVal sender As Object, _
  ByVal e As System.Windows.Forms.PaintEventArgs) Handles MyBase.Paint
    Dim txt As String = "The quick brown fox jumps over the lazy dog."
    Dim big_font As New Font("Times New Roman", 30, FontStyle.Bold)

    e.Graphics.TextRenderingHint = _
        System.Drawing.Text.TextRenderingHint.AntiAliasGridFit
    e.Graphics.DrawString(txt, big_font, Brushes.Black, 10, 10)
    e.Graphics.DrawEllipse(Pens.Black, 8, 8, 4, 4)
End Sub
```

Figure 21-1 shows the result. Notice that the text doesn't begin exactly at the point (10, 10). The text contains some leading space on the top and bottom that move it slightly right and downward from the starting point.

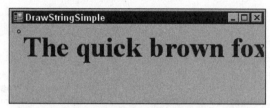

Figure 21-1: Text doesn't begin exactly at the starting point passed to the `DrawString` **method.**

Notice also that the text runs blithely off the edge of the form. The following section describes ways you can format text so it automatically provides alignment and wrapping as necessary.

`DrawString` automatically starts a new line when it encounters a Carriage Return/Line Feed pair in the text. It also advances to the next tab stop when it encounters a Tab character. The following code is similar to the previous version, except that the text includes Tab characters and Carriage Return/Line Feed pairs:

```
Private Sub Form1_Paint(ByVal sender As Object, _
  ByVal e As System.Windows.Forms.PaintEventArgs) Handles MyBase.Paint
    Dim txt As String = "The" & vbTab & "quick" & vbCrLf & _
        "brown" & vbTab & "fox" & vbCrLf & _
        "jumps" & vbTab & "over" & vbCrLf & _
        "the" & vbTab & "lazy" & vbCrLf & _
        "dog."
    Dim big_font As New Font("Times New Roman", 30, FontStyle.Bold)

    e.Graphics.TextRenderingHint = _
        System.Drawing.Text.TextRenderingHint.AntiAliasGridFit
    e.Graphics.DrawString(txt, big_font, Brushes.Black, 10, 10)
    e.Graphics.DrawEllipse(Pens.Black, 8, 8, 4, 4)
End Sub
```

Figure 21-2 shows the result.

Figure 21-2: `DrawString` **automatically processes Tab characters and Carriage Return/Line Feed pairs.**

Text Formatting

Some of the overloaded versions of the `Graphics` object's `DrawString` method take additional parameters that help format the text. The first of these parameters is a layout rectangle. This is a `RectangleF` structure that indicates the area where the text should be drawn. The second parameter is a `StringFormat` object that determines how the text is formatted.

The following code draws text inside a rectangle. It begins by defining the text, font, and the layout rectangle. It then creates a `StringFormat` object. It sets the object's `Alignment` property to `Center` to position each line of text centered horizontally in the layout rectangle. It sets the object's `LineAlignment` property to `Near`. That makes the text align vertically to the near vertical edge of the rectangle (its top). The program calls `DrawString` to draw the text and then uses `DrawRectangle` to display the layout rectangle.

The `Alignment` and `LineAlignment` properties both can take the values `Near`, `Center`, and `Far`. Using these values for both properties can make the properties somewhat confusing. On systems that draw right to left and top to bottom, the values are relative to a point in the upper-left corner of the text, so `Near` means left/top, `Center` means center/center, and `Far` means right/bottom.

```
Private Sub Form1_Paint(ByVal sender As Object, _
  ByVal e As System.Windows.Forms.PaintEventArgs) Handles MyBase.Paint
    Dim txt As String = "The quick brown fox jumps over the lazy dog."
    Dim big_font As New Font("Times New Roman", 30, FontStyle.Bold)

    Dim layout_rect As New RectangleF(10, 10, _
        Me.ClientSize.Width - 20, Me.ClientSize.Height - 20)
```

```
        Dim string_format As New StringFormat
        string_format.Alignment = StringAlignment.Center
        string_format.LineAlignment = StringAlignment.Near

        e.Graphics.DrawString(txt, big_font, Brushes.Black, layout_rect, string_format)

        e.Graphics.DrawRectangle(Pens.Black, Rectangle.Round(layout_rect))
    End Sub
```

Figure 21-3 shows the result. Notice that the text is centered horizontally and aligned to the top of the layout rectangle.

Figure 21-3: The `DrawString` method can use a layout rectangle and a `StringFormat` object to format text.

The `StringFormat` object provides several other properties and methods that you can use to position text. The following table describes the most useful of these.

Property or Method	Purpose
Alignment	Determines the text's horizontal alignment. This can be Near (left), Center (middle), or Far (right).
FormatFlags	Gets or sets flags that modify the `StringFormat` object's behavior. See the section "FormatFlags" later in this chapter for more information.
GetTabStops	Returns an array of Singles, giving the positions of tab stops. See the section "Tab Stops" later in this chapter for more information.

Property or Method	Purpose
HotkeyPrefix	Determines how the hotkey prefix character is displayed. (In a menu caption or label, the *hotkey* is underlined to show that pressing Alt-*<hotkey>* performs some special action. For example, in most applications Alt-F opens the File menu. A program specifies a control's hotkey character by placing an ampersand in front of it. For example, "&File" is displayed as "File.") If HotkeyPrefix is Show, any character that follows an ampersand is drawn as an underlined hotkey (a double ampersand is drawn as a single ampersand). If this is None, any ampersands are drawn as ampersands. If this is Hide, hotkey ampersands are hidden.
LineAlignment	Determines the text's vertical alignment. This can be Near (top), Center (middle), or Far (bottom).
SetMeasureableCharacterRanges	Sets an array of CharacterRange structures representing ranges of characters that will later be measured by the Graphics object's MeasureCharacterRanges method.
SetTabStops	Sets an array of Singles giving the positions of tab stops. See the section "Tab Stops" later in this chapter for more information.
Trimming	Determines how the text is trimmed if it cannot fit in the layout rectangle. See the section "Trimming" later in this chapter for more information.

The following sections describe some of the more complex formatting issues in greater detail.

FormatFlags

The StringFormat object's FormatFlags property determines the object's behavior. This property can take a bitwise combination of the values described in the following table.

FormatFlags Value	Purpose
DirectionRightToLeft	Indicates that the text is drawn from right to left.
DirectionVertical	Indicates that the text is drawn vertically.
FitBlackBox	Indicates that no character should extend beyond the layout rectangle. If this is not set, some characters in certain fonts may stick out a bit.
LineLimit	If the last line displayed in the layout rectangle is too tall to fit, this flag indicates that it should be omitted. By default, that line is clipped to show whatever parts will fit.

Table continued on following page

FormatFlags Value	Purpose
MeasureTrailingSpaces	Indicates that the Graphics object's MeasureString method should include spaces at the ends of lines. By default, it does not.
NoClip	Indicates that parts of characters that hang over the layout rectangle are not clipped.
NoFontFallback	If a character is missing from the selected font, the GDI+ normally looks for an equivalent character in another font. This flag prevents that and forces the character to be displayed as the font's missing character glyph (usually an open square).
NoWrap	Indicates that text should not be wrapped.

Figure 21-4 shows the difference between the default, NoClip, and LineLimit flags. If the last visible line won't fit within the layout rectangle, the default behavior is to clip the line to show whatever fits. If FormatFlags is NoClip, that line is displayed entirely. If FormatFlags is LineLimit, the line is omitted entirely.

Figure 21-4: The NoClip **and** LineLimit **flags change how a** StringFormat **object handles the text's last displayed line.**

The following code uses the DirectionVertical flag. After defining a string, font, and layout rectangle, it creates a StringFormat object. It sets the object's Alignment and LineAlignment properties to center the text and then sets its FormatFlags property to the combination of the values DirectionVertical and DirectionRightToLeft. Then the program draws the text as usual.

```
Private Sub Form1_Paint(ByVal sender As Object, _
  ByVal e As System.Windows.Forms.PaintEventArgs) Handles MyBase.Paint
    Dim txt As String = "The quick brown fox jumps over the lazy dog."
    Dim the_font As New Font("Times New Roman", 30, _
        FontStyle.Bold, GraphicsUnit.Pixel)
    Dim layout_rect As New RectangleF(0, 0, _
        Me.ClientSize.Width - 1, Me.ClientSize.Height - 1)

    Dim string_format As New StringFormat
    string_format.Alignment = StringAlignment.Center
    string_format.LineAlignment = StringAlignment.Center
    string_format.FormatFlags = _
        StringFormatFlags.DirectionVertical Or _
        StringFormatFlags.DirectionRightToLeft

    e.Graphics.TextRenderingHint = _
        System.Drawing.Text.TextRenderingHint.AntiAliasGridFit
    e.Graphics.DrawString(txt, the_font, Brushes.Black, layout_rect, string_format)
End Sub
```

Figure 21-5 shows the result.

This example sets the `FormatFlags` property to `DirectionVertical` plus `DirectionRightToLeft`. If you omit the second flag, the lines of text are drawn left to right. That means the line "The quick" appears on the left and the subsequent lines appear moving to the right, so the lines are drawn in the reverse of the order that you might expect.

Note that you can also draw vertical text by applying a transformation to the `Graphics` object that translates the text to the origin, rotates it, and translates the text back to where it belongs.

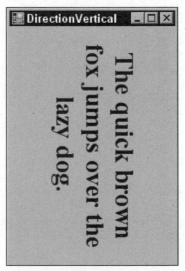

Figure 21-5: Setting the `StringFormat` object's `FormatFlags` property to `DirectionVertical` produces vertical text.

The following code demonstrates this technique. It defines its text and font and makes a layout rectangle. It uses the form's width to define the rectangle's height and the form's height to define the rectangle's width, so the rectangle will fit the form after it is rotated. The code creates a `StringFormat` object to center the text and applies the transformations to the `Graphics` object. Finally, the code draws the text. The result is similar to the text produced by the previous example.

```
Private Sub Form1_Paint(ByVal sender As Object, _
 ByVal e As System.Windows.Forms.PaintEventArgs) Handles MyBase.Paint
    ' Define the text and font.
    Dim txt As String = "The quick brown fox jumps over the lazy dog."
    Dim the_font As New Font("Times New Roman", 30, _
        FontStyle.Bold, GraphicsUnit.Pixel)

    ' Define the layout rectangle. It's slightly smaller
    ' than the form rotated 90 degrees so the rotated
    ' text will fit the form nicely.
    Dim rect_wid As Integer = Me.ClientSize.Height - 20
    Dim rect_hgt As Integer = Me.ClientSize.Width - 20
    Dim layout_rect As New RectangleF( _
        (Me.ClientSize.Width - rect_wid) \ 2, _
        (Me.ClientSize.Height - rect_hgt) \ 2, _
        rect_wid, rect_hgt)

    ' Set the StringFormat to center the text.
    Dim string_format As New StringFormat
    string_format.Alignment = StringAlignment.Center
    string_format.LineAlignment = StringAlignment.Center

    ' Translate to the origin, rotate, and translate back.
    e.Graphics.TranslateTransform( _
        -Me.ClientSize.Width \ 2, _
        -Me.ClientSize.Height \ 2, _
        MatrixOrder.Append)
    e.Graphics.RotateTransform(90, MatrixOrder.Append)
    e.Graphics.TranslateTransform( _
        Me.ClientSize.Width \ 2, _
        Me.ClientSize.Height \ 2, _
        MatrixOrder.Append)

    ' Draw the text and layout rectangle.
    e.Graphics.TextRenderingHint = _
        System.Drawing.Text.TextRenderingHint.AntiAliasGridFit
    e.Graphics.DrawString(txt, the_font, Brushes.Black, layout_rect, string_format)
    e.Graphics.DrawRectangle(Pens.Black, Rectangle.Round(layout_rect))
End Sub
```

This approach is a bit more complicated than the previous method of setting the `StringFormat` object's `FormatFlags` property to `DirectionVertical`, but it gives you more flexibility. Simply by changing the rotation transformation, you can draw text at any angle, not just rotated 90 degrees. Figure 21-6 shows this program with the angle of rotation changed from 90 to 60 degrees.

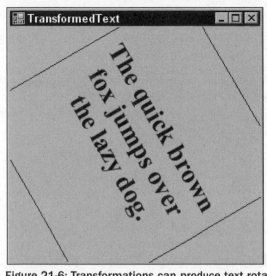

Figure 21-6: Transformations can produce text rotated at any angle.

Tab Stops

The `StringFormat` object's `GetTabStops` and `SetTabStops` methods let you get and set an array of `Singles` that determine the position of the layout rectangle's tab stops. Each entry in the array gives the distance between two tab stops. For example, the values {50, 50, 50} specify tab stops 50, 100, and 150 pixels from the left edge of the layout rectangle.

The following code shows how to use the `SetTabStops` method. It starts by creating a font, layout rectangle, and `StringFormat` object. It sets two tab stops 60 and 140 (60 + 80) pixels from the left edge of the layout rectangle. It then draws the rectangle and draws vertical lines showing the positions of the tab stops.

The program generates some random data, separating values on each row with Tab characters and separating each row with Carriage Return/Line Feed pairs. Finally, the program draws the text.

```
Private Sub Form1_Paint(ByVal sender As Object, _
 ByVal e As System.Windows.Forms.PaintEventArgs) Handles MyBase.Paint
    ' Define the font, layout rectangle, and StringFormat.
    Dim the_font As New Font("Times New Roman", 15, _
        FontStyle.Regular, GraphicsUnit.Pixel)
    Dim layout_rect As New RectangleF(10, 10, _
        Me.ClientSize.Width - 20, Me.ClientSize.Height - 20)
    Dim string_format As New StringFormat

    ' Set the tab stops.
    Dim tab_stops() As Single = {60, 80}
    string_format.SetTabStops(0, tab_stops)
```

```
' Draw the layout rectangle and tab stops.
e.Graphics.DrawRectangle(Pens.White, Rectangle.Round(layout_rect))
Dim x As Single = layout_rect.X
For i As Integer = 0 To tab_stops.Length - 1
    x += tab_stops(i)
    e.Graphics.DrawLine(Pens.White, x, layout_rect.Top, x, layout_rect.Bottom)
Next i

' Generate some random values.
Dim rnd As New Random
Dim txt As String = "Alpha" & vbTab & "Gamma" & vbTab & "Value" & vbCrLf
For r As Integer = 1 To 10
    txt &= rnd.Next(10, 99) & vbTab & _
        rnd.NextDouble.ToString("0.000000") & vbTab & _
        rnd.NextDouble.ToString("0.00") & vbCrLf
Next r

' Draw the text.
e.Graphics.TextRenderingHint = _
    System.Drawing.Text.TextRenderingHint.AntiAliasGridFit
e.Graphics.DrawString(txt, the_font, Brushes.Black, layout_rect, string_format)
End Sub
```

Figure 21-7 shows the result.

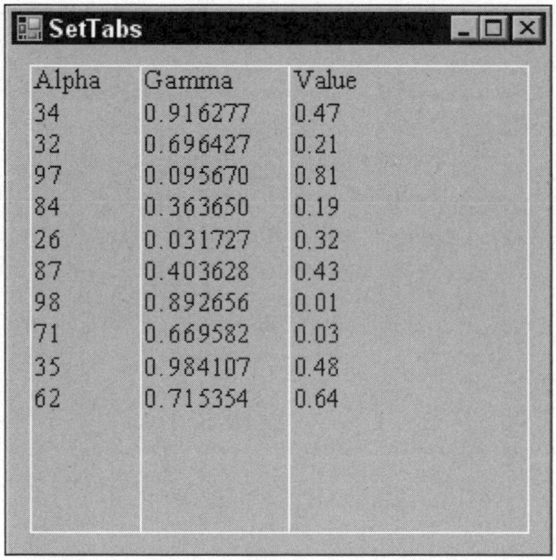

Figure 21-7: The SetTabStops method lets you easily align text.

Trimming

Normally, a string is wrapped as necessary until its layout rectangle is full. If there is still text that has not been displayed, the `Trimming` property determines how that text is handled. The following table describes the values this property can take.

Trimming Value	Purpose
Character	The text is trimmed to the nearest character.
EllipsisCharacter	The text is trimmed to the nearest character and an ellipsis is displayed at the end of the line.
EllipsisPath	The center of the line is removed and replaced with an ellipsis. This is sometimes a good choice when displaying file paths because it shows the beginning of the path and the file name. This method keeps as much of the last backslash (\) delimited part of the text as possible (it assumes that this is a file name).
EllipsisWord	The text is trimmed to the nearest word and an ellipsis is displayed at the end of the line.
None	The text is not trimmed. Instead, it is wrapped to the next line, which is hidden because it is below the bottom of the layout rectangle. If the last visible line contains a word break, the line will wrap after the last word that fits. That makes this seem similar to the Word setting.
Word	The text is trimmed to the nearest word.

The following code draws samples of the Trimming values. The form's Paint event handler calls subroutine DrawSample to draw samples of text that contain backslash (\) or space-delimited strings.

Subroutine DrawSample draws the name of the indicated Trimming value. It draws the sample text using the Trimming value in a specified layout rectangle, and then draws the rectangle so that you can see it. The routine finishes by incrementing its parameter Y, so the next sample is drawn below this one.

```
Public Class Form1
    Private Sub Form1_Load(ByVal sender As System.Object, _
      ByVal e As System.EventArgs) Handles MyBase.Load
        Me.ResizeRedraw = True
    End Sub

    Private Sub Form1_Paint(ByVal sender As Object, _
      ByVal e As System.Windows.Forms.PaintEventArgs) Handles MyBase.Paint
        Dim txt As String
        Dim the_font As New Font("Times New Roman", 30, _
            FontStyle.Bold, GraphicsUnit.Pixel)
        Dim layout_rect As RectangleF
        e.Graphics.TextRenderingHint = _
            System.Drawing.Text.TextRenderingHint.AntiAliasGridFit

        layout_rect = New RectangleF(100, 0, 180, 70)
        txt = "ABC\DEF\GHI\JKL\MNO\PQR\STU\VWX\YZ"
```

```
            DrawSample(e.Graphics, txt, the_font, layout_rect, _
                StringTrimming.Character)
            DrawSample(e.Graphics, txt, the_font, layout_rect, _
                StringTrimming.EllipsisCharacter)
            DrawSample(e.Graphics, txt, the_font, layout_rect, _
                StringTrimming.EllipsisPath)
            DrawSample(e.Graphics, txt, the_font, layout_rect, _
                StringTrimming.EllipsisWord)
            DrawSample(e.Graphics, txt, the_font, layout_rect, _
                StringTrimming.None)
            DrawSample(e.Graphics, txt, the_font, layout_rect, _
                StringTrimming.Word)

            layout_rect.X += layout_rect.Width + 10
            layout_rect.Y = 0
            txt = "ABC DEF GHI JKL MNO PQR STU VWX YZ"
            DrawSample(e.Graphics, txt, the_font, layout_rect, _
                StringTrimming.Character)
            DrawSample(e.Graphics, txt, the_font, layout_rect, _
                StringTrimming.EllipsisCharacter)
            DrawSample(e.Graphics, txt, the_font, layout_rect, _
                StringTrimming.EllipsisPath)
            DrawSample(e.Graphics, txt, the_font, layout_rect, _
                StringTrimming.EllipsisWord)
            DrawSample(e.Graphics, txt, the_font, layout_rect, _
                StringTrimming.None)
            DrawSample(e.Graphics, txt, the_font, layout_rect, _
                StringTrimming.Word)
        End Sub

        Private Sub DrawSample(ByVal gr As Graphics, ByVal txt As String, _
          ByVal the_font As Font, ByRef layout_rect As RectangleF, _
          ByVal string_trimming As StringTrimming)
            Dim string_format As New StringFormat
            string_format.Trimming = string_trimming

            gr.DrawString(string_trimming.ToString, Me.Font, _
                Brushes.Black, 0, layout_rect.Y + 5)

            gr.DrawString(txt, the_font, Brushes.Black, layout_rect, _
                string_format)
            gr.DrawRectangle(Pens.Black, Rectangle.Round(layout_rect))
            layout_rect.Y += layout_rect.Height + 10
        End Sub
    End Class
```

Figure 21-8 shows the results.

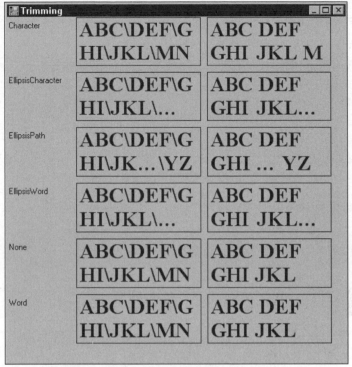

Figure 21-8: The `StringFormat` object's `Trimming` property determines how text is trimmed.

MeasureString

The `Graphics` object's `MeasureString` method returns a `SizeF` structure holding the string's width and height drawn in a particular font. You can use that information to arrange the text and other drawn objects on the form.

The following code shows how a program might center text on its form. It starts by defining the font it will use (in this case, a bold 40 pixel tall Times New Roman font). The code also defines the text it will draw. Next, the program uses the `Graphics` object's `MeasureString` method to get the string's size in that font. It uses the size to determine where it needs to draw the text to center it, and then draws the text. The code then makes a `Rectangle` object using the text's position and the size it got from `MeasureString`. It finishes by drawing the rectangle around the string.

```
Private Sub Form1_Paint(ByVal sender As Object, _
 ByVal e As System.Windows.Forms.PaintEventArgs) Handles MyBase.Paint
    ' Define the font and text we will use.
    Dim the_font As New Font("Times New Roman", 40, _
        FontStyle.Bold, GraphicsUnit.Pixel)
    Dim the_string As String = "MeasureString"

    ' Get the text's size.
    Dim string_size As SizeF = e.Graphics.MeasureString("MeasureString", the_font)

    ' Draw the text centered on the form.
    Dim x As Integer = (Me.ClientSize.Width - CInt(string_size.Width)) \ 2
    Dim y As Integer = (Me.ClientSize.Height - CInt(string_size.Height)) \ 2
    e.Graphics.DrawString(the_string, the_font, Brushes.Black, x, y)

    ' Draw a rectangle around the text.
    Dim string_rect As New Rectangle(x, y, _
        CInt(string_size.Width), CInt(string_size.Height))
    e.Graphics.DrawRectangle(Pens.Black, string_rect)
End Sub
```

Figure 21-9 shows the result. Notice that the rectangle includes some extra space above, below, and to the sides of the string. The section "Font Metrics" later in this chapter has more to say about this extra space.

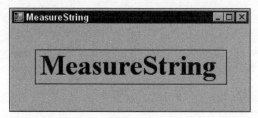

Figure 21-9: You can use the Graphics **object's** MeasureString **method to see how big a string will be when drawn in a particular font.**

Occasionally, it is useful to know where parts of a string will be drawn. For example, you might want to draw a box around certain words or know when the user has clicked on a particular letter.

The Graphics object provides a MeasureCharacterRanges method that returns an array of Regions representing the positions of ranges of characters within a string. To use MeasureCharacterRanges, the program must first create an array of CharacterRange objects defining the ranges of interest. It calls a StringFormat object's SetMeasurableCharacterRanges method passing it this array. Finally, it calls MeasureCharacterRanges.

The following code uses MeasureCharacterRanges to show the positions of all of the characters in a string. It begins by defining its text, font, layout rectangle, and StringFormat object as usual. It then creates an array of CharacterRange objects, one for each character in the string. It loops through this array, filling it with new CharacterRange objects, each of which represents a single character. When it has filled the array, the code passes it to the StringFormat object's SetMeasurableCharacterRanges method. The program then calls the `Graphics` object's `MeasureCharacterRanges` method to get `Region` objects representing the characters' positions. It loops through this array, calling each `Region`'s `GetBounds` method to convert the region into a `RectangleF` structure. It transforms the `RectangleF` into a `Rectangle` and draws it. Finally, the program draws the string.

```
Private Sub Form1_Paint(ByVal sender As Object, _
  ByVal e As System.Windows.Forms.PaintEventArgs) Handles MyBase.Paint
    Dim txt As String = "Great Galloping Giraffes"
    Dim the_font As New Font("Times New Roman", 50, _
        FontStyle.Bold, GraphicsUnit.Pixel)
    Dim layout_rect As New RectangleF(0, 0, _
        Me.ClientSize.Width, Me.ClientSize.Height)
    Dim string_format As New StringFormat
    string_format.LineAlignment = StringAlignment.Center
    string_format.Alignment = StringAlignment.Center

    e.Graphics.TextRenderingHint = _
        System.Drawing.Text.TextRenderingHint.AntiAliasGridFit

    ' Define an array of CharacterRange objects,
    ' one for each character.
    Dim character_ranges(txt.Length - 1) As CharacterRange
    For i As Integer = 0 To txt.Length - 1
        character_ranges(i) = New CharacterRange(i, 1)
    Next i

    ' Set the ranges in the StringFormat object.
    string_format.SetMeasurableCharacterRanges(character_ranges)

    ' Get the character range regions.
    Dim character_regions() As Region = _
        e.Graphics.MeasureCharacterRanges(txt, _
        the_font, layout_rect, string_format)

    ' Draw each region's bounds.
    For Each rgn As Region In character_regions
        ' Convert the region into a Rectangle.
        Dim character_bounds As RectangleF = rgn.GetBounds(e.Graphics)
        Dim character_rect As Rectangle = _
            Rectangle.Round(character_bounds)

        ' Draw the bounds.
        e.Graphics.DrawRectangle(Pens.White, character_rect)
    Next rgn

    ' Draw the text.
    e.Graphics.DrawString(txt, the_font, Brushes.Black, _
        layout_rect, string_format)
End Sub
```

Figure 21-10 shows the result.

Figure 21-10: The `Graphics` **object's** `MeasureCharacterRanges`
method shows where ranges of characters will be drawn in a string.

For some reason, the array of `CharacterRange` objects you pass to the `SetMeasurableCharacterRanges` method can hold at most 32 items. If the array is larger, `SetMeasurableCharacterRanges` raises an overflow error. Microsoft says this behavior is by design and they don't plan to change it. If you need to measure the positions of individual characters in a longer string, you should break the string into pieces smaller than 32 characters, probably at word boundaries, and arrange the pieces yourself.

Note that the characters do not necessarily actually stay within their assigned regions. Depending on the font, they may stick out slightly. Figure 21-11 shows the program used in the previous example with an italic bold Garamond font.

**Figure 21-11: Characters do not always
stay within their assigned regions.**

Many of the characters in this figure stray outside of their assigned regions. The "ll" and "ff" pairs are particularly shameless in their trespassing. The first "f" in the "ff" pair leans almost all the way across the second one's region.

Font Metrics

The `Graphics` object's `MeasureString` method tells you approximately how big a string will be when drawn on that object. Its `MeasureCharacterRanges` method enables you to get more information about the positioning of ranges within a string.

The `FontFamily` class provides some additional methods that a program can use to get more information about how characters are drawn. Before you can use these values, you must understand a bit of extra character anatomy.

Figure 21-12 shows how a font's internal leading, ascent, descent, and external leading values help determine a character's position.

The following table describes these font metrics.

Value	Meaning
Internal Leading	Extra space left above the characters but considered part of the string
Em Height	The height within which the characters are drawn
Ascent	The part of the character cell above the baseline
Descent	The part of the character cell below the baseline
Cell Height	The height of the character area including internal leading
External Leading	Extra space left below one line and above the next
Line Spacing	The distance between one line and the next

From the figure, you can verify the following relationships:

```
Cell Height = Ascent + Descent = Internal Leading + Em Height
Line Spacing = Cell Height + External Leading
```

The `FontFamily` object provides several methods for determining font metric values. These methods include `GetCellAscent`, `GetCellDescent`, `GetEmHeight`, and `GetLineSpacing`.

All of these methods return values in *font design units*. The key to converting them into some other unit is to realize that the `Font` object's `Size` property returns the font's em size in whatever units the font is currently using. For example, if you specify the font's size in pixels, then `Font.Size` returns the em size in pixels.

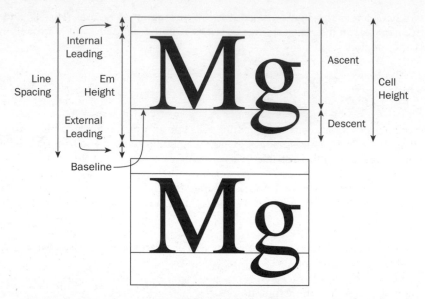

Figure 21-12: How text is positioned depends on many font metrics, including internal leading, ascent, descent, and external leading.

Using `Font.Size` and the value returned by the `FontFamily`'s `GetEmHeight` method, you can convert the other values into pixels. For example, the following equation shows how to calculate a font family's ascent in pixels.

```
Ascent Pixels = FontFamily.GetCellAscent * Font.Size / FontFamily.GetEmHeight
```

The following code draws the font metrics for some text in three different fonts. It starts by defining some text, a layout rectangle, and a `StringFormat` object. Then, for each of three fonts, the code creates the font and calls subroutine `MeasureCharacters` to display the font metrics. Subroutine `MeasureCharacters` defines an array of `CharacterRange` objects and initializes them so that they each refer to a single character in the string. It calls `SetMeasurableCharacterRanges` and then `MeasureCharacterRanges`, as described in section "MeasureString," earlier in this chapter. Next, the code calculates the font's em height, ascent, descent, cell height, internal leading, line spacing, and external leading. The program then loops through the `Regions` returned by `MeasureCharacterRanges`. It converts each `Region` into a `Rectangle` and draws it. It then draws lines showing the internal leading, ascent, and descent values and fills an area representing the external leading space. The subroutine finishes by drawing the text.

```
Private Sub Form1_Paint(ByVal sender As Object, _
 ByVal e As System.Windows.Forms.PaintEventArgs) Handles MyBase.Paint
    Dim txt As String = "Mgfi"
    Dim layout_rect As New RectangleF(0, 0, _
        Me.ClientSize.Width \ 3, Me.ClientSize.Height)
    Dim string_format As New StringFormat
    string_format.LineAlignment = StringAlignment.Center
    string_format.Alignment = StringAlignment.Center
    Dim the_font As Font
```

```
        e.Graphics.TextRenderingHint = _
            System.Drawing.Text.TextRenderingHint.AntiAliasGridFit

    the_font = New Font("Times New Roman", 80, FontStyle.Bold, GraphicsUnit.Pixel)
    MeasureCharacters(e.Graphics, the_font, txt, layout_rect, string_format)

    layout_rect.X += Me.ClientSize.Width \ 3
    the_font = New Font("Comic Sans MS", 80, FontStyle.Bold, GraphicsUnit.Pixel)
    MeasureCharacters(e.Graphics, the_font, txt, layout_rect, string_format)

    layout_rect.X += Me.ClientSize.Width \ 3
    the_font = New Font("Courier New", 80, FontStyle.Bold, GraphicsUnit.Pixel)
    MeasureCharacters(e.Graphics, the_font, txt, layout_rect, string_format)
End Sub

Public Sub MeasureCharacters(ByVal gr As Graphics, ByVal the_font As Font, _
 ByVal txt As String, ByVal layout_rect As RectangleF, _
 ByVal string_format As StringFormat)
    ' Define an array of CharacterRange objects,
    ' one for each character.
    Dim character_ranges(txt.Length - 1) As CharacterRange
    For i As Integer = 0 To txt.Length - 1
        character_ranges(i) = New CharacterRange(i, 1)
    Next i

    ' Set the ranges in the StringFormat object.
    string_format.SetMeasurableCharacterRanges(character_ranges)

    ' Get the character range regions.
    Dim character_regions() As Region = _
        gr.MeasureCharacterRanges(txt, _
        the_font, layout_rect, string_format)

    ' Get the font's ascent.
    Dim em_height As Integer = the_font.FontFamily.GetEmHeight(FontStyle.Bold)
    Dim em_height_pix As Single = the_font.Size
    Dim design_to_pixels As Single = the_font.Size / em_height
    Dim ascent As Integer = the_font.FontFamily.GetCellAscent(FontStyle.Bold)
    Dim ascent_pix As Single = ascent * design_to_pixels
    Dim descent As Integer = the_font.FontFamily.GetCellDescent(FontStyle.Bold)
    Dim descent_pix As Single = descent * design_to_pixels
    Dim cell_height_pix As Single = ascent_pix + descent_pix
    Dim internal_leading_pix As Single = cell_height_pix - em_height_pix
    Dim line_spacing As Integer = _
        the_font.FontFamily.GetLineSpacing(FontStyle.Bold)
    Dim line_spacing_pix As Single = line_spacing * design_to_pixels
    Dim external_leading_pix As Single = line_spacing_pix - cell_height_pix

    ' Draw each region's bounds.
    For Each rgn As Region In character_regions
        ' Convert the region into a Rectangle.
        Dim character_bounds As RectangleF = rgn.GetBounds(gr)
```

```
            Dim character_rect As Rectangle = _
                Rectangle.Round(character_bounds)

            ' Draw the bounds.
            gr.DrawRectangle(Pens.Black, character_rect)

            ' Draw the internal leading.
            gr.DrawLine(Pens.White, _
                character_rect.X, _
                character_rect.Y + internal_leading_pix, _
                character_rect.Right, _
                character_rect.Y + internal_leading_pix)

            ' Draw the ascent.
            gr.DrawLine(Pens.Yellow, _
                character_rect.X, _
                character_rect.Y + ascent_pix, _
                character_rect.Right, _
                character_rect.Y + ascent_pix)

            ' Draw the descent.
            gr.DrawLine(Pens.Orange, _
                character_rect.X, _
                character_rect.Y + ascent_pix + descent_pix, _
                character_rect.Right, _
                character_rect.Y + ascent_pix + descent_pix)

            ' Draw the external leading.
            gr.FillRectangle(Brushes.Red, _
                character_rect.X, _
                character_rect.Y + ascent_pix + descent_pix, _
                character_rect.Width, _
                external_leading_pix)
        Next rgn

        ' Draw the text.
        gr.DrawString(txt, the_font, Brushes.Black, _
            layout_rect, string_format)
    End Sub
```

Figure 21-13 shows the result.

Notice that the font metrics are not always rigidly followed. For example, sometimes a character may extend into the external leading space.

Figure 21-13: The `FontFamily` **and** `Font` **classes provide the methods you need to calculate font metrics.**

Summary

When you draw lines, rectangles, and other shapes, you can completely define the shape by giving its size and position. Text is different. Different fonts produce very different results, even for the same text. A single font sometimes even produces different results for a character, depending on the characters that surround it and the area in which it is drawn.

This chapter describes some of the methods you can use to position and measure text in Visual Basic. Layout rectangles and `StringFormat` objects let you easily draw text that is centered or aligned vertically and horizontally. The `DrawString` method automatically wraps text if necessary and can understand tabs and Carriage Return/Line Feed characters contained in the text.

The `StringFormat` object's flags let you determine how text is aligned, wrapped, and trimmed. The `StringFormat`'s methods let you read and define tab stops.

The `Graphics` object's `MeasureString` method lets you determine roughly how big a string will be when drawn on the object. Its `MeasureCharacterRanges` method lets you determine the placement of regions of text within a string.

With all of these methods at your disposal, you can position text almost exactly where you want it.

Chapters 20 and 21 explain how to draw objects such as lines, ellipses, and text at a relatively high level. When you draw a line from one point to another, you don't need to specify exactly how the pixels on the screen should be colored. You set values for higher-level properties such as the pen color and dash style, brush color and style, and so forth. Then Visual Basic figures out the details.

Chapter 22, "Image Processing," explains how you can read and manipulate images on a pixel-by-pixel basis. It tells how to load and save image files in different formats (such as BMP, GIF, JPEG, and PNG) and how to get and set the colors of individual pixels.

Image Processing

The `Graphics` class represents a drawing surface at a logical level. Below that level, a `Graphics` object is attached to a `Bitmap` or `Metafile` object. Those objects understand the slightly lower-level needs of managing more "physical" data structures. For example, a `Bitmap` object maps abstract drawing commands such as `DrawLine` and `DrawEllipse` to colored pixels that can be displayed on a `PictureBox` or saved into a file. Similarly, a `Metafile` maps the `Graphics` object's abstract commands into metafile records that you can play back on a drawing surface, or save in a graphical metafile.

This chapter describes the more down-to-earth classes `Bitmap` and `Metafile` classes. It explains methods for building, modifying, and manipulating these objects. It shows how to load and save them from graphics files and, in the case of `Bitmap`s, how to work with files saved in a variety of graphic formats such as BMP, GIF, JPEG, TIFF, and PNG.

Image

An `Image` object represents some sort of picture that you can draw on, copy, transform, and display. `Image` is an abstract (`MustInherit`) class, so you cannot create instances of this class directly. Instead you must make instances of its derived classes `Bitmap` and `Metafile`.

The `Image` class provides useful graphical methods that the `Bitmap` and `Metafile` classes inherit. Many other objects can work with any type of `Image` object, so you can pass them either a `Bitmap` or a `Metafile`. For example, the `Graphics` object's `FromImage` method takes an `Image` object as a parameter and returns a `Graphics` object attached to that `Image`. This parameter can be either a `Bitmap` or a `Metafile`. The following code creates a new `Bitmap` object, attaches a `Graphics` object to it, and then uses the `Graphics` object to draw a rectangle on the `Bitmap`.

```
Dim bm As New Bitmap(100, 100)
Dim gr As Graphics = Graphics.FromImage(bm)
gr.DrawRectangle(Pens.Black, 10, 10, 80, 80)
```

The `Image` class itself provides several useful methods, particularly `Load` and `Save`. The following table describes these and some of the class's other useful properties and methods.

Property or Method	Purpose
Dispose	Frees the resources associated with this image. See the sections "Loading Bitmaps" and "Saving Bitmaps" later in this chapter for more information.
Flags	Returns attribute flags for the image. These provide information such as whether the pixel data contains alpha values and whether the image is a gray scale. For more information, look in the online help for the ImageFlags enumeration.
FromFile	This shared function loads an image from a file as in bm = Bitmap.FromFile(file-name).
FromHbitmap	This shared function loads a Bitmap image from a Windows bitmap handle. (A *bitmap handle* is a 32-bit integer that gives a value associated with the bitmap in the GDI environment. Windows uses the handle to refer to the bitmap when it needs to manipulate it. In the .NET environment, you generally work with Bitmap and Image objects and don't need to worry about bitmap handles. It's useful to know about this method, however, in case you need to manipulate a bitmap loaded using older GDI routines.)
FromStream	This shared function loads an image from a data stream.
GetBounds	Returns a RectangleF structure representing the rectangle's bounds.
GetPixelFormatSize	Returns the color resolution (bits per pixel) for a specified PixelFormat.
GetThumbnailImage	Returns a thumbnail representation of the image.
Height	Returns the image's height.
HorizontalResolution	Returns the horizontal resolution of the image in pixels per inch.
IsAlphaPixelFormat	Returns True if the specified PixelFormat contains alpha information.
Palette	Determines the ColorPalette object used by the image.
PhysicalDimension	Returns a SizeF structure giving the image's dimensions in pixels for Bitmaps and 0.01 millimeter units for Metafiles.
PixelFormat	Returns the image's pixel format. This property can take such values as Format24bppRgb (24-bit red/green/blue data), Format32bppArgb (32-bit alpha/red/green/blue data), and Format8bppIndexed (8-bit index into a 256-color table). For more information, see the online help for the PixelFormat property and the PixelFormat enumeration.
RawFormat	Returns an ImageFormat object representing the image's raw format. The ImageFormat class has shared members for each of the standard image types. For example, the following code checks whether the Bitmap bm was loaded from a JPEG file.

```
If bm.RawFormat.Equals(ImageFormat.Jpeg) Then ...
```

Property or Method	Purpose
RotateFlip	Rotates, flips, or rotates and flips the image. The parameter indicates which combination of flips (vertical, horizontal, or both) and rotation (0, 90, 180, or 270 degrees) to use.
Save	Saves the image in a file or stream with a given data format (BMP, GIF, JPEG, and so forth). See the sections "Loading Bitmaps" and "Saving Bitmaps" later in this chapter for more information.
Size	Returns a Size structure containing the image's width and height in pixels.
VerticalResolution	Returns the vertical resolution of the image in pixels per inch.
Width	Returns the image's width.

Bitmap

The Bitmap class represents an image defined by pixel data. You can use a Bitmap to create, load, modify, and save image data to sources that display pixel data such as screen objects (PictureBoxes, Forms, UserControls, and so forth) and image files (BMP, GIF, JPEG, PNG, TIFF, and so forth).

Many of the Bitmap's most useful properties and methods are inherited from the Image class. These include Height, HorizontalResolution, Palette, RawFormat, Size, Width, GetThumbnailImage, RotateFlip, and Save. See the section "Image" earlier in this chapter for information about those and other inherited properties and methods.

The following table describes some of the most useful methods that the Bitmap class adds to those inherited from the Image class.

Method	Purpose
FromHicon	This shared function loads a Bitmap image from a Windows icon handle. (An *icon handle* is a 32-bit integer that gives a value associated with the icon in the GDI environment. Windows uses the handle to refer to the icon when it needs to manipulate it. In the .NET environment, you generally work with Icon objects and don't need to worry about icon handles. It's useful to know about this method, however, in case you need to manipulate an icon loaded using older GDI routines).
FromResource	This shared function loads a Bitmap image from a Windows resource.
GetPixel	Returns a specified pixel's Color.
LockBits	Locks the Bitmap's data in memory, so it cannot move until the program calls UnlockBits.

Table continued on following page

Method	Purpose
MakeTransparent	Makes all pixels with a specified color transparent by setting their alpha components to 0.
SetPixel	Sets a specified pixel's `Color` value.
SetResolution	Sets the `Bitmap`'s horizontal and vertical resolution in dots per inch (DPI).
UnlockBits	Unlocks the `Bitmap`'s data in memory so the system can relocate it if necessary.

For most applications, the `GetPixel` and `SetPixel` methods provide adequate performance when manipulating pixels, but there is some overhead in moving through the different layers between the program's code and the actual pixel data. For applications that work with very large images or that need to process pixel data on many images very quickly, performance may be an issue.

In cases where speed is an issue, you can access the pixel data more directly using so-called "unsafe" access. The program locks the `Bitmap`'s data, reads and updates the pixel values, and then unlocks the data. See the section "Pixel-by-Pixel Operations" later in this chapter for more information and examples.

Loading Bitmaps

Loading a `Bitmap` from a file is simple. Simply pass the file's name into the `Bitmap`'s constructor. The following code loads the bitmap file whose name is stored in the variable `file_name`, and then displays it in the `PictureBox` control named `picImage`.

```
Dim bm As New Bitmap(file_name)
picImage.Image = bm
```

Once you have loaded a `Bitmap`, you can attach a `Graphics` object to it, draw on it, display it, and save the results in a new bitmap file. The following code loads the bitmap file, attaches a `Graphics` object to it, uses that object to draw an ellipse, and displays the result in the `picImage` control.

```
Dim bm As New Bitmap(file_name)
Dim gr As Graphics = Graphics.FromImage(bm)
gr.DrawEllipse(Pens.White, 0, 0, bm.Width - 1, bm.Height - 1)
picImage.Image = bm
```

Unfortunately, the `Bitmap` object holds some sort attachment to the bitmap file. If you try to delete the file while the program is running and still using the `Bitmap`, the operating system complains that the file is locked by another process. Similarly, if you open the file in a program such as Microsoft Paint, make some changes, and try to save the file, the operating system complains about a sharing violation.

To release the file for other programs to use, you must dispose of the `Bitmap` object that opened it. However, if you assign the `Bitmap` to a property (such as a `PictureBox`'s `Image` property), the property keeps a reference to the `Bitmap` and will later generate an error when it tries to use the `Bitmap` that you have disposed.

One solution to this dilemma is to create a second `Bitmap` that is a copy of the first `Bitmap`, as shown in the following code. Then you can safely dispose of the first `Bitmap`. Because the second `Bitmap` was never associated with the bitmap file, the file is not locked.

```
' Load the bitmap file.
Dim bm As New Bitmap(file_name)

' Make a copy.
Dim new_bm As New Bitmap(bm)

' Dispose of the original Bitmap.
bm.Dispose

' Draw on the new Bitmap and display the result.
Dim gr As Graphics = Graphics.FromImage(new_bm)
gr.DrawEllipse(Pens.White, 0, 0, new_bm.Width - 1, new_bm.Height - 1)
picImage.Image = new_bm
```

Saving Bitmaps

You can use a `Bitmap` object's `Save` method to save the bitmap into a file or data stream. To save the `Bitmap` into a file, the `Save` method's first parameter should be the file's name. If you provide only the filename, the `Bitmap` is saved in PNG format no matter what extension you give the file. If you save the file in PNG format but the file's extension is something other than `.PNG`, such as `.BMP` or `.GIF`, you may become very confused later when Microsoft Paint refuses to open the file.

To save the `Bitmap` in some format other than PNG, pass the format as the `Save` method's second parameter. To avoid confusion, you should give the file the appropriate extension. If you save a BMP file, give the file a `.BMP` extension.

The following code generates a 256 × 256 pixel bitmap from scratch and saves it in a JPEG file:

```
' Make a 256x256 pixel Bitmap.
Dim bm As New Bitmap(256, 256)

' Draw on it.
Dim gr As Graphics = Graphics.FromImage(bm)
gr.Clear(Color.White)
gr.DrawEllipse(Pens.Red, 0, 0, bm.Width - 1, bm.Height - 1)
gr.DrawLine(Pens.Green, 0, 0, bm.Width - 1, bm.Height - 1)
gr.DrawLine(Pens.Blue, bm.Width - 1, 0, 0, bm.Height - 1)

' Save the result as a JPEG file.
bm.Save("C:\test.jpg", ImageFormat.Jpeg)
```

The `ImageFormat` enumeration includes the formats `Bmp`, `Emf`, `Exif`, `Guid`, `Icon`, `Jpeg`, `MemoryBmp`, `Png`, `Tiff`, and `Wmf`.

If you save a `Bitmap` image in the `Wmf` (Windows metafile) or `Emf` (Enhanced metafile) format, the `Save` method creates a metafile that contains a bitmapped image. If you create a metafile by using a `Metafile` object, on the other hand, the result is a metafile that contains records that draw lines, curves, text, and so forth. The difference can have a couple of important consequences.

First, if the image is large, the bitmapped version may take up a lot more space than the version that records only drawing commands. It may also take a lot longer to draw a large bitmap than it would to draw a few circles and lines.

Second, you can transform a metafile that contains commands more readily than you can transform a metafile that contains a bitmap. If you enlarge a metafile containing commands, the result contains enlarged lines, curves, and other output. If you enlarge a metafile containing a bitmap, the result is a relatively blocky enlarged bitmap. Anti-aliasing may help a little, but the metafile containing drawing commands will produce a much better result.

On the other hand, not all programs understand all metafile commands. You may load a metafile containing drawing commands into another application and find that your ellipses and text don't work. While a metafile containing a bitmap won't resize nicely, at least it should look similar to what you created.

See the section "Metafile Objects" later in this chapter for more information on metafiles.

Implementing AutoRedraw

In Visual Basic 6 and earlier versions, the `Form` and `PictureBox` objects had an `AutoRedraw` property. If you set this property to `True`, anything you drew on the object was automatically saved. If the object was later obscured and redrawn, the drawing was automatically restored.

This method required Visual Basic to allocate a chunk of internal memory to store the image, so it was not free. However, it could be a lot easier and faster than redrawing a complex image from scratch every time the drawing is exposed. For example, drawing a Mandelbrot set or other complex fractal may require hundreds or thousands of calculations per pixel in the image. Drawing a large image may take 10 or 20 seconds even on a relatively fast computer. Redrawing the image from scratch every time such a form was exposed would be impractical.

The bad news is that Visual Basic .NET has no `AutoRedraw` property. If you want similar functionality, you must implement it yourself. The good news is that Visual Basic .NET has a couple of controls that can display a persistent image, and they can do a lot of the work for you.

The `Form` object's `BackgroundImage` property holds an image that covers the form's background. If the image is too big to fit, it is cropped. If the image is too small to cover the whole form, it is repeated to tile the form.

The `PictureBox`'s `Image` property also displays a persistent image. The control's `SizeMode` property determines how Visual Basic uses the image to cover the control. This property can take the values `Normal` (the image is drawn at full scale in the upper-left corner of the `PictureBox` and is cropped if it is too big), `StretchImage` (the image is stretched or squashed to fit the control, possibly changing its shape), `AutoSize` (the `PictureBox` resizes to fit the image), and `CenterImage` (the image is drawn at full scale in the center of the `PictureBox` and is cropped if it is too big).

One relatively easy method for implementing `AutoRedraw` is to make a `Bitmap` and assign it to a `PictureBox`'s `Image` property. Then the `PictureBox` automatically redisplays the image whenever it is exposed. The following example demonstrates this approach.

This program's form contains a PictureBox named picCanvas with its Dock property set to Full, so it covers the entire form. When the form is loaded or resizes, its event handlers call the DrawDiamond subroutine.

DrawDiamond gets the PictureBox's size and makes a Bitmap that fits it. It makes a HatchBrush and uses it to fill the Bitmap. The code then defines the points needed to draw a diamond-shaped polygon on the form, fills the polygon with white, and outlines it in black.

The next statement is the key. It assigns the Bitmap to the PictureBox's Image property.

The code finishes by calling the HatchBrush and Graphics objects' Dispose methods to free their resources.

```
Private Sub Form1_Load(ByVal sender As Object, ByVal e As System.EventArgs) _
Handles MyBase.Load
    DrawDiamond()
End Sub

Private Sub Form1_Resize(ByVal sender As Object, ByVal e As System.EventArgs) _
Handles MyBase.Resize
    DrawDiamond()
End Sub

Private Sub DrawDiamond()
    ' Get the drawing surface's size.
    Dim wid As Integer = picCanvas.ClientSize.Width
    Dim hgt As Integer = picCanvas.ClientSize.Height

    ' Do nothing if we have no size.
    ' This happens, for example, if the form is minimized.
    If wid < 1 Or hgt < 1 Then Exit Sub

    ' Make a Bitmap and Graphics to fit.
    Dim bm As New Bitmap(wid, hgt)
    Dim gr As Graphics = Graphics.FromImage(bm)

    ' Fill the drawing area with a hatch pattern.
    Dim bg_brush As New HatchBrush(HatchStyle.HorizontalBrick, _
        Color.Blue, Color.Aqua)
    gr.FillRectangle(bg_brush, picCanvas.ClientRectangle)

    ' Draw a dimond.
    Dim pts() As Point = { _
        New Point(wid \ 2, 0), _
        New Point(wid, hgt \ 2), _
        New Point(wid \ 2, hgt), _
        New Point(0, hgt \ 2) _
    }
    gr.FillPolygon(Brushes.White, pts)
    gr.DrawPolygon(Pens.Black, pts)

    ' Display the result.
```

```
        picCanvas.Image = bm

        ' Free resources.
        bg_brush.Dispose()
        gr.Dispose()
    End Sub
```

Whenever this program is hidden and exposed, the `picCanvas` `PictureBox` automatically redisplays its image.

Some programs don't need to redraw their images when the form resizes. For example, a mapping application might display its map at a specific size. In that case, you don't need to redraw the map in the form's `Resize` event handler. Instead, you would probably add menus and buttons to let the user zoom in and out, and scroll to different parts of the map. In an application such as that one, the code would need to draw images only when the content changed. The rest is automatic.

Other applications draw in several routines and not just in the form's `Load` and `Resize` event handlers. For example, a drawing program might let the user draw various shapes (such as lines, rectangles, ellipses, and free-form curves). The program would need to add these shapes to a `Bitmap` as they were drawn and display the result.

In programs such as this, you can create `Bitmap` and `Graphics` objects at a module or application level and then use them whenever the user modifies the image.

The following code lets the user draw free-form curves. At the module level, it declares the variables `m_Bitmap` and `m_Graphics`, as well as some variables used while the user is drawing. When the form is loaded and when the user clicks the File menu's Clear command, the program calls the `MakeNewBitmap` subroutine.

`MakeNewBitmap` creates a new `Bitmap` to fit the form's `picCanvas` control and makes a `Graphics` object attached to it. It clears the `Bitmap` with the form's background color and displays the result by setting the `picCanvas` control's `Image` property to the `Bitmap`.

When the `picCanvas` control receives a `MouseDown` event, it records the mouse's X and Y coordinates and sets `m_Drawing` to `True` to indicate that a scribble is in progress.

The `picCanvas_MouseMove` event handler checks `m_Drawing` and, if it is `True`, draws a line connecting the mouse's previous position to its current location and saves the mouse's new X and Y coordinates for the next time. It then sets the `picCanvas` control's `Image` property to the `Bitmap` to display the new results.

Finally, the `picCanvas_MouseUp` event handler sets `m_Drawing` to `False` so that future `MouseMove` events don't draw on the `Bitmap`.

```
    ' The Bitmap and Graphics objects we will draw on.
    Private m_Bitmap As Bitmap
    Private m_Graphics As Graphics

    ' Used for scribbling.
    Private m_Drawing As Boolean
```

```
Private m_X As Integer
Private m_Y As Integer

' Make the initial blank image.
Private Sub Form1_Load(ByVal sender As Object, ByVal e As System.EventArgs) _
 Handles MyBase.Load
    MakeNewBitmap()
End Sub

' Make a new blank image.
Private Sub mnuFileClear_Click(ByVal sender As System.Object, _
 ByVal e As System.EventArgs) Handles mnuFileClear.Click
    MakeNewBitmap()
End Sub

' Make a new Bitmap to fit the canvas.
Private Sub MakeNewBitmap()
    ' Get the drawing surface's size.
    Dim wid As Integer = picCanvas.ClientSize.Width
    Dim hgt As Integer = picCanvas.ClientSize.Height

    ' Make a Bitmap and Graphics to fit.
    m_Bitmap = New Bitmap(wid, hgt)
    m_Graphics = Graphics.FromImage(m_Bitmap)

    ' Clear the drawing area.
    m_Graphics.Clear(Me.BackColor)

    ' Display the result.
    picCanvas.Image = m_Bitmap
End Sub

' Start scribbling.
Private Sub picCanvas_MouseDown(ByVal sender As Object, _
 ByVal e As System.Windows.Forms.MouseEventArgs) Handles picCanvas.MouseDown
    m_Drawing = True
    m_X = e.X
    m_Y = e.Y
End Sub

' Continue scribbling.
Private Sub picCanvas_MouseMove(ByVal sender As Object, _
 ByVal e As System.Windows.Forms.MouseEventArgs) Handles picCanvas.MouseMove
    If Not m_Drawing Then Exit Sub

    m_Graphics.DrawLine(Pens.Black, m_X, m_Y, e.X, e.Y)
    m_X = e.X
    m_Y = e.Y

    ' Display the result.
    picCanvas.Image = m_Bitmap
End Sub

' Stop scribbling.
```

623

```
Private Sub picCanvas_MouseUp(ByVal sender As Object, _
  ByVal e As System.Windows.Forms.MouseEventArgs) Handles picCanvas.MouseUp
    m_Drawing = False
End Sub
```

Figure 22-1 shows this program in action.

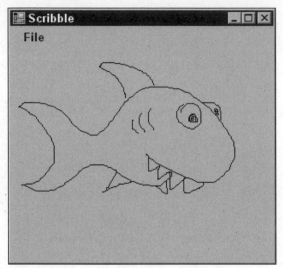

Figure 22-1: Program Scribble automatically redisplays its image when the form is hidden and exposed.

A final issue related to auto-redraw is resizing. If the user makes the form larger or smaller, you need to figure out what to do about the auto-redraw image. There are several approaches you can take, depending on your application.

The simplest approach is to not allow the user to resize the form or at least not to resize the `PictureBox` that displays the auto-redraw image. Then you can ignore the whole issue.

A second approach is to create a new `Bitmap` of the new correct size. Use a `Graphics` object's `Clear` method to erase the new `Bitmap`. Then use the object's `DrawImage` method to copy the contents of the old `Bitmap` into the new one.

In this approach, if the new `Bitmap` is larger than the old one, all of its data is saved. On the other hand, if the new `Bitmap` is smaller, then some of the old drawing is lost. You can preserve that information if you only allow the `Bitmap` to grow and never shrink. When the user resizes the form, you make the new `Bitmap`'s width and height the larger of the old `Bitmap`'s size and the form's new size.

Finally, if you think the program will often run maximized, you could just allocate a really big `Bitmap` when the program begins and forget the whole resizing issue.

Pixel-by-Pixel Operations

The `Bitmap` object provides two methods, `GetPixel` and `SetPixel`, that let a program easily read and write pixel values in the image. The following discussion describes an example that uses these methods to invert an image.

`GetPixel` and `SetPixel` are easy to use and fast enough for many applications. For high-performance graphics, however, they are relatively slow. The section "'Unsafe' Pixel Manipulation" later in this chapter explains how you can use "unsafe" methods to access pixel data more directly. This is a bit more difficult, but it is much faster for large images.

GetPixel and SetPixel

The `Bitmap` object's `GetPixel` method returns a `Color` structure for a pixel in a specific X and Y location. `SetPixel` sets the `Color` of a pixel at a particular position. These two methods are quite easy to use and provide good enough performance for many applications.

The following code shows how a program can use those methods to invert the pixel values in an image.

When the user selects the File menu's Open command and selects a file, the program loads the file into the `Bitmap` named bm. It copies the image into a new `Bitmap` named source_bm and disposes of the original `Bitmap` so that the image's file isn't locked. It then assigns source_bm to the `picSource` `PictureBox's` `Image` property to display the original image.

The program then arranges its controls nicely. The `picSource` control's `SizeMode` property is set to `AutoSize` so that it automatically resizes itself to fit the picture. The program gives the `picDest` `PictureBox` the same size, positions it to the right of `picSource`, and resizes the form to fit the two `PictureBoxes`.

Next, the program copies the source `Bitmap` into a new `Bitmap` named dest_bm and calls subroutine `InvertImage` to invert the pixels in that bitmap. When `InvertImage` returns, the program assigns the dest_bm `Bitmap` to the `picDest` control's `Image` property to display the result.

Subroutine `InvertImage` loops over all of the pixels in the image. It uses the bitmap's `GetPixel` function to get the color of each pixel. It inverts the red, green, and blue components of the pixel's color by subtracting them from the maximum allowed value 255. It then calls the destination `Bitmap's` `SetPixel` method to set the result pixel's value.

```
Private Sub mnuFileOpen_Click(ByVal sender As System.Object, _
  ByVal e As System.EventArgs) Handles mnuFileOpen.Click
    If dlgOpenImage.ShowDialog() = DialogResult.OK Then
        ' Load and display the image.
        Dim bm As New Bitmap(dlgOpenImage.FileName)
        Dim source_bm As New Bitmap(bm)
        bm.Dispose()
        picSource.Image = source_bm

        ' Arrange the controls.
        picDest.Size = picSource.Size

        ' Make the result Bitmap.
```

```
            Dim dest_bm As New Bitmap(source_bm)

            ' Invert the image's pixels.
            InvertImage(dest_bm)

            ' Display the results.
            picDest.Image = dest_bm
        End If
End Sub

Private Sub InvertImage(ByVal bm As Bitmap)
    ' Process the image's pictures.
    For y As Integer = 0 To bm.Height - 1
        For x As Integer = 0 To bm.Width - 1
            ' Get this pixel's color.
            Dim clr As Color = bm.GetPixel(x, y)

            ' Invert the color's components.
            clr = Color.FromArgb(255, _
                255 - clr.R, _
                255 - clr.G, _
                255 - clr.B)

            ' Set the result pixel's color.
            bm.SetPixel(x, y, clr)
        Next x
    Next y
End Sub
```

Figure 22-2 shows the result. The output image on the right is essentially the photographic negative of the original image on the left.

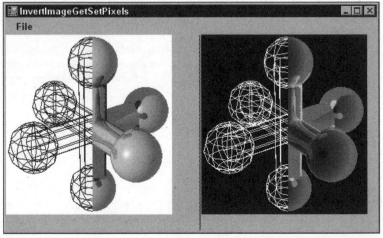

Figure 22-2: This program uses `GetPixel` and `SetPixel` to invert an image's pixel values.

"Unsafe" Pixel Manipulation

The GetPixel and SetPixel methods are very easy to use, and they are fast enough for many applications. For example, a program that generates fractals such as the Mandelbrot set spends a considerable amount of time calculating colors for each individual pixel. If it takes the program 5 seconds to generate the image and a tenth of a second of that time is spent by the SetPixel method, then SetPixel is probably fast enough. Using "unsafe" array methods may shave a few hundredths of a second off the total time, but the program's time is dominated by the code that calculates the pixels' colors, so it's hardly worth the extra complication.

However, suppose that you need to transform a series of images very quickly to display an animated sequence. In that case, the time spent by GetPixel and SetPixel may be significant. In that case, you may get much better performance using "unsafe" methods.

The basic idea is to directly access the array of bytes containing the red, green, and blue component values for the image's pixels. The Bitmap object's LockBits method copies the pixel data for a rectangular part of the image into a temporary buffer where you can manipulate it. Later, you call the UnlockBits method to copy any changes you made back into the bitmap.

Unfortunately the LockBits method returns the buffer of data as a pointer to memory and Visual Basic cannot work directly with that kind of pointer. To resolve this problem, you can use the Marshal class's Copy method to move the data into a Visual Basic array. You can then modify the data and, when you are finished, use Marshal.Copy to move the results back into the buffer.

The following code shows the BitmapBytesRGB24 class that makes this somewhat simpler for the main program. This class works with 24-bit image representations. Your call to LockBits can specify other formats, but this one is particularly easy to work with because it uses one byte for each of the pixels' red, green, and blue components.

The class's ImageBytes array will contain the pixel data stored as a one-dimensional array. Each pixel is represented by a byte for its blue component, a byte for its green component, and a byte for its red component, in that order.

The RowSizeBytes property tells how many bytes are stored in the array per row of pixels. The system may pad the array, so the number of bytes in each row is a multiple of four or some other number that is convenient for the operating system. Thus, RowSizeBytes may not always be three times the number of pixels in each row.

The constant PixelDataSize is 24 for this class because it works with 24-bit (3-byte) pixel data.

The class's constructor takes as a parameter a reference to a Bitmap and saves that reference for later use.

The class next declares a BitmapData object named m_BitmapData. This object will contain data describing the bitmap.

The LockBitmap method creates a Rectangle bounding the bitmap. This is the area in the bitmap that the routine will lock. This class doesn't mess around and simply locks the entire bitmap.

LockBitmap calls the Bitmap object's LockBits method, passing it the bounding Rectangle, a flag indicating that it wants to lock the data for reading and writing, and a flag indicating that we want to work with 24-bit pixel data. LockBits returns information about the bitmap in a BitmapData object, which the routine saves in m_BitmapData. The routine sets the RowSizeBytes value so that it is easy for the main program to use.

LockBitmap then calculates the total number of bytes needed to hold the pixel data, makes the ImageBytes array big enough, and calls Marshal.Copy to copy the pixel; data into the array.

The class's UnlockBitmap method copies the modified pixel data back into the bitmap. It recalculates the size of the array and uses Marshal.Copy to copy the data from the ImageBytes array back into the buffer allocated by LockBits. Finally, it calls the Bitmap object's UnlockBits method.

```vb
Imports System.Drawing.Imaging
Imports System.Runtime.InteropServices

Public Class BitmapBytesRGB24
    ' Provide public access to the picture's byte data.
    Public ImageBytes() As Byte
    Public RowSizeBytes As Integer
    Public Const PixelDataSize As Integer = 24

    ' A reference to the Bitmap.
    Private m_Bitmap As Bitmap

    ' Save a reference to the bitmap.
    Public Sub New(ByVal bm As Bitmap)
        m_Bitmap = bm
    End Sub

    ' Bitmap data.
    Private m_BitmapData As BitmapData

    ' Lock the bitmap's data.
    Public Sub LockBitmap()
        ' Lock the bitmap data.
        Dim bounds As Rectangle = New Rectangle( _
            0, 0, m_Bitmap.Width, m_Bitmap.Height)
        m_BitmapData = m_Bitmap.LockBits(bounds, _
            Imaging.ImageLockMode.ReadWrite, _
            Imaging.PixelFormat.Format24bppRgb)
        RowSizeBytes = m_BitmapData.Stride

        ' Allocate room for the data.
        Dim total_size As Integer = m_BitmapData.Stride * m_BitmapData.Height
        ReDim ImageBytes(total_size)

        ' Copy the data into the ImageBytes array.
        Marshal.Copy(m_BitmapData.Scan0, ImageBytes, _
            0, total_size)
    End Sub

    ' Copy the data back into the Bitmap
    ' and release resources.
    Public Sub UnlockBitmap()
```

```
            ' Copy the data back into the bitmap.
            Dim total_size As Integer = m_BitmapData.Stride * m_BitmapData.Height
            Marshal.Copy(ImageBytes, 0, _
                m_BitmapData.Scan0, total_size)

            ' Unlock the bitmap.
            m_Bitmap.UnlockBits(m_BitmapData)

            ' Release resources.
            ImageBytes = Nothing
            m_BitmapData = Nothing
        End Sub
    End Class
```

The following code shows how a main program can use the `BitmapBytesRGB24` class to invert an image's pixels. The code creates a new `BitmapBytesRGB24` object, passing the constructor the `Bitmap` that it wants to modify. It then calls the object's `LockBitmap` method to copy the pixel data into the object's `ImageBytes` array. Next, the program loops over the rows in the image. For each row, the code calculates the position in the pixel data that holds the row's first pixel's information. It then loops over the pixels in the row, modifying each pixel's blue, green, and red components. Remember that the components are in stored in the order blue, green, red. When it has finished modifying the pixel data, the program calls the `BitmapBytesRGB24` object's `UnlockBitmap` method to copy the results back into the bitmap.

```
' Invert the pixel values in this Bitmap.
Private Sub InvertImage(ByVal bm As Bitmap)
    ' Make a BitmapBytesRGB24 object.
    Dim bm_bytes As New BitmapBytesRGB24(bm)

    ' Lock the bitmap.
    bm_bytes.LockBitmap()

    Dim pix As Integer
    For y As Integer = 0 To bm.Height - 1
        pix = y * bm_bytes.RowSizeBytes
        For x As Integer = 0 To bm.Width - 1
            ' Blue component.
            bm_bytes.ImageBytes(pix) = CByte(255) - bm_bytes.ImageBytes(pix)
            pix += 1
            ' Green component.
            bm_bytes.ImageBytes(pix) = CByte(255) - bm_bytes.ImageBytes(pix)
            pix += 1
            ' Red component.
            bm_bytes.ImageBytes(pix) = CByte(255) - bm_bytes.ImageBytes(pix)
            pix += 1
        Next x
    Next y

    ' Unlock the bitmap.
    bm_bytes.UnlockBitmap()
End Sub
```

This is quite a bit more complicated than the previous program that uses GetPixel and SetPixel, so it's not the best method for simple applications. For high-performance image processing, however, the extra complication is worth it. In one set of tests on a 798-MHz Athlon 64 processor, the previous version using GetPixel and SetPixel took roughly 1.109 seconds to invert an 800 × 600 pixel image, while the version using the BitmapBytesRGB24 class took only 0.047 seconds.

Metafile Objects

The Metafile class represents image data defined by metafile records. These records encapsulate typical graphics commands that scale, rotate, draw lines, display text, and so forth. Using a Metafile object, you can build the metafile records and save them into a metafile, load a metafile, and "play" the metafile records on a display surface such as a Bitmap.

Many of the Metafile's most useful properties and methods are inherited from the Image class. These include Height, HorizontalResolution, Palette, RawFormat, Size, Width, GetThumbnailImage, RotateFlip, and Save. See the section "Image" earlier in this chapter for information about those and other inherited properties and methods.

The following table describes some of the most useful methods that the Metafile class adds to those inherited from the Image class.

Method	Purpose
GetMetafileHeader	Returns the MetafileHeader object associated with this Metafile. See the following text for more information on the MetafileHeader class.
PlayRecord	Plays a metafile record. To play the whole metafile, you can use a Graphics object's DrawImage method to copy the metafile's image onto a Bitmap and then display the Bitmap. PlayRecord lets you selectively play metafile records.

To build a Metafile, you create a Metafile object, attach a Graphics object to it, and then use drawing methods to draw into the metafile. In that respect, the Metafile behaves just like a Bitmap does.

The Graphics object also provides two special methods for working with its Metafile. AddMetafileComment adds a comment to the metafile. EnumerateMetafile sends the metafile's records to a callback subroutine one at a time. You can use that routine if you want to play back only some of the Metafile's records.

The following code shows how to make and use a metafile. It starts by calculating a file name for the metafile. If the file already exists, the program deletes it. Next the program makes a Graphics object to get a handle to its device context. It uses that handle as a parameter to the Metafile object's constructor. It also passes the constructor the name of the file, a RectangleF that defines the metafile's bounds, and the units used by the bounds.

After creating the Metafile object, the program attaches a Graphics object to it. It uses the Graphics object to clear the metafile in white and to draw a circle and two lines.

The program then disposes of the `Graphics` and `Metafile` objects. That closes the metafile.

The program then calls the `Metafile` constructor again, passing it the file's name. It makes a `Bitmap` and associated `Graphics` object, and defines source and destination `RectangleF` structures to use when copying the image. It enlarges the source rectangle slightly so the metafile doesn't crop off the circle's right and bottom pixels.

Next, the code uses the `Graphics` object's `DrawImage` method to copy the metafile onto the `Bitmap`. It then sets the `picOrig` control's `Image` property to the `Bitmap` to display the result.

The program then repeats these steps to display the metafile on the `picSmall` control. This time it makes the control half as large as the full-scale image and uses a scaling transformation to shrink the metafile data when it calls `DrawImage`.

```
Private Sub Form1_Load(ByVal sender As System.Object, _
  ByVal e As System.EventArgs) Handles MyBase.Load
    Const WID As Integer = 200
    Dim path_name As String = Application.StartupPath
    If path_name.EndsWith("\bin") Then _
        path_name = path_name.Substring(0, path_name.Length - 4)
    Dim file_name As String = path_name & "\test.wmf"

    ' Delete the file if it exists.
    If Len(Dir$(file_name)) > 0 Then Kill(file_name)

    ' Make a Graphics object so we can use its hDC as a reference.
    Dim me_gr As Graphics = Me.CreateGraphics
    Dim me_hdc As IntPtr = me_gr.GetHdc

    ' Make the Metafile, using the reference hDC.
    Dim bounds As New RectangleF(0, 0, WID, WID)
    Dim mf As New Metafile(file_name, me_hdc, _
        bounds, MetafileFrameUnit.Pixel)
    me_gr.ReleaseHdc(me_hdc)

    ' Make a Graphics object and draw.
    Dim gr As Graphics = Graphics.FromImage(mf)
    gr.PageUnit = GraphicsUnit.Pixel
    gr.Clear(Color.White)
    gr.DrawEllipse(Pens.Red, bounds)
    gr.DrawLine(Pens.Blue, 0, 0, WID, WID)
    gr.DrawLine(Pens.Blue, WID, 0, 0, WID)

    ' Close the metafile and free resources.
    gr.Dispose()
    mf.Dispose()

    ' Reload the metafile and copy it into a Bitmap.
    mf = New Metafile(file_name)
    Dim bm As New Bitmap(WID, WID)
    gr = Graphics.FromImage(bm)
    Dim dest_bounds As New RectangleF(0, 0, WID, WID)
    Dim source_bounds As New RectangleF(0, 0, WID + 1, WID + 1)
    gr.DrawImage(mf, bounds, source_bounds, GraphicsUnit.Pixel)
```

```
        picOrig.SizeMode = PictureBoxSizeMode.AutoSize
        picOrig.Image = bm
        gr.Dispose()
        mf.Dispose()


        ' Redisplay the result shrunk by 50%.
        mf = New Metafile(file_name)
        picSmall.SetBounds( _
            picOrig.Right + 10, picOrig.Top, _
            picOrig.Width \ 2, picOrig.Height \ 2)
        bm = New Bitmap( _
            picSmall.ClientSize.Width, _
            picSmall.ClientSize.Height)
        gr = Graphics.FromImage(bm)
        gr.ScaleTransform(0.5, 0.5)
        gr.DrawImage(mf, bounds, source_bounds, GraphicsUnit.Pixel)
        picSmall.Image = bm
        gr.Dispose()
        mf.Dispose()
    End Sub
```

Figure 22-3 shows the result.

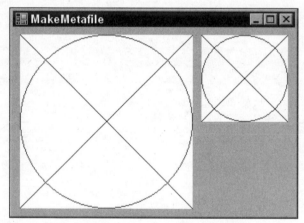

Figure 22-3: Program `MakeMetafile` **creates a metafile and then draws two copies of it.**

Summary

The `Image` class represents a generic image. Its two child classes `Bitmap` and `Metafile` represent specific file types.

The `Bitmap` class lets you manipulate pixel-oriented image data. Its `GetPixel` and `SetPixel` methods let you get and set a pixel's color. Those methods are fast enough for most applications, but when performance is really critical, you can use "unsafe" methods to access the pixel data more directly and manipulate

632

pixels much faster. When you are finished, you can use the `Bitmap`'s `Save` method to save the result in many different kinds of graphics files including BMP, EMF, EXIF, GUID, Icon, JPEG, MemoryBmp, PNG, TIFF, and WMF.

The `Metafile` class represents a collection of drawing commands. Metafiles are reasonably standardized, so you can use them to import and export graphic data between your application and external programs (such as Microsoft Word and CorelDRAW!).

Chapters 19 through 22 explain how to draw shapes, text, and images on the screen. Chapter 23, "Printing," shows how to generate similar output on a printer. The basic approach you use for generating shapes, text, and image is the same as it is for a screen, but when and where you generate printed output requires some new techniques.

Printing

Visual Basic .NET provides several good tools for printing. String formatting objects enable you to determine how text is wrapped and truncated if it won't fit in a printing area. Methods provided by `Graphics` objects enable you to easily scale, rotate, and translate drawing commands.

The basic process, however, seems somewhat backward to many programmers. Rather than issuing commands to a printer object, a program responds to requests to draw pages generated by a `PrintDocument` object. Instead of telling the printer what to do, the program responds to the `PrintDocument`'s requests for data.

In some cases, generating a printout using only Visual Basic commands can be difficult. The following section explains alternative methods for generating a printout and tells when you might want to use those methods. If you just want to print several pages of text, it's often easier to pull the text into Microsoft Word or some other application that specializes in formatting text rather than writing your own.

In other cases, however, you cannot take an easy way out. If the program generates very complex images and graphs, or produces text that is positioned and formatted in a complex manner, you probably need to work through Visual Basic's printing system. The rest of this chapter explains the techniques that you use to generate printouts in Visual Basic. It shows how to draw graphics and text on the printer and how to scale and center the results.

How Not to Print

While Visual Basic provides many tools for arranging graphics on a printout, it does not always provide the best approach to printing. The general method for printing in Visual Basic requires you to generate each page of output in turn. For simple documents (such as a line drawing containing a few lines and circles on a single page), this is easy.

On the other hand, suppose that you want to print several dozen pages of text interspersed with tables and pictures. Figuring out where each page break should be placed and how the text should flow around the tables and pictures could be a huge undertaking. To really do the job right, you might need to consider orphan lines (when the first line of a paragraph sits at the bottom of a page), widow lines (the last line of a paragraph sits at the top of a page), orphan and widow words (when the first or last word sits on a separate line), inserting extra space between words to make a line look nicer, page numbers, headers and footers, hyphenation, different left and right margins, mirrored margins, page gutters, bulleted lists, indentation and justification, different font sizes and styles, and a host of other issues.

Word processing and text-formatting applications such as Microsoft Word spend a great deal of effort on these issues — effort that you probably don't want to duplicate. In fact, Word is so good at handling these issues that you should consider using it to print your output instead of writing an elaborate Visual Basic program to do it.

If your output is simple text, you can drop it into a text file and then use Word to open, format, and print it. For printouts that you don't need to generate too frequently, and for printouts where the user may want to edit the results before printing anyway, this is a simple, flexible solution that doesn't require you to write, debug, and maintain a lot of complicated formatting code.

For more elaborate printouts, programs such as Word may still be useful. Using Visual Studio Tools for Office (VSTO), you can open a Microsoft Word application and control it from your Visual Basic program. Your program can use the Word object model to add text, insert pictures, build tables, set page printing options, and even print the result. You can then save the document for later use or discard it.

Using VSTO, not only can you control Microsoft Word, but you can also use the other Microsoft Office applications. For example, you can load information into Excel so that you can use its tools to analyze and graph the data, copy information into Access for analysis by other database applications, or compose email messages in Outlook.

VSTO is relatively complicated and outside of the scope of this book, so it isn't described here. For more information, see Microsoft's Web site or a book on Microsoft Office programming.

Basic Printing

The PrintDocument class sits at the heart of the printing process in Visual Basic. The program creates an instance of this class and installs event handlers to catch its events. When the object must perform printing-related tasks, it raises events to ask the program for help.

The PrintDocument object raises four key events:

❑   *BeginPrint* — The PrintDocument raises its BeginPrint event when it is about to start printing. The program can initialize data structures, load data, connect to databases, and perform any other chores it must do to get ready to print.

❑   *QueryPageSettings* — Before it prints a page, the PrintDocument object raises its QueryPageSettings event. A program can catch this event and modify the document's margins for the page that it is about to print.

❑   *PrintPage* — The PrintDocument object raises its PrintPage event to generate a page. The program must catch this event and use the Graphics object provided by the event handler's parameters to generate output. When it is finished, the event handler should set the value e.HasMorePages to True or False to tell the PrintDocument whether there are more pages to generate.

❑ *EndPrint* — Finally, when it has finished printing, the PrintDocument object raises its EndPrint event. The program can catch this event to clean up any resources it used while printing. It can free data structures, close data files and database connections, and perform any other necessary cleanup chores.

Having created a PrintDocument object and its event handlers, you can do three things with it. First you can call the object's Print method to immediately send a printout to the currently selected printer. The PrintDocument object raises its events as necessary as it generates the printout.

Second, you can set a PrintPreviewDialog's Document property to the PrintDocument object and then call the dialog's ShowDialog method. The PrintPreviewDialog displays the print preview window shown in Figure 23-1, using the PrintDocument object to generate the output it displays.

Figure 23-1: The PrintPreviewDialog **control lets the user zoom in and out and view the printout's various pages.**

The preview dialog's printer button on the left sends the printout to the printer. Note that this makes the PrintDocument object regenerate the printout using its events, this time sending the results to the printer instead of to the print preview dialog. The magnifying glass button displays a drop-down list where the user can select various scales for viewing the printout. The next five buttons let the user display one, two, three, four, or six of the printout's pages at the same time. The Close button closes the dialog and the Page up/down arrows let the user move through the printout's pages.

The PrintPreviewControl displays a print preview much as the PrintPreviewDialog control does, except that it sits on your form. It does not provide all the buttons that the dialog does, but it does provide methods that let you implement similar features. For example, it lets your program set the zoom level, number of columns in the display, and so forth.

The third thing you can do with a `PrintDocument` is assign it to a `PrintDialog`'s `Document` property and then call the dialog's `ShowDialog` method to display the dialog shown in Figure 23-2. The user can select the printer and set its properties (for example, selecting landscape or portrait orientation). When the user clicks Print, the dialog uses the `PrintDocument` object to send the printout to the printer.

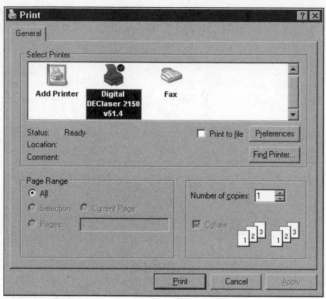

Figure 23-2: The `PrintDialog` **control lets the user send a printout to a printer.**

Your results could look different from those shown here. The print preview adjusts its appearance based on such factors as the type of printer you are using, its settings, the size of the paper you are using, and the paper's orientation.

The following code shows how a simple printing application can send output to the printer. This is just about the smallest program that demonstrates all three uses for a `PrintDocument` object: printing immediately, displaying a print preview dialog, and displaying a print dialog.

The code declares a `PrintDocument` object named `m_PrintDocument`. It uses the `WithEvents` keyword, so it can easily catch the object's events.

When the user clicks the Print Now button, the `btnPrintNow_Click` event handler assigns `m_PrintDocument` to a new `PrintDocument` object and calls its `Print` method.

If the user clicks the Print Preview button, the `btnPrintPreview_Click` event handler assigns `m_PrintDocument` to a new `PrintDocument` object, sets the `PrintPreviewDialog` object's `Document` property equal to the new object, and invokes the dialog's `ShowDialog` method.

The Print Dialog button works similarly. When the user clicks this button, the `btnPrintDialog_Click` event handler assigns `m_PrintDocument` to a new `PrintDocument` object, sets the `PrintDialog` object's `Document` property equal to the new object, and calls the dialog's `ShowDialog` method.

In all three cases, the PrintDocument object raises its PrintPage event when it is ready to print a page. The program's event handler creates a 10-pixel wide pen and defines an array of Point objects to define a diamond shape. It then calls the DrawPolygon method provided by the event handler's Graphics object to draw the diamond. It calls the pen's Dispose method to free resources and sets e.HasMorePages to False to tell the PrintDocument that the printout is complete.

```vb
Imports System.Drawing.Printing

Public Class Form1
    Private WithEvents m_PrintDocument As PrintDocument

    ' Print now.
    Private Sub btnPrintNow_Click(ByVal sender As System.Object, _
     ByVal e As System.EventArgs) Handles btnPrintNow.Click
        m_PrintDocument = New PrintDocument
        m_PrintDocument.Print()
    End Sub

    ' Display a print preview dialog.
    Private Sub btnPrintPreview_Click(ByVal sender As System.Object, _
     ByVal e As System.EventArgs) Handles btnPrintPreview.Click
        m_PrintDocument = New PrintDocument
        dlgPrintPreview.Document = m_PrintDocument
        dlgPrintPreview.ShowDialog()
    End Sub

    ' Display a print dialog.
    Private Sub btnPrintDialog_Click(ByVal sender As System.Object, _
     ByVal e As System.EventArgs) Handles btnPrintDialog.Click
        m_PrintDocument = New PrintDocument
        dlgPrint.Document = m_PrintDocument
        If dlgPrint.ShowDialog() = Windows.Forms.DialogResult.OK Then
            dlgPrint.Document.Print()
        End If
    End Sub

    ' Print a page with a diamond on it.
    Private Sub m_PrintDocument_PrintPage(ByVal sender As Object, _
     ByVal e As System.Drawing.Printing.PrintPageEventArgs) _
     Handles m_PrintDocument.PrintPage
        Dim the_pen As New Pen(Color.Black, 10)
        Dim pts() As Point = { _
            New Point(e.MarginBounds.Left + e.MarginBounds.Width \ 2, _
                e.MarginBounds.Top), _
            New Point(e.MarginBounds.Right, _
                e.MarginBounds.Top + e.MarginBounds.Height \ 2), _
            New Point(e.MarginBounds.Left + e.MarginBounds.Width \ 2, _
                e.MarginBounds.Bottom), _
            New Point(e.MarginBounds.Left, _
                e.MarginBounds.Top + e.MarginBounds.Height \ 2) _
        }
        e.Graphics.DrawPolygon(the_pen, pts)
        the_pen.Dispose()

        e.HasMorePages = False
    End Sub
End Class
```

The `PrintDocument`'s `PrintPage` event handler provides a parameter of type `PrintPageEventArgs` to let the program control the printout and to give information about the printer. This object's `PageBounds` and `MarginBounds` properties give the location of the printer's printable surface and the page's margins, respectively. Typically, the printable area might be a quarter inch smaller than the paper's physical size, and the margins might be an inch or more inside the paper's physical size.

Figure 23-3 shows these rectangles in a print preview. The `MarginBounds` are drawn with a thick line, and the `PageBounds` are shown with a thick dashed line.

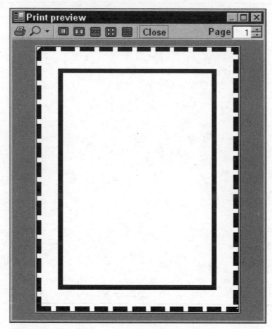

Figure 23-3: The `e.PageBounds` **and** `e.MarginBounds` **parameters give the paper's printable area and margins.**

Printing Text

The printing application described in the previous section is extremely simple. It prints a very straight-forward shape on a single page. You know the positions of the diamond before starting, so the program needs to perform little arranging and formatting. The only formatting it does is to make its diamond fit the page's margins.

This section describes a more useful example that prints a long series of paragraphs using different font sizes. The program must figure out how to break the text into pages. It also assumes that you will print the pages double-sided and then later bind the results into a booklet. To allow extra room for the binding, the program adds a *gutter* to the margin of edge of each page on the side where the binding will be. The program assumes that you will place the first page on the outside of the booklet, so it adds the gutter to the left margin on odd-numbered pages and to the right margin or even-numbered pages. Finally, the program displays a page number in the upper corner opposite the gutter.

Figure 23-4 shows the results displayed in a print preview dialog, so you can understand the goals. If you look closely, you can see that the left margins on the first and third pages and the right margin on the second page are enlarged to allow room for the gutter. You can also see that the page numbers are in the upper corner on the side that doesn't have the gutter. Imagine the second page printed on the back of the first, so their gutters lie on the same edge of the paper.

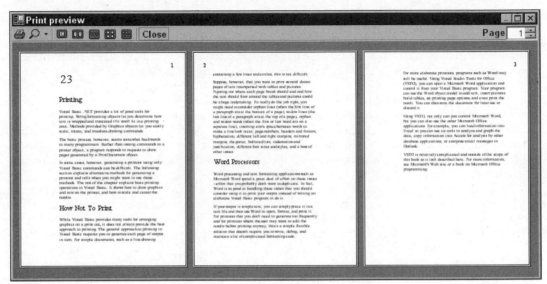

Figure 23-4: This preview shows text broken across pages with a gutter and displaying page numbers along the outside edges.

The following code shows the program generated this printout. The program begins by declaring a new `PrintDocument` object with the `WithEvents` keyword. The program uses `ParagraphInfo` structures to hold information about the paragraphs it will print. Each `ParagraphInfo` entry contains a font size and some text. The `m_Paragraphs` collection holds the `ParagraphInfo` objects that describe the program's text. The `m_ParagraphsToPrint` collection holds a copy of the text while the program is printing. The code uses this copy to keep track of the text that has yet to be printed. Variable `m_PagesPrinted` keeps track of the number of pages printed during the printing process. The code uses this value to display page numbers and to determine whether it is printing an odd or even page.

This little piece of code should have been omitted. When the program loads, the `Form1_Load` event handler attaches the program's print and print preview dialogs to the `PrintDocument` object. It then creates the `m_Paragraphs` collection and adds `ParagraphInfo` objects to it. This is just a bunch of data, so little of it is shown here.

When the user clicks the Print Preview or Print Dialog buttons, the corresponding event handlers simply display the appropriate dialogs. When the user clicks the Print Now button, the program calls the `PrintDocument` object's `Print` method.

More interesting differences between this program and the one described in the previous section come in the `PrintDocument`'s event handlers. The `BeginPrint` event handler sets `m_PagesPrinted` to zero. It then fills the `m_ParagraphsToPrint` collection with copies of the `ParagraphInfo` structures holding the program's text data. The program will use the objects in this collection to keep track of the paragraphs printed.

The `QueryPageSettings` event handler sets the margins for the page that the `PrintDocument` object is about the print. First, it sets the gutter size to 100 printer units (or one inch). Next, the program adjusts the margins based on the page number. If the page to be printed is the first page in the document, the program adds the gutter size to the left margin. If the page is some other odd-numbered page, the program moves the whole page to the right by increasing the left margin and decreasing the right margin. Finally, if the next page will be odd numbered, the program shifts the page to the left by decreasing the left margin and increasing the right margin.

The `PrintPage` event handler starts by incrementing the number of pages printed. It then includes commented code to draw a rectangle around the page's margins. When you are debugging a printing routine, drawing this rectangle can help you see where your drawing is in relation to the page's margins.

Next, the routine creates a font for the page number. Depending on whether this page is odd or even numbered, it calculates an X coordinate halfway between the nongutter margin and the edge of the printable page. It sets a `StringFormat` object's `Alignment` property to make numbers in the left margin left-justified and to make numbers in the right margin right-justified. It then draws the page number at the calculated X position, halfway between the top margin and the paper's top printable boundary.

The program then prepares to draw the text for this page. It sets the `StringFormat` object's properties so that the text is left-justified and lines wrap at word boundaries instead of in the middle of words. It sets the `FormatFlags` property to `LineLimit`. If only part of a line of text would fit vertically on the page, this makes Visual Basic not draw the line rather than drawing just the top halves of its letters.

After this preparation, the program sets variable `ymin` to the minimum Y coordinate where the routine can draw text. Initially, this is the top margin. It then enters a `Do` loop to process as much text as will fit on the page.

Inside the loop, the program takes the first `ParagraphInfo` structure from the `m_ParagraphsToPrint` collection and makes a font that has the right size for that paragraph. It creates a `RectangleF` representing the remaining area on the page. This includes the area between the left and right margins horizontally, and between `ymin` and the bottom margin vertically.

The program then uses the `e.Graphics` object's `MeasureString` method to see how much space the next piece of text will need. It passes `MeasureString` the layout rectangle's size and the `StringFormat` object so that Visual Basic can decide how it will need to wrap the paragraph's text when it prints it. The code also passes in the variables `characters_fitted` and `lines_filled`. These parameters are passed by reference, so `MeasureString` can fill in the number of characters and lines it could draw within the allowed size.

The routine then checks `characters_fitted` to see if any characters will fit in the available area. If any characters can fit, the program draws the paragraph. Commented code draws a rectangle around the text to help with debugging. The program increases `ymin` by the paragraph's printed height plus half of the font's height to provide a break between paragraphs.

Next, the program determines whether the entire paragraph fit in the allowed area. If some of the paragraph did not fit, the program stores the remaining text in the `ParagraphInfo` structure and puts the structure back at the beginning of the `m_ParagraphsToPrint` collection so that it can be printed on the next page. It then exits the `Do` loop because the current page is full.

When the page is full or the `m_ParagraphsToPrint` collection is empty, the `PrintPage` event handler is finished. It sets `e.HasMorePages` to `True` if `m_ParagraphsToPrint` is not empty.

Finally, when the `PrintDocument` has finished printing the whole document, the `EndPrint` event handler executes. This routine cleans up by setting the `m_ParagraphsToPrint` variable to `Nothing`, freeing up the collection object's memory. In this program, freeing the collection is a small matter. In a program that allocated more elaborate data structures, cleaning up in this event handler would be more important.

```vb
' The PrintDocument.
Private WithEvents m_PrintDocument As New PrintDocument

' Information about the paragraphs to print.
Private Structure ParagraphInfo
    Public FontSize As Integer
    Public Text As String
    Public Sub New(ByVal font_size As Integer, ByVal txt As String)
        FontSize = font_size
        Text = txt
    End Sub
End Structure

' The paragraphs.
Private m_Paragraphs As Collection
Private m_ParagraphsToPrint As Collection
Private m_PagesPrinted As Integer

' Load the paragraph info.
Private Sub Form1_Load(ByVal sender As Object, _
 ByVal e As System.EventArgs) Handles MyBase.Load
    ' Attach the PrintDocument to the
    ' PrintDialog and PrintPreviewDialog.
    dlgPrint.Document = m_PrintDocument
    dlgPrintPreview.Document = m_PrintDocument

    ' Make the text to print.
    m_Paragraphs = New Collection
    m_Paragraphs.Add(New ParagraphInfo(45, "23"))
    m_Paragraphs.Add(New ParagraphInfo(27, "Printing"))
    ... Code omitted...
End Sub

' Display the preview dialog.
Private Sub btnPrintPreview_Click(ByVal sender As System.Object, _
 ByVal e As System.EventArgs) Handles btnPrintPreview.Click
    dlgPrintPreview.WindowState = FormWindowState.Maximized
    dlgPrintPreview.ShowDialog()
End Sub

' Display the print dialog.
Private Sub btnPrintDialog_Click(ByVal sender As System.Object, _
 ByVal e As System.EventArgs) Handles btnPrintDialog.Click
If dlgPrint.ShowDialog() = Windows.Forms.DialogResult.OK Then
    dlgPrint.Document.Print()
End If
End Sub

' Print immediately.
Private Sub btnPrintNow_Click(ByVal sender As System.Object, _
 ByVal e As System.EventArgs) Handles btnPrintNow.Click
```

```
            m_PrintDocument.Print()
    End Sub

    ' Get ready to print pages.
    Private Sub m_PrintDocument_BeginPrint(ByVal sender As Object, _
     ByVal e As System.Drawing.Printing.PrintEventArgs) _
     Handles m_PrintDocument.BeginPrint
        ' We have not yet printed any pages.
        m_PagesPrinted = 0

        ' Make a copy of the text to print.
        m_ParagraphsToPrint = New Collection
        For Each para_info As ParagraphInfo In m_Paragraphs
            m_ParagraphsToPrint.Add(_
                New ParagraphInfo(para_info.FontSize, para_info.Text))
        Next para_info
    End Sub

    ' Set the margins for the following page.
    Private Sub m_PrintDocument_QueryPageSettings(ByVal sender As Object, _
     ByVal e As System.Drawing.Printing.QueryPageSettingsEventArgs) _
     Handles m_PrintDocument.QueryPageSettings
        ' Use a 1 inch gutter (printer units are 100 per inch).
        Const gutter As Integer = 100

        ' See if the next page will be the first, odd, or even.
        If m_PagesPrinted = 0 Then
            ' The next page is the first.
            ' Increase the left margin.
            e.PageSettings.Margins.Left += gutter
        ElseIf (m_PagesPrinted Mod 2) = 0 Then
            ' The next page will be odd.
            ' Shift the margins right.
            e.PageSettings.Margins.Left += gutter
            e.PageSettings.Margins.Right -= gutter
        Else
            ' The next page will be even.
            ' Shift the margins left.
            e.PageSettings.Margins.Left -= gutter
            e.PageSettings.Margins.Right += gutter
        End If
    End Sub

    ' Print the next page.
    Private Sub m_PrintDocument_PrintPage(ByVal sender As Object, _
     ByVal e As System.Drawing.Printing.PrintPageEventArgs) _
     Handles m_PrintDocument.PrintPage
        ' Increment the page number.
        m_PagesPrinted += 1

        ' Draw the margins (for debugging).
        'e.Graphics.DrawRectangle(Pens.Red, e.MarginBounds)

        ' Print the page number right justified
```

```
' in the upper corner opposite the gutter
' and outside of the margin.
Dim the_font As Font
Dim x As Integer
Dim string_format As New StringFormat
the_font = New Font("Times New Roman", _
    20, FontStyle.Regular, GraphicsUnit.Point)

' See if this is an odd or even page.
If (m_PagesPrinted Mod 2) = 0 Then
    ' This is an even page.
    ' The gutter is on the left.
    x = (e.MarginBounds.Left + e.PageBounds.Left) \ 2
    string_format.Alignment = StringAlignment.Near
Else
    ' This is an odd page.
    ' The gutter is on the right.
    x = (e.MarginBounds.Right + e.PageBounds.Right) \ 2
    string_format.Alignment = StringAlignment.Far
End If
e.Graphics.DrawString(m_PagesPrinted.ToString, _
    the_font, Brushes.Black, x, _
    (e.MarginBounds.Top + e.PageBounds.Top) \ 2, _
    string_format)

' Draw the rest of the text left justified,
' wrap at words, and don't draw partial lines.
string_format.Alignment = StringAlignment.Near
string_format.FormatFlags = StringFormatFlags.LineLimit
string_format.Trimming = StringTrimming.Word

' Draw some text.
Dim paragraph_info As ParagraphInfo
Dim ymin As Integer = e.MarginBounds.Top
Dim layout_rect As RectangleF
Dim text_size As SizeF
Dim characters_fitted As Integer
Dim lines_filled As Integer
Do While m_ParagraphsToPrint.Count > 0
    ' Print the next paragraph.
    paragraph_info = DirectCast(m_ParagraphsToPrint(1), ParagraphInfo)
    m_ParagraphsToPrint.Remove(1)

    ' Get the font.
    the_font = New Font("Times New Roman", _
        paragraph_info.FontSize, _
        FontStyle.Regular, GraphicsUnit.Point)

    ' Get the area available for this paragraph.
    layout_rect = New RectangleF( _
        e.MarginBounds.Left, ymin, _
        e.MarginBounds.Width, _
        e.MarginBounds.Bottom - ymin)
```

```
        ' Make sure the layout rectangle is at least 1 pixel tall
        ' to avoid confusing MeasureString.
        If layout_rect.Height < 1 Then layout_rect.Height = 1

            ' See how big the text will be and
            ' how many characters will fit.
            text_size = e.Graphics.MeasureString( _
                paragraph_info.Text, the_font, _
                New SizeF(layout_rect.Width, layout_rect.Height), _
                string_format, characters_fitted, lines_filled)

            ' See if any characters will fit.
            If characters_fitted > 0 Then
                ' Draw the text.
                e.Graphics.DrawString(paragraph_info.Text, _
                    the_font, Brushes.Black, _
                    layout_rect, string_format)

                ' Draw a rectangle around the text (for debugging).
                'e.Graphics.DrawRectangle(Pens.Green, _
                '    layout_rect.Left, _
                '    layout_rect.Top, _
                '    text_size.Width, _
                '    text_size.Height)

                ' Increase the location where we can start.
                ' Add a little interparagraph spacing.
                ymin += CInt(text_size.Height + _
                    e.Graphics.MeasureString("M", the_font).Height / 2)
            End If

            ' See if some of the paragraph didn't fit on the page.
            If characters_fitted < Len(paragraph_info.Text) Then
                ' Some of the paragraph didn't fit.
                ' Prepare to print the rest on the next page.
                paragraph_info.Text = paragraph_info.Text. _
                    Substring(characters_fitted)
                m_ParagraphsToPrint.Add(paragraph_info, Before:=1)

                ' That's all that will fit on this page.
                Exit Do
            End If
        Loop

        ' If we have more paragraphs, we have more pages.
        e.HasMorePages = (m_ParagraphsToPrint.Count > 0)
End Sub

' Clean up.
Private Sub m_PrintDocument_EndPrint(ByVal sender As Object, _
 ByVal e As System.Drawing.Printing.PrintEventArgs) _
 Handles m_PrintDocument.EndPrint
    m_ParagraphsToPrint = Nothing
End Sub
```

Centering Printouts

The previous section explained how to handle a common scenario: printing large amounts of text. Another common scenario is printing a picture centered on the printed page. To do that, you must move the drawing vertically and horizontally to put it at the correct position. You can do this by using the Graphics object's TranslateTransform method. That method defines a translation transformation for all the graphics drawn by the object. After you set the transformation, you can draw any graphics as usual, and the Graphics object automatically moves them to the correct position.

The CenterPictureInMargins subroutine shown in the following code defines a translation transformation that centers an area within some specified bounds. The routine begins by calling the Graphics object's ResetTransform method to remove any transformations that may already be defined. Next, the routine calculates the horizontal and vertical offsets by which it must translate the rectangle picture_bounds so that it will be centered within the rectangle margin_bounds. It calls the Graphics object's TranslateTransform method to make the translation.

```
' Transform the Graphics object to center the rectangle
' picture_bounds within margin_bounds.
Private Sub CenterPictureInMargins(ByVal gr As Graphics, _
 ByVal picture_bounds As RectangleF, ByVal margin_bounds As RectangleF)
    ' Remove any existing transformation.
    gr.ResetTransform()

    ' Apply the transformation.
    Dim dx As Single = _
        margin_bounds.Left - picture_bounds.Left + _
        (margin_bounds.Width - picture_bounds.Width) / 2
    Dim dy As Single = _
        margin_bounds.Top - picture_bounds.Top + _
        (margin_bounds.Height - picture_bounds.Height) / 2
    gr.TranslateTransform(dx, dy)
End Sub
```

You can use subroutine CenterPictureInMargins to prepare the e.Graphics object provided by the PrintPage event handler to center a drawing on a printout. For example, the following PrintPage event handler code draws a bar chart in the coordinate space $100 <= X <= 600$, $100 <= Y <= 400$. It begins with commented code that draws the page's margins for debugging purposes.

The code defines rectangles representing the area in which it will draw and the printed page's margin bounds. It passes those rectangles to the CenterPictureInMargins subroutine to prepare the Graphics object for centering.

Next, the program fills the picture area's rectangle with light gray and outlines it in black. It then calls subroutine DrawBar several times to draw five values for the bar chart. The event handler sets e.HasMorePages to False and ends.

Subroutine DrawBar draws a rectangle for the bar chart. It draws its rectangle at the X coordinate passed as a parameter, making it 100 units wide and hgt units tall. It fills the rectangle with a hatch pattern and then outlines it in black. The subroutine finishes by adding 100 to x, so the next call to DrawBar draws a rectangle to the right.

```
' Print the page.
Private Sub Print_PrintPage(ByVal sender As Object, _
  ByVal e As System.Drawing.Printing.PrintPageEventArgs)
    ' Draw the margins (for debugging). Be sure
    ' to do this before transforming the Graphics object.
    e.Graphics.DrawRectangle(Pens.Red, e.MarginBounds)

    ' This routine draws a bar chart for 5 values
    ' in printer coordinates between
    ' (100, 100) - (600, 400).
    ' Transform the Graphics object to center the results.
    Dim picture_rect As New RectangleF(100, 100, 600, 400)
    Dim margin_rect As New RectangleF( _
        e.MarginBounds.X, _
        e.MarginBounds.Y, _
        e.MarginBounds.Width, _
        e.MarginBounds.Height)
    CenterPictureInMargins(e.Graphics, picture_rect, margin_rect)

    ' Draw a rectangle around the chart.
    e.Graphics.FillRectangle(Brushes.LightGray, picture_rect)
    e.Graphics.DrawRectangle(Pens.Black, Rectangle.Round(picture_rect))

    ' Draw the values.
    Dim x As Integer = 100
    DrawBar(e.Graphics, x, 200, HatchStyle.BackwardDiagonal)
    DrawBar(e.Graphics, x, 280, HatchStyle.Vertical)
    DrawBar(e.Graphics, x, 240, HatchStyle.ForwardDiagonal)
    DrawBar(e.Graphics, x, 170, HatchStyle.Horizontal)
    DrawBar(e.Graphics, x, 290, HatchStyle.DiagonalCross)

    ' There are no more pages.
    e.HasMorePages = False
End Sub

' Draw a bar in (x, 400)-(x + 100, 400 - hgt).
Private Sub DrawBar(ByVal gr As Graphics, ByRef x As Integer, _
  ByVal hgt As Integer, ByVal hatch_style As HatchStyle)
    Dim rect As New Rectangle(x, 400 - hgt, 100, hgt)
    gr.FillRectangle( _
        New HatchBrush(hatch_style, Color.Black, Color.White), _
        rect)
    gr.DrawRectangle(Pens.Black, rect)
    x += 100
End Sub
```

Figure 23-5 shows the result. You can see in the picture that the bar chart is centered within the margins.

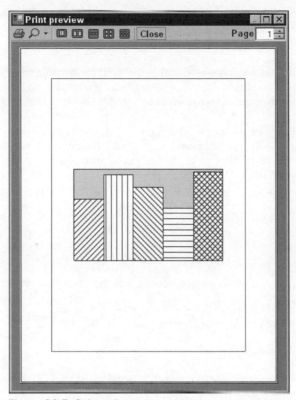

Figure 23-5: Subroutine `CenterPictureInMargins`
makes it easy to center a picture within a printed page.

Fitting Pictures to the Page

Another common scenario is drawing a picture as large as possible on the page without distorting it. You can use the same approach to this problem that was described in the previous section: Apply a transformation to the `PrintPage` event handler's `Graphics` object to make the picture fit the printed page.

The subroutine `FitPictureToMargins` shown in the following code makes this transformation. It begins by calling the `Graphics` object's `ResetTransform` method to remove any existing transformation. Next the subroutine translates to center the `picture_bounds` rectangle at the origin. Scaling an object centered at the origin is relatively simple because the object's center remains at the origin, so the program starts by centering `picture_bounds`.

The program compares aspect ratios (ratios of height/width) of the `picture_bounds` and `margin_bounds` rectangles. If `picture_bounds` has the greater aspect ratio, then it is relatively taller and thinner than `margin_bounds`. In that case, the program scales to make `picture_bounds` the same height as `margin_bounds` and sets its width appropriately.

If `picture_bounds` has the smaller aspect ratio, it is relatively wider and shorter than `margin_bounds`. In that case, the program scales to make `picture_bounds` the same width as `margin_bounds` and sets its height accordingly.

After calculating the scale factor it needs, the program calls the `Graphics` object's `ScaleTransform` method to add it to the `Graphics` object's transformation. It uses the `MatrixOrder.Append` parameter to make the object apply the scaling transformation after its first translation.

Finally, the subroutine applies another translation to move the center of the scaled `picture_bounds` rectangle from the origin to the center of `margin_bounds`. It again uses the `MatrixOrder.Append` parameter, so the new transformation is applied after the previous ones.

```
' Transform the Graphics object to fit the rectangle
' picture_bounds to margin_bounds and center it.
Private Sub FitPictureToMargins(ByVal gr As Graphics, _
 ByVal picture_bounds As RectangleF, ByVal margin_bounds As RectangleF)
    ' Remove any existing transformation.
    gr.ResetTransform()

    ' Translate to center picture_bounds at the origin.
    gr.TranslateTransform( _
        -(picture_bounds.Left + picture_bounds.Width / 2), _
        -(picture_bounds.Top + picture_bounds.Height / 2))

    ' Scale to make picture_bounds fit margin_bounds.
    ' Compare the aspect ratios.
    Dim margin_aspect As Single = margin_bounds.Height / margin_bounds.Width
    Dim picture_aspect As Single = picture_bounds.Height / picture_bounds.Width
    Dim scale As Single
    If picture_aspect > margin_aspect Then
        ' picture_bounds is relatively tall and thin.
        ' Make it as tall as possible.
        scale = margin_bounds.Height / picture_bounds.Height
    Else
        ' picture_bounds is relatively short and wide.
        ' Make it as wide as possible.
        scale = margin_bounds.Width / picture_bounds.Width
    End If
    ' Scale.
    gr.ScaleTransform(scale, scale, MatrixOrder.Append)

    ' Translate to move the origin to the center of margin_bounds.
    gr.TranslateTransform( _
        margin_bounds.Left + margin_bounds.Width / 2, _
        margin_bounds.Top + margin_bounds.Height / 2, _
        MatrixOrder.Append)
End Sub
```

A program can use subroutine `FitPictureToMargins` exactly as it can use subroutine `CenterPictureInMargins`. Figure 23-6 shows the result. This routine works whether the picture area is relatively short and wide (as in this case) or tall and thin. It will also shrink a picture that is bigger than the page.

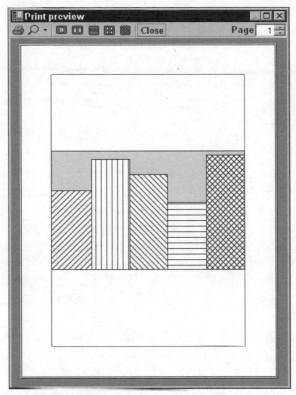

Figure 23-6: Subroutine `FitPictureToMargins`
**makes it easy to center a picture within a printed
page, making it as large as possible without distortion.**

Simplifying Drawing and Printing

Many applications draw some graphics, possibly with some user interaction, and then later print the same graphics, perhaps centered and scaled to fit the page.

You can make this process easier if you move all of the program's drawing code into subroutines that are independent of the drawing or printing surface. These drawing routines should take as a parameter a `Graphics` object on which to draw. Then it doesn't matter whether the program passes these routines the `Graphics` object provided by a `PrintPage` event handler or a control's `Paint` event handler. They can even use a `Graphics` object generated by control's `CreateGraphics` method.

The `DrawGraphics` subroutine shown in the following code encapsulates the drawing code used in the previous sections. It takes a `Graphics` object as a parameter, draws a background on it, and calls `DrawBar` to draw five hatched rectangles to form a bar chart.

```
' Draw the bar chart with world coordinate bounds (100, 100)-(600, 400).
Private Sub DrawGraphics(ByVal gr As Graphics)
    ' Draw a rectangle around the chart.
    Dim picture_rect As New Rectangle(100, 100, 500, 300)
    gr.FillRectangle(Brushes.LightGray, picture_rect)
    gr.DrawRectangle(Pens.Black, picture_rect)

    ' Draw the values.
    Dim x As Integer = 100
    DrawBar(gr, x, 200, HatchStyle.BackwardDiagonal)
    DrawBar(gr, x, 280, HatchStyle.Vertical)
    DrawBar(gr, x, 240, HatchStyle.ForwardDiagonal)
    DrawBar(gr, x, 170, HatchStyle.Horizontal)
    DrawBar(gr, x, 290, HatchStyle.DiagonalCross)
End Sub
```

Now the `PrintPage` event handler and other code can call this subroutine to draw the program's graphics. The following code shows how a program can use this routine to draw the bar chart on a `PictureBox` named `picCanvas`. The control's `Resize` event handler invalidates the control, so the `Paint` event handler can redraw the entire surface. The control's `Paint` event handler clears the `PictureBox`, calls `FitPictureToMargins` to fit the bar chart to the `PictureBox`'s surface (minus a 3-pixel margin), and calls `DrawGraphics` to draw the bar chart.

```
Private Sub picCanvas_Resize(ByVal sender As Object, _
 ByVal e As System.EventArgs) Handles picCanvas.Resize
    picCanvas.Invalidate()
End Sub
Private Sub picCanvas_Paint(ByVal sender As Object, _
 ByVal e As System.Windows.Forms.PaintEventArgs) Handles picCanvas.Paint
    ' Clear the picture.
    e.Graphics.Clear(picCanvas.BackColor)

    ' This routine draws a bar chart for 5 values
    ' in printer coordinates between
    ' (100, 100) - (600, 400).
    ' Transform the Graphics object to center the results.
    Dim picture_rect As New RectangleF(100, 100, 500, 300)
    Dim margin_rect As New RectangleF( _
        picCanvas.ClientRectangle.X + 3, _
        picCanvas.ClientRectangle.Y + 3, _
        picCanvas.ClientRectangle.Width - 6, _
        picCanvas.ClientRectangle.Height - 6)
    FitPictureToMargins(e.Graphics, picture_rect, margin_rect)

    ' Draw the bar chart.
    DrawGraphics(e.Graphics)
End Sub
```

Figure 23-7 shows the result.

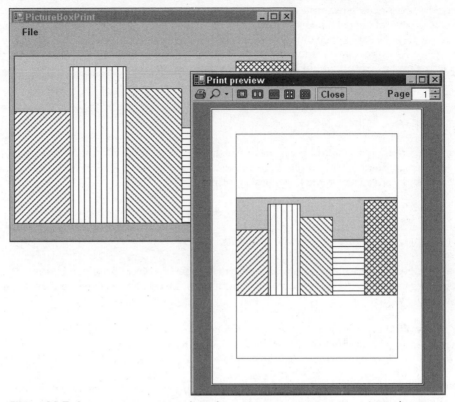

Figure 23-7: A program can use subroutine `FitPictureToMargins` to make a
picture fit a `PictureBox` as well as a printed page.

This technique minimizes the amount of drawing code. It lets the program share the same code for
drawing, printing, and print previewing. That means less code to debug and maintain. It also means that
you need only to modify the code in one place if you need to change it later.

By calling `FitPictureToMargins`, the program makes the bar chart fill the `PictureBox` as much as
possible without distorting it. If the control is anchored or docked so that it resizes when the form does,
the bar chart also resizes so that it is as big as possible, a fairly impressive feat at the cost of a single subroutine call.

While very useful, the technique of using a common routine to draw and print graphics is not appropriate for every application. Sometimes a program must take advantage of the particular characteristics of a
printer or screen object, and the results may not make sense for other types of devices.

For example, suppose that a program draws fractals by performing time-consuming calculations for
each pixel. It may make sense to show the results as the pixels are calculated on the screen. That would
take advantage of the fact that the user can immediately see the results of pixels drawn on the screen. On
the printer, however, the results aren't visible until the complete page is printed, so sending pixels to the
printer one at a time doesn't particularly help the user and may slow printing. It might make more sense
to draw the complete image on a `Bitmap` in memory and then send the result to the printer all at once by
using the `Graphics` object's `DrawImage` method.

Similarly, the text-printing example described earlier in this chapter prints a long series of paragraphs broken across several pages. It takes advantage of the printed page's exact size and margins. You might be able to display the same page data in a scrolling window on the screen, but that probably wouldn't make much sense. In that application, trying to force screen drawing and page printing routines to produce exactly the same result would probably be a waste of time.

Summary

The `PrintDocument` object sits at the heart of the standard Visual Basic printing process. A program makes a `PrintDocument` object and then responds to its `BeginPrint`, `QueryPageSettings`, `PrintPage`, and `EndPrint` events to generate a printout.

The `PrintDocument` object's `Print` method immediately generates a printout. You can also attach the `PrintDocument` to a `PrintDialog`, `PrintPreviewDialog`, or `PrintPreviewControl` and use those objects to display previews and generate printouts.

This chapter describes printing in general. Using the `Graphics` object provided by the `PrintDocument`'s `PrintPage` event, you can print lines, curves, text, images, and anything else you can draw to the screen.

One particular kind of printing is very common in business applications: reporting. While you can use the general printing techniques described in this chapter to draw your own reports, Visual Studio 2005 Professional Edition comes with a tool that simplifies many reporting tasks: Crystal Reports.

Crystal Reports can help you build, format, display, and print reports. It can automatically load data from a database and display it in tabular form complete with headers, sections, totals, subtotals, and graphs. Chapter 24, "Reporting," provides an introduction to Crystal Reports.

24

Reporting

Visual Studio 2005 Professional Edition and the higher editions come with Crystal Reports for Visual Studio 2005. Crystal Reports is a product that helps you build, display, and print reports in Visual Basic applications.

Crystal Reports is a large and complex application that provides a huge number of wizards, formats, charts, and other tools for building reports, so there isn't enough room here to do it justice. This chapter provides a quick introduction to using Crystal Reports to build a few simple examples. For more detailed information about particular topics, consult the online help at msdn.microsoft.com/library/en-us/crystlmn/html/crconcrystalreports.asp. The help includes several examples that show how to make reports with certain common formats.

You may also want to visit the Web site of Business Objects (the makers of Crystal Reports) at www.businessobjects.com and their Web page for Crystal Reports www.businessobjects.com/products/reporting/crystalreports/default.asp.

For more in-depth information, read a book that covers only Crystal Reports. Quite a few books about Crystal Reports are available for developers with all levels of experience, including *Professional Crystal Reports for Visual Studio .NET* (Wiley Publishing, 2004).

Report Objects

Normally, when you think of a report, you probably think of some sort of physical output, either on a computer screen or on paper. In Crystal Reports, a Report object represents the information needed to generate a report. It determines which fields are selected from what data source, how the fields are arranged and summarized, and any text that is displayed on the result.

A report is stored in a file with a .rpt extension. This file can be either included inside the application or loaded from a separate file. Each of these approaches has its advantages. Embedding a report in an application makes using and distributing the application somewhat easier. On the other hand, if an application loads a report from an external file, you can modify or replace the report file without recompiling the application.

At run time, a program can attach a report (either internal or external) to a data source and then use a `CrystalReportViewer` control to display the result. This control provides tools that enable the user to move between the report's different pages, zoom in and out, navigate through report groups using a tree view, view subreports, print or export the report, and so forth.

Building a Report

This section describes a simple example that uses an internal report to display student test scores. The report's data is taken from an Access database containing two tables.

The Students table contains the fields LastName, FirstName, and StudentId. The Scores table contains the fields StudentId, TestNumber, and Score. The StudentId field provides the link between the two tables.

Figure 24-1 shows the desired result. Each student's scores are grouped in a separate section that ends with the student's average score. The report as a whole ends by displaying the class average.

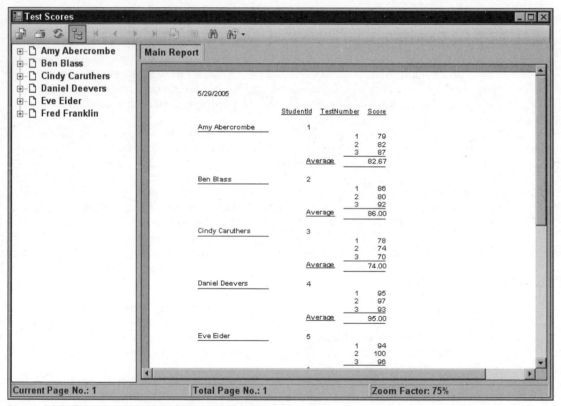

Figure 24-1: This report displays students' test scores.

To build the example program, start a new Windows application project. First you must define the report. Open the Project menu and select the Add New Item command. Select the Crystal Report template and enter a meaningful name for the report file, as shown in Figure 24-2.

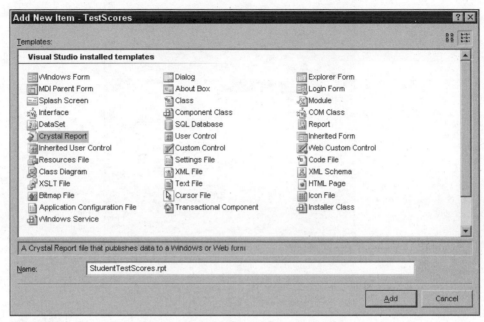

Figure 24-2: To create a report, select the Crystal Report template.

When you click Add, the Crystal Reports Gallery shown in Figure 24-3 appears (possibly after you accept a Crystal Reports license agreement). You can use the gallery to build a blank report, a report based on an existing report, or a report built by a wizard. For this example, select the "Using the Report Wizard" option and the Standard expert, and click OK.

The Standard Report Creation Wizard, shown in Figure 24-4, starts by letting you define the report's data source. Use the Available Data Sources display on the left to select the data source. To create a new data source, open the Create New Connection item. Then expand the appropriate connection type. For this example, which uses an Access database, you would expand the OLE DB (ADO) item.

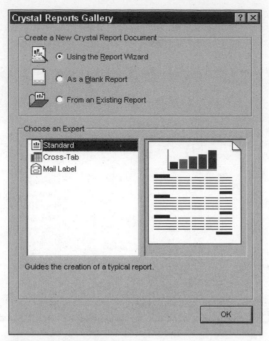

Figure 24-3: Select the report type from the
Crystal Reports Gallery.

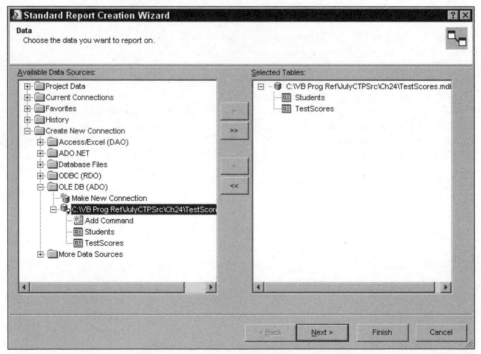

Figure 24-4: The Standard Report Creation Wizard's Data step lets you
define the report's data source.

If a connection item contains no connections, expanding it displays an appropriate connection wizard. If the item contains some previously built connections, expanding the item lists those connections and displays a Make New Connection item. Double-clicking this item also displays an appropriate connection wizard.

Figure 24-5 shows the connection wizard for an OLE DB (ADO) connection. Select the provider you want to use for the connection, and click Next. For an Access database, select Microsoft Jet 4.0 OLE DB Provider.

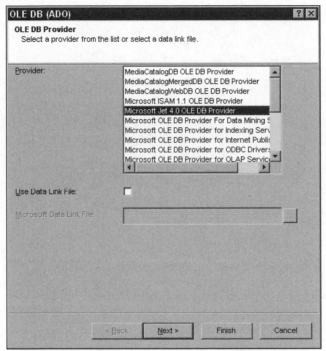

Figure 24-5: Use this wizard to define an OLE DB (ADO) connection.

When you click Next, the connection wizard asks you to enter the database name, as shown in Figure 24-6. Click the Browse button to search for the database. You can also select the database type from the drop-down list. In this example, the data comes from an Access database, but the provider can also read data from a number of other data sources such as dBASE, Excel, Lotus, Paradox, and text files.

After you enter the database name, click Finish to build the connection. The Standard Report Creation Wizard then lists the database's tables, as shown in Figure 24-4. Select the tables that contain the data you want to display and click the > button to add them to the Selected Tables list. In Figure 24-4, the Students and TestScores tables are selected.

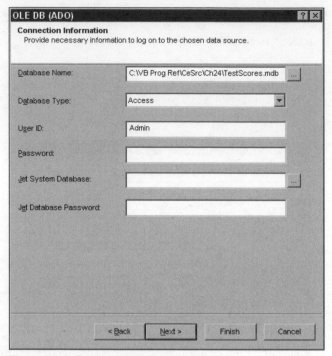

Figure 24-6: Enter the database' name.

When you click Next, the wizard displays the Link page shown in Figure 24-7. Drag the tables into convenient positions. Then click and drag the StudentId field from the Students table onto the StudentId field in the TestScores table. This defines the relationship between the two tables. If you click Auto-Arrange, the wizard will rearrange the tables so that it's easier to see the link.

Click Next to see the Fields page shown in Figure 24-8. Select the fields that you want to display and click the > button to move them to the "Fields to Display" list. In Figure 24-8, the Students table's FirstName, LastName, and StudentId fields are selected, together with the TestScores table's TestNumber and Score fields. The TestScores table's StudentId field is not selected because it duplicates the value in the Students table's StudentId field.

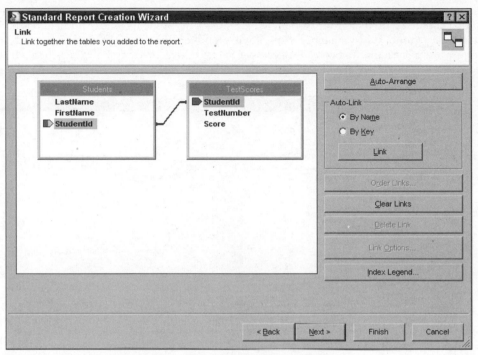

Figure 24-7: Use the Link page to define links between tables.

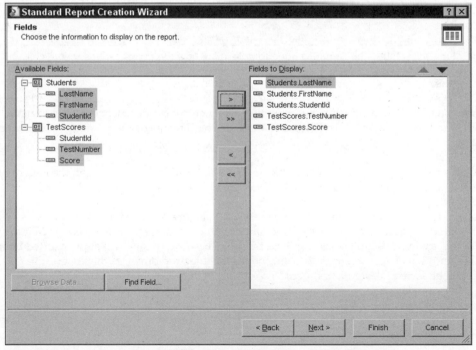

Figure 24-8: Use the Fields page to select the fields displayed by the report.

When you click Next, the wizard displays the Grouping page shown in Figure 24-9. Here, you can select fields that should be used to group results. In Figure 24-9, the Students.StudentId field has been selected as the primary group. When the report runs, it will group together all of the records for each student. The figure also selects the TestScores.TestNumber field. This ensures that the values in this field will be sorted.

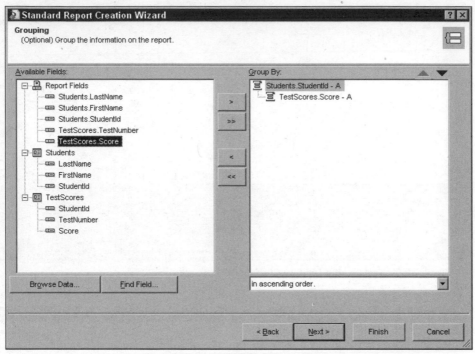

Figure 24-9: Use the Grouping page to determine how the report groups records.

Click Next to display the Summaries page shown in Figure 24-10. This page lets you add summary information to the report. Initially, the page displays some rather odd selections (including the sums of the StudentId, TestScore, and TestNumber values). It's hard to imagine wanting to add up all of the test numbers.

In the upper group, select the sum of TestScores.Score and use the drop-down on the lower right to select Average instead of Sum. Remove the other summary fields.

Click Next to display the Group Sorting page shown in Figure 24-11. You can use this page to sort groups based on their summary data. For example, you could sort students based on their average test scores. This example doesn't sort the groups by summary data, so they will appear sorted by the group field StudentId. (Go back to Figure 24-9 and notice that the drop-down on the lower right says that the group will be sorted in ascending order.)

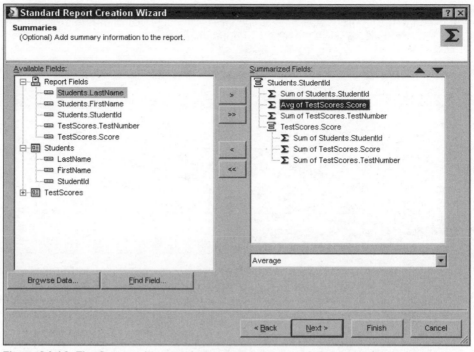

Figure 24-10: The Summaries page lets you add summary information to the report.

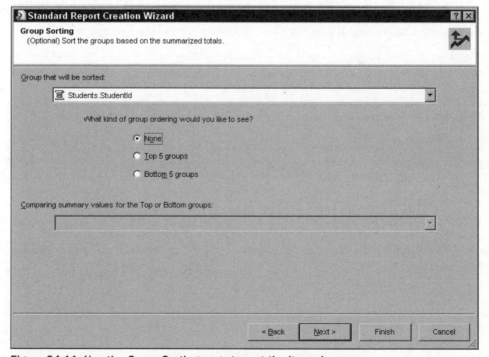

Figure 24-11: Use the Group Sorting page to sort the items in groups.

When you click Next, the wizard displays the Chart page shown in Figure 24-12. Select the type of chart you want to add to the report. Figure 24-12 is shown selecting a bar chart, but this example assumes that you don't want any chart, so select the No Chart option before continuing.

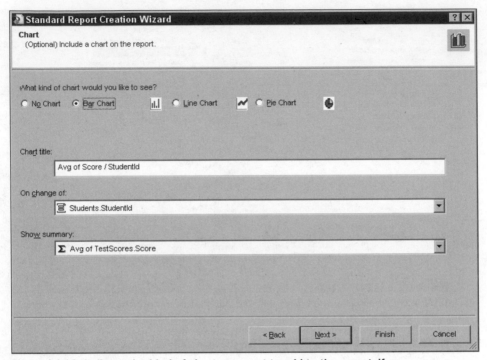

Figure 24-12: Indicate the kind of chart you want to add to the report, if any.

After you select a chart type, click Next to display the Record Selection page shown in Figure 24-13. This page lets you filter the records that are selected for the report. Move the fields you want to use to select records to the list on the right. Pick the selection operator you want to use in the drop-down below the list. If the operator requires extra data, additional fields appear below the drop-down.

For example, in Figure 24-13 the selection operator is "is less than or equal to." When you select this operator, another drop-down appears to let you enter a value to compare to the Students.LastName field. The wizard populates the drop-down with Students.LastName values taken from the database.

Figure 24-13 shows a record selection field selected, but this example assumes that you want all of the records, so remove this field before you continue.

When you click Next, the wizard displays its final page, the Report Style page shown in Figure 24-14. Select a style and click Finish.

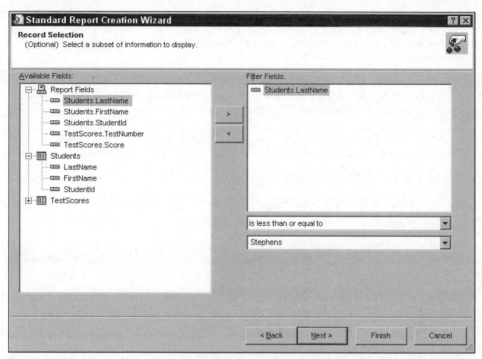

Figure 24-13: Use the Record Selection page to filter the records included in the report.

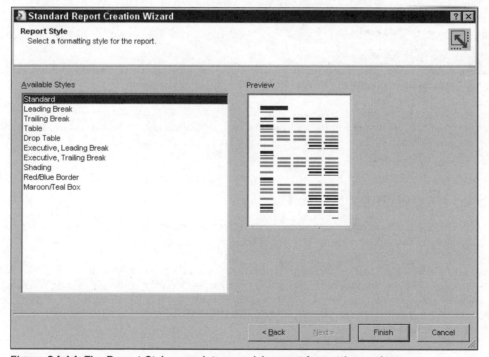

Figure 24-14: The Report Style page lets you pick report formatting options.

Figure 24-15 shows the resulting report in the development environment. The horizontal gray bars indicate the report's different sections. These include report headers and footers, page headers and footers, group headers and footers, and a details section inside the innermost group.

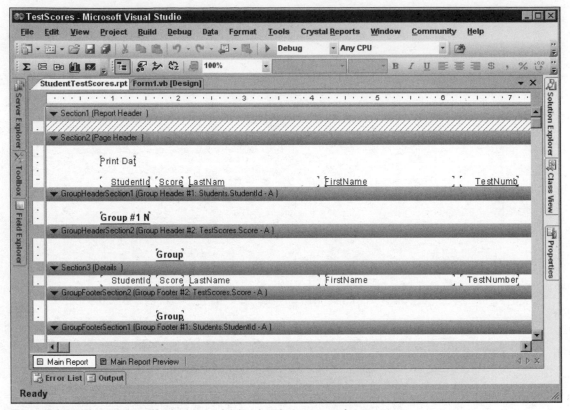

Figure 24-15: You can modify the report in the development environment.

Within each section, text surrounded by brackets indicates labels and text fields on the report. When the report executes, it will fill these in with values taken from the database.

CrystalReportViewer

At this point, the report is ready to generate output, but you still need to display the result somehow. One way to view the report is using a CrystalReportViewer control.

Open a form, select the Toolbox's Crystal Reports section, and add a CrystalReportViewer control to the form. Select the control, open the Properties window, click on the control's ReportSource property, and click the drop-down arrow on the right. Select the entry labeled TestScores.StudentTestScores. Here "TestScores" is the project's namespace and "StudentTestScores" is the name of the report you created in the previous section.

When you select this entry, Visual Basic makes an instance of the report, adds it to the form's component area, and attaches the `CrystalReportViewer` control to the new instance so the `CrystalReportViewer` displays the report. If you run the program now, you will see a result similar to the one shown in Figure 24-16.

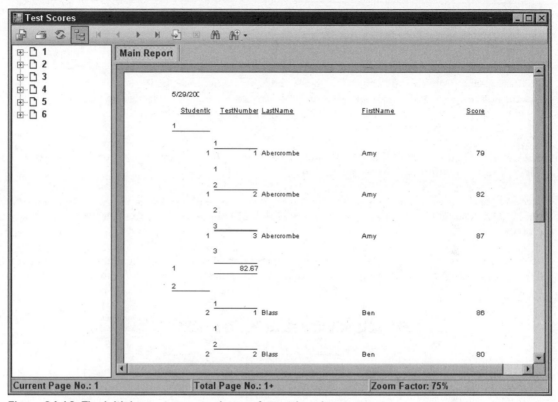

Figure 24-16: The initial report may need some formatting changes.

Customizing a Report

If you look closely at Figure 24-16, you can probably think of several ideas for improving the report. While the StudentId field groups records, it is probably not the value that you would use to locate a student's records. It would be more convenient to display the students' names instead.

The StudentId, LastName, and FirstName fields are repeated for every detail row, even though they are the same for each StudentId group.

The report also has some basic arrangement problems. The date field in the upper-left corner is also too small to show the entire date. Each student's average test score is shown, but the label to the left is the student's ID, not something meaningful. The average would also look better aligned below the students' scores. Finally, the columns are a lot wider than they probably need to be, making it hard to read the whole report.

Fortunately, it's relatively easy to customize the report. The basic idea is similar to using the Visual Studio development environment to customize a form. The Toolbox provides tools that you can place on the report just as you place controls on a form. When you select an object on the report, you can view and modify the object's properties in the Properties window.

While the basic idea is the same, some of the details are different. For example, you cannot change a Text Object's text in the Properties window. Instead you need to right-click on the object, select the Edit Text Object command, and enter the new text on the report.

Other properties have names that differ from those used by Visual Basic. For example, the HorAlignment property determines the object's horizontal alignment instead of Visual Basic's Alignment property, the Width and Height properties determine the object's size instead of Visual Basic's Size property, and the TextColor property determines the field's color instead of Visual Basic ForeColor property.

The details are different, but the ideas should be familiar to you and you should be able to achieve the effects you want with a little experimentation.

To make this example easier to read, start by opening the report in the development environment. Click on the Print Date field in the page header and use its drag handles to make the field wide enough to display the full date.

To change the text displayed by the first group from StudentId to the students' names, right-click on the Group Header #1 bar at the top of the first group and select the Group Expert command to display the Group Expert dialog shown in Figure 24-17.

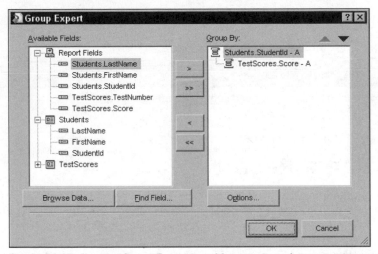

Figure 24-17: Use the Group Expert to add, remove, and rearrange groups.

Select the Students.StudentId field in the list on the right and click the Options button to see the dialog shown in Figure 24-18.

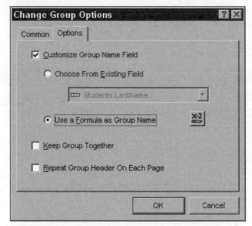

Figure 24-18: Use the Change Group Options
command to modify a group's properties.

Select the Options tab and check the "Customize Group Name Field" checkbox. Select the "Use a Formula as Group Name" option. Next click the X+2 button to the option button's right to display the Formula Workshop shown in Figure 24-19.

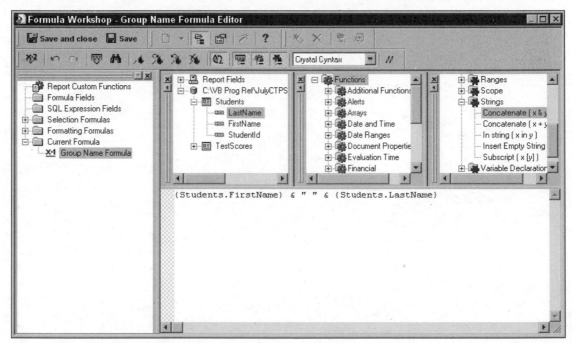

Figure 24-19: The Formula Workshop helps you define formulas for the report.

From the Formula Workshop's field tree (the second tree from the left with the LastName field high-lighted), drag the Students.FirstName and Students.LastName fields into the text box at the bottom. Add text to concatenate a space between the two fields as shown in Figure 24-19.

When you are finished, click the Save and close button at the upper left. Then close the Change Group Options dialog and the Group Expert. Now, when you run the report, this group's name includes the students' names. This value is displayed both in the group's header for each student and in the group tree display on the left of the `CrystalReportViewer` control.

Select the Group #1 Name field in the group's header, and use its grab handles to make it wide enough to display a reasonably long name.

Because the group header displays the students' first and last names, the report doesn't need them in the details section. Select those fields and delete them.

To prevent each student's test scores from appearing in a separate visible group, right-click on the Group Header #2 and select the Suppress (No Drill-Down) command. Then delete the Group #2 Name field from this section and resize the section to make it as short as possible. Similarly, remove the Group #2 Name field from the Group Footer #2 section and make that section as short as possible.

Next, remove the Group #1 Name field from the Group Footer #1 section. Then use the Toolbox to add a new Text Object to that section on the left of the existing Scores.Score control. Double-click on the control and set its text to "Average."

In the Report Footer section, right-click on the Grand Total field, select Edit Text Object, and change the control's text to "Class Average." Finally, drag the StudentId field from the Details section to the Group Header #1 section and drag all of the fields into more pleasing locations.

Figure 24-20 shows the rearranged report.

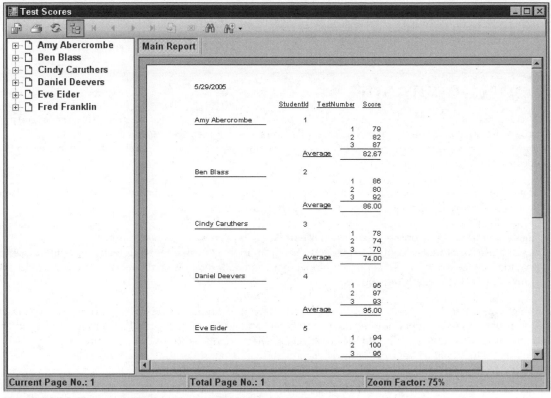

Figure 24-20: The rearranged report is much easier to read.

External Reports

The previous example uses a report that is embedded in the application. Using an external report is just as easy.

First, you must prevent Visual Basic from embedding the report in the project. In Solution Explorer, select the report. Then in the Properties window, set the report's Build Action property to None and set its Copy to Output Directory property to Copy if newer. Now, when you build the application, Visual Studio will copy the report file into the directory where it places the compiled application.

To load the report at run time, set the CrystalReportViewer control's ReportSource property to the report's location, as shown in the following code:

```
' Attach the report to the CrystalReportViewer.
Private Sub Form1_Load(ByVal sender As System.Object, _
 ByVal e As System.EventArgs) Handles MyBase.Load
    crvTestScores.ReportSource = Application.StartupPath & "\StudentTestScores.rpt"
End Sub
```

That's all there is to it. Now, if you must modify the report, you can distribute the new report file and the application will load the new version. You can also build a library of report files and let the application load whichever reports the user wants to see.

ReportDocument

The `CrystalReportViewer` control provides properties and methods for manipulating report output programmatically. For example, you can set the control's `DisplayGroupTree` and `ShowGroupTreeButton` properties to `False` to prevent the user from displaying the group tree on the control's left.

The `CrystalReportViewer` does not provide properties and methods that work with the report itself, however. For example, it cannot export the report into a file.

The `ReportDocument` object serves as an intermediate layer between a report and the `CrystalReportViewer` control to give your program more control over the report. `ReportDocument` provides access to a much larger object model that lets you interact with the report's sections, fields, data source, and other underlying entities.

When you create a `CrystalReportViewer` and attach it to a report as described earlier in this chapter, Visual Basic makes a typed `ReportDocument` object and adds it to the form. If you followed the earlier instructions carefully, you should see an object named StudentTestScores1 in the component tray below the form. The `CrystalReportViewer`'s `ReportSource` property is attached to this object.

Your code can access this object to manipulate the report. For example, the following code gets an object representing the report's field named TestNumber1. It displays the object's name and formula name.

```
' Manipulate the ReportDocument.
Dim field_object As FieldObject
field_object = DirectCast( _
    StudentTestScores1.ReportDefinition.ReportObjects("TestNumber1"), _
    FieldObject)
Debug.WriteLine("The " & field_object.Name & _
    " field has data source " & field_object.DataSource.FormulaName)
```

The following text shows the result:

```
The TestNumber1 field has data source {TestScores.TestNumber}
```

The following code exports a report into an Excel file:

```
' Export the report.
Dim output_file As String
output_file = Application.StartupPath & "\scores.xls"
StudentTestScores1.ExportToDisk( _
    CrystalDecisions.Shared.ExportFormatType.Excel, output_file)
```

The following example makes the GroupFooterSection1 section tall and gives it an aqua background. It then makes the AvgofScore1 field red and surrounded by a double line box with a drop shadow.

```
' Make GroupFooterSection1 tall and aqua.
Dim section1 As Section
section1 = DirectCast( _
    StudentTestScores1.ReportDefinition.Sections("GroupFooterSection1"), _
    Section)
section1.Height = 600
section1.SectionFormat.BackgroundColor = Color.Aqua

' Make the average score field red and surrounded by a box.
Dim avg_field_object As FieldObject
avg_field_object = DirectCast( _
    StudentTestScores1.ReportDefinition.ReportObjects("AvgofScore1"), _
    FieldObject)
avg_field_object.Color = Color.Red
avg_field_object.Top = (section1.Height - avg_field_object.Height) \ 2
With avg_field_object.Border
    .TopLineStyle = CrystalDecisions.Shared.LineStyle.DoubleLine
    .BottomLineStyle = CrystalDecisions.Shared.LineStyle.DoubleLine
    .LeftLineStyle = CrystalDecisions.Shared.LineStyle.DoubleLine
    .RightLineStyle = CrystalDecisions.Shared.LineStyle.DoubleLine
    .HasDropShadow = True
End With
```

Usually you can make formatting changes at design time but, as these examples show, you can manipulate the report's objects at run time if necessary.

Summary

Crystal Reports is a powerful tool for generating reports. It is so powerful, in fact, that it provides far too many features to describe in any detail here. This chapter only gives a glimpse into Crystal Reports. It shows how to build a relatively simple report and explains how to customize it a little.

See the online help for tips and examples, and for information about specific Crystal Reports objects such as the CrystalReportViewer control and the ReportDocument object. Read a good book on using Crystal Reports for a more tutorial and in-depth presentation.

A few chapters up to this point have shown how to interact with the operating system. Chapter 13, "Drag and Drop, and the Clipboard," explains how a Visual Basic program can interact with other programs through drag and drop and the clipboard. Chapter 23, "Printing," shows how a program can use the system's printer.

The chapters in the next part of the book explain more ways a program can interact with the system. Chapter 25, "Configuration and Resources," describes some of the ways that a Visual Basic program can store configuration and resource values for use at run time. Some of the most useful of these include environment variables, the Registry, configuration files, and resource files.

Configuration and Resources

A very simple application performs a well-defined task that changes minimally over time. You may not need to configure such an application for different circumstances.

Many more complex applications, however, must be configured differently to meet different conditions. For example, the application might display different data for different kinds of users (such as data-entry clerks, supervisors, managers, and developers). Similarly, you might configure an application for various levels of support. You might have different configurations for trial, basic, professional, and enterprise versions.

The application may also need to save state information between sessions. It might remember the types of forms that were last running, their positions, and their contents. The next time the program runs, it can restore those forms so that the user can get back to work as quickly as possible.

Visual Studio provides many ways to store and use application configuration and resource information. This chapter describes some of these tools. It starts by describing the My namespace that was invented to make these tools easier to find. It then tells how an application can use environment variables, the Registry, configuration files, resource files, and the `Application` object.

This chapter does not explain how to work with disk files more directly. Databases, XML files, text files, and other disk files are generally intended for storage of larger amounts of data, rather than simple configuration and resource information. Those topics are described more thoroughly in Chapter 11, "Database Controls and Objects," and Chapter 27, "File System Objects."

My

In previous versions of Visual Basic .NET, programmers discovered that many common tasks were difficult to perform. For example, many programs get the name of the user logged on to the computer, read a text file into a string, get the program's version number, or examine all of the application's currently loaded forms. While you can accomplish all of these tasks in previous versions of Visual Basic .NET, doing so is awkward.

To make these common tasks easier, Visual Basic 2005 introduced the My namespace to provide short-cuts for basic chores such as these. For example, to read the text in a file in Visual Basic .NET 2003, you must create some sort of object that can work with a file such as a `StreamReader`, use the object to read the file (the `ReadToEnd` method for a `StreamReader`), and the dispose of the object. The following code shows how you might do this in Visual Basic .NET 2003:

```
Dim stream_reader As New IO.StreamReader(file_name)
Dim file_contents As String = stream_reader.ReadToEnd()
stream_reader.Close()
```

This isn't too difficult, but it does seem more complicated than such a simple everyday task should be.

The My namespace provides a simpler method for reading a file's contents. The `Computer`
`.FileSystem.ReadAllText` method reads a text file in a single statement. The following statement reads the text in the file `C:\Temp\Test.txt` and displays it in a message box:

```
Dim file_contents As String = _
    My.Computer.FileSystem.ReadAllText("C:\Temp\Test.txt")
```

There is nothing new in the My namespace. All the tasks it performs you can already handle using exist-ing methods. The My namespace just makes some things easier.

This chapter describes the My namespace and the shortcuts it provides.

Me and My

Some programmers confuse the Me object and the My namespace. Me is a reference to the object that is currently executing code. If a piece of code is inside a particular class, Me is a reference to the class object that is running.

For example, if the class is a form, then within the form's code, Me returns a reference to the running form. If the form's code must change the form's `BackColor` property, it can use the Me object to explic-itly refer to its own form. It can also omit the keyword to refer to its form implicitly. That means the fol-lowing two statements are equivalent:

```
Me.BackColor = SystemColors.Control
BackColor = SystemColors.Control
```

If you build several instances of a class, the code in each instance gets a different value for Me. Each instance's Me object returns a reference to that instance.

On the other hand, My isn't an object at all. It is a namespace that contains objects, values, routines, and other namespaces that implement common functions. The My namespace is a single unique entity shared by all of the code throughout the application.

It may help if you try not to think of the My namespace as a thing in and of itself. The My namespace doesn't do anything all alone. It needs to be paired with something within the namespace. Think of My.Application, My.User, My.Computer, and so forth. It makes sense to think of My.Computer as repre-senting the computer.

My Sections

The following table briefly outlines the major sections within the My namespace. Later parts of this chapter and Appendix P describe these sections in greater detail.

Section	Purpose
My.Application	Provides information about the current application: current directory, culture, assembly information (such as program version number, log, splash screen, and forms)
My.Computer	Controls the computer hardware and system software: audio, clock, keyboard, clipboard, mouse, network, printers, Registry, and file system
My.Forms	Provides access to an instance of each type of Windows form defined in the application
My.Resources	Provides access to the application's resources: strings, images, audio, and so forth
My.Settings	Provides access to the application's settings
My.User	Provides access to information about the current user
My.WebServices	Provides access to an instance of each XML Web service referenced by the application

Environment

Visual Basic provides a couple of tools for working with the application's environment. The following sections describe two: the `Environ` function and the `System.Environment` object.

Environ

Environment variables are normally set on a systemwide basis before the program begins. In older operating systems, batch files such as `autoexec.bat` set these values. More recent systems provide Control Panel tools to set environment variables. In Windows XP, open the Control Panel, run the System applet, select the Advanced tab to see the page shown in Figure 25-1. Alternatively, you can right-click on My Computer and select Properties from the context menu.

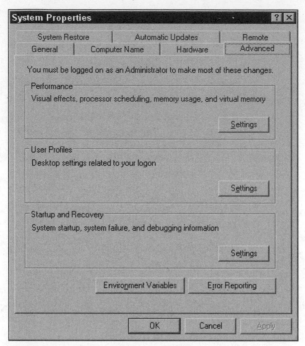

**Figure 25-1: Click the Advanced tab to see the
Environment Variables button.**

Click the Environment Variables button to display the dialog shown in Figure 25-2. Use the dialog to
add, modify, or remove environment variables.

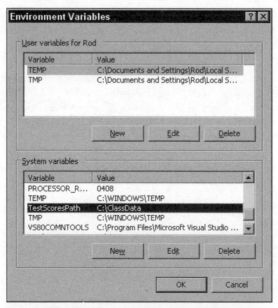

**Figure 25-2: Use this dialog to add, modify, and
delete environment variables.**

Environment variables are loaded when a process starts, and they are inherited by any process launched by the initial process. For Visual Basic development, that means the variables are loaded when you start Visual Studio and they are inherited by the program you are working on when you start it. That means if you make changes to the system's environment variables, you need to close and reopen Visual Studio before your program will see the changes.

At run time, a Visual Basic application can use the `Environ` function to retrieve environment variable values. If you pass this function a number, it returns a string giving the statement that assigns the corresponding environment variable. For example, `Environ(1)` might return the following string:

```
ALLUSERSPROFILE=C:\Documents and Settings\All Users
```

You should pass the function a number between 1 and 255. `Environ` returns a zero-length string if the number does not correspond to an environment variable. The following code uses this fact to list all the application's environment variables: When it finds a variable that has zero length, it knows it has read all of the variables with values.

```
For i As Integer = 1 To 255
    If Environ(i).Length = 0 Then Exit For
    Debug.WriteLine(Environ(i))
Next i
```

If you pass the `Environ` function the name of an environment variable, the function returns the variable's value or `Nothing` if the variable does not exist. The following code displays the value assigned to the `USERNAME` variable:

```
MessageBox.Show(Environ("USERNAME"))
```

System.Environment

The `Environ` function is easy to use, but it's not very flexible; it cannot create or modify variable values. Setting and modifying environment variables isn't as useful as it might seem, however, because each process has its own environment variables. If an application creates a new variable, other processes will not see it anyway. The only way another process will see the variable is if an application sets the variable's value and then starts the new process (for example, by using the `Shell` statement).

The `System.Environment` object provides methods for getting and setting environment variables. It also provides properties and methods for working with many other items in the application's environment. The following table describes the `Environment` object's most useful properties.

Property	Purpose
CommandLine	Returns the process's command line.
CurrentDirectory	Gets or sets the fully qualified path to the current directory.
ExitCode	Gets or sets the process's exit code. If the program starts from a `Main` function, that function's return value also sets the exit code.
HasShutdownStarted	Returns `True` if the common language run time is shutting down.

Table continued on following page

Property	Purpose
MachineName	Returns the computer's NetBIOS name.
NewLine	Returns the environment's defined new line string. For example, this might be a carriage return followed by a line feed.
OSVersion	Returns an OperatingSystem object containing information about the operating system. This object provides the properties ServicePack (name of the most recent service pack installed), Version (includes Major, Minor, Build, and Revision; ToString combines them all), VersionString (combines operating system name, version, and most recent service pack), and Platform, which can be Unix, Win32NT (Windows NT or later), Win32S (runs on 16-bit Windows to provide access to 32-bit applications), Win32Windows (Windows 95 or later), or WinCE.
ProcessorCount	Returns the number of processors on the computer.
StackTrace	Returns a string describing the current stack trace.
SystemDirectory	Returns the system directory's fully qualified path.
TickCount	Returns the number of milliseconds that have elapsed since the system started.
UserDomainName	Returns the current user's network domain name.
UserInteractive	Returns True if the process is interactive. This only returns False if the application is a service process or Web Service.
UserName	Returns the name of the user who started the process.
Version	Returns a Version object describing the Common Language Runtime. This object provides the properties Major, Minor, Build, and Revision. Its ToString method combines them all.
WorkingSet	Returns the amount of physical memory mapped to this process in bytes.

The following table describes the Environment object's most useful methods.

Method	Purpose
Exit	Ends the process immediately. Form Closing and Closed event handlers do not execute.
ExpandEnvironmentVariables	Replaces environment variable names in a string with their values. For example, the following code displays the current user's name. `MessageBox.Show("I am %username%.")`
GetCommandLineArgs	Returns an array of strings containing the application's command-line arguments. The first entry (with index 0) is the name of the program's executable file.

Method	Purpose
GetEnvironmentVariable	Returns an environment variable's value.
GetEnvironmentVariables	Returns an IDictionary object containing the names and values of all environment variables.
GetFolderPath	Returns the path to a system folder. This method's parameter is a SpecialFolder enumeration value such as Cookies, Desktop, SendTo, and Recent. See the online help for a complete list of available folders.
GetLogicalDrives	Returns an array of strings containing the names of the logical drives on the current computer.
SetEnvironmentVariable	Creates, modifies, or deletes an environment variable.

Registry

The System Registry is a hierarchical database that stores values for applications on the system. The hierarchy's root is named MyComputer and is divided into the six subtrees described in the following table.

Registry Branch	Contains
HKEY_CLASSES_ROOT	Definitions of types or classes, and properties associated with those types.
HKEY_CURRENT_CONFIG	Information about the system's current hardware configuration.
HKEY_CURRENT_USER	The current user's preferences (such as environment variable settings, program group information, desktop settings, colors, printers, network connections, and preferences specific to applications). Each user has separate HKEY_CURRENT_USER values. This is usually the subtree where a Visual Basic application stores and retrieves its settings.
HKEY_DYN_DATA	Performance data for Windows 95, 98, and Me.
HKEY_LOCAL_MACHINE	Information about the computer's physical state, including bus type, system memory, installed hardware and software, and network logon and security information.
HKEY_USERS	Default configuration information for new users and the current user's configuration.

Depending on your operating system, the Registry may also contain the unsupported keys HKEY_PERFORMANCE_DATA, HKEY_PERFORMANCE_NLSTEXT, and HKEY_PERFORMANCE_TEXT.

Visual Basic provides two main ways to access the Registry. First, you can use Visual Basic's native Registry methods: SaveSetting, GetSetting, GetAllSettings, and DeleteSetting. Second, you can use the tools in the My.Computer.Registry namespace. These two methods are described in the following sections.

You can also use API functions to manipulate the Registry. These are more complicated and not generally necessary (the My.Computer.Registry namespace contains some very powerful tools), so they are not described here.

Native Visual Basic Registry Methods

Visual Basic provides four methods for saving and reading Registry values for a particular application: SaveSetting, GetSetting, GetAllSettings, and DeleteSetting.

The SaveSetting method saves a value into a Registry key. This routine takes as parameters the name of the application, a section name, the setting's name, and the setting's value. For example, the following code saves the value stored in the m_CurrentDirectory variable in the ImageOrganizer application's Config section with the name CurrentDirectory:

```
SaveSetting("ImageOrganizer", "Config", "CurrentDirectory", m_CurrentDirectory)
```

SaveSetting automatically creates the application and section areas in the Registry if they don't already exist.

This value is saved at the following Registry location. This is all one name; it just doesn't fit on one line here.

```
HKEY_CURRENT_USER\Software\VB and VBA Program Settings\
    ImageOrganizer\Config\CurrentDirectory
```

If you use Visual Basic's SaveSetting, GetSetting, GetAllSettings, and DeleteSetting method, you don't need to worry about the first part of this Registry path. You need only to remember the application name, section name, and setting name.

The GetSetting function retrieves a Registry value. It takes as parameters the application name, section name, and setting name you used to save the value. It can optionally take a default value to return if the setting doesn't exist in the Registry. The following code displays the value saved by the previous call to SaveSetting. If no value is saved in the Registry, it displays the string "<none>."

```
MessageBox.Show( _
    GetSetting("ImageOrganizer", "Config", "CurrentDirectory", "<none>")
```

The GetAllSettings function returns a two-dimensional array of name and value pairs for a Registry section. The following code uses GetAllSettings to fetch the values stored in the ImageOrganizer application's Config section. It loops through the results, displaying the setting names and values.

```
Dim settings As String(,) = GetAllSettings("ImageOrganizer", "Config")
For i As Integer = 0 To settings.GetUpperBound(0)
    Debug.WriteLine(settings(i, 0) & " = " & settings(i, 1))
Next i
```

If an application needs to use all of the settings in a section, `GetAllSettings` may be faster than using `GetSetting` repeatedly.

The `DeleteSetting` method removes a setting, section, or an entire application's setting area from the Registry. The following code shows how to remove each of those kinds of items:

```
' Remove the ImageOrganizer/Config/CurrentDirectory setting.
DeleteSetting("ImageOrganizer", "Config", "CurrentDirectory")

' Remove the ImageOrganizer/Config section.
DeleteSetting("ImageOrganizer", "Config")

' Remove all of the ImageOrganizer application's settings.
DeleteSetting("ImageOrganizer")
```

As part of its uninstallation procedure, a program should remove any Registry entries it has made. All too often, programs leave the Registry cluttered with garbage. This not only makes it harder to figure out what real values the Registry contains, but it can also slow the system down.

In an attempt to combat this problem, Microsoft is promoting "XCopy compatibility," where applications store values in configuration files instead of the Registry. Then you can easily copy and remove these files rather than modifying the Registry.

My.Computer.Registry

The My.Computer.Registry namespace provides objects that manipulate the Registry. My.Computer.Registry has seven properties that refer to objects of type `RegistryKey`. The following table lists these objects and the corresponding Registry subtrees.

My.Computer.Registry Property	Registry Subtree
ClassesRoot	HKEY_CLASSES_ROOT
CurrentConfig	HKEY_CURRENT_CONFIG
CurrentUser	HKEY_CURRENT_USER
DynData	HKEY_DYNAMIC_DATA
LocalMachine	HKEY_LOCAL_MACHINE
PerformanceData	HKEY_PERFORMANCE_DATA
Users	HKEY_CURRENT_CONFIG

The program can use these `RegistryKey` objects to work with the corresponding Registry subtree. The following table describes the most useful properties and methods provided by the `RegistryKey` class.

Property or Method	Purpose
Name	Returns the key's Registry path.
Close	Closes the key and writes it to disk if it has been modified.
CreateSubKey	Creates a new subkey or opens an existing subkey within this key.

DeleteSubKey	Deletes the specified subkey. This method will delete the subkey if it contains values, but not if it contains other subkeys. The subkey to be deleted need not be a direct child of this key. For example, the following code uses the CurrentUser RegistryKey object to delete the descendant key Software\VB and VBA Program Settings\ImageOrganizer\Config.
	
	`My.Computer.Registry.CurrentUser.DeleteSubKey( _`
	`"Software\VB and VBA Program Settings\ImageOrganizer\Config")`

DeleteSubKeyTree	Recursively deletes a subkey and any child subkeys it contains. The subkey to be deleted need not be a direct child of this key. For example, the following code uses the CurrentUser RegistryKey object to delete all of the settings for the ImageOrganizer application.
	
	`My.Computer.Registry.CurrentUser.DeleteSubKeyTree( _`
	`"Software\VB and VBA Program Settings\ImageOrganizer")`

DeleteValue	Deletes a value from the key.
Flush	Writes any changes to the key into the Registry.
GetSubKeyNames	Returns an array of strings giving subkey names.
GetValue	Returns the value of a specified value within this key.
GetValueKind	Returns the type of a specified value within this key. This can be Binary, DWord, ExpandString, MultiString, QWord, String, or Unknown.
GetValueNames	Returns an array of strings giving the names of all of the values contained within the key.
OpenSubKey	Returns a RegistryKey object representing a descendant key. Parameters give the subkey name, and indicate whether the returned RegistryKey should allow you to modify the subkey.
SetValue	Sets a value within the key.
SubKeyCount	Returns the number of subkeys that are this key's direct children.
ToString	Returns the key's name.
ValueCount	Returns the number of values stored in this key.

The following example opens the HKEY_CURRENT_USER\Software\VB and VBA Program Settings\ImageOrganizer\Config key. It reads the CurrentDirectory value from that key using the default value "C:\" and saves the result in the variable `current_directory`. It closes the key and then uses the `DeleteSubKey` method to delete the ImageOrganizer application's `Config` section.

```
' Open the application's Config subkey.
Dim config_section As Microsoft.Win32.RegistryKey = _
    My.Computer.Registry.CurrentUser.OpenSubKey( _
        "Software\VB and VBA Program Settings\ImageOrganizer\Config\")

' Get the CurrentDirectory value.
Dim current_directory As String = _
    CType(config_section.GetValue("CurrentDirectory", "C:\"), String)

' Close the subkey.
config_section.Close()

' Delete the application's whole Config section.
My.Computer.Registry.CurrentUser. DeleteSubKey DeleteSubKey ( _
    "Software\VB and VBA Program Settings\ImageOrganizer\Config")
```

The following code shows the equivalent operations using Visual Basic's native Registry methods.

```
' Get the CurrentDirectory value.
Dim current_directory As String = _
    GetSetting("ImageOrganizer", "Config", "CurrentDirectory", "C:\")

' Delete the application's whole Config section.
DeleteSetting("ImageOrganizer", "Config")
```

It is generally easier to use Visual Basic's native Registry methods. Those methods work only with values in the HKEY_CURRENT_USER\Software\VB and VBA Program Settings Registry subtree, however. If you need to access keys and values outside of this subtree, you must use the My.Computer.Registry objects.

Configuration Files

Configuration files let you store information for a program to use at run time in a standardized external file. You can change the values in the configuration file, and the program will use the new value the next time it starts. That enables you to change some of the application's behavior without needing to recompile the executable program.

One way to use configuration files is through dynamic properties. Dynamic properties are automatically loaded from the configuration file at run time by Visual Basic.

Start by defining the settings you will bind to the dynamic properties. In Solution Explorer, double-click My Project and select the Settings tab to see the property page shown in Figure 25-3. Use this page to define the settings that you will load at run time.

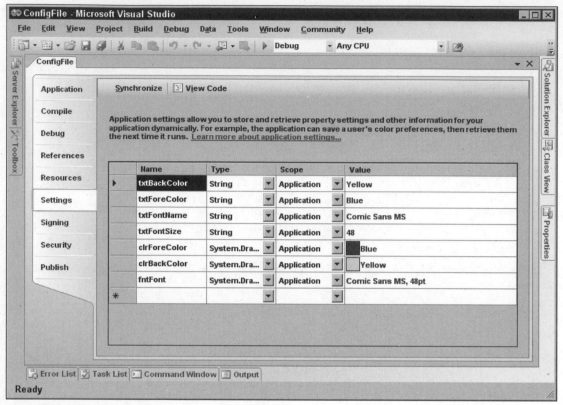

Figure 25-3: Use this page to define application settings.

Next, add a control to a form and select it. In Properties window, open the (ApplicationSettings) entry, click the PropertyBinding subitem, and click the ellipsis to the right to display a list of the control's properties.

Select the property that you want to load dynamically and click the drop-down arrow on the right to see a list of defined settings that you might assign to the property. Figue 25-4 shows the Application Setting dialog with this drop-down displayed. From the list, pick the setting that you want to assign to the property.

Visual Studio adds the setting to the program's configuration file. If you open Solution Explorer and double-click the `app.config` entry, you'll see the new dynamic property.

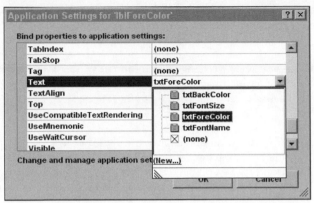

Figure 25-4: Use the drop-down to assign a setting to the dynamic property.

The following text shows the configuration setting sections of an `app.config` file. The userSettings section is empty. The applicationSettings section defines the settings shown in Figure 25-3.

```xml
<?xml version="1.0" encoding="utf-8" ?>
<configuration>
    ...
    <userSettings>
        <ConfigFile.Settings />
    </userSettings>
    <applicationSettings>
        <ConfigFile.Settings>
            <setting name="txtBackColor" serializeAs="String">
                <value>Yellow</value>
            </setting>
            <setting name="txtForeColor" serializeAs="String">
                <value>Blue</value>
            </setting>
            <setting name="txtFontName" serializeAs="String">
                <value>Comic Sans MS</value>
            </setting>
            <setting name="txtFontSize" serializeAs="String">
                <value>50</value>
            </setting>
            <setting name="clrForeColor" serializeAs="String">
                <value>Blue</value>
            </setting>
            <setting name="clrBackColor" serializeAs="String">
                <value>Yellow</value>
            </setting>
            <setting name="fntFont" serializeAs="String">
                <value>Comic Sans MS, 48pt</value>
            </setting>
        </ConfigFile.Settings>
    </applicationSettings>
</configuration>
```

When the application starts, Visual Basic loads the `app.config` file, reads the settings, and assigns their values to any properties bound to them.

So far, this is just a very roundabout way to set the control's property value. The real benefit of this method comes later when you want to change this setting. If you look in the compiled application's directory (normally the bin\Debug directory when you're developing the program), you'll find a file with the same name as the application but with a .config extension. If the application is called `ConfigFile.exe`, then this file is called `ConfigFile.exe.config`.

If you open this file with any text editor and change the value of the TheDynamicValue setting, the program uses the new value the next time it runs. Instead of recompiling the whole application, you only need to change this simple text file. If you have distributed the application to a large number of users, you need only to give them the revised configuration file and not a whole new executable.

When you make a new setting, Visual Basic automatically generates code that adds the setting to the My.Settings namespace. That makes the values easy for a program to read. The following code displays the values of the TheUserSetting and TheAppSetting settings:

```
MessageBox.Show(My.Settings.txtFontSize & "pt " & My.Settings.txtFontName)
```

The My.Settings namespace provides several other properties and methods that make working with settings easy. The following table summarizes the most useful My.Settings properties and methods.

Property or Method	Purpose
Item	A name-indexed collection of the values for the settings.
Properties	A name-indexed collection of `SettingsProperty` objects that contain information about the settings, including their names and default values.
Reload	Reloads the settings from the configuration file.
Save	Saves any modified settings into the configuration file. The program can modify settings with user scope. Settings with application scope are read-only.

The following example uses the `My.Settings.Properties` collection to list all of the application's settings and their values:

```
Imports System.Configuration

Public Class Form1
    Private Sub Form1_Load(ByVal sender As System.Object, _
    ByVal e As System.EventArgs) Handles MyBase.Load
        Dim txt As String = ""
        For Each settings_property As SettingsProperty In My.Settings.Properties
            txt &= settings_property.Name & " = " & _
                settings_property.DefaultValue.ToString & vbCrLf
```

```
          Next settings_property

          txtSettings.Text = txt
          txtSettings.Select(0, 0)
      End Sub
End Class
```

Resource Files

Resource files contain text, images, and other data for the application to load at run time. The intent of resource files is to let you easily replace one set of resources with another. One of the most common reasons for using resource files is to provide different resources for different languages. To create installation packages for different languages, you simply ship the executable and a resource file that uses the right language. Alternatively, you can ship resource files for all of the languages you support and then let the application pick the appropriate file at run time based on the user's computer settings.

Resource files are not intended to store application configuration information and settings. They are intended to hold values that you might want to change, but only infrequently. Configurations and settings, on the other hand, may change relatively often. You should store that kind of data in configuration files or the System Registry.

The distinction is small and frankly somewhat artificial. Both configuration files and resource files store data that you can swap without recompiling the application. Rebuilding resources files can be a little more complex, however, so perhaps the distinction that configuration and setting data changes more frequently makes some sense.

Resource files can also be embedded within a compiled application. In that case, you cannot swap the resource file without recompiling the application. While this makes embedded resource files less useful for storing frequently changing information, they still give you a convenient place to group resource data within the application. This is particularly useful if several parts of the application must use the same pieces of data. For example, if every form should display the same background image, it makes sense to store the image in a common resource file that they can all use.

The following sections describe the four most common types of resources: application, embedded, satellite, and localization.

Application Resources

To create application resources in Visual Basic, open Solution Explorer, double-click the My Project entry, and select the Resources tab. Use the drop-down on the left to select one of the resource categories Strings, Images, Icons, Audio, Files, or Other. Figure 25-5 shows the application's resources tab displaying the application's images.

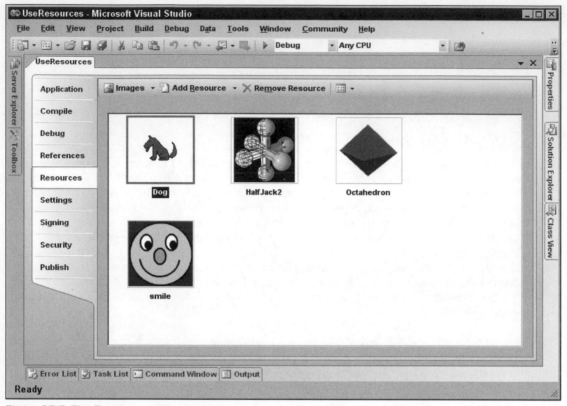

Figure 25-5: The Resources tab contains image resources used by the application.

If you double-click on an item, Visual Studio opens an appropriate editor. Figure 25-6 shows the Dog picture in the integrated bitmap editor.

Figure 25-7 shows the string resource editor. Click on an entry and type to create or modify a value. Click to the left of the Name column to select a row and then click the Remove button or press the Delete key to remove a string.

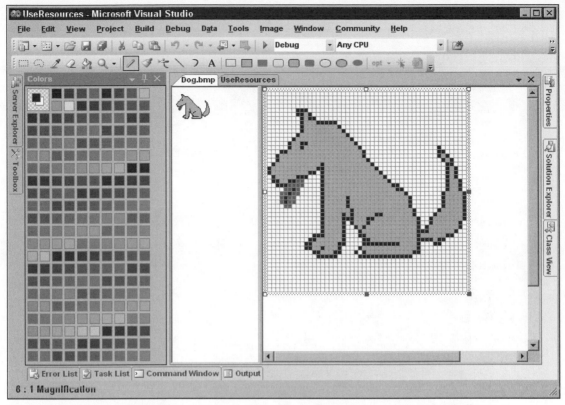

Figure 25-6: If you double-click on a resource, Visual Studio opens it in an appropriate editor.

Click the Add Resource drop-down and select the New String, New Image, New Icon, or New Text File commands to add new items to the resource file. The New Image item opens a cascading submenu that lets you create new PNG, bitmap, GIF, JPEG, and TIFF images.

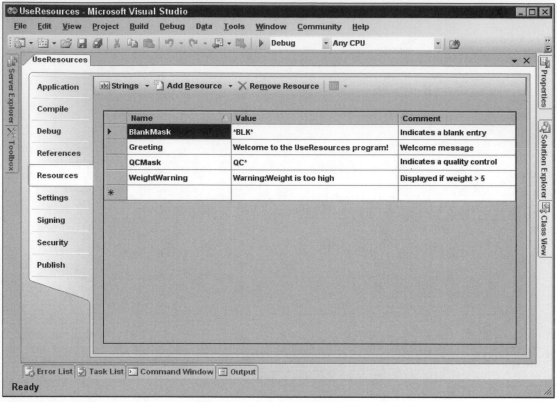

Figure 25-7: The string resource view lets you edit string resources in a grid.

Using Application Resources

When you create application resources, Visual Studio automatically generates code that adds strongly typed resource properties to the My.Resources namespace. If you open Solution Explorer and click the Show All Files button, you can see the file Resources.Designer.vb below the Resources.resx item. This file is highlighted in Figure 25-8.

For example, the following code shows the property that Resources.Designer.vb contains to retrieve the Octahedron image resource.

```
Friend ReadOnly Property Octahedron() As System.Drawing.Bitmap
    Get
        Return CType(ResourceManager.GetObject("Octahedron", _
            resourceCulture),System.Drawing.Bitmap)
    End Get
End Property
```

Figure 25-8: The file Resources.Designer.vb
contains strongly typed properties that fetch
resource values.

The following code shows how a program can use these My.Resources properties. It sets the
lblGreeting control's Text property to the string returned by the My.Resources.Greeting property.
Then it sets the form's BackgroundImage property to the image resource named Dog.

```
Private Sub Form1_Load(ByVal sender As System.Object, _
 ByVal e As System.EventArgs) Handles MyBase.Load
    lblGreeting.Text = My.Resources.Greeting
    Me.BackgroundImage = My.Resources.Dog
End Sub
```

Because these property procedures are strongly typed, IntelliSense can offer support for them. If you
type "My.Resources." IntelliSense lists the values defined in the application's resource file.

The strongly typed resources properties use a ResourceManager object to fetch the application's
resources. The My.Resources namespace exposes that object through its ResourceManager property, so
you can use that object directly to retrieve the application's resources. The following code does the same
things as the previous version, except is uses the ResourceManager directly. Note that the
ResourceManager 's GetObject method returns a generic Object, so the code uses CType to convert
the result into an Image before assigning it to the form's BackgroundImage property.

```
Private Sub Form1_Load(ByVal sender As System.Object, _
 ByVal e As System.EventArgs) Handles MyBase.Load
    lblGreeting.Text = My.Resources.ResourceManager.GetString("Greeting")
    Me.BackgroundImage = CType( _
        My.Resources.ResourceManager.GetObject("Dog"), _
        Image)
End Sub
```

Generally, you should use the automatically generated resource properties in the My.Resources namespace because they are easier to use and they are strongly typed. The ResourceManager class is much more useful when you use other embedded resource files.

Embedded Resources

In addition to storing resources in the application's resource file Resources.resx, you can add other resources files to the application. Open the Project menu and select the Add New item command. Pick the Resources File template, give the file a meaningful name, and click OK.

After you add a resource file to the project, you can double-click it in Solution Explorer to open it in the resource editor. Then you can add resources to the file exactly as you do for the application's resources file.

At run time, you can use a ResourceManager object to fetch the resources from the embedded file. The following code loads the Dog image from the file Images.resx and the string Greeting from the file StringResources.resx.

It starts by declaring a ResourceManager variable. It then initializes the variable, passing its constructor the resource file's path and the assembly containing the file. The file's path consists of the application's root namespace EmbeddedResources followed by the file's name Images.

The program then uses the ResourceManager's GetObject method to fetch the Dog image, converts the generic Object returned into an Image, and assigns the result to the form's BackgroundImage property.

Next, the code reinitializes the ResourceManager object so it represents the StringResources resource file. It calls the manager's GetString method to get the value of the Greeting resource and saves the result in the lblGreeting control's Text property.

```
Private Sub Form1_Load(ByVal sender As System.Object, _
 ByVal e As System.EventArgs) Handles MyBase.Load
    Dim resource_manager As ResourceManager

    ' Get the Dog image from Images.resx.
    resource_manager = New ResourceManager( _
        "EmbeddedResources.Images", _
        Me.GetType.Assembly)
    Me.BackgroundImage = CType( _
        resource_manager.GetObject("Dog"), _
        Image)

    ' Get the Greeting from StringResources.resx.
    resource_manager = New ResourceManager( _
        "EmbeddedResources.StringResources", _
        Me.GetType.Assembly)
    lblGreeting.Text = resource_manager.GetString("Greeting")
End Sub
```

Strongly Typed Embedded Resources

Just as it can generate code to provide properties that fetch application resources, Visual Studio can generate similar code for other embedded resource files. Select the file in Solution Explorer and open the Properties window. Set the file's Custom Tool property to VbMyResourcesResXFileCodeGenerator. Then set its Custom Tool Namespace property to the namespace that you want to contain the resource properties. For example, you might set this value for a string resource file to My.StringResources. The following code shows how the program could use the automatically generated `Greeting` property:

```
lblGreeting.Text = My.StringResources.Greeting
```

Setting the Custom Tool and Custom Tool Namespace properties requires some lengthy typing, but once you've set these values, using the strongly typed properties is much easier than fetching resources by using a `ResourceManager`.

Satellite Resources

Embedded resource files enable you to organize data in central locations. For example, you can keep all the images used by the application in a single resource file, and all of the program's forms can fetch the images from that file.

Rather than embedding a resource file in the application, you can load it at run time. Then if you must make changes to the resources, you can replace the resource file and the program will load the new resources the next time it runs.

To make switching resources easy, you can place them in a resource-only assembly. This "satellite assembly" contains data for the application but doesn't contain any program logic.

To make a resource-only satellite assembly, start a new Visual Basic project, selecting the Class Library template. Delete the project's initial class. Then, add resources to the project as you would add them to any other project. You can add resources to the project's resources or to embedded resource files. When you are finished adding resources, compile the project to build a `.dll` file.

You can then build an executable Windows application that loads resources from the assembly as shown in the following code. The program declares an `Assembly` object and uses the shared `Assembly.LoadForm` method to load information about the resource-only assembly `SatelliteResources.dll`. In this example, the file was copied into the executable program's startup directory so the program does not need to pass a complete path to the `LoadFrom` method.

Next, the program uses the `Assembly` object to create a `ResourceManager`. For the resource file's name, it passes the `ResourceManager`'s constructor the assembly's root namespace SatelliteResources, followed by the name of the resource file within the satellite project. In this case, the first resource is stored in the project's resources, so the file is `MyResources.resx`. Now the program uses the `ResourceManager`'s `GetString` method to fetch the Greeting resource.

The program then creates a new `ResourceManager` using the same `Assembly` object, this time using the resource file named `ImageResources.resx`. It uses the `GetObject` method to fetch the image named Dog, converts the result into an `Image`, and saves the result in the form's `BackgroundImage` property.

```
Private Sub Form1_Load(ByVal sender As System.Object, _
 ByVal e As System.EventArgs) Handles MyBase.Load
    ' Get the resource Assembly.
    Dim satellite_assembly As Assembly
    satellite_assembly = Assembly.LoadFrom("SatelliteResources.dll")

    ' Create a ResourceManager for the satellite's
    ' main resource file.
    Dim resource_manager As ResourceManager
    resource_manager = New ResourceManager( _
        "SatelliteResources.Resources", _
        satellite_assembly)

    ' Get the string resource from the satellite's
    ' main resource file.
    lblGreeting.Text = resource_manager.GetString("Greeting")

    ' Create a ResourceManager for the satellite's
    ' Images resource file.
    resource_manager = New ResourceManager( _
        "SatelliteResources.Images", _
        satellite_assembly)

    ' Get the form's background image from the satellite's
    ' Images resource file.
    Me.BackgroundImage = CType( _
        resource_manager.GetObject("Dog"), Image)
End Sub
```

Later, if you must change the value of the Greeting string or the Dog image, you can update the satellite project, build a new DLL file, and copy the DLL file into the executable program's startup directory. The next time you run the program, it will load the new resources.

Localization Resources

One of the most important reasons for inventing resources files was to allow localization: supporting different text, images, and other items for different languages and cultures. In Visual Studio .NET, localization is easy.

First, create a form using whatever language you typically use from day to day. For me, that's English as spoken in the United States. Open the form in the form designer and give it whatever controls you need. Set the form's and controls' properties as usual.

Next, set the form's Localizable property to True. Then set the form's Language property to the first language you want to support other than the default language that you have been working with so far. Modify the controls' properties for the new language.

As you modify a form, Visual Studio saves the changes you make into a new resource file attached to the form. Figure 25-9 shows the Solution Explorer for an application with a form that has English and German resources. Below the Form1.vb entry, you can see two resource files. The default file containing English resources is named Form1.resx. The resource file containing the German settings is named Form1.de.resx.

Figure 25-9: Visual Studio saves resources for different languages in separate resource files.

At run time, the application automatically checks the user's computer and selects the correct resource file based on the system's regional settings.

Normally, you should let the application pick the appropriate resource file automatically, but you can explicitly select a resource file for testing purposes. To do that, open the Solution Explorer and click the Show All Files button. Find the form's design file (for example, Form1.Designer.vb) and open it.

Give the form an empty constructor that sets the current thread's CurrentCulture and CurrentUICulture properties to the culture that you want to use. See the online help for the CultureInfo class to get a list of possible cultures such as en-US (US English) or de-DE (German). The result should look something like the following code:

```vb
Imports System.Threading
Imports System.Globalization

Public Class Form1
    Public Sub New()
        MyBase.New()

        ' Set the culture and UI culture to German.
        Thread.CurrentThread.CurrentCulture = New CultureInfo("de-DE")
        Thread.CurrentThread.CurrentUICulture = New CultureInfo("de-DE")

        'This call is required by the Windows Form Designer.
        InitializeComponent()
    End Sub
End Class
```

The rest is automatic. When the form's InitializeComponent method executes, it loads the resources it needs for the culture you selected.

ComponentResourceManager

The `ResourceManager` class provides tools for loading resources from resource file one at a time. The `ComponentResourceManager` class also provides `GetString`, and `GetObject` methods that work much as the `ResourceManager`'s methods do.

`ComponentResourceManager` also provides the `ApplyResources` method, which makes applying resources to an object easier. `ApplyResources` searches a resource file for items with a particular object name. It then applies any resources it finds to an object's properties.

For example, you could use `ApplyResources` to search for resources with the object name `ExitButton` and apply them to the `btnExit` control. If the resource file contained an item named `ExitButton.Text`, `ApplyResources` would apply it to the `btnExit` control's `Text` property. If the method found other resources (such as `ExitButton.Location` and `ExitButton.Size`), it would apply those properties to the control, too.

When you localize a form, Visual Studio automatically creates entries in the appropriate resource files for the form's controls. If you set the form's `Language` to German and set the `btnYes` button's `Text` property to "Ja," then Visual Studio adds a string entry named "btnYes.Text" with value "Ja" to the form's German resource file.

Visual Studio uses the special name "`$this`" to represent the form's properties. For example, if you set the form's `Text` property, the IDE adds a string resource named `$this.Text` to the appropriate resource file.

Figure 25-10 shows the German string resources for Form1 stored in the file `Form1.de.resx`. The resources define values for the form itself (`$this`), and the `radEnglish`, `radGerman`, and `lblPrompt` controls.

The following code uses `ComponentResourceManager` objects to load different localized resources. When the user clicks the `radEnglish` radio button, the program creates a new `CultureInfo` object representing United States English. It creates a `ComponentResourceManager` for the form's type, and uses its `ApplyResources` method to apply any English form resources to the form. It then loops through the form's controls, using `ApplyResources` to apply any English resources for the form's controls. When it is finished, the form and all of its controls are using the English resources. When the user clicks the `radGerman` radio button, the program similarly applies the German resources to the form and its controls.

```
' Select English.
Private Sub radEnglish_CheckedChanged(ByVal sender As System.Object, _
 ByVal e As System.EventArgs) Handles radEnglish.CheckedChanged
    Dim culture_info As New CultureInfo("en-US")
    Dim component_resource_manager As New ComponentResourceManager(Me.GetType)
    component_resource_manager.ApplyResources(Me, "$this", culture_info)
    For Each ctl As Control In Me.Controls
        component_resource_manager.ApplyResources(ctl, ctl.Name, culture_info)
```

```
        Ncxt ctl
    End Sub

    ' Select German.
    Private Sub radGerman_CheckedChanged(ByVal sender As System.Object, _
     ByVal e As System.EventArgs) Handles radGerman.CheckedChanged
        Dim culture_info As New CultureInfo("de-DE")
        Dim component_resource_manager As New ComponentResourceManager(Me.GetType)
        component_resource_manager.ApplyResources(Me, "$this", culture_info)
        For Each ctl As Control In Me.Controls
            component_resource_manager.ApplyResources(ctl, ctl.Name, culture_info)
        Next ctl
    End Sub
```

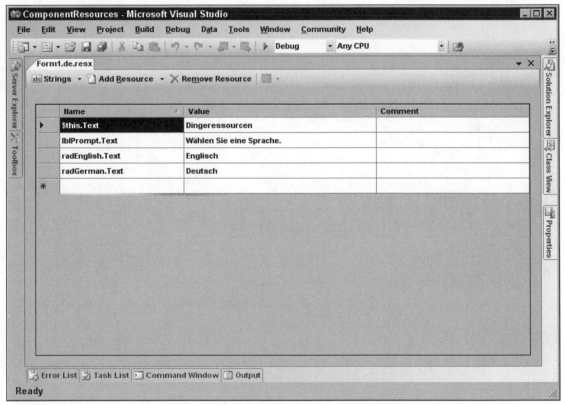

Figure 25-10: Locale-specific resource files include values for specific controls.

The following code shows a slightly different method for accomplishing the same tasks. Instead of passing a CultureInfo object into the ApplyResources method, the program sets the current thread's

CurrentCulture and CurrentUICulture properties. It then calls ApplyResources and lets it use those properties to figure out which resource file to use.

```
' Select English.
Private Sub radEnglish_CheckedChanged(ByVal sender As System.Object, _
 ByVal e As System.EventArgs) Handles radEnglish.CheckedChanged
    ' Set the current culture and UI culture.
    Thread.CurrentThread.CurrentCulture = New CultureInfo("en-US")
    Thread.CurrentThread.CurrentUICulture = New CultureInfo("en-US")

    ' Load resources.
    Dim component_resource_manager As New ComponentResourceManager(Me.GetType)
    component_resource_manager.ApplyResources(Me, "$this")
    For Each ctl As Control In Me.Controls
        component_resource_manager.ApplyResources(ctl, ctl.Name)
    Next ctl
End Sub

' Select German.
Private Sub radGerman_CheckedChanged(ByVal sender As System.Object, _
 ByVal e As System.EventArgs) Handles radGerman.CheckedChanged
    ' Set the current culture and UI culture.
    Thread.CurrentThread.CurrentCulture = New CultureInfo("de-DE")
    Thread.CurrentThread.CurrentUICulture = New CultureInfo("de-DE")

    ' Load resources.
    Dim component_resource_manager As New ComponentResourceManager(Me.GetType)
    component_resource_manager.ApplyResources(Me, "$this")
    For Each ctl As Control In Me.Controls
        component_resource_manager.ApplyResources(ctl, ctl.Name)
    Next ctl
End Sub
```

The program can later use the CurrentCulture and CurrentUICulture properties if it needs to remember which culture it is currently using.

Application

The Application object represents the running application at a very high level. It provides properties and methods to starting an event loop to process Windows messages, possibly for a form. It also provides methods for controlling and stopping the event loop.

Don't confuse the Application object with the My.Application namespace. The two have somewhat similar purposes but very different features.

The following sections describe the Application object's most useful properties, methods, and events.

Application Properties

The following table describes the Application object's most useful properties.

Property	Purpose
CommonAppDataPath	Returns the path where the program should store application data shared by all users. By default, this path has the form *base_path**company_name**product_name**product_version*. The *base_path* is typically C:\Documents and Settings\All Users\Application Data.
CommonAppDataRegistry	Returns the Registry key where the program should store application data shared by all users. By default, this path has the form HKEY_LOCAL_MACHINE\Software*company_name**product_name**product_version*.
CompanyName	Returns the application's company name.
CurrentCulture	Gets or sets the CultureInfo object for this thread.
CurrentInputLanguage	Gets or sets the InputLanguage for this thread.
ExecutablePath	Returns the fully qualified path to the file that started the execution, including the file name.
LocalUserAppDataPath	Returns the path where the program should store data for this local, nonroaming user. By default, this path has the form *base_path**company_name**product_name**product_version*. The *base_path* is typically C:\Documents and Settings*user_name*\Local Settings\Application Data.
MessageLoop	Returns True if the thread has a message loop. If the program begins with a startup form, this loop is created automatically. If it starts with a custom Sub Main, the loop doesn't initially exist and the program must start it by calling Application.Run.
OpenForms	Returns a collection holding references to all of the application's open forms.
ProductName	Returns the application's product name.
ProductVersion	Gets the product version associated with this application.
StartupPath	Returns the fully qualified path to the directory where the program starts.
UserAppDataPath	Returns the path where the program should store data for this user. By default, this path has the form *base_path**company_name**product_name**product_version*. The *base_path* is typically C:\Documents and Settings*user_name*\Application Data.
UserAppDataRegistry	Returns the Registry key where the program should store application data for this user. By default, this path has the form HKEY_CURRENT_USER\Software*company_name**product_name**product_version*.
UseWaitCursor	Determines whether this thread's forms display a wait cursor. Set this to True before performing a long operation, and set it to False when the operation is finished.

To set the `CompanyName`, `ProductName`, and `ProductVersion`, open Solution Explorer, double-click the My Project entry, and select the Application tab. Then click the Assembly Information button and enter the values on the Assembly Information dialog.

Application Methods

The following table describes the `Application` object's most useful methods.

Method	Purpose
AddMessageFilter	Adds a message filter to monitor the event loop's Windows messages. See the following text for an example.
DoEvents	Processes Windows messages that are currently in the message queue. If the thread is performing a long calculation, it would normally prevent the rest of the thread from taking action such as processing these messages. Calling `DoEvents` lets the user interface catch up with the user's actions. Note that you can often avoid the need for `DoEvents` if you perform the long task on a separate thread.
Exit	Ends the whole application. This is a rather abrupt halt and any forms that are loaded do not execute their `FormClosing` or `FormClosed` event handlers, so be certain that the application has executed any necessary clean-up code before calling `Application.Exit`.
ExitThread	Ends the current thread. This is a rather abrupt halt, and any forms running on the thread do not execute their `FormClosing` or `FormClosed` event handlers.
OnThreadException	Raises the `Application` object's `ThreadException` event, passing it an exception. If your application throws an uncaught exception in the IDE, the IDE halts. That makes it hard to test `Application.ThreadException` event handlers. You can call `OnThreadException` to invoke the event handler.
RemoveMessageFilter	Removes a message filter.
Run	Runs a message loop for the current thread. If you pass this method a form object, it displays the form and processes its messages until the form closes.
SetSuspendState	Makes the system suspend operation or hibernate. When the system hibernates, it writes its memory contents to disk. When you restart the system, it resumes with its previous desktop and applications running. When the system suspends operation, it enters low-power mode. It can resume more quickly than a hibernated system, but memory contents are not saved, so they will be lost if the computer loses power.

The following code gives a form a message filter that ignores left mouse button down messages. The `NoLeftDownMessageFilter` class provides the filter. It implements the `IMessageFilter` interface, which specifies the `PreFilterMessage` function.

`PreFilterMessage` examines a message and returns `True` if it wants to filter the message out of the form's message queue. In this example, it returns `True` if the message is `WM_LBUTTONDOWN`, indicating that the left button has been pressed down.

The form's `Load` event handler creates a new instance of the filter class and uses the `Application` object's `AddMessageFilter` method to install the filter object.

The form's `Click` event handler toggles the state of the `Application` object's `UseWaitCursor` property. This displays or hides the wait cursor.

When you left-click on the form, the message filter intercepts the left button down message, so the `Click` event doesn't occur. If you right-click on the form, the filter allows all messages through so the `Click` event occurs and the form displays or hides the wait cursor.

```
Public Class Form1
    ' Filter out left mouse button down messages.
    Public Class NoLeftDownMessageFilter
        Implements IMessageFilter

        Public Function PreFilterMessage(ByRef m As System.Windows.Forms.Message) _
            As Boolean Implements IMessageFilter.PreFilterMessage
            ' If the message is left mouse down, return True
            ' to indicate that the message should be ignored.
            Const WM_LBUTTONDOWN As Long = &H201
            Return (m.Msg = WM_LBUTTONDOWN)
        End Function
    End Class

    ' Install the message filter.
    Private Sub Form1_Load(ByVal sender As System.Object, _
     ByVal e As System.EventArgs) Handles MyBase.Load
        Dim no_left_down_message_filter As New NoLeftDownMessageFilter
        Application.AddMessageFilter(no_left_down_message_filter)
    End Sub

    ' Toggle the wait cursor.
    Private Sub Form1_Click(ByVal sender As Object, _
     ByVal e As System.EventArgs) Handles Me.Click
        Application.UseWaitCursor = Not Application.UseWaitCursor
    End Sub
End Class
```

Application Events

The `Application` object provides a few events that give you information about the application's state. The following table describes these events.

Event	Purpose
ApplicationExit	Occurs when the application is about to shut down.
Idle	Occurs when the application finishes executing some code and is about to enter an idle state to wait for events.
ThreadException	Occurs when the application throws an unhandled exception. See the following code for an example.
ThreadExit	Occurs when a thread is about to exit.

When you end an application by unloading its form, the program receives the events FormClosing, FormClosed, ThreadExit, and ApplicationExit, in that order.

If you end the application by calling the Application object's Exit method, the program only receives the ThreadExit and ApplicationExit events. If more than one thread is running, they each receive ThreadExit events, and then they each receive ApplicationExit events.

The following code uses a ThreadException event handler to catch all exceptions thrown by the application. When it starts, the form's Load event handler uses the Application object's AddHandler method to add the app_ThreadException subroutine as a handler for the Application's ThreadException event.

The app_ThreadException subroutine simply displays an error message so that you can tell that it executed. A real application would take different actions such as logging the error and a stack trace, restarting the application, and so forth.

When the user clicks the Throw button, the program throws an exception. If you are running the program in the development environment, Visual Studio halts at the Throw statement and tells you that it encountered an unhandled exception. If you run the compiled executable outside of the development environment, the application's ThreadException event occurs. The app_ThreadException routine catches the event and displays its message.

When the user clicks the OnThreadException button, the program calls the Application object's OnThreadException method, passing it an exception object. Whether you are running in the development environment or running the compiled executable, the application's ThreadException event occurs and the app_ThreadException routine catches it.

```
Imports System.IO

Public Class Form1
    ' Install the ThreadException event handler.
    Private Sub Form1_Load(ByVal sender As Object, _
      ByVal e As System.EventArgs) Handles Me.Load
        AddHandler Application.ThreadException, AddressOf Me.app_ThreadException
    End Sub

    ' Catch a ThreadException event.
    Private Sub app_ThreadException(ByVal sender As Object, _
```

```
        ByVal e As System.Threading.ThreadExceptionEventArgs)
            MessageBox.Show("Caught unhandled exception")
        End Sub

        ' Throw an InvalidDataException.
        Private Sub btnThrow_Click(ByVal sender As System.Object, _
         ByVal e As System.EventArgs) Handles btnThrow.Click
            Throw New InvalidDataException("Bad data! Bad!")
        End Sub

        ' Call the OnThreadException method.
        Private Sub btnOnThreadException_Click(ByVal sender As System.Object, _
         ByVal e As System.EventArgs) Handles btnOnThreadException.Click
            Application.OnThreadException(New InvalidDataException("Bad data! Bad!"))
        End Sub
    End Class
```

Summary

Visual Studio provides many ways to store and use application configuration and resource information. Some of the most useful of these include environment variables, the Registry, configuration files, and resource files. The My namespace and the `Application` object make working with some of these easier.

Store configuration information that may change relatively quickly in configuration files. Store resources that determine the application's appearance in resource files. If you will distribute the application in multiple languages, use localized resource files to manage the different languages. If necessary, you can change the data stored in configuration and resource files and redistribute them to your users without rebuilding the entire application.

You can store small pieces of information between program runs in the System Registry. Use databases, XML files, and other files to store larger amounts of data.

Using all of these techniques, you can make your application easily configurable. You can satisfy the needs of different kinds of users and customize the application without recompiling it.

This chapter explains ways that a program can save configuration and resource information using tools such as the Registry, environment variables, and resource files. Generally, these kinds of data are of relatively limited size. If an application needs to store larger amounts of data, it generally uses a database or file.

Chapter 26, "Streams," explains classes that a Visual Basic application can use to work with stream data in general, and files in particular. Using streams attached to files, a program can read and write large amounts of data without cluttering up the Registry, environment variables, or resource files.

26

Streams

At some very primitive level, all pieces of data are just piles of bytes. The computer doesn't really store invoices, employee records, and recipes. At its most basic level, the computer stores bytes of data (or even bits, but the computer naturally groups them in bytes). It is only when a program interprets those bytes that they acquire a higher-level meaning that is valuable to the user.

While you generally don't want to treat high-level data as undifferentiated bytes, there are times when thinking of the data as bytes lets you treat it in more uniform ways.

One type of bytelike data is the *stream*, an ordered series of bytes. Files, data flowing across a network, messages moving through a queue, and even the memory in an array all fit this description.

Defining the abstract idea of a stream lets applications handle these different types of objects uniformly. If an encryption or serialization routine manipulates a generic stream of bytes, it doesn't need to know whether the stream represents a file, a chunk of memory, or data flowing across a network.

Visual Studio provides several classes for manipulating different kinds of streams. It also provides higher-level classes for working with this kind of data at a more abstract level. For example, it provides classes for working with streams that happen to represent files and directories.

This chapter describes some of the classes you can use to manipulate streams. It explains lower-level classes that you may use only rarely and higher-level classes that let you read and write strings and files relatively easily.

#### Chapter 26

The following table summarizes the most useful stream classes.

Class	Use
FileStream	Read and write bytes in a file.
MemoryStream	Read and write bytes in memory.
BinaryReader, BinaryWriter	Read and write specific data types in a stream.
StringReader, StringWriter	Read and write text with or without new lines in a string.
StreamReader, StreamWriter	Read and write text with or without new lines in a stream (usually a file stream).

Stream

The Stream class defines properties and methods that derived stream classes must provide. These let the program perform relatively generic tasks with streams such as determining whether the stream allows writing.

The following table describes the Stream class's most useful properties.

Property	Purpose
CanRead	Returns True if the stream supports reading.
CanSeek	Returns True if the stream supports seeking to a particular position in the stream.
CanTimeout	Returns True if the stream supports timing out of read and write operations.
CanWrite	Returns True if the stream supports writing.
Length	Returns the number of bytes in the stream.
Position	Returns the stream's current position in its bytes. For a stream that supports seeking, the program can set this value to move to a particular position.
ReadTimeout	Determines the number of milliseconds that a read operation will wait before timing out.
WriteTimeout	Determines the number of milliseconds that a write operation will wait before timing out.

The following table describes the `Stream` class's most useful methods.

Method	Purpose
BeginRead	Begins an asynchronous read.
BeginWrite	Begins an asynchronous write.
Close	Closes the stream and releases any resources it uses (such as file handles).
EndRead	Waits for an asynchronous read to finish.
EndWrite	Ends an asynchronous write.
Flush	Flushes data from the stream's buffers into the underlying storage medium (device, file, memory, and so forth).
Read	Reads bytes from the stream and advances its position by that number of bytes.
ReadByte	Reads a byte from the stream and advances its position by one byte.
Seek	If the stream supports seeking, sets the stream's position.
SetLength	Sets the stream's length. If the stream is currently longer than the new length, it is truncated. If the stream is shorter than the new length, it is enlarged. The stream must support both writing and seeking for this method to work.
Write	Writes bytes into the stream and advances the current position by this number of bytes.
WriteByte	Writes one byte into the stream and advances the current position by one byte.

FileStream

The `FileStream` class provides a stream representation of a file.

The `FileStream's` parent class `Stream` defines most of its properties and methods. See the section "`Stream`" earlier in this chapter for descriptions of those properties and methods.

`FileStream` adds two useful new properties. First, `IsAsync` returns `True` if the `FileStream` was opened asynchronously. Second, the `Name` property returns the file name passed into the object's constructor.

The class also adds two new useful methods. The `Lock` method locks the file, so other processes can read it but not modify it. `Unlock` removes a previous lock.

Overloaded versions of the `FileStream's` constructor let you specify a file name or handle, the file mode (`Append`, `Create`, `CreateNew`, `Open`, `OpenOrCreate`, or `Truncate`), access mode (`Read`, `Write`, or `ReadWrite`), file sharing (`Inheritable`, which allows child processes to inherit the file handle; `None`, `Read`; `Write`; or `ReadWrite`), a buffer size, and file options (`Asynchronous`, `DeleteOnClose`, `Encrypted`, `None`, `RandomAccess`, `SequentialScan`, or `WriteThrough`).

The following code shows a small example that uses a `FileStream`. It creates a file and uses a Universal Transformation Format (UTF) `UTF8Encoding` object to convert a string into an array of bytes. It writes the bytes into the file and then closes the `FileStream`.

```
Dim file_name As String = Application.StartupPath & "\test.txt"
Dim file_stream As New FileStream(file_name, FileMode.Create)
Dim bytes As Byte() = New UTF8Encoding().GetBytes("Hello world!")

file_stream.Write(bytes, 0, bytes.Length)
file_stream.Close()
```

The 8-bit UTF encoding is the most popular type on the Web, although there are other encoding formats such as UTF-7 and UTF-16. For additional information, see `zsigri.tripod.com/fontboard/ cjk/unicode.html`*.*

As this example demonstrates, the `FileStream` class provides only low-level methods for reading and writing files. These methods let you read and write bytes, but not integers, strings, or the other types of data that you are more likely to want to use.

The `BinaryReader` and `BinaryWriter` classes let you read and write binary data more easily than the `FileStream` class does. The `StringReader` and `StringWriter` classes let you read and write string data more easily. See the section "`StringReader` and `StringWriter`," describing these classes, later in this chapter for more information.

MemoryStream

Like `FileStream`, the `MemoryStream` class inherits from the `Stream` class. This class represents a stream with data stored in memory. Like the `FileStream`, it provides only relatively simple methods for reading and writing data. Usually, you will want to attach a higher-level object to the `MemoryStream` to make using it easier.

The following code creates a `MemoryStream` object. It then creates a `BinaryWriter` attached to the `MemoryStream` and uses it to write some text into the stream. Next, the program creates a `BinaryReader` object attached to the same `MemoryStream`. It uses the stream's `Seek` method to rewind the stream to its beginning, and then uses the `BinaryReader` object's `ReadString` method to read the string out of the `MemoryStream`.

```
Dim memory_stream As New MemoryStream()
Dim binary_writer As New BinaryWriter(memory_stream)
binary_writer.Write("Peter Piper picked a peck of pickled peppers.")

Dim binary_reader As New BinaryReader(memory_stream)
memory_stream.Seek(0, SeekOrigin.Begin)
MessageBox.Show(binary_reader.ReadString())
binary_reader.Close()
```

The following example does the same things as the previous example, except that it uses the `StreamWriter` and `StreamReader` classes instead of `BinaryWriter` and `BinaryReader`. Note that this version must call the `StreamWriter`'s `Flush` method to ensure that all of the text is written into the `MemoryStream` before it can read the memory using the `StreamReader`.

```
Dim memory_stream As New MemoryStream()
Dim stream_writer As New StreamWriter(memory_stream)
stream_writer.Write("Peter Piper picked a peck of pickled peppers.")
stream_writer.Flush()

Dim stream_reader As New StreamReader(memory_stream)
memory_stream.Seek(0, SeekOrigin.Begin)
MessageBox.Show(stream_reader.ReadToEnd())
stream_reader.Close()
```

BufferedStream

The `BufferedStream` class adds buffering to another stream class. For example, you can create a `BufferedStream` attached to a network stream that communicates with another application through sockets. The `BufferedStream` class buffers data passing through the network connection.

Most programs don't need to explicitly create their own buffered streams, so this class isn't described further here. See the online help for more information.

BinaryReader and BinaryWriter

The `BinaryReader` and `BinaryWriter` classes are not stream classes. Instead, they are helper classes that work with stream classes. They let you read and write data in files using a specific encoding. For example, the `BinaryReader` object's `ReadInt32` method reads a 4-byte (32-bit) signed integer from the stream. Similarly, the `ReadUInt16` method reads a 2-byte (16-bit) unsigned integer.

These classes still work at a relatively low level, and you should generally use higher-level classes to read and write data. For example, you shouldn't tie yourself to a particular representation of an integer unless you really must.

`BinaryReader` and `BinaryWriter` objects are attached to stream objects that provide access to the underlying bytes. Both of these classes have a `BaseStream` property that returns a reference to the underlying stream. Note also that the `Close` method provided by each of these classes automatically closes the underlying stream.

The following table describes the `BinaryReader` class's most useful methods.

Method	Purpose
Close	Closes the `BinaryReader` and its underlying stream.
PeekChar	Reads the stream's next character but does not advance the reader's position, so other methods can still read the character later.
Read	Reads characters from the stream and advances the reader's position.
ReadBoolean	Reads a Boolean from the stream and advances the reader's position by 1 byte.
ReadByte	Reads a byte from the stream and advances the reader's position by 1 byte.
ReadBytes	Reads a number of bytes from the stream into a byte array and advances the reader's position by that number of bytes.
ReadChar	Reads a character from the stream, and advances the reader's position according to the stream's encoding and the character.
ReadChars	Reads a number of characters from the stream, returns the results in a character array, and advances the reader's position according to the stream's encoding and the characters.
ReadDecimal	Reads a decimal value from the stream and advances the reader's position by 16 bytes.
ReadDouble	Reads an 8-byte floating-point value from the stream and advances the reader's position by 8 bytes.
ReadInt16	Reads a 2-byte signed integer from the stream and advances the reader's position by 2 bytes.
ReadInt32	Reads a 4-byte signed integer from the stream and advances the reader's position by 4 bytes.
ReadInt64	Reads an 8-byte signed integer from the stream and advances the reader's position by 8 bytes.
ReadSByte	Reads a signed byte from the stream and advances the reader's position by 1 byte.
ReadSingle	Reads a 4-byte floating-point value from the stream and advances the reader's position by 4 bytes.
ReadString	Reads a string from the current stream and advances the reader's position past it. The string begins with its length.
ReadUInt16	Reads a 2-byte unsigned integer from the stream and advances the reader's position by 2 bytes.
ReadUInt32	Reads a 4-byte unsigned integer from the stream and advances the reader's position by 4 bytes.
ReadUInt64	Reads an 8-byte unsigned integer from the stream and advances the reader's position by 8 bytes.

The following table describes the `BinaryWriter` class's most useful methods.

Name	Description
Close	Closes the `BinaryWriter` and its underlying stream.
Flush	Writes any buffered data into the underlying stream.
Seek	Sets the position within the stream.
Write	Writes a value into the stream. This method has many overloaded versions that write characters, arrays of characters, integers, strings, unsigned 64-bit integers, and so forth.

TextReader and TextWriter

The `TextReader` and `TextWriter` classes are also not stream classes. They provide properties and methods for working with text, which is stream-related. In particular, the `StreamWriter` and `StreamReader` classes derived from `TextReader` and `TextWriter` are associated with streams.

`TextReader` and `TextWriter` are abstract (`MustInherit`) classes that define behaviors for derived classes that read or write text characters. For example, the `StringWriter` and `StreamWriter` classes derived from `TextWriter` let a program write characters into a string or stream, respectively. Normally, you would use these derived classes to read and write text, but you might want to use the `TextReader` or `TextWriter` classes to manipulate the underlying classes more generically. You may also encounter a method that requires a `TextReader` or `TextWriter` object as a parameter. In that case, you could pass the method either a `StringReader`/`StringWriter` or a `StreamReader`/`StreamWriter`. For more information on these, see the sections "`StringReader` and `StringWriter`" and "`StreamReader` and `StreamWriter`," which follow.

The following table describes the `TextReader`'s most useful methods.

Method	Purpose
Close	Closes the reader and releases any resources that it is using.
Peek	Reads the next character from the text without changing the reader's state, so other methods can read the character later.
Read	Reads data from the input. Overloaded versions of this method read a single character or an array of characters up to a specified length.
ReadBlock	Reads data from the input into an array of characters.
ReadLine	Reads a line of characters from the input and returns the data in a string.
ReadToEnd	Reads any remaining characters in the input and returns them in a string.

The TextWriter class has three useful properties. Encoding specifies the text's encoding (ASCII, UTF-8, Unicode, and so forth).

FormatProvider returns an object that controls formatting. For example, you can build a FormatProvider object that knows how to display numbers in different bases (such as hexadecimal or octal).

The NewLine property gets or sets the string used by the writer to end lines. Usually, this value is something similar to a carriage return or a carriage return plus a line feed.

The following table describes the TextWriter's most useful methods.

Method	Purpose
Close	Closes the writer and releases any resources it uses.
Flush	Writes any buffered data into the underlying output.
Write	Writes a value into the output. This method has many overloaded versions that write characters, arrays of characters, integers, strings, unsigned 64-bit integers, and so forth.
WriteLine	Writes data into the output followed by the new line sequence.

StringReader and StringWriter

The StringReader and StringWriter classes let a program read and write text in a string.

These classes are derived from TextReader and TextWriter and inherit the definitions of most of their properties and methods from those classes. See the section "TextReader and TextWriter" earlier in this chapter for details.

The StringReader provides methods for reading lines, characters, or blocks of characters from the string. Its ReadToEnd method returns any of the string that has not already been read. The StringReader's constructor takes as a parameter the string that it should process.

The StringWriter class lets an application build a string. It provides methods to write text into the string with or without a new-line character. Its ToString method returns the StringWriter's string.

The StringWriter stores its string in an underlying StringBuilder class. StringBuilder is designed to make incrementally building a string more efficient. For example, if an application needs to build a very large string by concatenating a series of long substrings, it may be more efficient to use a StringBuilder rather than adding the strings to a normal String variable. StringWriter provides a simple interface to the StringBuilder class.

The most useful method provided by StringWriter that is not defined by the TextWriter parent class is GetStringBuilder. This method returns a reference to the underlying StringBuilder object that holds the class's data.

The following code shows a simple example that uses the `StringWriter` and `StringReader` classes. It creates a `StringWriter` object and uses its `WriteLine` method to add two lines to the string. It then displays the result of the writer's `ToString` method. This method returns the writer's current contents. Next, the program creates a `StringReader`, passing its constructor the string from which it will read. It closes the `StringWriter` because it is no longer needed. The code displays the result of the `StringReader`'s `ReadLine` method. Because the `StringWriter` created the string as two separate lines, this displays only the first line, "The quick brown fox." Next, the code uses the `StringReader`'s `ReadToEnd` method to read and display the rest of the text, "jumps over the lazy dog." The code finishes by closing the `StringReader`.

```
' Use a StringWriter to write into a string.
Dim string_writer As New StringWriter()
string_writer.WriteLine("The quick brown fox")
string_writer.WriteLine("jumps over the lazy dog.")
MessageBox.Show(string_writer.ToString)

' Use a StringReader to read from the string.
Dim string_reader As New StringReader(string_writer.ToString)
string_writer.Close()
MessageBox.Show(string_reader.ReadLine())
MessageBox.Show(string_reader.ReadToEnd())
string_reader.Close()
```

StreamReader and StreamWriter

The `StreamReader` and `StreamWriter` classes let a program read and write data in a stream. The underlying stream is usually a `FileStream`. You can pass a `FileStream` into these class's constructors, or you can pass a file name and the object will create a `FileStream` automatically.

The `StreamReader` provides methods for reading lines, characters, or blocks of characters from the stream. Its `ReadToEnd` method returns any of the stream that has not already been read.

The `StreamWriter` class provides methods to write text into the stream with or without a new-line character.

`StreamReader` and `StreamWriter` are derived from the `TextReader` and `TextWriter` classes and inherit the definitions of most of their properties and methods from those classes. See the section "`TextReader` and `TextWriter`" earlier in this chapter for a description of these properties and methods.

The `StreamWriter` class adds a new `AutoFlush` property that determines whether the writer flushes its buffer after every write.

The following simple example shows how to use a `StreamReader` and `StreamWriter`. It generates a file name and passes it into a `StreamWriter`'s constructor. It uses the `StreamWriter`'s `Write` and `WriteLine` methods to place two lines of text in the file. It then closes the file. If you were to open the file now with a text editor, you would see the text. The program then creates a new `StreamReader`, passing its constructor the same file name. It uses the reader's `ReadToEnd` method to grab the file's contents and displays the results.

```
Dim file_name As String = Application.StartupPath & "\test.txt"
Dim stream_writer As New StreamWriter(file_name)
stream_writer.Write("The quick brown fox")
stream_writer.WriteLine(" jumps over the lazy dog.")
stream_writer.Close()

Dim stream_reader As New StreamReader(file_name)
MessageBox.Show(stream_reader.ReadToEnd())
stream_reader.Close()
```

This example would have been much more awkward using a FileStream object's lower-level Write and Read methods to manipulate byte arrays. Compare this code to the example in the "FileStream" section earlier in this chapter.

Custom Stream Classes

Visual Studio provides a few other stream classes with more specialized uses.

The CryptoStream class applies a cryptographic transformation to data that passes through it. For example, if you attach a CryptoStream to a file using a particular cryptographic transformation and then use it to write data, the CryptoStream automatically transforms the data and produces an encrypted file. Similarly, you can use a CryptoStream to read an encrypted file and recover the original text.

The NetworkStream class represents a socket-based stream over a network connection. You can use this class to make different applications communicate over a network.

Three other special uses of streams are standard input, standard output, and standard error. Console applications define these streams for reading and writing information to and from the console. An application can interact directly with these streams by accessing the Console.In, Console.Out, and Console.Error properties. It can change these streams to new stream objects such as StreamReaders and StreamWriters by calling the Console.SetIn, Console.SetOut, and Console.SetError methods.

Summary

Streams let a program consider a wide variety of data sources in a uniform way. If a subroutine takes a stream as a parameter, it doesn't care whether the stream is attached to a string, file, block of memory, or network connection.

Many applications use the StringReader and StringWriter classes to read and write text in strings, and the StreamReader and StreamWriter classes to read and write text in streams (usually files). The other stream classes are often used at lower levels or as more abstract classes to allow a routine to process different kinds of streams in a uniform way. If you focus on these four classes, you will quickly learn how to perform the most common stream operations.

Programs often use the StreamReader and StreamWriter classes to read and write files. Chapter 27, "File-System Objects," describes classes that let a Visual Basic application interact with the file system in other ways. These classes let a program examine, rename, move, and delete files and directories.

File-System Objects

Visual Basic includes a bewildering assortment of objects that you can use to manipulate drives, directories, and files. The stream classes described in Chapter 26 let you read and write files, but they don't really capture any of the special structure of the file system.

A Visual Basic application has two main choices for working with the file system: Visual Basic methods and .NET Framework classes. This chapter describes these two approaches and the classes that they use. It finishes by describing some of the My namespace properties and methods that you can use to access file-system tools more easily. For more information on the My namespace, see the section "My" in Chapter 25, "Configuration and Resources," and Appendix P, "The My Namespace."

Visual Basic Methods

Visual Basic provides a number of commands for manipulating the file system. These commands are relatively flexible and easy to understand. Most of them have been around since Visual Basic's youth, so many long-time Visual Basic developers prefer to use them rather than the newer .NET Framework methods.

One disadvantage to these methods is that they do not natively allow you to read and write non-standard data types. They can handle string, date, integer, long, single, double, and decimal data. They can also handle structures and arrays of those types. They cannot, however, handle classes themselves. You can use XML serialization to convert a class object into a string and then use these methods to read and write the result, but that requires an extra step with some added complexity.

The section "File-System Methods" later in this chapter describes Visual Basic's native file-system methods. The sections "Sequential-File Access," "Random-File Access," and "Binary-File Access," later in this chapter describe specific issues for working with sequential, random, and binary files.

File Methods

The following table describes the methods Visual Basic provides for working with files.

Function	Purpose
EOF	Returns True if a file open for reading is at the end of file. ("EOF" stands for End of File.)
FileClose	Closes an open file.
FileGet	Reads data from a file opened in Random and Binary mode into a variable.
FileGetObject	Reads data as an object from a file opened in Random and Binary mode into a variable.
FileOpen	Opens a file for reading or writing. Parameters indicate the mode (Append, Binary, Input, Output, or Random), access type (Read, Write, or Read-Write), and sharing (Shared, LockRead, LockWrite, or LockReadWrite).
FilePut	Writes data from a variable into a file opened for Random or Binary access.
FilePutObject	Writes an object from a variable into a file opened for Random or Binary access.
FreeFile	Returns a file number that is not currently associated with any file in this application. You should use FreeFile to get file numbers rather than using arbitrary numbers such as 1.
Input	Reads data written into a file by the Write method back into a variable.
InputString	Reads a specific number of characters from the file.
LineInput	Returns the next line of text from the file.
Loc	Returns the current position within the file.
LOF	Returns the file's length in bytes. ("LOF" stands for Length Of File.)
Print	Prints values into the file. Multiple values separated by commas are aligned at tab boundaries.
PrintLine	Prints values followed by a new line into the file. Multiple values separated by commas are aligned at tab boundaries.
Seek	Moves to the indicated position within the file.
Write	Writes values into the file, delimited appropriately so that they can later be read by the Input method.
WriteLine	Writes values followed by a new line into the file, delimited appropriately so that they can later be read by the Input method.

Many of Visual Basic's file methods use a file number to represent an open file. The file number is just a number used to identify the file. There's nothing magic about it. You just need to be sure not to use the same file number for more than one file at a time. The FreeFile method returns a number that is not in use so that you know it is safe to use as a file number.

The following example uses `FreeFile` to get an available file number. It uses `FileOpen` to open a file for reading. Then, while the `EOF` method indicates that the code hasn't reached the end of the file, the program uses `LineInput` to read a line from the file and it displays the line. When it finishes reading the file, the program uses `FileClose` to close it.

```
' Get an available file number.
Dim file_num As Integer = FreeFile()

' Open the file.
FileOpen(file_num, _
    "C:\Temp\test.txt", _
    OpenMode.Input, OpenAccess.Read, OpenShare.Shared)

' Read the file's lines.
Do While Not EOF(file_num)
    ' Read a line.
    Dim txt As String = LineInput(file_num)
    Debug.WriteLine(txt)
Loop

' Close the file.
FileClose(file_num)
```

File-System Methods

Visual Basic also provides several methods for working with the file system. The following table describes methods that manipulate directories and files.

Method	Purpose
ChDir	Changes the application's current working directory.
ChDrive	Changes the application's current working drive.
CurDir	Returns the application's current working directory.
Dir	Returns a file matching a directory path specification that may include wildcards, and matching certain file properties such as ReadOnly, Hidden, or Directory. The first call to Dir should include a path. Subsequent calls can omit the path to fetch the next matching file for the initial path. Dir returns file names without the path and returns Nothing when no more files match.
FileCopy	Copies a file to a new location.
FileDateTime	Returns the date and time when the file was created or last modified.
FileLen	Returns the length of a file in bytes.
GetAttr	Returns a value indicating the file's attributes. The value is a combination of the values vbNormal, vbReadOjnly, vbHidden, vbSystem, vbDirectory, vbArchive, and vbAlias.

Table continued on following page

Method	Purpose
Kill	Permanently deletes a file.
MkDir	Creates a new directory.
Rename	Renames a directory or file.
RmDir	Deletes an empty directory.
SetAttr	Sets the file's attributes. The attribute value is a combination of the values vbNormal, vbReadOjnly, vbHidden, vbSystem, vbDirectory, vbArchive, and vbAlias.

Sequential-File Access

With sequential file access, a program reads or writes the contents of a file byte by byte from start to finish with no jumping around. In contrast, in a random access file, the program can jump freely to any position in the file and write data wherever it likes.

A text file is a typical sequential file. The program can read the text in order, and read it one line at a time, but it cannot easily jump around within the file.

The Input, InputString, LineInput, Print, PrintLine, Write, and WriteLine methods provide sequential access to files.

The Print and PrintLine methods provide mostly unformatted results. If you pass these methods multiple parameters separated by commas, they align the results on tab boundaries. Write and WriteLine, on the other hand, delimit their output so that it can be easily read by the Input method.

A program cannot directly modify only part of a sequential file. For example, it cannot modify, add, or remove a sentence in the middle of a paragraph. If you must modify the file, you should read it into a string, make the changes you want, and the rewrite the file.

If you must frequently modify text in the middle of a file, you should consider using random or binary access, or storing the data in a database.

Random-File Access

A random-access file contains a series of fixed-length records. For example, you could make an employee file that contains a series of values defining an employee. Each record would have fixed-length fields to hold an employee's ID, first name, last name, street address, and so forth, as shown in the following structure definition:

```
Structure Employee
    Public Id As Long
    <VBFixedString(20)> Public FirstName As String
    <VBFixedString(20)> Public LastName As String
    <VBFixedString(40)> Public Street As String
    ...
End Structure
```

When you open a file for random access, you can jump to any record in the file. That makes certain kinds of file manipulation easier. For example, if the file is sorted, you can use a binary search to locate records in it.

You can overwrite the values in a record within the file, but you cannot add or remove records in the middle of the file. If you must make those sorts of changes, you must load the file into memory and then rewrite it from scratch.

The `FileGet`, `FileGetObject`, `FilePut`, and `FilePutObject` methods read and write records in random-access files. The following code demonstrates the `FilePut` and `FileGet` methods. First, it defines a structure named `Employee` to hold the data in a record. Notice how the code uses the `VBFixedString` attribute to flag the strings as fixed length. The structure must have a fixed length if you want to jump randomly through the file because Visual Basic calculates a record's position by multiplying a record's size by its index in the file. If records contained strings of unknown length, the calculation wouldn't work.

When the user clicks the Make Records button, the `btnMakeRecords_Click` event handler executes. This code declares a variable of the record type, `Employee`. It uses the `FreeFile` method to get an available file number and uses `FileOpen` to open the file for random access. The final parameter to `FileOpen` is the length of the file's records. To calculate this length, the program uses the `Len` function, passing it the `Employee` instance `emp`.

Next, the program uses the `FilePut` method to write six records into the file. It passes `FilePut` the file number and a new `Employee` structure. The structure's constructor makes initializing the new records easy.

The program then uses `FileGet` to retrieve the six records using their indexes as keys, fetching them out of numeric order to demonstrate random access. It then displays each record's data in the Output window.

There are two key points to notice here. First, the file numbers records starting with 1 not 0, so the first record in the file has index 1.

Second, the `FileGet` method does not have an overloaded version that takes an `Employee` structure as a parameter. Because this example has Option Strict set to On, the code must perform some shenanigans to pass `FileGet` a `ValueType` variable and then later convert it into an `Employee`.

If you set `Option Strict` to `Off`, you can pass an `Employee` object directly into `FileGet`. Turning off `Option Explicit` is generally a bad idea, because it can hide implicit data type conversions that may indicate a mistake. You can minimize the danger by placing as little code as possible in the file with `Option Explicit Off`. For example, if the code that uses `FileGet` is in a class, you can use the `Partial` keyword to move that code into a separate module. Then that module can turn off `Option Explicit` while the rest of the class's code keeps `Option Explicit On`.

After if it has read and displayed the records, the program uses `FileClose` to close the file.

```
Public Class Form1
    Public Structure Employee
        Public ID As Integer
        <VBFixedString(15)> Public FirstName As String
        <VBFixedString(15)> Public LastName As String

        Public Sub New(ByVal new_id As Integer, ByVal first_name As String, _
```

```
        ByVal last_name As String)
            ID = new_id
            FirstName = first_name
            LastName = last_name
        End Sub

        Public Overrides Function ToString() As String
            Return ID & ": " & FirstName & " " & LastName
        End Function
    End Structure

    Private Sub btnMakeRecords_Click(ByVal sender As System.Object, _
     ByVal e As System.EventArgs) Handles btnMakeRecords.Click
        ' Declare a record variable.
        Dim emp As New Employee

        ' Get an available file number.
        Dim file_num As Integer = FreeFile()

        ' Open the file.
        FileOpen(file_num, "MYFILE.DAT", OpenMode.Random, _
            OpenAccess.ReadWrite, OpenShare.Shared, _
            Len(emp))

        ' Make some records.
        FilePut(file_num, New Employee(1, "Alice", "Altanta"))
        FilePut(file_num, New Employee(2, "Bob", "Bakersfield"))
        FilePut(file_num, New Employee(3, "Cindy", "Chicago"))
        FilePut(file_num, New Employee(4, "Dan", "Denver"))
        FilePut(file_num, New Employee(5, "Erma", "Eagle"))
        FilePut(file_num, New Employee(6, "Fred", "Frisco"))

        ' Fetch and display the records.
        Dim obj As ValueType = DirectCast(emp, ValueType)
        For Each i As Integer In New Integer() {3, 1, 5, 2, 6}
            FileGet(file_num, obj, i)
            emp = DirectCast(obj, Employee)
            Debug.WriteLine(emp.ToString())
        Next i

        ' Close the file.
        FileClose(file_num)
    End Sub
End Class
```

The following text shows the result. Notice that the first names are padded with spaces to 15 characters, the length of the Employee structure's fixed-length strings. The last names are also padded to 15 characters, but it's less obvious from this display.

```
3: Cindy          Chicago
1: Alice          Altanta
5: Erma           Eagle
2: Bob            Bakersfield
6: Fred           Frisco
```

Binary-File Access

Binary access is similar to random access, except that it does not require its data to fit into neat records. You get control over pretty much every byte in the file, and you can jump to an arbitrary byte number in the file. If the items in the file are not fixed-length records, however, you cannot jump to a particular record because you cannot calculate where that record would begin.

.NET Framework Classes

The System.IO namespace provides several classes for working with the file system. The `Directory` and `File` classes provide shared methods that you can use to manipulate the file system without creating instances of helper objects.

The `DirectoryInfo` and `FileInfo` classes let you work with specific relevant file system objects. For example, a `FileInfo` object represents a particular file and provides methods to create, rename, delete, and get information about that file.

The following sections describe these and the other classes that the Framework provides to help you work with the file system.

Directory

The `Directory` class provides shared methods for working with directories. These methods let you create, rename, move, and delete directories. They let you enumerate the files and subdirectories within a directory, and get and set directory information such as the directory's creation and last access time.

The following table describes the `Directory` class's shared methods.

Method	Purpose
CreateDirectory	Creates a directory and any missing ancestors (parent, grandparent, and so forth).
Delete	Deletes a directory and its contents. It can recursively delete all subdirectories.
Exists	Returns `True` if the path points to an existing directory.
GetCreationTime	Returns a directory's creation date and time.
GetCreationTimeUtc	Returns a directory's creation date and time in Coordinated Universal Time (UTC).
GetCurrentDirectory	Returns the application's current working directory.
GetDirectories	Returns an array of strings holding the fully qualified names of a directory's subdirectories.
GetDirectoryRoot	Returns the directory root for a path (the path need not exist). For example, "C:\".

Table continued on following page

Method	Purpose
GetFiles	Returns an array of strings holding the fully qualified names of a directory's files.
GetFileSystemEntries	Returns an array of strings holding the fully qualified names of a directory's files and subdirectories.
GetLastAccessTime	Returns a directory's last access date and time.
GetLastAccessTimeUtc	Returns a directory's last access date and time in UTC.
GetLastWriteTime	Returns the date and time when a directory was last modified.
GetLastWriteTimeUtc	Returns the date and time in UTC when a directory was last modified.
GetLogicalDrives	Returns an array of strings listing the system's logical drives as in "A:\". The list only includes drives that are attached. For example, it lists an empty floppy drive and a connected flashdisk but doesn't list a flashdisk after you disconnect it.
GetParent	Returns a DirectoryInfo object representing a directory's parent.
Move	Moves a directory and its contents to a new location on the same disk volume.
SetCreationTime	Sets a directory's creation date and time.
SetCreationTimeUtc	Sets a directory's creation date and time in UTC.
SetCurrentDirectory	Sets the application's current working directory.
SetLastAccessTime	Sets a directory's last access date and time.
SetLastAccessTimeUtc	Sets a directory's last access date and time in UTC.
SetLastWriteTime	Sets a directory's last write date and time.
SetLastWriteTimeUtc	Sets a directory's last write date and time in UTC.

File

The File class provides shared methods for working with files. These methods let you create, rename, move, and delete files. They also make working with file streams a bit easier.

The following table describes the File class's most useful shared methods.

Method	Purpose
AppendAll	Adds text to the end of a file, creating it if it doesn't exist, and then closes the file.
AppendText	Opens a file for appending UTF-8 encoded text and returns a StreamWriter attached to it.
Copy	Copies a file.
Create	Creates a new file and returns a FileStream attached to it.
CreateText	Creates or opens a file for writing UTF-8 encoded text and returns a StreamWriter attached to it.
Delete	Permanently deletes a file.
Exists	Returns True if the specified file exists.
GetAttributes	Gets a file's attributes. This is a combination of flags defined by the FileAttributes enumeration: Archive, Compressed, Device, Directory, Encrypted, Hidden, Normal, NotContextIndexed, Offline, ReadOnly, ReparsePoint, SparseFile, System, and Temporary.
GetCreationTime	Returns a file's creation date and time.
GetCreationTimeUtc	Returns a file's creation date and time in UTC.
GetLastAccessTime	Returns a file's last access date and time.
GetLastAccessTimeUtc	Returns a file's last access date and time in UTC.
GetLastWriteTime	Returns a file's last write date and time.
GetLastWriteTimeUtc	Returns a file's last write date and time in UTC.
Move	Moves a file to a new location.
Open	Opens a file and returns a FileStream attached to it. Parameters let you specify the mode (Append, Create, CreateNew, Open, OpenOrCreate, or Truncate), access (Read, Write, or ReadWrite), and sharing (Read, Write, ReadWrite, or None) settings.
OpenRead	Opens a file for reading and returns a FileStream attached to it.
OpenText	Opens a UTF-8-encoded text file for reading and returns a StreamReader attached to it.
OpenWrite	Opens a file for writing and returns a FileStream attached to it.
ReadAllBytes	Returns a file's contents in an array of bytes.
ReadAllLines	Returns a file's lines in an array of strings.
ReadAllText	Returns a file's contents in a string.

Table continued on following page

Method	Purpose
Replace	This method takes three file paths as parameters, representing a source file, a destination file, and a backup file. If the backup file exists, the method permanently deletes it. It then moves the destination file to the backup file, and moves the source file to the destination file. For example, imagine a program that writes a log file every time it runs. It could use this method to keep three versions of the log: the current log (the method's source file), the most recent backup (the method's destination file), and a second backup (the method's backup file). This method throws an error if either the source or destination file doesn't exist.
SetAttributes	Sets a file's attributes. This is a combination of flags defined by the FileAttributes enumeration: Archive, Compressed, Device, Directory, Encrypted, Hidden, Normal, NotContextIndexed, Offline, ReadOnly, ReparsePoint, SparseFile, System, and Temporary.
SetCreationTime	Sets a file's creation date and time.
SetCreationTimeUtc	Sets a file's creation date and time in UTC.
SetLastAccessTime	Sets a file's last access date and time.
SetLastAccessTimeUtc	Sets a file's last access date and time in UTC.
SetLastWriteTime	Sets a file's last write date and time.
SetLastWriteTimeUtc	Sets a file's last write date and time in UTC.
WriteAllBytes	Creates or replaces a file, writes an array of bytes into it, and closes the file.
WriteAllLines	Creates or replaces a file, writes an array of strings into it, and closes the file.
WriteAllText	Creates or replaces a file, writes a string into it, and closes the file.

DriveInfo

A DriveInfo object represents one of the computer's drives. The following table describes the properties provided by this class. Note that some of these properties are available only when the drive is ready, as indicated in the Must Be Ready column. If you try to access them when the drive is not ready, Visual Basic throws an exception. The program should check the IsReady property to determine whether the drive is ready before trying to use the AvailableFreeSpace, DriveFormat, TotalFreeSpace, or VolumeLabel properties.

DriveInfo Property	Purpose	Must Be Ready
AvailableFreeSpace	Returns the amount of free space available on the drive in bytes.	True
DriveFormat	Returns the name of the file-system type such as NTFS (NT File System) or FAT32 (32-bit File Allocation Table). (For a comparison of these, see www.ntfs.com/ntfs_vs_fat.htm.)	True
DriveType	Returns a DriveType enumeration value indicating the drive type. This value can be CDRom, Fixed, Network, NoRootDirectory, Ram, Removable, or Unknown.	False
IsReady	Returns True if the drive is ready. Many DriveInfo properties are unavailable and raise exceptions if you try to access them while the drive is not ready.	False
Name	Return's the drive's name. This is the drive's root name (as in "A:\" or "C:\").	False
RootDirectory	Returns a DirectoryInfo object representing the drive's root directory. See the section "DirectoryInfo" later in this chapter for more information on this class.	False
TotalFreeSpace	Returns the total amount of free space on the drive in bytes.	True
VolumeLabel	Gets or sets the drive's volume label.	True

The DriveInfo class also has a public shared method GetDrives that returns an array of DriveInfo objects describing the system's drives.

DirectoryInfo

A DirectoryInfo object represents a directory. You can use its properties and methods to create and delete directories and to move through a directory hierarchy.

The following table describes the most useful public properties and methods provided by the DirectoryInfo class.

Property or Method	Purpose
Attributes	Gets or sets flags for the directory from the FileAttributes enumeration: Archive, Compressed, Device, Directory, Encrypted, Hidden, Normal, NotContentIndexed, Offline, ReadOnly, ReparsePoint, SparseFile, System, and Temporary.

Table continued on following page

Property or Method	Purpose
Create	Creates the directory. You can create a DirectoryInfo object, passing its constructor the fully qualified name of a directory that doesn't exist. You can then call the object's Create method to create the directory.
CreateSubdirectory	Creates a subdirectory within the directory and returns a Directory Info object representing it. The subdirectory's path must be relative to the DirectoryInfo's directory, but can contain intermediate subdirectories. For example, dir_info.CreateSubdirectory ("Tools\Bin") creates the Tools subdirectory and the Bin directory inside that.
CreationTime	Gets or sets the directory's creation time.
CreationTimeUtc	Gets or sets the directory's creation time in UTC.
Delete	Deletes the directory if it is empty. A parameter lets you tell the object to delete its contents, too, if it isn't empty.
Exists	Returns True if the directory exists.
Extension	Returns the extension part of the directory's name. Normally, this is an empty string for directories.
FullName	Returns the directory's fully qualified path.
GetDirectories	Returns an array of DirectoryInfo representing the directory's subdirectories. An optional parameter gives a pattern to match. This method does not recursively search the subdirectories.
GetFiles	Returns an array of FileInfo objects representing files inside the directory. An optional parameter gives a pattern to match. This method does not recursively search subdirectories.
GetFileSystemInfos	Returns a strongly typed array of FileSystemInfo objects, representing subdirectories and files inside the directory. The items in the array are DirectoryInfo and FileInfo objects, both of which inherit from FileSystemInfo. An optional parameter gives a pattern to match. This method does not recursively search subdirectories.
LastAccessTime	Gets or sets the directory's last access time.
LastAccessTimeUtc	Gets or sets the directory's last access time in UTC.
LastWriteTime	Gets or sets the directory's last write time.
LastWriteTimeUtc	Gets or sets directory's last write time in UTC.
MoveTo	Moves the directory and its contents to a new path.
Name	The directory's name without the path information.
Parent	Returns a DirectoryInfo object, representing the directory's parent. If the directory is its file system's root (for example, C:\), then this returns Nothing.

Property or Method	Purpose
Refresh	Refreshes the DirectoryInfo object's data. For example, if the directory has been accessed since the object was created, you must call Refresh to load the new LastAccessTime value.
Root	Returns a DirectoryInfo object representing the root of the directory's file system.
ToString	Returns the directory's fully qualified path and name.

FileInfo

A FileInfo object represents a file. You can use its properties and methods to create and delete directories and to move through a directory hierarchy.

The following table describes the most useful public properties and methods provided by the FileInfo class.

Property or Method	Purpose
AppendText	Returns a StreamWriter that appends text to the file.
Attributes	Gets or sets flags for the file from the FileAttributes enumeration: Archive, Compressed, Device, Directory, Encrypted, Hidden, Normal, NotContentIndexed, Offline, ReadOnly, ReparsePoint, SparseFile, System, and Temporary.
CopyTo	Copies the file and returns a FileInfo object, representing the new file. A parameter lets you indicate whether the copy should overwrite an existing file. If the destination path is relative, it is relative to the application's current directory, not to the FileInfo object's directory.
Create	Creates the file and returns a FileStream object attached to it. For example, you can create a FileInfo object, passing its constructor the name of a file that doesn't exist. Then you can call the Create method to create the file.
CreateText	Creates the file and returns a StreamWriter attached to it. For example, you can create a FileInfo object passing its constructor the name of a file that doesn't exist. Then you can call the Create-Text method to create the file.
CreationTime	Gets or sets the file's creation time.
CreationTimeUtc	Gets or sets the file's creation time in UTC.
Delete	Deletes the file.
Directory	Returns a DirectoryInfo object representing the file's directory.

Table continued on following page

Property or Method	Purpose
DirectoryName	Returns the name of the file's directory.
Exists	Returns True if the file exists.
Extension	Returns the extension part of the file's name, including the period. For example, the extension for game.txt is .txt.
FullName	Returns the file's fully qualified path and name.
IsReadOnly	Returns True if the file is marked read-only.
LastAccessTime	Gets or sets the file's last access time.
LastAccessTimeUtc	Gets or sets the file's last access time in UTC.
LastWriteTime	Gets or sets the file's last write time.
LastWriteTimeUtc	Gets or sets the file's last write time in UTC.
Length	Returns the number of bytes in the file.
MoveTo	Moves the file to a new location. If the destination uses a relative path, it is relative to the application's current directory, not to the FileInfo object's directory. When this method finishes, the FileInfo object is updated to refer to the file's new location.
Name	The file's name without the path information.
Open	Opens the file with various mode (Append, Create, CreateNew, Open, OpenOrCreate, or Truncate), access (Read, Write, or ReadWrite), and sharing (Read, Write, ReadWrite, or None) settings. This method returns a FileStream object attached to the file.
OpenRead	Returns a read-only FileStream attached to the file.
OpenText	Returns a StreamReader with UTF-8 encoding attached to the file for reading.
OpenWrite	Returns a write-only FileStream attached to the file.
Refresh	Refreshes the FileInfo object's data. For example, if the file has been accessed since the object was created, you must call Refresh to load the new LastAccessTime value.
Replace	Replaces a target file with this one, renaming the old target as a backup copy. If the backup file already exists, it is deleted and replaced with the target. You can use this method to save backups of logs and other periodically updated files.
ToString	Returns the file's fully qualified name.

FileSystemInfo

The FileSystemInfo class is the parent class for the FileInfo and DirectoryInfo classes. It is a MustInherit class so you cannot create instances of it directly, but some routines return this class rather than the more specific child classes. For example, the DirectoryInfo class's GetFileSystemInfos method returns an array of FileSystemInfo objects describing the files in the directory.

FileSystemWatcher

The FileSystemWatcher class keeps an eye on part of the file system and raises events to let your program know if something changes. For example, you could make a FileSystemWatcher monitor a work directory. For example, when a new file with a .job extension arrives, the watcher would raise an event and your application could process the file.

The FileSystemWatcher's constructor takes parameters that tell it which directory to watch and that give it a filter for selecting files to watch. For example, the filter might be "*.txt" to watch for changes to text files. The default filter is "*.*", which catches changes to all files that have an extension. Set the filter to the empty string ""to catch changes to all files.

The following table describes the FileSystemWatcher's most useful properties.

Property	Purpose
EnableRaisingEvents	Determines whether the component is enabled. Note that this property is False by default, so the watcher will not raise any events until you set it to True.
Filter	Determines the files for which the watcher reports events. You cannot watch for multiple file types as in *.txt and *.dat. Instead use multiple FileSystemWatchers. If you like, you can use AddHandler to make all of the FileSystemWatchers use the same event handlers.
IncludeSubdirectories	Determines whether the object watches subdirectories within the main path.
InternalBufferSize	Determines the size of the internal buffer. If the watcher is monitoring a very active directory, a small buffer may overflow.
NotifyFilter	Determines the types of changes that the watcher reports. This is a combination of values defined by the NotifyFilters enumeration and can include the values Attributes, CreationTime, DirectoryName, FileName, LastAccess, LastWrite, Security, and Size.
Path	Determines the path to watch.

The FileSystemWatcher class provides only two really useful methods. First, Dispose releases resources used by the component. When you are finished using a watcher, call its Dispose method to allow garbage collection to reclaim its resources more efficiently.

Second, the `WaitForChanged` method waits for a change synchronously (with an optional timeout). When a change occurs, the method returns a `WaitForChangedResult` object, giving information about the change that occurred.

When the `FileSystemWatcher` detects a change asynchronously, it raises an event to let the program know what has happened. The following table describes the class's events.

Name	Description
Changed	A file or subdirectory has changed.
Created	A file or subdirectory was created.
Deleted	A file or subdirectory was deleted.
Error	The watcher's internal buffer overflowed.
Renamed	A file or subdirectory was renamed.

The following simple example shows how to use a `FileSystemWatcher` to look for new files in a directory. The program uses the `WithEvents` keyword to declare a `FileSystemWatcher` object. When the program's main form loads, the `Form1_Load` event handler allocates this object. Its constructor sets the object's path to the program's startup directory's parent. It sets the object's filter to "`*.job`" so that the object will watch for changes to files that end with a `.job` extension.

The event handler sets the watcher's `NotifyFilter` to `FileName`, so it will raise its `Created` event if a new file name appears in the target directory. Unfortunately, the `NotifyFilter` values (`Attributes`, `CreationTime`, `DirectoryName`, `FileName`, `LastAccess`, `LastWrite`, `Security`, and `Size`) do not match up well with the events provided by the `FileSystemWatcher`, so you need to figure out which `NotifyFilter` values to set to raise different kinds of events.

The `Form1_Load` event handler finishes by setting the watcher's `EnableRaisingEvents` property to `True` so the object starts watching.

When a `.job` file's is created in the watcher's target directory, the program's `fswJobFiles_Created` executes. The program processes and then deletes the file. In this example, the program processes the file by displaying a message giving its fully qualified name. A more realistic example might read the file; parse fields, indicating the type of job this is; assign it to an employee for handling; and then e-mail it to that employee.

```
Private WithEvents fswJobFiles As FileSystemWatcher

Private Sub Form1_Load(ByVal sender As System.Object, _
  ByVal e As System.EventArgs) Handles MyBase.Load
    Dim watch_path As String = _
        FileSystem.GetParentPath(Application.StartupPath)
    fswJobFiles = New FileSystemWatcher(watch_path, "*.job")
    fswJobFiles.NotifyFilter = NotifyFilters.FileName
    fswJobFiles.EnableRaisingEvents = True
End Sub

Private Sub fswJobFiles_Created(ByVal sender As Object, _
```

```
    ByVal e As System.IO.FileSystemEventArgs) Handles fswJobFiles.Created
        ' Process the new file...
        MessageBox.Show("Process new job: " & e.FullPath)

        File.Delete(e.FullPath)
End Sub
```

Path

The Path class provides shared properties and methods that you can use to manipulate paths. Its methods return the path's file name, extension, directory name, and so forth. Other methods provide values that do not relate to a specific path. For example, they can give you the system's temporary directory path, or the name of a temporary file.

The following table describes the Path class's most useful public properties.

Property	Purpose
AltDirectorySeparatorChar	Returns the alternate character used to separate directory levels in a hierarchical path. Typically this is /.
DirectorySeparatorChar	Returns the character used to separate directory levels in a hierarchical path. Typically this is \ (as in C:\Tests\Billing\2005q2.dat).
InvalidPathChars	Returns a character array that holds characters that are not allowed in a path string. Typically, this array includes characters such as ", <, >, and |, as well as nonprintable characters such as those with ASCII values between 0 and 31.
PathSeparator	Returns the character used to separate path strings in environment variables. Typically this is ;.
VolumeSeparatorChar	Returns the character placed between a volume letter and the rest of the path. Typically this is : (as in C:\Tests\Billing\2005q2.dat).

The following table describes the Path class's most useful methods.

Method	Purpose
ChangeExtension	Changes a path's extension.
Combine	Returns two path strings concatenated.
GetDirectoryName	Returns a path's directory.
GetExtension	Returns a path's extension.
GetFileName	Returns a path's file name and extension.

Table continued on following page

Method	Purpose
GetFileNameWithoutExtension	Returns a path's file name without the extension.
GetFullPath	Returns a path's fully qualified value. This can be particularly useful for converting a partially relative path into an absolute path. For example, the statement `Path.Get-FullPath("C:\Tests\OldTests\Software\..\..\New\Code")` returns the string `"C:\Tests\New\Code"`.
GetInvalidFileNameChars	Returns an array listing characters that are invalid in file names.
GetInvalidPathChars	Returns an array listing characters that are invalid in file paths.
GetPathRoot	Returns a path's root directory string. For example, the statement `Path.GetPathRoot("C:\Invoices\Unpaid\Deadbeats")` returns the string `"C:\"`.
GetRandomFileName	Returns a random file name.
GetTempFileName	Creates a uniquely named, empty temporary file and returns its fully qualified path. Your program can open that file for scratch space, do whatever it needs to do, close the file, and then delete it. A typical file name might be `"C:\Documents and Settings\Rod\Local Settings\Temp\tmp19D.tmp"`.
GetTempPath	Returns the path to the system's temporary folder. This is the path part of the file names returned by `GetTemp-FileName`.
HasExtension	Returns `True` if a path includes an extension.
IsPathRooted	Returns `True` if a path is an absolute path. This includes "`\Temp\Wherever`" and "`C:\Clients\Litigation`," but not "`Temp\Wherever`" or "`..\Uncle`".

My.Computer.FileSystem

The `My.Computer.FileSystem` object provides tools for working with drives, directories, and files. The following table summarizes this object's properties.

Property	Description
CurrentDirectory	Gets or sets the fully qualified path to the application's current directory.
Drives	Returns a read-only collection of `DriveInfo` objects describing the system's drives. See the section "DriveInfo" earlier in this chapter for information about the `DriveInfo` class.

Property	Description
SpecialDirectories	Returns a SpecialDirectoriesProxy object that has properties giving the locations of various special directories (such as the system's temporary directory and the user's MyDocuments directory). See the section "My.Computer.FileSystem.SpecialDirectories" later in this chapter for more information.

The following list describes the My.Computer.FileSystem object's methods.

Method	Purpose
CombinePath	Combines a base path with a relative path reference and returns a properly formatted fully qualified path. For example, the following code displays the name of the directory that is the parent of the application's current directory:

```
MessageBox.Show( _
    My.Computer.FileSystem.CombinePath( _
        My.Computer.FileSystem.CurrentDirectory(), _
        "..")
```

Method	Purpose
CopyDirectory	Copies a directory. Parameters indicate whether to overwrite existing files, whether to display a progress indicator, and what to do if the user presses Cancel during the operation.
CopyFile	Copies a file. Parameters indicate whether to overwrite existing files, whether to display a progress indicator, and what to do if the user presses Cancel during the operation.
CreateDirectory	Creates a directory. This method will create ancestor directories if necessary. For example, if the C:\Temp directory contains no subdirectories, creating C:\Temp\Project\Data will automatically create C:\Temp\Project and C:\Temp\Project\Data.
DeleteDirectory	Deletes a directory. Parameters indicate whether to recursively delete subdirectories, prompt the user for confirmation, or move the directory into the Recycle Bin.
DeleteFile	Deletes a file. Parameters indicate whether to prompt the user for confirmation or move the file into the Recycle Bin, and what to do if the user presses Cancel while the deletion is in progress.
DirectoryExists	Returns True if a specified directory exists.
FileExists	Returns True if a specified file exists.
FindInFiles	Returns a read-only collection of strings listing files that contain a target string.
GetDirectories	Returns a string collection listing subdirectories of a given directory. Parameters tell whether to recursively search the subdirectories, and the wildcards to match.

Table continued on following page

Method	Purpose
GetDirectoryInfo	Returns a DirectoryInfo object for a directory. See the section "DirectoryInfo" earlier in this chapter for more information.
GetDriveInfo	Returns a DriveInfo object for a drive. See the section "DriveInfo" earlier in this chapter for more information.
GetFileInfo	Returns a FileInfo object for a file. See the section "FileInfo" earlier in this chapter for more information.
GetFiles	Returns a string collection holding the names of files within a directory. Parameters indicate whether the search should recursively search subdirectories, and give wildcards to match.
GetParentPath	Returns the fully qualified path of a path's parent. For example, this returns a file's or directory's parent directory.
MoveDirectory	Moves a directory. Parameters indicate whether to overwrite files that have the same name in the destination directory and whether to prompt the user when such a collision occurs.
MoveFile	Moves a file. Parameters indicate whether to overwrite a file that has the same name as the file's destination and whether to prompt the user when such a collision occurs.
OpenTextFieldParser	Opens a TextFieldParser object attached to a delimited or fixed-field file such as a log file. You can use the object to parse the file.
OpenTextFileReader	Opens a StreamReader object attached to a file. You can use the object to read the file.
OpenTextFileWriter	Opens a StreamReader object attached to a file. You can use the object to write into the file.
ReadAllBytes	Reads all of the bytes from a binary file into an array.
ReadAllText	Reads all of the text from a text file into a string.
RenameDirectory	Renames a directory within its parent directory.
RenameFile	Renames a file with its directory.
WriteAllBytes	Writes an array of bytes into a binary file. A parameter tells whether to append the data or rewrite the file.
WriteAllText	Writes a string into a text file. A parameter tells whether to append the string or rewrite the file.

My.Computer.FileSystem.SpecialDirectories

The `My.Computer.FileSystem.SpecialDirectories` property returns a `SpecialDirectoriesProxy` object that has properties giving the locations of various special directories (such as the system's temporary directory and the user's MyDocuments directory).

The following table describes these special directory properties.

Property	Purpose
AllUsersApplicationData	Application settings for all users.
CurrentUserApplicationData	Application settings for the current user.
Desktop	The current user's desktop directory.
MyDocuments	The current user's MyDocuments directory.
MyMusic	The current user's MyMusic directory.
MyPictures	The current user's MyPictures directory.
Programs	The current user's Start Menu\Programs directory.
Temp	The current user's temporary directory.

The following output shows typical examples of these directory paths. The first two are quite long, so they are broken into multiple lines, although the output from the methods is on a single line.

```
C:\Documents and Settings\All Users\Application Data\ShowSpecialDirectories\
    ShowSpecialDirectories\1.0.0.0
C:\Documents and Settings\Rod\Application Data\ShowSpecialDirectories\
    ShowSpecialDirectories\1.0.0.0
C:\Documents and Settings\Rod\Desktop
C:\Documents and Settings\Rod\My Documents
C:\Documents and Settings\Rod\My Documents\My Music
C:\Documents and Settings\Rod\My Documents\My Pictures
C:\Documents and Settings\Rod\Start Menu\Programs
C:\Documents and Settings\Rod\Local Settings\Temp
```

Summary

Visual Basic provides a native set of methods for reading and writing files, including `FreeFile`, `FileOpen`, `Input`, `LineInput`, `Print`, `Write`, and `FileClose`. It also provides method for working with the file system (such as `ChDir`, `MkDir`, `Kill`, and `RmDir`). If you have a lot of previous experience with Visual Basic, you may prefer these familiar methods.

The System.IO namespace offers many objects that provide even more powerful capabilities than Visual Basic's native methods. Classes such as `Directory`, `DirectoryInfo`, `File`, and `FileInfo` make it easy to create, examine, move, rename, and delete directories and files. The `File` class's methods make it particularly easy to read or write an entire file and to create streams attached to files for reading or writing.

The `FileSystemWatcher` class lets an application keep an eye on a file or directory and take action when it is changed. For example, a program can watch a spooling directory and take action when a new file appears in it.

The `Path` class provides miscellaneous support for working with paths. For example, it provides methods for examining a path's file name or extension.

The My.Computer.FileSystem namespace provides shortcuts to some of the more useful of the methods offered by the other file system classes. Its methods let you create, examine, and delete files and directories. The `SpecialDirectories` object also provides information about the locations of system directories.

There is considerable overlap among all of these tools, so you don't need to feel that you have to use them all. Take a good look so you know what's there, and then pick the tools that you find the most comfortable.

Many of the objects described in this chapter are in the System.IO or My namespaces. These namespaces are extremely useful when you need to examine and manipulate the file system. Chapter 28, "Useful Namespaces," describes some of the other useful namespaces defined by the .NET Framework. It provides a brief overview of some of the most important System namespaces and gives more detailed examples that demonstrate regular expressions, XML, cryptography, reflection, threading, and Direct3D.

Useful Namespaces

The .NET Framework is a library of classes, interfaces, and types that add extra power to Visual Studio .NET. These features go beyond what is normally provided by a programming language such as Visual Basic.

The .NET Framework is truly enormous. To make it more manageable, Microsoft has broken it into namespaces. The namespaces form a hierarchical catalog that groups related classes and functions in a meaningful way.

For example, the System namespace contains basic classes and methods that an application can use to perform common tasks. The System.Drawing namespace is the part of the System namespace that holds graphical tools. The System.Drawing.Design, System.Drawing.Drawing2D, System.Drawing.Imaging, System.Drawing.Printing, and System.Drawing.Text namespaces further subdivide System.Drawing into finer groupings.

Many of the Framework namespaces are essential for day-to-day programming. For example, many Visual Basic applications need to produce printouts, so they use the System.Drawing. Printing namespace. Different applications draw graphics or images on the screen, so they need to use other System.Drawing namespaces.

Because so much of the .NET Framework is used in everyday programming tasks, this book doesn't strongly differentiate between Visual Basic and .NET Framework functionality. Presumably, the book could have focused solely on the Visual Basic language and ignored the .NET Framework, but it would have been a much less useful book.

Although the book covers many useful .NET Framework features, there's a huge amount that it doesn't cover. Currently the .NET Framework defines more than 160 namespaces that define a huge number of classes, types, enumerated values, and other paraphernalia.

The following sections describe some of the highest-level and most useful namespaces provided by the .NET Framework.

High-Level Namespaces

The .NET Framework includes two root namespaces: Microsoft and System.

Your program may include references to many other namespaces. If you add references to development libraries, your program will have access to their namespaces. For example, you might have Amazon, Google, eBay, and other development toolkits installed and they come with their own namespaces. Later versions of Windows will also provide namespaces that you may want to reference.

Also note that the My namespace provides shortcuts that make common programming tasks easier. For more information on the My namespace, see the section "My" in Chapter 25, "Configuration and Resources," and Appendix P, "The My Namespace."

The Microsoft Namespace

The Microsoft root namespace contains Microsoft-specific items. In theory, any vendor can implement .NET languages that translate into Intermediate Language (IL) code. If you were to build such a language, the items in the Microsoft namespace would generally not apply to your language. Items in the System namespace described next would be as useful to users of your language as they are to programmers who use the Microsoft languages, but the items in the Microsoft namespace would probably not be as helpful.

The following table briefly describes the second-level namespaces contained in the Microsoft root namespace.

Namespace	Contains
Microsoft.Csharp	Items supporting compilation and code generation for C#.
Microsoft.JScript	Items supporting compilation and code generation for JScript.
Microsoft.VisualBasic	Items supporting compilation and code generation for Visual Basic. Some of the items in this namespace are useful to Visual Basic programmers, mostly for compatibility with previous versions of Visual Basic.
Microsoft.Vsa	Items supporting Visual Studio for Applications (VSA), which lets you including scripting in your application.
Microsoft.WindowsCE	Items supporting Pocket PC and Smartphone applications using the .NET Compact Framework.
Microsoft.Win32	Classes that handle operating system events and that manipulate the System Registry.

The System Namespace

The System namespace contains basic classes used to define fundamental data types. It also defines important event handlers, interfaces, and exceptions.

The following table briefly describes the second-level namespaces contained in the System root namespace.

Namespace	Contains
System.CodeDom	Classes for representing and manipulating source-code documents.
System.Collections	Interfaces and classes for defining various collection classes, lists, queues, hash tables, and dictionaries.
System.ComponentModel	Classes that control design-time and run-time behavior of components and controls. Defines several useful code attributes such as `Description`, `DefaultEvent`, `DefaultProperty`, and `DefaultValue`. Also defines some useful classes such as `ComponentResourceManager`.
System.Configuration	Classes and interfaces for working with configuration files.
System.Data	Mostly ADO.NET classes. Subnamespaces include features for specific kinds of databases and database technologies such as SQL Server, Oracle, OLE DB, and so forth.
System.Deployment	Classes that let you programmatically update ClickOnce deployments.
System.Diagnostics	Classes for working with system processes, performance counters, and event logs.
System.DirectoryServices	Classes for working with Active Directory.
System.Drawing	Classes for using GDI+ graphics routines to draw two-dimensional graphics, text, and images.
System.EnterpriseServices	Tools for working with COM+ and building enterprise applications.
System.Globalization	Classes that help with internationalization. Includes tools for customizing an application's language and resources, and for using localized formats such as date, currency, and number formats.
System.IO	Classes for reading and writing streams and files.
System.Management	Classes for system management and monitoring.
System.Messaging	Classes for working with message queues to send and receive messages across the network.
System.Net	Classes for working with network protocols.
System.Reflection	Classes for working with loaded types. A program can use these to learn about classes and their capabilities, and to invoke an object's methods.
System.Resources	Classes to create and manage culture-specific resources programmatically.

Table continued on following page

Namespace	Contains
System.Runtime	Classes for working with metadata for compilers, interop services (interoperating with unmanaged code), marshalling, remoting, and serialization.
System.Security	Classes for security and cryptography.
System.ServiceProcess	Classes that let you implement, install, and control Windows service processes.
System.Text	Classes representing various character encodings. Also contains the `StringBuilder` class, which lets you build large strings quickly, and classes for working with regular expressions.
System.Threading	Classes for multithreading.
System.Timers	Contains the `Timer` class.
System.Transactions	Classes for working with transactions involving multiple distributed components and multiphase notifications.
System.Web	Classes for Web programming and browser/server interactions.
System.Windows.Forms	Defines the Windows forms controls.
System.Xml	Classes that let you manipulate XML files.

Advanced Examples

Several chapters in this book have covered the many pieces of the .NET Framework namespaces in some detail. For example, Chapter 25, "Configuration and Resources," describes many of the most useful tools provided by the System.Globalization and System.Resources namespaces. Similarly, Chapters 19 through 23 explain many of the most useful drawing tools provided by the System.Drawing namespace.

Other parts of the .NET Framework namespaces are quite specialized, and you may never need to use their capabilities. Many developers can use fairly standard installation techniques, so they will never need to use the System.Deployment classes to programmatically update ClickOnce deployments.

A few namespaces bear some special mention here, however. They don't really fit into the rest of the book, but they are important enough that you may find a few examples helpful. The following sections give a few examples that use some of the more useful namespaces.

Regular Expressions

To most programmers, a *regular expression* is a series of symbols that represents a class of strings. A program can use regular expression tools to determine whether a string matches a regular expression or to extract pieces of a string that match an expression. For example, a program can use regular expressions to see if a string has the format of a valid phone number, Social Security number, ZIP code or other postal code, e-mail address, and so forth.

The following regular expression represents a 7- or 10-digit phone number in the United States:

```
^([2-9]{3}-)?[2-9]{3}-\d{4}$
```

The following table describes the pieces of this expression.

Subexpression	Meaning
^	(The caret symbol.) Matches the beginning of the string.
[2-9]	Matches the characters 2 through 9 (United States phone numbers cannot begin with 0 or 1).
{3}	Repeat the previous group ([2-9]) exactly three times.
-	Match a dash.
([2-9]{3}-)?	The parentheses group the items inside. The ? makes the expression match the previous item exactly zero or one times. Thus the subexpression ([2-9]{3}-)? matches three digits 2 through 9 followed by a dash, zero or one times.
[2-9]{3}-	Matches three digits 2 through 9 followed by a dash.
\d{4}	Matches any digit (0 through 9) exactly four times.
$	Matches the end of the string.

Taken together, this regular expression matches strings of the form NXX-XXXX and NXX-NXX-XXXX where N is a digit 2 through 9 and X is any digit.

A complete discussion of regular expressions is outside the scope of this book. Search the online help or Microsoft's Web site to learn about the rules for building regular expressions. The Web page msdn.microsoft.com/library/en-us/cpgenref/html/cpconregularexpressionslanguage elements.asp provides useful links to information about regular expression language elements. Another useful page is www.regexlib.com/RETester.aspx, which provides a regular expression tester and a library of useful regular expressions.

As you read the rest of this chapter and as you visit regular expression Web sites, be aware that there are a couple different types of regular expression languages and that they won't all work with every regular expression class.

The following code shows how a program can validate a text field against a regular expression. When the user changes the text in the txtTestExp control, its Changed event handler creates a new Regex object, passing its constructor the regular expression held in the txtRegExp text box. It then calls the Regex object's IsMatch method to see if the text matches the regular expression. If the text matches, the program sets the txtTestExp control's background color to white. If the text doesn't match the expression, the program makes the control's background yellow to indicate an error.

```
Private Sub txtTestExp_TextChanged(ByVal sender As System.Object, _
  ByVal e As System.EventArgs) Handles txtTestExp.TextChanged
    Dim reg_exp As New Regex(txtRegExp.Text)
    If reg_exp.IsMatch(txtTestExp.Text) Then
```

```
            txtTestExp.BackColor = Color.White
        Else
            txtTestExp.BackColor = Color.Yellow
        End If
    End Sub
```

The following example uses a `Regex` object's `Matches` method to retrieve a collection of `Match` objects that describe the places where a string matches a regular expression. It then loops through the collection, highlighting the matches in a Rich Text Box.

```
Private Sub btnGo_Click(ByVal sender As System.Object, _
 ByVal e As System.EventArgs) Handles btnGo.Click
    Dim reg_exp As New Regex(txtPattern.Text)
    Dim matches As MatchCollection
    matches = reg_exp.Matches(txtTestString.Text)

    rchResults.Text = txtTestString.Text
    For Each a_match As Match In matches
        rchResults.Select(a_match.Index, a_match.Length)
        rchResults.SelectionBackColor = Color.Black
        rchResults.SelectionColor = Color.White
    Next a_match
End Sub
```

Figure 28-1 shows the result. In this example, the regular expression is "`(in|or)`", so the program finds matches where the string contains "in" or "or."

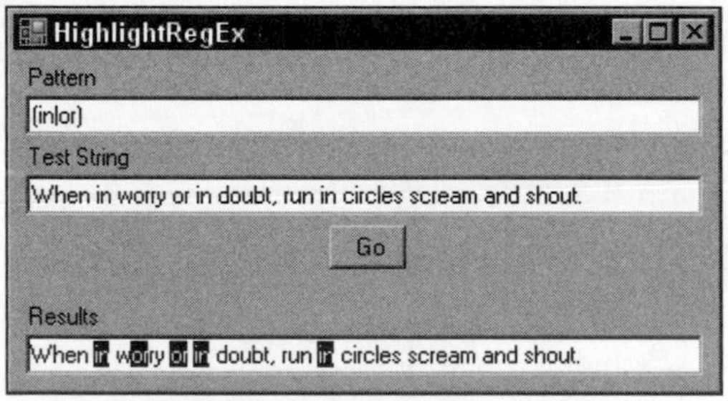

Figure 28-1: The `Regex` **object's** `Matches`
method returns a collection describing the
places where a string matches a regular
expression.

The following code uses a `Regex` object to make replacements in a string. It creates a `Regex` object, passing its constructor the `IgnoreCase` option to tell the object to ignore capitalization in the string. It then calls the object's Replace, passing it the string to modify and the pattern that it should use to make the replacement.

```
Dim reg_exp As New Regex(txtPattern.Text, RegexOptions.IgnoreCase)
lblResult.Text = reg_exp.Replace(Me.txtTestString.Text, txtReplacementPattern.Text)
```

Figure 28-2 shows an example that uses the regular expression "`[aeiou]`" to match vowels. It replaces the vowels with periods.

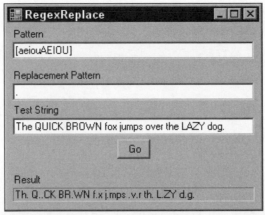

Figure 28-2: The `Regex` object's `Matches` method returns a collection describing the places where a string matches a regular expression.

The `Regex` class can perform much more complicated matches. For example, you can use it to find fields within each line in a multiline string and then build a string containing the fields reformatted or reordered. See the online help for more details.

XML

Extensible Markup Language (XML) is a simple language for storing data in a text format. It encloses data within tags that delimit the data. You can give those tags any names that you want. For example, the following text shows an XML file containing three Employee records.

```xml
<?xml version="1.0" encoding="utf-8" standalone="yes"?>
<Employees>
    <Employee>
        <FirstName>Albert</FirstName>
        <LastName>Anders</LastName>
        <EmployeeId>11111</EmployeeId>
    </Employee>
    <Employee>
        <FirstName>Betty</FirstName>
        <LastName>Beach</LastName>
        <EmployeeId>22222</EmployeeId>
    </Employee>
    <Employee>
        <FirstName>Chuck</FirstName>
        <LastName>Cinder</LastName>
        <EmployeeId>33333</EmployeeId>
    </Employee>
</Employees>
```

The System.Xml namespace contains classes for reading, writing, and manipulating XML data. Different classes let you process XML files in different ways. For example, the XmlDocument class lets you represent an XML document completely within memory. Using this class, you can perform complex manipulations of an XML file, adding and removing elements, searching for elements with particular attributes, and merging XML documents.

On the other hand, the XmlTextReader and XmlTextWriter classes let you read and write XML data in a fast, forward-only fashion. These classes can be more efficient than XmlDocument when you must quickly build or scan very large XML files that might not easily fit in memory all at once.

The following code shows one way a program can use the System.Xml namespace to generate the previous employee XML file. Note that Visual Basic programs do not initially contain a reference to the System.Xml namespace by default. To use the namespace, you must select the Project menu's Add Reference command and select the System.Xml.dll reference.

The code starts by creating an XmlTextWriter object. This class provides methods for efficiently writing items into of an XML file. The code sets the writer's Formatting and Indentation properties to make the object indent the resulting XML file nicely. If you don't set these properties, the file comes out all run together on a single line. That's fine for programs that process XML files but makes the file hard for humans to read.

The program calls the WriteStartDocument method to write the file's XML declaration, including the XML version, encoding, and standalone attribute. It calls WriteStartElement to write the starting <Employees> XML tag and then calls subroutine MakeEmployee to generate three Employee items. It calls the WriteEndElement method to write the </Employees> end tag, and calls WriteEndDocument to end the document. The program then closes the XmlTextWriter to close the file.

Subroutine MakeEmployee writes a starting <Employee> element into the file. It then uses the WriteStartElement, WriteString, and WriteEndElement methods to add the employee's FirstName, LastName, and EmployeeId elements to the document. The routine finishes by calling WriteEndElement to create the </Employee> end tag.

```
Private Sub btnGo_Click(ByVal sender As System.Object, _
  ByVal e As System.EventArgs) Handles btnGo.Click
    Dim xml_text_writer As _
        New XmlTextWriter("employees.xml", System.Text.Encoding.UTF8)

    ' Use indentation to make the result look nice.
    xml_text_writer.Formatting = Formatting.Indented
    xml_text_writer.Indentation = 4

    ' Write the XML declaration.
    xml_text_writer.WriteStartDocument(True)

    ' Start the Employees node.
    xml_text_writer.WriteStartElement("Employees")

    ' Write some Employee elements.
    MakeEmployee(xml_text_writer, "Albert", "Anders", 11111)
    MakeEmployee(xml_text_writer, "Betty", "Beach", 22222)
```

```
            MakeEmployee(xml_text_writer, "Chuck", "Cinder", 33333)

        ' End the Employees node.
        xml_text_writer.WriteEndElement()

        ' End the document.
        xml_text_writer.WriteEndDocument()

        ' Close the XmlTextWriter.
        xml_text_writer.Close()
    End Sub

    ' Add an Employee node to the document.
    Private Sub MakeEmployee(ByVal xml_text_writer As XmlTextWriter, _
     ByVal first_name As String, ByVal last_name As String, ByVal emp_id As Integer)
        ' Start the Employee element.
        xml_text_writer.WriteStartElement("Employee")

        ' Write the FirstName.
        xml_text_writer.WriteStartElement("FirstName")
        xml_text_writer.WriteString(first_name)
        xml_text_writer.WriteEndElement()

        ' Write the LastName.
        xml_text_writer.WriteStartElement("LastName")
        xml_text_writer.WriteString(last_name)
        xml_text_writer.WriteEndElement()

        ' Write the EmployeeId.
        xml_text_writer.WriteStartElement("EmployeeId")
        xml_text_writer.WriteString(emp_id.ToString)
        xml_text_writer.WriteEndElement()

        ' Close the Employee element.
        xml_text_writer.WriteEndElement()
    End Sub
```

Other classes within the System.Xml namespace let you load and manipulate XML data in memory, read XML data in a fast forward-only manner, and search XML documents for elements matching certain criteria. XML is quickly becoming a common language that allows unrelated applications to communicate with each other. Using the XML tools provided by the System.Xml namespace, your application can read, write, and manipulate XML data, too.

Cryptography

The System.Security namespace includes objects for performing various cryptographic operations. The four main scenarios supported by these objects include the following:

❑ *Secret-key encryption* — This technique encrypts data so you cannot read it unless you know the secret key. This is also called *symmetric cryptography*.

❑ *Public-key encryption* — This technique encrypts data using a public key that everyone knows. Only the person with a secret private key can read the data. This is useful when you want anyone to be able to send messages to you, but you should be able to read them. This is also called *asymmetric cryptography*.

747

❑ *Signing* — This technique signs data to guarantee that it really came from a specific party. For example, you can sign an executable program to prove that it's really your program and not a virus substituted by some hacker.

❑ *Hashing* — This technique maps a piece of data such as a document into a hash value in a way that guarantees that two different documents are unlikely to hash to the same value. If you know a document's hash value, you can later hash the document again and compare the values. If the calculated value matches the previously known value, it is very unlikely that anyone has modified the file since the first hashing.

The first example appearing later in this section encrypts and decrypts files. The basic idea is to create a CryptoStream object attached to a file stream opened for writing. As you write data into the CryptoStream, it encrypts or decrypts the data and sends the result to the output file stream.

While the classes provided by Visual Studio 2005 are easier to use than the routines contained in the underlying cryptography API, the details are still somewhat involved. To encrypt and decrypt files, you must first select an encryption algorithm. You need to pick a key size and block size that is supported by the corresponding encryption provider.

To use an encryption provider, you must pass it a key and initialization vector (IV). Each of these is a series of bytes that the encryption provider uses to initialize its internal state before it encrypts or decrypts files.

If you want to control the encryption with a textual password, you must convert it into a series of bytes that you can use for the key and initialization vector. You can do that with a PasswordDeriveBytes object, but that object also requires the name of the hashing algorithm that it should use to convert the password into the key and initialization vector bytes.

Working through the following example should make this less confusing. This example uses a triple DES encryption algorithm to encrypt and decrypt files. It uses the SHA384 hashing algorithm to convert a text password into key and initialization vector bytes.

Subroutine CryptFile encrypts or decrypts a file, saving the result in a new file. It takes as parameters a password string, the names of the input and output files, and a Boolean indicating whether it should perform encryption or decryption.

The routine starts by opening the input and output files. It then makes a TripleDESCryptoServiceProvider object to provide the encryption and decryption algorithms using triple DES.

Next, the program must find a key length that is supported by the encryption service provider. This code counts backward from 1,024 until it finds a value that the provider's ValidKeySize method approves. On my computer, the largest key size the provider supports is 128 bits.

The triple DES algorithm encrypts data in blocks. The program uses the provider's BlockSize property to see how big those blocks are. The program must generate an initialization vector that has this same size.

Next, the program calls the MakeKeyAndIV subroutine. This routine, which is described shortly, converts a text password into arrays of bytes for use as the key and initialization vector.

The program then makes an object to perform the encryption or decryption transformation, depending on whether the subroutine's encrypt parameter is `True` or `False`. The program uses the encryption provider's `CreateEncryptor` or `CreateDecryptor` method, passing it the key and initialization vector.

Now, the program makes a `CryptoStream` object attached to its output file stream. It passes the object's constructor and output file stream, the cryptographic transformation object, and a flag indicating that the program will write to the stream.

At this point, the program has set the stage and can finally begin processing data. It allocates a buffer to hold data and then enters a `Do` loop. In the loop, it reads data from the input file into the buffer. If it read no bytes, the program has reached the end of the input file, so it exits the loop. If it read some bytes, the program writes them into the `CryptoStream`. The `CryptoStream` uses its cryptographic transformation object to encrypt or decrypt the data and sends it on to its attached output file stream.

When it has finished processing the input file, the subroutine closes its streams.

Subroutine `MakeKeyAndIV` uses a text password to generate arrays of bytes to use as a key and initialization vector. It begins by creating a `PasswordDeriveBytes` object, passing its constructor the password text, the name of the hashing algorithm to use (SHA384), and the number of iterations the object should use to generate the key. The second parameter (which is set to `Nothing` in this example) is an array of bytes called a *salt*. This can be any array of bytes as long as it's the same when encrypting and decrypting the file. The salt can make it harder for an attacker to build a dictionary of key and initialization vector values for every possible password string.

Having built the `PasswordDeriveBytes` object, the subroutine calls its `GetBytes` method to get the proper number of bytes for the key and initialization vector.

```
' Encrypt or decrypt a file, saving the results
' in another file.
Private Sub CryptFile(ByVal password As String, ByVal in_file As String, _
 ByVal out_file As String, ByVal encrypt As Boolean)
    ' Create input and output file streams.
    Dim in_stream As New FileStream(in_file, FileMode.Open, FileAccess.Read)
    Dim out_stream As New FileStream(out_file, FileMode.Create, FileAccess.Write)

    ' Make a triple DES service provider.
    Dim des_provider As New TripleDESCryptoServiceProvider()

    ' Find a valid key size for this provider.
    Dim key_size_bits As Integer = 0
    For i As Integer = 1024 To 1 Step -1
        If des_provider.ValidKeySize(i) Then
            key_size_bits = i
            Exit For
        End If
    Next i
    Debug.Assert(key_size_bits > 0)

    ' Get the block size for this provider.
    Dim block_size_bits As Integer = des_provider.BlockSize

    ' Generate the key and initialization vector.
```

```
        Dim key As Byte() = Nothing
        Dim iv As Byte() = Nothing
        MakeKeyAndIV(password, key_size_bits, block_size_bits, key, iv)

        ' Make the encryptor or decryptor.
        Dim crypto_transform As ICryptoTransform
        If encrypt Then
            crypto_transform = des_provider.CreateEncryptor(key, iv)
        Else
            crypto_transform = des_provider.CreateDecryptor(key, iv)
        End If

        ' Attach a crypto stream to the output stream.
        Dim crypto_stream As New CryptoStream(out_stream, crypto_transform, _
            CryptoStreamMode.Write)

        ' Encrypt or decrypt the file.
        Const BLOCK_SIZE As Integer = 1024
        Dim buffer(BLOCK_SIZE) As Byte
        Dim bytes_read As Integer
        Do
            ' Read some bytes.
            bytes_read = in_stream.Read(buffer, 0, BLOCK_SIZE)
            If bytes_read = 0 Then Exit Do

            ' Write the bytes into the CryptoStream.
            crypto_stream.Write(buffer, 0, bytes_read)
        Loop

        ' Close the streams.
        crypto_stream.Close()
        in_stream.Close()
        out_stream.Close()
    End Sub

    ' Use the password to generate key bytes.
    Private Sub MakeKeyAndIV(ByVal password As String, _
     ByVal key_size_bits As Integer, ByVal block_size_bits As Integer, _
     ByRef key As Byte(), ByRef iv As Byte())
        Dim password_derive_bytes As New PasswordDeriveBytes( _
            txtPassword.Text, Nothing, "SHA384", 1000)

        key = password_derive_bytes.GetBytes(key_size_bits \ 8)
        iv = password_derive_bytes.GetBytes(block_size_bits \ 8)
    End Sub
```

The following code uses the `CryptFile` subroutine to encrypt and then decrypt a file. First it calls `CryptFile`, passing it a password, input and output file names, and the value `True` to indicate that the routine should encrypt the file. Next, the code calls `CryptFile` again, this time to decrypt the encrypted file.

```
' Encrypt the file.
CryptFile(txtPassword.Text, txtPlaintextFile.Text, txtCyphertextFile.Text, True)

' Decrypt the file.
CryptFile(txtPassword.Text, txtCyphertextFile.Text, txtDecypheredFile.Text, False)
```

See the online help for information about the other main cryptographic operations (secret-key encryption, public-key encryption, signing, and hashing). Other books may also provide additional insights into cryptography. For example, see *Applied Cryptography: Protocols, Algorithms, and Source Code in C, Second Edition* by Bruce Schneier (Hoboken, NJ: Wiley, 1996).

Reflection

Reflection lets a program learn about itself and other programming entities. It includes objects that tell the program about assemblies, modules, and types.

For example, the following code examines the program's form and displays a list of its properties, their types, and their values. The program starts by formatting the `ListView` control named `lvwProperties`. Next, the program defines an array of `PropertyInfo` objects named `properties_info`. It uses `GetType` to get type information about the `Form1` class and then uses the type's `GetProperties` method to get information about the properties. The program then loops through the `PropertyInfo` objects.

If the object's `GetIndexParameters` array contains no entries, the property is not an array. In that case, the program uses the `PropertyInfo` object's `GetValue` method to get the property's value. The code then displays the property's name, type, and value.

If the `PropertyInfo` object's `GetIndexParameters` array contains entries, the property is an array. In that case, the program displays the property's name, type, and the string "`<array>`."

The subroutine finishes by sizing `ListView` control's columns and then making the form fit the columns.

The helper subroutine `ListViewMakeRow` adds a row of values to the `ListView` control. It adds a new item to the control and then adds subitems to the item. The item appears in the control's first column and the subitems appear in the other columns.

```
Private Sub Form1_Load(ByVal sender As System.Object, _
  ByVal e As System.EventArgs) Handles MyBase.Load
    ' Make column headers.
    lvwProperties.View = View.Details
    lvwProperties.Columns.Clear()
    lvwProperties.Columns.Add("Property", 10, _
        HorizontalAlignment.Left)
    lvwProperties.Columns.Add("Type", 10, _
        HorizontalAlignment.Left)
    lvwProperties.Columns.Add("Value", 10, _
        HorizontalAlignment.Left)

    ' List the properties.
    Dim property_value As Object
    Dim properties_info As PropertyInfo() = _
```

```
                GetType(Form1).GetProperties()
        lvwProperties.Items.Clear()
        For i As Integer = 0 To properties_info.Length - 1
            With properties_info(i)
                If .GetIndexParameters().Length = 0 Then
                    property_value = .GetValue(Me, Nothing)
                    If property_value Is Nothing Then
                        ListViewMakeRow(lvwProperties, _
                            .Name, _
                            .PropertyType.ToString, _
                            "<Nothing>")
                    Else
                        ListViewMakeRow(lvwProperties, _
                            .Name, _
                            .PropertyType.ToString, _
                            property_value.ToString)
                    End If
                Else
                    ListViewMakeRow(lvwProperties, _
                        .Name, _
                        .PropertyType.ToString, _
                        "<array>")
                End If
            End With
        Next i

        ' Size the columns to fit the data.
        lvwProperties.Columns(0).Width = -2
        lvwProperties.Columns(1).Width = -2
        lvwProperties.Columns(2).Width = -2

        ' Size the form.
        Dim new_wid As Integer = 30
        For i As Integer = 0 To lvwProperties.Columns.Count - 1
            new_wid += lvwProperties.Columns(i).Width
        Next i
        Me.Size = New Size(new_wid, Me.Size.Height)
    End Sub

    ' Make a ListView row.
    Private Sub ListViewMakeRow(ByVal lvw As ListView, _
     ByVal item_title As String, ByVal ParamArray subitem_titles() As String)
        ' Make the item.
        Dim new_item As ListViewItem = lvw.Items.Add(item_title)

        ' Make the subitems.
        For i As Integer = subitem_titles.GetLowerBound(0) To _
            subitem_titles.GetUpperBound(0)
            new_item.SubItems.Add(subitem_titles(i))
        Next i
    End Sub
```

Figure 28-3 shows this code in action. It displays its form's properties, their types, and their values.

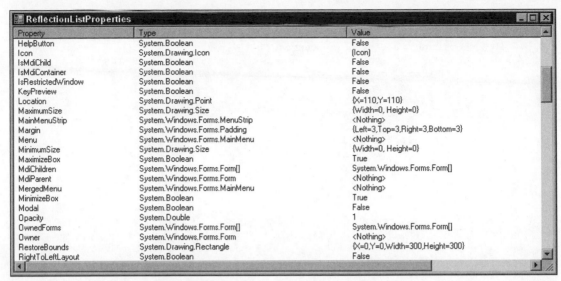

Figure 28-3: This program uses reflection to learn about its form's properties.

Using reflection to learn about your application is interesting, but not always necessary. After all, if you build an object, you probably know what its properties are.

However, reflection can also tell you a lot about other applications. The following example shows how a program can learn about another application. This program reads the assembly information in a file and lists the embedded resources that it contains. The user can then select a resource view it.

The user enters the name of the assembly to load in the `txtFile` text box. For example, this can be the name of a .NET executable.

When the user clicks the List button, the `btnList_Click` event handler uses the `Assembly` class's shared `LoadFile` method to load an `Assembly` object representing the indicated assembly. It then loops through the array of strings returned by the `Assembly` object's `GetManifestResourceNames` method adding the resource file names to the `ListBox` named `lstResourceFiles`.

When the user selects a resource file from the list, the `lstResourceFiles_SelectedIndexChanged` event handler displays a list of resources in the file. It uses the `Assembly` object's `GetManifestResourceStream` method to get a stream for the resources. It uses the stream to make a `ResourceReader` object and then enumerates the items found by the `ResourceReader`. It saves each object in a new `ResourceInfo` object (this class is descriebd shortly) and adds it to the `lstResources` list.

When the user selects a resource from `lstResources`, its `SelectedIndexChanged` event handler retrieves the selected `ResourceInfo` object, converts its `Value` property into an appropriate data type, and displays the result.The `ResourceInfo` class stores Key and Value information for a resource enumerated by a `ResourceReader`'s enumerator. It provides an oveloaded `ToString` that the `lstResources` list uses to represent the items.

```
Private m_TargetAssembly As Assembly

' List the target assembly's resources.
Private Sub btnList_Click(ByVal sender As System.Object, _
 ByVal e As System.EventArgs) Handles btnList.Click
    ' Get the target assembly.
    m_TargetAssembly = Assembly.LoadFile(txtFile.Text)

    ' List the target's manifest resource names.
    lstResourceFiles.Items.Clear()
    For Each str As String In m_TargetAssembly.GetManifestResourceNames()
        lstResourceFiles.Items.Add(str)
    Next str
End Sub

' List this file's resources.
Private Sub lstResourceFiles_SelectedIndexChanged(ByVal sender As System.Object, _
 ByVal e As System.EventArgs) Handles lstResourceFiles.SelectedIndexChanged
    lstResources.Items.Clear()

    Dim resource_reader As ResourceReader
    resource_reader = New ResourceReader( _
        m_TargetAssembly.GetManifestResourceStream(lstResourceFiles.Text))
    Dim dict_enumerator As IDictionaryEnumerator = resource_reader.GetEnumerator()
    While dict_enumerator.MoveNext()
        lstResources.Items.Add(New ResourceInfo( _
            dict_enumerator.Key, _
            dict_enumerator.Value))
    End While
    resource_reader.Close()
End Sub

' Display the selected resource.
Private Sub lstResources_SelectedIndexChanged(ByVal sender As System.Object, _
 ByVal e As System.EventArgs) Handles lstResources.SelectedIndexChanged
    lblString.Text = ""
    picImage.Image = Nothing

    Dim resource_info As ResourceInfo = _
        DirectCast(lstResources.SelectedItem, ResourceInfo)
    Select Case resource_info.Value.GetType.Name
        Case "Bitmap"
            picImage.Image = CType(resource_info.Value, Bitmap)
            lblString.Text = ""
        Case "String"
            picImage.Image = Nothing
            lblString.Text = CType(resource_info.Value, String)
    End Select
End Sub

Private Class ResourceInfo
    Public Key As Object
    Public Value As Object
    Public Sub New(ByVal new_key As Object, ByVal new_value As Object)
        Key = new_key
```

```
        Value = new_value
    End Sub
    Public Overrides Function ToString() As String
        Return Key.ToString & " (" & Value.ToString & ")"
    End Function
End Class
```

Figure 28-4 shows the result.

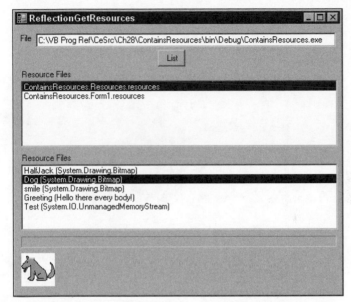

Figure 28-4: This application uses reflection to display another application's resources.

This is admittedly a fairly complex example, but it performs the fairly remarkable feat of pulling resources out of another compile application.

Reflection can provide a lot of information about applications, modules, types, methods, properties, events, parameters, and so forth. It lets a program discover and invoke methods at run time and build types at run time.

An application also uses reflection indirectly when it performs such actions as serialization, which uses reflection to learn how to serialize and deserialize objects.

Reflection is a very advanced and somewhat arcane topic, but it is extremely powerful.

> *Note that the behavior of some of these reflection routines changed fairly late in the Visual Basic 2005 beta process, so it's possible they will change again before the final release. Check the book's Web site* www.vb-helper.com/vb_prog_ref.htm *for updates.*

Direct3D

DirectX is a set of APIs that provide tools for high-performance multimedia applications. These APIs include tools for working with audio, music, input devices (such as joysticks and force-feedback devices), and other multimedia objects.

Direct3D is the three-dimensional drawing component provided by DirectX. Figure 28-5 shows a simple Direct3D application that displays an octahedron rotating around a vertical axis. Each of the octahedron's faces has a different color so that it's easy to see it rotating.

Figure 28-5: This Direct3D application displays a rotating octahedron.

Before an application can use the DirectX and Direct3D libraries, you must perform a few preliminary tasks. First, go to Microsoft's download Web site, `www.microsoft.com/downloads`, and download the latest DirectX development kit. As of this writing, the most recent version is DirectX 9.0b. After you download the toolkit, install it.

Next, start a new application. Use the Project menu's Add Reference command to add references to the Microsoft.DirectX and Microsoft.DirectX.Direct3D libraries.

The following code shows how the application works. The `OctahedronForm` class is a form that displays the Direct3D animation. The class begins by defining private constants giving the number of triangles it displays (8 triangles in an octahedron) and the number of vertices it needs to define the triangles (3 * 8 = 24). It also defines private variables to hold references to a `Device`, a `VertexBuffer`, and an array of `PresentParameters` items.

When the form loads, its `Load` event handler calls subroutine `InitializeGraphics` to prepare the Direct3D subsystem. If that succeeds, the program displays the form. It then enters a *rendering loop*. This loop calls the form's `Render` method to display an image and then calls `Application.DoEvents` to let the system respond to Windows events. For example, this lets the program respond if the user closes, resizes, or moves the form. The rendering loop runs as long as the form's Created property is True, indicating that the form has not been closed.

Subroutine InitializeGraphics sets some presentation parameters and creates a new Device object to represent the device on which the program will draw. The Windowed parameter means the device will sit within the form's window. The SoftwareVertexProcessing flag in the device's constructor means Direct3D should use software to process the data, rather than relying on special graphics hardware. Graphics hardware would produce a faster program, but the code would need to perform extensive checks to verify that the system actually had the necessary hardware.

The subroutine adds an event handler for the device's DeviceReset event. This event occurs when the device is reset, which happens if the form's window is recreated when it is maximized or restored. The subroutine calls subroutine CreateVertexBuffer to create the vertex buffer. It finishes by calling OnResetDevice to prepare the device for use.

Subroutine CreateVertexBuffer creates a buffer to hold data defining the octahedron's vertices. It passes the VertexBuffer class's constructor parameters giving the type of vertex (PositionColored means each entry gives the vertex's position and color), the number of vertices, the device, a usage flag (0 means no flags), the vertex format (position colored), and the memory pool that should contain the buffer memory.

The routine then adds an event handler for the buffer object's Created event. This event occurs when the buffer is recreated. That happens when the device is reset. Finally, the routine calls OnCreateVertexBuffer to initialize the vertex data.

When the device is reset, subroutine OnResetDevice prepares the device for use. In this example, the event handler disables Direct3D lighting. Lighting would allow the program to illuminate the scene with various light sources, but this example explicitly gives the colors of all of its vertices, so light sources are unnecessary.

When the vertex buffer is created, subroutine OnCreateVertexBuffer initializes it. The routine calls the buffer's Lock method to lock the vertex memory and retrieve an array containing a usable copy of the vetex data. The routine calls subroutine MakeTriangle eight times to initialize the vertices for the octahedron's eight faces. Then it calls the buffer's Unlock method to unlock the data.

Subroutine MakeTriangle simply initializes a triangle's vertices.

Subroutine Render draws the scene onto the graphics device. First, it clears the device's background. It calls the device's BeginScene method to tell Direct3D that it is about to draw objects. Next, the code calls subroutine SetupMatrices to build transformation matrices that define how the scene should be drawn. It sets the device's data source to the vertex buffer, tells the device the buffer's format, and calls subroutine DrawPrimatives to draw the triangles stored in the buffer. The routine finishes by calling the device's EndScene method to tell Direct3D that it is finished drawing and by calling its Present method to display the result.

Subroutine SetupMatrix defines the matrices that Direct3D uses to map three-dimensional objects onto the two-dimensional screen. The routine defines three matrices. The "world" matrix tells Direct3D how to transform the objects' coordinates before drawing. This could be an identity matrix (one that leaves the data unchanged) if you don't need to transform the data. In this example, this matrix rotates the points around the vertical axis. The code calculates the angle of rotation, so the data rotates around the axis completely every two seconds.

The second "view" matrix tells Direct3D how the program should view the data. You can think of this as the camera position. You can define this matrix by specifying the location where the viewer is standing, the direction the viewer is looking, and an "up" direction. For example, imagine a camera hanging from a boom, pointed toward some center of interest. The "up" direction tells which way the camera is rotated: right side up, upside down, sideways, and so forth. In this example, the camera is at position (0, 3, −10) looking toward the origin (0, 0, 0), and the "up" direction is in the normal up direction. In the Direct3D coordinate system, that's the direction of the positive Y axis.

The third matrix is a projection matrix that tells Direct3D how to project the three-dimensional data into two-dimensions. This example uses a perspective projection.

```vb
Imports Microsoft.DirectX
Imports Microsoft.DirectX.Direct3D

Public Class OctahedronForm
    Private Const NUM_TRIANGLES As Integer = 8
    Private Const NUM_POINTS As Integer = 3 * NUM_TRIANGLES

    Private m_Device As Device = Nothing
    Private m_VertexBuffer As VertexBuffer = Nothing
    Private m_PresentParams As New PresentParameters()

    ' Get started and enter the rendering loop.
    Private Sub OctahedronForm_Load(ByVal sender As System.Object, _
     ByVal e As System.EventArgs) Handles MyBase.Load
        ' Make a new form.
        'Dim frm As New OctahedronForm()

        ' Initialize Direct3D.
        If Not InitializeGraphics() Then
            MessageBox.Show("Error initializing Direct3D.")
            Return
        End If
        Show()

        ' Enter the rendering loop.
        While Created
            Render()
            Application.DoEvents()
        End While
    End Sub

    ' Initialize Direct3D.
    Public Function InitializeGraphics() As Boolean
        Try
            ' Initialize presentation parameters.
            m_PresentParams.Windowed = True
            m_PresentParams.SwapEffect = SwapEffect.Discard

            ' Make the device.
```

```vb
            m_Device = New Device(0, DeviceType.Hardware, _
                Me, CreateFlags.SoftwareVertexProcessing, _
                m_PresentParams)

            ' Add an event handler for DeviceReset.
            ' This event is called when the device is reset
            ' (you probably guessed that). That happens when
            ' the form is recreated when it is maximized
            ' or restored.
            AddHandler m_Device.DeviceReset, _
                AddressOf Me.OnResetDevice

            ' Call CreateVertexBuffer and OnResetDevice.
            Me.CreateVertexBuffer()
            Me.OnResetDevice(m_Device, Nothing)
            Return True
        Catch e As DirectXException
            Return False
        End Try
    End Function

' Create a vetex buffer for the device.
Public Sub CreateVertexBuffer()
    ' Create a vertex buffer.
    Dim dev As Device = CType(sender, Device)
    m_VertexBuffer = New VertexBuffer( _
        GetType(CustomVertex.PositionColored), _
        NUM_POINTS, m_Device, 0, CustomVertex.PositionColored.Format, _
        Pool.Default)

    ' Add an event handler for m_VertexBuffer.Created.
    ' This event occurs when the device is recreated
    ' and the vertex buffer is reinitialized.
    AddHandler m_VertexBuffer.Created, _
        AddressOf Me.OnCreateVertexBuffer

    ' Call m_VertexBuffer.Created to initialize
    ' the vertex data.
    Me.OnCreateVertexBuffer(m_VertexBuffer, Nothing)
End Sub

' Reset the device.
Public Sub OnResetDevice(ByVal sender As Object, ByVal e As EventArgs)
    ' Turn off D3D lighting because
    ' we set the vertex colors explicitly.
    Dim dev As Device = CType(sender, Device)
    dev.RenderState.Lighting = False
End Sub

' Define in the vertics.
Public Sub OnCreateVertexBuffer(ByVal sender As Object, ByVal e As EventArgs)
    Dim vb As VertexBuffer = CType(sender, VertexBuffer)

    ' Lock the vertex buffer.
    ' Lock returns an array of positionColored objects.
```

```
        Dim vertices As CustomVertex.PositionColored() = _
            CType(vb.Lock(0, 0), _
                CustomVertex.PositionColored())
        Dim start_index As Integer = 0

        Const WID As Single = 2
        MakeTriangle(vertices, start_index, Color.FromArgb(255, &HFF, 0, 0), _
            0, WID, 0, _
            0, 0, WID, _
            WID, 0, 0)
        ...
        MakeTriangle(vertices, start_index, Color.FromArgb(255, 0, 0, &H60), _
            0, -WID, 0, _
            0, 0, WID, _
            -WID, 0, 0)

        vb.Unlock()
    End Sub

    Private Sub MakeTriangle( _
        ByVal vertices As CustomVertex.PositionColored(), _
        ByRef start_index As Integer, ByVal clr As Color, _
        ByVal x1 As Single, ByVal y1 As Single, ByVal z1 As Single, _
        ByVal x2 As Single, ByVal y2 As Single, ByVal z2 As Single, _
        ByVal x3 As Single, ByVal y3 As Single, ByVal z3 As Single)

        With vertices(start_index)
            .X = x1
            .Y = y1
            .Z = z1
            .Color = clr.ToArgb()
        End With
        start_index += 1

        With vertices(start_index)
            .X = x2
            .Y = y2
            .Z = z2
            .Color = clr.ToArgb()
        End With
        start_index += 1

        With vertices(start_index)
            .X = x3
            .Y = y3
            .Z = z3
            .Color = clr.ToArgb()
        End With
        start_index += 1
    End Sub

    ' Render the scene.
    Private Sub Render()
        ' Do nothing if the device has not been created yet.
```

```
            If m_Device Is Nothing Then Return

        ' Clear the back buffer.
        m_Device.Clear(ClearFlags.Target, Color.White, 1, 0)

        ' Begin the scene.
        m_Device.BeginScene()

        ' Setup the world, view, and projection matrices.
        SetupMatrices()

        ' Set the device's data stream source
        ' (the vertex buffer).
        m_Device.SetStreamSource(0, m_VertexBuffer, 0)

        ' Tell the device the format of the vertices.
        m_Device.VertexFormat = CustomVertex.PositionColored.Format

        ' Draw the primitives in the data stream.
        m_Device.DrawPrimitives(PrimitiveType.TriangleList, 0, NUM_TRIANGLES)

        ' End the scene.
        m_Device.EndScene()

        ' Display the result.
        m_Device.Present()
End Sub

' Setup the world, view, and projection matrices.
Private Sub SetupMatrices()
    ' World Matrix:
    ' Rotate the object around the Y axis by
    ' 2 * Pi radians per 2000 ticks (2 seconds).
    Const TICKS_PER_REV As Integer = 2000
    Dim ms_rotated As Integer = Environment.TickCount Mod TICKS_PER_REV
    Dim angle As Double = ms_rotated * (2 * Math.PI) / TICKS_PER_REV
    m_Device.Transform.World = Matrix.RotationY(CSng(angle))

    ' View Matrix:
    ' This is defined by giving:
    '       An eye point            (0, 3, -10)
    '       A point to look at      (0, 0, 0)
    '       An "up" direction       <0, 1, 0>
    m_Device.Transform.View = Matrix.LookAtLH( _
        New Vector3(0, 3, -10), _
        New Vector3(0, 0, 0), _
        New Vector3(0, 1, 0))

    ' Projection Matrix:
    ' Perspective transformation defined by:
    '       Field of view           Pi / 4
    '       Aspect ratio            1
    '       Near clipping plane     Z = 1
    '       Far clipping plane      Z = 100
```

```
        m_Device.Transform.Projection = _
            Matrix.PerspectiveFovLH(Math.PI / 4, 1, 1, 100)
    End Sub
End Class
```

Setting all this up is a lot of work, but once it is running, it's not too hard to make changes. You can add, remove, or modify the vertex data. You can also change the view matrix to look at the data from different positions.

Direct3D is just one part of DirectX, and even that part is too complicated to describe completely here. For more information, see the online help, the examples, and the tutorials that come with the development kit. For more information about three-dimensional graphics in general, transformations, and the matrices that define transformations, you can also see a more theoretical three-dimensional graphics book such as *3D Computer Graphics*, Third Edition by Allan H. Watt (Boston: Addison Wesley, 2000). My book *Visual Basic Graphics Programming: Hands-On Applications and Advanced Color Development*, Second Edition (Hoboken, NJ: John Wiley & Sons, 1999) also covers three-dimensional graphics in addition to many other graphics topics. Unfortunately the examples use Visual Basic 6 code (although perhaps there will be a Visual Basic .NET edition at some point).

Summary

The .NET Framework defines more than 160 namespaces, and this chapter describes only a few. It provides a brief overview of some of the most important System namespaces and gives more detailed examples that demonstrate regular expressions, XML, cryptography, reflection, and Direct3D.

Even in these somewhat specialized areas, the examples can cover only a tiny fraction of the capabilities of the namespaces. However, the examples should give you an idea of the types of features that these namespaces can add to your application. If you need to do something similar, they will hopefully inspire you to do more in-depth research so that you can take full advantage of these powerful tools.

The chapters in this book cover a wide variety of Visual Basic programming topics. In the first part of the book, Chapters 1 through 13 explain basic topics of Visual Basic programming (such as the language itself, using standard controls, and draw and drop). In the second part of the book, Chapters 14 through 18 describe object-oriented concepts (such as class and structure declaration, namespaces, and generics). In the third part of the book, Chapters 19 through 24 cover graphical topics (such as how to draw shapes and text, image manipulation, printing, and report generation). In the fourth and final part of the book, Chapters 25 through 28 explain ways a program can interact with its environment by using such techniques as configuration files, the Registry, streams, and file system objects.

The rest of this book contains appendices that provide a categorized reference for Visual Basic .NET. You can use them to quickly review the syntax of a particular command, select from among several overloaded versions of a routine, or refresh your memory of what a particular class can do.

Useful Control Properties, Methods, and Events

A control interacts with a program or the user through properties, methods, and events. While each type of control provides different features, they are all derived from the Control class. This class provides many useful properties, methods, and events that other controls inherit, if they don't take special action to override them. The following sections describe some of the most useful of these inherited features.

Properties

The following table lists properties implemented by the Control class. All controls that inherit from this class inherit these properties unless they override the Control class's behavior.

Property	Purpose
AllowDrop	Determines whether the control allows drag and drop.
Anchor	Determines which of the control's edges are anchored to the edges of the control's container.
AutoSize	Determines whether the control automatically resizes to fit its contents.
BackColor	Determines the control's background color.
BackgroundImage	Determines the control's background image.
BackgroundImageLayout	Determines how the control's background image is used to fill the control. This can be Center, None, Tile, Stretch, and Zoom.

Table continued on following page

Property	Purpose
Bottom	Returns the distance between the top edge of the control's container and the bottom edge of the control. This is read-only. Modify the Top and Height properties to change this value.
Bounds	Determines the control's size and location, including nonclient areas.
CanFocus	Determines whether the control can receive the input focus. See also the Focus method.
CanSelect	Determines whether the control can select. For example, a TextBox can select some or all of its text. See also the Select method.
Capture	Determines whether the control has captured the mouse.
CausesValidation	Determines whether the control makes other controls validate when it receives the focus.
ClientRectangle	This Rectangle structure represents the control's client area.
ClientSize	This Size structure represents the control's height and width.
ContainsFocus	Indicates whether the control or one of its child controls has the input focus. This is read-only.
ContextMenu	Determines the context menu associated with the control.
ContextMenuStrip	Determines the context menu strip associated with the control.
Controls	This collection contains references to the controls contained within this control.
Cursor	Determines the cursor that the control displays when the mouse is over it.
DeteBindings	Gets the control's DataBindings, used to bind the control to a data source.
DefaultBackColor	Returns the control's default background color.
DefaultFont	Returns the control's default font.
DefaultForeColor	Returns the control's default foreground color.
DisplayRectangle	Returns a Rectangle structure giving the control's display area. Figure A-1 shows two GroupBoxes containing two Labels each. The Labels in the left GroupBox show the GroupBox's ClientRectangle and DisplayRectangles.
Dock	Determines the edge of the control's parent to which the control is docked.
Enabled	Determines whether the control will interact with the user.
Focused	Indicates whether the control has the input focus. This is read-only.

Property	Purpose
Font	Determines the control's font.
ForeColor	Determines the control's foreground color.
Handle	Returns the control's window handle. This is read-only.
HasChildren	Indicates whether the control holds any child controls. This is read-only. Also see the Controls property.
Height	Determines the control's height.
InvokeRequired	Returns True if the calling code is running on a thread different from the control's thread and therefore must use an invoke method to interact with the control.
Left	Determines the X coordinate of the control's left edge.
Location	This Point structure determines the position of the control's upper-left corner.
Margin	Determines the spacing between this control and another control's margin within an arranging container.
MaximumSize	Determines the control's largest allowed size.
MinimumSize	Determines the control's smallest allowed size.
ModifierKeys	Indicates what modifier keys (Shift, Ctrl, and Alt) are pressed. This is read-only.
MouseButtons	Indicates what mouse buttons (Left, Right, Middle, None) are pressed. This is read-only.
MousePosition	Returns a Point structure giving the mouse's current position in screen coordinates (the point (0, 0) is in the screen's upper-left corner). This is read-only.
Name	Determines the control's name.
Padding	Determines the spacing of the control's contents.
Parent	Determines the parent containing the control.
PreferredSize	Returns a size that is big enough to hold the control's contents.
Region	Determines the control's window region. This is the area in which the control may draw.
Right	Returns the distance between the left edge of the control's container and the right edge of the control. This is read-only. Modify the Left and Width properties to change this value.
Size	This Size structure determines the control's size including client and nonclient areas.

Table continued on following page

Property	Purpose
TabIndex	Determines the control's position in its container's tab order. If more than one control has the same TabIndex, they are traversed front-to-back using the stacking order.
TabStop	Determines whether the user can tab to the control.
Tag	This property can hold an object that you want to associate with the control.
Text	Determines the control's text.
Top	Determines the Y coordinate of the control's top edge.
TopLevelControl	Returns the control's top-level ancestor. Usually that is the outermost Form containing the control. This is read-only.
Visible	Determines whether the control is visible.
Width	Determines the control's width.

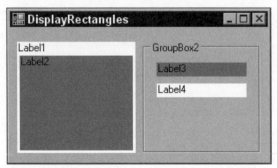

Figure A-1: The DisplayRectangle property gives the area in which you should normally place items within a control.

Methods

The following table lists useful methods implemented by the Control class. All controls that inherit from this class inherit these properties unless they override the Control class's behavior.

Method	Purpose
Sub BringToFront()	Brings the control to the front of the stacking order.
Function Contains(ByVal child As Control) As Boolean	Returns True if the control child is contained by this control.

Method	Purpose
`Function CreateGraphics() As Graphic`	Creates a `Graphic` object that you can use to draw on the control's surface.
`Function DoDragDrop(ByVal dragging_object As Object, ByVal allowed_effects As DragDropEffects)`	Starts a drag-and-drop operation.
`Sub DrawToBitmap(ByVal bm As Bitmap, ByVal rect As Rectangle)`	Draws an image of the control including an contained controls onto the `Bitmap` in the indicate `Rectangle`.
`Function FindForm() As Form`	Returns the `Form` that contains this control.
`Function Focus() As Boolean`	Gives the control the input focus.
`Function GetChildAtPoint(ByVal pt As Point) As Control`	Returns the control's child that contains the indicated point. If more than one control contains the point, the method returns the control that is higher in the stacking order.
`Function GetNextControl(ByVal ctl As Control, ByVal next As Boolean) As Control`	If next is `True`, returns the next control in the tab order of this control's children after control `ctl`. If next is `False`, returns the previous control in the tab order. Set `ctl = Nothing` to start from the start/end of the tab order. Returns `Nothing` when you reach the start/end.
`Function GetPreferredSize(ByVal proposed_size) As Size`	Returns a size that is big enough to hold the control's contents.
`Function GetType() As Type`	Returns a `Type` object representing the control's class. You can use this object to get information about the class.
`Sub Hide()`	Hides the control by setting its `Visible` property to `False`.
`Sub Invalidate()`	Invalidates some or all of the control and sends it a `Paint` event so that it redraws itself.
`Sub Invoke(ByVal delegate As Delegate)`	Invokes a delegate on the thread that owns the control.
`Function PointToClient(ByVal screen_point As Point) As Point`	Converts a `Point` in screen coordinates into the control's coordinate system.
`Function PointToScreen(ByVal control_point As Point) As Point`	Converts a `Point` in control coordinates into the screen coordinate system.
`Function RectangleToClient(ByVal screen_rect As Rectangle) As Rectangle`	Converts a `Rectangle` in screen coordinates into the control's coordinate system.

Table continued on following page

Method	Purpose
`Function RectangleToScreen(ByVal control_rect As Rectangle) As Rectangle`	Converts a `Rectangle` in control coordinates into the screen coordinate system.
`Sub Refresh()`	Invalidates the control's client area, so the control redraws itself and its child controls.
`Sub ResetBackColor()`	Resets the control's background color to its default value.
`Sub ResetCursor()`	Resets the control's cursor to its default value.
`Sub ResetFont()`	Resets the control's font to its default value.
`Sub ResetForeColor()`	Resets the control's foreground color to its default value.
`Sub ResetText()`	Resets the control's text to its default value.
`Sub Scale(ByVal scale_factor As Single)`	Scales the control and any contained controls by multiplying the `Left`, `Top`, `Width`, and `Height` properties by `scale_factor`.
`Sub Select()`	Moves the input focus to the control. Some controls have overloaded versions.
`Function SelectNextControl(ByVal ctl As Control, ByVal forward As Boolean, ByVal tab_stop_only As Boolean, ByVal include_nested As Boolean, ByVal wrap As Boolean) As Boolean`	Moves the input focus to the next control contained within this one.
`Sub SendToBack()`	Sends the control to the back of the stacking order.
`Sub SetBounds(ByVal x As Integer, ByVal y As Integer, ByVal width As Integer, ByVal height As Integer)`	Sets the control's position and size.
`Sub Show()`	Displays the control by setting its `Visible` property to `True`.
`Function ToString() As String`	Returns a textual representation of the control. This is generally the type of the control followed by its most commonly used property.
`Sub Update()`	Makes the control redraw any invalidated areas.

Events

The following table lists useful events implemented by the `Control` class. All controls that inherit from this class inherit these properties unless they override the `Control` class' behavior.

Event	Purpose
AutoSizeChanged	Occurs when the control's `AutoSize` property changes.
BackColorChanged	Occurs when the control's `BackColor` property changes.
BackgroundImageChanged	Occurs when the control's `BackgroundImage` property changes.
BackgroundImageLayoutChanged	Occurs when the control's `BackgroundImageLayout` property changes.
Click	Occurs when the user clicks on the control. This event is at a higher logical level than the `MouseClick` event, and it can be triggered by other actions than a mouse click (such as pressing the Enter key or a shortcut key).
ContextMenuChanged	Occurs when the control's `ContextMenu` property changes.
ContextMenuStripChanged	Occurs when the control's `ContextMenuStrip` property changes.
ControlAdded	Occurs when a new control is added to the control's contained child controls.
ControlRemoved	Occurs when a control is removed from the control's contained child controls.
CursorChanged	Occurs when the control's `Cursor` property changes.
DockChanged	Occurs when the control's `Dock` property changes.
DoubleClick	Occurs when the user double-clicks the control.
DragDrop	Occurs when the user drops something on the control in a drag-and-drop operation. This event handler should process the dropped information appropriately.
DragEnter	Occurs when the user drags something over the control in a drag-and-drop operation.
DragLeave	Occurs when the user drags something off of the control in a drag-and-drop operation.
DragOver	Occurs when the user has dragged something over the control in a drag-and-drop operation. This event fires repeatedly until the user drags off of the control, drops on the control, or cancels the drop.
EnabledChanged	Occurs when the control's `Enabled` property changes.

Table continued on following page

Event	Purpose
Enter	Occurs when the control is entered. This event fires before the GotFocus event.
FontChanged	Occurs when the control's Font property changes.
ForeColorChanged	Occurs when the control's ForeColor property changes.
GiveFeedback	Occurs during a drag-and-drop operation to let the drag source control take action.
GotFocus	Occurs when the control receives the input focus. This event fires after the Enter event. Generally, the Enter event is preferred.
HelpRequested	Occurs when the user requests help for the control. For example, if the user moves the focus to a TextBox and presses F1, the TextBox raises this event.
Invalidated	Occurs when part of the control is invalidated.
KeyDown	Occurs when the user presses a key while the control has the input focus.
KeyPress	Occurs when the user presses and releases a key while the control has the input focus.
KeyUp	Occurs when the user releases a key while the control has the input focus.
Layout	Occurs when the control should arrange its child controls. This event occurs before the Resize and SizeChanged events and is preferred for arranging child controls.
Leave	Occurs when the input focus leaves the control. This event fires before the LostFocus event.
LocationChanged	Occurs when the control's Location property changes. This event fires after the Move event fires.
LostFocus	Occurs when the input focus leaves the control. This event fires after the Leave event. Generally, the Leave event is preferred.
MarginChanged	Occurs when the control's Margin property changes.
MouseCaptureChanged	Occurs when the control loses a mouse capture.
MouseClick	Occurs when the user clicks the mouse on the control.
MouseDoubleClick	Occurs when the user double-clicks the mouse on the control.
MouseDown	Occurs when the user presses a mouse button down over the control.

Event	Purpose
MouseEnter	Occurs when the mouse enters the control.
MouseHover	Occurs when the mouse hovers over the control.
MouseLeave	Occurs when the mouse leaves the control.
MouseMove	Occurs when the mouse moves over the control.
MouseUp	Occurs when the user releases a mouse button over the control.
MouseWheel	Occurs when the user moves the mouse wheel while the control has the input focus.
Move	Occurs when the control is moved. This event fires before the LocationChanged event fires.
PaddingChanged	Occurs when the control's Padding property changes.
Paint	Occurs when the control must redraw itself. Normally the program draws on the control during this event (if it draws on the control at all).
ParentChanged	Occurs when the control's Parent property changes.
QueryContinueDrag	Occurs when something changes during a drag-and-drop operation so that the drag source can decide whether to modify or cancel the drag.
RegionChanged	Occurs when the control's Region property changes.
Resize	Occurs while the control is resizing. This event occurs after the Layout event, but before the SizeChanged event.
SizeChanged	Occurs while the control is resizing. This event occurs after the Layout and Move events.
SystemColorsChanged	Occurs when the system colors change. For instance, you might want to draw something using the same color that the operating system uses for active forms. If the user changes the system's color for borders, you can use this event to update your application.
TabIndexChanged	Occurs when the control's TabIndex property changes.
TabStopChanged	Occurs when the control's TabStop property changes.
TextChanged	Occurs when the control's Text property changes.
Validated	Occurs when the control has successfully finished validating its data.
Validating	Occurs when the control should validate its data.
VisibleChanged	Occurs when the control's Visible property changes.

Event Sequences

Several situations generate a series of events in a precise order.

Mouse Events

When you click on a control, the following events are raised in the order shown. The first instance of the `MouseMove` event can occur any number of times if you move the mouse while holding the mouse button down. The final `MouseMove` event occurs whether you move the mouse or not.

```
MouseDown

    [MouseMove]

Click

MouseClick

MouseUp

MouseCaptureChanged

MouseMove
```

When you double-click on a control, the following events are raised in the order shown.

```
MouseDown

    [MouseMove]

Click

MouseClick

MouseUp

MouseCaptureChanged

MouseMove

MouseDown

DoubleClick

MouseDoubleClick

MouseUp

MouseCaptureChanged

MouseMove
```

Resize Events

When you resize a control, the following events are raised in this order. These events are repeated as long as you are resizing the control.

```
Layout

Resize

SizeChanged
```

Form controls also provide `ResizeBegin` and `ResizeEnd` events that occur before and after the other events, respectively.

Move Events

When you move a control, the following events are raised in this order. These events are repeated as long as you are moving the control.

```
Move

LocationChanged
```

Form controls also provide `ResizeBegin` and `ResizeEnd` events that occur before and after the other events, respectively.

Variable Declarations and Data Types

This appendix provides information about variable declarations and data types.

Variable Declarations

The following code shows a standard variable declaration:

```
[attribute_list] [accessibility] [Shared] [Shadows] [ReadOnly] _
Dim [WithEvents] name [(bounds_list)] [As [New] type] [=
initialization_expression]
```

In this code, the following is true:

- ❏ *attribute_list* — A comma-separated list of attributes specific to a particular task. For example, <XmlAttributeAttribute(AttributeName:="Cost")>.

- ❏ *accessibility* — Public, Protected, Friend, Protected Friend, Private, or Static.

- ❏ *Shared* — Means that all instances of the class or structure containing the variable share the same variable.

- ❏ *Shadows* — Indicates that the variable hides a variable with the same name in a base class.

- ❏ *ReadOnly* — Indicates that the program can read, but not modify, the variable's value. You can set the value in an initialization statement or in an object constructor.

- ❏ *Dim* — Officially tells Visual Basic that you want to create a variable. You can omit the Dim keyword if you specify Public, Protected, Friend, Protected Friend, Private, Static, or ReadOnly.

- ❏ *WithEvents* — Tells Visual Basic that the variable is of a specific object type that may raise events that you will want to catch.

- ❏ *name* — Gives the name of the variable.

- ❏ *bounds_list* — Bounds for an array.

- ❏ *New* — Use New to make a new instance of an object variable. Include parameters for the class's constructor if appropriate.

- ❏ *type* — The variable's data type.

- ❏ *initialization_expression* — An expression that sets the initial value for the variable.

Visual Basic allows you to declare and initialize more than one variable in a single declaration statement, but that can make the code more difficult to read. To avoid possible later confusion, declare only variables of one type in a single statement.

Enumerated Type Declarations

The syntax for declaring an enumerated type is as follows:

```
[attribute_list] [accessibility] [Shadows] Enum name [As type]
    [attribute_list] value_name [= initialization_expression]
    [attribute_list] value_name [= initialization_expression]
    ...
End Enum
```

Most of these terms (including *attribute_list* and *accessibility*) are similar to those used by variable declarations. See the section "Variable Declarations" earlier in this appendix for more information.

Option Explicit and Option Strict

When Option Explicit is on, you must explicitly declare all variables before using them. When Option Explicit is off, Visual Basic creates a variable the first time it is encountered if is has not yet been declared. To make your code easier to understand, and to avoid problems such as Visual Basic creating a new variable because of a typographical error, you should always turn Option Explicit on.

When Option Strict is on, Visual Basic will not implicitly perform narrowing type conversions. For example, if you set an Integer variable equal to a String value, Visual Basic will raise an error. When Option Strict is off, Visual Basic will silently attempt narrowing conversions. It tries to convert the String value into an Integer and raises an error if the String doesn't contain an integral value. To avoid confusion and potentially slow conversions, always turn Option Strict on.

Data Types

The following table summarizes Visual Basic's data types.

Type	Size	Values
Boolean	2 bytes	True or False
Byte	1 byte	0 to 255 (unsigned byte)
SByte	1 byte	-128 to 127 (signed byte)
Char	2 bytes	0 to 65,535 (unsigned character)
Short	2 bytes	-32,768 to 32,767
UShort	2 bytes	0 through 65,535 (unsigned short)
Integer	4 bytes	-2,147,483,648 to 2,147,483,647
UInteger	4 bytes	0 through 4,294,967,295 (unsigned integer)
Long	8 bytes	-9,223,372,036,854,775,808 to 9,223,372,036,854,775,807
ULong	8 bytes	0 through 18,446,744,073,709,551,615 (unsigned long)
Decimal	16 bytes	0 to +/-79,228,162,514,264,337,593,543,950,335 with no decimal point.
		0 to +/-7.9228162514264337593543950335 with 28 places
Single	4 bytes	-3.4028235E+38 to -1.401298E-45 (negative values)
		1.401298E-45 to 3.4028235E+38 (positive values)
Double	8 bytes	-1.79769313486231570E+308 to -4.94065645841246544E-324 (negative values)
		4.94065645841246544E-324 through 1.79769313486231570E+308 (positive values)
String	variable	Depending on the platform, approximately 0 to 2 billion Unicode characters
Date	8 bytes	January 1, 0001 0:0:00 to December 31, 9999 11:59:59 pm
Object	4 bytes	Points to any type of data.
Structure	variable	Structure members have their own ranges.

Data Type Characters

The following table lists Visual Basic's data type characters.

Character	Data Type
%	Integer
&	Long

Table continued on following page

Character	Data Type
@	Decimal
!	Single
#	Double
$	String

Literal Type Characters

The following table lists Visual Basic's literal type characters.

Character	Data Type
S	Short
US	UShort
I	Integer
UI	UInteger
L	Long
IL	ULong
D	Decimal
F	Single (F for "floating point")
R	Double (R for "real")
c	Char (note that this is a lowercase "c")

Data Type Conversion Functions

The following table lists Visual Basic's data type conversion functions.

Function	Converts To
CBool	Boolean
CByte	Byte
CChar	Char
CDate	Date

Function	Converts To
CDbl	Double
CDec	Decimal
CInt	Integer
CLng	Long
CObj	Object
CSByte	SByte
CShort	Short
CSng	Single
CStr	String
CUInt	UInteger
CULng	ULong
CUShort	UShort

Remember that data types have their own parsing methods in addition to these data type conversion functions. For example, the following code converts the String variable a_string into an Integer value:

```
an_integer = Integer.Parse(a_string)
```

These methods are faster than using the corresponding data type conversion function (in this case, CInt).

Operators

Visual Basic's operators fall into five main categories: arithmetic, concatenation, comparison, logical, and bitwise. The following sections explain these categories and the operators they contain. The end of this appendix describes special Date and TimeSpan operators, as well as operator overloading.

Arithmetic Operators

The following table lists the arithmetic operators provided by Visual Basic.

Operator	Purpose	Example	Result
^	Exponentiation	2 ^ 3	(2 to the power 3) = 2 * 2 * 2 = 8.
–	Negation	–2	–2
*	Multiplication	2 * 3	6
/	Division	3 / 2	1.5
\	Integer division	17 \ 5	3
Mod	Modulus	17 Mod 5	2
+	Addition	2 + 3	5
–	Subtraction	3 – 2	1
<<	Bit left shift	10110111 << 1	01101110
>>	Bit right shift	10110111 >> 1	01011011

Visual Basic doesn't work with bits such as 10110111, so you must use decimal, hexadecimal, or octal in your code.

Concatenation Operators

Visual Basic provides two concatenation operators: + and &. Both join two strings together. Because the + symbol also represents an arithmetic operator, your code will be easier to read if you use the & symbol for concatenation.

Comparison Operators

The following table lists the comparison operators provided by Visual Basic.

Operator	Purpose	Example	Result
=	Equals	A = B	True if A equals B
<>	Not equals	A <> B	True if A does not equal B
<	Less than	A < B	True if A is less than B
<=	Less than or equal to	A <= B	True if A is less than or equal to B
>	Greater than	A > B	True if A is greater than B
>=	Greater than or equal to	A >= B	True if A is greater than or equal to B
Is	Equality of two objects	emp Is mgr	True if emp and mgr refer to the same object
IsNot	Inequality of two objects	emp IsNot mgr	True if emp and mgr refer to different objects
TypeOf...Is	Object is of a certain type	TypeOf(obj) Is Manager	True if obj points to a Manager object
Like	Matches a text pattern	A Like "###-####"	True if A contains three digits, a dash, and four digits

The following table lists characters with special meanings to the Like operator.

Character(s)	Meaning
?	Matches any single character
*	Matches any zero or more characters
#	Matches any single digit
[characters]	Matches any of the characters between the brackets
[!characters]	Matches any character not between the brackets
A-Z	When inside brackets, matches any character in the range A to Z

The following table lists some useful Like patterns.

Pattern	Meaning
[2-9]##-####	Seven-digit phone number
[2-9]##-[2-9]##-####	Ten-digit phone number including area code
1-[2-9]##-[2-9]##-####	Eleven-digit phone number beginning with 1 and area code
#####	Five-digit ZIP code
#####-####	Nine-digit ZIP+4 code
?*@?*.?*	E-mail address

Logical Operators

The following table summarizes Visual Basic's logical operators.

Operator	Purpose	Example	Result
Not	Logical or bitwise negation	Not A	True if A is false
And	Logical or bitwise And	A And B	True if A and B are both true
Or	Logical or bitwise Or	A Or B	True if A or B or both are true
Xor	Logical or bitwise exclusive Or	A Xor B	True if A or B but not both is true
AndAlso	Logical or bitwise And with short-circuit evaluation	A AndAlso B	True if A and B are both true
OrElse	Logical or bitwise Or with short-circuit evaluation	A OrElse B	True if A or B or both are true

Bitwise Operators

Bitwise operators work much as logical operators do, except that they compare values one bit at a time. Visual Basic provides bitwise versions of Not, And, Or, and Xor but not bitwise versions of AndAlso or OrElse.

Operator Precedence

The following table lists the operators in order of precedence. When evaluating an expression, the program evaluates an operator before it evaluates those lower than it in the list. When operators are on the same line, the program evaluates them from left to right.

Operator	Description
^	Exponentiation
-	Negation
*, /	Multiplication and division
\	Integer division
Mod	Modulus
+, -, +	Addition, subtraction, and concatenation
&	Concatenation
<<, >>	Bit shift
=, <>, <, <=, >, >=, Like, Is, IsNot, TypeOf...Is	All comparisons
Not	Logical and bitwise negation
And, AndAlso	Logical and bitwise And with and without short-circuit evaluation
Xor, Or, OrElse	Logical and bitwise Xor, and Or with and without short-circuit evaluation

Assignment Operators

The following table summarizes Visual Basic's assignment operators.

Operator	Example	Original Syntax Equivalent
=	A = B	A = B
^=	A ^= B	A = A ^ B
*=	A *= B	A = A * B
/=	A /= B	A = A / B
\=	A \= B	A = A \ B
+=	A += B	A = A + B
-=	A -= B	A = A - B
&=	A &= B	A = A & B

Date and TimeSpan Operators

The Date and TimeSpan data types are related through their operators. The following list shows the relationships between these two data types.

- ❏ Date − Date = TimeSpan
- ❏ Date + TimeSpan = Date
- ❏ TimeSpan + TimeSpan = TimeSpan
- ❏ TimeSpan − TimeSpan = TimeSpan

The following table lists convenience methods provided by the Date data type.

Syntax	Meaning
`result_date = date1.Add(timespan1)`	Returns `date1` plus `timespan1`
`result_date = date1.AddYears (num_years)`	Returns the date plus the indicated number of years
`result_date = date1.AddMonths (num_months)`	Returns the date plus the indicated number of months
`result_date = date1.AddDays (num_days)`	Returns the date plus the indicated number of days
`result_date = date1.AddHours (num_hours)`	Returns the date plus the indicated number of hours
`result_date = date1.AddMinutes (num_minutes)`	Returns the date plus the indicated number of minutes
`result_date = date1.AddSeconds (num_seconds)`	Returns the date plus the indicated number of seconds
`result_date = date1.AddMilliseconds (num_milliseconds)`	Returns the date plus the indicated number of milliseconds
`result_date = date1.AddTicks (num_ticks)`	Returns the date plus the indicated number of ticks (100 nanosecond units)
`result_timespan = date1. Subtract(date2)`	Returns the time span between `date2` and `date1`
`result_integer = date1. CompareTo(date2)`	Returns a value indicating whether `date1` is greater than, less than, or equal to `date2`
`result_boolean = date1.Equals(date2)`	Returns `True` if `date1` equals `date2`

Operator Overloading

The syntax for defining an operator for a class is:

```
[ <attributes> ] Public [ Overloads ] Shared [ Shadows ] _
  [ Widening | Narrowing ]  Operator symbol ( operands ) As type
    ...
End Operator
```

The operator's symbol can be +, -, *, /, \, ^, &, <<, >>, =, <>, <, >, <=, >=, Mod, Not, And, Or, Xor, Like, IsTrue, IsFalse, or CType.

Some operands come in pairs, and if you define one, you must define the other. The pairs are = and <>, < and >, <= and >=, and IsTrue and IsFalse.

If you define And and IsFalse, Visual Basic uses them to define the AndAlso operator. Similarly, if you define Or and IsTrue, Visual Basic automatically provides the OrElse operator.

Subroutine and Function Declarations

This appendix provides information about subroutine, function, and generic declarations. A property procedure includes a subroutine and function pair, so they are also described here.

Subroutines

The syntax for writing a subroutine is:

```
[attribute_list] [interitance_mode] [accessibility]
Sub subroutine_name [(parameters)] [ Implements interface.procedure ]
    [ statements ]
End Sub
```

The *inheritance_mode* can be one of the following values: Overloads, Overrides, Overridable, NotOverridable, MustOverride, Shadows, or Shared. These values determine how a subroutine declared within a class inherits from the parent class or how it allows inheritance in derived classes.

The *accessibility* clause can take one of the following values: Public, Protected, Friend, Protected Friend, and Private. These values determine which pieces of code can invoke the subroutine.

Functions

The syntax for writing a function is:

```
[attribute_list] [interitance_mode] [accessibility] _
Function function_name([parameters]) [As return_type] [ Implements
interface.function ]
    [ statements ]
End Function
```

This is the same as the syntax used for declaring a subroutine, except that a function includes a return type and ends with End Function.

The *inheritance_mode* can be one of the values Overloads, Overrides, Overridable, NotOverridable, MustOverride, Shadows, or Shared. These values determine how a subroutine declared within a class inherits from the parent class or how it allows inheritance in derived classes.

The *accessibility* clause can take one of the following values: Public, Protected, Friend, Protected Friend, and Private. These values determine which pieces of code can invoke the subroutine.

A function assigns its return value either by setting its name equal to the value or by using the Return statement. Using the Return statement may allow the compiler to optimize the code more, so it is generally preferred.

Property Procedures

The syntax for read/write property procedures is:

```
Property property_name() As data_type
    Get
        ...
    End Get
    Set(ByVal Value As data_type)
        ...
    End Set
End Property
```

The syntax for a read-only property procedure is:

```
Public ReadOnly Property property_name() As data_type
    Get
        ...
    End Get
End Property
```

The syntax for write-only property procedure is:

```
Public WriteOnly Property property_name() As data_type
    Set(ByVal Value As data_type)
        ...
    End Set
End Property
```

In all three of these cases, you don't need to remember all the declaration details. If you type the first line (including the ReadOnly or WriteOnly keywords if you want them) and press Enter, Visual Basic creates blank property procedures for you.

The Property Get procedures should all assign return values, as in property_name = return_value or by using the Return statement, as in Return return_value.

E

Control Statements

Control statements tell an application which other statements to execute under a particular set of circumstances. They control the path that execution takes through the code. They include statements that tell the program to execute some statements but not others and to execute certain statements repeatedly.

The two main categories of control statements are decision statements and looping statements. The following sections describe the decision and looping statements provided by Visual Basic .NET.

Decision Statements

A decision statement represents a branch in the program. It marks a place where the program can execute one set of statements or another or possibly no statements at all. These include `If` statements, `Choose`, and `Select Case` statements.

Single-Line If Then

A single-line `If Then` statement tests a condition and, if the condition is true, executes a piece of code. The code may include more than one simple statement separated by a colon.

Optional `Else If` clauses let the program evaluate other conditions and execute corresponding pieces of code. A final optional `Else` clause lets the program execute a piece of code if none of the previous conditions is true.

The syntax is:

```
If condition Then statement

If condition Then statement1 Else statement2

If condition1 Then statement1 Else If condition2 Then statement2 Else
statement3
```

```
If condition Then statement1 : statement2

If condition Then statement1 : statement2 Else statement3 : statement4
```

Multiline If Then

A multiline If Then statement is similar to the single-line version, except the pieces of code executed by each part of the statement can include multiple lines. Each piece of code ends before the following ElseIf, Else, or End If keywords. In complex code, this format is often easier to read than a complicated single-line If Then statement.

The syntax is:

```
If condition1 Then
    statements1...
ElseIf condition2
    statements2...
Else
    statements3...
End If
```

Select Case

A Select Case statement lets a program execute one of several pieces of code based on a test value. Select Case is equivalent to a long If Then Else statement.

The syntax is:

```
Select Case test_value
    Case comparison_expression1
        statements1
    Case comparison_expression2
        statements2
    Case comparison_expression3
        statements3
    ...
    Case Else
        else_statements
End Select
```

A comparison expression can contain multiple expressions separated by commas, can use the To keyword to specify a range of values, and can use the Is keyword to evaluate a logical expression using the test value. The following example's first case looks for a string in the range "A" to "Z" or "a" to "z." Its second and third cases look for values less than "A" and greater than "Z," respectively.

```
Select Case key_pressed
    Case "A" To "Z", "a" To "z"
        ...
    Case Is < "A"
        ...
    Case Is > "Z"
        ...
End Select
```

IIf

IIf takes a Boolean value as its first parameter. It returns its second parameter if the value is true, and it returns its third parameter if the value is false. IIf is often confusing and is slower than an If Then Else statement, so you should usually use If Then Else instead.

The syntax is:

```
variable = IIf(condition, value_if_false, value_if_true)
```

Choose

Choose takes an index value as its first parameter and returns the corresponding one of its other parameters.

The syntax is:

```
variable = Choose(index, value1, value2, value3, value4, ...)
```

Looping Statements

A looping statement makes the program execute a series of statements repeatedly. The loop can run for a fixed number of repetitions, run while some condition holds true, run until some condition holds true, or run indefinitely.

For Next

A For Next loop executes a piece of code while a loop control variable ranges from one value to another.

The syntax is:

```
For variable [As data_type] = start_value To stop_value [Step increment]
    statements
    [Exit For]
    statements
Next [variable]
```

For Each

A For Each loop executes a piece of code while a loop control variable ranges over all of the items contained in a group class such as a collection or array.

The syntax is:

```
For Each variable [As object_type] In group
    statements
    [Exit For]
    statements
Next [variable]
```

Do Loop

Do Loop statements come in three forms. First, if the statement has no While or Until clause, the loop repeats infinitely or until the code uses an Exit Do, Exit Sub, GoTo, or some other statement to break out of the loop.

The syntax is:

```
Do
    statements
    [Exit Do]
    statements
Loop
```

The other two forms of Do Loop statements execute as long as a condition is true (Do While condition) or until a condition is true (Do Until condition).

The second form of Do Loop statement tests its condition before it executes, so the code it contains is not executed even once if the condition is initially false.

The syntax is:

```
Do {While | Until} condition
    statements
    [Exit Do]
    statements
Loop
```

The third form of Do Loop statement tests its condition after it executes, so the code it contains is executed at least once even if the condition is initially false.

The syntax is:

```
Do
    statements
    [Exit Do]
    statements
Loop {While | Until} condition
```

While End

The While End loop executes a series of statements as long as a condition is true. It tests its condition before it executes, so the code it contains is not executed even once if the condition is initially false.

The syntax is:

```
While condition
    statements
    [Exit While]
    statements
End While
```

This statement is equivalent to the Do Loop:

```
Do While condition
     statements
     [Exit Do]
     statements
Loop
```

GoTo

GoTo performs an unconditional jump to a specified line.

The syntax is:

```
     GoTo line_label
     ...
line_label:
     ...
```

Because undisciplined use of GoTo can lead to "spaghetti code," which is difficult to understand, debug, and maintain, you should generally avoid using GoTo.

Error Handling

This appendix gives information about error handling.

Structured Error Handling

A `Try` block tries to execute some code and reacts to errors. The syntax is:

```
Try
    try_statements...
[Catch ex As exception_type_1
    exception_statements_1...]
[Catch ex As exception_type_2
    exception_statements_2...]
...
[Catch
    final_exception_statements...]
[Finally
    finally_statements...]
End Try
```

When an error occurs, the program examines the `Catch` statements until it finds one that matches the current exception. The program executes the *finally_statements* after the *try_statements* succeed or after any `Catch` block is done executing.

Throwing Exceptions

Use the `Throw` statement to throw an exception, as in the following code:

```
Throw New ArgumentException("Width must be greater than zero")
```

Custom Exceptions

You can derive your own custom exception classes from the System.ApplicationException class, as shown in the following example. By convention, the name of an exception class should end with "Exception." Also by convention, you should provide at least the first three constructors shown here.

```
Imports System.Runtime.Serialization

Public Class ObjectExpiredException
    Inherits System.ApplicationException

    ' No parameters. Use a default message.
    Public Sub New()
        MyBase.New("This object has expired")
    End Sub

    ' Set the message.
    Public Sub New(ByVal new_message As String)
        MyBase.New(new_message)
    End Sub

    ' Set the message and inner exception.
    Public Sub New(ByVal new_message As String, _
     ByVal inner_exception As Exception)
        MyBase.New(new_message, inner_exception)
    End Sub

    ' Include SerializationInfo object and StreamingContext objects.
    Public Sub New(ByVal info As SerializationInfo, _
     ByVal context As StreamingContext)
        MyBase.New(info, context)
    End Sub
End Class
```

Useful Exception Classes

The following table lists some useful exception classes.

Class	Purpose
AmbiguousMatchException	The program could not figure out which over-loaded object method to use.
ApplicationException	This is the ancestor class for all nonfatal application errors. When you build custom exception classes, you should inherit this class or one of its descendants.
ArgumentException	An argument is invalid.
ArgumentNullException	An argument that cannot be Nothing has value Nothing.

Class	Purpose
ArgumentOutOfRangeException	An argument is out of its allowed range.
ArithmeticException	An arithmetic, casting, or conversion operation has occurred.
ArrayTypeMismatchException	The program tried to store the wrong type of item in an array.
ConfigurationException	A configuration setting is invalid.
ConstraintException	A data operation violates a database constraint.
DataException	The ancestor class for ADO.NET exception classes.
DirectoryNotFoundException	A needed directory is missing.
DivideByZeroException	The program divided by zero.
DuplicateNameException	An ADO.NET operation encountered a duplicate name (for example, it tried to create a second table with the same name).
EvaluateException	Occurs when a DataColumn's Expression property cannot be evaluated.
FieldAccessException improperly.	The program tried to access a class property
FormatException	An argument's format doesn't match its required format. For example, Integer.Parse("Oops").
IndexOutOfRangeException	The program tried to access an item outside of the bounds of an array or other container.
InvalidCastException	The program tried to make an invalid conversion. For example, CInt("oops").
InvalidOperationException	The operation is not currently allowed.
IOException	The ancestor class for input/output (I/O) exception classes. A generic I/O error occurred.
EndOfStreamException	A stream reached its end.
FileLoadException	Error loading a file.
FileNotFoundException	Error finding a file.
InternalBufferOverflowException	An internal buffer overflowed.
MemberAccessException	The program tried to access a class member improperly.
MethodAccessException	The program tried to access a class method improperly.

Table continued on following page

Class	Purpose
MissingFieldException	The program tried to access a class property that doesn't exist.
MissingMemberException	The program tried to access a class member that doesn't exist.
MissingMethodException	The program tried to access a class method that doesn't exist.
NotFiniteNumberException	A floating-point number is PositiveInfinity, NegativeInfinity, or NaN (not a number). You can get these values from the floating-point classes as in Single.Nan or Double.PositiveInfinity.
NotImplementedException	The requested operation is not implemented.
NotSupportedException	The requested operation is not implemented. For example, the program might be asking a routine to modify data that was opened read-only.
NullReferenceException	The program tried to use an object reference that is Nothing.
OutOfMemoryException	There isn't enough memory. For example, if the user wants to generate a really huge data set, you may be able to predict how much memory the program will need, see if it is available, and throw this exception if it is not.
OverflowException	An arithmetic, casting, or conversion operation created an overflow. For example, if X is a Byte variable containing the value 100, then the statement X = X * X throws this error.
PolicyException	Policy prevents the code from running.
RankException	A routine is trying to use an array with the wrong number of dimensions.
ReadOnlyException	The program tried to modify read-only data.
ResourceException	A needed resource is missing.
SecurityException	A security violation occurred.
SyntaxErrorException	A DataColumn's Expression property contains invalid syntax.
UnauthorizedAccessException	The system is denying access because of an I/O or security error.

Classic Error Handling

The On Error statement controls error handlers in Visual Basic classic error handling. You can use structured and classic error handling in the same program but not in the same routine.

The following list briefly describes the On Error statement's four variations.

❑ *On Error GoTo* line — If an error occurs, the program enters error-handling mode and control jumps to the indicated line.

❑ *On Error Resume Next* — If an error occurs, the program ignores it. The code can use the Err object to see whether an error occurred and what error it was.

❑ *On Error GoTo 0* — This command disables any currently active error handler. If the program encounters an error after this statement, the routine fails and control passes up the call stack until the program finds an active error handler or the program crashes.

❑ *On Error GoTo -1* — This command is similar to On Error GoTo 0, except that it also ends error-handling mode if the program is in error-handling mode.

Visual Basic provides four ways to exit error-handling mode.

❑ *Exit Sub (or Exit Function)* — Ends error-handling mode and exits the current routine.

❑ *Resume* — Makes the program resume execution with the statement that caused the error. If the program has not taken some action to correct the problem, the error will occur again, triggering the error handler and possibly entering an infinite loop.

❑ *Resume Next* — Makes the program resume execution with the statement after the one that caused the error.

❑ *On Error GoTo -1* — Ends error-handling mode and lets execution continue with the statement that follows.

Using On Error GoTo -1 to end error-handling mode can be very confusing because it's hard to tell when the program is in error-handling mode and when it isn't. Usually, the code is easier to understand if all of the error-handling code is grouped at the end of the routine and if each block of error-handling code ends with one of the other methods (Exit Sub, Exit Function, Resume, or Resume Next).

G

Standard Controls and Components

This appendix describes the standard controls and components provided by Visual Basic .NET. Some of these are quite complicated, providing dozens or even hundreds of properties, methods, and events, so it would be impractical to describe them all completely here. Besides, the online help does a better job of explaining all of the controls' properties, methods, and events than a book can, covering all of the overloaded versions of the methods and providing hyperlinks to related topics.

The sections in this appendix describe the components' general purposes and give examples of what I believe to be their simplest, most common, and most useful usages. The idea is to help you decide which components to use for which purposes, and to give you some idea about the components' most commonly used properties, methods, and events. To learn more about a particular component, see the online help.

Note that all of these components inherit from the `Component` class, and the controls inherit from the `Control` class. Except where overridden, the components and controls inherit the properties, methods, and events defined by the `Component` and `Control` classes. Chapter 2, "Controls in General," discusses some of the more useful properties, methods, and events provided by the `Control` class, and many of those apply to these controls as well.

Figure G-1 shows the Visual Basic toolbox displaying the standard Windows forms controls.

Figure G-1: Visual Basic provides a large number of standard components and controls for Windows forms.

The following table lists the components shown in Figure G-1 in the same order in which they appear in the figure.

Pointer	BackgroundWorker	BindingNavigator	BindingSource
Button	CheckBox	CheckedListBox	ColorDialog
ComboBox	ContextMenuStrip	DataGridView	DataSet
DateTimePicker	DirectoryEntry	DirectorySearcher	DomainUpDown
ErrorProvider	EventLog	FileSystemWatcher	FlowLayoutPanel
FolderBrowserDialog	FontDialog	GroupBox	HelpProvider
HScrollBar	ImageList	Label	LinkLabel

ListBox	ListView	MaskedTextBox	MenuStrip
MessageQueue	MonthCalendar	NotifyIcon	NumericUpDown
OpenFileDialog	PageSetupDialog	Panel	PerformanceCounter
PictureBox	PrintDialog	PrintDocument	PrintPreviewControl
PrintPreviewDialog	Process	ProgressBar	PropertyGrid
RadioButton	RichTextBox	SaveFileDialog	SerialPort
ServiceController	SplitContainer	StatusStrip	TabControl
TableLayoutPanel	TextBox	Timer	ToolStrip
ToolStripContainer	ToolTip	TrackBar	TreeView
VScrollBar	WebBrowser		

Components' Purposes

By default, the Toolbox provides several tabs that group related components together. With such a large number of components at your fingertips, having categorized tabs sometimes makes finding a particular tool easier. Each tab also contains a Pointer tool.

The following table lists the tools in various Toolbox tabs. You can use this table to help decide which tool to use for a particular purpose.

Common Controls

Button	CheckBox	CheckedListBox	ComboBox
DateTimePicker	Label	LinkLabel	ListBox
ListView	MaskedTextBox	MonthCalendar	NotifyIcon
NumericUpDown	PictureBox	ProgressBar	RadioButton
RichTextBox	TextBox	ToolTip	TreeView
WebBrowser			

Containers

FlowLayoutPanel	GroupBox	Panel	SplitContainer
TabControl	TableLayoutPanel		

Menus & Toolbars

ContextMenuStrip	MenuStrip	StatusStrip	ToolStrip
ToolStripContainer			

Data

DataSet	DataGridView	BindingSource	BindingNavigatot
ReportViewer			

Components

BackgroundWorker	DirectoryEntry	DirectorySearcher	ErrorProvider
EventLog	FileSystemWatcher	HelpProvider	ImageList
MessageQueue	PerformanceCounter	Process	SerialPort
ServiceController	Timer		

Printing

PageSetupDialog	PrintDialog	PrintDocument	PrintPreviewControl
PrintPreviewDialog			

Dialogs

ColorDialog	FolderBrowserDialog	FontDialog	OpenFileDialog
SaveFileDialog			

One other section, General, is initially empty.

The following sections describe the tools shown in Figure G-1. Except for the generic pointer tool, all tools are presented in alphabetical order.

Pointer

Each of the Toolbox's sections begins with an arrow in its upper-left corner. This is the only tool shown in Figure G-1 that does not represent a type of control or component. Selecting the pointer deselects any other currently selected tool. You can then click the controls on the form to select them without creating a new control.

BackgroundWorker

The BackgroundWorker component simplifies multithreading. When a program invokes its RunWorkerAsync method, the component starts running on a new thread. It raises its DoWork method on the new thread, and the corresponding event handler should perform the necessary work. While it runs, the worker can call the component's ReportProgress method to raise a ProgressChanged event on the main thread to let the program know how it is progressing.

When the worker thread finishes, the component receives a RunWorkerCompleted event on the main thread.

The following code demonstrates the BackgroundWorker component. When the user clicks the Start button, the program disables its Start button, enables its Cancel button, and sets its ProgressBar's Value property to 0. It then prepares the bgrLongProcess BackgroundWorker component and calls its RunWorkerAsync method. If the user clicks the Cancel button while the worker is running, the program calls the BackgroundWorker's CancelAsync method to tell it to stop running. As the worker runs, it raises ProgressChanged events. When the main thread receives one of these events, it sets its ProgressBar's Value property to display the worker's progress. When the worker finishes, the RunWorkerCompleted event handler enables the Start button and disables the Cancel button.

All the code described so far runs on the main program thread. The worker's DoWork event handler runs on the worker thread. In this example, the code loops for several seconds. Each time through the loop, the program waits for one second. It then checks the worker component's CancellationPending property to see if the user clicked the Cancel button. If CancellationPending is True, then the event handler exits and the worker is done.

If CancellationPending is False, then the event handler calls the worker's ReportProgress method to tell the main thread how far it has gotten.

When the For loop ends, the event handler exits and the worker stops executing.

```
' Start the long process.
Private Sub btnStartProcess_Click(ByVal sender As System.Object, _
 ByVal e As System.EventArgs) Handles btnStartProcess.Click
    ' Get ready.
    btnStartProcess.Enabled = False
    btnCancel.Enabled = True
    prgLongProcess.Value = 0

    ' Start the worker.
    bgrLongProcess.WorkerReportsProgress = True
    bgrLongProcess.WorkerSupportsCancellation = True
    bgrLongProcess.RunWorkerAsync()
End Sub

' Cancel the long process.
Private Sub btnCancel_Click(ByVal sender As System.Object, _
 ByVal e As System.EventArgs) Handles btnCancel.Click
    bgrLongProcess.CancelAsync()
End Sub
```

```
' Display the progress.
Private Sub bgrLongProcess_ProgressChanged(ByVal sender As Object, _
 ByVal e As System.ComponentModel.ProgressChangedEventArgs) _
 Handles bgrLongProcess.ProgressChanged
    prgLongProcess.Value = e.ProgressPercentage
End Sub

' The worker is done.
Private Sub bgrLongProcess_RunWorkerCompleted(ByVal sender As Object, _
 ByVal e As System.ComponentModel.RunWorkerCompletedEventArgs) _
 Handles bgrLongProcess.RunWorkerCompleted
    btnStartProcess.Enabled = True
    btnCancel.Enabled = False
End Sub

' Do the work.
Private Sub bgrLongProcess_DoWork(ByVal sender As Object, _
 ByVal e As System.ComponentModel.DoWorkEventArgs) Handles bgrLongProcess.DoWork
    ' This example just wastes some time.
    Const NUM_SECONDS As Integer = 5
    For i As Integer = 1 To NUM_SECONDS
        ' Pause 1 second.
        Dim wait_until As Date = Now.AddSeconds(1)
        Do While Now < wait_until

        Loop

        ' If the user has canceled, stop.
        If bgrLongProcess.CancellationPending Then Exit Sub

        ' Report our progress.
        bgrLongProcess.ReportProgress(CInt(100 * i / NUM_SECONDS))
    Next i
End Sub
```

BindingNavigator

A BindingNavigator provides a user interface so the user can control a data source. It initially appears as a toolbar docked to the top of the form, although you can move it if you like. It contains navigation buttons that move to the beginning, previous record, next record, and end of the data source. It also contains a text box where you can enter a record number to jump to, a label showing the current record number, and buttons to add and delete records.

See Chapter 11, "Database Controls and Objects," for more information on BindingNavigator and other database controls.

BindingSource

A BindingSource provides control of bound data on a form. It provides programmatic methods for navigating through the data, adding items, deleting items, and otherwise managing the data at the code level.

Typically you attach the BindingSource to a data source. You then bind controls to the BindingSource. When the BindingSource changes its position in the data source, it automatically updates the bound controls. If you attach a BindingNavigator to the BindingSource, then the user can use the BindingNavigator to control the BindingSource.

See Chapter 11, "Database Controls and Objects," for more information on BindingNavigator and other database controls.

Button

The Button control is a simple push button. You can use it to let the user tell the program to do something.

A Button can display a textual caption, a picture, or both. Use the ImageAlign and TextAlign properties to determine where the caption and picture appear in the Button.

When the user clicks the Button, it raises its Click event. The program can take the appropriate action in the Button's Click event handler, as shown in the following code:

```
Private Sub btnValidatePhoneNumber_Click(ByVal sender As System.Object, _
  ByVal e As System.EventArgs) Handles btnValidatePhoneNumber.Click
    ValidatePhoneNumber(txtPhoneNumber.Text)
End Sub
```

You can use the control's ImageList and ImageIndex properties to assign an image to the Button.

If you set a form's AcceptButton property to a Button, the Button's Click event handler runs when the user pressed the Enter key while the form has focus. Similarly if you set a form's CancelButton property to a Button, the Button's Click event handler runs when the user pressed the Escape key while the form has focus.

CheckBox

A CheckBox displays a box that the user can check and uncheck. You can use it to let the user select and deselect options.

A CheckBox can display a textual caption, a picture, or both. Use the ImageAlign and TextAlign properties to determine where the caption and picture appear in the CheckBox.

You can also use the control's `ImageList` and `ImageIndex` properties to assign an image to the `CheckBox`.

Use the control's `CheckAlign` property to determine where the check box appears. Normally the box appears on the left, but you can make it appear on the right, center, upper-left corner, and so forth.

Usually a program uses the `CheckBox` control's `Checked` property to tell if it is checked. This property returns `True` if the `CheckBox` is checked and `False` if it is not. Your program can also set this property to `True` or `False` to check or uncheck the control.

While a `CheckBox` usually is either checked or not, this control also has a third "indeterminate" state. This state is represented as a grayed-out check in the box. Some applications use this state to represent a partial or unknown selection.

For example, some installation programs allow the user to select categories of files to install. Checking the box next to the "Images" choice would install all of the program's image files. Unchecking this box would tell the program not to install any images. Some programs allow you to click a plus sign or some other indicator to expand the "Images" category and select the specific files you want to install. In that case, the program displays the check box in the indeterminate state to indicate that you selected some but not all of the files.

If you want to allow the user to cycle through the three values (checked, indeterminate, and unchecked), set the control's `ThreeState` property to `True`.

Most programs use `CheckBoxes` to gather information and only process the information when the user clicks a button or selects a menu item, so they don't need to process any `CheckBox` events. The control does provide a `CheckedChanged` event, however, that fires whenever the control's value changes, either because the user clicked it or because your program's code changed the value. For example, the program could hide and display extra information that only applies when the box is checked, as shown in the following code:

```
Private Sub chkExtraInfo_CheckedChanged(ByVal sender As System.Object, _
 ByVal e As System.EventArgs) Handles chkExtraInfo.CheckedChanged
    grpExtraInfo.Visible = chkExtraInfo.Checked
End Sub
```

CheckedListBox

A `CheckedListBox` control displays a series of items with check boxes in a list format. This enables the user to pick and choose similar items from a list of choices. You can also use a `ListBox` to allow the user to select items in a list, but there are some differences between the two controls' behaviors.

First, in a `CheckedListBox`, previously checked items remain checked when the user clicks on another item. If the user clicks an item in a `ListBox`, the control deselects any previously selected items, although you can use the Shift and Ctrl keys to modify this behavior.

Second, the user must click each CheckedListBox item individually to select it. You can make a ListBox allow simple or extended selections. That means, for example, the user could Shift-click to select all of the items in a range. If the user is likely to want that type of selection, consider using a ListBox instead of a CheckedListBox.

If a CheckedListBox isn't big enough to display all of its items at once, it displays a vertical scroll bar to let the user see all the items. If some of the items are too wide to fit, set the control's HorizontalScrollBar property to True to display a horizontal scroll bar.

If you set the MultiColumn property to True, the control displays items in multiple columns.

By default, the user must click on an item and then click on its box to check the item. To allow the user to select an item with a single click, set the control's CheckOnClick property to True.

If the control's IntegralHeight property is True, the control will not display a partial item. For example, if the control is tall enough to display 10.7 items, it will make itself slightly shorter so that it can only display 10 items.

Set the control's Sorted property to True to make the control display its items in sorted order.

Use the control's Items.Add method to add an item to the list. This method has three overloaded versions. All three take a generic Object as the first parameter. The control uses this object's ToString method to generate the text that it displays to the user. The first overloaded version takes no extra parameters. The second version takes a Boolean parameter indicating whether the new item should be checked. The last version takes a parameter that indicates whether the new item should be checked, unchecked, or indeterminate.

For example, suppose that a program defines the following Employee class. The important part here is the ToString method, which tells the CheckedListBox how to display an Employee object, as shown in the following code:

```
Public Class Employee
    Public FirstName As String
    Public LastName As String

    Public Sub New(ByVal first_name As String, ByVal last_name As String)
        FirstName = first_name
        LastName = last_name
    End Sub

    Public Overrides Function ToString() As String
        Return FirstName & " " & LastName
    End Function
End Class
```

The following code shows how the program might add three items to the CheckedListbox named clbEmployees. It makes the first item checked, the second unchecked, and the third indeterminate.

```
Private Sub Form1_Load(ByVal sender As System.Object, _
 ByVal e As System.EventArgs) Handles MyBase.Load
    clbEmployees.Items.Add(New Employee("Alicia", "Anderson"), True)
    clbEmployees.Items.Add(New Employee("Brutus", "Bentley"), False)
    clbEmployees.Items.Add(New Employee("Cynthia", "Colefield"), _
        CheckState.Indeterminate)
End Sub
```

The `CheckedListBox`'s `CheckedItems` property returns a collection containing the objects that are checked, including those that are in the indeterminate state. The following code fragment displays the text values of the selected objects in the Output window:

```
Dim checked_items As CheckedListBox.CheckedItemCollection = _
    clbEmployees.CheckedItems

    For Each item As Object In checked_items
        Debug.WriteLine(item.ToString)
    Next item
```

The control's `CheckedIndices` property returns a collection of integers representing the items that are checked or indeterminate (numbered starting with zero).

ColorDialog

The `ColorDialog` component displays a dialog that enables the user to select a color from a standard palette or from a custom color palette. A program calls its `ShowDialog` method to display a color selection dialog. `ShowDialog` returns `DialogResult.OK` if the user selects a color and clicks OK. It returns `DialogResult.Cancel` if the user cancels. Figure G-2 shows the dialog in action.

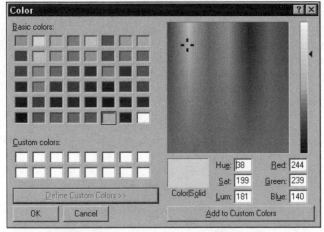

Figure G-2: The `ColorDialog` component enables the user to select a color.

The following code sets the dialog's Color property to the btnPickColor control's current background color. It displays the dialog and, if the user clicks OK, it sets the btnPickColor control's background color to the user's selection.

```
Private Sub btnPickColor_Click(ByVal sender As System.Object, _
  ByVal e As System.EventArgs) Handles btnPickColor.Click
    dlgColor.Color = btnPickColor.BackColor
    If dlgColor.ShowDialog() = DialogResult.OK Then
        btnPickColor.BackColor = dlgColor.Color
    End If
End Sub
```

On the right in Figure G-2, the dialog provides an area where the user can define custom colors. Set the component's AllowFullOpen property to True to allow the user access this area. Set the FullOpen property to True to make the dialog appear with this area already open (otherwise the user must click the Define Custom Colors button to show this area).

If you set the SolidColorOnly property to True, the dialog only allows the user to select solid colors. This applies only systems using 256 or fewer colors, where some colors are dithered combinations of other colors. All colors are solid on systems using more than 256 colors.

Dithering is the process of using dots or other shapes of various sizes to create the illusion of another color. For example, you can make orange by displaying a red area with tiny yellow dots or checks. On a system that uses a higher color model such as 24-bit color, the system can display every color directly. If you're using a lower color model system such as 8-bit color (256 colors), the system might dither to simulate colors that it cannot display directly.

The component's CustomColors property is an array of integers that determine the colors that the dialog displays in its custom colors area. These color values are a combination of red, green, and blue values between 0 and 255. In hexadecimal, the form of a value is *BBGGRR*, where *BB* is the blue component, *GG* is the green component, and *RR* is the red component.

For example, the color &HFF8000 has a blue component of &HFF = 255, a green component of &H80 = 128, and a red component of 0. This color is light blue. Unfortunately, the Color object's ToArgb method returns the color in the reversed format RRGGBB, so you cannot use that method to calculate these values. Instead, you need to calculate them yourself.

The following code initializes a color dialog's custom colors to a range of yellows and oranges with red component 255, blue component 0, and the green component ranging from 0 to 255:

```
' Initialize the color dialog's custom colors.
Dim colors() As Integer = { _
      &HFF, &H11FF, &H22FF, &H33FF, _
    &H44FF, &H55FF, &H66FF, &H77FF, _
    &H88FF, &H99FF, &HAAFF, &HBBFF, _
    &HCCFF, &HDDFF, &HEEFF, &HFFFF}
dlgColor.CustomColors = colors
```

ComboBox

The ComboBox control contains a text box where the user can enter a value. It also provides a list box or drop-down list where the user can select a value. How the text box, list box, and drop-down list work depends on the control's DropDownStyle property. Figure G-3 shows the three styles.

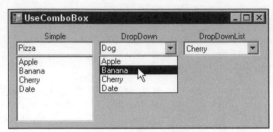

Figure G-3: The ComboBox **provides three different styles:** Simple, DropDown, **and** DropDownList.

When DropDownStyle is Simple, the ComboBox displays a text box and a list, as shown on the left in Figure G-3. The user can type a value in the text box, or select one from the list. The user can enter any text in the text box, even if it does not appear in the list.

When DropDownStyle is DropDown, the ComboBox displays a text box and a drop-down list, as shown in the middle in Figure G-3. The user can type a value in the text box. If the user clicks the drop-down arrow to the right of the text box, the control displays the list where the user can select an item. The user can enter any text in the text box, even if it does not appear in the list. In Figure G-3, the middle ComboBox's text box contains the value "Dog," which does not appear in the list.

When DropDownStyle is DropDownList, the ComboBox displays a noneditable text box and a drop-down list. If the user clicks on the control, the ComboBox displays a drop-down list exactly as it does when DropDownStyle is DropDown. The difference is that the user must select an item from the list. If the user sets focus to the control and types a letter, the control selects the next item in the list that begins with that letter. If the user presses the same letter again, the control moves to the next choice beginning with that letter.

Setting DropDownStyle to DropDownList restricts the user's choices the most and allows the least room for error. So, if you know all of the user's choices, you should use the DropDownList style. If you must allow the user to enter new values, you should use one of the other styles. The DropDown style takes less room on the form and is more familiar to most users, so that is often the better choice.

The control's DropDownWidth property determines how wide the drop-down list should be. It can sometimes be useful to make the drop-down area wider than the control. Then the control displays only the first part of the selected item, while the drop-down list can display extra detail. For example, you could make the items be state abbreviations, followed by some spaces, followed by state names as in "CA California." The user would see the abbreviation CA in the ComboBox, but would see the whole item (including the state name) in the drop-down list.

The `ComboBox`'s `MaxDropDownItems` property determines how many items the control displays in its drop-down list. For example, if you set this to 10 and the list contains more than 10 items, then the drop-down list displays a scroll bar to let the user find the additional items.

The `MaxLength` property lets you specify the maximum number of characters the user can type into the control's text box. Note, however, that the control will display a longer value if the user selects it from the control's list box or drop-down list. Set `MaxLength` to 0 to allow entries of any length.

If you set the control's `Sorted` property to `True`, the `ComboBox` lists its choices in sorted order.

The `ComboBox`'s `Text` property gets or sets the value displayed by the control's text box. If the control's `DropDownStyle` is `DropDownList`, this property does nothing at design time and the program can only set it to values that are in the control's list of allowed values at run time. Many programs use this property to see what value is selected in the control.

Like the `CheckedListBox` described earlier in this appendix, the items in a `ComboBox` can be any type of object and the control uses the objects' `ToString` methods to figure out what text to display to the user. As is the case with the `CheckedListBox`, you can use the `ComboBox`'s `Items.Add` method to add new objects to the control. See the "CheckedListBox" section earlier in this appendix for more information and an example that will also work with `ComboBox` controls.

If an item is selected, the `ComboBox`'s `SelectedItem` property returns the item's object. If no item is selected, this property returns `Nothing`.

If an item is selected, the `ComboBox`'s `SelectedIndex` property returns the item's index, numbered starting with zero. If no item is selected, this property returns -1.

Note that the `SelectedItem` and `SelectedIndex` properties return `Nothing` and -1, respectively, if the user types a new value into the text area, even if the user types a value that appears in the control's item list. If you want the user to select an item rather than typing some text, you should set the control's `DropDownStyle` property to `DropDownList`. Note that the control initially has no item selected when the program starts. If you want to ensure that something is always selected, select an item in the form's `Load` event handler, as shown in the following code:

```
' Select the first customer.
cboCustomer.SelectedIndex = 0

' Select the last employee.
cboEmployee.SelectedIndex = cboEmployee.Items.Count - 1
```

ContextMenuStrip

The `ContextMenuStrip` component represents a context menu. When you select it on the form at design time, the development environment displays the menu at the top of the form. Enter the menu's items, use the `Property` window to set their names and other properties, and double-click the items to edit their event handlers. See the section "MenuStrip" later in this appendix for information on menu item properties and events.

To use a ContextMenuStrip, you need to attach it to a control. Select the control that you want to use it. Open the Properties window, click the drop-down arrow to the right of the control's ContextMenuStrip property, and select your ContextMenuStrip component from the list. The rest is automatic. When the user right-clicks on this control at run time, Visual Basic automatically displays the ContextMenuStrip. If the user selects one of the menu's items, Visual Basic triggers the menu item's event handler.

DataGridView

The DataGridView control displays a tablelike grid display. The control's underlying data can come from a data source such as a DataSet or BindingSource, or the program can add rows and columns directly to the control. The DataGridView provides many properties for customizing the grid's appearance. For example, it lets you change column header styles, cell border styles, determine whether rows and columns are resizable, and determine whether the control displays tooltips and errors in data cells.

Visual Basic can automatically create a DataGridView bound to a BindingSource and associated with a BindingNavigator. To do this, create a data source and drag a table from the Data Sources window onto a form. For more information on this technique, or for information on using the control in general, see Chapter 11, "Database Controls and Objects."

DataSet

The DataSet component holds data in a relational format. It provides all the features you need to build, load, store, manipulate, and save data similar to that stored in a relational database. It can hold multiple tables related with complex parent/child relationships and uniqueness constraints. It provides methods for merging DataSets, searching for records that satisfy criteria, and saving data in different ways (such as into a relational database or an XML file).

One of the most common ways to use a DataSet is to load it from a relational database when the program starts, use various controls to display the data and let the user manipulate it interactively, and then save the changes back into the database when the program ends.

For more information on the DataSet component, see the online help and Chapter 11, "Database Controls and Objects."

DateTimePicker

The DateTimePicker control allows the user select a date and time. The control can display one of several styles, depending on its property values.

If the ShowUpDown property is True, the control displays small up and down arrows on its right, as shown at the top of Figure G-4. Click on part a date field (month, date, year) to select it and use the up and down arrow buttons to adjust that field.

Figure G-4: The DateTimePicker **control lets the user select a date and time.**

If ShowUpDown is False (the default), the control displays a drop-down arrow on its right, as shown in the second DateTimePicker in Figure G-4. If you click this arrow, the control displays the calendar shown under the control in Figure G-4. The right and left arrows at the top of the calendar let you move through months. If you click on the calendar's month, the control displays a pop-up menu listing the months so that you can quickly select one. If you click on the year, the control displays small up and down arrows that you can use to change the year. When you have found the month and year you want, click a date to select it and close the calendar.

If you get lost while scrolling through the calendar's months, you can click the Today entry at the bottom of the calendar to jump back to the current date. You can also right-click on the calendar and select the "Go to today" command.

Whether ShowUpDown is True or False, you can click on a date field (month, date, year) and then use the up and down arrow keys to adjust the field's value. You can also type a new value into numeric fields (such as the date and year).

The control's Format property determines the way in which the control displays dates and times. This property can take the values Long, Short, Time, and Custom. The results depend on the regional settings on the computer. The following table shows typical results for the Long, Short, and Time settings in the United States.

Format Property	Example
Long	Friday, February 20, 2004
Short	2/20/2004
Time	3:12:45 PM

When the Format property is set to Custom, the control uses the date and time format string stored in the control's CustomFormat property. For example, the DateTimePicker on the bottom in Figure G-4 has CustomFormat set to h:mm tt, MMM d, yyyy to display the time, abbreviated month, date, and year. See Appendix M, "Date and Time Format Specifiers," for information on date and time format specifiers.

If the control displays time (either because Format is set to Time or because a CustomFormat value includes time fields), then the user can click on a time field and use the arrow keys to adjust its value. You can also click on a numeric field or AM/PM designator and type a new value.

The DateTimePicker control's MinDate and MaxDate properties determine the first and last dates that the control will let the user select.

The control has several properties that determine the appearance of the calendar, if it displays one. These include CalendarFont, CalendarForeColor, CalendarMonthBackground, CalendarTitleBackColor, CalendarTitleForeColor, and CalendarTrailingForeColor.

The program can use the control's Value property to get or set the control's date and time.

DirectoryEntry

The DirectoryEntry component represents a node or object in an Active Directory hierarchy. Active Directory is a service that provides a common, hierarchical view of distributed resources and services on a network.

Active Directory is really a Windows operating system topic, not a Visual Basic topic, so it is not covered further here. For more information, see the DirectoryEntry class's Web page msdn.microsoft.com/ library/en-us/cpref/html/frlrfsystemdirectoryservicesdirectoryentryclasstopic.asp.

DirectorySearcher

The DirectorySearcher component performs searches on an Active Directory hierarchy. See the online help for more information on Active Directory and the DirectorySearcher component.

DomainUpDown

The DomainUpDown control displays a list of items that the user can select by clicking the up and down arrow buttons beside the control. For example, the control might let the user select one of the values High, Medium, and Low.

If the control's InterceptArrowKeys property is True, the user can also scroll through the items by using the up and down arrow keys. If InterceptArrowKeys is False, then the user must click the arrow buttons to change the value.

Normally, the control's `ReadOnly` property is set to `False` so the user can type text into the control's text area much as you can enter text in a `ComboBox`. If `ReadOnly` is `True`, then the user cannot type in this area and must use the arrow keys or buttons to pick one of the control's items. Unfortunately, setting `ReadOnly` to `True` gives the control a gray background, so it appears disabled unless you look closely and notice that the text is black rather than dark gray.

Like the `CheckedListBox` control, the `DomainUpDown` control can hold arbitrary objects as items. It displays the string returned by an object's `ToString` method. See the "CheckedListBox" section earlier in this appendix for more information about displaying objects in the control.

The control's `SelectedItem` property returns the object representing the item that is currently selected. Note that there may be no item selected if the user typed a value in the text area, rather than selecting a value from the list of items. The `SelectedIndex` property returns the index of the currently selected item or -1 if no choice is selected.

The control's `Text` property returns the text that the control is currently displaying. This property returns something meaningful whether the user typed a value or selected an item from the list.

When the control is first displayed, no item is selected. You can use the Properties window to give the control a `Text` value at design time but you cannot make it select an item, even if the `Text` value matches an item's text. If you want the control to begin with an item selected, you can use code similar to the following in the form's `Load` event handler:

```
' Select the first Priority value.
dudPriority.SelectedIndex = 0
```

If you set the control's `Sorted` property to `True`, then the control displays its items in sorted order.

If you set the `Wrap` property to `True`, then the control wraps its list of items around if the user moves past the beginning or end of the list.

ErrorProvider

The `ErrorProvider` component indicates to the user that another control has an error associated with it.

The following code shows how a program might use an `ErrorProvider` component. Suppose that the `TextBox` `txtZip` should contain a five-digit ZIP code. When the user enters a value and moves to another field, the control's `Validating` event handler, shown in the code, fires. The code uses a `Like` statement to see if the text contains exactly five digits.

If the text does not contain five digits, then the program calls the `ErrorProvider`'s `SetError` method to associate the error "Invalid ZIP code format" with the `TextBox`. At this point, the `ErrorProvider` displays an icon showing a little red circle containing a white exclamation mark next to the text box and makes the icon blink several times to draw the user's attention to the error. If the user hovers the mouse over the error icon, the component displays a tooltip showing the error message.

If the text does contain five digits, then the code calls the `ErrorProvider` component's `SetError` method to clear any error currently set for the `txtZip` TextBox. This makes the `ErrorProvider` remove any error icon it is currently displaying next to the control.

```
' Verify that this is a 5-digit ZIP code.
Private Sub txtZip_Validating(ByVal sender As Object, _
 ByVal e As System.ComponentModel.CancelEventArgs) Handles txtZip.Validating
    If Not (txtZip.Text Like "#####") Then
        ' It's invalid. Display an error.
        ErrorProvider1.SetError(txtZip, "Invalid ZIP code format")
    Else
        ' It's valid. Clear any error.
        ErrorProvider1.SetError(txtZip, "")
    End If
End Sub
```

The component's `BlinkRate` property determines how quickly the error icon blinks. The `BlinkStyle` property determines how it blinks.

If `BlinkStyle` is `BlinkIfDifferentError`, then the component makes the icon blink several times whenever the program sets a control's error message to a new nonblank value. Because the previous code uses the same error message whenever the ZIP code value does not contain exactly five digits, the message remains unchanged if the user changes the ZIP code to a new invalid value, so the icon does not blink again.

If `BlinkStyle` is `AlwaysBlink`, then the component makes the icon blink as long as the control has an associated error. The icon continues blinking, even if another application has the focus, until the user fixes the error and moves to a new field to trigger the `Validating` event handler again.

If `BlinkStyle` is `NeverBlink`, then the component displays the error icon without blinking.

The component's `Icon` property gives the icon that the component displays for an error. You can change this icon if you want to use a special error image.

Blinking text can be extremely irritating to users, so don't abuse it. The default behavior of blinking a couple of times and then stopping is probably reasonable, but a message that is constantly blinking very quickly is a bad idea. Note that the United States Accessibility code prohibits objects that blink faster than 2 Hz and slower than 55 Hz (see `508.nih.gov/saos/excerpted_stds.html`*).*

EventLog

The `EventLog` component enables an application to manipulate event logs. It provides methods to create logs, write and read log messages, and clear logs.

The following code demonstrates some of the `EventLog` component's features. Before a program can write into an event log, it must register with the log as an event source. When this program's form loads, it uses the `EventLog` class's shared `SourceExists` method to see if the `StatusSource` event source is defined. If the source is not defined, the program uses the `CreateEventSource` method to define it. The program sets the `logStatus EventLog` component's `Source` property to "`StatusSource`" and uses the component's `WriteEntry` method to place an entry in the log. It then calls the `ShowLog` subroutine described shortly to display the log entries. The form's `Closing` event handler writes a message into the log indicating that the program is closing.

When the user clicks the program's Add To Log button, the code writes the text in the `txtMessage` text box into the log, clears the text box, and calls `ShowLog` to display the log entries.

When the user clicks the Clear Log button, the program calls the `EventLog` component's `Clear` method to remove all of the entries from the log.

Finally, subroutine `ShowLog` clears the `lstLog` list box. It then loops through the `EventLogEntry` objects contained in the component's `Entries` collection, adding each object's message to the list box.

```
' Connect to the log.
Private Sub Form1_Load(ByVal sender As System.Object, _
 ByVal e As System.EventArgs) Handles MyBase.Load
    ' See if the log exists and create it if it doesn't.
    If Not EventLog.SourceExists("StatusSource") Then
        EventLog.CreateEventSource("StatusSource", "StatusLog")
        Debug.WriteLine("Creating event source")
    End If

    ' Set the EventLog component's source.
    logStatus.Source = "StatusSource"

    ' Write a Starting message to the log.
    logStatus.WriteEntry(Now & "> " & "Starting")
    ShowLog()
End Sub

' Write a Closing message to the log.
Private Sub Form1_FormClosing(ByVal sender As Object, _
 ByVal e As System.Windows.Forms.FormClosingEventArgs) Handles Me.FormClosing
    logStatus.WriteEntry(Now & "> " & "Closing")
End Sub

' Add an entry to the log.
Private Sub btnAddToLog_Click(ByVal sender As System.Object, _
 ByVal e As System.EventArgs) Handles btnAddToLog.Click
    logStatus.WriteEntry(Now & "> " & txtMessage.Text)
    txtMessage.Text = ""
    txtMessage.Select(0, 0)
    ShowLog()
End Sub

' Enable or disable btnAddToLog.
Private Sub txtMessage_TextChanged(ByVal sender As System.Object, _
 ByVal e As System.EventArgs) Handles txtMessage.TextChanged
    btnAddToLog.Enabled = (txtMessage.Text.Length > 0)
End Sub
```

```
' Clear the log.
Private Sub btnClearLog_Click(ByVal sender As System.Object, _
 ByVal e As System.EventArgs) Handles btnClearLog.Click
    logStatus.Clear()
    ShowLog()
End Sub

' List the items in the log.
Private Sub ShowLog()
    lstLog.Items.Clear()

    For Each log_entry As EventLogEntry In logStatus.Entries
        lstLog.Items.Add(log_entry.Message)
    Next log_entry
    lstLog.SelectedIndex = lstLog.Items.Count - 1
End Sub
```

FileSystemWatcher

The FileSystemWatcher component keeps an eye on part of the file system and raises events to let your program know if something changes. For example, it can notify your program if a file is created in a particular directory.

For more information on the FileSystemWatcher component, see Chapter 27, "File-System Objects," and Appendix R, "File-System Classes."

FlowLayoutPanel

The FlowLayoutPanel control displays the controls that it contains in rows or columns. For example, when laying out rows, it places controls next to each other horizontally in a row until it runs out of room, and then it starts a new row.

The FlowLayoutPanel is particularly useful for Toolboxes and in situations where the goal is to display as many of the contained controls as possible at one time, and the exact arrangement of the controls isn't too important.

The control's FlowDirection property determines the manner in which the control arranges its contained controls. This property can take the values LeftToRight, RightToLeft, TopDown, and BottomUp. Figure G-5 shows these different arrangements.

The control's AutoScroll property determines whether the control automatically provides scroll bars if its contents won't fit within the control all at once.

The Padding property determines how much space the control leaves between its edges and the controls it contains. Use the Margin properties of the contained controls to specify the spacing between the controls.

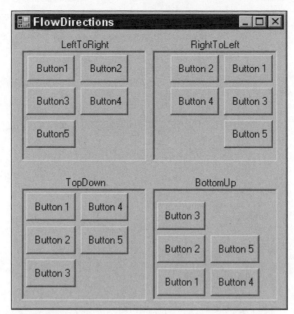

Figure G-5: The `FlowLayoutPanel` **control can arrange its contents from left to right, from right to left, top-down, or bottom-up.**

The `TableLayoutPanel` control also arranges contained controls, but in a grid. For information on that control, see the section, "`TableLayoutPanel`," later in this appendix.

FolderBrowserDialog

The `FolderBrowserDialog` component displays a dialog that lets the user select a folder (directory) in the file system. The program displays the dialog by calling the component's `ShowDialog` method.

The following code shows how a program can use the dialog. The program sets the dialog component's `Description` property to a string telling the user to select the folder containing configuration data and calls the component's `ShowDialog` method. If the user selects a folder and clicks OK, `ShowDialog` returns `DialogResult.OK`, and the program calls the `LoadConfiguration` subroutine, passing it the name of the folder that the user selected.

```
dlgFolder.Description = _
    "Select the folder that contains the configuration data XML files."
If dlgFolder.ShowDialog() = DialogResult.OK Then
    LoadConfiguration(dlgFolder.SelectedPath)
End If
```

Figure G-6 shows the dialog. Notice that the `Description` text is displayed above the folder area.

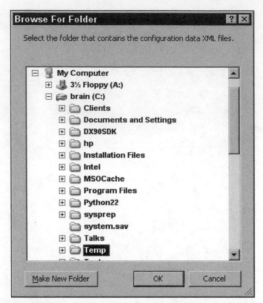

Figure G-6: The `FolderBrowserDialog` component lets the user select a directory.

The component's `SelectedPath` property returns the path selected by the user, but it also determines where the dialog begins browsing. If your code uses the dialog, does not change this value, and then uses the dialog again later, the dialog starts the second time where it left off the first time.

The program can also explicitly set the `SelectedPath` value to start browsing at a particular folder. For example, the following code makes the dialog begin browsing in the `C:\Temp` directory:

```
dlgFolder.SelectedPath = "C:\Temp"
```

Alternatively, you can use the component's `RootFolder` property to make the component start in one of the system folders. Set this property to one of the `Environment.SpecialFolder` values shown in the following table. For example, to start browsing in the `MyPictures` directory, set `RootFolder` to `Environment.SpecialFolder.MyPictures`.

ApplicationData	CommonApplicationData	CommonProgramFiles	Cookies
Desktop	DesktopDirectory	Favorites	History
InternetCache	LocalApplicationData	MyComputer	MyMusic
MyPictures	Personal	ProgramFiles	Programs
Recent	SendTo	StartMenu	Startup
System	Templates		

The dialog will not allow the user to leave the root folder. For example, if you set the `RootFolder` property to `Environment.SpecialFolder.ProgramFiles`, then the user will be able to browse through the Program Files hierarchy (normally, `C:\Program Files`), but will not be able to move to other parts of the system.

If you want to start browsing at a particular directory but want to allow the user to move to other parts of the directory hierarchy, leave the `RootFolder` with its default value of `Environment.SpecialFolder.Desktop` and then set the `SelectedPath` property appropriately. For example, the following code uses the `Environment` object's `SpecialFolder` method to make the browser start browsing at the Program Files folder:

```
dlgFolder.RootFolder = Environment.SpecialFolder.Desktop
dlgFolder.SelectedPath = _
    Environment.GetFolderPath(Environment.SpecialFolder.ProgramFiles)
```

FontDialog

The `FontDialog` component displays the dialog shown in Figure G-7 to let the user select a font. If the user selects a font and clicks OK, the `ShowDialog` method returns `DialogResult.OK`.

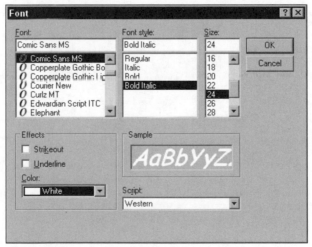

Figure G-7: The `FontDialog` **component lets the user select a font.**

The component has several properties that determine the options that the dialog displays and the types of fonts it will allow the user to select. The following table describes some of the most important of the component's properties.

Property	Purpose
AllowScriptChange	Determines whether the component allows the user to change the character set shown in the Script combo box (Western in Figure G-7). If this is False, the drop-down is still visible, but it only contains one choice.
AllowSimulations	Determines whether the component allows graphics device font simulations. For example, many fonts do not include bold or italics, but the graphics device interface (GDI) can simulate them.
AllowVectorFonts	Determines whether the component allows vector fonts. (Characters in a raster font are drawn as bitmaps. Characters in a vector font are drawn as a series of lines and curves. Vector fonts may provide a nicer look because they scale more easily than raster fonts, but vector fonts may take longer to draw.)
AllowVerticalFonts	Determines whether the component allows vertical fonts (such as Chinese).

Color	Sets or gets the font's color. Note that this is not part of the Font property, so if you want to let the user set a control's font and color, you must handle them separately, as shown in the following code:
	
	``
	dlgFont.Font = Me.Font
	dlgFont.Color = Me.ForeColor
	dlgFont.ShowColor = True
	If dlgFont.ShowDialog() = DialogResult.OK Then
	    Me.Font = dlgFont.Font
	    Me.ForeColor = dlgFont.Color
	End If
	``

FixedPitchOnly	Determines whether the dialog only allows fixed-pitch (fixed-width) fonts. (In a fixed-width font, all characters have the same width. For example, this sentence is in the Courier font, which is fixed-width. In a variable-width font, some characters such as "l" and "i" are thinner than other characters such as "W." This sentence is in the Times New Roman font, which has variable width.
Font	Sets or gets the font described by the dialog.
FontMustExist	Determines whether the component raises an error if the user tries to select a font that doesn't exist.
MaxSize	Determines the maximum allowed point size.
MinSize	Determines the minimum allowed point size.
ShowApply	Determines whether the dialog displays the Apply button. If you set this to True, you should catch the component's Apply event (as shown in the code example later in this section).
ShowColor	Determines whether the component allows the user to select a color.

Property	Purpose
ShowEffects	Determines whether the component displays the Effects group box that includes the Strikeout and Underline boxes and the Color drop-down.
ShowHelp	Determines whether the dialog displays the Help button. If you set this to True, you should catch the component's HelpRequest event. The event handler might explain to the user how the font will be used. For example, "Select the font to be used for item descriptions."

The following code shows how a program might use the dialog to let the user set a form's font. The btnSetFont_Click event handler runs when the user clicks the program's Set Font button. The code saves a copy of the form's current font and foreground color. It sets the dialog's ShowColor and ShowEffects properties to True so the user can select the font's color, Strikeout, and Underline values. It sets ShowApply to True to make the dialog display its Apply button.

Next, the program calls the dialog's ShowDialog method. If ShowDialog returns DialogResult.OK, then the user selected a font and clicked OK. In that case, the program sets the form's font by calling subroutine SetFormFont, passing it the dialog's current font and color.

If ShowDialog returns DialogResult.Cancel, then the user clicked Cancel. In that case, the program calls subroutine SetFormFont, passing it the form's original saved font and color to restore those values.

If the user clicks the dialog's Apply button, then the dlgFont_Apply event handler executes. That routine calls subroutine SetFormFont, passing it the dialog's current font and color to apply the current values.

Subroutine SetFormFont simply sets the form's font and foreground color.

```
' Let the user pick a new font for the form.
Private Sub btnSetFont_Click(ByVal sender As System.Object, _
  ByVal e As System.EventArgs) Handles btnSetFont.Click
    ' Save the current font and color.
    Dim old_font As Font = Me.Font
    Dim old_color As Color = Me.ForeColor

    dlgFont.ShowColor = True      ' Let the user select font color.
    dlgFont.ShowEffects = True    ' Let the user select Strikeout and Underline.
    dlgFont.ShowApply = True      ' Display the Apply button.
    dlgFont.Font = Me.Font        ' Set the initial font.

    ' Display the dialog.
    If dlgFont.ShowDialog() = DialogResult.OK Then
        ' The user clicked OK. Apply the new font.
        SetFormFont(dlgFont.Font, dlgFont.Color)
    Else
        ' The user canceled. Restore the old font.
        SetFormFont(old_font, old_color)
    End If
End Sub
```

```
' Apply the dialog's currently selected font.
Private Sub dlgFont_Apply(ByVal sender As Object, _
 ByVal e As System.EventArgs) Handles dlgFont.Apply
    Dim dlg As FontDialog = DirectCast(sender, FontDialog)
    SetFormFont(dlg.Font, dlg.Color)
End Sub

' Set the form's Font and ForeColor.
Private Sub SetFormFont(ByVal new_font As Font, ByVal new_color As Color)
    ' Set the form's font and color.
    Me.Font = new_font
    Me.ForeColor = new_color
End Sub
```

GroupBox

The GroupBox control displays a caption and a border. This control is mostly for decoration and provides a visually appealing method for grouping related controls on the form.

The GroupBox is also a control container, so you can place other controls inside it. If a GroupBox contains RadioButtons, those buttons form a group separate from any other RadioButtons on the form. If you click one of those buttons, the other buttons in the GroupBox deselect, but any selected RadioButtons outside of the GroupBox remain unchanged. This is important if you need to create more than one group of RadioButtons.

If you want to create multiple RadioButton groups, but you don't want to display a caption and border, use a Panel control instead of a GroupBox.

The GroupBox control provides a typical assortment of properties that determine its appearance (such as BackColor, BackgroundImage, and Font). These properties are straightforward.

If you set the control's Enabled property to False, then its caption is grayed out and any controls it contains are also disabled. This is a convenient way for a program to enable or disable a group of controls all at once.

The GroupBox's Controls property returns a collection containing references to the controls inside the GroupBox.

One of the few confusing aspects to working with GroupBox's in code is figuring out where to position controls within the GroupBox. The control's borders and caption take up room inside the control's client area, so deciding how to position controls without covering those decorations is not obvious. Fortunately, the control's DisplayRectangle property returns a Rectangle object that you can use to position items. This rectangle fills most of the control's area that isn't occupied by the caption and borders.

HelpProvider

The HelpProvider component displays help for other controls. You can associate a HelpProvider with a control. Then, if the user sets focus to the control and presses the F1 key, the HelpProvider displays help for the control. The `HelpProvider` either displays a small tooltip-like pop-up displaying a help string, or it opens a help file.

To assign a help string to a control at design time, open the form in the form designer and select the control. In the Properties window, look for a property named "`HelpString on HelpProvider1`," where *HelpProvider1* is the name of your `HelpProvider` component. If the form contains more than one `HelpProvider`, the control should have more than one "`HelpString on`" property.

Enter the text you want the `HelpProvider` to display in this property and you're finished. When the user sets focus to the control and presses F1, the `HelpProvider` displays the string automatically.

To set the help string programmatically, call the `HelpProvider`'s `SetHelpString` method passing it the control and the help string that it should display for the control. The following code defines help strings for a series of address text box controls:

```
HelpProvider1.SetHelpString(txtName, "Enter the customer's name.")
HelpProvider1.SetHelpString(txtStreet, _
    "Enter the customer's delivery street number and name, " & _
    "plus any apartment or suite number.")
HelpProvider1.SetHelpString(txtCity, "Enter the customer's delivery city.")
HelpProvider1.SetHelpString(txtState, "Enter the customer's delivery state.")
HelpProvider1.SetHelpString(txtZip, "Enter the customer's delivery ZIP code.")
```

To provide help using a help file, set the `HelpProvider` component's `HelpNamespace` property to the full name and path to the help file. Set the other control's "`HelpNavigator on HelpProvider1`" property to one of the values shown in the following table to tell the `HelpProvider` how to use the help file when the user asks for help on this control.

HelpNavigator Value	Purpose
AssociateIndex	Opens the help file's Index page and goes to the first entry that begins with the same letter as the control's "`HelpKeyword on HelpProvider1`" property.
Find	Opens the help file's Index tab.
Index	Opens the help file's Index tab and searches for the value entered in the control's "`HelpKeyword on HelpProvider1`" property.
KeywordIndex	Opens the help file's Index tab and searches for the value entered in the control's "`HelpKeyword on HelpProvider1`" property.
TableOfContents	Opens the help file's Table of Contents tab.
Topic	Displays the topic in the help file that has URL stored in the control's "`HelpKeyword on HelpProvider1`" property. For instance, the URL "`street_name.htm`" might contain the help file's page for the Street field.

To set a control's `HelpNavigator` value in code, call the `HelpProvider`'s `SetHelpNavigator` method passing it the control and the navigator method that you want to use. For example, the following code prepares to give help for the `btnSetColor` control. It sets the `HelpProvider1` component's help file to `C:\Tools\littledraw.chm`. It then sets the `btnSetColor` control's `HelpNavigator` method to `HelpNavigator.Topic`. Finally it sets the control's `HelpKeyword` to "select_color.htm." Now if the user sets focus to this control and presses F1, the `HelpProvider` opens the help file and displays the topic at "select_color.htm."

```
HelpProvider1.HelpNamespace = "C:\Tools\littledraw.chm"
HelpProvider1.SetHelpNavigator(btnSetColor, HelpNavigator.Topic)
HelpProvider1.SetHelpKeyword(btnSetColor, "select_color.htm")
```

A control's "ShowHelp on *HelpProvider1*" property indicates whether the control should use the `HelpProvider` to display its help.

HScrollBar

The `HScrollBar` control represents a horizontal scroll bar. The user can drag the scroll bar's "thumb" to select a number.

The control's `Value` property gets and sets its current numeric value. The `Minimum` and `Maximum` properties determine the range of values that the control can display. These are integer values, so the `HScrollBar` control is not ideal for letting the user select a nonintegral value (such as 1.25).

The control's `SmallChange` property determines how much the control's `Value` property changes when the user clicks the arrows at the scroll bar's ends. The `LargeChange` property determines how much the `Value` changes when the user clicks on the scroll bar between the thumb and the arrows.

Strangely, the control does not let the user to actually select the value given by its `Maximum` property. The program can select that value using code, but the largest value the user can select is `Maximum` − `LargeChange` + 1. For example, if `Maximum` is 100 and `LargeChange` is 10 (the default values), then the user can select values up to 100 − 10 + 1 = 91.

If you set the control's `TabStop` property to `True`, then the control can hold the input focus. While the control has the focus, you can use the arrow keys to change its value by the `SmallChange` amount.

The control's `Scroll` event fires when the user changes the control's value interactively. The `ValueChanged` event occurs when the control's value changes either because the user changed it interactively, or because the program changed it with code. The following code shows how a program can display the `hbarDays` control's `Value` property when the user or program changes it:

```
Private Sub hbarDays_ValueChanged(ByVal sender As Object, _
  ByVal e As System.EventArgs) Handles hbarDays.ValueChanged
    lblDays.Text = hbarDays.Value.ToString
End Sub
```

Note that many controls that might otherwise require scroll bars can provide their own. For example, the `ListBox`, `TextBox`, and `Panel` controls can display their own scroll bars when necessary, so you don't need to add your own.

ImageList

The `ImageList` component stores a series of images for use by other controls or by the program's code. For example, one way to display an image on a `Button` control is to create an `ImageList` component holding the image. Set the `Button`'s `ImageList` property to the `ImageList` component and set its `ImageIndex` property to the index of the image in the `ImageList`.

To add images to the component at design time, open the form designer, select the component, click on the `Images` property in the Properties window, and click the ellipsis (...) on the right. The Image Collection Editor that appears has buttons that let you add, remove, and rearrange the images.

The `ImageList` component's `ImageSize` property determines the size of the images. The component stretches any images of different sizes to fit the `ImageSize`. This means that a single `ImageList` component cannot provide images of different sizes. If you must store images of different sizes in the application, use another method such as multiple `ImageList` components, `PictureBoxes` (possible with `Visible` property set to `False`), or resources.

Label

The `Label` control displays some read-only text. Note that you cannot even select the text at run time so, for example, you cannot copy it to the clipboard. If you want to allow the user to select and copy text, but not modify it, use a `TextBox` with `ReadOnly` property set to `True`.

The `Label` control can display an image in addition to text. To display an image, either set the control's `Image` property to the image or set the control's `ImageList` and `ImageIndex` properties. Use the `ImageAlign` and `TextAlign` properties to determine where the image and text are positioned within the control.

If you set the `Label`'s `AutoSize` property to `True` (the default), then the control resizes itself to fit its text. This can be particularly useful for controls that contain text that changes at run time because it ensures that the control is always big enough to hold the text. Note that the control does not automatically make itself big enough to display any image it contains.

The `Label` control automatically breaks lines that contain embedded carriage returns. The following code makes a label display text on four lines:

```
lblInstructions.Text = "Print this message and either:" & vbCrLf & _
    "   - Mail it to the recipient" & vbCrLf & _
    "   - Fax it to the recipient" & vbCrLf & _
    "   - Throw it away"
```

Text that contains carriage returns confuses the control's `AutoSize` capabilities, however, so you should not use `AutoSize` with multiline text.

The `Label` control also automatically wraps to a new line if the text it contains is too long to fit within the control's width.

LinkLabel

The LinkLabel control displays a label that is associated with a hyperlink. By default, the label is blue and underlined, so it is easy to recognize as a link. It also displays a pointing hand cursor when the mouse moves over it, so it looks more or less like a link on a Web page.

When the user clicks a LinkLabel, the control raises its LinkClicked event. The program can catch the event and take whatever action is appropriate. For example, it could display another form, open a document, or open a Web page.

The following code shows how a program might display a Web page with URL stored in the LinkLabel's Tag property. The call to System.Diagnostics.Process.Start makes the operating system perform the default action for the string value stored in the Tag property. If that value is a URL, the system will normally open the URL with the system's default browser.

```
Private Sub llblBookUrl_LinkClicked(ByVal sender As System.Object, _
  ByVal e As System.Windows.Forms.LinkLabelLinkClickedEventArgs) _
  Handles llblBookUrl.LinkClicked
    System.Diagnostics.Process.Start(llblBookUrl.Tag.ToString)
End Sub
```

The LinkLabel control provides all the formatting properties that the Label control does. See the section "Label," earlier in this appendix for more information on formatting the control's label.

The control also provides several properties for determining the appearance of its link. The following table describes some of the most useful.

Property	Purpose
ActiveLinkColor	The color of an active link.
DisabledLinkColor	The color of a disabled link.
LinkArea	The piece of the control's text that is represented as a link. This includes a start position and a length in characters.
LinkBehavior	Determines when the link is underlined. This can take the values AlwaysUnderline, HoverUnderline, NeverUnderline, and SystemDefault.
LinkColor	The color of a normal link.
Links	A collection of objects representing the link(s) within the control's text.
LinkVisited	A Boolean that indicates whether the link should be displayed as visited.
VisitedLinkColor	The color of a visited link.

A `LinkLabel` can display more than one link within its text. For example, in the text "The quick brown fox jumps over the lazy dog," the control might display the text "fox" and "dog" as links and the rest as normal text. At design time, you can use the `LinkArea` property to specify only one link. To make "fox" the link, the program would set `LinkArea` to 16, 3 to start with letter 16 and include 3 letters.

At run time, the program can add other links to the control. The following code clears the `llblPangram` control's `Links` collection and then adds two new link areas. The program sets each of the new `Link` objects' `LinkData` property to a URL that the program should display when the user clicks that link.

```
Dim new_link As System.Windows.Forms.LinkLabel.Link

llblPangram.Links.Clear()
new_link = llblPangram.Links.Add(16, 3)
new_link.LinkData = "http://www.somewhere.com/fox.htm"
new_link = llblPangram.Links.Add(40, 3)
new_link.LinkData = "http://www.somewhere.com/dog.htm"
```

The following code shows how the program displays the URL corresponding to the link the user clicked. The code gets the appropriate `Link` object from the event handler's event arguments, converts the `Link` object's `LinkData` property into a string, and uses `System.Diagnostics.Process.Start` to open it with the system's default browser.

```
' Display the URL associated with the clicked link.
Private Sub llblPangram_LinkClicked(ByVal sender As System.Object, _
  ByVal e As System.Windows.Forms.LinkLabelLinkClickedEventArgs) _
  Handles llblPangram.LinkClicked
    System.Diagnostics.Process.Start(e.Link.LinkData.ToString)
End Sub
```

ListBox

The `ListBox` control displays a list of items that the user can select. The following table describes some of the control's most useful properties.

Property	Purpose
SelectionMode	Determines how the user can select text. See the following text for details.
MultiColumn	If this is `True`, the control does not display a vertical scroll bar. Instead, if there are too many items to fit, the control displays them in multiple columns. If the columns will not all fit, the control displays a horizontal scroll bar to let you see them all. The control's `ColumnWidth` property determines the width of the columns.
IntegralHeight	If this is `True`, the control will not display a partial item. For example, if the control is tall enough to display 10.7 items, it will shrink slightly so it can only display 10 items.

Table continued on following page

Property	Purpose
ScrollAlwaysVisible	If this is True, the control displays its vertical scroll bar even if all of its items fit. This can be useful if the program will add and remove items to and form the list at run time and you don't want the control to change size depending on whether the items all fit.
Sorted	Determines whether the control displays its items in sorted order.
SelectedItem	Returns a reference to the first selected item or Nothing if no item is selected. This is particularly useful if the control's SelectionMode is One.
SelectedIndex	Returns the zero-based index of the first selected item or -1 if no item is selected. This is particularly useful if the control's SelectionMode is One.
Text	Returns the text displayed for the first currently selected item, or an empty string if no item is selected. Your code can set this property to a string to make the control select the item that displays exactly that string.
SelectedItems	A collection containing references to all the items that are currently selected
SelectedIndices	A collection containing the indexes of all the items that are currently selected.
UseTabStops	Determines whether the control recognizes tabs embedded within its items' text. If UseTabStops is True, the control replaces tab characters with empty space. If UseTabStops is False, the control displays tab characters as thin black boxes.

The control's SelectionMode property determines how the user can select items. This property can take the values None, One, MultiSimple, or MultiExtended.

When SelectionMode is None, the user cannot select any items. This mode can be useful for displaying a read-only list. It can be particularly handy when the list is very long and the control's automatic scrolling is useful, allowing the user see all of the list's items.

When SelectionMode is One, the user can select a single item. When the user clicks on an item, any previously selected item is deselected.

When SelectionMode is MultiSimple, the user can select multiple items by clicking on them one at a time. When the user clicks on an item, the other items keep their current selection status. This mode is useful when the user needs to select multiple items that are not necessarily near each other in the list. It is less useful if the user must select a large number of items. For example, clicking 100 items individually would be tedious.

When `SelectionMode` is `MultiExtended`, the user can select multiple items in several ways. The user can click and drag to manipulate several items at once. If the first item clicks is not selected, then all of the items are selected. If the first item is already selected, then all of the items are deselected. If the user holds down the Ctrl key and clicks an item, the other items' selection status remains unchanged. If the user doesn't hold down the Ctrl key, any other items are deselected when the user selects new items. If the user clicks on an item and then clicks on another item while holding down the Shift key, all of the items between those two are selected. If the user holds down the Ctrl key at the same time, those items are selected and the other items' selection status remains unchanged.

The `MultiExtended` mode is useful when the user needs to select many items, some of which may be next to each other. This mode is quite complicated, however, so `MultiSimple` may be a better choice if the user doesn't need to select ranges of items or too many items.

Use the control's `Items.Add` method to add an object to the list. If the object isn't a string, the control uses the object's `ToString` method to determine the value it displays to the user.

The `ListBox`'s `FindString` method returns the index of the first item that begins with a given string. For example, the following code selects the first item that begins with the text "Code":

```
lstTask.SelectedIndex = lstTask.FindString("Code")
```

The `FindStringExact` method returns the index of the first item that matches a given string exactly.

ListView

The `ListView` control displays a list of items in one of five possible views, determined by the control's `View` property. The `View` property can take the following values:

❑ *Details* — For each item, displays a small icon, the item's text, and the subitems' text on a row.

❑ *LargeIcon* — Displays large icons above the item's text. Entries are arranged from left to right until they wrap to the next row.

❑ *List* — Displays small icons to the left of the item's text. Each entry is placed on its own row.

❑ *SmallIcon* — Displays small icons to the left of the item's text. Entries are arranged from left to right until they wrap to the next row.

❑ *Tile* — Displays large icons to the left of the item's text. Entries are arranged from left to right until they wrap to the next row.

Figure G-8 shows each of these views for the same list of items. The second tiled view shown in the lower right corner uses the control's `CheckBoxes` and `StateImageList` properties, and is described shortly.

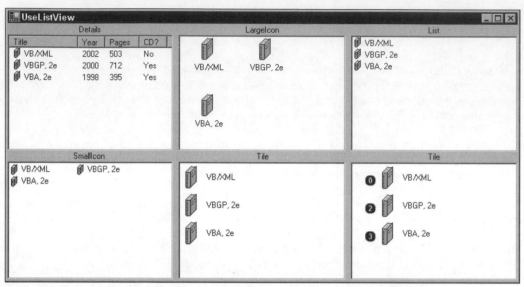

Figure G-8: The `ImageList` control can display four views.

Set the control's `LargeImageList` and `SmallImageList` properties to `ImageList` controls containing the images that you want to use for the `LargeIcon` and `SmallIcon` views.

Each of the `ListView` control's items may contain one or more subitems that are displayed in the Details view. To create the items and subitems, open the form designer, select the `ListView` control, click on the `Items` property in the Properties window, and click the ellipsis (...) to the right. This displays the `ListViewItem` Collection Editor shown in Figure G-9.

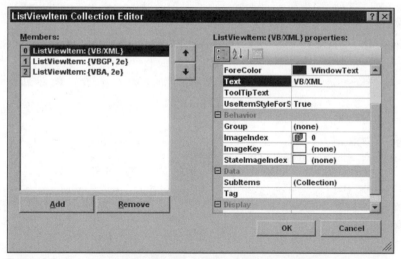

Figure G-9: Use the ListViewItem Collection Editor to define a `ListView` control's items at design time.

Click the Add button to make a new item. Set the item's `Text` property to the string you want the control to display. If you have attached `ImageList` controls to the `ListView`, set the new item's `ImageIndex` property to the index of the image you want to display for this item in the `LargeIcon` and `SmallIcon` views.

For example, the program in Figure G-8 contains two `ImageList` controls. The `imlBig` control contains 32×32 pixel images and the `imlSmall` control contains 16×16 pixel images. Each holds one image of a book. All of the items in the `ListView` items have `ImageIndex` set to 0, so they all display the first images in the `imlBig` and `imlSmall` controls.

To give an item subitems, select it in the `ListViewItem` Collection Editor, click on its `SubItems` property, and then click the ellipsis (...) to the right to display the `ListViewSubItem` Collection Editor shown in Figure G-10. Use the Add button to make subitems. Set the subitems' `Text` properties to determine what the Details view displays.

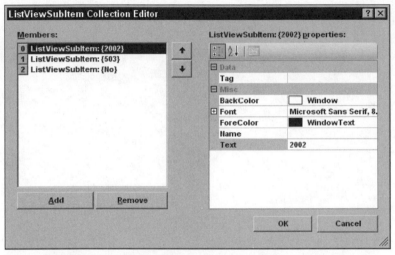

Figure G-10: Use the ListViewSubItem Collection Editor to define a `ListView` item's subitems.

If you set the `ListView` control's `CheckBoxes` property to `True`, the control displays check boxes next to its items. If you set the control's `StateImageList` property to an `ImageList` control, then the control displays the images in that list. When the user double-clicks on an item, the control toggles the image index between 0 and 1 and displays the first or second image. In Figure G-8, the `ListView` on the lower-right uses check box images that look like circles with numbers inside. If you set `CheckBoxes` to `True` but do not set the `ListView`'s `StateImageList` property, the control displays simple boxes containing checkmarks.

If CheckBoxes is True, the program can use the CheckedIndices or CheckedItems collections to see which items the user has "checked." If the StateImageList control holds more than two images, an item is considered checked if it is displaying any picture other than the first one. The following code lists the currently checked items in the lvwMeals ListView control:

```
For Each checked_item As ListViewItem In lvwMeals.CheckedItems
    Debug.WriteLine(checked_item.ToString)
Next checked_item
```

The control's SelectedIndices and SelectedItems collections let the program see which items the user has currently selected. The user can select items by clicking on them. If the user holds down the Ctrl key while clicking, any items that are already selected remain selected. If the user clicks an item, holds down the Shift key, and then clicks another item, the control selects all of the items in between the two.

If you are using the ListView in Details mode, you must define the control's columns. Open the form designer, select the control, click the Columns property in the Properties window, and click the ellipsis (...) to the right to display the ColumnHeader Collection Editor shown in Figure G-11.

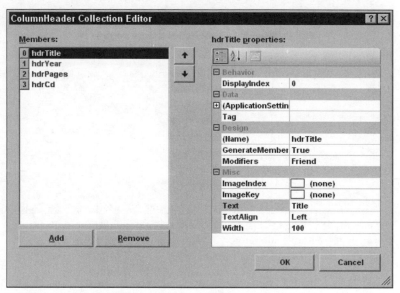

Figure G-11: Use the ColumnHeader Collection Editor to define the columns a ListView displays in Detail mode.

Use the Add button to create column headers and then set each header's text. If you don't define enough columns for all of the subitems, some of the subitems will not be visible to the user.

The LabelEdit control has several other properties that determine its appearance and how the control interacts with the user. The following table describes some of the most important of these.

Property	Purpose
AllowColumnReorder	If True, the user can rearrange the columns by dragging their column headers while in Detail mode.
FullRowSelect	If True, then clicking on an item or any of its subitems selects the item. If False, the user must click the item not a subitem to select the item. If AllowColumnReorder is True, you may want to set FullRowSelect to True also so the user doesn't need to figure out which rearranged column contains the item itself.
GridLines	If True, the control displays gray lines between the rows and columns while in Detail mode.
HeaderStyle	When in Detail mode, this can be None to not display column headers, Clickable to allow the user to click column headers, or Nonclickable to not let the user click column headers. If this is Clickable, the program can catch the control's ColumnClick event to learn the index of the column clicked. For example, you may want to sort the ListView's items using the clicked column.
LabelEdit	If True, the user can modify the items' labels. The user can never change the subitems' labels.
MultiSelect	If True, the user can use the Ctrl and Shift keys to select multiple items.
Sorting	Indicates whether the control displays its items sorted ascending, sorted descending, or not sorted.

ListView Helper Code

In addition to using the ListView control's collection property editors at design time, you can manipulate the control's items and subitems at run time using code.

The control's Columns collection contains ColumnHeader objects representing the control's column headers. You can use the collection's Add, Count, Remove, RemoveAt, and other methods to manage the text displayed above the columns.

The ListViewMakeColumnHeaders subroutine shown in the following code uses the Columns collection to define a ListView control's column headers. The routine takes as parameters a ListView control and a ParamArray of values that contain title strings, alignment values, and widths. The code clears the control's Columns collection and then loops through the ParamArray. For each triple of array entries, the control creates a column header using the title string, alignment value, and width.

```
' Make the ListView's column headers.
' The ParamArray entries should be triples holding
' column title, HorizontalAlignment value, and width.
Private Sub ListViewMakeColumnHeaders(ByVal lvw As ListView, _
 ByVal ParamArray header_info() As Object)
    ' Remove any existing headers.
    lvw.Columns.Clear()

    ' Make the column headers.
    For i As Integer = header_info.GetLowerBound(0) To _
                       header_info.GetUpperBound(0) Step 3
        Dim col_header As ColumnHeader = lvw.Columns.Add( _
            DirectCast(header_info(i), String), _
            -1, _
            DirectCast(header_info(i + 1), HorizontalAlignment))
        col_header.Width = DirectCast(header_info(i + 2), Integer)
    Next i
End Sub
```

The following code shows how a program might use subroutine `ListViewMakeColumnHeaders` to define the `lvwBooks` control's column headers. Because the Pages and Year columns contain numeric values, the control aligns them on the right of their columns.

```
' Make the ListView column headers.
ListViewMakeColumnHeaders(lvwBooks, _
    "Title", HorizontalAlignment.Left, 120, _
    "URL", HorizontalAlignment.Left, 120, _
    "ISBN", HorizontalAlignment.Left, 90, _
    "Picture", HorizontalAlignment.Left, 120, _
    "Pages", HorizontalAlignment.Right, 50, _
    "Year", HorizontalAlignment.Right, 40)
```

The `ListView` control's `Items` collection contains `ListViewItem` objects that represent the control's items. Each `ListViewItem` has a `SubItems` collection that represents the item's subitems. These collections provide the usual assortment of methods for managing collections: `Count`, `Add`, `Remove`, `RemoveAt`, and so forth.

The `ListViewMakeRow` subroutine shown in the following code uses these collections to add an item and its subitems to a `ListView`. The routine takes as parameters the `ListView` control, the name of the item, and a `ParamArray` containing the names of any number of subitems. The code uses the `ListView` control's `Items.Add` method to make the new item. It then loops through the subitem names, using the new item's `SubItems.Add` method to make the subitems.

```
' Make a ListView row.
Private Sub ListViewMakeRow(ByVal lvw As ListView, ByVal image_index As Integer, _
  ByVal item_title As String, ByVal ParamArray subitem_titles() As String)
    ' Make the item.
    Dim new_item As ListViewItem = lvw.Items.Add(item_title)
    new_item.ImageIndex = image_index
```

```
      ' Make the subitems.
      For i As Integer = subitem_titles.GetLowerBound(0) To _
                         subitem_titles.GetUpperBound(0)
          new_item.SubItems.Add(subitem_titles(i))
      Next i
  End Sub
```

If you set a `ListView` column's width to -1, the control automatically resizes the column so it is wide enough to displays all of its data. If you set a column's width to -2, the control makes the column wide enough to displays all of its data and its header text.

The `ListViewSizeColumns` subroutine shown in the following code sizes all of a `ListView` control's columns so that they fit their data. If the `allow_room_for_header` parameter is `True`, it also allows room for the column headers.

```
  ' Set column widths to -1 to fit data, -2 to fit data and header.
  Private Sub ListViewSizeColumns(ByVal lvw As ListView, _
   ByVal allow_room_for_header As Boolean)
      Dim new_wid As Integer = -1
      If allow_room_for_header Then new_wid = -2

      ' Set the width for each column.
      For i As Integer = 0 To lvw.Columns.Count - 1
          lvw.Columns(i).Width = new_wid
      Next i
  End Sub
```

These helper routines make working with `ListView` controls a bit easier.

Custom ListView Sorting

The `ListView` control's `Sorting` property enables you to sort items in ascending or descending order, but it only considers the items not the subitems. It doesn't even use the subitems to break ties when two items have the same values.

Fortunately, the `ListView` control's `ListViewItemSorter` property provides the flexibility to change the sort order in any way you like. To use this property, you must create a class that implements the `IComparer` interface. The `ListView` control will use an object of this type to decide which items to place before other items.

The following example shows how to use the `IComparer` interface. You can also find examples in the section "Array.Sort" in Chapter 17 and in the section "Derived Controls" in Chapter 12.

The `ListViewComparer` class shown in the following code allows a `ListView` to sort in ascending or descending order on any of its columns. The control uses private `m_ColumnNumber` and `m_SortOrder` variables to remember which column to sort and the direction in which to sort. The class's constructor initializes these values.

The key to the `IComparer` interface is the `Compare` function. This routine must compare two objects x and y. It should return a value less than zero, zero, or greater than zero, depending on whether object x should be considered as less than, equal to, or greater than object y according to the sort.

This version of the Compare function starts by converting the two generic objects x and y into ListViewItems. For each item, the code initializes a string to either the appropriate item or subitem's text, or to a blank string if the item does not have that subitem. For example, if the program is trying to sort using the fifth subitem, but an item only has two subitems, the code cannot try to access that item's fifth subitem.

After it has strings representing the two items, the code uses the String class's Compare method to compare them.

```
' Implements a comparer for ListView columns.
Class ListViewComparer
    Implements IComparer

    Private m_ColumnNumber As Integer
    Private m_SortOrder As SortOrder

    Public Sub New(ByVal column_number As Integer, ByVal sort_order As SortOrder)
        m_ColumnNumber = column_number
        m_SortOrder = sort_order
    End Sub

    ' Compare the items in the appropriate column
    ' for objects x and y.
    Public Function Compare(ByVal x As Object, ByVal y As Object) _
     As Integer Implements System.Collections.IComparer.Compare
        Dim item_x As ListViewItem = DirectCast(x, ListViewItem)
        Dim item_y As ListViewItem = DirectCast(y, ListViewItem)

        ' Get the subitem values.
        Dim string_x As String
        If item_x.SubItems.Count <= m_ColumnNumber Then
            string_x = ""
        Else
            string_x = item_x.SubItems(m_ColumnNumber).Text
        End If

        Dim string_y As String
        If item_y.SubItems.Count <= m_ColumnNumber Then
            string_y = ""
        Else
            string_y = item_y.SubItems(m_ColumnNumber).Text
        End If

        ' Compare them.
        If m_SortOrder = SortOrder.Ascending Then
            Return String.Compare(string_x, string_y)
        Else
            Return String.Compare(string_y, string_x)
        End If
    End Function
End Class
```

The following code shows how a program might use the `ListViewComparer` class to enable the user to sort in ascending or descending order on any column in `Details` view. The user can click on any column to sort on that column. If the user clicks on the same column again, the program reverses the sort order.

This code keeps track of the column that it is currently using for sorting in its `m_SortingColumn` variable.

When the user clicks on a column header, the `lvwBooks` control's `ColumnClick` event handler fires. The event handler begins by getting a reference to the column that the user clicked and determines the sort order it should use. If the current sorting column is `Nothing`, then the program sets the new sort order to `Ascending`.

If the current sorting column is not `Nothing`, then the program compares that column to the newly clicked column. If the two are the same, the program switches the sort order. It knows the current sort order because the sorting column begins with > if the program is sorting in ascending order, and < if the program is sorting in descending order.

If the current sorting column is not `Nothing` and the newly clicked column is different from the current sort column, then the program sorts in ascending order.

Having decided on a sport order, the program removes the > or < from the front of the current sorting column's header if the program is currently sorting on a column.

The code then saves a reference to the new sorting column and adds a > or < to its column header to indicate the direction of the sort. The program sets the `ListView` control's `ListViewItemSorter` property to a new `ListViewComparer` object that is initialized, so it sorts the correct column in the proper order. Finally, the program calls the control's `Sort` method to make it resort its items

```
' The column currently used for sorting.
Private m_SortingColumn As ColumnHeader

' Sort using the clicked column.
Private Sub lvwBooks_ColumnClick(ByVal sender As System.Object, _
 ByVal e As System.Windows.Forms.ColumnClickEventArgs) Handles lvwBooks.ColumnClick
    ' Get the new sorting column.
    Dim new_sorting_column As ColumnHeader = _
        lvwBooks.Columns(e.Column)

    ' Figure out the new sorting order.
    Dim sort_order As System.Windows.Forms.SortOrder
    If m_SortingColumn Is Nothing Then
        ' New column. Sort ascending.
        sort_order = SortOrder.Ascending
    Else
        ' See if this is the same column.
        If new_sorting_column.Equals(m_SortingColumn) Then
            ' Same column. Switch the sort order.
            If m_SortingColumn.Text.StartsWith("> ") Then
                sort_order = SortOrder.Descending
            Else
                sort_order = SortOrder.Ascending
            End If
        Else
```

```
            ' New column. Sort ascending.
              sort_order = SortOrder.Ascending
        End If

        ' Remove the old sort indicator.
        m_SortingColumn.Text = m_SortingColumn.Text.Substring(2)
    End If

    ' Display the new sort order.
    m_SortingColumn = new_sorting_column
    If sort_order = SortOrder.Ascending Then
        m_SortingColumn.Text = "> " & m_SortingColumn.Text
    Else
        m_SortingColumn.Text = "< " & m_SortingColumn.Text
    End If

    ' Create a comparer.
    lvwBooks.ListViewItemSorter = New ListViewComparer(e.Column, sort_order)

    ' Sort.
    lvwBooks.Sort()
End Sub
```

This example is rather complicated because it allows the user to sort on any column in either order. Building a comparer class that sorts the items in one order considering both the item values and the subitem values to break ties would be a bit simpler.

MaskedTextBox

The MaskedTextBox control is a text box that provides a mask that helps guide the user in entering a value in a particular format. The mask determines which characters are allowed at different positions in the text. It displays placeholder characters to help prompt the user and underscores where the user can enter characters. For example, an empty United States phone number field would appear as "(___)___-____" in the MaskedTextBox.

The control's Mask property uses the characters shown in the following table.

Character	Meaning
0	A required digit between 0 and 9.
9	An optional digit or space.
#	An optional digit, space, +, or -. If the user leaves this blank, this character appears as a space in the control's Text, InputText, and OutputText properties.

Character	Meaning
L	A required letter a–z or A–Z.
?	An optional letter a–z or A–Z.
&	A required nonspace character.
C	An optional character.
A	A required alpha-numeric character a–z, A–Z, or 0–9.
a	An optional alphanumeric character a–z, A–Z, or 0–9.
.	A decimal separator placeholder. The control automatically displays the appropriate decimal separator character for the current UI culture.
,	A thousands separator placeholder. The control automatically displays the appropriate thousands separator character for the current UI culture.
:	A time separator placeholder. The control automatically displays the appropriate time separator character for the current UI culture.
/	A date separator placeholder. The control automatically displays the appropriate date separator character for the current UI culture.
$	A currency symbol placeholder. The control automatically displays the appropriate currency symbol character for the current UI culture.
<	Automatically converts the characters that the user types after this point into lowercase.
>	Automatically converts the characters that the user types after this point into uppercase.
|	Disables the previous < or > character.
\	Escapes a character so it is displayed literally by the control even if the character would otherwise have special meaning. For example, \9 places a "9" in the output and \\ displays a "\."

All other characters appear as literals within the mask. Dashes and parentheses are common literal characters. For example, the Social Security number mask "000-00-0000" displays dashes as in " - ".

The control's MaskCompleted property returns True if the user has entered characters to satisfy all of the required pieces of the mask. For example, suppose that the control uses the mask "(999)000-0000" to represent a United States phone number. The control's MaskCompleted property returns True if the user enters "(123)456-7890" (here the parentheses and dashes are added automatically by the control). Because the first three digits are optional, the property is also True if the user enters "( )456-7890". Because the last seven digits are required, the MaskCompleted property returns False if the user enters "(123) -7890".

The following table shows the MaskTextBox control's most useful properties. Note that this control inherits from the TextBox control, so it inherits most of that control's properties, methods, and events. See the section "TextBox" later in this appendix for more information.

Property	Purpose
AllowPromptAsInput	Determines whether the user can enter the prompt character determined by the PromptChar property (normally an underscore).
AsciiOnly	Determines whether the control allows non-ASCII Unicode characters.
BeepOnError	Determines whether the control beeps whenever the user types an invalid keystroke.
EnableCutCopyLiterals	Determines whether literal characters such as the parentheses in the mask "(999)000-0000" are included when the user copies and pastes the control's text.
HidePromptOnLeave	Determines whether the control hides its prompt characters when it loses the focus.
IncludeLiterals	Determines whether the control includes literal characters in the Text and OutputText properties.
IncludePrompt	Determines whether the control includes the PromptChar character in the OutputText property.
InputText	Gets or sets the characters input by the user. This doesn't include any literal mask characters.
Mask	Gets or sets the mask.
MaskCompleted	Returns True if he user's input satisfies the required mask characters.
MaskFull	Returns True if the user has entered characters for all of the mask's required and optional elements.
OutputText	Returns the user's text modified by the IncludeLiterals and IncludePrompt properties.
PromptChar	Determines the character that the control uses as a placeholder for user input.
Text	Gets or sets the text as it is currently displayed to the user, including prompt and literal characters.

The following table describes the control's most useful events.

Event	Occurs When
InputTextChanged	The control's text has been modified.
MaskChanged	The control's mask changed.
MaskInputRejected	The user's input does not satisfy mask at the current position.
OutputTextChanged	The control's text has been modified.
TextChanged	The control's text has been modified.

Unfortunately, the MaskedTextBox control is relatively inflexible. It requires the user to enter exactly the right characters at the right positions, and there can be no variation in the format. For example, a single mask cannot let the user enter a telephone number in either of the formats "456-7890" or "(123)456-7890." The mask "(999)000-0000" makes the first three digits optional, but the user must enter spaces in those positions or skip over them. The mask also considers each character separately, so this mask accepts the value "(3)456-7890".

This inflexibility means the MaskedTextBox control is most useful when you know exactly what the user will need to enter. If you want the user to type a four-digit telephone extension, a seven-digit phone number, or a five-digit ZIP code, then the control works well. If the user might enter either a seven- or ten-digit phone number, a five-digit ZIP code or a nine-digit ZIP+4 code, or an arbitrary e-mail address, the control is much less useful. In these cases, you might want to use regular expressions to validate the user's input more precisely. For more information on regular expressions, see the "Regular Expressions" section in Chapter 28, "Useful Namespaces."

MenuStrip

The MenuStrip control represents a form's menus, submenus, and menu items. To make the form display the menu, its Menu property must be set to the MenuStrip control. The first time you add a MenuStrip control to the form, Visual Basic automatically sets the form's Menu property to the new control, so you usually don't need to worry about this. If you later delete the control and create a new MenuStrip, you may need to set this property yourself.

At design time, the MenuStrip control is visible both at the top of the form and in the component tray. Click on a menu entry and type to change the caption it displays. Place an ampersand in front of the character that you want to use as a keyboard accelerator. For example, to make the caption of the File menu display as "File," set the menu's text to &File. If you type Alt-F at run time, the program opens this menu.

To make a cascading submenu, click on a menu item and enter its caption. A ghostly text box appears to the right containing the text "Type Here." Click on this and enter the submenu's name.

When you select a menu item, the Properties window displays the menu item's properties. The following table describes the most useful menu item properties.

Property	Purpose
Checked	Indicates whether the item is checked. You can use this property to let the user check and uncheck menu items.
CheckOnClick	Determines whether the item should automatically check and uncheck when the user clicks it.
CheckState	Determines whether the item is checked, unchecked, or displayed as in an indeterminate state.
DisplayStyle	Determines whether the item displays text, an image, both, or neither. The image appears on the left where a check box would otherwise go. If the item displays an image, it draws a box around the image when the item is checked.
Enabled	Determines whether the menu item is enabled. If an item is disabled, its shortcut is also disabled and the user cannot open its submenu if it contains one.
Font	Determines the font used to draw the item.
MergeAction	Determines how Visual Basic merges MDI child and parent form menus. See the online help for more information.
MergeIndex	Determines the order in which Visual Basic merges MDI child and parent form menus. See the online help for more information.
Name	Gives the menu item's name.
ShortcutKeys	Determines the item's keyboard shortcut. For instance, if you set an item's Shortcut to F5, then the user can instantly invoke the item at run time by pressing the F5 key.
ShowShortcutKeys	Determines whether the menu displays its shortcut to the right at run time. Usually this should be True, so users can learn about the items' shortcuts.
Text	Gives the caption displayed by the item. Place an ampersand in front of the character you want to use as a keyboard accelerator as already described.
Visible	Determines whether the item is visible. An item's shortcut will still work even if the item is not visible. You can use that feature to provide keyboard shortcuts for functions that are not available in any menu.

When the user selects a menu item, the item raises a Click event. You can write an event handler to take whatever action is appropriate. For example, the following code shows how the File menu's Exit item closes the form:

```
Private Sub mnuFileExit_Click(ByVal sender As System.Object, _
 ByVal e As System.EventArgs) Handles mnuFileExit.Click
    Me.Close()
End Sub
```

To create a menu item event handler, open the item in the form editor and double-click it.

MessageQueue

The `MessageQueue` component provides access to a queue on a message-queuing server. An application can use a message queue to communicate with other applications. This is a fairly advanced and specialized topic, so it is not covered in detail here. See the online help for more information.

MonthCalendar

The `MonthCalendar` control displays a calendar that allows the user to select a range of dates. This calendar is similar to the one that the `DateTimePicker` control displays when its `ShowUpDown` property is `False` and you click the control's drop-down arrow. See the section "DateTimePicker," earlier in this appendix for more information on that control.

Figure G-12 shows a dialog that uses the `MonthCalendar` control. The right and left arrows at the top of the calendar let you move through months. If you click on the month, the control displays a pop-up menu listing the months so that you can quickly select one. If you click on the year, the control displays small up and down arrows that you can use to change the year. When you have found the month and year you want, click a date to select it.

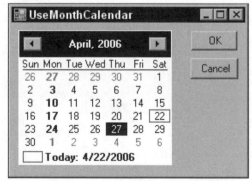

Figure G-12: The MonthCalendar control lets
the user select dates or a range of dates.

If you get lost scrolling through the calendar's months, you can click the Today entry at the bottom of the calendar to jump back to the current date. You can also right-click on the calendar and select the "Go to today" command.

The MonthCalendar control's MinDate and MaxDate properties determine the first and last dates that the control will let the user select.

The DateTimePicker control is designed to let the user select a single date. The MonthCalendar control is a bit more powerful. For example, this control can allow the user to select a range of dates by clicking and dragging across the calendar. The program can use the control's SelectionRange, SelectionStart, and SelectionEnd properties to see what dates the user has selected.

The following table describes the control's most useful properties for controlling its more advanced features.

Property	Purpose
AnnuallyBoldedDates	An array that specifies dates that should be bolded every year. For example, you can bold April 1 for every year displayed.
BoldedDates	An array that specifies specific dates that should be displayed in bold.
CalendarDimensions	Sets the number of columns and rows of months the control displays. Figure G-13 shows a MonthCalendar control with CalendarDimensions = 3, 2 (three columns and two rows).
FirstDayOfWeek	Sets the day of the week shown in the leftmost column of each month. Figure G-13 uses the default value Sunday.
MaxDate	The last date the user is allowed to select.
MaxSelectionCount	The maximum number of days the user can select.
MinDate	The first date the user is allowed to select.
MonthlyBoldedDates	An array that specifies dates that should be bolded every month. For example, you can bold the 13th of every month displayed.
SelectionEnd	A DateTime object representing the control's first selected date.
SelectionRange	A SelectionRange object representing the control's selected range of dates.
SelectionStart	A DateTime object representing the control's last selected date.
ShowToday	Determines whether the control displays today's date at the bottom.
ShowTodayCircle	Determines whether the control circles today's date (March 12, 2006 in Figure G-13). (Although on this system at least the date is "circled" with a rectangle.)
ShowWeekNumbers	Determines whether the control displays the number of each week in the year to the left of each week.

Property	Purpose
SingleMonthSize	Returns the minimum size needed to display a single month.
TodayDate	Determines the date displayed as today's date (March 12, 2006 in Figure G-13).
TodayDateSet	Boolean that indicates whether the control's TodayDate property has been explicitly set.

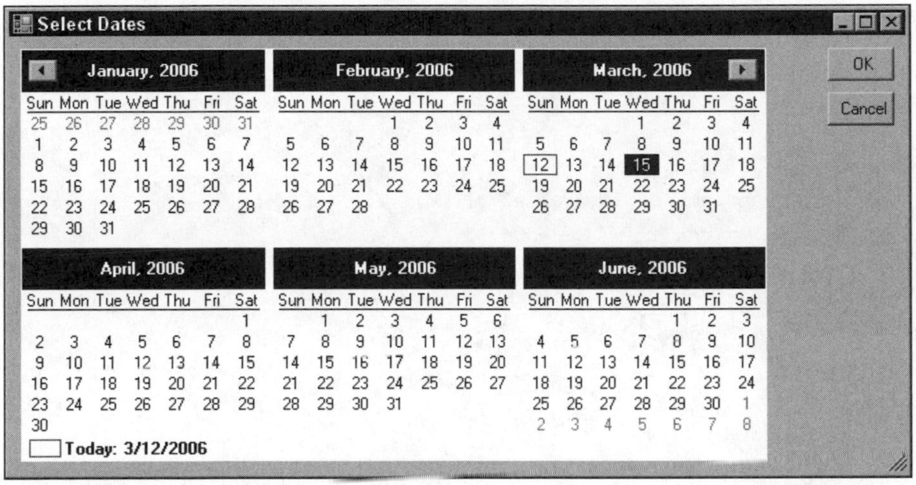

Figure G-13: The MonthCalendar control can display more than one month at a time.

The TodayDate property has an annoying side effect. If you set this value at design time and then set it back to the current day's date, the control's TodayDateSet property still returns True, indicating that you have set the TodayDate property. To clear TodayDate so that TodayDateSet returns False, right-click on the name (not the value) of the TodayDate property in the Properties window and select Reset.

The following code demonstrates several of these properties. It begins by initializing a DateTime variable to the first date allowed by the control. It checks the variable's day of the week and adds a number of days to move the variable to the following Monday. The code then builds an array of DateTime objects holding all of the Mondays between the first and last dates allowed by the MonthCalendar control and sets the control's BoldedDates property to this array. The program then sets the TodayDate property, and uses a new SelectionRange object to specify the dates that the control should initially display as selected.

```
' Get the first Monday in the allowed range.
Dim mon As DateTime
mon = CalReservation.MinDate
Select Case mon.DayOfWeek
    Case DayOfWeek.Tuesday
        mon = mon.AddDays(6)
    Case DayOfWeek.Wednesday
```

```
            mon = mon.AddDays(5)
        Case DayOfWeek.Thursday
            mon = mon.AddDays(4)
        Case DayOfWeek.Friday
            mon = mon.AddDays(3)
        Case DayOfWeek.Saturday
            mon = mon.AddDays(2)
        Case DayOfWeek.Sunday
            mon = mon.AddDays(1)
    End Select

    ' Make an array of the allowed Mondays.
    Dim num_mondays As Integer
    Dim mondays() As DateTime = Nothing
    Do While mon <= CalReservation.MaxDate
        num_mondays += 1
        ReDim Preserve mondays(num_mondays - 1)
        mondays(num_mondays - 1) = mon
        CalReservation.AddBoldedDate(mon)
        mon = mon.AddDays(7)
    Loop

    ' Bold the Mondays.
    CalReservation.BoldedDates = mondays

    ' Set today's date to 6/27/2005.
    CalReservation.TodayDate = New Date(2005, 6, 27)

    ' Start with the dates 7/28/2005 - 6/30/2005 selected.
    CalReservation.SelectionRange = _
        New SelectionRange( _
            New Date(2005, 6, 28), _
            New Date(2005, 6, 30))
```

The following code shows how the program can display the dates selected by the control. It presents a message box showing the control's `SelectionStart` and `SelectionEnd` properties. The result would be similar to "6/28/2005 to 6/30/2005."

```
Private Sub btnOK_Click(ByVal sender As System.Object, _
 ByVal e As System.EventArgs) Handles btnOK.Click
    MessageBox.Show( _
        calReservation.SelectionStart & " to " & _
        calReservation.SelectionEnd)
End Sub
```

The `MonthCalendar` control provides several useful methods. The following table describes the most useful.

Method	Purpose
AddAnnuallyBoldedDate	Adds a date to the control's array of annually bolded dates. You must call `UpdateBoldedDates` after using this method.

Method	Purpose
AddBoldedDate	Adds a date to the control's array of bolded dates. You must call UpdateBoldedDates after using this method.
AddMonthlyBoldedDate	Adds a date to the control's array of monthly bolded dates. You must call UpdateBoldedDates after using this method.
GetDisplayRange	Returns a SelectionRange object that indicates the range of dates currently displayed by the control. If this method's "visible" parameter is True, the SelectionRange includes only dates that are included in the months that are visible (1/1/2006 to 6/30/2006 in Figure G-13). If this parameter is False, the SelectionRange includes all of the displayed dates even if they are in the months before or after the first and last months displayed (12/26/2005 to 7/9/2006 in Figure G-13).
RemoveAllAnnuallyBoldedDates	Empties the control's array of annually bolded dates. You must call UpdateBoldedDates after using this method.
RemoveAllBoldedDates	Empties the control's array of bolded dates. You must call UpdateBoldedDates after using this method.
RemoveAllMonthlyBoldedDates	Empties the control's array of monthly bolded dates. You must call UpdateBoldedDates after using this method.
RemoveAnnuallyBoldedDate	Removes a specific annually bolded date. You must call UpdateBoldedDates after using this method.
RemoveBoldedDate	Removes a specific bolded date. You must call UpdateBoldedDates after using this method.
RemoveMonthlyBoldedDate	Removes a specific monthly bolded date. You must call UpdateBoldedDates after using this method.
SetCalendarDimensions	Sets the control's CalendarDimensions property.
SetDate	Selects the specified date.
SetSelectionRange	Selects the range defined by two dates.
UpdateBoldedDates	Makes the control update itself to show changes to its bolded dates.

The control's bolded dates, monthly bolded dates, and annually bolded dates are all tracked separately and the control displays any date that is listed in any of those groups as bold. That means, for instance, that the RemoveAllBoldedDates subroutine does not change the monthly bolded dates or annually bolded dates.

The following code sets April 1 as an annually bolded date and January 13 as a monthly bolded date. It then removes all of the nonspecific bolded dates and calls `UpdateBoldedDates`. The result is that April 1 in every year is bold and that the 13th of every month is bold.

```
calStartDate.AddAnnuallyBoldedDate(#4/1/2005#)
calStartDate.AddMonthlyBoldedDate(#1/13/2005#)
calStartDate.RemoveAllBoldedDates()
calStartDate.UpdateBoldedDates()
```

NotifyIcon

The `NotifyIcon` component is invisible at run time. A program can use the `NotifyIcon` to display an icon in the system tray. The system tray (also called the *status area*) is the little area holding small icons in the lower-left part of the taskbar. The program can use this icon to indicate the application's state.

Figure G-14 shows program `UseNotifyIcon`, which uses the `NotifyIcon` component to display an icon in the system tray. When you check the Happy box, this program displays the happy face shown in Figure G-14. When you check the Sad box, the program displays a sad face.

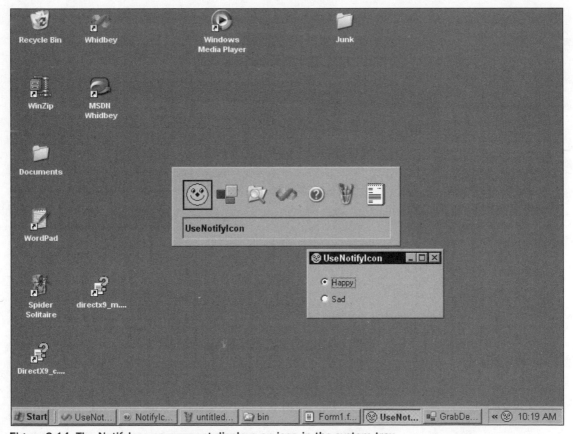

Figure G-14: The NotifyIcon component displays an icon in the system tray.

In Figure G-14, the icon shown by the NotifyIcon component is in the system tray on the lower-right near the time. The form's title bar, the system toolbar at the bottom of the screen, and the Task Manager also display a happy face. The pictures used for these come from the form's Icon property, not from the NotifyIcon component, so you can display different images for these and the one in the system tray.

Notification icons are particularly useful for programs that have no user interface or that run in the background. For example, a program that monitors the system's load could use its system tray icon to give the user an idea of the current load.

These sorts of programs, particularly those without normal user interfaces, often add a context menu to their tray icons so that the user can interact with them. This menu might include commands to minimize or restore the application if it has a user interface, or to make the application exit.

The NotifyIcon component only has a few interesting properties. Its Icon property determines the icon that the component displays. Its Text property sets the tooltip text that the component displays when the user hovers the mouse over the icon. The Visible property determines whether the icon is visible. Finally, the component's ContextMenuStrip property sets the ContextMenuStrip control that displays when the user right-clicks on the icon.

The following code shows how the UseNotifyIcon program works. The program includes four icon resources that are used by the program. The happy and sad icons contain happy and sad images at two sizes: 16×16 pixels and 32×32 pixels. The happy_small and sad_small icons contain only the smaller 16×16 pixel images.

When the user clicks the Happy button, the program sets the nicoStatus NotifyIcon component's Icon property to the happy_small icon and it sets the form's Icon property to the happy icon. It would be more convenient to use the same icon for both purposes. However, if you use the happy icon for both, the NotifyIcon component uses the 32×32 pixel image shrunk to a smaller size and the result looks bad. If you use the happy icon for both purposes, the Task Manager enlarges the 16×16 pixel image and that also looks bad.

When the user clicks the Sad button, the program similarly sets the nicoStatus NotifyIcon component's Icon property to the sad_small icon and it sets the form's Icon property to the sad icon.

At design time, a ContextMenuStrip was attached to the NotifyIcon component. When the user right-clicks on the icon, and then selects the menu's Exit command, the ExitToolStripMenuItem_Click event handler closes the program's form.

```
Public Class Form1
    ' Display the happy status icon.
    Private Sub radHappy_CheckedChanged(ByVal sender As System.Object, _
     ByVal e As System.EventArgs) Handles radHappy.CheckedChanged
        nicoStatus.Icon = My.Resources.happy_small
        Me.Icon = My.Resources.happy
    End Sub

    ' Display the sad status icon.
    Private Sub radSad_CheckedChanged(ByVal sender As System.Object, _
     ByVal e As System.EventArgs) Handles radSad.CheckedChanged
        nicoStatus.Icon = My.Resources.sad_small
        Me.Icon = My.Resources.sad
    End Sub
```

```
      ' Close the application.
      Private Sub ExitToolStripMenuItem_Click(ByVal sender As System.Object, _
       ByVal e As System.EventArgs) Handles ExitToolStripMenuItem.Click
          Me.Close()
      End Sub
  End Class
```

NumericUpDown

The NumericUpDown control displays a number with up and down arrows that you can use to change the number. If you click on an arrow and hold it down, the number changes repeatedly. After a small delay, the changes start happening faster, so you can make some fairly large changes in a reasonable amount of time. You can also change the number by clicking on it and typing in a new value.

The following table lists the control's most interesting properties.

Property	Purpose
DecimalPlaces	Determines the number of decimal places that the control displays. This has no effect when Hexadecimal is True.
Hexadecimal	Determines whether the control displays the number using a hexadecimal format as in A1C when the control's value is 2588 (decimal).
Increment	Determines the amount by which the values is modified when the user clicks an arrow.
InterceptArrowKeys	If this is True, then the user can also adjust the number's value using the up and down arrow keys.
Maximum	Determines the largest value that the control allows.
Minimum	Determines the smallest value that the control allows.
ReadOnly	Determines whether the user can type in a new value. Note that the arrow keys and arrow buttons still work when ReadOnly is True. You can disable them by setting InterceptArrowKeys to False and Increment to 0.
TextAlign	Determines whether the number is aligned on the left, right, or center of the control.
ThousandsSeparator	If this is True, then the control displays thousands separators when the value is greater than 999. This has no effect when Hexadecimal is True.
UpDownAlign	Determines whether the up and down arrows are positioned on the left or right.
Value	The control's numeric value.

The control's more important event, `ValueChanged`, fires whenever the control's numeric value changes, whether because the user changed it or because the program's code changed it.

The `Click` event handler is not as useful for deciding when the control's value has changed. It executes when the user changes the value by clicking an arrow button, but it does not execute if the user types a new value into the field or uses the arrow buttons. It also fires if the user clicks on the control's number but doesn't make any changes.

OpenFileDialog

The `OpenFileDialog` component displays a dialog that lets the user select a file to open. A program calls the component's `ShowDialog` method to display a file selection dialog. `ShowDialog` returns `DialogResult.OK` if the user selects a file and clicks OK, and it returns `DialogResult.Cancel` if the user cancels. The following code shows how a program might use the component to let the user select a configuration file:

```
If dlgConfigurationFile.ShowDialog() = DialogResult.OK Then
    ' Load the configuration information.
    ...
End If
```

Figure G-15 shows the dialog in action.

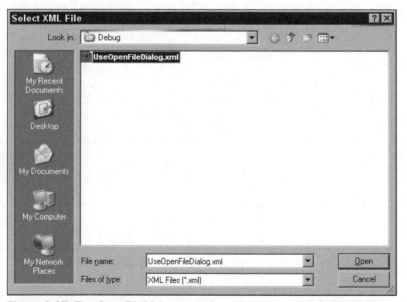

Figure G-15: The OpenFileDialog component lets the user select a file.

This component provides many properties for determining the kinds of files the user can select. The following table describes the most useful of these.

Property	Purpose
AddExtension	If True, then the component adds the default extension specified in the DefaultExt property to the file name if the user does not include an extension.
CheckFileExists	If True, then the component verifies that the file exists. If the user types in the name of a nonexistent file, then the component warns the user and refuses to close.
CheckPathExists	If True, then the component verifies that the file's directory path exists. If the user types in a file and path and the path doesn't exist, then the component warns the user and refuses to close.
DefaultExt	The default extension that the component adds to the file's name if the user omits the extension. This property should have a value such as "txt."
DereferenceLinks	If this is True and the user selects a shortcut file (.lnk), then the component returns the name of the file referenced by the shortcut rather than the link file.
FileName	Sets the first file selected when the dialog is initially displayed. When the user closes the dialog, this property returns the name of the file selected. The dialog retains this value so the next time it is displayed it begins with this file selected.
FileNames	Gets an array of all of the files selected (if the dialog allows multiple selections).
Filter	A string giving the filter that the dialog should use. This string holds pairs of display names (such as "Bitmaps") and their corresponding filter expressions (such as "*.bmp") separated by vertical bar characters (|). Separate multiple expressions within a filter entry with semicolons. For example, the value "GIFs|*.gif|JPGs|*.jpg;*.jpeg| Both|*.gif;*.jpg;*.jpeg|All Files|*.*" lets the user search for GIF files, JPG files, both GIFs and JPGs, or all files.
FilterIndex	Gives the index of the filter entry that the dialog initially displays. The indexes start with 1.
InitialDirectory	Determines the path where the dialog starts when it is displayed. If you later redisplay the same dialog, it will start at the path determined by its FileName property, so it continues where it last left off. If you want to change InitialDirectory to start in some other directory, you also need to set FileName = "".
MultiSelect	Determines whether the user can select multiple files.

Property	Purpose
ReadOnlyChecked	Determines whether the dialog's "Open as read-only" check box is initially selected. This has no effect unless ShowReadOnly is True. The dialog retains this value so that the next time it is displayed it has the value that the user selected. If you want the box checked every time the dialog appears, you must set ReadOnlyChecked to True before you display the dialog each time.
RestoreDirectory	If this value is True, then the dialog restores its initial directory after the user closes it, if the user has navigated to some other directory. However, if you later redisplay the same dialog, it will start at the path determined by its FileName property, so it continues where it last left off. That means if you want to restore the initial directory, you must also set FileName = "" before redisplaying the dialog.
ShowHelp	Determines whether the dialog displays a Help button. If you set this to True, then the application should catch the dialog's HelpRequest event and give the user some help.
ShowReadOnly	Determines whether the dialog displays an "Open as read-only" check box.
Title	Determines the dialog's title text.

The OpenFileDialog component raises its FileOk event when the user tries to accept a file. You can use an event handler to catch the event and perform extra validation. Set the event's e.Cancel value to True to stop the dialog from accepting the selection.

The following code allows the dlgBitmapFile dialog to accept only bitmap files. The code loops through the dialog's selected files. If it finds one with a name that doesn't end in ".bmp," then the program displays an error message, sets e.Cancel to True, and exits the function.

```
' Ensure that the user only selects bitmap files.
Private Sub dlgBitmapFile_FileOk(ByVal sender As System.Object, _
 ByVal e As System.ComponentModel.CancelEventArgs) Handles dlgBitmapFile.FileOk
    For Each file_name As String In dlgBitmapFile.FileNames
        ' See if this file name ends with .bmp.
        If Not file_name.EndsWith(".bmp") Then
            MessageBox.Show("File '" & file_name & "' is not a bitmap file", _
                "Invalid File Type", _
                MessageBoxButtons.OK, _
                MessageBoxIcon.Exclamation)
            e.Cancel = True
            Exit Sub
        End If
    Next file_name
End Sub
```

PageSetupDialog

The PageSetupDialog component displays a dialog that lets the user specify properties for printed pages. For example, the user can specify the printer's paper tray, page size, margins, and orientation (portrait or landscape). Figure G-16 shows the dialog in action.

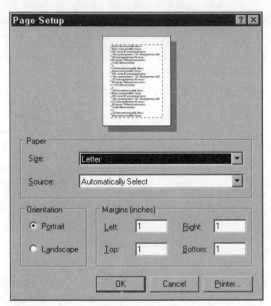

Figure G-16: The PageSetupDialog component lets the user specify printing settings.

Before you can display the dialog, you must assign it a PageSetting object to modify. You can do this in two ways. First, you can set the component's Document property to a PrintDocument object. If the user clicks OK, then the dialog modifies the PrintDocument's settings. This method is preferred because a PrintDocument object defines both page settings and printer settings.

Second, you can set the dialog's PageSettings property to a PageSettings object. If the user clicks OK, then the dialog modifies that object's settings.

Your program calls the component's ShowDialog method to display the dialog. ShowDialog returns DialogResult.OK if the user makes setting and clicks OK. It returns DialogResult.Cancel if the user cancels. Often, the program doesn't need to know whether the user accepted or canceled the dialog, however, because the dialog modifies a PageSettings object. The program can use that object when printing later, so it doesn't need to keep track of whether the user accepted or canceled the dialog.

The following code displays a PageSetupDialog attached to a PrintDocument object.

```
PageSetupDialog1.Document = New PrintDocument
PageSetupDialog1.ShowDialog()
```

The following table describes the `PageSetupDialog`'s most useful properties.

Property	Purpose
AllowMargins	Determines whether the dialog lets the user modify its margin settings.
AllowOrientation	Determines whether the dialog lets the user modify its orientation settings.
AllowPaper	Determines whether the dialog lets the user modify its paper settings.
AllowPrinter	Determines whether the dialog lets the user modify its printer settings.
Document	The `PrinterDocument` object that the dialog will modify.
MinMargins	Gives the smallest allowed margin values. `MinMargins` is a reference to a `Margins` object that has `Left`, `Right`, `Top`, and `Bottom` properties that you can use to specify each margin separately.
PageSettings	The `PageSettings` object that the dialog will modify.
PrinterSettings	The `PrinterSettings` object that the dialog will modify if the user clicks the Printer button. If you set the `Document` property, then the `PrinterDocument` object includes a `PrinterSettings` object.
ShowHelp	Determines whether the dialog displays a Help button. If you set this to `True`, then the application should catch the dialog's `HelpRequest` event and give the user some help.
ShowNetwork	Determines whether the dialog displays a Network button on the Printer setup dialog if the user clicks the Printer button.

Panel

The `Panel` control is a container of other controls. By setting the `Anchor` and `Dock` properties of the contained controls, you can make those controls arrange themselves when the `Panel` is resized.

You can use a `Panel` to make it easy to manipulate the controls it contains as a group. If you move the `Panel`, then the controls it contains move also. If you set the `Panel`'s `Visible` property to `False`, then the controls it contains are hidden. If you set the `Panel`'s `Enabled` property to `False`, then the controls it contains are also disabled.

Similarly, you can set the `Panel`'s other style properties such as `BackColor`, `ForeColor`, and `Font` and any controls contained in the `Panel` inherit these values (although a few controls insist on keeping their own values for some properties, such as the `TextBox`'s `ForeColor` and `BackColor` properties).

A `Panel` also defines a separate group for radio buttons. If you have two `Panel` controls, each containing several radio buttons, then the two groups of buttons work independently, so clicking a button in one `Panel` doesn't deselect the buttons in the other `Panel`.

The most advanced feature of the `Panel` control is its auto-scroll capability. If you set the `AutoScroll` property to `True`, then the control automatically provides working scroll bars if the controls that it contains won't fit. The `AutoScrollMargin` property lets you define extra space that the control should add around its contents when it is auto-scrolling.

Use the `AutoScrollMinSize` property to ensure that the control's scrolling area is at least a certain minimum size. For example, suppose that the `Panel` contains controls with coordinates between 0 and 100 in both the X and Y directions. Normally, the control would let you scroll over the area $0 <= X <= 100$, $0 <= Y <= 100$ so that you can see all of the controls. If you set `AutoScrollMinSize` to "200, 50," then the control would let you scroll over the area $0 <= X <= 200$, $0 <= Y <= 100$ so that you can see the controls plus the area defined by `AutoScrollMinSize`.

The `AutoScrollPosition` property lets your program get or set the scroll bars' position at run time. For example, the following code makes the `panMap` control scroll to make the upper-left corner of its contents visible.

```
panMap.AutoScrollPosition = New Point(0, 0)
```

If you set `AutoScrollPosition` to a point that is outside of the `Panel`'s display area, the control adjusts the point so that it lies within the area.

While a program often uses a `Panel` control as an invisible container for other controls, you can use its `BackColor` and `BorderStyle` properties to make it visible if you like.

PerformanceCounter

The `PerformanceCounter` component represents a Windows NT-style performance counter. You can use the component's methods to read, increment, and decrement the counters. This is a fairly advanced and specialized topic, so it is not covered in detail here. See the online help for more information.

PictureBox

The `PictureBox` control displays images. It also provides a `Graphics` object that you can use to draw lines, rectangles, ellipses, and other shapes at run time.

The control's `Image` property determines the picture that the control displays. Its `SizeMode` property determines how the image is sized to fit into the control. The following table describes the allowed `SizeMode` values.

Value	Meaning
Normal	The image is not resized. If it sticks off the edge of the `PictureBox`, the image is clipped.
StretchImage	The image is stretched to fill the control. This may change the image's shape, making it shorter and wider or taller and thinner than it should be.

Value	Meaning
AutoSize	The PictureBox adjusts its size to fit the image. If the control is displaying borders, it allows extra room for them.
CenterImage	The image is centered in the PictureBox at its normal size. If it sticks off the edge of the PictureBox, the image is clipped.

If you set the control's BackgroundImage property to a picture, the control tiles itself completely with copies of the picture. If you also set the Image property, then the background shows behind the image. If you have SizeMode set to StretchImage or AutoSize, then the image fills the entire control, so you will not see the background image.

The PictureBox control has several properties that deal with its size internally and externally. Its Size, Width, and Height properties give information about the size of the control, including its border if it has one. The ClientRectangle, ClientSize, and DisplayRectangle properties give information about the area inside the control, not including its border. You should use these properties when you draw on the control.

The PictureBox control's CreateGraphics method returns a Graphics object that represents the control's client area. Your code can use that object's methods to draw on the control.

The following code draws an ellipse on the picCanvas control when the user presses the btnDrawCircle button. It uses the PictureBox's CreateGraphics method to make the Graphics object and uses that object's DrawEllipse method to draw the ellipse. The code uses the PictureBox's DisplayRectangle property to get the dimensions of the PictureBox's interior. The code subtracts 1 from the rectangle's width and height so the ellipse will lie completely inside the control's display area.

```
Private Sub btnDrawCircle_Click(ByVal sender As System.Object, _
  ByVal e As System.EventArgs) Handles btnDrawCircle.Click
    Dim gr As Graphics = picCanvas.CreateGraphics()
    gr.DrawEllipse(Pens.Blue, _
        picCanvas.DisplayRectangle.X, _
        picCanvas.DisplayRectangle.Y, _
        picCanvas.DisplayRectangle.Width - 1, _
        picCanvas.DisplayRectangle.Height - 1)
End Sub
```

This routine draws an ellipse on a PictureBox, but it does not ensure that the drawing remains. If you hide the PictureBox with another form and then bring it back to the top, the ellipse is gone. There are two main approaches to keeping a drawing visible on a PictureBox.

First, you can place the drawing commands in the PictureBox's Paint event handler. The Paint event occurs any time part of the control needs to be refreshed. That happens if the control is covered and then uncovered, when its form is minimized and then restored, and when the control is enlarged so that a new part of its display area is exposed.

The following code draws an ellipse on the picCanvas PictureBox whenever it generates a Paint event. Notice that the even handler's e.Graphics parameter gives the Graphics object on which the routine should draw.

```
Private Sub picCanvas_Paint(ByVal sender As Object, _
 ByVal e As System.Windows.Forms.PaintEventArgs) Handles picCanvas.Paint
    e.Graphics.DrawEllipse(Pens.Red, _
        picCanvas.DisplayRectangle.X, _
        picCanvas.DisplayRectangle.Y, _
        picCanvas.DisplayRectangle.Width - 1, _
        picCanvas.DisplayRectangle.Height - 1)
End Sub
```

The second approach to keeping a drawing visible is to make a Bitmap that fits the PictureBox, draw on the Bitmap, and then set the control's Image property equal to the Bitmap. After that, the control automatically displays its image.

The following code shows how a program can make the picCanvas PictureBox permanently display an ellipse. It starts by creating a new Bitmap object with the same size as the PictureBox's display area. Next, it makes a Graphics object associated with the Bitmap. It uses that object's DrawEllipse method to draw the ellipse on the Bitmap. Finally, it sets the PictureBox's Image property to the Bitmap.

```
Private Sub Form1_Load(ByVal sender As System.Object, _
 ByVal e As System.EventArgs) Handles MyBase.Load
    ' Make a Bitmap to fit the PictureBox.
    Dim bm As New Bitmap( _
        picCanvas.DisplayRectangle.Width, _
        picCanvas.DisplayRectangle.Height)

    ' Get a Graphics object to draw on the Bitmap.
    Dim gr As Graphics = Graphics.FromImage(bm)

    ' Draw the ellipse.
    gr.DrawEllipse(Pens.Yellow, _
        picCanvas.DisplayRectangle.X, _
        picCanvas.DisplayRectangle.Y, _
        picCanvas.DisplayRectangle.Width - 1, _
        picCanvas.DisplayRectangle.Height - 1)

    ' Assign the Bitmap to the control's Image property.
    picCanvas.Image = bm
End Sub
```

This method takes more memory than the previous method of drawing in the control's Paint event handler. If the drawing is very complicated and takes a long time, however, it may be faster to generate the Bitmap once rather than redrawing the picture every time the control raises its Paint event.

The final PictureBox feature that is relevant to drawing is its Invalidate method. This method invalidates some or all of the control's display area and generates a Paint event. You can use this method to redraw the control if you have changed some data that will affect the drawing's appearance.

PrintDialog

The PrintDialog component displays the dialog shown in Figure G-17. A program calls the component's ShowDialog method to display the dialog.

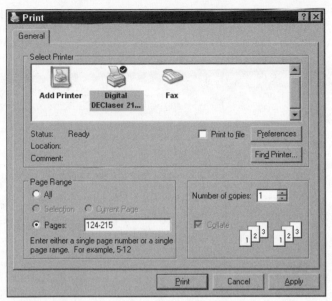

Figure G-17: The PrintDialog component lets the user specify
printing options.

The following table describes the dialog's most useful properties.

Property	Purpose
AllowPrintToFile	Determines whether the "Print to file" button is enabled.
AllowSelection	Determines whether the Selection radio button is enabled.
AllowSomePages	Determines whether the Pages radio button, as well as the From and To text boxes, are enabled.
Document	The PrintDocument object that provides the dialog with a PrinterSettings object.
PrinterSettings	The PrinterSettings object that the dialog modifies.
PrintToFile	Determines whether the "Print to file" box is checked.
ShowHelp	Determines whether the Help button is visible. If this is True, you should catch the component's HelpRequest event and give the user some help.
ShowNetwork	Determines whether the Network button is visible.

If the user clicks Print, the dialog returns DialogResult.OK. If the user clkicks Cancel, the dialog
returns DialogResult.Cancel. The program can use the dialog's PrintToFile property to see if the
user checked the "Print to file" box, and it can use the PrinterSettings object to learn about the user's
other selections.

The following table lists the PrinterSettings object's properties that are most useful for learning about the user's selections. You can set many of these properties before displaying the dialog to give it initial values. After the dialog closes, the properties indicate the user's selections.

Property	Purpose
CanDuplex	Indicates whether the printer can print in duplex.
Collate	Indicates whether the user checked the Collate box.
Copies	The number of copies the user selected.
Duplex	Indicates whether the user asked for duplex printing.
FromPage	The number the user entered in the From text box.
InstalledPrinters	Returns a collection listing the system's installed printers.
IsDefaultPrinter	True if the printer given by the PrinterName property is the default printer.
IsPlotter	True if the printer is a plotter device.
IsValid	True if the printer given by the PrinterName property is a valid printer.
LandscapeAngle	The angle at which the printout is rotated to produce landscape printing. The valid angles are 90 and 270 degrees, or 0 if the printer doesn't support landscape printing.
MaximumCopies	The maximum number of copies that the printer will let you print at a time.
MaximumPage	The largest value that the user is allowed to enter in the To and From boxes.
MinimumPage	The smallest value that the user is allowed to enter in the To and From boxes.
PaperSizes	Returns a collection of objects describing the paper sizes supported by the printer. These PaperSize objects have the properties Height, Width, PaperName, and Kind (for example, Letter).
PaperSources	Returns a collection of objects describing the paper trays provided by the printer. These PaperSource objects have the properties SourceName (for example, "Default tray") and Kind (for example, Upper).
PrinterName	Gets or sets the name of the printer to use.
PrinterResolutions	Returns a collection of PrinterResolution objects that describe the resolutions supported by the printer. PrinterResolution objects have the properties Kind (High, Medium, Low, Draft, or Custom), X, and Y. The X and Y properties return negative values for standard resolutions and the number of dots per inch (dpi) for custom resolutions.

Property	Purpose
PrintRange	Inndicates the pages that the user wants to print. This can have the values AllPages (print everything), Selection (print the current selection), or SomePages (print the pages between FromPage and ToPage).
PrintToFile	Indicates whether the "Print to file" box is checked.
SupportsColor	True if the printer supports color.
ToPage	The number the user entered in the To text box.

The FromPage and ToPage properties must lie between the MinimumPage and MaximumPage values before you display the dialog or the dialog raises an error. If the user enters a value outside of the range MinimumPage to MaximumPage and clicks Print, the dialog displays a message similar to "This value is not within the page range. Enter a number between 10 and 30." It then refuses to close.

Usually a program associates a PrintDialog with a PrintDocument object and that object provides the PrinterSettings object. You can either create the PrintDialog object at run time, or you can use the PrintDocument component described in the following section. If you create a PrintDocument component at design time, then you can also set the PrintDialog's Document property to that component at design time.

The following code shows how a program might print a document. In this example, the pdlgRectangle and pdlgRectangle components were created and pdlgRectangle.Document was set to pdlgRectangle at design time. When the user clicks the Print button, the program displays the PrintDialog. If the user clicks the dialog's Print button, then the code calls the PrintDocument object's Print method. When the PrintDocument object needs to generate a page for printing, it raises its PrintPage event. In this example, the event handler draws a rectangle and indicates that the document has no more pages to draw.

```
Imports System.Drawing.Printing

Public Class Form1
    ' Display the print dialog.
    Private Sub btnPrint_Click(ByVal sender As System.Object, _
     ByVal e As System.EventArgs) Handles btnPrint.Click
        If pdlgRectangle.ShowDialog() = Windows.Forms.DialogResult.OK Then
            ' Print the document.
            pdocRectangle.Print()
        End If
    End Sub

    ' Print a page of the document.
    Private Sub PrintDocument1_PrintPage(ByVal sender As Object, _
     ByVal e As System.Drawing.Printing.PrintPageEventArgs) _
     Handles pdocRectangle.PrintPage
        e.Graphics.DrawRectangle(Pens.Black, 100, 100, 600, 300)
        e.HasMorePages = False
    End Sub
End Class
```

For more information on the PrintDocument object, see the following section.

PrintDocument

The PrintDocument component represents an object that will be printed. Your program can use this object to send output to a printer.

The general procedure for printing using this object is to create the object, set its properties to determine how the printout is generated (the printer's name, paper tray, and so forth), and then call the object's Print method.

When the object needs to generate a page of output, it raises its PrintPage event. Your code catches that event, draws the page, and then sets the event handler's e.HasMorePages value to indicate whether that was the last page of output. See the previous section, "PrintDialog," for a small example.

The PrintDocument object provides only a few important properties itself. You set most of the values that describe the printing operation using the PrinterSettings object referenced by the component's PrinterSettings property. See the previous section, "PrintDialog," for information on the PrinterSettings object.

In addition to its PrinterSettings property, the PrintDocument object provides a DocumentName property that determines the name displayed for the document in printing-related dialogs such as the printer queue display.

This component also provides an OriginAtMargins property that determines whether each page's graphical origin begins at the page's margins. Setting OriginAtMargins to True makes it easier to draw relative to the left and top margins, rather than the upper-left corner of the physical page.

PrintPreviewControl

The PrintPreviewControl control (and yes, the word "Control" is part of the control's name, possibly to differentiate it from the PrintPreviewDialog control) displays a print preview within one of your forms. Usually, it is easier to use the PrintPreviewDialog control described in the next section to display a print preview dialog, but you can use this control to display a preview integrated into some other part of your application.

Figure G-18 shows a form displaying the PrintPreviewControl. This control and a PrintDocument control named pdocShapes were added to the form at design time and the PrintPreviewControl's Document property was set to pdocShapes.

The following code shows how the program works. The module-level variable m_PageNum indicates the next page that the pdocShapes object should draw. When it needs to generate a page, the pdocShapes object raises its PrintPage event. The event handler uses a Select Case statement to see which page it should geneate, and it draws an appropriate shape. It sets e.HasMorePages appropriately and increments the page number.

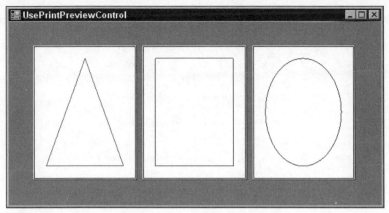

Figure G-18: The PrintPreviewControl control displays a print preview within your form.

```
Public Class Form1
    ' The number of the current page.
    Private m_PageNum As Integer = 1

    ' Generate the print document.
    Private Sub pdocShapes_PrintPage(ByVal sender As System.Object, _
     ByVal e As System.Drawing.Printing.PrintPageEventArgs) _
     Handles pdocShapes.PrintPage
        Select Case m_PageNum
            Case 1  ' Page 1. Draw a triangle.
                Dim pts() As Point = { _
                    New Point(e.MarginBounds.X + e.MarginBounds.Width \ 2, _
                              e.MarginBounds.Y), _
                    New Point(e.MarginBounds.X + e.MarginBounds.Width, _
                              e.MarginBounds.Y + e.MarginBounds.Height), _
                    New Point(e.MarginBounds.X, _
                              e.MarginBounds.Y + e.MarginBounds.Height) _
                }
                e.Graphics.DrawPolygon(Pens.Red, pts)
                e.HasMorePages = True
                m_PageNum += 1
            Case 2  ' Page 2. Draw a rectangle.
                e.Graphics.DrawRectangle(Pens.Green, e.MarginBounds())
                e.HasMorePages = True
                m_PageNum += 1
            Case 3  ' Page 3. Draw an ellipse.
                e.Graphics.DrawEllipse(Pens.Blue, e.MarginBounds())
                e.HasMorePages = False
                m_PageNum = 1
        End Select
    End Sub
End Class
```

That's all the code that the program needs. When the program starts, the PrintPreviewControl control uses pdocShapes to generate the pages it needs and it displays them.

The following table describes some of the `PrintPreviewControl`'s most useful properties.

Property	Purpose
AutoZoom	Determines whether the control automatically adjusts its `Zoom` property to make the display fill the control.
Columns	The number of columns of pages that the control displays. In Figure G-18, `Columns = 3`.
Document	The `PrintDocument` object that the control previews.
Rows	The number of rows of pages that the control displays. In Figure G-18, `Rows = 1`.
StartPage	The page number (starting with 0) displayed in the control's first page. Your code can use this property to change the pages displayed.
UseAntiAlias	Determines whether the control uses the system's anti-aliasing features to smooth the preview image. Setting this to `True` may make the image smoother, but it may also slow down the display.
Zoom	Determines the size of the pages within the control. The value 1.0 is full size, 0.5 is half-size, 2.0 is double size, and so forth. It's usually easier to just set `AutoZoom` to `True` and let the control make the pages as large as possible. If you set the scale so large that the page(s) won't fit, the control adds scroll bars so the user can see the results.

The control's `InvalidatePreview` method makes the control regenerate the print preview.

See the following section for information about the `PrintPreviewDialog` control. You can use that control to display a print preview without needing to build your own dialog.

PrintPreviewDialog

The `PrintPreviewDialog` component displays a dialog that shows what a print document will look like when it is printed. You can use this component to display a print preview dialog similar to the one shown in Figure G-19. This dialog contains a `PrintPreviewControl`, plus some extra tools to let the user control the preview.

The tools that run from left to right across the top of the dialog automatically give the user the following features:

❑ A Print button that prints the document

❑ A Zoom menu that lets the user zoom to scales between 10% and 500%, or to select Auto zoom

❑ Buttons that make the dialog display one, two, three, four, or six pages at a time

❑ A button that closes the dialog

❑ A text box and numeric up/down control that let the user select the number of the page to display

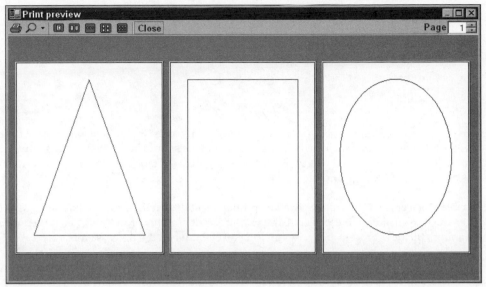

Figure G-19: The PrintPreviewDialog compmonent lets you easily display a full-featured print preview dialog.

The dialog's most important property is Document. This property determines the PrintDocument object that the dialog previews. See the earlier section "PrintDocument" for more information about this class.

The component's most important methods are Show, which displays the dialog, and ShowDialog, which displays the dialog modally.

Using this component is remarkably simple. Set its Document property and catch the PrintDocument object's PrintPage event as shown in the previous section. Display the dialog and print the document if the user clicks OK as in the following code:

```
If dlgPrintPreview.ShowDialog() = Windows.Forms.DialogResult.OK Then
    dlgPrintPreview.Document.Print()
End If
```

The rest is automatic. The dialog lets the user move through the document's pages, zoom in and out, and even print the document.

Process

The Process component provides access to the processes running on the computer. You can use this object to start, stop, and monitor processes. You can use the object to get information about a running process (such as its threads, the modules it has loaded, and the amount of memory it is using).

The following code shows how a program can start an excutable program. It creates a new Process object and sets values in its StartInfo property to define the application to run. This example sets the executable file name to the string contained in the txtFileName text box and sets the component's Verb to "Open" ("opening" an executable file makes it run). The program then calls the object's Start method.

```
' Start the process.
Private Sub btnRun_Click(ByVal sender As System.Object, _
 ByVal e As System.EventArgs) Handles btnRun.Click
    Dim new_process As New Process
    new_process.StartInfo.FileName = txtFileName.Text
    new_process.StartInfo.Verb = "Open"
    new_process.Start()
End Sub
```

The Process object's StartInfo property contains several values that tell the object how to start the new process. These values indicate whether the new process should be created without a window; what environment variables it should use; whether the new process's standard input, output, and error streams should be redirected; and the new process's working directory.

The Process object itself provides only a few properties at design time. Other than the StartInfo property, the most useful of these is EnableRaisingEvents. If this property is True, then the component monitors the new process and raises an Exited event when the process ends.

At run time, the Process object also provides read-only StandardInput, StandardOutput, and StandardError properties that the program can use to interact with the new process. It also provides methods for reading and writing with these streams, and properties for monitoring the process. For example, it lets you learn about the process's working set size, paged memory size, total processor time, and so forth.

This is a fairly advanced and specialized topic, so it is not covered in greater detail here. For more information, see the Process component's Web page msdn.microsoft.com/library/en-us/cpref/html/frlrfsystemdiagnosticsprocessclasstopic.asp.

ProgressBar

The ProgressBar control lets a program display a visible indication of its progress during a long task. As the task proceeds, the ProgressBar fills in from the left to the right. Ideally, the ProgressBar is completely full just as the task finishes.

The control's Minimum and Maximum properties determine the integers over which the ProgressBar's values will range. When the control's Value property equals its Minimum property, the control is completely blank. When its Value property equals its Maximum property, the control is completely filled.

By default, Minimum and Maximum are set to 0 and 100, respectively, so the Value property indicates the percentage of the task that is complete. However, you can set Minimum and Maximum to any values that make sense for the application. For example, if a program must back up some data by copying 173 files from one directory to another, you could set these properties to 0 and 173. As it copied each file, the program would set the ProgressBar's Value property to the number of files it has copied.

Instead of setting the control's Value property to indicate the task's status, you can set the Step property to indicate how much the control should update at each step. Then you can call the ProgressBar's PerformStep method to increment the Value by that amount.

Note that the Minimum, Maximum, Value, and Step properties are all integers. If the value you want to display has some other data type (such as Double or TimeSpan), you must convert the values into integers before you use them with the ProgressBar.

PropertyGrid

The PropertyGrid control displays information about an object in a format similar to the one used by the Properties window at design time. The control lets the user organize the properties alphabetically or by category, and lets the user edit the property values. Figure G-20 shows a PropertyGrid displaying information about an Employee object.

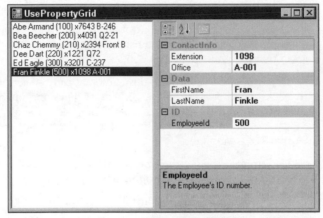

Figure G-20: The PropertyGrid control displays an object's properties.

The control's two most important properties are SelectedObject and SelectedObjects, which get or set the object(s) associated with the PropertyGrid.

The PropertyGrid control only displays object properties not public variables. It also only displays properties that are browsable. If you give a property the Browsable(False) attribute, the PropertyGrid will not display it.

For more information, see the PropertyGrid class's Web page msdn.microsoft.com/library/en-us/cpref/html/frlrfsystemwindowsformspropertygridclasstopic.asp.

RadioButton

A RadioButton control represents one of an exclusive set of options. For example, suppose that you want to let the user select between the choices Small, Medium, and Large. You could add three RadioButtons to a form with those captions. When the user clicks one button, Visual Basic selects it and deselects the others.

All the RadioButtons within a particular container are part of the same RadioButton group. If the user clicks a RadioButton, Visual Basic automatically deselects the others in the same group.

If you want to make more than one group on the same form, you must place the controls in separate containers (such as GroupBox or Panel controls). For example, you could put the Small, Medium, and Large buttons in one GroupBox and then put the Red, Green, and Blue buttons in another GroupBox. Then, when the user selects a size button, the other size buttons are deselected, but the color buttons are unaffected. When the user selects a color, the other colors are deselected, but the size buttons are unaffected.

RadioButton groups provide special navigation for the user. If one of the buttons in the group has the focus, then the user can press the arrow keys to move forward and backward through the group. If the user presses the Tab key, focus moves out of the group to the next control in the tab sequence.

The following table describes the RadioButton's most useful properties.

Property	Purpose
Appearance	Determines whether the control displays with its default appearance of a selection circle containing a black dot (Appearance = Normal) or a raised button (Appearance = Button).
AutoCheck	Determines whether the control automatically selects itself when the user clicks it. If this is False, the code must check and uncheck the control and any other controls in the RadioButton group. Usually it's better to use a CheckBox control instead if you don't want the button to behave like a normal RadioButton.
CheckAlign	Determines whether the control's selection circle is positioned in the bottom center, top center, middle right, and so forth.
Checked	Determines whether the control is selected.
Image	Determines the image that the control displays.
ImageAlign	Determines whether the control's image is positioned in the bottom center, top center, middle right, and so forth.
Text	Determines the text that the control displays.
TextAlign	Determines whether the control's text is positioned in the bottom center, top center, middle right, and so forth.

The RadioButton's most useful events are Click, which occurs when the user clicks the control, and CheckedChanged, which occurs when the control is checked or unchecked either because the user clicked a RadioButton in the group or because the code changed the button's state.

ReportViewer

The ReportViewer control displays a report generated by Crystal Reports. The control provides tools that let the user move between the report's different pages, zoom in and out, navigate through report groups using a tree view, view subreports, print or export the report, and so forth. See Chapter 24, "Reporting," for more information about Crystal Reports and this control.

RichTextBox

The `RichTextBox` control is a text box that supports "rich text" extensions. Those extensions let the control display text that is bold, underlined, italicized, indented, in different fonts, and that has other special visual properties.

The control can load and save its contents in plain-text files (in which case the formatting is lost) or in Rich Text Format (RTF) files (which preserve formatting).

A program can use the `RichTextBox`'s `Select` method to select some of its text. It can then use one of the control's properties to change the appearance of the selected text. For example, the following code selects the 10 characters starting with character 50 (the first character is number 0). It then sets the selection's color to red and makes its font bold.

```
rchNotes.Select(50, 10)
rchNotes.SelectionColor = Color.Red
rchNotes.SelectionFont = New Font(RichTextBox1.SelectionFont, FontStyle.Bold)
```

The following table lists the `RichTextBox`'s most useful properties.

Property	Purpose
AcceptsTab	For multiline controls, determines whether pressing the Tab key adds a Tab to the text, rather than moving to the next control in the tab sequence.
AutoSize	For single-line controls, determines whether the control automatically sets its height for the fonts it contains.
BulletIndent	Determines the number of pixels added after a bullet as indentation. If you make the selection a bulleted paragraph and then change this value, the paragraph's indentation is adjusted accordingly.
CanRedo	Indicates whether the control has any redo information that it can apply. See the discussion later in this section for an example.
CanUndo	Indicates whether the control has any undo information that it can apply. See the discussion later in this section for an example.
DetectUrls	Determines whether the control automatically recognizes Web URLs when they are typed. If some text looks like a URL, the control displays it in blue, underlines it, and displays a hyperlink cursor (pointing hand) when the mouse hovers over the text. If the user clicks a recognized link, the control raises its `LinkClicked` event.

Table continued on following page

Property	Purpose
Lines	An array of strings giving the lines of text (separated by carriage returns) that are displayed by the control. You can use this property to give the control more than one paragraph at design time.
MaxLength	The maximum number of characters the user can enter into the control.
MultiLine	Determines whether the control displays multiple lines.
PreferredHeight	Returns the height a single-line control would want for the font size.
ReadOnly	Determines whether the user can modify the control's text.
RedoActionName	The name of the action that will be redone if the program calls the control's Redo method (for example, "Typing" or "Delete"). You can use this property to show the user what the next redo action is.
RightMargin	Determines the control's right margin in pixels. The value 0 means there is no right margin.
Rtf	Determines the RTF codes for the control's text. This includes the text itself, font information, and paragraph information (such as indentation, bulleting, and so forth).
ScrollBars	Determines which scroll bars the control displays. The values Horizontal, Vertical, and Both make the control display the corresponding scroll bars only when they are needed. The values ForcedHorizontal, ForcedVertical, and ForcedBoth make the control display the corresponding scroll bars always. The value None makes the control display no scroll bars. Note that some of these values may not always be honored. For example, if WordWrap is True or RightMargin is nonzero, the control never displays horizontal scroll bars.
SelectedRtf	Determines the selected text's value and RTF formatting code.
SelectedText	Determines the selected text's value without RTF formatting codes.
SelectionAlignment	Determines the selected text's alignment (Left, Center, or Right).
SelectionBullet	Determines whether the selected text's paragraph is bulleted.
SelectionCharOffset	Determines the selected text's character offset above or below the baseline in pixels.
SelectionColor	Determines the selected text's color.

Property	Purpose
SelectionFont	Determines the selected text's font.
SelectionHangingIndent	Determines the selected text's hanging indent.
SelectionIndent	Determines the number of pixels by which subsequent lines are indented in the selected text's paragraph.
SelectionLength	Determines the length of the selected text. You can use SelectionStart and SelectionLength to selected text, or you can use the Select method.
SelectionProtected	Determines whether the selected text is protected so that the user cannot modify it.
SelectionRightIndent	Determines number of pixels by which the selected text's paragraph is indented on the right.
SelectionStart	Determines the start of the selection. You can use SelectionStart and SelectionLength to selected text, or you can use the Select method.
SelectionTabs	Determines the tabs for the selected text's paragraph. For example, the array {20, 40, 60} sets tabs 20, 40, and 60 pixels from the left margin.
ShowSelectionMargin	If True, the control adds a selection margin on the left. If the user clicks inside this margin, the control selects the text to the right.
Text	Determines the control's text, not including any formatting information. If you want to preserve formatting information, use the SelectedRtf property.
TextLength	Returns the length of the control's text.
UndoActionName	The name of the action that will be undone if the program calls the control's Undo method (for example, "Typing" or "Delete"). You can use this property to show the user what the next undo action is.
WordWrap	For multiline controls, determines whether the control wraps text to a new line if it is too long to fit.

The control also provides several important methods, as shown in the following table.

Method	Purpose
AppendText	Adds text to the end of the control's text.
CanPaste	Determines whether you can paste data of a specified format from the clipboard into the control.

Table continued on following page

Method	Purpose
Clear	Clears the control's text.
ClearUndo	Empties the control's undo list.
Copy	Copies the control's selection to the clipboard.
Cut	Copies the control's selection to the clipboard and removes it from the control's text.
Find	Finds and selects text. Overloaded versions let you search for one of a group of characters or a string, possibly with options (MatchCase, NoHighlight, Reverse, or WholeWord), and possibly within a range of characters.
GetCharFromPosition	Finds the character closest to a specified (X, Y) position.
GetCharIndexFromPosition	Finds the index of the character closest to a specified (X, Y) position.
GetLineFromCharIndex	Returns the number of the line containing the specified character index.
GetPositionFromCharIndex	Returns the (X, Y) position of the character as a specified index.
LoadFile	Loads an RTF or text file or a stream into the control.
Paste	Pastes the clipboard's contents into the control, replacing the current selection.
Redo	Reapplies the last action that was undone.
SaveFile	Saves the control's text into an RTF or text file or stream.
ScrollToCaret	Scrolls the text so the insertion position is visible.
Select	Selects the indicated text.
SelectAll	Selects all of the control's text.
Undo	Undoes the most recent action.

A program can use the CanUndo and CanRedo properties to determine when it should enable Undo and Redo buttons and menu items. The following code shows how a program can manage Undo and Redo buttons for the rchNotes control. When the control's contents change, the TextChanged event handler enables or disables the buttons, depending on which information the control has. The buttons simply call the control's Undo and Redo methods.

```
Private Sub rchNotes_TextChanged(ByVal sender As System.Object, _
  ByVal e As System.EventArgs) Handles rchNotes.TextChanged
    btnUndo.Enabled = rchNotes.CanUndo
    btnRedo.Enabled = rchNotes.CanRedo
End Sub
```

```
Private Sub btnUndo_Click(ByVal sender As System.Object, _
 ByVal e As System.EventArgs) Handles btnUndo.Click
    rchNotes.Undo()
End Sub

Private Sub btnRedo_Click(ByVal sender As System.Object, _
 ByVal e As System.EventArgs) Handles btnRedo.Click
    rchNotes.Redo()
End Sub
```

The following version of the TextChanged event handler adds the values returned by the UndoActionName and RedoActionName methods to the buttons' captions. For example, after the user deletes some text, the undo button's caption says "Undo Delete."

```
Private Sub rchNotes_TextChanged(ByVal sender As System.Object, _
ByVal e As System.EventArgs) Handles rchNotes.TextChanged
    btnUndo.Enabled = rchNotes.CanUndo
    btnRedo.Enabled = rchNotes.CanRedo

    If btnUndo.Enabled Then
        btnUndo.Text = "Undo " & rchNotes.UndoActionName
    Else
        btnUndo.Text = "Undo"
    End If

    If btnRedo.Enabled Then
        If btnRedo.Enabled Then btnRedo.Text = "Redo " & rchNotes.RedoActionName
    Else
        If btnRedo.Enabled Then btnRedo.Text = "Redo"
    End If
End Sub
```

The RichTextBox control's most useful event is TextChanged. You can use this event to take action when the user changes the control's text. For example, you can display a visible indication that the data has been modified or, as the previous examples show, you can enable and disable Undo and Redo buttons.

SaveFileDialog

The SaveFileDialog component displays a dialog that lets the user select a file for saving. The ShowDialog method returns DialogResult.OK if the user selects a file and clicks OK. It returns DialogResult.Cancel if the user cancels. The following code shows how a program might use the component to let the user select a file in which to save data.

```
If dlgSaveData.ShowDialog = DialogResult.OK Then
    ' Save the data.
    ...
End If
```

This component provides many properties for determining the kinds of files the user can specify. Most of these properties are the same as those provided by the OpenFileDialog component described earlier in this appendix. See the section "OpenFileDialog," earlier in this appendix for more information about those properties.

Unlike OpenFileDialog, this component does not provide the properties MultiSelect, ReadOnlyChecked, and ShowReadOnly because those properties don't make sense when the user is selecting a file for saving. The FileNames collection is also less useful for this component because the user will always select only one file, so you can use the FileName property instead.

The SaveFileDialog component provides one additional property not provided by the OpenFileDialog: CreatePrompt. If this property is True and the user enters the name of a file that doesn't exist, then the dialog asks the user if it should create the file. If the user clicks No, then the dialog continues letting the user select a different file.

Like the OpenFileDialog, this component raises its FileOk event when the user tries to accept a file. You can use an event handler to catch the event and perform extra validation. Set the event's e.Cancel value to True to stop the dialog from accepting the selection.

The following code only allows the dlgSaveData dialog to accept files that end with the .dat extension. If the dialog's selected file doesn't end with .dat, the event handler sets e.Cancel to True.

```vb
' Ensure that the user selects a .dat file.
Private Sub dlgSaveData_FileOk(ByVal sender As Object, _
 ByVal e As System.ComponentModel.CancelEventArgs) Handles dlgSaveData.FileOk
    If Not dlgSaveData.FileName.EndsWith(".dat") Then
        MsgBox("File " & dlgSaveData.FileName & _
            " is not a .dat file", _
            MsgBoxStyle.Exclamation, _
            "Invalid File Type")
        e.Cancel = True
    End If
End Sub
```

Note that the dialog adds its default extension if applicable before it raises the FileOk event. If the component has DefaultExt = "dat" and AddExtension = True, then this example would accept a file name with no extension.

SerialPort

The SerialPort component represents one of the computer's physical serial ports. It provides properties and methods for reading and configuring the port's baud rate, break signal, Data Set Ready (DSR) state, port name, parity, and stop bits. The class has methods to write data to the port and to read synchronously or asynchronously.

Serial communications is a fairly advanced and specialized topic that depends on your particular application, so it is not covered in detail here. See the online help for more information. If you plan to work extensively with serial communication, you might want to find a good book on the topic such as *Visual Basic Programmer's Guide to Serial Communications,* 4th Edition by Richard Grier (Stanwood, WA: Mabry Software, 2004).

ServiceController

The `ServiceController` component represents a Windows service process. It provides methods that let you connect to a running or stopped service to control it or get information about it.

The `ServiceController`'s `ServiceName` property gets or sets the name of the service associated with the component. To set this value at design time, select a `ServiceController` in the form designer. Then, click on the `ServiceName` property in the Properties window and click the drop-down arrow on the right to see a list of available services on the system. The class's methods let you start, pause, continue, or stop the service.

Windows services and their control is a relatively advanced topic, so it is not covered in detail here. For more information, see the `ServiceController` class's Web page `msdn.microsoft.com/library/en-us/cpref/html/frlrfsystemserviceprocessservicecontrollerclasstopic.asp`. For an introduction to Windows service applications, see `msdn.microsoft.com/library/en-us/vbcon/html/vbconintroductiontontserviceapplications.asp`. For a walkthrough that creates a Windows service application, see `msdn.microsoft.com/library/en-us/vbcon/html/vbwlkwalkthroughcreatingwindowsserviceapplication.asp`.

SplitContainer

The `SplitContainer` control represents are area divided into two regions either vertically or horizontally. The control contains a bar (called the splitter) that the user can drag to adjust the amount of space given to each region. A `SplitContainer` divides the form in Figure G-21 vertically into two regions that contain pictures.

Figure G-21: This SplitContainer control divides vertically.

879

Each of the SplitContainer's regions holds a Panel control. You can place other controls (such as the PictureBoxes used in Figure G-21) inside the Panels. You can also use the Panels' properties to affect their behavior. In Figure G-21, the Panels' AutoScroll properties were set to True so the Panels display scroll bars when either image cannot fit in its Panel.

The following table describes the SplitContainer's most useful properties.

Property	Purpose
BorderStyle	Determines the control's border style.
FixedPanel	Determines which panel keeps the same size when the control is resized.
IsSplitterFixed	Determines whether the user can drag the splitter.
Orientation	Determines whether the Panels are arranged vertically or horizontally.
Panel1	Returns a reference to the first panel (left or top depending on Orientation).
Panel1Collapsed	Determines whether the first Panel is collapsed. When collapsed, a Panel is completely hidden and the user cannot get it back by dragging the splitter.
Panel1MinSize	Determines the minimum size (width or height depending on Orientation) of the first Panel.
Panel2	Returns a reference to the second panel (right or bottom depending on Orientation).
Panel2Collapsed	Determines whether the second Panel is collapsed. When collapsed, a Panel is completely hidden and the user cannot get it back by dragging the splitter.
Panel2MinSize	Determines the minimum size (width or height depending on Orientation) of the second Panel.
SplitterDistance	Determines the distance from the control's left or top edge (depending on Orientation) to the splitter.
SplitterIncrement	Determines the number of pixels by which the splitter will move when dragged. For example, if SplitterIncrement is 10, the splitter jumps in 10 pixel increments are you drag it. The default is 1.
SplitterRectangle	Returns a Rectangle representing the splitter's current size and location within the SplitContainer.
SplitterWidth	Determines the splitter's width in pixels. The default is 4.

The SplitterContainer control's most interesting events are SplitterMoving and SplitterMoved. You can catch these events if you need to take action when the user drags the splitter. You can also use the Panels' sizing events Resize, ResizeBegin, ResizeEnd, and SizeChanged to take action when the Panels resize.

One rather confusing feature of the SplitterContainer is the way its contained Panel controls behave in the form designer. The drop-down at the top of the Properties window lets you select the controls on the form, including the SplitterContainer. The Panels are contained inside the SplitterContainer, so they are not always listed in this drop-down. If you click on one of the Panels, then the drop-down lists the Panel and the Properties window lets you view and edit the control's properties. If some other control is selected, however, the SplitterContainer is listed in the drop-down, but not its Panels.

StatusStrip

The StatusStrip control provides an area where the application can display brief status information. Usually the StatusStrip is at the bottom of the form, as shown in Figure G-22.

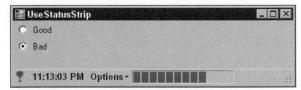

Figure G-22: The StatusStrip control allows a program to display status information.

The StatusStrip can contain several kinds of objects such as drop-down buttons, progress bars, and panels. These objects are represented by different kinds of controls contained in the form. For example, a progress bar is represented by a ToolStripProgressBar control.

You can edit a StatusStrip much as you edit a MenuStrip. When you click on the StatusStrip, a box appears that contains the text "Type Here." Enter the text that you want to display in on this object and press Enter. Click on an object and then click the little action arrow on the object's right edge to change the object's type (progress bar, panel, and so forth) and to configure the item.

You can also edit an object's properties in the Properties window. Simply click on the object and then use the Properties window to change its appearance.

The StatusStrip control provides access to the objects it contains through its Items collection. If you click the ellipsis to the right of this property in the Properties window, the Items Collection Editor shown in Figure G-23 appears.

To make new items, select the type of object you want to add from the drop-down in the upper left and click the Add button. Click on an item and use the other buttons to move or delete it. Use the properties grid on the right to modify the object's appearance.

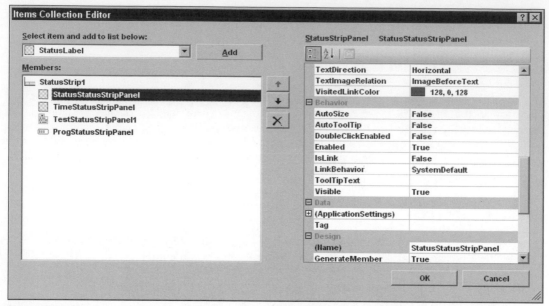

Figure G-23: The Items Collection Editor lets you edit the objects contained within a StatusStrip control.

The following table lists the types object objects you can add to a `StatusStrip` control.

StatusStripPanel	ToolStripButton	ToolStripComboBox
ToolStripDropDownButton	ToolStripLabel	ToolStripProgressBar
ToolStripSeparator	ToolStripSplitButton	ToolStripTextBox

See the online help for more information about these classes and the `StatusStrip` control.

TabControl

The `TabControl` control (for some reason, the word "Control" is part of the class's name) displays a series of tabs attached to separate pages. Each page is a control container and can hold whatever controls you want for that tab. When you click a tab at design time or the user clicks one at run time, the control displays the corresponding page.

Figure G-24 shows a `TabControl` displaying information about an employee. The tabs contain the employee's name and picture, personnel information (employee ID, Social Security number, and so on), home address, and office information (location and extension).

The control's tabs are represented programmatically by `TabPage` objects contained in the control's `TabPages` collection. To edit these objects interactively at design time, select the control's `TabPages` property and click the ellipsis on the right to display the collection editor shown in Figure G-25.

Figure G-24: A TabControl lets you easily display pages of related data.

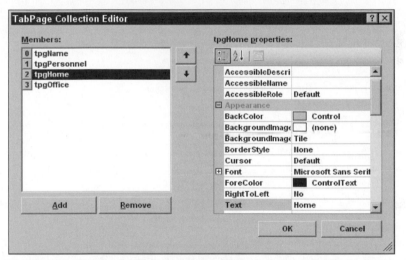

Figure G-25: Use the TabPage Collection Editor to define a TabControl's tabs.

The following table describes the TabPage object's most useful properties.

Property	Purpose
AutoScroll	If True, then the tab page automatically provides scroll bars if it is not big enough to display all of its contents.
BackColor	Determines the tab page's background color. This affects the tab's page, not the tab itself.
BackgroundImage	Determines the background image that tiles the tab page's. This affects the tab's page, not the tab itself.

Table continued on following page

Property	Purpose
BorderStyle	Determines the style of border around the tab's page. This can be None, FixedSingle, or Fixed3D.
Font	Determines the font used by the controls contained in the tab's page. To change the font used to draw the tabs, set the TabControl's Font property.
ImageIndex	If the TabControl's ImageList property is set to an ImageList control, this property determines the image within that list that the tab displays.
Text	Determines the text displayed on the tab.
ToolTipText	Determines the tooltip text displayed when the user hovers the mouse over the tab. This is ignored unless the TabControl's ShowToolTips property is True.

The TabPage object provides several events of its own. These include the usual assortment of events for a control container such events as Click, Layout, Resize, Paint, and various mouse events.

The TabControl provides several properties that are useful for arranging the tabs. The following table describes the most useful of these properties.

Property	Purpose
Alignment	Determines whether the control places its tabs on the Top, Bottom, Left or Right. If you set this to Left or Right, then the control rotates its tabs' text sideways. If a tab contains an image, the image is not rotated.
Appearance	Determines how the control displays its tabs. This property can take the values Normal, Buttons, or FlatButtons.
DrawMode	Determines whether the control draws the tabs automatically (DrawMode = Normal) or whether the code draws them (DrawMode = OwnerDrawFixed). See the discussion later in this section for an example.
Enabled	Determines whether the TabControl is enabled. If Enabled is False, then none of the tabs will respond to the user (although the tabs do not look disabled) and all of the controls on the tab pages are disabled.
Font	Determines the font that the control uses to draw its tabs. This does not affect the font used within the tab pages.
HotTrack	If this is True, then the tabs visually change when the mouse moves over them. For example, the tabs' text may change color.
ImageList	Determines the ImageList control that provides images for the tabs.
ItemSize	Determines the height of all of the tabs. Also determines the width of fixed-width tabs (see the SizeMode property) and owner-drawn tabs (see the DrawMode property).

Property	Purpose
MultiLine	Determines whether the control allows more than one line of tabs. If MultiLine is False and the tabs won't all fit, the control displays left-arrow and right-arrow buttons on the right to let the user scroll through the tabs.
Padding	Determines the horizontal and vertical space added around the tabs' text and images.
RowCount	Returns the current number of tab rows.
SelectedIndex	Sets or gets the index of the currently selected tab. At design time, you can simply click on the tab you want to select.
SelectedTab	Sets or gets the currently selected TabPage object. At design time, you can simply click on the tab you want to select.
ShowToolTips	Determines whether the control displays the TabPages' ToolTip values when the user hovers the mouse over the tabs.
SizeMode	Determines how the control sizes its tabs. This property can take the values Normal (tabs fit their contents), FillToRight (if the control needs more than one row of tabs, the tabs resize so each row fills the width of the control), and Fixed (all tabs have the same width).
TabCount	Returns the number of tabs.
TabPages	The collection of TabPage objects.

The TabControl's most useful event is SelectedIndexChanged, which fires when the control's selected tab index changes either because the user clicked a new tab, or because the code set the SelectedIndex or SelectedTab property.

The following code shows how a program can draw ellipses on owner-drawn tabs, assuming that the TabControl's DrawMode property is set to OwnerDrawFixed. The code uses the DrawItem event handler parameters to get the tab's bounds. It moves the bounding rectangle in from the upper-left corner and makes it a little smaller so it will fit completely inside the tab. The code outlines the ellipse on the selected tab with a wide line so it allows a little extra room if the tab it is drawing is currently selected. Next, the code checks the tab's index and fills a green, yellow, or red ellipse. Finally, the program checks the tab's state again and draws a black outline around the ellipse. If the tab is selected, it makes the outline four pixels wide.

```
' Draw ellipses in the tabs.
Private Sub tabProject_DrawItem(ByVal sender As Object, _
  ByVal e As System.Windows.Forms.DrawItemEventArgs) Handles tabProject.DrawItem
    ' Get the drawing bounds.
    Dim rect As Rectangle = e.Bounds
    If (e.State And DrawItemState.Selected) = DrawItemState.Selected Then
        ' Allow extra room for the selected tab.
        rect.X += 4
        rect.Y += 4
        rect.Width -= 8
        rect.Height -= 8
```

```
        Else
            rect.X += 2
            rect.Y += 2
            rect.Width -= 4
            rect.Height -= 4
        End If

        ' Fill the ellipse with the right color.
        Select Case e.Index
            Case 0
                e.Graphics.FillEllipse(Brushes.Green, rect)
            Case 1
                e.Graphics.FillEllipse(Brushes.Yellow, rect)
            Case 2
                e.Graphics.FillEllipse(Brushes.Red, rect)
        End Select

        ' Outline the ellipse in black.
        If (e.State And DrawItemState.Selected) = DrawItemState.Selected Then
            ' Use a thick line for the selected tab.
            e.Graphics.DrawEllipse( _
                New Pen(Color.Black, 3), _
                rect)
        Else
            e.Graphics.DrawEllipse(Pens.Black, rect)
        End If
End Sub
```

The TabControl is ideal for displaying multiple pages of related information in a limited amount of space. It works particularly well when the information is naturally categorized and each tab represents a category of data. It doesn't work as well if different tabs contain data that the user might want to compare to each other.

For example, suppose that the tabs contain information about a customer's orders. Having different orders' data on separate tabs makes it difficult for the user to compare two orders. If it is likely that the user will need to do that, you should consider some other method for displaying order data. For example, you could display orders in separate windows contained with an MDI container form.

TableLayoutPanel

The TableLayoutPanel control displays the controls that it contains in rows and columns. This makes it easy to build grids of regularly spaced controls.

Figure G-26 shows a form that uses a TableLayoutPanel running on top of the IDE displaying the same form. The TableLayoutPanel control displays prompts and data-entry controls displayed in two columns. The label at the top that says "Employee" is set to span both of the control's columns. The Form Designer in the background shows the control's rows and columns using dashed lines. In this example, the control doesn't draw its grid lines at run time.

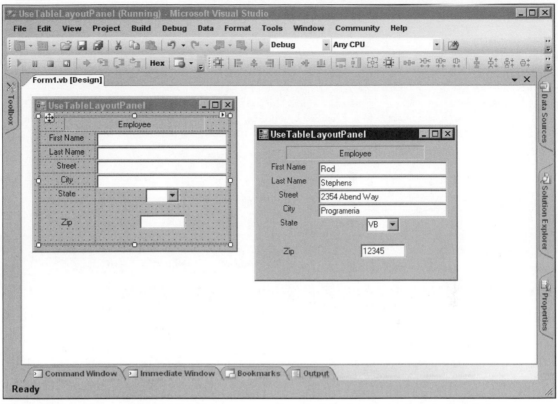

Figure G-26: In this example, the `TableLayoutPanel` control displays two columns of controls arranged in a grid.

The following table describes the `TableLayoutPanel` control's most useful properties.

Property	Purpose
AutoScroll	Determines whether the control automatically provides scroll bars if the controls it contains won't fit.
CellBorderStyle	Determines the cell border style. This can be None, NotSet (an appropriate style is selected based on the row and column styles), Inset (single sunken line), InsetDouble (double sunken line), Outset (single raised line), OutsetDouble (double raised line), OutsetPartial (single line containing a raised area), and Single (single line).
ColumnCount	Determines the number of columns.
ColumnStyles	A collection giving column styles.
ColumnWidths	An array of column widths.

Table continued on following page

Property	Purpose
Controls	A collection of controls contained within the control.
Enabled	Determines whether the control is enabled. If the TableLayoutPanel is disabled, then the controls it contains are also disabled.
GrowStyle	Determines how the control grows when you add new child controls to it. This can be AddRows, AddColumns, or FixedSize (the control throws an exception if you add more controls).
RowCount	Determines the number of rows.
RowHeights	An array of row heights.
RowStyles	A collection of row styles.
Visible	Determines whether the control and its contents are visible.

The following table describes the TableLayoutPanel control's most useful methods.

Method	Purpose
GetColumn	Returns a child control's column number.
GetColumnSpan	Returns the number of columns that a child control spans.
GetRow	Returns a child control's row number.
GetRowSpan	Returns the number of rows that a child control spans.
ScrollControlIntoView	If the TableLayoutPanel control has AutoScroll set to True, then this scrolls an indicated child control into view.
SetColumn	Sets a child control's column number.
SetColumnSpan	Sets a child control's column span.
SetRow	Sets a child control's row number.
SetRowSpan	Sets a child control's row span.

In addition to providing its own properties, the TableLayoutPanel acts as a property provider for its child controls. These properties include Column, ColumnSpan, Row, and RowSpan. For example, if you add a button to the TableLayoutPanel control named TableLayoutPanel1, then the button's Properties window will contain an entry labeled "Column on TableLayoutPanel1" that determines the button's column.

The TableLayoutPanel control also changes the meaning of its child controls' Anchor property. By default, a child control has Anchor property set to None, so it is centered in its table cell. If you set Anchor to "Left," then the control is moved to the left edge of the cell. If you set Anchor to "Left, Right," then both of the control's edges are attached to the cell's edges, so the control is stretched to fit the cell's width. The Top and Bottom Anchor settings work similarly.

The `FlowLayoutPanel` control also arranges contained controls, but not in a grid. It places controls one after another to fill either rows or columns. For information on that control, see the section "FlowLayoutPanel," earlier in this appendix.

TextBox

The `TextBox` control is a typical everyday text box. The user can enter and modify text, click and drag to select text, press Ctrl-C to copy the selected text to the clipboard, and so forth.

The `TextBox` control is much simpler than the `RichTextBox` control described earlier in this appendix. It can use only one font, background color, and foreground color for all of its text. It also cannot provide special formatting such as bullets, hanging indentation, and margins the way the `RichTextBox` can. If you need those extra features, use a `RichTextBox` instead of a `TextBox` control.

The following table describes the `TextBox` control's most useful properties.

Property	Purpose
AcceptsReturn	For multiline controls, determines whether pressing the Enter key adds a new line to the text rather than triggering the form's Accept button.
AcceptsTab	For multiline controls, determines whether pressing the Tab key adds a Tab to the text rather than moving to the next control in the tab sequence.
AutoSize	For single-line controls, determines whether the control automatically sets its height for the fonts it contains.
CharacterCasing	Determines whether the control automatically changes the case of text as it is entered. This property can take the values `Normal` (leave the case alone), `Upper` (uppercase), and `Lower` (lowercase). The control changes the text's case whether the user types or pastes it into the control, or if the program sets the control's text.
Lines	An array of strings giving the lines of text (separated by carriage returns) displayed by the control. You can use this property to give the control more than one paragraph at design time.
MaxLength	The maximum number of characters the user can enter into the control.
MultiLine	Determines whether the control displays multiple lines.
PasswordChar	Determines the password character displayed by a single-line `TextBox` control for each character it contains. For example, if you set `PasswordChar` to "*," then each character the user types appears as a "*" in the text box. The control's `Text` property returns the actual text to the program.

Table continued on following page

Property	Purpose
PreferredHeight	Returns the height a single-line control would want to use for the font size.
ReadOnly	Determines whether the user can modify the control's text. You can display read-only text in a label, but then the user cannot select it and copy it to the clipboard. If you want to display information that the user might want to copy, place it in a TextBox control and set ReadOnly to True.
ScrollBars	Determines which scroll bars the control displays. This property can take the values None, Vertical, Horizontal, and Both. The appropriate scroll bars are always displayed. although they are disabled when they are not needed. Note that some of these values may not always be honored. For example, if WordWrap is True, then the control never displays horizontal scroll bars.
SelectedText	Gets or sets the selected text's value.
SelectionLength	Gets the length of the selected text, or selects this number of letters. You can use SelectionStart and SelectionLength to selected text, or you can use the Select method.
SelectionStart	Gets or sets the start of the selection. You can use SelectionStart and SelectionLength to selected text, or you can use the Select method.
Text	Gets or sets the control's text.
TextAlign	Determines the text's alignment within the control. This can be Left, Right, or Center.
TextLength	Returns the length of the control's text.
WordWrap	For multiline controls, determines whether the control wraps text to a new line if it is too long to fit.

The control also provides several important methods described in the following table.

Method	Purpose
AppendText	Adds text to the end of the control's text.
Clear	Clears the control's text.
ClearUndo	Empties the control's undo list.
Copy	Copies the control's selection to the clipboard.
Cut	Copies the control's selection to the clipboard and removes it from the control's text.

Method	Purpose
Paste	Pastes the clipboard's contents into the control, replacing the current selection. This method does nothing if the clipboard doesn't contain textual data.
ScrollToCaret	Scrolls the text so the insertion position is visible.
Select	Selects the indicated text.
SelectAll	Selects all of the control's text.
Undo	Undoes the most recent action. The TextBox only stores information for one undo action, so calling Undo again undoes the undo. That also means that the TextBox doesn't need a Redo method because it would do the same thing as Undo.

The TextBox control's most useful event is TextChanged. You can use this event to take action when the user changes the control's text. For example, you can display a visible indication that the data has been modified.

Timer

The Timer component periodically raises a Tick event so the program can take action at specific intervals.

The component's Interval property determines the number of milliseconds (1000ths of a second) between events. This property is a 32-bit integer that must be greater than zero, so it can hold values between 1 and 2,147,483,647. If you set Interval to its maximum value 2,147,483,647, the component raises its Tick event roughly every 24.86 days.

The Timer component's Enabled property determines whether the Timer generates Tick events. The component continues raising its event as long as Enabled is True.

The component's Start and Stop methods simply set its Enabled property to True and False, respectively.

ToolStrip

The ToolStrip control displays a series of buttons, drop-downs, and other tools. The user can access these tools quickly without navigating through a series of menus, so they are most useful for performing frequently needed tasks. Menus are more appropriate for commands that are needed less often.

The following table lists the types of items that a ToolStrip may contain.

ToolStripButton	ToolStripComboBox	ToolStripDropDownButton	ToolStripLabel
ToolStripProgressBar	ToolStripSeparator	ToolStripSplitButton	ToolStripTextBox

Figure G-27 shows each of these tools. The mouse is hovering over the `ToolStripSplitButton` so that control is displaying its border and tooltip.

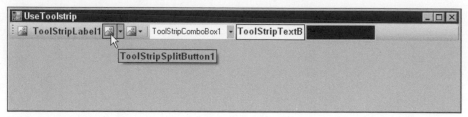

Figure G-27: The `ToolStrip` **component contains tools the user may want to use frequently.**

These tools are relatively straightforward. `ToolStripButton` is a button that sits on a `ToolStrip`, `ToolStripComboBox` is a combo box that sits on a `ToolStrip`, and so forth. The only tool that doesn't correspond to another type of control is the `SplitButton`. This control is a button with a drop-down area. If the user clicks the button, it raises a `Click` event. If the user clicks the drop-down arrow, the control displays a drop-down menu containing menu items that the user can select as usual. See the online help for more information on `SplitButton` and the other tool control classes.

The `ToolStrip` control stores its tools in its `Items` collection. At run time, a program can access the controls inside this collection, or it can refer to the tools directly by name. At design time, you can select a `ToolStrip`, click on its `Items` property in the Properties window, and click the ellipsis to the right to display the Items Collection Editor shown in Figure G-28.

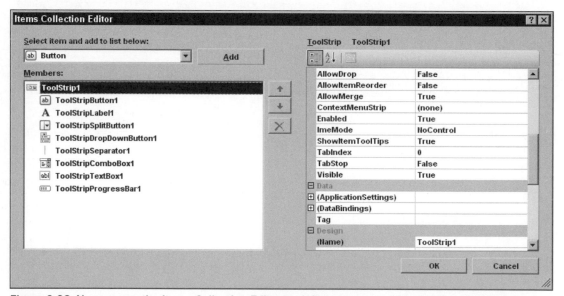

Figure G-28: You can use the Items Collection Editor to define a `ToolStrip`**'s tools at design time.**

You can also click on the `ToolStrip` and add items to it much as you edit a `MenuStrip` control.

The following table describes the `ToolStrip` control's most useful properties.

Property	Purpose
AllowItemReorder	Determines whether the user can drag-and-drop items to reorder them.
AllowMerge	Determines whether the `ToolStrip` can merge with others.
CanOverflow	Determines whether items can be sent to an overflow menu if the `ToolStrip` doesn't fit completely on the form.
GripDisplayStyle	Gets the orientation of the control's move handle.
GripMargin	Determines the space around the control's move handle.
GripRectangle	Gets the boundaries of the control's move handle.
GripStyle	Determines whether the control's move handle is visible or hidden.
Items	Returns a collection of `ToolStripItem` objects representing the control's tools.
OverflowButton	Returns a `ToolStripItem` representing the control's overflow button.
ShowItemToolTips	Determines whether the control's tool display their tooltips.

ToolStripContainer

The `ToolStripContainer` control contains a `ToolStripPanel` along each of its edges where a `ToolStrip` control can dock. The control's center is filled with another `ToolStripPanel` that can contain other controls that are not part of the menus.

The user can drag the `ToolStrips` around and position them inside of any of the `ToolStripPanel` controls much as you can move the menus in the Visual Basic development envirtonment. The user can drag the `ToolStrips` into multiple rows or columns within the panels.

Figure G-29 shows a form containing a ToolStripContainer with Dock property set to Fill so it fills the form. The lighter area in the middle is a PictureBox sitting inside the middle ToolStripPanel, also with Dock property set to Fill.

The ToolStripContainer holds five ToolStrip controls positioned in the container's various edge panels. The ToolStrip3 control's TextDirection property is set to Vertical90 so it sits along the right edge of the form. The ToolStrip1 and ToolStrip2 controls have been dragged into two rows at the top of the form. The ToolStrip1 and ToolStrip2 controls share a row at the bottom.

The control's `LeftToolStripPanel`, `RightToolStripPanel`, `TopToolStripPanel`, `BottomToolStripPanel`, and `ContentPanel` properties contain references to the `ToolStripPanel` controls that this control contains. Its `LeftToolStripPanelVisible`, `RightToolStripPanelVisible`, `TopToolStripPanelVisible`, and `BottomToolStripPanelVisible` properties let you show or hide specific panels. For example, you can hide the bottom or side panels if you don't want the user to drag `ToolStrips` there.

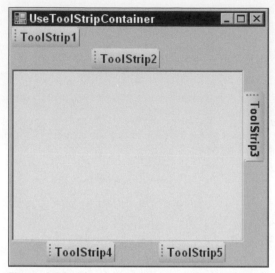

Figure G-29: The `ToolStripContainer` **control lets the user rearranged** `ToolStrip` **controls at run time.**

The ToolStripContainer's other properties are relatively straightforward. See the online help for more information.

ToolTip

The `ToolTip` component allows you to provide tooltip help when the user hovers the mouse over a control. After you add a `ToolTip` component to a form, the other controls on the form get a special `ToolTip` property. For example, suppose that you create a `ToolTip` component named `ttHint`. Then a button on the form would have a new property named "`ToolTip on ttHint`." Set that property to the text you want the `ToolTip` to display, and you are all set.

The following table describes the `ToolTip` component's most useful properties.

Property	Purpose
Active	Determines whether the component displays tooltips.
AutomaticDelay	Sets the `AutoPopDelay`, `InitialDelay`, and `ReshowDelay` properties to values that are appropriate for this value.
AutoPopDelay	The number of milliseconds before the tool tip disappears if the mouse remains stationary in the tooltip's area.
BackColor	Determines the tooltip's background color.
ForeColor	Determines the tooltip's foreground color.

Property	Purpose
InitialDelay	The number of milliseconds that the mouse must remain stationary inside the tooltip's area before the component displays the tooltip.
IsBalloon	Determines whether the tooltip is displayed as a balloon rather than a rectangle.
OwnerDraw	Determines whether your code will draw the tooltip. If you set this to True, catch the ToolTip component's Draw method and draw the tooltip. Parameters to the method give the Graphics object to use, the bounds of the area to draw, and the tooltip text. This property is ignored if IsBalloon is True.
ReshowDelay	The number of milliseconds before the next tooltip will display when the mouse moves from one tool tip area to another. The idea is that subsequent tooltips display more quickly if one is already visible.
ShowAlways	Determines whether the component still displays tooltips, even if the form does not have the focus. The mouse still must hover over the tooltip area as usual if ShowAlways is True.
StripAmpersands	Determines whether the component removes ampersand characters from tooltip text. This can be useful if the tooltip text looks like menu and label captions where ampersands are converted into underscores.
UseAnimation	Determines whether animation effects are used to show and hide the tooltip.
UseFading	Determines whether fading effects are used to show and hide the tooltip.

The ToolTip component's SetToolTip method lets a program associate a tooltip with a code at run time. The following code adds tooltip text to several address controls.

```
ttHint.SetToolTip(txtFirstName, "Customer first name")
ttHint.SetToolTip(txtLastName, "Customer last name")
ttHint.SetToolTip(txtStreet, "Mailing address street number and name")
ttHint.SetToolTip(txtCity, "Mailing address city")
ttHint.SetToolTip(cboState, "Mailing address state")
ttHint.SetToolTip(txtZip, "Mailing address ZIP code")
```

The following table lists the ToolTip component's most useful methods.

Method	Purpose
GetToolTip	Returns a control's associated tooltip text.
RemoveAll	Removes all tooltip text associated with this ToolTip component.
SetToolTip	Sets a control's associated tooltip text. Set the text to Nothing or an empty to remove that control's tooltip text.
Show	Displays a tooltip over a specific control. Different overloaded versions let you specify the tooltip's location and duration.

TrackBar

The TrackBar control allows the user to drag a pointer along a bar to select a numeric value. This control is very similar to a horizontal scroll bar, but with a different appearance.

The following table describes the control's most useful properties.

Property	Purpose
AutoSize	Determines whether the control automatically sets its height or width, depending on its Orientation property. For example, if the control's orientation is horizontal, then setting AutoSize to True makes the control pick a height that is appropriate for the control's width.
LargeChange	The amount by which the control's value changes when the user clicks on the TrackBar, but not on its pointer.
Maximum	The largest value that the user can select.
Minimum	The smallest value that the user can select.
Orientation	Determines the control's orientation. This can be Horizontal or Vertical.
SmallChange	The amount by which the control's value changes when the user presses an arrow key.
TickFrequency	The number of values between tick marks on the control.
TickStyle	Determines the position of tick marks on the control. This can be TopLeft (on the top if Orientation is Horizontal; on the left if Orientation is Vertical), BottomRight (on the bottom if Orientation is Horizontal; on the right if Orientation is Vertical), Both, or None.
Value	The control's current numeric value.

The control's Value, Minimum, Maximum, and TickFrequency properties are integer values, so the TrackBar control is not ideal for letting the user select a nonintegral value such as 1.25.

The control's Scroll event fires when the user changes the control's value interactively. The ValueChanged event occurs when the control's value changes either because the user changed it interactively or because the program changed it with code.

TreeView

The TreeView control displays a hierarchical data set graphically, as shown in Figure G-30.

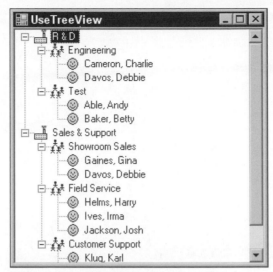

Figure G-30: The TreeView control displays hierarchical data graphically.

The TreeView control uses TreeNode objects to represent the items it contains. The control's Nodes collection contains references to the top-level objects called its *root nodes*. In Figure G-30, the "R & D" and "Sales & Support" items are the root nodes.

Each TreeNode object has a Nodes collection of its own that contains references to its child nodes. For example, in Figure G-30 the "R & D" root node has children labeled "Engineering" and "Test." Each of those nodes has child nodes representing employees.

You can assign each of the TreeNode objects icons to display. In Figure G-30, the nodes display images representing factories, workgroups, and people.

Your program can manipulate the TreeNode objects at run time, but you can also edit the tree data at design time. Select the TreeView control, select its Nodes property in the Properties window, and click the ellipsis to the right to make Visual Basic display the TreeNode Editor shown in Figure G-31.

Click Add Root to add a new root node to the tree. Select a node and click Add Child to give the node a new child. Select a node and click Delete to remove the node and any descendants it contains.

If the TreeView control's ImageList property is set to an ImageList control, then you can set a node's ImageIndex property to the index of the image in the ImageList that the node should display. Set the node's SelectedImageIndex to the index of the image that the control should display when the node is selected.

The following table describes the TreeView control's most useful properties.

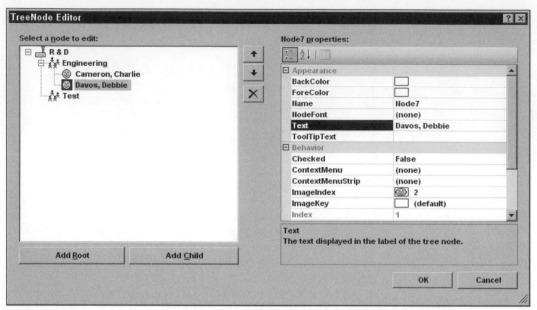

Figure G-31: The TreeNode Editor lets you edit a TreeView control's data at design time.

Property	Purpose
BorderStyle	Determines the control's border style.
CheckBoxes	Determines whether the control displays check boxes next to the nodes.
DrawMode	Determines whether your code draws nothing (the default), the nodes' text, or the nodes' text and lines.
FullRowSelect	Determines whether selection highlights span the whole width of the control.
HideSelection	Determines whether the selected node remains visibly highlighted even when the TreeView control loses the focus.
HotTracking	Determines whether node labels look like hyperlinks when the mouse moves over them.
ImageIndex	Determines the default image index for the nodes.
ImageList	Determines the ImageList control that contains the images used by the nodes.
Indent	Determines the indentation distance for each level in the tree.
ItemHeight	Determines the height of each node.
LabelEdit	Determines whether the user can edit the nodes' labels.
LineColor	Determines the color of the lines connecting the nodes.

Property	Purpose
Nodes	Returns the collection of tree nodes.
PathSeparator	Determines the delimiter string used to represent paths in the tree. For example, using the default separator "\", the path to the first person in Figure G-31 is "R & D\Engineering\Cameron, Charlie."
Scrollable	Determines whether the control displays scroll bars when necessary.
SelectedImageIndex	Determines the default image index for the selected nodes.
SelectedNode	Determines the currently selected node.
ShowLines	Determines whether the control draws lines connecting the nodes.
ShowNodeToolTips	Determines whether the control displays tooltips when the mouse hovers over a node. Use the TreeNode objects' ToolTipText properties to set the tooltip text.
ShowPlusMinus	Determines whether the control displays plus and minus signs next to tree nodes. The user can click the plus and minus signs or double-click the nodes to expand and collapse them.
ShowRootLines	Determines whether the control draws lines between the root nodes. In Figure G-31, ShowRootLines is True.
Sorted	Determines whether the control displays the nodes in sorted order.
TopNode	Returns the first node that is currently completely visible.
VisibleCount	Returns the number of nodes that could be fully visible. Fewer nodes may actually be visible if some are collapsed.

The TreeView control provides several methods that let your code manage the data at run time. The following table describes the most useful of these methods.

Method	Purpose
CollapseAll	Collapses all of the control's nodes.
ExpandAll	Expands all of the control's nodes. In the process, the control scrolls down, so the last node is visible and selects the topmost visible control. To select some other control, such as the topmost root node, set the control's SelectedNode property as in trvOrgChart.SelectedNode = trvOrg.Nodes(0).
GetNodeAt	Returns the TreeNode object at a specific (X, Y) location.
GetNodeCount	Returns the number of the tree's nodes. If the method's includeSubTrees parameter is False, the routine returns only the number of root nodes. If includeSubTrees is True, then the routine returns the total number of nodes in the tree.

The control provides a series of events that fire before and after the user takes certain actions. For example, when the user clicks a node's check box, the control raises its BeforeCheck event, changes the node's checked state, and then raises its AfterCheck event. The other actions that have similar Before and After event handlers are Collapse, Expand, LabelEdit, and Select.

Each of the Before event handlers provides a parameter that the code can set to cancel the event. For example, the following code shows how a program can prevent the user from editing the labels of the tree's root nodes. When the user tries to edit a node's label, the BeforeLabelEdit event fires. The value e.Node represents the node that the user is about to edit. Its FullPath property returns a delimited path showing the node's position in the tree.

The code searches this path for the path separator character (normally \). If the node is a root node, then the separator is not in the path so the IndexOf method returns -1 and the code sets e.CancelEdit to True so the edit never occurs. If IndexOf finds the path separator in the node's FullPath, the code leaves e.CancelEdit equal to False so the edit takes place as usual.

```
Private Sub trvOrgChart_BeforeLabelEdit(ByVal sender As Object, _
  ByVal e As System.Windows.Forms.NodeLabelEditEventArgs) _
  Handles trvOrgChart.BeforeLabelEdit
    e.CancelEdit = (e.Node.FullPath.IndexOf(trvOrgChart.PathSeparator) = -1)
End Sub
```

The TreeNode object also provides properties and methods if its own. The following table describes the TreeNode object's most useful properties.

Property	Purpose
Checked	Determines whether the node is checked, assuming that the TreeView control's CheckBoxes property is True.
FirstNode	Returns the node's first child node.
FullPath	Returns a string representing the node and its ancestors in the tree, delimited by the character specified by the TreeView control's PathSeparator property.
ImageIndex	Determines the index of the node's image in the ImageList control specified by the TreeView control's ImageList property.
Index	Returns the node's index within its parent node"s collection of children.
IsEditing	Indicates whether the user is editing the node's label.
IsExpanded	Indicates whether the node is expanded.
IsSelected	Indicates whether the node is selected.
IsVisible	Indicates whether the node is at least partly visible.
LastNode	Returns the node's last child node.
Level	Returns the node's level in the tree. Root nodes have level 0, their children have level 1, the children of those nodes have level 2, and so forth.

Property	Purpose
NextNode	Returns the node's next sibling node.
NextVisibleNode	Returns the next node that is not hidden because of a collapse. This may be a sibling, child, or some other node, depending on which nodes are expanded at the time. Note that this node may lie below the visible scrolling area, so it may not really be visible.
NodeFont	The font used to draw the node's text. If the node's font makes the text bigger than the TreeView control's Font property does, then the text is clipped.
Nodes	The collection of this node's child nodes.
Parent	Returns a reference to the node's parent node in the tree.
PrevNode	Returns the node's previous sibling node.
PrevVisibleNode	Returns the previous node that is not hidden because of a collapse. This may be a sibling, parent, or some other node, depending on which nodes are expanded at the time. Note that this node may be above the visible scrolling area, so it may not really be visible.
SelectedImageIndex	Determines the index of the node's selected image in the ImageList control specified by the TreeView control's ImageList property. The node displays this image while it is selected.
Text	Determines the text displayed in the node's label.
ToolTipText	Determines the node's tooltip text.
TreeView	Returns a reference to the TreeView control that contains the node.

The TreeNode object also provides several methods. The following table describes the most useful of these.

Method	Purpose
BeginEdit	Begins editing of the node's label. This raises an error if the TreeView control's LabelEdit property is False.
Clone	Copies the node and its entire subtree.
Collapse	Collapses the node's subtree.
EndEdit	Ends editing of the node's label.
EnsureVisible	Expands nodes and scrolls the TreeView as necessary to ensure that the node is visible.
Expand	Expands the node to display its children.
ExpandAll	Expands the node's whole subtree.

Table continued on following page

Method	Purpose
GetNodeCount	Returns the number of child nodes.
Remove	Removes the node and its subtree.
Toggle	Toggles the node between expanded and collapsed.

VScrollBar

The VScrollBar control is similar to the HScrollBar control, except that it is oriented vertically instead of horizontally. See the section "HScrollBar" earlier in this appendix for more information on the control.

WebBrowser

The WebBrowser control displays the contents of Web pages, XML documents, text files, and other documents understood by the browser. The control can automatically follow links that the user clicks in the document and provides a standard Web browser context menu, containing commands such as Back, Forward, Save Background As, and Print.

Using this control, you can easily add Web-based hypertext to your applications. For example, you could display an HTML help system or tutorial pages within the control.

The control provides several properties and methods for navigating to different documents. The following table describes the most useful of these.

Property/Method	Purpose
Url	Gets or sets the control's current Web address.
Navigate	Makes the control open a specific URL.
GoBack	Makes the control move to the URL it previously displayed.
GoForward	After a call to GoBack, makes the control move forward to the next URL it displayed.
GoHome	Makes the control go to the current user's home page.
GoSearch	Makes the control go to the current user's search page.

Whenever the control moves to a new document, it fires three events. The Navigating event fires before the control moves to the new document. The Navigated event occurs after the control has navigated to the new document and is loading it. The DocumentCompleted event occurs when the control has finished loading the document.

The control also supports a variety of other events that tells a program when something has changed. Some of the more useful of these notification events include CanGoBackChanged, CanGoForwardChanged, DocumentTitleChanged, NewWindow (the browser is about to open a new window), ProgressChanged (gives progress information on the download of a document), and StatusTextChanged.

After the control loads a document, the program can manipulate the document through the control's Document property. This property contains a reference to an HtmlDocument object that gives access to the document's images, forms, links, and other HTML document elements.

In addition to opening existing documents, a program can make the WebBrowser display a file generated within the application by setting its DocumentText or DocumentStream properties.

The WebBrowser control provides all of the power and flexibility of Internet Explorer. Unfortunately, that power and flexibility makes the control quite complicated, so it is not described further here. See the online help for more information.

Form Objects

This appendix describes the most useful properties, methods, and events provided by the Windows Form class.

The Form class inherits indirectly from the Control class (Control is Form's "great-grandparent"), so in many ways, a form is just another type of control. Except where overridden, Form inherits the properties, methods, and events defined by the Control class. Chapter 2, "Controls in General," discusses some of the more useful properties, methods, and events provided by the Control class and most of those apply to the Form class as well.

Properties

The following table describes some of the most useful Form properties.

Property	Description
AcceptButton	Determines the button that clicks when the user presses the Enter key. This button basically gives the form a default action. Most forms used as dialogs should have an Accept button and a Cancel button (see the CancelButton property described shortly). This makes the form more accessible to the visually impaired and is more efficient for users who prefer to use the keyboard.
ActiveControl	Gets the form's currently active control.
ActiveForm	Gets the application's currently active form. If an MDI child form is active, this returns the active form's MDI parent.
ActiveMdiChild	Gets the MDI parent form's currently active MDI child form.

Table continued on following page

Property	Description
AllowDrop	Determines whether the form processes drag and drop events. See Chapter 13, "Drag and Drop, and the Clipboard," for more information on drag and drop.
Anchor	Determines which edges of the form are anchored to the edges of its container. This lets MDI child forms resize with their MDI parents.
AutoScroll	Determines whether the form automatically provides scroll bars when it is too small to display all of the controls it contains.
AutoScrollMargin	If AutoScroll is True, then the control will provide scroll bars if necessary to display its controls plus this much margin.
AutoScrollPosition	Adjusts the AutoScroll scroll bars so this point on the form is placed at the upper-left corner of the visible area (if possible). For example, if a button has location (100, 20), the statement AutoScrollPosition = New Point(100, 20) scrolls the form so the button is in the upper-left corner of the visible area.
BackColor	Determines the form's background color.
BackgroundImage	Determines the image displayed in the form's background.
BackgroundImageLayout	Determines how the BackgroundImage is displayed. This can be None (the image is displayed at up to normal scale, or compressed, if necessary, to make it fit vertically or horizontally), Tile (the image is tiled to fill the form), Center (the image is centered on the form at up to normal scale, or compressed, if necessary, to make it fit vertically or horizontally), Stretch (the image is resized to fill the form exactly), or Zoom (the image is resized to fill the form as much as possible without distorting it).
Bottom	Returns the distance between the form's bottom edge and the top edge of its container.
Bounds	Determines the form's size and location within its container. These bounds include the form's client and nonclient areas (such as the borders and caption area).
CancelButton	Determines the button that clicks when the user presses the Escape key. This button basically gives the form a cancel action. If the form is being displayed modally, clicking this button either manually or by pressing Escape automatically closes the form.
Capture	Determines whether the form has captured mouse events. While this is True, all mouse events go to the form's event handlers. For example, pressing the mouse button sends the form a MouseDown event even if the mouse is over a control on the form or even if it is off of the form completely.

Property	Description
ClientRectangle	Returns a `Rectangle` object representing the form's client area.
ClientSize	Gets or sets a `Size` object representing the client area's size. If you set this value, the form automatically adjusts to make the client area this size while allowing room for its nonclient areas (such as borders and title bar). For example, the following statement makes the form just big enough to display the `txtNotes` control within the client area. ```Me.ClientSize = New Size(_ lblNotes.Left + lblNotes.Width, _ lblNotes.Top + lblNotes.Height)```
ContainsFocus	Returns `True` if the form or one of its controls has the input focus.
ContextMenuStrip	Gets or sets the form's context menu. If the user right-clicks on the form, Visual Basic automatically displays this menu. Note that controls on the form share this menu unless they have context menus of their own. Also note that some controls have their own context menus by default. For example, a `TextBox` displays a Copy, Cut, Paste menu, unless you explicitly set its `ContextMenu` property.
ControlBox	Determines whether the form displays a control box (the minimize, maximize, restore, and close buttons) on the right side of its caption area.
Controls	Returns a collection containing references to all the controls on the form. This includes only the controls contained directly within the form, and not controls contained within other controls. For example, if a form contains a `GroupBox` that holds several `TextBox` controls, then only the `GroupBox` is listed in the form's `Controls` collection. You would need to search the `GroupBox`'s `Controls` collection to find the `TextBoxes`.
Cursor	Determines the cursor displayed by the mouse when it is over the form.
DesktopBounds	Determines the form's location and size as a `Rectangle`.
DesktopLocation	Determines the form's location as a `Point`.
DialogResult	Gets or sets the form's dialog result. If code displays the form modally using its `ShowDialog` method, the method returns the `DialogResult` value the form has when it closes. Setting the form's `DialogResult` value automatically closes the dialog. Triggering the form's `CancelButton` automatically sets `DialogResult` to `Cancel` and closes the dialog.

Table continued on following page

Property	Description
DisplayRectangle	Gets a `Rectangle` representing the form's display area. This is the area where you should display things on the form. In theory, this might not include all of the client area and could exclude form decorations, although in practice it seems to be the same as `ClientRectangle`.
Enabled	Determines whether the form will respond to user events. If the form is disabled, all of its controls are disabled and drawn grayed out. The user can still resize the form and its controls' `Anchor` and `Dock` properties still rearrange the controls accordingly. The user can also click the form's Minimize, Maximize, Restore, and Close buttons. Note that you cannot display a form modally using `ShowDialog` if it is disabled.
Font	Determines the form's font.
ForeColor	Determines the foreground color defined for the form.
FormBorderStyle	Determines the form's border style. This can be `None`, `FixedSingle`, `Fixed3D`, `FixedDialog`, `Sizeable`, `FixedToolWindow`, and `SizeableToolWindow`.
Handle	Returns the form's integer window handle (hWnd). You can pass this value to API functions that work with window handles. Many of the API functions that are necessary in Visual Basic 6 are no longer needed in Visual Basic .NET because their functions have been incorporated into the .NET Framework, but there are still occasions when the form's handle is useful.
HasChildren	Returns `True` if the form contains child controls.
Height	Determines the form's height.
HelpButton	Determines whether the form displays a Help button displaying a question mark in the caption area to the left of the close button. The button is only visible if the `MaximizeBox` and `MinimizeBox` properties are both `False`. If the user clicks the Help button, the mouse pointer turns into a question mark arrow. When the user clicks on the form, Visual Basic raises the form's `HelpRequested` event. The form can provide help based on the location of the click and, if it provides help, it should set the event handler's `hlpevent.Handled` parameter to `True`.
Icon	Determines the form's icon displayed in the left of the form's caption area, in the taskbar, and by the Task Manager. Typically, this icon should contain images at the sizes 16×16 pixels and 32×32 pixels, so different displays can use an image with the correct size without resizing.

Property	Description
IsMdiChild	Returns `True` if the form is an MDI child form. To make an MDI application, set `IsMdiContainer = True` for the MDI parent form. Then display a child form, as shown in the following code. In the child form, `IsMdiChild` will return `True`. ```Dim child_form As New MyChildForm child_form.MdiParent = MdiParentForm child_form.Show```
IsMdiContainer	Returns `True` if the form is an MDI parent form. See the description of `IsMdiChild` for more information.
KeyPreview	Determines whether the form receives key events before they are passed to the control with the input focus. If `KeyPreview` is `True`, the form's key event handlers can see the key, take action, and hide the key from the control that would normally receive it, if necessary. For example, the following statement in a `KeyDown` event handler would close the form if the user presses Escape, no matter what control has the focus. ```If e.Keys = Keys.Escape Then Me.Close```
Left	Determines the distance between the form's left edge and the left edge of its container.
Location	Determines the coordinates of the form's upper-left corner.
MainMenuStrip	Gets or sets the form's main menu.
MaximizeBox	Determines whether the form displays a Maximize button on the right of its caption area.
MaximumSize	This `Size` object determines the maximum size the form can take.
MdiChildren	Returns an array of forms that are this form's MDI children.
MdiParent	Gets or sets the form's MDI parent form.
MinimizeBox	Determines whether the form displays a Maximize button on the right of its caption area.
MinimumSize	This `Size` object determines the minimum size the form can take.
Modal	Returns `True` if the form is displayed modally.
Name	Gets or sets the form's name. Initially, this is the form's class name, but your code can change it to anything, possibly even duplicating another form's name.
Opacity	Determines the form's opacity level between 0.0 (transparent) and 1.0 (opaque).

Table continued on following page

Property	Description
OwnedForms	Returns an array listing this form's owned forms. To make this form own another form, call this form's AddOwnedForm method, passing it the other form. Owned forms are minimized and restored with the owner and can never lie behind the owner. Typically, they are used for things like Toolboxes and search forms that should remain above the owner form.
Region	Gets or sets the region that defines the area that the form can occupy. Pieces of the form that lie outside of the region are clipped. For more information on regions, see Chapter 20, "Brushes, Pens, and Paths."
Right	Returns the distance between the form's right edge and the left edge of its container.
ShowIcon	Determines whether the form displays an icon in its title bar. If this is False, the system displays a default icon in the taskbar and Task Manager if ShowInTaskbar is True.
ShowInTaskbar	Determines whether the form is displayed in the taskbar and Task Manager.
Size	Gets or sets a Size object representing the form's size, including client and nonclient areas.
SizeGripStyle	Determines how the resize grip is shown in the form' lower-right corner. This can be Show, Hide, or Auto.
StartPosition	Determines the form's position when it is first displayed at run time. This can be Manual (use the size and position specified by the form's properties), CenterScreen (center the form on the screen taking the taskbar into account), WindowsDefaultLocation (use a default position defined by Windows and use the form's specified size), and WindowsDefaultBounds (use Windows default position and size).
Tag	Gets or sets an object associated with the form. You can use this for whatever purpose you see fit.
Text	Determines the text displayed in the form's caption.
Top	Determines the distance between the form's top edge and the top edge of its container.
TopMost	Determines whether the form is a topmost form. A topmost form always sits above all other nontopmost forms, even when the other forms have the input focus.

Property	Description
TransparencyKey	Gets or sets a color that determines the areas of the form that are shown as transparent. This applies to the form itself and any controls it contains. For example, if you set TransparencyKey to the default form and control color Colors.Control, then the whole form and the bodies of many of its controls are invisible, so you will see text and borders floating above whatever forms lie behind.
UseWaitCursor	Determines whether the form should is currently displaying the wait cursor.
Visible	Determines whether the form is visible. If the form is not visible, the user cannot interact with it. If you set Visible = False, the form's icon is also removed from the taskbar and Task Manager.
Width	Determines the form's width.
WindowState	Gets or sets the form's state. This can be Normal, Minimized, or Maximized.

Methods

The following table describes some of the most useful Form methods.

Method	Description
Activate	Activates the form and gives it the focus. Normally, this pops the form to the top. Note that forcing a form to the top takes control of the desktop away from the user, so you should use this method sparingly. For example, if the user dismisses one form, you might activate the next form in a logical sequence. You should not activate a form to get the user's attention every few minutes.
AddOwnedForm	Adds an owned form to this form. Owned forms are minimized and restored with the owner and can never lie behind the owner. Typically, they are used for things like Toolboxes and search forms that should remain above the owner form.
BringToFront	Brings the form to the top of the z-order. This applies only to other forms in the application. This form will pop to the top of other forms in this program, but not forms in other applications.
Close	Closes the form. The program can still prevent the form from closing by catching the FormClosing event and setting e.Cancel to True.

Table continued on following page

Method	Description
Contains	Returns True if a specified control is contained in the form. This includes controls inside GroupBoxes, Panels, and other containers, which are not listed in the form's Controls collection.
CreateGraphics	Creates a Graphics object that the program can use to draw on the form's surface. For example, the following code draws a circle when the user presses a button: ```Private Sub Button1_Click(ByVal sender As System.Object, _ ByVal e As System.EventArgs) Handles Button1.Click Dim gr As Graphics = Me.CreateGraphics() gr.FillEllipse(Brushes.Orange, 10, 10, 210, 220) gr.DrawEllipse(Pens.Red, 10, 10, 210, 220)End Sub``` Note that the Paint event handler provides a Graphics object in its e.Graphics parameter when the form needs to be redrawn. You should use that object rather than a new one returned by CreateGraphics while inside a Paint event handler. Otherwise, the Paint event handler's version will draw over anything that you draw using the object returned by CreateGraphics.
DoDragDrop	Begins a drag-and-drop operation. For more information on drag and drop, see Chapter 13, "Drag and Drop, and the Clipboard."
GetChildAtPoint	Returns a reference to the child control at a specific point. Note that the control is the outermost control at that point. For example, if a GroupBox contains a Button and you call GetChildAtPoint for a point above the Button, GetChildAtPoint returns the GroupBox. To find the Button, you would need to use the GroupBox's GetChildAtPoint method. Note also that the position of the Button within the GroupBox is relative to the GroupBox's origin, so you would need to subtract the GroupBox's position from the X and Y coordinates of the point relative to the form's origin.
GetNextControl	Returns the next control in the tab order. Parameters indicate the control to start from and whether the search should move forward or backward through the tab order.
Hide	Hides the form. This sets the form's Visible property to False.
Invalidate	Invalidates some or all of the form's area and generates a Paint event.

Method	Description
LayoutMdi	If this form is an MDI parent form, arranges its MDI child forms. This method can take the parameters ArrangeIcons, Cascade, TileHorizontal, and TileVertical. Typically, this command is used in a menu titled Window.
PointToClient	Converts a point from screen coordinates into the form's coordinate system.
PointToScreen	Converts a point from the form's coordinate system into screen coordinates.
RectangleToClient	Converts a rectangle from screen coordinates into the form's coordinate system.
RectangleToScreen	Converts a rectangle from the form's coordinate system into screen coordinates.
Refresh	Invalidates the form's client area and forces it to redraw itself and its controls.
RemoveOwnedForm	Removes an owned form from this form's OwnedForms collection.
ResetBackColor	Resets the form's BackColor property to its default value (Control). This change is adopted by any controls on the form that do not have their BackColor properties explicitly set.
ResetCursor	Resets the form's Cursor property to its default value (Default). This change is adopted by any controls on the form that do not have their Cursor properties explicitly set.
ResetFont	Resets the form's Font property to its default value (8-point regular Microsoft Sans Serif). This change is adopted by any controls on the form that do not have their Font properties explicitly set.
ResetForeColor	Resets the form's ForeColor property to its default value (ControlText). This change is adopted by any controls on the form that do not have their ForeColor properties explicitly set.
ResetText	Resets the form's Text property to its default value (an empty string).
Scale	Resizes the form and the controls it contains by a scale factor. A second overloaded version scales by different amounts in the X and Y directions. Note that this doesn't change the controls' font sizes, just their dimensions.

Table continued on following page

Method	Description
ScrollControlIntoView	If the form has AutoScroll set to True, this scrolls to make the indicated control visible.
SelectNextControl	Activates the next control in the tab order. Parameters indicate the control to start at, whether the search should move forward or backward through the tab order, whether the search should include only controls with TabStop set to True or all controls, whether to include controls nested inside other controls, and whether to wrap around to the first/last control if the search passes the last/first control.
SendToBack	Sends the form to the back of the z-order. This puts the form behind all other forms in all applications, although it *does not* remove the focus from this form.
SetAutoScrollMargin	If AutoScroll is True, this method sets the AutoScroll margin. The control will provide scroll bars if necessary to display its controls plus this much margin.
SetBounds	Sets some or all of the form's bounds: X, Y, Width, and Height.
SetDesktopBounds	Sets the form's position and size in desktop coordinates. See SetDesktopLocation for more information.
SetDesktopLocation	Sets the form's position in desktop coordinates. Desktop coordinates include only the screen's working area and do not include the area occupied by the taskbar. For example, if the taskbar is attached to the left edge of the screen, then the point (0, 0) in *screen coordinates* is beneath the taskbar. However the point (0, 0) in *desktop coordinates* is just to the right of the taskbar. If you set the form's location to (0, 0), part of the form is hidden by the taskbar. If you set the form's desktop location to (0, 0), then the form is visible just to the right of the taskbar.
Show	Displays the form. This has the same effect as setting the form's Visible property to True.
ShowDialog	Displays the form as a modal dialog. The user cannot interact with other parts of the application before this form closes. Note that some other processes may still be running. For example, a Timer control on another form still raises Tick events and the program can still respond to them.

Events

The following table describes some of the most useful Form events.

Event	Description
Activated	Occurs when the form activates.
Click	Occurs when the user clicks on the form. Normally, if the user clicks on a control, the control rather than the form receives the Click event. If the form's Capture property is set to True, however, the event goes to the form.
ControlAdded	Occurs when a new control is added to the form.
ControlRemoved	Occurs when a control is removed from the form.
Deactivate	Occurs when the form deactivates.
DoubleClick	Occurs when the user double-clicks on the form. Normally, if the user double-clicks on a control, the control rather than the form receives the DoubleClick event. If the form's Capture property is set to True, however, the first click goes to the form and the second goes to the control.
DragDrop	Occurs when the user drops data onto the form. The form should process the data in an appropriate way. See Chapter 13, "Drag and Drop, and the Clipboard," for more information on drag and drop.
DragEnter	Occurs when a drag-and-drop operation moves over the form. The form should indicate what drag operations it will allow and optionally display a visible indication that the drag is over it. See Chapter 13, "Drag and Drop, and the Clipboard," for more information on drag and drop.
DragLeave	Occurs when a drag-and-drop operation leaves the form. If the form is displaying a visible indicator of the pending drop, it should remove that indicator now. See Chapter 13, "Drag and Drop, and the Clipboard," for more information on drag and drop.
DragOver	Occurs repeatedly as long as a drag-and-drop operation is being performed over the form. The form can use this event to display a more complex visible indicator of the pending drop. For example, it might show where on the form the data will be dropped or it might highlight the area on the form under the mouse. See Chapter 13, Drag and Drop, and the Clipboard for more information on drag and drop.
FormClosed	Occurs when the form is closed. The program can still access the form's properties, methods, and controls, but it is going away. See also the FormClosing event. Note that if the program calls Application.Exit, then the form's FormClosed and FormClosing events do not occur. If you want the program to free resources before the form disappears, it should do so before calling Application.Exit.

Table continued on following page

Event	Description
FormClosing	Occurs when the form is about to close. The program can cancel the close (for example, if some data has not been saved) by setting the even handler's e.Cancel parameter to True.
GiveFeedback	Occurs when a drag moves over a valid drop target. The source can take action to indicate the type of drop allowed. For example, it might change the drag cursor displayed. See Chapter 13, "Drag and Drop, and the Clipboard," for more information on drag and drop.
GotFocus	Occurs when focus moves into the form.
HelpRequested	Occurs when the user requests help from the form, usually by pressing F1 or by pressing a context-sensitive Help button (see the HelpButton property) and then clicking a control on the form. Help requests move up through control containers until a HelpRequested event sets its hlpevent.Handled parameter to True. For example, suppose that the user sets focus to a TextBox contained in the form and presses F1. The TextBox's HelpRequested event handler executes. If that routine doesn't set hlpevent.Handled to True, the event bubbles up to the TextBox's container, the form, and its HelpRequested event handler executes.
KeyDown	Occurs when the user presses a keyboard key down.
KeyPress	Occurs when the user presses and releases a keyboard key.
KeyUp	Occurs when the user releases a keyboard key.
Layout	Occurs when the form should reposition its child controls. If your code needs to perform custom repositioning, this is the event where it should do so.
Load	Occurs after the form is loaded but before it is displayed. You can perform one-time initialization tasks here.
LostFocus	Occurs when the focus moves out of the form.
MdiChildActivate	Occurs when an MDI child form contained in this MDI parent form is activated or closed. This activation only applies to the MDI children within this form. For example, setting focus to a different form or application and then back to the MDI child does not raise this event, but switching back and forth between two MDI children does. This event basically occurs when the MDI parent's active MDI child changes. You can catch the event to update the MDI parent's menus or perform other actions when the active child changes.
MouseClick	Occurs when the user clicks on the form. You should consider the Click event to be on a logically higher level than MouseClick. For example, the Click event may be triggered by actions other than an actual mouse click (such as the user pressing the Enter key).

Event	Description
MouseDoubleClick	Occurs when the user double-clicks on the form. You should consider the DoubleClick event to be on a logically higher level than MouseDoubleClick.
MouseDown	Occurs when the user presses the mouse down over the form. Also see the Capture property.
MouseEnter	Occurs when the mouse first moves so that it is over the form. If the mouse moves over one of the form's controls, that counts as leaving the form, so when it moves back over an unoccupied part of the form, it raises a MouseEnter event.
MouseHover	Occurs when the mouse remains stationary over the form for a while. This event is raised once when the mouse first hovers and then is not raised again until the mouse leaves the form and returns. Note that the mouse moving over one of the form's controls counts as leaving.
MouseLeave	Occurs when the mouse leaves the form. Note that the mouse moving over one of the form's controls counts as leaving.
MouseMove	Occurs when the mouse moves while over the form.
MouseUp	Occurs when the user releases the mouse button. When the user presses a mouse button down, the form will capture subsequent mouse events until the user releases the button. While the capture is in place, the form receives MouseMove events, even if the mouse is moving off of the form. It will receive a MouseHover event, even if the mouse is off of the form, if no such event has been raised since the last time the mouse moved over the form. When the user finally releases the button, the form receives a MouseUp event and then, if the mouse is no longer over the form, a MouseLeave event.
MouseWheel	Occurs when the user moves the mouse wheel. The event's e.X and e.Y parameters give the mouse's current position. The e.Delta parameter gives the signed distance by which the wheel has been rotated. Currently, this is defined as 120 "detents" per notch of the wheel. Standards dictate that you should scroll data when the accumulated delta reaches plus or minus 120 detents, and that you should then scroll the data by the number of lines given by SystemInformation.MouseWheelScrollLines (currently this is 3). If higher-resolution mouse wheels are added some day, a notch might send a value smaller than 120, and you could update the data more often, but you should keep the same ratio: SystemInformation.MouseWheelScrollLines lines per 120 detents.
Move	Occurs when the form is moved.

Table continued on following page

Event	Description
Paint	Occurs when part of the form must be redrawn. You can use the e.ClipRectangle parameter to see what area needs to be drawn. For very complicated drawings, you may be able to draw more quickly if you only draw the area indicated by e.ClipRectangle. Note also that Visual Basic clips drawings outside of this rectangle and may clip some areas inside this rectangle that do not need to be redrawn. That makes drawing faster in some cases. The idea here is that part of the form has been covered and exposed so only that part must be redrawn. If you need to adjust the drawing when the form is resized, you should invalidate the form in the Resize event handler to force a redraw of the whole form.
QueryContinueDrag	Occurs during a drag-and-drop operation (with this form as the drag source) when the keyboard or mouse button state has changed. The form can decide to continue the drag, cancel the drag, or drop the data immediately. See Chapter 13, "Drag and Drop, and the Clipboard," for more information on drag and drop.
Resize	Occurs when the form is resized.
ResizeBegin	Occurs when the user starts resizing the form.
ResizeEnd	Occurs when the user has finished resizing the form.
SizeChanged	Occurs when the form is resized.

When focus moves into and out of a form, the sequence of events is: Activated, GotFocus, Deactivate, Validating, Validated, LostFocus.

Typically, when the user clicks on the form, the sequence of events is: MouseDown, Click, MouseClick, MouseUp.

Typically, when the user double-clicks on the form, the sequence of events is: MouseDown, Click, MouseClick, MouseUp, MouseDown, DoubleClick, MouseDoubleClick, MouseUp.

When code resizes the form, the sequence of events is: Resize, SizeChanged.

When the user resizes the form, the sequence of events is: ResizeBegin, Resize, SizeChanged, Resize, SizeChanged, . . ., ResizeEnd.

Property-Changed Events

The Form class provides several events that fire when certain form properties change. The name of each of these events has the form *PropertyName*Changed where *PropertyName* is the name of the corresponding property. For example, the BackColorChanged event fires when the form's BackColor property changes.

The following table lists these events.

BackColorChanged	BackgroundImageChanged	ContextMenuChanged
CursorChanged	DockChanged	EnabledChanged
FontChanged	ForeColorChanged	LocationChanged
MaximumSizeChanged	MinimumSizeChanged	ParentChanged
SizeChanged	StyleChanged	SystemColorsChanged
TextChanged	VisibleChanged	

The names of most of these controls are self-explanatory, so they are not described further here. The exception is the SystemColorsChanged event. This occurs when the system's colors are changed either by the user or programmatically.

For example, suppose that you want the form to draw using its ForeColor property and you want that property to match the active title bar text color. Then, you could use the following code to update ForeColor when the user changed the system colors:

```
Private Sub Form2_SystemColorsChanged(ByVal sender As Object, _
 ByVal e As System.EventArgs) Handles MyBase.SystemColorsChanged
    Me.ForeColor = SystemColors.ActiveCaptionText
End Sub
```

Note that Visual Basic invalidates the form after raising the SystemColorsChanged event, so the form immediately repaints itself using the new settings.

Classes and Structures

This appendix provides information about class and structure declarations.

Classes

The syntax for declaring a class is:

```
   [attribute_list] [Partial] [accessibility] [Shadows] [inheritance] _
 Class name[(Of type_list)]
    [Inherits parent_class]
    [Implements interface]
    statements
End Class
```

The *attribute_list* can include any number of attribute specifiers separated by commas.

The *accessibility* clause can take one of the values: Public, Protected, Friend, Protected Friend, and Private.

The Partial keyword indicates that this is only part of the class declaration and that the program may include other partial declarations for this class.

The Shadows keyword indicates that the class hides the definition of some other entity in the enclosing class's base class.

The *inheritance* clause can take the value MustInherit or NotInheritable.

The *type_list* clause defines type parameters for a generic class. For information on generics, see Chapter 18, "Generics," and Appendix J, "Generics."

The Inherits statement tells which class this class inherits from. A class can include at most one Inherits statement and, if present, this must be the first noncomment statement after the Class statement.

The `Implements` statement specifies an interface that the class implements. A class can implement any number of interfaces. You can specify interfaces in separate `Interface` statements or in a single statement separated by commas.

Structures

The syntax for writing a structure is:

```
   [attribute_list] [Partial] [accessibility] [Shadows] Structure name[(Of
type_list)]
       [Implements interface]
       statements
End Structure
```

The structure's *attribute_list*, `Partial`, *accessibility*, `Shadows`, *type_list*, and `Implements` statements are the same as those for classes. See the previous section for details.

The differences between a structure and a class are:

❑　Structures cannot use the `MustInherit` or `NotInheritable` keywords (because you cannot inherit from a structure).

❑　Structures cannot use the `Inherits` clause.

❑　Structures are *value types*, while classes are *reference types*. See Chapter 15, "Classes and Structures," for information on the consequences of this difference.

Constructors

A *constructor* is a special subroutine named `New`.

Class constructors can take any number of parameters. If you provide no constructors, Visual Basic allows a default empty constructor that takes no parameters. If you provide *any* constructor, Visual Basic does not provide a default empty constructor. If you want to allow the program to use an empty constructor in that case, you must either provide one or provide a constructor with all optional parameters.

Structure constructors are very similar to class constructors with two major exceptions. First, you cannot make an empty structure constructor. Second, Visual Basic always provides a default empty constructor, even if you give the structure other constructors.

Events

The syntax for declaring an event is:

```
   [accessibility] [Shadows] Event event_name(parameters)
```

The *accessibility* clause can take one of the values: Public, Protected, Friend, Protected Friend, and Private.

Use the Shadows keyword to indicate that the event shadows an item with the same name in the parent class. Any type of item can shadow any other type of item. For example, an event can shadow a subroutine, function, or variable. This would be rather bizarre and confusing, but it is possible.

The *parameters* clause specifies the parameters that you will pass when raising the event. An event handler catching the event will receive those parameters. Use ByRef parameters to allow the event handler to provide feedback to the code that raises the event.

The syntax for raising an event is:

```
RaiseEvent event_name(parameters)
```

The parameters that you pass to the event handler must match those declared in the Event statement.

Generics

The syntax for declaring a generic is:

```
[attribute_list] [Partial] [accessibility] [Shadows] [inheritance] _
Class name[(Of type_list)]
    [Inherits parent_class]
    [Implements interface]
    statements
End Class
```

All of these parts of the declaration are the same as those used by a normal (nongeneric) class. See Chapter 15, "Classes and Structures," and Appendix I, "Classes and Structures," for information about nongeneric classes.

The key to a generic class is the (Of type_list) clause. Here, type_list is a list of data types separated by commas that form the generic's parameter types. Each type can be optionally followed by the keyword As and a list of constraints that the corresponding type must satisfy. The constraint list can contain any number of interfaces and, at most, one class. It can also contain the New keyword to indicate that the corresponding type must provide an empty constructor. If a constraint list contains more than one item, the list must be surrounded by braces.

The following code defines the generic MyGeneric class. It takes three type parameters. The first is named Type1 within the generic's code and has no constraints. The second type, named Type2, must satisfy the IComparable interface. The third parameter, named Type3, must provide an empty constructor, must satisfy the IDisposable interface, and must inherit directly or indirectly from the Person class.

```
Public Class MyGeneric(Of _
  Type1, _
  Type2 As IComparable, _
  Type3 As {New, IDisposable, Person})
```

Graphics

This appendix provides information about graphics classes.

Graphics Namespaces

This section describes the most important graphics namespaces and their most useful classes, structures, and enumerated values.

System.Drawing

This namespace defines the most important graphics objects such as `Graphics`, `Pen`, `Brush`, `Font`, `FontFamily`, `Bitmap`, `Icon`, and `Image`. The following table describes the namespace's most useful classes and structures.

Classes and Structures	Purpose
Bitmap	Represents a bitmap image defined by pixel data.
Brush	Represents area fill characteristics.
Color	Defines a color's red, green, blue, and alpha components as values between 0 and 255. Alpha = 0 means the object is transparent; alpha = 255 means it is opaque.
Font	Represents a particular font (name, size, and style, such as italic or bold).
FontFamily	Represents a group of typefaces with similar characteristics.
Graphics	Represents a drawing surface. Provides methods to draw on the surface.

Table continued on following page

Classes and Structures	Purpose
Icon	Represents a Windows icon.
Image	Abstract base class from which Bitmap, Icon, and Metafile inherit.
Metafile	Represents a graphic metafile.
Pen	Represents line drawing characteristics (such as color, thickness, and dash style).
Pens	Provides a large number of predefined pens with different colors and width 1.
Point	Defines a point's X and Y coordinates.
PointF	Defines a point's X and Y coordinates with floating-point values.
Rectangle	Defines a rectangle using a Point and a Size.
RectangleF	Defines a rectangle using a PointF and a SizeF (with floating-point values).
Region	Defines a shape created from rectangles and paths for filling, hit testing, or clipping.
Size	Defines a width and height.
SizeF	Defines a width and height with floating-point values.
SolidBrush	Represents a solid brush.

System.Drawing.Drawing2D

This namespace contains classes for more advanced two-dimensional drawing. Some of these classes refine more basic drawing classes. For example, the HatchBrush class represents a specialized type of Brush that fills with a hatch pattern. Other classes define values for use by other graphics classes. For example, the Blend class defines color-blending parameters for a LinearGradientBrush.

The following table describes this namespace's most useful classes and enumerations.

Classes and Enumerations	Purpose
Blend	Defines blend characteristics for a LinearGradient-Brush
ColorBlend	Defines blend characteristics for a PathGradientBrush
DashCap	Enumeration that determines how the ends of a dash in a dashed line are drawn

Classes and Enumerations	Purpose
DashStyle	Enumeration that determines how a dashed line is drawn
GraphicsPath	Represents a series of connected lines and curves for drawing, filling, or clipping
HatchBrush	Defines a Brush that fills an area with a hatch pattern
HatchStyle	Enumeration that determines the hatch style used by a HatchBrush object
LinearGradientBrush	Defines a Brush that fills an area with a linear color gradient
LineCap	Enumeration that determines how the ends of a line are drawn
LineJoin	Enumeration that determines how lines are joined by a GDI method that draws connected lines
Matrix	Represents a transformation matrix
PathGradientBrush	Defines a Brush that fills an area with a color gradient that follows a path

System.Drawing.Imaging

This namespace contains objects that deal with more advanced bitmap graphics. It includes classes that define image file formats such as GIF and JPG, classes that manage color palettes, and classes that define metafiles. The following table describes this namespace's most useful classes.

Class	Purpose
ColorMap	Defines a mapping from old color values to new ones
ColorPalette	Represents a palette of color values
ImageFormat	Specifies an image's format (bmp, emf, gif, jpeg, and so forth)
Metafile	Represents a graphic metafile that contains drawing instructions
MetafileHeader	Defines the attributes of a Metafile object
MetaHeader	Contains information about a Windows metafile (WMF)
WmfPlaceableFileHeader	Specifies how a metafile should be mapped to an output device

System.Drawing.Text

This namespace contains only three classes for working with installed fonts. The following table describes these classes.

Class	Purpose
FontCollection	Base class for the derived InstalledFontCollection and PrivateFontCollection classes
InstalledFontCollection	Provides a list of the system's installed fonts
PrivateFontCollection	Provides a list of the application's privately installed fonts

System.Drawing.Printing

This namespace contains objects for printing and managing the printer's characteristics. The following table describes the most useful of these classes.

Class	Purpose
PageSettings	Defines the page settings for either an entire PrintDocument or for a particular page. This object has properties that are Margins, PaperSize, PaperSource, PrinterResolution, and PrinterSettings objects.
Margins	Defines the margins for the printed page.
PaperSize	Defines the paper's size.
PaperSource	Defines the printer's paper source.
PrinterResolution	Defines the printer's resolution.
PrinterSettings	Defines the printer's settings.

Drawing Classes

The following sections describe the most useful properties and methods provided by key drawing classes.

Graphics

The Graphics object represents a drawing surface. It provides many methods for drawing shapes, filling areas, and determining the appearance of drawing results.

The following table lists the Graphics object's drawing methods.

Drawing Method	Purpose
DrawArc	Draws an arc of an ellipse
DrawBezier	Draws a Bézier curve
DrawBeziers	Draws a series of connected Bézier curves
DrawClosedCurve	Draws a closed curve that connects a series of points, joining the final point to the first point
DrawCurve	Draws a smooth curve that connects a series of points
DrawEllipse	Draws an ellipse
DrawIcon	Draws an Icon onto the Graphics object's drawing surface
DrawIconUnstretched	Draws an Icon object onto the Graphics object's drawing surface without scaling
DrawImage	Draws an Image object onto the Graphics object's drawing surface
DrawImageUnscaled	Draws an Image object onto the drawing surface without scaling
DrawLine	Draws a line
DrawLines	Draws a series of connected lines
DrawPath	Draws a GraphicsPath object
DrawPie	Draws a pie slice taken from an ellipse
DrawPolygon	Draws a polygon
DrawRectangle	Draws a rectangle
DrawRectangles	Draws a series of rectangles
DrawString	Draws text on the drawing surface

The following table lists the Graphics object's area filling methods.

Filling Method	Purpose
FillClosedCurve	Fills a smooth curve that connects a series of points
FillEllipse	Fills an ellipse
FillPath	Fills a GraphicsPath object
FillPie	Fills a pie slice taken from an ellipse
FillPolygon	Fills a polygon
FillRectangle	Fills a rectangle
FillRectangles	Fills a series of rectangles
FillRegion	Fills a Region object

Appendix K

The following table lists other useful Graphics object properties and methods.

Properties and Methods	Purpose
AddMetafileComment	Adds a comment to a metafile
Clear	Clears the Graphics object and fills it with a specific color
Clip	Determines the Region object used to clip drawing on the Graphics surface
Dispose	Releases the resources held by the Graphics object
DpiX	Returns the horizontal number of dots per inch (DPI) for this object's surface
DpiY	Returns the vertical number of dots per inch (DPI) for this object's surface
ExcludeClip	Updates the Graphics object's clipping region to exclude the area defined by a Region or Rectangle
FromHdc	Creates a new Graphics object from a device context handle (hDC)
FromHwnd	Creates a new Graphics object from a window handle (hWnd)
FromImage	Creates a new Graphics object from an Image object
InterpolationMode	Controls anti-aliasing when drawing images
IntersectClip	Updates the Graphics object's clipping region to be the intersection of the current clipping region and the area defined by a Region or Rectangle
IsVisible	Returns True if a specified point is within the Graphics object's visible clipping region
MeasureCharacterRanges	Returns an array of Region objects that show where each character in a string will be drawn
MeasureString	Returns a SizeF structure that gives the size of a string drawn on the Graphics object with a particular font
MultiplyTransform	Multiplies the Graphics object's current transformation matrix by another transformation matrix
PageScale	Determines the amount by which drawing commands are scaled
PageUnit	Determines the units of measurement: Display (depends on the device, typically pixel for monitors and 1/100 inch for printers), Document (1/300 inch), Inch, Millimeter, Pixel, or Point (1/72 inch)
RenderingOrigin	Determines the point used as a reference when hatching

Properties and Methods	Purpose
ResetClip	Resets the object's clipping region so that the drawing is not clipped
ResetTransformation	Resets the object's transformation matrix to the identity matrix
Restore	Restores the Graphics object to a state saved by the Save method
RotateTransform	Adds a rotation to the object's current transformation
Save	Saves the object's current state
ScaleTransform	Adds a scaling transformation to the Graphics object's current transformation
SetClip	Sets or merges the Graphics object's clipping area to another Graphics object, a GraphicsPath object, or a Rectangle
SmoothingMode	Controls anti-aliasing when drawing lines, curves, or filled areas
TextRenderingHint	Controls anti-aliasing and hinting when drawing text
Transform	Gets or sets the Graphics object's transformation matrix
TransformPoints	Applies the object's current transformation to an array of points
TranslateTransform	Adds a translation transformation to the Graphics object's current transformation

Pen

The Pen object determines the appearance of drawn lines. It determines such properties as a line's width, color, and dash style. The following table lists the Pen object's most useful properties and methods.

Properties and Methods	Purpose
Alignment	Determines whether the line is drawn inside or centered on the theoretical perfectly thin line specified by the drawing routine.
Brush	Determines the Brush used to fill lines.
Color	Determines the lines' color.
CompoundArray	Lets you draw lines that are striped lengthwise.
CustomEndCap	Determines the line's end cap.
CustomStartCap	Determines the line's start cap.

Table continued on following page

Properties and Methods	Purpose
DashCap	Determines the cap drawn at the ends of dashes.
DashOffset	Determines the distance from the start of the line to the start of the first dash.
DashPattern	An array of Singles that specifies a custom dash pattern.
DashStyle	Determines the line's dash style.
EndCap	Determines the cap used at the end of the line.
LineJoin	Determines how lines are joined by a GDI method that draws connected lines.
MultiplyTransform	Multiplies the Pen's current transformation by another transformation matrix.
ResetTransform	Resets the Pen's transformation to the identity transformation.
RotateTransform	Adds a rotation transformation to the Pen's current transformation.
ScaleTransform	Adds a scaling transformation to the Pen's current transformation.
SetLineCap	This method takes parameters that let you specify the Pen's StartCap, EndCap, and LineJoin properties at the same time.
StartCap	Determines the cap used at the start of the line.
Transform	Determines the transformation applied to the initially circular "pen tip" used to draw lines.
Width	The width of the pen.

Brushes

The Brush class is an abstract class, so you cannot make instances of it. Instead, you must make instances of one of its derived classes: SolidBrush, TextureBrush, HatchBrush, LinearGradientBrush, and PathGradientBrush. The following table briefly describes these classes.

Class	Purpose
SolidBrush	Fills areas with a single solid color
TextureBrush	Fills areas with a repeating image
HatchBrush	Fills areas with a repeating hatch pattern
LinearGradientBrush	Fills areas with a linear gradient of two or more colors
PathGradientBrush	Fills areas with a color gradient that follows a path

GraphicsPath

The `GraphicsPath` object represents a path defined by lines, curves, text, and other drawing commands. You can use `Graphics` object methods to fill and draw a `GraphicsPath`, and you can use a `GraphicsPath` to define a clipping region. The following table lists the `GraphicsPath` object's most useful properties and methods.

Properties and Methods	Purpose
CloseAllFigures	Closes all open figures by connecting their last points with their first points and then starts a new figure.
CloseFigure	Closes the current figure by connecting its last point with its first point and then starts a new figure.
FillMode	Determines how the path handles overlaps when you fill it. This property can take the values `Alternate` and `Winding`.
Flatten	Converts any curves in the path into a sequence of lines.
GetBounds	Returns a `RectangleF` structure representing the path's bounding box.
GetLastPoint	Returns the last `PointF` structure in the `PathPoints` array.
IsOutlineVisible	Returns `True` if the indicated point lies beneath the path's outline.
IsVisible	Returns `True` if the indicated point lies in the path's interior.
PathData	Returns a `PathData` object that encapsulates the path's graphical data.
PathPoints	Returns an array of `PointF` structures giving the points in the path.
PathTypes	Returns an array of Bytes representing the types of the points in the path.
PointCount	Returns the number of points in the path.
Reset	Clears the path data and resets `FillMode` to `Alternate`.
Reverse	Reverses the order of the path's data.
StartFigure	Starts a new figure, so future data is added to the new figure.
Transform	Applies a transformation matrix to the path.
Warp	Applies a warping transformation defined by mapping a parallelogram onto a rectangle to the path.
Widen	Enlarges the curves in the path to enclose a line drawn by a specific pen.

StringFormat

The `StringFormat` object determines how text is formatted. It enables you to draw text that is centered vertically or horizontally, aligned on the left or right, and wrapped or truncated. The following table lists the `StringFormat` object's most useful properties and methods.

Properties and Methods	Purpose
Alignment	Determines the text's horizontal alignment. This can be `Near` (left), `Center` (middle), or `Far` (right).
FormatFlags	Gets or sets flags that modify the `StringFormat` object's behavior.
GetTabStops	Returns an array of Singles giving the positions of tab stops.
HotkeyPrefix	Determines how the hotkey prefix character is displayed. This can be `Show`, `Hide`, or `None`.
LineAlignment	Determines the text's vertical alignment. This can be `Near` (top), `Center` (middle), or `Far` (bottom).
SetMeasureableCharacterRanges	Sets an array of `CharacterRange` structures representing ranges of characters that will later be measured by the `Graphics` object's `MeasureCharacterRanges` method.
SetTabStops	Sets an array of Singles giving the positions of tab stops.
Trimming	Determines how the text is trimmed if it cannot fit within the layout rectangle.

Image

The `Image` class represents the underlying "physical" drawing surface hidden below the logical layer created by the `Graphics` class. `Image` is an abstract class, so you cannot directly create instances of it. Instead, you must create instances of its child classes `Bitmap` and `Metafile`.

The following table describes the `Image` class's most useful properties and methods, which are inherited by the `Bitmap` and `Metafile` classes.

Properties and Methods	Purpose
Dispose	Frees the resources associated with this image.
Flags	Returns attribute flags for the image.
FromFile	Loads an image from a file.
FromHbitmap	Loads a `Bitmap` image from a Windows bitmap handle.

Properties and Methods	Purpose
FromStream	Loads an image from a data stream.
GetBounds	Returns a RectangleF structure representing the rectangle's bounds.
GetPixelFormatSize	Returns the color resolution (bits per pixel) for a specified PixelFormat.
GetThumbnailImage	Returns a thumbnail representation of the image.
Height	Returns the image's height.
HorizontalResolution	Returns the horizontal resolution of the image in pixels per inch.
IsAlphaPixelFormat	Returns True if the specified PixelFormat contains alpha information.
Palette	Determines the ColorPalette object used by the image.
PhysicalDimension	Returns a SizeF structure giving the image's dimensions in pixels for Bitmaps and 0.01 millimeters for Metafiles.
PixelFormat	Returns the image's pixel format.
RawFormat	Returns an ImageFormat object representing the image's raw format.
RotateFlip	Rotates, flips, or rotates and flips the image.
Save	Saves the image in a file or stream with a given data format.
Size	Returns a Size structure containing the image's width and height in pixels.
VerticalResolution	Returns the vertical resolution of the image in pixels per inch.
Width	Returns the image's width.

Bitmap

The Bitmap class represents an image defined by pixel data. It inherits the Image class's properties and methods described in the previous section. The following table describes some of the most useful new properties and methods added by the Bitmap class.

Method	Purpose
FromHicon	Loads a Bitmap image from a Windows icon handle
FromResource	Loads a Bitmap image from a Windows resource
GetPixel	Returns a Color representing a specified pixel

Table continued on following page

Method	Purpose
LockBits	Locks the Bitmap's data in memory, so it cannot move until the program calls UnlockBits
MakeTransparent	Makes all pixels with a specified color transparent by setting the alpha component of those pixels to 0
SetPixel	Sets a specified pixel's Color value
SetResolution	Sets the Bitmap's horizontal and vertical resolution in DPI
UnlockBits	Unlocks the Bitmap's data in memory so that the system can relocate it, if necessary

Metafile

The Metafile class represents an image defined by metafile records. It inherits the Image class's properties and methods described in the earlier section "Image." The following table describes some of the most useful new properties and methods added by the Metafile class.

Method	Purpose
GetMetafileHeader	Returns the MetafileHeader object associated with this Metafile
PlayRecord	Plays a metafile record

Useful Exception Classes

When your program throws an exception, it's easy enough to use a `Try Catch` block to catch the exception and examine it to determine its class. When you want to throw your own exception, however, you must know what exception classes are available so that you can pick the right one. The following table lists some of Visual Basic .NET's most useful exception classes. You can raise one of these or create a new class of your own.

Class	Purpose
`AmbiguousMatchException`	The program could not figure out which overloaded object method to use.
`ApplicationException`	This is the ancestor class for all nonfatal application errors. When you build custom exception classes, you should inherit from this class, or from one of its descendants.
`ArgumentException`	An argument is invalid.
`ArgumentNullException`	An argument that cannot be `Nothing` has value `Nothing`.
`ArgumentOutOfRangeException`	An argument is out of its allowed range.
`ArithmeticException`	An arithmetic, casting, or conversion operation has occurred.
`ArrayTypeMismatchException`	The program tried to store the wrong type of item in an array.
`ConfigurationException`	A configuration setting is invalid.
`ConstraintException`	A data operation violates a database constraint.
`DataException`	The ancestor class for ADO.NET exception classes.

Table continued on following page

Class	Purpose
DirectoryNotFoundException	A needed directory is missing.
DivideByZeroException	The program tried to divide by zero.
DuplicateNameException	An ADO.NET operation encountered a duplicate name (for example, it tried to create a second table with the same name).
EvaluateException	Occurs when a DataColumn's Expression property cannot be evaluated.
FieldAccessException	The program tried to access a class property improperly.
FormatException	An argument's format doesn't match its required format.
IndexOutofRangeException	The program tried to access an item outside of the bounds of an array or other container.
InvalidCastException	The program tried to make an invalid conversion. For example, Integer.Parse("oops").
InvalidOperationException	The operation is not currently allowed.
IOException	The ancestor class for input/output (I/O) exception classes. A generic I/O error occurred.
EndOfStreamException	A stream reached its end.
FileLoadException	Error loading a file.
FileNotFoundException	Error finding a file.
InternalBufferOverflowException	An internal buffer overflowed.
MemberAccessException	The program tried to access a class member improperly.
MethodAccessException	The program tried to access a class method improperly.
MissingFieldException	The program tried to access a class property that doesn't exist.
MissingMemberException	The program tried to access a class member that doesn't exist.
MissingMethodException	The program tried to access a class method that doesn't exist.
NotFiniteNumberException	A floating-point number is PositiveInfinity, NegativeInfinity, or NaN (Not a Number). You can get these values from the floating-point classes (as in Single.Nan or Double.PositiveInfinity).

Class	Purpose
NotImplementedException	The requested operation is not implemented.
NotSupportedException	The requested operation is not supported. For example, the program might be asking a routine to modify data that was opened as read-only.
NullReferenceException	The program tried to use an object reference that is Nothing.
OutOfMemoryException	There isn't enough memory. Note that sometimes a program cannot recover from an OutOfMemoryException because it doesn't have enough memory to do anything useful. This exception is most useful if you can predict beforehand that you will run out of memory before you actually use up all of the memory and crash the program. For example, if the user wants to generate a really huge data set, you may be able to predict how much memory the program will need, see if it is available, and throw this error without actually allocating the data set.
OverflowException	An arithmetic, casting, or conversion operation created an overflow. For example, the program tried to assign a large Integer value to a Byte variable.
PolicyException	Policy prevents the code from running.
RankException	A routine is trying to use an array with the wrong number of dimensions.
ReadOnlyException	The program tried to modify read-only data.
SecurityException	A security violation occurred.
SyntaxErrorException	A DataColumn's Expression property contains invalid syntax.
UnauthorizedAccessException	The system is denying access because of an I/O or security error.

Date and Time Format Specifiers

A program uses date and time format specifiers to determine how dates and times are represented as strings. For example, the `Date` object's `ToString` method returns a string representing a date and time. An optional parameter to this method tells the object whether to format itself as in "2/20/2004, 02.20.04 A.D," or "Friday, February 20, 2004 2:37:18 PM."

Visual Basic provides two kinds of specifiers that you can use to determine a date and time value's format: standard format specifiers and custom format specifiers.

Standard Format Specifiers

A standard format specifier is a single character that you use alone to indicate a standardized format. For example, the format string "d" indicates a short date format (as in "2/20/2004").

The following table lists standard format specifiers that you can use to format date and time strings. The results depend on the regional settings on the computer. The examples shown in this table are for a typical computer in the United States.

Specifier	Meaning	Example
d	Short date.	2/20/2004
D	Long date.	Friday, February 20, 2004
t	Short time.	2:37 PM
T	Long time.	2:37:18 PM
f	"Full" date/time with short time.	Friday, February 20, 2004 2:37 PM

Table continued on following page

Specifier	Meaning	Example
F	"Full" date/time with long time.	Friday, February 20, 2004 2:37:18 PM
g	"General" date/time with short time.	2/20/2004 2:37 PM
G	"General" date/time with long time.	2/20/2004 2:37:18 PM
m or M	Month and date.	February 20
r or R	RFC1123 pattern. Formatting does not convert the time to Greenwich Mean Time (GMT), so you should convert local times to GMT before formatting.	Fri, 20 Feb 2004 14:37:18 GMT
s	Sortable ISO 8601 date/time.	2004-02-20T14:37:18
u	Universal sortable date/time. Formatting does not convert the time to universal time, so you should convert local times to universal time before formatting.	2004-02-20 14:37:18Z
U	Universal full date/time. This is the full universal time, not the local time.	Friday, February 20, 2004 9:37:18 PM
y or Y	Year and month.	February, 2004

Custom Format Specifiers

Custom format specifiers describe pieces of a date or time that you can use to build your own customized formats. For example, the specifier "ddd" indicates the abbreviated day of the week, as in "Wed."

The following table lists characters that you can use to build custom formats for date and time strings.

Specifier	Meaning	Example
d	Date of the month.	3
dd	Date of the month with two digits.	03
ddd	Abbreviated day of the week.	Wed
dddd	Full day of the week.	Wednesday
f	Fractions of seconds, one digit. Add additional f's for up to seven digits (fffffff).	8
g	Era.	A.D.
h	Hour, 12-hour clock with one digit, if possible.	1

Specifier	Meaning	Example
hh	Hour, 12-hour clock with two digits.	01
H	Hour, 24-hour clock with one digit, if possible.	13
HH	Hour, 24-hour clock with two digits.	07
m	Minutes with one digit, if possible.	9
mm	Minutes with two digits.	09
M	Month number (1–12) with one digit, if possible.	2
MM	Month number (1–12) with two digits.	02
MMM	Month abbreviation.	Feb
MMMM	Full month name.	February
s	Seconds with one digit, if possible.	3
ss	Seconds with two digits.	03
t	AM/PM designator with one character.	A
tt	AM/PM designator with two characters.	AM
y	Year with up to two digits, not zero-padded.	4
yy	Year with two digits.	04
yyyy	Year with four digits.	2004
z	Time zone offset (hours from GMT in the range –12 to +13).	–7
zz	Time zone offset with two digits.	-07
zzz	Time zone offset with two digits of hours and minutes.	-07:00
:	Time separator.	
/	Date separator.	
" . . . "	Quoted string. Displays the enclosed characters without trying to interpret them.	
' . . . '	Quoted string. Displays the enclosed characters without trying to interpret them.	
%	Displays the following character as a custom specifier. (See the following discussion.)	
\	Displays the next character without trying to interpret it.	

Some of the custom specifier characters in this table are the same as characters used by standard specifiers. For example, if you use the character "d" alone, Visual Basic interprets it as the standard specifier for short date. If you use the character "d" in a custom specifier, Visual Basic interprets it as the date of the month.

If you want to use a custom specifier alone, precede it with the "%" character. The following shows two queries and their results executed in the Immediate window:

```
?Now.ToString("d")
"2/20/2004"
?Now.ToString("%d")
"20"
```

Custom specifiers are somewhat sensitive to the computer's regional settings. For example, they at least know the local names and abbreviations of the months and days of the week.

The standard specifiers have even more information about the local culture, however. For example, the date specifiers know whether the local culture places months before or after days. The "d" specifier gives the result "2/20/2004" for the en-US culture (English, United States), and it returns "20/02/2004" for the culture en-NZ (English, New Zealand).

To simplify cultural differences, you should use the standard specifiers whenever they will satisfy your needs rather than building your own custom format specifiers. For example, use "d" instead of "M/d/yyyy."

Other Format Specifiers

A program uses format specifiers to determine how objects are represented as strings. For example, by using different format specifiers, you can make an integer's `ToString` method return a value as -12345, -12,345, (12,345), or 012,345-.

Visual Basic provides standard format specifiers in addition to custom specifiers. The standard specifiers make it easy to display values in often used formats (such as currency or scientific notation). Custom specifiers provide more control over how results are composed.

Standard Numeric Format Specifiers

Standard numeric format specifiers enable you to easily display commonly used numeric formats. The following table lists the standard numeric specifiers.

Specifier	Meaning
C or c	Currency. The exact format depends on the computer's internationalization settings. If a precision specifier follows the C, it indicates the number of digits that should follow the decimal point. On a standard system in the United States, the value −1234.5678 with the specifier "C" produces ($1,234.57).
D or d	Decimal. This specifier works only with integer types. It simply displays the number's digits. If a precision specifier follows the D, it indicates the number of digits the result should have, padding on the left with zeros, if necessary. If the value is negative, the result has a minus sign on the left. The value −1234 with the specifier "D6" produces −001234.

Table continued on following page

Specifier	Meaning
E or e	Scientific notation. The result always has exactly one digit to the left of the decimal point, followed by more digits, an E or e, a plus or minus sign, and at least three digits of exponent (padded on the left with zeros, if necessary). If a precision specifier follows the E, it indicates the number of digits the result should have after the decimal point. The value –1234.5678 with the specifier "e2" produces –1.23e+003.
F or f	Fixed point. The result contains a minus sign if the value is negative, digits, a decimal point, and then more digits. If a precision specifier follows the F, it indicates the number of digits the result should have after the decimal point. The value –1234.5678 with the specifier "f3" produces –1234.568.
G or g	General. Either scientific or fixed point notation depending on which is more compact.
N or n	Number. The result has a minus sign if the value is negative, digits with thousands separators, a decimal point, and more digits. If a precision specifier follows the N, it indicates the number of digits the result should have after the decimal point. The value –1234.5678 with the specifier "N3" produces –1,234.568.
P or p	Percentage. The value is multiplied by 100 and then formatted according to the computer's settings. If a precision specifier follows the P, it indicates the number of digits that should follow the decimal point. On a typical computer, the value 1.2345678 with the specifier "P" produces 123.46%.
R or r	Round trip. The value is formatted in such a way that the result can be converted back into its original value. Depending on the data type and value, this may require 17 digits of precision. The value 1/7 with the specifier "R" produces 0.14285714285714285.
X or x	Hexadecimal. This works for integer types only. The value is converted into hexadecimal. The case of the X or x determines whether hexadecimal digits above 9 are written in uppercase or lowercase. If a precision specifier follows the X, it indicates the number of digits the result should have, padding on the left with zeros, if necessary. The value 183 with the specifier "x4" produces 00b7.

Custom Numeric Format Specifiers

Custom numeric format specifiers describe how a number should be formatted. The following table lists characters that you can use to build custom numeric formats.

Specifier	Meaning
0	A digit or zero. If the number doesn't have a digit in this position, the specifier adds a 0. The value 12 with the specifier 000.00 produces 012.00.
#	A digit. If the number doesn't have a digit in this position, nothing is printed.

Specifier	Meaning
,	If used between two digits (either 0 or #), adds thousands separators to the result. The value 1234567 with the specifier "#,#" produces 1,234,567.
,	If used immediately to the left of the decimal point, the number is divided by 1000 for each comma. The value 1234567 with the specifier "#,#,." produces 1,234.
%	Multiplies the number by 100 and inserts the % symbol where it appears in the specifier. The value 0.123 with the specifier ".00%" produces 12.30%.
E0 (or e0)	Displays the number in scientific notation inserting an E (or e) between the number and its exponent. Use # and 0 to format the number before the exponent. The number of 0's after the E determines the number of digits in the exponent. If you place a + sign between the E and 0, the result's exponent includes a + or - sign. If you omit the + sign, the exponent only includes a sign if it is negative. The value 1234.5678 with the specifier "00.000E+000" produces 12.346E+002.
\	Displays the following character literally without interpreting it. Use \\ to display the \ character. The value 12 with the specifier "#\%" produces 12%, while the same value with the specifier "#%" produces 1200%.
'ABC' or "ABC"	Displays the characters in the quotes literally. The value 12 with the specifier "#'%'" (single quotes around the % symbol) produces 12%.

Numeric Formatting Sections

A numeric format specifier may contain one, two, or three sections separated by semicolons. If the specifier contains one section, the specifier is used for all numeric values.

If the specifier contains two sections, the first is used to format values that are positive or zero, and the second is used to format negative values.

If the specifier contains three sections, the first is used to format positive values, the second is used to format negative values, and the third is used to format values that are zero.

The following text shows output from the Immediate window for three values using the format specifier "#,#.00;<#,#.00>;ZERO":

```
?(1234.5678).ToString("#,#.00;<#,#.00>;ZERO")
1,234.57
?(-1234.5678).ToString("#,#.00;<#,#.00>;ZERO")
<1,234.57>
?(0).ToString("#,#.00;<#,#.00>;ZERO")
ZERO
```

Composite Formatting

The `String.Format`, `Console.WriteLine`, and `TextWriter.WriteLine` methods provide a different method for formatting strings. These routines can take a composite formatting string parameter that contains literal characters plus placeholders for values. Other parameters to the methods give the values.

The value placeholders have the following format:

```
{index[,alignment][:format_specifier]}
```

The *index* value gives the index numbered from 0 of the parameter that should be inserted in this placeholder's position.

The optional *alignment* value tells the minimum number of spaces the item should use and the result is padded with spaces, if necessary. If this value is negative, the result is left-justified. If the value is positive, the result is right-justified.

The *format_specifier* indicates how the item should be formatted.

For example, consider the following code:

```
Dim emp As String = "Crazy Bob"
Dim sales As Single = -12345.67
MessageBox.Show(String.Format("{0} {1:earned;lost} {1:c} this year", emp, sales))
```

The first placeholder refers to parameter number 0, which has value "Crazy Bob." The second placeholder refers to parameter number 1 and includes a two-part format specifier that displays "earned" if the value is positive or zero, and "lost" of the value is negative. The third placeholder refers to parameter number 1 again, this time formatted as currency.

The following text shows the result:

```
Crazy Bob lost ($12,345.67) this year
```

Enumerated Type Formatting

Visual Basic provides special formatting capabilities that can display the values of enumerated variables. For example, consider the following code:

```
Private Enum Dessert
    Cake = 1
    Pie = 2
    Cookie = 3
    IceCream = 4
End Enum
...
Dim dessert_choice As Dessert = Dessert.Cake
MessageBox.Show(dessert_choice.ToString)
```

This code displays the string "Cake."

For variables of an enumerated type such as dessert_choice, the ToString method can take a specifier that determines how the value is formatted.

The specifier G or g formats the value as a string if possible. If the value is not a valid entry in the Enum's definition, the result is the variable's numeric value. For example, the previous code does not define a Dessert enumeration for the value 7 so, if you set dessert_choice to 7, then dessert_choice .ToString("G") returns the value 7.

If you define an enumerated type with the Flags attribute, variables of that type can be a combination of the Enum's values, as shown in the following code:

```
<Flags()> _
Private Enum Dessert
    Cake = 1
    Pie = 2
    Cookie = 4
    IceCream = 8
End Enum
...
Dim dessert_choice As Dessert = Dessert.IceCream Or Dessert.Cake
MessageBox.Show(dessert_choice.ToString("G"))
```

In this case, the G format specifier returns a string that contains all of the flag values separated by commas. In this example, the result is "Cake, IceCream." Note that the values are returned in the order in which they are defined by the enumeration, not the order in which they are assigned to the variable.

If you do not use the Flags attribute when defining an enumerated type, the G format specifier always returns the variable's numeric value if it is a combination of values rather than a single value from the list. On the other hand, the F specifier returns a list of comma-separated values if it makes sense. If you omit the Flags attribute from the previous code, dessert_choice.ToString("G") would return 9, but dessert_choice.ToString("F") would return "Cake, IceCream."

The D or d specifier always formats the variable as a number.

The specifier X or x formats the value as a hexadecimal number.

The Application Class

The Application class provides static properties and methods for controlling the application. This appendix contains a summary of the Application class's most useful properties, methods, and events. Chapter 25, "Configuration and Resources," has a bit more to say about the Application class and provides some example code.

Properties

The following table describes the Application class's most useful properties.

Property	Purpose
CommonAppDataPath	Returns the path where the program should store application data that is shared by all users. By default, this path has the form *base_path**company_name**product_name**product_version*. The *base_path* is typically C:\\Documents and Settings\\All Users\\Application Data.
CommonAppDataRegistry	Returns the Registry key where the program should store application data that is shared by all users. By default, this path has the form HKEY_LOCAL_MACHINE\\Software*company_name**product_name**product_version*.
CompanyName	Returns the application's company name.
CurrentCulture	Gets or sets the CultureInfo object for this thread. The CultureInfo object specifies information about a specific culture (such its name, writing system, calendar, and its formats for dates, times, and numbers).

Table continued on following page

Property	Purpose
CurrentInputLanguage	Gets or sets the InputLanguage for this thread. The Input-Language object defines the layout of the keyboard for the culture. It determines how the keyboard keys are mapped to the characters in the culture's language.
ExecutablePath	Returns the fully qualified path to the file that started the execution, including the file name.
LocalUserAppDataPath	Returns the path where the program should store data for this local, nonroaming user. By default, this path has the form *base_path**company_name**product_name**product_version*. The *base_path* is typically C:\Documents and Settings*user_name*\Local Settings\Application Data.
MessageLoop	Returns True if the thread has a message loop. If the program begins with a startup form, this loop is created automatically. If it starts with a custom Sub Main, then the loop doesn't initially exist, and the program must start it by calling Application.Run.
OpenForms	Returns a collection holding references to all of the application's open forms.
ProductName	Returns the application's product name.
ProductVersion	Gets the product version associated with this application.
StartupPath	Returns the fully qualified path to the file that started the execution, including the filename.
UserAppDataPath	Returns the path where the program should store data for this user. By default, this path has the form *base_path**company_name**product_name**product_version*. The *base_path* is typically C:\Documents and Settings*user_name*\Application Data.
UserAppDataRegistry	Returns the Registry key where the program should store application data for this user. By default, this path has the form HKEY_CURRENT_USER\Software*company_name**product_name**product_version*.
UseWaitCursor	Determines whether this thread's forms display a wait cursor. Set this to True before performing a long operation, and set it to False when the operation is finished.

Methods

The following table describes the `Application` class's most useful methods.

Method	Purpose
AddMessageFilter	Adds a message filter to monitor the event loop's Windows messages. See the following text for an example.
DoEvents	Processes Windows messages that are currently in the message queue. If the thread is performing a long calculation, it would normally prevent the rest of the thread from taking action (such as processing these messages). Calling `DoEvents` lets the user interface catch up with the user's actions. Note that you can often avoid the need for `DoEvents` if you perform the long task on a separate thread.
Exit	Ends the whole application. This is a rather abrupt halt, and any forms do not execute their `FormClosing` or `FormClosed` event handlers, so be sure the application has executed any necessary clean-up code before calling `Application.Exit`.
ExitThread	Ends the current thread. This is a rather abrupt halt, and any forms on the thread do not execute their `FormClosing` or `FormClosed` event handlers.
OnThreadException	Raises the `Application` object's `ThreadException` event, passing it an exception. If your application throws an uncaught exception in the IDE, the IDE halts. That makes it hard to test `Application.ThreadException` event handlers. You can call `OnThreadException` to invoke the event handler.
RemoveMessageFilter	Removes a message filter.
Run	Runs a message loop for the current thread. If you pass this method a form object, it displays the form and processes its messages until the form closes.
SetSuspendState	Makes the system suspend operation or hibernate. When the system *hibernates*, it writes its memory contents to disk. When you restart the system, it resumes with its previous desktop and applications running. When the system *suspends* operation, it enters low-power mode. It can resume more quickly than a hibernated system, but memory contents are not saved, so they will be lost if the computer loses power.

Events

The following table describes the `Application` object's events.

Event	Purpose
ApplicationExit	Occurs when the application is about to shut down.
Idle	Occurs when the application finishes executing some code and is about to enter an idle state to wait for events.
ThreadException	Occurs when the application throws an unhandled exception.
ThreadExit	Occurs when a thread is about to exit.

The My Namespace

The My namespace provides shortcuts to make performing common tasks easier. The following sections describe the major items within the My namespace and describe the tools that they make available.

My.Application

My.Application provides information about the current application. It includes properties that tell you the program's current directory, culture, Log object, and splash screen. It also includes information about the application's assembly, including the program's version numbering.

The following table describes the most useful My.Application properties, methods, and events.

Item	Purpose
ApplicationContext	Returns an ApplicationContext object for the currently executing thread. It provides a reference to the thread's form. Its ExitThread method terminates the thread and its ThreadExit event fires when the thread is exiting.
ChangeCurrentCulture	Changes the thread's culture used for string manipulation and formatting.
ChangeCurrentUICulture	Changes the thread's culture used for retrieving resources.
CommandLineArgs	Returns a collection containing the command-line argument strings used when the application was started. The first entry (with index 0) is the fully qualified name of the executable application.

Table continued on following page

Item	Purpose
CurrentCulture	Returns a CultureInfo object that represents the settings used for culture-specific string manipulation and formatting. This includes calendar information, date and time specifications, the culture's name, keyboard layout, number formats for general numbers (for example, the thousands separator character and decimal character), currency, and percentages.
CurrentUICulture	Returns a CultureInfo object that represents the culture-specific settings used by the thread to retrieve resources. It determines the culture used by the Resource Manager and My.Resources.
Deployment	Returns the application's current ApplicationDeployment object used for ClickOnce deployment. Normally, you don't need to manage deployment yourself, but this object lets you check for updates, start an update synchronously or asynchronously, download files, and restart the updated application.
DoEvents	Makes the application process all of the Windows messages currently waiting in the message queue. Doing this allows controls to process messages and update their appearances while the program is performing a long calculation. Often, you can avoid using DoEvents by performing long calculations on a separate thread, so the user interface can continue running normally.
| GetEnvironmentVariable | Returns the value of the specified environment variable. For example, the following code displays the value of the PATH environment variable.<br><br>```
MessageBox.Show(My.Application.GetEnvironment
    Variable("PATH"))
```<br><br>This method raises an exception if the named environment variable doesn't exist. The method Environment.GetEnvironmentVariable performs the same function, except that it returns Nothing if the variable doesn't exist. |
| Info | Returns an AssemblyInfo object that provides information about the assembly such as assembly name, company name, copyright, trademark, and version. |
| IsNetworkDeployed | Returns True if the application was deployed over the network. You should check this property and only try to use the My.Application.Deployment object if it returns True. |
```

Item	Purpose
Log	An object of the class `MyLog`. You can use this object's `WriteEntry` and `WriteException` methods to log messages and exceptions.
MainForm	Gets or sets the application's main form.
NetworkAvailabilityChanged	The application raises this event when the network's availability changes.
OpenForms	Returns a collection containing references to all of the application's open forms.
Shutdown	The application raises this event when it is shutting down. This event occurs after all forms' `FormClosing` and `FormClosed` event handlers have finished.
SplashScreen	Gets or sets the application's splash screen.
Startup	The application raises this event when it is starting up.
StartupNextInstance	The application raises this event when the user tries to start a second instance of a single-instance application.
UICulture	Gets the thread's culture used for retrieving resources.
UnhandledException	The application raises this event if it encounters an unhandled exception.

The following table lists the `Info` object's properties.

Property	Purpose
AssemblyName	Gets the assembly's name.
CompanyName	Gets the assembly's company name.
Copyright	Gets the assembly's copyright information.
Description	Gets the assembly's description.
DirectoryPath	Gets the directory where the assembly is stored.
LoadedAssemblies	Returns a collection of Assembly objects for the application's currently loaded assemblies.
ProductName	Gets the assembly's product name.
StackTrace	Gets a stack trace.

Table continued on following page

Property	Purpose
Title	Gets the assembly's title.
Trademark	Gets the assembly's trademark information.
Version	Gets the assembly's version number.
WorkingSet	Gets the number of bytes mapped to the process context.

To set most of the Info values at design time, open Solution Explorer, double-click the My Project entry, select the Application tab shown in Figure P-1, and click the Assembly Information button.

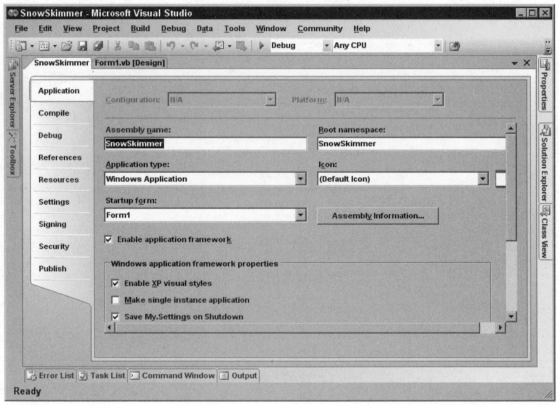

Figure P-1. Click the Assembly Information button to view and set assembly information.

Enter the assembly information in the dialog shown in Figure P-2 and click OK.

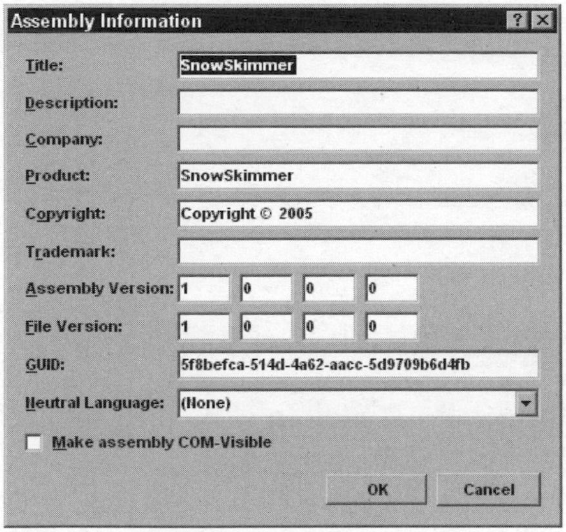

Figure P-2. Use this dialog to enter information that the program can later retrieve using `My.Application.AssemblyInfo.`

To place code in the `My.Application` object's `NetworkAvailabilityChanged`, `Shutdown`, `Startup`, `StartupNextInstance`, or `UnhandledException` event handlers, open Solution Explorer, double-click the My Project entry, select the Application tab, and click the View Application Events button at the bottom, as shown in Figure P-3.

Alternatively, you can open Solution Explorer, click the Show All Files button, expand the My Project entry, and open the file `ApplicationEvents.vb`.

To make the application a single-instance application, open the property page shown in Figure P-3 and check the "Make single instance application" box.

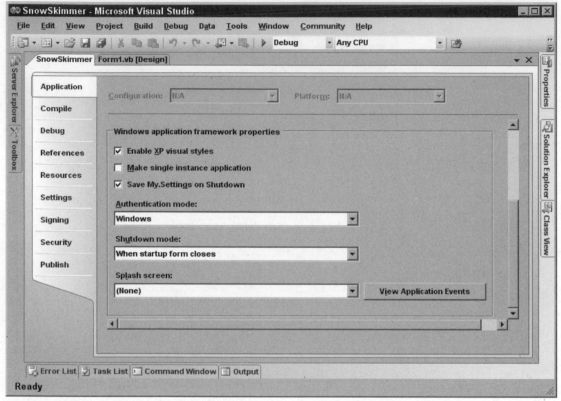

Figure P-3. Click the View Application Events button to add code to the My.Application object's `NetworkAvailabilityChanged`, `Shutdown`, `Startup`, `StartupNextInstance`, **or** `UnhandledException` **event handlers.**

My.Computer

`My.Computer` provides methods to understand and control the computer's hardware and the system software. It lets you work with the audio system, clock, keyboard, clipboard, mouse, network, printers, registry, and file system.

The following sections describe the properties, methods, and events available through `My.Computer` in detail.

Audio

This object provides access to the computer's audio system. Its methods let you play a .wav file synchronously or asynchronously, stop a file playing asynchronously, or play a system sound. For example, the following code plays the system's exclamation sound:

```
My.Computer.Audio.PlaySystemSound(SystemSounds.Exclamation)
```

The following table describes the Audio object's methods.

Method	Purpose
Play	Plays .wav data from a file, byte array, or stream. The second parameter can be Background (play asynchronously in the background), BackgroundLoop (play asynchronously in the background and repeat when it ends), or WaitToComplete (play synchronously).
PlaySystemSound	Plays a system sound. The parameter should be a member of the SystemSounds enumeration and can have the value Asterisk, Beep, Exclamation, Hand, or Question.
Stop	Stops the sound currently playing asynchronously.

Clipboard

The Clipboard object described in Chapter 13, "Drag and Drop, and the Clipboard," enables you to move data in and out of the system's clipboard. The My.Computer.Clipboard object provides extra tools that simplify some clipboard operations. The following table briefly summarizes the My.Computer.Clipboard object's methods.

Method	Purpose
Clear	Removes all data from the clipboard.
ContainsAudio	Returns True if the clipboard contains audio data.
ContainsData	Returns True if the clipboard contains data in a specific custom format.
ContainsFileDropList	Returns True if the clipboard contains a file drop list.
ContainsImage	Returns True if the clipboard contains image data.
ContainsText	Returns True if the clipboard contains textual data.

Table continued on following page

Method	Purpose
GetAudioStream	Gets audio data from the clipboard.
GetData	Gets data in a specific custom format from the clipboard.
GetDataObject	Gets a DataObject from the clipboard.
GetFileDropList	Gets a StringCollection holding the names of the files selected for drop from the clipboard.
GetImage	Gets image data from the clipboard.
GetText	Gets textual data from the clipboard.
SetAudio	Saves audio data to the clipboard.
SetData	Saves data in a specific custom format to the clipboard.
SetDataObject	Saves a DataObject to the clipboard.
SetFileDropList	Saves a StringCollection containing a series of fully qualified file names to the clipboard.
SetImage	Saves an image to the clipboard.
SetText	Saves textual data to the clipboard.

See Chapter 13 for more information about using the clipboard.

Clock

This property returns an object of type MyClock that you can use to learn about the current time. The following table describes this object's properties.

Property	Purpose
GmtTime	Returns a Date object that gives the current local date and time converted into Coordinated Universal Time (UTC) or Greenwich Mean Time (GMT).
LocalTime	Returns a Date object that gives the current local date and time.
TickCount	Returns the number of milliseconds since the computer started.

For example, suppose that you live in Colorado, which uses Mountain Standard Time (MST), seven hours behind Greenwich Mean Time. If My.Computer.Clock.LocalTime returns 2:03 PM, then My.Computer.Clock.GmtTime returns 9:03 PM.

If you must store a date and time for later use (for example, in a database), you should generally store it in UTC. Then you can meaningfully compare that value with other times stored on other computers in different time zones such as those across the Internet.

FileSystem

The `FileSystem` object provides tools for working with drives, directories, and files. The following table summarizes this object's properties and methods.

Item	Description
CombinePath	Returns a properly formatted combined path as a String.
CopyDirectory	Copies a directory.
CopyFile	Copies a file.
CreateDirectory	Creates a directory.
CurrentDirectory	Determines the fully qualified path to the application's current directory.
DeleteDirectory	Deletes a directory.
DeleteFile	Deletes a file.
DirectoryExists	Returns a Boolean indicating whether a directory exists.
Drives	Returns a read-only collection of `DriveInfo` objects describing the system's drives. See Chapter 27, "File-System Objects," for information about the `DriveInfo` class.
FileExists	Returns a Boolean indicating whether a file exists.
FindInFiles	Returns a collection holding names of files that contain a search string.
GetDirectories	Returns a String collection representing the path names of subdirectories within a directory.
GetDirectoryInfo	Returns a `DirectoryInfo` object for the specified path.
GetDriveInfo	Returns a `DriveInfo` object for the specified path.
GetFileInfo	Returns a `FileInfo` object for the specified path.
GetFiles	Returns a read-only String collection representing the names of files within a directory.
GetParentPath	Returns a String representing the absolute path of the parent of the provided path.
MoveDirectory	Moves a directory.
MoveFile	Moves a file.
OpenTextFieldParser	Opens a `TextFieldParser`.
OpenTextFileReader	Opens a `TextReader`.

Table continued on following page

Item	Description
OpenTextFileWriter	Opens a TextWriter.
ReadAllBytes	Reads from a binary file.
ReadAllText	Reads from a text file.
RenameDirectory	Renames a directory.
RenameFile	Renames a file.
SpecialDirectories	Returns a SpecialDirectoriesProxy object that has properties giving the locations of various special directories such as the systems temporary directory and the user's MyDocuments directory. See Chapter 27, "File System Objects," for more information.
WriteAllBytes	Writes to a binary file.
WriteAllText	Writes to a text file.

Info

The My.Computer.Info object provides information about the computer's memory and operating system. The following list describes this object's properties.

Property	Purpose
AvailablePhysicalMemory	Returns the computer's total amount of free physical memory in bytes.
AvailableVirtualMemory	Returns the computer's total amount of free virtual address space in bytes.
InstalledUICulture	Returns the current user-interface culture.
LoadedAssemblies	Returns a collection of the assemblies loaded by the application.
OSFullName	Returns the computer's full operating-system name as in "Microsoft Windows XP Home Edition".
OSPlatform	Returns the platform identifier for the operating system of the computer. This can be Unix, Win32NT (Windows NT or later), Win32S (runs on 16-bit Windows to provide access to 32-bit applications), Win32Windows (Windows 95 or later), or WinCE.
OSVersion	Returns the operating system's version in a string with the format *major.minor.build.revision*.
StackTrace	Returns a string containing the application's current stack trace.

Property	Purpose
TotalPhysicalMemory	Returns the computer's total amount of physical memory in bytes.
TotalVirtualMemory	Returns the computer's total amount of virtual address space in bytes.
WorkingSet	Returns the amount of physical memory mapped to the process context in bytes.

Keyboard

This object returns information about the current keyboard state. The following list describes this object's properties.

Property	Purpose
AltKeyDown	Returns True if the Alt key is down.
CapsLock	Returns True if Caps Lock is on.
CtrlKeyDown	Returns True if the Ctrl key is down.
NumLock	Returns True if Num Lock is on.
ScrollLock	Returns True if Scroll Lock is on.
ShiftKeyDown	Returns True if the Shift key is down.

The My.Computer.Keyboard object also provides one method named SendKeys. This method sends keystrokes to the currently active window just as if the user had typed them. You can use this method to provide some automated control over applications.

Mouse

The My.Computer.Mouse object provides information about the computer's mouse. The following table describes this object's properties.

Property	Description
ButtonsSwapped	Returns True if the functions of the mouse's left and right buttons have been switched. This can make using the mouse easier for left-handed users.
WheelExists	Returns True if the mouse has a scroll wheel.
WheelScrollLines	Returns a number indicating how much to scroll when the mouse wheel rotates one notch.

Name

The `My.Computer.Name` property simply returns the computer's name.

Network

The `My.Computer.Network` object provides a few simple properties and methods for working with the network. Its single property, `IsAvailable`, returns `True` if the network is available.

The following table describes the object's methods.

Method	Description
DownloadFile	Downloads a file from a remote computer. Parameters give such values as the file name, username, password, and connection timeout.
IsAvailable	Returns True if the network is available.
Ping	Pings a remote computer to see if it is connected to the network.
UploadFile	Uploads a file to a remote computer. Parameters give such values as the file name, username, password, and connection timeout.

This object also provides one event, `NetworkAvailabilityChanged`, that you can catch to learn when the network becomes available or unavailable.

Ports

This object provides one property and a single method. Its `SerialPortNames` property returns an array of strings listing the names of the computer's serial ports.

The `OpenSerialPort` method opens the serial port with a particular name (optional parameters give the baud rate, parity, data bits, and stop bits) and returns a reference to a `SerialPort` object.

The `SerialPort` class is much more complex than the `My.Computer.Ports` object. The following table describes the `SerialPort`'s most useful properties.

Property	Purpose
BaseStream	Returns the underlying `Stream` object.
BaudRate	Gets or sets the port's baud rate.
BreakState	Gets or sets the break signal state.
BytesToRead	Returns the number of bytes of data in the receive buffer.
BytesToWrite	Returns the number of bytes of data in the send buffer.

Property	Purpose
CDHolding	Returns the state of the port's Carrier Detect (CD) line.
CtsHolding	Returns the state of the port's Clear-to-Send (CTS) line.
DataBits	Gets or sets the standard length of data bits per byte.
DiscardNull	Determines whether null characters are ignored.
DsrHolding	Returns the state of the Data Set Ready (DSR) signal.
DtrEnable	Determines enabling of the Data Terminal Ready (DTR) signal.
Encoding	Determines the character encoding for text conversion.
Handshake	Determines the handshaking protocol.
IsOpen	Returns `True` if the port is open.
NewLine	Determines the end of line sequence for the `ReadLine` and `WriteLine` methods. This is a linefeed by default.
Parity	Determines the parity-checking protocol.
ParityReplace	Determines the character used to replace invalid characters when a parity error occurs.
PortName	Gets or selects the port.
ReadBufferSize	Determines the port's read buffer size.
ReadTimeout	Determines the read timeout in milliseconds.
ReceivedBytesThreshold	Determines the number of bytes in the input buffer before a `ReceivedEvent` is raised.
RtsEnable	Determines whether the Request to Transmit (RTS) signal is enabled.
StopBits	Determines the standard number of stop bits per byte.
WriteBufferSize	Determines the port's write buffer size.
WriteTimeout	Determines the write timeout in milliseconds.

The following table describes the `SerialPort` object's most useful methods.

Method	Purpose
Close	Closes the port.
DiscardInBuffer	Discards any data that is currently in the read buffer.
DiscardOutBuffer	Discards any data that is currently in the write buffer.

Table continued on following page

Method	Purpose
GetPortNames	Returns an array of strings holding the serial ports' names.
Open	Opens the port's connection.
Read	Reads data from the read buffer.
ReadByte	Synchronously reads one byte from the read buffer.
ReadChar	Synchronously reads one character from the read buffer.
ReadExisting	Reads all immediately available characters in both the stream and the read buffer.
ReadLine	Reads up to the next NewLine value in the read buffer.
ReadTo	Reads a string up to the specified value in the read buffer.
Write	Writes data into the port's write buffer.
WriteLine	Writes a string and a NewLine into the write buffer.

The SerialPort object also has a few events that you can use to learn about changes in the port's status. The following table describes the object's most useful events.

Event	Purpose
DataReceived	Occurs when the port receives data. The e.EventType parameter indicates the type of data and can be SerialData.Eof (end of file received) or SerialData.Chars (characters were received).
ErrorEvent	Occurs when the port encounters an error. The e.EventTytpe parameter indicates the type of error and can be Frame (framing error), Overrun (character buffer overrun), RxOver (input buffer overrun), RxParity (hardware detected parity error), or TxFull (output buffer full).
PinChangedEvent	Occurs when the port's serial pin changes. The e.EventTytpe parameter indicates the type of change and can be Break (break in the input), CDChanged (Receive Line Signal Detect, or RLSD, signal changed state), CtsChanged (CTS signal changed state), DsrChanged (DSR signal changed state), and Ring (detected a ring indicator).

Registry

My.Computer.Registry provides objects that manipulate the Registry. My.Computer.Registry has seven properties that refer to objects of type RegistryKey. The following table lists these objects and the corresponding Registry subtrees.

My.Computer.Registry Property	Registry Subtree
ClassesRoot	HKEY_CLASSES_ROOT
CurrentConfig	HKEY_CURRENT_CONFIG
CurrentUser	HKEY_CURRENT_USER
DynData	HKEY_DYNAMIC_DATA
LocalMachine	HKEY_LOCAL_MACHINE
PerformanceData	HKEY_PERFORMANCE_DATA
Users	HKEY_USERS

My.Computer.Registry also provides two methods, GetValue and SetValue, that get and set Registry values.

The program can use the RegistryKey objects to work with the corresponding Registry subtrees. The following table describes the most useful properties and methods provided by the RegistryKey class.

Property or Method	Purpose
Close	Closes the key and writes it to disk if it has been modified.
CreateSubKey	Creates a new subkey or opens an existing subkey within this key.
DeleteSubKey	Deletes the specified subkey.
DeleteSubKeyTree	Recursively deletes a subkey and any child subkeys it contains.
DeleteValue	Deletes a value from the key.
Flush	Writes any changes to the key into the Registry.
GetSubKeyNames	Returns an array of strings giving subkey names.
GetValue	Returns the value of a specified value within this key.
GetValueKind	Returns the type of a specified value within this key. This can be Binary, DWord, ExpandString, MultiString, QWord, String, or Unknown.
GetValueNames	Returns an array of strings giving the names of all of the values contained within the key.
Name	Returns the key's Registry path.
OpenSubKey	Returns a RegistryKey object representing a descendant key. A parameter indicates whether you need write access to the key.

Table continued on following page

Property or Method	Purpose
SetValue	Sets a value within the key.
SubKeyCount	Returns the number of subkeys that are this key's direct children.
ToString	Returns the key's name.
ValueCount	Returns the number of values stored in this key.

Visual Basic's native Registry methods SaveSetting and GetSetting are generally easier to use than My.Computer.Registry, although they don't provide access to the entire Registry.

Screen

The My.Computer.Screen property returns a Screen object representing the computer's main display. The following table describes the Screen object's most useful properties.

Property	Purpose
AllScreens	Returns an array of Screen objects representing all of the system's screens.
BitsPerPixel	Returns the screen's color depth in bits per pixel.
Bounds	Returns a Rectangle giving the screen's bounds in pixels.
DeviceName	Returns the screen's device name as in "\\.\DISPLAY1".
Primary	Returns True if the screen is the computer's primary screen.
PrimaryScreen	Returns a reference to a Screen object representing the system's primary display. For a single display system, the primary display is the only display.
WorkingArea	Returns a Rectangle giving the screen's working area bounds in pixels. This is the desktop area excluding taskbars, docked windows, and docked toolbars.

The following table describes the Screen class's most useful methods.

Method	Purpose
FromControl	Returns a Screen object representing the display that contains the largest piece of a specific control.
FromHandle	Returns a Screen object representing the display that contains the largest piece of the object with a given handle.

Method	Purpose
FromPoint	Returns a Screen object representing the display that contains a given point.
FromRectangle	Returns a Screen object representing the display that contains the largest piece of a given Rectangle.
GetBounds	Returns a Rectangle giving the bounds of the screen that contains the largest piece of a control, rectangle, or point.
GetWorkingArea	Returns a Rectangle giving the working area of the screen that contains the largest piece of a control, rectangle, or point.

The AllScreens and PrimaryScreen properties, and all of these methods, are shared members of the Windows.Forms.Screen class. If you refer to them using an instance of the class such as My.Computer .Screen, the IDE flags the code with a warning. You can avoid the warning by using the class itself (System.Windows.Forms.Screen) rather than an instance to refer to these properties as in the following code:

```
Debug.WriteLine(System.Windows.Forms.Screen.AllScreens(0).DeviceName)
Debug.WriteLine(System.Windows.Forms.Screen.PrimaryScreen.DeviceName)
```

The WorkingArea property does not update after you access the Screen object. If the user moves the system taskbar, the WorkingArea property does not show the new values.

The GetWorkingArea method retrieves the screen's current working area, however. If you must be certain that the user has not moved the taskbar or a docked object, use the GetWorkingArea method.

My.Forms

My.Forms provides properties that give references to an instance of each of the types of forms defined by the application. If the program begins with a startup form, then the corresponding My.Forms entry refers to that form. For example, suppose the program begins by displaying Form1. Then, My.Forms .Form1 refers to the startup instance of the Form1 class.

You can also refer to these forms directly. For example, the following two statements set the text and display the predefined instance of the Form2 class:

```
My.Forms.Form2.Text = "Hello!"
Form2.Show()
```

Other forms that you create using the New keyword are separate instances from those provided by My.Forms.

If you know you will only want one instance of a particular form, for example if the form is a dialog, you can use this instance instead of creating new instances of the class. If you will need to use more than one instance of the form at the same time, you must use New to create them.

You can set these properties to Nothing to dispose of the forms, but you can never set them to anything else. In particular, you cannot set them to new instances of their form classes later. Once you destroy one of these instances, it is gone forever. If you will need to reuse the form later, set its Visible property to False rather than setting it equal to Nothing. Alternatively, you can just create new instances of the class when you need them and ignore the forms in My.Forms.

My.Resources

My.Resources provides access to the application's resources. Its ResourceManager property returns a reference to a ResourceManager object attached to the project's resources. You can use this object to retrieve the application's resources.

My.Resources also provides strongly typed properties that return the application's resources. For example, if you create a string resource named Greeting, the following code sets the form's caption to that string's value:

```
Me.Text = My.Resources.Greeting
```

See Chapter 25, "Configuration and Resources," for more information on using My.Resources to access the application's resources.

My.User

My.User returns information about the current user. The following table describes the Screen object's most useful properties.

Property or Method	Purpose
CurrentPrincipal	Gets or sets an IPrincipal object used for role-based security.
InitializeWithWindowsUser	Sets the thread's principal to the Windows user who started it.
IsAuthenticated	Returns True if the user's identity has been authenticated.
IsInRole	Returns True if the user belongs to a certain role.
Name	Returns the current user's name in the format *domain\ user_name*.

Streams

Visual Studio provides several classes that treat data as a stream. These classes are not difficult to use, but they are similar enough to be confusing. This appendix summarizes the stream classes and describes their properties and their methods.

Stream Class Summary

The following table lists Visual Studio's stream classes. It can provide you with some guidance for selecting a stream class.

Class	Purpose
Stream	A generic stream class. This is a virtual (MustInherit) class, so you cannot create one directly. Instead, you must instantiate one of its subclasses.
FileStream	Represents a file as a stream. Usually, you can use a helper class such as BinaryReader or TextWriter to make working with a FileStream easier.
MemoryStream	Lets you read and write stream data in memory. This is useful when you need a stream but don't want to read or write a file.
BufferedStream	Adds buffering to another stream type. This sometimes improves performance on relatively slow underlying devices.
BinaryReader, BinaryWriter	Read and write data from an underlying stream using routines that manage specific data types (such as ReadDouble and ReadUInt16).
TextReader, TextWriter	These virtual (MustInherit) classes define methods that make working with text on an underlying stream easier.

Table continued on following page

Class	Purpose
StringReader, StringWriter	These classes inherit from TextReader and TextWriter. They provide methods for reading and writing text into an underlying string.
StreamReader, StreamWriter	These classes inherit from TextReader and TextWriter. They provide methods for reading and writing text into an underlying stream, usually a FileStream.
CryptoStream	Applies a cryptographic transformation to its data.
NetworkStream	Sends and receives data across a network connection.

Stream

The following table describes the Stream class's most useful properties.

Class	Purpose
CanRead	Returns True if the stream supports reading.
CanSeek	Returns True if the stream supports seeking to a particular position in the stream.
CanTimeout	Returns True if the stream supports timeouts.
CanWrite	Returns True if the stream supports writing.
Length	Returns the number of bytes in the stream.
Position	Returns the stream's current position in its bytes. For a stream that supports seeking, the program can set this value to move to a particular position.
ReadTimeout	Determines the stream's read timeout in milliseconds.
WriteTimeout	Determines the stream's write timeout in milliseconds.

The following table describes the Stream class's most useful methods.

Method	Purpose
BeginRead	Begins an asynchronous read.
BeginWrite	Begins an asynchronous write.
Close	Closes the stream and releases any resources it uses (such as file handles).
EndRead	Waits for an asynchronous read to finish.

Method	Purpose
EndWrite	Ends an asynchronous write.
Flush	Flushes data from the stream's buffers into the underlying storage medium (device, file, and so forth).
Read	Reads bytes from the stream and advances its position by that number of bytes.
ReadByte	Reads a byte from the stream and advances its position by 1 byte.
Seek	If the stream supports seeking, sets the stream's position.
SetLength	Sets the stream's length. If the stream is currently longer than the new length, it is truncated. If the stream is shorter than the new length, it is enlarged. The stream must support both writing and seeking for this method to work.
Write	Writes bytes into the stream and advances the current position by this number of bytes.
WriteByte	Writes 1 byte into the stream and advances the current position by 1 byte.

The FileStream and MemoryStream classes add few methods to those defined by the Stream class. The most important of those are new constructors specific to the type of stream. For example, the FileStream class provides constructors for opening files in various modes (append, new, and so forth).

BinaryReader and BinaryWriter

These are stream helper classes that make it easier to read and write data in specific formats onto an underlying stream. The following table describes the BinaryReader class's most useful methods.

Method	Purpose
Close	Closes the BinaryReader and its underlying stream.
PeekChar	Reads the reader's next character, but does not advance the reader's position, so other methods can still read the character later.
Read	Reads characters from the stream and advances the reader's position.
ReadBoolean	Reads a Boolean from the stream and advances the reader's position by 1 byte.
ReadByte	Reads a byte from the stream and advances the reader's position by 1 byte.
ReadBytes	Reads a number of bytes from the stream into a byte array and advances the reader's position by that number of bytes.

Table continued on following page

Method	Purpose
ReadChar	Reads a character from the stream and advances the reader's position according to the stream's encoding and the character.
ReadChars	Reads a number of characters from the stream, returns the results in a character array, and advances the reader's position according to the stream's encoding and the number of characters.
ReadDecimal	Reads a decimal value from the stream and advances the reader's position by 16 bytes.
ReadDouble	Reads an 8-byte floating-point value from the stream and advances the reader's position by 8 bytes.
ReadInt16	Reads a 2-byte signed integer from the stream and advances the reader's position by 2 bytes.
ReadInt32	Reads a 4-byte signed integer from the stream and advances the reader's position by 4 bytes.
ReadInt64	Reads an 8-byte signed integer from the stream and advances the reader's position by 8 bytes.
ReadSByte	Reads a signed byte from the stream and advances the reader's position by 1 byte.
ReadSingle	Reads a 4-byte floating-point value from the stream and advances the reader's position by 4 bytes.
ReadString	Reads a string from the current stream and advances the reader's position past it. The string begins with its length.
ReadUInt16	Reads a 2-byte unsigned integer from the stream and advances the reader's position by 2 bytes.
ReadUInt32	Reads a 4-byte unsigned integer from the stream and advances the reader's position by 4.
ReadUInt64	Reads an 8-byte unsigned integer from the stream and advances the reader's position by 8 bytes.

The following table describes the `BinaryWriter` class's most useful methods.

Name	Description
Close	Closes the `BinaryWriter` and its underlying stream.
Flush	Writes any buffered data into the underlying stream.
Seek	Sets the position within the stream.
Write	Writes a value into the stream. This method has many overloaded versions that write characters, arrays of characters, integers, strings, unsigned 64-bit integers, and so forth.

TextReader and TextWriter

These are stream helper classes that make it easier to read and write text data onto an underlying stream. The following table describes the TextReader class's most useful methods.

Method	Purpose
Close	Closes the reader and releases any resources that it is using.
Peek	Reads the next character from the text without changing the reader's state so other methods can read the character later.
Read	Reads data from the input. Overloaded versions of this method read a single character, or an array of characters up to a specified length.
ReadBlock	Reads data from the input into an array of characters.
ReadLine	Reads a line of characters from the input and returns the data in a string.
ReadToEnd	Reads any remaining characters in the input and returns them in a string.

The following table describes the TextWriter class's most useful properties.

Property	Purpose
Encoding	Specifies the data's encoding (ASCII, UTF-8, Unicode, and so forth).
FormatProvider	Returns an object that controls formatting.
NewLine	Gets or sets the stream's new-line sequence.

The following table describes the TextWriter class's most useful methods.

Method	Purpose
Close	Closes the writer and releases any resources it uses.
Flush	Writes any buffered data into the underlying output.
Write	Writes a value into the output. This method has many overloaded versions that write characters, arrays of characters, integers, strings, unsigned 64-bit integers, and so forth.
WriteLine	Writes data into the output followed by the new-line sequence.

StringReader and StringWriter

The StringReader and StringWriter classes let a program read and write text in a string. They implement the features defined by their parent classes TextReader and TextWriter. See the section "TextReader and TextWriter," earlier in this appendix, for a list of those features.

StreamReader and StreamWriter

The StreamReader and StreamWriter classes let a program read and write data in an underlying stream, often a FileStream. They implement the features defined by their parent classes TextReader and TextWriter. See the section,"TextReader and TextWriter," earlier in this appendix, for a list of the features.

Console Streams

Console applications define standard input, standard output, and standard error streams that the program can use to read and write information to and from the console. An application can also change these streams to new stream objects, thereby making the program read input and write output into the new streams.

File-System Classes

A Visual Basic application can take three basic approaches to file system manipulation: Visual Basic methods, System.IO Framework classes, and the My.Computer.FileSystem namespace. This appendix summaries the properties, methods, and events provided by these approaches.

Visual Basic Methods

The following table summarizes Visual Basic's methods for working with files. They let a program create, open, read, write, and learn about files.

Function	Purpose
EOF	Returns True if the file is at the end of file.
FileClose	Closes an open file.
FileGet	Reads data from a file opened in Random and Binary mode into a variable.
FileGetObject	Reads data as an object from a file opened in Random and Binary mode into a variable.
FileOpen	Opens a file for reading or writing. Parameters indicate the mode (Append, Binary, Input, Output, or Random), access type (Read, Write, or ReadWrite), and sharing (Shared, LockRead, LockWrite, or LockReadWrite).
FilePut	Writes data from a variable into a file opened for Random or Binary access.
FilePutObject	Writes an object from a variable into a file opened for Random or Binary access.

Table continued on following page

Function	Purpose
FreeFile	Returns a file number that is not currently associated with any file in this application. You should use FreeFile to get file numbers rather than using arbitrary numbers such as 1.
Input	Reads data written into a file by the Write method back into a variable.
InputString	Reads a specific number of characters from the file.
LineInput	Returns the next line of text from the file.
Loc	Returns the current position within the file.
LOF	Returns the file's length in bytes.
Print	Prints values into the file. Multiple values separated by commas are aligned at tab boundaries.
PrintLine	Prints values followed by a new line into the file. Multiple values separated by commas are aligned at tab boundaries.
Seek	Moves to the indicated position within the file.
Write	Writes values into the file, delimited appropriately so that they can later be read by the Input method.
WriteLine	Writes values followed by a new line into the file, delimited appropriately so that they can later be read by the Input method.

The following table describes Visual Basic methods that manipulate directories and files. They let an application list, rename, move, copy, and delete files and directories.

Method	Purpose
ChDir	Changes the application's current working directory.
ChDrive	Changes the application's current working drive.
CurDir	Returns the application's current working directory.
Dir	Returns a file matching a directory path specification that may include wildcards, and matching certain file properties such as ReadOnly, Hidden, or Directory. The first call to Dir should include a path. Subsequent calls can omit the path to fetch the next matching file for the initial path. Dir returns file names without the path and returns Nothing when no more files match.
FileCopy	Copies a file to a new location.
FileDateTime	Returns the date and time when the file was created or last modified.
FileLen	Returns the length of a file in bytes.

Method	Purpose
GetAttr	Returns a value indicating the file's attributes. The value is a combination of the values vbNormal, vbReadOjnly, vbHidden, vbSystem, vbDirectory, vbArchive, and vbAlias.
Kill	Permanently deletes a file.
MkDir	Creates a new directory.
Rename	Renames a directory or file.
RmDir	Deletes an empty directory.
SetAttr	Sets the file's attributes The value is a combination of the values vbNormal, vbReadOjnly, vbHidden, vbSystem, vbDirectory, vbArchive, and vbAlias.

Framework Classes

The System.IO namespace provides several classes for working with the file system. The following sections describe the properties, methods, and events provided by these classes.

FileSystem

The FileSystem class provides shared methods for working with the file system at a large scale. The following table describes its most useful properties and methods.

Property or Method	Purpose
CombinePath	Combines a base path with a relative child path and returns the resulting path. For example, the statement FileSystem.CombinePath("C:\Someplace\Lost", "..\Else") returns "C:\Someplace\Else."
CopyDirectory	Copies a directory and its contents to a new location. A parameter indicates whether you want to overwrite existing files that have the same names.
CopyFile	Copies a file to a new location, possibly overwriting an existing file.
CreateDirectory	Creates a new directory.
DeleteDirectory	Deletes an existing directory. Parameters indicate whether the method should recursively delete the directory's contents and whether the deleted files should be placed in the Recycle Bin or deleted permanently.

Table continued on following page

Property or Method	Purpose
DeleteFile	Deletes a file. A parameter indicates whether the file should be placed in the Recycle Bin or deleted permanently.
DirectoryExists	Returns True if the specified directory exists.
FileExists	Returns True if the specified file exists.
FindInFiles	Returns a collection holding names of files that contain a search string.
GetDirectories	Returns a read-only collection of strings giving the subdirectories within a specific directory. Parameters indicate whether the method should recursively search the subdirectories and whether the routine should allow wildcards.
GetDirectoryInfo	Returns a DirectoryInfo object representing a directory. Note that the directory need not exist yet. For example, you can create a DirectoryInfo object and then uses its Create method to create the directory.
GetDriveInfo	Returns a DriveInfo object representing a drive.
GetFileInfo	Returns a FileInfo object representing a file. Note that the file need not exist yet. For example, you can create a FileInfo object and then uses its Create method to create the file.
GetFiles	Returns a read-only collection of strings giving the names of files within a specific directory. Parameters indicate whether the method should recursively search the subdirectories and whether the routine should allow wildcards.
GetName	Returns the name portion of a file path.
GetParentPath	Returns a directory's parent directory path.
GetTempFileName	Creates a uniquely named empty file and returns its full path.
MoveDirectory	Moves a directory to a new parent directory. A parameter indicates whether you want to overwrite existing files with the same names.
MoveFile	Moves a file to a new directory. Parameters indicate whether the file should overwrite an existing file at the new location.
OpenTextFieldParser	Returns a TextFieldParser for a file. A TextFieldParser makes it easy to read fields from a delimited file or from a file with fixed-width field columns.
OpenTextFileReader	Returns a StreamReader attached to a file.
OpenTextFileWriter	Returns a StreamWriter attached to a file. A parameter indicates whether the StreamWriter should append to the file or create a new file.
ReadAllBytes	Returns a file's contents as an array of bytes.

Property or Method	Purpose
ReadAllText	Returns a file's contents as a string.
RenameDirectory	Changes a directory's name within its current parent directory.
RenameFile	Changes a file's name within its current directory.
WriteAllBytes	Writes a byte array into a file. A parameter indicates whether the method should append the bytes to the file or create a new file.
WriteAllText	Writes a string into a file. A parameter indicates whether the method should append the string to the file or create a new file.

Directory

The Directory class provides shared methods for working with directories. The following table summarizes its shared methods.

Method	Purpose
CreateDirectory	Creates all of the directories along a path.
Delete	Deletes a directory and its contents. It can recursively delete all subdirectories.
Exists	Returns True if the path points to an existing directory.
GetCreationTime	Returns a directory's creation date and time.
GetCreationTimeUtc	Returns a directory's creation date and time in Coordinated Universal Time (UTC).
GetCurrentDirectory	Returns the application's current working directory.
GetDirectories	Returns an array of strings holding the fully qualified names of a directory's subdirectories.
GetDirectoryRoot	Returns the directory root for a path, which need not exist (for example, "C:\").
GetFiles	Returns an array of strings holding the fully qualified names of a directory's files.
GetFileSystemEntries	Returns an array of strings holding the fully qualified names of a directory's files and subdirectories.
GetLastAccessTime	Returns a directory's last access date and time.
GetLastAccessTimeUtc	Returns a directory's last access date and time in UTC.
GetLastWriteTime	Returns the date and time when a directory was last modified.

Table continued on following page

Method	Purpose
GetLastWriteTimeUtc	Returns the date and time when a directory was last modified in UTC.
GetLogicalDrives	Returns an array of strings listing the system's logical drives as in "A:\." The list includes drives that are attached. For example, it lists an empty floppy drive and a connected flashdisk but doesn't list a flashdisk after you disconnect it.
GetParent	Returns a DirectoryInfo object representing a directory's parent directory.
Move	Moves a directory and its contents to a new location on the same disk volume.
SetCreationTime	Sets a directory's creation date and time.
SetCreationTimeUtc	Sets a directory's creation date and time in UTC.
SetCurrentDirectory	Sets the application's current working directory.
SetLastAccessTime	Sets a directory's last access date and time.
SetLastAccessTimeUtc	Sets a directory's last access date and time in UTC.
SetLastWriteTime	Sets a directory's last write date and time.
SetLastWriteTimeUtc	Sets a directory's last write date and time in UTC.

File

The File class provides shared methods for working with files. The following table summarizes its most useful shared methods.

Method	Purpose
AppendAllText	Adds text to the end of a file, creating it if it doesn't exist, and then closes the file.
AppendText	Opens a file for appending UTF-8 encoded text and returns a StreamWriter attached to it.
Copy	Copies a file.
Create	Creates a new file and returns a FileStream attached to it.
CreateText	Creates or opens a file for writing UTF-8 encoded text and returns a StreamWriter attached to it.
Delete	Permanently deletes a file.
Exists	Returns True if the specified file exists.

Method	Purpose
GetAttributes	Gets a file's attributes. This is a combination of flags defined by the FileAttributes enumeration, which defines the values Archive, Compressed, Device, Directory, Encrypted, Hidden, Normal, NotContextIndexed, Offline, ReadOnly, ReparsePoint, SparseFile, System, and Temporary.
GetCreationTime	Returns a file's creation date and time.
GetCreationTimeUtc	Returns a file's creation date and time in UTC.
GetLastAccessTime	Returns a file's last access date and time.
GetLastAccessTimeUtc	Returns a file's last access date and time in UTC.
GetLastWriteTime	Returns a file's last write date and time.
GetLastWriteTimeUtc	Returns a file's last write date and time in UTC.
Move	Moves a file to a new location.
Open	Opens a file and returns a FileStream attached to it. Parameters let you specify the mode (Append, Create, CreateNew, Open, OpenOrCreate, or Truncate), access (Read, Write, or ReadWrite), and sharing (Read, Write, ReadWrite, or None) settings.
OpenRead	Opens a file for reading and returns a FileStream attached to it.
OpenText	Opens a UTF-8 encoded text file for reading and returns a StreamReader attached to it.
OpenWrite	Opens a file for writing and returns a FileStream attached to it.
ReadAllBytes	Returns a file's contents in an array of bytes.
ReadAllLines	Returns a file's lines in an array of strings.
ReadAllText	Returns a file's contents in a string.
Replace	This method takes three file paths as parameters representing a source file, a destination file, and a backup file. If the backup file exists, the method permanently deletes it. It then moves the destination file to the backup file, and moves the source file to the destination file. For example, imagine a program that writes a log file every time it runs. It could use this method to keep three versions of the log: the current log (the method's source file), the most recent backup (the method's destination file), and a second backup (the method's backup file). This method throws an error if either the source or destination file doesn't exist.

Table continued on following page

Method	Purpose
SetAttributes	Sets a file's attributes. This is a combination of flags defined by the FileAttributes enumeration, which defines the values Archive, Compressed, Device, Directory, Encrypted, Hidden, Normal, NotContextIndexed, Offline, ReadOnly, ReparsePoint, SparseFile, System, and Temporary.
SetCreationTime	Sets a file's creation date and time.
SetCreationTimeUtc	Sets a file's creation date and time in UTC.
SetLastAccessTime	Sets a file's last access date and time.
SetLastAccessTimeUtc	Sets a file's last access date and time in UTC.
SetLastWriteTime	Sets a file's last write date and time.
SetLastWriteTimeUtc	Sets a file's last write date and time in UTC.
WriteAllBytes	Creates or replaces a file, writes an array of bytes into it, and closes the file.
WriteAllLines	Creates or replaces a file, writes an array of strings into it, and closes the file.
WriteAllText	Creates or replaces a file, writes a string into it, and closes the file.

DriveInfo

A DriveInfo object represents one of the computer's drives. The following table describes the properties provided by this class. The final column in the table indicates whether a drive must be ready for the property to work without throwing an exception. Use the IsReady property to see whether the drive is ready before using those properties.

Property	Purpose	Must Be Ready?
AvailableFreeSpace	Returns the amount of free space available on the drive in bytes. This value takes quotas into account, so it may not match TotalFreeSpace.	True
DriveFormat	Returns the name of the file system type (such as NTFS or FAT32).	True
DriveType	Returns a DriveType enumeration value indicating the drive type. This value can be CDRom, Fixed, Network, NoRootDirectory, Ram, Removable, and Unknown.	False

Property	Purpose	Must Be Ready?
IsReady	Returns True if the drive is ready. Many DriveInfo properties are unavailable and raise exceptions if you try to access them while the drive is not ready.	False
Name	Return's the drive's name. This is the drive's root name as in "A:\" or "C:\."	False
RootDirectory	Returns a DirectoryInfo object representing the drive's root directory. See the section "DirectoryInfo" later in this appendix for more information.	False
TotalFreeSpace	Returns the total amount of free space on the drive in bytes.	True
TotalSize	Returns the total amount of space on the drive in bytes.	True
VolumeLabel	Gets or sets the drive's volume label.	True

DirectoryInfo

A DirectoryInfo object represents a directory. The following table summarizes its most useful properties and methods.

Property or Method	Purpose
Attributes	Gets or sets flags from the FileAttributes enumeration for the directory. These flags can include Archive, Compressed, Device, Directory, Encrypted, Hidden, Normal, NotContentIndexed, Offline, ReadOnly, ReparsePoint, SparseFile, System, and Temporary.
Create	Creates the directory. You can create a DirectoryInfo object, passing its constructor the fully qualified name of a directory that doesn't exist. You can then call the object's Create method to create the directory.
CreateSubdirectory	Creates a subdirectory within the directory and returns a DirectoryInfo object representing it. The subdirectory's path must be relative to the DirectoryInfo's directory but can contain intermediate subdirectories. For example, the statement dir_info.CreateSubdirectory("Tools\Bin") creates the Tools subdirectory and the Bin directory inside that.
CreationTime	Gets or sets the directory's creation time.

Table continued on following page

Property or Method	Purpose
CreationTimeUtc	Gets or sets the directory's creation time in UTC.
Delete	Deletes the directory if it is empty. A parameter lets you tell the object to delete its contents, too, if it isn't empty.
Exists	Returns True if the directory exists.
Extension	Returns the extension part of the directory's name. Normally, this is an empty string for directories.
FullName	Returns the directory's fully qualified path.
GetDirectories	Returns an array of DirectoryInfo objects representing the directory's subdirectories. An optional parameter gives a pattern to match. This method does not recursively search the subdirectories.
GetFiles	Returns an array of FileInfo objects representing files inside the directory. An optional parameter gives a pattern to match. This method does not recursively search subdirectories.
GetFileSystemInfos	Returns a strongly typed array of FileSystemInfo objects representing subdirectories and files inside the directory. The items in the array are DirectoryInfo and FileInfo objects, both of which inherit from FileSystemInfo. An optional parameter gives a pattern to match. This method does not recursively search subdirectories.
LastAccessTime	Gets or sets the directory's last access time.
LastAccessTimeUtc	Gets or sets the directory's last access time in UTC.
LastWriteTime	Gets or sets the directory's last write time.
LastWriteTimeUtc	Gets or sets the directory's last write time in UTC.
MoveTo	Moves the directory and its contents to a new path.
Name	Returns the directory's name without the path information.
Parent	Returns a DirectoryInfo object representing the directory's parent. If the directory is its file system's root (for example, C:\), this returns Nothing.
Refresh	Refreshes the DirectoryInfo object's data. For example, if the directory has been accessed since the object was created, you must call Refresh to load the new LastAccessTime value.
Root	Returns a DirectoryInfo object representing the root of the directory's file system.
ToString	Returns the directory's fully qualified path and name.

FileInfo

A `FileInfo` object represents a file. The following table summarizes its most useful properties and methods.

Property or Method	Purpose
AppendText	Returns a `StreamWriter` that appends text to the file.
Attributes	Gets or sets flags from the `FileAttributes` enumeration for the file. These flags can include `Archive`, `Compressed`, `Device`, `Directory`, `Encrypted`, `Hidden`, `Normal`, `NotContentIndexed`, `Offline`, `ReadOnly`, `ReparsePoint`, `SparseFile`, `System`, and `Temporary`.
CopyTo	Copies the file and returns a `FileInfo` object representing the new file. A parameter lets you indicate whether the copy should overwrite an existing file if it already exists. If the destination path is relative, it is relative to the application's current directory, not to the `FileInfo` object's directory.
Create	Creates the file and returns a `FileStream` object attached to it. For example, you can create a `FileInfo` object passing its constructor the name of a file that doesn't exist. Then you can call the `Create` method to create the file.
CreateText	Creates the file and returns a `StreamWriter` attached to it. For example, you can create a `FileInfo` object passing its constructor the name of a file that doesn't exist. Then you can call the `CreateText` method to create the file.
CreationTime	Gets or sets the file's creation time.
CreationTimeUtc	Gets or sets the file's creation time in UTC.
Delete	Deletes the file.
Directory	Returns a `DirectoryInfo` object representing the file's directory.
DirectoryName	Returns the name of the file's directory.
Exists	Returns `True` if the file exists.
Extension	Returns the extension part of the file's name including the period. For example, the extension for `game.txt` is `.txt`.
FullName	Returns the file's fully qualified path and name.

Table continued on following page

Property or Method	Purpose
IsReadOnly	Returns True if the file is marked read-only.
LastAccessTime	Gets or sets the file's last access time.
LastAccessTimeUtc	Gets or sets the file's last access time in UTC.
LastWriteTime	Gets or sets the file's last write time.
LastWriteTimeUtc	Gets or sets the file's last write time in UTC.
Length	Returns the number of bytes in the file.
MoveTo	Moves the file to a new location. If the destination uses a relative path, it is relative to the application's current directory not to the FileInfo object's directory. When this method finishes, the FileInfo object is updated to refer to the file's new location.
Name	The file's name without the path information.
Open	Opens the file with different mode (Append, Create, CreateNew, Open, OpenOrCreate, or Truncate), access (Read, Write, or ReadWrite), and sharing (Read, Write, ReadWrite, or None) settings. This method returns a FileStream object attached to the file.
OpenRead	Returns a read-only FileStream attached to the file.
OpenText	Returns a StreamReader with UTF-8 encoding attached to the file for reading.
OpenWrite	Returns a write-only FileStream attached to the file.
Refresh	Refreshes the FileInfo object's data. For example, if the file has been accessed since the object was created, you must call Refresh to load the new LastAccessTime value.
Replace	Replaces a target file with this one, renaming the old target as a backup copy. If the backup file already exists, it is deleted and replaced with the target. You can use this method to save backups of logs and other periodically updated files.
ToString	Returns the file's fully qualified name.

FileSystemWatcher

The FileSystemWatcher class lets an application watch for changes to a file or directory. The following table summarizes its most useful properties.

Property	Purpose
EnableRaisingEvents	Determines whether the component is enabled. Note that this property is `False` by default, so the watcher will not raise any events until you set it to `True`.
Filter	Determines the files for which the watcher reports events. You cannot watch for multiple file types as in `*.txt` and `*.dat`. Instead, use multiple `FileSystemWatchers`. If you like, you can use `AddHandler` to make all of the `FileSystemWatchers` use the same event handlers.
IncludeSubdirectories	Determines whether the object watches subdirectories within the main path.
InternalBufferSize	Determines the size of the internal buffer. If the watcher is monitoring a very active directory, a small buffer may overflow.
NotifyFilter	Determines the types of changes that the watcher reports. This is a combination of values defined by the `NotifyFilters` enumeration and can include the values `Attributes`, `CreationTime`, `DirectoryName`, `FileName`, `LastAccess`, `LastWrite`, `Security`, and `Size`.
Path	Determines the path to watch.

The following table summarizes the `FileSystemWatcher`'s two most useful methods.

Method	Purpose
Dispose	Releases resources used by the object.
WaitForChanged	Synchronously waits for a change to the target file or directory.

The following table summarizes the class's events.

Name	Description
Changed	A file or subdirectory has changed.
Created	A file or subdirectory was created.
Deleted	A file or subdirectory was deleted.
Error	The watcher's internal buffer overflowed.
Renamed	A file or subdirectory was renamed.

Path

The Path class provides shared properties and methods that you can use to manipulate paths. The following table summarizes its most useful public properties.

Property	Purpose
AltDirectorySeparatorChar	Returns the alternate character used to separate directory levels in a hierarchical path (typically, /).
DirectorySeparatorChar	Returns the character used to separate directory levels in a hierarchical path (typically, \ ,as in C:\Tests\Billing\2005q2.dat).
InvalidPathChars	Returns a character array that holds characters that are not allowed in a path string. Typically, this array will include characters such as ", <, >, and |, as well as nonprintable characters such as those with ASCII values between 0 and 31.
PathSeparator	Returns the character used to separate path strings in environment variables (typically, ;).
VolumeSeparatorChar	Returns the character placed between a volume letter and the rest of the path (typically, :, as in C:\Tests\Billing\2005q2.dat).

The following table summarizes the Path class's most useful methods.

Method	Purpose
ChangeExtension	Changes a path's extension.
Combine	Returns two path strings concatenated. This does not simplify the result as the FileSystem.CombinePath method does.
GetDirectoryName	Returns a path's directory.
GetExtension	Returns a path's extension.
GetFileName	Returns a path's file name and extension.
GetFileNameWithoutExtension	Returns a path's file name without the extension.
GetFullPath	Returns a path's fully qualified value. This can be particularly useful for converting a partially relative path into an absolute path. For example, the statement Path.GetFullPath("C:\Tests\OldTests\ Software\..\..\New\Code") returns "C:\Tests\New\Code."

Method	Purpose
GetInvalidFileNameChars	Returns a character array that holds characters that are not allowed in a file names.
GetPathRoot	Returns a path's root directory string. For example, the statement Path.GetPathRoot("C:\Invoices\Unpaid\Deadbeats") returns "C:\".
GetRandomFileName	Returns a random file name.
GetTempFileName	Creates a uniquely named, empty temporary file, and returns its fully qualified path. Your program can open that file for scratch space, do whatever it needs to do, close the file, and then delete it. A typical file name might be "C:\Documents and Settings\Rod\Local Settings\Temp\tmp19D.tmp."
GetTempPath	Returns the path to the system's temporary folder. This is the path part of the file name returned by GetTempFileName.
HasExtension	Returns True if a path includes an extension.
IsPathRooted	Returns True if a path is an absolute path. This includes "\Temp\Wherever" and "C:\Clients\Litigation," but not "Temp\Wherever" or "..\Uncle."

My.Computer.FileSystem

The My.Computer.FileSystem object provides tools for working with drives, directories, and files. The following table summarizes this object's properties.

Property	Description
CurrentDirectory	Gets or sets the fully qualified path to the application's current directory.
Drives	Returns a read-only collection of DriveInfo objects describing the system's drives. See Chapter 27, "File-System Objects," for information about the DriveInfo class.
SpecialDirectories	Returns a SpecialDirectoriesProxy object that has properties giving the locations of various special directories such as the system's temporary directory and the user's My Documents directory. See the section "My.Computer. FileSystem.SpecialDirectories" later in this appendix for more information.

The following list summarizes the `My.Computer.FileSystem` object's methods.

Method	Purpose
CombinePath	Combines a base path with a relative path reference and returns a properly formatted fully qualified path.
CopyDirectory	Copies a directory. Parameters indicate whether to overwrite existing files, whether to display a progress indicator, and what to do if the user presses Cancel during the operation.
CopyFile	Copies a file. Parameters indicate whether to overwrite existing files, whether to display a progress indicator, and what to do if the user presses Cancel during the operation.
CreateDirectory	Creates all of the directories along a path.
DeleteDirectory	Deletes a directory. Parameters indicate whether to recursively delete subdirectories, prompt the user for confirmation, or move the directory into the Recycle Bin.
DeleteFile	Deletes a file. Parameters indicate whether to prompt the user for confirmation, or move the file into the Recycle Bin, and what to do if the user presses Cancel while the deletion is in progress.
DirectoryExists	Returns True if a specified directory exists.
FileExists	Returns True if a specified file exists.
FindInFiles	Returns a collection holding names of files that contain a search string.
GetDirectories	Returns a string collection listing subdirectories of a given directory. Parameters tell whether to recursively search the subdirectories, and wildcards to match.
GetDirectoryInfo	Returns a DirectoryInfo object for a directory. See the section "DirectoryInfo," earlier in this appendix for more information.
GetDriveInfo	Returns a DriveInfo object for a drive. See the section "DriveInfo," earlier in this appendix for more information.
GetFileInfo	Returns a FileInfo object for a file. See the section "FileInfo," earlier in this appendix for more information.
GetFiles	Returns a string collection holding the names of files within a directory. Parameters indicate whether the search should recursively search subdirectories and give wildcards to match.
GetParentPath	Returns the fully qualified path of a path's parent. For example, this returns a file's or directory's parent directory.
MoveDirectory	Moves a directory. Parameters indicate whether to overwrite files that have the same name in the destination directory and whether to prompt the user when such a collision occurs.

Method	Purpose
MoveFile	Moves a file. Parameters indicate whether to overwrite a file that has the same name as the file's destination and whether to prompt the user when such a collision occurs.
OpenTextFieldParser	Opens a TextFieldParser object attached to a delimited or fixed-field file (such as a log file). You can use the object to parse the file.
OpenTextFileReader	Opens a StreamReader object attached to a file. You can use the object to read the file.
OpenTextFileWriter	Opens a StreamReader object attached to a file. You can use the object to write into the file.
ReadAllBytes	Reads all the bytes from a binary file into an array.
ReadAllText	Reads all the text from a text file into a string.
RenameDirectory	Renames a directory within its parent directory.
RenameFile	Renames a file with its directory.
WriteAllBytes	Writes an array of bytes into a binary file. A parameter tells whether to append the data or rewrite the file.
WriteAllText	Writes a string into a text file. A parameter tells whether to append the string or rewrite the file.

My.Computer.FileSystem.SpecialDirectories

The My.Computer.FileSystem.SpecialDirectories property returns a SpecialDirectoriesProxy object that has properties giving the locations of various special directories (such as the system's temporary directory and the user's My Documents directory). The following table summarizes these special directory properties.

Property	Purpose
AllUsersApplicationData	The directory where applications should store settings for all users (typically, C:\Documents and Settings\All Users\Application Data\<company>\<product>\<version>).
CurrentUserApplicationData	The directory where applications should store settings for the current user (typically, C:\Documents and Settings\<user>\Application Data\<company>\<product>\<version>).

Table continued on following page

Property	Purpose
`Desktop`	The current user's desktop directory (typically, `C:\Documents and Settings\<user>\Desktop`).
`MyDocuments`	The current user's My Documents directory (typically, `C:\Documents and Settings\<user>\My Documents`).
`MyMusic`	The current user's My Music directory (typically, `C:\Documents and Settings\<user>\My Documents\My Music`).
`MyPictures`	The current user's My Pictures directory (typically, `C:\Documents and Settings\<user>\My Documents\My Pictures`).
`Programs`	The current user's Programs directory (typically, `C:\Documents and Settings\<user>\Start Menu\Programs`).
`Temp`	The current user's temporary directory (typically, `C:\Documents and Settings\<user>\Local Settings\Temp`).

Index

toolbars. *See also* **custom toolbars**
adding macros to, 41
overview, 4, 48
rearranging, 48
removing commands, 41
showing or hiding, 48
Toolbox. *See also* **components; controls;** *specific tools*
components listed by purpose, 803–804
double-clicking on controls, 70
dragging controls from, 70–71
overview, 4, 49–51
pointer, 804
right-click menu for, 50–51
setting icons for custom controls, 363
standard components (table), 802–803
using custom controls, 365–366
Windows forms controls in, 259–264
Tools menu
commands, 37–38
Customize command, 40
Macros submenu, 38–40
overview, 36
`Tools.Alias` **command, 33**
`ToolStrip` **control, 270–271, 891–893**
`ToolStripContainer` **control, 893–894**
`ToolTip` **component, 269, 894–895**
tooltips in code editor, 55–56, 58
`ToString` **method, 943–946**
TRACE constant, 113, 116
`TrackBar` **control**
for initiating action, 271
for making selections, 267
overview, 896
properties (table), 896
transaction objects
further information, 325–326
program demonstrating, 323–325
transaction defined, 322
transformations (graphical), 546
advanced, 551–556
basics, 546–551
combining, 547, 551
defined, 546
`Graphics` class methods for, 547, 551
mapping world coordinates to device coordinates, 553
matrices for, 546–547
order of applying, 549, 551
`Pen` class transformations, 569–571
for positioning drawings, 554–556
`Prepend` parameter for, 547–548
rotation, 548–549
rotation with translation, 549–551
saving and restoring graphics states, 556–558
scaling diamond around its center, 551–553
`TranslateTransform` **method, 647**
transparency properties for forms
`Opacity`, 275–277, 279
`TransparencyKey`, 277–279
`TransparencyKey` **property (** `Form` **object), 277–279**

`TreeNode` **objects**
methods (table), 901–902
overview, 897
properties (table), 900–901
`TreeView` **control**
methods (table), 899
overview, 896–902
properties (table), 898–899
`TreeNode` object methods (table), 901–902
`TreeNode` object properties (table), 900–901
`TreeNode` objects, 897
`Trimming` **property (** `StringFormat` **class), 602–605**
`Try` **block**
`Catch` statement, 239, 240–241
for structured error handling, 239–241, 795
syntax, 239, 795
`TypeOf` **operator, 171**
types. *See* **data types**
typographic code elements
line continuation, 126
line joining, 126–127
line labels, 127
normal comments, 121
overview, 120–121
XML comments, 122–125

U

`UniqueConstraint`, **345, 346–347**
unit scope of classes, 446–447
unmanaged resources
`Dispose` method for, 444–446
`Finalize` method for, 442–444
unplanned conditions. *See also* **error handling**
bugs versus, 233–234
catching, 235–238
defined, 234
Y2K problem, 233
`UserControl` **class**
for custom controls, 374, 380
customizing in executable projects, 381
inherited in executable projects, 381
UserControl Test Container, 363–364

V

validating data. *See also* **validation events**
`Assert` method for, 235
compiler constants for, 235
functions for, 237–238
need for, 234
regression testing tools and, 234
regular expressions for, 743–744
testing for unexpected conditions, 236–237
validation events
`CausesValidation` property for, 95, 97
deferred validation, 98–100
overview, 95
separated validation, 97–98
`Validated` events, 95, 97

1021